AN AMERICAN ALBUM

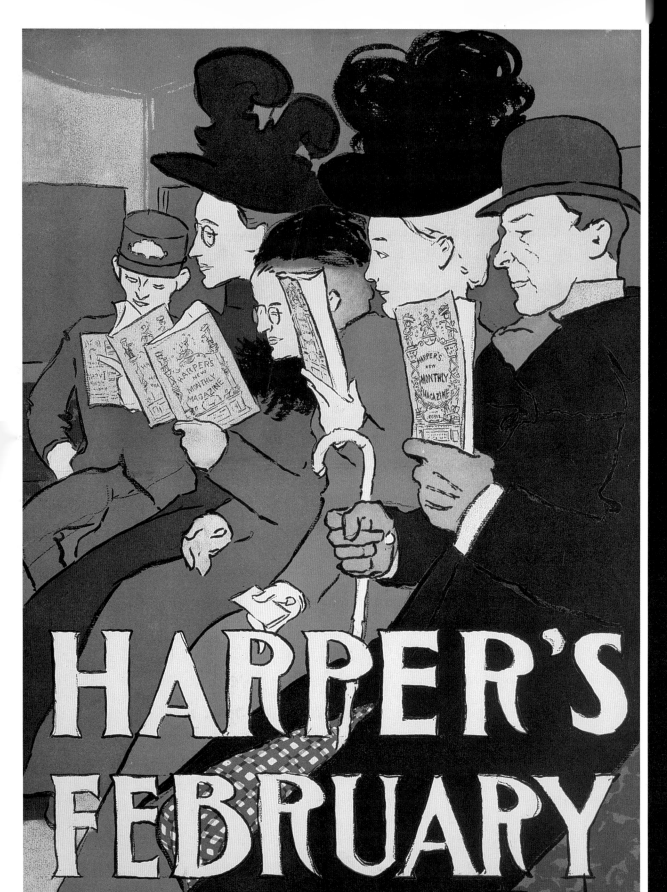

HARPER'S
FEBRUARY

Edward Penfield

AN AMERICAN ALBUM

ONE HUNDRED AND FIFTY YEARS OF

◆

HARPER'S

◆

MAGAZINE

Edited by Lewis H. Lapham & Ellen Rosenbush
Foreword by Arthur Schlesinger, Jr.

FRANKLIN SQUARE PRESS
A DIVISION OF HARPER'S MAGAZINE

CONTENTS

Foreword by Arthur Schlesinger, Jr. viii
Introduction by Lewis H. Lapham xi

1850's

Herman Melville, *The Town-Ho's Story* 2
Editor's Table: *Union Saving* 12
Nathaniel Hawthorne, *Uttoxeter* 17
The Siege of Fort Atkinson 20
Stephen A. Douglas, *The Dividing Line Between
Federal and Local Authority* 29

1860's

George F. Noyes, *The Battle of Antietam* 42
Hans Christian Andersen, *Psyche* 47
Robert Tomes, *The Fortunes of War* 53
Herman Melville, *The March to the Sea* 57
M. Schele de Vere, *The Freedman's Story* 59
Horace Greeley, *The Plains,
As I Crossed Them Ten Years Ago* 68

1870's

George William Curtis, Editor's Easy Chair: *Charles Dickens* 72
George Ward Nichols, *Down the Mississippi* 74
George William Curtis, Editor's Easy Chair:
Political Life in America 81
C. L. Brace, *The Little Laborers of New York City* 84
Panic in Wall Street 87
Walt Whitman, *Song of the Redwood-Tree* 93
Christina Rossetti, *A Song* 97
George William Curtis, Editor's Easy Chair: *Boss Tweed* 98

1880's

Henry James, *Washington Square* 102
George William Curtis, Editor's Easy Chair:
Women's Rights 106
Veeder B. Paine, *Our Public Land Policy* 108
George William Curtis, Editor's Easy Chair:
Ulysses S. Grant 113
George William Curtis, Editor's Easy Chair:
Strikes and Anarchy 115

1890's

James Russell Lowell, *His Ship* 118
Sarah Orne Jewett, *Fame's Little Day* 120
Theodore Roosevelt, *St. Clair's Defeat* 125

Frederic Remington, *With the Fifth Corps* 133
Stephen Crane, *The Angel Child* 140

1900's

Mark Twain, *Extracts from Adam's Diary and Eve's Diary* 146
Edith Wharton, *The Quicksand* 158
Grover Cleveland, *The Integrity of American Character* 166
Jack London, *The Sun-dog Trail* 168
Lewis Carroll, *Feeding the Mind* 175
Joseph Conrad, *The Informer* 178
Willa Sibert Cather, *The Enchanted Bluff* 189

1910's

Thomas Hardy, *Night in a Suburb* 196
Sherwood Anderson, *The Rabbit-pen* 197
William Allen White, *The Country Newspaper* 201
M. E. Ravage, *My Plunge into the Slums* 205
Theodore Dreiser, *The Country Doctor* 210
Don Marquis, The Lion's Mouth:
Mother Goose, Propagandist 217
William Dean Howells, *Eighty Years and After* 219

1920's

Rudyard Kipling, *The Gods of the Copybook Maxims* 226
Robert Frost, *Fire and Ice* 228
Carl Sandburg, *To the Ghost of John Milton* 229
Clarence S. Darrow, *Crime and the Alarmists* 230
Will Durant, *In Praise of Freedom* 235
Edward S. Martin, Editor's Easy Chair:
Re-discovering Europe 241
Sarah Comstock, *Aimee Semple McPherson* 243
Malcolm Cowley, *My Countryside, Then and Now* 251
Archibald MacLeish, *Not Marble nor
the Gilded Monuments* 256
Virginia Woolf, *The Lady in the Looking-Glass* 257

1930's

Walter Lippmann, *The Peculiar Weakness of Mr. Hoover* 262
Edna St. Vincent Millay, *Sonnet* 267
James Thurber, *"Listen to This, Dear"* 268
Stephen Vincent Benét, *A Death in the Country* 270
Leon Trotsky, *What Hitler Wants* 280
Emma Goldman, *Was My Life Worth Living?* 285
H. L. Mencken, *The Future of English* 290
John Steinbeck, *The Chrysanthemums* 295

Rainer Maria Rilke, *Solitude* 301
Pearl S. Buck, *America's Medieval Women* 302
E. B. White, One Man's Meat: *Walden Pond* 308
Frederick Lewis Allen, *Since Yesterday* 312

1 9 4 0's
Dorothy Thompson, *Who Goes Nazi?* 316
Eudora Welty, *The Wide Net* 321
Richard Wright, *What You Don't Know Won't Hurt You* 332
John Dos Passos, *The People at War* 336
Alfred Kazin, *Going Home* 343
John P. Marquand, *Iwo Jima Before H-Hour* 346
Eugene V. Rostow, *Our Worst Wartime Mistake* 352
Henry L. Stimson, *The Decision to Use the Atomic Bomb* 359
Katherine Anne Porter, *Gertrude Stein: A Self-Portrait* 365
Anne Morrow Lindbergh, *Anywhere in Europe* 372
E. M. Forster, *Art for Art's Sake* 375
John Cheever, *Vega* 379

1 9 5 0's
Bernard DeVoto, *The Century* 388
Joyce Cary, *Evangelist* 393
Thornton Wilder, *The Silent Generation* 396
Roald Dahl, *Lamb to the Slaughter* 399
John Kenneth Galbraith, *The Great Wall Street Crash* 404
Harold Brodkey, *The Sound of Moorish Laughter* 408
William Faulkner, *On Fear: The South in Labor* 414
Anne Sexton, *The Farmer's Wife* 417
Philip Roth, *Recollections from Beyond the Last Rope* 418

1 9 6 0's
Sylvia Plath, *Mushrooms* 426
John Updike, *Vermont* 427
James Baldwin, *The Dangerous Road
Before Martin Luther King* 428
George Plimpton, *Miami Notebook:
Cassius Clay and Malcolm X* 438
Richard Hofstadter, *The Paranoid Style in
American Politics* 445
Walker Percy, *Mississippi: The Fallen Paradise* 452
Langston Hughes, *Long View: Negro* 458
James Dickey, *The Celebration* 459
Barbara W. Tuchman, *History by the Ounce* 461
Tillie Olsen, *Silences: When Writers Don't Write* 465
Randall Jarrell, *The Player Piano* 472

Norman Mailer, *Miami Beach and Chicago* 473
John Fischer, Editor's Easy Chair: *Survival U* 478

1 9 7 0's
Seymour M. Hersh, My *Lai 4* 484
Arthur Schlesinger, Jr., *Is There a Place
for Morality in Foreign Affairs?* 509
Alice Walker, *Everyday Use* 515
Gabriel García Márquez, *The Death of
Salvador Allende* 520
Murray Kempton, *The Sound of Tinkling Brass* 526
Annie Dillard, *Innocence in the Galápagos* 530
Michael Harrington, *To the Disney Station* 537

1 9 8 0's
Walter Karp, *Liberty Under Siege* 546
Ryszard Kapuściński, *The Soccer War* 558
Nadine Gordimer, *The Moment Before
the Gun Went Off* 568
Salman Rushdie, *Untime of the Imam* 571
When You're a Crip (Or a Blood) 577
Gail Regier, *Users, Like Me* 586
Allan Gurganus, *Reassurance* 590
Tom Wolfe, *Stalking the Billion-Footed Beast* 595

1 9 9 0's
L. J. Davis, *Chronicle of a Debacle Foretold* 606
Richard Rodriguez, *Late Victorians* 620
Joyce Carol Oates, *Ladies and Gentlemen:* 628
David Mamet, *The Rake* 632
George Saunders, *The 400-Pound CEO* 635
Darcy Frey, *The Last Shot* 643
Mary Gaitskill, *On Not Being a Victim* 657
Lewis H. Lapham, Notebook: *Morte De Nixon* 663
David Foster Wallace, *Ticket to the Fair* 668
Pico Iyer, *Where Worlds Collide* 683
Fenton Johnson, *Beyond Belief* 690
Lewis H. Lapham, Notebook: *Exorcism* 699

Index 703
Illustration Credits 708
Copyright Acknowledgments 710

A year of Penfield color illustrations follows page 144

Copyright © 2000 Franklin Square Press

Published by Franklin Square Press, a division of
Harper's Magazine, 666 Broadway, New York, NY 10012

First edition
First printing 2000

Illustration credits and copyright acknowledgments
appear on pages 708–712.

LIBRARY OF CONGRESS CATALOGING-IN-PUBLICATION DATA

An American album : one hundred and fifty years of Harper's
magazine / edited by Lewis H. Lapham & Ellen Rosenbush ;
foreword by Arthur Schlesinger, Jr.
     p. cm.
     Includes index.
     ISBN 1-879957-53-1
     1. American literature—19th century. 2. United States—
Civilization—19th century—Miscellanea. 3. United
States—Civilization—20th century—Miscellanea. 4.
United States—Social life and customs—19th century—
Miscellanea. 5. United States—Social life and customs—
20th century—Miscellanea. 6. United States—Literary
collections. 7. American literature—20th century. I. Title:
Harper's magazine. II. Lapham, Lewis H. III. Rosenbush, Ellen.

PS509.U52 A39 2000
810.8'04—dc21   99-087125

Manufactured in the United States of America.

This book has been produced on acid-free paper.

Designed by Renée Khatami

2 4 6 8 10 9 7 5 3 1

Acknowledgments

The compilation of this book was a loving, though challenging task. For her help in patiently sorting through the wealth of material contained in 150 years of *Harper's Magazine*, the editors wish to thank our colleague Margaret Cordi. We also wish to thank *Harper's Magazine* publisher Rick MacArthur for his enthusiastic support and unfailing encouragement. We are extremely grateful to Renée Khatami, who designed the book; to Paul Reyes, Susan Burton, Rachel Monahan, Elizabeth Giddens, and Jason Smith for their help in proofreading the book; to Massoumeh Farman-Farmaian for her selection of historical photographs; and to Laura Lindgren and Celia Fuller for their expert arrangement of art and type. Thanks also to Lynn Carlson, Virginia Creeden, Susan Hayes, Anne Tardos, Tom Hopkins, Ellen Ryder, Margaret Ann Roth, and Arthur Rosenthal.

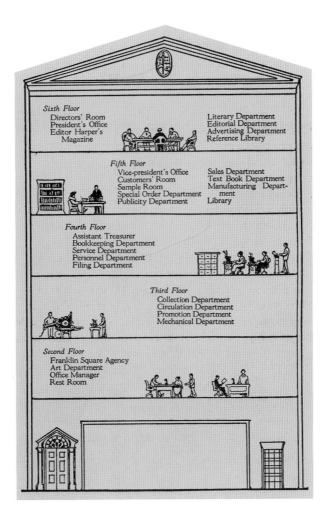

FOREWORD

BY ARTHUR SCHLESINGER, JR.

arper's *Magazine* has portrayed, reflected, and helped to shape the American literary landscape for two thirds of the life of the republic. When it made its debut in June 1850—its 144 pages illustrated by wood engravings, and a year's subscription offered for $3—the United States was a nation of twenty-three million people living in thirty states. As I write, a century and a half later, the population has increased twelvefold. The number of states has nearly doubled, and *Harper's Magazine* is today the longest-lived and most thoughtful periodical of general interest in the United States (its perennial rival, *The Atlantic Monthly*, is seven years younger).

Harper's New Monthly Magazine, as it was initially styled, was an immediate success. Taking advantage of the absence of an international copyright agreement, the first editors sailed for a season under the black flag of literary piracy, looting the British press for stories written by Charles Dickens, William Makepeace Thackeray, and Anthony Trollope. But Methodist consciences soon persuaded the Harper Brothers to pay British journals for advance sheets and to pay American authors as well, and by 1860 the magazine's circulation had reached what was then the impossibly high figure of 200,000.

The magazine during its early years expressed little interest in public affairs, but after the Civil War the transformation of America into an industrial society prompted the editors to take up the questions of political and economic theory and to commission articles dealing with foreign immigration, urban slums, municipal graft, the building of railroads, and the breaking of strikes.

By the turn of the century the magazine had become the most brilliant American periodical of its day—and for thirty-five cents a copy. It published serials by Henry James, William Dean Howells, and Mark Twain (for which the authors were paid $5,000—about $80,000 in our own inflated currency); short stories by Stephen Crane, Edith Wharton, Theodore Dreiser, and Sherwood Anderson; poetry by James Russell Lowell, Thomas Hardy, Robert Frost, and Carl Sandburg; history by Woodrow Wilson and Theodore Roosevelt. Howells argued famously for realism in American literature, and Howard Pyle and M. C. Wyatt provided vivid illustrations *in color*.

Then the Great War, known to later generations as World War I, transformed the literary climate. The old *Harper's Monthly Magazine*, with its sedate tone and its illustrated serials, seemed old-fashioned and irrelevant to the generation coming of age in what were known as the Roaring Twenties. Thomas Bucklin Wells, editor since 1919, deleted the serials and the illustrations as well as the word "Monthly" from the title, and in place of literary essays he substituted social commentary. The Great Depression and the Second World War sharpened the magazine's tone and enlarged its range of interest. Trotsky wrote on Hitler; Eugene Rostow condemned the internment of Japanese-Americans; Henry L. Stimson defended the decision to drop the atomic bomb. The historian Bernard DeVoto contributed polemics against the House Un-American Activities Committee, J. Edgar Hoover, and Joseph McCarthy. He also defended the national domain and the public lands against stockmen, timbermen, and miners intent upon despoiling the environment for short-term profit.

Since 1955, under editors as diverse as John Fischer, Willie Morris, and, since 1975, Lewis Lapham, *Harper's Magazine* has continued to reflect and comment upon the always changing nature of American society. It has prospered, moreover, in a time when the general-interest magazine has come under increasingly heavy competition from the "niche" magazines tailored for specialized audiences. Take a look at any newsstand, and you will find magazines for joggers, for rock fans, for evangelicals, for soccer players, for motorcyclists, for homosexuals, for computer hacks—but where are the magazines for the citizenry in general? The magazines of critical inquiry and appraisal, the magazines that deal broadly in ideas and issues, the magazines that stimulate debate on questions that bedevil us all? Where are the *American Mercury,* the *Scribner's,* and *The Century* of my youth? Where, for that matter, are *Life* and *Look, The Saturday Evening Post,* and *Collier's?*

In an age of niches, general-interest magazines—those few that remain—are all the more essential to the health of a democratic republic. In this time of identity politics, when people seem to rush to huddle with their own, there remain common afflictions and common prospects that ought to provoke us to reason together. *Harper's Magazine,* as this sampler shows, has been so provoking Americans for a century and a half, and much to the republic's benefit.

The Nation said of *Harper's Magazine* in 1866, "We may well consider it an index to the literary culture and general character of the nation." So it has been, as this volume so trenchantly and variously demonstrates.

HAZARDS OF NEW FORTUNE
BY LEWIS H. LAPHAM

At irregular but not infrequent intervals over the last twenty-odd years I've had occasion to search the back issues of *Harper's Magazine* for an essay or short story said to possess elements of historical or literary importance, and sometimes it takes me three days to reach the text in question. Idle curiosity saps the strength of scholarly resolve, and I succumb to the impulse to read at random. I begin to look for Woodrow Wilson's essay on George Washington, but I come across Henry James gathering his notebooks in Paris, and instead of attending to one American president's judgment of another, I accompany the expatriate novelist on an excursion through the south of France. I set out to find John Muir among the California redwoods or Captain A. T. Mahan's thoughts on naval warfare, but I never hear what either gentleman has to say because I stumble upon Horace Greeley, "The Plains, As I Crossed Them Ten Years Ago," or Leon Trotsky, "What Hitler Wants," or Pearl S. Buck, "America's Medieval Women."

The wealth of possibility attests both to the scale of the magazine's achievement over the span of the last 150 years and to the difficulties that confront an editor attempting to compile an anthology. Some of the articles have been reduced in length, but, even so, it would have been much easier to assemble a book at twice or four times the length of the one presently in hand, and the reader who finds no story by Owen Wister and no report from Richard Harding Davis (both reliable contributors to the magazine in the late 1890's) will, I hope, excuse their absence. The magazine consistently has published authors of large talent and deserved reputation, and the omission of Wister and Davis (like the omission of George Ward Nichols's interview with Wild Bill Hickok) merely suggests the extent of its enterprise, the size of its inventory, and the range of its interests.

Published without interruption since June 1850, the 1,800 issues of *Harper's Magazine* tell the story of a restless people fond of journeys and experiments. Their collected notes and observations bear comparison to the snapshots in a family album, the points of resemblance showing up in the war dispatches from Antietam and Iwo Jima, in the recurring sermons about a plutocracy too rich for its own good (the topic first introduced during the heyday of the Gilded Age, revised in the 1920's and then again in the 1980's), in the reports of new machines, new means of transport and communication, new advances in the sciences. Some of the authors are famous, others not well enough remembered, but all of them choose carefully their quarrels with Providence, and in the tumult of new fortunes coincident with the rise and fall of seven generations, their various remarks—on love, war, railroads, movie stars, barbed wire, atomic physics, lost dogs—add to the sum of what is meant by the American character and turn of mind. The inflections change and so does the construction of the prose, but the distinguishing tone of voice is that of a practical people interested in what they can see and make of the world, the voice of travelers in an always new country, optimistic and energetic, seeking to work the soil of the American experience into a cash crop, a grand hotel, a dream of heaven.

As fond of discoveries as their readers and authors, the magazine's eleven editors have proved themselves equally willing to make a new deal in new territory, and as American society over the last 150 years has repeatedly changed itself into something else, they have redrafted the magazine's format and adjusted its focus to meet the revised circumstances brought about by the transformation of an agrarian into an industrial economy, by six wars and as many sexual revolutions, by the translation of the vocabulary of print into the pictorial languages of the electronic media. The magazine owes its longevity to their collective sense of an historical narrative as closely bound to time future as to time past, the successive generations appearing on different stages but in the same repertory company, all of them caught up in the making of maps or metaphors with which to find the spirit of an age that they could recognize as their own.

The magazine's progenitors—the four brothers Harper, born in Brooklyn on a farm—operated a publishing company that by 1850 had become the largest in the world (nine five-story buildings in lower Manhattan, a force of several hundred people employed in the various printing trades), but it wouldn't have occurred to them to think that they were setting type for a literary monument. Frugal merchants and devout, side-whiskered Methodists, they had been successful booksellers for thirty years, the enterprise derived from the initiative of the eldest brother, James, who had rowed across the East River in 1810 and, at the age of sixteen, in what was still a small and predominantly maritime city found work as a printer's apprentice. Seven years later he set up his own printing establishment and was promptly joined in the venture by his three younger brothers, John, Wesley, and Fletcher. The business prospered, the brothers acquired wealth and reputation, and in 1844 James was elected mayor of what had become a gaslit metropolis inhabited by 300,000 people, the cobblestoned streets loud with the clatter of horses and wagons, the ships in the rivers crowding so close to the piers that their bowsprits pushed up against the upper windows of the waterfront taverns. Mayor Harper equipped the police with their first uniforms—notable for the copper buttons that gave currency to the term "cops"—and restricted the wandering of pigs (on which the city had depended to dispose of its refuse) to the alleys west of Fifth Avenue.

By 1850 the city's population had again doubled in size, the residential districts spreading north toward Forty-second Street, the traffic on lower Broadway prompting the British author William Makepeace Thackeray to remark on "a rush of life, such as I have never seen." In the excitement of what was perceived by all present as an era of immense promise, the Harper brothers conceived of their new magazine as a commercial opportunity and "a tender to our business," meant to drum up buyers for their books and occupy the downtime on the expensive steam presses newly installed in their factory on Franklin Square. Fletcher Harper, the more literary of the four brothers, told a biographer some years later that "the

atmosphere of the place did not suggest any special aesthetic refinement."

Neither did most other places in America in 1850. New York City boasted the comforts of sixteen first-class hotels, but at least half of the gentlemen in town were still blowing their noses in their fingers and eating with their knives. At all points of the American compass the inventors to whom Mark Twain once referred as "the creators of this world—after God" were busy tinkering with plows and motors and firing pins; the country was turning on its axis, the lines of communication and trade beginning to run east and west instead of north and south, and the old mercantile arrangements familiar to the dealers in rum and slaves being replaced by a commerce geared to the dynamo of the Industrial Revolution. Gold had been found in California, and victory in the war with Mexico had brought with it a new territory nearly as large as the one acquired in the Louisiana Purchase; banks were rising up on New York City street corners "like Aladdin palaces," the American steamer *Pacific* set a new record for a trans-Atlantic crossing (ten days, four hours, thirty minutes), and land on the frontier was still plentiful and "dog cheap." The travelers making their way west on the Oregon Trail—the vast caravan numbering as many as 42,000 immigrants in 1849—looked for a garden in a landscape that was mostly desert, for something glimpsed but not yet seen in a play of sunlight on a canyon wall or through a drift of rain in tall trees. The Indians on the Great Plains were still peaceable enough in the spring of 1850, more curious than belligerent, watching, in silence and from a distance, as the white man moved what they assumed were his villages to hunting grounds unknown.

The curtain was going up on a brave new world, but where did one look first, and what was the perspective that offered the clearest view? Harper & Brothers answered the question with a "compendium" for those of their customers who didn't have time to read through "scores and hundreds of magazines and journals, intermingled with much that is of merely local and transient interest, and are thus hopelessly excluded from the knowledge and the reach of readers at large." Expressing the wish "to remedy this evil," the advertisement on the first page of the first volume of *Harper's New Monthly Magazine* offered to place "within the reach of the great mass of the American people, an immense amount of useful and entertaining reading matter, to which, on account

James Harper

John Harper

Joseph Wesley Harper

Fletcher Harper

of the great number and expense of the books and periodicals in which it originally appears, they have hitherto had no access." A few pages later, under the rubric "A Word at the Start," the publishers defined the magazine as a means of general education:

> The Weekly and Daily journals of England, France, and America, [...] abound in the most brilliant contributions in every department of intellectual effort. The current of Political Events, in an age of unexampled political activity, can be traced only through their columns. Scientific discovery, Mechanical inventions, the creations of Fine Art, the Orations of Statesmen, all the varied intellectual movements of this most stirring and productive age, find their only record upon these multiplied and ephemeral pages.

The new periodical borrowed heavily from European journals and reviews because no copyright law hindered the reproduction of stories written by Dickens or Thackeray and because in the spring of 1850 the republic of American letters could scarcely be said to exist. Nathaniel Hawthorne published *The Scarlet Letter* in the summer of that year, the book selling 4,000 copies in ten days, but Poe had died in 1849, and Melville had drifted into an obscurity from which the publication of *Moby-Dick* in 1851 failed to rescue him. Thoreau had yet to write *Walden*, or Whitman, *Leaves of Grass*, and in New York an overly precious literary journal, *The Knickerbocker*, competed for readers against eleven newspapers, most of them fiercely partisan or as scurrilous as the *Sun*, "slimy and venomous...deadly in politics and groveling in morals."

To the position of the magazine's first managing editor the brothers Harper appointed Henry J. Raymond, who was then only thirty years old but of whom Horace Greeley already had said, "A cleverer, readier, more generally efficient journalist I never saw." Raymond in the 1840's had written most of Greeley's new newspaper, the *Tribune*, and in 1851, the year after he assumed the editorship of *Harper's New Monthly Magazine*, he founded the *New York Times*. A man of prodigious energy and talent, Raymond continued to edit both the periodical and the newspaper until 1856, and during those same five years he served as Speaker of the New York State Assembly in Albany and conducted a voluminous correspondence with most of the prominent politicians of the day, among them President Zachary Taylor, Senator William Henry Seward, and Thurlow Weed, eventual co-founder of the Republican Party. Believing that an editor should "see and examine everything" in the publication under his hand, Raymond in Albany required Harper & Brothers to send him manuscripts on the Hudson River steamboats. He was also an impressive orator, much in demand on platforms at Elmira and Buffalo as well as in New York City, widely known for his speeches on the question of slavery—"a moral, social and political evil, but its abolition a matter for the South, not the North to decide."

Raymond thought that the press should be used "to dissipate the fogs of error" that tended, unhappily all too often, to "cloud the public mind," and his idealism suited the purpose of the proprietors. They addressed their magazine to the educated reader, not to a broad or popular audience but to people blessed with both the leisure and the capacity to profit from an acquaintance with the writings of Anthony Trollope and Thomas De Quincey. Set before the public at the price of twenty-five cents, the first issue ran to the length of 144 octavo pages in double columns of eight-point type, the pale, tan cover decorated with drawings of cherubs blowing bubbles and strewing flowers, most of the text pirated from British sources—an appreciation of Thomas Babington Macaulay, three short stories from *Household Words* (the journal edited by Charles Dickens), an obituary of William Wordsworth (he had died in April), the *London Times* account of Pope Pius IX returning, not triumphantly, to Rome. The American contributions appeared at the back of the magazine, in the steerage-class space subsequent to page 122. Raymond supplied an eleven-page summary of current events, taking note of an ominous election in France as well as the talk in Washington about the prospect of admitting California to the Union of American States; the principal book review bestowed a favorable opinion on a volume just published by William Cullen Bryant; the final three pages presented engravings of feminine fashions in a magazine otherwise innocent of illustration or advertisement. The captions remarked on the preference for "dresses trimmed all over with puffings of net, lace and flowers" and applauded "the tendency this season to depart from simplicity of dress, and to adopt the extreme ornamental elegance of the Middle Ages."

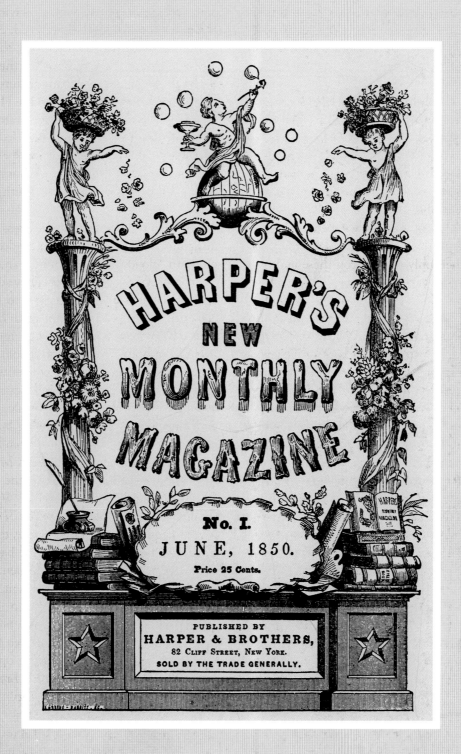

HARPER'S NEW MONTHLY MAGAZINE

No. I.

JUNE, 1850.

Price 25 Cents.

PUBLISHED BY

HARPER & BROTHERS,

82 CLIFF STREET, NEW YORK.

SOLD BY THE TRADE GENERALLY.

The magazine proved itself a success within six months, attracting 50,000 subscribers (an extraordinarily large number for the period), which confirmed the publishers in their good opinion of an American public, earnest and self-educating, devoted to the projects of enlightenment. The approaching shadow of civil war darkened the lamps of learning over the course of the next ten years—a massacre at Pottawatomie Creek in the Kansas Territory, stronger rumors of secession at Charleston, John Brown's raid on Harpers Ferry, Charles Sumner of Massachusetts nearly beaten to death by Preston Brooks of South Carolina on the floor of the United States Senate—but Harper & Brothers remained faithful to the cause of spiritual and intellectual advancement. Their magazine attracted subscribers on both sides of the Mason-Dixon Line, a "welcome messenger from the great world" found on Mississippi River steamboats, in sod houses on the Dakota prairie, on ships working their way around Cape Horn (eighty-nine days from Sandy Hook to San Francisco Bay, $400 for the passage), and in June 1858 the publishers posted their hope of resolving the slavery question in the form of an advertisement on the back cover—"Wise men and true patriots agree upon points far more numerous than those upon which they differ. The object of the magazine will be to unite rather than to separate the views and feelings of the people of the different sections of our common country."

The keeping of the editorial conscience Raymond assigned to George William Curtis, who in 1853 began to write the "Easy Chair," the monthly column that for the next 128 years embodied the magazine's abiding character and premise. Like Raymond, Curtis was a popular orator, a prolific author, and an idealist. As a young man he answered to the nineteenth-century description of a communist, forgoing the chance of a college education in favor of the Utopian experiment conducted in the 1830's by Ralph Waldo Emerson at Brook Farm. Emerson had wished to test the theory of a society erected on the blueprint of his transcendental philosophy, and with that project in view a small community of similarly high-minded souls applied themselves to the tasks of reading Plato and cultivating peas on 188 acres in West Roxbury, two miles south of Boston. Curtis later observed that the experiment's "economic failure was almost a foregone conclusion," but during his several semesters in Arcadia he taught himself the principal foreign languages and formed a durable acquaintance not only with Emerson but also with Hawthorne and Thoreau.

An anti-establishment figure, fervent in his advocacy of women's suffrage and civil service reform and strongly Abolitionist in the years prior to the Civil War, Curtis wrote mostly about politics, remarking on the ways in which politicians depended upon the nineteenth-century version of the sound bite ("whimsical and epigrammatic extravagance") but noticing also that "the crowd cheers the sayer of the good thing...not necessarily all that it may be made to mean."

When Raymond gave up his post as editor to attend more closely to the concerns of the *Times* (also to the presidential campaign of John Charles Frémont and to the writing of the document that formed the Republican Party at Pittsburgh in 1856), the publishers made good the loss of his judgment as a journalist by establishing, in 1857, a second and more topical journal under the title *Harper's Weekly*. The *Weekly* directed itself to the news of the day, and five years later its correspondents and sketch artists, among them Winslow Homer, were in the field with the armies of Northern Virginia and the Potomac; the *Monthly* continued to seek the higher ground occupied by writers on the order of Anne C. Lynch, who had traveled to Washington in the winter of 1852 to behold the marvel of the new building on Capitol Hill. The work wasn't finished, but Miss Lynch could see behind the scaffolding the embodiment of the American mission to civilize a continent and teach the lessons of democracy to the less fortunate nations of the earth:

> With the broadest principles of freedom for the foundation of our government—with a magnificent country, whose shores are washed by the great oceans, whose lakes are seas, whose rivers are the most majestic that water the earth, whose commerce whitens every sea, whose railroads and canals, like great arteries, intersect its whole surface, and carry life and activity to its remotest corner; whose "magnetic nerves," with the rapidity of thought, bear intelligence to its distant extremities; with a people springing from the fusion of many races, and whose energies are as inexhaustible as the resources of the country they inhabit, it would seem that here the human mind is destined to develop its highest powers, and that,

while on one side its influence will roll back upon the tottering monarchies of Europe, on the other its advancing tide of freedom and civilization will stretch across the Pacific, to the shores of Asia, and pour upon them its fertilizing flood.

The sense of the American mission survived the Civil War, and so did the high-flown rhetoric that filled the pages of *Harper's New Monthly Magazine* with what another of its writers identified as "the sweet and innocent search for daily bread and eternal wisdom." The readers took a keen interest in the world at large, and because most of them lacked the means or the occasion to travel more than fifty miles from their places of birth, the several forms of travel writing—reports of expeditions to Alaska or Arizona, notes on natural history, dispatches from the frontiers of applied science—made up the bulk of the editorial matter during the third quarter of the nineteenth century. The country was big and new, the citizens of the recombinant union returning to the tasks of their manifest destiny, the covered wagons still lumbering west from Missouri through "the untapped generosity of the soil...into a landscape unstained by history." Albert Guernsey, who succeeded Raymond and served as the magazine's editor from 1856 until 1869, sent correspondents to conduct surveys and mount investigations. They followed the progress of the transcontinental railroad building west from Omaha and east from Sacramento; reported on the exploits of William F. Cody (a.k.a. "Buffalo Bill"), a marksman and Indian scout who killed 4,000 buffalo in eight months to feed the Irish work gangs laying track in Nebraska and Wyoming; encountered hard and violent men on the Texas frontier, "men who could manage an estate, kill a bear, hang an Indian, yoke a team of oxen"; frequented gambling saloons in Virginia City to consort with silver miners, "bearded and dust-covered," holding "fiendish revels" under crystal pillars and gilded mirrors where "all is life, excitement, avarice, deviltry and enterprise."

The publishers added more illustration, and for those of their correspondents who could not furnish their own sketches, they provided a company of artists, among them the young Thomas Nast, seated at rows of desks in a high-ceilinged studio overlooking the avarice and deviltry walking in and out of New York's City Hall. It was an age in which everybody remarked on the obvious disparities between the rich (silk-waistcoated bankers in Boston and New York merchants sporting beaver hats) and the poor (who made their own clothes and seldom lived beyond the age of forty), but it was also an age that admired the trappings of wealth as marks of intelligence and grit. The rough company of expectant capitalists bore no socialist grudges; the successful stock fraud was seen as a "slick deal," the owner of a Colorado mining company deemed "mighty smart" if he could pay a pittance for his Chinese labor.

Guernsey's successor, Henry Mills Alden, enjoyed one of the longest careers known to the annals of American journalism. Appointed to the editorship in 1869, the first year of the Grant Administration, Alden held it for half a

Henry Mills Alden giving editorial counsel.

century, until 1919, the seventh year of the Wilson Administration. The country meanwhile passed through two generations of convulsive change—the stagecoach surpassed first by the railroad and then by the automobile and the airplane; the whaling ships gone over the horizon with the gold camps and the cowboys—and for most of his term in editorial office Alden managed to keep pace with the press of events. He was a classical scholar and a poet, educated for the ministry in rural Vermont and descended from an ancestor who arrived in Massachusetts on the *Mayflower*; he wore a full beard in the heavy Victorian manner, and he addressed his authors and subordinates in a voice they invariably remembered as courteous.

During the early years of Alden's tenure America was still largely pastoral, half the population at work on small farms, the sight lines in the cities still defined by the heights of the church spires. The "creators of this world—after God" were improving their inventions, figuring out new methods of steel production and a quicker mechanism for the Colt revolver, and Curtis in the "Easy Chair" mocked the corruptions of Manhattan's Tammany Hall gang in league with the bribery of Boss Tweed. Together with the writing of his column for *Harper's New Monthly* he took over the editing of the political pages in *Harper's Weekly*, and encouraged Thomas Nast, who drew the first Republican elephant and Democratic donkey, to become the most feared cartoonist of the age.

The country was coming into its industrial inheritance, and Alden in the 1870's continued Guernsey's practice of sending authors and sketch artists on journeys of discovery—to the Arctic Circle and Ceylon, as well as to the Black Hills of South Dakota, where the gold discovered in 1875 foreclosed the last mortgage that the United States had been willing to grant to the Sioux and the northern Cheyenne. The Indians refused to sell their land at the government price and assembled the following spring near the Little Bighorn River to consider the meagerness of their options. It was this encampment of 15,000 Indians, the largest ever seen in the history of the tribes, that Lt. Col. George A. Custer chose to attack, with a troop of 250 cavalrymen, on the morning of June 25, in the confident belief that he enjoyed the advantages of both superior numbers and surprise.

By 1885 the country was showing the signs of the triumphant prosperity allied with the splendors of the Gilded Age. Men who in 1853 had struck out for the Nevada Territory with a shovel and a mule were returning to New York to show off the proofs of their good fortune in rooms furnished with Italian marble and illuminated by the wonder of electric light. Alden shifted the magazine's emphasis to "visual description and interpretive sensibility," replacing "the literature of information with the literature of power." He assumed an audience of polite and fastidious readers, people of "wealth and importance" intent upon furnishing their minds with ornaments as sumptuous as those that decorated their fine new houses in Newport or on Fifth Avenue, and by way of appropriate illustration he commissioned the work of Howard Pyle, Frederic Remington, and Charles Dana Gibson, inviting them to submit variations on a tragic or sentimental theme rather than unadorned line drawings meant to supplement an expository text. The magazine no longer had space for "the merely topical." What was wanted was personality and the subjective point of view, authors as well as artists with whom a well-bred reader might enjoy a "genteel discourse" or enter into "a conjugation of minds in the world of imagination."

The conjugation was most happily arranged in the realm of fiction, and Alden crowded the magazine with short stories, sometimes as many as eight or ten in a single issue, by authors of the quality of Mark Twain, Willa Cather, Stephen Crane, Edith Wharton, Henry James. Alden thought stories more effective than articles or essays in their portrayal of "the moving drama" of "our modern life and thought," and his belief in the authority of literature (more comprehensive than anything available in the sciences) reversed the magazine's order of editorial priority—British fiction and plain reporting of the American scene replaced by American short stories and fanciful reporting of the European scene. Assuming that his readers took little notice of graft, crime, sports, or "the common amusements," Alden was especially admiring of those writers, many of them women, who provided tales of "domestic interest" and brought to their pages "agreeable, well-bred, intelligent, racy conversation of the higher kind." Two of his observations stand as a fair imprint of his temperament and prose style:

On the writing of Edward Everett Hale—"His stories always distinguished by some original turn of native wit, peculiar to the New England garden of genius in which they grew, and whose hardy shrubs often gave forth the same pungent aroma, quite distinct from the fragrance of some flowers which, though sheltered there, seemed exotic."

On the virtue of southern writers who had endured the trials of the Civil War—"The southern people, so completely absorbed in a losing venture, and so nearly losing all material possessions, were gainers in the spiritual sense."

By 1895 Alden's magazine and the publishing house of Harper & Brothers passed as synonyms for the highest grades of American literary ore. The reputation for refinement was grounded on the polite willingness to overlook the uglier and more brutal aspects of late nineteenth-century capitalism. Alden's readers didn't like to be reminded of the poverty and misfortune visited upon the imported proletariat working in the country's sweatshops, factories, and mines; didn't wish to inquire too closely into the slum conditions on Manhattan's Lower East Side (twelve people sleeping in a room ten feet square, paying five cents a night for the privilege of "a spot"), or into the cost of labor at Henry Clay Frick's satanic steel mill in Pittsburgh, where "fingers is going down . . . like bananas at a county fair." The subscribers preferred to follow the fortunes of the opulent plutocrats known to the newspapers as "nature's noblemen," and the magazine's correspondents brought reports of their uncommon amusements—the new craze for bicycle riding, the heroics of the Harvard-Yale game, the comings and goings of Mrs. Astor's carriage or Mr. Carnegie's golf ball.

The fashionable perspective contrived to overlook not only most of the political and financial chicanery of the period but also the garish competition offered by the suddenly numerous publications being set before the public at lower prices and less rarefied elevations of polite taste. *McClure's,* an upstart monthly selling for fifteen cents in 1895, promoted the popular stories of O. Henry and the muckraking journalism of Lincoln Steffens and Ida Tarbell. *Harper's New Monthly* sold for thirty-five cents, and the gradual decline of its circulation in conjunction with a falling off of the company's book sales forced Harper & Brothers into the margins of bankruptcy in the autumn of 1896. Appeal was made to J. P. Morgan, a friend of the proprietors and a patron of the arts known to take an interest in literature as well as painting. Morgan responded with a handsome compliment ("The

downfall of the House of Harper would be a national calamity") backed by substantial loans (several million dollars between 1896 and his death in 1913) for which he never sought repayment. What had been a family partnership became a public corporation, but the editorial direction of the magazine remained as it was, and in 1900 Alden persuaded William Dean Howells to write the "Easy Chair."

The column had fallen silent on Curtis's death in 1892, and Howells at the turn of the century was the acknowledged dean of American letters; his portrait appeared on cigar-box labels, and in literary circles his opinion of a new writer or an old book was equivalent to the word of God. An avowed socialist and a defender of anarchists, Howells was the son of an Ohio printer who shared with Curtis many of the attributes expected of a nineteenth-century sage—the lack of a college education, an autodidact who had taught himself the European languages, an advocate of women's rights, the author of a Lincoln campaign biography. In his youth he wrote occasional newspaper dispatches from Ohio for Raymond at the *Times,* who didn't think he showed much promise as a journalist. During the better part of the decade of the 1870's Howells served as editor of *The Atlantic Monthly,* but he resigned his office in 1881 and left Boston for New York to take up his long-deferred vocation as the originator, at least in its American form, of the realistic novel. He wrote his two most famous books, *The Rise of Silas Lapham* (1885) and *A Hazard of New Fortunes* (1890), while acting as literary adviser to Harper & Brothers, scouting manuscripts for the publishers and bringing to the magazine the essays of Mark Twain, an old friend with whom he sometimes played billiards. Howells in the "Easy Chair" expressed his disappointment with the coarsened texture of the "immediately modern condition," gazed sadly upon a literary landscape blighted by the lurid bloom of William Randolph Hearst's yellow journalism, worried about "that vast, half-taught, half-bred multitude, which has lately so increased," deplored the vulgarity of a publishing business in which "books are run like lines of dry-goods, and advertised like baking powders and patent medicines."

The magazine meanwhile continued to publish exceptional fiction (Edith Wharton's "The Quicksand," Jack London's "The Sun-dog Trail," Joseph Conrad's "The Informer"), but its reporting of the American

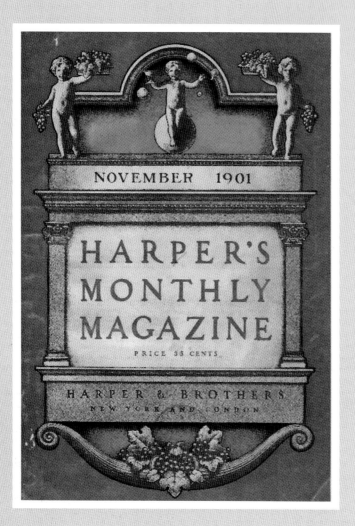

NOVEMBER   1901

HARPER'S
MONTHLY
MAGAZINE

PRICE 35 CENTS

HARPER & BROTHERS
NEW YORK AND LONDON

1919

HARPER'S
MAGAZINE

OCTOBER

How Uncle Sam Spends
Our Money
By Hon. JOSEPH G. CANNON

FOCH
As His Friends Know Him
By the Baron DE MARICOURT

Learning to Write
Before Learning to Read
By WILSON FOLLETT

scene was out of tune with an America in which Henry James, like Howells, could hear little else except the barbaric "rattle of gold." At Alden's invitation James in the summer of 1904 returned to the United States after an absence of more than twenty years to write an essay for the magazine setting forth his impressions of New York—what had become of the place and how it fared in comparison with Edwardian London and the French *Belle Époque*. The city's subway system opened in October of that year, and Mayor George B. McClellan invited 15,000 citizens, all of them presumably barbarians but many of them wearing top hats, to ride the first uptown trains from City Hall to West 145th Street. Workmen under the Hudson River completed the railroad tunnel joining the island of Manhattan to Jersey City and the American mainland, and in November Lt. Col. Teddy Roosevelt, lately of the Rough Riders and the victory at San Juan Hill, captured the White House and promptly announced his intention to chastise the malefactors of great wealth then resident in Wall Street.

James was predictably appalled by "the terrible town." Walking on lower Broadway in the vicinity of Franklin Square, he was moved to a feeling of pity for the "caged and dishonored condition" of Trinity Church mocked by the surrounding roar of commerce, "the new landmarks crushing the old quite as violent children stamp on snails and caterpillars." He gathered the impression of "dauntless power," of a pitiless energy so vast in scale that it dwarfed the literary imagination, and a "social sameness" that reduced all refinement of feeling or graciousness of manner to loud traffic in cheap publicity.

Alden and Howells approved the sentiment and mourned the loss. They remained in editorial office for another fifteen years (Alden dying in 1919, Howells in 1920), but their magazine was no match for the tide of events floating the brightly colored pavilions of their "genteel discourse" into the open sea of a new and violent century. The First World War began in August 1914; during the next twelve months *Harper's Magazine* refrained from publishing so much as a single paragraph about the unpleasantness on the Western Front.

In the spring of the year that Alden died, Woodrow Wilson was in Paris at the Peace Conference, and the well-to-do women in America were wearing clothes that wouldn't have been out of place in the first-class dining room of the *Titanic*. Their stately figures bound up in heavy silk and shaped by whalebone corsets to match the image of the "Gibson Girl," they had yet to receive the right to vote. Men wore high stiff collars, starched cuffs, top or bowler hats. Telephones were relatively rare, as were automobiles and houses furnished with the luxury of bathrooms. The dance orchestra at Delmonico's played "Dardanella" and "Shine on Harvest Moon," but if a young gentleman offered a young lady a cocktail, he stood instantly revealed as a scoundrel or a cad.

Two years later Warren Harding was president, and in the new speakeasies on New York's West Fifty-second Street, young girls in short dresses were drinking iced gin under potted palms, smoking Fatima cigarettes, and dancing to the music of Ted Snyder's "Sheik of Araby." Within the little span of what seemed like months, the "Roaring Twenties" came as suddenly to life as a showgirl rising from a cake. The war was over, and why not open the champagne.

Harding recommended a triumphant return to the noble truths of self-enrichment—"not revolution, but restoration; not agitation, but adjustment"—and the country was happy to take him at his word. The pitiless energy that had troubled Henry James found expression in record harvests of steel and grain, record outputs of tractors and Broadway musicals. Henry Ford's assembly lines delivered a new car every ten seconds, which was comparable to the rate of investment in stock market schemes guaranteed to put a chicken or a sucker in every American pot. Over the course of the decade corporate profits increased by 80 percent, the country doubled its miles of highway, Babe Ruth produced a record output of home runs, and on the newly sovereign silver screen Rudolph Valentino and Clara Bow bewitched a generation eager to give itself up as lost.

The presence of a new audience in what had become a new country obliged Thomas Bucklin Wells, the new editor of *Harper's Magazine,* to make revisions. The periodical was continuing to lose subscribers (down from 107,940 in 1915 to 76,675 in 1921), *Harper's Weekly* had ceased publication in 1916, and *The Saturday Evening Post,* the first American magazine to recruit a circulation of more than two million, was selling for five cents and supplying "visual description and interpretive sensibility" interleaved with advertisements for Coca-Cola instead of with cherubs blowing bubbles and strewing flowers.

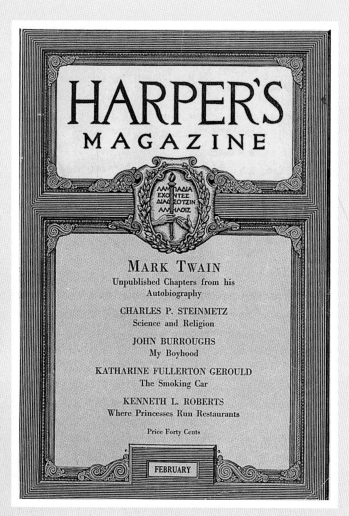

HARPER'S
MAGAZINE

MARK TWAIN
Unpublished Chapters from his
Autobiography

CHARLES P. STEINMETZ
Science and Religion

JOHN BURROUGHS
My Boyhood

KATHARINE FULLERTON GEROULD
The Smoking Car

KENNETH L. ROBERTS
Where Princesses Run Restaurants

Price Forty Cents

FEBRUARY

1922

Enter Atomic Power

June
Harpers
MAGAZINE

ENTER ATOMIC POWER
The Story of a Great Scientific Discovery
By JOHN J. O'NEILL

The Functions of a Teacher . . . . *Bertrand Russell*
Scorn and Comfort. *A Story* . . . . . . *Christopher La Farge*
He Flew in 1883 . . . . *Winsor Josselyn*
Social Security—Where Are We Now? . . . . *Abraham Epstein*
"They Write Worse and Worse" . . . . . *Adeline C. Bartlett*
   A Teacher of English Answers the Charge
J. D. Ross, Public Power Magnate . . . . *Carl Dreher*
Andy and the Village Virus. *A Story* . . . *Philip Curtiss*
The Millionth Map . . . . *Earl P. Hanson*
American Summer . . . . *Henry Seidel Canby*
A Small Boy in a Female College. *Part II* . . *John Andrew Rice*
Germany—The Voice from Within . . . . *Hans Schmidt*
   One Man's Meat . . . . *E. B. White*
   The Easy Chair—Ninetieth Anniversary . . *Bernard DeVoto*
   The New Books, by *John Chamberlain*; Personal and Otherwise

HARPER & BROTHERS, PUBLISHERS

Germany—the Voice from Within

1946

Wells chose to make virtue of necessity. Forty-four years old when he assumed responsibility for the magazine, Wells had been associated with Harper & Brothers since 1906 in the capacities of both editor and publisher. His interests were those of a journalist fluent in arithmetic, and guessing that it was pointless to chase the kind of polite reader likely to be satisfied with the genteel discourse as seen in *Vanity Fair* or *Vogue* (both publications new in the 1920's and shiny with Cecil Beaton's photographs of satin evening dresses), he imagined a conversation with people distinguished not only by their urbanity but also by what he defined, in an after-dinner speech, as their "concern for the national well-being"— i.e., readers apt to be familiar with the names of both Bertrand Russell and Cole Porter. He redrafted *Harper's Magazine* as a journal "primarily of appraisal and critical inquiry" (favoring the questions "Where are we, and what does it mean?" over "What is it, and how does it work?"), and in 1925 he deleted the illustrations, the rococo typography, and the cherubs. His sense of the market proved sound, as did his preference for authors as historically minded as H. G. Wells, Walter Lippmann, and Will Durant, and by 1929 the magazine had raised its circulation to 124,775 and its price to forty cents a copy. Harper & Brothers in the meantime had moved its several editorial offices from Franklin Square to a new six-story brick building on East Thirty-third Street, far enough uptown to allow Wells an easy walk to the Century Club for lunch with Edward Martin, the essayist in whose custody he had placed the writing of the "Easy Chair."

A former State Department official and founding editor of the *Harvard Lampoon*, Martin had been writing the column since 1920, addressing it to a broad range of public policy issues and presenting himself as "not a literary man." The disclaimer set him apart not only from Howells, his more famous predecessor, but also from the popular intellectual opinion of the day. The romance of a lost generation implicit in the novels of F. Scott Fitzgerald and Ernest Hemingway had prompted a good deal of posing in the attitudes of elegant despair, and the clumsy hypocrisies of the newly enriched business class (loud-mouthed, vulgar, badly dressed) offered easy occasions for the satires of Sinclair Lewis and Ezra Pound. Minor poets drinking absinthe in the bar of the Algonquin Hotel expressed their finer sensibilities with exquisite witticisms about America making the world safe for F. W. Woolworth and George Follansbee Babbitt.

Wells and Martin were more interested in what the idealistic Anne Lynch undoubtedly would have recognized as the advancing tide of civilization and the fertilizing flood of mass production. They looked upon the extravagance of the *nouveau riche* with cheerful irony, in much the same way they took for granted the cowardice of politicians and the enthusiasm of marathon dancers, but they didn't doubt the energy and inventiveness of the American people. The national political experiment they regarded as a work in progress, still subject to further amendment and not yet all that one might hope, but in the meantime "a school for democracy" that compelled its citizens to think for themselves, to train and educate their collective opinion in such a way that what "comes out of it shall be sound and wise and helpful." Martin objected to Prohibition because he thought it always a mistake to grant clergymen any kind of authority over the "lives and property of their fellow-creatures," and the crime and "calamitous disorder" associated with the traffic in bootleg whiskey he attributed to the folly of attempting "to remake the people to suit the laws." As construed by Martin and revised by Wells, the magazine reacquired the habit of constructive political thought and renewed Henry Raymond's effort to "dissipate the fogs of error" that still tended, even in the prosperous and enlightened 1920's, "to cloud the public mind." The optimistic intention provided the publication with its dominant editorial character during the nearly fifty years between the America that mourned the death of Woodrow Wilson and the America that assassinated Robert Kennedy and Martin Luther King.

The editors who succeeded Wells—Lee Foster Hartman (1931–1941), Frederick Lewis Allen (1941–1953), and John Fischer (1953–1967)—shared his understanding of their common enterprise as a set of improvisations on the theme of informed dissent. Revolutionary in the sense that they knew that all things change much more quickly than people like to suppose, they carried forward the American quarrel with Providence by questioning whatever temporary wisdom chanced to have been elected to political or literary office.

During the years in which the country was engaged with the sorrows of the Great Depression, the consequences of Franklin Roosevelt's "New Deal," and the conduct of the Second World War, the magazine found the clearest expression of its purpose in the voice of Bernard DeVoto, the essayist and historian who succeeded Martin in the "Easy Chair" in 1935. The author of fifteen books, among them *Mark Twain's America, Across the Wide Missouri,* and a five-volume history of the American West, for which he received both the Bancroft and the Pulitzer prizes, DeVoto wore his convictions on his sleeve. Not a man to mince words, he refused to cooperate with the investigations loosed upon the citizenry by the House Un-American Activities Committee in 1949 on the ground that "I like a country where it's nobody's damned business what magazine anybody reads, what he thinks, whom he has cocktails with. I like a country where we do not have to stuff the chimney against listening ears. . . . We had that kind of country only a little while ago and I'm for getting it back. It was a lot less scared than the one we've got now."

Born in 1897 in Ogden, Utah, under the western slope of the Wasatch Mountains, the son of a Mormon father and a Catholic mother (both apostate), DeVoto attended public high school and Harvard University before settling, in 1927, in Cambridge, Massachusetts. Like Raymond and Curtis, he took an active part in political affairs. Often in Washington to lobby Congress on behalf of the national forests and public lands, he wrote testimony for the Department of the Interior and policy papers for Adlai Stevenson's 1952 presidential campaign. His presence in the East strengthened his fierce affection for the West, and his writing is everywhere marked by poignant remembrance of western landscapes, western grasses, western animals and birds.

The composition of the "Easy Chair" DeVoto looked upon as the first of what he called his "private assignments." The column was remarkable not only for the broad range of its topics (the improper manufacture of kitchen knives and the proper blending of a martini, dust storms in Kansas and the fascist blueprint of Adolf Hitler's thousand-year Reich, the Mexican War, Huey Long, sagebrush, and the Normandy invasion) but also for the varied inflections of phrase (poetic, mocking, philosophical) with which DeVoto emptied the slops of ridicule on the heads of imbecile journalists and nervous politicians. He detested flag-waving patriots, thought Harry Truman too conservative in his politics and Thomas Wolfe too liberal with his adjectives, regarded Gertrude Stein's bleak and ornamental prose as "an art which floated freely in a medium of pure caprice sustained by nothing except its awareness of its own inner wondrousness." Usually at odds with his peers in the intellectual professions, especially those among them who complained about the crass materialism of American society, he once said, "There is something intrinsically absurd in the image of a literary man informing 120 million people that their ideals are base, their beliefs unworthy, their ideas vulgar, their institutions corrupt, and, in sum, their civilization too trivial to engage that literary man's respect."

Much of the same spirit that informed DeVoto's attitudes toward literature and politics showed up in the character of the magazine edited by Frederick Lewis Allen, who was also an historian, and whose chronicle of the 1920's, *Only Yesterday,* proved so successful that it set what has since become the standard style and form for the writing of popular history. A good many of Allen's contemporaries in the late 1930's translated the miseries of the Depression into an apology for Marxism, but he thought their arguments confounded "not by dogma, but by the logic of advanced capitalism itself; or, to put it another way, by capitalism turned to democratic ends." Impressed by the scale of the American achievement and fond of measuring the improved standards of living brought about by "a genius that was not static but venturesome," Allen thought the leftist side of the argument occupied by people "reacting angrily" to the news in the morning papers of 1901. As an editor he often rewrote manuscripts that he deemed insufficient to their purpose, and he tended to favor authors (among them John Kenneth Galbraith, Dorothy Thompson, James Thurber, and E. B. White) suspicious of ideological doctrine and revealed truth. *Harper's Magazine* in the late 1940's was selling for fifty cents a copy at a circulation of 145,000, and once when Allen was asked to speak to its bias, he said that it had little use for the public relations counselor and the official announcement, choosing to reserve its trust for the individual observer "who sits all by himself, unorganized, unrecognized, unorthodox and unterrified."

Allen died in 1954, DeVoto in 1955, and both the editorship of the magazine and the occupancy of the "Easy Chair" passed to John Fischer, who had been in charge of trade-book publishing at Harper & Brothers.

His long-standing friendship with his two predecessors was founded on common traits of character and qualities of mind. Like DeVoto, he had been born and raised west of the Mississippi River, on the high plains of the Texas and Oklahoma panhandles, where as a boy of ten he knew how to butcher cattle, string barbed wire, grease windmills, build barns; in the 1930's he had worked for Henry Wallace in the Department of Agriculture, during the Second World War for the American intelligence services in India and Washington. Admiring the same kind of enterprise in other people, Fischer crowded the magazine with what he regarded as useful suggestions from writers as different as Arnold Toynbee, Barbara Tuchman, and James Baldwin. Like Allen, he was a tinkerer with manuscripts and the models of human possibility, preferring the man who could accomplish a number of different tasks with a high degree of competence to the virtuoso who could perform only one trick with exceptional brilliance. On the frontier, virtuosos tended to be something of a nuisance. They seldom could shoe horses, and they weren't much good with common nouns.

Fischer knew enough about the workings of democracy to know that quite ordinary people had the tools in hand to better their lot if only they had the wit to understand them and the will to use them properly, and he liked to travel around the country as if he were riding circuit around a large farm, stopping here and there to inquire about the price of corn and the condition of the roads. If the people in Scranton, Pennsylvania, had found a way to improve their drainage or their schools, then perhaps there was a lesson to be learned for people in Mississippi or Michigan. More often than not, Fischer's "Easy Chair" essays read like a frontier scout's reports to the main party, and every December he published his "Christmas List," in which he celebrated the deeds of particular individuals who, in the previous year, had done something to make their fellow citizens "a little more comfortable, civilized, or light-hearted."

So generous a way of looking at the world didn't survive the shouting of the 1960's. Fischer found himself out of sympathy with street demonstrations and psychedelic flowers, also with Bob Dylan's harmonica and what was being touted as the genius of the New Journalism; knowing that the magazine's relevance depended upon its being attuned to the music of its times, he resigned as editor in 1967 and named Willie Morris, one of his younger associates, as his successor. Morris was thirty-two years old and already the much-praised author of a precocious autobiography, *North Toward Home*, in which he told the story of his childhood in Yazoo City, Mississippi, and his coming to the New York literary stage by way of the University of Texas and a Rhodes scholarship at Oxford. Fischer retired to a farmhouse in Connecticut, where he continued to write the "Easy Chair" and distribute his annual awards for good citizenship; Morris in Manhattan printed the investigative reporting of Seymour Hersh and David Halberstam as well as the confessions of Norman Mailer and William Styron. The magazine in the meantime had acquired a new owner, passing in 1965 from its parent publisher, by then known as Harper & Row, to the *Minneapolis Star and Tribune*. John Cowles, Jr., the principal stockholder in both the newspaper and the publishing house, established the magazine as a separate company and raised the newsstand price from sixty to seventy-five cents a copy and the circulation from 283,601 to 411,445 by acquiring the subscription list of another periodical, *The Reporter*, which had been forced into bankruptcy in the summer of 1968. A new cover design substituted full-bleed photographs for what had come to be seen as stodgy lines of print, and a spendthrift promotion budget bought poster space in Grand Central station and the commuter trains moving north toward Stamford and Darien.

The strategy matched the go-go expectations of the Age of Aquarius, and for two or three years it seemed to hold out the promise of astonishing success. Morris published Mailer's dispatches from the riots in Miami and Chicago, the literary criticism of Alfred Kazin and Irving Howe, Halberstam's excoriations of the deluded government officials (a.k.a. "The Best and the Brightest") mismanaging the war in Vietnam. The magazine was much talked about in New York, proclaimed a wonder of the age in drawing rooms on the Upper East Side. Elsewhere in the country the reviews were not so kind. West of the Hudson River subscribers departed in droves, the advertising revenue declined, most of the newsstand copies were being shredded or returned. The poor result reflected the several degrees of separation in the nation's attitude toward the Vietnam War, drugs, radical college students, black power, free-form feminists, and long hair.

The 1960's were about having it both ways—a reputation for principled objection and first-class hotel suites

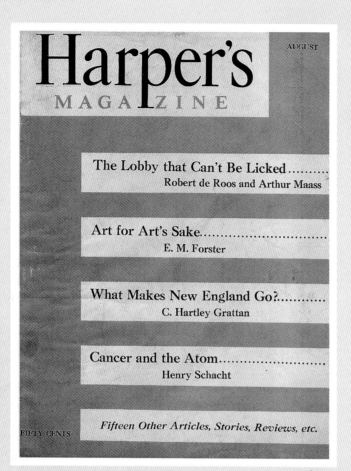

Harper's
MAGAZINE

AUGUST

The Lobby that Can't Be Licked..........
Robert de Roos and Arthur Maass

Art for Art's Sake....................
E. M. Forster

What Makes New England Go?...........
C. Hartley Grattan

Cancer and the Atom.........................
Henry Schacht

Fifteen Other Articles, Stories, Reviews, etc.

FIFTY CENTS

1949

FEBRUARY 1957 ▸ FIFTY CENTS

Harper's
magazine

HOW SAFE ARE THE NEW CARS? by Paul W. Kearney

Philadelphia Does It:
The Battle for Penn Center
James Reichley

Unnoticed Changes in America
D. W. Brogan

South Carolina's Incurable Aristocrats
William Francis Guess

Inside Russia's Treasure House
Sterling A. Callisen

1957

at the political conventions, a publisher's advance extended to six figures, and a blue work shirt signifying the author's contempt for money. The putative champions of liberty took up the cry of dissent only after it had become profitable and safe, denunciations of the Vietnam War when the students were already in the streets, sentiments in favor of the Civil Rights Movement when they had become the stuff of corporate advertising.

Most of the magazine's long-term subscribers assumed (as did Fischer, DeVoto, and Raymond) that intellectuals were indebted to society and therefore obliged to apply their knowledge to its service. Why else had they been sent to universities, and how else did they propose to find a use for books? Morris enlisted a company of writers who regarded the society's principal institutions (schools as well as government) as their natural enemies, which was a brave and noble pose and maybe even true, but not one that sold a lot of copies in Detroit. The accounting at the end of 1970 showed an annual loss of what was then the impressive sum of $700,000, the paid circulation well below 300,000, and the magazine reconstituted, for tax purposes, as a division of the *Minneapolis Star and Tribune*. Blaming Cowles for the unwelcome news, Morris abruptly resigned in March 1971, and for the next thirteen years the magazine drifted through a period of financial and editorial instability. Cowles retained ownership until 1980, but by then the losses were approaching two million dollars a year, and the managers of his newspaper no longer wished to pay the bills. They declared the magazine extinct in early June, but the MacArthur Foundation in Chicago—at the urging of John R. MacArthur, the founder's grandson and the present publisher—revived it in time to make the next month's deadlines. Two years later the publication was again reconstituted as the small and entirely independent entity, the nonprofit Harper's Magazine Foundation, now sustained by its own advertising and subscription revenues.

The several changes of management blurred the magazine's editorial focus and scattered the stores of memory accumulated by a succession of like-minded editors who learned from one another and tended to stay at their desks for at least ten years. Between 1967 and 1983 the magazine employed four editors of very different character—Morris, Robert Schnayerson (1971–1975), Lewis H. Lapham (1975–1981), Michael Kinsley (1981–1983)—none of whom remained on the premises long enough to form a clear understanding of what it was they were expected to do. It wasn't that they didn't know the difference between good writing and bad. The magazine during their collected tenure published the essays of Annie Dillard and Murray Kempton (also the observations of John Fowles, Alice Walker, Gabriel García Márquez, George Plimpton, Arthur Schlesinger, Jr., and Philip Roth), but it lacked a distinctive editorial character. To whom was the magazine addressed, and what could be found in its pages that couldn't be found on other racks in the same airport newsstand?

Some of the confusion followed from the magazine's financial trouble, but much of it was associated with the rapid series of changes that had begun to reshape the country's systems of communication during the decade of the 1960's. Prior to the election of President John F. Kennedy it was still possible to make distinctions between the various forms of what were then known as the lively arts. Their various audiences recognized the difference between journalism, opera, politics, and the movies, and a presidential candidate wasn't expected to run on stage in the costume of an actor or a clown. Over the next twenty years the distinctions dissolved into the alloys of "the media." Marshall McLuhan in 1964 published his famous book on the subject, observing that the grammar of print didn't bear literal translation into the electronic languages of television and cyberspace. Content followed form, and new ways of looking at the world gave rise to new structures of feeling and thought. As the lines between fact and fiction became as irrelevant as they were hard to distinguish, journalists began to claim the executive privileges of novelists *manqué*. The presumption allowed them to arrange the materials at hand (descriptions of scene, tones of voice, fragments of conversation, impressions of character, etc.) into whatever designs attracted the most applause and the highest fees. Substituting the veneer of style for the weight of evidence, and making few transitions between subject and object (the interviewer being as important as, often more important than, the interviewee), they presented their own advertisements for reality as literal renderings of the world of historical event.

News was entertainment and entertainment news, and a mixed media encouraged the telling of political fairy tales. Among his other gifts to a not always grateful

American people, the late President Richard M. Nixon had provided them with an abbreviation that came to stand as an acronym for any and all forms of government corruption. Twenty years after he was frog-marched out of the White House, the single word "Watergate" brought to mind not only the burglaries at the building of that name but also the subsequent impeachment proceedings in Congress, the failure of the Vietnam War, the assassinations of Robert Kennedy and Martin Luther King, Jr., and the general loss of belief in the decency of government and the goodness of politicians. Fondly remembered as a kind of film montage borrowing a series of images from the years 1968–1974 (the face of Sam Irvin superimposed on the faces of H. R. Haldeman and Archibald Cox, Henry Kissinger's voice mixed with the sound of incoming artillery at Da Nang, clouds of tear gas drifting across college lawns and the steps of the Pentagon), the sequence of meanings associated with Watergate added to the sum of innocence betrayed. Before Watergate the realm of politics was a land of orchards and sweet-running streams; after Watergate the realm of politics was a swamp inhabited by foul and crawling things.

Prior to 1968 most politicians were presumed trustworthy until proven guilty of fraud or discovered with a striptease dancer in a Virginia hotel. Maybe not all of them were as handsome as Jimmy Stewart in the movie *Mr. Smith Goes to Washington,* and quite possibly most of them couldn't qualify as Eagle Scouts, but, by and large and all things considered, they were thought to know the difference between the public interest and their own, and they weren't the kind of people who tapped telephones or volunteered to push their grandmothers in front of a bus. After 1974 it was assumed that any Mr. Smith who went to Washington brought with him the modus operandi of a racetrack tout and the morals of a stoat. The fashionable celebration of government became the equally fashionable abuse of government. The collective rapture of the Peace Corps gave way to the collective rapture of a race riot in Detroit, and the stagehands in the media theaters took down the brightly painted scenes of the Pax Americana and replaced them with the posters of Dylan and Che.

If the years between 1960 and 1968 established the thesis of the 1960's (Camelot), the years from 1968 to 1974 developed the antithesis (Watergate). The two periods presented mirror images of each other, and just as President John F. Kennedy embodied the persona of the American state as luminous romance, President Nixon embodied the persona of the American state as dismal melodrama. The split-screen technique set up a bull market for two kinds of rhetorical dry goods—the low-grade cynicism out of which the news media manufactured the proofs of political scandal and the equally low-grade moralism out of which a succession of would-be philosopher kings (university professors and radio-talk-show hosts) shaped the promises of political redemption.

Jimmy Carter in 1976 campaigned for the presidency in the robes of a Christian saint, barefoot and without guile, wandering around the country in search of a government as good as its people. His spiritualization of the issues argued that the business of governing the American republic mattered less than the mending of the American soul. In place of a vision of the future, Carter offered the memory of a nonexistent past, promising to restore the American supremacy, temporal as well as spiritual, to a condition of imaginary grace.

Before Carter had been in office for even one term, the television audience tired of his sermons and his constant fretting about the national "malaise." The voters turned away from him as if from a coroner's report and embraced their new savior in the person of Ronald Reagan, who also promised a triumphant return to a nonexistent past, but who did so with an actor's smile and the substitution of happy problems for sad problems. He presented himself as the candidate bringing hope, faith, freedom, and easy money to an electorate sorely in need of good news and foreign loans.

As the electronic media acquired authority over what once had been constituted as the republic of American letters, new means of production and distribution forced the reorganization of the book and magazine trades. Venerable publishing houses transformed themselves into film and television syndicates; *The Saturday Evening Post* ceased to exist, as did *Look* and *Collier's;* bookstores aspired to the excitement of county fairs; authors sought the approval not of critics but of talk-show hosts. Prominent scientific and political persons who in 1958 might have presented their opinions as long magazine articles converted their expression to the shorter forms of the television interview and the newspaper op-ed piece. The realm of the "public

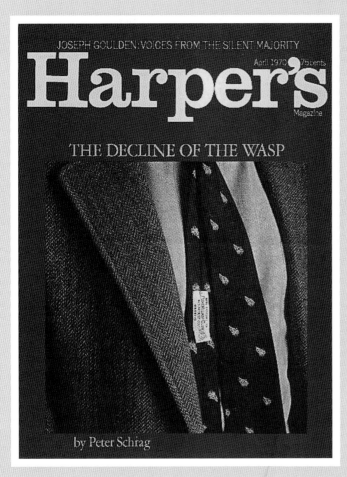

JOSEPH GOULDEN: VOICES FROM THE SILENT MAJORITY

Harper's
Magazine

April 1970 / 75 cents

THE DECLINE OF THE WASP

by Peter Schrag

1970

■ HARPER'S MAGAZINE   MARCH 1984   TWO DOLLARS ■

HARPER'S

DOES AMERICA STILL EXIST?
Looking for Reasons to Believe

Robert Stone   Louis L'Amour   Robert Nisbet
Michael Harrington, and others

GRENADA: AN ISLAND BETRAYED
By V.S. Naipaul

THE RISE OF THE VERBAL CLASS
By Joseph Epstein

SMALL TOWN GROTESQUES
By John Updike

Also: Remarks by Daniel Patrick Moynihan, Hugh Kenner,
Kurt Vonnegut, Leo Steinberg, and Tom Stoppard

interest" disintegrated into the provinces of special interest, each with its own newsletter, marketing plan, and subscription list. The theory of a "national discourse" didn't account for the deconstruction of what was once a common language spoken by Alden's polite audience (i.e., "people of wealth and importance") into regional dialects spoken by the sets and subsets of the "educated class"—historian to historian, weapons analyst to weapons analyst, divorce lawyer to divorce lawyer.

By the late summer of 1983, the year that I was granted a second chance to edit *Harper's Magazine*, the marvels of postmodern communication were dividing the whole spectrum of the country's political, literary, scientific, and business enterprise into remote images receding from one another literally at the speed of light. To what the magazine's first editors had seen as the "multiplied and ephemeral pages" of a periodical press "intermingled with much that is of merely local and transient interest," the newer forms of media had added not only cable channels, CD-ROM, and the beginnings of the Internet but also little kingdoms of virtual reality posted on blimps and office buildings. How then to address what the brothers Harper had perceived as the "commonwealth of shared meaning," and if the curtain was again going up on a brave new world, where did one look first, and what was the perspective that afforded the clearest view?

During my first term as editor I often had asked the questions of Jack Fischer, and he had encouraged me to study the history of *Harper's Magazine*, to become acquainted not only with the maxims of his tutors, Allen and DeVoto, but also with the earlier observations of Howells, Curtis, and Raymond. Their writings reflected a remarkably similar temperament, and in each of their voices I could hear overtones of all the others. Rebecca West, the British journalist briefly married to H. G. Wells, remarked on the effect in an essay that she wrote in 1950 for the magazine's centennial issue:

> The consistent character which *Harper's* has maintained through the century—it is as like itself as a man is at the different stages of a highly-accidented life—suggests that integrity is something which one can count on to be shown by some people in vastly different circumstances; and an agreeable flavor about that character suggests that maybe

these people cultivate integrity because they find it fun.

Since 1984 the fun mostly has been found in the discovery of individual observers, "unorthodox and unterrified," trying to tell the truth about the nature of their own experience, their own feeling, their own thought. Not the self-dramatizations of celebrity journalism but writers with courage enough to have made the acquaintance of their own minds and willing to undertake a close reading of the facts at hand. The task never has been as easy as it seems, but the accelerated data streams of the information and entertainment media add to the degrees of difficulty. The electronic forms of communication eliminate the dimensions of space and time and erode the presumption of cause and effect. In the lotusland of the eternal now all the world's joy and suffering is always and everywhere present (if not on CNN or *Oprah*, then on the *Sunday Night Movie*, at www.whitehouse.gov, or with a 900 number answering to the name of Domino), and the solo voice of the unorganized individual disappears into the void of a collective and corporate consciousness, which, as McLuhan well knew, doesn't "postulate consciousness of anything in particular."

The more efficient and expensive the machinery, the poorer and smaller the meaning. The future comes and goes as quickly as yesterday's headline, before anybody has time to remember what it was supposed to be about, and the news appears as such a familiar montage—the same footage, the same words, the same official spokesman—that we know that what was said last week will be said again this week, and then next week and once again six weeks from now. Only the camera angles change. Nor do the smaller journals of literary and political argument offer a much more imaginative view of events. They depend for their existence on their loyalty to the dogma espoused by their patrons, and they become as predictable in their apologetics as the sermons of Pat Robertson. The automatous media say everything and hear nothing, and behind their gaudy facades they can't quite hide their profound silence. The machines make a wonderful noise, but to whom do they speak, and in what language?

The wizards of Oz who operate the machinery of the omnipresent media come to imagine that they already know all the answers worth knowing, and they tend to choose images that match their prerecorded programs of the world. *Harper's Magazine* as it was redesigned in 1984 stands on the proposition that it knows not nearly enough about what its first editors described as "the varied intellectual movements of this most stirring and productive age." In line with the magazine's long-standing assumption that a working democracy requires as many questions as possible directed to the wisdoms in office, the authors appearing in its pages over the last sixteen years, among them Walter Karp, David Mamet, Mary Gaitskill, and Tom Wolfe, proceed on the premise that it is their business to open the view surprisingly out, not to wrap it neatly up. The revised compendium offers texts meant to incite acts of the imagination rather than facilitate the transfers of data, not to provide ready-made answers but to say, in effect, look at this, see how much more beautiful and strange and full of possibility is the world than can be dreamed of by the mythographers at NBC and *Time*.

As an editor subject to the arrivals of the mail, I have the chance every morning at ten o'clock to confront the spectacle of my own ignorance. The same opportunity undoubtedly presents itself to people in most other professions, but in a magazine office the encounter takes place at the moment when I sit down to a desk mobbed by five newspapers and as many as seven periodicals (three of them concerned with political affairs, the others with economic, environmental, or weapons systems), two books as yet unpublished (one of them about cyberspace, the other about feminism or Japan), a public-opinion poll sifting the national attitudes toward family values and assault weapons, three reports from charitable foundations—all of them about the meager funding available to one or another of the arts—and at least fifteen manuscripts, solicited and unsolicited, whose authors assure me in their accompanying letters that they have discovered, among other items of interest, the motive for the Kennedy assassinations and the secret of the universe.

Although I count myself a reasonably well-educated man, I cannot hope to make sense of each of these announcements, and so on first opening a book or looking into a manuscript I listen for the sound of a human voice. I think of all writing—whether cast in the form of the historical essay, the scientific treatise, or the minimalist poem—as an attempt to tell a story. Some stories are more complicated or beautiful than others. Some stories are immortal; many are false or incoherent. Homer told a story and so did Einstein; so does General Motors and Donald Duck. But no matter how well or how poorly we manage the narrative, we are all engaged in the same enterprise, all of us caught up in the making of metaphors, all of us seeking evocations or representations of what we can recognize as appropriately human.

Several years ago on the editorial page of the *New York Times* I noticed the complacent announcement that "great publications magnify beyond measure the voice of any single writer." The sentence employed the wrong verb. The instruments of the media multiply or amplify a voice, serving much the same purpose as a loudspeaker in a ballpark or a prison. What magnifies a voice is its human character, its compassion, honesty, and intelligence, and against the weight of things as they are the best resource is the imaginative labor of trying to tell the truth. Not, as has been said, an easy task, but the courage required of the teller, if he or she seriously attempts it—and the emotions called forth in the reader, if he or she recognizes the attempt as a serious one—increases, as the four brothers Harper long ago intended, the common stores of energy and hope.

1850's

THE TOWN-HO'S STORY

BY HERMAN MELVILLE

OCTOBER 1851

The Cape of Good Hope, and all the watery region round about there, is much like some noted four corners of a great highway, where you meet more travelers than in any other part.

It was not very long after speaking the Goney that another homeward-bound whaleman, the Town-Ho, was encountered. She was manned almost wholly by Polynesians. In the short gam that ensued she gave us strong news of Moby Dick. To some the general interest in the White Whale was now wildly heightened by a circumstance of the Town-Ho's story, which seemed obscurely to involve with the whale a certain wondrous, inverted visitation of one of those so called judgments of God which at times are said to overtake some men. This latter circumstance, with its own particular accompaniments, forming what may be called the secret part of the tragedy about to be narrated, never reached the ears of Captain Ahab or his mates. For that secret part of the story was unknown to the captain of the Town-Ho himself. It was the private property of three confederate white seamen of that ship, one of whom, it seems, communicated it to Tashtego with Romish injunctions of secresy, but the following night Tashtego rambled in his sleep, and revealed so much of it in that way, that when he was awakened he could not well withhold the rest. Nevertheless, so potent an influence did this thing have on those seamen in the Pequod who came to the full knowledge of it, and by such a strange delicacy, to call it so, were they governed in this matter, that they kept the secret among themselves so that it never transpired abaft the Pequod's mainmast. Interweaving in its proper place this darker thread with the story as publicly narrated on the ship, the whole of this strange affair I now proceed to put on lasting record.

For my humor's sake, I shall preserve the style in which I once narrated it at Lima, to a lounging circle of my

Editors' Note: This story appeared in Melville's novel Moby-Dick, which was then in the press of Harper & Brothers.

Spanish friends, one saint's eve, smoking upon the thick-gilt tiled piazza of the Golden Inn. Of those fine cavaliers, the young Dons, Pedro and Sebastian, were on the closer terms with me; and hence the interluding questions they occasionally put, and which are duly answered at the time.

"Some two years prior to my first learning the events which I am about rehearsing to you, gentlemen, the Town-Ho, Sperm Whaler of Nantucket, was cruising in your Pacific here, not very many days' sail eastward from the eaves of this good Golden Inn. She was somewhere to the northward of the Line. One morning upon handling the pumps, according to daily usage, it was observed that she made more water in her hold than common. They supposed a swordfish had stabbed her, gentlemen. But the captain, having some unusual reason for believing that rare good luck awaited him in those latitudes; and therefore being very averse to quit them, and the leak not being then considered at all dangerous, though, indeed, they could not find it after searching the hold as low down as was possible in rather heavy weather, the ship still continued her cruisings, the mariners working at the pumps at wide and easy intervals; but no good luck came; more days went by, and not only was the leak yet undiscovered, but it sensibly increased. So much so, that now taking some alarm, the captain, making all sail, stood away for the nearest harbor among the islands, there to have his hull hove out and repaired.

"Though no small passage was before her, yet, if the commonest chance favored, he did not at all fear that his ship would founder by the way, because his pumps were of the best, and being periodically relieved at them, those six-and-thirty men of his could easily keep the ship free; never mind if the leak should double on her. In truth, well nigh the whole of this passage being attended by very prosperous breezes, the Town-Ho had all but certainly arrived in perfect safety at her port without the occurrence of the least fatality, had it not been for the brutal overbearing of Radney, the

Pursuit of the sperm whale.

mate, a Vineyarder, and the bitterly provoked vengeance of Steelkilt, a Lakeman and desperado from Buffalo.

"'Lakeman!—Buffalo! Pray, what is a Lakeman, and where is Buffalo?' said Don Sebastian, rising in his swinging mat of grass.

"On the eastern shore of our Lake Erie, Don; but—I crave your courtesy—may be, you shall soon hear further of all that. Now, gentlemen, in square-sail brigs and three-masted ships, well nigh as large and stout as any that ever sailed out of your old Callao to far Manilla; this Lakeman, in the land-locked heart of our America, had yet been nurtured by all those agrarian freebooting impressions popularly connected with the open ocean. For in their interflowing aggregate, those grand fresh-water seas of ours—Erie, and Ontario, and Huron, and Superior, and Michigan—possess an ocean-like expansiveness, with many of the ocean's noblest traits; with many of its rimmed varieties of races and of climes. They contain round archipelagoes of romantic isles, even as the Polynesian waters do; in large part, are shored by two great contrasting nations, as the Atlantic is; they furnish long maritime approaches to our numerous territorial colonies from the East, dotted all round their banks; here and there are frowned upon by batteries, and by the goat-like craggy guns of lofty Mackinaw; they have heard the fleet thunderings of naval victories; at intervals, they yield their beaches to wild barbarians, whose red painted faces flash from out their peltry wigwams; for leagues and leagues are flanked by ancient and unentered forests, where the gaunt pines stand like serried lines of kings in Gothic genealogies; those same woods harboring wild Afric beasts of prey, and silken creatures whose exported furs give robes to Tartar Emperors; they mirror the paved capitals of Buffalo and Cleveland, as well as Winnebago villages; they float alike the full-rigged merchant ship, the armed cruiser of the State, the steamer, and the beech canoe; they are swept by Borean and dismasting blasts as direful as any that lash the salted wave; they know what shipwrecks are, for out of sight of land, however inland, they have drowned full many a midnight ship with all its shrieking crew. Thus, gentlemen, though an inlander, Steelkilt was wild-ocean born, and wild-ocean nurtured; as much of an audacious mariner as any. And for Radney, though in his infancy he may have laid him down on the lone Nantucket beach, to nurse at his maternal sea; though in after life he had long followed our austere Atlantic and your contemplative Pacific; yet was he quite as vengeful and full of social quarrel as the backwoods seaman, fresh from the latitudes of buck-horn handled Bowie-knives. Yet was this Nantucketer a man with some good-hearted traits; and this Lakeman, a mariner, who though a sort of devil indeed, might yet by inflexible firmness, only tempered by that common decency of human recognition which is the meanest slave's right; thus treated, this Steelkilt had long been retained harmless and docile. At all events, he had proved so thus far; but Radney was doomed and made mad, and Steelkilt—but, gentlemen, you shall hear.

"It was not more than a day or two at the furthest after pointing her prow for her island haven, that the Town-Ho's leak seemed again increasing, but only so as to require an hour or more at the pumps every day. You must know that in a settled and civilized ocean like our Atlantic, for example, some skippers think little of pumping their whole way across it; though of a still, sleepy night, should the officer of the deck happen to forget his duty in that respect, the probability would be that he and his shipmates would never again remember it, on account of all hands gently subsiding to the bottom. Nor in the solitary and savage seas far from you to the westward, gentlemen, is it altogether unusual for ships to keep clanging at their pump-handles in full chorus even for a voyage of considerable length; that is, if it lie along a tolerably accessible coast, or if any other reasonable retreat is afforded them. It is only when a leaky vessel is in some very out of the way part of those waters, some really landless latitude, that her captain begins to feel a little anxious.

"Much this way had it been with the Town-Ho; so when her leak was found gaining once more, there was in truth some small concern manifested by several of her company; especially by Radney the mate. He commanded the upper sails to be well hoisted, sheeted home anew, and every way expanded to the breeze. Now this Radney, I suppose, was as little of a coward, and as little inclined to any sort of nervous apprehensiveness touching his own person as any fearless, unthinking creature on land or on sea that you can conveniently imagine, gentlemen. Therefore when he betrayed this solicitude about the safety of the ship, some of the seamen declared that it was only on account of his being a part owner in her. So when they were working that evening at the pumps, there was on this head no small gamesomeness slily going on among them, as they stood with their feet continually overflowed by the rippling clear water; clear as any mountain spring, gentlemen—that bubbling from the pumps ran across the deck, and poured itself out in steady spouts at the lee scupperholes.

"Now, as you well know, it is not seldom the case in this conventional world of ours—watery or otherwise; that when a person placed in command over his fellow-men finds one of them to be very significantly his superior in general pride of manhood, straightway against that man he conceives an unconquerable dislike and bitterness; and if he have a chance he will pull down and pulverize that subaltern's tower, and make a little heap of dust of it. Be this conceit of mine as it may, gentlemen, at all events Steelkilt was a tall and noble animal with a head like a Roman, and a flowing golden beard like the tasseled housings of your last viceroy's snorting charger; and a brain, and a heart, and a soul in him, gentlemen, which had made Steelkilt Charlemagne, had he been born son to Charlemagne's father. But Radney, the mate, was ugly as a mule; yet as hardy, as stubborn, as malicious. He did not love Steelkilt, and Steelkilt knew it.

"Espying the mate drawing near as he was toiling at the pump with the rest, the Lakeman affected not to notice him, but unawed, went on with his gay banterings.

"'Ay, ay, my merry lads, it's a lively leak this; hold a cannikin, one of ye, and let's have a taste. By the Lord, it's worth bottling! I tell ye what, men, old Rad's investment must go for it! he had best cut away his part of the hull and tow it home. The fact is, boys, that sword-fish only began the job; he's come back again with a gang of ship-carpenters, saw-fish, and file-fish, and what not; and the whole posse of 'em are now hard at work cutting and slashing at the bottom; making improvements, I suppose. If old Rad were here now, I'd tell him to jump overboard and scatter 'em. They're playing the devil with his estate, I can tell him. But he's a simple old soul—Rad, and a beauty, too. Boys, they say the rest of his property is invested in looking-glasses. I wonder if he'd give a poor devil like me the model of his nose.'

"'Damn your eyes! what's that pump stopping for?' roared Radney, pretending not to have heard the sailors' talk. 'Thunder away at it!'

"'Ay, ay, sir,' said Steelkilt, merry as a cricket. 'Lively, boys, lively, now! And with that the pump clanged like fifty fire-engines; the men tossed their hats off to it, and ere long that peculiar gasping of the lungs was heard which denotes the fullest tension of life's utmost energies.

"Quitting the pump at last, with the rest of his band, the Lakeman went forward all panting, and sat himself down on the windlass; his face fiery red, his eyes bloodshot, and wiping the profuse sweat from his brow. Now what cozening fiend it was, gentlemen, that possessed Radney to meddle with such a man in that corporeally exasperated state, I know not; but so it happened. Intolerably striding along the deck, the mate commanded him to get a broom and sweep down the planks, and also a shovel, and remove some offensive matters consequent upon allowing a pig to run at large.

"Now, gentlemen, sweeping a ship's deck at sea is a piece of household work which in all times but raging gales is regularly attended to every evening; it has been known to be done in the case of ships actually foundering at the time. Such, gentlemen, is the inflexibility of sea-usages and the instinctive love of neatness in seamen; some of whom would not willingly drown without first washing their faces. But in all vessels this broom business is the prescriptive province of the boys, if boys there be aboard. Besides, it was the stronger men in the Town-Ho that had been divided into gangs, taking turns at the pumps; and being the most athletic seaman of them all, Steelkilt had been regularly assigned captain of one of the gangs; consequently he should have been freed from any trivial business not connected with truly nautical duties, such being the case with his comrades. I mention all these particulars so that you may understand exactly how this affair stood between the two men.

"But there was more than this: the order about the shovel was almost as plainly meant to sting and insult Steelkilt, as though Radney had spat in his face. Any man who has gone sailor in a whale-ship will understand this; and all this and doubtless much more, the Lakeman fully comprehended when the mate uttered his command. But as he sat still for a moment, and as he steadfastly looked into the mate's malignant eye and perceived the stacks of powder-casks heaped up in him and the slow match silently burning along toward them; as he instinctively saw all this, that strange forbearance and unwillingness to stir up the deeper passionateness in any already ireful being—a repugnance most felt, when felt at all, by really valiant men even when aggrieved—this nameless phantom feeling, gentlemen, stole over Steelkilt.

"Therefore, in his ordinary tone, only a little broken by the bodily exhaustion he was temporarily in, he answered him, saying that sweeping the deck was not his business, and he would not do it. And then, without at all alluding to the shovel, he pointed to three lads as the customary sweepers; who, not being billeted at the pumps, had done little or nothing all day. To this, Radney replied with an oath, in a most domineering and outrageous manner unconditionally reiterating his command; meanwhile advancing upon the still seated Lakeman, with an uplifted cooper's club hammer which he had snatched from a cask near by.

"Heated and irritated as he was by his spasmodic toil at the pumps, for all his first nameless feeling of forbearance the sweating Steelkilt could but ill brook this bearing in the mate; but somehow still smothering the conflagration within him, without speaking he remained doggedly rooted to his seat, till at last the incensed Radney shook the hammer within a few inches of his face, furiously commanding him to do his bidding.

"Steelkilt rose, and slowly retreating round the windlass, steadily followed by the mate with his menacing hammer, deliberately repeated his intention not to obey. Seeing, however, that his forbearance had not the slightest effect, by an awful and unspeakable intimation with his twisted hand he warned off the foolish and infatuated man; but it was to no purpose. And in this way the two went once slowly round the windlass; when, resolved at last no longer to retreat, bethinking him that he had now forborne as much as comported with his humor, the Lakeman paused on the hatches and thus spoke to the officer:

"'Mr. Radney, I will not obey you. Take that hammer away, or look to yourself.' But the predestinated mate coming still closer to him, where the Lakeman stood fixed, now shook the heavy hammer within an inch of his teeth; meanwhile repeating a string of insufferable maledictions. Retreating not the thousandth part of an inch; stabbing him in the eye with the unflinching poniard of his glance, Steelkilt, clenching his right hand behind him and creepingly drawing it back, told his persecutor that if the hammer but grazed his cheek he (Steelkilt) would murder him. But, gentlemen, the fool had been branded for the slaughter by the gods. Immediately the hammer touched the cheek; the next instant the lower jaw of the mate was stove in his head; he fell on the hatch spouting blood like a whale.

"Ere the cry could go aft Steelkilt was shaking one of the backstays leading far aloft to where two of his comrades were standing their mast-heads. They were both Canalers.

"'Canalers!' cried Don Pedro. 'We have seen many whaleships in our harbors, but never heard of your Canalers. Pardon: who and what are they?'

"Canalers, Don, are the boatmen belonging to our grand Erie Canal. You must have heard of it.

"'Nay, Senor; hereabouts in this dull, warm, most lazy, and hereditary land, we know but little of your vigorous North.'

"Ay? Well, then, Don, refill my cup. Your chicha's very fine; and, ere proceeding further, I will tell you what our Canalers are; for such information may throw side-light upon my story.

"For three hundred and sixty miles, gentlemen, through the entire breadth of the state of New York; through numerous populous cities and most thriving villages; through long, dismal, uninhabited swamps, and affluent, cultivated fields, unrivaled for fertility; by billiard-room and bar-room; through the holy-of-holies of great forests; on Roman arches over Indian rivers; through sun and shade; by happy hearts or broken; through all the wide contrasting scenery of those noble Mohawk counties; and especially by rows of snow-white chapels, whose spires stand almost like milestones, flows one continual stream of Venetianly corrupt and often lawless life. There's your true Ashantee, gentlemen; there howl your pagans; where you ever find them, next door to you; under the long-flung shadow, and the snug patronizing lee of churches. For by some curious fatality, as it is often noted of your metropolitan freebooters that they ever encamp around the halls of justice, so sinners, gentlemen, most abound in holiest vicinities.

"'Is that a friar passing?' said Don Pedro, looking downward into the crowded plaza, with humorous concern.

"'Well for our northern friend, Dame Isabella's Inquisition wanes in Lima,' laughed Don Sebastian. 'Proceed, Senor.'

"'A moment! Pardon!' cried another of the company. 'In the name of all us Limeese, I but desire to express to you, sir sailor, that we have by no means overlooked your delicacy in not substituting present Lima for distant Venice in your corrupt comparison. Oh! do not bow and look surprised; you know the proverb all along this coast—"Corrupt as Lima." It but bears out your saying, too; churches more plentiful than billiard-tables, and forever open—and "Corrupt as Lima." So, too, Venice; I have been there; the holy city of the blessed evangelist, St. Mark!—St. Dominic, purge it! Your cup! Thanks: here I refill; now, you pour out again.'

"Freely depicted in his own vocation, gentlemen, the Canaler would make a fine dramatic hero, so abundantly and picturesquely wicked is he. Like Mark Antony, for days and days along his green-turfed, flowery Nile, he indolently floats, openly toying with his red-cheeked Cleopatra, ripening his apricot thigh upon the sunny deck. But ashore, all this effeminacy is dashed. The brigandish guise which the Canaler so proudly sports; his slouched and gayly-ribboned hat betoken his grand features. A terror to the smiling innocence of the villages through which he floats; his swart visage and bold swagger are not unshunned in cities. Once a vagabond on his own canal, I have received good turns from one of those Canalers; I thank him heartily; would fain be not ungrateful; but it is often one of the prime redeeming qualities of your man of violence, that at times he has as stiff an arm to back a poor stranger in a strait, as to plunder a wealthy one. In sum, gentlemen, what the wildness of this canal life is, is emphatically evinced by this; that our wild whale-fishery contains so many of its most finished graduates, and that scarce any race of mankind, except Sydney men, are so much distrusted by our whaling captains. Nor does it at all diminish the curiousness of this matter, that to many thousands of our rural boys and young men born along its line, the probationary life of the Grand Canal furnishes the sole transition between quietly reaping in a Christian corn-field, and recklessly ploughing the waters of the most barbaric seas.

"'I see! I see!' impetuously exclaimed Don Pedro, spilling his chicha upon his silvery ruffles. 'No need to travel! The world's one Lima. I had thought, now, that at your temperate North the generations were cold and holy as the hills. But the story.'

"I left off, gentlemen, where the Lakeman shook the backstay. Hardly had he done so, when he was surrounded by the three junior mates and the four harpooners, who all crowded him to the deck. But sliding down the ropes like baleful comets, the two Canalers rushed into the uproar, and sought to drag their man out of it toward the forecastle. Others of the sailors joined with them in this attempt, and a twisted turmoil ensued; while standing out of harm's way, the valiant captain danced up and down with a whale-pike, calling upon his officers to manhandle that atrocious scoundrel, and smoke him along to the quarter-deck. At intervals, he ran close up to the revolving border of the confusion, and prying into the heart of it with his pike, sought to prick out the object of his resentment. But Steelkilt and his desperadoes were too much for them all; they succeeded in gaining the forecastle deck, where, hastily slewing about three or four large casks in a line with the windlass, these sea-Parisians entrenched themselves behind the barricade.

"'Come out of that, ye pirates!' roared the captain, now menacing them with a pistol in each hand, just brought to him by the steward. 'Come out of that, ye cut-throats!'

"Steelkilt leaped on the barricade, and striding up and down there, defied the worst the pistols could do; but gave the captain to understand distinctly, that his (Steelkilt's) death would be the signal for a murderous mutiny on the part of all hands. Fearing in his heart lest this might prove but too true, the captain a little desisted, but still commanded the insurgents instantly to return to their duty.

"'Will you promise not to touch us, if we do?' demanded their ringleader.

"'Turn to! turn to!—I make no promise; to your duty! Do you want to sink the ship, by knocking off at a time like this? Turn to!' and he once more raised a pistol.

"'Sink the ship?' cried Steelkilt. 'Ay, let her sink. Not a man of us turns to, unless you swear not to raise a rope-yarn against us. What say ye, men?' turning to his comrades. A fierce cheer was their response.

"The Lakeman now patrolled the barricade, all the while keeping his eye on the Captain, and jerking out such sentences as these: 'It's not our fault; we didn't want it; I told him to take his hammer away; it was boys' business: he might have known me before this; I told him not to prick the buffalo; I believe I have broken a finger here against his cursed jaw; ain't those mincing knives down in the forecastle there, men? look to those handspikes, my hearties. Captain, by God, look to yourself; say the word; don't be a fool; forget it all; we are ready to turn to; treat us decently, and we're your men; but we won't be flogged.'

"'Turn to! I make no promises: turn to, I say!'

"'Look ye, now,' cried the Lakeman, flinging out his arm toward him, 'there are a few of us here (and I am one of them) who have shipped for the cruise, d'ye see; now as you well know, sir, we can claim our discharge as soon as the anchor is down; so we don't want a row; it's not our interest; we want to be peaceable; we are ready to work, but we won't be flogged.'

"'Turn to!' roared the Captain.

"Steelkilt glanced round him a moment, and then said: 'I tell you what it is now, Captain, rather than kill ye, and be hung for such a shabby rascal, we won't lift a hand against ye unless ye attack us; but till you say the word about not flogging us, we don't do a hand's turn.'

"'Down into the forecastle then, down with ye, I'll keep ye there till ye're sick of it. Down ye go.'

"'Shall we?' cried the ringleader to his men. Most of them were against it; but at length, in obedience to Steelkilt, they preceded him down into their dark den, growlingly disappearing like bears into a cave.

"As the Lakeman's bare head was just level with the planks, the Captain and his posse leaped the barricade, and rapidly drawing over the slide of the scuttle, planted their group of hands upon it, and loudly called for the steward to bring the heavy brass padlock belonging to the companionway. Then opening the slide a little, the Captain whispered something down the crack, closed it, and turned the key upon them—ten in number—leaving on deck some twenty or more, who thus far had remained neutral.

"All night a wide-awake watch was kept by all the officers, forward and aft, especially about the forecastle scuttle and fore hatchway; at which last place it was feared the insurgents might emerge, after breaking through the bulkhead below. But the hours of darkness passed in peace; the men who still remained at their duty toiling hard at the pumps, whose clinking and clanking at intervals through the dreary night dismally resounded through the ship.

"At sunrise the Captain went forward, and knocking on the deck summoned the prisoners to work; but with a yell they refused. Water was then lowered down to them, and a couple of handfuls of biscuit were tossed after it; when again turning the key upon them and pocketing it, the Captain returned to the quarter-deck. Twice every day for three days this was repeated; but on the fourth morning a confused wrangling, and then a scuffling was heard, as the customary summons was delivered; and suddenly four men burst up from the forecastle, saying they were ready to turn to. The fetid closeness of the air, and a famishing diet, united perhaps to some fears of ultimate retribution, had constrained them to surrender at discretion. Emboldened by this, the Captain reiterated his demand to the rest, but Steelkilt shouted up to him a terrific hint to stop his babbling and betake himself where he belonged. On the fifth morning three others of the mutineers bolted up into the air from the desperate arms below that sought to restrain them. Only three were left.

"'Better turn to, now?' said the Captain with a heartless jeer.

"'Shut us up again, will ye!' cried Steelkilt.

"'Oh! certainly,' said the Captain, and the key clicked.

"It was at this point, gentlemen, that enraged by the defection of seven of his former associates, and stung by the mocking voice that had last hailed him, and maddened by his long entombment in a place as black as the bowels of despair; it was then that Steelkilt proposed to the two Canalers, thus far apparently of one mind with him, to burst out of their hole at the next summoning of the garrison; and armed with their keen mincing knives (long, crescentic, heavy implements with a handle at each end) run amuck from the bowsprit to the taffrail; and if by any devilishness of desperation possible, seize the ship. For himself, he would do this, he said, whether they joined him or not. That was the last night he should spend in that den. But the scheme met with no opposition on the part of the other two; they swore they were ready for that, or for any other mad thing, for any thing, in short, but a surrender. And what was more, they each insisted upon being the first man on deck, when the time to make the rush should come. But to this their leader as fiercely objected, reserving that priority for himself; particularly as his two comrades would not yield, the one to the other, in the matter; and both of them could not be first, for the ladder would but admit one man at a time. And here, gentlemen, the foul play of these miscreants must come out.

"Upon hearing the frantic project of their leader, each in his own separate soul had suddenly lighted, it would seem, upon the same piece of treachery, namely: to be foremost in breaking out, in order to be the first of the three, though the last of the ten, to surrender; and thereby secure whatever small chance of pardon such conduct might merit. But when Steelkilt made known his determination still to lead them to the last, they in some way, by some subtle chemistry of villainy, mixed their before secret treacheries together; and when their leader fell into a doze, verbally opened their souls to each other in three sentences; and bound the sleeper with cords, and gagged him with cords; and shrieked out for the Captain at midnight.

"Thinking murder at hand, and smelling in the dark for the blood, he and all his armed mates and harpooners rushed for the forecastle. In a few minutes the scuttle was opened, and, bound hand and foot, the still struggling ringleader was shoved up into the air by his perfidious allies, who at once claimed the honor of securing a man who had been fully ripe for murder. But all three were collared, and dragged along the deck like dead cattle; and, side by side, were seized up into the mizen rigging, like three quarters of meat, and there they hung till morning. 'Damn ye,' cried the Captain, pacing to and fro before them, 'the vultures would not touch ye, ye villains!'

"At sunrise he summoned all hands; and separating those who had rebelled from those who had taken no part in the mutiny, he told the former that he had a good mind to flog them all around—thought, upon the whole, he would do so—he ought to—justice demanded it; but, for the present, considering their timely surrender, he would let them go with a reprimand, which he accordingly administered in the vernacular.

"'But as for you, ye carrion rogues,' turning to the three men in the rigging—'for you, I mean to mince ye up for the try-pots;' and, seizing a rope, he applied it with all his might to the backs of the two traitors, till they yelled no more, but lifelessly hung their head sideways, as the two crucified thieves are drawn.

"'My wrist is sprained with ye!' he cried, at last; 'but there is still rope enough left for you, my fine bantam, that wouldn't give up. Take that gag from his mouth, and let us hear what he can say for himself.'

"For a moment the exhausted mutineer made a tremulous motion of his cramped jaws, and then painfully twisting round his head, said, in a sort of hiss, 'What I say is this—and mind it well—if you flog me, I murder you!'

"'Say ye so? then see how ye frighten me'—and the Captain drew off with the rope to strike.

"'Best not,' hissed the Lakeman.

"'But I must'—and the rope was once more drawn back for the stroke.

"Steelkilt here hissed out something, inaudible to all but the Captain; who, to the amazement of all hands, started back, paced the deck rapidly two or three times, and then suddenly throwing down his rope, said, 'I won't do it—let him go—cut him down: d'ye hear?'

"But as the junior mates were hurrying to execute the order, a pale man, with a bandaged head, arrested them—Radney the chief mate. Ever since the blow, he had lain in his berth; but that morning, hearing the tumult on the deck, he had crept out, and thus far had watched the whole scene. Such was the state of his mouth, that he could hardly speak; but mumbling something about *his* being willing and able to do what the Captain dared not attempt, he snatched the rope and advanced to his pinioned foe.

"'You are a coward!' hissed the Lakeman.

"'So I am, but take that.' The mate was in the very act of striking, when another hiss stayed his uplifted arm. He paused: and then pausing no more, made good his word, spite of Steelkilt's threat, whatever that might have been. The three men were then cut down, all hands were turned to, and, sullenly worked by the moody seamen, the iron pumps clanged as before.

"Just after dark that day, when one watch had retired below, a clamor was heard in the forecastle; and the two trembling traitors running up, besieged the cabin-door, saying they durst not consort with the crew. Entreaties, cuffs, and kicks could not drive them back, so at their own instance they were put down in the ship's run for salvation. Still, no sign of mutiny re-appeared among the rest. On the contrary, it seemed, that mainly at Steelkilt's instigation, they had resolved to maintain the strictest peacefulness, obey all orders to the last, and, when the ship reached port, desert her in a body. But in order to insure the speediest end to the voyage, they all agreed to another thing—namely, not to sing out for whales, in case any should be discovered. For, spite of her leak, and spite of all her other perils, the Town-Ho still maintained her mast heads, and her captain was just as willing to lower for a fish that moment, as on the day his craft first struck the cruising-ground, and Radney the mate was quite as ready to change his berth for a boat, and with his bandaged mouth seek to gag in death the vital jaw of the whale.

"But though the Lakeman had induced the seamen to adopt this sort of passiveness in their conduct, he kept his own counsel (at least till all was over) concerning his own proper and private revenge upon the man who had stung him in the ventricles of his heart. He was in Radney the chief-mate's watch; and as if the infatuated man sought to run more than half way to meet his doom, after the scene at the rigging, he insisted, against the express counsel of the captain, upon resuming the head of his watch at night. Upon this, and one or two other circumstances, Steelkilt systematically built the plan of his revenge.

"During the night, Radney had an unseamanlike way of sitting on the bulwarks of the quarter-deck, and leaning his arm upon the gunwale of the boat which was hoisted up there, a little above the ship's side. In this attitude, it was well known, he sometimes dozed. There was a considerable vacancy between the boat and the ship, and down between this was the sea. Steelkilt calculated his time, and found that his next trick at the helm would come round at two o'clock, in the morning of the third day from that in which he had been betrayed. At his leisure, he employed the interval in braiding something very carefully in his watches below.

"'What are you making there?' said a shipmate.

"'What do you think? what does it look like?'

"'Like a lanyard for your bag; but it's an odd one, seems to me.'

"'Yes, rather oddish,' said the Lakeman, holding it at arm's length before him; 'but I think it will answer. Shipmate, I haven't enough twine—have you any?'

"But there was none in the forecastle.

"'Then I must get some from old Rad;' and he rose to go aft.

"'You don't mean to go a-begging to him!' said a sailor.

"'Why not? Do you think he won't do me a turn, when it's to help himself in the end, shipmate?' and going to the mate, he looked at him quietly, and asked him for some twine to mend his hammock. It was given him—neither twine nor lanyard was seen again; but the next night an iron ball, closely netted, partly rolled from the pocket of the Lakeman's monkey-jacket, as he was tucking the coat into his hammock for a pillow. Twenty-four hours after, his trick at the silent helm—nigh to the man who was apt to doze over the grave always ready dug to the seaman's hand—that fatal hour was then to come; and in the fore-ordaining soul of Steelkilt, the mate was already stark and stretched as a corpse, with his forehead crushed in.

"But, gentlemen, a fool saved the would-be murderer from the bloody deed he had planned. Yet complete revenge he had, and without being the avenger. For by a mysterious fatality, Heaven itself seemed to step in to take out of his hands into its own the damning thing he would have done.

"It was just between daybreak and sunrise of the morning of the second day, when they were washing down the decks, that a stupid Teneriffe man, drawing water in the main-chains, all at once shouted out, 'There she rolls! there she rolls! Jesu! what a whale!' It was Moby Dick.

"'Moby Dick!' cried Don Sebastian; 'St. Dominic! Sir sailor, but do whales have christenings? Whom call you Moby Dick?'

"A very white, and famous, and most deadly immortal monster, Don; but that would be too long a story.

"'How? how?' cried all the young Spaniards, crowding.

"Nay, Dons, Dons—nay, nay! I can not rehearse that now. Let me get more into the air, sirs.

"'The chicha! the chicha!' cried Don Pedro; 'our vigorous friend looks faint; fill up his empty glass!'

"No need, gentlemen; one moment, and I proceed. Now, gentlemen, so suddenly perceiving the snowy whale within fifty yards of the ship—forgetful of the compact among the crew—in the excitement of the moment, the Teneriffe man had instinctively and involuntarily lifted his voice for the monster, though for some little time past it had been plainly beheld from the three sullen mast-heads. All was now a frenzy. 'The White Whale—the White Whale!' was the cry from captain, mates, and harpooners, who, undeterred by fearful rumors, were all anxious to capture so famous and precious a fish; while the dogged crew eyed askance, and with curses, the appalling beauty of the vast milky mass, that lit up by a horizontal spangling sun, shifted and glistened like a living opal in the blue morning sea. Gentlemen, a strange fatality pervades the whole career of these events, as if verily mapped out before the world itself was charted. The mutineer was the bowsman of the mate, and when fast to a fish, it was his duty to sit next him, while Radney stood up with his lance in the prow, and haul in or slacken the line, at the word of command. Moreover, when the four boats were lowered, the mate's got the start; and none howled more fiercely with delight than did Steelkilt, as he strained at his oar. After a stiff pull, their harpooner got fast, and, spear in hand, Radney sprang to the bow. He was always a furious man, it seems, in a boat. And now his bandaged cry was, to beach him on the whale's topmost back. Nothing loath, his bowsman hauled him up and up, through a blinding foam that blent two whitenesses together; till of a sudden the boat struck as against a sunken ledge, and keeling over, spilled out the standing mate. That instant, as he fell on the whale's slippery back, the boat righted, and was dashed aside by the swell, while Radney was tossed over into the sea, on the other flank of the whale. He struck out through the spray, and, for an instant, was dimly seen through that veil, wildly seeking to remove himself from the eye of Moby Dick. But the whale rushed round in a sudden maelstrom; seized the swimmer between his jaws; and rearing high up with him, plunged headlong again, and went down.

"Meantime, at the first tap of the boat's bottom, the Lakeman had slackened the line, so as to drop astern from the whirlpool; calmly looking on, he thought his own thoughts. But a sudden, terrific, downward jerking of the boat, quickly brought his knife to the line. He cut it; and the whale was free. But, at some distance, Moby Dick rose again, with some tatters of Radney's red woolen shirt, caught in the teeth that had destroyed him. All four boats gave chase again; but the whale eluded them, and, finally, wholly disappeared.

"In good time, the Town-Ho reached her port—a savage, solitary place—where no civilized creature resided. There, headed by the Lakeman, all but five or six of the foremast-men deliberately deserted among the palms; eventually, as it turned out, seizing a large double war-canoe of the savages, and setting sail for some other harbor.

"The ship's company being reduced to but a handful, the Captain called upon the Islanders to assist him in the laborious business of heaving down the ship to stop the leak. But to such unresting vigilance over their dangerous allies was this small band of whites necessitated, both by night and by day, and so extreme was the hard work they underwent, that upon the vessel being ready again for sea, they were in such a weakened condition that the captain durst not put off with them in so heavy a vessel. After taking counsel with his officers, he anchored the ship as far off shore as possible; loaded and ran out his two cannon from the bows; stacked his muskets on the poop; and warning the Islanders not to approach the ship at their peril, took one man with him, and setting the sail of his best whale-boat, steered straight before the wind for Tahiti, five hundred miles distant, to procure a reinforcement to his crew.

"On the fourth day of the sail, a large canoe was descried, which seemed to have touched at a low isle of corals. He steered away from it; but the savage craft bore down on him; and soon the voice of Steelkilt hailed him to heave to, or he would run him under water. The captain presented a pistol. With one foot on each prow of the yoked war-canoes, the Lakeman laughed him to scorn; assuring him that if the pistol so much as clicked in the lock, he would bury him in bubbles and foam.

"'What do you want of me?' cried the captain.

"'Where are you bound? and for what are you bound?' demanded Steelkilt; 'no lies.'

"'I am bound to Tahiti for more men.'

"'Very good. Let me board you a moment—I come in peace.' With that he leaped from the canoe, swam to the boat; and climbing the gunwale, stood face to face with the captain.

"'Cross your arm, sir; throw back your head. Now, repeat after me. As soon as Steelkilt leaves me, I swear to beach this boat on yonder island, and remain there six days. If I do not, may lightnings strike me!'

"'A pretty scholar,' laughed the Lakeman. 'Adios, Senor!' and leaping into the sea, he swam back to his comrades.

"Watching the boat till it was fairly beached, and drawn up to the roots of the cocoa-nut trees, Steelkilt made sail again, and in due time arrived at Tahiti, his own place of destination. There, luck befriended him; two ships were about to sail for France, and were providentially in want of precisely that number of men which the sailor headed. They embarked; and so forever got the start of their former captain, had he been at all minded to work them legal retribution.

"Some ten days after the French ships sailed, the whaleboat arrived, and the captain was forced to enlist some of the more civilized Tahitans, who had been somewhat used to the sea. Chartering a small native schooner, he returned with them to his vessel; and finding all right there, again resumed his cruisings.

"Where Steelkilt now is, gentlemen, none know; but upon the island of Nantucket, the widow of Radney still turns to the sea which refuses to give up its dead; still in dreams sees the awful white whale that destroyed him.

"'Are you through?' said Don Sebastian, quietly.

"I am, Don.

"'Then I entreat you, tell me if to the best of your own convictions, this your story is, in substance, really true? It is so passing wonderful! Did you get it from an unquestionable source? Bear with me if I seem to press.'

"'Also bear with all of us, sir sailor; for we all join in Don Sebastian's suit,' cried the company, with exceeding interest.

"Is there a copy of the Holy Evangelists in the Golden Inn, gentlemen?

"'Nay,' said Don Sebastian; 'but I know a worthy priest near by, who will quickly procure one for me. I go for it; but are you well advised? this may grow too serious.'

"'Will you be so good as to bring the priest also, Don?'

"'Though there are no Auto-da-Fés in Lima now,' said one of the company to another; 'I fear our sailor friend runs risk of the archiepiscopacy. Let us withdraw more out of the moonlight. I see no need of this.'

"Excuse me for running after you, Don Sebastian; but may I also beg that you will be particular in procuring the largest sized Evangelists you can.

"'This is the priest; he brings you the Evangelists,' said Don Sebastian, gravely, returning with a tall and solemn figure.

"Let me remove my hat. Now, venerable priest, further into the light, and hold the Holy Book before me that I may touch it.

"So help me Heaven, and on my honor, the story I have told ye, gentlemen, is, in substance and its great items, true. I know it to be true; it happened on this ball; I trod the ship; I knew the crew; I have seen and talked with Steelkilt since the death of Radney."

Editor's Table
Union Saving

August 1854

"Union saving" has for some time past been a by-word and a reproach. By a certain class of editors and political haranguers it has been employed as a base reflection upon some of our noblest men, as well as their noblest efforts for the perpetuation of our national strength and national glory. It was a taunt which barely spared the memory of Clay, and which haunted the patriot Webster to his grave. Their fears for the dissolution of the American Union were charged with hypocritical cant; their efforts for the aversion of such a calamity were characterized as the acts of unprincipled alarmists. But there can be no mistake about the matter now. That our national union, and along with it our proud national existence, is in the most imminent peril, the blindest must see, the most stupid must acknowledge. The proof of this comes not simply from turbulent Congressional debates, or inflammatory resolutions, or law-resisting riots. The most alarming evidence is in the tone of the press. Can any one be blind to that attitude of fierce defiance which is now assuming a form so sectionally distinct? Can we shut our ears to the furious invectives, the stinging reproaches of meanness and treachery on the one side, and of cowardice and fanaticism on the other—the vindictive taunts expressly designed to arouse the bitterest sectional animosities, and impart to them a virulence which no recollections of a common ancestry, of a common glorious history, can ever heal. The lover of peace, of union, of *compromise*—we will still use the term, although it has fallen into disrepute—might see nothing formidable in this, if regarded in itself or in its intrinsic weight of argument. Its dread significance lies in the fact that it is the sign of a people already divided, and whose hostile sections are beginning to hate each other with an intensity that no mere outward political connection can repress. The South is saying things of the North which no men at the North, whatever be their party ties, will bear. The North is hurling back upon the South vindictive taunts, which can not be for-

given, because they imply charges of what is even worse than corruption of blood, or any form of political dishonor. He who does not see this is blind indeed. We are already divided. The evidence is as direct as that England and Russia are now at war. In fact, we may well doubt whether there really exists between the hostile armies on the Danube, or the hostile fleets on the Baltic, as sore a feeling of personal and sectional rancor as the press is now spreading between the Northern and Southern portions of these United States.

Who is to blame for this most lamentable state of things? It may not be conducive to the great pacification for which every patriot should so earnestly strive, to examine too scrupulously the exact balance of criminations and recriminations. Let common sense, let a knowledge of history, above all, let Christian charity come in here. In all the world's annals have we ever read of a case like this of national strife in which one side was free from blame, while the whole, or even the great preponderance, of guilt was on the other? We know that this is a very old and trite solution, but trite truths are by no means of the least value. Sometimes, too, it requires more independence of thought to state them, and even more research to discover them, than is needed for those assumed occult causalities on account of which they are often neglected and cast out of sight.

But when we speak thus of both sides being to blame, we ought, perhaps, to qualify the declaration. If we have in view the great mass of the people, we might rather say that both sides are equally innocent. The bitter evils of this bitter and suicidal controversy can be mainly traced in their root to a few men at either extreme of the national and sectional scale, whose violence has been wickedly cherished, for the most corrupt purposes, by a still smaller class in the middle. Such are the parties on whom the future historian must visit the just condemnation of this sad work. They are the Northern fanatics who, twenty-five years ago, began to meddle with matters they had no right to touch, and to form treasonable combinations respecting interests with which they were expressly forbidden to interfere. We call them fanatical in the strictest sense of this much-abused term. They mingled a malevolent feeling with the profession of an abstract benevolence. They preached reform, as Christ and Paul had never preached it. We also say their designs were treasonable; for the result at which their combination aimed was the subversion, and not by legal means, of institutions which the political organization had placed exclusively in other and, to them, foreign jurisdictions. Here was one extreme. There were, on the other hand, Southern ultraists who, with equal fanaticism and equal treasonableness, sought to make that national which the Constitution, and the *compromises* of the Constitution, recognized as having a local existence depending on positive local law. Herein we can not help observing a wondrous agreement. Both insisted upon investing slavery with a national character; the one for the purpose of making an unconstitutional assault upon it, the other as the ground of its perpetual maintenance.

It is curious, too, to trace in other respects the striking parallel. One side commenced with false and forced interpretations of the Scriptures, and landed at last, after a series of struggles, in the most undisguised infidelity; the other, setting out with a false interpretation of history and political philosophy, and taking to itself a high conservative aspect, has terminated in that meanest of all species of radical anarchy, the practice and justification of filibustering. They discovered a wondrous excellency in what could be shown to have been the bane of the ancient republics. They made slavery the corner-stone of freedom. Of course, with such a dogma, they became as mad and as fanatical as their Northern counterparts. Each grew by the aliment afforded by the other, and hence the striking analogies presented in the whole course of these mischief-brooding factions. We have the spectacle of men everlastingly mouthing it about their higher law and higher morality, and yet recklessly undermining that only foundation on which the religion and morality of this world has ever yet been able to repose with any thing like a feeling of strength and security. Again,

Picking cotton.

we have seen men whose only title or only security for what may be called, to say the least, an anomalous species of property, rests on the sacredness of constitutions, compacts, compromises, judicial decisions, and national unity, ever the first to advocate nullification, secession, and resistance to law, wherever they supposed it to come in the way of their real or fancied interests. We have had in one latitude, those whose extreme progress had led them to doubt whether there is a real personality in the Deity, or at all events a real personal Providence, who could yet denounce upon their opponents a divine penal retribution with all the fury of a Mucklewrath or a Balfour. A few degrees further south there are to be found their moral and social antitypes—men who can coolly approve the most deliberate treaty-breaking, or what all civilized nations have characterized as the meanest of piracies, and yet these same moral and political anomalies can gravely rebuke the fanaticism of Northern mobs, can talk about the sanctity of law and constitutions, and above all, the inviolability of property, with all the conservative dignity of a Grotius or a Mansfield.

The sympathies and congenialities of these two apparent extremes might be discovered in the manner in which they sometimes mutually compliment each other, while jointly reviling all moderate men who stand in the way of their fanatical tendencies. In the rabid abolition conventicle it has been no uncommon thing to hear the praises of the "chivalrous South," the "high-minded" Southern gentleman—somewhat blinded by his position, but so much more worthy of respect than the cautious, time-serving conservative of the North. Thus Calhoun is lauded for his sterling honesty, while Webster is made the subject of the foulest abuse, and even John Quincy Adams sometimes charged with a hypocritical deficiency of "moral courage." Go to the nullifying Southern convention, or take up a fanatical Southern newspaper, and how fraternally do we find the compliment returned. How distinctly comes back the echo! "We like that man Parker—he is honest—he is consistent—he speaks right out."—"With all his errors, and bating a little fanaticism, that Wendell Phillips is really a noble orator."—"We like

these men, they tell the truth at all events about the North, and the hypocritical Northern churches, however much they may be mistaken in respect to the institutions of the South." "Give us such antagonists," cries out the "chivalry" on the one side.—"Give us such antagonists," responds the "moral courage" on the other. Give us such antagonists, say both these mischief-loving factions, rather than your sneaking conservatives, whether lay or clerical, or your "time-serving compromisers," as they characterize the peace-loving, law-loving, Union-loving men, whose position in these times is an exhibition of more true moral courage than was ever found in all the ranks of abolition or filibustering fanaticism. We have had abundant evidence of the fraternity of these apparent extremes in the course of the late exciting measure. The satisfaction of both parties, in prospect of the result, was too manifest to be mistaken. No denunciation could conceal the fact that the failure of the Nebraska Bill would have been as grievous a disappointment to the disunionists of Boston as to those of Charleston or New Orleans. This game of mutual laudation has been played long enough. It is beginning to be understood. It ought more and more to open the minds of thoughtful men to the true nature of the great question, and the utter unfitness of these two extreme classes to deal aright with so momentous a national issue.

And yet there are worse men than the abolitionists or the secessionists. Even with these, there would seem to be a species of honesty, of very shallow depth indeed, yet sufficient to acquit them of the charge of base hypocrisy. There is an unselfishness about the extreme anti-slavery position, which, however involved in passion, and carried away by personal vehemence of opinion, is still unselfishness when compared with the base characteristics that disclose themselves in the field of political party corruption. We repeat it—the wildest fanatic is a more respectable person, a higher being every way, than the party demagogue. Filibustering and ultra abolitionism, both seeking in their own mad ways what they would call the progress and higher law of humanity, are better things, more truthful, more manly, more noble every way, than the principles and proceedings that have been lauded under the names of regular nominations and party fidelity. [...]

There are those who say—there are many who say—no more compromises; but are they aware of what they are saying? Have they looked the issue steadily in the face? Can they not see that it is a question simply of compromise or

dissolution? Besides, we may charge upon many who use this language, that they directly cut the throat of their own argument. They tell us that this state of things has been brought about by a few political schemers, that the great mass of the people have had nothing to do with it, that the North has been opposed to it, that the South has not asked for it, that, twelve months ago, no man in any latitude would have thought of advocating the measure which has led to it. If this be so, what argument is there against further efforts at compromise by the great masses, North and South, who have been so grossly misrepresented? The opposition would seem to be to the idea itself, and if so, what charity can avoid the suspicion that the wish is father to the thought, and that some who clamor the loudest about the violation of the Missouri Compromise are the enemies of all compromises, and secretly rejoice in their destruction. [...]

Here are in our midst four millions of human beings of a race widely distinct—whether inferior or not we will not now say—and with whom it is admitted, for reasons we will not now discuss, that social union, social and domestic equality, is not to be thought of. Now put their present servile condition at the worst estimate that was ever made of it; they have in the continuance of the American Union some prospect of amelioration. They have it in the steady and powerful yet regulated sympathy of the North; they have it in that progress of humanity of the South, which is the result of well-established government, and from which there grows up in time a public sentiment giving to those in bondage rights and protection having all the force of law, and which no man would venture to violate who would not be deemed an outcast from humane society. Especially would this be the case in the absence of all angry and insulting intermeddling from without. History has abundantly shown that the servile condition, whether we take our examples from the ancient world, or from the serfdom of Europe, ever grows milder under the influences we have mentioned, ever assumes more and more the form of a state regulated by *general* law, which is the very essence of rational in distinction from licentious liberty—ever attains more and more of fixed personal rights, until it emerges into full civic freedom; or if any apparent shackles may yet remain, they are only the antiquarian memorials of a condition that has passed away.

Such is one aspect of the case; but should peculiar physiological differences be regarded as precluding the idea of complete social emancipation (which is but another name for that social equality and social liberty without which nominal political freedom is only an insult and a degradation), of complete social emancipation, we mean, with continuance on the same territory—then in union, and in union only, is the sole hope of any success in that mighty effort which will be required for the separation of the two races, and the exodus of one of them to some land, remote or near, where their elevation shall not be impeded by physical and social causes that are now so unsurmountable. We know that such an idea is offensive to both of our fanatical extremes. One has its higher law in the way, the other its "strict construction of the Constitution;" but much as the plan has been denounced, it may, in calmer times, and when men begin to see more clearly that they are responsible for expedient action as well as right abstract principle, unite every Christian and every patriot, North or South, in its hearty and successful support.

There is hope, we say, that one or the other of these results might take place in an unbroken union of these States. This once settled, that the Union *must* be preserved, and all irritating discussions being laid aside for higher and better work, as may reasonably be hoped when the exhaustive fruitlessness and positive mischief of such abstractions have been fully proved, the minds of men may be calmly brought to a consideration of what may be called emphatically *the great national problem*. We are strong in the belief that nothing would furnish so sure a beginning to the melioration of the condition of the African race, as some final settlement, or *compromise*, of the agitating sectional questions, which have hitherto resulted in evil, and evil only, to all parties, whether white or black.

And herein consists what seems to us the great evil of the late Nebraska Bill, and which far exceeds any mischievous advantage it may have afforded for the extension of slavery. It has greatly weakened, if not wholly destroyed, the only mode that seemed left to us of dealing with those aspects of the question which were not determined by the Constitution, and could not be so determined, because they have arisen out of circumstances that had no existence, and were not anticipated, when the national confederacy was first formed. The case is similar to that of new property and new domain accruing under old articles of partnership containing no provision for such an event. Nothing can be more absurdly foolish than to call such compromises unconstitutional. The nation forsooth may acquire foreign territory to any extent; for a change so vast and so vital as this, nothing more is required than simply a joint resolution of both Houses; but it has no power, say some of our Solons, to establish any rules for the regulation of such territory when acquired! It would certainly seem that if there were any doubt about the constitutionality it would much more strongly apply to that first act which produces all the necessity for the second. If we can acquire vast territories by purchase, or annex them by conquest, without thinking of the consent of the inhabitants, surely we may legislate, and in favor of freedom too, for what is yet an uninhabited wilderness. Thus grew up in our government the doctrine of compromises. We have had need of them, and shall have need of them again. There is no evading the issues out of which they arise. We must stop acquiring foreign territory, or we must continually amend the Constitution, or we must make compromises and observe them, or else familiarize ourselves at once with the ideas of anarchy and dissolution. In other words, we must come back to the old constitutional agreement which was never made for California or Cuba, or make new stipulations to meet the unanticipated emergency, or we must dissolve partnership. In the present state of our nation, so absolutely inseparable are these ideas of union and compromise, that, whatever they may say, we can not help regarding all who are openly the enemies of the one as being secretly hostile to the other.

But to return to our leading question, What would be the effect of the dissolution of the American Union upon the prospects of the African race? Can any sane man see in it the least ground of hope for their physical and moral elevation? Would it be more likely to be secured in a Southern Confederacy cut off from the North? Would a deluge of fugitive blacks in the Northern States be a desirable acquisition to our population; and would the intercourse between the two races, as far as past experience has shown us, tend to the moral elevation of the inferior? Or take another prospect; would anarchy and revolt, and San Domingan slaughter be the probable harbinger of future African progress? Judging form the history of Hayti and Jamaica, what may we rationally believe will be the condition of the future colored inhabitants of Carolina, when the Union is dissolved, the whites expelled, or some such anarchy in the ascendant as characterizes those charming tropical States with which our angry Southern cousins would seem so fond of forming unions for the conservation of the conservative institution? Can the prophetic eye of the most sanguine reformer see in such a state of things any prospect of more food, more clothing, more education, or any more hope of physical or moral elevation, of the unborn cultivators of the Southern rice-fields? Would these prospects be improved in a confederacy composed of Mexicans, Cubans, Creoles, Guatemalians, and South Americans? If servitude continues, would it be likely to become more mild by a dissolution of all connection with the North, and a *mixture*—we will not call it a *union*—with all these meaner elements? Or if a species of emancipation took place, and the two races continued to occupy the same territory, would there be any less toil, less degradation; or, on the other hand, would there probably be more of the family or social feeling, which is one of the bright aspects among the many dark features that characterize slavery as it now exists, and which would become tenfold darker amid the jealousies, the bitter animosities, the incurable anarchies that would follow the dissolution of the American Confederacy?

We see in this direction no cheering prospect for either race. The dissolution of the Union would be productive of the direst evils to the Negro, and no possible countervailing good. Instead of solving the great problem, such a prospect aggravates its difficulties a hundred fold. There yet stands the lowering and portentous issue, with all its physical and social difficulties—its ever-deepening shadow unrelieved by the least illumination growing out of any theory of the abstract rights of man. Whether we pass Nebraska bills or repeal them, it still frowns upon us in all its threatening significance. What shall be done with the four millions of Africans in our midst? Give them political freedom, says the abolitionist, and let them work out the problem for themselves. he ignores whatever comes in the way of his abstract conclusions. He has nothing to do, and he boasts he has nothing to do, with expediencies or consequences. If, however, political freedom with social degradation is a greater mockery of humanity than any form of regulated servitude, then have we not advanced a step? We are in fact further away than ever from the humane, in distinction from the mere political settlement of the question.

But we have not space to dwell on this. To the practical philanthropist there are but three conditions between which he is compelled to choose. We would present them in the briefest possible statement. There is—

1st. Servitude with its rights as well as duties defined by law instead of being left to the individual will—a servitude made as humane as legislation and the social circumstances of mankind can possibly render it, and with an eye to the moral and physical good of the serving race, as well as to the profit of the master—we may even say with a special regard to the former, as more imperatively demanded by the inferior and dependent condition. Such is the only form of slavery in which it can possibly be shielded from the reprobation of every enlightened conscience.

2d. Political freedom with social degradation arising inevitably from the antagonism of two races on the same soil, with social jealousies and contempts unmitigated by the ties of social dependence.

If we can not bear the first—if a true regard for human dignity makes intolerable the thought that *perpetual* servitude, even in its mildest form, should be the lot of any portion of the human race—if our souls still more revolt at the second as presenting the worst evils of slavery without any of its more humanizing counteracting traits, there is then but one condition left. We have to choose—

3d. The separation of the two races, and the exodus of one of them, at whatever expense of toil and treasure it may have to be accomplished. Removed to Africa they might acquire, form mere change of locality, a social and political energy that would make them the civilizers of that vast continent. Remaining where they are, they are a cause of degeneracy, and that too to both races. Whether in servitude, or in a nominal and degraded freedom, they have all the vices of civilization without any of the energies or virtues of barbarism. The only remedy, then, that reaches the very core of the evil is, that which is the reverse of the original wrong, in other words, the separation of races so unrighteously and so unnaturally combined; and for this there is needed the continuance of the American Union. If there were no other reason, this alone should secure for it the best counsels of every patriot statesman, the most ardent exertions of every enlightened philanthropist.

Uttoxeter*

by Nathaniel Hawthorne

April 1857

At Lichfield, in St. Mary's Square, I saw a statue of Dr. Johnson, elevated on a stone pedestal, some ten or twelve feet high. The statue is colossal (though perhaps not much more so than the mountainous Doctor), and sits in a chair, with a pile of big books underneath it, looking down upon the spectator with a broad, heavy, benignant countenance, very like Johnson's portraits. The figure is immensely massive—a vast ponderosity of stone, not finely spiritualized, nor, indeed, fully humanized, but rather resembling a great boulder than a man. On the pedestal are three bas-reliefs; in the first, Johnson is represented as a mere baby, seated on an old man's shoulders, resting his chin on the bald head which he embraces with his arms, and listening to the preaching of Dr. Sacheverell; in the second tablet he is seen riding to school on the backs of two of his comrades, while a third boy supports him in the rear. The third bas-relief possesses, to my mind, a good deal of pathos. It shows Johnson in the market-place of Uttoxeter, doing penance for an act of disobedience to his father, committed fifty years before. He stands bare-headed, very sad and woe-begone, with the wind and rain driving hard against

Nathaniel Hawthorne

him; while some market-people and children gaze awe-stricken into his face, and an aged man and woman, with clasped hands are praying for him. These latter personages, I fancy (though, in queer proximity, there are some living ducks and dead poultry), represent the spirits of Johnson's father and mother, lending what aid they can to lighten his half-century's burden of remorse.

I never heard of this statue before; it seems to have no reputation as a work of art, and very probably may deserve none. Yet I found it somewhat touching and effective, perhaps because my interest in the character of that sturdiest old Englishman has always been peculiarly strong; and especially the above-described bas-relief freshened my sense of a wonderful beauty and pathos in the incident which it commemorates. So, the next day, I left Lichfield for Uttoxeter, on a purely sentimental pilgrimage (by railway, however), to see the spot where Johnson performed his penance. Boswell, I think, speaks of the town (its name is pronounced Yute-oxeter) as being about nine miles from Lichfield, but the map would indicate a greater distance; and by rail, passing from one line to another, it is as much as eighteen. I have

* *"During the last visit which Doctor Johnson made to Lichfield, the friends with whom he was staying missed him one morning at the breakfast-table. On inquiring after him of the servants, they understood he had set off from Lichfield at a very early hour, without mentioning to any of the family whither he was going. The day passed without the return of the illustrious guest, and the party began to be very uneasy on his account, when, just before the supper-hour, the door opened, and the Doctor stalked into the room. A solemn silence of a few minutes ensued, nobody daring to inquire the cause of his absence, which was at length relieved by Johnson addressing the lady of the house in the following manner: 'Madam, I beg your pardon for the abruptness of my departure from your house this morning, but I was constrained to it by my conscience. Fifty years ago, madam, on this day, I committed a breach of filial piety, which has ever since lain heavy on my mind, and has not till this day been expiated. My father, you recollect, was a bookseller, and had long been in the habit of attending——market, and opening a stall for the sale of his books during that day. Confined to his bed by indisposition, he requested me, this time fifty years ago, to visit the market, and attend the stall in his place. But, madam, my pride prevented me from doing my duty, and I gave my father a refusal. To do away the sin of this disobedience, I this day went in a post-chaise to——, and going into the market at the time of high business, uncovered my head, and stood with it bare an hour before the stall which my father had formerly used, exposed to the sneers of the standers-by and the inclemency of the weather; a penance by which I trust I have propitiated Heaven for this only instance, I believe, of contumacy toward my father.' "—Boswell's Johnson.*

always had an idea of old Michael Johnson journeying thither on foot, on the morning of market-days, selling books through the busy hours, and returning home at night. This could not well have been.

Arriving at Uttoxeter station, the first thing I saw, in a convenient vicinity, was the tower and tall gray spire of a church. It is but a very short walk from the station up into the town. It had been my previous impression that the market-place of Uttoxeter lay immediately round about the church; and, if I remember the narrative aright, Johnson describes his father's book-stall as standing in the market-place, close beside the sacred edifice. But the church has merely a street of ordinary width passing around it; while the market-place, though near at hand, is not really contiguous; nor would its throng and bustle be apt to overflow their bounds and surge against the church-yard and the old gray tower. Nevertheless, a walk of a minute or two would bring a person from the centre of the market-place to the church-door; and Michael Johnson might very well have placed his stall, and have laid out his literary ware in the corner at the tower's base,—better there, perhaps, than in the busy centre of an agricultural market. But the picturesqueness and full impressiveness of the story require that Johnson, doing his penance, should have been the very nucleus of the crowd—the midmost man of the market-place—a central figure of Memory and Remorse, contrasting with, and overpowering the sultry materialism around him. I am resolved, therefore, that the true site of his penance was in the middle of the market-place.

This is a pretty, spacious, and irregular vacuity, surrounded by houses and shops, some of them old, with red-tiled roofs; others wearing a pretence of newness, but probably as old as the rest. In these ancient English towns you see many houses with modern fronts, but if you peep or penetrate inside, you often find an antique arrangement—old rafters, intricate passages, balustraded staircases; and discover that the spruce exterior is but a patch on some stalwart remnant of days gone by. England never gives up any thing old, as long as it is possible to patch it. The people of Uttoxeter seemed very idle in the warm summer day, and stood in little groups about the market-place; leisurely chatting and staring at me, as they would not stare if strangers were more plentiful. I question if Uttoxeter ever saw an American before. And as an American, I was struck by the number of old persons tottering about, and leaning on sticks; old persons in knee-breeches, and all the other traditional costume of the last century. Old places seem to produce old people, as by a natural propriety; or perhaps the secret is, that old age has a tendency to hide itself when it might otherwise be brought into contact with new edifices and new things, but comes freely forth, and meets the eye of man, amidst the sympathies of a decaying town. The only other thing that greatly impressed me in Uttoxeter, was the abundance of public-houses, one at every step or two; Red Lions, White Harts, Bull's Heads, Mitres, Cross Keys, and I know not what besides. These are, probably, for the accommodation of the agricultural visitors on market-day. At any rate, I appeared to be the only guest in Uttoxeter, on the day of my visit, and had but an infinitesimal portion of patronage to distribute among so many inns.

I stepped into one of these rustic hostelries, and got my dinner—bacon and greens, and a chop, and a gooseberry pudding—enough for six yeomen, besides ale; all for a shilling and sixpence. This hospitable inn was called the Nag's Head, and, standing beside the market-place, was as likely as any other to have entertained old Michael Johnson in the days when he used to come hither to sell books. He, perhaps, had eaten his bacon and greens, and drunk his ale and smoked his pipe, in the very room where I now sat; a low, ancient room, with a red-brick floor and a whitewashed ceiling, traversed by bare, rough beams; the whole in the rudest fashion, but extremely neat. Neither did the room lack ornament, the walls being hung with engravings of prize-oxen, and other pretty prints, and the mantle-piece adorned with earthenware figures of shepherdesses. But still, as I supped my ale, I glanced through the window into the sunny market-place, and wished that I could honestly fix on one spot rather than another as likely to have been the holy site where Johnson stood to do his penance.

How strange and stupid it is, that tradition should not have marked and kept in mind the very place! How shameful (nothing less than that) that there should be no local memorial of this incident, as beautiful and as touching a passage as can be cited out of any human life! no inscription of it, almost as sacred as a verse of Scripture, on the wall of the church! no statue of the venerable and illustrious penitent in the market-place, to throw a wholesome awe over its traffic, its earthliness, its selfishness! Such a statue, if the piety of man did not raise it, might almost have been expected to grow up out of the pavement of its own accord, on the spot that had been watered by Johnson's remorseful tears, and by the rain that dripped from him.

Well, my pilgrimage had not turned out a very successful one. There being no train till late in the afternoon, I spent I know not how many hours in Uttoxeter, and, to say the truth, was heartily tired of it; my penance being a great deal longer than Dr. Johnson's. Moreover, I forgot, until it was too late, to snatch the opportunity to repent of some of my own sins. While waiting at the station, I asked a boy who sat near me (a school-boy, some twelve or thirteen years old, whom I should take to be a clergyman's son)—I asked him whether he had ever heard the story of Dr. Johnson, how he stood an hour doing penance beside that church whose spire rose before us. The boy stared, and answered, "No." I inquired if no such story was known or talked about in Uttoxeter. "No," said the boy; "not that I ever heard of!" Just think of the absurd little town knowing nothing of its one memorable incident, which sanctifies it to the heart of a stranger from three thousand miles over the sea! Just think of the fathers and mothers of Uttoxeter never telling their children this sad and lovely story, which might have such a blessed influence on their young days, and spare them so many a pang hereafter!

But, personally, I had no right to find fault with these good people; for I myself had felt little or no impression from the scene; and my experience has been similar in many another spot, even of far deeper consecration than Uttoxeter. At Stratford-on-Avon—even at Westminster Abbey, on my first visit—I was as little moved as any stone on the pavement. These visits to the identical scenes of poetical or historic interest inevitably cause an encounter and a shock of the Actual with the Ideal, in which the latter—unless stronger than in my own case—is very apt to be overpowered. My emotions always come before, or afterward; and I can not help envying those happier tourists, who can time and tune themselves so accurately, that their raptures (as I presume from their printed descriptions) are sure to gush up just on the very spot, and precisely at the right moment.

The Siege of Fort Atkinson

October 1857

Next to Kit Carson, unquestionably the two most notorious characters in all the region of the Far West, at the present time, are Bill Bent and Yellow Bear, war-chief of the Arrapaho Indians. The name of Bent is too well known to require a card of introduction to the public. Yellow Bear has ever been Bent's warmest friend, and has saved that old trader's life for him time and time again. His influence is probably greater than that of any individual chief among all the Indian tribes, and it is due chiefly to him that Uncle Sam has been enabled to keep the peace for so many years with two of the most powerful nations of the plains—the Cheyennes and the Arrapahoes. In Yellow Bear, Cooper might have found his *beau ideal* of the red child of the forest; for, physically a *man* in the highest sense of the word, his intellectual capacity is all that could be expected from a mind without culture. Of great personal bravery, whether in battle or in the council, of profound sagacity and unshaken purpose, together with a rare modesty, a kindly disposition, and a magnanimous contempt of insult, his friends and allies worship him, while foes respect but fear him. Beneath the shadow of the Rocky Mountains, or along the banks of many a prairie creek and river, the wilderness has been the silent witness of scenes of strife and carnage that would curdle the blood and blanch the cheek; of which, betimes, some brief recital is borne eastward to shock incredulous ears. There is a startling history connected with the protracted siege of Bent's Fort during the winter just past, of which some half-distorted facts have been doled out in meagre parcels to readers of newspaper literature; and a moral, too, which if duly considered by those who have in charge the management of our Indian affairs, might be of practical benefit in the future. So, also, there is in every such event— which calls loudly for an amendment of the present policy as respects the Indian tribes. The following tritely-told incidents are fraught with illustrations bearing upon this point, and with this view are now for the first time recorded on the printed page.

It is some five years since the startling intelligence was brought from the Plains, by way of Independence, Missouri, that Fort Atkinson on the Arkansas River had been captured by the Indians, and its garrison massacred; and that Bent's and King's wagon-trains had also been intercepted, and every one of the party murdered. Fortunately the report afterward proved untrue, though it was by no means without foundation. It was in the month of July, 1852, the time for the distribution of the annuities and presents to the allied tribes of the Kiowas and Comanches, that the Indians of the aforesaid tribes were assembled in vast numbers in the vicinity of Fort Atkinson, impatiently awaiting the arrival of Charles Fitzpatrick, the agent for the Comanches, who, already behind time, was daily expected with the presents. There could not have been less than 10,000 in all, many of whom were encamped in the immediate vicinity of the fort; though the "big village" was some ten miles farther up the river, where the pasturage was better, and fire-wood more easily obtained.

The scarcity of fuel and grass is the chief inconvenience experienced by this fort, though in other respects it is by no means agreeably situated—its location having been chosen solely with a view to the accommodation of the neighboring Indian tribes and the protection of the Santa Fé trade. The Arkansas River flows within a few rods of its walls, having a depth of three or four feet at certain seasons of the year; but in summer, like most of the prairie streams, its bed is generally nearly dry. The surrounding country is a barren waste, without vegetation, save a few shrub bushes and the crispy buffalo grass, diversified only by innumerable sand hills. No wood is to be had within thirteen miles; and "buffalo chips," the dernier resort for fuel, once found in great abundance, are now quite scarce, the buffalo having almost entirely disappeared from this vicinity. The fort itself is of adobé, or sun-dried brick, roofed with canvas, containing fair accommodations for the garrison, and defended by a few small field-pieces and the usual armament. It has also a large *corral* on one side, five feet in height, for the protection of the animals. A garrison of ninety men (infantry, 6th regiment) and twenty B dragoons comprised the entire force at the date of our narrative—surprisingly deficient for so important a post.

Two weeks had nearly elapsed since the time appointed for the distribution of presents, but no agent yet made his appearance. The Indians had thus far borne the unwarrantable delay with remarkable patience, considering their naturally restless and irritable disposition, and the by-no-means-pleasing consciousness that they were, day by day, half-starving their horses on the sparse and abominable pasturage, and rapidly eating themselves out of all kinds of provisions—most of them, too, having traveled hundreds of miles to meet the agent at the time appointed. To this was added the suspicion of the red men (ever mistrustful of the whites) that they were to be cheated of their annuities. Thus, as day after day passed by, and still no agent came, they became more and more uneasy, and soon began to manifest unmistakable evidences of hostility. Indeed, the proposition was warmly espoused by many of the younger men that their treaty with the United States should be at once annulled, the annuities rejected, and an exterminating war declared; but the plan received little favor with the head men. They began now to gather around the fort in great numbers, threatening to annihilate the garrison if the presents were not speedily forthcoming, and occasionally endeavoring to force their way inside the gate. In vain the officers expostulated. They knew, they said, that "the Big Chief at Washington intended to cheat them out of their just dues. They were a heap mad; and if the presents did not arrive within ten days, they would not only take 'toll' from the first wagon train they met, but would wipe out every United States soldier and every white man on the plains who had any thing to do with the Government." [...]

In the present emergency, an attack being momentarily expected, and the garrison in the greatest excitement, it was determined to send to the States for aid. But instead of dispatching one of the common soldiers, the commanding officer imprudently undertook the commission himself, leaving the fort in charge of Second Lieutenant S——— and Sergeant R———, valiant men, but inadequate to the arduous and delicate duties assigned them. These now used every means in their power to keep the Indians quiet, and prevent them getting possession of the fort. Sentries were stationed at regular intervals near the gateway, with orders to shoot down any Indian that might attempt to pass; and every possible precaution was taken to guard against a sudden attack. Fortunately, however, for the present, matters did not assume a more threatening phase. It was not until the following day that the first direct attempt was made, when a gigantic Kiowa, six feet three in his moccasins, approached one of the sentries as he was patrolling his beat, and demanded permission to enter the fort. He was evidently the champion of several hundred Kiowas gathered in groups of twenties and fifties a few rods distant, who had deputized him to make the demand, and now stood eagerly awaiting the result. The soldier, a diminutive Celt, stood trembling as he regarded with no little apprehension the muscular form and threatening attitude of the savage confronting him; but putting as bold a face as possible upon the matter, he straightened himself up, and informed him in a tone decidedly military, that he "could not come in." The savage persisted. The sentry resisted, and presented his bayonet, whereupon the other deliberately knocked him down, and walked quietly toward the fort; the rest of the Indians following in a body. Of the remaining sentries, some fled precipitately within the walls as soon as they saw what was done, while the others stood motionless and dumbfounded, and permitted the Indians to pass in without opposing the least resistance.

Aside from this single act of violence the Indians seemed quite peaceable, and offered no injury to any of the troops, though they refrained from nothing by way of gesture, words, or supercilious bearing, to manifest their boldness and their supreme contempt, their object being apparently to show what they could do if disposed. There were altogether three or four hundred inside the fort, walking about the premises, and satisfying their curiosity by examining the barracks, officers' quarters, armory, and defenses, but taking nothing of value, being probably restrained by Ter-hausen (Little Mountain) their chief, with whom the officers were well acquainted. These, now recovering from their first alarm, and finding the Indians disposed to be peaceable, took especial pains to show them all the defenses of the fort, hoping thereby to intimidate them from making any subsequent attack. All this extra attention and civility the savages received with their wonted gravity, manifesting no surprise, but emitting a guttural "ugh" from time to time, expressive of their approbation or indifference, as the case might be. So, for the greater part of the day the fort remained thronged with these unwelcome visitors, causing the garrison no little anxiety; and when, at evening, the last of them withdrew his swarthy form from the place, and the gate was closed, a pleasurable sensation of relief came to each soldier as he exchanged congratulations with his fellow, thankful that they had been spared a tragedy like that which, years ago, made old Fort Mann a depopulated waste of ruins.*

II

No more trouble came that day or night; but the thin blue smoke curled silently and pleasingly from a myriad fires as the squaws prepared their evening meal, while the low drone of the camp, and the yelping and barking of a thousand gaunt and half-starved curs, were the only sounds that fell upon the ears of the distracted soldiers. Nevertheless, the garrison lay the whole night under arms. The next morning every thing was quiet and orderly, and comparatively few Indians were seen near the fort, the greater part of them having moved a few miles up the river, near the "big village." In this improved and gratifying state of affairs the confidence of the commanding officer partially returned, and he grew more and more courageous in proportion as the danger diminished. Remembering with shame and indignation the outrage committed upon one of his soldiers the day before by the audacious Kiowa, involving as it did a gross indignity upon the authority and honor of the United States Government as vested in its army, he determined to have the offender arrested at once, and properly punished, as an example to the rest. He would give them to understand that such outrages were not to be perpetrated with impunity! Accordingly he mustered his entire available force, and taking two pieces of artillery, marched up the river, leaving only *six* men in charge of the fort, to defend it, if need be, against the five hundred Indians who were prowling about. Most of these, however, followed in the trail of the troops, like a crowd of loafers in a large city at the tail of a procession, anticipating some fun or excitement.

In his zeal to bring the offender to justice, no thought of the danger and difficulties that attended the execution of his plans occurred to the valorous Lieutenant. He had not the least doubt that he could march up and take the Indian

---

* Fort Mann, once a thriving post, situated some twenty miles from Fort Atkinson, was attacked one night by an immense war-party of Pawnees, who stealthily scaled the walls while the guard slept, and put the inhabitants to death, sacking and burning the place. A confused mass of ruins now mark the spot, affording a startling memento of one of the many fearful tragedies enacted on this "Dark and Bloody Ground."

from his friends and his tribe without opposition on their part. He had only to state his demands, and the offender would be immediately surrendered; or, if they declined, the two field-pieces and his numerous force could not fail to effect what mere words would be unable to do. Awed by his imposing appearance, the red-skins would, no doubt, come to terms at once. It did occur to him, however, that it might have been better to have demanded the Indian of Ter-hausen the day before, when both were within the walls of the fort, instead of allowing the affair temporarily to blow over, and giving the offender an opportunity to escape; besides having now to contend with ten thousand Indians, instead of only four hundred, as would have been the case the day before.

No sooner had the troops formed in line outside the fort, preparatory to marching, than the Indians above were informed of their intentions, and prepared to receive them. The village turned out *en masse*, and when the troops came up, they at once surrounded them, so that they were completely flanked on either side, with the river in their rear. However, they made their way directly to the place where the chiefs were assembled awaiting their approach, the Indians meanwhile galloping around them in vast numbers, hooting, and yelling, and brandishing their weapons. In this dilemma the courage and ardor of the troops considerably abated, as they now expected nothing less than an attack; but the savages refrained from any act of violence. Arrived at the Council lodge, the Lieutenant immediately stated his demands, and the reasons therefor; having received which, the chiefs held a few moments' consultation. There were present, besides Ter-hausen the Kiowa chief, and Shaved-head, chief of the Comanches, and other minor chiefs of the two tribes, several Cheyenne chiefs, and Yellow Bear, the Arrapaho—all having considerable influence with the allies. These latter being friendly to the whites, earnestly dissuaded the others from molesting the troops, as any such act would bring upon them the vengeance of the United States Government, besides precluding every chance of their obtaining the presents they were so impatiently expecting. This well-timed advice had the effect to pacify them to a certain extent, and was no doubt the only thing that prevented the total annihilation of the troops. Nevertheless, the combined influence of the chiefs did not suffice to hold completely in check the passions of the excited braves, who now crowded close upon the soldiers, threatening to trample them beneath their horses' hoofs.

North American Indians and their ponies.

The prairie on fire.

After a short consultation the delinquent Kiowa was brought forward, led between two Kiowa braves, and surrounded by a host of his friends, who conducted him to the Lieutenant, and in a sarcastic manner told him, "Here is the rascal—take him!"

The Indians now thronged so closely upon the party within the little circle as to render it almost impossible to move, while the continual shouting and jeering rendered it difficult to hear a word that was said. It was evident to the Lieutenant that it was farthest from their intentions to give up the man, and that they had only employed this feint as a provocation to a fight, after the fashion of some "shoulder-hitters" in placing a chip upon a man's shoulder and daring another to knock it off. He was completely nonplussed. His men were drawn up in line, with the two field-pieces in front, bearing directly upon the densest body of the Indians, so that their first discharge, together with that of the musketry, could not fail to make dreadful havoc among them; but it required no great foresight to perceive that a resort to arms would be the height of folly, and that at the first onset they would be immediately overpowered and slaughtered to a man. To retreat was hazardous, for the Indians, perceiving their fear, would be encouraged to attack them; while, if they attempted to take the offender, they would, of course, be resisted. In this dilemma the officers looked despairingly at each other. They had evidently "caught a Tartar."

At length the Lieutenant, with more wit than valor, approached Ter-hausen, and extending his hand, graciously informed him that he was satisfied with his willingness to give up the culprit, and to have him properly punished; but he was confident that more good would be accomplished if the chiefs would punish him in their own way, rather than to have that unpleasant duty to perform himself. He would not, therefore, press the matter farther, but trust to them to have justice done. So saying, he shook hands with the chiefs, and affecting an air of *nonchalance*, turned to his men and gave the order to march.

But no sooner had he done this than the savages raised a triumphant shout, and charging upon the troops with deafening yells, forced them bodily down the gentle slope toward the river, but without using their weapons or attempting any greater violence; so that before the soldiers recovered from their first surprise sufficiently to comprehend the difficulty, they found themselves waist-deep in the river, with their guns and powder rendered useless by the water. Here the Indians jeered them to their hearts' content, and then suffered them to go on their way. Not a musket was fired by the troops, and no one attempted the least resistance. Indeed, all were so terribly frightened that they thought more of using their legs than their arms.

However, the Lieutenant at length succeeded in forming them in tolerable marching order, when they made good time to the fort, the Indians following them to the very gate, throwing sand and dirt at them, and using all manner of taunting epithets. It was not until the next day that the officers learned the full extent of the danger to which they had been exposed. Not only had the Indians invested them in front and on either side, but a party of not less than five hundred warriors lay secreted upon a reedy island in the river, ready to attack them on their rear. Thus if the Indians had been disposed, they might have not only destroyed them to a man, but also taken and plundered the fort, burned it, and returned to their own country before a single white man had been apprised of the fearful tragedy. Mangled corpses, smoking ruins, and utter devastation alone would have told the story to the first astounded traveler who passed that way. But a wise Providence ordered differently. The efforts of Yellow Bear and his few compatriots were unquestionably all that saved this country from a protracted Indian war.

III

A week subsequent to the occurrence above related, a train of fourteen white-tilted Conostoga wagons, to which were added a couple of light traveling-carriages—a rare phenomenon upon the prairies—were slowly rumbling along the bank of the Arkansas toward the fort, and distant about fourteen miles. The greater part of the wagons were drawn by mules, though to five of them oxen were attached, there being six to each wagon. These latter comprised the wagon-train of the notorious Bill Bent, who was now on his way from the States to St. Vrain's Fort on the South Platte, whither he had transferred his trading-post some years before, having burned and dismantled old Fort William (better known as Bent's Fort), it is said, to prevent its falling into the hands of the Government. This post was one of the best built and most eligibly situated in the whole Territory, and one much coveted by the Government for a military station—who offered Bent a considerable sum for its purchase, but not sufficient in the old trader's estimation. The eccentric old fellow, in a sudden freak of resentment, or from some inexplicable cause, accordingly demolished it.

The remaining wagons of the train, as also the two carriages, belonged to Mr. King's party, which was composed chiefly of young adventurers and valetudinarians, who had chosen this route of summer travel in preference to those more generally selected by fashionables and pleasure-seekers—choosing to run the risk of being eased of their money and valuables by the feather-bedizened and copper-colored thieves of the plains, rather than the civilized and more accomplished light-fingered gentry of the East. Fitzwilliam had also joined company, and was along with his men—all the camp-equipage and accoutrements of his party being secured upon the backs of pack-mules, hunter fashion. But by no means the least notable personage in the cavalcade was Yellow Bear, who had been waiting for Bent at Fort Atkinson, having agreed to meet him there; but being apprised of his approach, had hastened out stealthily to join him, fearful lest he should be attacked and massacred by the Comanches, as his was the first train along since the troubles commenced.

All those men not attached to the wagons were mounted on fine horses, and galloped along, rifle in hand, in front and rear and on either side, keeping a sharp look-out for Indians, and carefully guarding the pack animals and loose horses, of which there were some seventy in all. Altogether the train numbered about fifty persons; so that they presented quite an imposing appearance, as well as a formidable foe to Indian assailants.

Up to this time no Indians had been seen; but they had progressed but a short distance farther when a few stragglers were met. As they continued to advance, more were seen; and these gradually increased in number, until there were several hundred in the vicinity of the train, while reinforcements were continually arriving from above. It now became evident that the whole camp was apprised of their approach, and the situation of the little party became more critical every moment. However, no attempts were yet made to molest them, and they kept steadily on their way, but redoubling their precautions for safety. Bent's wagons were placed in front, and the animals between them and the remaining wagons, with a horse-guard on either side. As there were several women and children in the party, Bent also having his family with him, it was deemed advisable for their safety to send them on to the fort in advance, under the escort of Yellow Bear, as the object of the Indians now seemed to be plunder merely. Accordingly Bent, with his five wagons, the carriages, and a sufficient force for their protection, hastened forward with all possible speed, leaving the remaining wagons in charge of some sixteen men.

But no sooner were they fairly out of sight than the Indians gathered around the others in swarms, and commenced a series of manoeuvres, endeavoring, in every manner imaginable, to stampede the animals or to confuse and separate the men. Coursing around on every side, whooping and yelling and rattling their spears against their leathern shields, and making the most hideous din, they would charge suddenly upon the wagons, endeavoring to drive their horses between the men, and thus divide their ranks, when both men and wagons would at once become an easy prey. But most of the party were old teamsters and hunters, well versed in Indian strategy, and did not suffer themselves to be at all disconcerted by these proceedings. Moving in line, they always presented a bristling front of rifle-bores to their assailants, so that all their attempts to gain their purpose by such means proved quite ineffectual.* The Indians now essayed other expedients. Spurring furiously toward the now frightened animals, shaking their buffalo robes, hallooing loudly to each other, then suddenly rushing together in wild confusion, jabbering and gesticulating violently, as if engaged in most exciting conversation; then again breaking up with deafening yells, and riding furiously up and down the line, they strove to drive the frantic steeds outside the guard. But all to no purpose. The teamsters performed their duty manfully, and rendered all their attempts of no avail.

In this way the train advanced slowly until within eight miles of the fort, the constantly increasing numbers of the Indians rendering their situation momentarily more precarious. At length it became evident that, without speedy assistance, they must soon be overpowered, in spite of all their vigilance and untiring effort. There remained no alternative but to send to the fort for help, dangerous as the expedient was, and offering but a bare possibility of success; for the courier had a fearful gauntlet to run through such a multitude of savages, who, at once divining his intent, would attempt to cut him off. Nevertheless, a volunteer was immediately found in Tom Smith, a veteran trapper, who rode a noble mustang of the finest mettle.

---

* The Indian knows full well that the trigger of a hunter's rifle is seldom pulled in vain, and is exceedingly careful not to expose his body as a target to its aim, or to provoke the emptying of its contents; hence, a single man may often keep a host at bay, so long as his loaded rifle covers its mark.

"I'll risk it," he said. "Thar's good grit in old 'Lightfoot' yet, and she's seen red skin afore; eh, old gal?" and bending forward, he patted his favorite steed upon the neck, which salutation she returned with a low hinney of pleasure. Then drawing up the reins, he trotted her easily a few rods; then striking his spurs into her flanks, dashed on toward the fort with lightning speed. She was a noble beast. Many a time had she saved him from the vengeance of the savages, and now she bore him safely to the fort, distancing the few who attempted to pursue. Bent's wagons had but just arrived as Tom came up, having experienced but little trouble from the Indians, owing, no doubt, to the presence of Yellow Bear, who proved an excellent passport to the whites whom he befriended. Bent was busy unhitching the teams when the intelligence was brought. Muttering an angry oath, he dropped the yoke he held in his hand, and flinging himself upon the back of "Pigeon-toe," his favorite steed, drove his spurs to the rowels, and dashed headlong down the river, with oaths and threats of vengeance hissing on his lips. Mounting their horses with all possible haste, the rest of his men shot out from the fort one by one, and followed desperately after their leader. The Lieutenant, too, immediately ordered out his twenty dragoons, to send them after those already on their way to the scene of action. Hundreds of Comanches, instantly divining the difficulty, raised the war-cry from point to point, and dashed on in the headlong chase. All was excitement at the fort, and none doubted that, by this time, the scalps of the luckless teamsters were dangling from the spears of the victorious savages.

Meanwhile the beleaguered party down the river were struggling bravely on their way. But the Indians perceiving that they were gradually slipping through their fingers, became more courageous. A large party now came up, and lassoed a buffalo calf which the teamsters had with them, saying, "the whites had no right to such meat; it belonged to the Indians." This was only a ruse to divert attention from the horses and mules; and while it partially succeeded, others made a concerted attack upon the *cavallada*. But the teamsters, instantly recovering their self-possession, at once formed the wagons into a *corral* (made by driving them together in an elliptical form, resembling a horse-shoe), and surrounding the loose animals, drove them into it, excepting a few which the Indians succeeded in capturing; then taking their position behind this hastily-constructed but most effectual barricade, they stood with their rifles to their shoulders, ready to defend themselves to the last gasp.

But now a shout most fierce and loud came borne upon the wind; then a succession of stentorian whoops and yells, more fierce than the fiercest of Indian war-whoops, which caused them to turn suddenly in the direction of the sounds. The Indians heard it, too, and hastily drew off a little, in some degree of confusion. Glancing up the prairie, they descried the welcome form of the redoubtable Bent tearing down toward them at a furious rate, brandishing his rifle high over his head, and yelling loud threats of vengeance upon the audacious savages. A quarter of a mile behind him came Tom Smith and Yellow Bear, streaking it over the turf, while close at their heels followed another of the subsidiary party; then another and another at short intervals—the long and sinuous train stretching far away in the distance to where the last of the gallant fellows brought up the rear of the impetuous force.

The Indians, who seemed to regard Bent with a certain degree of awe, now fell back in a body, keeping a short distance behind. Bent was a terrible fellow when exasperated, and the Indians knew it. To them the fame of his might and deeds of daring was as wide as the prairie, and proud would be the trophy that "brave" would wear who won his scalp! No doubt it was this superstitious dread of their invincible foe that forced from them such circumspection, and caused them to refrain from their attack upon the wagons; though their odds were sufficient to have vanquished a force twenty times greater. As the old trader reined up his foaming steed, his rage could hardly find vent in words. One language would not suffice; but in a mingled jargon of Indian, English, French, and Spanish, he poured out his wrath upon the cowardly miscreants before him, swearing great oaths, alternately shaking his fist and his rifle, and daring them to the fight! Such was Bent when "a heap mad;" at other times a model of equanimity and calm decorum.

The whole of the relief party having now come in, with the exception of the dragoons, Bent presently gave the word to "put out." Once more the wagons were formed in the line of march, and the mules whipped into a brisk trot. Tom Smith, with half a dozen mounted men, led the van; eighteen more rode abreast behind the wagons, to guard their rear; while the remaining horsemen galloped along side. Thus they moved on for a couple of miles, the Indians following close behind, but not yet venturing an attack. But as they neared the fort, which now loomed up in the distance, and the chances of escape increased, they once more rallied to the onset, and forming in dense platoons, bristling with spears, came charging down upon the rear of the train with hideous yells. "*Hough-ough-ough-gh-gh!*" rang the deafening war-cry as they clattered over the ground—emitted in a series of prolonged yells which terminated with a whoop as abrupt as the halt they made when within fair pistol-shot of the wagons.

"Come on, you sneakin' varmints, if you're after har!" shouts old Bent, shaking his fist at the savages he could not see for the clouds of dust that now rose like a wall between him and them. "Come on, if you want shooting; but you can't come no such game as that on *this* child—for he's seen such doings afore, *he* has." Then turning away with an oath, he would hurry on the wagons, and they would speedily emerge from the region of dust. Again and again did the Indians attempt to disconcert the little party by similar feints—dashing furiously upon them, as if to crush them under their horses' feet, but always halting suddenly when within a few rods of them. At last old "Shaved-head" himself headed the onslaught. On they came, more furiously than before; but this time they slightly overmeasured their distance, and so impetuous was the charge, that the chief, who rode a mettlesome but tough-bitted steed, was unable to stop until he found himself in the very midst of his foes. Quick as thought sprang Bent and Yellow Bear together, and grasped the bridle of his horse, and he was at once made prisoner. A shout from the whites greeted their success.

Confounded at this sudden and unexpected misfortune, and alarmed for the safety of their favorite chief, the Indians at once became remarkably peaceable, and followed quietly behind, manifesting the greatest anxiety and uneasiness, and heedless of Bent's sarcastic banter, which he took no pains to spare.

Bent and the Bear rode one on either side of their captive, each holding a rein in his hand—Bent all the while shaking his fist in the Indian's face, and venting his spleen in great oaths and abusive language; while in marked contrast was the conduct of the dignified Yellow Bear, who cantered quietly along, saying nothing, but occasionally glancing into his captive's face with a calm, triumphant smile, singularly expressive, though scarcely noticeable. The rascals whom Bent so woefully berated were quite beneath his notice. Not once did the Comanches attempt to retake their chief, fearing the ready knife of the angry trader, which they knew he would not hesitate to use upon him if they attempted violence, as he had taken special pains to inform them. Thus, holding the key which kept securely locked an

earthly Pandemonium, they experienced no further trouble on their way to the fort.

Modern policemen are said to be always on hand when the danger is over. In like manner, the train had arrived within two miles of its destination, when ominous sounds attracted their attention, and they beheld the *dragoons* clattering over the prairie, on their way to render them the desired assistance—full two hours having elapsed since the first intimation of peril was received by the garrison! As they came up formed in regular military order, with their full panoply of jingling sabres, rattling trappings, and showy uniform, they really looked as though they might have done good service for Uncle Sam—always taking it for granted that they were not *two hours behind time*. But in the present instance they might as well have remained in their barracks, and left the teamsters to be massacred, as would have unquestionably been the case but for Bent's timely arrival.

The only cause assigned for such unwarrantable delay was, that but nineteen horses could be procured—one having been disabled the previous night. Their military discipline would not permit them to go without their full complement of men, and therefore they were forced to wait until they could send out and purchase an animal from the Indians. They seemed quite surprised to find all the men safe and arrived so soon, and—it may be well to add—heartily congratulated them upon their *fortunate* escape. So much for military tactics.

Absurdly ridiculous as the foregoing may appear, it is but one of a thousand similar cases which might be cited, explaining satisfactorily the causes of numerous failures and disasters apparently unaccountable to those unacquainted with the circumstances that occasioned them. It is an axiom which must sooner or later become perfectly lucid in the eyes of Congress, that methodical tactics, and armies of regulars ever so large, may frighten, but never subdue Indians. Put an experienced old "mountain-man," like Kit Carson or Bill Bent, at the head of thirty others like him, and they will accomplish more than a regiment of troops—especially in those cases where ambuscades and the wiles and cunning of the Indian are to be combated. In the open field the same is true. The Indians will never meet an enemy in open fight except with tremendous odds in their favor. Nowadays they are almost invariably mounted when on the war-trail or a thieving expedition. Of course *infantry* can do nothing, and are next to useless. If too numerous, the Indians will take good care to keep out of rifle-range; if too few, their fate is certain. Mounted men alone can effect any thing. Dragoons are better than infantry. If they can not conquer their foe, they can at least escape by running away. But of what possible use can even dragoons be if all their movements are to be regulated by such tactical machinery as requires them to move and act with an automatic precision which, in nine cases out of ten, prevents them from taking advantage of auspicious circumstances to strike an effective blow; allows the enemy to slip through their fingers unscathed; or, forsooth, permits a massacre of their own countrymen almost within hail of their voices?

The United States furnishes her cavalry with excellent horses, which, when mounted by men who know their business, and competent officers to command, could soon run the Indians out of the country, or punish them into good behavior and a proper regard for human life and the laws of *meum* and *tuum*. Let the *Ranger* system, then, be adopted in place of the old discipline—a system in which each man, acting in concert with his fellow, yet fights on his own hook; a system which would not prevent nineteen men from saving a massacre because a twentieth could not aid in the action—and government has found the true remedy for one of her greatest ills. [. . .]

The Attack.   *The Defeat.*

The Dividing Line Between Federal and Local Authority
Popular Sovereignty in the Territories

by Stephen A. Douglas

September 1859

Under our complex system of government it is the first duty of American statesmen to mark distinctly the dividing line between Federal and Local Authority. To do this with accuracy involves an inquiry, not only into the powers and duties of the Federal Government under the Constitution, but also into the rights, privileges, and immunities of the people of the Territories, as well as of the States composing the Union. The relative powers and functions of the Federal and State governments have become well understood and clearly defined by their practical operation and harmonious action for a long series of years; while the disputed question— involving the right of the people of the Territories to govern themselves in respect to their local affairs and internal polity—remains a fruitful source of partisan strife and sectional controversy. The political organization which was formed in 1854, and has assumed the name of the Republican party, is based on the theory that African slavery, as it exists in this country, is an evil of such magnitude—social, moral, and political—as to justify and require the exertion of the entire power and influence of the Federal Government to the full extent that the Constitution, according to their interpretation, will permit for its ultimate extinction. [...]

According to the theory of the Republican party there is an irrepressible conflict between freedom and slavery, free labor and slave labor, free States and slave States, which is irreconcilable, and must continue to rage with increasing fury until the one shall become universal by the annihilation of the other. [...]

Thus it will be seen, that under the auspices of a political party, which claims sovereignty in Congress over the subject of slavery, there can be no peace on the slavery question—no truce in the sectional strife—no fraternity between the North and South, so long as this Union remains as our fathers made it—divided into free and slave States, with the right on the part of each to retain slavery so long as it chooses, and to abolish it whenever it pleases.

On the other hand, it would be uncandid to deny that, while the Democratic party is a unit in its irreconcilable opposition to the doctrines and principles of the Republican party, there are radical differences of opinion in respect to the powers and duties of Congress, and the rights and immunities of the people of the Territories under the Federal Constitution, which seriously disturb its harmony and threaten its integrity. These differences of opinion arise from the different interpretations placed on the Constitution by persons who belong to one of the following classes:

First.—Those who believe that the Constitution of the United States neither establishes nor prohibits slavery in the States or Territories beyond the power of the people legally to control it, but "leaves the people thereof perfectly free to form and regulate their domestic institutions in their own way, subject only to the Constitution of the United States."

Second.—Those who believe that the Constitution establishes slavery in the Territories, and withholds from Congress and the Territorial Legislature the power to control it; and who insist that, in the event the Territorial Legislature fails to enact the requisite laws for its protection, it becomes the imperative duty of Congress to interpose its authority and furnish such protection.

Third.—Those who, while professing to believe that the Constitution establishes slavery in the Territories beyond the power of Congress or the Territorial Legislature to control it, at the same time protest against the duty of Congress to interfere for its protection; but insist that it is the duty of the Judiciary to protect and maintain slavery in the Territories without any law upon the subject.

By a careful examination of the second and third propositions, it will be seen that the advocates of each agree on the theoretical question, that the Constitution establishes slavery in the Territories, and compels them to have it whether they want it or not; and differ on the practical point, whether a right secured by the Constitution shall be protected by an act of Congress when all other remedies fail. The reason assigned for not protecting by law a right secured by the Constitution is, that it is the duty of the Courts to protect slavery in the Territories without any legislation upon the subject. How the Courts are to afford protection to slaves or any other property, where there is no law providing remedies and imposing penalties and conferring jurisdiction upon the Courts to hear and determine the cases as they arise, remains to be explained.

The acts of Congress, establishing the several Territories of the United States, provide that: "The jurisdiction of the several Courts herein provided for, both appellate and original, and that of the Probate Courts and Justices of the Peace, shall be as limited by law"—meaning such laws as the Territorial Legislatures shall from time to time enact. It will be seen that the judicial tribunals of the Territories have just such jurisdiction, and only such, in respect to the rights of persons and property pertaining to the citizens of the Territory as the Territorial Legislature shall see fit to confer; and consequently, that the Courts can afford protection to persons and property no further than the Legislature shall, by law, confer the jurisdiction, and prescribe the remedies, penalties, and modes of proceeding.

It is difficult to conceive how any person who believes that the Constitution confers the right of protection in the enjoyment of slave property in the Territories, regardless of the wishes of the people and of the action of the Territorial Legislature, can satisfy his conscience and his oath of fidelity to the Constitution in witholding such Congressional legislation as may be essential to the enjoyment of such right under the Constitution. Under this view of the subject it is impossible to resist the conclusion that, if the Constitution does establish slavery in the Territories, beyond the power of the people to control it by law, it is the imperative duty of Congress to supply all the legislation necessary to its protection; and if this proposition is not true, it necessarily results that the Constitution neither establishes nor prohibits slavery any where, but leaves the people of each State and Territory entirely free to form and regulate their domestic affairs to suit themselves, without the intervention of Congress or of any other power whatsoever. [...]

This dividing line between Federal and Local authority was familiar to the framers of the Constitution. It is clearly defined and distinctly marked on every page of history which records the great events of that immortal struggle between the American Colonies and the British Government, which resulted in the establishment of our national independence. In the beginning of that struggle the Colonies neither contemplated nor desired independence. In all their addresses to the Crown, and to the Parliament, and to the people of Great Britain, as well as to the people of America, they averred that as loyal British subjects they deplored the causes which impelled their separation from the parent country. They were strongly and affectionately attached to the Constitution, civil and political institutions and jurisprudence of Great Britain, which they proudly claimed as the birth-right of all Englishmen, and desired to transmit them unimpaired as a precious legacy to their posterity. For a long series of years they remonstrated against the violation of their inalienable rights of self-government under the British Constitution, and humbly petitioned for the redress of their grievances. [...]

The government of Great Britain had violated this inalienable right of local self-government by a long series of acts on a great variety of subjects. The first serious point of controversy arose on the slavery question as early as 1699, which continued a fruitful source of irritation until the Revolution, and formed one of the causes for the separation of the Colonies from the British Crown. [...]

The legislation of Virginia on this subject may be taken as a fair sample of the legislative enactments of each of the thirteen Colonies, showing conclusively that slavery was regarded by them all as a domestic question to be regulated and determined by each Colony to suit itself, without the intervention of the British Parliament or "the inhuman use of the Royal negative." Each Colony passed a series of enactments, beginning at an early period of its history and running down to the commencement of the Revolution, either protecting, regulating, or restraining African Slavery within its respective limits and in accordance with their wishes and supposed interests. North and South Carolina, following the example of Virginia, at first encouraged the introduction of slaves, until the number increased beyond their wants and necessities, when they attempted to check and restrain the further growth of the institution, by imposing a high rate of taxation upon all slaves which should be brought into those Colonies; and finally, in 1764, South

Carolina passed a law imposing a penalty of one hundred pounds (or five hundred dollars) for every negro slave subsequently introduced into that Colony.

The Colony of Georgia was originally founded on strict anti-slavery principles, and rigidly maintained this policy for a series of years, until the inhabitants became convinced by experience, that, with their climate and productions, slave labor, if not essential to their existence, would prove beneficial and useful to their material interests. Maryland and Delaware protected and regulated African Slavery as one of their domestic institutions. Pennsylvania, under the advice of William Penn, substituted fourteen years' service and perpetual adscript to the soil for hereditary slavery, and attempted to legislate, not for the total abolition of slavery, but for the sanctity of marriage among slaves, and for their personal security. New Jersey, New York, and Connecticut, recognized African Slavery as a domestic institution lawfully existing within their respective limits, and passed the requisite laws for its control and regulation.

Rhode Island provided by law that no slave should serve more than ten years, at the end of which time he was to be set free; and if the master should refuse to let him go free, or sold him elsewhere for a longer period of service, he was subject to a penalty of forty pounds, which was supposed at that period to be nearly double the value of the slave.

Massachusetts imposed heavy taxes upon all slaves brought into the Colony, and provided in some instances for sending the slaves back to their native land; and finally prohibited the introduction of any more slaves into the Colony under any circumstances.

When New Hampshire passed laws which were designed to prevent the introduction of any more slaves, the British Cabinet issued the following order to Governor Wentworth: "You are not to give your assent to, or pass any law imposing duties upon Negroes imported into New Hampshire."

While the legislation of the several Colonies exhibits dissimilarity of views, founded on a diversity of interests, on the merits and policy of slavery, it shows conclusively that they all regarded it as a domestic question affecting their internal polity in respect to which they were entitled to a full and exclusive power of legislation in the several provincial Legislatures. For a few years immediately preceding the American Revolution the African Slave-Trade was encouraged and stimulated by the British Government and carried on with more vigor by the English merchants than at any other period in the history of the Colonies; and this fact,

taken in connection with the extraordinary claim asserted in the Memorable Preamble to the act repealing the Stamp duties, that "Parliament possessed the right to bind the Colonies in all cases whatsoever," not only in respect to all matters affecting the general welfare of the empire, but also in regard to the domestic relations and internal polity of the Colonies—produced a powerful impression upon the minds of the colonists, and imparted peculiar prominence to the principle involved in the controversy.

Hence the enactments by the several colonial Legislatures calculated and designed to restrain and prevent the increase of slaves; and, on the other hand, the orders issued by the Crown instructing the Colonial Governors not to sign or permit any legislative enactment prejudicial or injurious to the African Slave-Trade, unless such enactment should contain a clause suspending its operation until the royal pleasure should be made known in the premises; or, in other words, until the King should have an opportunity of annulling the acts of the colonial Legislatures by the "inhuman use of the Royal negative."

Thus the policy of the Colonies on the slavery question had assumed a direct antagonism to that of the British Government; and this antagonism not only added to the importance of the principle of local self-government in the Colonies, but produced a general concurrence of opinion and action in respect to the question of slavery in the proceedings of the Continental Congress, which assembled at Philadelphia for the first time on the 5th of September, 1774. [...]

In the formation of the Constitution of the United States the Federal Convention took the British Constitution, as interpreted and expounded by the Colonies during their controversy with Great Britain, for their model—making such modifications in its structure and principles as the change in our condition had rendered necessary. They intrusted the Executive functions to a President in the place of a King; the Legislative functions to a Congress composed of a Senate and House of Representatives, in lieu of the Parliament consisting of the Houses of Lords and Commons; and the Judicial functions to a Supreme Court and such inferior Courts as Congress should from time to time ordain and establish.

Having thus divided the powers of government into the three appropriate departments, with which they had always been familiar, they proceeded to confer upon the Federal Government substantially the same powers which they as colonies had been willing to concede to the British Government, and to reserve to the States and to the people the

Stephen A. Douglas

formed the Constitution of the United States, to assume that they intended to confer upon Congress that unlimited and arbitrary power over the people of the American Territories, which they had resisted with their blood when claimed by the British Parliament over British Colonies in America? Did they confer upon Congress the right to bind the people of the American Territories in all cases whatsoever, after having fought the battles of the Revolution against a "Preamble" declaring the right of Parliament "to bind the Colonies in all cases whatsoever?"

If, as they contended before the Revolution, it was the birth-right of all Englishmen, inalienable when formed into political communities, to exercise exclusive power of legislation in their local legislatures in respect to all things affecting their internal polity—slavery not excepted—did not the same right, after the Revolution, and by virtue of it, become the birth-right of all Americans, in like manner inalienable when organized into political communities—no matter by what name, whether Colonies, Territories, Provinces, or new States?

Names often deceive persons in respect to the nature and substance of things. A signal instance of this kind is to be found in that clause of the Constitution which says:

> Congress shall have power to dispose of, and make all needful rules and regulations respecting the territory or other property belonging to the United States.

This being the only clause of the Constitution in which the word "territory" appears, that fact alone has doubtless led many persons to suppose that the right of Congress to establish temporary governments for the Territories, in the sense in which the word is now used, must be derived from it, overlooking the important and controlling facts that at the time the Constitution was formed the word "territory" had never been used or understood to designate a political community or government of any kind in any law, compact, deed of cession, or public document; but had invariably been used either in its geographical sense to describe the superficial area of a State or district of country, as in the Virginia deed of cession of the "territory or *tract of country*" northwest of the River Ohio; or as meaning land in its character as property, in which latter sense it appears in the clause of the Constitution referred to, when providing for the disposition of the "territory or other property belonging to the United States." These facts, taken in connection with

same rights and privileges which they as colonies had denied to the British Government during the entire struggle which terminated in our Independence, and which they had claimed for themselves and their posterity as the birth-right of all freemen, inalienable when organized into political communities, and to be enjoyed and exercised by Colonies, Territories, and Provinces as fully and completely as by sovereign States. Thus it will be seen that there is an organic feature or fundamental principle embodied in the Constitution of the United States which had not been familiar to the people of the Colonies from the period of their earliest settlement, and which had not been repeatedly asserted by them when denied by Great Britain during the whole period of their Colonial history.

Let us pause at this point for a moment, and inquire whether it be just to those illustrious patriots and sages who

the kindred one that during the whole period of the Confederation and the formation of the Constitution the temporary governments which we now call "Territories," were invariably referred to in the deeds of cession, laws, compacts, plans of government, resolutions of congress, public records, and authentic documents as "States," or "new States," conclusively show that the words "territory and other property" in the Constitution were used to designate the unappropriated lands and other property which the United States owned, and not the people who might become residents on those lands, and be organized into political communities after the United States had parted with their title.

It is from this clause of the Constitution alone that Congress derives the power to provide for the surveys and sale of the public lands and all other property belonging to the United States, not only in the Territories, but also in the several States of the Union. But for this provision Congress would have no power to authorize the sale of the public lands, military sites, old ships, cannon, muskets, or other property, real or personal, which belong to the United States and are no longer needed for any public purpose. It refers exclusively to property in contradistinction to persons and communities. It confers the same power "to make all needful rules and regulations" in the States as in the Territories, and extends wherever there may be any land or other property belonging to the United States to be regulated or disposed of; but does not authorize Congress to control or interfere with the domestic institutions and internal polity of the people (either in the States or the Territories) who may reside upon lands which the United States once owned. Such a power, had it been vested in Congress, would annihilate the sovereignty and freedom of the States as well as the great principle of self-government in the Territories, wherever the United States happen to own a portion of the public lands within their respective limits, as, at present, in the States of Alabama, Florida, Mississippi, Louisiana, Arkansas, Missouri, Illinois, Indiana, Ohio, Michigan, Wisconsin, Iowa, Minnesota, California, and Oregon, and in the Territories of Washington, Nebraska, Kansas, Utah, and New Mexico. The idea is repugnant to the spirit and genius of our complex system of government; because it effectually blots out the dividing line between Federal and Local authority which forms an essential barrier for the defense of the independence of the States and the liberties of the people against Federal invasion. With one anomalous exception, all the powers conferred on Congress are *Federal*, and not *Municipal*, in their character—affecting the general welfare of the whole country without interfering with the internal polity of the people—and can be carried into effect by laws which apply alike to States and Territories. The exception, being in derogation of one of the fundamental principles of our political system (because it authorizes the Federal government to control the municipal affairs and internal polity of the people in certain specified, limited localities), was not left to vague inference or loose construction, nor expressed in dubious or equivocal language; but is found plainly written in that Section of the Constitution which says:

Congress shall have power to exercise exclusive legislation in all cases whatsoever, over such district (not exceeding ten miles square) as may, by cession of particular States, and the acceptance of Congress, become the seat of the government of the United States, and to exercise like authority over all places purchased by the consent of the Legislature of the State in which the same shall be, for the erection of forts, magazines, arsenals, dock-yards, and other needful buildings.

No such power "to exercise exclusive legislation in all cases whatsoever," nor indeed any legislation in any case whatsoever, is conferred on Congress in respect to the municipal affairs and internal polity, either of the States or of the Territories. On the contrary, after the Constitution had been finally adopted, with its Federal powers delegated, enumerated, and defined, in order to guard in all future time against any possible infringement of the reserved rights of the States, or of the people, an amendment was incorporated into the Constitution which marks the dividing line between Federal and Local authority so directly and indelibly that no lapse of time, no partisan prejudice, no sectional aggrandizement, no frenzied fanaticism can efface it. The amendment is in these words:

The powers not delegated to the United States by the Constitution, nor prohibited by it to the States, are reserved to the States respectively, or to the people.

[...] The provision to authorize Congress to institute temporary governments for the new States or Territories, and to provide for their admission into the Union, appears in the Constitution in this form:

> New States may be admitted by the Congress into this Union.

The power to admit "*new States*," and "to make all laws which shall be necessary and proper" to that end, may fairly be construed to include the right to institute temporary governments for such new States or Territories, the same as Great Britain could rightfully institute similar governments for the Colonies; but certainly not to authorize Congress to legislate in respect to their municipal affairs and internal concerns, without violating that great fundamental principle in defense of which the battles of the Revolution were fought.

If judicial authority were deemed necessary to give force to principles so eminently just in themselves, and which form the basis of our entire political system, such authority may be found in the opinion of the Supreme Court of the United States in the Dred Scott case. In that case the Court say:

> This brings us to examine by what provision of the Constitution the present Federal Government, under its delegated and restricted powers, is authorized to acquire territory outside of the original limits of the United States, and what powers it may exercise therein over the person or property of a citizen of the United States, while it remains a Territory, and until it shall be admitted as one of the States of the Union.
>
> There is certainly no power given by the Constitution to the Federal Government to establish or maintain Colonies, bordering on the United States or at a distance, to be ruled and governed at its own pleasure; nor to enlarge its territorial limits in any way except by the admission of new States....
>
> The power to expand the territory of the United States by the admission of new States is plainly given; and in the construction of this power by all the departments of the Government, it has been held to authorize the acquisition of territory, not fit for admission at the time, but to be admitted as soon as its population and situation would entitle it to admission. It is acquired to become a State, and not to be held as a Colony and governed by Congress with absolute authority; and as

the propriety of admitting a new State is committed to the sound discretion of Congress, the power to acquire territory for that purpose, to be held by the United States until it is in a suitable condition to become a State upon an equal footing with the other States, must rest upon the same discretion.

[...] The power to acquire territory, as well as the right, in the language of Mr. Madison, "to institute temporary governments for the new States arising therein" (or Territorial governments, as they are now called), having been traced to that provision of the Constitution which provides for the admission of "new States," the Court proceed to consider the nature and extent of the power of Congress over the people of the Territories:

> All we mean to say on this point is, that, as there is no express regulation in the Constitution defining the power which the general Government may exercise over the person or property of a citizen in a Territory thus acquired, the Court must necessarily look to the provisions and principles of the Constitution, and its distribution of powers, for the rules and principles by which its decision must be governed.
>
> Taking this rule to guide us, it may be safely assumed that citizens of the United States, who emigrate to a Territory belonging to the people of the United States, can not be ruled as mere colonists, dependent upon the will of the general Government, and to be governed by any laws it may think proper to impose.... The Territory being a part of the United States, the Government and the citizen both enter it under the authority of the Constitution, with their respective rights defined and marked out; and the Federal Government can exercise no power over his person or property beyond what that instrument confers, nor lawfully deny any right which it has reserved.

Hence, inasmuch as the Constitution has conferred on the Federal Government no right to interfere with the property, domestic relations, police regulations, or internal polity of the people of the Territories, it necessarily follows, under the authority of the Court, that Congress can rightfully exercise no such power over the people of the Territories. For this reason alone, the Supreme Court were authorized and compelled to pronounce the eighth section of the Act approved March 6, 1820 (commonly called the Missouri Compromise), inoperative and void—there being no power delegated to Congress in the Constitution authorizing Congress to prohibit slavery in the Territories.

In the course of the discussion of this question the Court gave an elaborate exposition of the structure, principles, and powers of the Federal Government; showing that it possesses no powers except those which are delegated, enumerated, and defined in the Constitution; and that all other powers are either *prohibited* altogether or are *reserved* to the States, or to the people. In order to show that the prohibited, as well as the delegated powers are enumerated and defined in the Constitution, the Court enumerated certain powers which can not be exercised either by Congress or by the Territorial Legislatures, or by any other authority whatever, for the simple reason that they are forbidden by the Constitution.

Some persons who have not examined critically the opinion of the Court in this respect have been induced to believe that the *slavery question* was included in this class of prohibited powers, and that the Court had decided in the Dred Scott case that the Territorial Legislature could not legislate in respect to slave property the same as all other property in the Territories. A few extracts from the opinion of the Court will correct this error, and show clearly the class of powers to which the Court referred, as being forbidden alike to the Federal Government, to the States, and to the Territories. The Court say:

> A reference to a few of the provisions of the Constitution will illustrate this proposition. For example, no one, we presume, will contend that Congress can make any law in a Territory respecting the establishment of religion, or the free exercise thereof, or abridging the freedom of speech or of the press, or the right of the people of the Territory peaceably to assemble, and to petition the Government for the redress of grievances.
>
> Nor can Congress deny to the people the right to keep and bear arms, nor the right to trial by jury, nor compel any one to be a witness against himself in a criminal proceeding.... So too, it will hardly be contended that Congress could by law quarter a soldier in a house in a Territory without the consent of the owner in a time of peace; nor in time of war but in a manner prescribed by law. Nor could they by law forfeit the property of a citizen in a Territory who was convicted of treason, for a longer period than the life

of the person convicted, nor take private property for public use without just compensation.

The powers over persons and property, of which we speak, are not only not granted to Congress, but are in express terms denied, and they are forbidden to exercise them. And this prohibition is not confined to the States, but the words are general, and extend to the whole territory over which the Constitution gives it power to legislate, including those portions of it remaining under Territorial Governments, as well as that covered by States.

It is a total absence of power, every where within the dominion of the United States, and places the citizens of a Territory, so far as these rights are concerned, on the same footing with citizens of the States, and guards them as firmly and plainly against any inroads which the general Government might attempt, under the plea of implied or incidental powers. And if Congress itself can not do this—if it is beyond the powers conferred on the Federal Government—it will be admitted, we presume, that it could not authorize a Territorial government to exercise them. It could confer no power on any local government, established by its authority, to violate the provisions of the Constitution.

Nothing can be more certain than that the Court were here speaking only of *forbidden powers*, which were denied alike to Congress, to the State Legislatures, and to the Territorial Legislatures, and that the prohibition extends "every where within the dominion of the United States," applicable equally to States and Territories, as well as to the United States.

If this sweeping prohibition—this just but inexorable restriction upon the powers of government—Federal, State, and Territorial—shall ever be held to include the slavery question, thus negativing the right of the people of the States and Territories, as well as the Federal Government, to control it by law (and it will be observed that in the opinion of the Court "the citizens of a Territory, so far as these rights are concerned, are on the same footing with the citizens of the States"), then, indeed, will the doctrine become firmly established that the principles of law applicable to African slavery are *uniform throughout the dominion of the United States*, and that there "is an irrepressible conflict between opposing and enduring forces, which means that the United

States must and will, sooner or later, become either entirely a slave-holding nation or entirely a free labor nation."

Notwithstanding the disastrous consequences which would inevitably result from the authoritative recognition and practical operation of such a doctrine, there are those who maintain that the Court referred to and included the slavery question within that class of forbidden powers which (although the same in the Territories as in the States) could not be exercised by the people of the Territories.

If this proposition were true, which fortunately for the peace and welfare of the whole country it is not, the conclusion would inevitably result, which they logically deduce from the premises—that the Constitution by the recognition of slavery establishes it in the Territories beyond the power of the people to control it by law, and guarantees to every citizen the right to go there and be protected in the enjoyment of his slave property; and when all other remedies fail for the protection of such rights of property, it becomes the imperative duty of Congress (to the performance of which every member is bound by his conscience and his oath, and from which no consideration of political policy or expediency can release him) to provide by law such adequate and complete protection as is essential to the full enjoyment of an important right secured by the Constitution. If the proposition be true, that the Constitution establishes slavery in the Territories beyond the power of the people legally to control it, another result, no less startling, and from which there is no escape, must inevitably follow. The Constitution is uniform "every where within the dominions of the United States"—is the same in Pennsylvania as in Kansas—and if it be true, as stated by the President in a special Message to Congress, "that slavery exists in Kansas by virtue of the Constitution of the United States," and that "Kansas is therefore at this moment as much a slave State as Georgia or South Carolina," why does it not exist in Pennsylvania by virtue of the same Constitution?

If it be said that Pennsylvania is a Sovereign State, and therefore has a right to regulate the slavery question within her own limits to suit herself, it must be borne in mind that the sovereignty of Pennsylvania, like that of every other State, is limited by the Constitution, which provides that:

> This Constitution, and all laws of the United States which shall be made in pursuance thereof, and all treaties made, or which shall be made, under the authority of the United States, shall be the *supreme law of the land,* and the judges in every State shall be bound thereby, *any thing in the Constitution or laws of any State to the contrary notwithstanding.*

Hence, the State of Pennsylvania, with her Constitution and laws, and domestic institutions, and internal policy, is subordinate to the Constitution of the United States, in the same manner, and to the same extent, as the Territory of Kansas. The Kansas-Nebraska Act says that the Territory of Kansas shall exercise legislative power over "all rightful subjects of legislation consistent with the Constitution," and that the people of said Territory shall be left "perfectly free to form and regulate their domestic institutions in their own way, subject only to the Constitution of the United States." The provisions of this Act are believed to be in entire harmony with the Constitution, and under them the people of Kansas possess every right, privilege, and immunity, in respect to their internal polity and domestic relations which the people of Pennsylvania can exercise under their Constitution and laws. Each is invested with full, complete, and exclusive powers in this respect, "subject only to the Constitution of the United States."

The question recurs then, if the Constitution does establish slavery in Kansas or any other Territory beyond the power of the people to control it by law, how can the conclusion be resisted that slavery is established in like manner and by the same authority in all the States of the Union? And if it be the imperative duty of Congress to provide by law for the protection of slave property in the Territories upon the ground that "slavery exists in Kansas" (and consequently in every other Territory), "by virtue of the Constitution of the United States," why is it not also the duty of Congress, for the same reason, to provide similar protection to slave property in all the States of the Union, when the Legislatures fail to furnish such protection?

Without confessing or attempting to avoid the inevitable consequences of their own doctrine, its advocates endeavor to fortify their position by citing the Dred Scott decision to prove that the Constitution recognizes property in slaves—that there is no legal distinction between this and every other description of property—that slave property and every other kind of property stand on an equal footing—that Congress has no more power over the one than over the other—and, consequently, can not discriminate between them.

Upon this point the Court say:

Now as we have already said in an earlier part of this opinion, upon a different point, the right of property in a slave is distinctly and expressly affirmed in the Constitution.... And if the Constitution recognizes the right of property of the master in a slave, and makes no distinction between that description of property and other property owned by a citizen, no tribunal acting under the authority of the United States, whether it be legislative, executive, or judicial, has a right to draw such a distinction, or deny to it the benefit of the provisions and guarantees which have been provided for the protection of private property against the encroachments of the government.... And the government in express terms is pledged to protect it in all future time, *if the slave escapes from his owner*. This is done in plain words—too plain to be misunderstood. And no word can be found in the Constitution which gives Congress a *greater* power over slave property, or which entitles property of that kind to *less* protection than property of any other description. The only power conferred is the power coupled with the duty of guarding and protecting the owner in his rights.

The rights of the owner which it is thus made the duty of the Federal Government to guard and protect are those expressly provided for in the Constitution, and defined in clear and explicit language by the Court—that "the government, in express terms, is pledged to protect it (slave property) in all future time, *if the slave escapes from his owner*." This is the only contingency, according to the plain reading of the Constitution as authoritatively interpreted by the Supreme Court, in which the Federal Government is authorized, required, or permitted to interfere with slavery in the States or Territories; and in that case only for the purpose "of guarding and protecting the owner in his rights" to reclaim his slave property. In all other respects slaves stand on the same footing with all other property—"the Constitution makes no distinction between that description of property and other property owned by a citizen;" and "no word can be found in the Constitution which gives Congress a greater power over slave property, or which entitles property of that kind to less protection than property of any other description." This is the basis upon which all rights pertaining to slave property, either in the States or the Territories, stand under the Constitution as expounded by the Supreme Court in the Dred Scott case.

Inasmuch as the Constitution has delegated no power to the Federal Government in respect to any other kind of property belonging to the citizen—neither introducing, establishing, prohibiting, nor excluding it any where within the dominion of the United States, but leaves the owner thereof perfectly free to remove into any State or Territory and carry his property with him, and hold the same subject to the local law, and relying upon the local authorities for protection, it follows, according to the decision of the Court, that slave property stands on the same footing, is entitled to the same rights and immunities, and in like manner is dependent upon the local authorities and laws for protection.

The Court refer to that clause of the Constitution which provides for the rendition of fugitive slaves as their authority for saying that "the right of property in slaves is distinctly and expressly affirmed in the Constitution." By reference to that provision it will be seen that, while the word "slaves" is not used, still the Constitution not only recognizes the right of property in slaves, as stated by the Court, but explicitly states what class of persons shall be deemed slaves, and under what laws or authority they may be held to servitude, and under what circumstances fugitive slaves shall be restored to their owners, all in the same section, as follows:

> No person held to service or labor in one State, *under the laws thereof*, escaping into another, shall, in consequence of any law or regulation therein, be discharged from such service or labor, but shall be delivered up on claim of the party to whom such service or labor may be due.

Thus it will be seen that a slave, within the meaning of the Constitution, is a "person held to service or labor in one State, *under the laws thereof*"—not under the Constitution of the United States, nor by the laws thereof, nor by virtue of any Federal authority whatsoever, but under the laws of the particular State where such service or labor may be due.

It was necessary to give this exact definition of slavery in the Constitution in order to satisfy the people of the South as well as of the North. The slaveholding States would never consent for a moment that their domestic relations—and especially their right of property in their slaves—should be dependent upon Federal authority, or that Congress should have any power over the subject—either to extend, confine, or restrain it; much less to protect or regulate it—lest, under the pretense of protection and regulation, the Federal Government, under the influence of the strong and increasing anti-slavery sentiment which prevailed at that period, might destroy the institution, and divest those rights of property in slaves which were sacred under the laws and constitutions of their respective States so long as the Federal Government had no power to interfere with the subject.

In like manner the non-slaveholding States, while they were entirely willing to provide for the surrender of all fugitive slaves—as is conclusively shown by the unanimous vote of all the States in the Convention for the provision now under consideration—and to leave each State perfectly free to hold slaves under its own laws, and by virtue of its own separate and exclusive authority, so long as it pleased, and to abolish it when it chose, were unwilling to become responsible for its existence by incorporating it into the Constitution as a national institution, to be protected and regulated, extended and controlled by Federal authority, regardless of the wishes of the people, and in defiance of the local laws of the several States and Territories. For these opposite reasons the Southern and Northern States united in giving a unanimous vote in the Convention for that provision of the Constitution which recognizes slavery as a local institution in the several States where it exists, "under the laws thereof," and provides for the surrender of fugitive slaves.

It will be observed that the term "State" is used in this provision, as well as in various other parts of the Constitution, in the same sense in which it was used by Mr. Jefferson in his plan for establishing governments for the new States in the territory ceded and to be ceded to the United States, and by Mr. Madison in his proposition to confer on Congress power "to institute temporary governments for the *new States* arising in the unappropriated lands of the United States," to designate the political communities, Territories as well as States, within the dominion of the United States. The word "States" is used in the same sense in the ordinance of the 13th July, 1787, for the government of the territory northwest of the River Ohio, which was passed by the remnant of the Congress of the Confederation, sitting in New York while its most eminent members were at Philadelphia, as delegates to the Federal Convention, aiding in the formation of the Constitution of the United States.

In this sense the word "States" is used in the clause providing for the rendition of fugitive slaves, applicable to all political communities under the authority of the United States, including the Territories as well as the several States of the Union. Under any other construction the right of the owner to recover his slave would be restricted to the *States* of the Union, leaving the Territories a secure place of refuge for all fugitives. The same remark is applicable to the clause of the Constitution which provides that "a person charged in any *State* with treason, felony, or other crime, who shall flee from justice, and be found in *another State*, shall, on the demand of the executive authority of the *State* from which he fled, be delivered up to be removed to the State having jurisdiction of the crime." Unless the term "State," as used in these provisions of the Constitution, shall be construed to include every distinct political community under the jurisdiction of the United States, and to apply to Territories as well as to the States of the Union, the Territories must become a sanctuary for all the fugitives from service and justice, for all the felons and criminals who shall escape from the several *States* and seek refuge and immunity in the *Territories*.

If any other illustration were necessary to show that the political communities, which we now call Territories (but which, during the whole period of the Confederation and the formation of the Constitution, were always referred to as "States" or "New States"), are recognized as "States" in *some* of the provisions of the Constitution, they may be found in those clauses which declare that "no *State*" shall enter into any "treaty, alliance, or confederation; grant letters of marque and reprisal; coin money; emit bills of credit; make any thing but gold and silver coin a tender in payment of debts; pass any bill of attainder, *ex post facto* law, or law impairing the obligation of contracts, or grant any title of nobility."

It must be borne in mind that in each of these cases where the power is not expressly delegated to Congress the prohibition is not imposed upon the Federal Government, but upon the *States*. There was no necessity for any such prohibition upon Congress or the Federal Government, for the reason that the omission to delegate any such powers in the Constitution was of itself a prohibition, and so declared in express terms by the 10th amendment, which declares that "the powers not delegated to the United States by the Constitution, nor prohibited by it to the States, are reserved to the States respectively, or to the people."

Hence it would certainly be competent for the States and Territories to exercise these powers but for the prohibition contained in those provisions of the Constitution; and inasmuch as the prohibition only extends to the "States," the people of the "Territories" are still at liberty to exercise them, unless the Territories are included within the term *States*, within the meaning of these provisions of the Constitution of the United States. [...]

This exposition [...] shows conclusively that the authors of the Compromise Measures of 1850, and of the Kansas-Nebraska Act of 1854, as well as the members of the Continental Congress in 1774, and the founders of our system of government subsequent to the Revolution, regarded the people of the Territories and Colonies as political Communities which were entitled to a free and exclusive power of legislation in their Provincial legislatures, where their representation could alone be preserved, in all cases of taxation and internal polity. This right pertains to the people collectively as a law-abiding and peaceful community, and not to the isolated individuals who may wander upon the public domain in violation of law. It can only be exercised where there are inhabitants sufficient to constitute a government, and capable of performing its various functions and duties— a fact to be ascertained and determined by Congress. Whether the number shall be fixed at ten, fifteen, or twenty thousand inhabitants does not affect the principle.

The principle, under our political system, is *that every distinct political Community, loyal to the Constitution and the Union, is entitled to all the rights, privileges, and immunities of self-government in respect to their local concerns and internal polity, subject only to the Constitution of the United States.*

The Hyena, with much bitterness, rose to howl, etc.

Nothing to wear, 1857.

Illus. for William Allen Butler's poem
of the same name. Nov. 1857, p. 746.

1860's

THE BATTLE OF ANTIETAM

BY GEORGE F. NOYES

SEPTEMBER 1863

Wednesday, *September 17th.* Before retiring last night I had seen my horse safely stabled by my host, but, as General Sumner's cavalry escort had bivouacked all over the premises, and as I suspected that the distinction between meum and tuum in the matter of horseflesh was somewhat neglected in the code of cavalry morals, I took with me to sleep a half uneasy feeling, and was awakened by it before daybreak. Upon going to the stable I found all right; the cavalry-men were making coffee; and as soon as daylight came I mustered my squad, accomplished my errand, breakfasted in the tent of the officer whom I had come to seek, and was soon on my way back to the division.

By this time the incessant roar of artillery, apparently a couple of miles distant on the right, indicated that a battle was going forward; the dusty street of the little village was full of orderlies and staff officers, riding hither and thither on various duties; every house boiled over with excitement, and gathered upon its stoop a knot of half-frantic women, whose terror it was pitiful to behold. Of course my own thoughts were full of the impending conflict, of whose happy result to the good cause I could not doubt. We certainly had forced the enemy into a dangerous corner, and I felt sure that the music of these cannon was ushering in the salvation-day of the republic. Our victory at South Mountain had not lost its inspiration, and there was thus every reason for being hopeful and enthusiastic.

I was soon riding into the last night's camping ground of our division, but the ashes of their camp-fires were cold. Troops were, however, massed in the fields beyond, and thither I hastened, to be again disappointed. Presuming that they must have advanced still farther to the front, I rode on to find other troops drawn up in line of battle, but these also were strangers to me, and no one could give me the desired information. I was now on the battlefield of Antietam, and near the front of our centre. [...]

At the point where I now paused for a moment, just about the central point of our army, and on the east side of Antietam Creek, I saw no indications of a hostile force in the fields and woods opposite. Our forces were coming into position near me, but on the other side of the creek all was still. Very few missiles had yet come this way; but, as I rode away, I saw one shell burst in a group of our men, wounding two or three severely. A house upon a commanding elevation was pointed out to me as the head-quarters of General M'Clellan, and thither I at once proceeded, as the last resort for the information I sought. Here was the immense cavalry escort waiting in the rear, staff horses picketed by dozens around the house, while the piazza was crowded with officers seeking to read with their field-glasses the history of the battle at the right. On an elevation a couple of hundred yards in front, commanding a still better view, groups of officers, newspaper correspondents, and citizens were assembled, and I at once joined them, leaving my horse for a moment in the valley below.

It was only the usual battle panorama, and I could not distinguish a single battery, nor discern the movements of a single brigade, nor see a single battalion of the men in gray. Smoke-clouds leaped in sudden fury from ridges crowned with cannon, or lay thick and dim upon the valleys, or rose lazily up over the trees; all else was concealed; only the volleyed thunder was eloquent; and no man was so stolid, of all who now stood gazing down upon the field of death, but pictured in his excited imagination a scene with some at least of the features of the dread reality.

Only a short outlook was permitted me; for here I had discovered that beneath that smoky canopy my own division was engaged, having last evening been sent from the centre to the extreme left. It was necessary to return toward Keadysville, turn to the left over a road which crossed the Antietam by a stone bridge, and, after a two miles' ride, I had little need to inquire the way. It was now about nine o'clock, and already the ebb-tide which flows from every battle-field had fairly set in, bearing out some stragglers, but chiefly those of our wounded, whose injuries, being slight or in the upper portion of the body, permitted them to walk slowly back toward Keadysville, having already been bandaged in the field-hospitals. Ambulances bringing off the more desperately wounded, or returning for fresh freights of agony; pale-faced men looking up at me from the grassy wayside where they had paused to rest; a captain of our old brigade smilingly holding up both arms bandaged and bleeding, and assuring me that we were doing well on the right—such are some of the pictures left in my memory by that morning's ride.

And still, as I hastened on, the roar of the artillery and infantry grew more terrible, and I was soon passing a hospital sheltered in a low-lying valley on the verge of the battle-field. Farm-houses, barns, outhouses, all were tenanted, and still the stretcher-bearers brought in from the front a constantly fresh addition. I had no time to-day to visit this hospital, but, as I rode past the barn, a collection of amputated limbs lying outside the door attested the hurried and whole-sale character of the work going on within. At any other time such a sight would have shocked me, but to-day it came in naturally as part of the scene.

For now the ghastly procession of the wounded—some tottering along unsupported, some leaning upon their comrades, some borne upon stretchers, some carried in the arms of their friends, every step an agony—passed me almost continuously; full five hundred mangled and bleeding men, some of them with hardly life enough in them to reach the hospital. There were sights that day whose sad horrors can never be forgotten, too sad and horrible for any description here. And it was through this bloody avenue I must pass forward to the battle. It was no time to grow sick and faint, for into that hell of smoke and battle-din, out of which come these bleeding braves, I must enter, come what, come may. Let me admit that it was a terrible morning's ride.

I was now on the Hagerstown turnpike, across which cavalry were drawn up with drawn sabres to prevent the egress of stragglers from the battle-field. And now in what part of that awful hurly-burly of cloud and noise just ahead is my division? The cavalry-men were ignorant; none of the wounded could tell me; I must push on, and trust to fortune. As I rode down the turnpike, I passed under a hilly crest to its left, upon which a battery was posted, now hurling shot and shell over my head at a rebel battery opposite. On my right I saw troops drawn up in line of battle; on my left I

soon met other troops drawn up in a grove near the road; but still I heard nothing of my division, except that it was somewhere in front. And now I was passing between spots desperately fought over already this morning, when over the fields, or in the road just ahead, I was astonished to see some of our troops apparently falling back, and soon also I discovered the general.

We were now in rather too hot a place for the exchange of courtesies, but I saw at a glance that I had come at an inauspicious moment, and a word or two of hurried explanation told me the whole story. I had arrived just at the period when, General Hooker having been driven fainting with his wound from the field, our right wing, which had driven the enemy through these fields above us into a thick grove farther up the road, at least a mile, with great slaughter, had been compelled to fall back by the outnumbering force which the enemy, whose centre and right were left unattacked during all these morning hours, was able to concentrate against it. The bravest fighting could not withstand such fearful odds, especially as our old opponent, Stonewall Jackson, had sheltered his reserves behind rocky ledges waist-high, and wonderfully adapted for defense, had deepened natural depressions into rifle-pits, had laid up long lines of fence-rail breast-works, and so was all ready for a formidable resistance.

Our old brigade retained the position in which it was first posted in support of artillery, but the other brigades were falling back to a new position in excellent order, and the general and staff were overseeing the movement. A bitter disappointment all this to me, but how much worse to the men who had moved through such a storm of leaden rain up this turnpike, through yonder corn-field, close up to the rocky citadel—"slaughter-pen," as a friend designated it—where the rebels from behind stone bulwarks shot down our exposed ranks. But, though the anxious strain still rested on their features, there was not even a shadow of despair, and nowhere was there a single symptom of panic among our officers or men.

The division was soon halted, and drawn up in line of battle on both sides the Hagerstown turnpike; but the enemy did not follow up his temporary advantage, and the infantry fighting at this point was over. The artillery on both sides still filled the air with shot and shell, but not long after this ceased also; the general and staff dismounted, our horses were tethered on the west of the road, and there was a little rest. It was now about 10 A.M., and the right wing had been engaged since daybreak. The enemy, having over-powered our attack in this direction, was now able to give his undivided attention to his centre and right wing, which were to be attacked in turn later in the day.

After a brief interval under the trees, an orderly brought orders from General Meade, now in command of our corps since General Hooker's wound, to march the division on the east side of the turnpike, near our present locality, where we formed in line of battle behind several batteries, and the men were ordered to lie down on their arms. The woods and fields in front of this key-point of the right wing were now voiceless and still; not a grayback could be seen; not a battery saluted us; the scene of the late encounter seemed quiet and deserted. Thirty cannon of various calibre were silently looking toward the foe; grimly behind their pieces stood the gunners, peering out over field and wood, eager to get sight of the enemy. At any attempt to plant a rebel battery, any demonstration of rebel infantry, any symptom of advance, some of them took sight, and sent a shot or shell shrieking among the trees. One of these batteries of our division is well worth visiting; it has lost this day thirty-eight officers and men killed and wounded, and twenty-eight horses; but here it is now posted, every gun brought safely out of the fight, the ranks of its heroic gunners now recruited by infantry volunteers. If one half be true which the staff tell me as we stand around this battery, hundreds of rebels must have fallen this day before the hurricane of grape and canis-ter poured in a critical moment right into the face of the enemy from these wide-mouthed Napoleon guns.

Seated on this little summit, I listened to the deeply interesting recital of the events which occurred before I reached the field. How two of our staff appeased their hunger by a hoe-cake taken from the haversack of a dead rebel sol-dier; how one general of our division, at a doubtful moment, leaped toward a battery, ordered in double charges of grape and canister, and personally sighted the pieces into the enemy's teeth; how another general, not of our division, left his brigade to advance without him; how the horses of three of our orderlies were killed by a bursting shell as they rode behind the general, and yet no one was hurt seriously; how up to the last moment all was going well, when, just as our boys were pushing into some woods, leaving the corn-field behind them full of rebel dead and wounded, they found themselves confronted with fresh troops, fully fortified, who swept them with volleys so terrible that a retreat was unavoidable—these and the thousand and one little personal incidents, only

uttered into friendly ears, greatly interested me, though of course there was in my own mind a natural feeling of regret that I had lost all these new experiences.

But little did any of us imagine that for us the battle of Antietam was nearly over; this seemed to be only the first act of the tragedy, and every moment might lift the curtain for a new scene. On our left, toward the centre of our main line, the din of battle had long been heard, and ever and anon one or more of our own cannon in front spoke out its thunder. As an attack on our position was momentarily expected, one or the other of the staff was constantly engaged in sweeping with a glass the presumed locality of the enemy. Meantime our infantry rested on the ground in long lines—thin, broken ranks at best, giving one a pang at the heart to see how small were some of the regiments now gathered about the torn and bullet-riddled colors. On our right were the Pennsylvania Reserves, and other troops were gradually posted behind us to aid in resisting the expected attack, each brigade in turn stacking arms and then lying down.

Thus every moment was a moment of expectation; of anxiety as to the result of the battle in the centre, and later in the day on our extreme left; of the suppressed excitement of men liable at any moment to be called into battle, and yet of practical rest and idleness. I passed much of the time out among the batteries, whence we had a good view of the woods in which the enemy might lie concealed until the moment of attack, and of the corn-field, which afforded admirable covert for infantry. At times we saw little squads of men at the edge of the woods—rebel pickets, or persons curious like ourselves. A horseman on a white horse showed himself several times on a slight elevation beyond the corn-field, and we christened him Stonewall Jackson. I found that a powerful imagination helps out a picture wonderfully, for several times I was assured by others that large bodies of rebels could be seen *en masse* at the edge of the woods, while the glass gave me a view of nothing but trees.

During the day we were able to get up a wagon or two with provisions, which the regimental quarter-masters dis-tributed among the men. I was walking down the lines, when a regimental captain thus accosted me, holding up a great piece of pork on his sword: "Look here, captain, this is the allowance of pork for my company, and I shall have to eat it all, for I am the only one left." I paused to inquire about it, and found it was even so; no commissioned or non-commissioned officer, no private, not even a drummer-boy

Storming the Rebel position.

remained to him. We talk with sadness about the decimated ranks of a regiment or company; here was a company simply annihilated by sickness, wounds, and death.

During the day some of our boys brought in from the adjacent fields the dead bodies of some of their comrades, and buried them in the rear of our little elevation, placing at their heads strips of cracker-box-covers, with the name and regiment of the deceased in pencil. Horses were lying all about us just where they were killed, for over this spot the battle had at one time fiercely raged. Hour after hour of inaction slipped away, while the battle-field on our left was fought over fiercely, terribly, with a stubborn desperation on both sides rarely exhibited since the world began. For the truth of this statement I may safely appeal to the statistician when the records of this day's work are made up, and the lists of dead and wounded are completed, or to any one who may visit with me two days hence the field of battle and witness the fearful result.

Sometimes it seemed as if the fighting had drawn so near to us that it must be in the next wood, and that our turn must soon come, and then the din of battle would move off to the left, leaving us quiet as before. Of course rumor had full swing on such a day as this; victory, defeat, large Union reinforcements, the repulse of our left wing, the death of several of our prominent generals, the taking of

several thousand prisoners, all were in turn buzzed through the ranks, and relieved somewhat the tedious waiting of this long day. About 4 P.M. General M'Clellan, with his staff, rode along our lines, and was greeted with much enthusiasm by the troops. We had now learned that our centre and left had been partially successful, the enemy having been driven back with much loss, though still holding firmly their new position.

One of our orderlies brought us about this time from a neighboring farm-house a loaf of bread, with a modicum of butter ingeniously stored in a hole cut in the loaf, and we sat down to enjoy it, with a cup of coffee, for the men had been permitted to light fires and cook their rations. We began to think that the fighting for the day was over. But about 5 P.M., sudden as lightning out of a clear sky swept over us another tornado of rebel wrath, and the shot and shell began to strike and burst over and about us in all directions. In an instant we were in the saddle; but before we were fairly mounted our thirty guns, which had been impatiently awaiting this opportunity for hours, swept woods and cornfield with a deluge of shot and shell. Never before had I known how tremendous may be the roar of mingled artillery. Thirty guns, each discharged as fast as the men could load! they actually shook the hill; nay, the concussion seemed enough to shake the planet.

As the rebel projectiles were supposed to be introductory to an infantry attack, the troops in front were notified to be ready, while those in rear fell in, took arms, advanced closer to the crest of the hill, and also lay down, prepared for action at a moment's notice. The Reserves still remained as before, except that each commander was getting his men into thorough preparation; every wagon went off at full gallop; the right wing was all ready; and now we sat on our horses, looking earnestly down to see what was to be the next move. General Meade, who succeeded to the command of our corps after General Hooker was wounded, rode up to the crest where we were stationed, and reconnoitered the position of the enemy's batteries as coolly as if at a review. Already decorated with a bullet-hole in his cap as a trophy of to-day's battle, his almost nonchalant manner, and the quiet way in which, amidst the tornado of rebel wrath, he gave his orders to make ready for the storm, greatly impressed me. I saw the shot strike so close to our men as to fling the dust apparently over them; for perhaps ten minutes the enemy kept up a lively cannonade, but not a man was, to my knowledge, killed or wounded. This artillery firing at long range is terrible to hear, but is rarely fatal.

From some prisoners afterward captured we learned that it had been the intention of the enemy to attack with infantry, General Jackson's favorite time for flinging himself upon us seeming to be just before sunset. If this was his intention, the awful fire of our batteries must have admonished him of our thorough state of preparation, for in a brief period his batteries ceased to play, and our own thirty guns were silent also.

During a visit to one of our hospitals I heard from the lips of a German, who was severely wounded in to-day's battle, a thrilling account of his personal experiences during this ten minutes' cannonading. He was lying under a tree, desperately wounded and unable to stir, with several other Union soldiers and a number of rebels, all in the same condition, in the woods, where some of the hardest fighting had been, and through which now crashed our shot and shell. The ground had been taken from the enemy and occupied by our troops early in the day, but was retaken by the rebels, so that wounded men in blue and gray lay indiscriminately together. He suffered little pain, but was tortured with thirst, relieved from time to time by some generous Southerner, who, in passing, shared with him the contents of his canteen. When, however, the shot and shell from our own batteries, in this five o'clock duel, began to shriek among

the trees, killing some of our own wounded men, he described his sensations as truly horrible. Unable to move, planted by his wound just there, with these death-messengers crashing, bursting, striking sometimes within ten feet of him, what language could paint a scene so terrible! All that night, all the next day, and the next night also, he remained untended, only to be taken up at last when the enemy had retired and our own troops occupied the field. When I talked with him he was lying under a shelter-tent, outside a garden, every part of which was filled with the shelter-tent bedrooms of wounded rebels, waiting until his wound was sufficiently healed to enable him to be moved into the house. He told me that the surgeon had promised to save his leg, and added, in his broken way, a fervent hope that he might have one shot more at the enemy.

With this cannonading ended the fighting of the right wing for the day. The men were now permitted to bring in bundles of straw from the neighboring farms, with which they made themselves beds, and lay down in line of battle; the tired gunners made themselves similarly comfortable alongside their guns; pickets stood, with eye and ear open, close to the rebel lines, ready to give instant warning should a night-attack be attempted; and hardly had the darkness descended on hill and wood before we had also lain down on beds of corn-shooks and straw, pulled our blankets over us, and all was still. No one removed even his sword; our horses stood saddled and ready for instant use at the fence near by; all felt the importance of getting as much rest as possible while rest was permitted us.

There was no tree over our heads to shut out the stars, and as I lay looking up at these orbs moving so calmly on their appointed way, I felt, as never so strongly before, how utterly absurd in the face of high Heaven is this whole game of war, relieved only from contempt and ridicule by its tragic accompaniments, and by the sublime illustrations of man's nobler qualities incidentally called forth in its service. Sent to occupy this little planet, one among ten thousand worlds revolving through infinite space, how worse than foolish these mighty efforts to make our tenancy unhappy or to drive each other out of it. Within a space of four square miles lay two hundred thousand men, some stiff and stark, looking with visionless eyes up into the pitying heavens; some tossing on the beds of the hospital, or lying maimed and bleeding under the trees; some hugging in their sleep the deadly weapon with which, to-morrow, they may renew the work of death.

PSYCHE

BY HANS CHRISTIAN ANDERSEN

MAY 1864

t the dawn of day through the red atmosphere shines a large star, morning's clearest star; its ray quivers upon the white wall, as if it would there inscribe what it had to relate—what in the course of a thousand years it has witnessed here and there on our revolving earth.

Listen to one of its histories:

Lately (its *lately* is a century ago to us human beings) my rays watched a young artist; it was in the territory of the Pope, in the capital of the world—Rome. Much has changed there in the flight of years, but nothing so rapidly as the change which takes place in the human form between childhood and old age. The imperial city was then, as now, in ruins; fig-trees and laurels grew among the fallen marble pillars, and over the shattered bath-chambers, with their gold-enameled walls; the Colosseum was a ruin; the bells of the churches rang, incense perfumed the air, processions moved with lights and splendid canopies through the streets. The Holy Church ruled all, and art was patronized by it. At Rome lived the world's greatest painter, Raphael; there also lived the first sculptor of his age, Michael Angelo. The Pope himself paid homage to these two artists, and honored them by his visits. Art was appreciated, admired, and recompensed. But even then not all that was great and worthy of praise was known and brought forward.

In a narrow little street stood an old house; it had formerly been a temple, and there dwelt a young artist. He was poor and unknown; however, he had a few young friends, artists like himself, young in mind, in hopes, in thoughts. They told him that he was rich in talent, but that he was a fool, since he never would believe in his own powers. He always destroyed what he had formed in clay; he was never satisfied with any thing he did, and never had any thing finished so as to have it seen and known, and it was necessary to have this in order to make money.

"You are a dreamer," they said, "and therein lies your misfortune. But this arises from your never having lived yet, not having tasted life, enjoyed it in large exhilarating draughts, as it ought to be enjoyed. It is only in youth that one can do this. Look at the great master, Raphael, whom the Pope honors and the world admires: *he* does not abstain from wine and good fare."

"He dines with the baker's wife, the charming Fornarina," said Angelo, one of the liveliest of the young group.

They all talked a great deal, after the fashion of gay young men. They insisted on carrying the youthful artist off with them to scenes of amusement and riot—scenes of folly they might have been called—and for a moment he felt inclined to accompany them. His blood was warm, his fancy powerful; he could join in their jovial chat, and laugh as loud as any of them; yet what they called "Raphael's pleasant life" vanished from his mind like a morning mist. He thought only of the inspiration that was apparent in the great master's works. If he stood in the Vatican near the beautiful forms the masters of a thousand years before had created out of marble blocks, then his breast heaved; he felt within himself something so elevated, so holy, so grand and good, that he longed to chisel such statues from the marble blocks. He wished to give a form to the glorious conceptions of his mind; but how, and what form? The soft clay that was moulded into beautiful figures by his fingers one day was the next day, as usual, broken up.

Once, as he was passing one of the rich palaces, of which there are so many at Rome, he stepped within the large open entrance court, and saw arched corridors adorned with statues, inclosing a little garden full of the most beautiful roses. Great white flowers, with green juicy leaves, shot up the marble basin, where the clear waters splashed, and near it glided a figure, that of a young girl, the daughter of the princely house—so delicate, so light, so lovely! He had never beheld so beautiful a woman. Yes—painted by Raphael, painted as Psyche, in one of the palaces of Rome! Yes—there she stood as if living!

She also lived in his thoughts and heart. And he hurried home to his humble apartment, and formed a Psyche in clay; it was the rich, the high-born young Roman lady, and for the first time he looked with satisfaction on his work. It was life itself—it was herself. And his friends, when they saw it, were loud in their congratulations. This work was a proof of his excellence in art: that they had themselves already known, and the world should now know it also.

Clay may look fleshy and lifelike, but it has not the whiteness of marble, and does not last so long. His Psyche must be sculptured in marble, and the expensive block of marble required he already possessed: it had lain for many years, a legacy from his parents, in the courtyard. Broken bottles, decayed vegetables, and all manner of refuse, had been heaped on it and soiled it, but within it was white as the mountain snow. Psyche was to be chiseled from it.

One day it happened (the clear star tells nothing of this, for it did not see what passed, but we know it) a distinguished Roman party came to the narrow humble street. The carriage stopped near it. The party had come to see the young artist's work, of which they had heard by accident. And who were these aristocratic visitors? Unfortunate young man! All too happy young man, he might also well have been called. The young girl herself stood there in his studio; and with what a smile when her father exclaimed, "But it is you, you yourself to the life!" That smile could not be copied, that glance could not be imitated—that speaking glance which she cast on the young artist! It was a glance that fascinated, enchanted, and destroyed.

"The Psyche must be finished in marble," said the rich nobleman. And that was a life-giving word to the inanimate clay and to the heavy marble block, as it was a life-giving word to the young man.

"When the work is finished I will purchase it," said the noble visitor.

It seemed as if a new era had dawned on the humble studio; joy and sprightliness enlivened it now, and ennui fled before constant employment. The bright morning star saw how quickly the work advanced. The clay itself became as if animated with a soul, for even in it stood forth, in perfect beauty, each now well-known feature.

"Now I know what life is!" exclaimed the young artist, joyfully; "it is love. There is glory in the excellent, rapture in the beautiful. What my friends call life and enjoyment are corrupt and perishable—they are bubbles in the fermenting dregs, not the pure heavenly altar-wine that conse-

crates life." The block of marble was raised, the chisel hewed large pieces from it; it was measured, pointed, and marked. The work proceeded; little by little the stone assumed a form, a form of beauty—Psyche—charming as God's creation in the young female. The heavy marble became lifelike, dancing, airy, and a graceful Psyche, with the bright smile so heavenly and innocent, such as had mirrored itself in the young sculptor's heart.

The star of the rose-tinted morn saw it, and well understood what was stirring in the young man's heart—understood the changing color on his cheek, the fire in his eye—as he carved the likeness of what God had created.

"You are a master, such as those in the time of the Greeks," said his delighted friends. "The whole world will soon admire your Psyche."

"My Psyche!" he exclaimed. "Mine! Yes, such she must be. I too am an artist like these great ones of by-gone days. God has bestowed on me the gift of genius, which raises its possessor to a level with the high-born."

And he sank on his knees, and wept his thanks to God, and then forgot Him for *her*—for her image in marble. The figure of Psyche stood there, as if formed of snow, blushing rosy red on the morning sun.

In reality he was to see her, living, moving, her whose voice had sounded like the sweetest music. He was to go to the splendid palace to announce that the marble Psyche was

The sculptor's triumph.

finished. He went thither, passed through the open court to where the water poured, splashing from dolphins into the marble basin, around which the white flowers clustered, and the roses shed their fragrance. He entered the large lofty hall, whose walls and roof were adorned with armorial bearings and heraldic designs. Well-dressed, pompous-looking servants strutted up and down like sleigh-horses with their jingling bells; others of them, insolent-looking fellows, were stretched at their ease on handsomely-carved wooden benches; they seemed the masters of the house. He told his errand, and was then conducted up the white marble stairs, which were covered with soft carpets. Statues were ranged on both sides; he passed through handsome rooms with pictures and bright mosaic floors. For a moment he felt oppressed by all this magnificence and splendor—it nearly took away his breath. But he speedily recovered himself; for the princely owner of the mansion received him kindly, almost cordially, and, after they had finished their conversation, requested him, when bidding him adieu, to go to the apartments of the young Signora, who wished also to see him. Servants marshaled him through superb saloons and suits of rooms to the chamber where she sat, elegantly dressed and radiant in beauty.

She spoke to him. No *Miserere*, no tones of sacred music, could more have melted the heart and elevated the soul. He seized her hand and carried it to his lips; never was rose so soft. But there issued a fire from that rose—a fire that penetrated through him and turned his head; words poured forth from his lips, which he scarcely knew himself, like the crater pouring forth glowing lava. He told her of his love. She stood amazed, offended, insulted, with a haughty and scornful look, an expression which had been called forth instantaneously by his passionate avowal of his sentiments toward her. Her cheeks glowed, her lips became quite pale; her eyes flashed fire, and were yet as dark as ebon night.

"Madman!" she exclaimed; "begone! away!" And she turned angrily from him, while her beautiful countenance assumed the look of that petrified face of old with the serpents clustering around it like hair.

Like a sinking lifeless thing he descended into the street; like a sleep-walker he reached his home. But there he awoke to pain and fury; he seized his hammer, lifted it high in the air, and was on the point of breaking the beautiful marble statue, but in his distracted state of mind he had not observed that Angelo was standing near him. The latter caught his arm, exclaiming, "Have you gone mad? What would you do?"

They struggled with each other. Angelo was the younger of the two, and, drawing a deep breath, the young sculptor threw himself on a chair.

"What has happened?" asked Angelo. "Be yourself and speak."

But what could he tell? what could he say? And when Angelo found that he could get nothing out of him he gave up questioning him.

"Your blood thickens in this constant dreaming. Be a man like the rest of us, and do not live only in the ideal: you will go deranged at this rate. Take wine until you feel it get a little into your head; that will make you sleep well. Let a pretty girl be your doctor; a girl from the Campagna is as charming as a princess in her marble palace. Both are the daughters of Eve, and not to be distinguished from each other in Paradise. Follow your Angelo! Let me be your angel, the angel of life for you! The time will come when you will be old, and your limbs will be useless to you. Why, on a fine sunny day, when every thing is laughing and joyous, do you look like a withered straw that can grow no more? I do not believe what the priests say, that there is a life beyond the grave. It is a pretty fancy, a tale for children—pleasant enough if one could put faith in it. I, however, do not live in fancies only, but in the world of realities. Come with me! Be a man!"

And he drew him out with him; it was easy to do so at that moment. There was a heat in the young artist's blood, a change in his feelings; he longed to throw off all his old habits, all that he was accustomed to—to throw off his own former self—and he consented to accompany Angelo.

On the outskirts of Rome was a hostelry much frequented by artists. It was built amidst the ruins of an old bath-chamber; the large yellow lemons hung among their dark bright leaves, and adorned the greatest part of the old reddish-gilt walls. The hostelry was a deep vault, almost like a hole in the ruin. A lamp burned within it, before a picture of the Madonna; a large fire was blazing in the stove (roasting, boiling, and frying were going on there); on the outside, under lemon and laurel trees, stood two tables spread for refreshments.

Kindly and joyously were the two artists welcomed by their friends. None of them ate much, but they all drank a great deal; that caused hilarity. There was singing, and playing the guitar; Saltarello sounded, and the merry dance began. A couple of young Roman girls, models for the artists, joined in the dance, and took part in their mirth— two charming Bacchantes! They had not, indeed, the delicacy

The repulse.

of Psyche—they were not graceful lovely roses—but they were fresh, hardy, ruddy carnations.

How warm it was that day! Warm even after the sun had gone down—heat in the blood, heat in the air, heat in every look! The atmosphere seemed to be composed of gold and roses—life itself was gold and roses.

"Now at last you are with us! Let yourself be borne on the stream around you and within you."

"I never before felt so well and so joyous," cried the young sculptor. "You are right, you are all right; I was a fool, a visionary. Men should seek for realities, and not wrap themselves up in phantasies."

Amidst songs and the tinkling of guitars, the young men sallied forth from the hostelry, and took their way, in the clear starlit evening, through the small streets; the two ruddy carnations, daughters of the Campagna, accompanied them. In Angelo's room, amidst sketches and folios scattered about, and glowing voluptuous paintings, their voices sounded more subdued, but not less full of passion. On the floor lay many a drawing of the Campagna's daughters in various attractive attitudes: they were full of beauty, yet the originals were still more beautiful. The six-branched chandeliers were burning, and the light glared on the scene of sensual joy.

"Apollo! Jupiter! Into your heaven and happiness am I wafted. It seems as if the flower of life has in this moment sprung up in my heart."

Yes, it sprang up, but it broke and fell, and a deadening hideous sensation seized upon him. It dimmed his sight, stupefied his mind; perception failed, and all became dark around him.

He gained his home, sat down on his bed, and tried to collect his thoughts. "Fie!" was the exclamation uttered by his own mouth from the bottom of his heart. "Wretch! begone! away!" And he breathed a sigh full of the deepest grief.

"Begone! away!" These words of hers—the living Psyche's words—were re-echoed in his breast, re-echoed from his lips. He laid his head on his pillow; his thoughts became confused, and he slept.

At the dawn of day he arose, and sat down to reflect. What had happened? Had he dreamt it all—dreamt *her* words—dreamt his visit to the hostelry, and the evening with the flaunting carnations of the Campagna? No, all was reality—a reality such as he had never before experienced.

Through the purplish haze of the early morning shone the clear star; its rays fell upon him and upon the marble Psyche. He trembled as he gazed on the imperishable image; he felt that there was impurity in his look, and he threw a covering over it. Once only he removed the veil to touch the statue, but he could not bear to see his own work.

Quiet, gloomy, absorbed in his own thoughts, he sat the live-long day. He noticed nothing, knew nothing of what was going on about him, and no one knew what was going on within his heart.

Days, weeks passed; the nights were the longest. The glittering star saw him one morning, pale, shaking with fever, arise from his couch, go to the marble figure, lift the veil from it, gaze for a moment with an expression of deep devotion and sorrow on his work, and then, almost sinking under its weight, he dragged the statue out into the garden. In it there was a dried-up, dilapidated, disused well, which could only be called a deep hole; he sank his Psyche in it, threw in earth over it, and covered the new-made grave with brushwood and nettles.

"Begone! away!" was the short funeral service.

The star witnessed this through the rose-tinted atmosphere, and its ray quivered on two large tears upon the corpse-like cheeks of the young fever-stricken man—death-stricken they called him on his sick-bed.

The monk Ignatius came to see him as a friend and physician—came with religion's comforting words, and spoke to him of the Church's happiness and peace, of the sins of mankind, the grace and mercy of God.

And his words fell like warm sunbeams on the damp spongy ground; it steamed, and the misty vapors ascended from it, so that the thoughts and mental images which had received their shapes from realities were cleared, and he was enabled to take a more just view of man's life. The delusions of guilt abounded in it, and such there had been for him. Art was a sorceress that lured us to vanity and earthly lusts. We are false toward ourselves, false toward our friends, false toward our God. The serpent always repeats within us, *"Eat thereof; then your eyes shall be opened, and ye shall be as gods!"*

He seemed now for the first time to understand himself, and to have found the way to truth and rest. On the Church shone light from on high; in the monk's cell dwelt that peace amidst which the human tree might grow to flourish in eternity.

Brother Ignatius encouraged these sentiments, and the artist's resolution was taken. A child of the world became a servant of the Church: the young sculptor bade adieu to all his former pursuits, and went into a monastery.

How kindly, how gladly, was he received by the Brothers! What a Sunday fête was his initiation! The Almighty, it seemed to him, was in the sunshine that illumined the church. His glory beamed from the holy images and from the white cross. And when he now, at the hour of the setting sun, stood in his little cell, and, opening the window, looked out over the ancient Rome, the ruined temples, the magnificent but dead Colosseum—when he saw all this in the spring-time, when the acacias were in bloom, the evergreens were fresh, roses bursting from their buds, citrons and orange-trees shining, palms waving—he felt himself tranquilized and cheered as he had never been before. The quiet open Campagna extended toward the misty snow-decked hills, which seemed painted in the air. All, blended together, breathed of peace, of beauty, so soothingly, so dreamily—a dream the whole.

Yes, the world was a dream here. A dream may continue for an hour, and come again at another hour; but life in a cloister is a life of years, long and many.

He might have attested the truth of this saying, that from within comes much which taints mankind. What was that fire which sometimes blazed throughout him? What was that source from which evil, against his will, was always welling forth? He scourged his body, but from within came the evil yet again. What was that spirit within him, which, with the pliancy of a serpent, coiled itself up, and crept into his conscience under the cloak of universal love, and com-

forted him? The saints pray for us, the holy mother prays for us, Jesus Himself has shed His blood for us. Was it weakness of mind or the volatile feelings of youth that caused him sometimes to think himself received into grace, and made him fancy himself exalted by that—exalted over so many? For had he not cast from him the vanities of the world? Was he not a son of the Church?

One day, after the lapse of many years, he met Angelo, who recognized him.

"Man!" exclaimed Angelo. "Yes, surely it is yourself. Are you happy now? You have sinned against God, for you have thrown away His gracious gift, and abandoned your mission into this world. Read the parable of the confided talent. The Master who related it spoke the truth. What have you won or found? Have you not allotted to yourself a life of dreams? Is your religion not a mere coinage of the brain? What if all be but a dream—pretty yet fantastic thoughts?"

"Away from me, Satan!" cried the monk, as he fled from Angelo.

"There is a devil, a personified devil! I saw him to-day," groaned the monk. "I only held out a finger to him, and he seized my whole hand! Ah, no!" he sighed. "In myself there is sin, and in that man there is sin; but he is not crushed by it—he goes with brow erect, and lives in happiness. I seek my happiness in the consolations of religion. If only they were consolations—if all here, as in the world I left, were but pleasing thoughts! They are delusions, like the crimson skies of evening, like the beautiful sea-blue tint on the distant hills. Close by these look very different. Eternity, thou art like the wide, interminable, calm-looking ocean: it beckons, calls us, fills us with forebodings, and if we venture on it, we sink, we disappear, die, cease to exist! Delusions! Begone! away!"

And tearless, lost in his own thoughts, he sat upon his hard pallet: then he knelt. Before whom? The stone cross that stood on the wall? No, habit alone made him kneel there.

And the deeper he looked into himself the darker became his thoughts. "Nothing within, nothing without—a lifetime wasted!" And that cold snow-ball of thought rolled on, grew larger, crushed him, destroyed him.

"To none dare I speak of the gnawing worm within me; my secret is my prisoner. If I could get rid of it, I would be Thine, O God!"

And a spirit of piety awoke and struggled within him.

"Lord! Lord!" he exclaimed in his despair. "Be merciful, grant me faith! I despised and abandoned Thy gracious gift—my mission into this world. I was wanting in strength; Thou hadst not bestowed that on me. Immortal fame—Psyche—still lingers in my heart. Begone! away! They shall be buried like yonder Psyche, the brightest gem of my life. *That* shall never ascend from its dark grave."

The star in the rose-tinted morn shone brightly—the star that assuredly shall be extinguished and annihilated, while the spirits of mankind live amidst celestial light. Its trembling rays fell upon the white wall, but it inscribed no memorial there of the blessed trust in God, of the grace, of the holy love, that dwell in the believer's heart.

"Psyche within me can never die—it will live in consciousness! Can what is inconceivable be? Yes, yes! For I myself am inconceivable. Thou art inconceivable, O Lord! The whole of Thy universe is inconceivable—a work of power, of excellence, of love!"

His eyes beamed with the brightest radiance for a moment, and then became dim and corpse-like. The church bells rang their funeral peal over him—the dead; and he was buried in earth brought from Jerusalem, and mingled with the ashes of departed saints.

Some years afterward the skeleton was taken up, as had been the skeletons of the dead monks before him; it was attired in the brown cowl, with a rosary in its hand, and it was placed in a niche among the human bones which were found in the burying-ground of the monastery. And the sun shone outside, and incense perfumed the air within, and masses were said.

Years again went by.

The bones of the skeletons had fallen from each other, and become mixed together. The skulls were gathered and set up—they formed quite an outer wall to the church. There stood also *his* skull in the burning sunshine: there were so many, many death's-heads, that no one knew now the names they had borne, nor his. And see! in the sunshine there moved something living within the two eye-sockets. What could that be? A motley-colored lizard had sprung into the interior of the skull, and was passing out and in through the large empty sockets of the eye. There was life now within that head, where once grand ideas, bright dreams, love of art, and excellence had dwelt—from whence hot tears had rolled, and where had lived the hope of immortality. The lizard sprang forth and vanished; the skull mouldered away, and became dust in dust.

It was a century from that time. The clear star shone unchanged, as brightly and beautifully as a thousand years before; the dawn of day was red, fresh, and blushing as a rosebud.

Where once had been a narrow street, with the ruins of an ancient temple, stood now a convent. A grave was to be dug in the garden, for a young nun had died, and at an early hour in the morning she was to be buried. In digging the grave the spade knocked against a stone. Dazzling white it appeared—the pure marble became visible. A round shoulder first presented itself; the spade was used more cautiously, and a female head was soon discovered, and then the wings of a butterfly. From the grave in which the young nun was to be laid they raised, in the red morning light, a beautiful statue—Psyche carved in the finest marble. "How charming it is! how perfect—an exquisite work, from the most glorious period of art!" it was said. Who could have been the sculptor? No one knew that—none knew him except the clear star that had shone for a thousand years; *it* knew his earthly career, his trials, his weakness. But he was dead, returned to the dust. Yet the result of his greatest effort, the most admirable, which proved his vast genius—Psyche—that never can die; that might outlive fame. That was seen, appreciated, admired, and loved.

The clear star in the rosy-streaked morn sent its glittering ray upon Psyche, and upon the delighted countenances of the admiring beholders, who saw a soul created in the marble block.

All that is earthly returns to earth, and is forgotten; only the star in the infinite vault of heaven bears it in remembrance. What is heavenly obtains renown from its own excellence; and when even renown shall fade, Psyche shall still live.

The Fortunes of War
How They Are Made and Spent
by Robert Tomes

July 1864

The strangest and most frequently repeated boasts—for boasts we make, such is our national vanity, on all occasions whether of prosperity or adversity—is that *we don't feel this war*. Above the shock of battle, the groans of the wounded and dying, the sobs of the bereaved, the murmurs of defeat, and the shouts of victory, rises the triumphant exclamation, *We don't feel it!* Is this insensibility? Is it the delight in ruin? Is it indifference to failure or success? No! It is worse than either of these, for it embraces them all; it is the chuckling of gain over its pockets filling with the treasure of the country, while our brave soldiers are pouring out their blood in its defense.

We don't feel the war! is the exulting cry of the contractors, money-changers, and speculators, whose shouts of revel stifle the tearful voice of misery. It is in our large cities especially where this boasted insensibility to the havoc of war is found. It is there in the market-place and exchange, where fortunes are being made with such marvelous rapidity, and in the haunts of pleasure, where they are being spent with such wanton extravagance, that *they don't feel this war*. They are at a banquet of abundance and delight, from which they are not to be unseated, though the ghosts of the hundreds of thousands of their slaughtered countrymen shake their gory locks at them.

While the national wealth has been poured out with a profuse generosity in behalf of a cause dear to the national heart, there have been immense fortunes made by enterprising money-getters, seeking only to fill their own pockets.

When the war suddenly burst upon the nation, and before it was able to arouse its gigantic energies, the Government was so helpless that it besought aid at any cost. It was then, as our brave fellow-citizens came forward in multitudes to defend their country, there arose an urgent demand for arms, clothing, and subsistence. Every thing required for the use and consumption of the soldier was wanted, and wanted at once. Tents and blankets to protect him from the weather—clothes, from cap to shoe, to dress him—bread and meat and all the varied necessaries of the daily ration, even to the salt, to feed him—the knapsack, haversack, belt, and cartridge box, to equip him—muskets, pistols, cannon, swords, sabres, powder, shot, and percussion caps to fight with—horses and mules, wagons, railways, steam and sailing vessels of all kinds, for transportation.

A hundred thousand men or more in the immediate and continued want not only of all the ordinary necessaries of life, but of the many additional requirements for war, were to be provided for without delay. The Government, with a commissariat organized only for an army of some sixteen thousand soldiers, and suddenly called upon to clothe, arm, and subsist more than six times the number, could do nothing but appeal to the enterprise of trade to supply its pressing necessities. The appeal, with the treasure of the whole nation to sustain it, was not made in vain. Another army—the army of contractors—then came forward no less promptly than the hundred thousands of citizen soldiers. These with their lives as their offering asking nothing in exchange, and receiving only a bare subsistence; the former, no less liberal of the contents of their docks, ships, fields, stables, granaries, warehouses, and shops, demanding a great price, and getting it.

Think of the immense activity with which trade was inspired by the numerous and multifarious demands of the Government! Contractors for meat, contractors for bread, contractors for tents, contractors for clothing, contractors for arms, contractors for ammunition, contractors for equipments, contractors for wagons, contractors for horses, contractors for mules, contractors for forage, contractors for railway conveyance, contractors for steamers, contractors for ships, contractors for coal, contractors for hospitals, contractors for surgical instruments, contractors for drugs, and contractors for every thing else required for human use and consumption in order not only to sustain life but to destroy it, suddenly started into existence. The Government, pressed by a necessity which admitted of no hesitation in regard to time, character, quantity, quality, and cost, accepted almost every offer, and paid almost any price. It is true, that political allies and social friends and relatives were favored with the earliest information and the best places in the general race and scramble for the national treasure. That eager partisans and devoted brothers, cousins and brothers-in-law, having taken the shortest road, should come in ahead and grasp the first and biggest prizes, was not unnatural. There was one of these lucky favorites who made a fortune of a hundred thousand dollars or more as easily as these words which state the fact are written. Having secured a contract or agency for the purchase of transport steamers and other vessels, he fulfilled it with no more cost to himself than a cigar or two over the preliminary negotiation, and no greater effort than signing his name. The fortune was made by a minimum of personal labor given and a maximum of pay received.

The contractors of all kinds, with their contracts signed and sealed, hastened to pocket the profits. In many cases, with a mere dash of their pens, they transferred their bargains at an advance, and made snug fortunes, without the labor of an hour or the expense of a shilling. In other instances they fulfilled their contracts in a way more profitable to themselves than useful to the Government. The quality of the article they heeded little, provided it bore the name and the semblance of the thing, and could be had for almost nothing, or for much less than they were to receive for it. Thus *shoddy*, a villainous compound, the refuse stuff and sweepings of the shop, pounded, rolled, glued, and smoothed to the external form and gloss of cloth, but no more like the genuine article than the shadow is to the substance, was hastily got up, at the smallest expense, and supplied to the Government at the greatest. Our soldiers, on the first day's march, or in the earliest storm, found their clothes, over-coats, and blankets, scattering to the winds in rags, or dissolving into their primitive elements of dust under the pelting rain. Splendid looking warriors to-day, in their bran-new uniforms! To-morrow, in their rags and nakedness more pitiful objects than the ragged regiment of Falstaff, without a whole shirt among 'em! *Shoddy*, with the external gloss and form of a substantial thing but with the inherent weakness and solubility of its reflected image, has ever since become a word, in the vocabulary of the people, always quick in their forcible and incisive rhetoric to catch

and appropriate a simple and expressive figure to represent a familiar idea. [...]

It was not only in the contracts for clothing, but in those for almost every other supply that Government paying for the substance was mocked by the shadow. For sugar it often got sand; for coffee, rye; for leather, something no better than brown paper; for sound horses and mules, spavined beasts and dying donkeys; and for serviceable muskets and pistols the experimental failures of sanguine inventors, or the refuse of shops and foreign armories. There was, it is true, a show of caution on the part of the authorities in the form of a Governmental inspection; but the object of this was often thwarted by haste, negligence, collusion, or favoritism. [...]

There were fifty millions of dollars spent by the Government in a few months, at the beginning of the war, for arms alone. Out of this a dozen or more contractors enriched themselves for life. Poor men thus became rich between the rising and setting of the same day's sun; while the hundreds of thousands of dollars of the wealthy increased to millions in the same brief space of time. It is said that one of our great merchant princes gained from his transactions with Government two millions of dollars in a single year.

The proprietors of coal-mines came in for a large share of the national treasure. One company made such enormous profits from its supplies of coal to the Government, and the general rise in price in consequence of the increased demand, that it was enabled to declare, in a single year, dividends that, in the aggregate, amounted to two-thirds of its capital. Its stock, which a few years since could hardly tempt a purchaser at ten dollars a share, has arisen since the war to more than two hundred dollars, and is eagerly caught up at that price. One shareholder, in a twelvemonth, received in dividends no less than a hundred and fifty thousand dollars for a stock which cost him less than that sum, but which he could now sell for a million.

The "good time" of the contractors has, however, now gone. The Government, with the experience of three years' war, and with its commissariat thoroughly organized, is no longer at the mercy of the fraudulent and extortionate. In fact, it is said that in some later contracts the Government, more thanks to its luck than shrewdness, has, with the depreciation of the currency and the consequent rise in prices, got the best of the bargain.

As fortunes can be no longer made in a day out of the national treasury the eager money-seekers have taken to the stock exchange to make them out of each other. The rage of speculation—excitement is too mild a word—which has seized upon the community, and is fast making us a nation of stock-jobbers, has never been equaled since the days of John Law during the French regency of the Duc d'Orleans. The city exchanges and their approaches are already crowded with a frenzied throng of eager speculators, as was the *Rue de Quincampoix* of old. [...] The stranger goes to take a look at the speculators at the hour of exchange as he does at a collection of wild beasts at feeding-time, and comes away with the same impression, namely, that in their hunger to get their fill they are ready to devour each other. The prudent citizen turns the street, and shuns the place as dangerous to his morals and his person. If not tempted to risk his fortune, he is sure to be so hustled by the unruly crowd as to spoil his temper or his clothes, and perhaps endanger his limbs or life.

The passion for stock-gambling is fast extending to every class of society. Merchants, mechanics, and traders of all kinds are abandoning their counting-houses, their work-shops, and their stalls, and thronging into Wall Street. The daily industry, the constant self-denial, the vigilant prudence, and the patient expectation necessary to acquire a decent competence are scorned for the chances of making a fortune in a day. The number of brokers has more than quadrupled in a few months, such has been the enormous increase of stock-jobbing. Their aggregate business, in the city of New York alone, has arisen from twenty-five to more than a hundred millions a day. The transactions of several sum up to the amount of millions each in a morning, with a profit in commissions alone of more than a thousand dollars daily. There would be a cause of congratulation if this enormous business was an indication of the increased productive wealth of the nation; but it is nothing of the kind. It is only a proof of the passion for buying and selling, with the hope of benefiting by the fluctuations of price. [...]

The mania of speculation is wondrously contagious, especially among a people so gregarious and sympathetic as we are. What touches one is apt to be felt by all. As men of every class, age, and business are already thronging Wall Street, it may not be long before our women shall be seen, as in the times of John Law in France, and of the South Sea bubble in England, trailing their silks and satins in the dust of the exchange, and raising their voice in its din of excited barter. Already the spirit of speculation so pervades the community that the rise and fall of stocks is the most common topic of daily conversation in our houses during the hours of leisure, if hours of leisure we can be said to have when they are filled with the thoughts and talks of business. Some of our women are already infected with the prevailing passion of money-making as they have been long with that of spending it. "What's the price of gold to-day, my dear?" escapes from the pretty mouth of your wife before she has impressed the habitual kiss of connubial welcome upon your expectant lips. If you are a speculator, as you probably are in common with most of your fellow-citizens at this moment, and have made a good day of it, you answer blandly and don't complain of the loss of the conjugal embrace. If you have been unlucky and want consolation, and seek what you have a right to expect but don't find, you mourn over the loss, and conclude probably, with St. Paul, that money, or rather the love of it, is the root of all evil. [...]

It is obvious that when all are seeking to make their fortunes at others' expense that most will be disappointed. Each one, however, thinks that it will be his neighbor until he awakes some morning and finds it is himself who is ruined. There are some seductive examples undoubtedly of great success, of the rise of poverty to wealth in the course of a few weeks. There will be, too, with no less certainty before long, many striking instances of a fall from riches to beggary. [...]

The old proverb says: "That which comes easy goes easy." The suddenly enriched contractors, speculators, and stock-jobbers illustrate its truth. They are spending money with a profusion never before witnessed in our country, at no time remarkable for its frugality. Our great houses are not big enough for them; they pull them down and build greater. They, like the proud and wanton Caligula, construct stables of marble at a fabulous cost, in which their horses are stabled (some, doubtless, to be fed on gilded oats), with a luxury never hitherto indulged in by the most opulent of our fellow-citizens. Even the manure heaps lie upon more resplendent floors than are swept by the silken trains of our proudest dames. So magnificent are these structures that their proprietors have not hesitated to assemble within them "the best society" they could command of fine gentlemen and finer ladies, to hold a carnival of pleasure. The playing of Comedies, it is said, was a part of the programme, as if the presence of the *beau-monde*, seeking pleasure in a stable, was not in itself a sufficiently sorry farce. [...]

These Sybarites of "shoddy" buy finer furniture than was ever bought before, and dress in costlier cloths and silks than have been hitherto imported. No foreign luxury, even at the present enormous prices, is too dear for their exorbitant desires and swollen pockets. The importations of the country have arisen to the large amount of thirty millions of dollars a month, chiefly to satisfy the increased appetite for luxurious expense.

The ordinary sources of expenditure seem to have been exhausted, and these ingenious prodigals have invented new ones. The men button their waistcoats with diamonds of the first water, and the women powder their hair with gold and silver dust.

As excess, overflowing the natural channels of enjoyment, is always sure to take an irregular and perverted course for the indulgence of its unchecked vagaries, it is not surprising to find the boundless extravagance of the times assuming forms at variance with propriety and taste. Paris, provoked to excessive folly and wild extravagance by an imperial court willing to enervate the people by debauchery that they may become too languid for resistance to tyranny, has, among other forms of dissipations, invented a grotesque kind of fancy ball. In this the guests represent things instead of persons. For example, one presents herself as a kitchen, with her person hung all over with pots and kettles, wearing a saucepan for a helmet, like Sancho Panza, brandishing a shovel and tongs, and playing the part of a kitchen wench with probably a dish-clout hanging to her tail. Another of a more sentimental turn is a flower-garden, festooned with roses and bearing a spade and rake. A third is a pack of playing-cards, bedizened all over with clubs, diamonds, and hearts, and so on with every possible transformation of the human spiritual being (supposed to be rational) into the senseless, material thing.

This absurdity has been imported by our wealthy New Yorkers, together with other Parisian extravagances. Last winter, during which high carnival was held by our *nouveaux riches*, a dame who has traveled, and had the honor of fainting in the arms, it is said, of Imperial Majesty, in the course of which embrace she probably imbibed her high appreciation of imperial folly, got up one of these grotesque fancy balls. She herself appeared on the occasion as music, and bore upon her head an illuminated lyre supplied with genuine gas, from a reservoir and fixtures concealed somewhere under her clothes. "We don't feel this war," they say. We believe them. Nothing, we fear, while they are stupefying themselves in this whirl of absurd folly would bring them to their senses short of a shower of Greek fire. [...]

Are we deluding ourselves with the idea that this war is to be a continued carnival of abundance and pleasure? If so, we had better awaken at once to the fact that it is a sacrifice demanding the utmost effort of patient endurance. No noble cause, such as we are struggling for, was ever won by men while besotting themselves with excess and dallying pleasure. We must feel this war, and feel it resolutely, or we shall never triumph. Are we willing to prove ourselves worthy to triumph?

The Central Park: Carriages, toys, etc. en militaire

The March to the Sea
by Herman Melville

February 1866

Not Kenesaw high arching,
    Nor Allatoona's glen—
Though there the graves lie parching—
    Stayed Sherman's miles of men;
From charred Atlanta marching
    They launched the sword again.
        The columns streamed like rivers
            Which in their course agree,
        And they streamed until their flashing
            Met the flashing of the sea:
            It was glorious glad marching,
            That marching to the sea.

They brushed the foe before them
    (Shall gnats impede the bull?);
Their own good bridges bore them
    Over swamps or torrents full,
And the grand pines waving o'er them
    Bowed to axes keen and cool.
        The columns grooved their channels,
            Enforced their own decree,
        And their power met nothing larger
            Until it met the sea:
            It was glorious glad marching,
            A marching glad and free.

Kilpatrick's snare of riders
    In zigzags mazed the land,
Perplexed the pale Southsiders
    With feints on every hand;
Vague menace awed the hiders
    In forts beyond command.
        To Sherman's shifting problem
            No foeman knew the key;
        But onward went the marching
            Unpausing to the sea:
            It was glorious glad marching,
            The swinging step was free.

The flankers ranged like pigeons
    In clouds through field or wood;
The flocks of all those regions,
    The herds and horses good,
Poured in and swelled the legions,
    For they caught the marching mood.
        A volley ahead! They hear it;
            And they hear the repartee:
        Fighting was but frolic
            In that marching to the sea:
            It was glorious glad marching,
            A marching bold and free.

All nature felt their coming,
 The birds like couriers flew,
And the banners brightly blooming
 The slaves by thousands drew,
And they marched beside the drumming,
 And they joined the armies blue.
  The cocks crowed from the cannon
   (Pets named from Grant and Lee),
  Plumed fighters and campaigners
   In that marching to the sea:
    It was glorious glad marching,
    For every man was free.

The foragers through calm lands
 Swept in tempest gay,
And they breathed the air of balm-lands
 Where rolled savannas lay,
And they helped themselves from farm-lands—
 As who should say them nay?
  The regiments uproarious
   Laughed in Plenty's glee;
  And they marched till their broad laughter
   Met the laughter of the sea:
    It was glorious glad marching,
    That marching to the sea.

The grain of endless acres
 Was threshed (as in the East)
By the trampling of the Takers,
 Strong march of man and beast;
The flails of those earth-shakers
 Left a famine where they ceased.
  The arsenals were yielded;
   The sword (that was to be),
  Arrested in the forging,
   Rued that marching to the sea:
    It was glorious glad marching,
    But ah, the stern decree!

For behind they left a wailing,
 A terror, and a ban,
And blazing cinders sailing,
 And houseless households wan,
Wide zones of counties paling,
 And towns where maniacs ran.
  It was Treason's retribution
   (Necessity the plea);
  They will long remember Sherman
   And his streaming columns free—
    They will long remember Sherman
    Marching to the sea.

THE FREEDMAN'S STORY

BY M. SCHELE DE VERE

OCTOBER 1866

I have thought that a plain, unvarnished account of a servant's trials in his efforts to secure his freedom might not be uninteresting. It is given as nearly as possible in his own words. Oby is now with me, my dining-room servant. He has learned to read himself what I have written.

CHARLOTTESVILLE, VIRGINIA. M. S. DE V.

My name is Oby; they say it is because my father was an Obeah man, when he lived down South in Florida and drove a stage. I have heard him say, to the contrary, that he belonged, at the time I was born, to a man by the name of Overton, and that that is my true name. So when I went down to town the other day, and the Provost-Marshal asked me if I could sign my own name, I boldly wrote down "Mr. Overton Paragon." [...]

I was nearly grown—I may have been about nineteen or twenty years old—when the Yankees came right down upon us. We had been expecting them often before, and many is the time Uncle Henry came running in where mother was and cried out, "God be thanked, they are coming, they are coming!" And mother asked him, "Who are you talking about?" and he would say, "Our deliverers, the Yankees, whom God sends to make us all free!" But mother did not like his ways at all, and when he was gone she would take me and brother Henry by her little stool close to the fire and say: "Now, boys, don't you think you'll be so much better off when you are free. Folks have to work every where, free or slave, black or white; and it's much better for you to be with genteel folks, and go to church, [...] than to be way off, where you have not any body who cares for you."

Mother was mighty good to us, and I know she meant it all for the best, but, to save my life, I could not help thinking of what Uncle Henry said, and what a fine thing it would be to be free, and to have twelve dollars a month and nothing to do. So I went over to Colonel Wood's Aleck and we talked it over behind the wood-pile, where nobody could hear us, and he told me how he knew a plenty more who would go away as soon as ever the Yankees came. He said they were fighting for us, and if we wanted to go we need not run away by night, [...] but we might ride off on a fine horse, in the middle of the day, and our masters could not say a word against it for fear of the Yankees. So I promised I would join him, and when we heard that General Sheridan was coming this way, with a hundred thousand men, we knew that the Confederates could not stand before him, and we agreed we would go off all together. [...]

And so it did come about one fine, clear morning. On Monday a man in gray had come racing up the turnpike, looking right and left under his broad-brimmed, slouched hat, and gone into town. Uncle Henry had met him as he came up, and shook his head and said: "Now, I should not wonder if that was a real Yankee." They all laughed at him, and asked him if he did not see the Confederate gray and the ragged hat the man wore. But he shook his head and said: "Now, I'll tell you, boys, it may be so, and it may not be so; but that man there did not ride like one of our folks, and he had his eyes too busy and his hand too near his revolver to be one of our soldiers." That morning early there came two, and three, and at last a whole number of these gray-coats. [...]

On Tuesday, early in the morning, as soon as master had had his breakfast, we all slipped out and went down to the road, where we found a great many people standing about and talking of what the Yankees were going to do with the house, and the servants, and the town itself. Down by the lake, where the road from the house comes into the turn-pike, and not far from the little lodge, stood a heap of gentlemen, who had come up from town to beg pardon of the General, and to ask him not to burn them all out. They were mightily scared, and Mr. Fowler, the tailor, who is a great goose, as I have heard it said often and often, looked white and shook in all his limbs. It could not be from the cold, for although the rain had stopped overnight, it was quite mild in the morning. Alongside of them, but a little apart, stood master and some of his friends; I don't know if they had come too to ask the Yankees to spare the house. Soon one man came flying down the hill, and then another, and then three or four together, galloping right by us without ever stopping, and just crying one after another, "They are coming! they are coming!" [...] Every now and then somebody would cry out, "There they are!" and we all looked up to the top of the hill, behind which the road was hid, and when a man slowly rose over the brow and it turned out that he was on horseback, we thought sure enough there were the Yankees. So we stood hours and hours, and just when we thought they would not be coming that day, two men rode up the hill and down again slowly, then three more, then a dozen or more all in a body, with flags in their hands; and at last the whole turnpike was blue, and we knew for a certainty they were come. We just looked at one another, and I felt mighty queer; but Uncle Henry and all the others, who stood way down by the stile, looked exactly as if they were going to shout to the sky and to jump out of their skin. Aleck looked at me too, and winked, and shut his eyes, and shook all over, till I could not help myself, and I laughed, and they all laughed, and it set the others down at the stile a-laughing, and we held our sides and did not mind master and his friends looking at us as if they did not like it at all.

When the first officer came up to where Mr. Fowler stood, he rushed forward and came near falling between the horses' feet, and they all cried out together, I don't know what; but the tailor had the biggest mouth, and he talked loudest. So I suppose they heard him, and one of the officers said something about private property being spared, but public property must be given up.

Just then master walked up himself, like a real gentleman that he is, and although he was on foot and had not even a spur on his boot, he looked as good a man as the big officers on their fine horses. One of them told him he was not the General, but he would send up a guard as soon as they got into town. Then they moved on, and such a sight! They looked very different from our poor Confederate soldiers, with their sleek horses and bright swords, and there was not a ragged jacket or a bare foot among them all. They had, every one of them, a pile of good things strapped up behind and before their saddles, and a good many had a fine horse by their side with all sorts of packages and parcels strapped upon their back, ever so high, but nobody in the saddle. [...] We stood there and looked and looked until we were tired, for there was no end to the horses, and the big guns, and the wagons, and oh, they had every thing so nice and so whole, though they were bespattered from head to foot; I did not think soldiers could look so well. At last they were nearly all gone, and I and Aleck went back.

When we came to the other side of the lake we saw Miss Mary and some of the other young ladies standing by the window up stairs, and some of them were crying; but Miss Mary waved a little flag, such as our soldiers have, right in the face of the Yankees. But master looked up and gave her such a look! Miss Mary went away from the window, and when they sent for her to come down to dinner, she told Flora to tell master she had a bad headache and did not want any dinner. Soon after the bell rang, and when I went to the front-door there stood a big Yankee officer, with his sword by his side and the mud all over him, and he asked in a very soft voice if master was at home. I did not like much his talking of my master and he a Yankee, but I knew I must be polite to strangers, and I asked him to please walk in. He said he wanted to see master, would I request him to come to the front-door for a moment. I can't tell exactly what it was, but there was something in the officer's voice, and in the way he spoke to me, that made me feel a big man, and as if nobody ought to call me Oby any more. Master is mighty good to me, but he always talks to me as if I was a little baby and had not any sense at all. Now the officer spoke right sternly, though his voice was so soft, but somehow it did not hurt me in the least, and I felt all the better for it. I ran in and told master, who came out at once, not at all flurried but like a grand old gentleman, and he begged the officer very politely to walk in. But he would not come in, and merely told master that he was on General Sheridan's staff, and that he wished to know where he should place the guard. I wanted badly to hear what they were going to say to each other, but master sent me down stairs to tell Aunt Hannah to cook a big dinner for the soldiers. We had done that often enough when our poor Confederates came by, and there was not much left in the smoke-house; but when the folks in the kitchen heard it was for the Yankees they were going to cook they set to work with a will. Aunt Hannah said she would sit up all night to work for them blessed Yankees, and Flora laughed and cried out that she hoped there was a handsome captain coming to take her to Boston. [...]

[Then] there came such a pull at the door-bell that I jumped up and thought the Yankees were breaking into the house. I ran up the stairs as fast as I could, and as I was trying to unlock the door—we did not use to do it, and so the key would not turn very quickly—somebody rang and rang until I got frightened out of my wits. When I opened the door there stood Miss Polly, as red as a peony, her dress all in tatters, and her hair hanging about her as I had never seen a lady do in all my life, and rushes by me to master's study. Master had just come out to see what was the matter, and she ran nearly over him. Then she began telling him to come, for God's sake, to her house; how the Yankees had come there and broken every thing to pieces, and were misbehaving shamefully. I did not believe a word of it, for they had been very polite to us all and to master too; but he did not say a word, put on his hat, gave Miss Polly his arm, and walked right off with her. I followed him, for I thought he might want me, and I heard Miss Polly rattling away like a water-mill, telling him how the soldiers had come to the house, and first broken into the kitchen and eaten all the dinner that there was, and then came into the sitting-room and asked for whisky. Her brother, who had been shot in the Valley and was lying with a broken leg on a couch, had gotten very angry and called them names. The Yankees did not like that, and went to work smashing every thing in the house. So she ran over to our house to get help.

When we crossed the road—it was knee-deep in mud—we saw Miss Emma, with her three little children, sitting on the big oak stump right by the house, crying bitterly, and in the house all the windows and doors smashed, and such a row as I have not heard in my life. Master puts Miss Polly down by her sister's side, and tells her to sit quiet, and then he walks as boldly up to where the Yankees were as if he were General Sheridan himself. I was afraid to go after him, so I staid by the ladies, who, I thought, wanted somebody to protect them, and they were so full of the misfortune they told me every thing. All the silver was gone, and all the china was broken, and the pictures cut to pieces, and the books thrown out of the window; and as they were telling me the soldiers came out. Some had a pillow-case full of flour, another a tureen filled with meal, and still another had two big gold watches in his hand. At last one came out with a silver cup in his hand. When Miss Emma sees him she jumps up and catches hold of it, and says, "You sha'n't take away my poor baby's cup!" "But I will," says the soldier—a great big fellow with a sword by his side. "But you sha'n't!"

cries Miss Emma again, and the big tears ran down her cheeks. And there they pulled, she on one side and the gentleman on the other side, and I thought she was going to fall down, when master comes out and very quietly puts his hand upon the soldier's arm, and says, "You will surely oblige the lady and let her have the cup." The Yankee looked quite bewildered, but he had let go, and Miss Emma ran back to her seat with her baby in her arm; and the baby held the cup with her dumpy little fingers, as if she knew what she held, and master looked pleased and said: "I am glad, Sir, you can act so handsomely." I thought the soldier had a great mind to tell him he did not want any of his praise; but I know most men were rather afraid of master, he looked so stiff and so stately; and he went slowly away. [...]

Soon after the Yankees made a great uproar in the house, and then they came out, one by one, [a] red-haired man shoving them out with a laugh and a curse, until the house was clear again. I had been watching them, so that I did not hear what master said to the ladies, but just as the last one went down the hill I heard Miss Polly crying bitterly, and saying: "And would you believe it, Sir, one of these wretches told me I was the ugliest woman he had seen in the Confederacy; and as for Emma, she was too ugly to live?" I looked hard at master, to see what he would say to that, but I thought he was trying all he could not to laugh. Then he smiled and gave his arm to Miss Emma, and asked her when she had heard from her husband, and they all went back to the house.

The red-haired man came out and sat down on the bench in the veranda; and when he sees me standing there, he says, "Come here, man, and bring me some water; and, look here, bring me some whisky too, or I'll cut your head off!" I was certainly afraid he would do it, too, so I ran as fast as I could to Uncle Tony close by, who I knew had some apple brandy, and telling him that it was for a Yankee soldier he gave me some. I ran back to the Irish gentleman—for I knew him to be Irish, because we have so many of those folks around us, working on the canal—and brought him the whisky. I was running for the water too, but he called after me, and said he was not thirsty now, I need not go for water. So I sat down on the grass by his side, and looked up at him, and got hold of his sword, and made the little wheels on his spurs play as fast as they would go.

All of a sudden he looks at me and says: "Hallo, Cuffee, how would you like to have a fine horse and ride along with us all?" My heart jumped when I heard him make such an offer; but I did not know if he was in earnest, so I only laughed and laughed until he could not help himself and had to laugh too. But after a while he looked very sober, and said: "Nonsense, Cuffee, nonsense; don't laugh that way, but tell me soberly would not you like to go with me and become a soldier?" When I saw that he was really in earnest I jumped up and said, as loud as I could, "Yes, Sir, that I will, and I have long waited for the day; God be thanked it has come at last, and I shall be a free man!"

He told me then to follow him, and we went over to Burr's Hill, where the General had his head-quarters, and the red-haired man's regiment had their camp. When we got there I found out that he belonged to the artillery, and the whole wood was filled with guns, and wagons, and horses, and all about the hill were fires lit, and the men were sitting around them eating their supper. I felt all of a sudden as hungry as a rattlesnake, for there they had coffee, and white sugar, and lemons, and all the good things we had not seen at our house for ever so long. We went past them all, until we came close to the house, and there I saw a great number of colored gentlemen standing around in a circle, and in the middle were some Yankee soldiers. Just as we came up I heard one of them say, "Here is another fine lot; what's the bid?" I felt as if I was turning to stone, when I found out that he held Bob, my second cousin, by his right ear, and pushed him forward in the bright light. I thought sure enough it was all the old story over again, and we were not free yet, but to be sold just as we were before. Somebody cried out, "I'll give a ham!" and another, "I bid a loaf of sugar!" Now I wondered more than ever, for Bob was a powerful fellow, and could plow better than any man on the plantation, and that was no price at all, even in Confederate money. But I soon found out that they were only offering something for the right to choose their servants, and that we were really free, only we could not choose our masters, but they chose us.

When I understood that right, I turned round and said, very politely, "Master, I wish you would not offer me to any body but keep me yourself. I would rather be your servant than any body's else." He seemed to be quite pleased at being called Master, and slapped me on the shoulder, and said, "Well, Cuffee, if you wish it, you may do so." I did not like to be called Cuffee, which is not respectable for a nigger who moves in good society; so I said, "Master, my name is Oby; and if it is the same to you, I would rather you should call me by my name." [...]

My new master showed me a beautiful horse that I was to ride, and when the light came through the trees and I could see every thing clear, I saw it was Master William's great big stallion. I did not like to get on him, because every body about here knew him, he had stood so often down in town, but I was told to take him down to water, and I did not like to be bucked. [...] I went down to the spring, and I could not help thinking he was the handsomest horse I had ever laid eyes on, and it would be a great thing for me to ride alongside of all the gentlemen on such a fine horse. When I came back to the fire they showed me a quantity of bags and bales, all nicely fixed in white cotton sheets, which I had to strap on the horse; there was just enough room left between the pile in front and the pile behind to get into the saddle. They did not give me any breakfast either, but I did not mind that much, for soon the bugles sounded—it made me feel like a gentleman to be called by a bugle like all the others; and my new master, who was a corporal or a major, had some other gentlemen under him, and when the guns were all ranged in beautiful order, the Colonel came out and looked at us, and off we marched with the music at our head.

First came the Colonel and some officers, then came the music, with all sorts of instruments such as I had never seen before; after them came men who bore a number of flags, which I knew nothing of, and after them, before all the regiment, came we colored people, about fifty of us, all on fine horses, and the happiest boys ever you saw in your life. It was glorious. But when we got to the corner by the tobacco-house, where the gate has been out of order for many years and the lane is quite low and narrow, they all stopped and we could not go any farther. The mud was awful, and the horses could not pull the heavy guns and the wagons.

Just then who must come up but master. I felt mighty badly, but I could not run away, and I looked for my new master to stand by me and let them all know that I was free. When master's eye came slowly down the line and at last fell right upon me, I thought I was going to sink into the ground. It made me feel sick. When I looked up again he was making his way through the horses and the cannons right up to me, and did not mind the mud, and the way the soldiers all looked at him, and the horses that wanted to kick him. When he came up to where I sat on my horse, he just said, "Oh, Oby!" And before I knew what I was doing, I was out of the saddle and standing right before him, with my new cap in my hand. He said, in his quiet way, "Oby, you know you are not strong enough to sleep out in the open air;

you have not even a blanket, and it is not three weeks since you were sick with pneumonia. Come home, my boy, and don't distress your father and your mother. You know it will kill them!"

I knew that what he said was but too true; but then again, when I looked at the fine horse I was on, and all the gentlemen around me, I felt quite undecided. Master said again, very quietly, "Come home, Oby!" and I followed him, I did not know why. But just as we were getting out of the crowd, on the side of the road, my new master came dashing up to where we were, and with a terrible oath told me to mount my horse and be ready to start. I was so frightened I did not know what to do. Master never said a word, but just looked at me as if he pitied me from the bottom of his heart, and I could not stand that; I did not think of father and mother at home, nor of Flora, nor of the nice times we had had together in the fields at night, but I just looked at master and went away with him. But the soldier was not satisfied yet; he came straight up to us, and swearing worse than ever, he said to master, "How dare you, Sir, force that man away? Do you not know that he is free, and has a right to go where he will?" Master changed color; I knew he was not accustomed to be spoken to in that way, and I wished I had never thought of enlisting as a soldier. But he said nothing at all, and although the soldiers all turned around, and my new master pulled out his carbine and cocked it, he made his way between the horses and the guns, I following him close by, until we came out on the other side of the column, and then he said very quietly, "Now, Oby, go home and tell your father not to distress himself about you any farther." I was just running up the road, when I heard somebody galloping up, and as I turned round I saw it was a great officer, with a sword in his hand, who rode up to master and asked him what was the matter. I could not hear his answer, but the officer said, "We do not force servants to go with us, and if your boy wants to stay, let him stay."

When I came home I found father and mother, Uncle Henry, and all of them in mother's room, and when they saw me they all cried out, "Oh, Oby, what have you been doing?" Well, it made me right angry to be treated thus like a baby, and I went out into the yard. There stood Flora, and what must she do but come up to me in the prettiest way of the world and drop me a little courtesy, and say in a little lisping way, "Oho, Mr. Paragon, you had not the courage to go with your friends? Don't you look like a little whipped boy? Shall I ask Miss Lucy for some candy for you?" It made me mad to hear her talk so, when she had all the time been

telling me that I ought to stay, and not run away like the poor stupid field-hands. [...]

Late in the evening Uncle Bob came home, and such a sight he was! He had a double harness hanging over his shoulders, and a saddle on his head, and his hands full of bags and satchels, and a big gun under his arm. He looked very tired, and threw it all down; then he opened the door again and laughed, and when we went out there to see what it was, we found a nice carryall and two good, strong horses fastened to the fence. I knew the carriage well; it belonged to old Miss Mary Fitch, and the horses were Uncle Bob's master's. I did not like his goings on much, but he was an old man and I had no right to say any thing to him. When he had had his supper he lit his pipe and looked around him, and when he noticed me he opened his eyes wide, and said, "Why, Oby, I thought you had gone with the Yankees!" I felt mightily ashamed. I had to tell him all about it, and when I had done he called me out and whispered to me, "Now, look here, Oby, don't you make a fool of yourself, but come along with me to-night and be a man." He talked and talked, and before I knew exactly how it was, I had promised to go with him. He had a way about him that few could resist, and when he wanted you to do any thing he was sure to get you to do it.

It was a dark night, the moon was behind the clouds, and at times you could not see the hand before your eyes. Uncle Bob had hitched up and put Aunt Betsy and the four children inside the carryall; he sat on the box, and every corner behind and before was stuffed full with bags and parcels. I do not know why they took so much; but Aunt Betsy would take every thing; and there was her spinning-wheel, and her split-bottomed rocking-chair, and the cradle for the baby. [...] We walked pretty fast, and listened with all our might, for we thought we might meet some gentleman and he might stop us. But there was nobody about that night; every body was afraid of the Yankees, and kept very close. Besides, the roads were awful, and Uncle Bob's horses could hardly pull the carryall at a snail's pace. Every now and then they would stick fast in the mud, and then we had to take rails from the fence and put them under the wheels and help Uncle Bob. [...] At last we could not get any further, and just then we saw a light through the trees, and when we whipped the horses on both sides to get nearer to it we found an army wagon in the middle of the road, with the mud over the hubs of the wheels, and one of the mules half-dead and half-buried in the mud. The drivers and some of the escort had made a roaring fire in the woods, and we joined them. I was so sleepy I fell down where we stopped, and did not know what happened any more.

I was just dreaming of my young master's calling me to saddle his pony when somebody touched me on the shoulder. I could not wake up at once. It always went hard with me to wake in the morning, and then I heard somebody call my name. It sounded very sweet to me somehow, though I did not know where it came from, and when I got my eyes open at last I thought I was dreaming still. For there was Flora standing by my side, looking up at the top of the tree, as if she did not know I was lying right before her. After a while she turned her eyes all around her, and when they came back to me she cried out, "Why, Oby, if that is not you! Where on earth do you come from?" Now that was a nice question to ask me; so I just jumped up and laughed heartily; and then she began laughing too, and before I knew what I was doing my arm was round her waist and I had kissed her twice. She pretended to be very angry, but I only laughed the more, and at last she told me how she had heard from Uncle Bob's son, who stays at master's mill, that I had gone along with him. Then she had made a little bundle of her nicest clothes and had followed us all the way, never saying a word, until she felt so cold in the morning she could not stay away any longer from the fire. When I asked her what she had come for, she said: "You would not have me let Aunt Betsy go away with all those babies and no one to take care of them? And then, might not somebody have come and frightened Mr. Paragon out of his wits and sent him home again crying?" [...]

After a while I began to feel hungry, and when I looked at Flora in the bright daylight I thought she looked hungry too; at all events she was very pale and drooping, and I saw she had no shoes on, and could hardly walk. I went to help her, but she tried to hold up, and said it did not matter. I saw, though, it would matter pretty soon, for we had not a mouthful of bread nor meal among us, and, except Uncle Bob, who was rich enough, there was not one among us who had any money. And here we were alone, left by our natural friends and protectors, and not likely to be received on any plantation.

It seemed that all of our party felt the same way, for no one said a word. Every now and then one of the children would begin to whine and be told to hush up. Then some girl would laugh right out and suddenly stop short, as if she was frightened at the sound of her own voice. Uncle Bob, who knew best, had his hands full to drive his tired horses and to pull the carryall, with its heavy load, through the awfully bad roads. I walked steadily on, Flora right behind me, Indian file, and what with the cold, drizzling rain, wetting us to the skin, and the loads of mud that stuck to our feet, and the heavy thoughts that weighed on our minds, we did not make a very merry couple. I thought, every now and then, what a glorious time I would have at the North. I knew I could make as good a shoe as any white man, and I thought of a nice little shop I might have in Cincinnati, where Peter Hite went when he was made free, and of Flora being my good wife, really married, and the beautiful things I was going to buy for her, so that she might look a real lady. But in the midst of my thoughts I stumbled against a big, old root, or Flora sighed behind me, and then coughed a little to put me on a false track, or asked me some question, to show that she was not sad at all, and my dreams were gone in a moment, and I saw all our troubles clear before me again.

We tramped on until late in the evening, when we met an old field-hand, with a bag of potatoes on his back, who told us we were still eight miles from the canal, and that he had seen no Yankees any where. We asked him to let us have his potatoes, but he said he did not want to have any thing to do with runaway niggers, and was going away to leave us, when Uncle Bob came up and asked him what he would take for them in greenbacks. When he heard us speak of greenbacks he became very polite at once, and sold them for ninepence to Uncle Bob, who made him promise to bring some fat middling and some corn-meal up to the old tobacco house, where we meant to spend the night. We all went in there, and it was a nice enough place for us to get dry in; there was some hay in a lean-to on one side, and I made a nice little bed for Flora; but we did not dare make a large fire for fear they might see it at the house and send the overseer down to turn us out. Uncle Bob got his middling, and Aunt Betsy cooked all they had for herself and her children, asking me and Flora to come up and help ourselves. I did not like much going there, when there were so many others who had nothing at all to eat, but Uncle Bob told me to make no hesitation—he always loved big words—and to partake of his victuals. I took Flora by the hand and pulled her along with me to the fire. Aunt Betsy looked at us, and I thought she was going to have a hearty laugh, but somehow there was none of us that night could laugh heartily, and we ate just to satisfy our hunger, but it did not taste good. Then we had a chew of tobacco, and Uncle Bob proposed we should sing a psalm about the mansions in the sky, and hallelujah, but we

Fugitives in the swamps.

broke down pretty soon, and then we all lay down, one here, one there, as we were sitting. I was tired enough, but I could not sleep; the thoughts would come into my head. I could not drive father and mother out of my head, and every time I saw them in my mind they looked so sad it made me feel very badly. Then the children cried and moaned and asked for something to eat; and some of the old ones groaned too, and cried out: "O Lord, O Lord a-mercy!"—it was very hard to hear it all and not be able to help them in any way. So I was right glad when the mist broke in the morning and the sun rose, first red, like blood, and looking as if it were angry at us, and then clear and bright, like the dayspring from on high. [...]

The road was worse than ever, for Sheridan's men had been right ahead of us, and they had trampled the mud knee-deep, and if the carryall once got into the ruts the army wagons had made, there was hardly any way to get it out again. We were soon left behind, for we had to pull the horses out when they stuck fast, and to mend the harness, that was all the time breaking, and take the rails from the fence and pry the carriage up to let the poor starved horses pull it out again.

At last we came to a sandy stretch in the pine woods, where it was a little better, and as we turned round a corner, there, right in the fence, lay Aunt Phoebe, and by her side

two of her little babies, the one three years old and the other about nine months, and never a word did any one of them say. I went up to Aunt Phoebe and shook her, and asked her what was the matter. At first she would not answer at all; at last, when Flora came up and whispered into her ear, and begged her to speak to her, she said, very faintly, that she could not possibly go a step further, and that she had not a drop of milk left for her baby. [...] I asked Uncle Bob if he thought she would die? He did not look at me at all, but just said in his beard, "I don't know; maybe she will, maybe she won't; perhaps it's better for her to die than to live on as she has done."

After that we were sadder than ever before. Poor Flora lost her big shoes every other step, and most of the ladies had to throw away their bundles, and even then they could hardly get along. Whenever we met a colored man we asked him how far it still was to the canal, for we knew we would meet the Yankees there sure enough, and they would not let us starve, but give us all rations. It seemed as if we were never getting nearer to it, for every time we asked it was still some four or five miles, maybe six. We met some white gentlemen, too, on the road, but they just looked at us with stern faces and rode by. Once we came to a little bit of a house by the way-side, and saw an old lady sitting by the door, with a cat lapping up the milk in a gourd she held on her lap. I could not stand seeing that, so I walk up to her and make her a polite bow, and say, "Oh, Missis, I see you are a mighty good lady, won't you be so kind as to give me a little of that milk for a poor girl who is half dead over yonder?" The old lady looked at me and then at Flora, who was standing at the gate, staring with her big eyes at the gourd as if she had never seen milk in her life. After a while she said, "Well, I don't care; take it if you want it." I was just taking the gourd by the handle, being careful not to spill a drop, when a great big man in a gray uniform and a large revolver in his hand comes out of the passage, and swearing at me, as they did in the army, says, "Now, you rascal, you clear out here or I'll shoot you down like a dog!" I felt so mad I would have liked to run up to him and snatch the pistol out of his hand and shoot him myself; but I did not have the courage, that is the truth of it, and I knew also I must not get my friends into trouble before we got to the soldiers again. When I came back to where Flora stood I saw she had dropped down upon a big rock they used to get on horseback by, and when I spoke to her she said she could not get any further. That finished me, and I swore to God Almighty I would have something for her or take a man's life. But just then something came between me and her, and when I looked up there was the old lady with the gourd in her hand and a piece of corn-bread I had not seen before, and she said: "Never mind my son, boy; he is in bad humor because all our servants have left us in a body yesterday and taken our horses with them. Poor child, what is the matter with her?" And then she took Flora's hand in hers and rubbed it, and told her to sit up and eat and not to cry any more. I talked to her too, and after a while she did sit up, and the way the milk and the bread went! It would have been a pleasure to me to see how she enjoyed it; but I was terribly hungry myself, and I counted every mouthful she took and every gulp that went down. When she had done, she stood up and looked much better, and then she thanked the old lady, as she had learned to do from Miss Lucy. The old lady had big tears in her eyes and looked mighty sad; she said something about God's Providence, which I did not understand, and about somebody's being ground between the upper and the nether millstone, which, I think, is somewhere in the Bible.

We had to walk fast enough to overtake the others, who had gotten far ahead of us, and it was late in the evening when we saw them all standing in a crowd together on a high place. The sun was just about setting, and the sky was golden, and as we looked at them we could see every ray of their clothes and every hair on their head. They all talked very loud, even Uncle Bob, who seemed to be very angry. We came up slowly, for we were terribly tired, and Flora could hardly drag one foot after the other. When we came up to where they stood, we saw we were on the side of the canal, and there on the tow-path sat Aunt Hannah, crying and screaming all together, and the others stood around her and looked as angry as could be. We pressed close up to Aunt Betsy, and I asked her in a whisper what was the matter. "Oh, Oby!" she said, "just think of it, Aunt Hannah was the first to see the canal, and she walks right up to where we now are and takes her poor little baby—it was not more than two months old—and before we knew what she was about she had thrown it into the water, and there it lies now. Oh, Oby, these are awful times! God have mercy upon us!" […]

Flora got up and followed me, but she did not say a word. The tears were just running down her cheeks, and she did not mind it in the least. Uncle Bob was driving along on the tow-path, and we all followed in a long string, very slowly. At last we came to another turn, and there, right before us, lay a big mill, and behind it the town. On the mill-race stood a soldier in blue, and I could have shouted aloud, for now I knew our troubles would surely be at an end. I do not know what made me so bold, but I walked right up to the soldier and asked him if he did not know somebody that wanted a really good servant. He looked at me and then at Flora, who was standing behind me, and said: "You mean two good servants, don't you? I can't afford keeping a servant, but there is the sutler; I heard him inquire a little while ago for a handy fellow, who understood horses and knew how to make coffee and such things."

I hardly let him finish, for that was exactly what I was good for, and Flora made beautiful coffee. I just asked him where the sutler was, and when he showed me some way down the street a splendid team of four gray mules, standing before a large, fine house, and said that was the sutler's wagon, I took hold of Flora's hand and ran down as fast as I could. But when I came between the mules and the house I saw a whole crowd of servants standing around the door and crying out: "Take me, master, take me!" I thought it was all over, and I had lost my first and last chance, when Flora suddenly let go my hand and fell down like a log of wood, right between the wheels of the wagon. I tried to lift her up, but there was such a crowd, and the mules began to kick, and I thought she was going to die right away. Just then a man who had been inside the wagon popped his head out, and seeing Flora lying there, he asked: "Hallo, what is the matter, my man?" I told him as well as I could, and begged him for mercy's sake to help me, for Flora was sure enough dying. He laughed and stepped down leisurely over the swingletrees, with a piece of hard tack in one hand and a bottle in the other. He poured some out of the bottle into his hand and rubbed her head with it, then he poured some down between her teeth, and when I could see next, she was sitting up with her head leaning against the wheel, opening her eyes as if she had been fast asleep, and munching a little bread in her mouth. I thanked the gentleman for having saved her life, but he only laughed the more. Then he asked me if I was not hungry too; and before I could say a word he pushed a whole pile of crackers into my hands. When Flora was all right again, he asked us what we were going to do with ourselves, and we told him as fast as we could, for we were both mighty grateful to him for his kindness. Then he told us that he was the sutler himself, and that if we promised to do well and be faithful servants to him he might find something to do for us both. He called to his clerk, who was in the house, and told him to see to it that we got a place to sleep in and some supper. When I looked a little around me I saw they had a beautiful flag flying from the top of the house, and that was the first night I slept under the Stars and Stripes, a free man.

THE PLAINS, AS I CROSSED THEM TEN YEARS AGO

BY HORACE GREELEY

MAY 1869

The Mississippi is the King of Rivers. Taking rise almost on the northern limit of the temperate zone, it pursues its majestic course nearly due south to the verge of the tropic, with its tributaries washing the Alleghanies on the one hand and the Rocky Mountains on the other, throughout the entire length of those great mountain chains.

The Amazon, or La Plata, may possibly bear to the sea an equal volume of waters; the Nile flows through more uniformly genial climates, and ripples over grander and more ancient relics of the infancy of mankind; the Ganges, or the Hoang-ho, may be intimately blended with the joys and griefs, the fears and hopes, of more millions of human beings; while the Euphrates, the Danube, or the Rhine, is far richer in historic associations and bloody, yet glorious, memories: but the Mississippi still justifies its proud appellation of "The Father of Waters."

Its valley includes more than one million square miles of the richest soil on earth, and is capable of sustaining in plenty half the population of the globe; its head-springs are frozen half the year, while cane ripens and frost is rarely seen at its mouth; and a larger and richer area of its surface is well adapted at once to Indian corn, to wheat, and to grass—to the apple, the peach, and the grape—than of any other commensurate region of earth. Its immense prairies are gigantic natural gardens, which need but the plow to adapt them to the growth of the most exacting and exhausting plants. It is the congenial and loved home of the choicest animals: I judge that more game is now roving at will over its immeasurable wilds and pastures than is found on an equal area all the world besides. It is the geographic heart of North America, and probably contains fully half the arable land in the New World north of the Isthmus of Darien.

Its recent progress in industry and civilization has been rapid beyond parallel. At the birth of this century, its only city was a village; its total white population was less than one million. To-day, it has five cities, averaging two hundred thousand inhabitants each, and its civilized population exceeds fifteen millions.

And to its luxuriant and still unpeopled expanse all nations, all races, are yet eagerly flocking. The keen-eyed sons of cold and hard New England there meet the thrifty Dutchmen of Pennsylvania, the disinherited children of Scandinavia, of Northern Germany, and of the British Isles. From every quarter, every civilized land, the hungry, the portionless, the daring, hie to the Great Valley, there to forget the past buffets of niggard fortune and hew out for their offspring the homes of plenty and comfort denied to their own rugged youth. Each year, as it flits, sees the cultivated portion of the Great Valley expand; sees the dominion of the brute and the savage contracted and driven back; sees the aggregate product of its waving fields and fertile glades dilate and increase. Another century, if signalized by no unforeseen calamity, will witness the Great Valley the home of one hundred millions of energetic, efficient, intelligent farmers and artisans, and its chief marts the largest inland cities of the globe.

The Mississippi and its eastern tributaries are among the most placid, facile, tractable of rivers. A single fall wholly arrests navigation on the former; the Ohio rolls its bright volume a thousand miles unbroken by one formidable cataract. If half the steam vessels on earth are not found on these waters, the proportion is not much less than that. It may almost be said that steam navigation and the development of the Great Valley have hitherto gone hand in hand, and that the former is the vital impulse, the indispensable main-spring, of the latter.

There is no eastern affluent of the Great River whose sands have not been plowed by adventurous keels almost to their sources; and the spectacle of a steamboat pilot backing his engine to let a yoke of oxen and cart ford unharmed ahead of his stern-wheeled, light-drawing craft, is probably

Breaking a herd.

peculiar to this region. The Ohio River captain who averred that his boat drew so little that she could get on by the help of a moist surface or a smart dew was less extravagant than he would have been in uttering the same hyperbole any where else.

But, the moment the Great River is crossed, all this is changed. The turbid, resistless Missouri waters a far larger area than the other "inland sea" of Mr. Calhoun, wherewith it blends at St. Louis; yet its tonnage is but a fraction when compared with that of the latter; and, while boats of liberal size are overshadowed by the Alleghanies at almost each day's journey along their western base, the rays of no setting sun were ever yet intercepted on their way to a steamboat deck by the peaks of the Rocky Mountains.

Time will doubtless multiply the keels plying on the Missouri and its affluents; but human genius can never wholly overcome the obstacles to secure and speedy navigation presented by the nature of that resistless current, or rather of the country it traverses. The eager thousands pressing westward overland each summer to the shores of the Pacific find no relief from the length, the weariness, of their tedious journey in the shrill but welcome whistle of the fire-propelled, floating caravanserai. For weeks, they stalk in dusty, sombre array, beside the broad, impetuous Platte: finding obstruction, not furtherance, in its rippling, treacherous current; this moment scarcely knee-deep, and the next far over head; only their thirst, with that of their fainting beasts, is assuaged thereby. For all other uses, its bed might as well—perhaps better—be a stretch of uniformly thirsty, torrid sand.

For the wide PLAINS, which slope imperceptibly, regularly upward from the bluffs of the Missouri to the bases of the Rocky Mountains, are unlike any other region of earth. They labor under what, with no reference to our current politics, may be fitly characterized as a chronic deficiency of *back-bone*. Rock, to be sure, is sometimes seen here in place; but very rarely, save in the *buttes*, or perpendicular faces of hills, which are mainly confined to the vicinity of mountains, and are obviously a sort of natural *adobe*—a modern product of sun and rain and wind, out of the mingled clay and sand which form the subsoil of all this region. [...]

Drouth is, throughout each summer, the master scourge of the Plains. No rain—or next to none—falls on them from May till October. By day, hot suns bake them; by night, fierce winds sweep them; parching the earth to cavernous depths; withering the scanty vegetation, and causing fires to run wherever a thin vesture of dead herbage may have escaped the ravages of the previous autumn.

Of course, no young tree escapes destruction, unless it cowers behind the perpendicular, herbless bank of some gullying, washing stream, or stands in the low, wet, narrow bottom of some unfailing creek. Even here, the slender belt of scanty, indifferent timber—usually the elsewhere worthless cotton-wood—is often set upon by a fierce prairie-fire, driven through the dead grass to windward by some resistless gale, and is charred and blackened to lifelessness, save at the roots. Yet from those roots springs a new growth of luxuriant shoots, and, if no fresh disaster is encountered, these shoots develop rapidly into trees, while their predecessors fall, decay, and are forgotten. But, let the fires ravage them for two or three seasons successively, the vigor of the roots is exhausted, and the trees disappear forever.

Hence, as prairie-fires are kindled far more frequently and wantonly by white men than by Indians, timber on the Plains has visibly been diminishing throughout the last fifty years, and threatens at no remote day to disappear altogether.

The bleached skeletons of dead cotton-woods, and, as you approach the Rocky Mountains, of pines also, still linger beside creek-beds where no living tree has been seen for an age; while the thin screens of timber along many streams have for miles been swept away by the relentless axe of camping teamster or emigrant.

Rivers sink and are lost for miles in beds where water was formerly visible nearly through the summer; what were once perennial brooks are now for months but stretches of thirsty, scorching sand. Grass now springs but in patches, in hollows wherein the drifted snow lies deep far into spring, where it formerly overspread miles of hill and glade. And the predominant tendency, as wherever matters are left to the anarchical caprice and short-sighted greed of coarse, selfish men, is from bad to worse.

The prevalent impression made on the stranger's mind by the Plains is one of loneliness—of isolation. You press on, day after day, without seeing a house, a fence, a cultivated field, or even a forest—nought but a few shy wild beasts at intervals, or undelightful birds, and rarely a scanty, niggard stream, with a few mean, low, scrubby trees thinly

strewn along its banks—often one of them only; and, as you go farther west, even these disappear, or are only seen in thin patches, miles apart.

If you are traveling along a river, you are amazed at the sparseness, the feebleness, of its tributaries, the dryness of their beds, the bareness of their banks. At length, the river itself disappears, or is only seen in pools and in hollows along its bed, where a deep excavation has been gullied under one of its banks; at last, the necessary, but not particularly inviting, fluid has wholly vanished, and you are compelled to make your way hurriedly over the long "divide" that separates this stream from one, often less considerable, but which heads in or near a range of mountains, and, therefore, maintains its current nearly or quite through the summer. This "divide" may be thirty, fifty miles across—it may be a hundred—wood and grass upon it, and, in summer, water also, are out of the question; only a few straggling weeds, with the worthless shrubs here known as grease-wood and sage-brush, relieve the monotony of the sterile, dreary waste.

What wonder if the patient ox, weary, famished, footsore, should here lie down to his long rest, leaving his master and more pitiable mate to get on without him as they may?

It would be rather Hibernian to pronounce dead oxen the only signs of life to be encountered during many days' journey on the Plains; but I have no doubt that the carcasses of fifty thousand cattle are now slowly decomposing aboveground on the arid, treeless, dewless stretches which separate Kansas and Nebraska from California and Oregon.

Verily, the carrion-crow is lord of the Plains—the only ample feeder in those famished regions—quick-sighted, impudent, and, though gorged to heaviness, abundantly able to take care of himself. I can not guess where he finds nest-accommodation; probably in the face of some high, perpendicular creek-bank, the brow of some *butte*, not too remote from the emigrant trail to enable him to gorge his young ones as he gorges himself. He is as decorously jolly as an undertaker in cholera-time, and sports a grave demeanor and a black coat professionally, and with no thought of evincing sorrow, or exciting sympathy, still less of mortifying the flesh. On the Plains, the crow is general executor and universal heir. [...]

1870's

Editor's Easy Chair
Charles Dickens

by George William Curtis

August 1870

The death of Dickens was a shock, but probably not altogether a surprise, to those who knew him most intimately. It was the peculiarity of his temperament that he seemed always to be under full headway. Whatever he did with his hands or his head he did with his heart also. There are people who never seem to get so far as to be wholly alive. They are like fires that never quite burn, but smoke and smoulder away; or candles that feebly flicker, but never spring into a clear, bright flame. Others burn and blaze warmly and cheerfully from the first, and therefore are sooner exhausted. The very intensity of Dickens's nature should have announced the probability of a comparatively brief career. How busy he was in many ways all the world knows. But how equally devoted in many other ways of private beneficence only those know who came nearest to him.

Even those who did not personally know him well, of whom the Easy Chair is one, may recall many a pleasant instance of his heartiness and profuse humor. One bright June day in London, several years ago, there was a little dinner at Cattermole's, the artist, at which Dickens had promised to be present. The company assembled, and every thing went pleasantly until the dinner hour arrived. There was then some pause of expectation, for Mr. Dickens had not come. Conversation became a little more difficult; and as the conviction gradually seized the party that perhaps he would not come at all, there was a very obvious disappointment. When it was impossible to wait longer the dinner was served, and the guests descended to the dining-room; but it was curious to remark the blight

that had overspread the feast. There was the usual gay murmur of a dinner all around the table, but it seemed as if every body were secretly looking for something or somebody else. Suddenly, when the business was well advanced, there was a loud ring at the door, which every body heard, and the cloud instantly lifted. "There's Dickens!" said several of the guests, with an air of delight and relief; and those who did not say it looked it. The next moment a noise was heard in the hall above, merry voices, pleasant laughter; and then there seemed to be a charge of school-boys or light cavalry down the stairs, and Dickens and his friend John Forster burst into the dining-room, each loudly excusing himself, and accusing the other as having caused the delay.

Dickens seated himself by the mistress of the house, and instantly, as it were, took up the conversation, and carried it along with little sallies of fun; and his "carrying on" with the waiter when he wanted a piece of bread was like a rollicking scene from "Pickwick." It was the overflow of the highest animal spirits, and was as electrical in his manner as it is in his books. He felt entirely at home; and the feeling that the solemn English waiter would be confounded by such antics— which, however, did not in the least turn him into ridicule— was part of the humor. Dickens made a mock apology for his delay, founded upon a promise to attend a picnic in the earlier part of the day given by the manager of the Opera, at which Grisi and the other singers, with the dancers, had been present. He sketched them all with a word and a smile. They were all vividly before the company. He took the dinner guests also, as it were, to the picnic. "But oh! the eating!" exclaimed he. "Dear Madame, do you know the eating at an operatic picnic—I mean, of course," he added, with a solemn sly twinkle in the eye, "when the ladies of the ballet attend?" It was sheer extravaganza; and however foolish and flat it seems in the tame telling, it was delightful and memorable. After dinner, when the ladies went up stairs and the children peeped in, Dickens beckoned to them; and seating one on each knee, took a slate and pencil, and drew the most grotesque figures as illustrations of the most absurd story; then sent the young folks away as merry as the elders.

What he did at that table he did in the world. He told the most delightful stories, he made the most harmless fun; and all his story-telling and fun-making were morally healthful. He was a great civilizing and Christianizing power during thirty years. He was one of the men of the most unquestionable genius and positive influence that have appeared in English literature, and meanwhile it was almost as good as his own fun to hear the comments that were made upon the man and upon his works. [. . .] There were those who thought him a caricaturist—a writer of mere extravaganzas, no artist; a kind of newspaper reporter on the great scale. That last criticism Dickens himself would undoubtedly have accepted. For the business of the great novelist is to report human life and character as they daily appear; but his genius makes his reports the best of literature. [. . .] [H]owever broad and coarse the touch of Dickens may seem, the effect is wholly lifelike, and the proof is the universal acceptance of the type. Common conversation and current literature reflect the humor and the wisdom of this genius as the streams and lakes reflect the bright sky. [. . .]

It is true that the fashion of story-tellers passes away. Every history of literature is a body of dismal proof of that truth. But the influence and the admiration of great genius do not pass away. The mere novelist, the delineator of the temporary forms of society and of persons as affected by them, will gradually become curious as he becomes obsolete. But the story-teller who deals with human nature itself, and who paints human character, which does not lose its freshness with the lapse of time, although he may direct his force at a particular and even transitory object, is not the prey of a changing fashion nor of a whimsical taste. [. . .]

When it is said that Dickens was the people's story-teller, how much is said! The word people describes a universal range of sympathy. It signifies no class, but means all classes. It includes, as the old alliterative phrase was, the peer and the peasant. And how immense the service to the general faith in each other which we all really wish to cherish, is that of a man who shows, as Dickens did, that the greatest and most universal popularity, the favor of the most ignorant and of the most educated, may be won without pandering to a single mean impulse, without the least ridicule of noble and generous emotion, without any touch of baseness! What work is so truly lofty as that which, while morally cheering and strengthening all men, also inspires and justifies a deeper mutual confidence? This is the service of Dickens. If he was not a great artist, so be it. If he was a caricaturist, so be it. If he was not a gentleman, again so be it. But he was the most popular author of a time when reading was universal, and popular without a hint of impurity. He was more widely loved than any author has ever been in his time; and he left no man living whose death would be so sore and personal a grief to the English-speaking race as his has been.

Farewell, kind master! generous heart! How many and many in America or in England, gathering roses in that solemn week of June, did not wish that they could lay them upon his grave! For even so, sweet and perennial as June roses, full of all summer warmth and beauty, shall be the memory of the man whose tender touch still makes, and will yet make, summer in a thousand, thousand lives.

Down the Mississippi

by George Ward Nichols

November 1870

We were a party of six—three ladies and three gentlemen. Two of these only were husband and wife, so it can easily be believed we all got on very well together.

We were to take our point of departure from the city of St. Louis, not because the would-be capital of all the States is particularly interesting in itself, but because it is easily reached from any where else; and because one may be sure to find here large and comfortable steamboats, which go all the way to New Orleans.

Steamboats of the largest size, such as the *Thompson Dean, Great Republic, Richmond,* and others, do not go above St. Louis, neither do they ascend the Ohio, except for a short distance, because of shoal water and rapids, and therefore they do not invite freights. On a "full river," however, they can pass over all of these, and then these monster craft appear at the levee of Cincinnati.

St. Louis is the greatest transfer dépôt on the river. Steamboats bring to this point freights from the Upper Missouri and Mississippi and all the rivers which empty into these largest of the water-courses, and thus there is abundance of business for the great export mart of New Orleans.

To St. Louis, therefore, we repaired in search of the steamboat *Thompson Dean,* whose reputation for size and safety was so well assured as to gain the confidence of us timid travelers. [...] The boat we were to take was advertised to start at ten o'clock in the morning. An hour before that time we were on board, and had settled ourselves in the plain but large and comfortable state-room, which had been previously engaged for us through the medium of the telegraph. There were no evidences of haste nor press of business about the gangway of the boat. What freight there was had been stowed away, and the passengers who were to accompany us dropped in quietly. At the hour appointed the lines were cast loose, and we backed easily out from among the crowd of steamers which lay at the levee. There

was a raw wind from the north, and the sun shone cold and cheerless through the gray and white clouds which covered the sky. [...] Very soon we were fairly out into the river, and, with head down stream, with choking gasps from the steampipes, and bulging columns of smoke from the huge lofty smokestacks, and swift revolutions of the large paddlewheels, we sped away toward our destination.

At the risk of telling many of your readers what they will know as well as I, let me give a brief sketch of a Mississippi River steamboat. It is one of the most striking, as well as most original forms of our altogether original American architecture. Whenever our people attempt to build public edifices, such as churches, state-houses, and private dwellings, after their own invention, they are pretty sure to make a frightful botch of it; but American steamboat architecture, which has grown out of the needs of our commerce, is not only original to us in its form of construction, but it is sometimes splendid in appearance. This is a noble craft which bears us safely over the turbid waters of the great river. Her actual carrying capacity is thirty-two hundred tons. She is some two hundred and ninety feet in length, and fifty-six in breadth. From her keel to the roof of the upper cabin she includes forty feet. Above that is the "Texas," as it is called, which is an upper row of cabins, where the officers' quarters are, and upon the top of which is imposed the pilothouse. The main cabin is plainly but well furnished, with large state-rooms on either side. Below it is the main-deck, where the big boilers and furnaces and engines are. Below this deck again there is a deep, spacious hold, where a thousand or fifteen hundred tons of freight may be stowed away. [...]

Pretty nearly all the incidents which go to make up human life and society are represented on this steamboat of ours; and there are some which are exceptional, and find no parallel elsewhere. During some ten days which were occupied in our trip to New Orleans I passed a good deal of time in the pilot-house, and came to have a deeply interested admiration for the men who guide these noble vessels upon their devious journey.

Of all that belongs to life on our great Western rivers, the business and experiences of the pilots interest me most; and, as they are to have our lives in keeping for twelve hundred miles to come, it is worth our while to know all about them. No class of public servants stand in a position of greater trust and responsibility than theirs. The captain of our boat, for example, has supreme command, and is held responsible for the doings of all those within his control, but his authority is, in fact, limited in the pilot-house; for, although he has the power of directing the action of the pilot, yet, so far as taking this or that direction is concerned, he seldom exercises it. I can not conceive of a more arduous and dangerous business than that of guiding one of these gigantic steamboats along the twisting, shifting, treacherous channel of the river. The ocean steamship, whatever may happen, has the refuge of the open sea. The direction to be pursued is well known, and the compass points the way, while, if the vessel is deprived of the use of steam, she can resort to canvas, and, beyond delay, but little injury occurs. The man who directs the movement of the locomotive may, by the slightest carelessness, cause the death of hundreds of his fellow-beings; yet most accidents by railroad happen from exterior and accidental causes. There are many other stations in life where the safety of human beings and of property is dependent upon the judgment and good conduct of a single man. But in neither one nor all of them is there any such grave responsibility as that resting upon the pilot of the Western river. Truly must he be a man of rare natural gifts of memory of localities, quick observing comprehension, a sure hand, rapid judgment, determination of will, iron nerve, even temper, and good habits. [...]

From St. Louis to Cairo is what the pilots call a "bad piece of river." To me the river all the way down is "bad"— that is to say, difficult of navigation. I stand by the side of our pilot, and watch with curious interest the movement of the boat. To my eye the surface of the water is all the same, and there appears no reason why a course should not be pursued straight down the stream to the point a mile away, where the cotton-wood trees dip toward the gray horizon; but suddenly

Riverboat pilot.

the large wheel whirls swiftly around, and the bow of the boat points directly in shore at a right angle to the course of the stream. In an instant we are close under the bank, where the water is whirling and tearing along, where big roots of trees, like snakes, are crawling out from the yellow, crumbling earth. On the bank, near a log-hut, there stands a yellow-visaged man, who moves not, but stares at us with lack-lustre eyes. I see all this, so near are we to the bank; in fact, one might jump ashore, but one had rather be left on a desert island than in that dark forest. The man we saw will stay there but a little while. He has "squatted" there for the purpose of cutting wood for the steamers. He owns neither land nor wood, and, after earning a few dollars, will either move to another place, or go to some city on the river, where he can drink and gamble his money away. But we have left him far behind, and pushed out again into the middle of the river, not in a straight course, but winding hither and thither, as if led by some fitful sprite. First one side, and then the other, until your wits are fairly puzzled, and you are almost willing to believe that the pilot is a sham, or that he has some insight beyond that of human ken, which permits him to pursue his dangerous way among snags and shoals and sand-bars with perfect certainty and safety. You can comprehend how the direction might be taken from certain landmarks on the shore, although that would require a prodigious effort of the memory in these hundreds of miles; but between St. Louis and where the Ohio River joins the Mississippi the channel changes daily. We passed the wreck of the steamer *Lady Gay*. A few days ago an ugly snag went on an exploring expedition in her hold. The water followed it, and the steamer sank. Three or four other steamers had met with the same fate from this same snag; but in two days the channel shifted across, a mile away, to the other side of the stream.

"You see where that bit of brush-wood lies in the water?" said the pilot to me, as he pointed to a spot some half a mile from the shore. "When we came up three days ago the channel ran the other side of it, and up toward that sand-bar; but I see it has changed, and has gone away over to the other shore."

Again the wheel whirled about, and the swift-speeding steamboat shot across with as much certainty as if she were off Sandy Hook, and all the world of water before her.

"I have watched and searched for some sign by which you can find your way, and give it up. It is a mystery I can't fathom," I remarked to the pilot.

"Well, it's sort of instinct," he replied. "I can tell something by the color of the water, something by its motion, and something in the habits of the beast; and between 'em all I manage to find my way." [...]

However brave the pilots may be wherever human agencies are concerned, they are as superstitious as any Jack Tar who has seen the *Flying Dutchman*. A story is told of an adventure that happened many years ago to a pilot on the steamer *St. Louis*. It was in the summer, and on a trip up the river. A corpse had been taken on board at Memphis, and for safety's sake, and because it was cooler there, it was placed in the pilot-house. The pilot was not altogether temperate. In fact, a cocktail was necessary to his happiness at least every half hour, and he had made an arrangement with the bar-keeper by which, after midnight, he had possession of the key to the bar, so that he could go or send down for his own cocktail. As midnight approached he began to get rather nervous about this corpse, and all the ghost-stories he had ever heard came thronging before him with intense reality. Now and then he would look over his shoulder at the coffin, which stood upright against the window, and the sight did not reassure him.

Suddenly, for an instant, he turned his eyes from the river, and at his very elbow he saw a figure in white which held up a bony finger, as if in warning, while ghostly, hollow eyes stared into his. That one look was enough; for, fully possessed with the belief that the ghost of the man dead in the coffin stood beside him, he gave one frantic scream, and, at a single jump, sprang over the wheel and through the window on to the roof of the cabin, twenty feet below.

It subsequently required the presence of the ghost in person to persuade our poor pilot that he was only the bar-keeper, who had forgotten to send up the key of the bar until after he had gone to bed, and so came up, silently, in his bare feet, shirt, and drawers.

But we have been listening to the stories of our friends in the pilot-house while the boat is rapidly passing points of interest on the riverbank. Here is St. Genevieve, an old French settlement, where, for many generations, the people have cultivated a large extent of land, covering a thousand acres or more, in common. I do not learn that these people are disciples of Fourier or of any of the celebrated communists; but it is certain that they work together, and, by some mutual arrangement, divide the proceeds of their labor. It is said that this community increases slowly, is not very wealthy, and its members do not quarrel among themselves nor with their neighbors. It would be interesting to know more of the city of St. Genevieve.

The scenery on this part of the river is not at all startling. On the one side we pass low swamp lands filled with forests of cotton-wood. On the other, low bluffs arise, whose red and yellow earths frequently indicate the presence of one or another kind of mineral. This character of scenery is interrupted at Grand Tower, which takes its name from rocks some forty feet high, which have been worn by the action of the water into a circular shape. A railroad strikes the river at this point, and brings coal from a place called Carbondale. It is said to be much better and cheaper than the Illinois coal, and at St. Louis and along the river is largely used.

Cape Girardeau is another town of prominence, but at this, as well as at a dozen and more stopping-places between St. Louis and Cairo, there is little or nothing to attract the attention of the traveler. But grand old nature ever presents glorious spectacles to the reverent eye, and nowhere do the clouds and sky and atmospheric effects take on more exquisite changes of beauty than in the valley of the Mississippi. As the first day of our voyage was closing into evening the sun went down toward the western tree-tops in glowing splendor. We were all gazing in love and delight, when out from the paler rosy-gray of the eastern horizon there came a line of dark, which each instant increased in size and length until the sky was filled with flocks of birds, flying toward us and into the sunlight. At first we thought them flocks of ducks or wild-geese, but as they neared us, beating the singing air with their white wings, we found that they were the beautiful swan; and, as if to do us greatest pleasure, one by one, as gracefully as a feather falls in the quiet air, they settled down upon a bar of golden sand which ran far out into the now darkening waters of the river. A more fascinatingly lovely sight I never beheld, as tens and fifties and hundreds and thousands of these aerial visitors swept round and round as they neared the earth, their snow-white plumage taking on infinite tints of beauty as it glanced and fluttered in the ruby rays of the setting sun.

When the darkness came on the boat went into port for the night. Our wise and careful captain refuses to risk the lives of his passengers and the safety of the boat by running

A night landing.

on this part of the river after nightfall. They call this route between St. Louis and Cairo a "bad piece of river," for more accidents and loss have occurred here than in the remaining thousand odd miles to New Orleans.

When near Cairo we bothered ourselves little about currents and snags and sand-bars, but steered in a straight course from point to point. At times it seemed as if we were crossing large lakes; and when, near nightfall, we rounded a group of trees, and directed our course toward some far-distant lights upon the edge of the horizon, it was hard to realize that we were not upon some large inland sea, instead of the river whose course upon the map is indicated by a crooked black line.

We laid over at Cairo a day and a night. A more disheartening place I never beheld than this same Cairo, which, from its location at the junction of the Ohio and Mississippi rivers, many people professed to believe would become a large city. I would not like to prophesy as to its future beyond that of a third-class graveyard, but to-day it is the vilest hole above-ground, if the streets formed by intro-

ducing foreign soil can be said to be above-ground; for the open lots formed by the streets were partially filled with water covered with green scum, and which was also the receptacle for offal, dead animals, and other offensive refuse. Turn which way you would the sight was unspeakably disgusting. The streets were knee-deep in mud, and it seemed impossible to transact business upon them when horses and wagons were required.

"It must be very sickly here in the summer," I remarked to one of the store-keepers.

"Not at all, Sir," he stoutly replied. "We never have chills and fever nor cholera here. One of the healthiest places on the river, Sir. Bound to be a big city, Sir."

The yellow skin and hollow cheeks of the speaker were more eloquent reporters as to the health of the city than his tongue; while in every shop window hung placards of "Chills and Fever Specific," "Jones's Fever Cure," "Osgood's India Collaghouge," and so on. All the day and into the night the loading of our steamboat progressed. Thousands of barrels of flour were rolled into the hold, which lies under the main-deck, until it seemed as if not another stave could find place. Then the cars came in from the north, and several hundred "head" of mules and horses came on board, and were put somewhere. Subsequently there came coops filled with geese, turkeys, and chickens, and the air was filled with braying, neighing, bleating, crowing, cackling, and gobbling, until one began really to believe they could appreciate the feelings of Noah when he was loading up for that little excursion he took in the ark. [...]

The morning after leaving Cairo we came upon deck, and, gazing about, we no longer recognized the river Mississippi, of which we have just now used opprobrious epithets.

In the presence of this vast flood of water rushing resistlessly along we stand in awe and wonder.

What the river people here call a rise, in Europe would be an inundation, which would carry havoc in its path. It is not so much what the eye takes in upon the surface of drifting trees and logs and houses, but it is the hidden force which, rushing and whirling and eating underneath, undermines the giant trees of the forest; they tumble as if smitten with the hand of death, and plunge into the stream to be whirled and turned hither and thither like twigs in a whirlwind. Then secret currents dig and dig at the base of some high bluff, and, in an instant, acres of rock and earth and forest sink into the waters, and before your very eyes the solid land is engulfed and disappears. As the steamboat with assured pace steams quickly past the forest of cotton and cypress, with their solemn depth made more than melancholy by their long drapings of hanging moss, as you pass swamps and cultivated fields, you will detect a break in the brimful bank, and in a second the flood is upon the land, not with a rush and a roar, giving the poor farmer with his wife and children yonder in his cabin notice of its approach, but, with silent fatal speed, it covers and envelops field and cabin, and fortunate is its human prey should he escape the deathly embrace.

All along this great river the water overruns the banks, extending far inland, uniting, by bayou and lagoon and lake, thousands of miles of country in one vast flood.

Now that we are fairly on our way, let us see who are our companions. It is after dinner—that is to say, about three in the afternoon. The cold wind from the north takes on a keener edge as the sun begins to decline, and most all the passengers are indoors. The young gentleman and lady on the sofa yonder came aboard with us at St. Louis. There is a neat, natty look about them, especially the young lady, which has the manner of New York. All her wardrobe is of the latest fashion. Her boots are close, firm-fitting, and have that nice look which suggests a fashionable shoemaker; and so with the looped skirt of the dress, the jaunty hat; and about the *ensemble* there is a nameless something of nicety which breathes the atmosphere of the metropolis. The remark has been made that these people are bride and bridegroom on a wedding trip. Why young people should always be thus accused I know not, but any lady and gentleman traveling together, who have not turned forty, are always subject to this charge. [...]

In the forward cabin, usually gathered about the big stove or at the tables playing cards, there is a motley group of men. There are two sprucely dressed young fellows from Baltimore who are going to Texas on a sporting expedition. Somewhere in the interior of that vast country they have a place well furnished with dogs, guns, and ammunition; the game, they say, comes of itself, of all sorts, and in any quantity, from black bear to quail.

Half a dozen quiet, orderly men I see day by day moving around; these appear to be merchants, farmers, or traders. But of altogether another sort is a part of our invoice from Cairo. Four of these are tall, muscular young fellows, from Kentucky I think, who, in the old time, when it was not honorable in the South to labor, would have turned out first-class ruffians. As it is, they have all the swagger and dare-devil manner which characterizes the cut-throat and bravo. All of this party carry pistols, a strange sight nowadays. One of them wears a Confederate gray coat, and a look into whose eyes reveals a story of adventure.

There is another gang in the forward cabin who are not even as respectable as those we have just described; these last are gamblers. We had heard that this feature of steamboat life in the West had, since the war, disappeared. In truth, it has—or, at least, its character has changed.

You can not see now, as we did ten years ago, the cabin tables surrounded by planters, merchants, and politicians, calling themselves gentlemen, who would gamble from morning till night, and again till morning, staking, and often losing, their entire fortunes. We do not now encounter the elegant, gentlemanly, professional gambler, who was accomplished in every way, and not least in the use of the pistol and bowie-knife. Well-educated, fascinating gentlemen were they, whose hands were again and again stained with the blood of their fellow-creatures. All this class of men are hardly to be found in the Southwest in this goodly year of

our Lord 1870. The war did splendid scavenger-work in sweeping them into the other world. And the young men now coming up into life, who would have been such as they, find a better existence in working for their daily bread. The gang of gamblers who are our companions on this trip belong to altogether another class than those whose places they fill. [...] It is amusing for your experienced traveler to watch the tricks and schemes of these miserable wretches. One of these is short, rather fat, dressed in black broadcloth, and carries under his plug hat a cunning, greasy, smooth-shaven face, which has small, ferrit-like eyes in it, and a red snub nose, like a carbuncle, imposed upon it. This man is called the "Judge," and is, I believe, the leader of the gang, although another fellow in common clothes, with a wolfish, cowardly countenance, gives the cue to all their doings. The third thief of the party is small in stature, with black mustache, and an assumed wobegone look. It is he who, in their make-believe games, bets wildly and largely, who most always loses, gets angry, and appeals to the lookers-on. The fourth of the squad looks like an honest tradesman, who ought to be in better business than betting. [...]

Below stairs on the main-deck, among the corn-sacks, mules, and deck hands, there are other travelers, going I know not whither. Filthy, hungry, forlorn wretches are they; men, women, and children on the same errand which hurries us all onward, forward, somewhere; the struggle of humanity, whether on the lower deck or in the cabin, in the hovel or the palace, life, life, to live.

The state-rooms, or sleeping-chambers, on the boat are quite large; they have double berths, wash-basins, and mirrors, and all of this is kept in good, cleanly order. Of course there is a door opening out upon the guards. This doorway has blinds, and a printed notice on the wall tells you there are very good life-preservers, in the event of a burst up, or other accident. It is rather uncomfortably significant to see these means of saving life, and the constant call upon your attention, so prominent; but it is well to know that these and other means of safety, which also include cork life-preservers, are at hand. By-the-way, if there should be an accident, I prefer, as a matter of choice, one of the blinds. [...]

The cabin of our boat is so large that we are able to have tables placed across as well as lengthwise. Thus, instead of three fearfully long tables, where every thing is in confusion and all is in common, the passengers are divided up into parties of six and ten, to the convenience and comfort of all. The food provided is very palatable.

Take it all in all, the scenery of the lower Mississippi is monotonous. Bluffs rise here and there, but they vary but little from the flat, far-stretching corn and cotton fields and the border of cotton-wood forests. From Memphis to Cape Girardeau is found the most fruitful corn lands in the world. They raise from sixty to one hundred bushels to the acre. Sometimes we passed corn-fields which extended continuously for miles along the river and for a long distance inland. Many of these places were situated upon the shore of some shoot or side channel of the river, which could not be approached by our steamboat but for the high water. But now she entered fearlessly these side channels. All along the bank would be found piles of corn. A signal from its owner would cause our boat to swing round and take the pile of three or ten hundred sacks on board. Again and again and many times was this done, until we ceased to wonder at the receptive capacity of the vessel, and came to believe that there was no limit to her space. [...] At Memphis we took on board a party of twenty negroes, who had come all the way from Virginia, and were en route for the Red River country. I was told that it was easier to get these people over all the remainder of the long journey than through this city of Memphis, where they are waylaid, robbed, and maltreated. If the representations are true, Memphis is a thriving cut-throat hole, a shade worse even than the city of New York.

From Memphis down the river cotton is raised. The plantations are very large, or they were extensive before the war. Now and then we came upon plantations which seemed to be working a large number of hands, and the far-spreading fields were under cultivation; but most often we passed by lands which ten years ago were valued at hundreds of dollars per acre, but which were now overgrown with weeds, or perhaps the neglected levee had been worn away, and the mad waters were pouring swiftly in to lay waste the land.

At Helena we made quite a halt, in order to take on three hundred bales of cotton. We smiled derisively at the suggestion, but had the pleasure of seeing them piled up twenty feet high on the forward deck. We were to take this cotton to New Orleans; but at this point, and higher up, cotton usually goes up stream, and is forwarded east by railroad at Memphis or Evansville, on the Ohio. [...]

At Red River the gang of negroes from Virginia left us. It was after dark when we made our landing at the wharfboat. As usual, when we made a night landing, the iron cages at the bow of the boat were filled with blazing pitch-pine knots, which threw a lurid light upon the immediately surrounding objects. Beyond those all was deep darkness. Out from the shadows of the between decks crept these poor wanderers. Some bore upon their backs bundles of bedding, clothing, cooking utensils, and children. Out of the darkness they came, men and women, young and old; in the glare of the torches they hobbled across the plank, and then disappeared in a deeper darkness. Some said the scene was significant of the history and fate of the negro race; while others, more hopeful, said, "Nonsense, the history of the negro has just begun."

Vicksburg we came upon in the night. It was a pretty sight to gaze upon the many lights blinking and sparkling on the hillside; and one could imagine the magnificent spectacle of the passage of the forts and batteries by the fleet during the war. [...]

Neither Natchez under the hill nor Natchez on top of the hill served to arrest our now rapid journey toward the Crescent City. It was on the ninth day of our journey after we left St. Louis that we arrived on the "coast," as that part of the river is termed which is fenced in with levees, behind which lie magnificent plantations of sugar. I had had but little idea of the extent of these sugar plantations. When they were in operation, and many are not, each place with its grand house and manufactory and negro cabins formed a village in itself. I was told that some of the establishments for converting the cane into sugar cost as high as three hundred thousand dollars. [...]

It was in the afternoon of a glorious sunny day that we were presented to the Crescent City, the commercial metropolis of the Southwest. Past groves of orange-trees filled with their rich yellow fruit, past elegant villas surrounded with the waving palm and far-spreading oak, past gardens and fields clothed in fresh tints of green, past all that was charming and refreshing to the vision which a few days before had rested only upon snow and ice, we came upon the city of New Orleans.

The sun was going down behind us, and its golden light illuminated each roof-top and wall and spire. So that all the length and breadth of this great city was bathed in splendid radiance. It was a noble presentation, and afforded a happy termination of our journey "down the Mississippi."

EDITOR'S EASY CHAIR
POLITICAL LIFE IN AMERICA

BY GEORGE WILLIAM CURTIS

DECEMBER 1870

The letter of Vice-President Colfax, in which he states his intention to retire from public life, has occasioned some surprise upon the part of those who imagine that official distinction is happiness. But the Vice-President, although his career has been singularly successful and his character irreproachable, declares that he withdraws without regret, and that he rejoices at his prospective release from the exactions, the cares, and the misrepresentations of political life. It is not all happiness, then? The glory has its shadow?

Political life is a curious study. In England the most dazzling prizes are political. In the English novels political success is represented as the greatest triumph. However illustrious in rank a man may be, however rich, the real crown of his life is political distinction. It is very much so in fact. Men of the highest culture, of the utmost refinement and delicacy of nature, enter the lists. Parliament, to the young and accomplished English gentleman of to-day, is what the tournament and the field were to his ancestor. The church, the army, and political life are the three careers open to a "gentleman." And of these the highest in general estimation is unquestionably the last. It is hardly less so in France. The hero in the vaudeville, which is a picture of contemporary life, triumphs at last in receiving his appointment as embassador. Upon the actual stage of life scholars, historians, *savans*, are politicians and statesmen also. [...]

To cross the Atlantic to America is to reverse the fact altogether. The American "gentleman" upon his travels, who remembers with more real pride than any other incident of his tour the fact that he was invited to dinner by the Prime Minister in England, or by the Foreign Minister in France, in his own country wonders that any gentleman can dabble in the dirty pool of politics. [...]

De Tocqueville observed that the tendency of the better men in the United States was to avoid politics. He did not find what Thackeray says was believed in England, that sagacious politicians had their eyes upon the universities, and selected the most promising youths as candidates for political honors. Yet, at an earlier period, our own custom was the same as in England. In the first Conventions and Congresses there were men of a corresponding elevation and accomplishment with the best elsewhere. Lord Chatham's compliment to the Continental Congress is historical, and the political history of any State seventy or eighty years ago presents the finest figures. Nor do they seem so only because they are of the past. The essential ability of Alexander Hamilton, for instance, or the moral dignity and power of John Jay, are as evident as the pure patriotism and sagacity of Washington. In explanation of the fact which he observes De Tocqueville suggests that a government of the numerical majority is a government of ignorant men who will be swayed by arguments and appeals to which the better kind of citizens will disdain to condescend. Consequently the danger of our system, he thought, would be the continually greater prominence and influence of unprincipled politicians. Whether his prescience has been vindicated every man will decide for himself.

That the mass of people in any country have been generally ignorant is true. But the promising conditions of popular government when it was established in this country were these: its wide separation from the immediate contact of other states; the great extent of our territory, avoiding the perils of a close population, and a climate favorable to industry; the homogeneity of the population of the colonies, its general thrift and intelligence; familiarity with the forms of popular government; and beyond all these the social truth, of which in various ways history is the ample verification, that in regard to the general welfare, not in every case but upon the whole, every body knows more or better than any body. With this moral conviction, with these material advantages, with the clear perception of the vital relation of the schools to the state, and with the sensible belief that a popular government was not an ideal system, but the best under all the circumstances, our republic was founded. The difficulty which De Tocqueville mentions was to be obviated, first, by constantly enlightening the people; and secondly, by the fact that a fairly educated people would really choose more wisely for themselves than any class among them could possibly choose. Because, plainly, if they were sensible enough to choose the best citizens for legislators, it was all that was necessary. If they were not sagacious enough to do it, how would the best get appointed? Would chance or gunpowder or the guillotine or an order of aristocracy select any more wisely?

It follows, therefore, that interest in politics, which may be in other countries a privilege, is in this country an imperative duty. The American "gentleman," who is amazed that his refined and educated neighbor is "active in politics," must understand that his neighbor is merely doing his duty—is only paying the tax of time and attention and knowledge which it is indispensable for a good government that every decent man should pay. His neighbor is doing all that he can do to enlighten the public opinion, which is the real government of the country, and to direct its action. For nothing can be plainer to every thoughtful man than that if good men do not interest themselves in politics, bad men will. If the tone of politics and the general character of public men have deteriorated, it is greatly due to the feeling that there is something essentially degrading in political life, or in any degree of participation in political affairs. And, therefore, the difficulty has fed itself. The methods of politics have now become so repulsive, the corruption is so open, the intrigues and personal hostilities are so shameless, that it is very difficult to engage in them without a sense of humiliation. But the deeper this feeling is, the more supreme should the sense of duty be.

On the other hand, every man who does his duty in the matter will find that there are great multitudes who are obeying a similar feeling. We are apt to speak of the dirty pool of politics; but a man is amazed, after hearing his neighbor declaim against the rascals and traders and swindlers, to find such troops of honest, generous, and enlightened men who are "in politics" only that they may serve the common welfare. Indeed, if they were not there—if he were the only intelligent and sincere man who went to the caucus or the primary meeting—anarchy and revolution would be close at hand. And every party, however corrupt its management may be, or unprincipled its leaders, acknowledges its conviction of the public respect for hon-

esty by generally avoiding in its nominations for high office men of notoriously bad character. The most venal party managers are conscious that a spotless name strengthens the ticket. And to make that consciousness deeper and deeper by constantly improving public sentiment, it is a patriotic duty to engage in practical politics so far as to discuss public questions upon the loftiest principles; to assist in the selection of the best men for office; and, where it can be honorably done with a just regard for all other duties, to make what is to so many men of a certain temperament the sacrifice of taking office.

But if any body supposes that a political career is happiness, he has only to read a few chapters in history, or to reflect upon the letter of the Vice-President. His political life, as we said, has been successful and distinguished, and few men who have been for eighteen years in public position have made so few enemies. It is not to be supposed, of course, that he retires from interest in public affairs, nor that he intends to desert the political duties of a private citizen. But he thinks, and justly, that he has given as much of his life to public office as ought to be demanded, unless he wishes to continue in it. And in withdrawing he mentions the real sting of an honest official career, the misrepresentations which accompany it. For it is only when a man takes office, or is proposed for it, that he feels the full fury of party spirit. And never is a human being so ludicrously contemptible as when he is, not severely criticising the culpable conduct of a political opponent, but indulging party malignity. This malignity would be infinitely funny if it were not so ferocious. It is one of the chief impediments to civilization, for this, among many other reasons, that it so utterly perplexes judgment by its enormous falsehoods. The philosophers say that Nature is so intent upon certain results that she overcharges certain instincts and passions, so as to be superfluously sure of them. And this is also the law of party spirit, which burns a house down to roast a pig.

The ingenuity with which the simplest facts are distorted by party spirit into the most baleful significance is exquisitely comical. The most familiar details of life are invested with awful mystery. If a distinguished gentleman is seen going North or South or East or West—what is he going for? If he wears a red cravat—he is secretly a *sansculotte*. If he wears a yellow waistcoat—he is no friend of Ireland. The distinguished Mr. Jones meets his friend Smith, and they have a chat about the weather. Party spirit publishes the interesting fact that Mr. Jones and Mr. Smith were closeted in earnest conversation, and begs a naturally indignant people to keep calm at all hazards, and entreats the judicious, upon retiring at night, to look under their beds for torpedoes. The minister in the Feejee Islands or at Behring Straits sends a telegram, and to save money signs it Short or Long, omitting the Tobias and Timothy. "Ah ha!" snorts the watchful spirit of party, "behold the demoralization of foreign courts! Kings and noblemen call themselves merely William, or Charles, or Wellington, or De Broglie; so this debased American, whose soul is eaten up by flunkeyism, and who grovels in spirit before the proud upstarts of an effete despotism, signs himself Short instead of Tobias Short, and Long, forsooth, instead of Timothy Long! Faugh! Out upon such spaniels!" Bless your soul, dear Cato, they only do it to save a sixpence!

These are the absurdities; but there are the malignities also. What a spectacle it is, that of a really clever man sitting down to tax his wits for the most caustic and elaborate misrepresentation of something which he perfectly well knows to be simple and intelligible! Laboriously to increase the misunderstanding and falsehood and ill feeling in the world is certainly the most pitiful of human tasks. But it is one which party spirit relentlessly requires. The man whose views of public policy differ from yours you must make ridiculous and odious if you possibly can. "We have no case," said the defendant's senior counsel to his junior; "so abuse the plaintiff's attorney." Take, for instance, in this country, the question of revenue. Let us suppose that there are two general views: one, that the revenue should be raised by direct, the other that it should be raised by indirect taxation. Or let there be one opinion, that domestic industry should be protected; another, that such a policy is unsound. Apparently here is a question to be decided upon careful consideration of facts and arguments. But the debate is a Donnybrook fair. There is but one rule on both sides. Wherever you see a head, hit it. The great object is to make the opponent personally ridiculous; to smear him with lies and slanders and jibes; to denounce him as a fool or a knave. It is not enough to show the unsoundness of his opinions, to prove them injurious to the public welfare, to state truly the dangerous tendency or the humiliating history of the opposing party, but you must stigmatize by name those who belong to it, or whom circumstances make prominent, as caitiffs, cowards, and contemptible donkeys.

Of course, when their conduct justifies the severest censure, it is not to be spared. It is often the plainest duty to speak of official persons by name, and to contrast their general professions, or their tacit claims of respectability, with their unprincipled conduct. Indeed, the press does no greater service than when it shows that a man who privately is not a scoundrel may be politically or officially a rascal. But to contemplate every act solely with the intention of ridiculing it is a capital crime against the country, because it tends to repel from the public service the very men who are most wanted in it. The more fierce and bitter party spirit becomes, the more venal and perilous will be our politics; and no hero of the Revolution, whose name and memory we reverence, is more worthy of profound regard, as a patriot, than the honest and able citizen who takes office under the government.

Playing poker.

THE LITTLE LABORERS OF NEW YORK CITY

BY C. L. BRACE

AUGUST 1873

One of the most touching facts to any one examining the lower strata of New York is the great number of young children toiling in factories and shops. With the children of the fortunate classes there are certain years of childhood which every parent feels ought to be freed from the burdens and responsibilities of life. The "struggle for existence," the labor of money-making, the toil for support, and all the cares and anxieties therewith, will come soon enough. And the parent is glad that the first years at least should be buoyant and free from care, with no shadow of after-life upon them. He knows how heavy the burden must be which the child will soon be forced to carry, and he is pleased that a few years can be left cheerful and happy and free from anxiety. But the father of the poor child can indulge in no such sentiments. He is compelled to harness the little one very early to the car of labor, or if he be not forced to this, he is indifferent to the child's natural growth and improvement, and believes that his boy ought to pass through the same hard experience which he had himself. He is struggling with poverty, and eager for every little addition which he can make to his income. The child's wages seem to him important, and, indeed, it requires a character of more disinterestedness and a mind of more scope of view than we usually find among the laboring class to be able to forego present profit for the future benefit of the little one. The laborer sees the daily earnings, and does not think much of the future advantages which the child may win by being educated now. The father, accordingly, of a poor boy is found in all countries to be willing to neglect his education, if he can put him at profitable work. Neither his affection for his offspring nor his unselfishness can be relied upon as guarding his child's future. The law is forced to protect the minor. [...]

It is difficult to obtain minute or accurate information in relation to children employed in factories in New York City, and more difficult still to gain access to the factories, owing to the reluctance of employers to admit strangers. The manufacturers naturally suspect some sinister motives on the part of the inquirers. They are jealous of one another, and desirous of keeping their various patents and modes of work secret from their competitors. There have been not infrequent instances of covert attempts by the members of one firm to get possession of the secrets of another, and they are consequently all somewhat suspicious of strangers making inquiries.

It is estimated on trustworthy grounds that over 100,000 children are at work in the factories of New York and the neighboring districts, while from 15,000 to 20,000 are "floaters," drifting from one factory to another. Of these the envelope factories employ about 8000 children, one-quarter of whom are under fifteen years of age. The average earnings of the little workers are $3 per week. The ventilation in these factories is generally good. The gold-leaf factories employ a large number of children, though the exact statistics of the number can not be given. This occupation requires much skill and delicacy of touch; it is not severe, but demands constant attention. The outside air is carefully excluded from these factories, owing to the fragile nature of the material used. The girls employed are mostly over fifteen years of age. The burnishing of gold, silver, and china-ware is mostly done by girls, some of whom are under thirteen years of age. Singularly enough, it is said that men in this business require to wear breastplates, in order to prevent injury from the steel instruments employed, while the girls who labor at it sit at long tables, their undefended breasts pressing against the handles of the frame.

Paper-collar factories are a very important branch of children's labor. Fully 8000 girls from twelve to sixteen years of age are employed in it. A girl can count and box 18,000 collars in a day of ten hours.

Paper-box factories, embracing all sorts and sizes, from a match to a work box, employ at least 10,000 children.

These become very expert, and often invent new patterns. The material being cheap, the children are permitted to take home enough to do extra work, and are thus, in fact, excluded from night school.

In regard to factories for making artificial flowers it is extremely difficult to obtain trustworthy information, as access to the shops is rigidly refused. After considerable investigation, it seems to us that from 10,000 to 12,000 children are engaged in them, of whom nearly 8000 are under twelve years of age. Many are only five and seven years old. The latter are employed preparing and cutting feathers for coloring. Employers claim this to be a healthy business, but, judging from the pale and sickly countenances of the girls, we doubt the assertion.

Another important industry employing children in the city is the manufacture of tobacco. The tobacco factories contain fully 10,000 children, of whom 5000 at least are under fifteen years. The youngest child we saw employed in them was four years of age. He was engaged in stripping tobacco, and his average earnings were about one dollar per week. Many laborers work all their lives in these factories. We saw persons as old as eighty years in them. A man seventy years of age told us he had spent thirty years in one factory. His two boys had entered the factory with him at the age of ten and twelve years, and were now at work as men in the same shop. Another, the foreman, and general workshop manager, had entered that factory thirty-five years ago, when a boy ten years of age. In some of these factories boys under fifteen years are employed in dusky cellars and basements, preparing, brining, and sweetening the weed preliminary to "stemming." The under-ground life in these damp, cavernous places tends to keep the little workers stunted in body and mind. Other boys from ten to twelve years were squatting on the floors, whetting the knives of the cutting machines with a mixture of rum and water applied with a sponge. The rapidity with which the girls work is wonderful. A girl of sixteen years can put up thirteen gross of packages of chewing tobacco in tin-foil, and twenty-two gross in paper, in one day. Girls and boys from twelve to fourteen years earn in this business from four to five dollars per week. Some little girls only eight years of age earn $3 per week. The fact is that these children are often able to perform the same amount of this light labor as adults, while they only receive a portion of the pay given to older laborers. Thus the children who ought to be in school are made to deprive older laborers of their employment and remuneration.

Still another branch absorbs a great number of children—the twine factories. No accurate estimate can be obtained of the number of little laborers in these, but it is known to be very large. In one up-town factory alone, 200 children, mostly girls, are employed. This work is dangerous. The "hackling machines" are generally tended by boys from ten to fifteen years of age. Their attention must be riveted on the machinery, and can not relax for a moment, or the danger to life or limb is imminent. The "twisting machines," attended to by girls, are equally dangerous. Many have lost their fingers, or joints of them, that were caught in the twine. Only great presence of mind has saved many of these girls from losing the whole hand. We knew in one instance, in a single night school in New York, five factory girls who

Little tobacco strippers.

had each lost a finger or thumb. It is evident that strict legislation is needed here, as it has been in England, to protect these young workers from dangerous machinery. The air of these twine factories is filled with floating particles of cotton and flax, and must be exceedingly unhealthful.

It will be seen from these condensed statistics what an immense population of children in this city are the little slaves of capital. How intense and wearying is their daily toil, and how much of their health and education is sacrificed in these early years and premature labor! The evil in New York is evidently enormous, and most threatening to our future. These children, stunted in body and mind, are growing up to be our voters and legislators. There are already over 60,000 persons in New York who can not read or write. These little overworked operatives will swell this ignorant throng. Fortunately this great abuse has not escaped the attention of humane men.

There is one well-known benevolent organization in New York which has been especially the friend of working children—the Children's Aid Society. This has established in various parts of the city "industrial schools," where the children of the working classes are taught habits of industry, order, and cleanliness, together with common-school lessons and some industrial branch, and are then forwarded to places in the country. Besides these well-known institutions, which contain now during the year some nine thousand children, they have also founded night schools in destitute quarters, where boys and girls who labor all day can acquire a little education at night. The eagerness of these hard-working youths after a day of severe toil to obtain the rudiments of education is one of the most pathetic experiences in the field of the society's work. In one school, the Park School, near Sixty-eighth Street, young girls and lads, who have been working from seven o'clock till six, have been known to go without their supper in order not to miss the evening lessons. The stormiest weather and the worst walking do not keep them from these schools. In the various night schools of the Children's Aid Society will be found hundreds of little ones from six to thirteen who have been working very hard the whole day, and who are now just as eager to learn their little tasks. Their occupations are innumerable. Thus we learn from a recent report from one of the society's visitors that at the school at 98 Crosby Street "there were some hundred children. Their occupations were as follows: They put up insect powder, drive wagons, tend oyster saloons; are tin-smiths, engravers, office-boys; in type-foundries, at screws, in blacksmith shops; make cigars, polish, work at packing tobacco; in barber shops, at paper stands; are cash-boys, light porters, make artificial flowers, work at hair; are errand-boys, make ink, are in Singer's sewing-machine factory, and print-ing-offices; some post bills, some are paint scrapers, some peddlers; they pack snuff, attend poultry stands at market, in shoe stores and hat stores, tend stands, and help painters and carpenters. [...]

This association [...] are now especially laboring to prevent the evil of overwork in factories. An act has been drawn up by their counsel, Charles E. Whitehead, Esq., and is now before the Legislature, designed for the protection of factory children. By this law no child under the age of ten years is allowed to be employed at all in a manufactory, and no child under the age of twelve, unless he can intelligibly read.

No child under the age of sixteen years is allowed to be employed more than sixty hours in one week, while four public holidays are secured to him. We think a humane amendment to this provision would have been the limiting of the day's work of children to eight hours. Other sections of a very stringent character secure to every factory child between the ages of ten and sixteen a certain proportion of education, either in night schools, half-time day schools, or by three months' annual schooling. Judicious exceptions are made in cases where a poor family is dependent on the labor of its children, in permitting such children to attend the night school instead of the usual day school.

Careful registers are required to be kept by the manufacturers or employers, showing the amount of schooling enjoyed by each child, the time of his labor in the factory, and other facts important for the execution of the law.

Humane provisions are also included in the act for the promotion of the good sanitary condition of the factories, and to protect the children from dangerous machinery. Under the proposed law a new official has to be appointed by the Governor, to be called the "Inspector of Factory Children." Such an officer, acting under so wise and humane a law, can not but accomplish immense good throughout the State. [...]

Panic in Wall Street

December 1873

It has been estimated that for several years we have been investing from four to five hundred millions in the construction of new and the extension of old railways. Now it needs no argument to show that the people of the United States had no such sum as this to spend in any such manner. At least four-fifths of this money was borrowed, mostly by the sale of bonds abroad, and the rest by temporary loans at home. To thoughtful observers, the danger of the situation had been apparent long before last September. It was obvious that the European market for American bonds was not unlimited, and that sooner or later it would be glutted. It was likewise clear that railway companies could not go on forever floating their acceptances, and procuring temporary advances on unsalable bonds, in our own money centres; that some day or other people would want their money, and that in all probability every body would want it simultaneously, and just at the time when it was most difficult to obtain. The first contingency occurred some months ago. As long since as in May last some of our most skillful financiers failed utterly to place in the European markets as good issues of bonds as were ever printed. The simple fact was, there was no more loose money in Europe seeking such investments. It had all been absorbed. There was no more help to be expected from this source until the industrious people of Europe had had time to earn and save more money for investment—in other words, for two or three years. From the hour this discovery was made it was inevitable that certain great unfinished railways, which were large absorbers of money, and had not yet begun to yield returns on the investment, must go to the wall, and carry with them the banking houses which had acted as their financial agents, and had advanced them money in anticipation of the sale of bonds that were now unsalable. Prominent among these were the Midland Railway Company of New York, the Canada Southern, the Northern Pacific, the Missouri, Kansas, and Texas, and the Chesapeake and Ohio. Of these the first named went to protest six weeks before the panic began. Confidence was somewhat unsettled by the event, but the company's bankers, Messrs. George Opdyke and Co., managed to weather the storm, and Broad Street comforted itself with the delusion that this was an isolated case of weakness.

In the first week of September the wheat crop—three weeks earlier than usual—began to call money from New York. Sight exchange on New York fell at Chicago to $1.50 discount, currency was shipped in large amounts, and money became scarce. We shall refer presently to the currency question; in this place it is enough to say that, with the first approach of monetary stringency, railroad acceptances with bankers' indorsement became unsalable. By dint of great sacrifices of property the evil hour was postponed for a few days, but at length alarm began to spread, depositors began to withdraw their money, and the Canada Southern, the Northern Pacific, and the Chesapeake and Ohio Railway companies, with their bankers, Robinson, Cox, and Co., Jay Cooke and Co., and Fisk and Hatch, were forced to suspend. This was on 17th, 18th, and 19th September, and from those days dates the crisis. [. . .]

The next great disaster was the failure of the Union Trust Company. [. . .] The Union Trust Company was managed carelessly, it is true, and the chief executive officer, Carlton, was allowed to rob it of a large part of its surplus. But there is no reason at this hour (October 6) to suspect that it is either ruined, or that even its capital will be seriously impaired, if its affairs are wound up with judgment. So with the Commonwealth Bank, which closed its doors on the day before the failure of the Trust Company. It is believed at present that the depositors will not lose a dollar.

Still, the failure of these two institutions [. . .] aggravated general distrust to such a pitch that the Stock Exchange appeared to be smitten with paralysis. Stocks had fallen within a few days from twenty-five to fifty per cent., and bonds were almost wholly unsalable. Thirty-five houses, comprising many of the leading dealers at the board, had reported themselves suspended. On Saturday, September 20, at twelve o'clock, the panic had reached such a height that it was impossible to get a bid for any stock. Under the rules of the Stock Exchange, when a member fails, the stocks he can not pay for are sold out at auction ("under the rule," it is called) by the presiding officer. On this Saturday at noon the presiding officer was offering stocks, and no one dared to bid. If he had gone on, it is not at all impossible that Central might have sold at 50, and Western Union at 25, or even less, in which case every house in active business would have failed. Happily there was sense enough among the members to avert this. The Governing Committee were hastily called together, and the Stock Exchange was closed until further notice. Thus a breathing-time was secured.

Let us now turn to the currency question and the banks. The National Banking law requires national banks in the city of New York to hold twenty-five per cent. of their aggregate liabilities—*i.e.,* deposits and circulation—in greenbacks or gold. This is called the "legal reserve." During the summer months currency usually accumulates at New York, and from May to September the banks generally hold from ten to twenty millions in excess of the required legal reserve. When the Western crops begin to move, currency is drawn from New York, and by the time it returns, with the approach of the close of navigation, it is required at the South to move the cotton crop, so that in ordinary years our city banks are kept bare of currency from the beginning of October till the early spring, when money begins to return from the South. During the fall of 1872 and the winter of 1872–73 the drain of currency was so severe that the banks were crippled for six consecutive months. Many ingenious reasons were given for this unexampled stringency. The simple fact was that the country in nine years of general activity had outgrown the currency system which was quite adequate for its wants in 1864, just as a boy of eighteen has outgrown the coat which fitted him at nine.

Care must be taken not to confound money with currency. Money is not necessarily currency, though currency always represents money. Money is the accumulated profits of labor or trade. Currency is its representative. When confidence prevails, money may be easy though currency is scarce. When confidence is shaken or banking facilities are scarce, currency is the only acceptable representative of money. At the great financial centres hundreds of millions of money change hands without the use of a dollar of currency. But at the West and South the banking system is as yet so undeveloped that the crops can not be moved without the actual intervention of greenbacks. Under a better system the farmer would receive pay for his produce in a draft or bank credit, which he would presently hand over to his country merchant in payment for dry-goods, groceries, and farm implements. Now he wants to handle the actual bank-notes for which his wheat and corn have been sold. Hence our city banks have always looked forward to a drain of twenty millions or more during the months of September and October "to move the crops." During the past six years they have generally entered upon the fall months with a reserve of from fifty to sixty-five millions of legal tenders, out of which they could spare this sum. But the gradual growth of the country and the absorption of legal tender notes by the South and West reduced them in the first week of September, 1873, to thirty-eight millions of greenbacks. During the second week they lost nearly three millions more. During the third week, if all had gone well in Wall Street, they would probably have lost two or three millions more. But the failures we have mentioned, and a gradual destruction of confidence throughout the country, led to a general run upon them for greenbacks, and they lost, not three, but ten millions.

On Sunday, 21st September, General Grant met the principal financiers of New York at the Fifth Avenue Hotel. The leading features of the situation were explained to him, and he was urged to place the legal tender reserve of the government—forty-four millions—at the service of the banks, as he had done in October, 1872. He replied that he could not see his way to do so without violating the law, and after conferences which lasted from ten in the morning till nine at night he declined to accede to the request of the bankers, but directed the Assistant Treasurer to buy all the United States bonds which were offered, up to twelve millions of dollars.

During the ensuing week the government bought the twelve millions of bonds, and then stopped. Not one dollar of the greenbacks thus disbursed went into the banks. On the contrary, notwithstanding the purchases of the government, the banks lost during the week, being the fourth week of September, eleven millions of greenbacks, and their reserve ran down from thirty-eight millions on the 6th to twelve millions on the 27th, and their deposits from

Winslow Homer etching of lodgers in a police station following the panic of 1873.

$200,000,000 to $150,000,000. People had begun to hoard greenbacks, and they already commanded a premium of three to four per cent. In the first week of October the country had three currencies, gold, legal tender notes, and money, this last consisting of certified checks and certificates of deposit. The banks of Boston, Philadelphia, Chicago, St. Louis, and Cincinnati followed the example of the banks of New York, and refused to pay out greenbacks. Individuals and companies employing workmen found it difficult to obtain currency for their weekly pay. Employers buying greenbacks for the purpose discovered that the bank suspension practically involved an increase of three to four per cent. in the wages of their operatives. Early in October greenbacks commanded a premium of three to five per cent. in New York, and as much as eight per cent. at New Orleans. For the purchase of cotton on the plantations or wheat on the Western farms bank drafts were useless, and

agents were dispatched daily West and South with bundles of currency purchased in New York at the premium mentioned. A scarcity of small notes was soon developed. To meet the emergency the city of Chicago issued city shinplasters for five and ten dollars each, and the necessity of issuing certificates of deposit for ten and twenty dollars each was strongly urged upon the banks of New York.

Among these latter no harmony prevailed. With many, years of uninterrupted prosperity had led to lax administration. There were some which were unquestionably sound in any event; there were others which were decidedly shaky; and there were a great many whose soundness depended upon the value of the collaterals they held. When the crisis occurred there was an attempt to separate the sheep from the goats. The strong banks kicked at being held responsible for the weak ones. The strong bank *par excellence*, the Chemical, whose stock is worth several hundred per cent.

premium, and which has no depositors requiring discounts, insisted on retiring from the Clearing-house.

"Very well," said its colleagues, "we shall collect all checks on you in greenbacks."

And the Chemical staid. No bank in the world can pay its depositors in greenbacks on demand and live.

Tired of fighting with each other, the banks then combined to carry the merchants through. Many said that the panic was an affair of stock speculators, and that the banks should not help them out. They would discount all the legitimate business paper that was offered, paying their way with Clearing-house certificates largely based on stock collateral, but they would not lend to brokers. At the time we write it is too soon to pronounce the issue of this policy.

In the mean time the Stock Exchange remained closed. Every body was afraid of its reopening, except a few who had no contracts and no stocks, and were eager to purchase at panic prices. To men of foresight the resumption of business at the Exchange, and the enforcement of its cast-iron rules, seemed certain to drive helpless debtors into a corner, and to provoke appeals to the courts, which would develop such loop-holes in the ordinary customs of trade as could hardly fail to damage the brokerage interest and terrify moneylenders. Hence a general desire for further delay, in order to give time for voluntary settlements. But though the Exchange was not in session, a market always existed. During the interregnum, which lasted from Monday, 22d September, to Tuesday, 30th, a dense crowd thronged Broad Street. By the law of the Exchange, its members can not transact business in the street, or in any other place than on Change or in their offices. During the closing of the Exchange, therefore, the business was done by "outside" brokers—that is to say, persons not members of the Exchange. They reaped a handsome harvest. Thousands of shares were sold by brokers who were determined to preserve their credit at any cost, and were bought by small capitalists in search of bargains. Men arrived by each train from the North and South and East and West, from Canada, and even from Havana, with their wallets full of greenbacks, which they exchanged for low-priced stocks. A room was hired by some suspended members of the board, and an "Independent Exchange" established. But the suspension of business was too brief for this new concern to take root. During the week of its existence, however, it was the theatre of large transactions, and many men hereafter will date the beginning of their fortunes from the cheap stocks they bought there.

At length, on Tuesday, September 30, the Stock Exchange reopened. It was rather a solemn event. Though the rules had been suspended for three days, so that no contracts could be enforced by the compulsory process of the Exchange, a committee had been appointed to see to it that creditors who had unsatisfied claims should be made secure by deposits of money or securities with the committee. The extremely small number of applications for security gave evidence of the great extent to which liquidation had been effected. All day long the transactions were of the same monotonous character. Stocks were sold by brokers to raise money, and bought by investors who could pay for them. The Exchange was crowded by a swarm of new faces. Men came from every part of the city—nay, every part of the Union—with their pockets full of money to buy cheap stocks. And brokers, determined to save their commercial standing and to pay their debts, supplied the demand, no matter at what sacrifice.

After the lapse of three days the regular rules were once more enforced. But there was no slaughter of securities, as had been apprehended. The great house in default, G. Bird Grinnell and Co., was thrown into bankruptcy by a creditor, and its contracts were thus authoritatively held in suspense. No one else proved unable to respond. It was soon evident that "the street" had been relieved of securities to an extent which placed the remaining solvent houses almost out of danger. During the two weeks of panic no less than thirty-six thousand shares of Rock Island and twenty-five thousand shares of Central were said to have passed into the hands of investors—never, probably, to see Broad Street again. If, as is probable, a similar absorption went on in other stocks, the brokers must have been relieved of millions of securities. This was soon proved by the condition of the loan market. On 2d October the banks began to curtail their Clearing-house certificates, and to call in the few loans they had made to brokers. This policy, of course, tended to increase the stringency in money. But so generally had brokers lightened ship by throwing cargo overboard that, notwithstanding the diminished supply of money, the demand had decreased even more rapidly, and rates declined from one-quarter per cent. a day to seven per cent. per annum. Business began again, in short, under very conservative auspices. The volume of stocks offered for sale was small, because almost every body had sold already, while the investment demand continued. On the other hand, the difficulty of obtaining loans, and the conservative policy of the banks in certifying brokers' checks, effectually damped any tendency to reckless speculation. People who had been in the habit of buying a thousand shares now contented themselves with a hundred, and brokers generally declined to execute orders to buy unless the customer provided the money to pay his purchases. [. . .] When a broker fails he makes up his accounts, and finds that he can pay fifty, twenty-five, or ten cents on the dollar. He makes a list of his creditors, and goes round with his paper. He rarely meets with a rebuff. His creditors are all aware that a broker's life is full of vicissitudes, and that prosperity to-day is often followed by adversity to-morrow. Each treats his debtor as he would be treated himself when his hour of trial comes. In many cases brokers cling to their position until they have paid out their last dollar, and so, when they fail, have nothing to give their creditors. But if they have conducted themselves honestly, they need not despair of obtaining a release. It is an axiom among brokers that it is bad policy to keep an active, honest fellow out of the board because he has been unfortunate. Let him get back, and who knows but he may make money, and the sting of conscience may induce him to pay debts which were forgiven him long ago? The late Jacob Little used to say that he could paper his private office with the notes he had forgiven to members of the board.

Speculators in Wall Street are known as "bulls," that is, speculators for the rise, and "bears," or speculators for the fall. The heaviest operators in the street, Commodore Vanderbilt, Daniel Drew, Jay Gould, John Steward, Jun., the late Horace Clark, etc., have never been members of the board, but have bought and sold through their respective brokers. Of these Mr. Vanderbilt stands apart from all others. He is never a bear. He never sells that which he has not got. In the old days of Nicaragua Transit he used, when he had quarreled with the Pacific Mail, to sell a few thousand shares of that stock "short." But this was more in the light of a formal declaration of war, an Indian war-whoop, than a speculation looking to profit. Of late years he has been a steady and persistent bull, but only in the stocks which he has controlled himself. People who have followed him, and have not bought more stock than they could carry through panics, have always made money. During the Black Friday panic of 1868 New York Central fell from 218 to 145, and a vast array of the Commodore's followers, being unable to stand so heavy a fall, were compelled to sell out, and were ruined.

"If you had bought a hundred shares instead of a thousand," said the veteran, when they went to him for consolation, "you could have held on. Never be in too great a hurry to get rich."

The great power of the Commodore is derived from his enormous income, and from his habit of concentrating his strength on one object at a time. It has been estimated that his surplus income at present is not less than six millions of dollars. Now he is not buying a foot of real estate or a single bond of any kind. He invests the whole of this income in the stock which happens to be his favorite at the time. Thus in the course of a year he retires six millions of this stock from the market. Panics may depress his favorites for a time, but a steady absorption of this kind must tell in the long-run, and it is not surprising that he should always win in the end.

Mr. Jay Gould, who is the greatest operator in the street next to Mr. Vanderbilt, is alternately a bull and a bear, as his judgment of the market prompts him. He was a bear before the Chicago fire, which accident yielded him a harvest of over a million. He was a bull immediately afterward, and made money again on the rise. He was a bear on general principles before the panic of September, and again a bull afterward, realizing handsome profits on both sides of the game. Like all great operators, he loses as well as wins. In his great campaign in gold in the summer of 1873 he lost a good deal of money. But whether he loses or wins he is always the same, cool, imperturbable, and apparently unconcerned. Much more conservative than the street generally supposes, he gets the credit of doing far more than he does. He is often charged with tying up money when he has not had a thought of the kind, or buying or selling large lines of stock when he is really doing nothing at all. Though not nearly so rich as Commodore Vanderbilt, he has contrived, whenever they have contended together, to come off victor in the contest, and the veteran Commodore loves him accordingly.

It is needless to mention by name the minor operators of the day. Some of them are always bulls, sanguine, hopeful men who see every thing on the bright side; others are always bears, being prone to look at the dark shadows of life, and to scrutinize the flaws which exist in all human institutions; many, like Mr. Gould, are bulls and bears alternately, according to their judgment of the market. It does not always follow that a bull is a genial, whole-souled fellow, or that a bear is cross-grained and cantankerous. Some chronic bulls are not remarkable for geniality, while many inveterate bears are liberal, good-natured, and universally popular. Of late years the staple argument of the bulls has been the steady growth of the country, and the increased traffic on the railways, which has enabled several of them to water their stock profusely, and to pay dividends on the increased capital. On the other side, the bears point to the growing distrust of watered stocks, and the muttered discontent of the people at the power of railway monopolies—a feeling which they are sure will culminate sooner or later in legislative interference. They rely too, in a great measure, upon such monetary disturbances as precipitated the panic of last September, arguing that with a currency so inadequate as ours, periods of intolerable monetary stringency are sure to occur at regular intervals. As a general thing, each side has its "innings" once or twice a year. Stocks are pretty sure to be low toward the end of the year, unless there has been a panic in September or October; and they are generally high in May and June, unless the "spring rise" culminates, as it sometimes does, in April. But it is a pretty sound maxim that if speculators exercise a fairly sound judgment, do not operate beyond their capital, and have patience to wait, they are almost sure to win at last, no matter which side they have embraced, or at what season of the year they have bought or sold.

THE SILENT MAJORITY.

SONG OF THE REDWOOD-TREE
BY WALT WHITMAN

FEBRUARY 1874

A CALIFORNIA *song!*
A prophecy and indirection—a thought impalpable, to breathe, as air;
A chorus of dryads, fading, departing—or hamadryads departing;
A murmuring, fateful, giant voice, out of the earth and air,
Voice of a mighty dying tree in the redwood forest dense.

Farewell, my brethren,
Farewell, O earth and sky—farewell, ye neighboring waters;
My time has ended, my term has come.

Along the northern coast,
Just back from the rock-bound shore, and the caves,
In the saline air from the sea, in the Mendocino country,
With the surge for bass and accompaniment low and hoarse,
With crackling blows of axes, sounding musically, driven by strong arms,
Riven deep by the sharp tongues of the axes—there in the redwood forest dense,
I heard the mighty tree its death-chant chanting.

Editors' Note: This poem appeared in Whitman's Leaves of Grass.

The choppers heard not—the camp shanties echoed not;
The quick-ear'd teamsters, and chain and jack-screw men heard not,
As the wood-spirits came from their haunts of a thousand years, to join the refrain;
But in my soul I plainly heard.

Murmuring out of its myriad leaves,
Down from its lofty top, rising over a hundred feet high,
Out of its stalwart trunk and limbs—out of its foot-thick bark,
That chant of the seasons and time—chant not of the past only, but the future.

You untold life of me,
And all you venerable and innocent joys,
Perennial, hardy life of me, with joys, 'mid rain and many a summer sun,
And the white snows, and night, and the wild winds;
O the great patient, rugged joys! my soul's strong joys, unreck'd by man;
(For know I bear the soul befitting me—I too have consciousness, identity,
And all the rocks and mountains have—and all the earth;)
Joys of the life befitting me and brothers mine,
Our time, our term has come.

Nor yield we mournfully, majestic brothers,
We who have grandly fill'd our time;
With Nature's calm content, and tacit, huge delight,
We welcome what we wrought for through the past,
And leave the field for them.

For them predicted long,
For a superber race—they too to grandly fill their time,
For them we abdicate—in them ourselves, ye forest kings!
In them these skies and airs—these mountain peaks—Shasta—Nevadas,
These huge, precipitous cliffs—this amplitude—these valleys grand—Yosemite,
To be in them absorb'd, assimilated.

Then to a loftier strain,
Still prouder, more ecstatic, rose the chant,
As if the heirs, the Deities of the west,
Joining, with master-tongue, bore part.

Not wan from Asia's fetiches,
Nor red from Europe's old dynastic slaughter-house,
(Area of murder-plots of thrones, with scent left yet of wars and scaffolds every where,)
But come from Nature's long and harmless throes—peacefully builded thence,
These virgin lands—Lands of the Western Shore,
To the new Culminating Man—to you, the Empire New,
You, promis'd long, we pledge, we dedicate.

You occult, deep volitions,
You average Spiritual Manhood, purpose of all, pois'd on yourself—giving, not
    taking law,
You Womanhood divine, mistress and source of all, whence life and love, and aught
    that comes from life and love,
You unseen Moral Essence of all the vast materials of America, (age upon age, working
    in Death the same as Life,)
You that, sometimes known, oftener unknown, really shape and mould the New
World, adjusting it to Time and Space,
You hidden National Will, lying in your abysms, conceal'd, but ever alert,
You past and present purposes, tenaciously pursued, maybe unconscious of yourselves,
Unswerv'd by all the passing errors, perturbations of the surface;
You vital, universal, deathless germs, beneath all creeds, arts, statutes, literatures,
Here build your homes for good—establish here—These areas entire, Lands of the
    Western Shore,
We pledge, we dedicate to you.

For man of you—your characteristic race,
Here may he hardy, sweet, gigantic grow—here tower, proportionate to Nature,
Here climb the vast, pure spaces, unconfined, uncheck'd by wall or roof,
Here laugh with storm or sun—here joy—here patiently inure,
Here heed himself, unfold himself (not others' formulas heed)—here fill his time,
To duly fall, to aid, unreck'd at last,
To disappear to serve.

Thus on the northern coast,
In the echo of teamsters' calls, and the clinking chains, and the music of choppers' axes,
The falling trunk and limbs, the crash, the muffled shriek, the groan,
Such words combined from the redwood-tree—as of wood-spirits' voices ecstatic, ancient and
    rustling,
The century-lasting, unseen dryads, singing, withdrawing,
All their recesses of forests and mountains leaving,
From the Cascade range to the Wasatch—or Idaho far, or Utah,
To the deities of the modern henceforth yielding,
The chorus and indications, the vistas of coming humanity—the settlements, features all,
In the Mendocino woods I caught.

The flashing and golden pageant of California!
The sudden and gorgeous drama—the sunny and ample lands;
The long and varied stretch from Puget Sound to Colorado south;
Lands bathed in sweeter, rarer, healthier air! valleys and mountain cliffs!
The fields of Nature long prepared and fallow—the silent, cyclic chemistry;
The slow and steady ages plodding—the unoccupied surface ripening—the rich ores forming
    beneath;
At last the New arriving, assuming, taking possession,

A swarming and busy race settling and organizing every where;
Ships coming in from the whole round world, and going out to the whole world,
To India and China and Australia, and the thousand island paradises of the Pacific;
Populous cities—the latest inventions—the steamers on the rivers—the railroads—with
     many a thrifty farm, with machinery,
And wool and wheat and the grape—and diggings of yellow gold.

But more in you than these, Lands of the Western Shore!
(These but the means, the implements, the standing-ground,)
I see in you, certain to come, the promise of thousands of years, till now deferr'd,
Promis'd, to be fulfill'd, our common kind, the race.

The New Society at last, proportionate to Nature;
In Man of you, more than your mountain peaks, or stalwart trees imperial,
In Woman more, far more, than all your gold, or vines, or even vital air.

Fresh come, to a New World indeed, yet long prepared,
I see the Genius of the modern, child of the real and ideal,
Clearing the ground for broad Humanity, the true America, heir of the past so grand,
To build a grander future.

A Song

by Christina Rossetti

April 1878

O Roses for the flush of youth,
　And laurel for the perfect prime;
But pluck an ivy branch for me
　Grown old before my time.

O violets for the grave of youth,
　And bay for those dead in their prime;
Give me the withered leaves I chose
　Before in the old time

EDITOR'S EASY CHAIR
BOSS TWEED

BY GEORGE WILLIAM CURTIS

JUNE 1878

There was nothing in Tweed besides his enormous thefts to make him a person of any importance, but his death was an event which the newspapers treated at length as if he had been a hero or statesman, or a poet, or a famous man. The reason is obvious. Tweed was the type of a system of fraud and peculation which was felt with alarm to be corrupting the moral forces of the republic, and it was seen with dismay that it needed no ability to push it to monstrous results. The Tammany Ring was the sorriest set of rogues that ever menaced a great community with great dangers. It was utterly unredeemed by talent, by capacity, or even by the vulgar romance of Dick Turpin or Jack Sheppard. It was a plot for sheer stealing, and it was successful. The reason of its great success may be partly seen in the feeling of sympathy for the only one of the band who was imprisoned, and a half complaint at the inequality of his punishment—a feeling which at bottom insisted that as the others had gotten off, he ought to have escaped also.

Another illustration of the same feeling of good-humored indifference which made the crimes of the Ring possible was the way in which Tweed's gift of fifty thousand dollars to the poor of the city was received. This was one of the most impudent acts of his career. Mr. Robert Macaire having robbed a traveller of his fortune, benevolently gave his widowed daughter a gold watch. There was a murmur of admiration among the spectators, and an exclamation that Mr. Macaire, after

Thomas Nast's rendering of the Boss Tweed ring.

all, had a good heart, and that although his acquisitions of money were perhaps irregular, yet his bounty made him somehow a public benefactor in disguise. So when the end came, and Tweed died in comfortable quarters in jail, where it appears he paid seventy-five dollars a week, indulging in "luxuries and delicacies" as they took his fancy, and amusing himself at games with old boon companions, there was the same kind of remark that there were quite as bad men as he out of jail, as if because all who deserve to be imprisoned are not caught, those who are caught should be released. It was added that he was a "poor old man" who could do no more harm, who had been sufficiently punished, and from whom nothing more could be obtained. He was a man of fifty-five years, and nobody knew how much of his plunder he had indirectly retained, and there was certainly no more reason for releasing him than any other known offender. There was, under the law, one, and one only, sufficient reason for remitting his punishment, and that was evidence which he only could give, and which would enable some of the money that he and his confederates had stolen to be restored. It was supposed that he had furnished this evidence in his confession. But the Attorney-General decided, and decided justly, that he had not, and the resolution with which Mr. Fairchild held that position in the face of the most powerful and unscrupulous political hostility, commends him to public approval and sympathy.

The *World*, the morning after Tweed's death, drew a very just distinction between men of great political ability who use base methods because they are the easiest for their public purposes, and men who use them merely for gross personal enjoyment and emolument. It cites Sir Robert Walpole as a type of the first class, and thus of necessity brings his name into ludicrous proximity with that of Tweed. Walpole's political morality was certainly no higher than that of his time; but his recent biographer, Mr. Ewald, and Mr. Lecky, in his *History of the Eighteenth Century*, show that the most famous remark attributed to him has been misrepresented. He did not say, however the condition of things around him might have justified the remark, that "all men have their price;" but he said of a particular group of members, "All these men have their price," which he doubtless knew to be true. Walpole, however, did unquestionably, as Lecky says, organize corruption as a system, a process of Parliamentary government. But Walpole also, despite the fatal influence of his methods, rendered great services to England. Of course the two men are not mentioned together except to show how one man can turn enormous political corruption to the mere gratification of his private pleasure, while another will not scruple to use it to secure beneficial public results, without the least personal gain. It is fortunate for public morality that Tweed's career ended as it did. For those whom his final success would have emboldened for any knavery are the very class to be admonished by his total miscarriage.

illus—
Harper's Weekly
Sept. 23, 1871
see Keller [123]

Two readers of Harper's *depicted by Edwin A. Abbey.*

"Two Readers of 'Harper.'" illus. to S.S. Cox's "American Humor." April 1875, p. 692

1880's

WASHINGTON SQUARE

BY HENRY JAMES

SEPTEMBER 1880

XIV

D r. Sloper] wrote his frank letter to Mrs. Montgomery, who punctually answered it, mentioning an hour at which he might present himself in the Second Avenue. She lived in a neat little house of red brick, which had been freshly painted, with the edges of the bricks very sharply marked out in white. It has now disappeared, with its companions, to make room for a row of structures more majestic. There were green shutters upon the windows, without slats, but pierced with little holes, arranged in groups; and before the house was a diminutive "yard," ornamented with a bush of mysterious character, and surrounded by a low wooden paling, painted in the same green as the shutters. The place looked like a magnified baby-house, and might have been taken down from a shelf in a toy-shop. Doctor Sloper, when he went to call, said to himself, as he glanced at the objects I have enumerated, that Mrs. Montgomery was evidently a thrifty and self-respecting little person—the modest proportions of her dwelling seemed to indicate that she was of small stature—who took a virtuous satisfaction in keeping herself tidy, and had resolved that, since she might not be splendid, she would at least be immaculate. She received him in a little parlor, which was precisely the parlor he had expected: a small unspeckled bower, ornamented with a desultory foliage of tissue-paper, and with clusters of glass drops, amid which—to carry out the analogy—the temperature of the leafy season was maintained by means of a cast-iron stove, emitting a dry blue flame, and smelling strongly of varnish. The walls were embellished with engravings swathed in pink gauze, and the tables ornamented with volumes of extracts from the poets, usually bound in black cloth stamped with florid designs in jaundiced gilt. The Doctor had time to take cognizance of these details; for Mrs. Montgomery, whose conduct he pronounced under the circumstances inexcusable, kept him waiting some ten minutes before she appeared. At last, however, she rustled in, smoothing down a stiff poplin dress, with a little frightened flush in a gracefully rounded cheek.

She was a small, plump, fair woman, with a bright, clear eye, and an extraordinary air of neatness and briskness. But these qualities were evidently combined with an unaffected humility, and the Doctor gave her his esteem as soon as he had looked at her. A brave little person, with lively perceptions, and yet a disbelief in her own talent for social, as distinguished from practical, affairs—this was his rapid mental *résumé* of Mrs. Montgomery, who, as he saw, was flattered by what she regarded as the honor of his visit. Mrs. Montgomery, in her little red house in the Second Avenue, was a person for whom Dr. Sloper was one of the great men, one of the fine gentlemen of New York; and while she fixed her agitated eyes upon him, while she clasped her mittened hands together in her glossy poplin lap, she had the appearance of saying to herself that he quite answered her idea of what a distinguished guest would naturally be. She apologized for being late; but he interrupted her.

"It doesn't matter," he said; "for while I sat here I had time to think over what I wish to say to you, and to make up my mind how to begin."

"Oh, do begin," murmured Mrs. Montgomery.

"It is not so easy," said the Doctor, smiling. "You will have gathered from my letter that I wish to ask you a few questions, and you may not find it very comfortable to answer them."

"Yes, I have thought what I should say. It is not very easy."

Editors' Note: This chapter is part of James's novel Washington Square, *which was serialized in* Harper's Magazine.

"But you must understand my situation—my state of mind. Your brother wishes to marry my daughter, and I wish to find out what sort of a young man he is. A good way to do so seemed to be to come and ask you, which I have proceeded to do."

Mrs. Montgomery evidently took the situation very seriously; she was in a state of extreme moral concentration. She kept her pretty eyes, which were illumined by a sort of brilliant modesty, attached to his own countenance, and evidently paid the most earnest attention to each of his words. Her expression indicated that she thought his idea of coming to see her a very superior conception, but that she was really afraid to have opinions on strange subjects.

"I am extremely glad to see you," she said, in a tone which seemed to admit, at the same time, that this had nothing to do with the question.

The Doctor took advantage of this admission. "I didn't come to see you for your pleasure; I came to make you say disagreeable things—and you can't like that. What sort of a gentleman is your brother?"

Mrs. Montgomery's illuminated gaze grew vague, and began to wander. She smiled a little, and for some time made no answer, so that the Doctor at last became impatient. And her answer, when it came, was not satisfactory. "It is difficult to talk about one's brother."

"Not when one is fond of him, and when one has plenty of good to say."

"Yes, even then, when a good deal depends on it," said Mrs. Montgomery.

"Nothing depends on it, for you."

"I mean for—for—" and she hesitated.

"For your brother himself. I see."

"I mean for Miss Sloper," said Mrs. Montgomery.

The Doctor liked this; it had the accent of sincerity. "Exactly; that's the point. If my poor girl should marry your brother, everything—as regards her happiness—would depend on his being a good fellow. She is the best creature in the world, and she could never do him a grain of injury. He, on the other hand, if he should not be all that we desire, might make her very miserable. That is why I want you to throw some light upon his character, you know. Of course you are not bound to do it. My daughter, whom you have never seen, is nothing to you; and I, possibly, am only an indiscreet and impertinent old man. It is perfectly open to you to tell me that my visit is in very bad taste, and that I had better go about my business. But I don't think you will

do this, because I think we shall interest you, my poor girl and I. I am sure that if you were to see Catherine, she would interest you very much. I don't mean because she is interesting in the usual sense of the word, but because you would feel sorry for her. She is so soft, so simple-minded, she would be such an easy victim. A bad husband would have remarkable facilities for making her miserable; for she would have neither the intelligence nor the resolution to get the better of him, and yet she would have an exaggerated power of suffering. I see," added the Doctor, with his most insinuating, his most professional, laugh, "you are already interested."

"I have been interested from the moment he told me he was engaged," said Mrs. Montgomery.

"Ah! he says that—he calls it an engagement?"

"Oh, he has told me you didn't like it."

"Did he tell you that I don't like *him*?"

"Yes, he told me that too. I said I couldn't help it," added Mrs. Montgomery.

"Of course you can't. But what you can do is to tell me I am right; to give me an attestation, as it were." And the Doctor accompanied this remark with another professional smile.

Mrs. Montgomery, however, smiled not at all; it was obvious that she could not take the humorous view of his appeal. "That is a good deal to ask," she said at last.

"There can be no doubt of that; and I must, in conscience, remind you of the advantages a young man marrying my daughter would enjoy. She has an income of ten thousand dollars in her own right, left her by her mother. If she marries a husband I approve, she will come into almost twice as much more at my death."

Mrs. Montgomery listened in great earnestness to this splendid financial statement; she had never heard thousands of dollars so familiarly talked about. She flushed a little with excitement. "Your daughter will be immensely rich," she said, softly.

"Precisely—that's the bother of it."

"And if Morris should marry her, he—he—" And she hesitated timidly.

"He would be master of all that money? By no means. He would be master of the ten thousand a year that she has from her mother; but I should leave every penny of my own fortune, earned in the laborious exercise of my profession, to my nephews and nieces."

Mrs. Montgomery dropped her eyes at this, and sat for some time gazing at the straw matting which covered her floor.

"I suppose it seems to you," said the Doctor, laughing, "that in so doing I should play your brother a very shabby trick?"

"Not at all. That is too much money to get possession of so easily, by marrying. I don't think it would be right."

"It's right to get all one can. But in this case your brother wouldn't be able. If Catherine marries without my consent, she doesn't get a penny from my own pocket."

"Is that certain?" asked Mrs. Montgomery, looking up.

"As certain as that I sit here."

"Even if she should pine away?"

"Even if she should pine to a shadow, which isn't probable."

"Does Morris know this?"

"I shall be most happy to inform him," the Doctor exclaimed.

Mrs. Montgomery resumed her meditations, and her visitor, who was prepared to give time to the affair, asked himself whether, in spite of her little conscientious air, she was not playing into her brother's hands. At the same time he was half ashamed of the ordeal to which he had subjected her, and was touched by the gentleness with which she bore it. "If she were a humbug," he said, "she would get angry: unless she be very deep indeed. It is not probable that she is as deep as that."

"What makes you dislike Morris so much?" she presently asked, emerging from her reflections.

"I don't dislike him in the least as a friend, as a companion. He seems to me a charming fellow, and I should think he would be excellent company. I dislike him, exclusively, as a son-in-law. If the only office of a son-in-law were to dine at the paternal table, I should set a high value upon your brother. He dines capitally. But that is a small part of his function, which, in general, is to be a protector and caretaker of my child, who is singularly ill adapted to take care of herself. It is there that he doesn't satisfy me. I confess I have nothing but my impression to go by; but I am in the habit of trusting my impression. Of course you are at liberty to contradict it flat. He strikes me as selfish and shallow."

Mrs. Montgomery's eyes expanded a little, and the Doctor fancied he saw the light of admiration in them. "I wonder you have discovered he is selfish!" she exclaimed.

"Do you think he hides it so well?"

"Very well indeed," said Mrs. Montgomery. "And I think we are all rather selfish," she added, quickly.

"I think so too; but I have seen people hide it better than he. You see, I am helped by a habit I have of dividing people into classes, into types. I may easily be mistaken about your brother as an individual, but his type is written on his whole person."

"He is very good-looking," said Mrs. Montgomery.

The Doctor eyed her a moment. "You women are all the same. But the type to which your brother belongs was made to be the ruin of you, and you were made to be its handmaids and victims. The sign of the type in question is the determination—sometimes terrible in its quiet intensity—to accept nothing of life but its pleasures, and to secure these pleasures chiefly by the aid of your complaisant sex. Young men of this class never do anything for themselves that they can get other people to do for them, and it is the infatuation, the devotion, the superstition of others that keeps them going. These others, in ninety-nine cases out of a hundred, are women. What our young friends chiefly insist upon is that some one else shall suffer for them; and women do that sort of thing, as you must know, wonderfully well." The Doctor paused a moment, and then he added, abruptly, "You have suffered immensely for your brother!"

This exclamation was abrupt, as I say, but it was also perfectly calculated. The Doctor had been rather disappointed at not finding his compact and comfortable little hostess surrounded in a more visible degree by the ravages of Morris Townsend's immorality; but he had said to himself that this was not because the young man had spared her, but because she had contrived to plaster up her wounds. They were aching there, behind the varnished stove, the festooned engravings, beneath her own neat little poplin bosom; and if he could only touch the tender spot, she would make a movement that would betray her. The words I have just quoted were an attempt to put his finger suddenly upon the place; and they had some of the success that he looked for. The tears sprang for a moment to Mrs. Montgomery's eyes, and she indulged in a proud little jerk of the head.

"I don't know how you have found that out," she exclaimed.

"By a philosophic trick—by what they call induction. You know you have always your option of contradicting me. But kindly answer me a question. Don't you give your brother money? I think you ought to answer that."

"Yes, I have given him money," said Mrs. Montgomery.

"And you have not had much to give him?"

She was silent a moment. "If you ask me for a confession of poverty, that is easily made. I am very poor."

"One would never suppose it from your—your charming house," said the Doctor. "I learned from my sister that your income was moderate, and your family numerous."

"I have five children," Mrs. Montgomery observed; "but I am happy to say I can bring them up decently."

"Of course you can—accomplished and devoted as you are! But your brother has counted them over, I suppose?"

"Counted them over?"

"He knows there are five, I mean. He tells me it is he that brings them up."

Mrs. Montgomery stared a moment, and then, quickly, "Oh, yes; he teaches them—Spanish."

The Doctor laughed out. "That must take a great deal off your hands! Your brother also knows, of course, that you have very little money."

"I have often told him so," Mrs. Montgomery exclaimed, more unreservedly than she had yet spoken. She was apparently taking some comfort in the Doctor's clairvoyance.

"Which means that you have often occasion to, and that he often sponges on you. Excuse the crudity of my language; I simply express a fact. I don't ask you how much of your money he has had; it is none of my business. I have ascertained what I suspected—what I wished." And the Doctor got up, gently smoothing his hat. "Your brother lives on you," he said, as he stood there.

Mrs. Montgomery quickly rose from her chair, following her visitor's movements with a look of fascination. But then, with a certain inconsequence, "I have never complained of him," she said.

"You needn't protest—you have not betrayed him. But I advise you not to give him any more money."

"Don't you see it is in my interest that he should marry a rich person?" she asked. "If, as you say, he lives on me, I can only wish to get rid of him, and to put obstacles in the way of his marrying is to increase my own difficulties."

"I wish very much you would come to me with your difficulties," said the Doctor. "Certainly, if I throw him back on your hands, the least I can do is to help you to bear the burden. If you will allow me to say so, then, I shall take the liberty of placing in your hands, for the present, a certain fund for your brother's support."

Mrs. Montgomery stared; she evidently thought he was jesting; but she presently saw that he was not, and the complication of her feelings became painful. "It seems to me that I ought to be very much offended with you," she murmured.

"Because I have offered you money? That's a superstition," said the Doctor. "You must let me come and see you again, and we will talk about these things. I suppose that some of your children are girls?"

"I have two little girls," said Mrs. Montgomery.

"Well, when they grow up, and begin to think of taking husbands, you will see how anxious you will be about the moral character of these husbands. Then you will understand this visit of mine."

"Ah, you are not to believe that Morris's moral character is bad!"

The Doctor looked at her a little, with folded arms. "There is something I should greatly like—as a moral satisfaction. I should like to hear you say, 'He is abominably selfish.'"

The words came out with the grave distinctness of his voice, and they seemed for an instant to create, to poor Mrs. Montgomery's troubled visage, a material image. She gazed at it an instant, and then she turned away. "You distress me, sir!" she exclaimed. "He is, after all, my brother, and his talents—his talents—" On these last words her voice quavered, and before he knew it she had burst into tears.

"His talents are first-rate," said the Doctor. "We must find the proper field for them." And he assured her most respectfully of his regret at having so greatly discomposed her. "It's all for my poor Catherine," he went on. "You must know her, and you will see."

Mrs. Montgomery brushed away her tears, and blushed at having shed them. "I should like to know your daughter," she answered. And then, in an instant, "Don't let her marry him!"

Doctor Sloper went away with the words gently humming in his ears—"Don't let her marry him!" They gave him the moral satisfaction of which he had just spoken, and their value was the greater that they had evidently cost a pang to poor little Mrs. Montgomery's family pride. [. . .]

Editor's Easy Chair
Women's Rights
by George William Curtis

February 1885

There is one "right" of woman which the most unreasonable conservative will not deny, and that is the right of earning her own living by her own industry and skill. This kind of conservative will see, therefore, with pleasure that there was a department in the New Orleans Exposition reserved for the "work of women." Mrs. Julia Ward Howe is very properly the president of this department, and the collection will furnish adequate evidence of the comparative skill and ingenuity of women.

It is the constant remark of those who are vexed by the agitation for "woman's rights" that they have the right to mind their homes and their children, and they are vigorously exhorted to remember their "sphere" and to stick to it. The mocking-birds of every kind and degree who echo and re-echo this familiar cry may well alight for a moment upon the window-sills of hundreds of factories of every kind in the city of New York alone, and, looking in, they will feel the utter folly of their parrot scream. They will see thousands and thousands of women busily occupied all day long in a hundred industries to earn their living. Could there be any twaddle so ineffable as a solemn charge to these women to betake themselves to the care of their homes and their children? Except for their work in these rooms, and hard work and constant work, they would have no homes, and the larger part of them are unmarried and have no children. Their homes are cared for by themselves or by their parents. But their "sphere," that is to say, the sphere which is not fixed for them by nature, is the employment by which they can live.

The efforts of women to extend the range and variety of those employments, or to secure the guarantees for them which men secure, can not be honorably met by the exhortation to stick to their sphere and to mind their homes. Such women are doing both those things in the efforts they make and the lives they lead. And the twittering mocking-birds can not escape the pitiless logic. If women are within their "sphere," which is undeniable, when engaged in any form of honest manual labor, they can not be out of it when exercising any special gift or talent, whether of invention, of vocalism, of oratory, or whatever it may be. There is many an excellent man who hears with delight Jenny Lind or some other renowned singer standing upon a platform and singing "I know that my Redeemer liveth." The hearing is an inspiration, and he no more thinks the woman to be unsphered than an angel in the celestial choir whose

> divinely warbled voice,
> Answering the stringed noise,

would take his soul in blissful rapture. Why is it that a woman standing upon the same platform and solemnly reading the same words affects him unpleasantly, as if she were "out of her sphere," and doing something not quite womanly? There is no good reason for it whatever. It is simply custom.

No man could possibly object to the display at New Orleans of specimens of every production of the skill of women, unless he thinks that a woman who invents or is manually dexterous has wandered from her sphere and has become unwomanly. At the meeting in New York to consider what could be done to promote the success of the women's department there were very interesting statements made of the variety of products of womanly talent and skill. There are works in embroidery, moulding, wood-carving; in the finest surgical instruments; in bolts, screws, nails, locks; in applying bronze to wall-papers—in which branch it appears that a German woman in this city makes $18,000 a year—in painting, drawing, modelling, designing, and repoussé. Whatever good work women can accomplish in any of these branches, or in any other handicraft, every man of sense will gladly welcome. The results of intellectual ability or works of genius could not be less welcome.

"Spring Blossoms," by Howard Pyle.

Such activities are the incontestable "rights" of woman. What, then, is the significance of the antipathy to what is called the woman's rights movement? The secret? responds a friend of the "spheres" of the sexes; why, the secret of the antipathy is that the movement does not concern inventions and abilities, but demands political enfranchisement, and that is intolerable and unnatural. Yet if a woman be conceded to be equally with a man a responsible moral agent and a laborer making her own living by her own industry, and if it be perfectly seemly for a man to promote his advantage as such a worker by the privilege of voting, why should not such a woman—not necessarily a woman whose livelihood is otherwise assured, but a woman working side by side with a man to earn her living—have every defense and protection that he has?

Is it perhaps because men are weaker and less able to help themselves? or is it possibly because they are physically stronger and can insist upon their own way? The Woman's Department at New Orleans will be a gallery of meditation as well as of admiration.

Our Public Land Policy

by Veeder B. Paine

October 1885

here is no branch of our political economy more worthy of careful study, of more immediate and vital importance to the people, about which they know so little, and to which they show so much indifference, as that of the management of our public lands. Dignified dissertations, dry as dust, treating of the public domain, are hurriedly glanced over by the reading portion of the public, and laid aside with a vague feeling of helplessness, and a groundless hope that some one will rise up and set the matter right. We read in the newspapers of gigantic land swindles by scheming speculators, whose audacity is equalled only by their success. We read, and turn the page; and yet the most careless observer of public affairs will hardly fail to notice that, however large the slice those who are parcelling out among themselves the public lands may choose, in homely phrase, to bite off, their facilities for mastication and the very efficient aids to digestion which they receive in various ways at some local land offices are so considerable that they chew with ease and swallow with impunity; and if by any mischance the mouthful prove too large, and local practitioners fail in their treatment of the case, then the great healer at Washington may be called upon to prescribe a remedy. A new ruling for the General Land Department, the reversal of some former decision, unusual dispatch in issuing patents, suppression of reports of irregularities practiced in certain cases, and in a twinkling, by a kind of legerdemain, vast areas of fertile prairie or virgin pine forest disappear within the capacious maw of some soulless, unapproachable, unknowable something termed a syndicate.

The laws governing individual titles to real property, while of a nature so dry in the abstract, so difficult to follow, that only those who probe to the bottom may be sure of the condition of the title to any given description, and an expert alone can tell when the bottom is reached, are yet certain and well settled. Not so, however, with our public lands. Titles to these are subject to the dictation of changing officials, to rules and regulations of different Secretaries of Interior, to acts of Congress, and are, in consequence, within the influence of wealthy corporations, and involved in obscurity and uncertainty.

Notable instances bear witness to the truth of this, some of which it will be well to consider. Let us first regard the unsettled ownership of millions of acres of unearned and, by contract terms, forfeitable, if not forfeited, grants to railroads.

In some instances these roads have been partially constructed, in others no attempt has been made to build, yet in all cases the entire grant is claimed, and the lands thus covered are withheld from settlement. The Supreme Court of the United States having decided that "a failure to complete the road within the time fixed in the grant does not forfeit the grant," the lands thus withheld must remain so until by act of Congress the respective unearned grants are declared forfeited. It has been truly affirmed "that title to nearly one hundred million acres of land, rightfully belonging to the people of this country, is in a condition that it may, by crafty entanglement of law, be confirmed in the interest of grasping and corporate monopolies; yet Congress remains passive, refusing to assert the rights of the people, although well advised of the imperative necessity for action."

A fair illustration that the government is or has been in danger of losing these lands is the case of the "Backbone" grant, made in 1871 to the New Orleans, Vicksburg, and Baton Rouge Railroad. One of the conditions of the grant was that the road should be completed in five years. Not a yard of earth was ever moved by this company. They did, however, issue and sell bonds, then transferred the grant to the New Orleans and Pacific road, which company sold its charter rights to the Texas Pacific, reserving its assigned grant, and transferring it to the American Improvement Company. The "Backboners" have repeatedly importuned

Congress for confirmation, always meeting with refusal. The culmination of this affair shows how great the power and how little the care exercised by high officials in disposing of or protecting the public lands. During the last few weeks of the retiring administration there was great and unusual animation noticeable in the General Land Department. Extra clerks were busy night and day filling out papers with precipitous haste; and when the present Secretary assumed control of the office the mill was still in full blast, grinding out what proved to be patents for lands of this "Backbone" grant, seven hundred thousand acres of which were already deeded, every revolution of the wheels severing from the public domain, without adequate, if any, compensation, great tracts of land. At once the machinery was ordered stopped, saving to the government thousands of acres, and inaugurating, it is to be hoped, a new era in the methods of disposing of that portion of our public domain which still remains.

The wanton and wholesale plunder of our public lands the past twenty years furnishes material for the most astounding chapter of American history.

In what terms may we fitly characterize a system which permits one man, by questionable methods, to secure a grant of lands covering a narrow strip extending for miles along the banks of a large stream with all its tributaries, comprising in its self a small acreage, but rendering inaccessible to others, and depriving the government of the sale of, millions of acres of the adjacent lands (a notable instance of this kind occurring in New Mexico)—a system which winks at the building of fences by cattle kings around vast areas, excluding therefrom the honest settler, putting up in effect a barrier to the progress of civilization, and which enables railroad corporations, after receiving patents to over fifty-three million acres, still to set up, with fair prospect of success, claims for one hundred and two millions more?

A second example of uncertainty is the Oklahoma lands, of which so much has been said and written, and about which so little is known, either as to their boundaries or the title, that to the masses they are extremely mythical, while hundreds of people are hovering on the outskirts of this promising but not yet promised land, anxiously awaiting a settlement of the vexed question.

By some arrangement known only to the high contracting parties several cattle companies were permitted to go in and possess the land, pasturing thereon their immense flocks and herds without molestation by the government, while the hardy settler, bent on securing a home for his family, was held back at the point of the bayonet. This fact has undoubtedly led to much of the persistence of the so-called boomers; and who shall say that injustice has not been done by such discrimination against them?

The recent order to the cattle men to withdraw has apparently satisfied the would-be settlers that the administration intends to be fair, and treat all classes alike, and they have quietly dispersed, or wait with patience final action of the government in acquiring undisputed title.

Thirdly comes to our notice the case of the Winnebago and Crow Creek Indian reservations, comprising a large body of fertile lands in southwestern Dakota, which by a ruling of the outgoing Secretary of the Interior, rendered in February last, and by Presidential proclamation, were declared open to settlement. On the authority of such ruling and proclamation over three thousand families went upon the lands, made their selections, and stuck their stakes for a home, only to find themselves confronted by angry and threatening Indians, whose title has not yet been legally extinguished; and, by what is still worse for the settler, though undoubtedly proper and justifiable, a ruling from the Department suspending further settlement, and an order from the Executive to retire from the reservation. In this conduct there must have been a blunder somewhere.

Fourthly, we note the thousands of acres of pine and mineral lands in Michigan and other States, for which certificates for patents have been issued by registers of local government land districts, in violation of instructions, and contrary to the rules and regulations of the General Land Department at Washington. This has been done for the benefit of favored syndicates, who were permitted to purchase at private entry, for cash, at one dollar and twenty-five cents per acre, lands to which the general public were denied access by the known rules of the office, which required the lands to be proclaimed in market by the President, and to be offered at public auction. During the last session of Congress a Michigan Senator undertook to secure the passage of a bill confirming these titles, and by taking it on as an amendment to House Bill 7004 "to repeal the present pre-emption law," and by arousing the fears of the honest farmers of the State that all titles were in danger, succeeded in getting it through the Senate by a majority of two; but when it reached the House the members had been aroused to the situation, and the amended bill was left on the Speaker's table.

Dakota wheat fields.

In relation to these lands thus held by virtue of such irregular sales the former Secretary of the Interior rendered various and conflicting opinions, the very latest being in the last week of his term, and in favor of issuing the patents, but leaving the question involved in such obscurity that the present Secretary has very properly suspended all action affecting these lands until an investigation is had. Meanwhile the lands are being stripped as rapidly as possible of their valuable pine timber.

Fifthly, the fraudulent practices permitted under the "Timber Act," which applies only to the timbered lands of the States of Oregon, Nebraska, California, and the Territory of Washington, demand investigation. The conditions of this act are that the land shall be chiefly valuable for timber and unfit for cultivation; that no one person or association shall be permitted to enter more than one hundred and sixty acres; that the entry shall not be made for speculation nor for the benefit of any other person than the party making the entry. The applicant is required to swear, among other things, that he has made no contract or agreement by which the title that he may receive from the United States shall enure to the benefit of any person except himself. These provisions are hardly noticed. Large operators cause their employés and procure other persons to make affidavits, enter the lands, and then convey to their employers. In this manner large tracts of timber lands are secured and controlled by individuals and firms contrary to the intention of the statute. Some wealthy corporation advances the money to pay for the making of a government survey of some well-timbered township, having their men engaged and ready to file their claims on the choicest selections as soon as the surveyor runs the lines, and before outsiders, as other people are termed, know anything about the lands. The money

advanced to make the survey is paid back in land. A tract of five hundred million feet secured in this manner is not unusual; so that by reason of inefficient laws, or through the connivance of officials in the execution thereof, the government, in this as in all other cases, parts with its choicest lands for the merest trifle to scheming speculators by unfair and unlawful means.

Sixthly, there are the abuses practiced under the pre-emption law. This law grew out of the "log-cabin, hard-cider, and 'coon-skin" campaign of 1840. Within the State of Minnesota alone, during the past three years, over 150,000 acres of government lands were taken under this act fraudulently, investigation showing that out of one hundred and seventy-four claims, in two only had even the forms of the law been complied with, and this in a region mainly valuable for its timber, and, in the meaning of the law, not subject to pre-emption. Yet somehow these pre-emptors hold, and the lands are lost to the government. [...]

There is urgent need of a thorough overhauling and complete revision of the present system, and a change in measures and methods. Our present Secretary of Interior has already shown a determination to enter upon this great work, and his efforts in that direction should meet with proper encouragement from the people. The first thing, then, to do is to withdraw from market all offered lands. Next, we should repeal the pre-emption, timber-culture, desert-land, timber, and stone acts, and revise the homestead laws. Then we should cause to be made by practical and experienced woodsmen such careful examination and appraisal as an individual owner would do of all the surveyed lands. At a cost not to exceed five cents per acre, the Department of the Interior can be furnished with a complete record and description of each forty-acre lot in the whole seventy millions of timber area it now owns—such reports showing in detail the nature of the soil; variety, quality, and quantity of timber; whether watered by stream, lake, or springs; if pine timber, the facilities for bringing logs to market, either by stream or by rail—in short, every item necessary to enable the Department to arrive at its actual value.

A scale of prices should then be placed on the timbered or mineral lands, on the basis of their relative and ascertained value. No homestead entry should be permitted where the value of the land is in the timber standing thereon, only lands suitable for agriculture and pasturage being open to such entry; none of these lands to be sold for cash without actual occupancy, the object of the government with reference to these being not to realize their value in money, but to reserve them for cultivation and permanent homes for the people.

Such amendment to the homestead law should be made that at any time after a continuous residence of not less than two years the settler may receive patent for his location by paying therefor one dollar per acre, and that no matter how long he might continue to reside thereon, no patent should ever issue until such sum be paid.

The conditions which existed at the time the present laws were enacted, and made them necessary and proper, are changed throughout the entire country. Then the pioneer was obliged to encounter dangers and endure hardships and privations without stint, and the home he rescued from the howling wolf or prowling Indian, and carved out of the unbroken forest, was dearly bought, though free. Long pilgrimages, hundreds of miles by ox team, were made; the family lived for years isolated from friends or neighbors; children were denied the privilege of schools and churches. Now all is changed. A whole neighborhood pack their household effects and live stock into a train of comfortable cars, and in forty-eight hours are unloaded within a few miles, and perhaps in plain view, of their homestead entry, on a broad expanse of fertile prairie, which has "only to be tickled with a hoe to laugh with a harvest." Any man who, after having the use of 160 acres of such land for, say, five years, free of rent, taxes, or interest, is unwilling to pay the government the small sum of one dollar per acre for a title in fee-simple, does not merit a home, and if unable, unless by reason of misfortune, has certainly mistaken his calling.

As most of the surveyed public lands have been at one time or another for some cause withdrawn from sale, it has been since 1820 the custom of the Land Department to restore them to market as occasion seemed to require, by Presidential proclamation and public auction sale, with an established minimum price of one dollar and twenty-five cents per acre, and this without regard to its real value, no examination having been made prior to sale. Commencing at a corner township of the advertised tract, the government subdivisions are read over by the Register of the Land Office in the district where the lands lie. As the reading progresses, bids are receivable; and after the entire list has been read, any and all lands embraced therein remaining unsold are subject to private purchase at the minimum price. As the intent of advertising is to give all the people an equal chance to secure lands, and the auction sale is to enable the government to realize by active competition among buyers something like their value, let us attend one of these sales, observe the manner in which they are conducted, and note the result in dollars to the United States Treasury. We must, however, understand that several weeks or months before the public are notified, it has come, in some mysterious manner, to the knowledge of a few capitalists that certain townships of land are soon to be restored in the usual way. At once they are actively though quietly engaged, sending off crews of two or three men each, practiced land-lookers, on whose judgment they can rely, to make careful examination and report on each forty-acre lot, each crew working within separate and prescribed limits.

After the proclamation other individuals or firms undertake, in like manner, similar examinations, so far as the limited time will admit or their means justify.

On the night preceding the day of sale those who are regarded as bidders at the so-called auction are assembled at the village hotel, and the scene is one of extreme though cautious activity. Verily, says the outside spectator, "on the morrow the bidding will be spirited, and the choice lots will be run up to a high figure." We enter the throng, and learn something of its purpose. That sleek-looking, self-contained gentleman engaged so earnestly in conversation with the smooth-visaged young man, with the twenty-four inch head and Napoleonic physique, is the representative of a New York syndicate of unlimited capital, having an estimate of each forty acres to be offered, and hungry for pine. The younger man is recognized as the shrewdest land-dealer in Michigan, and is well informed about the lands. They are now "sizing" each other up as to information and ability to purchase. Here, again, is a man whose whole exterior tells of hardship and exposure, a land-examiner who has been in the woods for weeks exploring on his own account, and who has a pocketful of "minutes," which he is ready to sell for cash, or an interest in the lands, the latter preferred. His information is probably reliable and of value. This glib-tongued, red-nosed person, with the uncertain eye and anxious look, is also a land-examiner with information for sale. Beware of him. He is on the watch for tenderfeet. His minutes are made up from hearsay and his general knowledge of the country, and compiled at his lodgings. As he "draws on his imagination for his facts," he describes only the choicest selections, holds them at a good round price, and sells for what he can get. Notice the gentleman who in his general "make-up" reminds one of the "briefless barrister." He wanders about, listening closely, and occasionally dropping with well-assumed carelessness a word to indicate his intention to invest heavily on the morrow. His plan is to hold aloof, refuse to join any combination, hoping that some one will be weak enough to buy him off from bidding at all. And if he has the courage to run up the price on a few pieces at the opening of the sale, he will succeed. Some one will be deputized to induce him to retire; he names his price, transfers his bids, and gracefully abandons the unequal contest. To the efforts of this adventurer is the government generally indebted for whatever it may realize at the sale above the minimum price. All the other conflicting interests having made the best terms possible, and agreed not to bid against each other—in fact, conspired against the interests of the public—the sale is a sham. The choicest lands are gone at the lowest figure, the remainder left on hand, subject to purchase at the same price.

Another evil requiring prompt and vigorous action is the constantly increasing encroachments on the public lands by timber trespassers, who have been treated with great lenity, and undoubtedly encouraged thereby to continue their depredations. Of late years it has been the practice of the Land Department to send out "special timber agents" to look after these trespassers, and although a vast amount of property is reported taken and carried away, the Treasury is not the gainer thereby. The men employed are either incompetent or worse. Note the result of their labors for the years 1881–2:

For 1881 these agents reported trespass to the value of $225,472. The government received on account thereof $41,679.97, at an expense of $40,000.

For the year 1882 there were 817 cases reported, recapitulating as follows:

Feet of lumber	222,734,585
Number of railroad ties	2,434,525
Sticks of square timber	1,926
Cords of bark	650
Posts	11,050
Hop poles	20,000
Shingles	575,000
Cords of wood	79,139
Sugar-pine shakes	1,110,000
Pickets	65,000
Estimated market value	$2,044,277.92
Realized on the above through the courts and paid to receivers	38,583.27
Unaccounted for	$2,005,694.65

Such a result would discourage the most persistent stickler for his rights. There is a bad leak somewhere, which can and should be stopped. It is hardly to be wondered at that the Commissioner of Lands under the administration just closed recommended the discontinuance of this branch of the service. The honorable Commissioner offers as a further reason that "such a system of espionage is not in keeping with the spirit of the republic," and says, "everything which might appear like oppression of the people has been carefully avoided." Truly a very convenient system for the timber thief.

By what code of morals, or on what grounds of public policy, should the citizens of a country be thus encouraged to steal? Undoubtedly the Commissioner meant well, but was not his sympathy bestowed on the wrong class of people? Equal justice to all is not oppression.

Our public officers are in charge of a public trust to be administered for the benefit of the whole people. A sentimentalism which looks on and permits the wholesale and wanton destruction and waste of that trust is, we hope, a thing of the past.

By no means should we abandon a strict surveillance of the public lands. The special timber agents should be continued. It should be made a part of their duty to make such examination and appraisal as are indicated in this article, and only men who are competent and practical woodsmen should be appointed to such office.

The time has come when, as affecting our land policy, all sentiment should be laid aside, and a policy adopted vigorous in protecting and conservative in disposing of the public domain. There are strong indications that such a policy is soon to be inaugurated, "and your petitioners, the people, will ever pray."

Editor's Easy Chair
Ulysses S. Grant
by George William Curtis

October 1885

In the recent warm July day when the bells tolling from ocean to ocean across the continent announced the death of Grant, a great multitude, as it listened, recalled the solemn day of Lincoln's death, and a few octogenarians, still hale, may have remembered the famous Fourth of July when Adams and Jefferson died. The singular coincidence of that event, however, was not known until some time afterward, and they were buried before a large part of the country knew that they were dead.

General Grant, by the greatness of his patriotic service, belongs with the most famous Americans. But like every great actor in great events, and especially when a man takes an eminent part in political affairs, he was enveloped, like Adams and Jefferson and Washington and Lincoln, in the clouds and darkness of partisan rancor. Already, however,

that cloud is passing away. The pathetic dignity of his last days, when, patient and gentle in extreme suffering, he awaited the end, yet felt and spoke so wisely and generously of those of his countrymen whom he had opposed in arms, invests the end with a kind of patriotic sanctity, and the soldier whose sword had maintained the Union, and whose magnanimity had softened the asperity of baffled secession, died, as it were, with uplifted hands, blessing a reunited people.

It has been often thought and said that it is unfortunate for his fame that he should have been President, and that he was great only as a soldier. The truer thing to say is that he was great only as a patriot. He was bred a soldier, and he had a soldierly nature and character. He was unfamiliar with politics, and he had nothing of the politician. Yet in all impor-

Grant's funeral procession.

tant affairs his cool judgment and good sense greatly availed. He was not a cultivated man in the ordinary sense, as Washington was not, and his range of sympathies was not large. He was doubtless susceptible, also, in some instances, to strong prejudices. But in all situations, upon the field as in the cabinet, his supreme self-possession, his simplicity and rectitude, never failed him; and when a victorious general at the head of an enormous army, or the chief of a great and dominant political party, and clothed with the highest official authority, liberty and law and the established order were as absolutely secure in his keeping as they were with Washington.

In his eulogy upon Mr. Seward before the Legislature of New York, Mr. Charles Francis Adams speaks of the danger of selecting for the Presidency a man comparatively new to such duties, like Lincoln, rather than a trained and able and experienced public man like Mr. Seward. In point of fact, however (and certainly with no depreciation of the high qualities of Mr. Seward), no man regrets that the choice fell upon Mr. Lincoln. Whatever the reason of his selection— whether it were chance or intrigue or the happy instinct which so often makes the many wiser than the few—there

is no doubt that it was what is called a Providential act, and no man can to-day point out any other man then living in the United States who was so singularly fitted for that tremendous trust at that time as Abraham Lincoln.

General Grant was less trained in politics and public affairs than Mr. Lincoln. But in a popular government the military chief of a war which has saved the state is a popular hero whom the people can not be withheld from honoring. And when to this inevitability in the case of any such general there are added a magnanimity, a simplicity, and a freedom from personal ambition even greater than the military genius, and when the long civil disturbance has been exasperated by mingled ambition, recklessness, and folly in the actual Executive, the selection is no less fortunate for the country, even if with many details of administration there must be just dissatisfaction, and even when certain tendencies of administration must be deplored. The great consideration at such a time is that the President himself is the earnest of an immutable purpose, a fact which, under such circumstances, clears the political atmosphere and produces a pacification which is indispensable. [...]

Photographer's advertisement, 1883.

EDITOR'S EASY CHAIR
STRIKES AND ANARCHY
BY GEORGE WILLIAM CURTIS

NOVEMBER 1886

The prolonged railway strikes, the sudden prominence of the Knights of Labor, the boycotts, the bloody riots in Chicago and Milwaukee, and the verdict of death against seven of the anarchists in Chicago, have been the chief events in our American year, and are full of interest and suggestion. A man by the name of Most, an immigrant from Germany or Bohemia, has been in the country for three or four years, living upon the proceeds of lectures in beer saloons and elsewhere, in which he sets forth the tyranny of society, and preaches murder and anarchy as the remedy. Most established a paper to disseminate his cheerful doctrines, but his talk was so wild, and seemed to be so clearly the shift of a lazy vagabond to live without labor, that it was wholly disregarded until the Chicago massacre. It was then seen to be important, and upon a charge of inciting to riot and crime the man was caught hiding under his paramour's bed, and after due trial was sentenced to prison.

While Most has preached anarchy in tours about the country, there has been in Chicago an organization of anarchists. The population of Chicago is largely foreign, and recent events have disclosed the fact that Poles, Bohemians, and the people of countries from which the emigration to this country was not supposed to be large, supply some of the worst elements of our population. From time to time it has been reported that societies of these foreigners were drilling with arms, and were constantly taught the use of destructives, and were ready at a moment's notice to reduce to practice the doctrines which were constantly set forth in their papers. But those doctrines to the American mind were so absurd, and the methods of European conspirators are so foreign to Americans, and there is so just an indisposition to interfere with any freedom until it actually attacks the general welfare, that the stories were assumed to be exaggerated, and serious trouble was not apprehended.

But the great railroad strikes had excited the public mind, and the conduct of some authorities in the State of Illinois and in the city of Chicago was not such as to intimidate criminal designs, and during an outbreak, which the police of that city were trying to suppress, dynamite bombs were thrown, and there was a massacre of policemen, who displayed a cool intrepidity and undaunted heroism which could not be surpassed. The whole country rose in a cry of consternation and indignation at the crime of European anarchists upon American soil. It was a crime at once monstrous

Haymarket riots in Chicago.

and causeless. It struck at liberty and justice and order. It was perpetrated by the most worthless of men, who are pests everywhere, and whose presence in this country American generosity had tolerated. In this country and under our institutions the crime of the anarchists was unpardonable, and nothing could more clearly vindicate the spirit of Americans and the worth of those institutions than the fact of the conviction of the ringleaders after a prolonged trial, in which every ruling of the judge was passionless and merciful to the prisoners.

The strikes and the anarchist massacres taken together show that there is not only great discontent, but also the will and the skill to organize discontent into revolution. The discontent is not the political discontent from which revolution has usually proceeded. But it is similar in kind. Political discontent is a protest against the political organization known as government when it has oppressed the great body of the people, who have had no voice in the government. But the discontent here is a protest against the huge industrial organizations known as corporations, which, in the judgment of the protestants, like unjust governments, abridge the rights of their employés. The instinctive American reply to this protest is that the majority of the people live by their daily labor, and, if injustice is done, the majority can secure justice through the law, and there is no plea whatever for disorder. But the rejoinder to this reply is this, that however true such a statement may be in our normal condition, yet it is a fact that the oppressive corporations illicitly control the government by bribing the law-makers and the judges, as the old barons overawed the king. It is therefore, says the rejoinder, mere mockery to refer the discontented to the ballot-box.

But this rejoinder is fatally defective, because it is not true that the legislature and the judiciary are generally corrupt. Venal legislators and corrupt judges there may be, but they are few. Moreover, there is a general American love of fair play and an instinctive sympathy for the oppressed. Any strike upon a railroad or in a shop which states plainly and promptly its reason is immediately supported by the press if the reason be obviously fair. If, however, the strikers complaining of oppression instantly proceed to oppress, and claiming the right to decide upon what terms they will labor, deny that right to others, the same instinctive love of fair play intervenes, and again befriends the oppressed as against the oppressor. A corporation of labor can be quite as unjust as a corporation of capital, and the striker who hurls his rightful complaint against the company must take great care that his conduct does not make the complaint a boomerang which will suddenly turn about and smite him in the forehead.

Every striker, however he may be stung by what he feels to be brutal tyranny, ought to see that while public sympathy will support his lawful action, it will not sustain courses which threaten public calamity. If it is proposed to settle differences between employers and employés not by appeal to the law, but to lawlessness and disorder, the issue proposed is anarchy against society, and the American verdict upon that appeal will certainly repeat the Chicago verdict against the anarchists.

1890's

His Ship

by James Russell Lowell

December 1891

"O watcher on the Minster Hill,
　Look out o'er the sloping sea;
Of the tall ships coming, coming still,
　Is never one for me?

"I have waited and watched (the weary years!)
　When I to the shore could win,
Till now I cannot see for tears
　If my ship be coming in.

"Eyes shut, I see her night and day,
　No inch of canvas furled,
As a swan full-breasted push her way
　Up out of the underworld.

"'Tis but her wraith! And all the time
　These cheated eyes grow dim.
Will her tardy topmasts never climb
　Above the ocean's rim?

"The minster tower is goldener grown
　With lichens the sea winds feed,
Since first I came; each bleak head-stone
　Grows hard and harder to read.

"Think! There's a dearer heart that waits,
   And eyes that suffer wrong,
As the fruitless seasons join their mates
   While my ship delays so long!"

"From among so many pennons bright
   On which the sunshine pours,
From among so many wings of white,
   Say, how shall I single yours?"

"By her mast that's all of the beaten gold,
   By her gear of the silk so fine,
By the smell of spices in her hold,
   Full well may you know mine."

"O some go west and some go east;
   Their shadows lighten all the sea;
'Tis a blessing of God to see the least,
   So stately as they be.

"Their high-heaped sails with the wind are round;
   The sleek waves past them swirl;
As they stoop and straighten without a sound,
   They crush the sea to pearl.

"Wind-curved the rainbow signals stream,
   Green, yellow, blue, and red,
But never a ship with the glory and gleam
   Of the tokens you have said."

"My ship of dreams I may never see
   Slide swan-like to her berth,
With her lading of sandal and spicery
   Such as never grew on earth.

"But from peril of storm and reef and shoal,
   From ocean's tumult and din,
My ship, her freight a living soul,
   Shall surely erelong come in.

"With toll of bells to a storm-proof shore,
   To a haven landlocked and still,
Where she shall lie with so many more
   In the lee of the Minster Hill.

"In God's good time she shall 'scape at last
   From the waves' and the weather's wrong,
And the rattle of her anchor cast
   There's a heart shall hear life-long."

FAME'S LITTLE DAY

BY SARAH ORNE JEWETT

MARCH 1895

Nobody ever knew, except himself, what made a foolish young newspaper reporter, who happened into a small old-fashioned hotel in New York, notice Mr. Abel Pinkham with deep interest, listen to his talk, ask a question or two of the clerk, and then go away and make up an effective personal paragraph for one of the morning papers. He must have had a heart full of fun, this young reporter, and something honestly rustic and pleasing must have struck him in the guest's demeanor, for there was a flavor in the few lines he wrote that made some of his fellows seize upon the little paragraph, and copy it, and add to it, and keep it moving. Nobody knows what starts such a thing in journalism, or keeps it alive after it is started, but on a certain Thursday morning the fact was made known to the world that among the notabilities then in the city, Abel Pinkham, Esq., a distinguished citizen of Wetherford, Vermont, was visiting New York on important affairs connected with the maple-sugar industry of his native State. Mr. Pinkham had expected to keep his visit unannounced, but it was likely to occasion much interest in business and civic circles. This was something like the way that the paragraph started, but here and there a kindred spirit of the original journalist caught it up and added discreet lines about Mr. Pinkham's probable stay in town, his occupation of an apartment on the fourth floor of the Ethan Allen Hotel, and other circumstances so uninteresting to the reading public in general that presently, in the next evening edition, one city editor after another threw out the item, and the young journalists, having had their day of pleasure, passed on to other things.

Mr. and Mrs. Pinkham had set forth from home with many forebodings, in spite of having talked all winter about taking this journey as soon as the spring opened. They would have caught at any reasonable excuse for giving it up altogether, because when the time arrived it seemed so much easier to stay at home. Mrs. Abel Pinkham had never seen New York; her husband himself had not been to the city for a great many years; in fact, his reminiscences of the former visit were not altogether pleasant, since he had foolishly fallen into many snares, and been much gulled in his character of honest young countryman. There was a tarnished and worthless counterfeit of a large gold watch still concealed between the outer boarding and inner lath and plaster of the lean-to bedroom which Mr. Abel Pinkham had occupied as a bachelor; it was not the only witness of his being taken in by city sharpers, and he had winced ever since at the thought of their wiles. But he was now a man of sixty, well-to-do, and of authority in town affairs; his children were all well married and settled in homes of their own, except a widowed daughter, who lived at home with her young son, and was her mother's lieutenant in household affairs.

The boy was almost grown, and at this season, when the maple sugar was all made and shipped, and it was still too early for spring work on the land, Mr. Pinkham could leave home as well as not, and here he was in New York, feeling himself to be a stranger and foreigner to city ways. If it had not been for that desire to appear well in his wife's eyes, which had buoyed him over the bar of many difficulties, he could have found it in his heart to take the next train back to Wetherford, Vermont, to be there rid of his best clothes and the stiff rim of his heavy felt hat. He could not let his wife discover that the noise and confusion of Broadway had the least power to make him flinch: he cared no more for it than for the woods in snow-time. He was as good as anybody, and she was better. They owed nobody a cent; and they had come on purpose to see the city of New York.

They were sitting at the breakfast table in the Ethan Allen Hotel, having arrived at nightfall the day before. Mrs. Pinkham looked a little pale about the mouth. She had been kept awake nearly all night by the noise, and had enjoyed but little the evening she had spent in the stuffy parlor of the hotel, looking down out of the window at what seemed to her but garish scenes, and keeping a reproachful and suspicious eye upon some unpleasantly noisy young women of forward behavior who were her only companions. Abel himself was by no means so poorly entertained in the hotel office and smoking-room. He felt much more at home than she did, being better used to meeting strange men than she was to strange women, and he found two or three companions who had seen more than he of New York life. It was there, indeed, that the young reporter found him, hearty and country-fed, and loved the appearance of his best clothes, and the way Mr. Abel Pinkham brushed his hair, and loved the way that he spoke in a loud and manful voice the belief and experience of his honest heart.

In the morning at breakfast-time the Pinkhams were depressed. They missed their good bed at home; they were troubled by the roar and noise of the streets, that hardly stopped overnight before it began again in the morning.

The waiter did not put what mind he may have had to the business of serving them; and Mrs. Abel Pinkham, whose cooking was the triumph of parish festivals at home, had her own opinion about the beefsteak. She was a woman of imagination, and now that she was fairly here, spectacles and all, it really pained her to find that the New York of her dreams, the metropolis of dignity and distinction, of wealth and elegance, did not seem to exist. These poor streets, these unlovely people, were the end of a great illusion. They did not like to meet each other's eyes, this worthy pair. The man began to put on an unbecoming air of assertion, and Mrs. Pinkham's face was full of lofty protest.

"My gracious me, Mary Ann! I *am* glad I happened to get the *Tribune* this mornin'," said Mr. Pinkham, with sudden excitement. "Just you look here! I'd like well to know how they found out about our comin'!" and he handed the paper to his wife across the table. "There—there 'tis; right by your thumb," he insisted. "Can't you see it?" and he smiled

"There 'tis, right by your thumb."

like a boy as she finally brought her large spectacles to bear upon the important paragraph.

"I guess they think somethin' of us, if you don't think much o' them," continued Mr. Pinkham, grandly. "Oh, they know how to keep the run o' folks who are somebody to home! Draper and Fitch knew we was comin' this week: you know I sent word I was comin' to settle with them myself. I suppose they send folks round to the hotels, these newspapers, but I shouldn't thought there'd been time. Anyway, they've thought 'twas worth while to put us in!"

Mrs. Pinkham did not take the trouble to make a mystery out of the unexpected pleasure. "I want to cut it out an' send it right up home to daughter Sarah," she said, beaming with pride, and looking at the printed names as if they were flattering photographs. "I think 'twas most too strong to say we was among the notables. But there! 'tis their business to dress up things, and they have to print somethin' every day. I guess I shall go up and put on my best dress," she added, inconsequently—"this one's kind of dusty; it's the same I rode in."

"Le' me see that paper again," said Mr. Pinkham, jealously. "I didn't more'n half sense it, I was so taken aback. Well, Mary Ann, you didn't expect you was goin' to get into the papers when you come away. 'Abel Pinkham, Esq., o' Wetherford, Vermont.' It looks well, don't it? But you might have knocked me down with a feather when I first caught sight of them words."

"I guess I will put on my other dress," said Mrs. Pinkham, rising, with quite a different air from that with which she had sat down to her morning meal. "This one looks a little out o' style, as Sarah said, but when I got up this mornin' I was so homesick it didn't seem to make any kind o' difference. I expect that saucy girl last night took us to be nobodies. I'd like to leave the paper round where she couldn't help seein' it."

"Don't take no notice of her," said Abel, in a dignified tone. "If she can't do what you want an' be civil, we'll go somewheres else. I wish I'd done what we talked of at first an' gone to the Astor House, but that young man in the cars told me 'twas remote from the things we should want to see. The Astor House was the top o' everything when I was here last, but I expected to find some changes. I want you to have the best there is," he said, smiling at his wife as if they were just making their wedding journey. "Come, let's be stirrin'; 'tis long past eight o'clock," and he ushered her to the door, newspaper in hand.

II

Later that day the guests walked up Broadway, holding themselves erect, and feeling as if every eye was upon them. Abel Pinkham had settled with his correspondents for the spring consignments of maple sugar, and a round sum in bank-bills was stowed away in his breast pocket. One of the partners had been a Wetherford boy, and when there came a renewal of interest in maple sugar, and the best confectioners were ready to do it honor, and the finest quality was at a large premium, this partner remembered that there never was any sugar made in Wetherford of such melting and delicious flavor as that from the trees on the old Pinkham farm. He had now made a good bit of money for himself on this private venture, and was ready that morning to pay Mr. Abel Pinkham cash down, and to give him a handsome order for the next season for all he could make. Mr. Fitch was also generous in the matter of such details as freight and packing; he was immensely polite and kind to his old friends, and begged them to come out to stay with him and his wife, where they lived now, in a not far distant New Jersey town.

"No, no, sir," said Mr. Pinkham, promptly. "My wife has come to see the city. Our time is short. Your folks 'll be up this summer, won't they? An' we can visit then."

"You must certainly take Mrs. Pinkham up to the Park," said the commission merchant. "I wish I had time to show you round myself. I suppose you've been seeing some things already, haven't you? I noticed your arrival in the *Herald*."

"The *Tribune* it was," said Mr. Pinkham, blushing through a smile and looking round at his wife.

"Oh no; I never read the *Tribune*," said Mr. Fitch. "There was quite an extended notice in my paper. They must have put you and Mrs. Pinkham into the *Herald* too." And so the friends parted, laughing. "I am much pleased to have a call from such distinguished parties," said Mr. Fitch, by way of final farewell, and Mr. Pinkham waved his hand grandly in reply.

"Let's get the *Herald*, then," he said, as they started up the street. "We can go an' sit over in that little square that we passed as we came along, and rest an' talk things over about what we'd better do this afternoon. I'm tired out a-trampin' and standin'. I'd rather have set still while we were there, but he wanted us to see his store. Done very well, Joe Fitch has, but 'tain't a business I should like."

There was a lofty look and sense of behavior about Mr. Pinkham of Wetherford. You might have thought him a great politician as he marched up Broadway, looking neither to right hand nor left. He felt himself to be somebody very particular.

"I begin to feel sort of at home myself," said his wife, who always had a certain touch of simple dignity about her. "When we was comin' yesterday New York seemed to be 'way off, and there wasn't nobody expectin' us. I feel now just as if I'd been here before."

They were now on the edge of the better-looking part of the town; it was still noisy and crowded, but noisy with fine carriages instead of drays, and crowded with well-dressed people. The hours for shopping and visiting were beginning, and more than one person looked with appreciative and friendly eyes at the comfortable pleased-looking elderly man and woman who went their easily beguiled and loitering way. The pavement peddlers detained them, but the cabmen beckoned them in vain; their eyes were busy with the immediate foreground. Mrs. Pinkham was embarrassed with the recurring reflection of herself in the great windows.

"I wish I had seen about a new bonnet before we came," she lamented. "They seem to be havin' on some o' their spring things."

"Don't you worry, Mary Ann. I don't see anybody that looks any better than you do," said Abel, with boyish and reassuring pride.

Mr. Pinkham had now bought the *Herald,* and also the *Sun,* well recommended by an able newsboy, and presently they crossed over from that corner by the Fifth Avenue Hotel which seems like the very heart of New York, and found a place to sit down on the square—an empty bench, where they could sit side by side and look the papers through, reading over each other's shoulder, and being impatient from page to page. The paragraph was indeed repeated, with trifling additions. Ederton of the *Sun* had followed the *Tribune* man's lead, and fabricated a brief interview, a marvel of art and discretion, but so general in its allusions that it could create no suspicion; it almost deceived Mr. Pinkham himself, so that he found unaffected pleasure in the fictitious occasion, and felt as if he had easily covered himself with glory. Except for the bare fact of the interview's being imaginary, there was no discredit to be cast upon Mr. Abel Pinkham's having said that he thought the country near Wetherford looked well for the time of year, and promised a fair hay crop, and that his income was augmented one-half to three-fifths by his belief in the future of maple sugar. It was likely to be the great coming crop of the

Green Mountain State. Ederton suggested that there was talk of Mr. Pinkham's presence in the matter of a great maple-sugar trust, in which much of the capital of Wall Street would be involved.

"How they do hatch up these things, don't they?" said the worthy man at this point. "Well, it all sounds well, Mary Ann."

"It says here that you are a very personable man," smiled his wife, "and have filled some of the most responsible town offices" (this was the turn taken by Goffey of the *Herald*). "Oh, and that you are going to attend the performance at Barnum's this evening, and occupy reserved seats! Why, I didn't know—who have you told about that? who was you talkin' to last night, Abel?"

"I never spoke o' goin' to Barnum's to any livin' soul," insisted Abel, flushing. "I only thought of it two or three times to myself that perhaps I might go an' take you. Now that is singular; perhaps they put that in just to advertise the show."

"Ain't it a kind of a low place for folks like us to be seen in?" suggested Mrs. Pinkham, timidly. "People seem to be payin' us all this attention, an' I don't know's 'twould be dignified for us to go to one o' them circus places."

"I don't care; we sha'n't live but once. I ain't comin' to New York an' confine myself to evenin' meetin's," answered Abel, throwing away discretion and morality together. "I tell you I'm goin' to spend this sugar-money just as we've a mind to. You've worked hard, an' counted a good while on comin', an' so've I; an' I ain't goin' to mince my steps an' pinch an' screw for nobody. I'm goin' to hire one o' them hacks an' ride up to the Park."

"Joe Fitch said we could go right up in one o' the elevated railroads for five cents, an' return when we was ready," protested Mary Ann, who had a thriftier inclination than her husband; but Mr. Pinkham was not to be let or hindered, and they presently found themselves going up Fifth Avenue in a somewhat battered open landau. The spring sun shone upon them, and the spring breeze fluttered the black ostrich tip on Mrs. Pinkham's durable winter bonnet, and brought the pretty color to her faded cheeks.

"There! this is something like. Such people as we are can't go meechin' round; it ain't expected. Don't it pay for a lot o' hard work?" said Abel; and his wife gave him a pleased look for her only answer. They were both thinking of their gray farm-house on a long western slope, with the afternoon sun full in its face, the old red barn, the pasture, the shaggy woods that stretched far up the higher mountain-side.

"I wish Sarah an' little Abel was here to see us ride by," said Mary Ann Pinkham, presently. "I can't seem to wait to have 'em get that newspaper. I'm so glad we sent it right off before we started this mornin'. If Abel goes to the post-office comin' from school, as he always does, they'll have it to read to-morrow before supper-time."

III

This happy day in two plain lives ended, as might have been expected, with the great Barnum show. Mr. and Mrs. Pinkham found themselves in possession of countless advertising cards and circulars next morning, and these added somewhat to their sense of responsibility. Mrs. Pinkham became afraid that the hotel-keeper would charge them double. "We've got to pay for it some way, an' I don't know but I'm more'n willin'," said the good soul. "I never did have such a splendid time in all my life. Findin' you so respected 'way off here is the best of anything; an' then seein' them dear little babies in their splendid carriages, all along the streets and up to the Central Park! I never shall forget them beautiful little creatur's. And then the houses, an' the hosses, an' the store windows, an' all the rest of it! Well, I

can't make my country pitcher hold no more, an' I want to get home an' think it over, goin' about my house-work."

They were just entering the door of the Ethan Allen Hotel for the last time, when a young man met them and bowed cordially. He was the original reporter of their arrival, but they did not know it, and the impulse was strong within him to formally invite Mr. Pinkham to make an address before the members of the Produce Exchange on the following morning; but he had been a country boy himself, and their look of seriousness and self-consciousness appealed to him unexpectedly. He wondered what effect this great experience would have upon their after-life. The best fun, after all, would be to send marked copies of his paper and Ederton's to all the weekly newspapers in that part of Vermont. He saw before him the evidence of their happy increase of self-respect, and he would make all their neighborhood agree to do them honor. Such is the dominion of the press.

"Who was that young man?—he kind of bowed to you," asked the lady from Wetherford, after the journalist had meekly passed; but Abel Pinkham, Esq., could only tell her that he looked like a young fellow who was sitting in the office the night that they came to the hotel. The reporter did not seem to these distinguished persons to be a young man of any consequence.

Bicycle advertisement, 1895.

St. Clair's Defeat

by Theodore Roosevelt

February 1896

The attitude of the United States and Great Britain, as they faced each other in the Western wilderness at the beginning of the year 1791, was one of scarcely veiled hostility. The British held the lake posts at Detroit, Mackinaw, and Niagara, and more or less actively supported the Indians in their efforts to bar the Americans from the Northwest. Nominally they held the posts because the Americans had themselves left unfulfilled some of the conditions of the treaty of peace; but this was felt not to be the real reason, and the Americans loudly protested that their conduct was due to sheer hatred of the young republic. The explanation was simpler. The British had no far-reaching design to prevent the spread and growth of the English-speaking people on the American continent. They cared nothing, one way or the other, for that spread and growth, and it is unlikely that they wasted a moment's thought on the ultimate future of the race. All that they desired was to preserve the very valuable fur trade of the region round the Great Lakes for their own benefit. They were acting from the motives of self-interest that usually control nations; and it never entered their heads to balance against these immediate interests the future of a nation many of whose members were to them mere foreigners.

The majority of the Americans on their side were exceedingly loath to enter into aggressive war with the Indians, but were reluctantly forced into the contest by the necessity of supporting the backwoodsmen. The frontier was pushed westward not because the leading statesmen of America or the bulk of the American people foresaw the continental greatness of this country or strove for such greatness, but because the bordermen of the West and the adventurous land-speculators of the East were personally interested in acquiring new territory, and because, against their will, the governmental representatives of the nation were finally forced to make the interests of the Westerners their own. The people of the seaboard, the leaders of opinion in the coast towns and old-settled districts, were inclined to look eastward rather than westward. They were interested in the quarrels of the Old World nations; they were immediately concerned in the rights of the fisheries they jealously shared with England, or the trade they sought to secure with Spain. They did not covet the Indian lands. They had never heard of the Rocky Mountains—nobody had as yet; they cared as little for the Missouri as for the Congo, and they thought of the Pacific slope as a savage country, only to be reached by an ocean voyage longer than the voyage to India. They believed that they were entitled, under the treaty, to the country between the Alleghanies and the Great Lakes; but they were quite content to see the Indians remain in actual occupancy, and they had no desire to spend men and money in driving them out. Yet they were even less disposed to proceed to extremities against their own people, who in very fact were driving out the Indians; and this was the only alternative, for in the end they had to side with one or the other set of combatants.

The governmental authorities of the newly created republic shared these feelings. They felt no hunger for the Indian lands; they felt no desire to stretch their boundaries, and thereby add to their already heavy burdens and responsibilities. They wished to do strict justice to the Indians; the treaties they held with them were carried on with scrupulous fairness, and were honorably lived up to by the United States officials. They strove to keep peace, and made many efforts to persuade the frontiersmen to observe the Indian boundary lines, and not to intrude on the territory in dispute; and they were quite unable to foresee the rapidity of the nation's westward growth. Like the people of the Eastern seaboard, the men high in governmental authority were apt to look upon the frontiersmen with feelings dangerously kin to dislike and suspicion. Nor were these feelings wholly unjustifiable. The men who settle in a new country and begin subduing the wilderness plunge back into the very conditions from which the race has raised itself by the slow toil of ages. The conditions cannot but tell upon them. Inevitably, and for more than one lifetime—perhaps for several generations—they tend to retrograde, instead of advancing. [...]

Yet it was these Western frontiersmen who were the real and vital factors in the solution of the problems which so annoyed the British monarchy and the American republic. They eagerly craved the Indian lands; they would not be denied entrance to the thinly peopled territory, wherein they intended to make homes for themselves and their children. Rough, masterful, lawless, they were neither daunted by the prowess of the red warriors whose wrath they braved, nor awed by the displeasure of the government whose solemn engagements they violated. The enormous extent of the frontier dividing the white settler from the savage, and the tangled inaccessibility of the country in which it everywhere lay, rendered it as difficult for the national authorities to control the frontiersmen as it was to chastise the Indians.

If the separation of interests between the thickly settled East and the sparsely settled West had been complete, it may be that the East would have refused outright to support the West, in which case the advance would have been very slow and halting. But the separation was not complete. The frontiersmen were numerically important in some of the States, as in Virginia, Georgia, and even Pennsylvania and New York, and under a democratic system of government this meant that these States were more or less responsive to their demands. It was greatly to the interest of the frontiersmen that their demands should be gratified, while other citizens had no very concrete concern in the matter one way or the other. In addition to this, and even more important, was the fact that there were large classes of the population everywhere who felt much sense of identity with the frontiersmen, and sympathized with them. The fathers or grandfathers of these people had themselves been frontiersmen, and they were still under the influences of the traditions which told of a constant march westward through the vast forests, and a no less constant warfare with a hostile savagery. Moreover, in many of the communities there were people whose kinsmen or friends had gone to the border, and the welfare of these adventurers was a matter of more or less interest to those who had staid behind. Finally, and most important of all, though the nation might be lukewarm originally, and might wish to prevent the settlers from trespassing on the Indian lands or entering into an Indian war, yet when the war had become of real moment, and when victory was doubtful, the national power was sure to be used in favor of the hard-pressed pioneers. At first the authorities at the national capital would blame the whites, and try to temporize and make new treaties, or even threaten to drive back the settlers with a strong hand; but when the ravages of the Indians had become serious, when the bloody details were sent to homes in every part of the Union by letter after letter from the border, when the little newspapers began to publish accounts of the worst atrocities, when the county lieutenants of the frontier counties were clamoring for help, when the Congressmen from the frontier districts were appealing to Congress, and the Governors of the States whose frontiers were molested were appealing to the President—then the feeling of race and national kinship rose, and the government no longer hesitated to support in every way the hard-pressed wilderness vanguard of the American people.

The situation had reached this point by the year 1791. For seven years the Federal authorities had been vainly endeavoring to make some final settlement of the question by entering into treaties with the Northwestern and Southwestern tribes. In the earlier treaties the delegates from the Continental Congress asserted that the United States were invested with the fee of all the land claimed by the Indians. In the later treaties the Indian proprietorship of the lands was conceded. This concession at the time seemed important to the whites; but the Indians probably never understood that there had been any change of attitude; nor did it make any practical difference, for, whatever the theory might be, the lands had eventually to be won, partly by whipping the savages in fight, partly by making it better worth their while to remain at peace than to go to war.

The Federal officials under whose authority these treaties were made had no idea of the complexity of the problem. In 1789 the Secretary of War, the New-Englander Knox, solemnly reported to the President that if the treaties were only observed and the Indians conciliated, they would become attached to the United States, and the expense of managing them for the next half-century would be only some fifteen thousand dollars a year. He probably represented not unfairly the ordinary Eastern view of the matter. He had not the slightest conception of the rate at which the settlements were increasing. Though he expected that tracts of Indian territory would from time to time be acquired, he made no allowance for a growth so rapid that within the half-century a dozen populous States were to stand within the Indian-owned wilderness of his day. He utterly failed to grasp the central feature of the situation, which was that the settlers needed the land, and were bound to have it within a few years, and that the Indians would not give it up, under no matter what treaty, without an appeal to arms. [...]

In the Northwest matters culminated sooner than in the Southwest. The Georgians and the settlers along the Tennessee and Cumberland were harassed rather than seriously menaced by the Creek war parties; but in the North the more dangerous Indians of the Miami, the Wabash, and the lakes gathered in bodies so large as fairly to deserve the name of armies. Moreover, the pressure of the white advance was far heavier in the North. The pioneers who settled in the Ohio basin were many times as numerous as those who settled on the lands west of the Oconee or north of the Cumberland, and were fed from States much more populous. The advance was stronger, the resistance more desperate; naturally the open break occurred where the strain was most intense.

There was fierce border warfare in the South. In the North there were regular campaigns, and pitched battles were fought between Federal armies as large as those commanded by Washington at Trenton or Greene at Eutaw Springs, and bodies of Indian warriors more numerous than had ever yet appeared on any single field.

The newly created government of the United States was very reluctant to make formal war on the Northwestern Indians. Not only were President Washington and the national Congress honorably desirous of peace, but they were hampered for funds, and dreaded any extra expense. Nevertheless, they were forced into war. Throughout the years 1789 and 1790 an increasing volume of appeals for help came from the frontier countries. The Governor of the Northwestern Territory, the Brigadier-General of the troops on the Ohio, the members of the Kentucky Convention, all the county lieutenants of Kentucky, the lieutenants of the frontier counties of Virginia proper, the representatives from the counties, the field-officers of the different districts, the General Assembly of Virginia—all sent bitter complaints and long catalogues of injuries to the President, the Secretary of War, and the two Houses of Congress. [...] With heavy hearts the national authorities prepared for war.

Their decision was justified by the redoubled fury of the Indian raids during the early part of 1791. [...] Until this year the war was not general. One of the most bewildering

problems to be solved by the Federal officers on the Ohio was to find out which tribes were friendly and which hostile. Many of the inveterate enemies of the Americans were as forward in professions of friendship as the peaceful Indians, and were just as apt to be found at the treaties, or lounging about the settlements; and this widespread treachery and deceit made the task of the army officers puzzling to a degree. As for the frontiersmen, who had no means whatever of telling a hostile from a friendly tribe, they followed their usual custom, and lumped all the Indians, good and bad, together, for which they could hardly be blamed. [...] A long course of aggressions and retaliations resulted, by the year 1791, in all the Northwestern Indians going on the war-path. The hostile tribes had murdered and plundered the frontiersmen; the vengeance of the latter, as often as not, had fallen on friendly tribes; and these justly angered friendly tribes usually signalized their taking the red hatchet by some act of treacherous hostility directed against settlers who had not molested them.

In the late winter of 1791 the hitherto friendly Delawares, who hunted or traded along the western frontiers of Pennsylvania and Virginia proper, took this manner of showing that they had joined the open foes of the Americans. A big band of warriors spread up and down the Alleghany for about forty miles, and on the 9th of February attacked all the outlying settlements. The Indians who delivered this attack had long been on intimate terms with the Alleghany settlers, who were accustomed to see them in and about their houses; and as the savages acted with seeming friendship to the last moment, they were able to take the settlers completely unawares, so that no effective resistance was made. Some settlers were killed and some captured. [...]

The chief interest of the British was to preserve the fur trade for their merchants, and it was mainly for this reason that they clung so tenaciously to the lake posts. For their purposes it was essential that the Indians should remain lords of the soil. They preferred to see the savages at peace with the Americans, provided that in this way they could keep their lands; but, whether through peace or war, they wished the lands to remain Indian, and the Americans to be barred from them. While they did not at the moment advise war, their advice to make peace was so faintly uttered and so hedged round with conditions as to be of no weight, and they furnished the Indians not only with provisions, but with munitions of war. [...]

Peace could only be won by the unsheathed sword. Even the national government was reluctantly driven to this view. As all the Northwestern tribes were banded in open war, it was useless to let the conflict remain a succession of raids and counter-raids. Only a severe stroke delivered by a formidable army could cow the tribes. It was hopeless to try to deliver such a crippling blow with militia alone, and it was very difficult for the infant government to find enough money or men to equip an army composed exclusively of regulars. Accordingly preparations were made for a campaign with a mixed force of regulars, special levies, and militia; and St. Clair, already Governor of the Northwestern Territory, was put in command of the army as Major-General.

Before the army was ready the Federal government was obliged to take other measures for the defence of the border. Small bodies of rangers were raised from among the frontier militia, being paid at the usual rate for soldiers in the army—a net sum of about two dollars a month while in service. In addition, on the repeated and urgent request of the frontiersmen, a few of the most active hunters and best woodsmen, men like Brady, were enlisted as scouts, being paid six or eight times the ordinary rate. These men, because of their skill in woodcraft and their thorough knowledge of Indian fighting, were beyond comparison more valuable than ordinary militia or regulars, and were prized very highly by the frontiersmen. [...]

St. Clair himself was broken in health; he was a sick, weak, elderly man, high-minded, and zealous to do his duty, but totally unfit for the terrible responsibilities of such an expedition against such foes. The troops were of wretched stuff. There were two small regiments of regular infantry, the rest of the army being composed of six months levies and of militia ordered out for this particular campaign. The pay was contemptible. Each private was given three dollars a month, from which ninety cents were deducted, leaving a net payment of two dollars and ten cents a month. Sergeants netted three dollars and sixty cents, while the lieutenants received twenty-two, the captains thirty, and the colonels sixty dollars. The mean parsimony of the nation in paying such low wages to men about to be sent on duties at once very arduous and very dangerous met its fit and natural reward. Men of good bodily powers and in the prime of life, and especially men able to do the rough work of frontier farmers, could not be hired to fight Indians in unknown forests for two dollars a month. Most of the recruits were from the streets and prisons of the seaboard cities. They were hurried into a campaign against peculiarly formidable foes before they had acquired the rudiments of a soldier's training, and of course they never even understood what woodcraft meant. The officers were men of courage, as in the end most of them showed by dying bravely on the field of battle, but they were utterly untrained themselves, and had no time in which to train their men. Under such conditions it did not need keen vision to foretell disaster. [...]

As the raw troops straggled to Pittsburg they were shipped down the Ohio to Fort Washington; and St. Clair made the headquarters of his army at a new fort some twenty-five miles northward, which he christened Fort Hamilton. During September the army slowly assembled— two small regiments of regulars, two of six months levies, a number of Kentucky militia, a few cavalry, and a couple of small batteries of light guns. After wearisome delays, due mainly to the utter inefficiency of the quartermaster and contractor, the start for the Indian towns was made on October the 4th.

The army trudged slowly through the deep woods and across the wet prairies, cutting out its own road, and making but five or six miles a day. On October 13th a halt was made to build another little fort, christened in honor of Jefferson. There were further delays, caused by the wretched management of the commisariat department, and the march was not resumed until the 24th, the numerous sick being left in Fort Jefferson. Then the army once more stumbled northward through the wilderness. The regulars, though mostly raw recruits, had been reduced to some kind of discipline, but the six months levies were almost worse than the militia. Owing to the long delays, and to the fact that they had been enlisted at various times, their terms of service were expiring day by day, and they wished to go home, and tried to, while the militia deserted in squads and bands. Those that remained were very disorderly. Two who attempted to desert were hanged, and another, who shot a comrade, was hanged also; but even this severity in punishment failed to stop the demoralization.

With such soldiers there would have been grave risk of disaster under any commander, but St. Clair's leadership made the risk a certainty. There was Indian sign, old and new, all through the woods, and the scouts and stragglers occasionally interchanged shots with small parties of braves, and now and then lost a man killed or captured. It was therefore certain that the savages knew every movement of the army, which, as it slowly neared the Miami towns, was putting itself within easy striking range of the most formidable Indian confederacy in the Northwest. The density of the forest was such that only the utmost watchfulness could prevent the foe from approaching within arm's-length unperceived. [. . .] But St. Clair was broken down by the worry and by continued sickness; time and again it was doubtful whether he could do so much as stay with the army. The second in command, Major-General Richard Butler, was also sick most of the time, and, like St. Clair, he possessed none of the qualities of leadership save courage. The whole burden fell on the Adjutant-General, Colonel Winthrop Sargent, an old Revolutionary officer; without him the expedition would probably have failed in ignominy even before the Indians were reached; and he showed not only cool courage, but ability of a good order; yet in the actual arrangements for battle he was of course unable to remedy the blunders of his superiors.

St. Clair should have covered his front and flanks for miles around with scouting parties; but he rarely sent any out, and, thanks to letting the management of those that did go devolve on his subordinates, and to not having their reports made to him in person, he derived no benefit from what they saw. He had twenty Chickasaws with him, but he sent these off on an extended trip, lost touch of them entirely, and never saw them again until after the battle. He did not seem to realize that he was himself in danger of attack. When some fifty miles or so from the Miami towns, on the last day of October, sixty of the militia deserted; and he actually sent back after them one of his two regular regiments, thus weakening by one-half the only trustworthy portion of his force.

On November 3d the doomed army, now reduced to a total of about fourteen hundred men, camped on the eastern fork of the Wabash, high up, where it was but twenty yards wide. There was snow on the ground, and the little pools were skimmed with ice. The camp was on a narrow rise of ground, where the troops were cramped together, the artillery and most of the horse in the middle. On both flanks and along most of the rear the ground was low and wet. All about the wintry woods lay in frozen silence. In front the militia were thrown across the creek, and nearly a quarter of a mile beyond the rest of the troops. Parties of Indians were seen during the afternoon, and they skulked around the lines at night, so that the sentinels frequently fired at them;

yet neither St. Clair nor Butler took any adequate measures to ward off the impending blow. It is improbable that, as things actually were at this time, they could have won a victory over their terrible foes, but they might have avoided overwhelming disaster.

On November 4th the men were under arms, as usual, by dawn, St. Clair intending to throw up intrenchments and then make a forced march in light order against the Indian towns. But he was forestalled. Soon after sunrise, just as the men were dismissed from parade, a sudden assault was made upon the militia, who lay unprotected beyond the creek. The unexpectedness and fury of the onset, the heavy firing, and the wild whoops and yells of the throngs of painted savages threw the militia into disorder. After a few moments' resistance they broke and fled in wild panic to the camp of the regulars, among whom they drove in a frightened herd, spreading dismay and confusion.

The drums beat, and the troops sprang to arms as soon as they heard the heavy firing at the front, and their volleys for a moment checked the onrush of the plumed woodland warriors. But the check availed nothing. The braves filed off to one side and the other, completely surrounded the camp, killed or drove in the guards and pickets, and then advanced close to the main lines.

A furious battle followed. After the first onset the Indians fought in silence, no sound coming from them save the incessant rattle of their fire as they crept from log to log, from tree to tree, ever closer and closer. The soldiers stood in close order in the open; their musketry and artillery fire made a tremendous noise, but did little damage to a foe they could hardly see. Now and then, through the hanging smoke, terrible figures flitted, painted black and red, the feathers of hawk and eagle braided in their long scalp locks; but, save for these glimpses, the soldiers knew the presence of their sombre enemy only from the fearful rapidity with which their comrades fell dead and wounded in the ranks. They never even knew the numbers or leaders of the Indians. At the time it was supposed that they outnumbered the whites; but it is probable that the reverse was the case, and it may even be that they were not more than half as numerous. It is said that the chief who led them, both in council and battle, was Little Turtle the Miami. At any rate there were present all the chiefs and picked warriors of the Delawares, Shawnees, Wyandots, and Miamies, and all the most reckless and adventurous young braves from among the Iroquois and the Indians of the upper lakes, as well as many of the ferocious whites and half-breeds who dwelt in the Indian villages.

The Indians fought with the utmost boldness and ferocity, and with the utmost skill and caution. Under cover of the smoke of the heavy but harmless fire from the army they came up so close that they shot the troops down as hunters slaughter a herd of standing buffalo. Watching their chance, they charged again and again with the tomahawk, gliding in to close quarters, while their bewildered foes were still blindly firing into the smoke-shrouded woods. The men saw no enemy as they stood in the ranks to load and shoot; in a moment, without warning, dark faces frowned through the haze, the war-axes gleamed, and on the frozen ground the weapons clattered as the soldiers fell. As the comrades of the fallen sprang forward to avenge them, the lithe warriors vanished as rapidly as they had appeared, and once more the soldiers saw before them only the dim forests and the shifting smoke wreaths, with vague half-glimpses of the hidden foe, while the steady singing of the Indian bullets never ceased, and on every hand the bravest and steadiest fell, one by one. [...]

Instead of being awed by the bellowing artillery, the Indians made the gunner a special object of attack. Man after man was picked off, until every officer was killed but one, who was wounded, and most of the privates also were slain or disabled. The artillery was thus almost silenced; and the Indians, emboldened by success, swarmed forward and seized the guns, while at the same time a part of the left wing of the army began to shrink back. But the Indians were now on comparatively open ground, where the regulars could see them and get at them, and under St. Clair's own leadership the troops rushed fiercely at the savages with fixed bayonets, and drove them back to cover. By this time the confusion and disorder were great, while from every hollow and grass-patch, from behind every stump and tree and fallen log, the Indians continued their fire. Again and again the officers led forward the troops in bayonet charges, and at first the men followed them with a will. Each charge seemed for a moment to be successful, the Indians rising in swarms and running in headlong flight from the bayonets. [...]

The charging troops could accomplish nothing permanent. The men were too clumsy and ill trained in forest warfare to overtake their fleet, half-naked antagonists. The latter never received the shock; but though they fled, they were nothing daunted, for they turned the instant the battalion did, and followed firing. They skipped out of reach of

The men saw no enemy as they stood in the ranks.

the bayonets and came back as they pleased, and they were only visible when raised by a charge. [...]

As the officers fell, the soldiers, who at first stood up bravely enough, gradually grew disheartened. No words can paint the hopelessness and horror of such a struggle as that in which they were engaged. They were hemmed in by foes who showed no mercy, and whose blows they could in no way return. If they charged they could not overtake the Indians, and the instant the charge stopped the Indians came back. If they stood, they were shot down by an unseen enemy; and there was no stronghold, no refuge, to which to flee. The Indian attack was relentless, and could neither be avoided, parried, nor met by counter-assault. For two hours or so the troops kept up a slowly lessening resistance, but by degrees their hearts failed. [...]

There was but one thing to do. If possible the remnant of the army must be saved, and it could only be saved by instant flight, even at the cost of abandoning the wounded. The broad road by which the army had advanced was the only line of retreat. The artillery had already been spiked and abandoned. Most of the horses had been killed, but a few were still left, and on one of these St. Clair mounted. He gathered together those fragments of the different battalions which contained the few men who still kept heart and head, and ordered them to charge and regain the road from which the savages had cut them off. Repeated orders were necessary before some of the men could be roused from their stupor sufficiently to follow the charging party, and they were only induced to move when told that it was to retreat.

Colonel Darke and a few officers placed themselves at the head of the column, the coolest and boldest men drew up behind them, and they fell on the Indians with such fury as to force them back well beyond the road. [...] The Indians were surprised by the vigor of the charge, and puzzled as to its object; they opened out on both sides, and half the men had gone through before they fired more than a chance shot or two. They then fell on the rear and began a hot pursuit. [...]

There never was a wilder rout. As soon as the men began to run, and realized that in flight there lay some hope of safety, they broke into a stampede, which became uncontrollable. Horses, soldiers, and the few camp-followers and the women who had accompanied the army were all mixed together. Neither command nor example had the slightest weight; the men were abandoned to the terrible selfishness of utter fear. They threw away their weapons as they ran. They thought of nothing but escape, and fled in a huddle, the stronger and the few who had horses trampling their way to the front through the old, the weak, and the wounded, while behind them raged the Indian tomahawk. Fortunately the attraction of plundering the camp was so overpowering that the savages only followed the army about four miles; otherwise hardly a man would have escaped. [...]

Before reaching Fort Jefferson the wretched army encountered the regular regiment which had been so unfortunately detached a couple of days before the battle. The most severely wounded were left in the fort, and then the flight was renewed, until the disorganized and half-armed rabble reached Fort Washington and the mean log huts of Cincinnati. Six hundred and thirty men had been killed, and over two hundred and eighty wounded; less than five hundred, only about a third of the whole number engaged in the battle, remained unhurt. But one or two were taken prisoners, for the Indians butchered everybody, wounded or unwounded, who fell into their hands. There is no record of the torture of any of the captives, but there was one singular instance of cannibalism. The savage Chippewas from the far-off North devoured one of the slain soldiers, probably in a spirit of ferocious bravado; the other tribes expressed horror at the deed. The Indians were rich with the spoil. They got horses, tents, guns, axes, powder, clothing, and blankets—in short, everything their hearts prized. Their loss was comparatively slight; it may not have been one-twentieth that of the whites. They did not at the moment follow up their victory, each band going off with its own share of the booty. But the triumph was so overwhelming and the reward so great that the war spirit received a great impetus in all the tribes. The bands of warriors that marched against the frontier were more numerous, more formidable, and bolder than ever.

In the following January Wilkinson with a hundred and fifty mounted volunteers marched to the battle-field to bury the slain. The weather was bitterly cold; snow lay deep on the ground, and some of the volunteers were frost-bitten. Four miles from the scene of the battle, where the pursuit had ended, they began to find the bodies on the road, and close alongside in the woods, whither some of the hunted creatures had turned at the last to snatch one more moment of life. Many had been dragged from under the snow and devoured by wolves. The others lay where they had fallen, showing as mounds through the smooth white mantle that covered them. On the battle-field itself the slain lay thick, scalped, and stripped of all their clothing which the conquerors deemed worth taking. The bodies, blackened by frost and exposure, could not be identified, and they were buried in a shallow trench in the frozen ground. The volunteers then marched home.

When the remnant of the defeated army reached the banks of the Ohio. St. Clair sent his aide, Denny, to carry the news to Philadelphia, at that time the national capital. The river was swollen, there were incessant snow-storms, and ice formed heavily, so that it took twenty days of toil and cold before Denny reached Wheeling and got horses. For ten days

On the battlefield itself the slain lay thick.

more he rode over the bad winter roads, reaching Philadelphia with the evil tidings on the evening of December 19th. It was thus six weeks after the defeat of the army before the news was brought to the anxious Federal authorities.

The young officer called first on the Secretary of War; but as soon as the Secretary realized the importance of the information he had it conveyed to the President. Washington was at dinner, with some guests, and was called from the table to listen to the tidings of ill fortune. He returned with unmoved face, and at the dinner and at the reception which followed he behaved with his usual stately courtesy to those whom he was entertaining, not so much as hinting at what he had heard. But when the last guest had gone, his pent-up wrath broke forth in one of those fits of volcanic fury which sometimes shattered his iron outward calm. Walking up and down the room, he burst out in wild regret for the rout and

disaster, and bitter invective against St. Clair, reciting how in that very room he had wished the unfortunate commander success and honor, and had bidden him above all things beware of a surprise. "He went off with that last solemn warning thrown into his ears," spoke Washington, as he strode to and fro, "and yet to suffer that army to be cut to pieces, hacked, butchered, tomahawked, by a surprise, the very thing I guarded him against! Oh God! Oh God! he's worse than a murderer! How can he answer it to his country?" Then, calming himself by a mighty effort, "General St. Clair shall have justice . . . he shall have full justice." And St. Clair did receive full justice, and mercy too, from both Washington and Congress. For the sake of his courage and honorable character they held him guiltless of the disaster, for which his lack of capacity as a general was so largely accountable.

WITH THE FIFTH CORPS

TEXT AND ILLUSTRATIONS BY FREDERIC REMINGTON

NOVEMBER 1898

I approach this subject of the Santiago campaign with awe, since the ablest correspondents in the country were all there, and they wore out lead-pencils most industriously. I know I cannot add to the facts, but I remember my own emotions, which were numerous, interesting, and, on the whole, not pleasant. I am as yet unable to decide whether sleeping in a mud-puddle, the confinement of a troop-ship, or being shot at is the worst. They are all irritating, and when done on an empty stomach, with the object of improving one's mind, they are extravagantly expensive. However, they satisfied a life of longing to see men do the greatest thing which men are called on to do.

The creation of things by men in time of peace is of every consequence, but it does not bring forth the tumultuous energy which accompanies the destruction of things by men in war. He who has not seen war only half comprehends the possibilities of his race. Having thought of this thing before, I got a correspondent's pass, and ensconced myself with General Shafter's army at Tampa. [...]

So the transports gathered to Port Tampa, and the troops got on board, and the correspondents sallied down to their quarters, and then came a wait. A Spanish war-ship had loomed across the night of some watch-on-deck down off the Cuban coast. Telegrams flew from Washington to "stop where you are." The mules and the correspondents were unloaded, and the whole enterprise waited.

Here I might mention a series of events which were amusing. The exigencies of the service left many young officers behind, and these all wanted, very naturally, to go to Cuba and get properly shot, as all good soldiers should. They used their influence with the general officers in command; they begged, they implored, and they explained deviously and ingeniously why the expedition needed their particular services to insure success. The old generals, who appreciated the proper spirit which underlay this enthusiasm, smiled grimly as they turned "the young scamps" down.

I used to laugh to myself when I overheard these interviews, for one could think of nothing so much as the schoolboy days, when he used to beg off going to school for all sorts of reasons but the real one, which was a ball-game or a little shooting-trip.

Presently the officials got the Spanish war-ship off their nerves, and the transports sailed. Now it is so arranged in the world that I hate a ship in a compound, triple-expansion, forced-draught way. Barring the disgrace, give me "ten days on the island." Do anything to me, but do not have me entered on the list of a ship. It does not matter if I am to be the lordly proprietor of the finest yacht afloat, make me a feather in a sick chicken's tail on shore, and I will thank you. So it came about that I did an unusual amount of real suffering in consequence of living on the *Segurança* during the long voyage to Cuba. I used to sit out on the after-deck and wonder why, at my time of life, I could not so arrange my affairs that I could keep off ships. I used to consider seriously if it would not be a good thing to jump overboard and let the leopard-sharks eat me, and have done with a miserable existence which I did not seem to be able to control.

When the first landing was made, General Shafter kept all the correspondents and the foreign military attachés in his closed fist, and we all hated him mightily. We shall probably forgive him, but it will take some time. He did allow us to go ashore and see the famous interview which he and Admiral Sampson held with Garcia, and for the first time to behold the long lines of ragged Cuban patriots, and I was convinced that it was no mean or common impulse which kept up the determination of these ragged, hungry souls.

Then on the morning of the landing at Daiquiri the soldiers put on their blanket rolls, the navy boats and launches lay by the transports, and the light ships of Sampson's fleet ran slowly into the little bay and "turned everything loose" on the quiet, palm-thatched village. A few fires were burning in the town, but otherwise it was quiet. After severely pounding the coast, the launches towed in the long lines of boats deep laden with soldiery, and the correspondents and foreigners saw them go into the overhanging smoke. We held our breath. We expected a most desperate fight for the landing. After a time the smoke rolled away, and our people were on the beach, and not long after some men climbed the steep hill on which stood a block-house, and we saw presently the stars and stripes break from the flag-staff. "They are Chinamen!" said a distinguished foreign soldier; and he went to the other side of the boat, and sat heavily down to his reading of our artillery drill regulations.

We watched the horses and mules being thrown overboard, we saw the last soldiers going ashore, and we bothered General Shafter's aid, the gallant Miley, until he put us all on shore in order to abate the awful nuisance of our presence.

No one had any transportation in the campaign, not even colonels of regiments, except their good strong backs. It was for every man to personally carry all his own hotel accommodations; so we correspondents laid out our possessions on the deck, and for the third time sorted out what little we could take. I weighed a silver pocket-flask for some time, undecided as to the possibility of carriage. It is now in the woods of Cuba, or in the ragged pack of some Cuban soldier. We had finally three days of crackers, coffee, and pork in our haversacks, our canteens, rubber ponchos, cameras, and six-shooter—or practically what a soldier has.

I moved out with the Sixth Cavalry a mile or so, and as it was late afternoon, we were ordered to bivouac. I sat on a hill, and down in the road below saw the long lines of troops pressing up the valley toward Siboney. When our troops got on the sand beach, each old soldier adjusted his roll, shouldered his rifle, and started for Santiago, apparently by individual intuition.

The troops started, and kept marching just as fast as they could. They ran the Spaniards out of Siboney, and the cavalry brigade regularly marched down their retreating columns at Las Guasimas, fought them up a defile, out-flanked, and sent them flying into Santiago. I think our army would never have stopped until it cracked into the

The biggest thing in Shafter's army was my pack.

doomed city in column formation, if Shafter had not discovered this unlooked-for enterprise, and sent his personal aide on a fast horse with positive orders to halt until the "cracker-line" could be fixed up behind them.

In the morning I sat on the hill, and still along the road swung the hard-marching columns. The scales dropped from my eyes. I could feel the impulse, and still the Sixth was held by orders. I put on my "little hotel equipment," bade my friends good-by, and "hit the road." The sides of it were blue with cast-off uniforms. Coats and overcoats were strewn about, while the gray blankets lay in the camps just where the soldiers had gotten up from them after the night's rest. This I knew would happen. Men will not carry what they can get along without, unless they are made to; and it is a bad thing to "make" American soldiers, because they know what is good for them better than any one who sits in a roller-chair. In the tropics mid-day marching under heavy kits kills more men than damp sleeping at night. I used to think the biggest thing in Shafter's army was my pack.

It was all so strange, this lonely tropic forest, and so hot. I fell in with a little bunch of headquarters cavalry orderlies, some with headquarters horses, and one with a mule dragging two wheels, which I cannot call a cart, on which General Young's stuff was tied. We met Cubans loitering along, their ponies loaded with abandoned soldier-clothes. Staff-officers on horseback came back and said that there had been a fight on beyond, and that Colonel Wood was killed and young Fish shot dead—that the Rough Riders were all done to pieces. There would be more fighting, and we pushed forward, sweating under the stifling heat of the jungle-choked road. We stopped and cracked cocoanuts to drink the milk. Once, in a sort of savanna, my companions halted and threw cartridges into their carbines. I saw two or three Spanish soldiers on ahead in some hills and brush. We pressed on; but as the Spanish soldiers did not seem to be concerned as to our presence, I allowed they were probably Cubans who had taken clothes from dead Spanish soldiers, and so it turned out. The Cubans seem to know each other by scent, but it bothered the Northern men to make a distinction between Spanish and Cuban, even when shown Spanish prisoners in order that they might recognize their enemy by sight. If a simple Cuban who stole Spanish soldier clothes could only know how nervous it made the trigger fingers of our regulars, he would have died of fright. He created the same feeling that a bear would, and the impulse to "pull up and let go" was so instinctive and sudden with our men that I marvel more mistakes were not made.

At night I lay up beside the road outside of Siboney, and cooked my supper by a soldier fire, and lay down under a mango-tree on my rubber, with my haversack for a pillow. I could hear the shuffling of the marching troops, and see by the light of the fire near the road the white blanket rolls glint past its flame—tired, sweaty men, mysterious and silent too, but for the clank of tin cups and the monotonous shuffle of feet.

In the early morning the field near me was covered with the cook-fires of infantry, which had come in during the night. Presently a battery came dragging up, and was greeted with wild cheers from the infantry, who crowded up to the road. It was a great tribute to the guns; for here in the face of war the various arms realized their interdependence. It is a solace for cavalry to know that there is some good steady infantry in their rear, and it is a vast comfort for infantry to feel that their front and flanks are covered, and both of them like to have the shrapnel travelling their way when they "go in."

At Siboney I saw the first wounded Rough Riders, and heard how they had behaved. From this time people began to know who this army doctor was, this Colonel Wood. Soldiers and residents in the Southwest had known him ten years back. They knew Leonard Wood was a soldier, skin, bones, and brain, who travelled under the disguise of a doctor, and now they know more than this.

Then I met a fellow-correspondent, Mr. John Fox, and we communed deeply. We had not seen this fight of the cavalry brigade, and this was because we were not at the front. We would not let it happen again. We slung our packs and most industriously plodded up the Via del Rey until we got to within hailing distance of the picket posts, and he said: "Now, Frederic, we will stay here. They will pull off no more fights of which we are not a party of the first part." And stay we did. If General Lawton moved ahead, we went up and cultivated Lawton; but if General Chaffee got ahead, we were his friends, and gathered at his mess fire. To be popular with us it was necessary for a general to have command of the advance.

But what satisfying soldiers Lawton and Chaffee are! Both seasoned, professional military types. Lawton, big and long, forceful, and with iron determination. Chaffee, who never dismounts but for a little sleep during the darkest hours of the night, and whose head might have been presented to him by one of William's Norman barons. Such a head! We used to sit around and study that head. It does not belong to the period; it is remote, when the race was young and strong; and it has "warrior" sculptured in every line. It may seem trivial to you, but I must have people "look their part." That so many do not in this age is probably because men are so complicated; but "war is a primitive art," and that is the one objection I had to von Moltke, with his simple student face. He might have been anything. Chaffee is a soldier.

The troops came pouring up the road, reeking under their packs, dusty, and with their eyes on the ground. Their faces were deeply lined, their beards stubby, but their minds were set on "the front"—"on Santiago." There was a suggestion of remorseless striving in their dogged stepping along, and it came to me that to turn them around would require some enterprise. I thought at the time that the Spanish commander would do well to assume the offensive, and marching down our flank, pierce the centre of the straggling column; but I have since changed my mind, because of the superior fighting ability which our men showed. It must be carefully remembered that, with the exception of three regiments of Shafter's army, and even these were "picked volunteers," the whole command was our regular army—trained men, physically superior to any in the world, as any one will know who understands the requirements of our enlistment as against that of conscript troops; and they were expecting attack, and praying devoutly for it. Besides, at Las Guasimas we got the *moral* on the Spanish.

Then came the "cracker problem." The gallant Cabanais pushed his mules day and night. I thought they would go to pieces under the strain, and I think every "packer" who worked on the Santiago line will never forget it. Too much credit cannot be given them. The command was sent into the field without its proper ratio of pack-mules, and I hope the blame of that will come home to some one some day. That was the *direct* and *only* cause of all the privation and delay which became so notable in Shafter's operations. I cannot imagine a man who would recommend wagons for a tropical country during the rainy season. Such a one should not be censured or reprimanded; he should be spanked with a slipper.

So while the engineers built bridges, and the troops made roads behind them, and until we got "three days' crackers ahead" for the whole command, things stopped. The men were on half-rations, were out of tobacco, and it rained, rained, rained. We were very miserable.

Mr. John Fox and I had no cover to keep the rain out, and our determination to stay up in front hindered us from making friends with any one who had. Even the private soldiers had their dog-tents, but we had nothing except our two rubber ponchos. At evening, after we had "bummed" some crackers and coffee from some good-natured officer, we repaired to our neck of woods, and stood gazing at our mushy beds. It was good, soft, soggy mud, and on it, or rather in it, we laid one poncho, and over that we spread the other.

"Say, Frederic, that means my death; I am subject to malaria."

"Exactly so, John. This cold of mine will end in congestion of the lungs, or possibly bronchial consumption. Can you suggest any remedy?"

"The fare to New York," said John, as we turned into our wallow.

At last I had the good fortune to buy a horse from an invalided officer. It seemed great fortune, but it had its drawback. I was ostracized by my fellow-correspondents.

All this time the reconnaissance of the works of Santiago and the outlying post of Caney was in progress. It was rumored that the forward movement would come, and being awakened by the bustle, I got up in the dark, and went gliding around until I managed to steal a good feed of oats for my horse. This is an important truth as showing the demoralization of war. In the pale light I saw a staff-officer who was going to Caney, and I followed him. We overtook others, and finally came to a hill overlooking the ground which had been fought over so hard during the day. Capron's battery was laying its guns, and back of the battery were staff-officers and correspondents eagerly scanning the country with field-glasses. In rear of these stood the hardy First Infantry, picturesquely eager and dirty, while behind the hill were the battery horses, out of harm's way.

The battery opened and knocked holes in the stone fort, but the fire did not appear to depress the rifle-pits. Infantry in the jungle below us fired, and were briskly answered from the trenches.

I had lost my canteen and wanted a drink of water, so I slowly rode back to a creek. I was thinking, when along

came another correspondent. We discussed things, and thought Caney would easily fall before Lawton's advance, but we had noticed a big movement of our troops toward Santiago, and we decided that we would return to the main road and see which promised best. Sure enough, the road was jammed with troops, and up the hill of El Poso went the horses of Grimes's battery under whip and spur. Around El Poso ranch stood Cubans, and along the road the Rough Riders—Roosevelt's now, for Wood was a brigadier.

The battery took position, and behind it gathered the foreigners, naval and military, with staff-officers and correspondents. It was a picture such as may be seen at a manoeuvre. Grimes fired a few shells toward Santiago, and directly came a shrill screaming shrapnel from the Spanish lines. It burst over the Rough Riders, and the manoeuvre picture on the hill underwent a lively change. It was thoroughly evident that the Spaniards had the range of everything in the country. They had studied it out. For myself, I fled, dragging my horse up the hill, out of range of Grimes's inviting guns. Some as gallant soldiers and some as daring correspondents as it is my pleasure to know did their legs proud there. The tall form of Major John Jacob Astor moved in my front in jack-rabbit bounds. Prussian, English, and Japanese correspondents, artists, all the news, and much high-class art and literature, were flushed, and went straddling up the hill before the first barrel of the Dons. Directly came the warning scream of No. 2, and we dropped and hugged the ground like star-fish. Bang! right over us it exploded. I was dividing a small hollow with a distinguished colonel of the staff.

"Is this thing allowed, Colonel?"

"Oh, yes, indeed!" he said. "I don't think we could stop those shrapnel."

And the next shell went into the battery, killing and doing damage. Following shells were going into the helpless troops down in the road, and Grimes withdrew his battery for this cause. He had been premature. All this time no one's glass could locate the fire of the Spanish guns, and we could see Capron's smoke miles away on our right. Smoky powder belongs with arbalists and stone axes and United States ordnance officers, which things all belong in museums with other dusty rust.

Then I got far up on the hill, walking over the prostrate bodies of my old friends the Tenth Cavalry, who were hugging the hot ground to get away from the hotter shrapnel. There I met a clubmate from New York, and sundry good foreigners, notably the Prussian (Von Goetzen), and that lovely "old British salt" Paget, and the Japanese major, whose name I could never remember. We sat there. I listened to much expert artillery talk, though the talk was not quite so impressive as the practice of that art.

But the heat—let no man ever attempt that after Kipling's "and the heat would make your blooming eyebrows crawl."

This hill was the point of vantage; it overlooked the flat jungle, San Juan hills, Santiago, and Caney, the whole vast country to the mountains which walled in the whole scene. I heard the experts talk, and I love military science, but I slowly thought to myself this is not my art—neither the science of troop movement nor the whole landscape. My art requires me to go down in the road where the human beings are who do these things which science dictates, in the landscape which to me is overshadowed by their presence. I rode slowly, on account of the awful sun. Troops were standing everywhere, lying all about, moving regularly up the jungle road toward Santiago, and I wound my way along with them, saying, "Gangway, please." [. . .]

War, storms at sea, mountains, deserts, pests, and public calamities leave me without words. I simply said "Gangway" as I wormed my way up the fateful road to Santiago. Fellows I knew out West and up North and down South passed their word to me, and I felt that I was not alone. A shrapnel came shrieking down the road, and I got a drink of water from Colonel Garlington, and a cracker. The soldiers were lying alongside and the staff-officers were dismounted, also stopping quietly in the shade of the nearest bush. The column of troops was working its way into the battle-line.

"I must be going," I said, and I mounted my good old mare—the colonel's horse. It was a tender, hand-raised trotting-horse, which came from Colorado, and was perfectly mannered. We were in love.

The long columns of men on the road had never seen this condition before. It was their first baby. Oh, a few of the old soldiers had, but it was so long ago that this must have come to them almost as a new sensation. Battles are like other things in nature—no two the same.

I could hear noises such as you can make if you strike quickly with a small walking-stick at a very few green leaves. Some of them were very near and others more faint. They were the Mausers, and out in front through the jungle I could hear what sounded like a Fourth of July morning, when the boys are setting off their crackers. It struck me as new, strange, almost uncanny, because I wanted the roar of battle, which same I never did find. These long-range, smokeless bolts are so far-reaching, and there is so little fuss, that a soldier is for hours under fire getting into the battle proper, and he has time to think. That is hard when you consider the seriousness of what he is thinking about. The modern soldier must have moral quality; the guerilla is out of date. This new man may go through a war, be in a dozen battles, and survive a dozen wounds without seeing an enemy. This would be unusual, but easily might happen. All our soldiers of San Juan were for the most part of a day under fire, subject to wounds and death, before they had even a chance to know where the enemy was whom they were opposing. To all appearance they were apathetic, standing or marching through the heat of the jungle. They flattened themselves before the warning scream of the shrapnel, but that is the proper thing to do. Some good-natured fellow led the regimental mascot, which was a fice, or a fox-terrier. Really, the dog of war is a fox-terrier. Stanley took one through Africa. He is in all English regiments, and he is gradually getting into ours. His flag is short, but it sticks up straight on all occasions, and he is a vagabond. Local ties must set lightly on soldiers and fox-terriers.

Then came the light as I passed out of the jungle and forded San Juan River. The clicking in the leaves continued, and the fire-crackers rattled out in front. "Get down, old man; you'll catch one!" said an old alkali friend, and I got down, sitting there with the officers of the cavalry brigade. But promptly some surgeons came along, saying that it was the only safe place, and they began to dig the sand to level it. We, in consequence, moved out into the crackle, and I tied my horse with some others.

"Too bad, old fellow," I thought; "I should have left you behind. Modern rifle fire is rough on horses. They can't lie down. But, you dear thing, you will have to take your chances." And then I looked at the preparation for the field hospital. It was altogether too suggestive. A man came, stooping over, with his arms drawn up, and hands flapping downward at the wrists. That is the way with all people when they are shot through the body, because they want to hold the torso steady, because if they don't it hurts. Then the oncoming troops poured through the hole in the jungle which led to the San Juan River, which was our line of battle, as I supposed. I knew nothing of the plan of battle, and I have an odd conceit that no one else did, but most all the line-officers were schooled men, and they were able to put two and two together mighty fast, and in

The temporary hospital, Bloody Ford.

most instances faster than headquarters. When educated soldiers are thrown into a battle without understanding, they understand themselves.

As the troops came pouring across the ford they stooped as low as they anatomically could, and their faces were wild with excitement. The older officers stood up as straight as on parade. They may have done it through pride, or they may have known that it is better to be "drilled clean" than to have a long ranging wound. It was probably both ideas which stiffened them up so.

Then came the curious old tube drawn by a big mule, and Borrowe with his squad of the Rough Riders. It was the dynamite-gun. The mule was unhooked and turned loose. The gun was trundled up the road and laid for a shot, but the cartridge stuck, and for a moment the cheerful grin left the red face of Borrowe. Only for a moment; for back he came, and he and his men scraped and whittled away at the thing until they got it fixed. The poor old mule lay down with a grunt and slowly died. The fire was now incessant. The bullets came like the rain. The horses lay down one after another as the Mausers found their billets. I tried to

take mine to a place of safety, but a sharp-shooter potted at me, and I gave it up. There was no place of safety. For a long time our people did not understand these sharp-shooters in their rear, and I heard many men murmur that their own comrades were shooting from behind. It was very demoralizing to us, and on the Spaniards' part a very desperate enterprise to lie deliberately back of our line; but of course, with bullets coming in to the front by the bucketful, no one could stop for the few tailing shots. The Spaniards were hidden in the mango-trees, and had smokeless powder.

Now men came walking or were carried into the temporary hospital in a string. One beautiful boy was brought in by two tough, stringy, hairy old soldiers, his head hanging down behind. His shirt was off, and a big red spot shone brilliantly against his marblelike skin. They laid him tenderly down, and the surgeon stooped over him. His breath came in gasps. The doctor laid his arms across his breast, and shaking his head, turned to a man who held a wounded foot up to him, dumbly imploring aid, as a dog might. It made my nerves jump, looking at that grewsome hospital, sand-covered, with bleeding men, and yet it seemed to have fascinated me; but I gathered myself and stole away. I went down the creek, keeping under the bank, and then out into the "scrub," hunting for our line; but I could not find our line. The bullets cut and clicked around, and a sharp-shooter nearly did for me. The thought came to me, what if I am hit out here in the bush while all alone? I shall never be found. I would go back to the road, where I should be discovered in such case; and I ran quickly across a space that my sharp-shooting Spanish friend did not see me. After that I stuck to the road. As I passed along it through an open space I saw a half-dozen soldiers sitting under a tree. "Look out—sharp-shooters!" they sang out. "Wheet!" came a Mauser, and it was right next to my ear, and two more. I dropped in the tall guinea-grass, and crawled to the soldiers, and they studied the mango-trees; but we could see nothing. I think that episode cost me my sketch-book. I believe I lost it during the crawl, and our friend the Spaniard shot so well I wouldn't trust him again.

From the vantage of a little bank under a big tree I had my first glimpse of San Juan hill, and the bullets whistled about. One would "tumble" on a tree or ricochet from the earth, and then they shrieked. Our men out in front were firing, but I could not see them. I had no idea that our people were to assault that hill—I thought at the time such an attempt would be unsuccessful. I could see with my powerful glass the white lines of the Spanish intrench-ments. I did not understand how our men could stay out there under that gruelling, and got back into the safety of a low bank.

A soldier said, while his stricken companions were grunting around him, "Boys, I have got to go one way or the other, pretty damn quick." Directly I heard our line yelling, and even then did not suppose it was an assault.

Then the Mausers came in a continuous whistle. I crawled along to a new place and finally got sight of the fort, and just then I could distinguish our blue soldiers on the hill-top, and I also noticed that the Mauser bullets rained no more. Then I started after. The country was alive with wounded men—some to die in the dreary jungle, some to get their happy home-draft, but all to be miserable. Only a handful of men got to the top, where they broke out a flag and cheered. "Cheer" is the word for that sound. You have got to hear it once where it means so much, and ever after you will grin when Americans make that noise. [...]

THE ANGEL CHILD

BY STEPHEN CRANE

AUGUST 1899

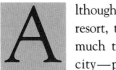lthough Whilomville was in no sense a summer resort, the advent of the warm season meant much to it, for then came visitors from the city—people of considerable confidence—alighting upon their country cousins. Moreover, many citizens who could afford to do so escaped at this time to the seaside. The town, with the commercial life quite taken out of it, drawled and drowsed through long months, during which nothing was worse than the white dust which arose behind every vehicle at blinding noon, and nothing was finer than the cool sheen of the hose sprays over the cropped lawns under the many maples in the twilight.

One summer the Trescotts had a visitation. Mrs. Trescott owned a cousin who was a painter of high degree. I had almost said that he was of national reputation, but, come to think of it, it is better to say that almost everybody in the United States who knew about art and its travail knew about him. He had picked out a wife, and naturally, looking at him, one wondered how he had done it. She was quick, beautiful, imperious, while he was quiet, slow, and misty. She was a veritable queen of health, while he, apparently, was of a most brittle constitution. When he played tennis, particularly, he looked every minute as if he were going to break.

They lived in New York, in awesome apartments wherein Japan and Persia, and indeed all the world, confounded the observer. At the end was a cathedral-like studio. They had one child. Perhaps it would better to say that they had one CHILD. It was a girl. When she came to Whilomville with her parents, it was patent that she had an inexhaustible store of white frocks, and that her voice was high and commanding. These things the town knew quickly. Other things it was doomed to discover by a process.

Her effect upon the children of the Trescott neighborhood was singular. They at first feared, then admired, then embraced. In two days she was a Begum. All day long her voice could be heard directing, drilling, and compelling those free-born children; and to say that they felt oppression would be wrong, for they really fought for records of loyal obedience.

All went well until one day was her birthday.

On the morning of this day she walked out into the Trescott garden and said to her father, confidently, "Papa, give me some money, because this is my birthday."

He looked dreamily up from his easel. "Your birthday?" he murmured. Her envisioned father was never energetic enough to be irritable unless some one broke through into that place where he lived with the desires of his life. But neither wife nor child ever heeded or even understood the temperamental values, and so some part of him had grown hardened to their inroads. "Money?" he said. "Here." He handed her a five-dollar bill. It was that he did not at all understand the nature of a five-dollar bill. He was deaf to it. He had it; he gave it; that was all.

She sallied forth to a waiting people—Jimmie Trescott, Dan Earl, Ella Earl, the Margate twins, the three Phelps children, and others. "I've got some pennies now," she cried, waving the bill, "and I am going to buy some candy." They were deeply stirred by this announcement. Most children are penniless three hundred days in the year, and to another possessing five pennies they pay deference. To little Cora waving a bright green note these children paid heathenish homage. In some disorder they thronged after her to a small shop on Bridge Street hill. First of all came ice-cream. Seated in the comic little back parlor, they clamored shrilly over plates of various flavors, and the shopkeeper marvelled that cream could vanish so quickly down throats that seemed wide open, always, for the making of excited screams.

These children represented the families of most excellent people. They were all born in whatever purple there was to be had in the vicinity of Whilomville. The Margate twins, for example, were out-and-out prize-winners. With their long golden curls and their countenances of similar vacuity, they shone upon the front bench of all Sunday-school functions, hand in hand, while their uplifted mother felt about her the envy of a hundred other parents, and less heavenly children scoffed from near the door.

Then there was little Dan Earl, probably the nicest boy in the world, gentle, fine-grained, obedient to the point where he obeyed anybody. Jimmie Trescott himself was, indeed, the only child who was at all versed in villany, but in these particular days he was on his very good behavior. As a matter of fact, he was in love. The beauty of his regal little cousin had stolen his manly heart.

Yes, they were all most excellent children, but, loosened upon this candy-shop with five dollars, they resembled, in a tiny way, drunken revelling soldiers within the walls of a stormed city. Upon the heels of ice-cream and cake came chocolate mice, butter-scotch, "everlastings," chocolate cigars, taffy-on-a-stick, taffy-on-a-slate-pencil, and many semi-transparent devices resembling lions, tigers, elephants, horses, cats, dogs, cows, sheep, tables, chairs, engines (both railway and for the fighting of fire), soldiers, fine ladies, odd-looking men, clocks, watches, revolvers, rabbits, and bed-steads. A cent was the price of a single wonder.

Some of the children, going quite daft, soon had thought to make fight over the spoils, but their queen ruled with an iron grip. Her first inspiration was to satisfy her own fancies, but as soon as that was done she mingled prodigality with a fine justice, dividing, balancing, bestowing, and sometimes taking away from somebody even that which he had.

It was an orgy. In thirty-five minutes those respectable children looked as if they had been dragged at the tail of a chariot. The sacred Margate twins, blinking and grunting, wished to take seat upon the floor, and even the most durable Jimmie Trescott found occasion to lean against the counter, wearing at the time a solemn and abstracted air, as if he expected something to happen to him shortly.

Of course their belief had been in an unlimited capacity, but they found there was an end. The shopkeeper handed the queen her change.

"Two seventy-three from five leaves two twenty-seven, Miss Cora," he said, looking upon her with admiration.

She turned swiftly to her clan. "O-oh!" she cried, in amazement. "Look how much I have left!" They gazed at the coins in her palm. They knew then that it was not their capacities which were endless; it was the five dollars.

The queen led the way to the street. "We must think up some way of spending more money," she said, frowning. They stood in silence, awaiting her further speech.

Suddenly she clapped her hands and screamed with delight. "Come on!" she cried. "I know what let's do." Now behold, she had discovered the red and white pole in front of the shop of one William Neeltje, a barber by trade.

It becomes necessary to say a few words concerning Neeltje. He was new to the town. He had come and opened a dusty little shop on dusty Bridge Street hill, and although the neighborhood knew from the courier winds that his diet was mainly cabbage, they were satisfied with that meagre data. Of course Riefsnyder came to investigate him for the local Barbers' Union, but he found in him only sweetness and light, with a willingness to charge any price at all for a shave or a hair-cut. In fact, the advent of Neeltje would have made barely a ripple upon the placid bosom of Whilomville if it were not that his name was Neeltje.

At first the people looked at his signboard out of the eye corner, and wondered lazily why any one should bear the name of Neeltje; but as time went on, men spoke to other men, saying, "How do you pronounce the name of that barber up there on Bridge Street hill?" And then, before any could prevent it, the best minds of the town were splintering their lances against William Neeltje's signboard. If a man had a mental superior, he guided him seductively to this name, and watched with glee his wrecking. The clergy of the town even entered the lists. There was one among them who had taken a collegiate prize in Syriac, as well as in several less opaque languages, and the other clergymen—at one of their weekly meetings—sought to betray him into this ambush. He pronounced the name correctly, but that mattered little, since none of them knew whether he did or did not; and so they took triumph according to their ignorance. Under these arduous circumstances it was certain that the town should look for a nickname, and at this time the nickname was in process of formation. So William Neeltje lived on with his secret, smiling foolishly toward the world.

"Come on," cried little Cora. "Let's all get our hair cut. That's what let's do. Let's all get our hair cut! Come on! Come on! Come on!" The others were carried off their feet by the fury of this assault. To get their hair cut! What joy! Little did they know if this were fun; they only knew that their small leader said it was fun. Chocolate-stained but confident, the band marched into William Neeltje's barber shop.

"We wish to get our hair cut," said little Cora, haughtily.

Neeltje, in his shirt sleeves, stood looking at them with his half-idiot smile.

"Hurry, now!" commanded the queen. A dray-horse toiled step by step, step by step, up Bridge Street hill; a far woman's voice arose; there could be heard the ceaseless hammers of shingling carpenters; all was summer peace. "Come on, now. Who's goin' first? Come on, Ella; you go first. Gettin' our hair cut! Oh, what fun!"

Little Ella Earl would not, however, be first in the chair. She was drawn toward it by a singular fascination, but at the same time she was afraid of it, and so she hung back, saying: "No! You go first! No! You go first!" The question was precipitated by the twins and one of the Phelps children. They made simultaneous rush for the chair, and screamed and kicked, each pair preventing the third child. The queen entered this mêlée, and decided in favor of the Phelps boy. He ascended the chair. Thereat an awed silence fell upon the band. And always William Neeltje smiled fatuously.

He tucked a cloth in the neck of the Phelps boy, and taking scissors, began to cut his hair. The group of children came closer and closer. Even the queen was deeply moved. "Does it hurt any?" she asked, in a wee voice.

"Naw," said the Phelps boy, with dignity. "Anyhow, I've had m' hair cut afore."

When he appeared to them looking very soldierly with his cropped little head, there was a tumult over the chair. The Margate twins howled; Jimmie Trescott was kicking them on the shins. It was a fight.

But the twins could not prevail, being the smallest of all the children. The queen herself took the chair, and ordered Neeltje as if he were a lady's-maid. To the floor there fell proud ringlets, blazing even there in their humiliation with a full fine bronze light. Then Jimmie Trescott, then Ella Earl (two long ash-colored plaits), then a Phelps girl, then another Phelps girl; and so on from head to head. The ceremony received unexpected check when the turn came to Dan Earl. This lad, usually docile to any rein, had suddenly grown mulishly obstinate. No, he would not, he would not. He himself did not seem to know why he refused to have his hair cut, but, despite the shrill derision of the company, he remained obdurate. Anyhow, the twins, long held in check, and now feverishly eager, were already struggling for the chair.

And so to the floor at last came the golden Margate curls, the heart treasure and glory of a mother, three aunts, and some feminine cousins.

All having been finished, the children, highly elate, thronged out into the street. They crowed and cackled with pride and joy, anon turning to scorn the cowardly Dan Earl.

Ella Earl was an exception. She had been pensive for some time, and now the shorn little maiden began vaguely to weep. In the door of his shop William Neeltje stood watching them, upon his face a grin of almost inhuman idiocy.

It now becomes the duty of the unfortunate writer to exhibit these children to their fond parents. "Come on, Jimmie," cried little Cora, "let's go show mamma." And they hurried off, these happy children, to show mamma.

The Trescotts and their guests were assembled indolently awaiting the luncheon-bell. Jimmie and the angel child burst in upon them. "Oh, mamma," shrieked little Cora, "see how fine I am! I've had my hair cut! Isn't it splendid? And Jimmie too!"

The wretched mother took one sight, emitted one yell, and fell into a chair. Mrs. Trescott dropped a large lady's journal and made a nerveless mechanical clutch at it. The painter gripped the arms of his chair and leaned forward, staring until his eyes were like two little clock faces. Dr. Trescott did not move or speak.

To the children the next moments were chaotic. There was a loudly wailing mother, and a pale-faced, aghast mother; a stammering father, and a grim and terrible father. The angel child did not understand anything of it save the voice of calamity, and in a moment all her little imperialism went to the winds. She ran sobbing to her mother. "Oh, mamma! mamma! mamma!"

The desolate Jimmie heard out of this inexplicable situation a voice which he knew well, a sort of colonel's voice, and he obeyed like any good soldier. "Jimmie!"

He stepped three paces to the front. "Yes, sir."

"How did this—how did this happen?" said Trescott.

Now Jimmie could have explained how had happened anything which had happened, but he did not know what had happened, so he said, "I—I—nothin'."

"And, oh, look at her frock!" said Mrs. Trescott, brokenly.

The words turned the mind of the mother of the angel child. She looked up, her eyes blazing. "Frock!" she repeated. "Frock! What do I care for her frock? Frock!" she choked out again from the depths of her bitterness. Then she arose suddenly, and whirled tragically upon her husband. "Look!" she declaimed. "All—her lovely—hair—all her lovely hair—gone—gone!" The painter was apparently in a fit; his jaw was set, his eyes were glazed, his body was stiff and straight. "All gone—all—her lovely hair—all gone—my poor little darlin'—my—poor—little—darlin'!" And the angel child

"Look!" she declaimed.

added her heart-broken voice to her mother's wail as they fled into each other's arms.

In the mean time Trescott was patiently unravelling some skeins of Jimmie's tangled intellect. "And then you went to this barber's on the hill. Yes. And where did you get the money? Yes. I see. And who besides you and Cora had their hair cut? The Margate twi—Oh, lord!"

Over at the Margate place old Eldridge Margate, the grandfather of the twins, was in the back garden picking pease and smoking ruminatively to himself. Suddenly he heard from the house great noises. Doors slammed, women rushed up stairs and down stairs calling to each other in voices of agony. And then full and mellow upon the still air arose the roar of the twins in pain.

Old Eldridge stepped out of the pea-patch and moved toward the house, puzzled, staring, not yet having decided that it was his duty to rush forward. Then around the corner of the house shot his daughter Mollie, her face pale with horror.

"What's the matter?" he cried.

"Oh, father," she gasped, "the children! They—"

Then around the corner of the house came the twins, howling at the top of their power, their faces flowing with tears. They were still hand in hand, the ruling passion being strong even in this suffering. At sight of them old Eldridge took his pipe hastily out of his mouth. "Good God!" he said.

And now what befell one William Neeltje, a barber by trade? And what was said by angry parents of the mother of such an angel child? And what was the fate of the angel child herself?

There was surely a tempest. With the exception of the Margate twins, the boys could well be eliminated form the affair. Of course it didn't matter if their hair was cut. Also the two little Phelps girls had had very short hair, anyhow, and their parents were not too greatly incensed. In the case of Ella Earl, it was mainly the pathos of the little girl's own grieving; but her mother played a most generous part, and called upon Mrs. Trescott, and condoled with the mother of the angel child over their equivalent losses. But the Margate contingent! They simply screeched.

Trescott, composed and cool-blooded, was in the middle of a giddy whirl. He was not going to allow the mobbing of his wife's cousins, nor was he going to pretend that the spoliation of the Margate twins was a virtuous and beautiful act. He was elected, gratuitously, to the position of a buffer.

But, curiously enough, the one who achieved the bulk of the misery was old Eldridge Margate, who had been picking pease at the time. The feminine Margates stormed his position as individuals, in pairs, in teams, and *en masse*. In two days they may have aged him seven years. He must destroy the utter Neeltje. He must midnightly massacre the angel child and her mother. He must dip his arms in blood to the elbows.

Trescott took the first opportunity to express to him his concern over the affair, but when the subject of the disaster was mentioned, old Eldridge, to the doctor's great surprise, actually chuckled long and deeply. "Oh, well, look-a-here," he said. "I never was so much in love with them there damn curls. The curls was purty—yes—but then I'd a darn sight rather see boys look more like boys than like two little wax figgers. An', ye know, the little cusses like it themselves. *They* never took no stock in all this washin' an' combin' an' fixin' an' goin' to church an' paradin' an' showin' off. They stood it because they was told to. That's all. Of course this here Neel-te-gee, er whatever his name is, is a plumb dumb ijit, but I don't see what's to be done, now that the kids is full well cropped. I might go and burn his shop over his head, but that wouldn't bring no hair back onto the kids. They're even kicking on sashes now, an' that's all right, 'cause what fer does a boy want a sash?"

Whereupon Trescott perceived that the old man wore his brains above his shoulders, and Trescott departed from him rejoicing greatly that it was only women who could not know that there was finality to most disasters, and that when a thing was fully done, no amount of door-slammings, rushing up stairs and down stairs, calls, lamentations, tears, could bring back a single hair to the heads of twins.

But the rains came and the winds blew in the most biblical way when a certain fact came to light in the Trescott household. Little Cora, corroborated by Jimmie, innocently remarked that five dollars had been given her by her father on her birthday, and with this money the evil had been wrought. Trescott had know it, but he—thoughtful man—had said nothing. For her part, the mother of the angel child had up to that moment never reflected that the consummation of the wickedness must have cost a small sum of money. But now it was all clear to her. He was the guilty one—he! "My angel child!"

The scene which ensued was inspiriting. A few days later, loungers at the railway station saw a lady leading a shorn and still undaunted lamb. Attached to them was a husband and father, who was plainly bewildered, but still more plainly vexed, as if he would be saying: "Damn 'em! Why can't they leave me alone?"

"In the Diplomats' Gallery," by Charles Dana Gibson.

A PENFIELD YEAR

Edward Penfield: Self-portrait

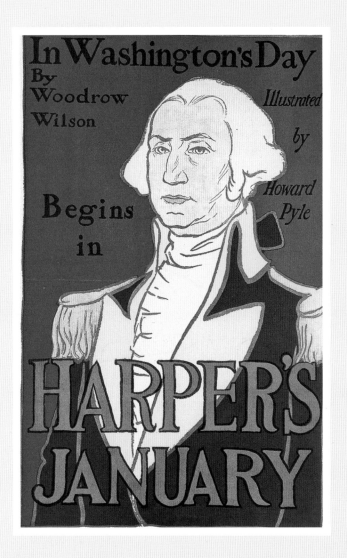

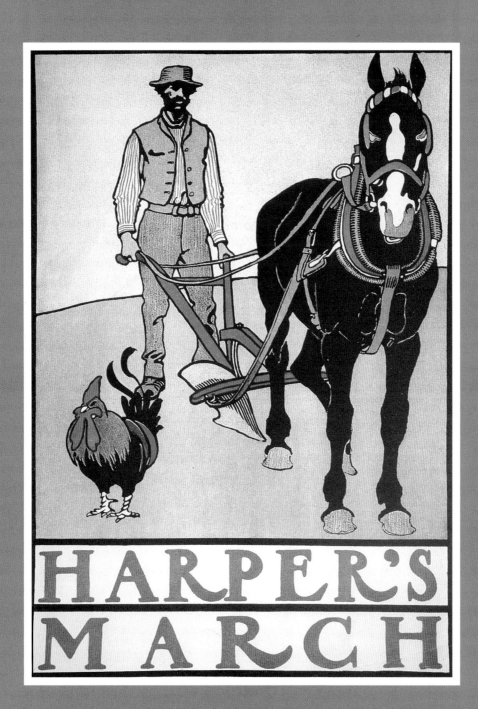

HARPER'S
MARCH

HARPER'S
SEPTEMBER

Three Gringos in Central America
    RICHARD HARDING DAVIS
Mental Telegraphy Again.
            MARK TWAIN
The German Struggle for Liberty
        POULTNEY BIGELOW
The Evolution of the Cow-Puncher
            OWEN WISTER
Arabia—Islam and the Eastern Question
        DR. WILLIAM H. THOMSON
Short Stories by THOMAS A. JANVIER
        IAN MACLAREN, and
            JULIAN RALPH
&c., &c., &c.

HARPER'S
OCTOBER

HARPER'S NOV'BR

BRISEIS — A New Novel
    By WILLIAM BLACK
COMEDY —
    By WILLIAM DEAN HOWELLS
SHORT STORIES —
    By BRANDER MATTHEWS — KATE
    DOUGLAS WIGGIN — AND OTHERS
ON SNOW-SHOES TO THE BARREN GROUNDS
    By CASPAR W. WHITNEY
THE PARIS OF SOUTH AMERICA
    By RICHARD HARDING DAVIS
PICTURES   By HOWARD PYLE — F.V. DUMOND —
FREDERIC REMINGTON — W.T. SMEDLEY — ALBERT E.
STERNER — R. CATON WOODVILLE — AND OTHERS

HARPER'S
CHRISTMAS

EDWARD PENFIELD
1895

1900's

EXTRACTS FROM ADAM'S DIARY

TRANSLATED FROM THE ORIGINAL MS.

BY MARK TWAIN

APRIL 1901

MONDAY.—This new creature with the long hair is a good deal in the way. It is always hanging around and following me about. I don't like this; I am not used to company. I wish it would stay with the other animals.... Cloudy today, wind in the east; think we shall have rain.... *We?* Where did I get that word?.... I remember now,—the new creature uses it.

TUESDAY.—Been examining the great waterfall. It is the finest thing on the estate, I think. The new creature calls it Niagara Falls—why, I am sure I do not know. Says it *looks* like Niagara Falls. That is not a reason; it is mere waywardness and imbecility. I get no chance to name anything myself. The new creature names everything that comes along, before I can get in a protest. And always that same pretext is offered—it *looks* like the thing. There is the dodo, for instance. Says the moment one looks at it one sees at a glance that it "looks like a dodo." It will have to keep that name, no doubt. It wearies me to fret about it, and it does no good, anyway. Dodo! It looks no more like a dodo than I do.

WEDNESDAY.—Built me a shelter against the rain, but could not have it to myself in peace. The new creature intruded. When I tried to put it out it shed water out of the holes it looks with, and wiped it away with the back of its paws, and made a noise such as some of the other animals make when they are in distress. I wish it would not talk; it is always talking. That sounds like a cheap fling at the poor creature, a slur; but I do not mean it so. I have never heard the human voice before, and any new and strange sound intruding itself here upon the solemn hush of these dreaming solitudes offends my ear and seems a false note. And this new sound is so close to me; it is right at my shoulder, right at my ear, first on one side and then on the other, and I am used only to sounds that are more or less distant from me.

FRIDAY.—The naming goes recklessly on, in spite of anything I can do. I had a very good name for the estate, and it was musical and pretty—GARDEN-OF-EDEN. Privately, I continue to call it that, but not any longer publicly. The new creature says it is all woods and rocks and scenery, and therefore has no resemblance to a garden. Says it *looks* like a park, and does not look like anything *but* a park. Consequently, without consulting me, it has been new-named—NIAGARA FALLS PARK. This is sufficiently high-handed, it seems to me. And already there is a sign up:

> KEEP OFF THE GRASS

My life is not as happy as it was.

SATURDAY.—The new creature eats too much fruit. We are going to run short, most likely. "We" again—that is *its* word; mine too, now, from hearing it so much. Good deal of fog this morning. I do not go out in the fog myself. The new creature does. It goes out in all weathers, and stumps right in with its muddy feet. And talks. It used to be so pleasant and quiet here.

SUNDAY.—Pulled through. This day is getting to be more and more trying. It was selected and set apart last November as a day of rest. I already had six of them per week, before. This morning found the new creature trying to clod apples out of that forbidden tree.

MONDAY.—The new creature says its name is Eve. That is all right, I have no objections. Says it is to call it by when I want it to come. I said it was superfluous, then. The word evidently raised me in its respect; and indeed it is a large, good word, and will bear repetition. It says it is not an It, it is a She. This is probably doubtful; yet it is all one to me; what she is were nothing to me if she would but go by herself and not talk. [...]

FRIDAY.—She has taken to beseeching me to stop going over the Falls. What harm does it do? Says it makes her shudder. I wonder why. I have always done it—always liked the plunge, and the excitement, and the coolness. I supposed it was what the Falls were for. They have no other use that I can see, and they must have been made for something. She says they were only made for scenery—like the rhinoceros and the mastodon.

I went over the Falls in a barrel—not satisfactory to her. Went over in a tub—still not satisfactory. Swam the Whirlpool and the Rapids in a fig-leaf suit. It got much damaged. Hence, tedious complaints about my extravagance. I am too much hampered here. What I need is change of scene.

SATURDAY.—I escaped last Tuesday night, and travelled two days, and built me another shelter, in a secluded place, and obliterated my tracks as well as I could, but she hunted me out by means of a beast which she has tamed and calls a wolf, and came making that pitiful noise again, and shedding that water out of the places she looks with. I was obliged to return with her, but will presently emigrate again, when occasion offers. She engages herself in many foolish things: among others, trying to study out why the animals called lions and tigers live on grass and flowers, when, as she says, the sort of teeth they wear would indicate that they were intended to eat each other. This is foolish, because to do that would be to kill each other, and that would introduce what, as I understand it, is called "death"; and death, as I have been told, has not yet entered the Park. Which is a pity, on some accounts.

SUNDAY.—Pulled through.

MONDAY.—I believe I see what the week is for: it is to give time to rest up from the weariness of Sunday. It seems a good idea.... She has been climbing that tree again. Clodded her out of it. She said nobody was looking. Seems to consider that a sufficient justification for chancing any dangerous thing. Told her that. The word justification moved her admiration—and envy too, I thought. It is a good word.

THURSDAY.—She told me she was made out of a rib taken from my body. This is at least doubtful, if not more than that. I have not missed any rib.... She is in much trouble about the buzzard; says grass does not agree with it; is afraid she can't raise it; thinks it was intended to live on decayed flesh. The buzzard must get along the best it can

Illustration of Mark Twain, by Edward Penfield.

with what is provided. We cannot overturn the whole scheme to accommodate the buzzard. [...]

TUESDAY.—She has taken up with a snake now. The other animals are glad, for she was always experimenting with them and bothering them; and I am glad, because the snake talks, and this enables me to get a rest.

FRIDAY.—She says the snake advises her to try the fruit of that tree, and says the result will be a great and fine and noble education. I told her there would be another result, too—it would introduce death into the world. That was a mistake—it had been better to keep the remark to myself; it only gave her an idea—she could save the sick buzzard, and furnish fresh meat to the despondent lions and tigers. I advised her to keep away from the tree. She said she wouldn't. I foresee trouble. Will emigrate.

WEDNESDAY.—I have had a variegated time. I escaped that night, and rode a horse all night as fast as he could go, hoping to get clear out of the Park and hide in some other country before the trouble should begin; but it was not to be. About an hour after sunup, as I was riding through a flowery plain where thousands of animals were grazing, slumbering, or playing with each other, according to their wont, all of a sudden they broke into a tempest of frightful noises, and in one moment the plain was in a frantic commotion and every beast was destroying its neighbor. I knew what it meant—Eve had eaten that fruit, and death was come into the world.... The tigers ate my horse, paying no attention when I ordered them to desist, and they would even have eaten me if I had staid—which I didn't, but went away in much haste.... I found this place, outside the Park, and was fairly comfortable for a few days, but she has found me out. Found me out, and has named the place Tonawanda—says it *looks* like that. In fact I was not sorry she came, for there are but meagre pickings here, and she brought some of those apples. I was obliged to eat them, I was so hungry. It was against my principles, but I find that principles have no real force except when one is well fed.... She came curtained in boughs and bunches of leaves, and when I asked her what she meant by such nonsense, and snatched them away and threw them down, she tittered and blushed. I had never seen a person titter and blush before, and to me it seemed unbecoming and idiotic. She said I would soon know how it was myself. This was correct. Hungry as I was, I laid down the apple half eaten—certainly the best one I ever saw, considering the lateness of the season—and arrayed myself in the discarded boughs and branches, and then spoke to her with some severity and ordered her to go and get some more and not make such a spectacle of herself. She did it, and after this we crept down to where the wild-beast battle had been, and collected some skins, and I made her patch together a couple of suits proper for public occasions. They are uncomfortable, it is true, but stylish, and that is the main point about clothes. . . . I find she is a good deal of a companion. I see I should be lonesome and depressed without her, now that I have lost my property. Another thing, she says it is ordered that we work for our living hereafter. She will be useful. I will superintend.

TEN DAYS LATER.—She accuses *me* of being the cause of our disaster! She says, with apparent sincerity and truth, that the Serpent assured her that the forbidden fruit was not apples, it was chestnuts. I said I was innocent, then, for I had not eaten any chestnuts. She said the Serpent informed her that "chestnut" was a figurative term meaning an aged and mouldy joke. I turned pale at that, for I have made many jokes to pass the weary time, and some of them could have been of that sort, though I had honestly supposed that they were new when I made them. She asked me if I had made one just at the time of the catastrophe. I was obliged to admit that I had made one to myself, though not aloud. It was this. I was thinking about the Falls, and I said to myself, "How wonderful it is to see that vast body of water tumble down there!" Then in an instant a bright thought flashed into my head, and I let it fly, saying, "It would be a deal more wonderful to see it tumble *up* there!"—and I was just about to kill myself with laughing at it when all nature broke loose in war and death, and I had to flee for my life. "There," she said, with triumph, "that is just it; the Serpent mentioned that very jest, and called it the First Chestnut, and said it was coeval with the creation." Alas, I am indeed to blame. Would that I were not witty; oh, would that I had never had that radiant thought!

NEXT YEAR.—We have named it Cain. She caught it while I was up country trapping on the North Shore of the Erie; caught it in the timber a couple of miles from our dug-out—or it might have been four, she isn't certain which. It resembles us in some ways, and may be a relation. That is what she thinks, but this is an error, in my judgment. The difference in size warrants the conclusion that it is a different and new kind of animal—a fish, perhaps, though when I put it in the water to see, it sank, and she plunged in and snatched it out before there was opportunity for the experiment to determine the matter. I still think it is a fish, but she is indifferent about what it is, and will not let me have it to try. I do not understand this. The coming of the creature seems to have changed her whole nature and made her unreasonable about experiments. She thinks more of it than she does of any of the other animals, but is not able to explain why. Her mind is disordered—everything shows it. Sometimes she carries the fish in her arms half the night when it complains and wants to get to the water. At such times the water comes out of the places in her face that she looks out of, and she pats the fish on the back and makes soft sounds with her mouth to soothe it, and betrays sorrow and solicitude in a hundred ways. I have never seen her do like this with any other fish, and it troubles me greatly. She used to carry the young tigers around so, and play with them, before we lost our property; but it was only play; she never took on about them like this when their dinner disagreed with them.

SUNDAY.—She doesn't work, Sundays, but lies around all tired out, and likes to have the fish wallow over her; and she makes fool noises to amuse it, and pretends to chew its paws, and that makes it laugh. I have not seen a fish before that could laugh. This makes me doubt. . . . I have come to like Sunday myself. Superintending all the week tires a body so. There ought to be more Sundays. In the old days they were tough, but now they come handy.

WEDNESDAY.—It isn't a fish. I cannot quite make out what it is. It makes curious devilish noises when not satisfied, and says "goo-goo" when it is. It is not one of us, for it doesn't walk; it is not a bird, for it doesn't fly; it is not a frog, for it doesn't hop; it is not a snake, for it doesn't crawl; I feel sure it is not a fish, though I cannot get a chance to find out whether it can swim or not. It merely lies around, and mostly on its back, with its feet up. I have not seen any other animal do that before. I said I believed it was an enigma, but she only admired the word without understanding it. In my judgment it is either an enigma or some kind of a bug. If it dies, I will take it apart and see what its arrangements are. I never had a thing perplex me so.

Three Months Later.—The perplexity augments instead of diminishing. I sleep but little. It has ceased from lying around, and goes about on its four legs, now. Yet it differs from the other four-legged animals in that its front legs are unusually short, consequently this causes the main part of its person to stick up uncomfortably high in the air, and this is not attractive. It is built much as we are, but its method of travelling shows that it is not of our breed. The short front legs and long hind ones indicate that it is of the kangaroo family, but it is a marked variation of the species, since the true kangaroo hops, whereas this one never does. Still it is a curious and interesting variety, and has not been catalogued before. As I discovered it, I have felt justified in securing the credit of the discovery by attaching my name to it, and hence have called it *Kangaroorum Adamiensis*.... It must have been a young one when it came, for it has grown exceedingly since. It must be five times as big, now, as it was then, and when discontented is able to make from twenty-two to thirty-eight times the noise it made at first. Coercion does not modify this, but has the contrary effect. For this reason I discontinued the system. She reconciles it by persuasion, and by giving it things which she had previously told it she wouldn't give it. [...]

Three Months Later.—The kangaroo still continues to grow, which is very strange and perplexing. I never knew one to be so long getting its growth. It has fur on its head now; not like kangaroo fur, but exactly like our hair, except that it is much finer and softer, and instead of being black is red. I am like to lose my mind over the capricious and harassing developments of this unclassifiable zoological freak. If I could catch another one—but that is hopeless; it is a new variety, and the only sample; this is plain. But I caught a true kangaroo and brought it in, thinking that this one, being lonesome, would rather have that for company than have no kin at all, or any animal it could feel a nearness to or get sympathy from in its forlorn condition here among strangers who do not know its ways or habits, or what to do to make it feel that it is among friends; but it was a mistake—it went into such fits at the sight of the kangaroo that I was convinced it had never seen one before. I pity the poor noisy little animal, but there is nothing I can do to make it happy. If I could tame it—but that is out of the question; the more I try, the worse I seem to make it. It grieves me to the heart to see it in its little storms of sorrow and passion. I wanted to let it go, but she wouldn't hear of it. That seemed cruel and not like her; and yet she may be

right. It might be lonelier than ever; for since I cannot find another one, how could *it*?

Five Months Later.—It is not a kangaroo. No, for it supports itself by holding to her finger, and thus goes a few steps on its hind legs, and then falls down. It is probably some kind of a bear; and yet it has no tail—as yet—and no fur, except on its head. It still keeps on growing—that is a curious circumstance, for bears get their growth earlier than this. Bears are dangerous—since our catastrophe—and I shall not be satisfied to have this one prowling about the place much longer without a muzzle on. I have offered to get her a kangaroo if she would let this one go, but it did no good—she is determined to run us into all sorts of foolish risks, I think. She was not like this before she lost her mind.

A Fortnight Later.—I examined its mouth. There is no danger yet; it has only one tooth. It has no tail yet. It makes more noise now than it ever did before—and mainly at night. I have moved out. But I shall go over, mornings, to breakfast, and to see if it has more teeth. If it gets a mouthful of teeth it will be time for it to go, tail or no tail, for a bear does not need a tail in order to be dangerous.

Four Months Later.—I have been off hunting and fishing a month, up in the region that she calls Buffalo; I don't know why, unless it is because there are not any buffaloes there. Meantime the bear has learned to paddle around all by itself on its hind legs, and says "poppa" and "momma." It is certainly a new species. This resemblance to words may be purely accidental, of course, and may have no purpose or meaning; but even in that case it is still extraordinary, and is a thing which no other bear can do. This imitation of speech, taken together with general absence of fur and entire absence of tail, sufficiently indicates that this is a new kind of bear. The further study of it will be exceedingly interesting. Meantime I will go off on a far expedition among the forests of the North and make an exhaustive search. There must certainly be another one somewhere, and this one will be less dangerous when it has company of its own species. I will go straightway; but I will muzzle this one first.

Three Months Later.—It has been a weary, weary hunt, yet I have had no success. In the mean time, without stirring from the home estate, she has caught another one! I never saw such luck. I might have hunted these woods a hundred years, I never should have run across that thing.

Next Day.—I have been comparing the new one with the old one, and it is perfectly plain that they are the same breed. I was going to stuff one of them for my collection, but she is prejudiced against it for some reason or other; so I have relinquished the idea, though I think it is a mistake. It would be an irreparable loss to science if they should get away. The old one is tamer than it was, and can laugh and talk like the parrot, having learned this, no doubt, from being with the parrot so much, and having the imitative faculty in a highly developed degree. I shall be astonished if it turns out to be a new kind of parrot; and yet I ought not to be astonished, for it has already been everything else it could think of, since those first days when it was a fish. The new one is as ugly now as the old one was at first; has the same sulphur-and-raw-meat complexion and the same singular head without any fur on it. She calls it Abel.

TEN YEARS LATER.—They are boys; we found it out long ago. It was their coming in that small, immature shape that puzzled us; we were not used to it. There are some girls now. Abel is a good boy, but if Cain had staid a bear it would have improved him. After all these years, I see that I was mistaken about Eve in the beginning; it is better to live outside the Garden with her than inside it without her. At first I thought she talked too much; but now I should be sorry to have that voice fall silent and pass out of my life. Blessed be the chestnut that brought us near together and taught me to know the goodness of her heart and the sweetness of her spirit!

Eve's Diary

TRANSLATED FROM THE ORIGINAL MS.

BY Mark Twain

December 1905

SATURDAY.—I am almost a whole day old, now. I arrived yesterday. That is as it seems to me. And it must be so, for if there was a day-before-yesterday I was not there when it happened, or I should remember it. It could be, of course, that it did happen, and that I was not noticing. Very well; I will be very watchful, now, and if any day-before-yesterdays happen I will make a note of it. It will be best to start right and not let the record get confused, for some instinct tells me that these details are going to be important to the historian some day. For I feel like an experiment, I feel exactly like an experiment, it would be impossible for a person to feel more like an experiment than I do, and so I am coming to feel convinced that that is what I *am*—an experiment; just an experiment, and nothing more.

Then if I am an experiment, am I the whole of it? No, I think not; I think the rest of it is part of it. I am the main part of it, but I think the rest of it has its share in the matter. Is my position assured, or do I have to watch it and take care of it? The latter, perhaps. Some instinct tells me that eternal vigilance is the price of supremacy. [That is a good phrase, I think, for one so young.]

Everything looks better to-day than it did yesterday. In the rush of finishing up yesterday, the mountains were left in a ragged condition, and some of the plains were so cluttered with rubbish and remnants that the aspects were quite distressing. Noble and beautiful works of art should not be subjected to haste; and this majestic new world is indeed a most noble and beautiful work. And certainly marvellously near to being perfect, notwithstanding the shortness of the time. There are too many stars in some places and not enough in others, but that can be remedied presently, no doubt. The moon got loose last night, and slid down and fell out of the scheme—a very great loss; it breaks my heart to think of it. There isn't another thing among the ornaments and decorations that is comparable to it for beauty and finish. It should have been fastened better. If we can only get it back again—

But of course there is no telling where it went to. And besides, whoever gets it will hide it; I know it because I would do it myself. I believe I can be honest in all other matters, but I already begin to realize that the core and centre of my nature is love of the beautiful, a passion for the beautiful, and that it would not be safe to trust me with a moon that belonged to another person and that person didn't know I had it. I could give up a moon that I found in the daytime, because I should be afraid some one was looking; but if I found it in the dark, I am sure I should find some kind of an excuse for not saying anything about it. For I do love moons, they are so pretty and so romantic. I wish we had five or six; I would never go to bed; I should never get tired lying on the moss-bank and looking up at them.

Stars are good, too. I wish I could get some to put in my hair. But I suppose I never can. You would be surprised to find how far off they are, for they do not look it. When they first showed, last night, I tried to knock some down with a pole, but it didn't reach, which astonished me; then I tried clods till I was all tired out, but I never got one. It was because I am left-handed and cannot throw good. Even when I aimed at the one I wasn't after I couldn't hit the other one, though I did make some close shots, for I saw the black blot of the clod sail right into the midst of the golden clusters forty or fifty times, just barely missing them, and if I could have held out a little longer maybe I could have got one.

So I cried a little, which was natural, I suppose, for one of my age, and after I was rested I got a basket and started for a place on the extreme rim of the circle, where the stars were close to the ground and I could get them with my hands, which would be better, anyway, because I could gather them tenderly then, and not break them. But it was farther than I thought, and at last I had to give it up; I was so tired I couldn't drag my feet another step; and besides, they were sore and hurt me very much.

I couldn't get back home; it was too far and turning cold; but I found some tigers and nestled in amongst them and was most adorably comfortable, and their breath was sweet and pleasant, because they live on strawberries. I had never seen a tiger before, but I knew them in a minute by the stripes. If I could have one of those skins, it would make a lovely gown.

To-day I am getting better ideas about distances. I was so eager to get hold of every pretty thing that I giddily grabbed for it, sometimes when it was too far off, and sometimes when it was but six inches away but seemed a foot—alas, with thorns between! I learned a lesson; also I made an axiom, all out of my own head—my very first one: *The scratched Experiment shuns the thorn.* I think it is a very good one for one so young.

I followed the other Experiment around, yesterday afternoon, at a distance, to see what it might be for, if I could. But I was not able to make out. I think it is a man. I had never seen a man, but it looked like one, and I feel sure that that is what it is. I realize that I feel more curiosity about it than about any of the other reptiles. If it is a reptile, and I suppose it is; for it has frowsy hair and blue eyes, and looks like a reptile. It has no hips; it tapers like a carrot; when it stands, it spreads itself apart like a derrick; so I think it is a reptile, though it may be architecture.

I was afraid of it at first, and started to run every time it turned around, for I thought it was going to chase me; but by and by I found it was only trying to get away, so after that I was not timid any more, but tracked it along, several hours, about twenty yards behind, which made it nervous and unhappy. At last it was a good deal worried, and climbed a tree. I waited a good while, then gave it up and went home.

To-day the same thing over. I've got it up the tree again.

SUNDAY.—It is up there yet. Resting, apparently. But that is a subterfuge: Sunday isn't the day of rest; Saturday is appointed for that. It looks to me like a creature that is more interested in resting than in anything else. It would tire me to rest so much. It tires me just to sit around and watch the tree. I do wonder what it is for; I never see it do anything.

They returned the moon last night, and I was *so* happy! I think it is very honest of them. It slid down and fell off again, but I was not distressed; there is no need to worry when one has that kind of neighbors; they will fetch it back. I wish I could do something to show my appreciation. I would like to send them some stars, for we have more than we can use. I mean I, not we, for I can see that the reptile cares nothing for such things.

It has low tastes, and is not kind. When I went there yesterday evening in the gloaming it had crept down and was trying to catch the little speckled fishes that play in the pool, and I had to clod it to make it go up the tree again and let them alone. I wonder if *that* is what it is for? Hasn't it any heart? Hasn't it any compassion for those little creatures? Can it be that it was designed and manufactured for such ungentle work? It has the look of it. One of the clods took it back of the ear, and it used language. It gave me a thrill, for it was the first time I had ever heard speech, except my own. I did not understand the words, but they seemed expressive.

When I found it could talk I felt a new interest in it, for I love to talk; I talk all day, and in my sleep, too, and I am very interesting, but if I had another to talk to I could be twice as interesting, and would never stop, if desired.

If this reptile is a man, it isn't an *it,* is it? That wouldn't be grammatical, would it? I think it would be *he.* I think so. In that case one would parse it thus: nominative, *he;* dative, *him;* possessive, *his'n.* Well, I will consider it a man and call it he until it turns out to be something else. This will be handier than having so many uncertainties.

NEXT WEEK SUNDAY.—All the week I tagged around after him and tried to get acquainted. I had to do the talking, because he was shy, but I didn't mind it. He seemed pleased to have me around, and I used the sociable "we" a good deal, because it seemed to flatter him to be included.

WEDNESDAY.—We are getting along very well indeed, now, and getting better and better acquainted. He does not try to avoid me any more, which is a good sign, and shows that he likes to have me with him. That pleases me, and I study to be useful to him in every way I can, so as to increase his regard. During the last day or two I have taken all the work of naming things off his hands, and this has been a great relief to him, for he has no gift in that line, and is evidently very grateful. He can't think of a rational name to save him, but I do not let him see that I am aware of his defect. Whenever a new creature comes along I name it before he has time to expose himself by an awkward silence. In this way I have saved him many embarrassments. I have no defect like his. The minute I set eyes on an animal I know what it is. I don't have to reflect a moment; the right name comes out instantly, just as if it were an inspiration, as no doubt it is, for I am sure it wasn't in me half a minute before. I seem to know just by the shape of the creature and the way it acts what animal it is.

When the dodo came along he thought it was a wild-cat—I saw it in his eye. But I saved him. And I was careful not to do it in a way that could hurt his pride. I just spoke up in a quite natural way of pleased surprise, and not as if I was dreaming of conveying information, and said, "Well, I do declare if there isn't the dodo!" I explained—without seeming to be explaining—how I knew it for a dodo, and although I thought maybe he was a little piqued that I knew the creature when he didn't, it was quite evident that he admired me. That was very agreeable, and I thought of it more than once with gratification before I slept. How little a thing can make us happy when we feel that we have earned it.

THURSDAY.—My first sorrow. Yesterday he avoided me and seemed to wish I would not talk to him. I could not believe it, and thought there was some mistake, for I loved to be with him, and loved to hear him talk, and so how could it be that he could feel unkind toward me when I had not done anything? But at last it seemed true, so I went away and sat lonely in the place where I first saw him the morning that we were made and I did not know what he was and was indifferent about him; but now it was a mournful place, and every little thing spoke of him, and my heart was very sore. I did not know why very clearly, for it was a new feeling; I had not experienced it before, and it was all a mystery, and I could not make it out.

But when night came I could not bear the lonesomeness, and went to the new shelter which he has built, to ask him what I had done that was wrong and how I could mend it and get back his kindness again; but he put me out in the rain, and it was my first sorrow.

Rockwell Kent

SUNDAY.—It is pleasant again, now, and I am happy; but those were heavy days; I do not think of them when I can help it.

I tried to get him some of those apples, but I cannot learn to throw straight. I failed, but I think the good intention pleased him. They are forbidden, and he says I shall come to harm; but so I come to harm through pleasing him why shall I care for that harm?

MONDAY.—This morning I told him my name, hoping it would interest him. But he did not care for it. It is strange. If he should tell me his name, I would care. I think it would be pleasanter in my ears than any other sound.

He talks very little. Perhaps it is because he is not bright, and is sensitive about it and wishes to conceal it. It is such a pity that he should feel so, for brightness is nothing; it is in the heart that the values lie. I wish I could make him understand that a loving good heart is riches, and riches enough, and that without it intellect is poverty.

Although he talks so little he has quite a considerable vocabulary. This morning he used a surprisingly good word. He evidently recognized, himself, that it was a good one, for he worked it in twice afterward, casually. It was not good casual art, still it showed that he possesses a certain quality of perception. Without a doubt that seed can be made to grow, if cultivated.

Where did he get that word? I do not think I have ever used it. [. . .]

TUESDAY.—All the morning I was at work improving the estate; and I purposely kept away from him in the hope that he would get lonely and come. But he did not.

At noon I stopped for the day and took my recreation by flitting all about with the bees and the butterflies and revelling in the flowers, those beautiful creatures that catch the smile of God out of the sky and preserve it! I gathered them, and made them into wreaths and garlands and clothed myself in them whilst I ate my luncheon—apples, of course; then I sat in the shade and wished and waited. But he did not come.

But no matter. Nothing would have come of it, for he does not care for flowers. He calls them rubbish, and cannot tell one from another, and thinks it is superior to feel like that. He does not care for me, he does not care for flowers, he does not care for the painted sky at eventide—is there anything he does care for, except building shacks to coop himself up in from the good clean rain, and thumping the melons, and sampling the grapes, and fingering the fruit on the trees, to see how those properties are coming along?

I laid a dry stick on the ground and tried to bore a hole in it with another one, in order to carry out a scheme that I had, and soon I got an awful fright. A thin, transparent bluish film rose out of the hole, and I dropped everything and ran! I thought it was a spirit, and I *was* so frightened! But I looked back, and it was not coming; so I leaned against a rock and rested and panted, and let my limbs go on trembling until they got steady again; then I crept warily back, alert, watching, and ready to fly if there was occasion; and when I was come near, I parted the branches of a rose-bush and peeped through—wishing the man was about, I was looking so cunning and pretty—but the sprite was gone. I went there, and there was a pinch of delicate pink dust in the hole. I put my finger in, to feel it, and said *ouch!* and took it out again. It was a cruel pain. I put my finger in my mouth; and by standing first on one foot and then the other, and grunting, I presently eased my misery; then I was full of interest, and began to examine.

I was curious to know what the pink dust was. Suddenly the name of it occurred to me, though I had never heard of it before. It was *fire!* I was as certain of it as a person could be of anything in the world. So without hesitation I named it that—fire.

I had created something that didn't exist before; I had added a new thing to the world's uncountable properties; I realized this, and was proud of my achievement, and was going to run and find him and tell him about it, thinking to raise myself in his esteem,—but I reflected, and did not do it. No—he would not care for it. He would ask what it was good for, and what could I answer? for if it was not *good* for something, but only beautiful, merely beautiful—

So I sighed, and did not go. For it wasn't good for anything; it could not build a shack, it could not improve melons, it could not hurry a fruit crop; it was useless, it was a foolishness and a vanity; he would despise it and say cutting words. But to me it was not despicable; I said, "Oh, you fire, I love you, you dainty pink creature, for you are *beautiful*—and that is enough!" and was going to gather it to my breast. But refrained. Then I made another maxim out of my own head, though it was so nearly like the first one that I was afraid it was only a plagiarism: "*The burnt Experiment shuns the fire.*"

I wrought again; and when I had made a good deal of fire-dust I emptied it into a handful of dry brown grass, intending to carry it home and keep it always and play with it; but the wind struck it and it sprayed up and spat out at me fiercely, and I dropped it and ran. When I looked back the blue spirit was towering up and stretching and rolling away like a cloud, and instantly I thought of the name of it—*smoke!*—though, upon my word, I had never heard of smoke before.

Soon, brilliant yellow and red flares shot up through the smoke, and I named them in an instant—*flames!*—and I was right, too, though these were the very first flames that had ever been in the world. They climbed the trees, they flashed splendidly in and out of the vast and increasing volume of tumbling smoke, and I had to clap my hands and laugh and dance in my rapture, it was so new and strange and so wonderful and so beautiful!

He came running, and stopped and gazed, and said not a word for many minutes. Then he asked what it was. Ah, it was too bad that he should ask such a direct question. I had to answer it, of course, and I did. I said it was fire. If it annoyed him that I should know and he must ask, that was not my fault; I had no desire to annoy him. After a pause he asked,

"How did it come?"

Another direct question, and it also had to have a direct answer.

"I made it."

The fire was travelling farther and farther off. He went to the edge of the burnt place and stood looking down, and said,

"What are these?"

"Fire-coals."

He picked up one to examine it, but changed his mind and put it down again. Then he went away. *Nothing* interests him.

But I was interested. There were ashes, gray and soft and delicate and pretty—I knew what they were at once. And the embers; I knew the embers, too. I found my apples, and raked them out, and was glad; for I am very young and my appetite is active. But I was disappointed; they were all burst open and spoiled. Spoiled apparently; but it was not so; they were better than raw ones. Fire is beautiful; some day it will be useful, I think.

FRIDAY.—I saw him again, for a moment, last Monday at nightfall, but only for a moment. I was hoping he would praise me for trying to improve the estate, for I had meant well and had worked hard. But he was not pleased, and turned away and left me. He was also displeased on another account: I tried once more to persuade him to stop going over the Falls. That was because the fire had revealed to me a new passion—quite new, and distinctly different from love, grief, and those others which I had already discovered—*fear*. And it is horrible!—I wish I had never discovered it; it gives me dark moments, it spoils my happiness, it makes me shiver and tremble and shudder. But I could not persuade him, for he has not discovered fear yet, and so he could not understand me.

TUESDAY—WEDNESDAY—THURSDAY—and to-day: all without seeing him. It is a long time to be alone; still, it is better to be alone than unwelcome.

I *had* to have company—I was made for it, I think,—so I made friends with the animals. They are just charming, and they have the kindest disposition and the politest ways; they never look sour, they never let you feel that you are intruding, they smile at you and wag their tail, if they've got one, and they are always ready for a romp or an excursion or anything you want to propose. I think they are perfect gentlemen. All these days we have had such good times, and it hasn't been lonesome for me, ever. Lonesome! No, I should say not. Why, there's always a swarm of them around—sometimes as much as four or five acres—you can't count them; and when you stand on a rock in the midst and look out over the furry expanse it is so mottled and splashed and gay with color and frisking sheen and sun-flash, and so rippled with stripes, that you might think it was a lake, only you know it isn't; and there's storms of sociable birds, and hurricanes of whirring wings; and when the sun strikes all that feathery commotion, you have a blazing up of all the colors you can think of, enough to put your eyes out.

We have made long excursions, and I have seen a great deal of the world; almost all of it, I think; and so I am the first traveller, and the only one. When we are on the march, it is an imposing sight—there's nothing like it anywhere. For comfort I ride a tiger or a leopard, because it is soft and has a round back that fits me, and because they are such pretty animals; but for long distance or for scenery I ride the elephant. He hoists me up with his trunk, but I can get off myself; when we are ready to camp, he sits and I slide down the back way.

The birds and animals are all friendly to each other, and there are no disputes about anything. They all talk, and they all talk to me, but it must be a foreign language, for I cannot make out a word they say; yet they often understand me when I talk back, particularly the dog and the elephant. It makes me ashamed. It shows that they are brighter than I am, and are therefore my superiors. It annoys me, for I want to be the principal Experiment myself—and I intend to be, too.

I have learned a number of things, and am educated, now, but I wasn't at first. I was ignorant at first. At first it used to vex me because, with all my watching, I was never smart enough to be around when the water was running up-hill; but now I do not mind it. I have experimented and experimented until now I know it never does run up-hill, except in the dark. I know it does in the dark, because the pool never goes dry; which it would, of course, if the water didn't come back in the night. It is best to prove things by actual experiment; then you *know*; whereas if you depend on guessing and supposing and conjecturing, you will never get educated. [...]

At first I couldn't make out what I was made for, but now I think it was to search out the secrets of this wonderful world and be happy and thank the Giver of it all for devising it. I think there are many things to learn yet—I hope so; and by economizing and not hurrying too fast I think they will last weeks and weeks. I hope so. When you cast up a feather it sails away on the air and goes out of sight; then you throw up a clod and it doesn't. It comes down, every time. I have tried it and tried it, and it is always so. I wonder why it is? Of course it *doesn't* come down, but why should it *seem* to? I suppose it is an optical illusion. I mean, one of them is. I don't know which one. It may be the feather, it may be the clod; I can't prove which it is, I can only demonstrate that one or the other is a fake, and let a person take his choice.

By watching, I know that the stars are not going to last. I have seen some of the best ones melt and run down the sky. Since one can melt, they can all melt; since they can all melt, they can all melt the same night. That sorrow will come—I know it. I mean to sit up every night and look at them as long as I can keep awake; and I will impress those sparkling fields on my memory, so that by and by when they are taken away I can by my fancy restore those lovely myriads to the black sky and make them sparkle again, and double them by the blur of my tears.

AFTER THE FALL

When I look back, the Garden is a dream to me. It was beautiful, surpassingly beautiful, enchantingly beautiful; and now it is lost, and I shall not see it any more.

The Garden is lost, but I have found *him*, and am content. He loves me as well as he can; I love him with all the strength of my passionate nature, and this, I think, is proper to my youth and sex. If I ask myself why I love him, I find I do not know, and do not really much care to know; so I suppose that this kind of love is not a product of reasoning and statistics, like one's love for other reptiles and animals. I think that this must be so. I love certain birds because of their song; but I do not love Adam on account of his singing—no, it is not that; the more he sings the more I do not get reconciled to it. Yet I ask him to sing, because I wish to learn to like everything he is interested in. I am sure I can learn, because at first I could not stand it, but now I can. It sours the milk, but it doesn't matter; I can get used to that kind of milk.

It is not on account of his brightness that I love him— no, it is not that. He is not to blame for his brightness, such as it is, for he did not make it himself; he is as God made him, and that is sufficient. There was a wise purpose in it, *that* I know. In time it will develop, though I think it will not be sudden; and besides, there is no hurry; he is well enough just as he is.

It is not on account of his gracious and considerate ways and his delicacy that I love him. No, he has lacks in these regards, but he is well enough just so, and is improving.

It is not on account of his industry that I love him—no, it is not that. I think he has it in him, and I do not know why he conceals it from me. It is my only pain. Otherwise he is frank and open with me, now. I am sure he keeps nothing from me but this. It grieves me that he should have a secret from me, and sometimes it spoils my sleep, thinking of it, but I will put it out of my mind; it shall not trouble my happiness, which is otherwise full to overflowing.

It is not on account of his education that I love him— no, it is not that. He is self-educated, and does really know a multitude of things, but they are not so.

It is not on account of his chivalry that I love him—no, it is not that. He told on me, but I do not blame him; it is a peculiarity of sex, I think, and he did not make his sex. Of course I would not have told on him, I would have perished first; but that is a peculiarity of sex, too, and I do not take credit for it, for I did not make my sex.

Then why is it that I love him? *Merely because he is masculine*, I think.

At bottom he is good, and I love him for that, but I could love him without it. If he should beat me and abuse me, I should go on loving him. I know it. It is a matter of sex, I think.

He is strong and handsome, and I love him for that, and I admire him and am proud of him, but I could love him without those qualities. If he were plain, I should love him; if he were a wreck, I should love him; and I would work for him, and slave over him, and pray for him, and watch by his bedside until I died.

Yes, I think I love him merely because he is *mine*, and is *masculine*. There is no other reason, I suppose. And so I think it is as I first said: that this kind of love is not a product of reasonings and statistics. It just *comes*—none knows whence—and cannot explain itself. And doesn't need to.

It is what I think. But I am only a girl, and the first that has examined this matter, and it may turn out that in my ignorance and inexperience I have not got it right.

FORTY YEARS LATER

It is my prayer, it is my longing, that we may pass from this life together—a longing which shall never perish from the earth, but shall have place in the heart of every wife that loves, until the end of time; and it shall be called by my name.

But if one of us must go first, it is my prayer that it shall be I; for he is strong, I am weak, I am not so necessary to him as he is to me—life without him would not be life; how could I endure it? This prayer is also immortal, and will not cease from being offered up while my race continues. I am the first wife; and in the last wife I shall be repeated.

AT EVE'S GRAVE

ADAM: Wheresoever she was, *there* was Eden.

THE QUICKSAND
BY EDITH WHARTON

JUNE 1902

s Mrs. Quentin's victoria, driving homeward, turned from the Park into Fifth Avenue, she divined her son's tall figure walking ahead of her in the twilight. His long stride covered the ground more rapidly than usual, and she had a premonition that, if he were going home at that hour, it was because he wanted to see her.

Mrs. Quentin, though not a fanciful woman, was sometimes aware of a sixth sense enabling her to detect the faintest vibrations of her son's impulses. She was too shrewd to fancy herself the one mother in possession of this faculty, but she permitted herself to think that few could exercise it more discreetly. If she could not help overhearing Alan's thoughts, she had the courage to keep her discoveries to herself, the tact to take for granted nothing that lay below the surface of their spoken intercourse: she knew that most people would rather have their letters read than their thoughts. For this superfeminine discretion Alan repaid her by—being Alan. There could have been no completer reward. He was the key to the meaning of life, the justification of what must have seemed as incomprehensible as it was odious, had it not all-sufficingly ended in himself. He was a perfect son, and Mrs. Quentin had always hungered for perfection.

Her house, in a minor way, bore witness to the craving. One felt it to be the result of a series of eliminations: there was nothing fortuitous in its blending of line and color. The almost morbid finish of every material detail of her life suggested the possibility that a diversity of energies had, by some pressure of circumstance, been forced into the channel of a narrow dilettanteism. Mrs. Quentin's fastidiousness had, indeed, the flaw of being too one-sided. Her friends were not always worthy of the chairs they sat in, and she overlooked in her associates defects she would not have tolerated in her bric-à-brac. Her house was, in fact, never so distinguished as when it was empty; and it was at its best in the warm fire-lit silence that now received her.

Her son, who had overtaken her on the door-step, followed her into the drawing-room, and threw himself into an armchair near the fire, while she laid off her furs and busied herself about the tea table. For a while neither spoke; but glancing at him across the kettle, his mother noticed that he sat staring at the embers with a look she had never seen on his face, though its arrogant young outline was as familiar to her as her own thoughts. The look extended itself to his negligent attitude, to the droop of his long fine hands, the dejected tilt of his head against the cushions. It was like the moral equivalent of physical fatigue: he looked, as he himself would have phrased it, dead-beat, played out. Such an air was so foreign to his usual bright indomitableness that Mrs. Quentin had the sense of an unfamiliar presence, in which she must observe herself, must raise hurried barriers against an alien approach. It was one of the drawbacks of their excessive intimacy that any break in it seemed a chasm.

She was accustomed to let his thoughts circle about her before they settled into speech, and she now sat in motionless expectancy, as though a sound might frighten them away.

At length, without turning his eyes from the fire, he said: "I'm so glad you're a nice old-fashioned intuitive woman. It's painful to see them think."

Her apprehension had already preceded him. "Hope Fenno—?" she faltered.

He nodded. "She's been thinking—hard. It was very painful—to me, at least; and I don't believe she enjoyed it: she said she didn't." He stretched his feet to the fire. "The result of her cogitations is that she won't have me. She arrived at this by pure ratiocination—it's not a question of feeling, you understand. I'm the only man she's ever loved—but she won't have me. What novels did you read when you were young, dear? I'm convinced it all turns on that. If she'd been brought up on Trollope and Whyte-Melville, instead of Tolstoi and Mrs. Ward, we should have now been vulgarly sitting on a sofa, trying on the engagement-ring."

Mrs. Quentin at first was kept silent by the mother's instinctive anger that the girl she has not wanted for her son should have dared to refuse him. Then she said, "Tell me, dear."

"My good woman, she has scruples."

"Scruples?"

"Against the paper. She objects to me in my official capacity as owner of the *Radiator*."

His mother did not echo his laugh.

"She had found a solution, of course—she overflows with expedients. I was to chuck the paper, and we were to live happily ever afterward on canned food and virtue. She even had an alternative ready—women are so full of resources! I was to turn the *Radiator* into an independent organ, and run it at a loss to show the public what a model newspaper ought to be. On the whole, I think she fancied this plan more than the other—it commended itself to her as being more uncomfortable and aggressive. It's not the fashion nowadays to be good by stealth."

Mrs. Quentin said to herself, "I didn't know how much he cared!" Aloud she murmured, "You must give her time."

"Time?"

"To move out the old prejudices and make room for new ones."

"My dear mother, those she has are brand-new; that's the trouble with them. She's tremendously up-to-date. She takes in all the moral fashion-papers, and wears the newest thing in ethics."

Her resentment lost its way in the intricacies of his metaphor. "Is she so very religious?"

"You dear archaic woman! She's hopelessly irreligious; that's the difficulty. You can make a religious woman believe almost anything: there's the habit of credulity to work on. But when a girl's faith in the Deluge has been shaken, it's very hard to inspire her with confidence. She makes you feel that, before believing in you, it's her duty as a conscientious agnostic to find out whether you're not obsolete, or whether the text isn't corrupt, or somebody hasn't proved conclusively that you never existed, anyhow."

Mrs. Quentin was again silent. The two moved in that atmosphere of implications and assumptions where the lightest word may shake down the dust of countless stored impressions; and speech was sometimes more difficult between them than had their union been less close.

Presently she ventured, "It's impossible?"

"Impossible?"

She seemed to use her words cautiously, like weapons that might slip and inflict a cut. "What she suggests."

Her son, raising himself, turned to look at her for the first time. Their glance met in a shock of comprehension. He was with her against the girl, then! Her satisfaction overflowed in a murmur of tenderness.

"Of course not, dear. One can't change—change one's life...."

"One's self," he emended. "That's what I tell her. What's the use of my giving up the paper if I keep my point of view?"

The psychological distinction attracted her. "Which is it she minds most?"

"Oh, the paper—for the present. She undertakes to modify the point of view afterward. All she asks is that I shall renounce my heresy: the gift of grace will come later."

Mrs. Quentin sat gazing into her untouched cup. Her son's first words had produced in her the hallucinated sense of struggling in the thick of a crowd that he could not see. It was horrible to feel herself hemmed in by influences imperceptible to him; yet if anything could have increased her misery it would have been the discovery that her ghosts had become visible.

As though to divert his attention, she precipitately asked, "And you—?"

His answer carried the shock of an evocation. "I merely asked her what she thought of *you*."

"Of me?"

"She admires you immensely, you know."

For a moment Mrs. Quentin's cheek showed the lingering light of girlhood: praise transmitted by her son acquired something of the transmitter's merit. "Well—?" she smiled.

"Well—you didn't make my father give up the *Radiator*, did you?"

His mother, stiffening, made a circuitous return: "She never comes here. How can she know me?"

"She's so poor! She goes out so little." He rose and leaned against the mantel-piece, dislodging with impatient fingers a slender bronze wrestler poised on a porphyry base, between two warm-toned Spanish ivories. "And then her mother—" he added, as if involuntarily.

"Her mother has never visited me," Mrs. Quentin finished for him.

He shrugged his shoulders. "Mrs. Fenno has the scope of a wax doll. Her rule of conduct is taken from her grandmother's sampler."

"But the daughter is so modern—and yet—"

"The result is the same? Not exactly. *She* admires you—oh, immensely!" He replaced the bronze and turned to his mother with a smile. "Aren't you on some hospital committee together? What especially strikes her is your way of doing good. She says philanthropy is not a line of conduct, but a state of mind—and it appears that you are one of the elect."

As, in the vague diffusion of physical pain, relief seems to come with the acuter pang of a single nerve, Mrs. Quentin felt herself suddenly eased by a rush of anger against the girl. "If she loved you—" she began.

His gesture checked her. "I'm not asking you to get her to do that."

The two were again silent, facing each other in the disarray of a common catastrophe—as though their thoughts, at the summons of danger, had rushed naked into action. Mrs. Quentin, at this revealing moment, saw for the first time how many elements of her son's character had seemed comprehensible simply because they were familiar: as, in reading a foreign language, we take the meaning of certain words for granted till the context corrects us. Often as, in a given case, her maternal musings had figured his conduct, she now found herself at a loss to forecast it; and with this failure of intuition came a sense of the subserviency which had hitherto made her counsels but the anticipation of his wish. Her despair escaped in the moan, "What *is* it you ask me?"

"To talk to her."

"Talk to her?"

"Show her—tell her—make her understand that the paper has always been a thing outside your life—that hasn't touched you—that needn't touch *her*. Only, let her hear you—watch you—be with you—she'll see . . . she can't help seeing . . ."

His mother faltered. "But if she's given you her reasons—?"

"Let her give them to you! If she can—when she sees you. . . ." His impatient hand again displaced the wrestler. "I care abominably," he confessed.

II

On the Fenno threshold a sudden sense of the futility of the attempt had almost driven Mrs. Quentin back to her carriage; but the door was already opening, and a parlor-maid who believed that Miss Fenno was in led the way to the depressing drawing-room. It was the kind of room in which no member of the family is likely to be found except after dinner or after death. The chairs and tables looked like poor relations who had repaid their keep by a long career of grudging usefulness: they seemed banded together against intruders in a sullen conspiracy of discomfort. Mrs. Quentin, keenly susceptible to such influences, read failure in every angle of the upholstery. She was incapable of the vulgar error of thinking that Hope Fenno might be induced to marry Alan for his money; but between this assumption and the inference that the girl's imagination might be touched by the finer possibilities of wealth, good taste admitted a distinction. The Fenno furniture, however, presented to such reasoning the obtuseness of its black-walnut chamferings; and something in its attitude suggested that its owners would be as uncompromising. The room showed none of the modern attempts at palliation, no apologetic draping of facts; and Mrs. Quentin, provisionally perched on a green-reps Gothic sofa with which it was clearly impossible to establish any closer relations, concluded that, had Mrs. Fenno needed another seat of the same size, she would have set out placidly to match the one on which her visitor now languished.

To Mrs. Quentin's fancy, Hope Fenno's opinions, presently imparted in a clear young voice from the opposite angle of the Gothic sofa, partook of the character of their surroundings. The girl's mind was like a large light empty place, scantily furnished with a few massive prejudices, not designed to add to any one's comfort but too ponderous to be easily moved. Mrs. Quentin's own intelligence, in which its owner, in an artistically shaded half-light, had so long moved amid a delicate complexity of sensations, seemed in comparison suddenly close and crowded; and in taking refuge there from the glare of the young girl's candor, the older woman found herself stumbling in an unwonted obscurity. Her uneasiness resolved itself into a sense of irritation against her listener. Mrs. Quentin knew that the momentary value of any argument lies in the capacity of the mind to which it is addressed; and as her shafts of persuasion spent themselves against Miss Fenno's obduracy, she said to herself that, since conduct is governed by emotions rather than ideas, the really strong people are those who mistake their sensations for opinions. Viewed in this light, Miss Fenno was certainly very strong: there was an unmistakable ring of finality in the tone with which she declared,

"It's impossible."

Mrs. Quentin's answer veiled the least shade of feminine resentment. "I told Alan that, where he had failed, there was no chance of my making an impression."

Hope Fenno laid on her visitor's an almost reverential hand. "Dear Mrs. Quentin, it's the impression you make that confirms the impossibility."

Mrs. Quentin waited a moment: she was perfectly aware that, where her feelings were concerned, her sense of humor was not to be relied on. "Do I make such an odious impression?" she asked at length, with a smile that seemed to give the girl her choice of two meanings.

"You make such a beautiful one! It's too beautiful—it obscures my judgment."

Mrs. Quentin looked at her thoughtfully. "Would it be permissible, I wonder, for an older woman to suggest that, at your age, it isn't always a misfortune to have what one calls one's judgment temporarily obscured?"

Miss Fenno flushed. "I try not to judge others—"

"You judge Alan."

"Ah, *he* is not others," she murmured, with an accent that touched the older woman.

"You judge his mother."

"I don't; I don't!"

Mrs. Quentin pressed her point. "You judge yourself, then, as you would be in my position—and your verdict condemns me."

"How can you think it? It's because I appreciate the difference in our point of view that I find it so difficult to defend myself—"

"Against what?"

"The temptation to imagine that I might be as *you* are—feeling as I do."

Mrs. Quentin rose with a sigh. "My child, in my day love was less subtle." She added, after a moment, "Alan is a perfect son."

"Ah, that again—that makes it worse!"

"Worse?"

"Just as your goodness does, your sweetness, your immense indulgence in letting me discuss things with you in a way that must seem almost an impertinence."

Mrs. Quentin's smile was not without irony. "You must remember that I do it for Alan."

"That's what I love you for!" the girl instantly returned; and again her tone touched her listener.

"And yet you're sacrificing him—and to an idea!"

"Isn't it to ideas that all the sacrifices that were worth while have been made?"

"One may sacrifice one's self."

Miss Fenno's color rose. "That's what I'm doing," she said gently.

Mrs. Quentin took her hand. "I believe you are," she answered. "And it isn't true that I speak only for Alan. Perhaps I did when I began; but now I want to plead for you too—against yourself." She paused, and then went on with a deeper note: "I have let you, as you say, speak your mind to me in terms that some women might have resented, because I wanted to show you how little, as the years go on, theories, ideas, abstract conceptions of life, weigh against the actual, against the particular way in which life presents itself to us—to women especially. To decide beforehand exactly how one ought to behave in given circumstances is like deciding that one will follow a certain direction in crossing an unexplored country. Afterward we find that we must turn out for the obstacles—cross the rivers where they're shallowest—take the tracks that others have beaten—make all sorts of unexpected concessions. Life is made up of compromises: that is what youth refuses to understand. I've lived long enough to doubt whether any real good ever came of sacrificing beautiful facts to even more beautiful theories. Do I seem casuistical? I don't know—there may be losses either way...but the love of the man one loves...of the child one loves...that makes up for everything...."

She had spoken with a thrill which seemed to communicate itself to the hand her listener had left in hers. Her eyes filled suddenly, but through their dimness she saw the girl's lips shape a last desperate denial:

"Don't you see it's because I feel all this that I mustn't—that I can't?"

III

Mrs. Quentin, in the late spring afternoon, had turned in at the doors of the Metropolitan Museum. She had been walking in the Park, in a solitude oppressed by the ever-present sense of her son's trouble, and had suddenly remembered that some one had added a Beltraffio to the collection. It was an old habit of Mrs. Quentin's to seek in the enjoyment of the beautiful the distraction that most of her acquaintances appeared to find in each other's company. She had few friends, and their society was welcome to her only in her more superficial moods; but she could drug anxiety with a picture as some women can soothe it with a bonnet.

During the six months that had elapsed since her visit to Miss Fenno she had been conscious of a pain of which she had supposed herself no longer capable: as a man will continue to feel the ache of an amputated arm. She had fancied that all her centres of feeling had been transferred to Alan; but she now found herself subject to a kind of dual suffering, in which her individual pang was the keener in that it divided her from her son's. Alan had surprised her: she had not foreseen that he would take a sentimental rebuff so hard. His disappointment took the uncommunicative form of a sterner application to work. He threw himself into the concerns of the *Radiator* with an aggressiveness that almost betrayed itself in the paper. Mrs. Quentin never read the *Radiator*, but from the glimpses of it reflected in the other journals she gathered that it was at least not being subjected to the moral reconstruction which had been one of Miss Fenno's alternatives.

Mrs. Quentin never spoke to her son of what had happened. She was superior to the cheap satisfaction of avenging his injury by depreciating its cause. She knew that in sentimental sorrows such consolations are as salt in the wound. The avoidance of a subject so vividly present to both could not but affect the closeness of their relation. An invisible presence hampered their liberty of speech and thought. The girl was always between them; and to hide the sense of her intrusion they began to be less frequently together. It was then that Mrs. Quentin measured the extent of her isolation. Had she ever dared to forecast such a situation, she would have proceeded on the conventional theory that her son's suffering must draw her nearer to him; and this was precisely the relief that was denied her. Alan's uncommunicativeness extended below the level of speech, and his mother, reduced to the helplessness of dead-reckoning, had not even the solace of adapting her sympathy to his needs. She did not know what he felt: his course was incalculable to her. She sometimes wondered if she had become as incomprehensible to him; and it was to find a moment's refuge from the dogging misery of such conjectures that she had now turned in at the Museum.

The long line of mellow canvases seemed to receive her into the rich calm of an autumn twilight. She might have been walking in an enchanted wood where the footfall of care never sounded. So deep was the sense of seclusion that, as she turned from her prolonged communion with the new Beltraffio, it was a surprise to find she was not alone.

A young lady who had risen from the central ottoman stood in suspended flight as Mrs. Quentin faced her. The older woman was the first to regain her self-possession.

"Miss Fenno!" she said.

The girl advanced with a blush. As it faded, Mrs. Quentin noticed a change in her. There had always been something bright and bannerlike in her aspect, but now her look drooped, and she hung at half-mast, as it were. Mrs. Quentin, in the embarrassment of surprising a secret that its possessor was doubtless unconscious of betraying, reverted hurriedly to the Beltraffio.

"I came to see this," she said. "It's very beautiful."

Miss Fenno's eye travelled incuriously over the mystic blue reaches of the landscape. "I suppose so," she assented; adding, after another tentative pause, "You come here often, don't you?"

"Very often," Mrs. Quentin answered. "I find pictures a great help."

"A help?"

"A rest, I mean . . . if one is tired or out of sorts."

"Ah," Miss Fenno murmured, looking down.

"This Beltraffio is new, you know," Mrs. Quentin continued. "What a wonderful background, isn't it? Is he a painter who interests you?"

The girl glanced again at the dusky canvas, as though in a final endeavor to extract from it a clue to the consolations of art. "I don't know," she said at length; "I'm afraid I don't understand pictures." She moved nearer to Mrs. Quentin and held out her hand.

"You're going?"

"Yes."

Mrs. Quentin looked at her. "Let me drive you home," she said, impulsively. She was feeling, with a shock of surprise, that it gave her, after all, no pleasure to see how much the girl had suffered.

Miss Fenno stiffened perceptibly. "Thank you; I shall like the walk."

Mrs. Quentin dropped her hand with a corresponding movement of withdrawal, and a momentary wave of antagonism seemed to sweep the two women apart. Then, as Mrs. Quentin, bowing slightly, again addressed herself to the picture, she felt a sudden touch on her arm.

"Mrs. Quentin," the girl faltered, "I really came here because I saw your carriage." Her eyes sank, and then fluttered back to her hearer's face. "I've been horribly unhappy!" she exclaimed.

Mrs. Quentin was silent. If Hope Fenno had expected an immediate response to her appeal, she was disappointed. The older woman's face was like a veil dropped before her thoughts.

"I've thought so often," the girl went on precipitately, "of what you said that day you came to see me last autumn. I think I understand now what you meant—what you tried to make me see...Oh, Mrs. Quentin," she broke out, "I didn't mean to tell you this—I never dreamed of it till this moment—but you *do* remember what you said, don't you? You must remember it! And now that I've met you in this way, I can't help telling you that I believe—I begin to believe—that you were right, after all."

Mrs. Quentin had listened without moving; but now she raised her eyes with a slight smile. "Do you wish me to say this to Alan?" she asked.

The girl flushed, but her glance braved the smile. "Would he still care to hear it?" she said fearlessly.

Mrs. Quentin took momentary refuge in a renewed inspection of the Beltraffio; then, turning, she said, with a kind of reluctance: "He would still care."

"Ah!" broke from the girl.

During this exchange of words the two speakers had drifted unconsciously toward one of the benches. Mrs. Quentin glanced about her: a custodian who had been hovering in the doorway sauntered into the adjoining gallery, and they remained alone among the silvery Vandykes and flushed bituminous Halses. Mrs. Quentin sank down on the bench and reached a hand to the girl.

"Sit by me," she said.

Miss Fenno dropped beside her. In both women the stress of emotion was too strong for speech. The girl was still trembling, and Mrs. Quentin was the first to regain her composure.

"You say you've suffered," she began at last. "Do you suppose *I* haven't?"

"I knew you had. That made it so much worse for me—that I should have been the cause of your suffering for Alan!"

Mrs. Quentin drew a deep breath. "Not for Alan only," she said. Miss Fenno turned on her a wondering glance. "Not for Alan only. *That* pain every woman expects—and knows how to bear. We all know our children must have such disappointments, and to suffer with them is not the deepest pain. It's the suffering apart—in ways they don't understand." She breathed deeply. "I want you to know what I mean. You were right—that day—and I was wrong."

"Oh," the girl faltered.

Mrs. Quentin went on in a voice of passionate lucidity. "I knew it then—I knew it even while I was trying to argue with you—I've always known it! I didn't want my son to marry you till I heard your reasons for refusing him; and then—then I longed to see you his wife!"

"Oh, Mrs. Quentin!"

"I longed for it; but I knew it mustn't be."

"Mustn't be?"

Mrs. Quentin shook her head sadly, and the girl, gaining courage from this mute negation, cried with an uncontrollable escape of feeling:

"It's because you thought me hard, obstinate, narrow-minded? Oh, I understand that so well! My self-righteousness must have seemed so petty! A girl who could sacrifice a man's future to her own moral vanity—for it *was* a form of vanity; you showed me that plainly enough—how you must have despised me! But I am not that girl now—indeed I'm not. I'm not impulsive—I think things out. I've thought this out. I know Alan loves me—I know *how* he loves me—and I believe I can help him—oh, not in the ways I had fancied before—but just merely by loving him." She paused, but Mrs. Quentin made no sign. "I see it all so differently now. I see what an influence love itself may be—how my believing in him, loving him, accepting him just as he is, might help him more than any theories, any arguments. I might have seen this long ago in looking at *you*—as he often told me—in seeing how you'd kept yourself apart from—from—Mr. Quentin's work and his—been always the beautiful side of life to them—kept their faith alive in spite of themselves—not by interfering, preaching, reforming, but by—just loving them and being there—" She looked at Mrs. Quentin with a simple nobleness. "It isn't as if I cared for the money, you know; if I cared for that, I should be afraid—"

"You will care for it in time," Mrs. Quentin said suddenly.

Miss Fenno drew back, releasing her hand. "In time?"

"Yes; when there's nothing else left." She stared a moment at the pictures. "My poor child," she broke out, "I've heard all you say so often before!"

"You've heard it?"

"Yes—from myself. I felt as you do, I argued as you do, I acted as I mean to prevent your doing, when I married Alan's father."

The long empty gallery seemed to reverberate with the girl's startled exclamation— "Oh, Mrs. Quentin—"

"Hush; let me speak. Do you suppose I'd do this if you were the kind of pink-and-white idiot he ought to have married? It's because I see you're alive, as I was, tingling with beliefs, ambitions, energies, as I was—that I can't see you walled up alive, as I was, without stretching out a hand to save you!" She sat gazing rigidly forward, her eyes on the pictures, speaking in the low precipitate tone of one who tries to press the meaning of a lifetime into a few breathless sentences.

"When I met Alan's father," she went on, "I knew nothing of his—his work. We met abroad, where I had been living with my mother. That was twenty-six years ago, when the *Radiator* was less—less notorious than it is now. I knew my husband owned a newspaper—a great newspaper—and nothing more. I had never seen a copy of the *Radiator*; I had no notion what it stood for, in politics—or in other ways. We were married in Europe, and a few months afterward we came to live here. People were already beginning to talk about the *Radiator*. My husband, on leaving college, had bought it with some money an old uncle had left him, and the public at first was merely curious to see what an ambitious, stirring young man without any experience of journalism was going to make out of his experiment. They found first of all that he was going to make a great deal of money out of it. I found that out too. I was so happy in other ways that it didn't make much difference at first; though it was pleasant to be able to help my mother, to be generous and charitable, to live in a nice house, and wear the handsome gowns he liked to see me in. But still it didn't really count— it counted so little that when, one day, I learned what the *Radiator* was, I would have gone out into the streets barefooted rather than live another hour on the money it brought in...." Her voice sank, and she paused to steady it. The girl at her side did not speak or move. "I shall never forget that day," she began again. "The paper had stripped bare some family scandal—some miserable bleeding secret that a dozen unhappy people had been struggling to keep out of print—that *would* have been kept out if my husband had not—Oh, you must guess the rest! I can't go on!"

She felt a hand on hers. "You mustn't go on, Mrs. Quentin," the girl whispered.

"Yes, I must—I must! You must be made to understand." She drew a deep breath. "My husband was not like Alan. When he found out how I felt about it he was surprised at first—but gradually he began to see—or at least I fancied he saw—the hatefulness of it. At any rate he saw how I suffered, and he offered to give up the whole thing— to sell the paper. It couldn't be done all of a sudden, of

course—he made me see that—for he had put all his money in it, and he had no special aptitude for any other kind of work. He was a born journalist—like Alan. It was a great sacrifice for him to give up the paper, but he promised to do it—in time—when a good opportunity offered. Meanwhile, of course, he wanted to build it up, to increase the circulation—and to do that he had to keep on in the same way—he made that clear to me. I saw that we were in a vicious circle. The paper, to sell well, had to be made more and more detestable and disgraceful. At first I rebelled—but somehow—I can't tell you how it was—after that first concession the ground seemed to give under me: with every struggle I sank deeper. And then—then Alan was born. He was such a delicate baby that there was very little hope of saving him. But money did it—the money from the paper. I took him abroad to see the best physicians—I took him to a warm climate every winter. In hot weather the doctors recommended sea air, and we had a yacht and cruised every summer. I owed his life to the *Radiator*. And when he began to grow stronger the habit was formed—the habit of luxury. He could not get on without the things he had always been used to. He pined in bad air; he drooped under monotony and discomfort; he throve on variety, amusement, travel, every kind of novelty and excitement. And all I wanted for him his inexhaustible foster-mother was there to give!

"My husband said nothing, but he must have seen how things were going. There was no more talk of giving up the *Radiator*. He never reproached me with my inconsistency, but I thought he must despise me, and the thought made me reckless. I determined to ignore the paper altogether—to take what it gave as though I didn't know where it came from. And to excuse this I invented the theory that one may, so to speak, purify money by putting it to good uses. I gave away a great deal in charity—I indulged myself very little at first. All the money that was not spent on Alan I tried to do good with. But gradually, as my boy grew up, the problem became more complicated. How was I to protect Alan from the contamination I had let him live in? I couldn't preach by example—couldn't hold up his father as a warning, or denounce the money we were living on. All I could do was to disguise the inner ugliness of life by making it beautiful outside—to build a wall of beauty between him and the facts of life, turn his tastes and interests another way, hide the *Radiator* from him as a smiling woman at a ball may hide a cancer in her breast! Just as Alan was entering college his father died. Then I saw my way clear. I had loved my husband—and yet I drew my first free breath in years. For the *Radiator* had been left to Alan outright—there was nothing on earth to prevent his selling it when he came of age. And there was no excuse for his not selling it. I had brought him up to depend on money, but the paper had given us enough money to gratify all his tastes. At last we could turn on the monster that had nourished us. I felt a savage joy in the thought—I could hardly bear to wait till Alan came of age. But I had never spoken to him of the paper, and I didn't dare speak of it now. Some false shame kept me back, some vague belief in his ignorance. I would wait till he was twenty-one, and then we should be free.

"I waited—the day came, and I spoke. You can guess his answer, I suppose. He had no idea of selling the *Radiator*. It wasn't the money he cared for—it was the career that tempted him. He was a born journalist, and his ambition, ever since he could remember, had been to carry on his father's work, to develop, to surpass it. There was nothing in the world as interesting as modern journalism. He couldn't imagine any other kind of life that wouldn't bore him to death. A newspaper like the *Radiator* might be made one of the biggest powers on earth, and he loved power, and meant to have all he could get. I listened to him in a kind of trance. I couldn't find a word to say. His father had had scruples—he had none. I seemed to realize at once that argument would be useless. I don't know that I even tried to plead with him—he was so bright and hard and inaccessible! Then I saw that he was, after all, what I had made him—the creature of my concessions, my connivances, my evasions. That was the price I had paid for him—I had kept him at that cost!

"Well—I *had* kept him, at any rate. That was the feeling that survived. He was my boy, my son, my very own— till some other woman took him. Meanwhile the old life must go on as it could. I gave up the struggle. If at that point he was inaccessible, at others he was close to me. He has

"What shall I tell Alan?" she said.

always been a perfect son. Our tastes grew together—we enjoyed the same books, the same pictures, the same people. All I had to do was to look at him in profile to see the side of him that was really mine. At first I kept thinking of the dreadful other side—but gradually the impression faded, and I kept my mind turned from it, as one does from a deformity in a face one loves. I thought I had made my last compromise with life—had hit on a *modus vivendi* that would last my time.

"And then he met you. I had always been prepared for his marrying, but not a girl like you. I thought he would choose a sweet thing who would never pry into his closets—he hated women with ideas! But as soon as I saw you I knew the struggle would have to begin again. He is so much stronger than his father—he is full of the most monstrous convictions. And he has the courage of them, too—you saw last year that his love for you never made him waver. He believes in his work; he adores it—it is a kind of hideous idol to which he would make human sacrifices! He loves you still—I've been honest with you—but his love wouldn't change him. It is you who would have to change—to die gradually, as I have died, till there is only one live point left in me. Ah, if one died completely— that's simple enough! But something persists—remember that—a single point, an aching nerve of truth. Now and then you may drug it—but a touch wakes it again, as your face has waked it in me. There's always enough of one's old self left to suffer with. . . ."

She stood up and faced the girl abruptly. "What shall I tell Alan?" she said.

Miss Fenno sat motionless, her eyes on the ground. Twilight was falling on the gallery—a twilight which seemed to emanate not so much from the glass dome overhead as from the crepuscular depths into which the faces of the pictures were receding. The custodian's step sounded warningly down the corridor. When the girl looked up she was alone.

The Integrity of American Character

by Grover Cleveland

December 1905

It will doubtless be generally confessed that the departures of the American people from the way originally ordained for them were never so common and never so disquieting as now. In official circles offences of malfeasance and corrupt breaches of public trust are alarmingly frequent. The old landmarks of integrity and faithfulness to duty which once indicated our nation's course of safety are rashly neglected; and public extravagance, no longer universally condemned as a disgrace to official stewardship, is flaunted before our people as evidence of the splendor of our nationality. In business and social circles the pursuit of money has become heartless and rapacious; the deference to those who have won great fortunes has grown in many quarters to be so unquestioning and so obsequious as to amount to scandalous servility, while the envy of the rich among the struggling poor is more than ever bitter and menacing. In politics there is far too often concealed behind a pretence of devotion to the public weal the sly promotion of disreputably selfish and personal advantages; and in the industrial field there is no longer found the generous and contented cooperation between employer and employee which should insure the prosperity and happiness of both. In addition to all this, there is sadly apparent among those who undertake trusteeship a tendency to complacently venture upon bold and rank violations of duty, only explained by the prevalence of lax and flippant conceptions of the sacredness of fiduciary obligations. [...]

It is doubtful if ordinary crimes were ever more certainly detected and punished than at the present time. And, what is more to the purpose, we have daily before our eyes instances of the discovery and punishment not only of public and official offences, but of other misfeasances which, though not in a strict sense of a public or official nature, affect interests hardly less important and far-reaching. United States Senators and Representatives in Congress who, relying on the loose ideas of honesty pervading their environment, have betrayed the trust of the people, find that no perverted sentiment and no disguise or dazzle of high position avails to save them from the fate of common malefactors. Those also who, while intrusted with important duties in the executive branches of government, national and State, have taken advantage of easy opportunity to filch public funds or have lent themselves to the pilfering schemes of others, wofully realize, behind prison bars and in the depths of irredeemable disgrace, that American justice and decent American sentiment are no more ready to condone stealing from the public than from an individual.

Offences against the political rights of the people, involving the corruption of their suffrage and the sale in places high and low of official patronage and favor, are overtaken by exposure and punishment in every part of our land. Many who have indulged in these crimes, impudently assuming that the universality of our people's indifference to political affairs and public administration gives promise of immunity, have of late had a rude awakening to the fact that an easy-going disuse of political privileges by honest citizens falls far short of a willingness on their part to overlook or tolerate a vile traffic in votes or an abominable bartering away of the people's interests in places of trust.

A startling exposure lately made of the reckless management of some of our leading life-insurance companies has not only laid bare overt acts of wrong-doing, but has made public in ugly relief an astonishing heedlessness and disregard of the duties of trusteeship. Searching investigation and hints of legal persuasion have already resulted in the restitution of large sums rightfully belonging to one of these companies, and nearly all who were directors at the time the misfeasances occurred have been summoned into court to give an account of their stewardship.

The recital thus made, showing activity and certainty of punishment, correction, and restitution, where specific wrongful acts have affected the public, or other widely extended interests, furnishes pregnant evidence that no adverse conditions thus far developed have weakened the strength or resilience of American character. We shall better appreciate the reach and value of the evidence adduced in support of this proposition if we take into account not only the direct effect of punitive and corrective action on the wrong-doers themselves, but also its indirect and deterrent effect upon those inclined to similar transgressions. [...]

While there can be no doubt that the elements of safety in our character as a people still remain adequate to our country's salvation, it would, nevertheless, be inexcusable folly to assume that there are no debilitating and destructive germs in our national atmosphere. As a vitiated environment may undermine the strongest constitution, so unwholesome moral conditions in our social, political, and business surroundings cannot be neglected without inviting perilous enfeeblement of our nation's strength and vigor. The dangers we have most to fear are not those which arise from the direct attack of palpable and discoverable wrongs, nor yet those arising from the deleterious influence of false standards of conduct which are open to patriotic watchfulness. They are, instead, those which are the progeny of a stealthy and insidious growth which little by little poisons the atmosphere and distorts the moral vision.

We need have no quarrel with wealth. In a country offering such boundless opportunities as ours, its accumulation cannot be forbidden nor its apportionment decreed. We should not, however, be unmindful of the fact that the getting of riches is apt to lead to the adoption of a code of morals which though suited to its purposes, does not furnish the best guarantee of national security and the general welfare and happiness of our people. Such a code should be ameliorated and softened by an admixture of higher, better sentiment. The rich, instead of disparaging education and religious teaching as irksome restraints upon their especial activities, should be willing to recognize them as countervailing or balancing forces fitly mitigating the harsh creed of money-getting. It would mean much in the way of our country's reassurance if our wealthy men would more generally contribute—not niggardly, but on a decent, liberal scale—to the maintenance and the highest usefulness of the educa-

tional and religious agencies that have been potential in producing the conditions of peace and steadiness which have made the possession and enjoyment of their wealth possible. [...]

Without attempting to enumerate all the insidious influences and tendencies which, if disregarded and unchecked, may seriously menace American character or stand in the way of its saving power, the list should not be closed without mentioning, as the most dangerous, deep-seated, and inexcusable of all, the indifference of a vast number of our decent and otherwise patriotic people to political movements, and their consequent neglect of duty as voting citizens. This evil has already spread to every part of our land, and infects all classes of our population. Thousands in the mad pursuit of riches see no profitable relationship between good government and their intents or designs. And, what is infinitely worse, thousands of our citizens of the ultra-respectable sort superciliously regard politics as an unclean thing, while too many of our educated men shun political duty as foreign to their intellectual superiority. Of course a majority of reputable Americans interest themselves in public affairs; but there ought to be no exceptions. To the extent that intelligent, thoughtful citizens fail to vote and to give impress to the politics of their country and their neighborhood, they give opportunity which the base and unprincipled will not be slow to improve. American character may be as robust and sound as can be desired, and yet it may entirely fail to save us from disaster if the practical duties of citizenship— the avenues through which it must reach its beneficent end—are disregarded. No one can make good his claim to patriotism who begrudges the time necessary to the discharge of these duties, or harbors the thought that the touch of things that further the prosperity and welfare of the American people can defile or degrade him.

The American character has received no disabling wounds or hurts. It can be relied upon to save our institutions, if its moral fibre is not further weakened by the creeping corrosion of greed or wicked neglect. And these cannot occur if the masses of the American people are watchful, faithful to their great trust, and in all things patriotic.

THE SUN-DOG TRAIL

BY JACK LONDON

DECEMBER 1905

Sitka Charley smoked his pipe and gazed thoughtfully at the newspaper illustration on the wall. For half an hour he had been steadily regarding it, and for half an hour I had been slyly watching him. Something was going on in that mind of his, and, whatever it was, I knew it was well worth knowing. He had lived life, and seen things, and performed that prodigy of prodigies, namely, the turning of his back upon his own people, and, in so far as it was possible for an Indian, becoming a white man even in his mental processes. As he phrased it himself, he had come into the warm, sat among us, by our fires, and become one of us.

We had struck this deserted cabin after a hard day on trail. The dogs had been fed, the supper dishes washed, the beds made, and we were now enjoying that most delicious hour that comes each day, on the Alaskan trail, when nothing intervenes between the tired body and bed save the smoking of the evening pipe.

"Well?" I finally broke the silence.

He took the pipe from his mouth and said, simply, "I do not understand."

He smoked on again, and again removed the pipe, using it to point at the illustration.

"That picture—what does it mean? I do not understand."

I looked at the picture. A man, with a preposterously wicked face, his right hand pressed dramatically to his heart, was falling backward to the floor. Confronting him, with a face that was a composite of destroying angel and Adonis, was a man holding a smoking revolver.

"One man is killing the other man," I said, aware of a distinct bepuzzlement of my own and of failure to explain.

"Why?" asked Sitka Charley.

"I do not know," I confessed.

"That picture is all end," he said. "It has no beginning."

"It is life," I said.

"Life has beginning," he objected.

"Look at that picture," I commanded, pointing to another decoration. "It means something. Tell me what it means to you."

He studied it for several minutes.

"The little girl is sick," he said, finally. "That is the doctor looking at her. They have been up all night—see, the oil is low in the lamp, the first morning light is coming in at the window. It is a great sickness; maybe she will die; that is why the doctor looks so hard. That is the mother. It is a great sickness, because the mother's head is on the table and she is crying."

"And now you understand the picture," I cried.

He shook his head, and asked, "The little girl—does it die?"

It was my turn for silence.

"Does it die?" he reiterated. "You are a painter-man. Maybe you know."

"No, I do not know," I confessed.

"It is not life," he delivered himself, dogmatically. "In life little girl die or get well. Something happen in life. In picture nothing happen. No, I do not understand pictures."

"Pictures are bits of life," I said. "We paint life as we see it. For instance, Charley, you are coming along the trail. It is night. You see a cabin. The window is lighted. You look through the window for one second, or for two seconds; you see something, and you go on your way. You see maybe a man writing a letter. You saw something without beginning or end. Nothing happened. Yet it was a bit of life

Jack London

you saw. You remember it afterward. It is like a picture in your memory. The window is the frame of the picture."

For a long time he smoked in silence. He nodded his head several times, and grunted once or twice. Then he knocked the ashes from his pipe, carefully refilled it, and, after a thoughtful pause, he lighted it again.

"Then have I, too, seen many pictures of life," he began; "pictures not painted but seen with the eyes. I have looked at them like through the window at the man writing the letter. I have seen many pieces of life, without beginning, without end, without understanding."

With a sudden change of position he turned his eyes full upon me and regarded me thoughtfully.

"Look you," he said; "you are a painter-man. How would you paint this which I saw, a picture without beginning, the ending of which I do not understand, a piece of life with the northern lights for a candle and Alaska for a frame?"

"It is a large canvas," I murmured.

"There are many names for this picture," he said. "But in the picture there are many sun-dogs, and it comes into my mind to call it 'The Sun-dog Trail.' It was seven years ago, the fall of '97, when I saw the woman first time. At Lake Linderman I had one canoe. I came over Chilcoot Pass with two thousand letters for Dawson. Everybody rush to Klondike at that time. Many people on trail. Many people chop down trees and make boats. Last water, snow in the air, snow on the ground, ice on the lake, on the river. Every day more snow, more ice, any day maybe freeze-up come; then no more water, all ice, everybody walk; Dawson six hundred miles; long time walk. Boat go very quick. Everybody want to go boat. Everybody say, 'Charley, two hundred dollars you take me in canoe,' 'Charley, three hundred dollars,' 'Charley, four hundred dollars.' I say no; all the time I say no. I am letter-carrier.

"In the morning I get to Lake Linderman; I walk all night and am much tired. I cook breakfast, I eat, then I sleep on the beach three hours. I wake up. It is ten o'clock. Snow is falling. There is wind, much wind that blows fair. Also, there is a woman who sits in the snow alongside. She is white woman, she is young, very pretty; maybe she is twenty years old, maybe twenty-five years old. She look at me. I look at her. She is very tired. She is no dance-woman. I see that right away. She is good woman, and she is very tired.

"'You are Sitka Charley,' she says. 'I go to Dawson,' she says. 'I go in your canoe—how much?'

"I do not want anybody in my canoe. I do not like to say

no. So I say, 'One thousand dollars.' She look at me very hard, then she says, 'When you start?' I say right away. Then she says all right, she will give me one thousand dollars.

"What can I say? I do not want the woman, yet have I given my word that for one thousand dollars she can come. And that woman, that young woman, all alone on the trail, there in the snow, she take out one thousand dollars in greenbacks, and she put them in my hand. I look at money, I look at her. What can I say? I say: 'No; my canoe very small. There is no room for outfit.' She laugh. She says: 'I am great traveller. This is my outfit.' She kick one small pack in the snow. It is two fur robes, canvas outside, some woman's clothes inside. I pick it up. Maybe thirty-five pounds. I am surprised. She take it away from me. She says, 'Come, let us start.' She carries pack into canoe. What can I say? I put my blankets into canoe. We start.

"And that is the way I saw the woman first time. The wind was fair. I put up small sail. The canoe went very fast. The woman was much afraid. 'What for you come Klondike much afraid?' I ask. She laugh at me, a hard laugh, but she is still much afraid. Also she is very tired. I run canoe through rapids to Lake Bennett. Water very bad, and woman cry out because she is afraid. We go down Lake Bennett. Snow, ice, wind like a gale, but woman is very tired and go to sleep.

"That night we make camp at Windy Arm. Woman sit by fire and eat supper. I look at her. She is pretty. She fix hair. There is much hair, and it is brown; also sometimes it is like gold in the firelight when she turn her head, so, and flashes come from it like golden fire. The eyes are large and brown. When she smile—how can I say?—when she smile I know white man like to kiss her, just like that, when she smile. She never do hard work. Her hands are soft like a baby's hand. She is not thin, but round like a baby; her arm, her leg, her muscles, all soft and round like baby. Her waist is small, and when she stand up, when she walk, or move her head or arm, it is—I do not know the word—but it is nice to look at, like—maybe I say she is built on lines like the lines of a good canoe, just like that,—and when she move she is like the movement of the good canoe sliding through still water or leaping through water when it is white and fast and angry. It is very good to see.

"I ask her what is her name. She laugh, then she says, 'Mary Jones; that is my name.' But I know all the time that Mary Jones is not her name.

"It is very cold in canoe, and because of cold sometimes she not feel good. Sometimes she feel good and she sing.

Her voice is like a silver bell, and I feel good all over like when I go into church at Holy Cross Mission, and when she sing I feel strong and paddle like hell. Then she laugh and says, 'You think we get to Dawson before freeze-up, Charley?' Sometimes she sit in canoe and is thinking far away, her eyes like that, all empty. She does not see Sitka Charley, nor the ice, nor the snow. She is far away. Sometimes, when she is thinking far away, her face is not good to see. It looks like a face that is angry, like the face of one man when he want to kill another man.

"Last day to Dawson very bad. Shore-ice in all the eddies, mush-ice in the stream. I cannot paddle. The canoe freeze to ice. All the time we go down Yukon in the ice. Then ice stop, canoe stop, everything stop. 'Let us go to shore,' the woman says. I say no; better wait. By and by everything start down-stream again. There is much snow; I cannot see. At eleven o'clock at night everything stop. At one o'clock everything start again. At three o'clock everything stop. Canoe is smashed like egg-shell, but it is on top of ice and cannot sink. I hear dogs howling. We wait; we sleep. By and by morning come. There is no more snow. It is the freeze-up, and there is Dawson. Canoe smash and stop right at Dawson. Sitka Charley has come in with two thousand letters on very last water.

"The woman rent a cabin on the hill, and for one week I see her no more. Then, one day, she come to me. 'Charley,' she says, 'how do you like to work for me? You drive dogs, make camp, travel with me.' I say that I make too much money carrying letters. She says, 'Charley, I will pay you more money.' I tell her that pick-and-shovel man get fifteen dollars a day in the mines. She says, 'That is four hundred and fifty dollars a month.' And I say, 'Sitka Charley is no pick-and-shovel man.' Then she says: 'I understand, Charley. I will give you seven hundred and fifty dollars each month.' It is a good price, and I go to work for her. I buy for her dogs and sled. We travel up Klondike, up Bonanza and Eldorado, over to Indian River, to Sulphur Creek, to Dominion, back across divide to Gold Bottom and to Too Much Gold, and back to Dawson. All the time she look for something; I do not know what.

"She has a small revolver, which she carries in her belt. Sometimes, on trail, she makes practice with revolver.

"At Dawson comes the man. Which way he come I do not know. Only do I know he is che-cha-quo—what you call tenderfoot. His hands are soft. He never do hard work. At first I think maybe he is her husband. But he is too young.

He is maybe twenty years old. His eyes blue, his hair yellow; he has a little mustache which is yellow. His name is John Jones. Maybe he is her brother. I do not know.

"One night I am asleep at Dawson. He wake me up. He says, 'Get the dogs ready; we start.' No more do I ask questions, so I get the dogs ready and we start. We go down the Yukon. It is night-time, it is November, and it is very cold—sixty-five below. She is soft. He is soft. The cold bites. They get tired. They cry under their breaths to themselves. By and by I say better we stop and make camp. But they say that they will go on. After that I say nothing. All the time, day after day, it is that way. They are very soft. They get stiff and sore. They do not understand moccasins, and their feet hurt very much. They limp, they stagger like drunken people, they cry under their breaths; and all the time they say: 'On! on! We will go on!'

"We make Circle City. That for which they look is not there. I think now that we will rest, and rest the dogs. But we do not rest; not for one day do we rest. 'Come,' says the woman to the man, 'let us go on.' And we go on. We leave the Yukon. We cross the divide to the west and swing down into the Tanana Country. There are new diggings there. But that for which they look is not there, and we take the back trail to Circle City.

"It is a hard journey. December is 'most gone. The days are short. It is very cold.

"We limp into Circle City. It is Christmas eve. I dance, drink, make a good time, for to-morrow is Christmas day and we will rest. But no. It is five o'clock in the morning—Christmas morning. I am two hours asleep. The man stand by my bed. 'Come, Charley,' he says; 'harness the dogs. We start.' I harness the dogs, and we start down the Yukon.

"They are very weary. They have travelled many hundreds of miles, and they do not understand the way of the trail. Besides, their cough is very bad—the dry cough that makes strong men swear and weak men cry. Every day they go on. Never do they rest the dogs. Always do they buy new dogs. At every camp, at every post, at every Indian village, do they cut out the tired dogs and put in fresh dogs. They have much money, money without end, and like water they spend it. They are crazy? Sometimes I think so, for there is a devil in them that drives them. They cry aloud in their sleep at night. And in the day, as they stagger along the trail, they cry under their breaths.

"We pass Fort Yukon. We pass Fort Hamilton. We pass Minook. January has come and nearly gone. The days are very short. At nine o'clock comes daylight. At three o'clock comes night. And it is cold. And even I, Sitka Charley, am tired. Will we go on forever this way without end? I do not know. But always do I look along the trail for that which they try to find. There are few people on the trail. Sometimes we travel one hundred miles and never see a sign of life. The northern lights flame in the sky, and the sun-dogs dance, and the air is filled with frost-dust.

"I am Sitka Charley, a strong man. I was born on the trail, and all my days have I lived on the trail. And yet have these two baby wolves made me tired. Their eyes are sunk deep in their heads, bright sometimes as with fever, dim and cloudy sometimes like the eyes of the dead. Their cheeks are black and raw from many freezings. Sometimes it is the woman in the morning who says: 'I cannot get up. I cannot move. Let me die.' And it is the man who stands beside her and says, 'Come, let us go on.'

"Sometimes, at the trading-posts, the man and woman get letters. I do not know what is in the letters. But it is the scent that they follow; these letters themselves are the scent. One time an Indian gives them a letter. I talk with him privately. He says it is a man with one eye who gives him the letter—a man who travels fast down the Yukon. That is all. But I know that the baby wolves are after the man with the one eye.

"It is February, and we have travelled fifteen hundred miles. We are getting near Bering Sea, and there are storms and blizzards. The going is hard. We come to Anvig. I do not know, but I think sure they get a letter at Anvig, for they are much excited, and they say, 'Come, hurry; let us go on.' But I say we must buy grub, and they say we must travel light and fast. Also, they say that we can get grub at Charley McKeon's cabin. Then do I know that they take the big cut-off, for it is there that Charley McKeon lives where the Black Rock stands by the trail.

"Before we start I talk maybe two minutes with the priest at Anvig. Yes, there is a man with one eye who has gone by and who travels fast. And I know that for which they look is the man with the one eye. We leave Anvig with little grub, and travel light and fast. We take the big cut-off, and the trail is fresh. The baby wolves have their noses down to the trail, and they say, 'Hurry!' All the time do they say: 'Hurry! Faster! Faster!' It is hard on the dogs. We have not much food and we cannot give them enough to eat, and they grow weak. Also, they must work hard. The woman has true sorrow for them, and often, because of them, the tears are in her eyes. But the devil in her that drives her on will not let her stop and rest the dogs.

"And then we come upon the man with the one eye. He is in the snow by the trail and his leg is broken. Because of the leg he has made a poor camp, and has been lying on his blankets for three days and keeping a fire going. When we find him he is swearing. Never have I heard a man swear like that man. I am glad. Now that they have found that for which they look, we will have a rest. But the woman says: 'Let us start. Hurry!'

"I am surprised. But the man with the one eye says: 'Never mind me. Give me your grub. You will get more grub at McKeon's cabin to-morrow. Send McKeon back for me. But do you go on.' So we give him our grub, which is not much, and we chop wood for his fire, and we take his strongest dogs and go on. We left the man with one eye there in the snow, and he died there in the snow, for Mc-Keon never went back for him.

"That day and that night we had nothing to eat, and all next day we travelled fast, and we were weak with hunger. Then we came to the Black Rock, which rose five hundred feet above the trail. It was at the end of the day. Darkness was coming, and we could not find the cabin of McKeon. We slept hungry, and in the morning looked for the cabin. It was not there, which was a strange thing, for everybody knew that McKeon lived in a cabin at Black Rock. We were near to the coast, where the wind blows hard and there is much snow. Everywhere were there small hills of snow where the wind had piled it up. I have a thought, and I dig in one and another of the hills of snow. Soon I find the walls of the cabin, and I dig down to the door. I go inside. McKeon is dead. Maybe two or three weeks he is dead. A sickness had come upon him so that he could not leave the cabin. He had eaten his grub and died. I looked for his cache, but there was no grub in it.

"'Let us go on,' said the woman. Her eyes were hungry, and her hand was upon her heart, as with the hurt of something inside. She swayed back and forth like a tree in the wind as she stood there.

"'Yes, let us go on,' said the man. His voice was hollow, like the klonk of an old raven, and he was hunger-mad. His eyes were like live coals of fire, and as his body rocked to and fro, so rocked his soul inside. And I, too, said, 'Let us go on.' For that one thought, laid upon me like a lash for every mile of fifteen hundred miles, had burned itself into my soul, and I think that I, too, was mad. Besides, we could only go on, for there was no grub. And we went on, giving no thought to the man with the one eye in the snow.

"The snow had covered the trail, and there was no sign that men had ever come or gone that way. All day the wind blew and the snow fell, and all day we travelled. Then the woman began to fall. Then the man. I did not fall, but my feet were heavy, and I caught my toes and stumbled many times.

"That night is the end of February. I kill three ptarmigan with the woman's revolver, and we are made somewhat strong again. But the dogs have nothing to eat. They try to eat their harness, which is of leather and walrus-hide, and I must fight them off with a club and hang all the harness in a tree. And all night they howl and fight around that tree. But we do not mind. We sleep like dead people, and in the morning get up like dead people out of our graves and go on along the trail.

"That morning is the 1st of March, and on that morning I see the first sign of that after which the baby wolves are in search. It is clear weather, and cold. The sun stay longer in the sky, and there are sun-dogs flashing on either side, and the air is bright with frost-dust. The snow falls no more upon the trail, and I see the fresh sign of dogs and sled. There is one man with that outfit, and I see in the snow that he is not strong. He, too, has not enough to eat. The young wolves see the fresh sign, too, and they are much excited. 'Hurry!' they say. All the time they say: 'Hurry! Faster, Charley, faster!'

"We make hurry very slow. All the time the man and the woman fall down. When they try to ride on sled, the dogs are too weak, and the dogs fall down. Besides, it is so cold that if they ride on the sled they will freeze. It is very easy for a hungry man to freeze. When the woman fall down, the man help her up. Sometimes the woman help the man up. By and by both fall down and cannot get up, and I must help them up all the time, else they will not get up and will die there in the snow. This is very hard work, for I am greatly weary, and as well I must drive the dogs, and the man and woman are very heavy, with no strength in their bodies. So, by and by, I, too, fall down in the snow, and there is no one to help me up. I must get up by myself. And always do I get up by myself, and help them up, and make the dogs go on.

"That night I get one ptarmigan, and we are very hungry. And that night the man says to me, 'What time start to-morrow, Charley?' It is like the voice of a ghost. I say, 'All the time you make start at five o'clock.' 'To-morrow,' he says, 'we will start at three o'clock.'

"And we start at three o'clock. It is clear and cold, and there is no wind. When daylight comes we can see a long way off. And it is very quiet. We can hear no sound but the beat of our hearts, and in the silence that is a very loud sound. We are like sleep-walkers, and we walk in dreams until we fall down; and then we know we must get up, and we see the trail once more and hear the beating of our hearts.

"In the morning we come upon the last-night camp of the man who is before us. It is a poor camp, the kind a man makes who is hungry and without strength. On the snow there are pieces of blanket and of canvas, and I know what has happened. His dogs have eaten their harness, and he has made new harness out of his blankets. The man and woman stare hard at what is to be seen. Their eyes are toil-mad and hunger-mad, and burn like fire deep in their heads. Their faces are like the faces of people who have died of hunger, and their cheeks are black with the dead flesh of many freezings. We come to where we can see a long way over the snow, and that for which they look is before them. A mile away there are black spots upon the snow. The black spots move. My eyes are dim, and I must stiffen my soul to see. And I see one man with dogs and a sled. The baby wolves see, too. They can no longer talk, but they whisper: 'On, on! Let us hurry!'

"And they fall down, but they go on. The man who is before us, his blanket harness breaks often and he must stop and mend it. Our harness is good, for I have hung it in trees each night. At eleven o'clock the man is half a mile away. At one o'clock he is a quarter of a mile away. He is very weak. We see him fall down many times in the snow.

"Now we are three hundred yards away. We go very slow. Maybe in two, three hours we go one mile. We do not walk. All the time we fall down. We stand up and stagger two steps, maybe three steps, then we fall down again. And all the time I must help up the man and woman. Sometimes they rise to their knees and fall forward, maybe four or five times before they can get to their feet again, and stagger two or three steps and fall. But always do they fall forward. Standing or kneeling, always do they fall forward gaining on the trail each time by the length of their bodies.

"Sometimes they crawl on hands and knees like animals that live in the forest. We go like snails—like snails that are dying we go so slow. And yet we go faster than the man who is before us. For he, too, falls all the time, and there is no Sitka Charley to lift him up. Now he is two hundred yards away. After a long time he is one hundred yards away.

"It is a funny sight. I want to laugh out loud, Ha! ha! just like that, it is so funny. It is a race of dead men and dead dogs. It is like in a dream when you have a nightmare and run away very fast for your life and go very slow. The man who is with me is mad. The woman is mad. I am mad. All the world is mad. And I want to laugh, it is so funny.

"The stranger man who is before us leaves his dogs behind and goes on alone across the snow. After a long time we come to the dogs. They lie helpless in the snow, their harness of blanket and canvas on them, the sled behind them, and as we pass them they whine to us and cry like babies that are hungry.

"Then we, too, leave our dogs and go on alone across the snow. The man and the woman are nearly gone, and they moan and groan and sob, but they go on. I, too, go on. I have but the one thought. It is to come up to the stranger man. Then it is that I shall rest, and not until then shall I rest, and it seems that I must lie down and sleep for a thousand years, I am so tired.

"The stranger man is fifty yards away, all alone in the white snow. He falls and crawls, staggers, and falls and crawls again. By and by he crawls on hands and knees. He no longer stands up. And the man and woman no longer stand up. They, too, crawl after him on hands and knees. But I stand up. Sometimes I fall, but always do I stand up again.

"On either side the sun are sun-dogs, so that there are three suns in the sky.

"After a long time the stranger man crawls no more. He stands slowly upon his feet and rocks back and forth. Also does he take off one mitten and wait with revolver in his hand, rocking back and forth as he waits. His face is skin and bones, and frozen black. It is a hungry face. The eyes are deep-sunk in his head, and the lips are snarling. The man and woman, too, get upon their feet, and they go toward him very slowly. And all about is the snow and the silence. And in the sky are three suns, and all the air is flashing with the dust of diamonds.

"And thus it was that I, Sitka Charley, saw the baby wolves make their kill. No word is spoken. Only does the stranger man snarl with his hungry face. Also does he rock

"And thus I, Sitka Charley, saw the baby wolves make their kill."

to and fro, his shoulders drooping, his knees bent, and his legs wide apart so that he does not fall down. The man and the woman stop maybe fifty feet away. Their legs, too, are wide apart so that they do not fall down, and their bodies rock to and fro. The stranger man is very weak. His arm shakes, so that when he shoots at the man his bullet strikes in the snow. The man cannot take off his mitten. The stranger man shoots at him again, and this time the bullet goes by in the air. Then the man takes the mitten in his teeth and pulls it off. But his hand is frozen and he cannot hold the revolver, and it falls in the snow. I look at the woman. Her mitten is off, and the revolver is in her hand. Three times she shoot, quick, just like that. The hungry face of the stranger man is still snarling as he falls forward in the snow.

"They did not look at the dead man. 'Let us go on,' they said. And we went on. But now that they have found that for which they look, they are like dead. The last strength has gone out of them. They can stand no more upon their feet. They will not crawl, but desire only to close their eyes and sleep. I see not far away a place for camp. I kick them. I have my dog-whip, and I give them the lash of it. They cry aloud, but they must crawl. And they do crawl to the place for camp. I build fire so that they will not freeze. Then I go back for sled. Also, I kill the dogs of the stranger man so that we may have food and not die. I put the man and woman in blankets and they sleep. Sometimes I wake them up and give them little bit of food. They are not awake, but they take the food. The woman sleep one day and a half. Then she wake up and go to sleep again. The man sleep two days and wake up and go to sleep again. After that we go down to the coast at St. Michaels. And when the ice goes out of Bering Sea the man and woman go away on a steamship. But first they pay me my seven hundred and fifty dollars a month."

"But why did they kill the man?" I asked.

Sitka Charley delayed reply until he had lighted his pipe. He glanced at the illustration on the wall and nodded his head at it familiarly. Then he said, speaking slowly and ponderingly:

"I have thought much. I do not know. It is something that happened. It is a picture I remember. It is like looking in at the window and seeing the man writing a letter. They came into my life and they went out of my life, and the picture is, as I have said, without beginning, the end without understanding."

"You have painted many pictures in the telling," I said.

"Ay,"—he nodded his head. "But they were without beginning and without end."

"The last picture of all had an end," I said.

"Ay," he answered. "But what end?"

"It was a piece of life," I said.

"Ay," he answered. "It was a piece of life."

Feeding the Mind

AN ESSAY HITHERTO UNPUBLISHED

by (the late) Lewis Carroll

May 1906

Breakfast, dinner, tea; in extreme cases, breakfast, luncheon, dinner, tea, supper, and a glass of something hot at bedtime. What care we take about feeding the lucky body! Which of us does as much for his mind? And what causes the difference? Is the body so much the more important of the two?

By no means; but life depends on the body being fed, whereas we can continue to exist as animals (scarcely as men) though the mind be utterly starved and neglected. Therefore Nature provides that, in case of serious neglect of the body, such terrible consequences of discomfort and pain shall ensue as will soon bring us back to a sense of our duty; and some of the functions necessary to life she does for us altogether, leaving us no choice in the matter. It would fare but ill with many of us if we were left to superintend our own digestion and circulation. "Bless me!" one would cry, "I forgot to wind up my heart this morning! To think that it has been standing still for the last three hours!" "I can't walk with you this afternoon," a friend would say, "as I have no less than eleven dinners to digest. I had to let them stand over from last week, being so busy—and my doctor says he will not answer for the consequences if I wait any longer!"

Well it is, I say, for us, that the consequences of neglecting the body can be clearly seen and felt; and it might be well for some if the mind were equally visible and tangible—if we could take it, say, to the doctor and have its pulse felt.

"Why, what have you been doing with this mind lately? How have you fed it? It looks pale, and the pulse is very slow."

"Well, doctor, it has not had much regular food lately. I gave it a lot of sugar-plums yesterday."

"Sugar-plums! What kind?"

"Well, they were a parcel of conundrums, sir."

"Ah! I thought so. Now just mind this: if you go on playing tricks like that, you'll spoil all its teeth, and get laid up with mental indigestion. You must have nothing but the plainest reading for the next few days. Take care now! No novels on any account!"

Considering the amount of painful experience many of us have had in feeding and dosing the body, it would, I think, be quite worth our while to try and translate some of the rules into corresponding ones for the mind.

First, then, we should set ourselves to provide for our mind its *proper kind* of food; we very soon learn what will, and what will not, agree with the body, and find little difficulty in refusing a piece of the tempting pudding or pie which is associated in our memory with that terrible attack of indigestion, and whose very name irresistibly recalls rhubarb and magnesia; but it takes a great many lessons to convince us how indigestible some of our favorite lines of reading are, and again and again we make a meal of the unwholesome novel, sure to be followed by its usual train of low spirits, unwillingness to work, weariness of existence—in fact by mental nightmare.

Then we should be careful to provide this wholesome food in *proper amount*. Mental gluttony, or overreading, is a dangerous propensity, tending to weakness of digestive power, and in some cases to loss of appetite; we know that bread is a good and wholesome food, but who would like to try the experiment of eating two or three loaves at a sitting?

I have heard of a physician telling his patient—whose complaint was merely gluttony and want of exercise—that "the earliest symptom of hypernutrition is a deposition of adipose tissue," and no doubt the fine long words greatly consoled the poor man under his increasing load of fat.

I wonder if there is such a thing in nature as a *fat mind*? I really think I have met with one or two minds which could not keep up with the slowest trot in conversation, could not jump over a logical fence to save their lives, always got stuck fast in a narrow argument, and, in short, were fit for nothing but to waddle helplessly through the world.

Then, again, though the food be wholesome and in proper amount, we know that we must not consume *too many kinds at once*. Take the thirsty haymaker a quart of beer, or a quart of cider, or even a quart of cold tea, and he will probably thank you (though not so heartily in the last case!). But what think you his feelings would be if you offered him a tray containing a little mug of beer, a little mug of cider, another of cold tea, one of hot tea, one of coffee, one of cocoa, and corresponding vessels of milk, water, brandy-and-water, and buttermilk? The sum total might be a quart, but would it be the same thing to the haymaker?

Having settled the proper kind, amount, and variety of our mental food, it remains that we should be careful to allow *proper intervals* between meal and meal, and not swallow the food hastily without mastication, so that it may be thor-

Lewis Carroll telling a story to the Liddell sisters.

oughly digested; both which rules for the body are also applicable at once to the mind.

First as to the intervals: these are as really necessary as they are for the body, with this difference only, that while the body requires three or four hours' rest before it is ready for another meal, the mind will in many cases do with three or four minutes. I believe that the interval required is much shorter than is generally supposed, and from personal experience I would recommend any one who has to devote several hours together to one subject of thought to try the effect of such a break, say once an hour—leaving off for five minutes only, each time, but taking care to throw the mind absolutely "out of gear" for those five minutes, and to turn it entirely to other subjects. It is astonishing what an amount of impetus and elasticity the mind recovers during those short periods of rest.

And then as to the mastication of the food: the mental process answering to this is simply *thinking over* what we read. This is a very much greater exertion of mind than the mere passive taking in the contents of our author—so much greater an exertion is it, that, as Coleridge says, the mind often "angrily refuses" to put itself to such trouble—so much greater, that we are far too apt to neglect it altogether, and go on pouring in fresh food on the top of the undigested masses already lying there, till the unfortunate mind is fairly swamped under the flood. But the greater the exertion, the more valuable, we may be sure, is the effect; one hour of steady thinking over a subject (a solitary walk is as good an opportunity for the process as any other) is worth two or three of reading only. And just consider another effect of this thorough digestion of the books we read; I mean the arranging and "ticketing," so to speak, of the subjects in our minds, so that we can readily refer to them when we want them. Sam Slick tells us that he has learned several languages in his life, but somehow "couldn't keep the parcels sorted" in his mind; and many a mind that hurries through book after book, without waiting to digest or arrange anything, gets into that sort of condition, and the unfortunate owner finds himself far from fit really to support the character all his friends give him.

"A thoroughly well-read man. Just you try him in any subject, now. You can't puzzle him!"

You turn to the thoroughly well-read man: you ask him a question, say, in English history (he is understood to have just finished reading Macaulay); he smiles good-naturedly, tries to look as if he knew all about it, and proceeds to dive into his mind for the answer. Up comes a handful of very promising facts, but on examination they turn out to belong to the wrong century, and are pitched in again; a second haul brings up a fact much more like the real thing, but unfortunately along with it comes a tangle of other things—a fact in political economy, a rule in arithmetic, the ages of his brother's children, and a stanza of Gray's "Elegy"; and among all these the fact he wants has got hopelessly twisted up and entangled. Meanwhile every one is waiting for his reply, and as the silence is getting more and more awkward, our well-read friend has to stammer out some half-answer at last, not nearly so clear or so satisfactory as an ordinary schoolboy would have given. And all this for want of making up his knowledge into proper bundles and ticketing them!

Do you know the unfortunate victim of ill-judged mental feeding when you see him? Can you doubt him? Look at him drearily wandering round a reading-room, tasting dish after dish—we beg his pardon, book after book—keeping to none. First a mouthful of novel—but no, faugh! he has had nothing but that to eat for the last week, and is quite tired of the taste; then a slice of science, but you know at once what the result of that will be—ah, of course, much too tough for *his* teeth. And so on through the old weary round, which he tried (and failed in) yesterday, and will probably try, and fail in, to-morrow.

Mr. Oliver Wendell Holmes, in his very amusing book *The Professor at the Breakfast-table*, gives the following rule for knowing whether a human being is young or old. "The crucial experiment is this. Offer a bulky bun to the suspected individual just ten minutes before dinner. If this is easily accepted and devoured, the fact of youth is established." He tells us that a human being, "if young, will eat anything at any hour of the day or night."

To ascertain the healthiness of the *mental* appetite of a human animal, place in its hands a short, well-written, but not exciting treatise on some popular subject—a mental *bun*, in fact. If it is read with eager interest and perfect attention, *and if the reader can answer questions on the subject afterwards*, the mind is in first-rate working order; if it be politely laid down again, or perhaps lounged over for a few minutes, and then, "I can't read this stupid book! Would you hand me the second volume of *The Mysterious Murder?*" you may be equally sure that there is something wrong in the mental digestion.

If this paper has given you any useful hints on the important subject of reading, and made you see that it is one's duty no less than one's interest to "read, mark, learn, and inwardly digest" the good books that fall in your way, its purpose will be fulfilled.

NOTE.—The manuscript of this address was given to the Rev. W. H. Draper, of Adel, Yorkshire, England, by the author, and is now printed for the first time, with the consent of his executor and family.

The Informer

by Joseph Conrad

December 1906

M
r. X came to me with a letter of introduction from a good friend of mine in Paris, specifically to see my collection of Chinese bronzes and porcelain.

My friend in Paris is a collector too. He collects neither porcelain, nor bronzes, nor pictures, nor medals, nor stamps, nor anything that could be profitably dispersed under an auctioneer's hammer. He would reject, with unaffected surprise, the name of a collector. Nevertheless, that is what he is by temperament. He collects acquaintances. It is a delicate work. He brings to it the patience, the passion, the determination of a true collector of curiosities. His collection does not contain any royal personages. I don't think he considers them sufficiently rare and interesting; but, with that exception, he has met and talked with every one worth knowing on any conceivable ground. He observes them, listens to them, penetrates them, measures them, and puts the memory away in the galleries of his mind. He has schemed, plotted, and travelled all over Europe in order to add to his collection of distinguished personal acquaintances.

As he is wealthy, well connected, and unprejudiced, his collection is pretty complete, including objects (or should I say subjects?) whose value is unappreciated by the vulgar, and often unknown to popular fame. Of those specimens my friend is naturally the most proud.

He wrote to me of X. "He is the greatest insurgent (révolté) of modern times. The world knows him as a revolutionary writer whose savage irony has laid bare the rottenness of the most respectable institutions. He has scalped every venerated head, and has mangled at the stake of his wit every received opinion and every recognized principle of conduct and policy. Who does not remember those flaming red revolutionary pamphlets whose sudden swarmings used to overwhelm the powers of every Continental police like a sudden plague of crimson gadflies? But this extreme writer has been also a man of action, the inspirer of secret societies, the mysterious unknown Number One of desperate conspiracies suspected and unsuspected, matured or baffled. And the world at large has never had an inkling of that fact. This accounts for him going about amongst us to this day, a veteran of many subterranean campaigns, standing aside now, safe within his reputation of merely the greatest destructive publicist that ever lived."

Thus wrote my friend, adding that Mr. X was an enlightened connoisseur of bronzes and china, and asking me to show him my collection.

X turned up in due course. My treasures are disposed in three large rooms without carpets and curtains. There is no other furniture than the glass cases and the étagères whose contents shall be worth a fortune to my heirs. I allow no fires to be lighted, for fear of accidents, and a fire-proof door separates them from the rest of the house.

It was a bitter cold day. We kept on our overcoats and hats. Middle-sized and spare, his eyes alert in a long, Roman-nosed countenance, X walked on neat little feet, with short steps, and looked at my collection intelligently. I hope I looked at him intelligently too. A snow-white mustache and imperial made his nut-brown complexion appear darker than it really was. In his fur coat and shiny tall hat that terrible man looked fashionable. I believe he belonged to a noble family, and could have called himself Vicomte X de la Z if he chose. We talked nothing but bronzes and porcelain. He was remarkably appreciative. We parted on cordial terms.

Where he was staying I don't know. I imagine he must have been a lonely man. Anarchists, I suppose, have no families—not, at any rate, as we understand that social relation. Organization into families may answer to a need of human nature, but in the last instance it is based on law, and therefore must be something odious and impossible to an anarchist. But, indeed, I don't understand anarchists. Does a man of that—of that—persuasion still remain an anarchist when alone, quite alone and going to bed, for instance? Does he lay his head on the pillow, pull his bed-clothes over him, and go to sleep with the necessity of the *chambardement général*, as the French slang has it, of the general blow-up, always present to his mind? And if so, how can he? I am sure that if such a faith (or such a fanaticism) once mastered my thoughts I would never be able to compose myself sufficiently to sleep or eat or perform any of the routine acts of daily life. I would want no wife, no children; I could have no friends, it seems to me; and as to collecting bronzes or china, that, I should say, would be quite out of the question. But I don't know. All I know is that Mr. X took his meals in a very good restaurant which I frequented also.

I used to sit with him at a little table. With his head uncovered, the silver topknot of his brushed-up hair completed the character of his physiognomy, all bony ridges and sunken hollows, clothed in a perfect impassiveness of expression. His meagre brown hands emerging from large white cuffs came and went breaking bread, pouring wine, and so on, with quiet mechanical precision. His head and torso above the table-cloth had a rigid immobility. This fire-brand, this great agitator, exhibited the least possible amount of warmth and animation. His voice was rasping, cold, and monotonous in a low key. He could not be called a talkative personality; but with his detached calm manner he appeared as ready to keep the conversation going as to drop it at any moment.

And his conversation was by no means commonplace. To me, I own there was some excitement in talking quietly across a dinner-table with a man whose venomous pen-stabs had sapped the vitality of at least one monarchy. That much was a matter of public knowledge. But I knew more. I knew of him—from my friend—as a certainty what the guardians of social order in Europe had at most only suspected, or dimly guessed at.

He had had what I may call his underground life. And as I sat, evening after evening, facing him at dinner, a curiosity in that direction would naturally arise in my mind. I am a quiet and peaceable product of civilization, and know no passion other than the passion for collecting things which are rare, and must remain exquisite even if approaching to the monstrous. Some Chinese bronzes are monstrously precious. And here (out of my friend's collection), here I had before me a kind of rare monster. It is true that this monster was polished and in a sense even exquisite. His beautiful

unruffled manner was that. But then he was not of bronze. He was not even Chinese, which would have enabled one to contemplate him calmly across the gulf of racial difference. He was alive and European; he had the manner of good society, wore a coat and hat like mine, and had pretty near the same taste in cooking. It was too frightful to think of.

One evening he remarked, casually, in the course of conversation, "There's no amendment to be got out of mankind except by terror and violence."

You can imagine the effect of such a phrase out of such a man's mouth upon a person like myself, whose whole scheme of life had been based upon a suave and delicate discrimination of social and artistic values. Just imagine! Upon me, to whom all sorts and forms of violence appeared as unreal as the giants, ogres, and seven-headed hydras whose activities affect, fantastically, the course of legends and fairy-tales!

I seemed suddenly to hear above the festive bustle and clatter of the brilliant restaurant the mutter of a hungry and seditious multitude.

I suppose I am impressionable and imaginative. I had a disturbing vision of darkness, full of lean jaws and wild eyes, amongst the hundred electric lights of the place. But somehow this vision made me angry, too. The sight of that man, so calm, breaking bits of his bread, exasperated me. And I had the audacity to ask him how it was that the hungry proletariat of Europe to whom he had been preaching revolt and violence had not been made indignant and angry by his openly luxurious life. "At all this," I said, pointedly, with a glance round the room and at the bottle of champagne we generally shared between us at dinner.

He remained unmoved.

"Do I feed on their toil and their heart's blood? Am I a speculator or a capitalist? Did I steal my fortune from a starving people? No! They know this very well. And they envy me nothing. The miserable mass of the people is generous to its leaders. What I have acquired has come to me through my writings; not from the millions of pamphlets distributed gratis to the hungry and the oppressed, but from the hundreds of thousands of copies sold to the well-fed bourgeois. You know that my writings were at one time the rage, the fashion—the thing to read with wonder and horror, to turn your eyes up at my pathos . . . or else to laugh in ecstasies at my wit."

"Yes," I admitted. "I remember, of course; and I confess frankly that I could never understand that infatuation."

"Don't you know yet," he said, "that an idle and selfish class loves to see mischief being made, even if it is made at its own expense? Its own life being all a matter of vestment and gesture, it is unable to realize the power and the danger of real ache and of words that have no sham meaning. It is all fun and sentiment. It is sufficient, for instance, to point out the attitude of the old French aristocracy towards the philosophers whose words were preparing the Great Revolution. Even in England, where you have some common sense, a demagogue has only to shout loud enough and long enough to find some backing in the very class he is shouting at. You too like to see mischief being made. The demagogue gets the amateurs of emotion with him. Amateurism in this, that, and the other thing is a delightfully easy way of killing time, and of feeding one's own vanity—the silly vanity of being abreast with the ideas of the day after to-morrow. Just as good and otherwise harmless people will join you in ecstasies over your collection without having the slightest notion in what its marvellousness really consists."

I hung my head. It was a crushing illustration of the sad truth he advanced. The world is full of such people. And that instance of the French aristocracy before the Revolution was extremely telling, too. I could not traverse his statement, though its cynicism—always a distasteful trait—took off much of its value, to my mind. However, I admit I was impressed. I felt the need to say something which would not be in the nature of assent and yet would not invite discussion.

"You don't mean to say," I observed, airily, "that extreme revolutionists have ever been actively assisted by the infatuation of such people?"

"I did not mean exactly that by what I said just now. I generalized. But since you ask me, I may tell you that such help has been given to revolutionary activities, more or less consciously, in various countries. And even in this country."

"Impossible!" I protested with firmness. "We don't play with fire to that extent."

"And yet you can better afford it than others, perhaps. But let me observe that most women, if not always ready to play with fire, are generally eager to play with a loose spark or so."

"Is that a joke?" I asked, smiling.

"If it is, I am not aware of it," he said, woodenly. "I was thinking of an instance. Oh! mild enough in a way...."

I became all expectation at this. I had tried many times to approach him on his underground side, so to speak. The very word had been pronounced between us. But he had always met me with his impenetrable calm.

"And at the same time," Mr. X continued, "it will give you a notion of the difficulties that may arise in what you are pleased to call underground work. It is sometimes difficult to deal with them. Of course there is no hierarchy amongst the affiliated. No rigid system."

My surprise was great, but short-lived. Of course amongst the extreme anarchists there could be no hierarchy; nothing in the nature of a law of precedence. The idea of anarchy ruling among anarchists was comforting, too. It could not possibly make for efficiency.

Mr. X startled me by asking, abruptly, "You know Hermione Street?"

I nodded doubtful assent. Hermione Street has been, within the last three years, improved out of any man's knowledge. The name exists still, but not one brick or stone of the old Hermione Street is left now. It was the old street he meant, for he said:

"There was a row of two-storied brick houses on the left, with their backs against the wing of a great public building—you remember. Would it surprise you very much to hear that one of these houses was for a time the centre of anarchist propaganda and of what you would call underground action?"

"Not at all," I protested. Hermione Street had never been particularly respectable, as I remembered it.

"The house was the property of a distinguished government official," he added, sipping his champagne.

"Oh, indeed!" I said, this time not believing a word of it.

"Of course he was not living there," Mr. X continued. "But from ten till four he sat next door to it, the dear man, in his well-appointed private room in the wing of the public building I've mentioned. To be strictly accurate, I must explain that the house in Hermione Street perhaps did not really belong to him. It belonged to his grown-up children—a daughter and a son. The girl, a fine figure, was by no means vulgarly pretty. To more personal charm than mere youth could account for, she added the seductive appearance of enthusiasm, of independence, of courageous thought. I suppose she put them on as she put on her picturesque dresses and for the same reason: to assert her individuality at any cost. You know, women would go to any length almost for such a purpose. She went to a great length. She had acquired all the appropriate gestures of revolutionary convictions;—the gestures of pity, of anger, of indignation against the anti-humanitarian vices of the social class to which she belonged herself. All this sat on her striking personality as well as her slightly original costumes. Very slightly original; just enough to mark a protest against the philistinism of the overfed taskmasters of the poor. Just enough, and no more. It would not have done to go too far in that direction—you understand. But she was of age, and nothing stood in the way of her offering her house to the revolutionary workers."

"You don't mean it!" I cried.

"I assure you," he affirmed, "that she made that extremely effective gesture. How else could they have got hold of it? The cause is not rich. And, moreover, there would have been difficulties with any ordinary house-agent, who would have wanted references and so on. The group she came in contact with through going about in the poor quarters of the town (you know the gesture of charity and personal service which was so fashionable some years ago) accepted with gratitude. The first advantage was that Hermione Street is, as you know, miles away from the suspect part of the town, specially watched by the police.

"The ground floor consisted of a little Italian restaurant, of the flyblown sort. There was no difficulty in buying the proprietor out. A woman and a man belonging to the group took it on. The man had been a cook. The comrades could get their meals there, unnoticed amongst the other customers. This was another advantage. The first floor was occupied by a shabby Variety Artists' Agency—an agency for performers in inferior music-halls, you know. A fellow called Bomm, I remember. He was not disturbed. It was rather favorable than otherwise to have a lot of foreign-looking people, jugglers, acrobats, singers of both sexes, and so on, going in and out all day long. The police paid no attention to new faces, you see. The top floor happened, most conveniently, to stand empty then."

X interrupted himself to attack impassively, with measured movements, a *bombe glacée* which the waiter had just set down on the table. He swallowed carefully a few spoonfuls of the iced stuff, and asked me, "Did you ever hear of Stone's Dried Soup?"

"Hear of what?" I asked, completely put off.

"It was," X pursued evenly, "a comestible article, once rather prominently advertised in the dailies, but which never, somehow, gained the favor of the public. The enter-prise fizzled out, as you say here. Parcels of their stock could be picked up at auctions at considerably less than a penny a pound. The group bought some of it, and an agency for Stone's Dried Soup was started on the top floor. A perfectly respectable enterprise. The stuff, a yellow powder of extremely unappetizing aspect, was put up in large square tins, of which six went to a case. If anybody ever came to give an order, it was, of course, executed. But the advantage of the powder was this, that things could be concealed in it very conveniently. Now and then a special case got put on a van and sent off to be exported abroad under the very nose of the policeman on duty at the corner. You understand?"

"Perfectly," I said, with an expressive nod at the remnants of the *bombe* melting slowly in the dish.

"Exactly. But the cases were useful in another way, too. In the basement, or in the cellar at the back, rather, two printing-presses were established. A lot of revolutionary literature of the most extreme kind was got away from the house in Stone's Dried Soup cases. The brother of our anarchist young lady found some occupation there. He wrote articles, helped to set up type and pull off the sheets, and generally assisted the man in charge, a very able young fellow called Sevrin.

"The guiding spirit of that group was a fanatic of social revolution. He is dead now. He was an engraver and etcher of genius. You must have seen his work. It is much sought after by certain amateurs now. But he began by being revolutionary in his art, and ended by becoming a revolutionist, after his wife and child had died in want and misery. He used to say that the bourgeois, the smug overfed lot, had killed them. That was his real belief. He still worked at his art and led a double life. He was tall, gaunt and swarthy, with a dark beard and deep-set eyes. You must have seen him. His name was Horne."

At this I was really amazed. Of course years ago I used to meet Horne about. He looked like a powerful, rough gipsy, with a red muffler round his throat and buttoned up in a long, shabby overcoat. He talked of art with exaltation, and gave one the impression of being strung up to the verge of insanity. A small group of connoisseurs appreciated his work. Who would have thought that this man. . . . Amazing! And yet it was not, after all, so difficult to believe.

"As you see," X went on, "this group was in a position to pursue its work of propaganda, and the other kind of work too, under very advantageous conditions. They were all resolute, experienced men of a superior stamp. And yet we became struck at length by the fact that plans prepared in Hermione Street almost invariably failed."

"Who were 'we'?" I asked pointedly.

"Some of us in Brussels—at the centre," he said hastily. "Whatever vigorous action originated in Hermione Street seemed doomed to failure. Something always happened to baffle the best-planned manifestations in every part of Europe. It was a time of general activity. You must not imagine that all our failures are of a loud sort, with arrests and trials. That is not so. Often the police work quietly, contenting themselves by defeating our combinations by a sort of counterplotting. No arrests, no noise, no alarming of the public mind and inflaming the passions. It is a wise procedure. But at that time the police were too uniformly successful from the Mediterranean to the Baltic. It was annoying and began to look dangerous. At last we in Brussels came to the conclusion that there must be some untrustworthy elements amongst the London groups. And I came over to see what could be done quietly.

"My first step was to call upon our young Lady Patroness of anarchism at her private house. She received me in a flattering way. I judged that she knew nothing of the chemical and other operations going on at the top of the house in Hermione Street. The printing of anarchist literature was the only 'activity' she seemed to be aware of there. She was displaying very strikingly the usual signs of severe enthusiasm, and had already written many sentimental articles with ferocious conclusions. I could see she was enjoying herself hugely, with all the gestures and grimaces of deadly earnestness. They suited her big-eyed, broad-browed face and the good carriage of her shapely head. Her black hair was done in an unusual and becoming style. Her brother was there, a serious youth, with arched eyebrows and wearing a red necktie, who struck me as being absolutely in the dark about everything in the world, including himself. By and by a tall young man came in. He was clean-shaved, with a strong jaw and something of the air of a taciturn actor or of a fanatical priest: the type with heavy black eyebrows—you know. But he was very presentable indeed. He shook hands at once vigorously with each of us in turn. The young lady came up to me and murmured sweetly, 'Comrade Sevrin.'

"I had never seen him before. He had little to say to us, but sat down by the side of the girl, and they fell at once into earnest conversation. She leaned forward in her deep armchair, and took her nicely rounded chin in her beautiful white hand. He looked attentively into her eyes. It was the attitude of love-making, serious, intense, as if on the brink of the grave. I suppose she felt it necessary to round and complete her assumption of advanced ideas, of revolutionary lawlessness, by falling in love with an anarchist. And this one, I repeat, was extremely presentable, notwithstanding his fanatical black-eyed aspect. After a few stolen glances in their direction, I had no doubt that he was in earnest. As to the lady, her gestures were unreproachable, better than the very thing itself in the blended suggestion of dignity, sweetness, condescension, fascination, surrender, and reserve. She interpreted her conception of what that precise sort of love-making should be with consummate art. And so far, she too, no doubt, was in earnest. Gestures—but so perfect!

"After I had been left alone with our Lady Patroness I informed her guardedly of the object of my visit. I hinted at our suspicions. I wanted to hear what she would have to say, and half expected some perhaps unconscious revelation. All she said was, 'That's serious,' looking delightfully concerned and grave. But there was a sparkle in her eyes which meant plainly, 'How exciting!' After all, she knew little of anything except of words. Still, she undertook to put me in communication with Horne, who was not easy to find except in Hermione Street, where I did not wish to show myself just then.

"I met Horne. This was another kind of a fanatic altogether. I exposed to him the conclusion we in Brussels had arrived at, and pointed out to him the significant series of failures. To this he answered with exaltation:

"'I have something in hand that shall not fail to strike terror into the heart of these gorged brutes.'

"And then I learned that by excavating in one of the cellars of the house he and some companions had made their way into the vaults under the great public building I have mentioned before. The blowing up of a whole wing was a certainty as soon as the materials were ready.

"I was not so appalled at the stupidity of that move as I might have been had not the usefulness of our centre in Hermione Street become already very problematical. In fact, in my opinion it was much more of a police trap by now than anything else.

"What was necessary now was to discover what, or rather who, was wrong, and I managed at last to get that idea into Horne's head. He glared, perplexed, his nostrils working as if he were sniffing treachery in the air.

"And here comes a piece of work that will no doubt strike you as a sort of theatrical expedient. And yet what else could have been done? I wished to find out the untrustworthy member of the group. But no suspicion could be fastened on one more than another. To set a watch upon them all was not very practicable. Besides, that proceeding often fails. In any case, it takes time, and the danger was pressing. I felt certain that the premises in Hermione Street would be ultimately raided, though the police had evidently such confidence in the informer that the house, for the time being, was not even watched. Horne was positive about that point. Under the circumstances it was a bad symptom. Something had to be done quickly.

"I decided to organize a raid myself upon the group. Do you understand? A raid of other trusty comrades personating the police. A conspiracy within a conspiracy. You see the object of it, of course. When apparently about to be arrested I hoped the informer would betray himself in some way or other; either by some unguarded act or simply by his unconcerned demeanor, for instance. Of course there was the risk of complete failure and the no lesser risk of some fatal accident in the course of resistance, perhaps, or in the efforts at escape. For, as you will easily see, the Hermione Street group had to be actually and completely taken unawares, as I was sure they would be by the real police before very long. The informer was amongst them, and Horne alone could be let into the secret of my plan.

"I will not enter into the detail of my preparations. It was not very easy to arrange, but it was done very well, with a really amazing effect. The sham police invaded the restaurant, whose shutters were immediately put up. The surprise was perfect. Most of the Hermione Street party were found in the second cellar, enlarging the hole communicating with the vaults of the great public building. At the first alarm, several comrades bolted through impulsively into the aforesaid vault, where, of course, had this been a genuine raid, they would have been hopelessly trapped. We did not bother about them for the moment. They were harmless enough. The top floor caused considerable anxiety to Horne and myself. There, surrounded by tins of Stone's Dried Soup, a comrade, nicknamed the Professor (he was an ex-science student), was engaged in perfecting some new detonators. He was an abstracted, vaguely smiling, sallow little man, armed with large round spectacles, and we were afraid that under a mistaken impression he would blow himself up and wreck the house about our ears. I rushed up-stairs and found him already at the door on the alert, listening, as he said, to 'suspicious noises down below.' Before I had quite

finished explaining to him what was going on, he shrugged his shoulders and turned away to his balances and test-tubes. His was the true spirit of an extreme revolutionist. Explosives were his faith, his hope, his weapon, and his shield. He perished a couple of years afterwards in a secret laboratory through the premature explosion of one of his improved detonators.

"Hurrying down again, I found an impressive scene in the vast gloom of the big cellar. The man who personated the inspector (he was no stranger to the part) was speaking harshly, and giving bogus orders to his bogus subordinates for the removal of his prisoners. Evidently nothing enlightening had happened so far. Horne, saturnine and swarthy, waited with folded arms, and his patient, moody expectation had an air of stoicism well in keeping with the situation. I detected in the shadows one of the Hermione Street group surreptitiously chewing up and swallowing a small piece of paper. Some compromising scrap, I suppose; perhaps just a note of a few names and addresses. He was a true and faithful 'companion.' But the fund of secret malice which lurks at the bottom of our sympathies caused me to feel amused at that perfectly uncalled-for performance.

"In every other respect the risky experiment, the theatrical *coup*, if you like to call it so, seemed to have failed. The deception could not be kept up much longer; the explanation would bring about a very embarrassing and even grave situation. The man who had eaten the paper would be furious. The fellows who had bolted away would be angry too.

"To add to my vexation, the door communicating with the other cellar, where the printing-presses were, was flung open, and our young lady revolutionist appeared, a black silhouette in a close-fitting dress and a large hat, with the blaze of gas flaring in there at her back. Over her shoulder I perceived the arched eyebrows and the red necktie of her brother.

"The last people in the world I wanted to see then! They had gone that evening to some amateur concert for the delectation of the poor people, you know; but she had insisted on leaving early on purpose to call in Hermione Street on the way home, under the pretext of having some work to do. Her usual task was to correct the proofs of the Italian and French editions of the *Alarm Bell* and the *Firebrand*." . . .

"Heavens!" I murmured. I had been shown once copies of these publications. Nothing, in my opinion, could have been less fit for the eyes of a young lady. They were the most advanced things of the sort; advanced, I mean, beyond all bounds of reason and decency. One of them preached the dissolution of all social ties; the other advocated systematic murder. To think of a young girl calmly tracking printers' errors all along the sort of abominable sentences I remembered was intolerable to my sentiment of womanhood. And Mr. X, after giving me a glance, pursued steadily:

"I think, however, that she came mostly to exercise her fascinations upon Sevrin, and to receive his homage in her queenly and condescending way. She was aware of both—fascination and homage—and enjoyed them with, I dare say, complete innocence. And we have no ground in expediency or morals to quarrel with her on that account. Charm in woman and exceptional intelligence in man are a law unto themselves. Is it not so?"

I refrained from expressing my abhorrence of that licentious doctrine because of my curiosity.

"But what happened then?" I hastened to ask.

X went on crumbling slowly a small piece of bread with a careless left hand.

"What happened, in effect," he confessed, "is that she saved the situation."

"She gave you an opportunity to end your rather sinister farce," I suggested.

"Yes," he said, preserving his impassive bearing. "The farce was bound to end soon. And it ended in a very few minutes. And it ended well. It might have ended badly had she not come in. Her brother, of course, did not count. They had slipped into the house quietly some time before. The printing-cellar had an entrance of its own. Not finding any one there, she sat down to her proofs, expecting Sevrin to return to his work at any moment. He did not do so. She grew impatient, heard through the door the sounds of a commotion, and naturally went to see.

"Sevrin had been with us. At first he had seemed to me the most amazed of the whole raided lot. He appeared for an instant as if paralyzed with astonishment. He stood rooted to the spot. He never moved a limb. A solitary gas-jet flared near his head; all the other lights had been put out at the first alarm. And presently, from my dark corner, I observed on his shaven actor's face an expression of puzzled, vexed watchfulness, with a knitting of his heavy eyebrows. The corners of his mouth dropped scornfully. He was angry. Most likely he had seen through the game, and I regretted I had not taken him from the first into my complete confidence.

"But with the appearance of the girl he became obviously alarmed. It was plain. I could see it grow. The change of his expression was swift and startling. All other sensations and emotions were swept away by a wave of sheer terror. And I did not know why. The reason never occurred to me. I was merely astonished at the extreme alteration of the man's face. Of course he had not been aware of her presence in the other cellar. But that did not explain the shock her advent had given him. For a moment he seemed to have been scared into imbecility. He opened his mouth as if to shout, or perhaps only to gasp. At any rate, it was somebody else who shouted. This somebody else was the heroic comrade whom I had detected swallowing a piece of paper. With laudable presence of mind he let out a warning yell.

"'It's the police! Back! Back! Run back, and bolt the door behind you.'

"It was an excellent hint; but instead of retreating, the girl for whom it was meant continued to advance, followed by her long-faced brother in his knickerbocker suit, in which he had been singing comic songs for the entertainment of a joyless proletariat. She advanced not as if she had failed to understand—the word 'police' has an unmistakable sound—but rather as if she could not help herself. She did not advance with the free gait and expanding presence of a distinguished amateur anarchist amongst poor, struggling professionals, but with slightly raised shoulders, and her elbows pressed close to her body, as if trying to shrink within herself. Her eyes were fixed immovably upon Sevrin. Sevrin the man, I fancy; not Sevrin the anarchist. But she advanced. And that was natural. For all their assumption of independence, girls of that class are used to the feeling of being specially protected, as, in fact, they are. This feeling accounts for nine-tenths of their audacious gestures. Her face had gone completely colorless. Ghastly. Fancy having it brought home to her so brutally that she was the sort of person who must run away from the police! I believe she was pale with indignation, mostly, though there was, of course, also the concern for her intact personality, a vague dread of some sort of rudeness. And, naturally, she turned to a man, to the man on whom she had a claim of fascination and homage—the man who could not conceivably fail her at any juncture."

"But," I cried, amazed at this analysis, "if it had been serious, real, I mean—as she thought it was—what could she expect him to do for her?"

X never moved a muscle of his face.

"Goodness knows. I imagine that this charming, generous, and independent creature had never known in her life a single genuine thought; I mean a single thought detached from small human vanities, or whose source was not in some conventional perception. All I know is that after advancing a few steps she extended her hand towards the motionless Sevrin. And that at least was no gesture. It was a natural movement. As to what she expected him to do, who can tell? The impossible. But whatever she expected, it could not have come up, I am safe to say, to what he had made up his mind to do, even before that entreating hand had appealed to him so directly. It had not been necessary. From the moment he had seen her enter that cellar, he had made up his mind to sacrifice his future usefulness, to throw off the impenetrable solidly fastened mask it had been his pride to wear—"

"What do you mean?" I interrupted, puzzled. "Was it Sevrin, then, who was—"

"He was. The most persistent, the most dangerous, the craftiest, the most systematic of informers. A genius amongst betrayers. Fortunately for us, he was unique. The man was a fanatic, I have told you. Fortunately, again, for us, he had fallen in love with the accomplished and innocent gestures of that girl. An actor in desperate earnest himself, he must have believed in the absolute value of conventional signs. As to the grossness of the trap into which he fell, the explanation must be that two sentiments of such absorbing magnitude cannot exist simultaneously in one heart. The danger of that other and unconscious comedian robbed him of his vision, of his perspicacity, of his judgment. Indeed, it did at first rob him of his self-possession. But he regained that through the necessity—as it appeared to him imperiously—to do something at once. To do what? Why, to get her out of the house as quickly as possible. He was desperately anxious to do that. I have told you he was terrified. It could not be about himself. He had been surprised and annoyed at a move quite unforeseen and premature. I may even say he had been furious. He was accustomed to arrange the last scene of his betrayals with a deep, subtle art which left his revolutionist reputation untouched. But it seems clear to me that at the same time he had resolved to make the best of it, to keep his mask resolutely on. It was only with the discovery of her being in the house that everything—the forced calm, the restraint of his fanaticism, the mask—all came off together in a kind of panic. Why panic, do you ask? The answer is very simple.

He remembered—or, I dare say, he had never forgotten the Professor alone at the top of the house, pursuing his researches, surrounded by tins upon tins of Stone's Dried Soup. There was enough in some few of them to bury us all where we stood under a heap of bricks. Sevrin, of course, was aware of that. And we must believe, also, that he knew the exact character of the man, apparently. He had gauged so many such characters! Or perhaps he only gave the Professor credit for what he himself was capable of. But, in any case, the effect was produced. And suddenly he raised his voice in authority.

"'Get the lady away at once.'

"It turned out that he was as hoarse as a crow. Result, no doubt, of the intense emotion. It passed off in a moment. But these fateful words issued forth from his contracted throat in a discordant, ridiculous croak. They required no answer. The thing was done. However, the man personating the inspector judged it expedient to say roughly:

"'She shall go soon enough, together with the rest of you.'

"These were the last words belonging to the comedy part of this affair.

"Oblivious of everything and everybody, Sevrin strode towards him and seized the lapels of his coat. Under his thin bluish cheeks one could see his jaws working with passion.

"'You have men posted outside. Get the lady taken home at once. Do you hear? Now. Before you try to get hold of the man up-stairs.'

"'Oh! There is a man up-stairs,' scoffed the other, openly. 'Well, he shall be brought down in time to see the end of this.'

"But Sevrin, beside himself, took no heed of the tone.

"'Who's the imbecile meddler who sent you blundering here? Didn't you understand your instructions? Don't you know anything? It's incredible. Here—'

"He dropped the lapels of the coat he had been shaking. He plunged his hand into his breast and jerked feverishly at something under his shirt. At last he produced a small square pocket of soft leather, which must have been hanging like a scapulary from his neck by the tape, whose broken ends dangled from his fist.

"'Look inside,' he spluttered, flinging it in the other's face. And instantly he turned round towards the girl. She stood just behind him, perfectly still and silent. Her set, white face gave an illusion of placidity. Only her staring eyes seemed to have grown bigger and darker.

"He spoke to her rapidly, with nervous assurance. I heard him distinctly promise to make everything as clear as daylight presently. But that was all I caught. He stood close to her and never raised his hand, never attempted to touch her even with the tip of his little finger. And she stared at him stupidly. For a moment, however, her eyelids descended slowly, pathetically, and then, with the long black eyelashes lying on her white cheeks, she looked as if she were about to fall headlong in a swoon. But she never even swayed where she stood. He urged her loudly to follow him without losing an instant, and walked towards the door at the bottom of the cellar stairs without looking behind him. And, as a matter of fact, she did move after him a pace or two. But, of course, he was not allowed to reach the door. There were angry exclamations, the tumult of a short, fierce scuffle. Flung away violently, he came flying backwards upon her. She threw out her arms in a gesture of dismay and stepped aside, just clear of his head, which struck the ground heavily near her shoe.

"He grunted with the shock. By the time he had picked himself up, slowly, dazedly, he was awake to the reality of things. The man into whose hands he had thrust the leather case had extracted therefrom a narrow strip of bluish paper. He held it up above his head, and, as after the scuffle an expectant uneasy stillness reigned once more, he threw it down disdainfully with the words, 'I think, comrades, that this proof was hardly necessary.'

"Quick as thought, the girl stooped after the fluttering slip. Holding it spread out in both hands, she looked at it; then, without raising her eyes, opened her fingers slowly and let it fall.

"I examined that curious document afterwards. It was signed by a very high personage, and stamped and countersigned by other high officials in various countries of Europe. In his trade—or shall I say, in his mission?—that sort of talisman might have been necessary, no doubt, for even to the police itself—all but the heads—he had been known only as Sevrin the noted anarchist.

"He hung his head, biting his lower lip. A change had come over him, a sort of thoughtful, absorbed calmness. Nevertheless, he panted. His sides worked visibly, and his nostrils expanded and collapsed in weird contrast with his sombre aspect of a fanatical monk in a meditative attitude, but with something, too, in his face of an actor intent upon the terrible exigencies of his part. Before him Horne declaimed, haggard and bearded, like an inspired denuncia-

"She threw out her arms in dismay and stepped aside."

tory prophet from a wilderness. Two fanatics. They were made to understand each other. Does this surprise you? I suppose you think that such people are given to foaming at the mouth and snarling at each other?"

I protested hastily that I was not surprised in the least; that I thought nothing of the kind; that anarchists in general were simply inconceivable to me mentally, morally, logically, sentimentally, and even physically. X received this declaration with his usual woodenness and went on.

"Horne had burst out into eloquence. While pouring out scornful invective, he let tears escape from his eyes. They fell down his black beard unheeded. Sevrin panted quicker and quicker. When he opened his mouth to speak, every one hung on his words.

"'Don't be a fool, Horne,' he began. 'You know very well that I have done this for none of the reasons you are throwing at me.' And in a moment he became outwardly as steady as a rock under the other's livid stare. 'I have been thwarting, deceiving and betraying you—from conviction.'

"He turned his back on Horne, and, looking intently at the girl, repeated the words, 'From conviction.'

"It's extraordinary how cold she looked. I suppose she could not think of an appropriate gesture. There can have been few precedents indeed for such a situation.

"'Clear as daylight,' he added. 'Do you understand? From conviction.'

"And still she did not stir. She did not know how to respond. But the luckless wretch was about to give her the opportunity for a beautiful and correct gesture.

"'And I had in me the power to make you share it,' he protested, ardently. He had forgotten himself. He made a step towards her. Perhaps he stumbled. To me he seemed only to be stooping low before her with an extended hand. And then the appropriate gesture came. She snatched her skirt away from his polluting touch and turned her head from him with an upward tilt. It was magnificently done, this gesture of conventionally unstained honor, of an unblemished high-minded amateur.

"Nothing could have been better. And he seemed to think so, too, for once more he turned away. But this time he faced no one. He was again panting frightfully, while he fumbled hurriedly in his waistcoat pocket, and then raised his hand to his lips. There was something furtive in this movement, but directly his bearing changed visibly. His labored breathing gave him a resemblance to a man who had just run a desperate race; a curious air of detachment, of sudden and profound indifference, replaced the strain of the striving effort. I did not want to see what would happen next. I was only too well aware. I tucked the young lady's arm under mine without a word, and made my way with her to the stairs.

"Her brother walked behind us. Halfway up she seemed unable to lift her feet high enough, and we had to pull and push to get her to the top. In the passage she dragged herself along, hanging on my arm, helplessly bent like an impotent old woman. We issued into an empty street through a half-open door, staggering like besotted revellers. At the corner we stopped a four-wheeler, and the ancient driver looked round from his box with morose contempt at our efforts to get her in. Twice during the drive I felt her collapse on my shoulder in a half faint. Facing us, the youth in knicker-bockers remained as mute as a fish, and, till he jumped out with the latch-key, more still than I would have believed it possible.

"At the door of their drawing-room she left my arm and walked in first, catching at the chairs and tables. She unpinned her hat, then, as if exhausted with the effort, her cloak still hanging from her shoulders; she flung herself into the deep arm-chair, sideways, her face half buried in a cushion. The good brother appeared silently with a glass of water. She motioned it away. He drank it himself and walked to a distant corner of the room—behind the grand piano, somewhere. All was still in this room where I had seen, for the first time, Sevrin, the anti-anarchist, captivated and spellbound by the consummate and hereditary grimaces that in a certain sphere of life take the place of feelings with an excellent effect. I suppose her thoughts were busy with the same memory. Her shoulders were shaken by dry sobs. A pure attack of nerves. When it quieted down she murmured drearily, 'What will they do to him?'

"'Nothing. They can do nothing to him,' I assured her, with perfect truth. I was pretty certain he had died in less than twenty minutes from the moment his hand had gone to his lips. For if his fanatical anti-anarchism went even as far as carrying poison in his pocket, only to rob his adversaries of their legitimate vengeance, I knew he would take care to provide something that would not fail him when required.

"She sighed deeply. There were red spots on her cheeks and a feverish brilliance in her eyes while she exhaled her characteristic plaint.

"'What an awful, terrible experience, to be so basely, so abominably, so cruelly deceived by a man to whom one has given one's whole confidence!' She gulped down a pathetic sob. 'If I ever felt sure of anything, it was of Sevrin's high-mindedness.'

"Then she began to weep quietly, which was good for her. Then through her flood of tears, half resentful, 'What was it he said to me?—"From conviction!" It seemed worse than anything. What could he mean by it?'

"'That, my dear young lady,' I said gently, 'is more than I or anybody else can explain to you.'"

Mr. X flicked a crumb off the front of his coat.

"And that was strictly true as to her. Though Horne, for instance, understood very well; and so did I, especially after we had been to Sevrin's lodging in a dismal back street of an intensely respectable quarter. Horne was known there as a friend, and we had no difficulty in being admitted, the slatternly girl merely remarking, as she let us in, that 'Mr. Sevrin had not been home that night.' We forced a couple of drawers in the way of duty, and found a little useful information. The most interesting part was his diary; for this man, engaged in such deadly work, had the weakness to keep a record of the most damnatory kind. There were his acts and also his thoughts laid bare to us. But the dead don't mind that. They don't mind anything.

"'From conviction.' Yes. The vague but ardent humanitarianism which had urged him in his first youth to embrace the extreme revolutionary doctrines had ended in a sudden revulsion of feeling. You have heard of converted atheists. These turn often into dangerous fanatics. But the soul remains the same, after all. After he had got acquainted with the girl, there are to be met in that diary of his, mingled with amorous rhapsodies, bizarre, piously worded aspirations for her conversion. He took her sovereign grimace with deadly seriousness. But all this cannot interest you. For the rest, I don't know if you remember—it is a good many years ago now—the journalistic sensation of the 'Hermione Street Mystery'; the finding of a man's body in the cellar of an empty house; the inquest; some arrests; many surmises—then silence—the usual end for many obscure martyrs and confessors. The fact is, he was not enough of an optimist.

You must be a savage, determined, pitiless, thick-and-thin optimist, like Horne, for instance, to make a good revolutionist of the extreme type."

He rose from the table. A waiter hurried up with his overcoat; another held his hat in readiness.

"But what became of the young lady?" I asked.

"I happen to know," he said, buttoning himself up carefully. "I confess to the small malice of sending her Sevrin's diary. She went into retirement; then she went to Rome; then she went into a convent. I don't know where she will go next. What does it matter? Gestures! Gestures! Mere gestures of her class."

He fitted on his glossy high hat with extreme precision, and casting a slight glance round the room, full of well-dressed people, innocently dining, muttered between his teeth,

"And nothing else! That is why their kind is fated to perish."

I never saw Mr. X again after that evening. I took to dining elsewhere. On my next visit to Paris I found my friend all impatience to hear of the effect produced on me by this rare item of his collection. I told him all the story, and he beamed on me with the pride of his distinguished specimen.

"Isn't X well worth knowing?" he bubbled over in great delight. "He's unique, amazing, absolutely terrific."

His enthusiasm grated upon my finer feelings. I told him curtly that the man's cynicism was simply abominable.

"Oh, abominable! abominable!" my friend asserted effusively. "And then, you know, he likes to have his little joke sometimes," he added in a confidential tone.

I fail to understand the connection of this last remark. I have been utterly unable to discover where in all this the joke comes in.

THE ENCHANTED BLUFF
BY WILLA SIBERT CATHER

APRIL 1909

e had our swim before sundown, and while we were cooking our supper the oblique rays of light made a dazzling glare on the white sand about us. The translucent red ball itself sank behind the brown stretches of corn field as we sat down to eat, and the warm layer of air that had rested over the water and our clean sand-bar grew fresher and smelled of the rank iron-weed and sunflowers growing on the flatter shore. The river was brown and sluggish, like any other of the half-dozen streams that water the Nebraska corn lands. On one shore was an irregular line of bald clay bluffs where a few scrub-oaks with thick trunks and flat, twisted tops threw light shadows on the long grass. The western shore was low and level, with corn fields that stretched to the sky-line, and all along the water's edge were little sandy coves and beaches where slim cottonwoods and willow saplings flickered.

The turbulence of the river in springtime discouraged milling, and, beyond keeping the old red bridge in repair, the busy farmers did not concern themselves with the stream; so the Sandtown boys were left in undisputed possession. In the autumn we hunted quail through the miles of stubble and fodder land along the flat shore, and, after the winter skating season was over and the ice had gone out, the spring freshets and flooded bottoms gave us our great excitement of the year. The channel was never the same for two successive seasons. Every spring the swollen stream undermined a bluff to the east, or bit out a few acres of corn field to the west and whirled the soil away to deposit it in spumy mud banks somewhere else. When the water fell low in mid-summer, new sand-bars were thus exposed to dry and whiten in the August sun. Sometimes these were banked so firmly that the fury of the next freshet failed to unseat them; the little willow seedlings emerged triumphantly from the yellow froth, broke into spring leaf, shot up into summer growth, and with their mesh of roots bound together the

moist sand beneath them against the batterings of another April. Here and there a cottonwood soon glittered among them, quivering in the low current of air that, even on breathless days when the dust hung like smoke above the wagon road, trembled along the face of the water.

It was on such an island, in the third summer of its yellow green, that we built our watch-fire; not in the thicket of dancing willow wands, but on the level terrace of fine sand which had been added that spring; a little new bit of world, beautifully ridged with ripple marks, and strewn with the tiny skeletons of turtles and fish, all as white and dry as if they had been expertly cured. We had been careful not to mar the freshness of the place, although we often swam out to it on summer evenings and lay on the sand to rest.

This was our last watch-fire of the year, and there were reasons why I should remember it better than any of the others. Next week the other boys were to file back to their old places in the Sandtown High School, but I was to go up to the Divide to teach my first country school in the Norwegian district. I was already homesick at the thought of quitting the boys with whom I had always played; of leaving the river, and going up into a windy plain that was all windmills and corn fields and big pastures; where there was nothing wilful or unmanageable in the landscape, no new islands, and no chance of unfamiliar birds—such as often followed the watercourses.

Other boys came and went and used the river for fishing or skating, but we six were sworn to the spirit of the stream, and we were friends mainly because of the river. There were the two Hassler boys, Fritz and Otto, sons of the little German tailor. They were the youngest of us; ragged boys of ten and twelve, with sunburned hair, weather-stained faces, and pale blue eyes. Otto, the elder, was the best mathematician in school, and clever at his books, but he always dropped out in the spring term as if the river could not get on without him. He and Fritz caught the fat, horned catfish and sold them about the town, and they lived so much in the water that they were as brown and sandy as the river itself.

There was Percy Pound, a fat, freckled boy with chubby cheeks, who took half a dozen boys' story-papers and was always being kept in for reading detective stories behind his desk. There was Tip Smith, destined by his freckles and red hair to be the buffoon in all our games, though he walked like a timid little old man and had a funny, cracked laugh. Tip worked hard in his father's grocery store every afternoon, and swept it out before school in the morning. Even his recreations were laborious. He collected cigarette cards and tin tobacco-tags indefatigably, and would sit for hours humped up over a snarling little scroll-saw which he kept in his attic. His dearest possessions were some little pill-bottles that purported to contain grains of wheat from the Holy Land, water from the Jordan and the Dead Sea, and earth from the Mount of Olives. His father had bought these dull things from a Baptist missionary who peddled them, and Tip seemed to derive great satisfaction from their remote origin.

The tall boy was Arthur Adams. He had fine hazel eyes that were almost too reflective and sympathetic for a boy, and such a pleasant voice that we all loved to hear him read aloud. Even when he had to read poetry aloud at school, no one ever thought of laughing. To be sure, he was not at school very much of the time. He was seventeen and should have finished the High School the year before, but he was always off somewhere with his gun. Arthur's mother was dead, and his father, who was feverishly absorbed in promoting schemes, wanted to send the boy away to school and get him off his hands; but Arthur always begged off for another year and promised to study. I remember him as a tall, brown boy with an intelligent face, always lounging among a lot of us little fellows, laughing at us oftener than with us, but such a soft, satisfied laugh that we felt rather flattered when we provoked it. In after-years people said that Arthur had been given to evil ways even as a lad, and it is true that we often saw him with the gambler's sons and with old Spanish Fanny's boy, but if he learned anything ugly in their company he never betrayed it to us. We would have followed Arthur anywhere, and I am bound to say that he led us into no worse places than the cattail marshes and the stubble fields. These, then, were the boys who camped with me that summer night upon the sand-bar.

After we finished our supper we beat the willow thicket for driftwood. By the time we had collected enough, night had fallen, and the pungent, weedy smell from the shore increased with the coolness. We threw ourselves down about the fire and made another futile effort to show Percy Pound the Little Dipper. We had tried it often before, but he could never be got past the big one.

"You see those three big stars just below the handle, with the bright one in the middle?" said Otto Hassler; "that's Orion's belt, and the bright one is the clasp." I crawled behind Otto's shoulder and sighted up his arm to the star that seemed perched upon the tip of his steady forefinger. The Hassler boys did seine-fishing at night, and they knew a good many stars.

Percy gave up the Little Dipper and lay back on the sand, his hands clasped under his head. "I can see the North Star," he announced, contentedly, pointing toward it with his big toe. "Any one might get lost and need to know that."

We all looked up at it.

"How do you suppose Columbus felt when his compass didn't point north any more?" Tip asked.

Otto shook his head. "My father says that there was another North Star once, and that maybe this one won't last always. I wonder what would happen to us down here if anything went wrong with it?"

Otto and Fritz caught the fat, horned catfish.

Arthur chuckled. "I wouldn't worry, Ott. Nothing's apt to happen to it in your time. Look at the Milky Way! There must be lots of good dead Indians."

We lay back and looked, meditating, at the dark cover of the world. The gurgle of the water had become heavier. We had often noticed a mutinous, complaining note in it at night, quite different from its cheerful daytime chuckle, and seeming like the voice of a much deeper and more powerful stream. Our water had always these two moods: the one of sunny complaisance, the other of inconsolable, passionate regret.

"Queer how the stars are all in sort of diagrams," remarked Otto. "You could do most any proposition in geometry with 'em. They always look as if they meant something. Some folks say everybody's fortune is all written out in the stars, don't they?"

"They believe so in the old country," Fritz affirmed.

But Arthur only laughed at him. "You're thinking of Napoleon, Fritzey. He had a star that went out when he began to lose battles. I guess the stars don't keep any close tally on Sandtown folks."

We were speculating on how many times we could count a hundred before the evening star went down behind the corn fields, when some one cried, "There comes the moon, and it's as big as a cart wheel!"

We all jumped up to greet it as it swam over the bluffs behind us. It came up like a galleon in full sail; an enormous, barbaric thing, red as an angry heathen god.

"When the moon came up red like that, the Aztecs used to sacrifice their prisoners on the temple top," Percy announced.

"Go on, Perce. You got that out of *Golden Days*. Do you believe that, Arthur?" I appealed.

Arthur answered, quite seriously: "Like as not. The moon was one of their gods. When my father was in Mexico City he saw the stone where they used to sacrifice their prisoners."

As we dropped down by the fire again some one asked whether the Mound-Builders were older than the Aztecs. When we once got upon the Mound-Builders we never willingly got away from them, and we were still conjecturing when we heard a loud splash in the water.

"Must have been a big cat jumping," said Fritz. "They do sometimes. They must see bugs in the dark. Look what a track the moon makes!"

There was a long, silvery streak on the water, and where the current fretted over a big log it boiled up like gold pieces.

"Suppose there ever *was* any gold hid away in this old river?" Fritz asked. He lay like a little brown Indian, close to the fire, his chin on his hand and his bare feet in the air. His brother laughed at him, but Arthur took his suggestion seriously.

"Some of the Spaniards thought there was gold up here somewhere. Seven cities chuck full of gold, they had it, and Coronado and his men came up to hunt it. The Spaniards were all over this country once."

Percy looked interested. "Was that before the Mormons went through?"

We all laughed at this.

"Long enough before. Before the Pilgrim Fathers, Perce. Maybe they came along this very river. They always followed the watercourses."

"I wonder where this river really does begin?" Tip mused. That was an old and a favorite mystery which the map did not clearly explain. On the map the little black line stopped somewhere in western Kansas; but since rivers generally rose in mountains, it was only reasonable to suppose that ours came from the Rockies. Its destination, we knew, was the Missouri, and the Hassler boys always maintained that we could embark at Sandtown in flood-time, follow our noses, and eventually arrive at New Orleans. Now they took up their old argument. "If us boys had grit enough to try it, it wouldn't take no time to get to Kansas City and St. Joe."

We began to talk about the places we wanted to go to. The Hassler boys wanted to see the stock-yards in Kansas City, and Percy wanted to see a big store in Chicago. Arthur was interlocutor and did not betray himself.

"Now it's your turn, Tip."

Tip rolled over on his elbow and poked the fire, and his eyes looked shyly out of his queer, tight little face. "My place is awful far away. My uncle Bill told me about it."

Tip's Uncle Bill was a wanderer, bitten with mining fever, who had drifted into Sandtown with a broken arm, and when it was well had drifted out again.

"Where is it?"

"Aw, it's down in New Mexico somewheres. There aren't no railroads or anything. You have to go on mules, and you run out of water before you get there and have to drink canned tomatoes."

"Well, go on, kid. What's it like when you do get there?"

Tip sat up and excitedly began his story.

"There's a big red rock there that goes right up out of the sand for about nine hundred feet. The country's flat all around it, and this here rock goes up all by itself, like a monument. They call it the Enchanted Bluff down there, because no white man has ever been on top of it. The sides are smooth rock, and straight up, like a wall. The Indians say that hundreds of years ago, before the Spaniards came, there was a village away up there in the air. The tribe that lived there had some sort of steps, made out of wood and bark, hung down over the face of the bluff, and the braves went down to hunt and carried water up in big jars swung on their backs. They kept a big supply of water and dried meat up there, and never went down except to hunt. They were a peaceful tribe that made cloth and pottery, and they went up there to get out of the wars. You see, they could pick off any war party that tried to get up their little steps. The Indians say they were a handsome people, and they had some sort of a queer religion. Uncle Bill thinks they were Cliff-Dwellers who had got into trouble and left home. They weren't fighters, anyhow.

"One time the braves were down hunting and an awful storm came up—a kind of waterspout—and when they got back to their rock they found their little staircase had been all broken to pieces, and only a few steps were left hanging away up in the air. While they were camped at the foot of the rock, wondering what to do, a war party from the north came along and massacred 'em to a man, with all the old folks and women looking on from the rock. Then the war party went on south and left the village to get down the best way they could. Of course they never got down. They starved to death up there, and when the war party came back on their way north, they could hear the children crying from the edge of the bluff where they had crawled out, but they didn't see a sign of a grown Indian, and nobody has ever been up there since."

We exclaimed at this dolorous legend and sat up.

"There couldn't have been many people up there," Percy demurred. "How big is the top, Tip?"

"Oh, pretty big. Big enough so that the rock doesn't look nearly as tall as it is. The top's bigger than the base. The bluff is sort of worn away for several hundred feet up. That's one reason it's so hard to climb."

I asked how the Indians got up, in the first place.

"Nobody knows how they got up or when. A hunting party came along once and saw that there was a town up there, and that was all."

Otto rubbed his chin and looked thoughtful. "Of course there must be some way to get up there. Couldn't people get a rope over someway and pull a ladder up?"

Tip's little eyes were shining with excitement. "I know a way. Me and Uncle Bill talked it all over. There's a kind of rocket that would take a rope over—life-savers use 'em—and then you could hoist a rope-ladder and peg it down at the bottom and make it tight with guy-ropes on the other side. I'm going to climb that there bluff, and I've got it all planned out."

Fritz asked what he expected to find when he got up there.

"Bones, maybe, or the ruins of their town, or pottery, or some of their idols. There might be 'most anything up there. Anyhow, I want to see."

"Sure nobody else has been up there, Tip?" Arthur asked.

"Dead sure. Hardly anybody ever goes down there. Some hunters tried to cut steps in the rock once, but they didn't get higher than a man can reach. The Bluff's all red granite, and Uncle Bill thinks it's a boulder the glaciers left. It's a queer place, anyhow. Nothing but cactus and desert for hundreds of miles, and yet right under the bluff there's good water and plenty of grass. That's why the bison used to go down there."

Suddenly we heard a scream above our fire, and jumped up to see a dark, slim bird floating southward far above us—a whooping-crane, we knew by her cry and her long neck. We ran to the edge of the island, hoping we might see her alight, but she wavered southward along the rivercourse until we lost her. The Hassler boys declared that by the look of the heavens it must be after midnight, so we threw more wood on our fire, put on our jackets, and curled down in the warm sand. Several of us pretended to doze, but I fancy we were really thinking about Tip's Bluff and the extinct people. Over in the wood the ring-doves were calling mournfully to one another, and once we heard a dog bark, far away. "Somebody getting into old Tommy's melon patch," Fritz murmured, sleepily, but nobody answered him. By and by Percy spoke out of the shadow.

"Say, Tip, when you go down there will you take me with you?"

"Maybe."

"Suppose one of us beats you down there, Tip?"

"Whoever gets to the Bluff first has got to promise to tell the rest of us exactly what he finds," remarked one of the Hassler boys, and to this we all readily assented.

Somewhat reassured, I dropped off to sleep. I must have dreamed about a race for the Bluff, for I awoke in a kind of fear that other people were getting ahead of me and that I was losing my chance. I sat up in my damp clothes and looked at the other boys, who lay tumbled in uneasy attitudes about the dead fire. It was still dark, but the sky was blue with the last wonderful azure of night. The stars glistened like crystal globes, and trembled as if they shone through a depth of clear water. Even as I watched, they began to pale and the sky brightened. Day came suddenly, almost instantaneously. I turned for another look at the blue night, and it was gone. Everywhere the birds began to call, and all manner of little insects began to chirp and hop about in the willows. A breeze sprang up from the west and brought the heavy smell of ripened corn. The boys rolled over and shook themselves. We stripped and plunged into the river just as the sun came up over the windy bluffs.

When I came home to Sandtown at Christmas time, we skated out to our island and talked over the whole project of the Enchanted Bluff, renewing our resolution to find it.

Although that was twenty years ago, none of us have ever climbed the Enchanted Bluff. Percy Pound is a stockbroker in Kansas City and will go nowhere that his red touring-car cannot carry him. Otto Hassler went on the railroad and lost his foot braking; after which he and Fritz succeeded their father as the town tailors.

Arthur sat about the sleepy little town all his life—he died before he was twenty-five. The last time I saw him, when I was home on one of my college vacations, he was sitting in a steamer-chair under a cottonwood tree in the little yard behind one of the two Sandtown saloons. He was very untidy and his hand was not steady, but when he rose, unabashed, to greet me, his eyes were as clear and warm as ever. When I had talked with him for an hour and heard him laugh again, I wondered how it was that when Nature had taken such pains with a man, from his hands to the arch of his long foot, she had ever lost him in Sandtown. He joked about Tip Smith's Bluff, and declared he was going down there just as soon as the weather got cooler; he thought the Grand Cañon might be worth while, too.

I was perfectly sure when I left him that he would never get beyond the high plank fence and the comfortable shade of the cottonwood. And, indeed, it was under that very tree that he died one summer morning.

Tip Smith still talks about going to New Mexico. He married a slatternly, unthrifty country girl, has been much tied to a perambulator, and has grown stooped and gray from irregular meals and broken sleep. But the worst of his difficulties are now over, and he has, as he says, come into easy water. When I was last in Sandtown I walked home with him late one moonlight night, after he had balanced his cash and shut up his store. We took the long way around and sat down on the schoolhouse steps, and between us we quite revived the romance of the lone red rock and the extinct people. Tip insists that he still means to go down there, but he thinks now he will wait until his boy, Bert, is old enough to go with him. Bert has been let into the story, and thinks of nothing but the Enchanted Bluff.

"Truth Went on Her Way Alone," by Howard Pyle.

From Dec, 1900
P. 13
where dis w
col

1910's

Night in a Suburb

(Near Tooting Common)

by Thomas Hardy

December 1911

While rain, with eve in partnership,
    Descended darkly, drip, drip, drip,
Beyond the last lone lamp I passed
        Walking slowly, whispering sadly,
Two linked loiterers, wan, downcast;
Some heavy thought constrained each face,
And made them blank to time and place.

The pair seemed lovers, yet absorbed
In mental scenes no longer orbed
By love's young light. Each countenance
        As it slowly, as it sadly
Caught the lamplight's yellow glance,
Held in suspense a misery
At things which might, or might not, be.

When I retrod that watery way
Some hours beyond the death of day,
Still I found pacing there the twain
        Just as slowly, just as sadly,
Heedless of the night and rain.
One could but wonder who they were,
And what wild woe detained them there.

Though thirty years of blur and blot
Have flown since I beheld that spot,
And saw in curious converse there
        Moving slowly, moving sadly,
That mysterious tragic pair,
Its olden look may linger on—
All but the couple; they have gone.

Whither? Who knows, indeed!... And yet
To me, when nights are weird and wet,
Without those comrades there at tryst
        Creeping slowly, creeping sadly,
That lone lane does not exist.
Still they seem brooding on their pain,
And will, while such a lane remain.

The Rabbit-pen

by Sherwood Anderson

July 1914

In a wire pen beside the gravel path, Fordyce, walking in the garden of his friend Harkness and imagining marriage, came upon a tragedy. A litter of new-born rabbits lay upon the straw scattered about the pen. They were blind; they were hairless; they were blue-black of body; they oscillated their heads in mute appeal. In the center of the pen lay one of the tiny things, dead. Above the little dead body a struggle went on. The mother rabbit fought the father furiously. A wild fire was in her eyes. She rushed at the huge fellow again and again.

The man who had written two successful novels stood trembling in the path. He saw the father rabbit and the furious little mother struggling in the midst of the new life scattered about the pen, and his hands shook and his lips grew white. He was afraid that the mother of the litter would be killed in the struggle. A cry of sympathy broke from his lips. "Help here! Help! There is murder being done!" he shouted.

Out at the back door of the house came Gretchen, the housekeeper. She ran rapidly down the gravel path. Seeing the struggle going on in the wire pen, she knelt, and, tearing open a little door, dragged the father rabbit out of the pen. In her strong grasp the father rabbit hung by his ears, huge and grotesque. He kicked out with his heels. Turning, she flung him through an open window into a child's play-house standing amid the shrubbery beside the path.

Fordyce stood in the path, looking at the little dead rabbit in the center of the pen. He thought that it should be taken away, and wondered how it might be done. He tried to think of himself reaching through the little door into the cage and taking the little blue-black dead thing into his hand; but the housekeeper, coming from the child's play-house with a child's shovel in her hand, reached into the pen and threw the body over the shrubbery into the vegetable-garden beyond.

Fordyce followed her—the free-walking, straight-backed Gretchen—into the stable at the end of the gravel path. He heard her talking, in her bold, quick way, to Hans, the stableman. He wondered what she was saying that made Hans smile. He sat on a chair by the stable door, watching her as she walked back to the house.

Hans, the stableman, finished the righting of things in the home of the rabbits. The tragedy was effaced; the dead rabbit buried among the cabbages in the garden. Into the wire pen Hans put fresh, new straw. Fordyce wondered what Gretchen had said to Hans in that language. He was overcome by her efficiency. "She knew what to do, and yet, no doubt, like me, she knew nothing of rabbits," he thought, lost in wonder.

Hans came back into the stable and began again polishing the trimmings of a harness hanging on the wall. "He was trying to kill the young males," he explained in broken English.

Fordyce told Harkness of the affair of the rabbit-pen. "She was magnificent," he said. "She saved all of that new life while I stood by, trembling and impotent. I went up to my room and sat thinking of her. She should be spending her days caring for new life, making it fine and purposeful, and not be counting sheets and wrangling with the iceman for an old, worn-out newspaper hack like you."

Joe Harkness had laughed. "Same old sentimental, susceptible Frank," he had shouted, joyously. "Romancing about every woman you see, but keeping well clear of them, just the same."

Sitting on the wide veranda in the late afternoon, Fordyce read a book. He was alone, so it was his own book. As he read, he wondered that so many thousands of people had failed to buy and appreciate it. Between paragraphs he became entangled in one of his own fancies—the charming fancies that never became realities. He imagined himself the proud husband of Gretchen, the housekeeper.

Fordyce was always being a proud husband. Scarcely a week passed without the experience. It was satisfying and complete. He felt now that he had never been prouder husband to a more beautiful or more capable woman than Gretchen. Gretchen was complete. She was a Brünnhilde. Her fine face, crowned by thick, smooth hair, and her quiet, efficient manner, brought a thrill of pride. He saw himself getting off the train in the evening at some Chicago suburb and walking through the shady streets to the frame house where Gretchen waited at the door.

Glancing up, his eyes rested on the wide emerald lawn. In the shrubbery, Hans, the stableman, worked with a pair of pruning-shears. Fordyce began thinking of the master of the house and its mistress, Ruth—the brown-eyed, soft-voiced Ruth with the boyish freckles. Joe, comrade of the struggling newspaper days, was married to pretty Ruth and her fortune, and went off to meetings of directors in the city, as he had done this afternoon. "Good old Joe," thought Fordyce, with a wave of tenderness. "For him no more uncertainties, no more heartaches."

From the nursery at the top of the house came the petulant voices of the children. They were refusing to be off to bed at the command of their mother, refusing to be quiet, as they had been refusing her commands all afternoon. They romped and shouted in the nursery, throwing things about. Fordyce could hear the clear, argumentative voice of the older boy.

"Don't be obstinate, mother," said the boy; "we will be quiet after a while."

The man sitting on the veranda could picture the gentle mother. She would be standing in the doorway of the nursery—the beautiful children's room with the pictures of ships on the walls—and there would be the vague, baffled, uncertain look in her eyes. She would be trying to make herself severe and commanding, and the children would be defying her. The listening man closed his book with a bang. A shiver of impatience ran through him. "Damn!" he said, swiftly. "Damn!"

From below-stairs came the sharp, clicking sound of footsteps. A voice, firm and purposeful, called up to the nursery. "*Schweig!*" commanded the voice of Gretchen, the housekeeper.

Above-stairs all became quiet. The mother, coming slowly down, joined Fordyce on the veranda. They sat together discussing books. They talked of the work of educators among children.

"I can do nothing with my own children," said Ruth Harkness. "They look to that Gretchen for everything."

In the house Fordyce could hear the housekeeper moving about, up and down the stairs, and in and out of the living-room; he could see her through the windows and the open doors. She went about silently, putting the house in order. Above in the nursery all was peace and quiet.

Fordyce stayed on as a guest at Cottesbrooke, finishing his third book. With him stayed Gretchen, putting the house in order for the winter; Harkness, with Ruth, the two boys and the servants, had gone to the city home. It was autumn, and the brown leaves went dancing through the bare shrubbery on the lawn. In his overcoat Frank now sat on the veranda and looked at the hurrying leaves. He was being one of the leaves.

"I am dead and brown and without care, and that is I now being blown by the wind across the dead grass," he told himself.

At the end of the veranda, near the carriage entrance, stood his trunk. His brown bag was by his feet.

Out through the door of the house came Gretchen. She stood by the railing at the edge of the veranda, talking. "I am not satisfied with this family," she said. "I shall be leaving them. There is too much money."

She turned, waving her hand and talking vehemently. "It is of no account to save," she declared. "I am best at the saving. In this house all summer I have made the butter for the table from cream that has spoiled. Things were wasted in the kitchen and I have stopped that. It has passed unnoticed. I know every sheet, every towel. Is it appreciated? Master Harkness and mistress—they do not know that I know, and do not care. The sour cream they would see thrown to the pig. Uh!—It is of no use to be saving here."

Fordyce thought that he was near to being a real husband. It came into his mind to spring from his chair and beseech this frugal woman to come and save the soured cream in a frame house in a Chicago suburb. While he hesitated, she turned and disappeared into the house. "*Auf Wiedersehen!*" she called to him over her shoulder.

He went along the veranda and climbed into the carriage. He went slowly, looking back at the door through which she had disappeared. He was thinking of the day in the green summer when he had stood in the gravel path by the wire rabbit-pen, watching her straighten out the affair in the family of the rabbits. As on that day, he now felt strangely impotent and incapable. "I should be taking things into my own hands," he reflected, while Hans drove the carriage along the road under the bare trees.

Now it was February, with the snow lying piled along the edges of the city streets. Sitting in the office of his friend

"Kuerner's Farm," 1916, by Newell Wyeth.

Harkness, Fordyce, looking through the window, could see the lake, blue and cold and lonely.

Fordyce turned from the window to his friend, at work among the letters on the desk. "It is of no avail to look sternly and forbiddingly at me," he said. "I will not go away. I have sold the book I wrote at your house, and have money in my pocket. Now I will take you to dine with me, and after the dinner I will get on a train and start on a trip to Germany. There is a reason why I should learn to speak the German language. I hear housekeepers talking to stablemen about the doings of rabbits in pens, and it gets into my mind that I don't know what they say. They may whisper secrets of life in that language. I have a wish to know everything, and I shall begin by knowing the German language. Perhaps I shall get me a wife over there and come home a proud and serious husband. It would be policy for you to drop letter-signing and come to dine with me while yet I am a free man."

In the restaurant they had come to the cigars, and Harkness was talking of life in his house. He was talking intimately, as a man talks only to one who is near and dear to him.

"I have been unhappy," said Harkness. "A struggle has gone on in which I have lost."

His friend said nothing. Putting down his cigar, he fingered the thin stem of the glass that sat before him.

"In Germany I engaged Gretchen," said Harkness, talking rapidly. "I got her for the management of our house and for the boys. They were unruly, and Ruth could do nothing with them. Also we thought it would be well for them to know the German language.

"In our house, after we got Gretchen, peace came. The boys stayed diligently at their lessons. When in the schoolroom at the top of the house they were unruly, Gretchen came to the foot of the stairs, '*Schweig!*' she shouted, and they were intent upon their lessons.

"In the house Gretchen went about quietly. She did the work of the house thoroughly. When I came home in the evening the toys of the children no longer were scattered about underfoot. They were gathered into the boxes put into the nursery for the purpose.

"Our two boys sat quietly with us at the evening meal. When they had been well-mannered they looked for approval to Gretchen, who talked to them in German. Ruth did not speak German. She sat at the table, looking at the boys and at Gretchen. She was unhappy in her own home, but I did not know why.

"One evening when the boys had gone up-stairs with Gretchen she turned to me, saying intensely, 'I *hate* German!' I thought her over-tired. 'You should see a physician for the nerves,' I said.

"And then came Christmas. It was a German Christmas with German cakes and a tree for each of the boys. Gretchen and I had planned it one evening when Ruth was in bed with a headache.

"The gifts on our Christmas trees were magnificent. They were a surprise to me. Ruth and I had not believed in costly gifts, and now Ruth had loaded the trees with them. The trees were filled with toys, costly mechanical toys for each of our two boys. With them she had planned to win the boys.

"The boys were beside themselves with joy. They ran about the room shouting. They played with the elaborate toys upon the floor.

"Ruth took the gifts from the trees. In the shadow by the door stood Gretchen. She was silent. When the boys got the packages from the trees they ran to her, shouting, '*Mach' es auf! Mach' es auf! Tante Gretchen!*'

"I was happy. I thought we were having a beautiful Christmas. The annoyance I had felt at the magnificence of Ruth's gifts passed away.

"And then, in one moment, the struggle that had smoldered under the surface of the lives of the two women in my house burst forth. Ruth, my gentle Ruth, ran out into the middle of the floor, shouting in a shrill, high voice, 'Who is mother here? Whose children are these?'

"The two boys clung to the dress of Gretchen. They were frightened and cried. Gretchen went out of the room, taking them with her. I could hear her quick, firm footsteps on the stairs.

"Gretchen put the two boys into their white beds in the nursery. At her word they ceased weeping.

"In the center of the room they had left, lighted only by the little electric bulbs in the branches of the Christmas trees, stood Ruth. She stood in silence, looking at the floor, and trembling.

"I looked at the door through which our boys had gone at the command of Gretchen. I did not look at Ruth. A flame of indignation burned in me. I felt that I should like to take her by the shoulders and shake her."

Fordyce had never seen his friend so moved. Since his visit to Cottesbrooke he had been thinking of his old comrade as a man in a safe harbor—one peacefully becalmed behind the breakwater of Ruth and her fortune, passing his days untroubled, secure in his happiness.

"My Ruth is wonderful," declared Harkness, breaking in on these reflections. "She is all love and truth. To me she had been more dear than life. We have been married all these years, and still like a lover I dream of her at night. Sometimes I get out of bed and creep into her room, and, kneeling there in the darkness, I kiss the strands of her hair that lie loose upon the pillow.

"I do not understand why it is not with our boys as it is with me," he said, simply. "To myself I say, 'Her love should conquer all.'"

Before the mind of Fordyce was a different picture—the picture of a strong, straight-backed woman running down a gravel path to a wire rabbit-pen. He saw her reach through the door, and, taking the father rabbit by the ears, throw him through the window of the child's play-house. "She could settle the trouble in the rabbit's pen," he thought; "but this was another problem."

Harkness talked again. "I went to where Ruth stood trembling and took her in my arms," he said. "I made up my mind that I would send Gretchen back to Germany. It was my love for Ruth that had made my life. In a flash I saw how she had been crowded out of her place in her own home by that able, quiet, efficient woman."

Harkness turned his face away from the eyes of his friend. "She lay in my arms and I ran my hand over her hot little head," he said. "'I couldn't keep it back any longer, Joe; I couldn't help saying it,' she cried. 'I have been a child, and I have lost a fight. If you will let me, I will try now to be a woman and a mother.'"

Fordyce took his eyes from the face of his friend. For relief he had been feeding an old fancy. He saw himself walking up a gravel path to the door of a German house. The house would be in a village, and there would be formal flower-plots by the side of the gravel path.

"To what place in Germany did she go, this Gretchen?" he demanded.

Harkness shook his head. "She married Hans, the stableman, and they went away together," he said. "In my house the mechanical toys from the Christmas tree lie about underfoot. We are planning to send our boys to a private school. They are pretty hard to control."

THE COUNTRY NEWSPAPER

BY WILLIAM ALLEN WHITE

MAY 1916

The country town is one of those things we have worked out for ourselves here in America. Our cities are not unlike other cities in the world; the trolley and the omnibus and the subway, the tender hot-house millionaire and the hardy, perennial crook are found in all cities. Class lines extend from city to city well around the globe. And American aversion to caste disappears when the American finds himself cooped in a city with a million of his fellows. But in the country town—the political unit larger than the village and smaller than the city, the town with a population between three and one hundred thousand—we have built up something distinctively American. Physically, it is of its own kind; the people for the most part live in detached wooden houses on lots with fifty feet of street frontage, and from one hundred to one hundred and fifty feet in depth. Grass is the common heritage of all the children—grass and flowers. A kitchen-garden smiles in the back yard, and the service of public utilities is so cheap that in most country towns in America electricity for lighting and household power, water for the kitchen sink and the bath-room, gas for cooking, and the telephone with unlimited use may be found in every house. In the town where these lines are written there are more telephones than there are houses, and as many water intakes as there are families, and more electric lights than there are men, women, and children. Civilization brings its labor-saving devices to all the people of an American country town. The uncivilized area is negligible, if one measures civilization by the use of the conveniences and luxuries that civilization has brought.

In the home, the difference between the rich and the poor, in these towns, is denoted largely by the multiplication of rooms; there is no very great difference in the kinds of rooms in the houses of those who have much and those who have little. And, indeed, the economic differences are of no consequence. The average American thinks he is saving for his children, and for nothing else. But if the child of the rich man and the child of the poor man meet in a common school, graduate from a common high-school, and meet in the country college or in the state university—and they do associate thus in the days of their youth—there is no reason why parents should strain themselves for the children; and they do not strain themselves. They relax in their automobiles, go to the movies, inhabit the summer boarding-house in the mountains or by the sea, and hoot at the vulgarity and stupidity of those strangers who appear to be rich and to be grunting and sweating and saving and intriguing for more money, but who really are only well-to-do middle-class people.

In the American country town the race for great wealth has slackened down. The traveler who sees our half-dozen great cities, who goes into our industrial centers, loafs about our pleasure resorts, sees much that is significantly American. But he misses much also if he fails to realize that there are in America tens of thousands of miles of asphalted streets arched by elms, bordered by green lawns, fringed with flowers marking the procession of the seasons, and that back from these streets stand millions of houses owned by their tenants—houses of from five to ten rooms, that cost from twenty-five hundred to twenty-five thousand dollars, and that in these houses live a people neither rural nor urban, a people who have rural traditions and urban aspirations, and who are getting a rather large return from civilization for the dollars they spend. Besides the civilization that comes to these people in pipes and on wires, they are buying civilization in the phonograph, the moving picture, the automobile, and the fifty-cent reprint of last year's fiction success. The Woman's City Federation of Clubs is bringing what civic beauty it can lug home from Europe and the Eastern cities; the opportune death of the prominent citizen is opening playgrounds and hospitals and parks; and the country college, which has multiplied as the sands of the sea, supplements the state schools of higher learning in the work of bringing to youth opportunities for more than the common-school education.

Now into this peculiar civilization comes that curious institution, the country newspaper. The country newspaper is the incarnation of the town spirit. The newspaper is more than the voice of the country-town spirit; the newspaper is in a measure the will of the town, and the town's character is displayed with sad realism in the town's newspapers. A newspaper is as honest as its town, is as intelligent as its town, as kind as its town, as brave as its town. And those curious phases of abnormal psychology often found in men and women, wherein a dual or multiple personality speaks, are found often in communities where many newspapers babble the many voices arising from the disorganized spirits of the place. For ten years and more the tendency in the American country town has been toward fewer newspapers. That tendency seems to show that the spirit of these communities is unifying. The disassociated personalities of the community—the wrangling bankers, the competing public utilities, the wets and the drys, the Guelfs and the Ghibellines in a score of guises that make for discord in towns—are slowly knitting into the spirit of the place. So one newspaper in the smaller communities—in communities under fifteen thousand, let us say—is becoming the town genus! And in most of the larger towns—so long as they are towns and not cities—one newspaper is rising dominant and authoritative because it interprets and directs the community. The others are merely expressions of vagrant moods; they are unhushed voices that are still uncorrelated, still unbridled in the community's heart.

It is therefore the country newspaper, the one that speaks for the town, that guides and cherishes the town, that embodies the distinctive spirit of the town, wherein one town differeth from another in glory—it is that country newspaper, which takes its color from a town and gives color back, that shall engage our attention at present. That newspaper shall be our vision.

Of old in this country the newspaper was a sort of poor relation in the commerce of a place. The newspaper required support, and the support was given, somewhat in charity, more or less in return for polite blackmail, and the rest for business reasons. The editor was a tolerated person. He had to be put on the chairmanship of some important committee in every community enterprise to secure his help. In times of social or political emergency, he sold stock in his newspaper company to statesmen. That was in those primeval days before corporations were controlled; so the editor's trusty job-press never let the supply of stock fall behind the demand. Those good old days were the days when the editor with the "trenchant pen" stalked to glory through libel-suits and shooting scrapes, and when most American towns were beset by a newspaper row as by a fiendish mania.

But those fine old homicidal days of the newspaper business are past, or are relegated to the less civilized parts of the land. The Colonel and the Major have gone gallantly to dreams of glory, perhaps carrying more buckshot with them to glory than was needed for ballast on their journey; but still they are gone, and their race has died with them. The newspaper man of to-day is of another breed. How the Colonel or the Major would snort in derision at the youth who pervades the country newspaper office to-day. For this young man is first of all a manufacturer! The shirt-tail full of type and the cheese press, which in times past were held as emblems of the loathed contemporary's plant, have now grown even in country villages to little factories. The smallest offices now have their typesetting-machines. The lean, sad-visaged country printer, who had tried and burned his wings in the editorial flight, is no more. Instead we have a keen-eyed, dressy young man who makes eyes at the girls in the front office, and can talk shows with the drummer at the best hotel, or books with the high-school teacher in the boarding-house. This young gentleman operates the typesetting-machine. Generally he is exotic; frequently he is a traveler from far countries, but he rides in the Pullman and the clay of no highway ever stains his dainty feet. In the country town, in the factory that makes even the humblest of our country dailies, the little six and eight page affairs, all unknown, unhonored, and unsung, three or four and sometimes half a dozen of the smart, well-fed, nattily dressed machine operators are hired, and the foreman—the dear old pipe-smoking, unshaven foreman who prided himself in a long line of apprentice printers, the foreman who edited copy, who wrote the telegraph heads and ruled the reporters in the front office with an iron rod of terror, the foreman who had the power of life and death over every one around the building but the advertising man, the foreman who spent his princely salary of fifteen dollars a week buying meals for old friends drifting through with the lazy tide of traffic between the great cities, the foreman who could boast that he once held cases on the *Sun* and knew old Dana—

that foreman is gone; in his place we know the superintendent. And, alas! the superintendent is not interested in preserving the romance of a day that is past. He is not bothered by the touch of a vanished hand. When the vanished hand tries to touch the superintendent of the country newspaper office to-day, a ticket to the Associated Charities' woodyard is his dull response. The superintendent is interested largely in efficiency. The day of romance is past in the back room of the country newspaper.

But in the front room, in the editorial offices, in the business office even, there abides the spirit of high adventure that is incarnate in these marvelous modern times. Never before were there such grand doings in the world as we are seeing to-day. Screen the great war from us, and still we have a world full of romance, full of poetry, full of an unfolding progress that is like the gorgeous story of some enchanter's spell. Where in all the tales of those *Arabian Nights' Entertainments* is anything so wonderful as wireless telegraphy, so weird and uncanny as talking over the seas without wires? What is Cinderella and her romance compared with the Cinderella story to-day—the story that tells us how the world is turning into her prince, shortening her hours of work, guaranteeing her a living wage, keeping her little brothers and sisters away from the factory and in school, and pensioning her widowed mother that she may care for her little flock! How tame is the old Cinderella story beside this! And Sindbad is losing his load, too—slowly, as the years form into decades, Sindbad is sloughing off the old man of the sea; the twelve-hour day is almost gone, and the eight-hour day is coming quickly; the diseases and accidents of labor are falling from his shoulders, being assumed by his employer; his bank savings are guaranteed by his government; his food is no longer poisoned; his tenement is ceasing to be a pit of infection; his shop is no longer a place of torture. And every day the newspaper brings some fresh and inspiring chapter of these great stories to their readers. Stories of progress are the magnificent tales of sorcery and wizarding that come gleaming in celestial light across the pages

"Well, sir, which part of my paper would you like to read next?"

of our newspapers every day. And in our country papers we rejoice in them, because we know the heroes. [...] We open the country paper and say, "How blessed on the mountains are the feet of them that bring glad tidings," and so we read it, every line. It is the daily chronicle of the doings of our friends.

Of course our country papers are provincial. We know that as well as any one. But then, so far as that goes, we know that all papers are provincial. How we laugh at the provincialisms of the New York and Boston and Chicago papers when we visit the cities! For the high gods of civilization, being jealous of the press, have put upon all newspapers this spell: that every one must be limited in interest to its own town and territory. There can be no national daily newspaper, for before it reaches the nation its news is old and dull and as clammy as a cold pancake. News does not keep. Twelve hours from the press it is stale, flat, and highly unprofitable. However the trains may speed, however the organization of the subscription department and the press-room may perfect itself, the news spoils before the ink dries, and there never may be in our land a cosmopolitan press. So the cities' papers find that they must fill up those spaces, which in a nation-wide paper should be filled with the news from the far corners of our land, with city news. Thus in every country paper we have the local gossip of its little world. And our country papers are duplicated on a rather grander scale in the cities. What we do in six or eight or ten or twelve pages in the country, the city papers do in twenty or forty pages. What they do with certain prominent citizens in the social and criminal and financial world, we do also with our prominent citizens in their little worlds. [...]

But the beauty and the joy of our papers and their little worlds is that we who live in the country towns know our own heroes. Who knows Murphy in New York? Only a few. Yet in Emporia we all know Tom O'Connor—and love him. Who knows Morgan in New York? One man in a hundred thousand. Yet in Emporia who does not know George Newman, our banker and merchant prince? Boston people pick up their morning papers and read with shuddering horror of the crimes of their daily villain, yet read without that fine thrill that we have when we hear that Al Ludorph is in jail

again in Emporia. For we all know Al; we've ridden in his hack a score of times. And we take up our paper with the story of his frailties as readers who begin the narrative of an old friend's adventures. [...]

Our papers, our little country papers, seem drab and miserably provincial to strangers; yet we who read them read in their lines the sweet, intimate story of life. And all these touches of nature make us wondrous kind. It is the country newspaper, bringing together daily the threads of the town's life, weaving them into something rich and strange, and setting the pattern as it weaves, directing the loom, and giving the cloth its color by mixing the lives of all the people in its color-pot—it is this country newspaper that reveals us to ourselves, that keeps our country hearts quick and our country minds open and our country faith strong.

When the girl at the glove-counter marries the boy in the wholesale house, the news of their wedding is good for a forty-line wedding-notice, and the forty lines in the country paper give them self-respect. When in due course we know that their baby is a twelve-pounder, named Grover or Theodore or Woodrow, we have that neighborly feeling that breeds the real democracy. When we read of death in that home we can mourn with them that mourn. When we see them moving upward in the world, into a firm, and out toward the country club neighborhood, we rejoice with them that rejoice. Therefore, men and brethren, when you are riding through this vale of tears upon the California Limited, and by chance pick up the little country newspaper with its meager telegraph service of three or four thousand words—or, at best, fifteen or twenty thousand; when you see its array of countryside items; its interminable local stories; its tiresome editorials on the waterworks, the schools, the street railroad, the crops, and the city printing, don't throw down the contemptible little rag with the verdict that there is nothing in it. But know this, and know it well: if you could take the clay from your eyes and read the little paper as it is written, you would find all of God's beautiful sorrowing, struggling, aspiring world in it, and what you saw would make you touch the little paper with reverent hands.

MY PLUNGE INTO THE SLUMS

BY M. E. RAVAGE

APRIL 1917

It seems to be assumed by the self-complacent native that we immigrants are at once and overwhelmingly captivated by America and all things American. The mere sight of this new world, he fancies, should fill our hearts with the joy of dreams realized and leave us in a state of surfeited contentment empty of all further desire. Why, he would ask, if the doubt were ever to occur to him—why should we not be happy? Have we not left our own country because we were in one way or another discontented there? And if we have chosen America, it is quite clear that we must have been attracted by what she offered us in substitution. Besides, no man with eyes could fail to see right off the superiority of this great republic to every other country on the face of the earth. Witness how the tide of immigration is forever flowing—and always in one direction. If the alien were dissatisfied with America, would he not be taking the first steamer back instead of inviting his friends and family to follow him?

And yet, in spite of logic and appearances, the truth remains that the immigrant is almost invariably disappointed in America. At any rate, of this much I am certain: I myself was very bitterly disappointed in America. And, unless observation has been altogether astray with me, I think I am justified in the generalization that nearly all other newcomers are at least as disappointed as I was. It was not that this land of my aspirations had failed to come up to my dream of it, although in a measure it did fall short there. Neither was my disillusionment due to the dreariness, the sordidness, and the drudgery of immigrant life, although this, too, may have entered into the equation. All these things came only later. I am writing of the first impact of America—or of that small fraction of it which was America to me—of the initial shock that came to me when I first set foot on American soil. And I say that long before I had had time to find out what my own fate would be in this new world, I experienced a revulsion of feeling of the most distressful sort.

What were the reasons for it? Well, there were a variety of them: The alien who comes here from Europe is not the raw material that Americans suppose him to be. He is not a blank sheet to be written on as you see fit. He has not sprung out of nowhere. Quite the contrary. He brings with him a deep-rooted tradition, a system of culture and tastes and habits—a point of view which is as ancient as his national experience and which has been engendered in him by his race and his environment. And it is this thing—this entire Old World soul of his—that comes in conflict with America as soon as he has landed. Not, I beg you to observe, with America of the Americans. Of that greater and remoter world in which the native resides we immigrants are hardly aware. What rare flashes of it do come within range of our blurred vision reveal a planet so alien and far removed from our experience that they strike us as merely comical or fantastic—a set of phenomena so odd that we can only smile over them but never be greatly concerned with them.

I needed sadly to readjust myself when I arrived in New York. But the incredible thing is that my problem was to fit myself in with the people of Vaslui and Rumania, my erstwhile fellow-townsmen and my fellow-countrymen. It was not America in the large sense, but the East Side Ghetto that upset all my calculations, reversed all my values, and set my head swimming. New York at first sight was, after all, not so very unlike many other large cities that I had traveled through. I viewed it from the upper deck as my steamer plowed into the harbor and up the river, and was not the least bewildered by the sight. I cannot remember whether I thought it was ugly or beautiful. What did it matter? From the pier I was hustled with hundreds of others of my kind into a smaller boat and taken to Ellis Island. There I was put through a lot of meaningless maneuvers by uniformed, rough officials. I was jostled and dragged and shoved and shouted at. I took it philosophically. I had been through the performance many times before—at the Hungarian border, at Vienna, in Germany, in Holland. It did not touch me, and I have forgotten all about it.

But I have not forgotten and I never can forget that first pungent breath of the slums which were to become my home for the next five years. [...] I shall never forget how depressed my heart became as I trudged through those littered streets, with the rows of push-carts lining the sidewalks and the centers of the thoroughfares, the ill-smelling merchandise, and the deafening noise. My pretty little cousin, elegant in her American tailored suit, was stepping along beside me, apparently oblivious to the horrible milieu that was sickening me well-nigh into fainting. So this was America, I kept thinking. This was the boasted American freedom and opportunity—the freedom for respectable citizens to sell cabbages from hideous carts, the opportunity to live in those monstrous, dirty caves that shut out the sunshine. And when we got beyond Grand Street and entered the Rumanian section my cousin pointed out to me several of my former fellow-townspeople—men of worth and standing they had been in Vaslui—bargaining vociferously at one kind of stand or another, clad in an absurd medley of Rumanian sheep-pelts and American red sweaters. Here was Jonah Gershon, who had been the chairman of the hospital committee in Vaslui and a prominent grain merchant. He was dispensing soda-water and selling lollypops on the corner of Essex Street. This was Shloma Lobel, a descendant of rabbis and himself a learned scholar. In America he had attained to a basket of shoe-strings and matches and candles. I myself recognized young Layvis, whose father kept the great drug-store in Vaslui, and who, after two years of training in medicine at the University of Bucharest, was enjoying the blessings of American liberty by selling newspapers on the streets.

Here and there were women, too, once neighbors of ours, mothers of sons, and mistresses of respectable households. And what were they doing here in this diabolical country? Well, here was one selling pickles from a double row of buckets placed on a square cart, yelling herself hoarse to an insensible world in a jargon of Yiddish and "English," and warming her hands by snatches over an outlandish contraption filled with glowing coals. Farther on I came upon another, laboriously pushing a metal box on wheels and offering baked potatoes and hot *knishes* to the hungry, cold-bitten passers-by. And all the while there was the dainty little figure of Cousin Betty walking airily beside me, unaware

of the huge tragedy of it all. She had herself arrived no more than a year before, but how callous America had already made her! I asked myself whether I, too, would harden and forget the better days I had known, and I fervently hoped not.

Ah, the blessed life we had left behind! [...] A family occupied but one room, or two at the most; but the houses were individual and sufficient, and the yard was spacious and green in summer, filled with trees and flowers to delight the senses. Business men scarcely earned in a week what a peddler or an operator made here in a day, but they were free men and had a standing in the community, and with God's help they supported their families in decency. They were not unattached, drifting nobodies, as every one was here. Life ran along smoothly on an unpretentious plane. There was no ambition for extravagance, and therefore no unhappiness through the lack of luxuries. Homes in Vaslui were not furnished with parlor sets of velvet, and the womenfolks did not wear diamonds to market; but, on the other hand, they did not have to endure the insolence of the instalment agent, who made a fearful scene whenever he failed to receive his weekly payment. No one was envious because his neighbor's wife had finer clothes and costlier jewels than his own had. The pride of a family was in its godliness and in its respected forebears. Such luxury as there was consisted in heavy copper utensils and solid silver candelabra, which were passed on as heirlooms from generation to generation—substantial things, not the fleeting vanities of dress and upholstery.

As those first weeks rolled on I became more and more overwhelmed with the degeneration of my fellow-countrymen under their shabby existence in America. Even their names had become emasculated and devoid of either character or meaning. Mordecai—a name full of romantic association—had been changed to the insipid monosyllable Max. Rebecca—mother of the race—was in America Becky. Samuel had been shorn to Sam, Abraham to Abe, Israel to Izzy. The surprising dearth in their vocabulary of the precious words, rich in poetic suggestion, betrayed a most lamentable lack of imagination. Whole battalions of people were called Joe; the Harrys alone could have repopulated Vaslui; and of Morrises there was no end. With the womenfolks matters went even worse. It did not seem to matter at all what one had been called at home. The first step toward Americanization was to fall into one or the other of the two great tribes of Rosies and Annies.

This distressing transformation, I discovered before long, went very much deeper than occupation and the externals of fashion. It pervaded every chamber of their life. Cut adrift suddenly from their ancient moorings, they were floundering in a sort of moral void. Good manners and good conduct, reverence and religion, had all gone by the board, and the reason was that these things were not American. A grossness of behavior, a loudness of speech, a certain repellent "American" smartness in intercourse, were thought necessary, if one did not want to be taken for a greenhorn and a boor. The younger folk, in particular, had undergone an intolerable metamorphosis. As they succeeded in picking up English more speedily than their elders, they assumed a defiant attitude toward their parents, which the latter found themselves impotent to restrain and, in too many cases, secretly approved as a step toward the emancipation of their offspring. Parents, indeed, were altogether helpless under the domination of their own children. There prevailed a superstition in the quarter to the effect that the laws of America gave the father no power over the son, and that the police stood ready to interfere in behalf of the youngsters, if any attempt to carry out the barbarous European notion of family relations were made.

Thus the younger generation was master of the situation, and kept the older in wholesome terror of itself. Mere slips of boys and girls went around together and called it love after the American fashion. The dance-halls were thronged with them. The parks saw them on the benches in pairs until all hours of the morning, and they ran things in their parents' homes to suit themselves, particularly when their families were partially dependent on them for support. Darker things than these were happening. These were the shameful days when Allen Street, in the heart of Little Rumania, was honeycombed with houses of evil repute, and the ignorant, untamed daughters of immigrants furnished the not always unwilling victims. And for the first time in history Jewish young men by the score were drifting into the ranks of the criminal.

A market on the Lower East Side.

The young, however, were not the only offenders. The strong wine of American freedom was going to the heads of all ages alike. The newspapers of the Ghetto were continually publishing advertisements and offering rewards for the arrest of men who had deserted their wives and children. Hundreds of husbands who had parted from their families in Europe with tears in their eyes, and had promised, quite sincerely, to send for them as soon as they had saved up enough money, were masquerading as bachelors and offering themselves in wedlock to younger women for love or for money. Very often the entanglement reached that screaming stage which lies on the borderland of tragedy and farce, when the European wife, having been secretly and hurriedly sent for by her American relatives, appeared on the scene and dragged the culprit before the rabbi or the law-court.

The prices of things in America were extortionate. The rental per month for a dark, noisome "apartment" on Rivington Street would have paid for a dwelling in Vaslui for an entire year. A shave cost ten cents, which was half a franc; if we had had to pay that much for it in Vaslui the whole community would have turned barbers. When I asked my cousin landlady how much my room-rent would come to, she told me that every one paid fifty cents a week. Two francs fifty! I tried to calculate all the possible things that my parents could buy for that vast sum at home if I were to desist from the extravagance of living in a house, and I resolved that as soon as I found work I would try to devise some substitute, and send the money home where it could be put to some sane use.

My Americanized compatriots were not happy, by their own confession. As long as they kept at work or prospered at peddling, they affected a hollow gaiety and delighted in producing a roll of paper dollars (which they always carried loose in their pockets, instead of keeping them securely in purses as at home) on the least provocation, and frequented the coffee-houses, and indulged in high talk about their abilities and their prosperity, and patronizingly inquired of the greenhorn how he liked America, and smiled in a knowing way when the greenhorn replied by cursing Columbus. But no sooner did he lose his job or fail in the business of peddling than he changed his tone and sighed for the flesh-pots of his native home, and hung his head when asked how he was getting on, and anathematized America, and became interested in socialism. At such times it was very apparent that America's hold on his affections was very precarious—a thing that needed constant reinforcing by means of very definite, material adhesives to keep it from ignominious collapse.

As a greenhorn I got my share of the ridicule and the condescension and the bullying that fell to the lot of my kind. I was laughed at for calling things by their right names instead of by their English equivalents, as my Americanized friends did, even while conversing in Rumanian. In my cousin's house I was constantly meeting Americanized young men who came to call on the girls, and invariably I must submit to the everlasting question and its concomitant, the idle grin: "How do you like America?" Well, after what I have given you of my impressions, you may readily guess that I did not like America; that, indeed, I very emphatically hated America. In my most courageous moments, which usually came to me when my young gentleman questioner was particularly insistent and particularly stupid, I declared so openly and with great stress, which declaration of mine was regularly met with loud peals of superior laughter, interspersed with phrases of that miserable gibberish which the Americanized of the foreign colony fondly regard as English, and which, even in those first days, I recognized for the sham it was. After such encounters I came away hating America more than ever.

Yes, I hated America very earnestly on my first acquaintance with her. And yet I must confess here and now that for a whole year every letter that came from my parents in Vaslui was an offer to return home, and that I steadily refused to accept it. [...] And in the mean time the East Side Ghetto *was* my America, a theater within a theater, as it were. No, it was even more circumscribed than that. The outsider may imagine that the Ghetto is a unified, homogeneous country, but a little more intimate acquaintance will rectify that mistake. There are in it strata and substrata, each with a culture, a tradition, and a method of life peculiar to itself. The East Side is not a colony; it is a miniature federation of semi-independent, allied states. To be sure, it

is a highly compact union, territorially. One traverses a square, and lo! he finds himself in a new polity. The leap in civilization from Ridge Street to Madison Street is a much wider one than that between Philadelphia and Seattle. The line of demarcation is drawn sharply, even to the point of language—the most obvious of national distinctions. The Jew from Austrian Poland will at first hardly understand his coreligionist from Lithuania. The dialects they speak differ enormously in accent and intonation and very appreciably in vocabulary; and each separate group entertains a humorous, kindly contempt for the speech and the manners and the foibles of all the others.

As I had come from Vaslui, it was my lot to settle in that odd bit of world which I have referred to as Little Rumania. It was bounded on the east by Clinton Street, with Little Galicia extending on the other side to the East River; by Grand Street on the south, with the Russians and Lithuanians beyond; and on the north lay the untracked wilds surrounding Tompkins Square Park, which to me was the vast dark continent of the "real Americans." Even as far back as 1900 this Little Rumania was beginning to assume a character of its own. Already it had more restaurants than the Russian quarter—establishments with signs in English and Rumanian, and platters of liver-paste, chopped egg-plant, and other distinctive edibles in the windows. On Rivington Street and on Allen Street the Rumanian delicatessen store was making its appearance, with its goose-pastrama and kegs of ripe olives and tubs of salted vine-leaves (which, when wrapped around ground meat, make a most delicious dish), and the moon-shaped cash-caval cheese made of sheep's milk, and, most important of all, the figure of an impossible American version of a Rumanian shepherd in a holiday costume, with a flute at his waxen lips, standing erect in the window. Unlike the other groups of the Ghetto, the Rumanian is a *bon vivant* and a pleasure-lover; therefore he did not long delay to establish the pastry-shop (while his Russian neighbor was establishing the lecture platform), whither of a Saturday afternoon after his nap he would betake himself with his friends and his ladies and consume dozens of dainty confections with ice-cold water. [...]

Of the broader life and the cleaner air of that vast theater within which this miniature stage was set I was hardly aware. What I knew of it came to me vaguely by hearsay in occasional allusions to a hazy, remote world called variously "up-town" and "the South," to which the more venturesome of my fellows now and then resorted, only to find their spunk failing them, and to return forthwith. In addition, there was the policeman, who made life miserable for the peddler, while accepting his bribe. He was a representative of "up-town," for as soon as his tyrannical day's work was over he vanished into the mysteries of that uncharted region. There was likewise the school-teacher, with her neat figure and sweet smile, and a bevy of admiring little children always clinging to her skirts as she tried to make her way from the corner of Eldridge Street "up-town." Now and then in my search for work I wandered into Broadway and across Fifth Avenue, and stared at the extravagant displays in the shop-windows and the obvious wealth (judging from their clothes) of the passers-by. But altogether I remained untouched by the life of greater America. It merely brushed me in passing, but it was too far removed from my sphere to affect me one way or the other.

One thing that did impress me right early was the almost ludicrous liberality of American life, and a certain generous confidence that was in the air. Every one was sufficiently dressed in the streets of New York. At home people who were thought of as in comfortable circumstances usually wore their clothes and shoes away past the patch stage and thought nothing of it. In America nobody, except the newly landed and a certain recognizable type styled a bum, wore patched garments. [...] Indeed, one of the most curious things in America was the fact that, if you went merely by their dress, you could not tell a bank president from his office-boy.

I was employed for a brief period as assistant to a milk-driver, and it made me marvel to see how our customers left bottles with money in them at the doors, where anybody could have taken them, and how we in turn left the milk in the same places. Somehow they never were taken—or at least I never heard of it. Imagine, I used to say to myself— imagine doing business after that fashion in Vaslui. Once a newspaper-wagon sped by and dropped a bundle of magazines right at my feet. I picked it up and was walking away with it when a man emerged from a stationery-shop and politely, though smilingly, informed me that it belonged to him. I gave it up, of course, in confusion, but I thought that if that had happened at home the case would have gone to the courts before the owner could have proved his right to

the goods. And we were honest people in Vaslui; only our ideas were different. This undiscriminating confidence in God and man was a distinctly American peculiarity.

In my adventures with the outer world I made another discovery. Bargaining was discouraged. I stopped in front of a grocery-store to buy a basket of what I thought were plums of a species I particularly liked. The man asked ten cents; I offered him six, and he calmly put the basket back in its place and proceeded to walk into the store. I called him back and suggested splitting the difference. Whereupon his face assumed a threatening shade, and I handed over my dime. When I reached home I discovered that my plums were tomatoes. I set to work to prepare a long and convincing speech which opened in the petitionary vein and ended in menace. Then I marched back to the store with my heart thumping. I had scarcely opened my mouth when the salesman, divining my mission, took the package out of my hand and handed me back my ten cents.

These rare ventures into the world beyond the Ghetto were revelations that usually amused and sometimes inspired me. They served to give me a glimpse of that greater destiny which somehow even in my darkest days I felt was awaiting me in America. But for a long time to come the Ghetto remained at once my home and my exile. To its life and to its culture I must adjust myself or perish. Before the year was past, I had succeeded in wearing into my place there, after a fashion. Something of my early repulsion to it may here and there have clung to me. The memories of my native home did not for a long time leave me. To a degree I always remained a foreigner in the slums, but time and habit softened and mellowed the first rude impressions. In time I learned to carry money loose in my pockets and to think no longer of it in terms of francs. I came to accept a lot of horrid things as being altogether in the order of nature— the cramped quarters, the filthy, impassable streets, the fine furniture on the instalment plan, the Sunday holiday with the showy American clothes. And when the next time I chanced to meet a fresh arrival I was wont self-complacently to ask him, "How do you like America?" and to smile knowingly when he cursed Columbus in reply. I had run my first lap in the race toward America. I had become quite "Americanized."

THE COUNTRY DOCTOR

BY THEODORE DREISER

JULY 1918

How well I remember him—the tall, grave, slightly bent figure, the head like Plato's or that of Diogenes, peering, all too kindly, into the faces of dishonest men, the mild, brown-gray eyes. In addition, he wore long, full, brown-gray whiskers, in winter a long gray overcoat (soiled and patched toward the last), a soft black hat that hung darkeningly over his eyes. But what a doctor! And how simple, and often non-drug-storey, were so many of his remedies!

"My son, your father is very sick. Now, I'll tell you what you can do for me. You go out here along the Cheevertown road about a mile or two and ask any farmer this side of the creek to let you have a good big handful of peach sprigs—about so many—see? Say that Doctor Gridley said he was to give them to you for him. Then, Mrs. ——, when he brings them, you take a few, not more than seven or eight, and break them up and steep them in hot water until you have an amber-colored tea. Give Mr. —— about three or four teaspoonfuls of that every three or four hours, and I hope we'll find he'll do better. This kidney case is severe, I know, but he'll come around all right."

And he did. My father had been very ill, so weak at last that we thought he was sure to die. The house was so somber at the time—an atmosphere of depression and fear, with pity for the sufferer, and groans of distress on his part; and then the solemn visits of the doctor, made pleasant by his wise, kindly humor and his hopeful predictions, and ending in this mild prescription, which resulted, in this case, in a cure. He was seemingly so remote at times, in reality so near, and wholly thoughtful.

On this occasion I went out along the long, cold, country road of a March evening. I was full of thoughts of his importance as a doctor. He seemed so necessary to us, as to everybody. I knew nothing about medicine or how lives were saved, but I felt sure that he did and that he would save my father in spite of his always conservative, speculative, doubtful manner. What a wonderful man he must be to know all these things—that peach sprouts, for instance, were an antidote to the agony of gall-stones!

As I walked along, the simplicity of country life and its needs and deprivations were impressed upon me, even though I was so young. So few here could afford to pay for expensive prescriptions—ourselves especially—and Doctor Gridley knew that and took it into consideration, so rarely did he order anything from a drug-store. Most often what he prescribed he took out of a case, compounded, as it were, in our presence.

A brisk wind had fluttered snow in the morning, and now the ground was white, with a sinking red sun shining across it, a sense of spring in the air. Being unknown to these farmers, I wondered if any one of them would really cut me a double handful of fresh young peach sprigs or suckers from their young trees, as the doctor had said. Did they really know him? Some one along the road—a home-driving farmer—told me of an old Mr. Mills who had a five-acre orchard farther on. In a little while I came to his door and was confronted by a thin, gaunt, bespectacled woman, who called to a man inside:

"Henry, here's a little boy says Doctor Gridley said you were to cut him a double handful of peach sprigs."

Henry now came forward—a tall, bony farmer in high boots and an old wool-lined leather coat and a cap of wool.

"Doctor Gridley sent cha, did he?" he observed, eying me most critically.

"Yes, sir."

"What's the matter? What does he want with 'em? Do ya know?"

"Yes, sir. My father's sick with kidney trouble, and Doctor Gridley said I was to come out here."

"Oh, all right. Wait 'll I git my big knife," and back he went, returning later with a large, horn-handled knife, which he opened. He preceded me out through the barn lot and into the orchard beyond.

"Doctor Gridley sent cha, did he, huh?" he asked as he went. "Well, I guess we all have ter comply with whatever the doctor orders. We're all apt ter git sick now an' ag'in," and, talking trivialities of a like character, he cut me an armful, saying: "I might as well give ya too many as too few. Peach sprigs! Now, I never heered o' them bein' good fer anythin', but I reckon the doctor knows what he's talkin' about. He usually does—or that's what we think around here, anyhow."

In the dusk I trudged home with my armful, my fingers cold. The next morning, the tea having been brewed and taken, my father was better. In a week or two he was up and around, as well as ever, and during this time he commented on the efficacy of this tea, a strange remedy, something new to him, which caused the whole incident to be impressed upon my mind. The doctor had told him that if at any time in the future he was so troubled again and could get fresh young peach sprigs for a tea, he would find that it would help him. And the expense for drugs was exactly nothing.

In later years I came to know him better—this thoughtful, crusty, kindly soul, always so ready to come at all hours when his cases permitted, so anxious to see that his patients were not taxed beyond their resources financially.

I remember once, one of my sisters being very ill, so ill that we were beginning to fear death, one and another of us had to take turns sitting up with her at night to help and to give her medicine regularly. During one of the nights when I was sitting up, dozing, reading, and listening to the wind in the pines outside, she seemed to get worse persistently. Her fever rose, and she complained of such aches and pains that finally I had to go and call my mother. A consultation with her finally resulted in my being sent for Doctor Gridley—no telephones in those days—to tell him, although she hesitated so to do, how she felt, and ask him if he would not come.

I was only fourteen. The street along which I had to go was quite dark, the town lights being put out at 2 A.M., by reason of thrift, perhaps. There was a high wind that cried in the trees. My shoes on the boardwalks here and there sounded like the thuds of a giant. I recall progressing in a shivery, ghost-like sort of way, expecting at any step to encounter goblins of the most approved form, until finally the well-known outlines of the house of the doctor on the main street—yellow, many-roomed, a wide porch in front—came, because of a very small lamp in a very large glass case to one side of the door, into view.

Here I knocked, and then knocked more. No reply. I then made a still more forceful effort. Finally, through one of the red-glass panels which graced either side of the door I saw at the head of the stairs the lengthy figure of the doctor, arrayed in a long white nightshirt, and carrying a small glass hand-lamp. His feet were in gray-flannel slippers, and his whiskers stuck out most discordantly.

"Wait! Wait!" I heard him call. "I'll be there! I'm coming! Don't make such a fuss! It seems as though I never get a real good night's rest any more."

He came on, opened the door, and looked out.

"Well," he demanded, a little fussily for him, "what's the matter now?"

"Doctor," I began, and proceeded to explain all my sister's aches and pains, winding up by saying that my mother said, "Wouldn't he please come at once?"

"Your mother!" he grumbled. "What can I do if I do come down? Not a thing. Feel her pulse and tell her she's all right. That's every bit I can do. Your mother knows that as well as I do. That disease has to run its course." He looked at me as though I were to blame, then added, "Calling me up this way at three in the morning!"

"But she's in such pain, Doctor," I complained.

"All right—everybody has to have a little pain! You can't be sick without it."

"I know," I replied, disconsolately, believing sincerely that my sister might die, "but she's in such awful pain, Doctor."

"Well, go on," he replied, turning up the light. "I know it's all foolishness, but I'll come. You go back and tell your mother that I'll be there in a little bit, but it's all nonsense, nonsense. She isn't a bit sicker than I am right this minute, not a bit—" and he closed the door and went up-stairs.

To me this seemed just the least bit harsh for the doctor, although, as I reasoned afterward, he was probably half asleep and tired—dragged out of his bed, possibly, once or twice more in the same night.

In due time the doctor came. The seizure was apparently nothing which could not have waited until morning. However, he left some new cure, possibly clear water in a bottle, and departed. But the night trials of doctors and their patients, especially in the country, were fixed in my mind then. [...]

One of the truly interesting things about Doctor Gridley, as I early began to note, was his profound indifference to what might be called his material welfare. Why, I have often asked myself, should a man of so much genuine ability choose to ignore the gauds and plaudits and pleasures of the gayer, smarter world outside, in which he might readily have shone, to thus devote himself and all his talents to a simple rural community? For that he was an extremely able physician there was not the slightest doubt. Other physicians from other towns about, and even so far away as Chicago, were repeatedly calling him into consultation. That he knew life—much of it—as only a priest or a doctor of true wisdom can know it, was evident from many incidents, of which I subsequently learned, and yet here he was, hidden away in this simple rural world, surrounded probably by his Rabelais, his Burton, his Frazer, and his Montaigne, and dreaming what dreams—thinking what thoughts?

"Say," an old patient, friend, and neighbor of his once remarked to me years later when we had both removed to another city, "one of the sweetest recollections of my life is to picture old Doctor Gridley, Ed Boulder who used to run the hotel over at Sleichertown, Congressman Barr, and Judge Morgan, sitting out in front of Boulder's hotel over there of a summer evening, and haw-hawing over the funny stories which Boulder was always telling, while they were waiting for the Pierceton bus. Doctor Gridley's laugh, so soft to begin with, but growing in force and volume until it was a jolly shout. And the green fields all around. And Mrs. Calder's drove of geese over the way honking, too, as geese will whenever people begin to talk or laugh. It was delicious."

One of the most significant traits of his character, as might have been predicated from the above, was his absolute indifference to actual money, the very cash, one would think, with which he needed to buy his own supplies. During his life his wife, who was a thrifty, hard-working woman, used frequently, as I learned after, to comment on this; but to no result. He could not be made to charge where he did not need to, nor collect where he knew the people were poor.

"Once he became angry at my uncle," his daughter once told me, "because he offered to collect for him for three per cent., dunning his patients for their debts, and another time he dissolved a partnership with a local physician who insisted that he ought to be more careful to charge and collect."

This generosity on his part frequently led to some very interesting results. On one occasion, for instance, when he was sitting out on his front lawn in Warsaw, smoking, his chair tilted back against a tree and his legs crossed in the fashion known as "jack-knife," a poorly dressed farmer without a coat came up and, after saluting the doctor, began to explain that his wife was sick and that he had come to get the doctor's advice. He seemed quite disturbed and every now and then wiped his brow, while the doctor listened with an occasional question or gently accented "Uh-huh, uh-huh!" until the story was all told and the advice ready to be received. When this was given in a low, reassuring tone, he took from his pocket his little book of blanks and wrote out a prescription, after which he handed it to the man and began talking again. The latter took out a silver dollar and handed it to him, the which he turned idly between his fingers for a few seconds, then searched in his pocket for a mate to it, and, playing with them awhile as he talked, finally handed back the dollar to the farmer.

"You take that," he said, pleasantly, "and go down to the drug-store and have the prescription filled. I think your wife will be all right."

When he had gone the doctor sat there a long time, meditatively puffing the smoke from his cob pipe and turning his own dollar over in his hand. After a time he looked up at his daughter, who was present, and said:

"I was just thinking what a short time it took me to write that prescription and what a long time it took him to earn that dollar. I guess he needs the dollar more than I do."

In the same spirit of this generosity, he was one day sitting in his yard of a summer day, sunning himself and smoking, a favorite pleasure of his, when two men rode up to his gate from opposite directions and simultaneously hailed him. He arose and went out to meet them. His wife, who was sewing just inside the hall, as she usually was when her husband was outside, leaned forward in her chair to see through the door, and took note of who they were. Both were men in whose families the doctor had practised for years. One was a prosperous farmer who always paid his "doctor's bills," and the other was a miller, a ne'er-do-well, with a delicate wife and a family of sickly children, who never asked for a statement and never had one sent him, and who only occasionally and at great intervals handed the doctor a dollar in payment for his many services. Both men talked to him a little while and then rode away, after which he returned to the house, calling to Enoch, his old negro servant, to bring his horse, and then went into his study to prepare his medicine-case. Mrs. Gridley, who was naturally interested in his financial welfare and who at times had to plead with him not to let his generosity stand wholly in the way of his judgment, inquired of him as he came out:

"Now, Doctor, which of those two men are you going with?"

"Why, Miss Susan," he replied—a favorite manner of addressing his wife, the note of apology in his voice showing that he knew very well what she was thinking about, "I'm going with W——."

"I don't think that is right," she replied, with mild emphasis. "Mr. N—— is as good a friend of yours as W——, and he always pays you."

"Now, Miss Susan," he returned, coaxingly, "N—— can go to Pierceton and get Doctor Bodine, and W—— can't get any one but me. You surely wouldn't have left him without any one?"

What the effect of such an attitude was may be judged when it is related that there was scarcely a man, woman, or child in the entire county who had not at some time or other been directly or indirectly benefited by the kindly wisdom of this Samaritan. He was nearly everybody's doctor, in the last extremity, either as consultant or otherwise. Everywhere he went, by every lane and hollow that he fared, he was constantly being called into service by some one—the well-to-do as well as by those who had nothing; and in both cases he was equally keen to give the same degree of painstaking skill, finding something in the very poor—a humanity and possibly an art interest—which detained and fascinated him. The very, very poor were as much his patients as, if not more so than, the well-to-do, although his repute was such that all felt that they needed and demanded him. If anything, he was a little more prone to linger at the bedside of the very poor and neglected than anywhere else.

"He was always doing it," said his daughter, "and my mother used to worry over it. She declared that of all things earthly, papa loved an unfortunate person; the greater the misfortune, the greater his care."

In our town was an old and very distinguished colonel, comparatively rich, and very crotchety, who had won considerable honors for himself during the Civil War. He was a figure, and very much looked up to by all. People were, in the main, overawed by and highly respectful of him. Plainly, he was one born to command, as I used to think—a remote, stern soul—yet to Doctor Gridley he was little more than a child or school-boy—one to be bossed on occasion and made to behave. Plainly, the doctor had the conviction that all of us, great and small, were very much in need of sympa-

thy and care and that he, the doctor, was the one to provide it. At any rate, the latter had known the colonel long and well, and in a public way—at the principal street corner, for instance, or in the post-office where we school-children were wont to congregate—it was not at all surprising to hear him take the old colonel, who was quite frail now, to task for not taking better care of himself—coming out, for instance, without his rubbers or his overcoat in wet or chilly weather, and in other ways misbehaving himself.

"There you go again!" I once heard him call to the colonel, as the latter was leaving the post-office and he was entering (there was no rural free delivery in those days), "walking around without your rubbers, and no overcoat! You want to get me up in the night again, do you?"

"It didn't seem so damp when I started out, Doctor."

"And of course it was too much trouble to go back! You wouldn't feel that way if you couldn't come out at all, perhaps."

"I'll put 'em on! I'll put 'em on! Only, please don't fuss, Doctor. I'll go back to the house and put 'em on."

The doctor merely stared after him quizzically, like an old schoolmaster, as the rather stately colonel marched off.

Another of his patients was an old Mr. Pegram, a large, kind, big-hearted man, who was very fond of the doctor, but who had an exceedingly irascible temper, and who was the victim of some obscure malady which medicine apparently failed at times to relieve. This seemed to increase his irritability a great deal, so much so that the doctor had at last discovered that if he could get Mr. Pegram angry enough the malady would occasionally disappear. This sometimes seemed as good a remedy as any, and in consequence he was occasionally inclined to try it.

Among other things this old gentleman was the possessor of a handsome buffalo-robe which, according to a story that long went the rounds locally, he once promised to leave to the doctor when he died. At the same time all reference to death both pained and irritated him greatly—a fact which the doctor knew. Finding the old gentleman in a most complaining and hopeless mood one night, not to be dealt with, indeed, in any reasoning way, the doctor returned to his home and early the next day without any other word sent old Enoch, his negro servant, around to get, as he said, the buffalo-robe—a request which would indicate, of course, that the doctor had concluded that old Mr. Pegram had died—or was about to—a hopeless case. When ushered into the latter's presence, Enoch began innocently enough:

"De doctah say dat now dat Mr. Peg'am hab subspired, he was to hab dat ba-ba-buffalo-robe."

"What!" shouted the old irascible, rising and clambering out of his bed. "What's that? Buffalo-robe! By God! You go back and tell old Doc Gridley that I ain't dead yet by a damned sight! No, sir!" and forthwith he dressed himself and was out and around the same day.

Persons who met the doctor, as I heard years later from his daughter and from others who had known him, were frequently asking him, just in a social way, what to do for certain ailments, and he would as often reply in a humorous and half-vagrom manner that if he were in their place he would do or take so-and-so, not meaning really that they should do so, but merely to get rid of them, and indicating, of course, any one of a hundred harmless things—never one that could really have proved injurious to any one. Once, according to his daughter, as he was driving into town from somewhere, he met a man on a lumber-wagon whom he scarcely knew, but who knew him well enough, who stopped him and, showing him a sore on the upper tip of his ear, asked him what he would do for it.

"Oh," said the doctor, idly and jestingly, "I think I'd cut it off."

"Yes," said the man, very much pleased with this free advice; "with what, Doctor?"

"Oh, I think I'd use a pair of scissors," he replied, amusedly, scarcely assuming that his jesting would be taken seriously.

The driver jogged on and the doctor did not see or hear of him again until some two months later, when, meeting him in the street, the driver smilingly approached him and enthusiastically exclaimed:

"Well, Doc, you see I cut 'er off, and she got well!"

"Yes," replied the doctor, solemnly, not remembering anything about the case, but willing to appear interested—"what was it you cut off?"

"Why, that sore on my ear up here, you know. You told me to cut it off, and I did."

"Yes," said the doctor, becoming curious and a little amazed; "with what?"

"Why, with a pair of scissors, Doc, just like you said."

The doctor stared at him, the whole thing coming gradually back to him.

"But didn't you have some trouble in cutting it off?" he inquired, in disturbed astonishment.

"No, no," said the driver; "I made 'em sharp, all right. I spent two days whettin' 'em up, and Bob Hart cut 'er off fer me. They cut, all right, but I tell you she hurt when she went through the gristle."

He smiled in pleased remembrance of his surgical operation, and the doctor smiled also, but, according to his daughter, he decided to give no more idle advice of that kind. [...]

Although a sad man at times, as I understood, the doctor was not a hypochondriac, and in many ways, both by practical jokes and the humoring of odd characters, sought relief from the intense emotional strain which the large practice of his profession put upon him. One of his greatest reliefs was the carrying out of these same practical jokes, and he had been known to go to no little trouble at times to work up a good laugh. [...]

Only those, however, who knew Doctor Gridley in the sick-room and knew him well, ever discovered the really finest trait of his character—a keen, unshielded sensibility to, and sympathy for, all human suffering, that could not bear to inflict the slightest additional pain. He was really, in the main, a man of soft tones and unctuous laughter, of gentle touch and gentle step, and a devotion to duty that carried him far beyond his interests or his personal well-being. One of his chief compunctions, according to his daughter, was the telling friends or relatives of any stricken person that there was no hope. Instead, he would use every delicate shade of phrasing and tone in imparting the fateful words, in order to give less pain, if possible. "I remember in the case of my father," said one of his friends, "when the last day came and knowing the end was near, he was compelled to make some preliminary discouraging remark, I bent over with my ear against my father's chest and said: 'Doctor Gridley, the disease is under control, I think. I can hear the respiration to the bottom of the lungs.'

"'Yes, yes,' he answered me, sadly, but now with an implication which could by no means be misunderstood, 'it is nearly always so. The failure is in the recuperative energy. Vitality runs too low.' It meant from the first, 'Your father will not live.'"

In the case of a little child with meningitis, the same person was sent to him to ask what of the child—better or worse. His answer was, "He is passing as free from pain as ever I knew a case of this kind."

In yet another case of a dying woman, one of her relatives inquired, "Doctor, is this case dangerous?" "Not in the nature of the malady, madam," was his sad and sympathetic reply, "but fatal in the condition it meets. Hope is broken. There is nothing to resist the damage." [...]

His love for his old friends and familiar objects was striking, and he could no more bear to see an old friend depart than he could to lose one of his patients. One of his oldest friends was a fine old Christian lady by the name of Weeks, who lived down in Louter Creek bottoms and in whose household he had practised for nearly fifty years. During the latter part of his life, however, this family began to break up, and finally, when there was no one left but the mother, she decided to move over into Whitley County where she could stay with her daughter. Just before going, however, she expressed a wish to see Doctor Gridley and he called in upon her. A little dinner had been prepared in honor of his coming. After it was over and the old times were fully discussed, the little visit was fairly concluded and he was about to take his leave when Mrs. Weeks disappeared from the room and then returned shortly bearing upon her arm a beautiful yarn-spread which she held out before her, and, in her nervous, feeble way getting the attention of the little audience, said:

"Doctor, I am going up to Whitley now to live with my daughter and I don't suppose I will get to see you very often any more. Like myself, you are getting old and it will be too far for you to come. But I want to give you this spread that I wove with my own hands since I have been sixty years of age. It isn't very much, but it is meant for a token of the love and esteem I bear you and in remembrance of all that you have done for me and mine."

Her eyes were wet as she concluded, and her voice quivering as she brought it forward. The doctor, who had been wholly taken by surprise by this kindly manifestation of regard, had risen during her impromptu address and now stood before her, dignified and emotionally grave, his own eyes wet with tears of appreciation.

Balancing the homely gift upon his extended hands, he waited until the force of his own sentiment had slightly subsided, when he replied:

"Madam, I appreciate this gift with which you have chosen to remember me as much as I honor the sentiment which has produced it. There are, I know, threads of feeling woven into it stronger than any cords of wool and more enduring than all the fabrics of this world. I have been your physician now for fifty years and have been a witness of your joys and sorrows. But, as much as I esteem you and as highly as I prize this token of your regard, I can accept it but upon

one condition, and that is, Mrs. Weeks, that you promise me that, no matter how dark the night, how stormy the sky, or how deep the waters that intervene, you will not fail to send for me in your hour of need. It is both my privilege and my pleasure and I should not rest content unless I knew it were so."

When the old lady had promised, he took his spread and, going out to his horse, mounted and rode away to his own home, where he related this incident and ended with, "Now I want this put on my bed."

His daughter, who lovingly humored his every whim, immediately complied with his wish, and from that day to the hour of his death the spread was never out of his service. [...]

One of the sweetest and most interesting of all his mental phases was, as I have reason to know, his attitude toward the problem of suffering and death, an attitude so full of the human qualities of wonder, sympathy, tenderness, and trust that he could scarcely view them without exhibiting the emotion he felt. He was a constant student of the phenomena of dissolution, and in one instance calmly declared it as his belief that when a man was dead he was dead, and that was the end of him, consciously. At other times he modified his view to one of an almost prayerful hope, and in reading Emily Brontë's somewhat morbid story of *Wuthering Heights*, his copy of which I long had in my possession, I noted that he had annotated numerous passages relative to death and a future life with interesting comments of his own. To one of these passages, which reads:

> I don't know if it be a peculiarity with me, but I am seldom otherwise than happy while watching in the chamber of death, provided no frenzied or despairing mourner shares the duty with me. I see a repose that neither earth nor hell can break; and I feel an assurance of the endless and shadowless hereafter—the eternity they have entered—where life is boundless in its duration, and love in its sympathy, and joy in its fullness.

he had added on the margin:

> How often I have felt this very emotion. How natural I know it to be. And what a consolation in the thought!

Writing a final prescription for a young clergyman who was dying, there being no longer any hope, and for whom he had been most tenderly solicitous, he added to the list of drugs he had written in Latin the lines:

> In life's closing hour, when the trembling soul flies
>   And death stills the heart's last emotion,
> Oh, then may the angel of mercy arise
>   Like a star on eternity's ocean!

When he himself was upon his deathbed, he greeted his old friend Colonel Dyer—he of the absent overcoat and overshoes—with:

"Dyer, I'm almost gone. I am in the shadow of death. I am standing upon the very brink. I cannot see clearly, I cannot speak coherently, the film of death obstructs my sight; I know what this means. It is the end, but all is well with me. I have no fear. I have said and done things that would have been better left unsaid and undone, but I have never wilfully wronged a man in my life. I have no concern for myself. I am concerned only for those I leave behind. I never saved money and I die as poor as when I was born. We do not know what there is in the future now shut out from our view by a very thin veil. It seems to me there is a hand somewhere that will lead us safely across, but I cannot tell. No one can tell."

This interesting speech, made scarcely a day before he closed his eyes in death, was typical of his whole generous, trustful, philosophical point of view.

"If there be green fields and placid waters beyond the river that he so calmly crossed," so ran an editorial in the local county paper edited by one of his most ardent admirers, "reserved for those who believe in and practise upon the principle of 'Do unto others as you would have them do unto you,' then this Samaritan of the medical profession is safe from all harm. If there be no consciousness, but only a mingling of that which was gentleness and tenderness here with the earth and the waters, then the greenness of the one and the sparkling limpidity of the other are richer for that he lived, and wrought, and returned unto them so trustfully again."

THE LION'S MOUTH
MOTHER GOOSE, PROPAGANDIST
BY DON MARQUIS

AUGUST 1919

Mother Goose has never had the recognition which she deserves for the part she has played in making the world unsafe for anti-democracy.

A young fellow who will be four years old by the time he is half a year older, asked me the other day just what a crown is. I explained that it is a style of head-dress affected by kings, in their more formal and regal moods and tenses.

He accepted the explanation so readily that I wondered what he knew about kings, and asked him.

Kings, he told me, were persons who stole things. They stole meal and made puddings out of it. Queens were the same as cooks.

Queens fry things for breakfast. He had known about kings and their thieving propensities for a long time. Kings were the same as Arfurs. There was a picture of a king who was an Arfur in his Mother Goose Book stealing a bag of meal.

My own introduction to kings was the same as this young person's.... The King Arthur in my Mother Goose Book who stole three pecks of barley meal to make a bag pudding was the first king I ever knew. I am no Bolshevist by temperament or trade, but to this day I cannot think of kings as quite honest persons. Even the jovial King Cole did not quite reassure me with regard to kings; I seemed to see a something cunning in his eye. While ostensibly occupied with his pipe, his bowl, and his fiddlers three, he was likely thinking up some scheme to purloin edibles. The king who sat in his counting-house, counting out his money, after having had the four-and-twenty blackbirds baked within a pie, all but confirmed my youthful suspicion of kings as a class.... I was sure that the money really belonged to some one else; he counted it, in the picture, with a guilty air. Possibly he had stolen the blackbirds, to begin with.

"Mother Goose," by Arthur Rackham.

Later, when I read Lanier's version of the Arthurian legend, I was still unable to banish the thought of King Arthur as a fat rogue with a sack of meal slung over his shoulder and a hang-dog eye beneath his crown.

Still later, Tennyson could do nothing for me. The Tennysonian Arthur was very pure and noble and brave, to the eye, but beneath the royal mail there was a horrid secret; disguise himself as he would, I knew that he had once been a meal-stealer; for me, he could never live it down. It influenced me in my judgment of him and Guinevere. I felt that Guinevere was unable to forget it, too, and that she justified, in some measure, her relations with Lancelot, with the reflection that the Arthur whom she deceived had, after all, the soul of a pudding-thief under his splendid exterior.

As for Guinevere herself, I could never feel so very sorry for her when she was flung from her place beside the king and compelled to enter a convent and scar her dainty fingers embroidering heavy tapestries for the Camelot trade; she had done rough work before, and she could do rough work again, and get no pity of mine. I remembered her from the old kitchen days; at one time in her career she had fried mush for breakfast—stolen mush—with her hair straggling unqueenly down from her coronet, and with a look upon her face that showed her glad enough to get that mush to fry.

A friend and I once paid a visit to the Eden Musee, and in the Chamber of Horrors we saw two females showing the great gouts of blood and severed heads to their offspring, nine or ten in number, and all between the ages of three and eight. The little boys and girls were in a state of agreeable hysteria, evidently supposing all this blood to be real; nothing in after-life would make the impression upon them that this shambles was making. "The mind of youth," quoted my friend, eying the group reflectively, "is wax to receive and marble to retain." It is possible that young Hohenzollerns were trained in a similar manner.

It took me a long time to live down an impression of Welshmen, gained from the same source as the notion about kings...and even now, when I contemplate Mr. Lloyd George and the list of things that he is taking home from Paris, I murmur that the hand is quicker than the eye. But what I started out to say was that the world of to-morrow is not being made in the school-rooms of to-day; it is being made before the children get as far as the school-rooms. I warn all kings that Mother Goose will bear watching.

"Now, children, don't play near any submarines—remember the depth bombs!"

EIGHTY YEARS AND AFTER
BY WILLIAM DEAN HOWELLS

DECEMBER 1919

All my life I have been afraid of death. I think the like is true of every one, and I think it is also true that now, when old and nearer death, in the order of life, than ever before, I am less afraid of dying than when I was young and naturally far from it. I believe this again is true of all men, but it may not be at all true of others. Perhaps in age, as in sickness, when the vital forces are lowered we lose something of that universal and perpetual dread, until, as observation, if not experience, teaches, we survive it altogether and make the good end common to the dying.

Apparently the fear of death does not always mount with the loss of faith in a life hereafter, but sometimes the contrary. Until I was thirty-five years old I had no question but if I died I should live again; yet the swift loss of that faith, through the almost universal lapse of it in the prevailing agnosticism of the eighteen-seventies and 'eighties, was a relief from that fear. I had hitherto felt that, being a sinner, as I did not doubt I was, I should suffer for my sins after death; yet, now that the fear of hell was effectively gone, a certain stress was lifted from me which had weighed upon my soul. When I was a well-grown boy I used to pray before I slept at night that I might not die before morning and that I might not go to hell, but neither of my petitions had been inspired by the wise and kind doctrine of Swedenborg which I had been taught from my earliest years, and so I must suppose that my terror was a remnant of the ancestral, the anthropoidal fear which once possessed all human life.

In age, in youth, most people believe in God because they cannot deny the existence of a cause of things. The uni-

verse did not happen of itself, though we may, in middle life, say so sometimes. Even then I felt that there was a Creator of Heaven and Earth, but I had not the sense of a Father in Heaven, though I prayed to Him every night by that name. I had not the sense of loving Him, though I feared Him because I knew myself a wrong-doer in my thoughts and deeds, and imagined Him a just judge. The fear of His judgment has passed from me more and more as I have grown older; but at no time have I thought irreverently of Him or spoken so of Him. Still I have not affectionately prayed to Him outside of the Scriptural words. I have not praised Him in the terms of flattery which must, if He is the divine consciousness we imagine Him, make Him sick at heart. I do not say this is the case with other old men, but I note it in my own case with whatever humility the utmost piety would have.

My fear of Him has not grown upon me; neither do I think it has lessened, as it seems to me my fear of death has. There is apparently no reason for this diminishing dread, and I do not account for it as a universal experience. There seems to be a shrinkage of the emotions as of the forces from youth to age. When we are young life fills us full to the verge of being and leaves us no vantage-point from which we have any perspective of ourselves. For instance, I cannot recall inquiring what I was at twenty, thirty, forty, fifty, and hardly at sixty, as I am now inquiring what I am at eighty-two, though I have always been keenly interested in the analysis of life and character. But experience grows with age, and the study of it may be the last stage of introspection, though hardly, I should say, could it prevail till ninety or after.

The greatest and most dramatic shrinkage of consciousness is, of course, that which follows from the cooling of the passions, and is something apparently quite physical. Love at its best means marriage, and is altogether the most beautiful thing in life. It is never self-consciously ridiculous, though often ridiculous enough to the witness. Its perversion is the ugliest thing in life and the shamefulest, but for a day, for an hour of its bliss, one would give all one's other years; yet it does not escape the imperfection which mars everything. The best of existence, the home and the children, proceed from it; without it there can be no death, and the rending of the dearest ties and the anguish of grief come from love, too; the grave as well as the home awaits it.

There are faults which age redeems us from, and there are virtues which turn to vices with the lapse of years. The worst of these is thrift, which in early and middle life it is wisdom and duty to practise for a provision against destitution. As time goes on this virtue is apt to turn into the ugliest, cruelest, shabbiest of the vices. Then the victim of it finds himself hoarding past all probable need of saving for himself or those next him, to the deprivation of the remoter kindred of the race. In the earlier time when gain was symbolized by gold or silver, the miser had a sensual joy in the touch of his riches, in hearing the coins clink in their fall through his fingers, and in gloating upon their increase sensible to the hand and eye. Then the miser had his place among the great figures of misdoing; he was of a dramatic effect, like a murderer or a robber; and something of this bad distinction clung to him even when his specie had changed to paper currency, the clean, white notes of the only English bank, or the greenbacks of our innumerable banks of issue; but when the sense of riches had been transmuted to the balance in his favor at his banker's, or the bonds in his drawer at the safety-deposit vault, all splendor had gone out of his vice. His bad eminence was gone, but he clung to the lust of gain which had ranked him with the picturesque or histrionic wrong-doers, and which only ruin from without could save him from, unless he gave his remnant of strength to saving himself from it. Most aging men are sensible of all this, but few have the frankness of that aging man who once said that he who died rich died disgraced, and died the other day in the comparative penury of fifty millions.

Few old men have the strength to save themselves from their faults, perhaps because they have no longer the resilience of youth in any sort. It would be interesting to know when this ceases in mind or body; but without calling other dotards to witness, I will record that, physically, it had ceased in me half-way through my seventies, as I once found when I jumped from a carriage at the suggestion of the young driver who said he did not like the way the horse was acting. I myself saw nothing wrong in the horse's behavior, but I reasoned that a driver so young must know better, and I struck the ground with the resilience of an iron casting of the same weight.

Yet any time within the seventies I should say that one still felt young in body if not in mind; after that one feels young oftenest in spirit; a beautiful morning will go far to find the joy of youth in the octogenarian, as a gloomy sunset will find the pathos of it. I imagine, in fact, that youth lurks about in holes and corners of us as long as we live, but we must not make too free with it. We may go for a good long walk in the forenoon, and feel the fresher; but we must not be tempted to another walk in the afternoon, lest the next morning find us fully as old as we are. Exercise is not for age unless it is the carriage exercise which used to be prescribed by the physicians of the rich; certainly not motor exercise, which is almost as bad as walking exercise. A stick helps out, but it will not do so much as it promises on an up-hill way. In the summer, for instance, I live in a valley with the sea at either end of it, and I can traverse the intervening meadows with refreshment, or at least without exhaustion, but in front there has grown up since I was seventy a hill which was not there before and is as surprising as the effect of some recent volcanic upheaval. When I begin to climb this strange acclivity I find my stick a very lively leg, but as I mount it falters and goes lame; and before I reach the top I think I should almost be better without it. Before a certain time in my later seventies I was a quite indefatigable pedestrian, but one night, coming out of a theater in Boston, I boldly crossed the Common toward my hotel on Beacon Hill till it began to rise under me. There I began to sink under it, and before I reached the top I despaired in a deadly fatigue which was probably in part the effect of sitting unmoved through several hours in the theater. I should like to warn all octogenarians to beware of resting too much; there is such a thing as that and it is a very serious thing.

After sixty one must not take too many chances with one's self; but I should say that the golden age of man is between fifty and sixty, when one may safely take them. One has peace then from the different passions; if one has been tolerably industrious one is tolerably prosperous; one has fairly learned one's trade or has mastered one's art; age seems as far off as youth; one is not so much afraid of death as earlier; one likes joking as much as ever and loves beauty and truth as much; family cares are well out of the way; if one has married timely one no longer nightly walks the floor with even the youngest child; the marriage ring is then a circle half rounded in eternity. It is a blessed time; it is indeed the golden age, and no age after it is more than silvern. The best age after it may be that between eighty and ninety, but one cannot make so sure of ninety as of seventy in the procession of the years, and that is where the gold turns silver. But silver is one of the precious metals, too, and it need not have any alloy of the baser ones. I do not say how it will be in the years between ninety and a hundred; I am not yet confronted with that question. Still, all is not gold between eighty and ninety as it is between fifty and sixty. In that time, if one has made oneself wanted in the world, one is still wanted; but between eighty and ninety, if one is still wanted, is one wanted as much as ever? It is a painful question, but one must not shirk it; and in trying for the answer one must not do less than one's utmost, at a time when one's utmost will cost more effort than before. This is a disadvantage of living so long, but we cannot change the conditioning if we wish to live. [. . .]

The young mostly think the old are subjectively dull because they seem objectively dull, but they may often seem so because youth, not life, is uninteresting. I have known only one octogenarian who was not interested in any phase of life, who no longer cared to hear or tell of a new thing, who turned from books as jadedly as from men. This might have been because he had known the best of both to satiety. If one is of the reading habit as this sad sage was of, one has, by eighty and after, read most of the best books. In my own case, though, I have not been a measureless consumer of literature; I have devoured so much of it that every now and then when I propose myself some novelty, I cannot find the desired freshness in books which I have read only two or three times before, or even never before. Yet, not counting the latest poetry and fiction, I have ignored many of the things which most people have read—some very signal things, in fact. I have been rather fond of reading things many times over; they do not tire; certain passages of Shakespeare which I got by heart when I was a boy—say Henry V's heartless snub of Falstaff when the new King must call his joke-fellow off, or things out of "Macbeth" or "Othello." Tennyson does not bear re-reading like Keats, though long as much my favorite; and Heine does not, though he was once my greatest favorite. Yet within my eighty-second year I have read Don Quixote with as much zest as in my twelfth year; and the other day I read Milton's "Lycidas" with as rich a woe as the first time.

Literature is a universe where we poor planets swim about as if we were each no greater than the Earth which is well-nigh lost in its own little solar system. The question should be of one's continuing interest in public questions, and of one's value in treating of them. If I were boasting here of senility or its signal usefulness I would allege that of the octogenarian who seems to me the first of those publicists among us in addressing the sense and conscience of his countrymen since the German war on mankind began.

The attitude of amaze in comparative youth at mere superannuation is one of the hardest things which the old have to bear from their juniors, far harder than the insult of Hamlet's mockery of Polonius. Every old man knows the truth about physical age, and it can only hurt him the more to be told that he is looking better than ever, to be forced to smirk in the acceptance or refusal of the false homage offered his years in the effort to discount them for him. Let us alone, I say, and we can bear our burden; do not add the weight of your gross kindness to it. We know that we have wonderful alleviations and even advantages; we are at least not dead, and there we are at least equal with younger men, for at the end of the ends no grade of juniority can claim more.

I have met many old people, and I am glad that when I was younger I did not wish to praise their youthfulness or exalt their abounding health and vigor. When I once sat next to Emerson and heard him asking his other next-hand neighbor who I was when I had just told him who that neighbor was, I did not praise his wonderful memory. I must have been saved by somehow realizing that time would do all the needful remembering of him and eternity for him. Loss of memory is almost the first infirmity of noble minds, and I am proud to recall that when I was little more than thirty I clung to the hand of a fellow-citizen and tried for his familiar name, a name as idle as could well be. I had it as soon as our backs were turned, and I have never since lost it, or been the richer for it. I was young then, but when I was really beginning to be old I found myself at Rome, in returning to the use of my earlier Italian, often failing of a word before I realized that I had first failed of the English of it. Now I wander in a whirl of lost words which I can find only by first defining their uses to myself. Then the name wonderfully appears and I keep it a longer or shorter time; but meanwhile I have suffered. [...] Tolstoy says that remembering is hell, and nothing can be more terrible than remembering everything, as those newly arrived spirits do in the life to come, when their inner memories are explored for the things which have been dropped into their outer memories and comfortably forgotten. But if it is a blessing to forget, what a torment it is to fail of the thing we want to remember!

Titian outlived his ninety-nine years and kept on painting almost to the last. I have not found any critic to say how well he continued to paint, though I dare say there is more than one such critic. I can well believe that he wrought as greatly then from his exhaustless soul as in his prime. At ninety-nine he was working hard at Venice, in the intimacy of another Venetian master, the great sculptor and architect Sansovino, who was, however, only ninety-three. I used to view his Renaissance work with as great pleasure as my subservience to Ruskin's Gothic tyranny would let me, but I did not try to distinguish the later work in it from the earlier, and I cannot say from my personal knowledge that his mastery held out to the last. It is only now that from the Encyclopedia Britannica I have learned that "his masterpiece, the bronze doors of the sacristy in St. Mark's," was done when he was eighty-five, and that at eighty-eight "he completed a small bronze gate with a graceful relief of Christ surrounded by angels." Titian and he lived in great jollity together, and were of a gaiety which is rather characteristic of the old, though their younger friends are apt to think otherwise. [...]

There is a common superstition of old people's severity, and even surliness, which I should here like to combat, for I have oftenest found age kind and sweet. I have not known so many nonagenarians as to have lost count of any, and I recall one dear lady whom I first saw when I was still twenty-nine and met a second time when I was thirty and she ninety-seven. "You remember Mr. H., mother?" her daughter suggested. "Yes," she chirped in answer, "but he won't remember *me*." Think of one's not remembering a lady of ninety-seven! After an interval of more than half a century I met my second nonagenarian, who was indeed only ninety-five, but who came tripping down-stairs to greet me in his parlor like a light-footed youth of thirty-five, and who said, as if to excuse his delay, that his wife was not very well, though only ninety. Soon afterward she died, and then he died, too, but that day he was as much alive as need be. His face showed few marks of age, though his eyes, which were bright, were narrowed to little more than a fine gleam. It was in Cambridge, and of course we talked books with the back thought in my own mind that I must not tire him. Will the reader believe that before I was aware I *did* tire him? I am so fond of talking books! I shall always be ashamed of that inadvertence, though I almost rushed away. At seventy-three I could still rush a little.

Once in Boston, long before that, I lunched with a brave gentleman of ninety-four, who was still in the office-practice of the law, and went to his office every day. He did not brag of this, but his son did, in a proud aside to me. As to octogenarians there is simply no end to them; they swarm, they get in one's way. I recall notably the first I met on my way to Europe. I had left my father at home in his eighty-eighth year; he had always been alive, and I did not think his age strange; but my fellow-voyager had perhaps never been very much alive, and I observed him with question whether people were usually so dull at eighty. Now I do not think they usually are; they seem rather a sprightly generation, and rightly resentful of the sympathy of people who regard them as infirm and in the need of being told that they are looking wonderfully well, and younger than ever. So, perhaps, they are; but why rub it in?

When I met this octogenarian I am speaking of, I was making the first of five or six successive transatlantic voyages in ten or twelve years—after remaining homebound for nigh twenty years; now I hope, as soon as the terms of universal peace are fixed, to begin going to Europe again. "I cannot rest from travel," as Ulysses says in the words of Tennyson. It involves some risks, but is not it the only escape from death, for the time being? [...]

Among the things that the octogenarian must guard against is that solitude which is liable to grow upon him through the fault of other octogenarians. I do not know that they are apt to die out of proportion to other mortals; but certainly they seem to die more noticeably and to leave their contemporaries lonelier than people who have not lived so long. Perhaps this is an effect of the stir which is made about their dying at such an advanced age—as if, having lived so long, they ought to have lived longer. But I cannot say what is to be done about it, if anything; the solitude is inevitable; and yet, I cannot pretend that I miss other old people much. This is possibly because we octogenarians are not so much in the habit of seeing one another as septuagenarians and sexagenarians are. Perhaps there is a remote feeling of relief when we hear of one another going; we realize that those others were often rather dull company. Still, we are lonelier, till the solitude accumulated upon us ceases to be a conscious fact. I have no remedy to suggest unless it is the rather mechanical device of cultivating the acquaintance of the young. But then the young are often so dull, too, and they cumber one with kindness, more than the old; you do not see *us* helping the old on with their overcoats, or putting them chairs. The best thing would be to be born of a copious generation, with lots of brothers and sisters, and no end of cousins. There is comfort in the next of kin, such as comes from no other propinquity, though there is now and then a painful sense of responsibility for our blood-relations if they are rather fitter for the kingdom of heaven in their pecuniary circumstances than for the best society of a democratic republic. If they are somewhat silly one feels that one would rather have them criminal.

Quite apart from these digressions, and only because his case comes into the chapter of octogenarian loneliness, I wish to speak of a very gentle old man whose acquaintance I made in sharing with him a wayside seat, several years ago, when we were still within our seventies. We began at once with those intimate topics which strangers enter upon so promptly, and he told me that he had left his farm and was passing his widower-years in the family of his son, where they were all very kind to him. He casually mentioned that he always went to bed at six o'clock, and when I showed some surprise at this he explained that he did not wish to disturb the wonted course of the family life, or to put his children and grandchildren to the trouble of entertaining him. He seemed to imply that he was less lonely in withdrawing from them than if he had kept about with them. He sweetly touched upon differences in the young and old which no good-will or affection could annul. "But," he added, "there is an old lady coming to visit us, and then I shall keep about. We shall have more to say to each other, and be more sociable." I ventured to ask how old this lady was, and he said sixty; he did not seem to think the space between this and his eightieth year any great matter. In fact, upon reflection, I could not feel it so, either, considering how far the sympathy of women can go in bridging such intervals.

I recall that when I was a very small boy—small, but of fixed opinions—I unspeakably preferred old ladies to old men, as I saw them about our house in the character of guests, for the day or the dinner. They were mostly of Quakerly guise and cult, apparently, but the one old gentleman who visited us was of our small sect and perhaps came for the comfort of the little-friended doctrine which we shared with him. He must have stayed overnight, for I have still the vision of his movable teeth in the tumbler of water, where he kept them while he slept, and where they remained while he scraped a sweet apple for luncheon before the noonday dinner. He was somehow dreadful to me for these facts, and I contrasted him in my mind with those old ladies, to their infinite advantage. [...]

There is a matter so personal to people at all times of life that I must not fail to speak of it in the case of people in their eighties, and that is dreaming. It was once held (and may still be held) that dreams are of such instantaneousness that they might be said to take no time at all in their lapse; but if the psychologists no longer contend for this I may say that I have spent a large part of my life in the conscious cerebration of sleep. There have been nights of mine almost as busy as my days, in even more varied experiences, among persons from the other world as well as this; and it is so yet, but I think that I do not dream so much as formerly, though less than a week before this writing I dreamed of occurrences where my father and mother, dead for near twenty and fifty years, figured no more nor less lovingly than certain entire strangers.

A few paragraphs back I treated of failing memory, especially in the reluctance of this or that word to come when we wanted it, though it was ready enough when not wanted; and now I should like to inquire of other old men whether they are equally forgetful in other matters. Of course we all forget where we have put things, and are astounded to find them in places where we would like to be sworn we never put them. I have not happened to see dotards of my acquaintance going about crowned with the spectacles which they were ransacking the house for, and almost cursing and swearing in their failure to find, though I have heard of them often; and I have myself wandered in parallel oblivion till I had to abandon the search in despair. Yet if I have been charged by myself or others with duties, I never forget them, and I should like to think that no fellow-dotard of mine has failed in the like point. [...]

In the rashness which I have never paid dearly enough for yet, I am here, at the end of my sheet, as the old-time letter-writer used to say, tempted to hold that the first failure of memory to give us the name of the person who has lost it, is the first token of death, the first falling leaf of autumn, the first flake of the winter's snow. But who knows? Whence is death, and out of what awful void or whither? All along the line of living, from the moment of birth, when we first catch our breath and cry out in terror of life, death has set his signals, beckoning us the way which we must go. Kind Science knows them, but will not let us believe they are what they are, and Nature laughs them to scorn, because she is our fond mother. "Oh, that is nothing, is it, Science?" she cries at our alarm, and Science echoes, "Nothing at all, Nature; or if it is anything it is proof of superabounding vigor, of idiosyncratic vitality." Very likely; but quite the same, all the men born of women must die in a destined course; every man of eighty and after must die as certainly as the new-born babe, or often sooner, or if not, certainly in the event. It will not avail against the fact whether we pray and praise, or whether we eat and drink; the merciless morrow is coming. But why call it merciless? No one knows whether it is merciless or not. We know that somewhere there is love, the love that welcomed us here, the love that draws us together in our pairing, that our children may live, the love in our children which shall see that their fathers and mothers do not die before their time, even if their time shall be delayed till eighty and after.

1920's

THE GODS OF THE COPYBOOK MAXIMS
BY RUDYARD KIPLING

JANUARY 1920

As I pass through my incarnations in every age and race,
I make my proper prostrations to the Gods of the Market Place;
Peering through reverent fingers, I watch them flourish and fall,
And the Gods of the Copybook Maxims, I notice, outlast them all.

We were living in trees when they met us. They showed us each in turn
That Water would certainly wet us as Fire would certainly burn:
But we found them lacking in Uplift, Vision, and Breadth of Mind,
So we left them to teach Gorillas while we followed the March of Mankind.

We moved as the Spirit listed. They never altered their pace,
Being neither Cloud nor Wind borne like the Gods of the Market Place,
But they always caught up with our progress, and usually word would come
That a tribe had been wiped off its ice-field or Creation crashed at Rome.

With the Hopes that our World is built on they were utterly out of touch.
They denied the Moon was Stilton, they denied she was even Dutch.
They denied that Wishes were horses; they denied that a Pig had Wings.
So we worshiped the Gods of the Market Who promised these beautiful things.

When the Cambrian marshes were forming, they promised perpetual peace,
They swore, if we gave them our weapons, that the wars of the tribes would cease.
And when we disarmed they sold us and delivered us bound to our foe
And the Gods of the Copybook Maxims said:—"Stick to the Devil you know."

On the first Feminian Sandstones we were promised the Fuller Life
(Which started by loving our neighbor and ended by loving his wife)
Till our women had no more children and the men lost reason and faith,
And the Gods of the Copybook Maxims said:—"The Wages of Sin is Death."

In the Carboniferous Epoch we were promised abundance for all,
By robbing selected Peter to pay for collective Paul;
And, though we had plenty of money, there was nothing our money would buy.
And the Gods of the Copybook Maxims said:—"If you don't work you die."

Then the Gods of the Market tumbled, and their smooth-tongued Wizards withdrew,
And the hearts of the meanest were humbled and began to believe it was true
That All is not Gold that Glitters, and Two and Two make Four—
And the Gods of the Copybook Maxims limped up to explain it once more!

As it will be in "The Future," it was at the birth of Man—
There are only four things certain since the Larger Primates began:
That the Dog returns to his Vomit and the Sow returns to her Mire,
And the burnt Fool's bandaged finger goes wabbling back to the fire.

And after this is accomplished, and the brave new world begins
Where all men insist on their merits and no one desists from his sins,
As surely as Water will wet us, as surely as Fire will burn,
The Gods of the Copybook Maxims with terms and slaughters return!

FIRE AND ICE
BY ROBERT FROST

DECEMBER 1920

Some say the world will end in fire,
    Some say in ice.
From what I've tasted of desire
I hold with those who favor fire.
        But if it had to perish twice,
I think I know enough of hate
        To know that for destruction ice
Is also great,
        And would suffice.

To the Ghost of John Milton
by Carl Sandburg

November 1924

If I should pamphleteer twenty years against royalists,
With rewards offered for my capture dead or alive,
And jails and scaffolds always near,

And then my wife should die and three ignorant daughters
Should talk about their father as a joke, and steal the
Earnings of books, and the poorhouse always reaching for me,

If I then lost my eyes and the world was all dark and I
Sat with only memories and talk—

I would write "Paradise Lost," I would marry a second wife
And on her dying I would marry a third pair of eyes to
Serve my blind eyes, I would write "Paradise Regained," I
Would write wild, foggy, smoky, wordy books—

I would sit by the fire and dream of hell and heaven,
Idiots and kings, women my eyes could never look on again,
And God Himself and the rebels God threw into hell.

CRIME AND THE ALARMISTS

BY CLARENCE S. DARROW

OCTOBER 1926

Readers of newspapers and periodicals are constantly regaled with lurid stories of crime. From time to time with great regularity these tales are pieced together to produce the impression that waves of crime are sweeping across the land. Long rows of figures generally go with these tales which purport to tabulate the number of murders, hold-ups, burglaries, etc., in given areas, and sometimes comparisons are drawn with other countries and with other periods. The general effect is always to arouse anger and hatred, to induce legislatures to pass more severe laws, to fill the jails and penitentiaries, and to furnish more victims for the electric chair and gallows. It is a commonplace that cruel and hard punishments cannot be inflicted unless the populace is moved by hatred and fear. The psychology of fighting crime is the same as the psychology of fighting wars: the people must be made to hate before they will kill. This state of mind prevents any calm study of facts or any effort to seek causes or even to consider whether causes for crime may exist.

No one need be surprised that crime is so seldom the subject of objective study. It has not been very long since men thought that the whole physical world was operated by miracles. The motion of the earth and sun, the procession of day and night, the seasons of the year, the waves and wind, the flood and drought, the seed time and the harvest—all were defined by no natural laws, but all were dependent upon the whim and caprice of some other-worldly power. Even when some natural law of causation was believed to account for the phenomena of the physical world, the conduct of man was still supposed to lie outside this realm. Sickness and disease meant the possession of the individual by devils, and these could be driven out only by punishments and incantations. The ordinary treatment of disease was by magic and sorcery. For eighteen centuries, over most of Europe, medical men were punished often in the most terrible ways for seeking to find out the causes of disease and for attempting to treat illness by scientific methods. It was the greatest heresy to deny that sickness was due to sin and that pestilence and plague came as a divine visitation of angry gods to afflicted communities. And yet, in spite of restrictive measures and stern persecutions, the doctors persisted, until now no one questions that disease and pestilence are due to natural causes which must and can be removed if the patients are to be cured and infection prevented.

Insanity, too, was for many centuries thought of as possession by devils, and the punishment of the afflicted individual was the favorite treatment for driving out the demon. Hundreds of thousands of unfortunate insane men and women have been put to the severest tortures even down to the most recent times. Sorcery, witchcraft, and magic were the only methods of treatment permitted and the physician was obliged to risk his liberty and life in treating insanity as a disease, and seeking to understand the causes back of the phenomenon.

To-day, no one doubts that disease and insanity can be traced to natural causes and that both can be cured only by discovering the cause and applying the remedies which have been arrived at by careful and objective study of the disease.

The realm of miracle and magic has constantly grown smaller as natural law has come to be better understood. Crime, like insanity and sickness, is a departure from ordinary conduct; but most of the world clings to the belief that it can only be treated as a manifestation outside the realm of natural law. The old indictments read that "John Smith, being possessed of the devil, did wilfully kill," etc., etc. The modern indictments do not mention the devil, yet we still believe that crime is not due to causes, but is an arbitrary act unrelated to the criminal's past. We believe that the criminal should be made to suffer punishment for his act as a matter of "justice" and likewise that the only way to deter others from crime is to make them fear punishment.

In support of the theory that severe punishment with all its attendant horrors, and the psychology of general fear which goes with it, is the only admissible treatment of crime, tables of so-called statistics are always freely called into play. What these figures would prove in this behalf, even if they were dependable, is not easy to conceive.

It is only during a few years that any effort has been made in the United States to gather statistics on the subject of crime. From the nature of our political organization, this movement began with isolated states and cities, and even up to the present time statistics can be obtained from relatively only few and small areas. In the main these figures have been collected by police departments, coroners' offices, clerks of courts, Grand Juries, prison superintendents, and sometimes by outside agencies. In short, as the system was built up the methods of gathering statistics have developed in a hit or miss fashion. Naturally, as in all similar cases, the additional work thrown upon the various officials was done carelessly and imperfectly. As time has gone on, however, the collection of data has been improved. The growing care in gathering statistics in itself might easily lead to the conclusion that crime in the United States is on the increase. But still in very few places has there been any attempt to place the collection of data in the hands of intelligent people trained for such a task.

Every student of crime who has commented on these statistics gathered by various agencies has reached the conclusion that in their present state they are of little if any value. In no field has it been more clearly shown that there is a vast difference between the mere gathering of figures and an *intelligent interpretation* of the statistics after they have been collected. Public speakers, magazine writers, and newspapers are periodically presenting long arrays of figures to prove that there is an epidemic of crime in some part of the United States. As a rule there is not the slightest relation between the figures and the conclusions drawn. For example, the figures which are sometimes quoted with regard to the increase of the crime of rape are noteworthy illustrations of the care that must be taken in interpreting criminal statistics. Any one reading the startling statement that in New York state 146 persons were convicted of rape in the decade between 1880 and 1889, while 1297 were convicted of rape in the decade between 1910 and 1919 would be amazed if not horrified at the increase in the sexual passion and its manifestations in this period. Still, their condemnation of their fellows may be somewhat abated

when they learn that in the decade showing the largest number of convictions for rape the age of consent had been raised from ten years of age to eighteen. Let us take another case: 991 persons were found guilty of violating motor laws in Michigan in the three-year period from 1906 to 1909. The number increased to 29,393 in the three-year period from 1919 to 1922. Before reaching the conclusion that this is positive evidence of the increasing recklessness of automobile owners and drivers or of the younger generation it might be well to consider the increase in the general use of automobiles from 1909 to 1922.

Alarmists also forget that the number of violators of law has something to do with the number of laws. Every new criminal statute brings a new grist of crimes. This is well illustrated in the Volstead Act and the state legislation covering the same subject. Prisons are now filled with inmates who have only done something which a few years ago was perfectly legal.

Or, again, it is freely asserted that the late comers to the United States commit more crimes than the descendants of the earlier settlers. Those who make this statement forget to take into account the fact that practically all of the later immigrants live in our large cities and industrial centers. It is beyond question that our large urban areas produce more disorder, maladjustment, and crime than our rural communities. And this is true, irrespective of the race or nationality of the people who live under these crime-breeding conditions.

Likewise, the colored population is charged with a share in the commission of crime quite out of proportion to their number. This, too, should always be considered in connection with the fact that in the North they live in industrial centers and in restricted, crowded areas and that colored people, owing to race prejudice and poverty, are much more apt to be accused and convicted than whites.

All this amounts to saying that the agencies which gather statistics of crime and those who quote these statistics in our newspapers and magazines use all sorts of standards and definitions and overlook explanatory facts which make their conclusions valueless. For instance, in classifying murders some agencies base their conclusions on the police reports, some on the coroner's inquests, some on indictments, and others on convictions. Statistics taken from these various sources differ so widely that they seem almost to have no relation to each other. As a rule, the people who quote statistics to prove their theories simply cite figures without giving their source and without in any way analyzing them to find out what they mean. [...]

One thing is certainly clear—no intelligent person can examine carefully the statistics which are at present available and come to any satisfactory or defensible conclusion as to the number of crimes committed in the United States, or whether they are increasing or diminishing in proportion to the population, or the cause of any increase or diminution. The study of statistics in regard to crime, as in many other matters, leaves one in a hopeless maze. It will take years of careful preparation and thorough, unbiased gathering of objective statistics before any general conclusion can be reached in this way. It is, however, safe to say that statistics do not show that there is an increasing trend of crime in America. On the whole, it probably remains fairly stationary—with variations up and down now and then due to all sorts of reasons. Probably, on the whole, there is a tendency downward, especially if allowance is made for the new crimes that are constantly being created by statute and which add materially to the tables of law violation.

The growing use of the automobile has had a positive tendency to increase crime materially. It is a new lure that is hard to withstand. Men and women mortgage their homes and their beds to get them, and of course boys borrow and steal them. The indiscriminate use of the automobile in crowded cities has added largely to the coroner's returns, and many accidents appear in the tables as murders, although the only element even of homicide is careless or reckless driving. Sometime life may adjust itself to the automobile, but it will be a long time before men, women, and children can withstand the lure and before the accidents incident to the use of the automobile be materially reduced.

The Volstead Act and kindred state laws have furnished a great many additions to the reports of crimes. Many of these are classed as murders, many others as unlawful buying and selling. It is inevitable, in a mixed people like ours, with their diversity of habits and customs, that a drastic, tyrannical law, which makes criminal acts that carry with them no feeling of wrong, can have any other effect than to add to the list of crimes. Prohibition will continue to reap this harvest until it is settled whether the government shall recognize the habits of its citizens or whether the people shall be compelled by brute force to yield what they have long believed to be their rights.

Those who believe in sterner laws and harsher treatment of criminals are always drawing comparisons between America and England. [...] Other things being equal, all new countries have a higher crime rate than old ones. This is due to many reasons, not all of which apply in all new countries. The residents of England are a homogeneous people. This is true of all old countries. They lack many of the inducing causes that lead to crime. The English people have been made alike by centuries of molding and welding. They have from long association formed common customs, habits, and views of life; in other words, folkways—which make them one people. An old country inevitably develops a sort of caste system; each person takes his place without hope of change or advancement. The individual grows to accept his lot in life.

When we remember that crime means the violation of law, which in turn means getting out of the beaten path, it is easy to see why it is more common in new countries, where the paths are faint and not strongly marked, than in old countries where the paths are deep. It is only one hundred and fifty years since the United States gained its independence. It then had some 3,000,000 people. Since that time it has grown to about 115,000,000. This necessarily means that it has drawn from almost every country of the earth. These people have brought all kinds of religions, social customs, political ideas, temperaments, and ambitions. Probably no such heterogeneous combination was ever before brought together upon the earth. Most of these people came here to improve their condition, to get out of their caste. Their children are still hopeful that they may rise. The subduing of natural resources has built our great cities and filled them with a babel of tongues and a medley of temperaments, and with every religious, social, and political idea in the world. The higher wages and better opportunities have made the people venturesome and aggressive. The larger individual freedom and greater independence of individual action have made collisions more inevitable and severe.

Most of the crime in the United States comes from our industrial centers. Our cities have always been settled by a mixture of the peoples of the world with varied feelings and emotions, and with the individual customs and habits of their native lands. In the main these have been the poor of Europe. They have come with new hopes and ambitions, moved by intense desires. The industrial cities have been alternately prosperous and idle. Aside from the natural emotions of love and fear and hate, there has been the constant battle with employers and between union and non-union men. Such a medley of conflicting peoples and emotions has always been a prolific soil out of which violations of habits, customs, and laws inevitably grow. No other country has ever had so many antagonisms, such a fertile soil for combat and discontent. Australia and Canada, although new countries, have in the main a homogeneous people and a rural population. The statistics of crime of the rural communities of the United States are not unlike the statistics of rural communities in Canada and the other countries of the world. [...]

It is not the terror of brutal punishment that holds the units of society in their place. It is customs and habits. It is long familiarity with the beaten paths. People think and act and live as they are wont. They stay in grooves. Any sudden change jolts them from their ways and sets them loose to find or make other paths. To believe that men are kept in a certain line by fear is a crude conception at variance with experience and psychology alike.

Imperfect as all our statistics are confessed to be, it is doubtless true that the dangerous age for boys in reference to crime is constantly growing younger. It is safe to say that almost all crimes are committed by boys in their early teens or by those who began in effect a criminal career at that age. Saving criminals is, in the last analysis, only saving children; and saving children means not only saving criminals but their victims, too. Most of the criminals come from the cities and most of them were born and reared in the poor and crowded districts where they had little chance to develop into anything but criminals. A little knowledge of biology, psychology, and life makes this plain to understand. No well-informed person believes that one is born a criminal or with even a tendency to crime. If so, crime would not be of the individual's own choosing nor his end be due to his own volition. No child is born a criminal. He may be born weak or strong and, therefore, his power of resistance be more or less; but the course he takes is due to training, opportunity, and environment. The protection of the child or the grown person comes from habit. Religion may teach precepts, but this means nothing without habits. The school may give a certain kind of education, but unless this creates habits which fit the child for life it is of no avail.

Most of those who follow a criminal career have had little education and cared little for books. Most of them could not be fitted for professions by education; their only chance was some sort of work. They passed the school age without becoming scholars, and the schools have given them nothing in the place of what is generally called an education. When very young they began a life that almost inevitably leads to crime. If it is the duty of the state or any organized institution to provide for the education of the youth, then the most important thing is to fit them for the job of living. Many boys come to the adolescent age with only scant education in books and no education that fits them for any self-reliant life. For the large class who have no taste for books society furnishes no training in the schools. These boys are thrown on their own resources with no occupation that will furnish them a chance to live. The schools could as well teach manual trades as books, and a large part of those who cannot succeed with books could do well in working with their hands. There is no more reason why schools should prepare one to succeed in a profession than why they should teach certain ones a useful trade. Most boys like to use their hands, and the proper training for trades should be begun when very young. It is seldom that a mechanic enters on a life of crime. He forms habits that keep him safe.

The child is born with the same instincts that move all other animals. When he wants something he feels the urge to take it in the easiest way. It is only training that teaches him that he may get things one way, but not another. His training must be developed into habits. The life of a child is a conflict between primal emotions and social restrictions, and he must be fortified, not alone by teaching, but by habits, if he is to live by the rules that society lays down. Intelligent teachers and wise parents know what this means. It is only rarely that a boy carefully trained and fitted for life is sent to jail.

More and more the teacher and the psychologist are learning the importance of early training. Habits are formed when the child is young; these are easily fixed and hard to change. All statistics, if carefully gathered and thoroughly studied, lead to this conclusion, and logic and experience likewise show that this is true. To believe any other theory would be to deny the efficacy of moral and religious teaching and the effect of education and habit in the formation of character.

It is not difficult for the student to find the causes of crime. When they are found, it is not hard to prescribe for their cure. To ignore reason and judgment and all the finer sentiments that move men, to follow blind force and cruelty in the hope that fear will prevent crime and make all people safe, is bad in practice, philosophy, and ethics.

"Give us ten cents worth of animal crackers—all lions and tigers."
"What's the idea?"
" 'Cause they scare the baby."

In Praise of Freedom
by Will Durant

June 1927

It is a marvel inadequately noted that the contemporary victory of conservatism in the politics and economics of the world has been accompanied by the triumph of liberalism in religion and morals, in science and philosophy, in literature and art.

We have selected for our rulers gentlemen who reverently represent the established gods of industry; and we have put behind us, for the while, all thought of experiment in the relations of master and man. We have conferred a mystic popularity upon officials whose only virtue is their timidity; while our scorn of rebels and reformers is so great that we have ceased to persecute them. The capitals and governments of the world are in the hands of caution; and change comes over them only in the night, unseen.

Yet, bewilderingly simultaneous with this virtuous avoidance of the new in the official world, behold in our cities such a riot of moral and literary innovation, such an exuberant rejection of ancient faith and discipline, as makes every gray head shake with sociological tremors, and every aged finger point to corrupt Imperial Rome. Science thinks it has won its battle with the antediluvians; in the exhilaration of its victory it marches gayly into a mechanical dogmatism that does justice to everything but life. Literature violates every rule and every precedent; the boldest experiment is applauded by the most respectable critics; no one dares admire the classics any more; and to be a revolutionist in poetry and painting is as fashionable as to vote for mediocrity and reaction. The stage has suddenly discovered the mysterious beauty of the female form divine; the cabaret is devoting itself aesthetically to "artistic nudity"; and sculpture, which decayed as clothing grew, may be expected to flourish happily again. It is a remarkable synthesis of the omnipotent state and the liberated individual.

How shall we explain this humorous anomaly? Partly it is a corollary of our wealth: the same riches that make us timidly conservative in politics make us bravely liberal in morals; it is as difficult to be ascetic with full pockets as it is, with full pockets, to be a revolutionist. Puritanism did not die from bichloride of *Mercury*, it was poisoned with silver and gold.

Partly the situation issues from a contradiction in our hearts: it is the same soul that hungers for the license of liberty and the security of order; the same mind that hovers, in its fluctuating strength and fear, between pride in its freedom and admiration for the police. There are moments when we are anarchists, and moments when we are Prussians. In America above all—in this land of the brave and this home of the free—we are a little fearful of liberty. Our forefathers were free in politics, and stoically stern in morals; they respected the Decalogue, and defied the State. But we deify the State, and riddle the Decalogue; we are Epicureans in morals, but we submit to all but one of a hundred thousand laws; we are slaves in politics, and free only in our cups.

It is revealing that when an American speaks of liberty's decay he has reference to his stomach rather than to his mind. A convention of the American Federation of Labor threatened a revolution some years ago: because of the open shop?—certainly not; but because of the closed saloon. All the liberalism of the respectable American to-day confines itself to making alcohol the first necessity of a gentleman, and broadmindedness the first requisite of a lady. [. . .] What does it matter that freedom to think is lost, if freedom to drink remains? *Primum est bibere, deinde philosophari.*

It is not law that takes our freedom from us, it is the innocuous desuetude of our minds. Standardized education, and the increasing power of mass suggestion in an increasing mass, rob us of personality and character and independent thought; as crowds grow, individuals disappear. Ease of communication facilitates imitation and assimilation; rapidly we all become alike; visibly we joy in becoming as much as possible alike—in our dress, our manners, and our morals, in the interior decoration of our homes, our hotels, and our minds. God knows—perhaps even our moral freedom is a form of imitation.

Yet some rebellion is better than none; and possibly our thirst for liberty will go to the head, and dare to include thought. It is good that men should resist wholesale moralization by the law; to forbid the use of stimulating and consoling liquors because some men abuse them shows the amateurish weakness of a government that does not know how to control the fools without making fools of all. Civilization without wine is impossible. Civilization without restraint is impossible; and there can be no restraint where there is no liberty. [...]

What shall we say of this brave religion of liberty? How far is social order natural, and how long can it maintain itself without the prop of law? How far is freedom possible to man?

In human affairs (to spoil a perfect phrase of Santayana's) everything artificial has a natural origin, and everything natural has an artificial development. Expression is natural, language is artificial; religion is natural, the Church is artificial; society is natural, the state is artificial. Like language and theology, obedience to law comes through social transmission and individual learning rather than through impulses native to mankind. Hence the perpetual conflict, within the self, between the desires of one's heart and fear of the policeman; and hence the joy which triumphant rebels find in violating, with social approval and comparative impunity, some artificial and irksome prohibition. We are anarchists by nature, and citizens by suggestion.

But though in the secret sanctuaries of our souls we are lawless savages, we are not indisposed by nature to a moderate measure of spontaneous order and decency. Society is older than man, and older than the vertebrates. The protozoa have their colonies, with a division of labor between reproductive and nutritive cells; and the ants and bees bring this specialization of function to the point of physiologically differentiating the organism for its social task. Even the carnivores, whose tusks and hides and claws are individualistic substitutes for the strength and security of social order, include those gentle-eyed dogs who can be more sociable than a salesman and more loyal than a rural editor. "The Hamadryas baboons," says Darwin, "turn over stones to find insects; and when they come to a large one, as many as can stand round it, turn it over together, and share the booty.... Bull bisons, when there is danger, drive the cows and calves into the middle of the herd, while they defend the outside." Imperiled horses gather head to head, heels outward, forming a *cordon sanitaire*, as the Gauls put their women at the center when they engaged the foe. It was in such unions for defense, presumably, that animal society had its origin, and through them that it established a heritage of social impulse for humanity.

Add to this spontaneous sociability the formative co-operation of the family, and the case for a purely natural order simulates plausibility. "The social instinct," says Darwin, "seems to be developed by the young remaining a long time with their parents." The brotherhood of man is in this sense as old as history; it vitalizes a thousand secret societies and forms of fellowship; there hardly lives the brute with soul so dead that he has not thrilled at times with a sense of his almost physical solidarity with mankind. Along with natural fraternity a beneficent spread of parental tenderness helps us to mutual aid; and altruism, which the Enlightenment (in Taine's phrase) reduced to virtue furnished with a spy-glass, is as natural as love and as universal as maternity. Kant marveled that there was so much kindness in the world, and so little justice; perhaps it is because kindness is spontaneous sympathy, while justice is bound up with judgment and reasoning. Women, in consequence, are a little less than just, and infinitely more than kind.

Finally, society itself, supported on these instinctive and economic props, develops in the individual certain social habits which become as powerful as any second nature, and constitute a pledge of order far more reliable than law. The longer we live the more gregarious we become; the more susceptible to the opinions of our neighbors; the more imitative and respectable; the more attached to custom and convention; the more reconciled to those restraints upon desire which make civilization depend upon habit rather than upon force.

Every organized psychological power strives to complete this taming and socialization of the individual. The church sets up, almost at his birth, a bombardment of moral exhortations from which some gentle influence remains even when their theological basis has passed away. As parental and ecclesiastical authority wane, the school replaces them more and more; it pretends to prepare the individual for economic and artistic victories; but quietly and subtly it molds him, as Aristotle advised, "to suit the form of govern-

"The Precipice," by Rockwell Kent.

ment under which he lives"; it pours into his receptive constitution the peculiar habits and morals of his group; and it modestly covers the naked truth of history with such a glorification of the nation's past that the young graduate is ready to spur his neighbors to any sacrifice for the enhancement of his country's power. If the school fails in this socializing strategy, or the individual eludes it by immigrating when adult, the press will carry on the work; mechanical invention co-operates with urban aggregation to bring every mind within reach of that ancient thing called "news," and that delicate indoctrination which lurks between the lines.

When these molding forces are viewed in summary, the drive to good behavior seems so irresistible that one might reasonably question the necessity of laws that would regulate morality. In a large measure it is society that exists, and not the individual; [...] By biological heredity we are bound to our animal past; by social heredity—through our imitative and educational absorption of the traditions and morals of our group—we are bound to our human past; and the forces of stability, so rooted in our impulses and our habits, leave precious little in us that requires the unnatural morality of the state.

Since these forming influences act upon us in our tenderest and most suggestive years, we hardly overcome them except at the cost of a struggle that involves our very sanity. A miserable nostalgia visits us when we depart from the *mores* of our country and our time; and when we settle down in life it is most often into one or another of the grooves that the past has dug. Contented people are usually those who adopt without question the manners, customs, morals, and grammar of their group, becoming indistinguishable molecules in the social mass, and sinking into a restful peace of self-surrender that rivals the lassitude of love. The greater the society, the stronger will be the pressure upon the individual to divest himself of individuality even in those fashionable novelties which delight the modest soul because they are felt to be not really innovations, but respectful variations on an ancestral theme. In the final result a large population becomes an almost immovable body; the natural conservatism of society outreaches the chauvinism of the state. The individual, made in the image of the whole, becomes so docile and well behaved that the compulsions and punishments of law appear as a gratuitous extravagance; and we are for a moment tempted to sign our names defiantly to the doctrine of those fearful anarchists whom we exclude, or deport, or vilify, or imprison, or hang.

Let us reassure ourselves: there are defects in this philosophy of freedom. For first, it underestimates the violence of the strong: the same ruthless domination that makes the state would rule with more visible and direct force, and with more suffering and chaos, if there were no state at all. Civilization is in part the establishment of order and custom in the use of the weak by the strong. The precariousness of international law reveals the imminence of violence among the mighty; only little states are virtuous. [...] Every invention strengthens the strong and the unscrupulously clever in their manipulation of the unintelligent, the scrupulous, and the weak; every development in the complexity of life widens the gap and makes resistance harder. It is a bitter thing to realize; but society is founded not on the ideals but on the nature of man. His ideals are as like as not an attempt to conceal his nature from himself or from the world.

Again, the social dispositions upon which a natural order rests are far less deeply rooted in us than those individualistic impulses of acquisition and accumulation, of pugnacity and mastery which underlie our economic life.

Even the cry for liberty comes from a heart that secretly hungers for power; it is because of that hunger in the human beast of prey that liberty is limited and bound. In some measure it is the weak who by the pressure of majority ideas curtail the freedom of the individual, lest unshackled strength should so widen the gap between itself and the unfortunate that the social organism would burst, like a growing cell, into revolution. The first condition of freedom is its limitation; life is a balance of interferences, like the suspension of the earth in space. Men are so diverse in capacity and courage that without restraints their natural differences would breed and multiply through a thousand artificial inequalities into a stagnant and hopeless stratification of mankind. The French loved Napoleon because, with all his despotism, he kept careers open to all talents wherever born, and gave men in unprecedented abundance that equality which timid souls love a little more than freedom.

Ages of liberty, therefore, are transitions, brave interludes between eras of custom and order. They last while rival systems of order struggle for ascendancy; when either system wins, freedom melts away. Nothing is so disastrous to liberty as a successful revolution; the greatest tragedy that can befall an ideal is its fulfillment.

Why is it that wherever there has appeared in history the spontaneous order that rests solely on the natural sociability of mankind, as in primitive societies, or in the California of forty-nine, or in the Alaska of the nineties, it has passed eventually into the artificial and compulsory order of the state? It is a large question, for which a single answer will not suffice; no formula can do justice to the infinite variety of truth. Doubtless part of the cause lies in the passage from the family to the individual as the unit of production and society. Visibly the family loses its functions, even to the care of the child; filial respect and fraternal loyalty give way to a patriotism that becomes the only piety of the modern soul. Divested of its functions the family rots away; nothing remains but centrifugal individuals, magnificently independent in a common slavery. For slavery looks much like freedom when the master is never seen.

Meanwhile the aggregation of people in cities breaks down neighborhood morality as a source of spontaneous order; every egoistic impulse is free in the protecting anonymity of the crowd. Where natural order is still powerful, as in simple rural communities, little law is necessary; where natural order is weak, as in our sprawling cities, legislation grows. The state replaces spontaneous society as the corporation replaces the small dealer, or as the great railroad system replaces the stage-coach of picturesque individualistic days. The developing complexity of life has bound us into a highly integrated whole, and taken from us that independence of the parts which once was possible when each family was economically a self-sufficient sovereignty. Political and economic liberty decays for the same reason again that moral laxity increases: because the family and the church have ceased to function adequately as sources of social order, and legal compulsion insinuates itself into the growing gaps in natural restraint. Freedom has left industry and the state, and survives only in the gonads.

If the implements of production had remained as in days of barbaric simplicity—a spade and a plot of land—the state would not have swollen into the monster that now dwarfs our petty lives. For then each man might have owned his tools and controlled the conditions of his earthly life; his freedom would have kept its necessary economic support, and political liberty would not have become, like political equality, a baseless sham. But invention made tools more complex and more costly; it differentiated and evaluated men according to their capacity to use or direct or acquire the subtler or larger mechanisms; and in the end, by the most natural process in the world, the ownership of tools was centered in a few, self-sufficiency disappeared, and freedom became a politician's phrase, an honored relic commemorated annually like the rest of our noble dead.

On every side, then, we are caught in a current of development in which ancient and natural liberties are swept away. Our industrial relations are too intricate to be left entirely to "economic law"; certain functions, like transport and communication, are so strategically powerful that without legal limitation they would bestride all industry like some colossal beast of prey. All in all, it is well that these processes should fall under regulation by the state, incompetent and partial and corrupt as every state must, in our generations, be. Perhaps all the main channels of the economic life should be under such national control, and every vital artery between producer and consumer should be withdrawn from the strangling dominance of entrenched and irresponsible individuals. When all the avenues of distribution welcome every user on equal terms, production and consumption will be as free as human lust will tolerate; and industry—cured of that arteriosclerosis, that narrowing and pinching of the arteries of exchange by multiplying intermediaries, which threatens our economic health in the very heyday of our wealth—would sprout and flourish like an unbound plant; the initiative and enterprise of individual ownership would be liberated rather than enchained; cooperatives would find some protection from the hostile lords of our distributive machinery; and freedom, so pruned and trained, might in the outcome be deeper and richer than before.

All this is a grudging concession; for the Jeffersonian ideal of the government that governs least still grips the heart with its simple lure, and every added law desecrates the sovereignty of the soul. Order is a means to liberty, and not an end; liberty is priceless, for it is the vital medium of growth. "In the end," as old Goethe said, "only personality counts." The state was made for man, and not man for the state. Heredity was invented to preserve variations; and every custom began as a broken precedent. Evolution feeds on difference and change; social development demands innovation and experiment as well as order and law; history moves through genius and invention as well as through impersonal forces and unthinking crowds.

If we let our economic lives be limited we ought to guard a hundred times more jealously the freedom of the mind. Mental liberty should be at least as dear to us as liberty of body to an animal; caught and caged, it never reconciles itself to captivity, and paces about forever on the watch for a way to freedom. Perhaps it is because we can bear to see such pitiful prisoners, and can look without remorse into eyes deepened and softened with the longing for liberty, that we are unworthy of the freedom our fathers had when they met the animal on equal terms, and killed it in fair fight instead of imprisoning it as a pleasant sight for a Sunday afternoon. But we ourselves are caged, and do not complain; how can we understand the hunger of the fettered beast?

There is a Chinese proverb to the effect that when a nation begins to have many laws it is slipping into senility. The ancient Thurians provided a halter for every unsuccessful proponent of new laws, suggesting his fit punishment for mutilating liberty. Our legislatures in America, one hears, pass some six thousand laws per week; if this is so, we are a nation of thieves, and we need not laws but education. Sessions of Congress are a source of national apprehension, to rich and poor alike; and perhaps the quiet esteem in which the present executive is widely held is due to the fact that he is a *roi fainéant*, who may be relied upon, like an English king, to do nothing but draw his salary. Even his vetoes are gratefully received; what if the bills they nullify should by strange chance be good?—even a good law is a law, and so far bad. There is not so sharp a contradiction as we supposed between the unpopularity of virtue in our cities and the popularity of an abstemious president; in either case it is liberty that is served.

If this appears to imply that our current moral laxity is not so unmixed an evil as those of us suppose who soothe our consciences by making other people virtuous, the presumption is correct. Much of our immorality takes the form of honesty; we oldsters were as lax as we could afford in our guarded and impecunious youth; and when we sinned we sinned in silence, and carried pious faces into meeting. The growing generation is not so skilled in secrecy, and likes to boast of greater crimes than it commits. Its sins are superficial and will be washed away in the confessional of time; experience will make men mature enough to love modesty again. Meanwhile of what moment is it that in our youth our grandmothers smoked malodorous pipes respectably, while in our desuetude our daughters smoke whatever satisfies? How shall we dissuade youth from making *vade mecums* of whiskey flasks (whose contents they manfully pretend to enjoy), except by ceasing to forbid it? What does it matter that nudity can be seen more readily and less furtively than in our hooped and petticoated days, that undue stimulation replaces morbid brooding? Habit will correct the evil gently by dulling sensitivity, and clothing will have to be restored to generate again the illusions of desire.

Against this magnificent uprising of the young the old can only think of laws. Every timid and jealous voice calls upon the immaculate assemblymen of America to come to the rescue of morality. Because some sleek panders have made filthy lucre by exposing God's handiwork upon the stage, tired people demand that policemen be empowered to revise all pictures and dramas before their public unveiling. But one supposed the police had full power to stop indecency by pre-existing legislation. One supposed that the police had the power to put an end at once to any spectacle that violated the statutes against obscenity. Possibly there is no need to resort again to indiscriminate prohibition; possibly public opinion, if it is the public's opinion, would suffice to condemn excess, and might prove (as it does in the case of drink) more effective than any law. It would stamp us indelibly as a provincial and infantile nation if we relapsed into the strait-jackets of Puritanism at the very time when

America begins to create its own literature, its own drama, and its own art. Better a Charles II than a Cromwell.

Luckily for us, life is on the side of youth in these matters, and youth is on the side of life. Our heirs may commit suicide, and prefer baseball to epistemology, and forget to say grace before drinking, but these diversions must not obscure for us the buoyant health and bright good-nature of contemporary adolescence. Let the young be happy; soon enough they will be old; and the lassitude of the flesh will make them virtuous. If morals are transiently too lax, they will correct themselves as knowledge and wisdom grow; in the end, as Socrates suggested, we must instruct rather than forbid. Every vice was once a virtue, necessary for existence, and every virtue was once a vice, developed beyond need; not laws but public opinion hewed them into social form. If we wish to improve other people's morals let us improve our own; example speaks so loud that precept is unheard. The best thing we can do for the community is not to fetter it with laws, but to straighten our own lives with tolerance and honor. A gentleman will have no morals but his own.

The time must come (for the world does move) when men will understand that the highest function of government is not to legislate but to educate, to make not laws but schools. The greatest statesman, like the subtlest teacher, will guide and suggest through information, rather than invite pugnacity with prohibitions and commands. The state, which began as the conquest and taxation of peaceful peasants by marauding herdsmen, will become again, as it was for a moment under the Antonines, the leadership of a great nation by great men. We need not so despair of our race as to believe that government will be in the hands of politicians forever. Day by day the level of intelligence rises; generation after generation the ennobling heritage of culture grows, and finds transmission to a larger minority of mankind; soon men will not tolerate the charlatans whom we have suffered so patiently and so long. Our children's children, lifted up by our care, will choose their rulers more wisely than we chose. They will ask not for lawmakers but for creative teachers; they will submit not to regimentation but to knowledge; they will achieve peace and order not through violence and compulsion, but through the advance and spread and organization of intelligence. And perhaps— who knows?—as their knowledge mounts they will deserve, and therefore get, at last, the best of all governments— which will govern not at all.

EDITOR'S EASY CHAIR

RE-DISCOVERING EUROPE

BY EDWARD S. MARTIN

AUGUST 1927

It was a real fairy story, that story of Lindbergh—something between the Arabian Nights and Hans Andersen or Laboulaye: Prince Charming dropping out of the sky and allaying all the rows and making everybody happy. Even two months afterwards it may not be too late to talk about it, for really it is an astonishing subject.

The miracle of Lindbergh was not so much in his getting across to Paris as in the extraordinary effect that his exploit seemed to have had on the human race. The human race—hardly less—for when the newspapers and the radios and all the picture-taking machines and the movies and the loud speakers got through with Lindbergh's exploit, the bigger part of mankind must surely have heard of it. Here was a most individual feat, something done by that youth primarily out of his own head, with only so much consultation with others as was necessary to convert them to the idea that his thought was feasible and offered a good chance for success. Charles did the stunt himself but, of course, he had organization back of him and under him at every turn. It made his engine, it made his plane, it made the noise he started with, and amplified and distributed the resounding acclamation of his landing on Bourget Field. [...]

Now then, what may we hope that Charles will accomplish which will be worth all this immense noise made about him and which we do not wish to see go to waste?

He has taken us out from under the spell of the movie idols and the fisticuff champions, and lighted up our minds by contemplation of an achievement of a higher order. A newspaper writer, Mr. Garrett, has said (in the *World*) that he has

lifted up men's respect for mankind as it has not been done since his predecessors died in war.

So he has, and it is a very great achievement and most timely.

In doing so he has acquired immense influence. How will he use that?

So far as one can judge, he will use it to quicken the development of aviation in these States.

And that may be immensely important, not primarily for commercial reasons, but to increase our efficiency in war, and so our influence and power as a factor in keeping the peace of the world and saying our say in international concerns at a time when great changes are making, and still greater ones impending.

My very accomplished friend Weston was talking the other day about the immediate future of the world and of wars to come, and doped it out something like this. "What I go by," he said, "is this: A nation that is ashamed of itself recovers its self-respect *through war*. The French had disgraced themselves by the Revolution and were very grateful to Napoleon for giving them *glory*. The Germans never got over the humiliation that Napoleon subjected them to through war. The Italians have never quite got over the humiliation of their centuries of division under Austria. They have had the inferiority complex. Mussolini relies on that. Russia for the same reason will follow." So he figured out that "Italy will make war in 1934 and Russia in 1950."

All that is interesting in a way. The year 1934 is only seven years ahead of us and some people now living may survive till 1950. But Lindbergh's hop and its astonishing emotional consequences [...] are fit to remind

Foreign travel leaves its mark.

Dec. 1908, p. 166
by A. B. Walker

betters that it is the unexpected that usually happens. Weston's forecasts seem to be based on conditions of life that existed before the Great War. There are now tremendous motives for the maintenance of peace and terrific objections to large-scale war of which humanity was certainly not so conscious before 1914. One can understand how an inferiority complex turns to glory. One can also understand that it was a comfort to many minds who were tired of having debt collection the chief subject of discussion between their country and Europe to see that subject suddenly swept out of notice by the appearance in Paris of a young man in an airplane. [...]

All the same, while interest in aviation in general has been wonderfully increased [...], and while the commercial possibilities of air service to Europe are now actively discussed, a very lively detail—perhaps the predominant one—of the talk about these hopes is their relation to war—the next war, the thought of which no one is willing to countenance, but which few reflecting people can yet dismiss from their minds. The flights have made the world smaller. [...] It is a small world when you can go from New York to Paris on one load of gasoline in a day and a half, and these machines steadily progressing in efficiency and safety can be turned to missile-carriers if occasion calls for it. They can drop their bad bombs on far-off places. It has all made the people whose minds are on war think harder than ever on that subject.

But it has seemed to help to tie together Western Europe and the United States, and that is very valuable, even though the tie made seems no more than sentimental; for a sentimental tie may be very strong—indeed, the strongest kind.

When we think about war, another Great War, of course we think about Germany and whether she will tie up with Russia to beat France and Britain, or tie up with Western Europe to stand off Muscovy and anything that might threaten in Asia. [...]

Mussolini's Italy is a political conundrum. Which way will that cat jump? Turkey is another. But the big one is Russia. There are very active minds in that great country nowadays and they seem to practice day and night for the realization of purposes that run constantly through them to produce extremely radical changes in this world. The changes they are concerned about are not the evolutionary ones that are going on everywhere, but changes, apparently, that are geared to a plan; a tremendous plan to make Russia off-hand the dominant political and economic influence in human life. If that plan ever runs strong enough to be recognized as an imminent world peril, what is the United States going to do about it? It has refused diplomatic relations with Russia. It has done that much already. Britain, who needed them and somewhat reluctantly accepted them, has had to give them up. That was evidence as far as it went of like-mindedness between the British government and ours. What should we do if we saw another irrepressible conflict, not merely between nations of Western Europe, but between Western Europe and those minds that plan at Moscow, and all the backing they could gather? It is not necessary to say what the United States would do; but as one thinks about it, these airplane exploits take on a new significance that is quite comforting. For if there is another big disturbance in the world, the armies of the sky are going to count enormously, and the influence of the United States may be vitally increased by the reputation of its airmen and the provision of means on a large scale to make their proficiency effective. [...]

It is almost as if they had discovered a new world, and in so far as it is that, the discovery is very, very timely. For how very unreal our present world is, particularly to the elders in it! The young who never knew a different one, probably do not feel this unreality, but the changes that have come in the twentieth century have been enormous, and minds that go back of them and to nineteenth-century habits and standards seem to themselves to be living in a sort of dreamland—much of it quite delectable, but a lot of it pretty well passing understanding. Does anyone, do you suppose, look upon our present world, our present life, with any sense of its permanency? Is everybody waiting for something to drop, or only meditating elders and international politicians? Most curious times, times apparently of preparation and subject evidently to unexpected thrills.

AIMEE SEMPLE MCPHERSON
PRIMA DONNA OF REVIVALISM
BY SARAH COMSTOCK

DECEMBER 1927

There is a blare of trumpets, and the murmur of more than five thousand people hushes sharply. A baton flickers—"The Stars and Stripes" flings itself in long red and white streamers of sound. Glances swing abruptly toward a staircase which comes down to the flower-decked platform. A figure descends—plump, tripping, balancing an armload of roses.

"There she is! That's her!"

"That's *her!*"

The plump one trips forward to center stage, lifts the bouquet, her face wreathed in a garland of interwoven roses and smiles. Upon it plays the calcium—violet light, pink light, blue light, golden light. And now the vast gathering rises to its feet, breaks into clapping. The plump one bows to this side, to that, a focussed center of roses, smiles, light, delight, applause, while the band fairly bursts its brass to hail her.

No. It is not a famous prima donna's opening night. It is not the entrance of a world-renowned tragedienne or of a queen of the flying trapeze or the tightrope. It is she who outstrips all of these. It is "Sister."

This was my first sight of Aimee Semple McPherson. From it I received the impression, strengthened on many following occasions, that in this unique house of worship called Angelus Temple in the city of Los Angeles the Almighty occupies a secondary position. He plays an important part in the drama, to be sure; but center stage is taken and held by Mrs. McPherson. It is in her praise that the band blares, that flowers are piled high, that applause splits the air. It is to see her and hear her that throngs travel, crushed in the aisles of electric cars, thrust, elbow, and bruise one another as they shove at the doors of her Temple. Ropes protect the several entrances; hundreds strain and struggle to be first when these are released. A whistle sounds, the ropes give way, a large detachment of the crowd surges through, as many as

the ushers can handle. Then up go the ropes again, and a fresh front presses forward, ready to surge in at the next signal. Over the great lower floor and two balconies attendants are hurrying to seat the mob, a full hour before the entrance of the star. Men and women stand against the wall, they sit upon the steps of the aisles, and still, when the final whistle blows, there are thousands turned away, thousands who stand for two, three, four hours on the street and in the nearby park, to listen to the concert and the inspired utterances as they scream themselves forth from the loud speaker outside the building. All the people are making a joyful noise, in very truth; bringing hither the timbrel and blowing up the trumpet in the new moon; but the primary object of this mighty demonstration is not that of the Psalmist's.

Rather, it is an ample lady of early middle years, her soft curves concealing muscles like steel; a lady of flashing eye and quick movements and conspicuous reddish hair and ever-busy smile; a lady who, gazing forth with satisfaction upon the assemblage come to do her homage, has the right to honest pride. Sunday after Sunday the same phenomenon is seen. Thousands travel to Angelus Temple, packing the street cars and mobbing the doors, standing with aching feet in the hope of gaining admittance. And this happens not for a brief period of hysteria, it is no nine-days' wonder; for several years it has been going on, with ever-growing enthusiasm, and bids fair to continue. Aimee Semple McPherson is staging, month after month and even year after year, the most perennially successful show in the United States.

In the weeks that I spent in Los Angeles and observed her with growing wonder, I probably fell far short of learning all her accomplishments. But this much I did grasp: that as a show-producer with unflagging power to draw she knows no equal. She is playwright, producer, director, and star performer in one; she keeps all her assistants, from call-boy and property man up to her leads, on their toes; and, in their midst, she plays her own role with an abandon that sweeps her hearers by hundreds to the altar. Many a revivalist of the past has played upon his audience by the old methods of sensational preaching; but Mrs. McPherson has methods of her own. Her Sunday evening service is a complete vaudeville program, entirely new each week, brimful of surprises for the eager who are willing to battle in the throng for entrance. In this show-devouring city no entertainment compares in popularity with that of Angelus Temple; the audience, whether devout or otherwise, concede it the best for the money (or for no money) in town.

Take a typical Sunday evening. The spectators arrive to find the stage set with an ocean background, rolling green waves flanked by rocks. At one side rises a lofty lighthouse of the kind known technically as "practical." From time to time its windows flash, its door stands ready to open.

An hour of orchestral music, then the singers file in, from fifty to a hundred of them, ranging themselves in a loft over the speaker's platform, facing the people and creating the illusion of a heavenly choir just above the inspired one's head. Their costumes, for this particular evening of nautical entertainment, are in sailor effect, navy and white, jaunty caps atilt. When at length the leading lady enters in the role of rear admiral, she is gallant in a swinging cape over a white uniform, her red-gold coils surmounted by an all-but-official cap.

And now, after the round of applause, after the usual greetings and opening hymns and congratulations, after the request that everyone shake hands with four neighbors and say, "The Lord bless you!" the program begins. It is announced that Christopher Columbus will recite Joaquin Miller's poem. The lighthouse door opens and America's discoverer, in full costume of the fifteenth century and with impressive whiskers, emerges.

"Look at that, will yuh! If that ain't Chris to the life!"

"*I'll* say it's him!"

Delighted murmurs accompany him as he rolls forth. "Sail on!" in baritone billows of elocution, while the organ assists.

The next performer will be a musician who plays upon a tin whistle and a set of chimes, perhaps a few other instruments. Again the lighthouse door opens, forth he comes, a Gloucester fisherman in full rubber attire to protect him from the nor'easter of tribulation. While Mrs. McPherson informs Radio Land upon the microphone (which is her constant care) that, "He's got just a little tin whistle, folks,

just like a little child'd play on," the artist chirps forth "Listen to the Mocking Bird," and in the audience many a horny-handed son of the Iowa farm nudges his neighbor and observes delightedly, "By gum! I used to whistle that when I was *so* high!"

"The Mocking Bird" is followed by "The Old Oaken Bucket," and delight waxes. But the act must be quickly finished. Rarely is the request for an encore acknowledged by more than a bow. The director knows the value of rapid movement, of the quick shift that anticipates boredom. The Gloucester fisherman is hustled off to make way for a sailor boys' quartette in which there is much business of tugging at the ropes, climbing the mast hand-over-hand, heave-hoing, rocking, and rolling.... Next an organ solo, a descriptive piece in which a storm at sea is depicted by creaks, roars, crashes, and groans of the instrument and terrific flashes of electric lightning. There are more songs by sailors and sailoresses, and at length, when the appetite for vaudeville is fairly appeased, comes the headliner, the great act of the evening—Sister's message.

It is in what she terms "illustrations" that she gives full vent to her showman's genius. These are her master effort, a novel and highly original use that she makes of properties, lights, stage noises, and mechanical devices to point her message. Heaven and Hell, sinner and saint, Satan, the fleshpots of Egypt, angels of Paradise and temptations of a bejazzed World are made visual by actors, costumes, and theatrical tricks of any and every sort that may occur to her ingenious mind—a mind which must work twenty-four hours to the day to pave the way for the lady's activities.

On this particular evening her analogy pertains to the sea.

"Look at the little pleasure boat!" She turns to the background of tossing waves. "Here it comes, sailing along, having a grand time!"

Forth sails the little boat, which represents the gay and reckless one who ignores the warning to repent. It crosses the background of painted waves somewhat jerkily, but entirely to the satisfaction of the rapturous spectators.

"Yes, it's having a grand time, all right. But here comes the pirate ship—oh, the old pirate'll get you, little pleasure boat! I'm sorry for you, but it's too late!"

And now the pirate ship, emblem of Satan, hurries forward, overtakes the gay craft. A struggle—then down goes the victim, crashing, capsizing, while a rejoicing mob applauds—not the triumph of Evil, but the triumph of Sister the Showman.

A ship of commerce follows and goes upon the pasteboard rocks. "You men that don't think about anything but money, money, can't you make some more money! Oh, you'll find yourself on the rocks!" ... Finally the submarine; it is compared to those infamous ones who attack Angelus Temple and its high priestess. Her devoted adherents laugh victoriously as the submarine fails in its deadliest efforts at destruction.

The sensation of the season was the spectacle called "Life, Death, and Eternity," which one member of the church described to me as "the grandest show I ever seen. Once when I was in New York I went to the Hippodrome, but it wan't nothin' to this." A huge world, presumably pasteboard, occupied the center of the stage. The actors in the drama appeared ranged, at one side as angels in heavenly white, on the other, as sinners in purgatorial black.

"Oh, the rich man wants to hold on to his wealth and his fine house—he holds on mighty tight, don't he?"

Now, at this stage of the performance I had not been able to get near enough to see exactly what happened, and I was obliged to visualize the tragedy of Dives through the report of a breathless spectator.

"Say, the rich man was carryin' a big toy house to the door o' Heaven—what d'yuh know about that? An' there was an angel stood there, she had grand wings, an' she was holdin' the door open. Well, the rich man he started to step in, but he wanted to take his fine house along, an' he couldn't get it through the door. He tried an' tried, but it stuck. Say, he had to leave it behind, all right!"

One by one the frivolous and the sinful were seen to pass into outer darkness, Mrs. McPherson herself enacting the idle lady of wealth who squanders the fleeting hours over the tea-table. Incidentally, she indulged in a few jazz steps across the stage to enforce her point, and performed them with notable facility. So on, to the grand climax. Suddenly out burst a conflagration—"It was real fire, for sure!" one of the marvelling reported—the flames fell rapaciously upon the world, embracing it, destroying. The sinners had left for lower and unseen regions, the world had vanished.

And now, slowly descending from the top of the dome, appeared a huge painted scene of the Celestial City, sparkling with lights as it placed itself in the center just above Sister. Never having seen an authentic view of it before in any travelogue, I observed its architecture and streets with deep interest; the impression gained was that, in its tinted stucco effects and palm-lined boulevards, it strikingly resembles a realtor's depiction of Los Angeles. A mighty murmur rose; as stated in *The Foursquare Crusader* (the church's official news organ), "over 5,300 pairs of eyes watched one of the most spectacular illustrations ever presented on this platform."

Sister's resources are as the widow's cruse. She is never at a loss for novelty nor does she spare labor or cost. Many a theatrical producer would shrink from the outlay involved in staging such scenes. It is said that the lighting expenditure for one Sunday evening performance would make safe the streets of a dark village. Scene designers and painters are constantly employed. There have been "illustrations" such as a spectacle of brilliant red streamers carried by white-clad Crusaders in a vast interweaving design which must have suggested a ballet figure, the ribbon ends being finally gathered up at a central altar. Harpists were employed to interrupt from time to time her sermon on "The Song of Songs." I have been told that a peacock once strutted upon her platform to represent the proud before their fall.

The baptism by immersion is perhaps the greatest spectacle of all. Every Thursday evening there are fifty to one hundred and fifty converts who don white robes and become "dead to sin." "Oh, what a happy funeral!" cries the priestess. Curtains part upon an elaborate scene of palms, flowers, and grassy banks, below which the water ripples enticingly. Mrs. McPherson and one of the Brothers, standing waist-deep, immerse one, two, even five at a time; it is then that the steel muscle within that softly rounded arm displays itself. I have seen her, with only slight assistance, baptize three powerfully built young women with their arms linked, and have marvelled at the physical ease with which she so quickly raised them.

[...] Healing takes place on Saturday evenings, at which service Sister is aided by her associate, Brother Smith Wigglesworth, an English evangelist and author of *Worthy Words from Wigglesworth*, or *Tidbits for All on the Word of God*. Scores hasten (or limp, or creep, or are carried) to the altar. Discarded canes, crutches, and wheel-chairs are seen in the foyer. When Sister heals she lays hands upon the afflicted spot and prays. Brother's method is more athletic: he strips off his coat, advances to the front, squaring as though about to enter the ring. "This woman (crippled from rheumatism) hasn't knelt down for eight years. When I get through with her *she'll kneel*!" She knelt three times after his

The Angelus Temple in Los Angeles.

manipulations upon her body, so forceful that an assistant had to support her lest she topple over. "I curse you, disease; I command you to leave this woman!"

Those who witness the healing by hands, sometimes by oil, are of many opinions. The majority watch open-mouthed and round-eyed. "*I'll* say it's a miracle!" "Look at Gran'pa throw away his cane, will yuh!" A grasshopperish oldster is breaking forth in whoops of joy and prancing across the platform, kicking like a member of the Follies, waving his arms, and shouting hallelujahs, while Sister beholds with beaming pride.... "Aw, they been rehearsin' him for that act!" whispers a skeptic behind me.... One thing is patent: Brother Wigglesworth's pugilistic manner of handling Satan makes an excellent foil for the tripping and dimpling femininity which led an enraptured follower to sigh, "Sometimes Sister's such a cutie I think she'd leave Mary Pickford behind if she'd give up religion for the screen!"

One of the first questions raised by the observant and non-partisan visitor concerns the audience. Who are they that pack a huge building week after week, who have been doing so more and more ever since it was opened, almost five years ago?

Obviously, a great number are those scorned by the priestess as "curiosity seekers." Thousands of the transient population of the Southwest drift in and out because they "have heard of her." But there are other thousands who attend faithfully, a large part of them as signed members of this Church of the Foursquare Gospel, which claims, including its branches, to number ten thousand.

A uniformed member of the staff told me that it is estimated that two-thirds come into membership through healing. This seems likely in a land that has always been the sick man's Mecca, where flourishes every kind of physician, from the orthodox practitioner to the veriest charlatan. The rest drift in, from other denominations or none.

A glance about shows that they are largely represented by the Middle West farmer or small-townsman and his family who have come to form so large a proportion of Los Angeles' population. On every hand are old men and women, seamed, withered, shapeless, big jointed from a lifetime of hard labor with corn and pigs. The men wear what would be their Sunday-best in Iowa. The women are often gaudy in the short, tight, adolescent garb that some salesperson has foisted upon them, and their gray hair is bobbed.

The couples drag tired old bones to the Temple and listen as if at the gates of Heaven itself.

Often the young people are quite as zealous. One sees earnestness, admiration, even exaltation now and then. One woman, I remember, held my eyes by her beauty, her rapture; throwing back her head, lifting her hands high, she was singing:

> "Speak, my Lord, speak to me,
> Speak, and I will be quick to answer Thee!"

She was not on earth; she was translated. [...]

But although, after sitting in various parts of the auditorium and talking with many individuals, I was convinced that the majority are more or less ignorant, credulous, and susceptible to cheap emotionalism, nevertheless, I have met a few intelligent and educated persons who believe thoroughly in Sister's inspired leadership. Indeed, the conflicting opinions within the organization itself create one of its remarkable features. No doubt, most of the members worship at her feet and regard those enemies who criticize her private life and question her disposition of the funds as Satan's own host. But there are some who, strangely enough, go so far as to join the church with tongue in cheek. "Yes, I belong," a certain woman told me. "I work for the poor, too. There's a lot o' money spent for charity. But that ain't accountin' for all of it. Oh, I ain't no fool!" The city is rife with gossip concerning her alleged personal extravagances; incidentally I may observe that I never felt warmly prompted to rally to the defense of Mrs. McPherson except when told by the scandalized that it is said she buys the most expensive lingerie in the best shops. For my part I fail to see why one cannot serve the Lord as well in pink silk as in red flannel.

But this astounding inconsistency, this mingling of belief and disbelief, I have never seen in any similar following. Apparently, the congregation worship not a prophet of the Lord, but a theatrical idol. For whatever their opinions may be, they revel in the entertainment which Sister provides. They treat the performance, whether a child-wonder's recitation, a negro's tune on the piccolo, an opera singer's solo, or an actor's delineation, with a sort of admiring familiarity. "Here comes Chris!" they say at Columbus' appearance. "My land, ain't the sinners great!" they exclaim during the Heaven and Hell spectacle. This is similar to the family interest which a stock company wins in time, with a happy anticipation of each week's novelty.

Aimee Semple McPherson at her revival's twenty-fifth anniversary pageant.

"It's a good show, anyway—we always get our money's worth," they say. The price is their own. "Don't stop at nickels and dimes—make it dollars for the Lord!" they are urged. Many small coins do, however, rub elbows with large greenbacks. Nevertheless, the sum total must be very large.

You may believe Aimee Semple McPherson to be a messenger direct from God Almighty to save His erring world. Or you may believe her to be the most unblushing fraud in the public eye today. Some do one, some the other; and there is every shade of opinion between. But the one fact that stands out is that her influence is incredible, that it carries as that of few evangelists has ever carried, that she is to-day one of the most amazing phenomena of power in this feverish, power-insane United States, and that the curious would like to know how, in popular parlance, the lady puts it over.

One of the most remarkable evidences of her hold upon men and women is the fact that she has been able to remain, and to keep on growing, in the *same place*. Most revivalists move on, as enthusiasm wanes. Mrs. McPherson came to Los Angeles more than a half dozen years ago, I understand, shaking her tambourine in a little tent to a handful of worshippers. It is said that she was a Holy Roller, and traveled in Canada and the United States with this tent which she sewed up with her own bleeding fingers whenever it blew down. To-day she is head of a tremendous organization, and her sermons are heard not only by thousands inside and outside the Temple, but by thousands more who tune in regularly on KFSG.

Most remarkable of all is the fact that she accomplishes what she does by means of such vehicles as her own sermons. Every successful preacher of the kind, as far as I can recall, has possessed some cleverness and originality in discourse, no matter how crude its expression. A certain coarse humor, sometimes rising to wit, has informed the utterances of the acrobatic Billy Sunday. But let Mrs. McPherson's deliverances be divorced from Mrs. McPherson's personality, and they fall to the depths of the banal. I have heard a number of her sermons, and I have before me a packet of seventeen of the most famous, in pamphlet form. To quote at random:

"How wonderful are the forces of nature! How mighty!"

"You and I are gardens, like trees of the planting of the Lord."

"Little butterfly flitting hither and yon—little humming birds that come humming around to get what honey you can—where are you when the storm comes?"

"A mother with trembling hands was stroking back the dampened yellow curls from a marble-white brow."

"A tear trickled down the weather-beaten face and hung like a sparkling jewel in the rough-looking beard."

The ancient phrases, the ancient platitudes. Now and then they are enlivened by slang, as, when the wife of Potiphar was accusing Joseph, "She surely framed him up." Or, "Will you follow Him? Oh, men and women, this is brought to a show-down!" But it is not the slang of wit, which attracts a certain type of listener; rather, it carries the impression of being an unconscious lapse into the vernacular. Broadly humorous anecdotes are sometimes brought in, as, for instance, when during her frequent "stunt" of throwing Testaments for individuals in the audience to catch (a performance more skilful than any I have ever seen outside the circus) she relates in her curious nasal twang:

"One night I was doing this in San Francisco, and there was a lady there who was just a curiosity seeker. She didn't care about the Lord. But one of the Bibles missed the man I meant it for and it hit that lady right in the head. And what do you think she did? She dropped right down on her knees, and she said, 'Lord, take me! I never was so hard hit before, and I give up! I'm Yours!'"

But in the main her sermons are without even such diversion; they are mired hopelessly in a slough of analogy and metaphor (frequently much mixed), in hackneyed phrases, and in the type of sentimentalism styled as "sob sister." "The Scarlet Thread" is "considered to be the most magnificent of all Sister McPherson's superb sermons" according to its own foreword. It is a mass of commonplaces, melodrama, tawdriness, and cheap emotionalism. Her voice is noticeably damaged by years of strain, breaking in sharp nicks along its edge. Her "r" has the sound of a machine-drill. Hearing thus delivered a sermon utterly commonplace in itself, even to the least fastidious intellect, one marvels more and more at the power of the personality.

One grants that there are very wide "varieties of religious experience," and that different methods appeal to different tastes. Those who would never be even touched by a Handel composition on the organ of King's at Cambridge, or by a La Farge painting above the altar of the Ascension in New York may be plucked from the gutter and saved by far less subtle means. Furthermore, it is for us to admit, and not grudgingly, that certain niceties of the tongue have no connection with righteousness. "He would call to Mother and I," "Let everybody ketch the Temple spirit" may offend the finicky, but will never offend the Lord, we may well be thankful to say. But other preachers with great followings have been possessed of a stimulating freshness of thought; they have, according to their lights, had something to say and in a novel manner.

Aimee McPherson's power lies not here. Rather, it is the remarkable combination of showman and actress in her gifts which attracts and holds the multitude. As a director she is incomparable. While others are performing, she never for an instant permits interest to flag; at the first sign of restlessness she steps forward. "All join in with him now! 'Sail on!'" If a young singer's voice proves weak and, therefore, uninspiring, Sister snatches her own tambourine and drives home the rhythm. Let a recitation be dull, she will advance beaming to inquire if it isn't grand. Always she senses, with that swift, uncanny perception of hers, the slightest waning of attention; always, in emergency, she lifts those pink palms, flashes her infectious smile, and breaks into a hymn, catching back her hearers before they discover that they are slipping.

This complete control over the mood of her audience she exercises from the instant she arrives upon the platform. Nothing gets away from her. Her grasp, from the first moment, is as tight and as all-inclusive as that of a violinist upon his instrument or a chariot racer upon his reins. Her hands tell the tale of nervous tension—her hands alone. For the rest she appears completely relaxed. Her chest is full with big breathing, her movements are swingingly free. But watch her hands while others are performing; they play restlessly, interlacing, touching a lock of hair, adjusting a cuff, collar, wrist-watch. They never relax except as she forces them to do so. [...]

She does for herself what a manager is accustomed to do; she creates an overwhelming "Sister consciousness." Not only by keeping herself in the newspapers, but by a multitude of other means, she impresses the image. Large banners on the Temple cry, "Welcome to our Sister!" when she returns from a mission. Her photographs in countless poses appear on cards, bookmarks, pamphlets, and the like, which are sold in the foyer. On a page of the church's newspaper I counted the number of times that her name occurred: fifteen, to the Almighty's nine.

Every advertiser knows the psychological effect of ceaseless repetition. But no personality can long be impressed unless the personality is in itself remarkable. And Mrs. McPherson's magnetism is of that inexplicable sort which occurs but rarely in a puzzled world. In appearance she is wholesome, freshly groomed, comely—no more. But the glance of her companionable eye, the flash of her comprehending smile possess the electrical quality to an all-conquering degree. I confess to having felt it like a warm and overcoming current. My intellect may have sat back disdainfully. But I was relieved when the lady broke her appointment with me; had I met and talked with her as I intended, I am far from sure that I should have been able to write this article dispassionately. Her gift for taking everyone, from the individual to the vast audience, into her confidence, is incomparable; and it includes the Almighty as well. She will suddenly run forward, throw up her expressive hands, cry impulsively, "Oh, say, folks, you know I think God is (her voice catches)—oh, say, I think He's *just simply wonderful*, don't you?" It swoops them up. Here is the genius of intimacy. By these spontaneous, convincing outbursts she gathers together those five thousand people, draws the Lord down into their midst, holds them all there, together, tight, in a swift melting of emotion which brings men and women crowding to the altar with a weeping outburst of "Hallelujahs!" Hers may be assumed emotion, but the infectiousness of it is immense. Down she goes on her nimble knees, imploring Heaven...sobs are heard on every side.... I have seen an athletic youth rise shrieking in the audience, pallid, clutching the air and crying upon God—an able-looking boy who ought to be at some sane work or play instead of wrought to this delirium of "getting the Spirit" by an intoxicant far more dangerous than that taken from him by Volstead. "Talking in tongues" usually accompanies these attacks of hysteria, and at times the assistance of sturdy ushers is required to handle the converts.

Mrs. McPherson's creed is clearly defined. Heaven is an "indescribably glorious habitation" where the righteous will be presented at the Throne "without spot or wrinkle"; and "wherein hosts of attending angels sweep their harps." Hell is "a place of outer darkness, and there into a lake that burns with fire and brimstone shall be cast the unbelieving, the abominable, the murderers, sorcerers, idolaters, and liars." It is needless to say in what light she regards Mr. Darwin. One trembles for him. Garden of Eden, serpent and apple are her origin of species, and her pictures of the Hereafter are authoritative. There is no hope of escape from either one or the other of those two dreadful futures—the lake of brimstone, or the eternal twanging of a harp. Her world consists of all-black sinners and all-white saints, and whichever one is he must pay a horrible penalty.

Her church does relief work among the poor. A staff of workers daily visits from house to house, carrying food, money, clothing, and "the Word." There have been cases of outcasts saved, especially from the drug habit. A woman who had worked in this social service said to me, "There's no question that a lot of money is spent to help the needy. Gossip says that a lot more is never accounted for. The whole organization looks to me like a queer mixture of good and bad." Sister is not restrained, at any rate, by over-delicacy in the matter of asking for funds. She always calls for "dollars for the Lord," and she does not blush to take up a second offering after a service, holding the plate herself while greenbacks take on legs and run down the aisles to her. In her published by-laws it is stated that each applicant for membership "must declare his loyalty to and willingness to assist in the support of this association, both with his substance as well as his undivided effort."

Whatever she has won she has worked for—worked in a ruthless drive, with no pity for her own fatigue. Six days a week she preaches, often more than once a day, hurling her tremendous force into every word she speaks. She utters platitudes in a way that gives them the guise of inspiration. And this is only a fraction of her labor. She organizes and manages a great business enterprise in the Temple. She writes articles, books. She plans and directs the weekly vaudeville with its ever-fresh "illustrations." She teaches in her Bible School, she marries, baptizes, heals, buries. Breathless with wonder, you ask how one human being ever accomplishes it all. "It's the Lord working in her," reply the faithful. "She sure is on the job. She'll retire a millionaire," retort the scoffers.

There is nothing ambiguous about her statement of authority. [...] One by one she casts off those who impede her progress of power; at last she has broken free even from the business partnership in which she and her mother labored in "the great white-heated flame of soul-winning"; at the height of her prowess she marches forward alone to her goal. It has been stated that her Lighthouse symbol represents a Salvation Navy which she visualizes, world-wide, rivalling the Army and sweeping souls to repentance over the ocean of sin. And it is very certain that, if this comes to pass, Mrs. McPherson herself will be the one ceaselessly celebrated upon an instrument of ten strings and upon the lute, upon a loud instrument and upon the harp.

My Countryside, Then and Now
A Study in American Evolution
by Malcolm Cowley

January 1929

It is not an abstraction for politicians, a capitalized immensity like the Middle West, the South, New England, the Prairie States. My country is tangible, small, immediate: a Pennsylvania valley, or rather a high tableland cut by ravines, lying between Chestnut Ridge on the west and Laurel Hill on the east and south. By climbing to the highest branches of a pine tree on the knob behind our barn, one can survey the whole of my country, from the one steeple of Bethel to the stone house at Nolo, and from the high ground in the north, around Nicktown, to where, in the south, the coke-ovens of Vintondale cut the horizon with a wall of smoke.

Last summer, after twelve years of absence broken by a few hasty visits, I returned to my country to find it the same and not the same. It had changed physically and socially; it had changed in fashions peculiar to itself and in other fashions that were typical of a whole cycle in American rural life.

When I went away, in 1916, it had the look of something ravished and deserted. The Vinton Lumber Company had cut the second-growth pine, the first-growth hemlock, the sugar-maple and, leaving birch and beech as unworthy of attention, had torn up its twenty miles of railroad track and moved into Kentucky. Fires had followed the lumbermen, turning thousands of acres into black meadows where ashes stirred in the breeze like the pollen of infernal flowers. Mine-tipples and culm-banks were toadstools on the bare hills. The poisoned creeks ran orange with sulphur water. It was as if my country had been occupied by an invading army which had wasted the resources of the hills, ravaged the forests with fire and steel, fouled the waters, and now was slowly retiring, without booty.

For one by one, the settlers were drifting away. Young men, the flower of their generation, tramped off to Pittsburgh or Johnstown to look for work in the mills. Some of them went farther west. They helped to open the new mines of West Virginia; they followed the harvest northward, week by week, from Oklahoma into Saskatchewan; they toiled in Oregon sawmills or Michigan factories, and grew into landless men, trees without roots—the homeless peasants of the machine.

My country was becoming a region of old people and children. The minority of young men who stayed behind had yielded to the yoke of women and the past; or rather, their future had been decided in a fashion somewhat more casual. There were, during the summer, barn dances, hay rides, church festivals (pronounced "festibbles") and picnics. In winter there were husking bees and sociables. Chaperons were unknown. Boys and girls drove home together, wrapped in lap robes, pressed body to body in narrow sleighs. Early in these essentially puritan lives there had come one or two years of candid paganism. Soon they ended; Vida or Irma was "in trouble"; there was generally a marriage; and a boy of nineteen, kept from migration, settled down to his father's life of plowing for rye in September, for buckwheat in June; of cutting mine-props in winter and, as time went on, of driving his family to church, with his six or eight children crowded in a surrey, on the circuit-rider's alternate Sundays. What magnificent families they raised in my country! And how sallow and toothless the women were at thirty!

Life there was hard and in its essentials tragic. Youth was a hurried episode. The few distractions of manhood were taken seriously: a keg of beer, a few raucous songs, a fight; soon a man went down; the victor knelt over him, swinging his great arms rhythmically, like a reaper; somewhere in the crowd a woman was screaming. In the morning all the drinkers except one would return to their battle against starvation.

It was a battle in which there were many casualties. Men died in accidents; men died in the mines, under a hundred tons of rock, or in the woods under a fallen tree; there were women who had outlived four husbands. There were men who had killed three wives with milking, child-bearing, housework. And each of these tragedies was purely a family affair. Social feeling was almost lacking; each man worked alone, for his own salvation; and the lack of responsibility to the community was shown in bad roads, in primitive schools, in trout streams poisoned by sawmills, in churches that were never painted or reshingled, in forest fires that no one bothered to fight.

My country blossomed a little in its old men. Those who survived the hardships and accidents of middle age acquired a sort of exhausted calm, a faded whiteness like that of rain-washed lilacs. They sat in the sun, whittling and chewing tobacco with an air of unalterable dignity. They talked, choosing their words slowly, in the drawling singsong of the Pennsylvania mountains. My country has no dialect of its own, but it has a verbal melody which is unmistakable; and the speech of these old men was a sort of chant that rose and fell like the slow Allegheny ridges. They spoke of the days when the hills were covered with first-growth

pine, when water grist mills hummed in all the valleys, when panthers slunk after white-tailed deer, when every creek and run (there are no brooks in western Pennsylvania) was full of shadowy trout.

My country, for all its unsocial harshness, for all its emigrants, had then, and still preserves, a fund of local patriotism which is symbolized by trout, white pine, and deer. The old men used to say, "Them days we alluz come home with a string of trout as heavy as a ham.... I c'n mind when every pine we cut would saw two thousand foot of boards.... It was nice, I tell ye, to go huntin' atter deer." They tried to hide their enthusiasm under these practical judgments, but it was obvious that these fish, these trees, these beasts had more than a practical value: they were the totems of a tribe. To catch a trout, to cut a virgin pine, or to shoot a twelve-tined buck was almost a ritual act: it was like sacrificing a white bull to the god Mithra.

There were no longer any deer in my country. The white pines which once had covered it were reduced to a few weevily saplings. The trout had been poisoned by sawmills or sulphur from the mines. The young men were dispersing, the farms were neglected, and soon my country would be a fire-blackened wilderness with a few old houses crumbling in the midst of overgrown fields. So at least it seemed to me in the summer of 1916.

I was to see many deserted countrysides during the next twelve years. In Vermont, on the wooded slopes of the Green Mountains, I would find stone fences precisely marking the boundaries of non-existent fields, and clumps of lilacs to show where villages had stood. In tidewater Virginia I would see whole townships abandoned to scrub pine and sassafras. There, thinking of General Sheridan's boast that after he left the Shenandoah Valley a crow flying through it would have to carry his own provisions, I reflected that peace was often no less destructive than war. That year an old Pennsylvania farmer had told me of driving for twenty miles in Armstrong County, through what had been a prosperous farming district, and of finding not so much as a forkful of hay to feed his horses.

When I returned to my country last summer I half expected to encounter the same condition. Instead, the population had increased. The nearest village was crowded with new houses. The farms, though few of them seemed prosperous, at least were occupied. The roads were admirable. It was obvious that the women had improved their own position; they looked somehow less weary, less indifferent, and even the boys who played by the roadside were rather less unkempt. A new brick high school was rising near the site of the little building where sixty of us children, a turbulent roomful divided into five classes, had recited turn by turn to the same discouraged teacher.

However, the change in my country was not confined to its physical appearance: the social attitude of our neighbors had developed like their roads and schools. I soon discovered that the old individualism of life on lonely farms had almost disappeared. People there, as elsewhere in the country, had come to regard themselves as members of a collectivity: a village, a township, a lodge, a church. They judged actions by their social effects, and spoke of a successful man as being "a credit to the town." Formerly they would have said, with the same note of admiration, "Milt knows how to take care of hisself."

It was this new collectivism which smoothed the way for the organizers of the Ku Klux Klan when they appeared in my country five years ago last summer. They were aided also by a sort of particularism, a regional pride; for there was hardly a man of twenty-one in the upland villages—as distinguished from the mining towns of the valley—who was not white, Protestant, and for three generations a native. There was hardly a man who did not take the Klan oath; and the local sentiment was so unanimous that there was practically no attempt at concealment. Everybody knew that Squire Adam Diffenbaugh had been the first to join, and that Preacher Cameron, who was almost the last, had become the most fanatical member. In the Hemphill family there were seven Klansmen. If wash day happened to follow a Klan meeting, all seven robes would hang on the Hemphill line, in full view of every automobile that passed along the state highway.

The robes hang there no longer. By the summer of 1928 the Klan was practically dead in my country. It had died in a series of quarrels over money, in the defalcation of a treasurer, in a feud between the Diffenbaughs and Preacher Cameron, and also to some extent in the growth of rival orders. The forces which produced the Klan were perhaps as strong as ever, but fortunately the group instinct and the spirit of regionalism were being directed toward less questionable ends.

They were directed toward the building of new schools, the resurfacing of the roads, the better enforcement of the forest and game laws. Local pride, as expressed in these improvements, has raised the taxes nearly two hundred per cent. Government and law are beginning to play a vaster part in the life of the community. In my day they were represented almost solely by a constable and a squire; now, in addition, I found game wardens, fire wardens, state troopers, prohibition agents, inspectors of various sorts, forest rangers.... And the effects of all this supervision were beginning to be seen.

There have been no forest fires in my country this year or last, for the first time in three decades. Deer have become so plentiful that in some places they have stripped the underbrush of bark and leaves to the height of a man's head. Stray dogs and cats, the most dangerous enemies of game, are exterminated systematically. Sawmills are almost violently encouraged not to pollute the waters. A fishing club of farmers and miners, formed three years ago, has stocked several streams, and in these one can catch nearly as many trout as in my grandfather's day. Even the white pines are coming back, though more slowly: they are creeping into the deserted fields; the edge of the forest shows a line of deeper green.

And my country, now that its local symbols have been restored, no longer lives in the past. It has found salvation of a sort, even though its economic problems remain unsolved. Migration to the cities has almost ceased; perhaps, in this era of collectivism, it has come to be regarded as desertion, as a guilty form of disloyalty. At any rate, the young men are staying at home. [...]

For most of them the problem of finding work has proved none too easy. They are compensated, however, by the privilege of living in their own country, among friends; and a few have even made opportunities for themselves which might have been closed to them in a city. Elmer Moody, at thirty-five, has just retired with a comfortable fortune after fifteen years of selling automobiles. Merton Ward, whom I remember as the bad boy of the second-reader class, is one of the few rural storekeepers who have adjusted themselves to new conditions; his business is growing. Milt Peters has become a lumberman. Starting after the War with no capital except his government bonus, he has acquired a sawmill, two motor trucks, a reputation for thoroughness, and several valuable tracts of timber. He leaves no waste behind him; he is bent on making a fortune out of tops and branches which the Vinton Lumber Company would have left to rot. And he is employing nearly a dozen men of his own age and his own locality.

To-day, as in other country districts, it is the aged who are leaving their homes. Old J. L. Edwards, the only man of wealth in the township, has bought a farm in Georgia where the winters are less severe. Bill George, formerly a sergeant in the Army of the West, wounded at Chickamauga, prisoner at Andersonville, has gone to live with his eldest son, a clerk in the War Department. He returned last summer for a brief visit, but it may be his last; I hear that in his eighty-seventh year he is looking "purty dauncy."

With the young men working at home and the old men moving away, my country has become what America is always supposed to be, and very seldom is—a land of youth.

On the second day of my visit I went to the swimming hole in Blacklick Creek, a hundred yards below the White Mill Dam.

I remembered it as a pool in the deep woods, black and still, with a school of minnows floating at the surface of the water, in the sunlight, and hummingbirds moving from flower to flower along the bank. Usually it was the haunt of silence. At infrequent intervals it was invaded by half a dozen boys who stood shivering and naked in the water, one or two of them able to venture a few strokes and all of them splashing and shouting as if the stillness were an enemy to be conjured away.

This time the swimming hole was crowded with young men, children, girls in their teens, and middle-aged women who had never worn a bathing suit before. All of the boys could swim and a few were really skilful. However, it was the presence of women that astonished me. No one familiar with the position of farm wives in my country could fail to gasp at finding them here in the water, under the trees, at a time when there were socks to mend and dewberries to preserve.

Their right to the swimming hole—a right significant of all the little revolutions by which the life of American country women is being transformed—had not been won without a struggle. I heard that Preacher Cameron had declaimed against it on three successive Sundays.

Reverend Elisha Cameron, as he signed his letters, was a powerful figure, the father, by two wives, of fifteen children, twelve of whom were living. He was known throughout the township for his deer-stalking and his skill in catching trout. To the improvement of roads and schools, to the rights of women, and the comforts of life he was hostile or indifferent: he was an individualist, drawing a personal

inspiration from the Bible; hunting, fishing, damning, and exhorting with the same vehemence, the same lonely fire. In some ways he typified the older standards of the country.

He was envied for his bags of game. He was respected for his fecundity no less than for his picturesque faith. There had always been many to follow him even when, as in the dispute over the swimming hole, he was opposing popular new customs. But his prestige was threatened by a series of minor disagreements; it was seriously compromised by his failure to repay a loan; and it finally disappeared in a curious affair which brought two instincts of my country into opposition.

Milt Diffenbaugh, killed in a mine accident, had married the preacher's second daughter. He was buried with some pomp in the graveyard overlooking the valley of the Blacklick. There was a quarrel, however, between the Diffenbaugh clan and Milt's young widow, in which Preacher Cameron took his daughter's side. Milt's body was exhumed from the Diffenbaugh plot, with the preacher helping the undertaker, and carried to a lonely burying ground in Centre County. From that day the preacher's influence disappeared. He, the official representative of Protestantism in my country, the local head of what was almost an Established Church, had outraged our instinctive reverence for the dead, had committed a sacrilege. And, in Preacher Cameron's defeat, the causes he supported were compromised: the Klan lost other members; card parties and dances were held for high school students; part of the past was swept away. The swimming hole was opened to country wives.

Standing knee-deep in the muddy water that afternoon was Millie Armstrong, the preacher's eldest daughter, the mother of six children at twenty-nine, and a rebel against his patriarchal standards.

The new pastor arrived a few days later. He was a young man: brisk, tolerant, rather sentententious, and eager to work for what he called "the spiritual and moral welfare of the community." Obviously he would lead no crusade against the swimming hole. After a short conversation he invited me to a picnic and conference at which plans for community service would be discussed.

I liked the young pastor for his easy enthusiasms, but strangely I regretted old Cameron's lean shoulders, his bitter faith, his blue eyes quick to spy out a deer or a sinner. I was glad to see the village improved; I admired the new spirit of collectivism less for itself than for its effects; but still I could not help looking backwards. My country had once possessed a tragic power, a sort of cold majesty that was melting in this more genial age. I felt like seeking the past. And so on the morning of the picnic, which fell on the day before my visit ended, I did not drive to town; instead, I went rambling through the pasture-lot. After a time I reached the top of the knob and climbed the old pine tree from which all my country is visible.

It stands some distance behind the farmhouse, alone in a bare field, with its branches twisted northward in the direction of the prevailing winds. Branch after branch they spread like Egyptian fans of ostrich feathers or separate terraces of moss, hiding the ground from the watcher who has climbed to the top. There, a perpetual breeze creeps through the needles, exhaling the odor of dried herbs and a rustle of heavy silk.

Perched on the highest branch, I looked southward to the road, once known as the Clay Pike and now transformed into the Benjamin Franklin Highway. It rippled with an unbroken stream of motor cars, bound east to the mines of Nant-y-glo, bound for the picnic, bound west beyond the ridges, bound nowhere in particular. South of the highway was the deep ravine where the Blacklick flowed, its orange water sometimes visible between the trees. The horizon west of the valley was closed by Duncan's Knob, the limit of the lands that my great-great-uncle had claimed. South and southeast was a file of parallel mountains, ridge on ridge, growing bluer and fainter as they marched into the sky. Bands of lightning were playing over the last ridge.

In the nearer distance I began to distinguish familiar sites. A crumbling chimney in a pasture lot was all that remained of the cabin which James Duncan, the deerslayer and pine-butcher, had hewn from the forest log by log. He lay buried near-by, under a blasted tree. It was his son Thomas who built the White Mill, first of the water grist mills along our streams, now standing idle as a memorial to the days of more prosperous farming. Empty also was the clearing where the Vinton sawmills had devoured the hardwood and hemlock of twenty thousand acres. A rash on a distant hillside, lividly gleaming in an island of sunlight among the clouds, was the culm-bank and abandoned tipple of what had been Mine No. 6.

The history of my country, like that of so many American districts, and perhaps like that of the nation as a whole, had been a slow exhausting of resources. The men in coonskin caps, the fierce Scotch-Irish of the frontier, had driven away the larger game. Their sons, who cleared the fields, had cut almost the last of the virgin forest, and the next two generations had worn out the arable soil. My country to-day was fed with minerals, but the coal in time would be exhausted, and then? . . . I had no fear for what would come. The hills had shown a power of recuperation; the trees were creeping back into the desolate choppings where fire had raged; the fields were resting for other tasks under a blanket of white-top and goldenrod. The people, too, were preparing for the future; they felt a common aim; they would find other resources inevitably.

Out of the village, borne by the low winds that precede a storm, came the ring of hammers from the carpenters at work on the new school.

Not Marble nor the Gilded Monuments

by Archibald MacLeish

September 1929

The praisers of women in their proud and beautiful poems,
Naming the grave mouth and the hair and the eyes,
Boasted those they loved should be forever remembered.
These were lies.

The words sound, but the face in the Istrian sun is forgotten.
The poet speaks, but to her dead ears no more.
The sleek throat is gone and the breast that was troubled to listen:
Shadow from door.

Therefore, I will not praise your knees and your fine walking,
Telling you men shall remember your name as long
As lips move or breath is spent or the iron of English
Rings from a tongue.

I shall say you were young and your arms straight and your
    mouth scarlet.
I shall say you will die, and none will remember you;
Your arms change and none remember the swish of your garments
Nor the click of your shoe.

Not with my hands' strength, not with difficult labor
Springing the obstinate words to the bones of your breast
And the stubborn line to your young stride and the breath to
    your breathing
And the beat to your haste,
Shall I prevail on the hearts of unborn men to remember.

What is a dead girl but a shadowy ghost,
Or a dead man's voice but a distant and vain affirmation
Like dream words most?

Therefore, I will not speak of the undying glory of women.
I shall say you were young and straight and your skin fair—
And you stood in the door, and the sun was a shadow of leaves
    on your shoulders,
And a leaf on your hair.

I will not speak of the famous beauty of dead women.
I shall say the shape of a blown leaf lay on your hair.
Till the world ends and the sun is out and the sky broken
Look! It is there!

Archibald MacLeish and his wife, 1933.

The Lady in the Looking-Glass
A Reflection

by Virginia Woolf

December 1929

People should not leave looking-glasses hanging in their rooms any more than they should leave open check books or letters confessing some hideous crime. One could not help looking, that summer afternoon, in the long glass that hung outside in the hall. Chance had so arranged it. From the depths of the sofa in the drawing-room one could see reflected in the Italian glass not only the marble-topped table opposite, but a stretch of the garden beyond. One could see a long grass path leading between banks of tall flowers until, slicing off an angle, the gold rim cut it off.

The house was empty, and one felt, since one was the only person in the drawing-room, like one of those naturalists who, covered with grass and leaves, lie watching the shyest animals—badgers, otters, kingfishers—moving about freely, themselves unseen. The room that afternoon was full of such shy creatures, lights and shadows, curtains blowing, petals falling—things that never happen, so it seems, if someone is looking. The quiet old country room with its rugs and stone chimney pieces, its sunken book-cases and red and gold lacquer cabinets, was full of such nocturnal creatures. They came pirouetting across the floor, stepping delicately with high-lifted feet and spread tails and pecking allusive beaks as if they had been cranes or flocks of elegant flamingoes whose pink was faded, or peacocks whose trains were veiled with silver. And there were obscure flushes and darkenings too, as if a cuttlefish had suddenly suffused the air with purple; and the room had its passions and rages and envies and sorrows coming over it and clouding it, like a human being. Nothing stayed the same for two seconds together.

But, outside, the looking-glass reflected the hall table, the sunflowers, the garden path so accurately and so fixedly that they seemed held there in their reality unescapably. It was a strange contrast—all changing here, all stillness there. One could not help looking from one to the other.

Meanwhile, since all the doors and windows were open in the heat, there was a perpetual sighing and ceasing sound, the voice of the transient and the perishing, it seemed, coming and going like human breath, while in the looking-glass things had ceased to breathe and lay still in the trance of immortality.

Half an hour ago the mistress of the house, Isabella Tyson, had gone down the grass path in her thin summer dress, carrying a basket, and had vanished, sliced off by the gilt rim of the looking-glass. She had gone presumably into the lower garden to pick flowers; or as it seemed more natural to suppose, to pick something light and fantastic and leafy and trailing, travelers' joy, or one of those elegant sprays of convolvulus that twine round ugly walls and burst here and there into white and violet blossoms. She suggested the fantastic and the tremulous convolvulus rather than the upright aster, the starched zinnia, or her own burning roses alight like lamps on the straight posts of their rose trees. The comparison showed how very little, after all these years, one knew about her; for it is impossible that any woman of flesh and blood of fifty-five or sixty should be really a wreath or a tendril. Such comparisons are worse than idle and superficial—they are cruel even, for they come like the convolvulus itself trembling between one's eyes and the truth. There must be truth; there must be a wall. Yet it was strange that after knowing her all these years one could not say what the truth about Isabella was; one still made up phrases like this about convolvulus and travelers' joy. As for facts, it was a fact that she was a spinster; that she was rich; that she had bought this house and collected with her own hands—often in the most obscure corners of the world and at great risk from poisonous stings and Oriental diseases—the rugs, the chairs, the cabinets which now lived their nocturnal life before one's eyes. Sometimes it seemed as if they knew more about her than we, who sat on them, wrote at them, and trod on them so carefully were allowed to know. In each of these cabinets were many little drawers, and each almost certainly held letters, tied with bows of ribbon, sprinkled with sticks of lavender or rose leaves. For it was another fact—if facts were what one wanted—that Isabella had known many people, had had many friends; and thus if one had the audacity to open a drawer and read her letters, one would find the traces of many agitations, of appointments to meet, of upbraidings for not having met, long letters of intimacy and affection, violent letters of jealousy and reproach, terrible final words of parting—for all those interviews and assignations had led to nothing—that is, she had never married, and yet, judging from the mask-like indifference of her face, she had gone through twenty times more of passion and experience than those whose loves are trumpeted forth for all the world to hear. Under the stress of thinking about Isabella, her room became more shadowy and symbolic; the corners seemed darker, the legs of chairs and tables more spindly and hieroglyphic.

Suddenly these reflections were ended violently and yet without a sound. A large black form loomed into the looking-glass; blotted out everything, strewed the table with a packet of marble tablets veined with pink and gray, and was gone. But the picture was entirely altered. For the moment it was unrecognizable and irrational and entirely out of focus. One could not relate these tablets to any human purpose. And then by degrees some logical process set to work on them and began ordering and arranging them and bringing them into the fold of common experience. One realized at last that they were merely letters. The man had brought the post.

There they lay on the marble-topped table, all dripping with light and color at first and crude and unabsorbed. And then it was strange to see how they were drawn in and arranged and composed and made part of the picture and granted that stillness and immortality which the looking-glass conferred. They lay there invested with a new reality and significance and with a greater heaviness too, as if it would have needed a chisel to dislodge them from the table. And, whether it was fancy or not, they seemed to have become not merely a handful of casual letters but to be tablets graven with eternal truth—if one could read them, one would know everything there was to be known about Isabella, yes, and about life too. The pages inside those marble-looking envelopes must be cut deep and scored thick with meaning. Isabella would come in, and take them, one

by one, very slowly, and open them, and read them carefully word by word, and then with a profound sigh of comprehension, as if she had seen to the bottom of everything, she would tear the envelopes to little bits and tie the letters together and lock the cabinet drawer in her determination to conceal what she did not wish to be known.

The thought served as a challenge. Isabella did not wish to be known—but she should no longer escape. It was absurd, it was monstrous. If she concealed so much and knew so much one must prize her open with the first tool that came to hand—the imagination. One must fix one's mind upon her at that very moment. One must fasten her down there. One must refuse to be put off any longer with sayings and doings such as the moment brought forth—with dinners and visits and polite conversations. One must put oneself in her shoes. If one took the phrase literally, it was easy to see the shoes in which she stood, down in the lower garden, at this moment. They were very narrow and long and fashionable—they were made of the softest and most flexible leather. Like everything she wore, they were exquisite. And she would be standing under the high hedge in the lower part of the garden, raising the scissors that were tied to her waist to cut some dead flower, some overgrown branch. The sun would beat down on her face, into her eyes; but no, at the critical moment a veil of cloud covered the sun, making the expression of her eyes doubtful—was it mocking or tender, brilliant or dull? One could only see the indeterminate outline of her rather faded, fine face looking at the sky. She was thinking, perhaps, that she must order a new net for the strawberries; that she must send flowers to Johnson's widow; that it was time she drove over to see the Hippesleys in their new house. Those were the things she talked about at dinner certainly. But one was tired of the things that she talked about at dinner. It was her profounder state of being that one wanted to catch and turn to words, the state that is to the mind what breathing is to the body, what one calls happiness or unhappiness. At the mention of those words it became obvious, surely, that she must be happy. She was rich; she was distinguished; she had many friends; she traveled—she bought rugs in Turkey and blue pots in Persia. Avenues of pleasure radiated this way and that from where she stood with her scissors raised to cut the trembling branches while the lacy clouds veiled her face.

Here with a quick movement of her scissors she snipped the spray of travelers' joy and it fell to the ground. As it fell, surely some light came in too, surely one could penetrate a

"The Violet Kimono," by Robert Reid. c. 1910

little farther into her being. Her mind then was filled with tenderness and regret.... To cut an overgrown branch saddened her because it had once lived, and life was dear to her. Yes, and at the same time the fall of the branch would suggest to her how she must die herself and all the futility and evanescence of things. And then again quickly catching this thought up, with her instant good sense, she thought life had treated her well; even if fall she must, it was to lie on the earth and molder sweetly into the roots of violets. So she stood thinking. Without making any thought precise—for she was one of those reticent people whose minds hold their thoughts enmeshed in clouds of silence—she was filled with thoughts. Her mind was like her room, in which lights advanced and retreated, came pirouetting and stepping delicately, spread their tails, pecked their way; and then her whole being was suffused, like the room again, with a cloud of some profound knowledge, some unspoken regret, and then she was full of locked drawers, stuffed with letters, like her cabinets. To talk of "prizing her open" as if she were an oyster, to use any but the finest and subtlest and most pliable tools upon her was impious and absurd. One must imagine—here was she in the looking-glass. It made one start.

She was so far off at first that one could not see her clearly. She came lingering and pausing, here straightening a rose, there lifting a pink to smell it, but she never stopped; and all the time she became larger and larger in the looking-glass, more and more completely the person into whose mind one had been trying to penetrate. One verified her by degrees—fitted the qualities one had discovered into this visible body. There were her gray-green dress, and her long shoes, her basket, and something sparkling at her throat. She came so gradually that she did not seem to derange the pattern in the glass, but only to bring in some new element which gently moved and altered the other objects as if asking them, courteously, to make room for her. And the letters and the table and the grass walk and the sunflowers which had been waiting in the looking-glass separated and opened out so that she might be received among them. At last there she was, in the hall. She stopped dead. She stood by the table. She stood perfectly still. At once the looking-glass began to pour over her a light that seemed to fix her; that seemed like some acid to bite off the unessential and superficial and to leave only the truth. It was an enthralling spectacle. Everything dropped from her—clouds, dress, basket, diamond—all that one had called the creeper and convolvulus. Here was the hard wall beneath. Here was the woman herself. She stood naked in that pitiless light. And there was nothing. Isabella was perfectly empty. She had no thoughts. She had no friends. She cared for nobody. As for her letters, they were all bills. Look, as she stood there, old and angular, veined and lined, with her high nose and her wrinkled neck, she did not even trouble to open them.

People should not leave looking-glasses hanging in their rooms.

Maxfield Parrish

1930's

The Peculiar Weakness of Mr. Hoover

by Walter Lippmann

June 1930

In telling the story of a private life it is usually enough to describe the interaction of the hero's character with the circumstances in which he lived. But in the history of a public man there is a third element. That is the public character of the hero, the character, that is to say, which the public ascribes to him.

The triangle of fate, character, and reputation is peculiarly important in considering Mr. Hoover's first year of office. For to a greater degree than would be true, I think, of any other President, his reputation is a work of art. Mr. Hoover's ascent to the Presidency was planned with great care and assisted throughout by a high-powered propaganda of the very latest model. He is, in fact, the first American President whose whole public career has been presented through the machinery of modern publicity. The Hoover legend, the public stereotype of an ideal Hoover, was consciously contrived. By arousing certain expectations, the legend has established a standard by which the public judgment has estimated him; if, as I think most observers would admit, his first year ended in an atmosphere of mild disappointment, the cause in some measure at least was the inability of the real Hoover to act up to the standards of the ideal Hoover. Thus Mr. Hoover is blamed for not achieving things which nobody would ever have expected Mr. Coolidge to do.

In saying that Mr. Hoover's reputation was a work of art, I do not mean, of course, that it is a lie. I mean that it is an idealization, a portrait not of the man as he is but of his finest intentions and his greater abilities abstracted from the confusions of the flesh. The idealized Hoover exists in Mr. Hoover much as a play exists in the mind of a playwright before he has written it for production on Broadway.

The ideal Hoover was established by an efficient propaganda, and without the propaganda it is inconceivable that the miracle of Mr. Hoover's nomination could have been effected. The real man at the core of this idealization was not known to the American people at large, for he had never participated in the kind of political fighting which displayed his qualities. His great activities during the War were carried on in the abnormally uncritical atmosphere of wartime; in his subsequent career as Secretary of Commerce he was concerned with matters that are wholly mysterious to the mass of the people. Thus the real Hoover went to the White House accompanied by the ideal Hoover of the popular legend. In the White House the real Hoover struggling with sour circumstances and unmanageable passions must occasionally wish that his idealized reputation were at the bottom of the sea. For the ideal picture presents him as the master organizer, the irresistible engineer, the supreme economist. In the actuality these speculations deposited by the propaganda are like the toastmaster's introduction saying that John Smith will now get up and make the wittiest speech you have ever heard. It is depressing to be elevated too high, and it is depressing to be a master organizer with a disobedient Congress on your hands, or to be an irresistible engineer with wets and drys on the rampage, or a supreme economist at the tail end of a bull market. It is better to be lucky and unpretentious and to be admired, like Mr. Coolidge, for your deficiencies than to have to wear the hairshirt of your own idealism. The Woodrow Wilsons and the Herbert Hoovers who reach very high and arouse great expectations tempt the ironies of fate, and unless they do brilliantly well and have lots of luck, are often as much the victims of their disappointed admirers as of their avowed opponents.

The deliberation and the contrivance which went into creating the idealized Hoover are thoroughly consistent with Mr. Hoover's outlook on life. He has the peculiarly modern, in fact, the contemporary American, faith in the power of the human mind and will, acting through organization, to accomplish results. Mr. Hoover once delivered some semi-philosophical lectures in which he celebrated in orthodox

Hooverville, New York City, 1930.

fashion the traditional American laissez-faire individualism. He is, however, no true believer in letting nature take its course. He has not the piety, the skepticism, or the complacency which all true believers in laissez-faire have in some degree or other. In his world there must be a remedy for every wrong, a solution for every problem; there must always be something to do about everything. He may not know the remedies and solutions, he may even find it inexpedient to apply them, but he believes they can and will be found. He is a devotee of the religion of progress, of the faith that man can be master of his fate by studying, inventing, and arranging things. There have been other reformers in the White House but none, I think, who has had his peculiar reliance upon the power of the applied intelligence: the traditional American reformer is an apostle of the ancient righteousness like Roosevelt or of the messianic hope like Wilson. The popular acclaim which greeted the advent of an "engineer" to the Presidency was a recognition that at last a man had gone to the White House who believed that politics could be conducted by the kind of intelligence which has produced such excellent motor cars, airplanes, and refrigerators.

The faith that statesmanship could be made a branch of engineering would, of course, be more congenial to an engineer who had moved mountains of matter than to an experienced statesman who had tried to move mankind out of its ancient habits. The religion of progress is, in fact, a creed inspired by the history of man's triumphant conflict with matter plus a certain subconscious belief that as a source book of wisdom the history of man himself is bunk. The idea that human societies can be fabricated, that they can be rationally conceived, deliberately planned, and efficiently executed is one for which there is a ready market in contemporary America. Many circumstances conspired to make Mr. Hoover the embodiment of that idea. He is an idealist who has studied applied science rather than history, a successful man who has lived on the frontiers of civilization, a promoter and engineer who has organized obedient subordinates, a public official baptized under the war dictatorship. Why should he not have entered office believing that human problems can be managed and arranged by the conferences of key men? The portrait of the ideal Hoover man was drawn from this model, and the difficulties of the real Hoover are in large measure due to the refusal of circumstances to fit the specifications.

Mr. Hoover's first year in office was marked by a series of major events which simply did not happen according to plan. He planned a limited revision of the tariff. He is getting a general revision. He planned a continuation of the prosperity which he had celebrated with a symphony of statistics. He got a first-class panic and depression. He planned to have prohibition quietly studied, largely ignored, and ultimately solved. He got an agitation which has made prohibition the paramount issue in those parts of the country where it hurts the most. In the light of the campaign talk, such an outcome is full of the most embarrassing ironies; and the Democrats cannot be blamed if they make the most of it. But there is a more interesting speculation than to dwell upon the contrast between promise and performance, and that is to ask why it is that events have so spectacularly eluded the control of a man who with fine purposes and high abilities had set himself the ideal of controlling them.

My own notion is that a close examination of Mr. Hoover's conduct in the critical matters will disclose a strange weakness which renders him indecisive at the point where the battle can be won or lost; further examination would show too, I think, that this weakness appears at the point where in order to win he would have to intervene in the hurly-burly of conflicting wills which are the living tissue of popular government; that he is baffled and worried, and his action paralyzed by his own inexperience in the very special business of democracy. When the decision lies in his own hands, he is happy and effective; in the questions which are not controversial, in making appointments which are not seriously challenged, he acts easily and with high intelligence. If his Administration were to be judged by these standards, it would rank among the most distinguished of our generation. But it is in the controversial questions that the real test comes.

The difficulty which most affects his immediate political fortunes is, of course, the depression in business. Mr. Hoover was elected when the boom was near its peak and the stock speculation was still rising to greater and greater heights. He took office at a time when the most experienced business men, bankers, and economists were pointing out the symptoms of extreme danger. Their voices were drowned out, of course, in the frenzied speculation; nevertheless, at the center, in the heart of the financial district, in the Federal Reserve Bank of New York, the unpopular but sound view predominated, and, as we now know, efforts were made by that bank to stop the financial hysteria before the inevitable collapse occurred. The record recently disclosed shows that these efforts were vetoed from Washington during the early months of Mr. Hoover's administration, and that preventive measures were not authorized until it was too late to avert the crash.

These vetoes came from a board of which Mr. Hoover's Secretary of the Treasury is a member, a board so constituted that it could hardly fail to listen to any clear leadership from the President. One need not underestimate the risks of such leadership; under the circumstances a bold policy of deflation of stock prices would have made the administration intensely unpopular among a people the majority of whom seemed to be committed to bullish speculation. I do not know of any President who would have taken the risks of such a policy, but we have had no President, on the other hand, who made quite the same claims to an understanding of how to maintain prosperity. We must assume that Mr. Hoover saw the dangers in the spring of 1929; to assume the opposite would be to doubt his reputation for economic wisdom. We must assume that he knew what steps ought to be taken to stop the speculation before it got completely out of hand, for the steps were laid before the Board on which Mr. Mellon sits. We are compelled to conclude that he shrank from facing the uproar and that he let matters drift until the fever had run so high in the late summer that action designed to avert the crash then appeared simply to bring it on. Except by the standards of the ideal Hoover, this indecision cannot be criticized too severely. For it would have taken a political superman to break a boom when almost everybody thought he was making money. No statesman in time of peace could have faced a severer test, and few indeed could have met it.

Mr. Hoover began to function on the maintenance of prosperity after prosperity had disappeared. He then improvised an impressive emergency relief organization. Then there was no controversy to face out. The post-panic situation was one in which he was thoroughly at home. Party lines, sectional lines, class lines were wiped out for the moment. It was like the days following the floods, the famines, the earthquakes amid which Mr. Hoover had his schooling in public affairs. I do not know, I do not suppose it is possible to know, how effective his emergency actions were. They certainly steadied people's nerves and undoubtedly prevented the panic from spreading. At any rate, he applied decisively the remedies which economic science prescribed. More than that could not be asked of any man. If they were not altogether effective, the fault lies not with Mr. Hoover but with the state of economic science.

The real point is that when economic knowledge could be applied only at the risk of a terrific controversy, Mr. Hoover shrank from applying it; when there was no controversy, but only a unanimity of feeling that something should be done, Mr. Hoover applied the teaching of economic science without further hesitation.

The same dualism appears in his attitude toward farm relief. When it was a question of laying down principles he was clear and decisive and confident in his own theoretical wisdom. "Certain vital principles," he said, "must be adhered to." There must be no undermining of private initiative, there must be no buying or selling or price-fixing through any government agency, there must be no lending of government funds or duplication of facilities where credit and facilities are already available at reasonable rates, there must be no activities which would result in increasing the surplus production. This was the plan in April. A few weeks later Congress passed the Agricultural Marketing Act providing for a Federal Farm Board. The President selected an able Board. In October cotton and grain prices fell below the prices obtaining when the Board was established. The powerful Farm Bloc demanded action. It demanded what it has always demanded—governmental price-fixing. Here was a direct challenge to Mr. Hoover's principles, plans, and economic philosophy. The principles, plans, philosophy were scrapped, and the Farm Board embarked on a policy which was nothing less than the use of Treasury funds for a gigantic speculation aimed at price-fixing of commodities. Every one of Mr. Hoover's "vital principles" was ignored. For Mr. Hoover had no taste for a head-on collision with the Farm Bloc. [...]

The north pole in the realm of unreason is, of course, the prohibition question. Mr. Hoover began, when he first had to deal with the question as a candidate, with what in his philosophy would be a highly reasonable proposal. Let us, he said, regard prohibition as an experiment aimed to achieve a noble purpose. Let us concede that the experiment has developed grave abuses. Let us, therefore, agree to examine all the facts and then proceed to solve the problem. It did not take him long to discover that this reasonable procedure had no genuine connection with the actual prohibition problem, and that, in truth, prohibition was a gigantic conflict of wills. The forces engaged are fired with a zeal that puts them upon a wholly different plane from that on which reasonable inquiry can be conducted; in that conflict reason is a weapon of war and not an instrument of truth. The problem presented by this conflict of wills is just the kind of problem for which Mr. Hoover has the greatest

distaste and the least native equipment. My own impression is that he regards both wets and drys as substantially insane, that he regards passionate conviction about prohibition as foolish, and that what he would best like to do about prohibition is to do nothing, since there is nothing he can do without getting into a brawl. But popular government being what it is, brawling about prohibition is the order of the day.

By the rough judgments of politics Mr. Hoover finds himself set down as an irresolute and easily frightened man. His opponents believe that he shrinks from attack and that he will not fight back. They feel that the faction which first takes the offensive boldly will force his consent, that he fears denunciation and immediate criticism more than the ultimate defeat of his policies. Thus, because he shrinks from attack he invites it; though he occupies the most powerful office in the world, he does not impress the politicians with whom he deals as formidable. [...]

Yet Mr. Hoover, though his conduct in office is that of a weak man, is not really a weak man. His public career for the last fifteen years is that of a man willing to face the most difficult tasks and to shoulder responsibilities that would terrify most men. A timid man would have shrunk from the risks of the Belgian relief; a weak and calculating man would have sought some other task in the War than that of reducing the popular consumption of food. Mr. Hoover at the Peace Conference, Mr. Hoover in the post-war relief operations, Mr. Hoover developing the Department of Commerce, Mr. Hoover taking on the disagreeable extra jobs during the Harding administration, may be subject to criticism for this or that; but that he was bold and self-confident beyond the ordinary cannot, I think, be questioned.

The weakness Mr. Hoover has displayed as President is a specific, not a general, weakness. He is weak in the presence of politics and politicians. Even during the War, when his fame was worldwide and his prestige incalculably great, it was known in Washington that the attack of a relatively obscure man like Senator Reed of Missouri could rattle him for days. He can face with equanimity almost any of the difficulties of statesmanship except the open conflict of wills; he falters only when he has to act in the medium of democracy.

Mr. Hoover, in spite of his vast experience of many things, has had very little experience in the art of government. He has never before been elected to any office. He has never been a legislator, a mayor, a governor. His weakness seems to me to be due to just the kind of uncertainty which might be expected of a man who suddenly finds himself in a strange environment, especially a conscientious, tender-minded, thin-skinned man to whom the behavior of the crowd is alarming because it is alien. Such a man would find it difficult to function at his full capacity until he had accustomed himself to the weird atmosphere of politics, had grown used to its maneuvers, its intrigue, and its special scale of values, and had got over the first impression that politicians, the press, the undifferentiated crowd are lions, tigers, and a stampede of wild elephants.

If intelligence and the capacity to learn are enough, Mr. Hoover may master this weakness of inexperience. If it is possible to acquire the art of politics late in life by rational induction, instead of through one's pores, as the natural politicians like Roosevelt and Al Smith acquire the art, then Mr. Hoover's first year may turn out to have been, not a mere series of considerable failures, but a very intensive, rather expensive, political education.

Should this happen it will be a conclusive demonstration of the fallaciousness of the popular notion that the art of governing is something which any competent business man, lawyer, or engineer can do better than an experienced politician. It is true, of course, that a politician who is ignorant of business, law, and engineering will move in a closed circle of jobs and unrealities. It is also true—and the history of the Hoover legend illustrates it—that governing human societies is a thing in itself, with its own aptitudes, its own kind of training, its own fund of wisdom and tradition. The popular notion that administering a government is like administering a private corporation, that it is just business, or housekeeping, or engineering, is a misunderstanding. The political art deals with matters peculiar to politics, with a complex of material circumstances, of historic deposit, of human passion, for which the problems of business or engineering as such do not provide an analogy.

It is, I think, a realization that he has not yet mastered the political art which accounts for Mr. Hoover's peculiar weakness in meeting the controversial issues of his first year.

the devices by which men can harm one another, such as private property, are removed and if the worship of authority can be discarded, co-operation will be spontaneous and inevitable, and the individual will find it his highest calling to contribute to the enrichment of social well-being.

Anarchism alone stresses the importance of the individual, his possibilities and needs in a free society. Instead of telling him that he must fall down and worship before institutions, live and die for abstractions, break his heart and stunt his life for taboos, Anarchism insists that the center of gravity in society is the individual—that he must think for himself, act freely, and live fully. The aim of Anarchism is that every individual in the world shall be able to do so. If he is to develop freely and fully, he must be relieved from the interference and oppression of others. Freedom is, therefore, the cornerstone of the Anarchist philosophy. Of course, this has nothing in common with a much boasted "rugged individualism." Such predatory individualism is really flabby, not rugged. At the least danger to its safety it runs to cover of the state and wails for protection of armies, navies, or whatever devices for strangulation it has at its command. Their "rugged individualism" is simply one of the many pretenses the ruling class makes to unbridled business and political extortion.

Regardless of the present trend toward the strong-armed man, the totalitarian states, or the dictatorship from the left, my ideas have remained unshaken. In fact, they have been strengthened by my personal experience and the world events through the years. I see no reason to change, as I do not believe that the tendency of dictatorship can ever successfully solve our social problems. As in the past, so I do now insist that freedom is the soul of progress and essential to every phase of life. I consider this as near a law of social evolution as anything we can postulate. My faith is in the individual and in the capacity of free individuals for united endeavor.

The fact that the Anarchist movement for which I have striven so long is to a certain extent in abeyance and overshadowed by philosophies of authority and coercion affects me with concern, but not with despair. It seems to me a point of special significance that many countries decline to admit Anarchists. All governments hold the view that while parties of the right and left may advocate social changes, still they cling to the idea of government and authority. Anarchism alone breaks with both and propagates uncompromising rebellion. In the long run, therefore, it is Anarchism which is considered deadlier to the present regime than all other social theories that are now clamoring for power.

Considered from this angle, I think my life and my work have been successful. What is generally regarded as success—acquisition of wealth, the capture of power or social prestige—I consider the most dismal failures. I hold when it is said of a man that he has arrived, it means that he is finished—his development has stopped at that point. I have always striven to remain in a state of flux and continued growth, and not to petrify in a niche of self-satisfaction. If I had my life to live over again, like anyone else, I should wish to alter minor details. But in any of my more important actions and attitudes I would repeat my life as I have lived it. Certainly I should work for Anarchism with the same devotion and confidence in its ultimate triumph.

THE FUTURE OF ENGLISH
BY H. L. MENCKEN

APRIL 1935

The English tongue is of small reach, stretching no further than this island of ours, nay not there over all.

This was written in 1582. The writer was Richard Mulcaster, headmaster of the Merchant Taylors' School, teacher of prosody to Edmund Spenser, and one of the earliest of English grammarians. At the time he wrote, English was spoken by between four and five millions of people, and stood fifth among the European languages, with French, German, Italian, and Spanish ahead of it in that order, and Russian following. Two hundred years later Italian had dropped behind but Russian had gone ahead, so that English was still in fifth place. But by the end of the Eighteenth Century it began to move forward, and by the middle of the Nineteenth it had forced its way into first place. To-day it is so far in the lead that it is probably spoken by as many people as the next two languages—Russian and German—combined.

It is not only the first—and, in large part, the only—language of both of the world's mightiest empires; it is also the second language of large and populous regions beyond their bounds. Its teaching is obligatory in the secondary schools of countries as diverse as Germany and Argentina, Turkey and Denmark, Estonia and Japan. Three-fourths of all the world's mail is now written in it; it is used in printing more than half the world's newspapers, and it is the language of three-fifths of the world's radio stations. No ship captain can trade upon the oceans without some knowledge of it; it is the common tongue of all the great ports, and likewise of all the maritime Bad Lands, from the South Sea islands to the Persian Gulf. Every language that still resists its advance outside Europe—for example, Spanish in Latin America, Italian in the Levant, and Japanese in the Far East—holds out against it only by making large concessions to it. That is to say, all of them show a large and ever larger admixture of English words and phrases; indeed in Japanese they become so numerous that

special dictionaries of them begin to appear. Finally, English makes steady inroads upon French as the language of diplomacy and upon German as the language of science.

How many people speak it to-day? It is hard to answer with any precision, but an approximation is nevertheless possible. First, let us list those to whom English is their native tongue. They run to about 112,000,000 in the continental United States, to 42,000,000 in the United Kingdom, to 6,000,000 in Canada, 6,000,000 in Australia, 3,000,000 in Ireland, 2,000,000 in South Africa, and probably 3,000,000 in the remaining British colonies and the possessions of the United States. All these figures are very conservative, but they foot up to 174,000,000. Now add the people who, though born to some other language, live in English-speaking communities and speak English themselves in their daily business, and whose children are being brought up to it—say 13,000,000 for the United States, 1,000,000 for Canada (where English is gradually ousting French), 1,000,000 for the United Kingdom and Ireland, and 2,000,000 for the rest of the world—and you have a grand total of 191,000,000. [...]

Altogether, it is probable that English is now spoken as a second language by at least 20,000,000 persons throughout the world—very often, to be sure, badly, but nevertheless understandably. It has become a platitude that one may go almost anywhere with no other linguistic equipment and get on almost as well as in New York. I have visited since the War sixteen countries in Europe, five in Africa, three in Asia, and three in Latin America, beside a large miscellany of islands, but I don't remember ever encountering a situation that English could not resolve. I have heard it spoken with reasonable fluency in a Lithuanian village, in an Albanian fishing port, and at the edge of the Libyan Desert.

In part, of course, its spread has been due to the extraordinary dispersion of the English-speaking peoples. They have been the greatest travelers of modern times, and the most adventurous merchants, and the most assiduous colonists. Moreover, they have been, on the whole, poor linguists, and so they have dragged their language with them, and forced it upon the human race. Wherever it has met with serious competition, as with French in Canada, with Spanish along our southwestern border, and with Dutch in South Africa, they have compromised with its local rival only reluctantly, and then sought every opportunity, whether fair or unfair, to break the pact. If English is the language of the sea, it is largely because there are more English ships on the sea than any other kind, and English ship captains refuse to learn what they think of as the barbaric gibberishes of Hamburg, Rio, and Marseilles.

But there is more to the matter than this. English, brought to close quarters with formidable rivals, has won very often, not by force of numbers and intransigence, but by the sheer weight of its merit. "In wealth, wisdom, and strict economy," said the eminent Jakob Grimm a century ago, "none of the other living languages can vie with it." To which the eminent Otto Jespersen was adding only the other day: "It seems to me positively and expressly masculine. It is the language of a grown-up man, and has very little childish or feminine about it." Dr. Jespersen goes on to specifications: English is simple, it has clear sounds, it packs its words closely together, it is logical in their arrangement, and it is free from all pedantic flubdub, by Latin out of the languages of Babel. What an immense advantage lies in a single thing: its lack of grammatical gender! (I spent the years from 1887 to 1892 trying to remember whether *Hund* and *Katze* were *der, die* or *das*, and I can't tell you to this day.) And what another in its reduction of all the pronouns of the second person nominative to the single *you*!

When American pedagogues discourse on the virtues of English they almost always begin by hymning its enormous vocabulary, which is at least twice as large as that of any other language. But this is not what enchants the foreigner; on the contrary, the vast reaches of the vocabulary naturally alarm him, and he keeps as close as he may to its elements. The thing that really wins him is the succinctness and simplicity of those elements. We use, for all our store of Latin polysyllables, a great many more short words than long ones, and we are always trying to make the long ones short. What began as *mobile vulgus* in the Eighteenth Century, two words and both Latin, is *mob* to-day, one word and that one as English as *cat*. What was once *pundigrion* is now *pun*; what was *gasoline* only

yesterday is already *gas*. No other European language has so many three-letter words, nor so many four-letter words, whether decorous or naughty. And none other can say its say with so few of them. "First come, first served"—that is typically English, for it is bold, plain, and short. In French, as Dr. Jespersen reminds us, the same homely proverb is stretched out and toned down to *"Premier venu, premier moulu"*; in German it is mauled and hammered into *"Wer zuerst kommt, mahlt zuerst,"* and in Danish it reaches the really appalling form of *"Den der kommer først til mølle, får først malet."*

Several years ago an American philologian, Dr. Walter Kirkconnell, undertook to count the number of syllables needed to translate the Gospel of Mark into forty Indo-European languages, ranging from Persian and Hindustani to English and French. He found that, of all of them, English was the most economical, for it took but 29,000 syllables to do the job, whereas the average for all the Teutonic languages was 32,650, that for the Slavic group 36,500, that for the Latin group 40,200, and that for the Indo-Iranian group (Bengali, Persian, Sanskrit, etc.) 43,100. It is commonly believed that French is a terse language and, compared to its cousins, Italian and Spanish, it actually is, but compared to English it is garrulous, for it takes 36,000 syllables to say what English says in 29,000. Dr. Kirkconnell did not undertake to determine the average size of the syllables he counted, but I am confident that if he had done so he would have found those of English shorter, taking one with another, than those of any other language.

To most educated foreigners it seems so simple that it strikes them as almost a kind of baby-talk. To be sure, when they proceed from trying to speak it to trying to read and write it they are painfully undeceived, for its spelling is almost as irrational as that of French or Swedish, but so long as they are content to tackle it *viva voce* they find it strangely loose and comfortable, and at the same time very precise. The Russian, coming into it burdened with his six cases, his three genders, his palatalized consonants, and his complicated pronouns, luxuriates in a language which has only two cases, no grammatical gender, a set of consonants which (save only *r*) maintain their integrity in the face of any imaginable rush of vowels, and an outfit of pronouns so simple that one of them suffices to address the President of the United States or a child in arms, a lovely female creature *in camera* or the vast radio hordes of a Father Coughlin. And the German, the Scandinavian, the Italian, and the Frenchman, though the change for them is measurably less sharp, nevertheless find it grateful too. Only the Spaniard brings with him a language comparable to English for logical clarity, and even the Spaniard is afflicted with grammatical gender.

As I have said, the huge English vocabulary is likely to make the foreigner uneasy, but he soon finds that nine-tenths of it lies safely buried in the dictionaries, and is never drawn on for everyday use. Its richness in synonyms is hardly his concern; he is not trying to write English poetry but to speak plain English prose. That it may be spoken intelligibly, and even gracefully, with very few words has been demonstrated by Dr. C. K. Ogden, the English psychologist. Dr. Ogden believes, indeed, that 850 words are sufficient for all ordinary purposes, and he has devised a form of simplified English, called by him Basic, which uses no more. Of his 850 words no less than 600 are the names of things, which leaves only 250 for the names of qualities and actions, and for all the linguistic hooks and eyes that hold sentences together.

Does this seem too few? Then it is only to those who have forgotten one of the prime characteristics of English—its capacity for getting an infinity of meanings out of a single word by combining it with simple modifiers. Consider, for example, the difference between the verbs *to get, to get going, to get by, to get on to, to get wise, to get off, to get ahead of,* and *to get over.* Dr. Ogden proposes to rid the language of a great many verbs—some of them irregular, and hence difficult—by substituting such compounds for them. Why, for example, should a foreigner be taught to say that he has *disembarked* from a ship? Isn't it sufficient for him to say that he has *got off?* And why should he be taught to say that he has *recovered* from the flu, or *escaped* the police, or *obtained* a job? Isn't it enough to say that he has *got over* the first, *got away from* the second, and simply *got* the third?

Dr. Ogden is not much upset by the incongruities and irrationalities of English spelling. For one thing, his list of 850 words, being made up mainly of the commonest coins of speech, avoids most of them; for another thing, he believes that the very eccentricity of the spelling of some of the rest will help the foreigner to remember them. Every schoolboy, as we all know, seizes upon such bizarre forms as *through, straight,* and *island* with fascinated eagerness, and not infrequently he masters them before he masters such phonetically-spelled words as *first, to-morrow,* and *engineer.* In my own youth, far away in the dark backward and abysm of time, the glory of every young American was *phthisic,* with the English proper name, *Cholmondeley,* a close second. Dr.

Ogden proposes to let the foreigners attempting Basic share the joy of hunting down such basilisks. For the rest, he leaves the snarls of English spelling to the judgments of a just God, and the natural tendency of all things Anglo-Saxon to move toward an ultimate perfection. [...]

But as English spreads, will it be able to maintain its present form? Probably not. But why should it? The notion that anything is gained by fixing a language in a groove is cherished only by pedagogues, perhaps the stupidest class of literate men on earth. Every successful effort at standardization, as Dr. Ernest Weekley has well said, results in nothing better than emasculation. "Stability in language," he adds, "is synonymous with *rigor mortis.*" But such efforts, fortunately, seldom succeed. The schoolma'am has been trying since the Revolution to bring American English to her rules, but it goes on sprouting and coruscating in spite of her, like the vigorous organism it is. My guess is that it will eventually conquer the English of England, and so spread its gaudy inventions round the globe. When Macaulay's New Zealander stands at last upon the ribs of London Bridge, it will be in lusty American, not in embalmed London (or Oxford) English, that he will voice his polite regrets.

This guess indeed is rather too easy to be quite sporting. English has been yielding to American for fifty years past, and since the turn of the century it has been yielding at a constantly accelerated rate. The flow of novelties in vocabulary, in idiom, even in pronunciation, is now overwhelmingly eastward. We seldom borrow an English word or phrase any more, though we used to borrow many; but the English take in our inventions almost as fast as we can launch them. The American movie, I suppose, is largely responsible for this change, but there are unquestionably deeper causes too. English, subjected to a violent policing in the Eighteenth Century, has scarcely recovered; it is still a bit tight, a bit stiff, more than a little artificial. But American, having escaped that policing and become quickly immune to the subsequent schoolma'am, has gone on developing with almost Elizabethan prodigality. All the processes of word-formation that were in operation in Shakespeare's England are still in operation here, and they produce a steady stream of neologisms that he would have relished as joyfully as he relished the novelties actually produced in his time, for example, *lonely, multitudinous, dwindle,* and *bump.*

The English, from the Age of Anne onward, have resisted the march of American with a mixture of patriotic watchfulness and moral indignation, albeit with steadily decreasing effectiveness. When Francis Moore in his *Voyage to Georgia* (1744) denounced our use of the noun *bluff* (in the topographical sense) as "barbarous" he lined out a hymn that is still being sung stridently by many an English pedant. After the Revolution it rose to a roar, with the quarterly reviews leading, and Southey, Landor, Wordsworth, Tom Moore, and other such lights of letters carrying the bass. The main attack began in 1787, when the *European Review* fell upon the English of Thomas Jefferson's *Notes on the State of Virginia*, and especially upon his use of *to belittle*, apparently his own invention. Thus it roared:

> *Belittle!* What an expression! It may be an elegant one in Virginia, and even perfectly intelligible; but for our

part, all we can do is to *guess* at its meaning. [A fling at another Americanism.] For shame, Mr. Jefferson! Why, after trampling upon the honor of our country— why trample also upon the very grammar of our language? ... Freely, good sir, will we forgive all your attacks, impotent as they are illiberal, upon our national character; but for the future spare—O spare, we beseech you, our mother-tongue!

The *Gentleman's Magazine* joined the charge with sneers for the "uncouth localities" [localisms?] in the "Yankey dialect" of Noah Webster's *Sentimental and Humorous Essays,* and soon all the other English reviews of the time, and especially the *Edinburgh,* the *Monthly Mirror,* the *Critical,* the *Annual,* and the *British Critic,* were heavily

H. L. Mencken selling banned issue of the American Mercury *magazine in Boston.*

engaged. The *Annual,* borrowing the adjective of Francis Moore, denounced "the torrent of barbarous phraseology" that was pouring from the new republic, and the *Monthly Mirror,* forgetting the Treaty of Paris, moaned and beat its breast over "the corruptions and barbarities which are hourly obtaining in the speech of our trans-Atlantic *colonies.*" But the most violent of all the periodical alarmists was the *Edinburgh,* then edited by the bitterly anti-American William Gifford. In almost every issue Gifford warned his readers that the toleration of Americanisms would ruin the English language irrevocably, and it was also he, I believe, who spread the story that the Americans were preparing to abandon English altogether, and to use Hebrew (or Greek, or some unnamed Indian language) in its stead.

The English travelers who began to swarm in America after 1800, and especially after the War of 1812, gave willing aid in this benign work, and scarcely one of them failed to record his horror over the new American words that he encountered, and the unfamiliar American pronunciation. Captain Basil Hall, who was here in 1827 and 1828, went to the length of making a call upon Noah Webster, then a septuagenarian, to lodge his protest.

"Surely," he said, "such innovations are to be deprecated?"

"I don't know that," replied Webster stoutly. "If a word becomes universally current in America, why should it not take its station in the language?"

"Because," answered Hall, with a magnificent resort to British complacency, "there are words enough already."

This hostility continues into our own day. At regular intervals the London dailies and weeklies break into sonorous complaints against the American invasion. The latest inventions of the Hollywood gag-writers are seized upon as proofs that the language is fast going to pot in this country, along with the sub-species of the human race that speaks it. Even the relatively cautious and plainly useful simplicities of American spelling (as in the *-or* words, for example) are sometimes denounced with great rancor. But it is really too late for the English to guard the purity of their native tongue, for so many Americanisms have already got into it that, on some levels at least, it is now almost an American dialect. It has often amused me to count the Americanisms in articles written to put them down. There are hundreds of them in daily use in England, and many have become so familiar that an Englishman, on being challenged for using them, will commonly argue that they are actually English.

Thus a note of despair reveals itself in the current objurgations, and there are Englishmen who believe that the time has come to compromise with the invasion, and even to welcome it. The father of this pro-American party seems to have been the late William Archer, who was saying so long ago as 1899 that Americans had "enormously enriched the language, not only with new words, but (since the American mind is, on the whole, quicker and wittier than the English) with apt and luminous colloquial metaphors." The late Dr. Robert Bridges, Poet Laureate from 1913 until his death in 1930, was of like mind with Archer, and of late there have been influential recruits to the party—among them, Richard Aldington, Wyndham Lewis, Edward Shanks, and Virginia Woolf. "In England," said Mrs. Woolf not long ago, "the word-coining power has lapsed.... When we want to freshen our speech we borrow from American—*poppycock, rambunctious, flip-flop, booster, good mixer.* All the expressive, ugly, vigorous slang which creeps into use among us, first in talk, later in writing, comes from across the Atlantic."

I turn to Dr. Ogden's list of fifty "international" nouns for the Basic vocabulary—and find that no less than nine of them are American, not English. I turn to Professor Ichikawa's list of English words that have been taken into Japanese—and Americanisms bristle from every page. Plainly enough, the conquest of the world by English, if it ever comes off, will really be a conquest by American.

The Chrysanthemums

by John Steinbeck

October 1937

The high gray-flannel fog of winter closed the Salinas Valley from the sky and from all the rest of the world. On every side it sat like a lid on the mountains and made of the great valley a closed pot. On the broad, level land floor the gang plows bit deep and left the black earth shining like metal where the shares had cut. On the foot-hill ranches across the Salinas River the yellow stubble fields seemed to be bathed in pale cold sunshine; but there was no sunshine in the valley now in December. The thick willow scrub along the river flamed with sharp and positive yellow leaves.

It was a time of quiet and of waiting. The air was cold and tender. A light wind blew up from the southwest so that the farmers were mildly hopeful of a good rain before long; but fog and rain do not go together.

Across the river, on Henry Allen's foot-hill ranch there was little work to be done, for the hay was cut and stored and the orchards were plowed up to receive the rain deeply when it should come. The cattle on the higher slopes were becoming shaggy and rough-coated.

Elisa Allen, working in her flower garden, looked down across the yard and saw Henry, her husband, talking to two men in business suits. The three of them stood by the tractor shed, each man with one foot on the side of the Little Fordson. They smoked cigarettes and studied the machine as they talked.

Elisa watched them for a moment and then went back to her work. She was thirty-five. Her face was lean and strong and her eyes were as clear as water. Her figure looked blocked and heavy in her gardening costume, a man's black hat pulled low down over her eyes, clodhopper shoes, a figured print dress almost completely covered by a big corduroy apron with four big pockets to hold the snips, the trowel and scratcher, the seeds and the knife she worked with. She wore heavy leather gloves to protect her hands while she worked.

She was cutting down the old year's chrysanthemum stalks with a pair of short and powerful scissors. She looked down toward the men by the tractor shed now and then. Her face was eager and mature and handsome; even her work with the scissors was over-eager, over-powerful. The chrysanthemum stems seemed too small and easy for her energy.

She brushed a cloud of hair out of her eyes with the back of her glove, and left a smudge of earth on her cheek in doing it. Behind her stood the neat white farmhouse with red geraniums close-banked round it as high as the windows. It was a hard-swept looking little house, with hard-polished windows, and a clean mat on the front steps.

Elisa cast another glance toward the tractor shed. The stranger men were getting into their Ford Coupé. She took off a glove and put her strong fingers down into the forest of new green chrysanthemum sprouts that were growing round the old roots. She spread the leaves and looked down among the close-growing stems. No aphids were there, no sow bugs nor snails nor cut worms. Her terrier fingers destroyed such pests before they could get started.

Elisa started at the sound of her husband's voice. He had come near quietly and he leaned over the wire fence that protected her flower garden from cattle and dogs and chickens.

"At it again," he said. "You've got a strong new crop coming."

Elisa straightened her back and pulled on the gardening glove again. "Yes. They'll be strong this coming year." In her tone and on her face there was a little smugness.

"You've got a gift with things," Henry observed. "Some of those yellow chrysanthemums you had last year were ten inches across. I wish you'd work out in the orchard and raise some apples that big."

Her eyes sharpened. "Maybe I could do it too. I've a gift with things all right. My mother had it. She could stick anything in the ground and make it grow. She said it was having planters' hands that knew how to do it."

"Well, it sure works with flowers," he said.

"Henry, who were those men you were talking to?"

"Why, sure, that's what I came to tell you. They were from the Western Meat Company. I sold those thirty head of three-year-old steers. Got nearly my own price too."

"Good," she said. "Good for you."

"And I thought," he continued, "I thought how it's Saturday afternoon, and we might go into Salinas for dinner at a restaurant and then to a picture show—to celebrate, you see."

"Good," she repeated. "Oh, yes. That will be good."

Henry put on his joking tone. "There's fights to-night. How'd you like to go to the fights?"

"Oh, no," she said breathlessly. "No, I wouldn't like fights."

"Just fooling, Elisa. We'll go to a movie. Let's see. It's two now. I'm going to take Scotty and bring down those steers from the hill. It'll take us maybe two hours. We'll go in town about five and have dinner at the Cominos Hotel. Like that?"

"Of course I'll like it. It's good to eat away from home."

"All right then. I'll go get up a couple of horses."

She said, "I'll have plenty of time to transplant some of these sets, I guess."

She heard her husband calling Scotty down by the barn. And a little later she saw the two men ride up the pale-yellow hillside in search of the steers.

There was a little square sandy bed kept for rooting the chrysanthemums. With her trowel she turned the soil over and over and smoothed it and patted it firm. Then she dug ten parallel trenches to receive the sets. Back at the chrysanthemum bed she pulled out the little crisp shoots, trimmed off the leaves of each one with her scissors, and laid it on a small orderly pile.

A squeak of wheels and plod of hoofs came from the road. Elisa looked up. The country road ran along the dense bank of willows and cottonwoods that bordered the river, and up this road came a curious vehicle, curiously drawn. It was an old spring-wagon, with a round canvas top on it like the cover of a prairie schooner. It was drawn by an old bay horse and a little gray-and-white burro. A big stubble-bearded man sat between the cover flaps and drove the crawling team. Underneath the wagon, between the hind wheels, a lean and rangy mongrel dog walked sedately. Words were painted on the canvas in clumsy, crooked letters. "Pots, pans, knives, scissors, lawn mowers, Fixed." Two rows of articles, and the triumphantly definitive "Fixed" below. The black paint had run down in little sharp points beneath each letter.

Elisa, squatting on the ground, watched to see the crazy loose-jointed wagon pass by. But it didn't pass. It turned into the farm road in front of her house, crooked old wheels skirling and squeaking. The rangy dog darted from beneath the wheels and ran ahead. Instantly the two ranch shepherds flew out at him. Then all three stopped, and with stiff and quivering tails, with taut straight legs, with ambassadorial dignity, they slowly circled, sniffing daintily. The caravan pulled up to Elisa's wire fence and stopped. Now the newcomer dog, feeling outnumbered, lowered his tail and retired under the wagon with raised hackles and bared teeth.

The man on the wagon seat called out, "That's a bad dog in a fight when he gets started."

Elisa laughed. "I see he is. How soon does he generally get started?"

The man caught up her laughter and echoed it heartily. "Sometimes not for weeks and weeks," he said. He climbed stiffly down over the wheel. The horse and the donkey dropped like unwatered flowers.

Elisa saw that he was a very big man. Although his hair and beard were graying, he did not look old. His worn black suit was wrinkled and spotted with grease. The laughter had disappeared from his face and eyes the moment his laughing voice ceased. His eyes were dark and they were full of the brooding that gets in the eyes of teamsters and of sailors. The calloused hands he rested on the fence were cracked, and every crack was a black line. He took off his battered hat.

"I'm off my general road, ma'am," he said. "Does this dirt road cut over across the river to the Los Angeles highway?"

Elisa stood up and shoved the thick scissors in her apron pocket. "Well, yes, it does, but it winds around and then fords the river. I don't think your team could pull through the sand."

He replied with some asperity, "It might surprise you what them beasts can pull through."

"When they get started?" she asked.

He smiled for a second. "Yes. When they get started."

"Well," said Elisa, "I think you'll save time if you go back to the Salinas road and pick up the highway there."

He drew a big finger down the chicken wire and made it sing. "I ain't in any hurry, ma'am. I go from Seattle to San Diego and back every year. Takes all my time. About six months each way. I aim to follow nice weather."

Elisa took off her gloves and stuffed them in the apron pocket with the scissors. She touched the under edge of her man's hat, searching for fugitive hairs. "That sounds like a nice kind of a way to live," she said.

He leaned confidentially over the fence. "Maybe you noticed the writing on my wagon. I mend pots and sharpen knives and scissors. You got any of them things to do?"

"Oh, no," she said quickly. "Nothing like that." Her eyes hardened with resistance.

"Scissors is the worst thing," he explained. "Most people just ruin scissors trying to sharpen 'em, but I know how. I got a special tool. It's a little bobbit kind of thing and patented. But it sure does the trick."

"No. My scissors are all sharp."

"All right then. Take a pot," he continued earnestly, "a bent pot or a pot with a hole. I can make it like new so you don't have to buy no new ones. That's a saving for you."

"No," she said shortly. "I tell you I have nothing like that for you to do."

His face fell to an exaggerated sadness. His voice took on a whining undertone. "I ain't had a thing to do to-day. Maybe I won't have no supper to-night. You see I'm off my regular road. I know folks on the highway clear from Seattle to San Diego. They save their things for me to sharpen up because they know I do it so good and save them money."

"I'm sorry," Elisa said irritably. "I haven't anything for you to do."

His eyes left her face and fell to searching the ground. They roamed about until they came to the chrysanthemum bed where she had been working. "What's them plants, ma'am?"

The irritation and resistance melted from Elisa's face. "Oh, those are chrysanthemums, giant whites and yellows. I raise them every year, bigger than anybody around here."

"Kind of a long-stemmed flower? Looks like a quick puff of colored smoke?" he asked.

"That's it. What a nice way to describe them."

"They smell kind of nasty till you get used to them," he said.

"It's a good bitter smell," she retorted, "not nasty at all."

He changed his tone quickly. "I like the smell myself."

"I had ten-inch blooms this year," she said.

The man leaned farther over the fence. "Look. I know a lady down the road a piece has got the nicest garden you ever seen. Got nearly every kind of flower but no chrysantheums. Last time I was mending a copper-bottom wash tub for her (that's a hard job but I do it good), she said to me, 'If you ever run acrost some nice chrysantheums I wish you'd try to get me a few seeds.' That's what she told me."

Elisa's eyes grew alert and eager. "She couldn't have known much about chrysanthemums. You *can* raise them from seed, but it's much easier to root the little sprouts you see there."

"Oh," he said. "I s'pose I can't take none to her then."

"Why yes, you can," Elisa cried. "I can put some in damp sand, and you can carry them right along with you. They'll take root in the pot if you keep them damp. And then she can transplant them."

"She'd sure like to have some, ma'am. You say they're nice ones?"

"Beautiful," she said. "Oh, beautiful." Her eyes shone. She tore off the battered hat and shook out her dark pretty hair. "I'll put them in a flower pot, and you can take them right with you. Come into the yard."

While the man came through the picket gate Elisa ran excitedly along the geranium-bordered path to the back of the house. And she returned carrying a big red flower pot. The gloves were forgotten now. She kneeled on the ground by the starting bed and dug up the sandy soil with her fingers and scooped it into the bright new flower pot. Then she picked up the little pile of shoots she had prepared. With her strong fingers she pressed them into the sand and tamped round them with her knuckles. The man stood over her. "I'll tell you what to do," she said. "You remember so you can tell the lady."

"Yes, I'll try to remember."

"Well, look. These will take root in about a month. Then she must set them out, about a foot apart in good rich earth like this, see?" She lifted a handful of dark soil for him to look at. "They'll grow fast and tall. Now remember this. In July tell her to cut them down, about eight inches from the ground."

"Before they bloom?" he asked.

"Yes, before they bloom." Her face was tight with eagerness. "They'll grow right up again. About the last of September the buds will start."

She stopped and seemed perplexed. "It's the budding that takes the most care," she said hesitantly. "I don't know how to tell you." She looked deep into his eyes searchingly. Her mouth opened a little, and she seemed to be listening. "I'll try to tell you," she said. "Did you ever hear of planting hands?"

"Can't say I have, ma'am."

"Well, I can only tell you what it feels like. It's when you're picking off the buds you don't want. Everything goes right down into your fingertips. You watch your fingers work. They do it themselves. You can feel how it is. They pick and pick the buds. They never make a mistake. They're with the plant. Do you see? Your fingers and the plant. You can feel that, right up your arm. They know. They never make a mistake. You can feel it. When you're like that you can't do anything wrong. Do you see that? Can you understand that?"

She was kneeling on the ground looking up at him. Her breast swelled passionately.

The man's eyes narrowed. He looked away self-consciously. "Maybe I know," he said. "Sometimes in the night in the wagon there—"

Elisa's voice grew husky. She broke in on him, "I've never lived as you do, but I know what you mean. When the night is dark—the stars are sharp-pointed, and there's quiet. Why, you rise up and up!"

Kneeling there, her hand went out toward his legs in the greasy black trousers. Her hesitant fingers almost touched the cloth. Then her hand dropped to the ground.

He said, "It's nice, just like you say. Only when you don't have no dinner it ain't."

She stood up then, very straight, and her face was ashamed. She held the flower pot out to him and placed it gently in his arms. "Here. Put it in your wagon, on the seat, where you can watch it. Maybe I can find something for you to do."

At the back of the house she dug in the can pile and found two old and battered aluminum sauce pans. She carried them back and gave them to him. "Here, maybe you can fix these."

His manner changed. He became professional. "Good as new I can fix them." At the back of his wagon he set a little

Dust Bowl migrant, California, 1935.

anvil, and out of an oily tool box dug a small machine hammer. Elisa came through the gate to watch him while he pounded out the dents in the kettles. His mouth grew sure and knowing. At a difficult part of the work he sucked his under-lip.

"You sleep right in the wagon?" Elisa asked.

"Right in the wagon, ma'am. Rain or shine I'm dry as a cow in there."

"It must be nice," she said. "It must be very nice. I wish women could do such things."

"It ain't the right kind of a life for a woman."

Her upper lip raised a little, showing her teeth. "How do you know? How can you tell?" she said.

"I don't know, ma'am," he protested. "Of course I don't know. Now here's your kettles, done. You don't have to buy no new ones."

"How much?"

"Oh, fifty cents'll do. I keep my prices down and my work good. That's why I have all them satisfied customers up and down the highway."

Elisa brought him a fifty-cent piece from the house and dropped it in his hand. "You might be surprised to have a rival sometime. I can sharpen scissors too. And I can beat the dents out of little pots. I could show you what a woman might do."

He put his hammer back in the oily box and shoved the little anvil out of sight. "It would be a lonely life for a woman, ma'am, and a scary life, too, with animals creeping under the wagon all night." He climbed over the singletree, steadying himself with a hand on the burro's white rump. He settled himself in the seat, picked up the lines. "Thank you kindly, ma'am," he said. "I'll do like you told me; I'll go back and catch the Salinas road."

"Mind," she called, "if you're long in getting there, keep the sand damp."

"Sand, ma'am?—Sand? Oh, sure. You mean around the chrysantheums. Sure I will." He clucked his tongue. The beasts leaned luxuriously into their collars. The mongrel dog took his place between the back wheels. The wagon turned and crawled out the entrance road and back the way it had come, along the river.

Elisa stood in front of her wire fence watching the slow progress of the caravan. Her shoulders were straight, her head thrown back, her eyes half-closed, so that the scene came vaguely into them. Her lips moved silently, forming the words "Good-by—good-by." Then she whispered,

"That's a bright direction. There's a glowing there." The sound of her whisper startled her. She shook herself free and looked about to see whether anyone had been listening. Only the dogs had heard. They lifted their heads toward her from their sleeping in the dust, and then stretched out their chins and settled asleep again. Elisa turned and ran hurriedly into the house.

In the kitchen she reached behind the stove and felt the water tank. It was full of hot water from the noonday cooking. In the bathroom she tore off her soiled clothes and flung them into the corner. And then she scrubbed herself with a little block of pumice, legs and thighs, loins and chest and arms, until her skin was scratched and red. When she had dried herself she stood in front of a mirror in her bedroom and looked at her body. She tightened her stomach and threw out her chest. She turned and looked over her shoulder at her back.

After a while she began to dress slowly. She put on her newest underclothing and her nicest stockings and the dress which was the symbol of her prettiness. She worked carefully on her hair, pencilled her eyebrows, and rouged her lips.

Before she was finished she heard the little thunder of hoofs and the shouts of Henry and his helper as they drove the red steers into the corral. She heard the gate bang shut and set herself for Henry's arrival.

His step sounded on the porch. He entered the house calling, "Elisa, where are you?"

"In my room, dressing. I'm not ready. There's hot water for your bath. Hurry up. It's getting late."

When she heard him splashing in the tub, Elisa laid his dark suit on the bed, and shirt and socks and tie beside it. She stood his polished shoes on the floor beside the bed. Then she went to the porch and sat primly and stiffly down. She looked toward the river road where the willow-line was still yellow with frosted leaves so that under the high gray fog they seemed a thin band of sunshine. This was the only color in the gray afternoon. She sat unmoving for a long time.

Henry came banging out of the door, shoving his tie inside his vest as he came. Elisa stiffened and her face grew tight. Henry stopped short and looked at her. "Why—why, Elisa. You look so nice!"

"Nice? You think I look nice? What do you mean by 'nice'?"

Henry blundered on. "I don't know. I mean you look different, strong and happy."

"I am strong? Yes, strong. What do you mean 'strong'?"

He looked bewildered. "You're playing some kind of a game," he said helplessly. "It's a kind of a play. You look strong enough to break a calf over your knee, happy enough to eat it like a watermelon."

For a second she lost her rigidity. "Henry! Don't talk like that. You didn't know what you said." She grew complete again. "I am strong," she boasted. "I never knew before how strong."

Henry looked down toward the tractor shed, and when he brought his eyes back to her, they were his own again. "I'll get out the car. You can put on your coat while I'm starting."

Elisa went into the house. She heard him drive to the gate and idle down his motor, and then she took a long time to put on her hat. She pulled it here and pressed it there. When Henry turned the motor off she slipped into her coat and went out.

The little roadster bounced along on the dirt road by the river, raising the birds and driving the rabbits into the brush. Two cranes flapped heavily over the willow-line and dropped into the river-bed.

Far ahead on the road Elisa saw a dark speck in the dust. She suddenly felt empty. She did not hear Henry's talk. She tried not to look; she did not want to see the little heap of sand and green shoots, but she could not help herself. The chrysanthemums lay in the road close to the wagon tracks. But not the pot; he had kept that. As the car passed them she remembered the good bitter smell, and a little shudder went through her. She felt ashamed of her strong planter's hands, that were no use, lying palms up in her lap.

The roadster turned a bend and she saw the caravan ahead. She swung full round toward her husband so that she could not see the little covered wagon and the mismatched team as the car passed.

In a moment they had left behind them the man who had not known or needed to know what she said, the bargainer. She did not look back.

To Henry she said loudly, to be heard above the motor, "It will be good, to-night, a good dinner."

"Now you're changed again," Henry complained. He took one hand from the wheel and patted her knee. "I ought to take you in to dinner oftener. It would be good for both of us. We get so heavy out on the ranch."

"Henry," she asked, "could we have wine at dinner?"

"Sure. Say! That will be fine."

She was silent for a while; then she said, "Henry, at those prize fights do the men hurt each other very much?"

"Sometimes a little, not often. Why?"

"Well, I've read how they break noses, and blood runs down their chests. I've read how the fighting gloves get heavy and soggy with blood."

He looked round at her. "What's the matter, Elisa? I didn't know you read things like that." He brought the car to a stop, then turned to the right over the Salinas River bridge.

"Do any women ever go to the fights?" she asked.

"Oh, sure, some. What's the matter, Elisa? Do you want to go? I don't think you'd like it, but I'll take you if you really want to go."

She relaxed limply in the seat. "Oh, no. No. I don't want to go. I'm sure I don't." Her face was turned away from him. "It will be enough if we can have wine. It will be plenty." She turned up her coat collar so he could not see that she was crying weakly—like an old woman.

SOLITUDE

BY RAINER MARIA RILKE

TRANSLATED BY C. F. MACINTYRE

JANUARY 1938

Solitude is like a rain.
It rises from the sea to meet the night;
It rises from the dim far-distant plain
Toward the sky (as by an old birthright),
And thence falls on the city from the height.

It falls like rain in that gray doubtful hour
When all the streets are turning toward the dawn,
And when those bodies, with all hope foregone
Of what they sought, are sorrowfully alone;
And when all men, that hate each other, creep
Together in one common bed for sleep:

Flows solitude, a river black and deep.

America's Medieval Women

by Pearl S. Buck

August 1938

I am an American woman but I had no opportunity until a few years ago to know women in America. Living as I did in China, it is true that I saw a few American women; but that is not the same thing. One was still not able to draw many conclusions from them about American women. I gathered, however, that they felt that girls in China had a hard time of it, because there every family liked sons better than daughters, and, in the average family, did not give them the same education or treatment. In America, however, they said people welcomed sons and daughters equally and treated them the same. This, after years in a country which defines a woman's limitations very clearly, seemed nothing short of heaven—if true.

When I came to America to live therefore I was interested particularly in her women. And during these immediate past years I have come to know a good many of them—women in business, artists, housewives in city and country, women young and old. I have taken pains to know them. More than that, I have made my own place as a woman in America. And I find that what I anticipated before I came here is quite wrong. It seems to me that women are very badly treated in America. A few of them know it, more of them dimly suspect it, and most of them, though they know they ought to be glad they live in a Christian country where women are given an education, do not feel as happy in their lonely hearts as they wish they did. The reason for this unhappiness is a secret sense of failure, and this sense of failure comes from a feeling of inferiority, and the feeling of inferiority comes from a realization that actually women are not much respected in America.

I know quite well that any American man hearing this will laugh his usual tolerant laughter, though tolerant laughter is the cruelest form of contempt. He always laughs tolerantly when the subject of women is broached, for that is the attitude in which he has been bred. And immaturely, he judges the whole world of women by the only woman he knows at all—his wife. Nor does he want the sort of wife at whom he cannot laugh tolerantly. I was once amazed to see a certain American man, intelligent, learned, and cultivated, prepare to marry for his second wife a woman as silly and unfit for him as the first one had been, whom he had just divorced. I had to exclaim before it was too late, "Why do you do the same thing over again? She's merely younger and prettier than the other one—that's all. And even those differences are only temporary." To which he growled, "I do not want a damned intelligent woman in the house when I come home at night. I want my mind to rest."

What he did not see of course—though he found it out later—was that there could be no rest for him of any kind. He was irritated by a thousand stupidities and follies and beaten in the end by his own cowardice. He died a score of years too soon, exhausted not by work but by nervous worry. His two wives go hardily on, headed for a hundred, since he left them what is called "well provided for." Neither of them has ever done an honest day's work in her life, and he literally sacrificed his valuable life to keep them alive.

And yet, going home that day from his funeral and wondering how it could have been helped, I knew it could not have been helped. He was doomed to the unhappiness, or at least to the mediocre happiness, with which many if not most American men must be satisfied in their relationships with their women. For if he had been married to an intelligent superior woman he would have been yet more unhappy, since, with all his brilliance as a scientist, he belonged to that vast majority of American men who still repeat to-day the cry of traditional male pride, "I don't want *my* wife to work."

That is, he wanted a woman who would contain herself docilely within four walls. And he could not have seen that an intelligent, energetic, educated woman cannot be kept in four walls—even satin-lined, diamond-studded walls—without discovering sooner or later that they are still a

prison cell. No home offers scope enough to-day for the trained energies of an intelligent modern woman. Even children are not enough. She may want them, need them and have them, love them and enjoy them, but they are not enough for her, even during the short time they preoccupy her. Nor is her husband, however dear and congenial, enough for her. He may supply all her needs for human companionship, but there is still more to life than that. There is the individual life. She must feel herself growing and becoming more and more complete as an individual, as well as a wife and mother, before she can even be a good wife and mother. I heard a smug little gray-haired woman say last week, "No, I don't know anything about politics. It takes all my time to be a good wife and mother. I haven't time to keep up with other things." Unfortunately, her husband, successful doctor that he is, has time to keep up not only with his business and with being what she calls a "wonderful husband and father," but with another woman as well. But that too is one of the things she knows nothing about.... Yet who can blame him? He is clever and full of interest in many things, and his wife is dulled with years of living in the four walls he put round her. It is a little unfair that he so encouraged her to stay in the walls that she came to believe in them completely as her place.

But tradition is very strong in this backward country of ours. We Americans are a backward nation in everything except in the making and using of machines. And we are nowhere more backward than we are in our attitude toward our women. We still, morally, shut the door of her home on a woman. We say to her, "Your home ought to be enough for you if you are a nice woman. Your husband ought to be enough—and your children." If she says, "But they aren't enough—what shall I do?", we say, "Go and have a good time, that's a nice girl. Get yourself a new hat or something, or go to the matinée or join a bridge club. Don't worry your pretty head about what is not your business." [...]

And yet, vicious circle that it is, I cannot blame Americans for distrusting the ability of their women. For if the intelligent woman obeys the voice of tradition and limits herself to the traditional four walls she joins the vast ranks of the nervous, restless, average American women whose whimsies torture their families, who spoil the good name of all women because they are often flighty, unreliable, without good judgment in affairs, and given to self-pity. In short, she becomes a neurotic, if not all the time, a good deal of the time. Without knowing it or meaning it she falls too often to being a petty dictator in the home, a nag to her husband and children, and a gossip among her women friends. Too often too she takes no interest in any matters of social importance and refuses all responsibility in the community which she can avoid. She may be either a gadabout and extravagant or she may turn into a recluse and pride herself on being a "home woman." Neither of these escapes deceives the discerning. When will American men learn that they cannot expect happiness with a wife who is not her whole self? A restless unfulfilled woman is not going to be a satisfied wife or satisfactory lover. It is not that "women are like that." Anyone would be "like that" if he were put into such circumstances—that is, trained and developed for opportunity later denied.

"Plenty of men like that too nowadays," someone may murmur.

Yes, but the times have done it, and not tradition. There is a difference. And one man has as good a chance as another to win or lose, even in hard times. But no woman has a man's chance in hard times, or in any times.

I am not so naïve, however, as to believe that one sex is responsible for this unfortunate plight of the American woman. I am not a feminist, but I am an individualist. I do not believe there is any important difference between men and women—certainly not as much as there may be between one woman and another or one man and another. There are plenty of women—and men, for that matter—who would be completely fulfilled in being allowed to be as lazy as possible. If someone will ensconce them in a pleasant home and pay their bills they ask no more of life. It is quite all right for these men and women to live thus so long as fools can be found who will pay so much for nothing much in return. Gigolos, male and female, are to be found in every class and in the best of homes. But when a man does not want to be a gigolo he has the freedom to go out and work and create as well as he can. But a woman has not. Even if her individual husband lets her, tradition in society is against her.

For another thing we Americans cannot seem to believe or understand is that women—some women, any woman, or as I believe, most women—are able to be good wives, ardent lovers, excellent mothers, and yet be themselves too. This seems strange, for as a nation we have fitted woman to be an individual as well as a woman by giving her a physical and mental education and a training superior to that of women in any other nation. But when she comes eagerly to life, ready to contribute her share, not only to home, but to government, sciences, and arts, we raise the old sickening cry of tradition, "This isn't your business! Woman's place is in the home—" and we shut the door in her face.

I am aware that at this point American men will be swearing and shouting, "You don't know what you're talking about! Why, we give our women more than any women on earth have!" With that I perfectly agree. American women are the most privileged in the world. They have all the privileges—far too many. They have so many privileges that a good many of them are utterly spoiled. They have privileges but they have no equality. "Nobody keeps them back," the American man declares. Ah, nobody, but everybody! For they are kept back by tradition expressed through the prejudices not only of men but of stupid, unthinking, tradition-bound women. Here is what I heard a few days ago.

A young woman wanted a new book to read and her father offered to send it to her. "What do you want?" he asked.

"Anything, only not one by a woman," she said carelessly. "I have a prejudice against books written by women."

Ignoring the rudeness, I asked, "Why?"

"Oh, I dislike women," she said. What she really meant was she despised women so much that she actually disliked women who did anything beyond the traditional jobs that the average women do. There are thousands of women who uphold medieval tradition in America more heartily than do men—just as in China it is the ignorant tradition-bound women who have clung to foot binding for themselves and their daughters.... No, women have many enemies among women. It goes back of course to the old jealous sense of general female inferiority. Tradition, if it binds one, should bind all, they feel.

Sometimes, I confess, I do not see how American men can endure some of their women—their imperiousness, their peevishness, their headstrongness, their utter selfishness, their smallness of mind and outlook, their lack of any sense of responsibility toward society, even to be pleasant. And their laziness—look at the motion-picture houses, the theaters, the lecture halls—crowded all day with women! The average house, even with no servant, can be no full-time job or they wouldn't be there in such hordes—they couldn't be there. But children go to school as soon as they stop being babies, and electricity cleans and washes the house and clothing, and husbands are away all day. So what is there for the restless woman to do? She goes to the show—and comes home, if she has any sense, to wonder what life is for, and to think that marriage isn't so much after all, though if she hadn't been married she would have been ashamed of herself. For tradition is there too, and it would have made her seem, if unmarried, unsuccessful as a female.

"But what are we going to do?" the harassed American man cries. "There aren't enough jobs now to go round. And women are getting into industries more and more."

This is nonsense and a masculine bugaboo, though merely getting a job is not what I mean. The truth is the number of women in industries is increasing at so slow a rate that it is shocking when one considers how long they have had an equal chance with men for education and training. In the past fifty years—that is, half a century, during which education for women has enormously increased—the percentage of women in industry and the professions has increased from fourteen per cent only to twenty-two per cent. That means millions of women have been made ready for work they either had no chance to do or never wanted to do.

As to what men are going to do with women, I do not pretend to know. But I know I have never seen in any country—and I have seen most of the countries of the world—such unsatisfactory personal relationships between men and women as are in America—no, not even in Japan, where women as a class are depressed. For the Japanese are wiser in their treatment of women than we Americans are. They keep them down from the beginning so that they never hope for or expect more than life is to give them. They are not restless or neurotic or despotic, nor are they spoiled children. They have not been trained for equality and they do not expect it. They know they are upper servants, and they fulfil their duties gracefully and ably, and are happier on the whole than women in America. To know what one can have and to do with it, being prepared for no more, is the basis of equilibrium.

No, what is wrong in America is this matter of educating women. Life for the American woman is still controlled by old traditions. Men think of women, if at all, in the old simple traditional ways. Then women ought to be prepared for this sort of life and shaped through childhood and girlhood for what is to come. The root of the discontent in American women is that they are too well educated. What is the use of it? They do not need college educations nor even high school educations. What they ought to have is a simple course in reading, writing, and arithmetic—and advanced courses in cosmetics, bridge, sports, how to conduct a club meeting gracefully, how to be an attractive hostess, with or without servants, and how to deal with very young children in the home. This last course, obviously, should be purely optional.

But all this higher present education is unfortunate. It has led American women into having ideas which they can never realize when they come to maturity. A college education may, for instance, persuade a girl to become interested in biology, which may lead her into wanting to become a doctor. And yet she will never have the chance to become a first-rate doctor, however gifted she is by birth. People will not allow it—not only men, but women will not allow it. They will look at her tentative little shingle and shrug their shoulders and say, "I don't feel I'd *trust* a woman doctor as I would a man." So after a while, since she has to earn something, she takes her shingle down and accepts a secondary position in a hospital or a school or goes into baby-clinic work, supplemented by magazine articles on child care—or she just marries a doctor. But inside herself she knows she still wants to *be* a doctor, only she cannot. Tradition does not allow it.

Or a college education may lead a girl into wanting to be a banker. It is natural for women to be interested in finance since they own about seventy per cent of America's money. But it is unfortunate if a woman thinks she can be a real banker. I have talked with a good many women who work in our American banking system. Not one is where she hoped to be when she began, and a fair percentage are not where they should be with their high executive ability, or where they would be if they were men. As one of the most brilliant of them said to me bitterly, "I know if I were a man I should now, at the age of fifty, and after thirty years of experience, be a bank president. But I'll never be anything but an assistant to a vice-president. I reached the top—for a woman—years ago. I'll never be allowed to go on."

"Why can't you?" I inquired, being then too innocent.

"They say no one would want to put money in a bank run by a woman," she said.

I pondered this. I had then just come from Shanghai, where one of the best modern banks was run and controlled entirely by modern Chinese women. It was a prosperous bank because most people there thought women were probably more honest than men and more practical in the handling of money. So the Chinese women bankers did very well.

A good deal is said too about the profession of teaching for women. There are a great many women teachers in America—many more in proportion to men than in other countries. Men here, it seems, allow women to teach in lower schools because they themselves do not want to teach in anything less than a college. And even the best men do not like to teach in women's colleges nor in co-educational colleges. The finest teaching in America, I am told, is done by men for men.

As for the arts, I know very well that the odds are strongly against the woman. Granted an equally good product, the man is given the favor always. Women artists in any field are not often taken seriously, however serious their work. It is true that they often achieve high popular success. But this counts against them as artists. American men critics may show respect to a foreign woman artist, feeling that perhaps the foreign women are better than their own. But they cannot believe that the fools they see in department stores, in the subways and buses, or running to the movies and lectures, or even in their own homes, can amount to anything in the arts. Indeed they cannot think of a woman at all, but only of "women." And the pathetic efforts of American women to improve their minds by reading and clubs have only heightened the ridicule and contempt in which their men hold them. To educate women, therefore, to think, so that they need the personal fulfillment of activity and participation in all parts of life is acute cruelty, for they are not allowed this fulfillment. They should be educated not to think beyond the demands of simple household affairs or beyond the small arts and graces of pleasing men who seem always to want mental rest. The present method is not only cruel; it is extremely wasteful. Good money is spent teaching women to do things for which there will be no need. Men strain themselves to furnish educations for their daughters which they would be happier without, and not only happier but better women because they would be more contented women.

It is not only wasteful but dangerous. To educate women as we do for our present state of traditionalism is to put new wine into old bottles. A good deal of ferment is going on. And if we keep this up more will come of it. No one knows the effect upon children, for instance, of so many discontented women as mothers. Amiable, ignorant, bovine women make much better mothers than neurotic college graduates. And a woman does not need to complain aloud to let her children know she is unhappy. The atmosphere about her is gray with her secret discontent and children live deprived of that essential gayety in which they thrive as in sunshine. So few American women are really gay. This must have an effect. [...]

Of course there is the chimeralike possibility that we might change tradition. But I do not see anyone capable of changing it. Men certainly will not. They do not even want to talk about it. They do not want the woman question stirred up, having as they say, "enough on their hands already." To them, of course, women "stirred up" simply means nervous, illogical, clamoring children who must be placated in one way or another. They cannot conceive of woman as a rational being, equal to themselves and not always fundamentally connected with sex. Emotionally, as it has been truly said, many American men are adolescents—kind, delightful, charming adolescents. "He's just like a boy" seems to be considered a compliment to a man in America. It ought to be an insult. This horrible boyishness lingering in persons who should be adult is as dismaying as mental retardation. It is responsible for our childish tendencies to "jazz things up," to make "whoopee," to think of being drunk, of removing "inhibitions," of playing the clown, as the only way to have a good time, to the complete destruction of adult conversation and real wit and subtler humor. It certainly is responsible for wanting women to be nothing but wives, mothers, or leggy relaxations for tired business men. Even a pretty college girl said despairingly not long ago in my presence, "You can't get anywhere with men if you show any brains. I have to make myself a nit-wit if I want dates. Oh, well, that's the way they are!" There are too many nice and rather sad American women who patiently accept even their middle-aged and old men as perennial "boys." "Men are like that," they say, at least as often as men say, "women are like that."

Nothing could show a greater misunderstanding between the sexes than this frequent fatalistic remark. Neither men nor women are like that if "that" means what they now seem to each other. It is a strange fact that in new America, as in old India or China, the real life of each sex is not with each other but away from each other. Men and women in America meet stiffly for social functions, drink together in an earnest effort to feel less inhibited, play the fool guardedly and feel queer about it afterward. Or they meet for physical sex, in the home or out. And they jog along in family life. Of the delight of exploring each other's differing but equally important personalities and points of view, of the pleasure of real mutual comprehension and appreciation and companionship, there is almost none, inside the home or out. Tradition decrees that after marriage real companionship between persons of opposite sex must cease except between husband and wife. Tradition decrees that all companionship indeed between men and women is tinged with sex. Such an idea as interest in each other as persons, aside from sex, is almost unknown. Women, talking of this among themselves, say, "Men don't want anything else." I am inclined to think they are right. The average American man demands amazingly little from his women—nothing much except to look as pretty as possible on as little money as possible, to run the home economically with as little trouble as possible to the man when he comes home tired. What educated, intelligent, clever, gifted woman is going to be satisfied with that? What average woman would be satisfied even? Ask the average man if he would change places with a woman—any woman. The idea horrifies him. Yet women are far more like him than he knows or wants to know, and modern times have done everything to make her more so.

No, our men, perennial boys, most of them, will not do anything about changing tradition. They do not know how, absorbed as they are in the game of business, abashed as they are in the presence of sex as anything except simply physical, and afraid as they are of women. They are, naturally, afraid of women or they would not cling so to tradition. They were afraid of their mothers when they were children, their imperious, discontented mothers, and that fear carries over into fear of their wives and fear of all women, in industry as well as at home. It leads to the attitude of petty deception which so many perennially boyish men maintain toward their women.

So, naturally enough, men do not want women "getting too smart." I heard a carpenter working in my home say pontifically to his assistant about to be married, "And why would you want a woman eddicated? Says I, if I want eddication I can go to the public library. A woman should know just so much as when it rains she stands on the sheltered side of the street. It's enough." And after a moment he added solemnly, "You don't want a woman what can talk smart. You want one what can keep quiet smart."

The voice of America's perennial boys, I thought—speaking out in a carpenter, but heard as clearly in the embarrassed reserves of an after-dinner circle in a drawing-room. And yet, I do not blame them. There are so many women who chatter without thought, who stop all attempts at conversation with continual commonplaces uttered with all the petty authority of ignorance. And the fetters of another tradition—that of chivalry—still hang upon American men. Foolish, haughty women, standing in crowded buses, staring at a tired man in a seat, accepting favors as their right; peevish, idle women, wasting their husbands' money; dogmatic women talking ignorantly about practical important matters—men must try to be polite to them all alike. I do not blame American men, except for not seeing that not all women are the same. [...]

ONE MAN'S MEAT
WALDEN POND
BY E. B. WHITE

AUGUST 1939

Miss Nims, take a letter to Henry David Thoreau. Dear Henry: I thought of you the other afternoon as I was approaching Concord doing fifty on Route 62. That is a high speed at which to hold a philosopher in one's mind, but in this century we are a nimble bunch.

On one of the lawns in the outskirts of the village a woman was cutting the grass with a motorized lawn mower. What made me think of you was that the machine had rather got away from her, although she was game enough, and in the brief glimpse I had of the scene it appeared to me that the lawn was mowing the lady. She kept a tight grip on the handles, which throbbed violently with every explosion of the one-cylinder motor, and as she sheered around bushes and lurched along at a reluctant trot behind her impetuous servant, she looked like a puppy who had grabbed something that was too much for him. Concord hasn't changed much, Henry; the farm implements and the animals still have the upper hand.

I may as well admit that I was journeying to Concord with the deliberate intention of visiting your woods; for although I have never knelt at the grave of a philosopher nor placed wreaths on moldy poets, and have often gone a mile out of my way to avoid some place of historical interest, I have always wanted to see Walden Pond. The account which you left of your sojourn there is, you will be amused to learn, a document of increasing pertinence; each year it seems to gain a little headway, as the world loses ground. We may all be transcendental yet, whether we like it or not. As our common complexities increase, any tale of individual simplicity (and yours is the best written and the cockiest) acquires a new fascination; as our goods accumulate, but not our well-being, your report of an existence without material adornment takes on a certain awkward credibility.

My purpose in going to Walden Pond, like yours, was not to live cheaply or to live dearly there, but to transact some private business with the fewest obstacles. Approaching Concord, doing forty, doing forty-five, doing fifty, the steering wheel held snug in my palms, the highway held grimly in my vision, the crown of the road now serving me (on the righthand curves), now defeating me (on the lefthand curves), I began to rouse myself from the stupefaction which a day's motor journey induces. It was a delicious evening, Henry, when the whole body is one sense, and imbibes delight through every pore, if I may coin a phrase. Fields were richly brown where the harrow, drawn by the stripped Ford, had lately sunk its teeth; pastures were green; and overhead the sky had that same everlasting great look which you will find on Page 144 of the Oxford Pocket Edition. I could feel the road entering me, through tire, wheel, spring, and cushion; shall I not have intelligence with earth too? Am I not partly leaves and vegetable mold myself?—a man of infinite horsepower, yet partly leaves.

Stay with me on 62 and it will take you into Concord. As I say, it was a delicious evening. The snake had come forth to die in a bloody S on the highway, the wheel upon its head, its bowels flat now and exposed. The turtle had come up too to cross the road and die in the attempt, its hard shell smashed under the rubber blow, its intestinal yearning (for the other side of the road) forever squashed. There was a sign by the way-side which announced that the road had a "cotton surface." You wouldn't know what that is, but neither, for that matter, did I. There is a cryptic ingredient in many of our modern improvements—we are awed and pleased without knowing quite what we are enjoying. It is something to be traveling on a road with a cotton surface.

The civilization round Concord to-day is an odd distillation of city, village, farm, and manor. The houses, yards, fields look not quite suburban, not quite rural. Under the bronze beech and the blue spruce of the departed baron grazes the milch goat of the heirs. Under the porte-cochère stands the reconditioned station wagon; under the grape arbor sit the puppies for sale. (But why do men degenerate ever? What makes families run out?)

It was June and everywhere June was publishing her immemorial stanza: in the lilacs, in the syringa, in the freshly edged paths and the sweetness of moist beloved gardens, and the little wire wickets that preserve the tulips' front. Farmers were already moving the fruits of their toil into their yards, arranging the rhubarb, the asparagus, the strictly fresh eggs on the painted stands under the little shed roofs with the patent shingles. And though it was almost a hundred years since you had taken your ax and started cutting out your home on Walden Pond, I was interested to observe that the philosophical spirit was still alive in Massachusetts: in the center of a vacant lot some boys were assembling the framework of a rude shelter, their whole mind and skill concentrated in the rather inauspicious helter-skeleton of studs and rafters. They too were escaping from town, to live naturally, in a rich blend of savagery and philosophy.

That evening, after supper at the inn, I strolled out into the twilight to dream my shapeless transcendental dreams and see that the car was locked up for the night (first open the right front door, then reach over, straining, and pull up the handles of the left rear and the left front till you hear the click, then the handle of the right rear, then shut the right front but open it again, remembering that the key is still in the ignition switch, remove the key, shut the right front again with a bang, push the tiny keyhole cover to one side, insert key, turn, and withdraw). It is what we all do, Henry. It is called locking the car. It is said to confuse thieves and keep them from making off with the laprobe. Four doors to lock behind one robe. The driver himself never uses a laprobe, the free movement of his legs being vital to the operation of the vehicle; so that when he locks the car it is a pure and unselfish act. I have in my life gained very little essential heat from laprobes, yet I have ever been at pains to lock them up.

The evening was full of sounds, some of which would have stirred your memory. The robins still love the elms of New England villages at sundown. There is enough of the thrush in them to make song inevitable at the end of day, and enough of the tramp to make them hang round the dwellings of men. A robin, like many another American, dearly loves a white house with green blinds. Concord is still full of them.

Your fellow-townsmen were stirring abroad—not many afoot, most of them in their cars; and the sound which they made in Concord at evening was a rustling and a whispering. The sound lacks steadfastness and is wholly unlike that of a train. A train, as you know who lived so near the Fitchburg line, whistles once or twice sadly and is gone, trailing a memory in smoke, soothing to ear and mind. Automobiles, skirting a village green, are like flies that have gained the inner ear—they buzz, cease, pause, start, shift, stop, halt, brake, and the whole effect is a nervous polytone curiously disturbing.

As I wandered along, the toc toc of ping pong balls drifted from an attic window. In front of the Reuben Brown house a Buick was drawn up. At the wheel, motionless, his hat upon his head, a man sat, listening to Amos and Andy on the radio (it is a drama of many scenes and without an end). The deep voice of Andrew Brown, emerging from the car, although it originated more than two hundred miles away, was unstrained by distance. When you used to sit on the shore of your pond on Sunday morning, listening to the church bells of Acton and Concord, you were aware of the excellent filter of the intervening atmosphere. Science has attended to that, and sound now maintains its intensity without regard for distance. Properly sponsored, it goes on forever.

A fire engine, out for a trial spin, roared past Emerson's house, hot with readiness for public duty. Over the barn roofs the martins dipped and chittered. A swarthy daughter of an asparagus grower, in culottes, shirt, and bandanna, pedalled past on her bicycle. It was indeed a delicious evening, and I returned to the inn (I believe it was your house once) to rock with the old ladies on the concrete veranda.

Next morning early I started afoot for Walden, out Main Street and down Thoreau, past the depot and the Minuteman Chevrolet Company. The morning was fresh, and in a bean field along the way I flushed an agriculturalist, quietly studying his beans. Thoreau Street soon joined Number 126, an artery of the State. We number our highways nowadays, our speed being so great we can remember little of their quality or character and are lucky to remember their number. (Men have an indistinct notion that if they keep up this activity long enough all will at length ride somewhere, in next to no time.) Your pond is on 126.

I knew I must be nearing your woodland retreat when the Golden Pheasant lunchroom came into view—Sealtest ice cream, toasted sandwiches, hot frankfurters, waffles, tonics, and lunches. Were I the proprietor, I should add rice,

Thoreau's Cove at Walden Pond.

Indian meal, and molasses—just for old time's sake. The Pheasant, incidentally, is for sale: a chance for some nature lover who wishes to set himself up beside a pond in the Concord atmosphere and live deliberately, fronting only the essential facts of life on Number 126. Beyond the Pheasant was a place called Walden Breezes, an oasis whose porch pillars were made of old green shutters sawed into lengths. On the porch was a distorting mirror, to give the traveler a comical image of himself, who had miraculously learned to gaze in an ordinary glass without smiling. Behind the Breezes, in a sun-parched clearing, dwelt your philosophical descendants in their trailers, each trailer the size of your hut, but all grouped together for the sake of congeniality. Trailer people leave the city, as you did, to discover solitude and in any weather, at any hour of the day or night, to improve the nick of time; but they soon collect in villages and get bogged deeper in the mud than ever. The camp behind Walden Breezes was just rousing itself to the morning. The ground was packed hard under the heel, and the sun came through the clearing to bake the soil and enlarge the wry smell of cramped housekeeping. Cushman's bakery truck

had stopped to deliver an early basket of rolls. A camp dog, seeing me in the road, barked petulantly. A man emerged from one of the trailers and set forth with a bucket to draw water from some forest tap.

Leaving the highway I turned off into the woods toward the pond, which was apparent through the foliage. The floor of the forest was strewn with dried old oak leaves and *Transcripts*. From beneath the flattened popcorn wrapper (*granum explosum*) peeped the frail violet. I followed a footpath and descended to the water's edge. The pond lay clear and blue in the morning light, as you have seen it so many times. In the shallows a man's waterlogged shirt undulated gently. A few flies came out to greet me and convoy me to your cove, past the No Bathing signs on which the fellows and the girls had scrawled their names. I felt strangely excited suddenly to be snooping around your premises, tiptoeing along watchfully, as though not to tread by mistake upon the intervening century. Before I got to the cove I heard something which seemed to me quite wonderful: I heard your frog, a full, clear *troonk*, guiding me, still hoarse and solemn, bridging the years as the robins had bridged them in the sweetness of the village evening. But he soon quit, and I came on a couple of young boys throwing stones at him.

Your front yard is marked by a bronze tablet set in a stone. Four small granite posts, a few feet away, show where the house was. On top of the tablet was a pair of faded blue bathing trunks with a white stripe. Back of it is a pile of stones, a sort of cairn, left by your visitors as a tribute I suppose. It is a rather ugly little heap of stones, Henry. In fact the hillside itself seems faded, brow-beaten; a few tall skinny pines, bare of lower limbs, a smattering of young maples in suitable green, some birches and oaks, and a number of trees felled by the last big wind. It was from the bole of one of these fallen pines, torn up by the roots, that I extracted the stone which I added to the cairn—a sentimental act in which I was interrupted by a small terrier from a nearby picnic group, who confronted me and wanted to know about the stone.

I sat down for a while on one of the posts of your house to listen to the blue-bottles and the dragonflies. The invaded glade sprawled shabby and mean at my feet, but the flies were tuned to the old vibration. There were the remains of a fire in your ruins, but I doubt that it was yours; also two beer bottles trodden into the soil and become part of earth. A young oak had taken root in your house, and two or three ferns, unrolling like the ticklers at a banquet. The only other furnishings were a DuBarry pattern sheet, a page torn from a picture magazine, and some crusts in wax paper.

Before I quit I walked clear round the pond and found the place where you used to sit on the N. E. side to get the sun in the fall, and the beach where you got sand for scrubbing your floor. On the eastern side of the pond, where the highway borders it, the State has built dressing rooms for swimmers, a float with diving towers, drinking fountains of porcelain, and rowboats for hire. The pond is in fact a State Preserve, and carries a twenty-dollar fine for picking wild flowers, a decree signed in all solemnity by your fellow-citizens Walter C. Wardwell, Erson B. Barlow, and Nathaniel I. Bowditch. There was a smell of creosote where they had been building a wide wooden stairway to the road and the parking area. Swimmers and boaters were arriving; bodies splashed vigorously into the water and emerged wet and beautiful in the bright air. As I left, a boatload of town boys were splashing about in mid-pond, kidding and fooling, the young fellows singing at the tops of their lungs in a wild chorus:

> Amer-ica, A-mer-i-ca, God shed his grace on thee,
> And crown thy good with brotherhood
> From sea to shi-ning sea!

I walked back to town along the railroad, following your custom. The rails were expanding noisily in the hot sun, and on the slope of the roadbed the wild grape and the blackberry sent up their creepers to the track.

The expense of my brief sojourn in Concord was:

Canvas shoes	$1.95	
Baseball bat	.25	gifts to take
Left-handed fielder's glove	1.25	back to a boy
Hotel and meals	4.25	
In all	$7.70	

As you see, this amount was almost what you spent for food for eight months. I cannot defend the shoes or the expenditure for shelter and food: they reveal a meanness and grossness in my nature which you would find contemptible. The baseball equipment, however, is the sort of impediment with which you were never on even terms. You must remember that the house where you practiced the sort of economy which I respect was haunted only by mice and squirrels. You never had to cope with a shortstop.

Since Yesterday
The Social Climate of the Nineteen-Thirties
by Frederick Lewis Allen

November 1939

A t thirty-two and a half minutes past three (Mountain Time) in the afternoon of the 5th of December, 1933, the roll call in the ratification convention in Utah was completed, and Utah became the 36th State to ratify the Twenty-first Amendment to the Constitution, repealing the Prohibition Amendment. A telegram went off to Washington, and presently the Acting Secretary of State and the President declared that prohibition was at an end, after a reign of nearly fourteen years.

Crowds of men and women thronged the hotels and restaurants waiting for the word to come through that the lid was off, and when at last it did, drank happily to the new era of legal liquor. They thronged too to those urban speakeasies which had succeeded in getting licenses, and joyfully remarked how readily the front door swung open wide at the touch of the door-bell. But the celebration of the coming of repeal was no riot, if only because in most places the supply of liquor was speedily exhausted: it took time for the processes of distribution to get into motion. And as for the processes of legal manufacture—which for distilled liquors are supposed to include a long period of aging—these were so unready that an anomalous situation developed. The available liquor was mostly in the

Revenue agents during raid on a speakeasy.

hands of bootleggers; even the legal liquor was mostly immature. Among the people who, during the first days and months of repeal, rejoiced in at last being able to take a respectable drink of "good liquor" instead of depending upon "this bootleg stuff," thousands were consuming whisky which consisted simply of alcohol acceptably tinted and flavored. To a public whose taste had been conditioned for years by bootleg liquor, good bush needed no wine.

Drinking, to be sure, did not become legal everywhere. Eight States remained dry—all of them Southern except North Dakota, Kansas, and Oklahoma. (These States received—at least in the years immediately following repeal—precious little assistance from the Federal government in protecting their aridity.) Fifteen States made the selling of liquor a State monopoly—though seven of these permitted private sale under varying regulations, most of which, in a determined effort to prevent "the return of the saloon," forbade perpendicular drinking and insisted—at least for a time—that drinkers be seated at restaurant tables.

Despite these qualifications, the change in the American *mores* which began in 1933 was tremendous.

Hotels and restaurants blossomed with cocktail lounges and tap-rooms and bars, replete with chromium fittings, mirrors, bright-colored modern furniture, Venetian blinds, bartenders taken over from the speakeasies, and bartenders who for years had been serving at the oyster bar or waiting on table, and now, restored to their youthful occupation, persuaded the management to put on the wine-list such half-forgotten triumphs of their ancient skill as Bronx and Jack Rose cocktails. So little building had been going on during the Depression that the architects and decorators had had almost no chance for years to try out the new principles of functional design and bright color and simplified furniture; now at last they had it, in the designing of cocktail lounges—with the odd result that throughout the nineteen-thirties most Americans instinctively associated modern decoration with eating and drinking.

Hotels in cities which in days gone by would have frowned upon the very notion of a night club now somewhat hesitantly opened night clubs with floor shows—and found they were a howling success. Neat new liquor stores opened—in some States operated by government authority, in others under private ownership; it took some time for customers to realize that it was no longer necessary for a man carrying home a package of rum to act the part of a

man carrying home a shoe-box. Restaurants which in pre-prohibition days would never have dreamed of selling liquor installed bars and made prodigious sales; the tea-room proprietor wrestled with her conscience and applied for a license, and even the Childs' restaurants, unmindful of their traditional consecration to dairy products, pancakes, and calories, opened up slick circular bars and sold Manhattans and old-fashioneds. And if most of the metropolitan speakeasies withered and died, if the speakeasy cards grew dog-eared in the pocket-book of the man-about-town and at last were thrown away, if the hip-flask became a rarity, if the making of bathtub gin became a lost art in metropolitan apartment houses, and the business executive no longer sallied forth to the trade convention with two bottles of Scotch in his golf-bag, so many bright new bars appeared along the city streets that drinking seemed to have become not only respectable but ubiquitous.

For a time there was a wishful thought among those of gentle tastes that when good wines became more accessible a good many Americans would acquire fastidious palates. G. Selmer Fougner, Julian Street, Frank Schoonmaker, and other experts in the detection and savoring of rare vintages preached their gospel of deference to the right wine of the right year, and for a time ladies and gentlemen felt themselves to be nothing better than boors if they did not warm inwardly to the story of how somebody found a little French inn where the Armagnac de Nogaro was incomparable. But the crass American nature triumphed; pretty soon it was clear that even in the politest circles whisky was going to be the drink in greatest demand.

Whether there was more drinking after repeal than before cannot be determined statistically, owing to the obvious fact that the illicit sale of liquor was not measured. The consensus of opinion would seem to be that drinking pretty surely increased during the first year or two, and perhaps increased in quantity thereafter, but that on the whole it decreased in stridency.

"Less flamboyant drinking is the present-day rule," said the *Fortune* survey of youth in college in 1936; "there is no prohibition law to defy, hence one can drink in peace." There were signs here and there of a reaction against drinking among the boys and girls of college age; observers reported some of them, at least, to be less interested in alcohol than their elders, and were amazed at the volume of their consumption of Coca Cola and milk (Coca Cola, long the standard soft drink of the South, had followed its invasion of the campuses of the Middle West by extending its popularity among the young people in the Northeast as well). The American Institute of Public Opinion, taking a poll in 1936 as to whether conditions were "better" or "worse" since repeal, or showed no significant change, arrived at a singularly inconclusive result: 36 per cent of the voters thought things were better, 33 per cent thought they were worse, 31 per cent saw no significant change: not only was the division almost even, but there was no way of knowing what each voter may have meant in his heart by "conditions" being "better."

One change was manifest: there was now more mixed drinking than ever. In fact, a phenomenon which had been conspicuous during the nineteen-twenties, when women smokers invaded the club cars of trains and women drinkers invaded the speakeasies, appeared to be continuing: there were fewer and fewer bars, restaurants, smoking cars, and other haunts set apart for men only: on the whole men and women were spending more of their time in one another's company and less of their time segregated from one another. Perhaps it was not an altogether unrelated fact that most men's clubs were still somewhat anxiously seeking members throughout the nineteen-thirties (a survey of seventy-five prominent clubs throughout the country showed their memberships in 1936 to be even smaller than in 1932, and much smaller than in 1929), and that many of the lodges were in dire straits. Was it not possible to infer that the male sex was enjoying mixed company too well to want very urgently to get away from it? Perhaps the cause of feminism was triumphing in a way which the earnest suffragists of a generation before would never have expected—and at which they might have been dismayed.

And what became of the bootleggers? Some of them went into the legitimate liquor business or other legitimate occupations, some of them went into business rackets and gambling rackets, some joined the ranks of the unemployed—and a large number of them went right on bootlegging. For one of the most curious facts about the post-repeal situation was that the manufacture and smuggling and wholesaling of illicit liquor continued in great volume. The Federal government and the States, in their zeal to acquire revenue from the sale of liquor, had clapped upon it such high taxes that the inducement to dodge them was great. Year after year the Internal Revenue agents continued to seize and destroy stills at the rate of something like 15,000 a year, and straightway new ones sprang up. In his report for the fiscal year ending June 30, 1938, the Commissioner of Internal Revenue, reporting that only 11,407 stills had been seized, noted, "This is the first year since the enactment of the Twenty-first Amendment that there has been a decline in illicit distillery seizures." Likewise rum-running—or, to be more accurate, the smuggling of alcohol—continued to provide a headache for the customs officers and the Coast Guard; in February, 1935, more than a year after repeal, the Coast Guard found twenty-two foreign vessels lying at sea *at one time* beyond our customs waters, waiting for a chance to sneak in.

So easy was it to operate illicit stills, to store bottles and counterfeit labels and counterfeit revenue stamps and alcohol cans in separate places, bottle the illicit liquor, transport it in trucks or automobiles equipped with traps, and offer a liquor-store or saloon-keeper a consignment of spurious liquor at a bargain, that a year or two after repeal the best expert opinion was that anywhere from fifteen to sixty per cent of the liquor consumed in the United States was bootleg.

Were the American people glad that they had ended prohibition? Apparently they were. A *Fortune* Quarterly Survey made late in 1937 showed that only 15.1 per cent of the men of the country and 29.7 per cent of the women wanted complete prohibition back again. Even combining with this dry group those who were in favor of prohibition of hard liquors but would permit the sale of wine and beer, there was still approximately a two-thirds majority in favor of a wet regime. Americans might or might not think "conditions" were "better," but they did not—most of them—want to re-open the question. What had been a burning issue till 1933 had dropped almost completely out of the focus of general public attention, as if settled once and for all.

Could it really have been true, the men and women of 1939 asked themselves, that in 1929 prohibition had been the topic of hottest and angriest debate in American public life?

WHO GOES NAZI?

BY DOROTHY THOMPSON

AUGUST 1941

It is an interesting and somewhat macabre parlor game to play at a large gathering of one's acquaintances: to speculate who in a showdown would go Nazi. By now, I think I know. I have gone through the experience many times—in Germany, in Austria, and in France. I have come to know the types: the born Nazis, the Nazis whom democracy itself has created, the certain-to-be fellow-travelers. And I also know those who never, under any conceivable circumstances, would become Nazis.

It is preposterous to think that they are divided by any racial characteristics. Germans may be more susceptible to Nazism than most people, but I doubt it. Jews are barred out, but it is an arbitrary ruling. I know lots of Jews who are born Nazis and many others who would heil Hitler to-morrow morning if given a chance. There are Jews who have repudiated their own ancestors in order to become "Honorary Aryans and Nazis"; there are full-blooded Jews who have enthusiastically entered Hitler's secret service. Nazism has nothing to do with race and nationality. It appeals to a certain type of mind.

It is also, to an immense extent, the disease of a generation—the generation which was either young or unborn at the end of the last war. This is as true of Englishmen, Frenchmen, and Americans as of Germans. It is the disease of the so-called "lost generation."

Sometimes I think there are direct biological factors at work—a type of education, feeding, and physical training which has produced a new kind of human being with an imbalance in his nature. He has been fed vitamins and filled with energies that are beyond the capacity of his intellect to discipline. He has been treated to forms of education which have released him from inhibitions. His body is vigorous. His mind is childish. His soul has been almost completely neglected.

At any rate, let us look round the room.

The gentleman standing beside the fireplace with an almost untouched glass of whiskey beside him on the man-

tel-piece is Mr. A, a descendant of one of the great American families. There has never been an American Blue Book without several persons of his surname in it. He is poor and earns his living as an editor. He has had a classical education, has a sound and cultivated taste in literature, painting, and music; has not a touch of snobbery in him; is full of humor, courtesy, and wit. He was a lieutenant in the World War, is a Republican in politics, but voted twice for Roosevelt, last time for Willkie. He is modest, not particularly brilliant, a staunch friend, and a man who greatly enjoys the company of pretty and witty women. His wife, whom he adored, is dead, and he will never remarry.

He has never attracted any attention because of outstanding bravery. But I will put my hand in the fire that nothing on earth could ever make him a Nazi. He would greatly dislike fighting them, but they could never convert him.... Why not?

Beside him stands Mr. B, a man of his own class, graduate of the same preparatory school and university, rich, a sportsman, owner of a famous racing stable, vice-president of a bank, married to a well-known society belle. He is a good fellow and extremely popular. But if America were going Nazi he would certainly join up, and early.

Why?... Why the one and not the other?

Mr. A has a life that is established according to a certain form of personal behavior. Although he has no money, his unostentatious distinction and education have always assured him a position. He has never been engaged in sharp competition. He is a free man. I doubt whether ever in his life he has done anything he did not want to do or anything that was against his code. Nazism wouldn't fit in with his standards and he has never become accustomed to making concessions.

Mr. B has risen beyond his real abilities by virtue of health, good looks, and being a good mixer. He married for money and he has done lots of other things for money. His

Hitler Youth at a rally.

code is not his own; it is that of his class—no worse, no better. He fits easily into whatever pattern is successful. That is his sole measure of value—success. Nazism as a minority movement would not attract him. As a movement likely to attain power, it would.

The saturnine man over there talking with a lovely French émigrée is already a Nazi. Mr. C is a brilliant and embittered intellectual. He was a poor white-trash Southern boy, a scholarship student at two universities where he took all the scholastic honors but was never invited to join a fraternity. His brilliant gifts won for him successively government positions, partnership in a prominent law firm, and eventually a highly paid job as a Wall Street adviser. He has always moved among important people and always been socially on the periphery. His colleagues have admired his brains and exploited them, but they have seldom invited him—or his wife—to dinner.

He is a snob, loathing his own snobbery. He despises the men about him—he despises, for instance, Mr. B—because he knows that what he has had to achieve by relentless work men like B have won by knowing the right people. But his contempt is inextricably mingled with envy. Even more than he hates the class into which he has insecurely risen, does he hate the people from whom he came. He hates his mother and his father for *being* his parents. He loathes everything

that reminds him of his origins and his humiliations. He is bitterly anti-Semitic because the social insecurity of the Jews reminds him of his own psychological insecurity.

Pity he has utterly erased from his nature, and joy he has never known. He has an ambition, bitter and burning. It is to rise to such an eminence that no one can ever again humiliate him. Not to rule but to be the secret ruler, pulling the strings of puppets created by his brains. Already some of them are talking his language—though they have never met him.

There he sits: he talks awkwardly rather than glibly; he is courteous. He commands a distant and cold respect. But he is a very dangerous man. Were he primitive and brutal he would be a criminal—a murderer. But he is subtle and cruel. He would rise high in a Nazi regime. It would need men just like him—intellectual and ruthless.

But Mr. C is not a born Nazi. He is the product of a democracy hypocritically preaching social equality and practicing a carelessly brutal snobbery. He is a sensitive, gifted man who has been humiliated into nihilism. He would laugh to see heads roll.

I think young D over there is the only *born* Nazi in the room. Young D is the spoiled only son of a doting mother. He has never been crossed in his life. He spends his time at the game of seeing what he can get away with. He is constantly arrested for speeding and his mother pays the fines. He has been ruthless toward two wives and his mother pays the alimony. His life is spent in sensation-seeking and theatricality. He is utterly inconsiderate of everybody. He is very good-looking, in a vacuous, cavalier way, and inordinately vain. He would certainly fancy himself in a uniform that gave him a chance to swagger and lord it over others.

Mrs. E would go Nazi as sure as you are born. That statement surprises you? Mrs. E seems so sweet, so clinging, so cowed. She is. She is a masochist. She is married to a man who never ceases to humiliate her, to lord it over her, to treat her with less consideration than he does his dogs. He is a prominent scientist, and Mrs. E, who married him very young, has persuaded herself that he is a genius, and that there is something of superior womanliness in her utter lack of pride, in her doglike devotion. She speaks disapprovingly of other "masculine" or insufficiently devoted wives. Her husband, however, is bored to death with her. He neglects her completely and she is looking for someone else before whom to pour her ecstatic self-abasement. She will titillate with pleased excitement to the first popular hero who proclaims the basic subordination of women.

On the other hand, Mrs. F would never go Nazi. She is the most popular woman in the room, handsome, gay, witty, and full of the warmest emotion. She was a popular actress ten years ago; married very happily; promptly had four children in a row; has a charming house, is not rich but has no money cares, has never cut herself off from her own happy-go-lucky profession, and is full of sound health and sound common sense. All men try to make love to her; she laughs at them all, and her husband is amused. She has stood on her own feet since she was a child, she has enormously helped her husband's career (he is a lawyer), she would ornament any drawing-room in any capital, and she is as American as ice cream and cake.

How about the butler who is passing the drinks? I look at James with amused eyes. James is safe. James has been butler to the 'ighest aristocracy, considers all Nazis parvenus and communists, and has a very good sense for "people of quality." He serves the quiet editor with that friendly air of equality which good servants always show toward those they consider good enough to serve, and he serves the horsy gent stiffly and coldly.

Bill, the grandson of the chauffeur, is helping serve tonight. He is a product of a Bronx public school and high school, and works at night like this to help himself through City College, where he is studying engineering. He is a "proletarian," though you'd never guess it if you saw him without that white coat. He plays a crack game of tennis—has been a tennis tutor in summer resorts—swims superbly, gets straight A's in his classes, and thinks America is okay and don't let anybody say it isn't. He had a brief period of Youth Congress communism, but it was like the measles. He was not taken in the draft because his eyes are not good enough, but he wants to design airplanes, "like Sikorsky." He thinks Lindbergh is "just another pilot with a build-up and a rich wife" and that he is "always talking down America, like how we couldn't lick Hitler if we wanted to." At this point Bill snorts.

Mr. G is a *very* intellectual young man who was an infant prodigy. He has been concerned with general ideas since the age of ten and has one of those minds that can scintillatingly rationalize everything. I have known him for ten years and in that time have heard him enthusiastically explain Marx, social credit, technocracy, Keynesian economics, Chestertonian distributism, and everything else one can imagine. Mr. G will never be a Nazi, because he will never be anything. His brain operates quite apart from the rest of his apparatus. He will certainly be able, however, fully to explain and apologize for Nazism if it ever comes along. But Mr. G is always a "deviationist." When he played with communism he was a Trotskyist; when he talked of Keynes it was to suggest improvement; Chesterton's economic ideas were all right but he was too bound to Catholic philosophy. So we may be sure that Mr. G would be a Nazi with purse-lipped qualifications. He would certainly be purged.

H is an historian and biographer. He is American of Dutch ancestry born and reared in the Middle West. He has been in love with America all his life. He can recite whole chapters of Thoreau and volumes of American poetry, from Emerson to Steve Benét. He knows Jefferson's letters, Hamilton's papers, Lincoln's speeches. He is a collector of early American furniture, lives in New England, runs a farm for a hobby and doesn't lose much money on it, and loathes parties like this one. He has a ribald and manly sense of humor, is unconventional and lost a college professorship because of a love affair. Afterward he married the lady and has lived happily ever afterward on the wages of sin.

H has never doubted his own authentic Americanism for one instant. This is his country, and he knows it from Acadia to Zenith. His ancestors fought in the Revolutionary

War and in all the wars since. He is certainly an intellectual, but an intellectual smelling slightly of cow barns and damp tweeds. He is the most good-natured and genial man alive, but if anyone ever tries to make this country over into an imitation of Hitler's, Mussolini's, or Petain's systems H will grab a gun and fight. Though H's liberalism will not permit him to say it, it is his secret conviction that nobody whose ancestors have not been in this country since before the Civil War really understands America or would really fight for it against Nazism or any other foreign ism in a show-down.

But H is wrong. There is one other person in the room who would fight alongside H and he is not even an American citizen. He is a young German émigré, whom I brought along to the party. The people in the room look at him rather askance because he is so Germanic, so very blond-haired, so very blue-eyed, so tanned that somehow you expect him to be wearing shorts. He looks like the model of a Nazi. His English is flawed—he learned it only five years ago. He comes from an old East Prussian family; he was a member of the post-war Youth Movement and afterward of the Republican "Reichsbanner." All his German friends went Nazi—without exception. He hiked to Switzerland penniless, there pursued his studies in New Testament Greek, sat under the great Protestant theologian, Karl Barth, came to America through the assistance of an American friend whom he had met in a university, got a job teaching the classics in a fashionable private school; quit, and is working now in an airplane factory—working on the night shift to make planes to send to Britain to defeat Germany. He has devoured volumes of American history, knows Whitman by heart, wonders why so few Americans have ever really read the Federalist papers, believes in the United States of Europe, the Union of the English-speaking world, and the coming democratic revolution all over the earth. He believes that America is the country of Creative Evolution once it shakes off its middle-class complacency, its bureaucratized industry, its tentacle-like and spreading government, and sets itself innerly free.

The people in the room think he is not an American, but he is more American than almost any of them. He has discovered America and his spirit is the spirit of the pioneers. He is furious with America because it does not realize its strength and beauty and power. He talks about the workmen in the factory where he is employed.... He took the job "in order to understand the real America." He thinks

the men are wonderful. "Why don't you American intellectuals ever get to them; talk to them?"

I grin bitterly to myself, thinking that if we ever got into war with the Nazis he would probably be interned, while Mr. B and Mr. G and Mrs. E would be spreading defeatism at all such parties as this one. "Of course I don't like Hitler but..."

Mr. J over there is a Jew. Mr. J is a very important man. He is immensely rich—he has made a fortune through a dozen directorates in various companies, through a fabulous marriage, through a speculative flair, and through a native gift for money and a native love of power. He is intelligent and arrogant. He seldom associates with Jews. He deplores any mention of the "Jewish question." He believes that Hitler "should not be judged from the standpoint of anti-Semitism." He thinks that "the Jews should be reserved on all political questions." He considers Roosevelt "an enemy of business." He thinks "It was a serious blow to the Jews that Frankfurter should have been appointed to the Supreme Court."

The saturnine Mr. C—the real Nazi in the room—engages him in a flatteringly attentive conversation. Mr. J agrees with Mr. C wholly. Mr. J is definitely attracted by Mr. C. He goes out of his way to ask his name—they have never met before. "A very intelligent man."

Mr. K contemplates the scene with a sad humor in his expressive eyes. Mr. K is also a Jew. Mr. K is a Jew from the South. He speaks with a Southern drawl. He tells inimitable stories. Ten years ago he owned a very successful business that he had built up from scratch. He sold it for a handsome price, settled his indigent relatives in business, and now enjoys an income for himself of about fifty dollars a week. At forty he began to write articles about odd and out-of-the-way places in American life. A bachelor, and a sad man who makes everybody laugh, he travels continually, knows America from a thousand different facets, and loves it in a quiet, deep, unostentatious way. He is a great friend of H, the biographer. Like H, his ancestors have been in this country since long before the Civil War. He is attracted to the young German. By and by they are together in the drawing-room. The impeccable gentleman of New England, the country-man-intellectual of the Middle West, the happy woman whom the gods love, the young German, the quiet, poised Jew from the South. And over on the other side are the others.

Mr. L has just come in. Mr. L is a lion these days. My hostess was all of a dither when she told me on the telephone,

"…and L is coming. You know it's *dreadfully* hard to get him." L is a *very* powerful labor leader. "My dear, he is a man of the people, but really *fascinating*."

L is a man of the people and just exactly as fascinating as my horsy, bank vice-president, on-the-make acquaintance over there, and for the same reasons and in the same way. L makes speeches about the "third of the nation," and L has made a darned good thing for himself out of championing the oppressed. He has the best car of anyone in this room; salary means nothing to him because he lives on an expense account. He agrees with the very largest and most powerful industrialists in the country that it is the business of the strong to boss the weak, and he has made collective bargaining into a legal compulsion to appoint him or his henchmen as "labor's" agents, with the power to tax pay envelopes and do what they please with the money. L is the strongest natural-born Nazi in this room. Mr. B regards him with contempt tempered by hatred. Mr. B will use him. L is already parroting B's speeches. He has the brains of Neanderthal man, but he has an infallible instinct for power. In private conversation he denounces the Jews as "parasites." No one has ever asked him what are the creative functions of a highly paid agent, who takes a percentage off the labor of millions of men, and distributes it where and as it may add to his own political power.

It's fun—a macabre sort of fun—this parlor game of "Who Goes Nazi?"

And it simplifies things—asking the question in regard to specific personalities.

Kind, good, happy, gentlemanly, secure people never go Nazi. They may be the gentle philosopher whose name is in the Blue Book, or Bill from City College to whom democracy gave a chance to design airplanes—you'll never make Nazis out of them. But the frustrated and humiliated intellectual, the rich and scared speculator, the spoiled son, the labor tyrant, the fellow who has achieved success by smelling out the wind of success—they would all go Nazi in a crisis.

Believe me, nice people don't go Nazi. Their race, color, creed, or social condition is not the criterion. It is something in them.

Those who haven't anything in them to tell them what they like and what they don't—whether it is breeding, or happiness, or wisdom, or a code, however old-fashioned or however modern, go Nazi.

It's an amusing game. Try it at the next big party you go to.

THE WIDE NET

BY EUDORA WELTY

MAY 1942

William Wallace Jamieson's wife Hazel was going to have a baby. But this was October, and it was six months away, and she acted exactly as though it would be to-morrow. When he came in the room she would not speak to him but would look as straight at nothing as she could, with her eyes glowing. If he only touched her she stuck out her tongue or ran round the table. So one night he went out with two of the boys down the road and stayed out all night. But that was the worst thing yet, because when he came home in the early morning Hazel had vanished. He went through the house not believing his eyes, balancing with both hands out, his yellow cowlick rising on end, and then he turned the kitchen inside out looking for her, but it did no good. Then when he got back to the front room he saw she had left him a little letter in an envelope. That was doing something behind someone's back. He took out the letter, pushed it open, held it out at a distance from his eyes.... After one look he was scared to read the exact words, and he crushed the whole thing in his hand instantly, but what it had said was that she could not put up with him after that and was going to the river to drown herself.

"Drown herself... but she's in mortal fear of the water!"

He ran out front, his face red like the red of the picked cotton field he ran over, and down in the road he gave a loud shout for Virgil Thomas, who was just going in his own house, to come out again. He had almost got in, he had one foot inside the door.

They met half-way between the farms, under the shade tree.

"Haven't you had enough of the night?" asked Virgil. There they were, their pants all covered with the dust and dew, and they had had to carry the third man home flat between them.

"I've lost Hazel, she's vanished, she went to drown herself."

"Why, that ain't like Hazel," said Virgil.

William Wallace reached out and shook him. "You heard me. Don't you know we have to drag the river?"

"Right this minute?"

"You ain't got nothing to do till spring."

"Let me go set foot inside the house and speak to my mother and tell her a story and I'll come back."

"This will take the wide net," said William Wallace. His eyebrows gathered, and he was talking to himself.

"How come Hazel to go and do that way?" asked Virgil as they started out.

William Wallace said, "I reckon she got lonesome."

"That don't argue—drown herself for getting lonesome. My mother gets lonesome."

"Well," said William Wallace. "It argues for Hazel."

"How long is it now since you and her was married?"

"Why, it's been a year."

"It don't seem that long to me. A year!"

"It was this time last year. It seems longer," said William Wallace, breaking a stick off a tree in surprise. They walked along, kicking at the flowers on the road's edge. "I remember the day I seen her first and that seems a long time ago. She was coming along the road holding a little frying-size chicken from her grandma under her arm, and she had it real quiet. I spoke to her with nice manners. We knowed each other's names, being bound to, just didn't know each other to speak to.

"I says, 'Where are you taking the fryer?' and she says, 'Mind your manners,' and I kept on till after a while she says, 'If you want to walk me home take littler steps.' So I didn't lose time. It was just four miles across the field and full of blackberries, and from the top of the hill there was Dover below, looking sizeable-like and clean, spread out between the two churches like that. When we got down, I says to her, 'What kind of water's in this well?' and she says, 'The best water in the world.' So I drew a bucket and took out a dipper and she drank and I drank. I didn't think it was that remarkable, but I didn't tell her."

"What happened that night?" asked Virgil.

"We ate the chicken," said William Wallace, "and it was tender. Of course that wasn't all they had. The night I was trying their table out, it sure had good things to eat from one end to the other. Her mama and papa sat at the head and foot and we was face to face with each other across it with, I remember, a pat of butter between. They had real sweet butter with a tree drawed down it, elegant-like. Her mama eats like a man. I had brought her a whole hatful of berries and she didn't even pass them to her husband. Hazel, she would leap up and take a pitcher of new milk and fill up the glasses. I had heard how they couldn't have a singing at the church without a fight over her."

"Oh, she's a pretty girl, all right," said Virgil. "It's a pity for the ones like her to grow old, and get like their mothers."

"Another thing will be that her mother will get wind of this and come after me," said William Wallace.

"Her mother will eat you alive," said Virgil.

"She's just been watching her chance," said William Wallace. "Why did I think I could stay out all night?"

"Just something come over you."

"First it was just a carnival at Carthage, and I had to let them guess my weight...and after that..."

"It was nice to be sitting on your neck in a ditch singing," prompted Virgil, "there in the moonlight. And playing on the harmonica like you can play."

"Even if Hazel did sit home knowing I was drunk that wouldn't kill her," said William Wallace. "What she knows ain't ever killed her yet.... She's smart too for a girl," he said.

"She's a lot smarter than her cousins in Beula," said Virgil. "And especially Edna Earle, that never did get to be what you'd call a heavy thinker. Edna Earle could sit and ponder all day on how the little tail of the 'C' got through the 'L' in a Coca-Cola sign."

"Hazel *is* smart," said William Wallace. They walked on. "You ought to see her pantry shelf—it looks like a hundred jars when you open the door. I don't see how she could turn around and jump in the river."

"It's a woman's trick."

"I always behaved before. Till the one night—last night."

"Yes, but the one night," said Virgil. "And she was waiting to take advantage."

"She jumped in the river because she was scared to death of the water and that was to make it worse," he said. "She remembered how I used to have to pick her up and carry her

over the oak-log bridge, how she'd shut her eyes and make a dead-weight and hold me round the neck, just for a little creek. I don't see how she brought herself to jump."

"Jumped backward," said Virgil. "Didn't look."

When they turned off it was still early in the pink and green fields. The fumes of morning, sweet and bitter, sprang up where they walked. The insects ticked softly, their strength in reserve; butterflies chopped the air, going to the east, and the birds flew carelessly and sang by fits and starts, not the way they did in the evening, in sustained and drowsy songs.

"It is a pretty *day* for sure," said William Wallace. "It's a pretty *day* for it."

"I don't see a sign of her ever going along here," said Virgil.

"Well," said William Wallace, "she wouldn't have dropped anything. I never saw a girl to leave less signs of where she's been."

"Not even a plum seed," said Virgil, kicking the grass.

In the grove it was so quiet that once William Wallace gave a jump, as if he could almost hear a sound of himself wondering where she had gone. A descent of energy came down on him in the thick of the woods and he ran at a rabbit and caught it in his hands.

"Rabbit...rabbit..." He acted as if he wanted to take it off to himself and hold it up and talk to it. He laid a palm against its pushing heart. "Now...there now..."

"Let her go, William Wallace, let her go." Virgil, chewing on an elderberry whistle he had just made, stood at his shoulder. "What do you want with a live rabbit?"

William Wallace squatted down and set the rabbit on the ground but held it under his hand. It was a little, old, brown rabbit. It did not try to move. "See there?"

"Let her go."

"She can go if she wants to, but she don't want to."

Gently he lifted his hand. The round eye was shining at him sideways in the green gloom.

"Anybody can freeze a rabbit that wants to," said Virgil. Suddenly he gave a far-reaching blast on the whistle, and the rabbit went in a streak. "Was you out catching cottontails or was you out catching your wife?" he said, taking the turn to the open fields. "I come along to keep you on the track."

"Who'll we get now?" They stood on top of a hill and William Wallace looked critically over the countryside. "Any of the Malones?"

"I was always scared of the Malones," said Virgil. "Too many *of* them."

"This is my day with the net, and they would have to watch out," said William Wallace. "I reckon some Malones and the Doyles will be enough. The six Doyles and their dogs, and you and me, and two little nigger boys is enough, with just a few Malones."

"That ought to be enough," said Virgil, "no matter what."

"I'll bring the Malones and you bring the Doyles," said William Wallace, and they separated at the spring.

When William Wallace came back, with a string of Malones just showing behind him on the hilltop, he found Virgil with the two little Rippen boys waiting behind him, solemn little towheads. As soon as he walked up, Grady, the one in front, lifted his hand, as if to signal silence and caution to his brother Brucie, panting merrily and untrustworthily behind him.

Brucie bent readily under William Wallace's hand-pat and gave him a dreamy look out of the tops of his round eyes, which were pure green-and-white, like clover tops. William Wallace gave him a nickel. Grady hung his head; his white hair lay in a little tail in the nape of his neck.

"Let's let them come," said Virgil.

"Well, they can come then, but if we keep letting everybody come it is going to be too many," said William Wallace.

"They'll appreciate it, those little old boys," said Virgil. Brucie held up at arm's length a long red thread with a bent pin tied on the end; and a look of helpless and intense interest gathered Grady's face like a drawstring; his eyes, one bright with a sty, shone pleadingly under his white bangs, and he snapped his jaw and tried to speak. . . . "Their papa was drowned in the Pearl River," said Virgil.

There was a shout from the gully.

"Here come all the Malones," cried William Wallace. "I asked four of them would they come, but the rest of the family invited themselves."

"Did you ever see a time when they didn't?" said Virgil. "And yonder from the other direction comes the Doyles, still with biscuit crumbs on their cheeks, I bet, now it's nothing to do but eat, as their mother said."

"If two little niggers would come along now, or one big nigger," said William Wallace. And the words were hardly out of his mouth when two little Negro boys came along, going somewhere, one behind the other, stepping high and gay in their overalls, as though they waded through honeydew to the waist.

"Come here, boys. What's your names?"

"Sam and Robbie Bell."

"Come along with us, we're going to drag the river."

"You hear that, Robbie Bell?" said Sam.

They smiled.

The Doyles came noiselessly, their dogs made all the fuss. The Malones, eight giants with great long black eyelashes, were already stamping the ground and pawing one another, ready to go. Everybody went up together to see Doc.

Old Doc owned the wide net. He had a house on top of the hill and he sat and looked out from a rocker on the front porch.

"Climb the hill and come in!" he began to intone across the valley. "Harvest's over . . . slipped up on everybody . . . cotton's picked, gone to the gin . . . hay cut . . . molasses made around here. . . . Big explosion's over, supervisors elected, some pleased, some not. . . . We're hearing talk of war!"

When they got closer he was saying, "Many's been saved at revival, twenty-two last Sunday, including a Doyle, ought to counted two. Hope they'll be a blessing to Dover community besides a shining star in Heaven. Now what?" he asked, for they had arrived and stood gathered in front of the steps.

"If nobody else is using your wide net could we use it?" asked William Wallace.

"You just used it a month ago," said Doc. "It ain't your turn."

Virgil jogged William Wallace's arm and cleared his throat. "This time is kind of special," he said. "We got reason to think William Wallace's wife Hazel is in the river, drowned."

"What reason have you got to think she's in the river drowned?" asked Doc. He took out his old pipe. "I'm asking the husband."

"Because she's not in the house," said William Wallace.

"Vanished?" and he knocked out the pipe.

"Plum vanished."

"Of course a thousand things could have happened to her," said Doc and he lighted the pipe.

"Hand him up the letter, William Wallace," said Virgil. "We can't wait around till Doomsday for the net while Doc sits back thinkin'."

"I tore it up, right at the first," said William Wallace.

"But I know it by heart. It said she was going to jump straight in the Pearl River and that I'd be sorry."

"Where do you come in, Virgil?" asked Doc.

"I was in the same place William Wallace sat on his neck in, all night, and done as much as he done, and come home the same time."

"You-all were out cuttin' up, so Lady Hazel has to jump in the river, is that it? Cause and effect. Anybody want to argue with me? Where do these others come in, Doyles, Malones, and what not?"

"Doc is the smartest man around," said William Wallace, turning to the stolidly waiting Doyles, "but it sure takes time."

"These are the ones that's collected to drag the river for her," said Virgil.

"Of course I am not going on record to say so soon that *I* think she's drowned," Doc said, blowing out blue smoke.

"Do you think..." William Wallace went up a step, and his hands both went into fists. "Do you think she was *carried off?*"

"Now that's the way to argue, see it from all sides," said Doc promptly. "But who by?"

Some Malone whistled, but not so you could tell which one.

"There's no booger around the Dover section that goes around carrying off young girls that's married," stated Doc.

"She was always scared of the gypsies." William Wallace turned scarlet. "She'd sure turn her ring around on her finger if she passed one, and look in the other direction so they couldn't see she was pretty and carry her off. They come in the end of summer."

"Yes, there are the gypsies, kidnappers since the world began. But was it to be you that would pay the grand ransom?" asked Doc. He pointed his finger. They all laughed then at how clever old Doc was and clapped William Wallace on the back. But that turned into a scuffle and they fell to the ground.

"Stop it, or you can't have the net," said Doc. "You're scaring my wife's chickens."

"It's time we was gone," said William Wallace.

The big barking dogs jumped to lean their front paws on the men's chests.

"My advice remains, Let well enough alone," said Doc. "Whatever this mysterious event will turn out to be, it has kept one woman from talking a while. However, Lady Hazel is the prettiest girl in Mississippi, a golden-haired girl; you've never seen a prettier one and you never will." He got

to his feet with the nimbleness that was always his surprise, and said, "I'll come along with you."

The path they always followed was the Old Natchez Trace. It took them through the deep woods and led them out down below on the Pearl River, where they could begin dragging it upstream to a point near Dover. They walked in silence round William Wallace, not letting him carry anything, but the net dragged heavily and the buckets were full of clatter in a place so dim and still.

Once they went through a forest of cucumber trees and came up on a high ridge. Grady and Brucie who were running ahead all the way stopped in their tracks; a whistle had blown, and far down and far away a long freight train was passing. It seemed like a little festival procession, moving with the slowness of ignorance or a dream, from distance to distance, the tiny pink and gray cars like secret boxes. Grady was counting the cars to himself, as if he could certainly see each one clearly, and Brucie watched his lips, hushed and cautious, the way he would watch a bird drinking. Tears suddenly came to Grady's eyes, but it could only be because a tiny man walked along the top of the train, walking and moving on top of the moving train.

They went down again and soon the smell of the river spread over the woods, cool and secret. Every step they took among the great walls of vines and among the passionflowers started up a little life, a little flight.

"We're walking along in the changing-time," said Doc. "Any day now the change will come. It's going to turn from hot to cold, and we can kill the hog that's ripe and have fresh meat to eat. Come one of these nights and we can wander down here and tree a nice possum. Old Jack Frost will be pinching things up. Old Mr. Winter will be standing in the door. Hickory tree there will be yellow. Sweet-gum red, hickory yellow, dogwood red, sycamore yellow." He went along rapping the tree trunks with his knuckle. "Magnolia and live oak never die. Remember that. Persimmons will all get fit to eat, and the nuts will be dropping like rain all through the woods here. And run, little quail, run, for we'll be after you too."

They went on and suddenly the woods opened upon light, and they had reached the river. Everyone stopped, but Doc talked on ahead as though nothing had happened. "Only to-day," he said, "to-day, in October sun, it's all gold—sky and tree and water. Everything just before it changes looks to be made of gold."

William Wallace looked down as though he thought of

Hazel with the shining eyes, sitting at home and looking straight before her, like a piece of pure gold, too precious to touch.

Below them the river was glimmering, narrow, soft and skin-colored, and slowed nearly to stillness. The shining willow trees hung round them. The net that was being drawn out, so old and so long-used, it too looked golden, strung and tied with golden threads.

Standing still on the bank, all of a sudden William Wallace, on whose word they were waiting, spoke up in a voice of surprise. "What is the name of this river?"

They looked at him as if he were crazy not to know the name of the river he had fished in all his life. But a deep frown was on his forehead, as if he were compelled to wonder what people had come to call this river, or to think there was a mystery in the name of a river they all knew so well, the same as if it were some great far torrent of waves that dashed through the mountains somewhere, and almost as if it were a river in some dream, for they could not give him the name of that.

"Everybody knows Pearl River is named the Pearl River," said Doc.

A bird note suddenly bold was like a stone thrown into the water to sound it.

"It's deep here," said Virgil, and jogged William Wallace. "Remember?"

William Wallace stood looking down at the river as if it were still a mystery to him. There under his foot which hung over the bank it was transparent and yellow like an old bottle lying in the sun, filling with light.

Doc clattered all his paraphernalia.

Then all of a sudden all the Malones scattered jumping and tumbling down the bank. They gave their loud shout. Little Brucie started after them, and looked back.

"Do you think she jumped?" Virgil asked William Wallace.

Since the net was so wide when it was all stretched, it reached from bank to bank of the Pearl River, and the weights would hold it all the way to the bottom. Juglike sounds filled the air, splashes lifted in the sun, and the party began to move upstream. The Malones with great groans swam and pulled near the shore, the Doyles swam and pushed from behind with Virgil to tell them how to do it best; Grady and Brucie with his thread and pin trotted along the sandbars hauling buckets and lines. Sam and Robbie Bell, naked and bright, guided the old oarless rowboat that always drifted at the shore, and in it, sitting up tall with his hat on, was Doc—he went along without ever touching water and without ever taking his eye off the net. William Wallace himself did everything but most of the time he was out of sight, swimming about under water or diving, and he had nothing to say any more.

The dogs chased up and down, in and out of the water and in and out of the woods.

"Don't let her get too heavy, boys," Doc intoned regularly every few minutes, "and she won't let nothing through."

"She won't let nothing through, she won't let nothing through," chanted Sam and Robbie Bell, one at his front and one at his back.

The sandbars were pink or violet drifts ahead. Where the light fell on the river, in a wandering from shore to shore, it was leaf-shaped spangles that trembled softly, while the dark of the river was calm. The willow trees leaned overhead and their trailing leaves hung like waterfalls in the morning air. The thing that seemed like silence must have been the endless cry of all the crickets and locusts in the world, rising and falling.

Every time William Wallace took hold of a big eel that slipped the net, the Malones all yelled, "Rassle with him, son!"

"Don't let her get too heavy, boys," said Doc.

"This is hard on catfish," William Wallace said once.

There were big and little fishes, dark and light, that they caught, good ones and bad ones, the same old fish.

"This is more shoes than I ever saw got together in any store," said Virgil when they emptied the net to the bottom. "Get going!" he shouted in the next breath.

The little Rippens who had stayed ahead in the woods stayed ahead on the river. Brucie, leading them all, made small jumps and hops as he went, sometimes on one foot, sometimes on the other.

The winding river looked old sometimes, when it ran wrinkled and deep under high banks where the roots of trees hung down, and sometimes it seemed to be only a young creek, shining with the colors of wildflowers. Sometimes sandbars in the shapes of fishes lay nose to nose, without the track of even a bird.

"Here comes some alligators," said Virgil. "Let's let them by."

They drew out on the shady side of the water, and three big alligators and four middle-sized ones went by, taking their own time.

"Look at their great big old teeth!" called a shrill voice. It was Grady making his only outcry, and the alligators were not showing their teeth at all.

"The better to eat folks with," said Doc from his boat, looking at him severely.

"Doc, you are bound to declare all you know," said Virgil. "Get going!"

When they started off again the first thing they caught in the net was the baby alligator.

"That's just what we wanted!" cried the Malones.

They set the little alligator down on a sandbar and he squatted perfectly still; they could hardly tell when it was he started to move. They watched with set faces his incredible mechanics, while the dogs after one bark stood off in inquisitive humility, until he winked.

"He's ours!" shouted all the Malones. "We're taking him home with us!"

"He ain't nothing but a little old baby," said William Wallace.

The Malones only scoffed, as if he might be only a baby but he looked like the oldest and worst lizard.

"What are you going to do with him?" asked Virgil.

"Keep him."

"I'd be more careful what I took out of this net," said Doc.

"Tie him up and throw him in the bucket," the Malones were saying to one another, while Doc was saying, "Don't come running to me and ask me what to do when he gets big."

They kept catching more and more fish, as if there was no end in sight.

"Look, a string of lady's beads," said Virgil. "Here, Sam and Robbie Bell."

Sam wore them round his head, with a knot over his forehead and loops round his ears, and Robbie Bell walked behind and stared at them.

In a shadowy place something white flew up. It was a heron and it went away over the dark treetops. William Wallace followed it with his eyes and Brucie clapped his hands, but Virgil gave a sigh, as if he knew that when you go looking for what is lost everything is a sign.

An eel slid out of the net.

"Rassle with him, son!" yelled the Malones. They swam like fiends.

"The Malones are in it for the fish," said Virgil.

It was about noon that there was a little rustle on the bank.

"Who is that yonder?" asked Virgil, and he pointed to a little undersized man with short legs and a little straw hat, who was following along on the other side of the river.

"Never saw him and don't know his brother," said Doc. Nobody had ever seen him before.

"Who invited you?" cried Virgil hotly. "Hi…!" and he made signs for the little undersized man to look at him, but he would not.

Stan Fellows

"Looks like a crazy man from here," said the Malones.

"Just don't pay any attention to him and maybe he'll go away," advised Doc.

But Virgil had already swum across and was up on the other bank. He and the stranger could be seen exchanging a word apiece and then Virgil put out his hand the way he would pat a child and patted the man to the ground. The little man got up again just as quickly, lifted his shoulders, turned round, and walked away with his hat tilted over his eyes.

When Virgil came back he said, "Little old man claimed he was harmless as a baby. I told him to just try horning in on this river and anything in it."

"What did he look like up close?" asked Doc.

"I didn't study how he looked," said Virgil. "But I don't like anybody to come looking at me that I am not familiar with." And he shouted, "Get going!"

"Things are moving in too great a rush," said Doc.

Brucie darted ahead and ran looking into all the bushes, lifting up the branches and peeping underneath.

"Not one of the Doyles has spoke a word," said Virgil.

"That's because they're not talkers," said Doc.

All day William Wallace kept diving to the bottom. Once he dived down and down into the dark water, where it was so still that nothing stirred, not even a fish, and so dark that it was no longer the muddy world of the upper river but the dark clear world of deepness, and he must have believed this was the deepest place in the whole Pearl River, and if she was not here she would not be anywhere. He was gone such a long time that the others stared hard at the surface of the water, through which the bubbles came from below. So far down and all alone, had he found Hazel? Had he suspected down there, like some secret, the real, the true trouble that Hazel had fallen into, about which words in a letter could not speak . . . how (who knew?) she had been filled to the brim with that elation that they all remembered, like their own secret, the elation that comes of great hopes and changes, sometimes simply of the harvest time, that comes with a little course of its own like a tune to run in the head, and there was nothing she could do about it—they knew—and so it had turned into despair? It could be nothing but the old trouble that William Wallace was finding out, reaching and turning in the gloom of such depths.

"Look down yonder," said Grady softly to Brucie.

He pointed to the surface, where their reflections lay colorless and still side by side. He touched his brother gently as though to impress him.

"That's you and me," he said.

Brucie swayed precariously over the edge, and Grady caught him by the seat of his overalls. Brucie looked, but showed no recognition. Instead, he backed away, and seemed all at once unconcerned and spiritless and pressed the nickel William Wallace had given him into his palm, rubbing it into his skin. Grady's inflamed eyes rested on the brown water. Without warning he saw something . . . perhaps the image in the river seemed to be his father, the drowned man—with arms open, eyes open, mouth open . . . Grady stared and blinked, again something wrinkled up his face.

And when William Wallace came up it was in an agony from submersion, which seemed an agony of the blood and of the very heart, so woeful he looked. He was staring round in astonishment, as if a long time had gone by, away from the pale world where the brown light of the sun and the river and the little party watching him trembled before the eyes.

"What did you bring up?" somebody called—was it Virgil?

One of his hands was holding fast to a little green ribbon of plant, root and all. He was surprised and let it go.

It was afternoon. The trees spread softly, the clouds hung wet and tinted. A buzzard turned a few slow wheels in the sky, and drifted upward. The dogs promenaded the banks.

"It's time we ate fish," said Virgil.

On a wide sandbar on which seashells lay they dragged up the haul and built a fire.

Then for a long time among clouds of odors and smoke, all half-naked except Doc, they cooked and ate catfish. They ate until the Malones groaned and all the Doyles stretched out on their faces, though for long after Sam and Robbie Bell sat up to their own little table on a cypress stump and ate on and on. Then they all were silent and still and one by one fell asleep.

"There ain't a thing better than fish," muttered William Wallace. He lay stretched on his back in the glimmer and shade of trampled sand. His sunburned forehead and cheeks seemed to glow with fire. His eyelids fell. The shadow of a willow branch dipped and moved over him. "There is nothing in the world as good as . . . fish. The fish of Pearl River." Then slowly he smiled. He was asleep.

But it seemed almost at once that he was leaping up, and one by one up sat the others in their ring and looked at him, for it was impossible to stop and sleep by the river.

"You're feeling as good as you felt last night," said Virgil, setting his head on one side.

"The excursion is the same when you go looking for your sorrow as when you go looking for your joy," said Doc.

But William Wallace answered none of them anything, for he was leaping all over the place and all over them and the feast and the bones of the feast, trampling the sand, up and down, and doing a dance so crazy that he would die next. He took a big catfish and hooked it to his belt-buckle and went up and down, so that they all hollered, and the tears of laughter streaming down his cheeks made him put his hand up, and the two days' growth of beard began to jump out, bright red.

But all of a sudden there was an even louder cry, something almost like a cheer, from everybody at once, and all pointed fingers moved from William Wallace to the river. In the center of three light-gold rings across the water was lifted first an old hoary head ("It has whiskers!" a voice cried) and then in an undulation loop after loop and hump after hump of a long dark body, until there were a dozen rings of ripples, one behind the other, stretching all across the river, like a necklace.

"The King of the Snakes!" cried all the Malones at once, in high tenor voices and leaning together.

"The King of the Snakes," intoned old Doc, alone in his profound bass.

"He looked you in the eye."

William Wallace stared back at the King of the Snakes with all his might.

It was Brucie that darted forward, dangling his little thread with the pin tied to it, going toward the water.

"That's the King of the Snakes!" cried Grady, who always looked after him.

Then the snake went down.

The little boy stopped with one leg in the air, spun around on the other, and sank to the ground.

"Git up," Grady whispered. "It was just the King of the Snakes. He went off whistling. Git up. It wasn't a thing but the King of the Snakes."

Brucie's green eyes opened, his tongue darted out, and he sprang up; his feet were heavy, his head light, and he rose like a bubble coming to the surface.

The thunder like a stone loosened and rolled down the bank.

They all stood unwilling on the sandbar, holding the net. In the eastern sky were the familiar castles and the round towers to which they were used, gray, pink, and blue, growing darker and filling with thunder. Lightning flickered in the sun along their thick walls. But in the west the sun shone with such a violence that in an illumination like a long-prolonged glare of lightning the heavens looked black and white; all color left the world, the goldenness of everything was like a memory, and only heat, a kind of glamour and oppression, lay on their heads. The thick heavy trees on the other side of the river were brushed with mile-long streaks of silver, and a wind touched each man on the forehead. At the same time there was a very long roll of thunder that began behind them, came up and down mountains and valleys of air, passed over their heads, and left them listening

still. With a small, near noise a mockingbird followed it, the little white bars of its body flashing over the willow trees.

"We are here for a storm now," Virgil said. "We will have to stay until it's over."

They retreated a little, and hard drops fell in the leathery leaves at their shoulders and about their heads.

"Magnolia's the loudest tree there is in a storm," said Doc.

Then the light changed the water, until all about them the woods in the rising wind seemed to grow taller and blow inward together and suddenly turn dark. The rain struck heavily. A huge tail seemed to lash through the air and the river broke in a wound of silver. In silence the party crouched and stooped beside the trunk of the great tree, which in the push of the storm rose full of a fragrant and unyielding weight. Where they all stared, past their tree was another tree, and beyond that another and another, all the way down the bank of the river, all towering and darkened in the storm.

"The outside world is full of endurance," said Doc. "Full of endurance."

Robbie Bell and Sam squatted down low and embraced each other from the start.

"Runs in our family to get struck by lightnin'," said Robbie Bell. "Lightnin' drawed a pitchfork right on our grandpappy's cheek, stayed till he died. Pappy got struck by some bolts of lightnin' and was dead three days, dead as that-there axe."

There was a succession of glares and crashes.

"This'n's goin' to be either me or you," said Sam. "Here come a little bug. If he go to the left, it's me, and to the right, it's you."

But at the next flare a big tree on the hill seemed to turn into fire before their eyes, every branch, twig, and leaf, and a purple cloud hung over it.

"Did you hear that crack?" asked Robbie Bell. "That were its bones."

"Why do you little niggers talk so much!" said Doc. "Nobody's profiting by this information."

"We always talks this much," said Sam, "but now everybody so quiet, they hears us."

The great tree, split and on fire, fell roaring to earth. Just at its moment of falling, a tree like it on the opposite bank split wide open and fell in two parts.

"Hope they ain't goin' to be no balls of fire come rollin' over the water and fry all the fishes with they scales on," said Robbie Bell.

The water in the river had turned purple and was filled with sudden currents and whirlpools. The little willow trees bent almost to its surface, bowing one after another down the bank and breaking under the storm. A great curtain of wet leaves was borne along before a blast of wind, and every human being was covered.

"Now us got scales," wailed Sam. "Us is the fishes."

"Shut up, little old colored children," said Virgil. "This isn't the way to act when somebody takes you out to drag a river."

"Poor lady's ghost, I bet it is scareder than us," said Sam.

"All I hoping is, us don't find her!" screamed Robbie Bell.

William Wallace bent down and knocked their heads together. After that they clung silently in each other's arms, the two black heads resting with wind-filled cheeks and tight-closed eyes one upon the other, until the storm was over.

"Right over yonder is Dover," said Virgil. "We've come all the way. William Wallace, you have walked on a sharp rock and cut your foot open."

In Dover it had rained and the town looked somehow like new. The wavy heat of late afternoon came down from the water tank and fell over everything like shiny mosquito-netting. At the wide place where the road was paved and patched with tar it seemed newly embedded with Coca-Cola tops. A few wet wagons and cars stood like a sparkling puzzle down the middle of the street. The old circus posters on the store were nearly gone, only bits, the snowflakes of white horses, clinging to its side. Morning-glory vines started almost visibly to grow over the roofs and cling round the ties of the railroad track, where bluejays lighted on the rails, and umbrella chinaberry trees hung heavily over the whole town dropping their first fall berries on to the tin roofs.

Each with his counted fish on a string, the members of the river-dragging party walked through the town. They went toward the town well, and there was Hazel's mother's house, but no sign of her yet, coming out. They all drank a dipper of the water, and still there was not a soul on the street. Even the bench in front of the store was empty.

But something told them somebody had come, for after one moment people began to look out of the store and out of the post office. All the bird dogs woke up to see such a large number of men and boys materialize suddenly with such a big catch of fish, and they ran out barking. The blue-jays flashed up from the track and screeched above the town, whipping through their tunnels in the chinaberry trees. In the café a nickel clattered inside a music-box and a love song began to play. The whole town of Dover began to throb in its wood and tin, like an old tired heart, when the men walked through once more, coming around again and going down the street carrying the fish, so drenched, exhausted, and muddy that no one could help but admire them.

William Wallace walked through the town as though he did not see anybody or hear anything. Yet he carried his great string of fish held high where it could be seen by all. Virgil came next, imitating William Wallace exactly, then the modest Doyles crowded by the Malones, who were holding up their alligator, tossing it in the air, even, like a father tossing his child. Following behind and pointing authoritatively at the ones in front strolled Doc, with Sam and Robbie Bell still chanting in his wake. In and out of the whole little line Grady and Brucie jerked about. Grady, with his head ducked, and stiff as a rod, walked with a springy limp; it made him look forever angry and unapproachable. Under his breath he was whispering, "Sty, sty, git out of my eye, and git on somebody passing by." He traveled on with narrowed shoulders, and kept his eye unerringly upon his little brother, wary and at the same time proud, as though he held a flying June bug on a string. Brucie, making a twanging noise with his lips, had shot forth again, and he was darting rapidly everywhere at once, delighted and tantalized, running in circles round William Wallace pointing to his fish. A frown of pleasure like the print of a bird's foot was stamped between his faint brows, and he trotted in some unknown realm of delight.

"Did you ever see so many fish?" said the people in Dover.

"How much are your fish, mister?"

"Would you sell your fish?"

"Is that all the fish in Pearl River?"

"How much you sell them all for? Everybody's?"

"Three dollars," said William Wallace suddenly.

The Malones were upon him and shouting, but it was too late.

And just as William Wallace was taking the money in his hand, Hazel's mother walked solidly out of her front door and saw it.

"You can't head her mother off," said Virgil. "Here she comes in full bloom."

But William Wallace turned his back on her, and on them all, for that matter, and that was the breaking-up of the party.

Just as the sun went down, Doc climbed his back steps, sat in his chair on the back porch where he sat in the evenings, and lighted his pipe. William Wallace hung out the net and came back and Virgil was waiting for him, so they could say good-evening to Doc.

"All in all," said Doc, when they came up, "I've never been on a better river-dragging, or seen better behavior. If it took catching catfish to move the Rock of Gibraltar, I believe this outfit could move it."

"We didn't catch Hazel Jamieson," said Virgil.

"What did you say?" asked Doc.

"He don't really pay attention," said Virgil. "I said, 'We didn't catch Hazel.'"

"Who says she was to be caught?" asked Doc. "She wasn't in there. Girls don't like the water—remember that. Girls don't just haul off and go jumping in rivers to get back at their husbands. They got other ways."

"Didn't you ever think she was in there?" asked William Wallace.

"Not once," said Doc.

"He's just smart," said Virgil, putting his hand on William Wallace's arm. "It's only because we didn't find her that he wasn't looking for her."

"I'm beholden to you for the net, anyway," said William Wallace.

"You're welcome to borry it again," said Doc.

On the way home Virgil kept saying, "Calm down, calm down, William Wallace."

"If he wasn't such an old skinny man I'd have wrung his neck for him," said William Wallace. "He had no business coming."

"He's too big for his britches," said Virgil. "Don't nobody know everything. And just because it's his net. Why does it have to be his net?"

"If it wasn't for being polite to old men, I'd have skinned him alive," said William Wallace.

"I guess he don't really know nothing about wives at all; his wife's so deaf," said Virgil.

"He don't know Hazel," said William Wallace. "I'm the only man alive knows Hazel: would she jump in the river or not, and I say she would. She jumped in because I was sitting on the back of my neck in a ditch singing, and that's

just what she ought to done. Doc ain't got no right to say one word about it."

"Calm down, calm down, William Wallace," said Virgil.

"If it had been you that talked like that I'd have broke every bone in your body," said William Wallace. "Just let you talk like that. You're my age and size."

"But I ain't going to talk like that," said Virgil. "What have I done the whole time but keep this river-dragging going straight and running even, without no hitches? You couldn't have drug the river a foot without me."

"What are you talking about!" cried William Wallace. "This wasn't your river-dragging! It wasn't your wife!" He jumped on Virgil and they began to fight.

"Let me up." Virgil was breathing heavily.

"Say it was my wife. Say it was my river-dragging."

"Yours!" Virgil was on the ground with William Wallace's hand putting dirt in his mouth.

"Say it was my net."

"Your net!"

"Get up then."

They walked along getting their breath. On a hill William Wallace looked down, and at the same time there went drifting by the sweet sounds of music outdoors. They were having the Sacred Harp Sing on the grounds of an old white church glimmering there at the crossroads, far below. He stared away as if he saw it minutely, as if he could see a lady in white take the flowered cover off the organ, which was set on a little slant in the shade, dust the keys, and start to pump and play. . . . He smiled faintly, as he would at his mother, and at Hazel, and at the singing women in his life, now all one young girl standing up to sing under the trees the oldest and longest ballads there were.

Virgil told him good-night and went into his own house and the door shut on him.

When he got to his own house, William Wallace saw to his surprise that it had not rained at all. But there, curved over the roof, was something he had never seen before as long as he could remember, a rainbow at night. In the light of the moon, which had risen again, it looked small and of gauzy material, like a lady's summer dress, a faint veil through which the stars showed.

He went up on the porch and in at the door, and all exhausted he had walked through the front room and through the kitchen when he heard his name called. After a moment he smiled, as if no matter what he might have hoped for in his wildest heart, it was better than that to hear his name called out in the house. The voice came out of the bedroom.

"What do you want?" he yelled, standing stock-still.

Then she opened the bedroom door with the old complaining creak and there she stood. She was not changed a bit.

"How do you feel?" he said.

"I feel pretty good. Not too good," Hazel said, looking mysterious.

"I cut my foot," said William Wallace, taking his shoe off to show the blood.

"How in the world did you do that?" she cried, with a step back.

"Dragging the river. But it don't hurt any longer."

"You ought to have been more careful," she said. "Supper's ready and I wondered if you would ever come home, or if it would be last night all over again. Go and make yourself fit to be seen," she said and ran away from him.

After supper they sat on the front steps a while.

"Where were you this morning when I came in?" asked William Wallace when they were ready to go in the house.

"I was hiding," she said. "I was still writing on the letter. And then you tore it up."

"Did you watch me when I was reading it?"

"Yes, and you could have put out your hand and touched me, I was so close."

But he bit his lip and gave her a little tap and slap and then turned her up and spanked her.

"Do you think you will do it again?" he asked.

"I'll tell my mother on you for this!"

"Will you do it again?"

"No!" she cried.

"Then pick yourself up off my knee."

It was just as if he had chased her and captured her again. She lay smiling in the crook of his arm. It was the same as any other chase at the end.

"I will do it again if I get ready," she said. "Next time will be different too."

Then she was ready to go in and rose up and looked out from the top step, out across the yard where the chinaberry tree was and beyond, into the dark fields where the lightning-bugs flickered away. He climbed to his feet too and stood beside her, with the frown on his face, trying to look where she looked. And after a few minutes she took him by the hand and led him into the house, smiling as if she were smiling down on him.

WHAT YOU DON'T KNOW WON'T HURT YOU
A BELATED REPORT ON THE PROGRESS OF MEDICAL RESEARCH

BY RICHARD WRIGHT

DECEMBER 1942

In the winter of 1932 I was employed by the Michael Reese Hospital, one of the largest and wealthiest hospitals in Chicago. I had obtained the job through a WPA placement agency and had been detailed to work as a porter in the Medical Research Institute. Along with three other Negro porters, I scrubbed floors, cleaned up the leavings of diabetic dogs, shaved the bellies of rabbits to prepare them for Aschheim-Zondek tests, administered diets to cancerous and tubercular rats and mice, sterilized dishes and cages, and fed lettuce to guinea pigs that would be used in Wassermann tests.

Of the other three Negroes who worked with me, one was a boy of about my own age, Fred, who was either sleepy or drunk most of the time. The other two Negroes were elderly and had been employed in the research institute for fifteen years or more. One was Homer, a short, black, morose bachelor; the other was Allen, a tall, yellow, spectacled fellow who spent his spare time keeping track of world events through the Chicago *Daily Tribune*. In fact, it was Allen's love of the accuracy of the news stories in the *Tribune* that formed the basis for a near murder and one of the weirdest upsets to medical research in the history of the United States.

We four Negroes worked in a huge room filled with many rows of high steel tiers. Perched upon each of these tiers were layers of steel cages containing the dogs, rats, mice, rabbits, and guinea pigs. Each cage was labeled in some indecipherable scientific jargon. Along the walls of the room were long charts with zigzagging red and black lines. As we four went about our duties we would often gape in wonder at doctors examining the animals and tracing complicated lines upon the charts, but none of us had any notion of the meaning of the experiments. Once or twice I asked a doctor what was wrong with a certain animal and the doctor replied, "Bring me the next rat, please."

The labors of the doctors proceeded on a plane far beyond our consciousness. Of course, we knew vaguely that certain rabbits were being used in Aschheim-Zondek tests to determine the possible pregnancy of women, or that certain cages contained cancerous and tubercular rats and mice, or that certain dogs were diabetic, or that certain guinea pigs were being used in Wassermann tests, and so on. But we were never concerned if the animals died or got well; all of them looked more or less alike to us and for the most part we ignored them.

Now amid this ordered progress of medical research, Homer and Allen carried on an old feud, the origin and cause of which neither Fred nor I could guess. We had been told that during the early years of their employment they had been great pals, but of late they had grown to hate each other so much that they could scarcely endure each other's presence. I can account for their mutual hate only on the basis of boredom, vague resentment at their dull lives, and a general feeling of futility. It seemed that they felt a causeless anger toward something they could not see or touch, and they turned upon each other like those dogs that snap at the air and whirl in circles when an aimless pain strikes them....

The tug of war between the two elderly men reached a climax at noon one winter day. It was incredibly cold and an icy gale swept up and down the Chicago streets with blizzard force. The door of the animal-filled room was locked, for we had always insisted that we be allowed one hour in which to eat and rest. Fred and I were sitting on wooden boxes, eating our lunches out of paper bags. Homer was washing his hands at the sink. Allen was sitting upon a rickety stool, munching an apple and reading the Chicago *Daily Tribune*.

Now and then a devocalized dog (to keep the dogs from howling, their vocal cords had been slit) would lift his nose to the ceiling and gape soundlessly. The lonely piping of guinea pigs floated unheeded about us. Hay rustled as a rabbit leaped restlessly about its pen. A rat scampered about its steel prison. Allen tapped the newspaper for attention.

"It says here," Allen mumbled through a mouthful of apple, "that this is the coldest day since 1888."

Fred and I sat unconcerned. Homer chuckled softly.

"What in hell you laughing at?" Allen demanded of Homer.

"You can't believe that damn *Tribune*," Homer said.

"How come I can't?" Allen demanded. "It's the world's greatest newspaper."

Homer did not reply; he shook his head pityingly and chuckled again.

"Stop laughing at me!" Allen said angrily.

"I laugh as much as I wanna," Homer said. "You don't know what you talking about. The *Herald-Examiner* says it's the coldest day since 1873."

"But the *Trib* oughta know," Allen countered. "It's older'n that *Examiner*."

"That damn *Trib* tells lies!" Homer drowned out Allen's voice.

"How in hell do *you* know?" Allen asked with rising anger.

The argument waxed until Allen shouted that if Homer didn't shut up he was going to "cut his black throat."

Homer whirled from the sink, his hands dripping soapy water, his eyes blazing.

"Take that back," Homer said.

"I take nothing back! What you wanna do about it?" Allen taunted.

The two elderly Negroes glared at each other. I wondered if the quarrel was really serious, or if it would turn out harmlessly as so many others had.

Suddenly Allen dropped the Chicago *Daily Tribune* and pulled a long knife from his pocket; his thumb pressed a button and a gleaming steel blade leaped out. Homer stepped back quickly and seized an ice pick that was stuck in a wooden board above the sink.

"Put down that knife," Homer said.

"Stay 'way from me, or I'll cut your throat," Allen warned.

Homer lunged with the ice pick. Allen dodged out of range. They circled each other like fighters in a prize-ring. The cancerous and tubercular rats and mice leaped about their cages. The guinea pigs whistled in fright. The diabetic dogs bared their teeth in our direction. The Aschheim-Zondek rabbits flopped their ears and tried to hide in the corners of their pens. Allen now crouched and sprang forward with the knife. Homer retreated. The eyes of both men were hard and unblinking; they breathed deeply.

"Say, cut it out!" I called in alarm.

"Them damn fools is really fighting," Fred said in amazement.

Slashing at each other, Homer and Allen surged up and down the aisles of steel tiers. Suddenly Homer uttered a bellow and charged into Allen and swept him violently backward. Allen grasped Homer's hand to keep the ice pick from sinking into his chest. Homer broke free and charged Allen again, sweeping him into an animal-filled steel tier. The tier balanced itself on its edge for an indecisive moment, then toppled.

Like kingpins, one steel tier lammed into another, then they all crashed to the floor with a sound as of the roof falling. The whole aspect of the room altered quicker than the eye could follow. Homer and Allen stood stock-still, their eyes fastened upon each other, their pointed weapons raised; but they were dimly conscious of the havoc that churned about them.

The steel tiers lay jumbled; the doors of the cages swung open; and the rats and mice and dogs and rabbits moved over the floor in wild panic. The Wassermann guinea pigs were squealing as though judgment day had come. Here and there an animal had been crushed beneath a cage.

All four of us looked at one another. We knew what this meant. We might lose our jobs. Fred rushed to the door to make sure that it was locked. I glanced at the clock and saw that it was 12:30. We had one half-hour of grace.

"Come on," Fred said uneasily, "we got to get this place cleaned."

Homer and Allen stared at each other, both doubting.

"Give me your knife, Allen," I said.

"Naw! Take Homer's ice pick *first*," Allen said.

"The hell you say!" Homer said. "Take his knife *first*!"

A knock sounded on the door.

"Sssshh," Fred said.

We waited. We heard footsteps going away. We'll all lose our jobs, I thought.

Persuading the fighters to surrender their weapons was a difficult task, but at last it was done and we could begin to right things. Slowly Homer stooped and tugged at one of the steel tiers. Allen stooped to help him. Both men seemed to be acting in a dream. Soon, however, all four of us were working frantically, watching the clock.

As we labored we conspired to keep the fight a secret; we agreed to tell the doctors—if any should ask—that we had not been in the room during our lunch hour; we felt that that lie would explain why no one had unlocked the door when the knock had come.

We righted the tiers and replaced the cages; then we were faced with the impossible job of sorting the cancerous and tubercular rats and mice, the diabetic dogs, the Aschheim-Zondek rabbits, and the Wassermann guinea pigs. Whether we kept our jobs or not depended upon how shrewdly we could cover up all evidences of the fight. It was pure guesswork, but we had to try to put the animals back into their correct cages. We knew from memory that certain rats or mice went into certain cages, but we did not know *what* rat or mouse went into *what* cage. We didn't know a tubercular mouse from a cancerous mouse....

First we sorted the dogs; that was fairly easy, for we could remember the size and color of most of them. But the rats and mice and guinea pigs baffled us completely.

We put our heads together and pondered. It was a strange scientific conference; the fate of the entire Medical Research Institute rested in our hands.

As we remembered the number of rats, mice, or guinea pigs that went into a given cage, we supplied the number helter-skelter from those animals we could catch on the floor. We discovered that many rats, mice, and guinea pigs were missing; they had been killed in the scuffle. We solved that problem by taking healthy stock from other cages and putting them into cages with sick animals. We repeated this process until we were certain that, numerically at least, all of the animals were accounted for.

The rabbits came last. We broke the rabbits down into two groups: those that had fur on their bellies and those that did not. We knew that all of those rabbits that had shaven bellies were undergoing Aschheim-Zondek tests. But in what pen did a given rabbit belong? We did not know. I solved the problem very simply. I counted the shaven rabbits; they numbered seventeen. I counted the pens labeled "Aschheim-Zondek," then proceeded to drop a shaven rabbit into each pen at random. And again we were numerically successful.

Lastly we wrapped all of the dead animals in newspapers and hid their bodies in a garbage can.

At a few minutes to one the room was in order; that is, the kind of order that we four Negroes could figure out. I unlocked the door and we sat waiting, whispering, vowing secrecy, wondering what the reaction would be.

Finally a doctor came, gray-haired, white-coated, spec-

Loren MacIver

tacled, efficient, serious, taciturn, bearing a tray upon which lay a bottle of mysterious fluid, and a hypodermic needle.

"My rats, please."

Allen shuffled forward to serve him. We held our breath. Allen got the cage which he knew the doctor always asked for at that hour and brought it forward. One by one, Allen took out the rats and held them as the doctor solemnly injected the mysterious fluid under their skins.

"Thank you, Allen," the doctor murmured.

"Not at all, sir," Allen mumbled with a suppressed gasp.

When the doctor had gone we looked at one another, hardly daring to believe that our secret would be kept. We were so anxious that we did not know whether to curse or laugh. Another doctor came.

"Give me A-Z rabbit number 14."

"Yes, sir," I said.

I brought him the rabbit and he took it upstairs to the operating rooms. We waited for repercussions. None came.

Throughout the afternoon the doctors came and went. We waited upon them with tense, forced smiles, watching their faces closely. But we could detect nothing. At quitting time we felt almost triumphant.

"They won't never know," Allen boasted in a whisper.

I saw Homer stiffen. I knew that he was aching to dispute Allen's optimism, but the memory of the fight he had just had was so fresh in his mind that he could not move or speak.

Another day went by and nothing happened. Then still another day. The doctors examined the animals and wrote in their little black books and continued to trace red and black lines upon the charts.

A week passed and we felt out of danger. Not one question had been asked.

Of course we were much too modest to make our contribution known, but we often wondered what went on in the laboratories after that secret disaster. Was some scientific hypothesis, well on its way to validation and ultimate public use, discarded because of unexpected findings on that cold winter morning? Was some tested principle given a new and strange refinement because of fresh, remarkable evidence? Did some brooding researcher get a wild, if brief, glimpse of a new scientific truth? At any rate we never heard.

THE PEOPLE AT WAR
DOWNEASTERS BUILDING SHIPS
BY JOHN DOS PASSOS

MARCH 1943

The whistle blows. At the wide sliding doors of the long building shaped like a shoebox, with oblong windows stained dark blue, figures appear. One man runs out, then two, then three, cantering across the broad stretch of cinders in the windy winter sunlight. More follow until hurrying lines are converging on the low shed where they punch their time-cards. The morning shift is off.

A black dense crowd now is pushing slowly out through the gates. Their faces are gray and yellowish under the dirt of eight hours' work. They wear visored caps pulled down over their foreheads, heavy gloves well grimed, thick clothes bunched at the waist under coveralls, or woolen trousers tucked into arctics or lumbermen's boots. There are a few red-checked breeches or green-and-red plaid shirts, and occasional red deer hunters' caps that have a look of the north woods. They all wear their pictures on oval identification badges pinned to their caps or to the breasts of their shirts. They are in a hurry. It's cold. Their bodies, baggy with sweaters and heavy woolen pants, move sluggishly. As they flow in a packed mass out the gate and across the railroad track you begin to make out the difference in faces. The clothes, the boots, the caps, the gloves are more or less interchangeable, but faces are sharp or blunt, ruddy or pale, old or young. They all have a fixed intent look. Some of them are women. It's surprising how many women. Middle-aged women. Young girls. They wear the same clothes, their faces are bleared under the same grime. It's hard to tell them from the men and boys.

As the crowd reaches the sidewalk it dissolves suddenly into brisk individuals hurrying in different directions, threes

Westinghouse ad, 1940's.

and fours chatting as they turn off on the sidewalks, or stand stamping their feet waiting along the counter of the hotdog stand or jam the doors of the shabby lunchroom across the street. They line up for busses. They scatter among the parked cars that are ranked in all the open lots and line all the streets as far as you can see. The streets that were empty a few minutes before are jammed now with slow-moving strings of cars. A procession of cars two abreast fills the right lane of the tall soaring girder-work bridge that crosses the great tidal river swirling brown and silvery past rocks rimmed with ice under the high bank tufted with bright white birches and green firs on the other side.

The cars are packed tight with bodies in bulky clothes. As the cars cross the bridge every face turns to look downstream at the long buildings and the iron spiderwebs of the ways and at the destroyers lying alongside the wharf, spare gray pointed hulls still streaked and checkered with yellow underpaint, narrow decks encumbered with temporary housing where the shipfitters are at work. The boat that shows a string of red, white, yellow, blue bunting fluttering in the sharp wind was launched only yesterday. That is the end product of their work.

They are in a hurry to get home. More than half of them still live out from town, in big, white, oldtime farm-houses linked by a kitchen wing and a woodshed to their great barns, standing back from the road maybe at the top of a rolling grass lot, with the woods behind them, or in rough board shacks with belching stovepipes in clearings in the woods, or in the small gray-gabled houses grouped sedately round the seaweedy rocks of old fishing coves where dories and power-boats are anchored off worm-eaten wharves.

Some of them live in gingerbread bungalows with scalloped composition roofing beside filling stations along highways, or in half-slums of gawky, long-unpainted, red and yellow four-family houses that radiate from shoe factories and old textile mills in the patchwork industrial towns at the falls of the rivers. A third of them have moved in near their work and are camping in tourist cabins and in rows of silvery trailers nailed down to the ground with tar paper to keep the drafts out from under, or in the rooming houses and boarding houses of the shipyard town itself, or in the moderately comfortable dwellings left over from the last war, or in the carefully designed colonies of well-equipped brick houses that were laid out a couple of years ago in the last flicker of social ardor of New Deal housing, or in the rows of prefabricated barracks on stilts that are now being slapped together with little regard for the climate or the standard of living. [...]

For many of the men, women, and boys the work is novel and exciting. Out of more than twenty thousand employees only a couple of thousand ever worked in a shipyard before. They are making good money, they are learning new skills, and every twenty-one days now they see the end product of their work slide off the ways into the brown river.

Two great revolutions have occurred in the shipbuilding industry since the last war. One is that assembly-line methods have been made easier by the use of welding to replace most riveting as a method of gluing steel plates together, and the other is the employment of women, which started on a large scale only in the fall of this past year. With the payment of equal wages to women who do the same work as men, one of the aims of the bitter social struggles of the past twenty-five years has quietly been attained. There have been no headlines or brass bands. Equal wages have not spread through other than war-production industries yet, but the results have been so surprisingly good that I think it is safe to say that the principle has at last been established.

At this shipyard the women's personnel director told me that in the three months during which they had been hiring women only twenty out of four hundred that started training had had to be dropped for any reason at all. [...]

The personnel director talked enthusiastically about the work of the women in the yard. "These Maine women have so much stuff," she kept saying. It was expected that they would be useful as messengers and for winding asbestos covering on steam pipes and for cleaning up and painting

and similar light work, but it was a surprise to everybody that they should turn out to be first-rate welders, that there would be three women dressing tools in the blacksmith shop, or that they would be running lathes and drill presses, or doing complicated layout work and operating a plate-rolling machine. "In this yard women work in every department, from the tool room to shipfitting on board the launched hulls."

"Where do they come from?"

Well, about a third of them were young wives of men in the service who had to support themselves and wanted to make their work count.... A great many of them were hardworking farmers' wives, a lot were millhands from textile and shoe factories. Some of them were tough little numbers from juke joints and dance halls. Of course the management was very much afraid of allure, afraid that sex would raise its grisly head; but actually some of the best welders were from among these tough little girls. On the whole, women with some sort of artistic or craft-working skill and jitterbugs made the best welders. The little girls were particularly useful for getting into tight corners in shipfitting. In fact in some shipyards it was said they were trying to get midgets. The stout old biddies were harder to train and usually ended up cleaning or painting. "And let me tell you that it takes stuff to handle a welding arc all day long—stuff and skill. They are most of them scared to death of it at first on account of the roar and splutter and the fumes, but after three or four days they get used to it and will weld two steel plates together as coolly as they'd sew a hem on a dress."

The only change that has been made in the plant to accommodate the growing female contingent has been the installing of new washrooms and toilets for women, with a matron or industrial nurse in charge of each. As they couldn't buy plumbing, they had been using the orchid-colored fittings for the bathrooms of a wealthy glamour boy's yacht that had been under construction in the yard when the war began. The girls thought they were great.

Naturally the men have been quicker to break in, as most of them were what the manager called "Yankee mechanics" to begin with: part-time farmers and fishermen who were accustomed to tinkering with their own cars and farming machinery and marine engines, or else garage men and filling-station attendants, men from building trades and from textile mills, with a sprinkling of schoolteachers, clerks from stores, and office workers. All of them, almost without exception, came from inside the State, and the great majority from within a radius of thirty miles around the shipyard. It's surprising how many old men have come out. Many of them had been foremen or skilled operators in shipyards during the last war. It's the old men who contribute the traditional knowhow and form the backbone of the training system that is turning shoe clerks, filling-station attendants, and farmhands into efficient operators of machine tools, so fast that even under the constant crippling loss of trained men to the draft, with the coupling of new methods with old skills the efficiency of the yard has been increasing month by month.

Though the old men have played a part in the building of steel ships, it is in the small yards that have sprung up along the coast to build barges and tugs and minesweepers out of wood that they have really come into their own. Outside of a few yachts and fishing boats, there had been no wooden ships built along the New England coast since the over-size schooners built during the last war. At the yard I visited they told me that when its promoters, who up to last spring operated only a small marine railway, came back from Washington with the money to build wooden ships, they couldn't find a man who knew how to handle an adze.

Only gradually, out of lobstermen's shacks and fishing coves and farmhouses, the old ship carpenters began to show their grizzled and mustached faces. They knew how to shape oak timbers. From the laying of the first keel they made building the ship a training school for the medley of lumbermen, granite workers, house carpenters, farmers, and fishermen who were attracted to the growing yard by an average wage of seventy-eight cents an hour—not a high wage by some standards but more than they could make felling trees in the woods. As they worked the science of building wooden hulls had to be invented all over again. They had the government orders and the financial setup and the great oaks ready marked to be cut in the forested river valleys, but they couldn't go ahead until they got the knowhow out of the heads of the old men. They never managed to get together more than a hundred real ship carpenters. The youngsters of them were in their sixties. The oldest in the yard I visited was eighty-four.

Shaping oak timbers with an adze takes a very special skill and is heavy work besides. Most of the men taken on for training were handy with an axe and accustomed to lumbering and carpenter work. They learned fast. In this yard

they have about nine hundred men at work and forty girls. They could use five hundred more hands any day if they could get them. They are starting to work out a system of half-time work for poultry raisers and farmers and even local business people who could take four hours a day off from their own affairs to help in the yard.

Here the women paint and sew on pipe covering and spin oakum for calking and drive in the wooden bungs that cover the heads of the bolts that hold the joints together. You can see them perched up along with the men on the scaffolding that surrounds the huge oaken skeletons of the barges. They have an air of going at their new work with a great deal of zest. They are learning how to build boats, and the lumbermen and house carpenters are learning how to build boats, and the management and office force made up of a yachtsman and some ship-chandlers and salesmen and an architectural draftsman and a retired banker and miscellaneous business men are learning how to build boats, and they show every sign of enjoying it.

It was a magnificent day—a slaty sky full of cotton clouds and a bright sunlight that shimmered on the blue-steel bay so full of islands densely set with dark spruce and blue balsam. A sharp wind ruffled the scalloped waves to indigo with speeding cat's-paws. The air smelled of cold sea water and rankly of fresh-sawed green oak and steamed planking. From the sawmill up the hill there came the muffled whir of buzz saws. Above every other sound rose the clear ringing crack of the adze on sound timber. The ribs of the row of big coal barges stood up along the edge of the water, a glistening cold yellow from out of crisscrossed scaffolding and runways. The bustle of men in lumbermen's clothes about the oaken skeletons of the ships, and the old red brick of the buildings across the narrow shining tongue of the harbor, and the white gables and the church spire of the old Downeast town climbing up a spur of a big wooded hill gave you the feeling of being in a steel engraving of a hundred years ago.

They were getting ready to launch a minesweeper. The pennants run up in a string fore and aft from the spar above the pilot-house were fluttering briskly over the tubby vessel shining with new gray paint. Two men in a sharp-pointed little ochre-colored dory that danced prettily on the small sparkling waves were hammering at the forward part of the cradle. Then they drew away with a couple of strokes of the oars and the gray boat started to slide gently forward. The bow bit into the water as she gathered speed, rose for a sort of nod; then the minesweeper, gliding free of the tangled

timbers of the cradle, went skimming smoothly as a duck out into the bay.

Meanwhile work went on on the other hulls. Outside of a small group from the management and a few invited guests muffled up against the cold, stamping their feet on the dock round the bashful figure of the little girl who had broken the bottle on the ship's prow, no one had even looked round. A few months back all shipyards used to shut down for the day and serve out beer to all hands when they launched a ship, but now they launch too many of them to bother about it.

At the big yard up the coast where they build freighters, speed of production has reached such a point that you can see a steel ship grow before your eyes as the huge sections are put together. The whole process to a layman seems strangely simple, like putting models together out of children's construction toys. That probably accounts for the fascination shipyards have always had for men who worked in them. In a shipyard you can see what you are producing.

Sitting in a glassed-in office that looked out on acres of new barracks under construction, I was asking a member of the management whether in his opinion the day-to-day news of the war had any effect on the efficiency of the workers. He couldn't see that it did. [...]

I asked about labor-management committees. On the whole they were working out pretty well, he said. This was a union yard and you had to be careful not to let the union run away with the committee. About a quarter of the suggestions made through the committee were really worth while. Yes, there were suggestions as to the technique of production, but not many of the men knew enough about it yet to have much to offer; most suggestions were about safety precautions, methods of fighting absenteeism and lateness, and ideas for posters and slogans.

In this part of the world unions are still a subject nobody wants to be quoted on. There's a background of bitter anti-union prejudice, not entirely confined to management. But even here there certainly isn't the bitterness there used to be. [...] Teamwork between the unions and management with production as the only aim is far from being perfect yet. High wages still cause management pain, even though they know the government is paying the bill, and when working men are told that capital isn't making enormous profits they simply don't believe it. But whether you ask the personnel manager or the union organizer he'll roll back his eyes and tell you that perfect harmony exists. [...]

In a famous old shipyard in Massachusetts the secretary of the labor-management committee gave me, as he talked about his work, management's picture of a harmonious arrangement with labor. He was evidently an old shipbuilder himself. He was a ruddy-faced man with a clear skin younger than his years, and clear gray eyes. What he enjoyed most in life, you could see, was getting ships built. He talked with pleasure of the great expansion of the yard in the past ten years since naval building had started up again. That had meant a labor force doubling and tripling and expanding almost indefinitely. In spite of that the oldtimers still dominated the yard. It pleased him that so many of the men who had worked in the yard during the expansion of the last war had come back, and that their sons were coming to work, and that, now that girls and women were being employed, most of them were the wives and daughters of old employees who had been drafted. Of course some troublemakers and union-minded mavericks had come in—among so many you had to have some bad eggs—but on the whole they had been able to keep it in the family.

In fact, the majority of their workers still lived within a fifteen-mile radius. Several thousand families had moved into the adjoining towns, to be sure, but surprisingly few of them came from outside of the State or even from very far. I asked if the government would put up housing for them. He shook his head. I got to laughing. I'd been asking about that up at the town square, and had been left with no doubts as to how the local business men felt. They dreaded government housing as much as the managers of industries dreaded national labor organizations. I had been told that all available houses were just about full now and that some more houses would have to be built before the shipyard reached the peak of employment which was expected sometime next spring. Private enterprise was taking care of the matter. No, sir, there'd be no over-building. They'd learned their lesson in the last war; they weren't going to get stung this time.

This was a densely populated area of sprawling towns that were all one another's suburbs, fairly well linked up by trains, busses, and streetcars. Streets and streets of big glum houses left over from the real estate booms of the past. Along the beaches and rocky necks of the shore there were thousands of vacant seaside cottages. At the Chamber of Commerce they were planning to fill them up with shipyard workers. Everybody was very proud that this region contained such a wealth of housing as well as of skilled labor. If outsiders only kept their noses out, they said, they could handle their war problems very nicely by themselves. [...]

When I asked him my stock question as to whether what they read in the papers or heard over the radio had any effect on the men's efficiency and enthusiasm he said it was a poser. He guessed not many of 'em took much stock in the newspapers. Sure they listened to the radio, but most of it went in one ear and out the other. No, he never heard much talk about the news. Of course Pearl Harbor had

given us all a shock. We knew we were in for it then; we knew the war had to be won, in fact we couldn't imagine not winning it. No, not even the North African landings had caused much of a ripple. "But I'll tell you what does: when one of the ships we built ourselves is sunk, that has an effect.... That aircraft carrier, now, the men sure felt her loss. There are men in the yard who knew every bolt and rivet on that ship. They knew the crews too. Skeleton crews are attached to the ships as soon as they are started. Losing that carrier really brought the thing home. There wasn't a man here who wasn't crazy to get to work on a new one. They circulated a petition and sent it to the Navy Department asking to have the new one called the *Pearl Harbor*."

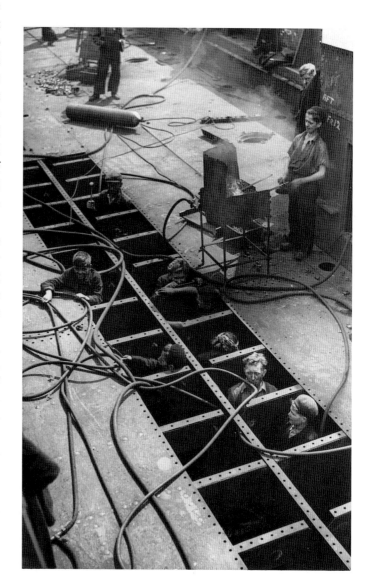

As this was a man who had spent his life in shipbuilding I asked him finally how the workers they had now compared with those who had come into the yards during the last war. His idea was that there had been a great improvement. Of the young men who came as apprentices and trainees more had had at least a year of high school; they learned quicker, dressed better, were generally better behaved—a higher type of man than the bunch of raw laborers who couldn't speak English who had flocked there to work twenty-five years ago. [...]

The question on everybody's lips in these parts is how the rest of the economy is going to be able to continue in operation when most of its manpower, and especially the most energetic and enterprising slice of it, has been siphoned off into war production and the armed services. High wages are doing very little to keep the regular economy going. The more you ask the less you know about where money is going. In one town they tell you that retail sales are only up thirty per cent while the payroll has been multiplied by fifty. Except for the increased money spent everywhere on food and drink, increased rents that are giving landlords and rooming-house keepers a profit, and the large turnover of novelty goods of the cheapest and trashiest type, there's no great sign of the dreaded boom in consumption. In the cities there has been a big sale of women's furs. Clothing stores are doing well, lunchrooms and restaurants thrive as more housewives go into industry and give up cooking meals at home, but none of the increase amounts to enough to compare with the vastly enlarged earnings. Nor do bank deposits or bond sales. "By gum," said the secretary of one Chamber of Commerce, "I think they are putting it in their socks."

Wherever you talk to them the attitude of men in retail and service businesses can only be described as inert. Business men in the Northeast have been so long encouraged to blame Washington for everything that goes wrong that they seem to have lost the ability to strike out for themselves. Now that they have an opportunity to reap a harvest they haven't the initiative left to work their way through the red tape and the obstacles, not at all insurmountable, that stand in the way of finding something to sell and inducing somebody to buy it. [...]

In the small towns you have a feeling that the economic life of the community has lost its roots. It is only the giant heavy-industry concerns, through which money is piped directly from Washington into production, that have sap in them. Typical of small business men was a man I met who was driving a taxi down in Maine. At home, in another Downeast town that had had no war industries to keep it alive, he had run a hardware store for many years and before that had edited the newspaper. He was a dignified, portly man with steel-gray hair, the very type of successful Rotarian. When he had found he couldn't make both ends meet at home (he had two boys in the Army and their leaving had made things kind of empty) he had driven his car up here and licensed it as a taxi. Yes, he'd been making quite a lot of money transporting war workers and service men, but after the first of January he understood taxis were to be allowed only three gallons of gas a day. He wouldn't be able to make a living at that and would have to find some other job. A reporter for the local newspaper was in the cab. As we were getting out the driver turned to him and said, "Say, how about getting me a job on your paper?"

It was a sunny winter afternoon. In the rosy haze off the bay the quiet streets of stately old mansarded houses and the bare elms and the old brick warehouses had that familiar remembered look of being in a weathered steel engraving. Roaming around the town I turned down a street that led to the wharves and came upon an old-time barber college. The dingy chairs were empty and covered with dust. Gone were the strapping lady barbers and the bleary-eyed youths who in the old days would have been standing in a row rasping the fur off the chins of hungry bindlestiffs or drunken lumberjacks who had blown in their pay, or cutting their hair and putting their ears and noses in jeopardy with flashing razors and clickclacking scissors. No shabby men were lolling in the chairs waiting for a fifteen-cent shave. The soap had dried in the mugs; the mirrors, streaked brown, were murky with grime. Only in the darkest corner an elderly man in his shirtsleeves was laboriously scraping the upturned cheek of another tattered relic of the Hoovervilles of the past. I guess there was nobody else in town broke enough to be there. The cut-rate shave was another casualty of high wages.

Up on the hill the shopping streets were full of midday bustle. Women with bundles were shoving in and out of shops. People were holding small children up to the show windows of a department store to see a big dummy Santa Claus continually shake with mechanized laughter. Candy stores, restaurants, and soda fountains were full of sailors from the nearby Naval Base. As I still had a couple of hours before train time, I set out to find a cocktail lounge to settle down to read the paper in. Cocktail lounges there were, but so lugubriously untenanted that I decided to go somewhere else. Sauntering farther along the main street, I came to a vaudeville theater that advertised "Songs from the Gay Nineties." People were filing past the ticket office. The stout young woman in a fur neckpiece and a shovel-shaped black hat who was in line ahead of me cried out in surprise when she reached the window. "You?... Why, goodness, how long have you been working here?"

"Three days," the black-eyed girl inside said rather proudly.

"Why on earth don't you go to the shipyard? Lil's there and everybody."

The girl, who evidently thought better than that of herself, flashed her eyes as she rattled the change-making machine and said resentfully, "To hell with the shipyard."

"I bet you are not making your car-fare."

The girl behind the window didn't answer. She dropped her eyes to her tickets.

The stout young woman tossed her shovel-shaped hat and chanted as she flounced off into the theater: "You'd be doing better for yourself, dearie."

Going Home

by Alfred Kazin

April 1945

Rain fell just as they left Chicago; by the time the train swept past the mills at Gary, the smoke over the lakefront had turned yellow and green in the downpour and the twilight. Great fires licked upward from the furnaces, and the stacks were so funneled, huge, and curled that they made him think of his mother's Victorian lampshades standing massively on a hill. He looked at the rain trudging against the windows, the Negro girl who had fallen asleep in the next seat with her mouth open, took a deep breath of the steamed air in the car, and sighed with relief. He was looking forward to the drink and dinner he could buy on the train out of his discharge pay, and when he thought of the hours he had lain on a bench in the Chicago waiting room, he felt he deserved a good one. Christ, peace again. He was out of the Army, out of Chicago at last, and now out of the rain. It would be good to get home.

The train rattled and curved along the tracks like a tail looking for its body. Five o'clock. The rain was coming down hard, and it was suddenly all black outside. When he looked at the windows he could see only the white disks in the car ceilings and his own thoughts. Ruth came into the window and as quickly went away; he could not find her anywhere now. Then he saw, like lost goods dredged from the sea, the maroon Army bathrobe with its worn lettering, AUSMD, the files in Ward C-7, an open notebook, a hypodermic of sodium amytal, and the dark, almost stupidly shy face of Captain Danziger looking at him with the greatest attention. It seemed to him that the psychiatrist was sitting at a table with his chin thoughtfully in his hands, the open notebook before him, and that *he* was under the table with his knees up to his face.

"Locomotive," by Edward Hopper.

Danziger was looking for him. By God, he could look far. All that was over.

Danziger would not go away. Danziger made him think of the hospital, and the hospital made him think of the wire fencing between the kitchen and Ward C-7. He heard the recurrent clang of the locks and gates that went on all day between the hospital and the camp; suddenly it all went bad again. He felt as if he were made of the grime that lay on the window ledge; it was hard to believe that he was traveling at all. He looked at the Negro girl beside him, but her sleeping open mouth made it worse. She was too far away. The car lights swam revolvingly in the windows, a red-faced Marine just in front of him snored, and as the train jolted and screeched its way forward it seemed to him that the rattle of the wheels was asking the question he had in his mind: where?

He turned on his side, pressed his nose against the cold window, and thought how good it would be to fall asleep. But his mind kept turning with the disks shining back from the windows, and when he peered out he could see nothing but trees, farms already dead in the night, and the lights of an automobile winking its way down a small-town street. His loneliness lay in his stomach like the hard weight of something he had eaten and disliked, and when he fingered his rough new overcoat and looked down at his Army shoes, the mixed clothes he was in laughed back at him like the mixed state he was in—not a soldier, not free yet—and he suddenly wished he were back in bed in Ward C-7. It was not so bad, once they put away the sodium amytal and closed the notebook. It was only the notebook that had ever frightened him, for he had dreamed, the night his talk had been first taken down, that his veins were open dripping blood into the notebook, and that behind it Danziger's dark, secret face was piling up notes like a bank teller behind his cage. Danziger was writing a book. Hadn't the bastard told it around himself? He was writing a book out of endless drinks out of the veins of patients under the influence of sodium amytal in Ward C-7. He was frightened when he thought of the book. It stood like the memory of impotence between him and Ruth. Once in public school he had done something wrong and they had given him a red C on his report card: C for Bad Conduct. Of course it wasn't right for an Army psychiatrist to flaunt his private research in the hearing of his patients, but a man bubbled up serenely from his unconscious after seven and a half grains of sodium amytal, and this was a chance no Danziger, full of *his* post-war plans, would miss. The sodium amytal went into the veins. In the dream Danziger drank the veins. Yes, he had been let out at last: discharged, cut off the tree, a red crack down his service papers telling its own story to anyone who could know, but glad to be out. But Danziger had no right! He had no right!

He lifted himself past the Negro girl, sauntered down the aisle, and drank three cups of water very quickly. The car was full of sailors and soldiers, weary middle-aged women with cheap luggage and service stars on their coats. He wondered if they would see his Army shoes and realize, at least, that he had been in. He still had his long Army underwear, shoes, and shirt, but they were all inside. Like him. Would they know? They would never know? The curse of being something apart was now as sharp in his mind as it had been from the day they had put him to bed in Ward C-7, and he could hear, lying there, the beer parties on Friday nights at the Non-Commissioned Officers' Club while the clang of the doors in the ward rang in their laughter. So they were laughing. And? Plenty of men, good men, had been turned down or back when the going got too rough. No disgrace. In uniform or out he was as good as any of them. He remembered Major Rosenberger saying comfortingly, when he had wept that first time, that even Lincoln had been a little neurotic; and impatient with himself went forward to the dining car.

It was full of officers he didn't want to sit with. Foolishly, he had brought his cap in with him, the cap he had bought with such defiance and nostalgia in the Chicago station when he thought of all his good clothes waiting for him

at home, and he could see that the steward wanted to snub him. He deliberately put on his cap and ate his meal at a table with three sailors who looked at each other in frigid silence. When he had gulped the last of the cold coffee he was too nervous to wait for the check and left two dollar bills on the cloth and ran back to his seat.

The Negro girl had fallen in her sleep all over his seat, and he could just barely wedge himself in past her. He pulled the shade down, lowered the cap over his eyes, and imagined that he was climbing into bed at home with Ruth waiting for him. After fifteen months away and thirteen weeks without letters, he could no longer see her clearly, and he was afraid now to make love to her even in his mind. All his fears, mistakes, and quarrels swam between him and her body, and when he tried violently to possess her, as he had so often possessed a woman in reverie before falling asleep, he saw her eyes staring ahead with such bafflement and longing that he could not bear it. Too nervous; both of them always in flight and running in parallel lines of dismay. In his reveries the women were always sleek and big and later kissed his hand. Ruth was always afraid. A man needed strengthening from the outside, by God; by God he did. Ruth whimpered and her rabbit eyes floated at the bottom of a stream. He swung back from his fretful pictures of her and meditated that it was foolish, maybe, not to let her know. But over and over, lying on the bench in the Chicago station, he had planned it as the violent surprise that would dissolve the past. Now he was afraid again. His heart rocked and puffed in his chest like the train on its tracks, a whistle blew, and he wondered what it would be like. Morning after morning he had lain awake at four in Ward C-7, listening to the change of the guard and spelling out his life to himself in the early morning dark like a pilot peering ahead between rocks. Some mornings it had seemed possible. He had imagined himself flying into the apartment, flying back into Ruth's body to awaken her, embracing with violent love and tenderness all his old clothes, the three Van Gogh prints on the wall, the massed linen in the closet. What was over was over. Always a human being got damaged somewhere and somehow. Life was full of damage. And always there was the chance of renewal. Damage and renewal was the personal equation Rosenberger had drummed into him at the end, and he had believed it. He believed it now. It had to work.

The whistle blew into his head like Army bugles in the morning. They were drinking up ahead and laughing. A Negro corporal broke out an accordion and people sang.

The floating music of the accordion brought into his mind water and country ferries on which a blind man with a stick tapped around for pennies when the music was over. The boat nuzzled against the pier walls like a calf, and people rushed for home. It was not all gone! It was not all gone! The ferry was home and the pier embraced it in love and bound it to itself in warm iron chains. He fell asleep.

When he awoke it was two o'clock. They would be getting into Buffalo soon. There was the taste of coal in his mouth and the Negro girl had left. He went to the toilet, washed his hands and face, got his barracks bag off the rack, and held it between his legs to hide his nervousness. On a sudden impulse he took off the cap and threw it out of a window, and when the train coughed its way into the station he felt happy, standing beside the half-open door with the wind in his face. Rain swept along the deserted platform. He ran through it with the barracks bag in front of him like a basket of wash, got a nickel out of his pocket, and leaped into a booth to call Ruth. He was so nervous that he could not find the switch to light up the booth, and he panted in the dark cell for a moment, unable to move with the bag against the wall. Two-thirty. Could he awake her at this hour? He was afraid to go in without telling her first. He found the light, heard the hollow echo of his coin in the slot, and thought that the clang would awake the town. The ring of his telephone five miles away seemed foreign, and suddenly he wondered if he had not dialed a wrong number. He put the receiver back on its hook, closed his eyes for a moment, and tried again. Sweat rolled into his eyes and down his nose, his coat was suffocating, and he hung over the sound of the phone, his heart beating loudly to every ring. There was no answer.

He sat on a bench outside and let the rain fall on him. Saturday night. She was out somewhere. The darkness was all around him like the past and the world in which a splinter fell off the tree. They took a man and put him into the Army, told him nothing but yelled at him and fed him and marched him, and he fell like a splinter off the tree. The tree was always there, and there were millions in it still, even if they told them nothing. But a splinter off the tree. Ruth, he said to the rain, Ruth. Where? If it had been so bad before, what would it be now? The rain washed him and he cried with it in the dark. A local train came along the platform and threw its doors open. He thought for a moment, shouldered his barracks bag, and got in.

Iwo Jima Before H-Hour

by John P. Marquand

May 1945

Life on a battleship is largely conducted against a background of disregarded words. For example, upon leaving Saipan, the radio loudspeaker on the open bridge produced a continuous program somewhat along the following lines:

"This is Peter Rabbit calling Audacity One—Peter Rabbit calling Audacity One—over... Audacity One calling Peter Rabbit...Come in, Peter Rabbit—over...Peter Rabbit to Audacity One—Shackle. Charley. Abel. Oboe. Noel Coward. Unshackle—over...Audacity One to Peter Rabbit—Continue as directed. Over...Peter Rabbit to Audacity One—Roger. Over..."

Sometimes these guarded code conversations, all conducted with flawless diction in clear unemotional tones, would reach a degree of subtlety that bordered on the obvious.

"Tiger Two is now in a position to give the stepchildren a drink. Will Audacity One please notify the stepchildren?... Bulldog calling Turtle. A pilot is in the water, southeast of Hot Rock. Pick him up. I repeat: In the water, southeast of Hot Rock. Pick him up...."

There was never any way of telling whether or not the stepchildren received the drinks which Tiger was kind enough to offer, or whether or not the pilot was rescued from the slightly chilly waters off that unpleasant island of Iwo. Moreover, no one seemed particularly to care. The Admiral and the Captain sat upon the bridge in comfortable highchairs, not unlike those used by patrons in a billiard parlor. Their staff officers stood near them, and behind the staff officers stood the men with earphones and mouthpieces tethered by long insulated cords, and next came the Marine orderlies with their .45 automatics. Occasionally a Filipino mess boy would appear from the small kitchenette below—doubtless called a galley—with sandwiches and coffee for the Admiral and the Captain. He would carry these on a tray, sparkling with bright silver, china, and napery, up two dark companion ladders to the open bridge. Once when the main battery of 14-inch guns was firing, some freak of concussion lifted him a good six inches off the deck. But guns or not, no one appeared to listen to the voices on that radio. [...]

"If you write this thing just the way you see it," an officer said, "maybe it might mean something to people back home. They might see what we're going through. They might understand—they never understand back home."

That was what nearly everyone aboard said. They all had a pathetic desire for people at home to know. Of course, if they had thought about it, they would have realized that this was impossible. There was too great a gap between civilian and naval life. There were too few common values. The life aboard a ship in enemy waters was even more complex and difficult of explanation than the life of troops ashore. There was a combination of small personal comforts and of impending danger verging on calamity that was ugly and incongruous. The living quarters of the crew were overcrowded, but they had hot water and soap, hot showers, and all sorts of things you would never get ashore. There were clean clothes, and all the coffee you wanted day and night, and red meat and other hot food, and butter and ice cream. Yet, at the same time, the sense of danger was more intense. You could not run away from it as you could on land. It might come at any minute of the day and night from torpedoes, from the air, from a surface engagement. Almost any sort of blow meant casualties and damage. Even a light shell on the superstructure might cause complications incomparable to the results of a similar blow on land.

There had been some hope that the task force of battleships, cruisers, and destroyers that was scheduled to bombard Iwo Jima for three days before the transports and the amphibious craft appeared, might arrive there undetected, but the force was spotted by an enemy plane on the evening of February 15th. No one aboard saw that speck in the dark sky.

In the Pacific Theater, 1945.

In the junior officers' wardroom there was a complete collection of all the intelligence which had been gathered regarding the island of Iwo. Nothing was a secret any longer. It was possible to scan the latest airplane photographs, which had been taken early in the month. There were maps showing the target areas assigned every unit, with batteries, pillboxes, and anti-aircraft installations marked in red. There were reports on the soil of the island. The beach would be coal-black lava sand, and the land rose up from it quite sharply in terraces. Each terrace had been a former beach, since in the past few years the island had been rising from the sea. As one moved in from the water's edge the soil was a soft sand of volcanic ash, almost barren of vegetation and exceedingly difficult for any sort of vehicle to negotiate. Higher on the island were the cliffs of brown volcanic stone, suitable for construction of underground galleries. There were patches of coarse grass full of the mites that cause scrub typhus. There were hot springs, and there was the sulphur mine from which Iwo draws its name (Sulphur Island), and

a small sugar plantation to the north near a single town called Motoyama. There were believed to be fifteen hundred troops on the island. The defensive installations were all underground or carefully camouflaged. There was only one practical beach on which to land and there was no chance for tactical subtlety.

The most interesting unit of this informational material was a large relief map made out of soft, pliable rubber, that gave a bird's-eye view of the island we were approaching. Every contour of it was there in scale—the cliffs to the northward, the vegetation, the roads, the air strips (two finished and one nearing completion), and Mount Suribachi, the low, brown volcanic cone on the southern tip.

There have already been a good many ingenious descriptions of the shape of Iwo Jima, including comparisons to a mutton chop and a gourd. The whole thing was about five miles long. Mount Suribachi, to the south, was a walled-in crater. Its northern slope was known to be studded with pillboxes and with artillery. Bushes and boulders on this slope ran down to the lowest and narrowest stretch on the island, which had beaches on the east and west. (The west beach, however, would not permit landing operations on account of the prevailing winds.) From here the land gradually rose upward, and the island broadened until it finally reached a width of two and one-half miles. The air strips were on its central spine. The northern shores came down to the sea in cliffs. There were only eight square miles of this bleak, unpromising, and porous dry land.

Anyone could tell that the plans for the seizure of Iwo Jima must have been the main occupation of a large group of specialists for a long, long time. Heaps of secret orders showed the disposition at any given moment of every one of the hundreds of craft that would take part in the invasion. The thousands of pages made a scenario for an operation which might take place in an hour or a minute. Veterans of other invasions were not impressed by the infinite detail. They spoke of the plans for Normandy and the south of France, or they discussed the arrangements for Guam and Saipan.

"If you've seen one of them," they said, "you've seen them all."

No one spoke much on the bridge. It was chilly and rain was falling before daylight. We were a silent, blacked-out ship, moving slowly, and as far as one could tell, alone—except for voices on the bridge radio.

"Battleaxe One," the radio was saying, "Area Zebra. Shackle. Charley. Oswald. Henry. Abel. Unshackle."

"We'll start firing at about ten thousand yards," someone said.

Then the first daylight began to stir across the water and we were among the shadows of other heavy ships, moving very slowly.

"Look," someone said, "there's the mountain."

There was a faint, pinkish glow on the rain clouds above the horizon and the first faint rays of an abortive sunrise struggling against the rain fell on a rocky mass some five miles dead ahead. It was the cone of Suribachi emerging from a misty haze of cloud, and cloud vapor covered the dark mass of the rest of Iwo Jima. After one glance at its first vague outlines, it would have been hard to have mistaken it for anything but a Japanese island, for it had the faint delicate colors of a painting on a scroll of silk.

Our spotting plane was warming up on the catapult aft and you could hear the roar of the motor clearly over the silent ship. Then there was a flat explosion as the plane shot over the water. When it circled for altitude and headed for the island, there was already light enough to see the faces on the bridge.

The Captain dropped his binoculars and lighted a cigarette. The clouds were gradually lifting above the island. It was unexpectedly tedious waiting and wondering when we would begin to fire. The island lay there mute and watchful. A bell was ringing. "Stand by," someone said, and seconds later one of our 14-inch projectiles was on its way to Iwo Jima. The noise was not as bad as the concussion, for your chest seemed to be pushed by invisible hands when the big guns went off. There was a cloud of yellow smoke, not unlike the color of Mount Suribachi. Then everyone crowded forward to gaze at the island. It seemed a very long while before a cloud of smoke and gray sand rose up almost like water from land. Then another ship fired. The bombardment of Iwo Jima had begun and the island lay there in the dingy, choppy sea, taking its punishment stoically without a sound.

Even at a distance of five miles, which somehow does not seem as far at sea as it does on land, one had the inescapable impression that Iwo Jima was ready for it and accustomed to taking a beating. This was not strange, as we had bombed it from the air for successive dozens of days, and fleet units had already shelled it twice. Nevertheless, this lack of reaction was something that you did not expect, even though common sense told you that there would not possibly be any land fire until we closed the range.

Another aspect of that three-day bombardment before D-day was even more unexpected, especially when one retained memories of the heavy and continuous fire by land batteries upon prepared positions in the last World War. The bombardment turned out to be a slow, careful probing for almost invisible targets, with long dull intervals between the firing. Occasionally one could see a cloud of drab smoke arise from another ship, and a long while afterward the sound of the explosion would come almost languidly across the water, and then there would be another plume of dust and rubble on another target area of Iwo Jima. Sometimes, when the breeze was light, the smoke from the big guns of another ship would rise in the air in a huge perfect ring. Of course common sense again gave the reason for this deliberate firing. The fleet had come too long a distance to waste its limited ammunition, and consequently the effect of every shot had to undergo careful professional analysis. [...]

The slow approach on Iwo Jima was somewhat like the weaving and feinting of a fighter watching for an opening early in the first round. To put it another way, our task force was like a group of big-game hunters surrounding a slightly wounded but dangerous animal. They were approaching him slowly and respectfully, endeavoring to gauge his strength and at the same time trying to tempt him into action. We moved all through the day, nearer and nearer to Iwo Jima. Planes from the carrier force came from beyond the horizon, peeling off through the clouds and diving toward the air strip; but except for an occasional burst of automatic fire and a few black dots of flak, the enemy was very listless. Our minesweeps, small, chunky vessels, began operating very close to the island. There were a few splashes near them, but that was all. The Japanese commander was too good a soldier to show his hand.

As the day wore on, we crowded close and objects loomed very large ashore. You could see the coal-black strip of beach where our assault waves would land, and the sea broke on the rusting hulls of a few old wrecks. Above the beach were the gray terraces we had read about, mounting in gradual, uneven steps to the air strip. Beside the air strip there was a tangle of planes, smashed by our bombings and pushed carelessly aside, like rubbish on a city dump. To the north were the quarries which had been mentioned by the Intelligence. You could see caves to the south on Mount Suribachi. We were very close for a battleship and we knew the enemy had 8-inch coast defense guns.

We continued firing at pillboxes and at anti-aircraft emplacements, but there was no return fire and no trace of life upon the island. We stayed there until the light grew dim, and then we turned to leave the area until next morning. Twelve hours of standing on the bridge and the concussion of the guns left everyone very tired. We must have done some damage but not enough to hurt.

It was different the next morning—D-day minus two. When we returned to the dull work the island was waiting with the dawn. Today the sky was clearer and the sea was smoother, and the ships closed more confidently with the shore. The schedule showed that there was to be a diversion toward the middle of the morning, and the force was obviously moving into position.

"We're going to reconnoiter the beach with small craft," an officer explained. "And the LCI's will strafe the terraces with rockets."

It was hard to guess where the LCI's had come from, for they had not been with us yesterday—but there they were just behind us, on time and on order, like everything else in amphibious war. The sun had broken through the cloud ceiling and for once the sea was almost blue. The heavy ships had formed a line, firing methodically. Two destroyers edged their way past us and took positions nearer shore.

"Here come the LCI's," someone said. [...] They were small vessels that had never been designed for heavy combat. They had been built only to carry infantry ashore, but in the Pacific they were being put to all sorts of other uses—as messenger ships to do odd jobs for the fleet, as gunboats, and as rocket ships. Each had a round tower amidships where the commanding officer stood. Each had open platforms with light automatic guns, and now they were also fitted with brackets for the rockets. They were high and narrow, about a hundred feet overall, dabbed with orange and green paint in jungle camouflage. They were a long way from jungle shores, however, as they moved toward the beach of Iwo Jima.

Suddenly the scene took concrete shape. They would approach within a quarter of a mile of shore under the cover of our guns. Without any further protection their crews stood motionless at their stations.

Afterward a gunner from one of the LCI's spoke about it.

"If we looked so still," he said, "it was because we were scared to death. But then everyone had told us there was nothing to be scared of. They told us the Japs never bothered to fire at LCI's."

They were wrong this time, probably because the small craft that followed gave the maneuver the appearance of a landing. For minutes the LCI's moved in and nothing happened. They had turned broadside to the beach, with small boats circling around them like water beetles, before the enemy tipped his hand and opened up his batteries. Then it became clear that nothing we had done so far had contributed materially to softening Iwo Jima. The LCI's were surrounded with spurts of water, and spray and smoke. They twisted and backed to avoid the fire, but they could not get away. It all seemed only a few yards off, directly beneath our guns. Then splashes appeared off our own bows. The big ships themselves were under fire.

"The so-and-so has taken a hit," someone said. "There are casualties on the such-and-such." He was referring to the big ships, but at the moment it did not seem important. All you thought of were the LCI's just off the beach. We were inching into line with the destroyers.

It appeared later that when we had been ordered to withdraw we had disregarded the order, and thus all at once we were in a war of our own, slugging it out with the shore. There had been a great deal of talk about our gunnery and the training of our crews. There was no doubt that they knew their business when they began firing with everything that could bear. The 14-inch guns and the 5-inch batteries were firing as fast as they could load. The breeze from the shore blew the smoke up to the bridge in bilious clouds. The shore line of Iwo Jima became cloaked in white smoke as we threw in phosphorus. Even our 40-millimeters began to fire. It was hard to judge the lapse of time, but the LCI's must have let off their rockets according to the schedule while the Japanese were blinded by the smoke and counterfire. When the LCI's began to withdraw, we also moved off slowly. It was the first mistake the enemy had made, if it was a mistake—revealing those batteries, for the next day was mainly occupied in knocking them out. [...]

The first Japanese soldier to be taken prisoner on Iwo Jima, May 16, 1945.

That evening the Japanese reported that they had beaten off two landings on Iwo Jima and that they had sunk numerous craft, including a battleship and a destroyer. There was a certain basis of fact in this, since what had happened must have looked like a landing. One LCI was sinking, waiting for a demolition charge, as disregarded as a floating can.

After the reconnaissance of the beach had been accomplished, the pounding of Iwo Jima continued through the afternoon and through the whole next day. Planes drove in with bomb loads, while the ring of ships kept up their steady fire. At night the "cans," as the destroyers were called, continued a harassing fire. Incendiary bombs were dumped on the slopes of Suribachi. Rockets were thrown at it from the air. Fourteen-inch shells pounded into its batteries. The ship to starboard of us attacked the battery to the north on the lip of the quarry. The earth was blown away, exposing the naked concrete gun emplacements, but now that the nov-

elty had worn off it was all a repetition of previous hours. The scene grew dull and very fatiguing, but the voices on the radio loudspeaker continued tirelessly.

"Dauntless reports a contact.... Bulldog is ready to give a drink to any of our pigeons that may need it. Audacity One to Tiger—I repeat: Did you get our message? Over...."

The island lay still, taking it. No visible life appeared until the last day, when an installation was blown up and a few men staggered out from it. Some of us on the bridge saw them and some did not. One Japanese ran a few steps and seemed to stop and stoop to pick up something. Then he was gone. We had probably seen him dying.

The Japanese commander was playing his cards close to his chest, revealing no more targets by opening fire. It was clear that he also had his plan, less complicated than ours, but rational. He might damage our heavy ships, but he could not sink them, or conceivably prevent the inevitable landing. He had clearly concluded to wait and take his punishment, to keep his men and weapons under cover, until our assault waves were on the beach. Then he would do his best to drive them off, and everyone at Iwo knows it was not such a bad plan, either. He did not come so far from doing it when he opened up his crossfire on the beach. Some pessimists even admit that he might have succeeded if it had not been for that coarse, light sand which embedded the mortar shells as they struck, so that they only killed what was very near them.

At the end of D-day minus one our task force was still there, without many new additions, but it was different the next morning. At dawn on D-day the waters of Iwo looked like New York harbor on a busy morning. The transports were there with three divisions of Marines—a semicircle of gray shipping seven miles out. Inside that gray arc the sea, turned choppy by the unsettled weather, was dotted by an alphabet soup of ships. [...]

At nine o'clock exactly the first assault wave was due to hit the beach, but before that Iwo Jima was due to receive its final polishing. Its eight square miles were waiting to take everything we could pour into them, and they must have already received a heavier weight of fire than any navy in the world had previously concentrated upon so small an area.

Anyone who has been there can shut his eyes and see the place again. It never looked more aesthetically ugly than on D-day morning, or more completely Japanese. Its silhouette was like a sea monster with the little dead volcano for the head, and the beach area for the neck, and all the rest of it with its scrubby, brown cliffs for the body. It also had the minute, fussy compactness of those miniature Japanese gardens. Its stones and rocks were like those contorted, wind-scoured, water-worn boulders which the Japanese love to collect as landscape decorations. "I hope to God," a wounded Marine said later, "that we don't get to go on any more of those screwy islands."

An hour before H-hour it shook and winced as it took what was being dished out to it. In fact, the whole surface of the island was in motion as its soil was churned by our shells and by the bombs from the carrier planes that were swooping down across its back. Every ship was firing with a rising tempo, salvo after salvo, with no more waiting for the shellburst to subside. Finally Iwo Jima was concealing itself in its own debris and dust. The haze of battle had become palpable, and the island was temporarily lost in a gray fog. [. . .]

The amphibious vehicles, churning up the sea into foaming circles, organized themselves in lines, each line following its leader. Then the leaders moved out to the floating flags, around which they gathered in circling groups, waiting for their signal to move ashore. The gray landing craft with the Marines had left the transports some time before for their own fixed areas and they also were circling, like runners testing their muscles before the race. The barrage which had been working over the beach area had lifted, and the beach, with the smoldering terraces above it, was visible again. It was time for the first wave to be starting.

It was hard to pick the first wave out in that sea of milling craft, but suddenly a group of the barges broke loose from its circle, following its leader in a dash toward shore. Close to land the leader turned parallel to the beach, and kept on until the whole line was parallel. Then the boats turned individually and made a dash for it. The Navy had landed the first wave on Iwo Jima—at nine o'clock on the dot—or, at least, not more than a few seconds after nine.

OUR WORST WARTIME MISTAKE

BY EUGENE V. ROSTOW

SEPTEMBER 1945

Time is often needed for us to recognize the great miscarriages of justice. The Dreyfus case had lasted four years before public opinion was fully aroused. The trials of Sacco and Vanzetti endured six years. As time passes, it becomes more and more plain that our wartime treatment of the Japanese and the Japanese-Americans on the West Coast was a tragic and dangerous mistake. That mistake is a threat to society, and to all men. Its motivation and its impact on our system of law deny every value of democracy.

In the perspective of our legal tradition, the facts are almost incredible.

During the bleak spring of 1942, the Japanese and the Japanese-Americans who lived on the West Coast of the United States were taken into custody and removed to camps in the interior. More than one hundred thousand men, women, and children were thus exiled and imprisoned. More than two-thirds of them were American citizens.

These people were taken into custody as a military measure on the ground that espionage and sabotage were especially to be feared from persons of Japanese blood. The whole group was removed from the West Coast because the military authorities thought it would take too long to conduct individual investigations on the spot. They were arrested without warrants and were held without indictment or a statement of charges, although the courts were open and freely functioning. They were transported to camps far from their homes, and kept there under prison conditions, pending investigations of their "loyalty." Despite the good intentions of the chief relocation officers, the centers were little better than concentration camps.

If the evacuees were found "loyal," they were released only if they could find a job and a place to live, in a community where no hoodlums would come out at night to chalk up anti-Japanese slogans, break windows, or threaten riot. If

found "disloyal" in their attitude to the war, they were kept in the camps indefinitely—although sympathy with the enemy is no crime in the United States (for white people at least) so long as it is not translated into deeds or the visible threat of deeds. On May 1, 1945, three years after the program was begun, about 70,000 persons were still in camps. While it is hoped to have all these people either free, or in more orthodox confinement, by January 1, 1946, what is euphemistically called the Japanese "relocation" program will not be a closed book for many years.

The original program of "relocation" was an injustice, in no way required or justified by the circumstances of the war. But the Supreme Court, in three extraordinary decisions, has upheld its main features as constitutional. This fact converts a piece of wartime folly into national policy—a permanent part of the law—a doctrine enlarging the power of the military in relation to civil authority. It is having a sinister impact on the minority problem in every part of the country. It is giving aid to reactionary politicians who use social division and racial prejudice as their tools. The precedent is being used to encourage attacks on the civil rights of both citizens and aliens. As Mr. Justice Jackson has said, the principle of these decisions "lies about like a loaded weapon ready for the hand of any authority that can bring forward a plausible claim of an urgent need." All in all, the case of the Japanese-Americans is the worst blow our liberties have sustained in many years. Unless repudiated, it may support devastating and unforeseen social and political conflicts.

What was done in the name of military precaution on the West Coast was quite different from the security measures taken in Hawaii or on the East Coast, although both places were active theaters of war in 1942.

On the East Coast enemy aliens were controlled without mass arrests or evacuations, despite their heavy concentration in and near shipping and manufacturing centers. Aliens had been registered, and the police had compiled information about fascist sympathizers, both aliens and citizens. "On the night of December 7, 1944," Attorney General Biddle reported, "the most dangerous of the persons in this group were taken into custody; in the following weeks a number of others were apprehended. Each arrest was made on the basis of information concerning the specific alien taken into custody. We have used no dragnet techniques and have conducted no indiscriminate, large-scale raids." General regulations were issued, somewhat restricting the freedom of all enemy aliens over fourteen years of age. They were forbidden to enter military areas; they had to get the District Attorney's permission before traveling; they were forbidden to own or use firearms, cameras, short-wave radio sets, codes, ciphers, or invisible ink. This control plan kept security officers informed, but otherwise allowed the aliens almost their normal share in the work and life of the community.

Enemy aliens under suspicion, and those who violated the regulations, were subject to summary arrest, and were then promptly examined by one of the special Alien Enemy Hearing Boards. These boards could recommend that the individual alien be interned, paroled, or released unconditionally. The examinations were smoothly conducted, and they did nothing to lower prevailing standards of justice. Of the 1,100,000 enemy aliens in the country, 9,080 had been examined by the end of June 1943, about 4,000 of them being interned. By June 30, 1944, the number interned had been reduced to approximately 2,500.

In Hawaii a different procedure was followed, but one less drastic than the evacuation program pursued on the West Coast, although Hawaii was certainly a more active theater of war. Immediately after Pearl Harbor, martial law was installed in Hawaii, and the commanding general assumed the role of military governor. Yet, although about one-third the population of Hawaii is of Japanese descent, and although the tension was great after the Pearl Harbor raid, there was no mass roundup on the islands. Fewer than 800 Japanese aliens were sent to the mainland for internment, and fewer than 1,000 persons of Japanese ancestry, 912 of them being citizens, were sent to relocation centers on the mainland. Many of the latter group were families of interned aliens, transferred voluntarily. Those arrested in Hawaii were taken into custody on the basis of individual suspicion, resting on previous examination or observed behavior. Even under a regime of martial law, men were arrested as individuals, and not because of the color of their skins. Safety was assured without mass arrests, or needless hardship.

On the West Coast the security program was something else again. Immediately after Pearl Harbor there were no special regulations for persons of Japanese extraction. Known enemy sympathizers among the Japanese, like white traitors and enemy agents, were arrested. There was no sabotage by persons of Japanese ancestry. There was no reason to suppose that the 112,000 persons of Japanese descent on the West Coast, less than 2 per cent of the population, constituted a greater menace than such persons in Hawaii, where they were 32 per cent of the population.

After a month's silence, the organized minority whose business it has been to exploit racial tensions on the West Coast went to work. They had strong support in the Hearst press and its equivalents. Politicians, fearful of an unknown public opinion, spoke out for white supremacy. West Coast Congressional delegations led by Senator Hiram Johnson, urged the administration to exclude all persons of Japanese blood from the coast states. Anti-Oriental spokesmen appeared before special hearings of the Tolan Committee, and explained the situation as they conceived it to Lieutenant General J. L. DeWitt, commanding the Western Defense Command. Tension was intensified, and doubters, worried about the risks of another Pearl Harbor, remained silent, preferring too much caution to too little. An opinion crystallized in favor of evacuating the Japanese.

After some hesitation, General DeWitt proposed the policy of exclusion on grounds of military need. The War Department backed him up. No one in the government took the responsibility for opposing or overruling him.

Despite the nature of the emergency, the Army's lawyers wanted more legal authority before action was taken. The President issued an Executive Order in February 1942, and in March Congress passed a statute, authorizing military commanders to designate "military areas" and to prescribe the terms on which any persons could enter, leave, or remain in such areas. A policy of encouraging the Japanese to move away individually had shown signs of producing confusion. It was therefore decided to establish a compulsory system of detention in camps, to simplify the process of resettlement, and to afford the fullest measure of security.

The history of law affords nothing more fantastic than the evidence which is supposed to justify this program. General DeWitt's final recommendation to the Secretary of War, dated February 14, 1942, but not made public until early in 1944, explains the basis of his decision.

"In the war in which we are now engaged," he said, "racial affinities are not severed by migration. The Japanese race is an enemy race and while many second and third generation Japanese born on United States soil, possessed of United States citizenship, have become 'Americanized,' the racial strains are undiluted." From the premise of a war of "races," the general had no difficulty reaching his conclusion. There is "no ground for assuming," he said, that Japanese-Americans will not turn against the United States. So much for the idea that men are presumed innocent until proved guilty, and that American citizens stand on an equal footing before the law without regard for race, color, or previous condition of servitude! "It therefore follows," the general added, "that along the vital Pacific Coast over 112,000 potential enemies, of Japanese extraction, are at large today. There are disturbing indications that these are organized and ready for concerted action at a favorable opportunity. The very fact that no sabotage has taken place to date is a disturbing and confirming indication that such action will be taken."

There was somewhat more evidence than the absence of sabotage to prove its special danger. The Japanese lived closely together, often concentrated around harbors and other strategic areas. Japanese clubs and religious institutions played an important part in their segregated social life. Japanese language schools existed, to preserve for the American born something of the cultural heritage of Japan. The Japanese government, like that of many other countries, asserted a doctrine of nationality different from our own, which gave rise to possible claims of dual citizenship. Thus a long-standing conflict in international law, involving many countries other than Japan, was invoked to cast special doubt on the loyalty of American citizens of Japanese descent.

Much of the suspicion inferentially based on these statements disappears on closer examination. In many instances the concentration of Japanese homes around strategic areas had come about years before, and for entirely innocent reasons. Japanese cannery workers, for example, had had to live on the waterfront in order to be near the plants in which they worked. Japanese truck gardeners had rented land in the industrial outskirts of large cities to be close to their markets. They had rented land for gardening under high tension lines—regarded as a very suspicious cir-

cumstance—because the company could not use the land for other purposes; the initiative in starting this practice had come from the utility companies, not from the Japanese.

Despite discrimination against the Japanese, many had done well in America. They were substantial property owners. Their children participated normally and actively in the schools and universities of the West Coast. Their unions and social organizations had passed resolutions of loyalty in great number, before and after Pearl Harbor. It is difficult to find real evidence that either religious or social institutions among the Japanese had successfully fostered Japanese militarism or other dangerous sentiments. The Japanese language schools, which the Japanese-Americans themselves had long sought to put under state control, seem to represent little more than the familiar desire of many immigrant groups to keep alive the language and tradition of the "old country"; in the case of Japanese-Americans, knowledge of the Japanese language was of particular economic importance, since so much of their working life was spent with other Japanese on the West Coast.

Some elements among the Japanese were, of course, suspect. They were known to the authorities, who had for several years been checking on the Japanese-American population. Many had been individually arrested immediately after Pearl Harbor, and the others were under constant surveillance.

It is also true that a considerable percentage of the evacuees later gave negative answers to loyalty questions in the questionnaires they were asked to fill out while in camps. Many of those answers were expressly based upon the treatment the individuals had received; the same shock of evacuation and confinement undoubtedly was responsible indirectly for many more. Basically, however, the issue of abstract loyalty is irrelevant. Disloyalty, even in the aggravated form of enthusiastic verbal support for the Axis cause, is not a crime in the United States. At most, it is a possible ground for interning enemy aliens. Citizens must do more than talk or think disloyal thoughts before being arrested and jailed.

Apart from the members of the group known to be under suspicion, there was no evidence beyond the vaguest fear to connect the Japanese on the West Coast with the unfavorable military events of 1941 and 1942. Both at Pearl Harbor and in sporadic attacks on the West Coast the enemy had shown that he had knowledge of our dispositions. There was some signaling to enemy ships at sea, both by radio and by lights, along the West Coast. There were several episodes

Japanese-Americans being rounded up for detention in California, 1942.

of shelling the coast by submarine—although two of the three such cases mentioned by General DeWitt as tending to create suspicion of the Japanese-Americans took place *after* their removal from the coast. (These were the only such items in his report which were not identified by date.) And those subsequently arrested as Japanese agents in the Pearl Harbor area were all white men.

The most striking comment on the quality of the evidence produced by General DeWitt to support his proposal was made by Solicitor General Fahy, whose job it was to defend the general's plan before the Supreme Court. He relied upon the general's report "only to the extent that it relates" statistics and other details concerning the actual evacuation and the events which took place after it. But the briefs that he himself presented were identical in the substance of their argument. The Japanese-Americans were an unknown, unknowable, foreign group, living together, and moving in mysterious ways, inscrutable to puzzled white

men. Therefore, let them be imprisoned; let their property be taken into custody, sold off at bargain prices, dissipated, and lost; let their roots be torn up, let their children suffer the irreparable shock of life in a concentration camp; let their relation to society be distorted by the searing memory of humiliation, rejection, and punishment.

The evidence supports one conclusion only: the dominant element in the development of our relocation policy was race prejudice, not a military estimate of a military problem.

By the time the issues raised by this program reached the Supreme Court, the crisis which was supposed to justify it had passed. The first cases came up in June 1943, the second and third in December 1944. The course of the war had changed completely; the Japanese were no longer prowling off California, but fighting defensively among the islands of the Western Pacific.

The problem presented to the Supreme Court was thus completely different from that which confronted worried soldiers, legislators, and executive officials in the melancholy months after Pearl Harbor. Invalidation of the relocation scheme would do no possible harm to the prosecution of the war. The Supreme Court could afford to view the issues in perspective, giving full weight to its own special responsibilities for the development of constitutional law as a whole.

Moreover, the issue for the court was infinitely more complex than that which faced General DeWitt in 1942. The court had to decide not only whether General DeWitt had acted within the scope of his permissible authority, but whether it should validate what had been done. As many episodes in our constitutional history attest, those are different issues. The court could not escape the fact that it was the Supreme Court, arbiter of a vast system of customs, rules, habits, and relationships. Its decision inevitably would have far-reaching effects—on the power of the military, on our developing law of emergencies, on the future of those demagogues and political groups which live by attacking minorities, and on the future decision of cases in lower courts and police stations, involving the rights of citizens and aliens, the availability of habeas corpus, and like questions.

The question of how and on what grounds the Supreme Court should dispose of the cases also was one of broad political policy. Would a repudiation of Congress, the President, and the military in one aspect of their conduct of the war affect the people's will to fight? Would it create a campaign issue for 1944? Would it affect the power and prestige of the Supreme Court as a political institution?

In a bewildering and unimpressive series of opinions, relieved only by the dissents of Justice Roberts and Justice Murphy in one of the three cases—*Korematsu* v. *United States*—the court chose to assume that the main issues did not exist. In avoiding the risks of overruling the government on an issue of war policy, it weakened society's control over military power—one of the controls on which the whole organization of our society depends. It failed to uphold the most ordinary rights of citizenship, making Japanese-Americans into second-class citizens, who stand before the courts on a different legal footing from other Americans. It accepted and gave the prestige of its support to dangerous racial myths about a minority group, in arguments which can easily be applied to any other minority in our society.

The reasoning of the court was simple and direct. The problem was the scope of the war power of the national government. Both Congress and the executive seemed to have decided that special measures were required because espionage and sabotage were especially to be feared from persons of Japanese descent on the West Coast in the spring of 1942. It was not the job of the Supreme Court to decide such questions for itself. Its task was that of judicial review—to uphold the judgment of the officers directly responsible for fighting the war if, the court said, there was "any substantial basis" in fact for the conclusion that protective measures were necessary.

Two propositions which the court accepted as "facts" were held to afford a sufficiently "rational basis" for military decision. The first was that in time of war "residents having ethnic affiliations with an invading enemy may be a greater source of danger than those of different ancestry"—a doctrine which belongs with the race theories of the Nazis and, moreover, is contrary to the experience of American society in both our World Wars. (The weight of scientific evidence is that the most important driving urge of such minority groups is to conform, not to rebel.) The second was that on the West Coast in 1942 there was no time to isolate and examine the suspected Japanese on an individual basis—although of the 110,000 persons subject to the exclusion orders, 43 per cent were over fifty or under fifteen years old; they had lived in California without committing sabotage for five months after Pearl Harbor; in the country as a whole, thousands of aliens were examined individually without substantial delay; and in Britain 74,000 enemy aliens were checked in a few months.

By accepting the military judgment on these two points, without any evidence in the record to back it up, without requiring any testimony from the military, and even without adequate discussion by the court itself, the court has taken "judicial notice" of doubtful and controversial propositions of fact, as if they were as well-established as the census statistics or the tide tables. The court could have sent the cases back for a full trial on the justification for General DeWitt's decision. Instead, it upheld his ruling. Thus it created a profound question as to the position of the military power in our public life. [...]

The history of this question in the Supreme Court is unmistakable. The earlier decisions of the court had vigorously asserted that "what are the allowable limits of military discretion, and whether or not they have been overstepped in a particular case, are judicial questions"; and that there must be evidence enough to satisfy the court as to the need for the action taken. They had made it clear that the law is not neutral in such issues, but has a positive preference for protecting civil rights where possible, and a long-standing suspicion of the military mind when acting outside its own sphere.

Yet in the Japanese-American cases there was literally no evidence whatever by which the court might test the responsibility of General DeWitt's action. Dozens of Supreme Court decisions had said that the court would not pass on serious constitutional questions without a record before it, establishing the essential facts. Those cases were all ignored. One hundred thousand persons were sent to concentration camps on a record which wouldn't support a conviction for stealing a dog.

The earlier cases not only established the rule that there must be an independent judicial examination of the justification for a military act. They went much further. They declared a simple rule-of-thumb as a guide in handling cases involving military discretion, in which the military undertook to arrest, hold, or try people. So long as the civil courts were open and functioning, the Supreme Court had previously held, there could be no military necessity for allowing generals to hold, try, or punish people. The safety of the country could be thoroughly protected against treason, sabotage, and like crimes by ordinary arrest and trial in the civil courts, unless the courts were shut by riot, invasion, or insurrection.

That was the moral of the great case of *Ex Parte Milligan*, decided in 1866. *Ex Parte Milligan* is a monument in the democratic tradition, and until now it has been the animating force in this branch of our law. [...] Milligan was convincingly charged with active participation in a fifth column plot worthy of Hitler. A group of armed and determined men planned to seize federal arsenals at Columbus, Indianapolis, and at three points in Illinois, and then to release Confederate prisoners of war held in those states. Thus they would create a Confederate army behind the Union lines in Tennessee. Milligan and his alleged co-conspirators acted in Indiana, Missouri, Illinois, and in other border states. Their strategy had a political arm. The Union was to be split politically, and a Northwest Confederation was to be declared, friendly to the South, and embracing six states. This was not an idle dream. It was sponsored by a well-financed society,

the Sons of Liberty, thought to have 300,000 members, many of them rich and respectable, and the planned uprising would coincide with the Chicago convention of the Democratic Party, which was then sympathetic to abandoning the war and recognizing the Confederacy.

The unanimous court which freed Milligan for civil trial was a court of fire-eating Unionists. Mr. Justice Davis, who wrote for the majority, was one of President Lincoln's closest friends. The Chief Justice, who wrote for the concurring minority, was a valiant supporter of the war, whatever his shortcomings in other respects. Yet the court had no difficulty in freeing Milligan, and facing down the outcry provoked by the decision.

The court held in Milligan's case that it was unconstitutional to try him before a military commission, rather than a court of law. There was little doubt of his guilt. But it was beyond the powers of the military to measure or punish it. [...]

Yet in the cases of the Japanese-Americans the Supreme Court held the precedent of *Ex Parte Milligan* inapplicable. The reasoning is extraordinarily dangerous. The Japanese-Americans, the court said, were detained by a civilian agency, not by the Army. The program was not exclusively a matter for military administration, and it was enforceable under a statute by ordinary criminal remedies. Therefore, it did not present the question of the power of military tribunals to conduct trials under the laws of war.

But the Japanese-Americans were ordered detained by a general, purporting to act on military grounds. The military order was enforceable, on pain of imprisonment. While a United States marshal, rather than a military policeman, assured obedience to the order, the ultimate sanction behind the marshal's writ is the same as that of the military police: the bayonets of United States troops. It is hardly a ground for distinction that the general's command was backed by the penalty of civil imprisonment, or that he obtained civilian aid in running the relocation camps. The starting point for the entire program was a military order, which had to be obeyed.

In *Ex Parte Milligan* the Supreme Court had said that the military could not constitutionally arrest, nor could a military tribunal constitutionally try, civilians charged with treason and conspiracy to destroy the state by force, at a time when the civil courts were open and functioning. Yet under the plan considered in the Japanese-American cases, people not charged with crime are imprisoned without even a military trial, on the ground that they have the taint of Japanese blood. It would seem clear that if it is illegal to arrest and confine people after an unwarranted military trial, it is surely even more illegal to arrest and confine them without any trial at all. But the Supreme Court says that the issues of the *Milligan* case were not involved in this case because the evacuees were committed to camps by military orders, not by military tribunals, and because their jailers did not wear uniforms! [...]

As for the Japanese *aliens* involved in the evacuation program, the constitutional problem is different. In time of war, the government possesses great powers over enemy aliens, which are to be exercised, the courts say, for the "single purpose" of preventing enemy aliens from aiding the enemy. They may be interned if dangerous and their property in the United States may be taken into custody. Yet they are entitled to our general constitutional protections of individual liberty—to trial by jury, the writ of habeas corpus, and the other basic rights of the person. Is it permissible to intern all the Japanese who live on the West Coast, but to allow German and Italian aliens, and Japanese who live elsewhere, general freedom? Surely the control and custody of enemy aliens in wartime should be reasonably equal and even-handed. [...]

We believe that the German people bear a common political responsibility for outrages secretly committed by the Gestapo and the SS. What are we to think of our own part in a program which violates every principle of our common life, yet has been approved by the President, Congress, and the Supreme Court?

Three chief forms of reparation are available, and should be pursued. The first is the inescapable obligation of the federal government to protect the civil rights of Japanese-Americans against organized and unorganized hooliganism. If local law enforcement fails, federal prosecutions under the national Civil Rights Act should be undertaken.

Secondly, generous financial indemnity should be sought. Apart from the sufferings of their imprisonment, the Japanese-Americans have sustained heavy property losses from their evacuation.

Finally, the basic issues should be presented to the Supreme Court again, in an effort to obtain a prompt reversal of these wartime cases. The Supreme Court has often corrected its own errors in the past, especially when that error was occasioned by the excitement of a tense moment. [...P]ublic expiation in the case of the Japanese-Americans would be good for the court, and for the country.

The Decision to Use the Atomic Bomb
by Henry L. Stimson

February 1947

I t was in the fall of 1941 that the question of atomic energy was first brought directly to my attention. At that time President Roosevelt appointed a committee consisting of Vice President Wallace, General Marshall, Dr. Vannevar Bush, Dr. James B. Conant, and myself. The function of this committee was to advise the President on questions of policy relating to the study of nuclear fission which was then proceeding both in this country and in Great Britain. For nearly four years thereafter I was directly connected with all major decisions of policy on the development and use of atomic energy, and from May 1, 1943, until my resignation as Secretary of War on September 21, 1945, I was directly responsible to the President for the administration of the entire undertaking; my chief advisers in this period were General Marshall, Dr. Bush, Dr. Conant, and Major General Leslie R. Groves, the officer in charge of the project. At the same time I was the President's senior adviser on the military employment of atomic energy.

The policy adopted and steadily pursued by President Roosevelt and his advisers was a simple one. It was to spare no effort in securing the earliest possible successful development of an atomic weapon. The reasons for this policy were equally simple. The original experimental achievement of atomic fission had occurred in Germany in 1938, and it was known that the Germans had continued their experiments. In 1941 and 1942 they were believed to be ahead of us, and it was vital that they should not be the first to bring atomic weapons into the field of battle. Furthermore, if we should be the first to develop the weapon, we should have a great new instrument for shortening the war and minimizing destruction. At no time, from 1941 to 1945, did I ever hear it suggested by the President, or by any other responsible member of the government, that atomic energy should not be used in the war. All of us of course understood the terrible responsibility involved in our attempt to unlock the doors to such a devastating weapon; President Roosevelt particularly spoke to me many times of his own awareness of the catastrophic potentialities of our work. But we were at war, and the work must be done. I therefore emphasize that it was our common objective, throughout the war, to be the first to produce an atomic weapon and use it. The possible atomic weapon was considered to be a new and tremendously powerful explosive, as legitimate as any other of the deadly explosive weapons of modern war. The entire purpose was the production of a military weapon; on no other ground could the wartime expenditure of so much time and money have been justified. The exact circumstances in which that weapon might be used were unknown to any of us until the middle of 1945, and when that time came, as we shall presently see, the military use of atomic energy was connected with larger questions of national policy. [...]

[T]he Interim Committee was charged with the function of advising the President on the various questions raised by our apparently imminent success in developing an atomic weapon. I was its chairman, but the principal labor of guiding its extended deliberations fell to George L. Harrison, who acted as chairman in my absence. It will be useful to consider

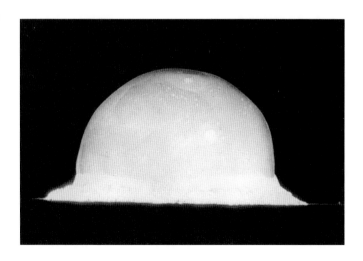

the work of the committee in some detail. Its members were the following, in addition to Mr. Harrison and myself:

James F. Byrnes (then a private citizen) as personal representative of the President.

Ralph A. Bard, Under Secretary of the Navy.

William L. Clayton, Assistant Secretary of State.

Dr. Vannevar Bush, Director, Office of Scientific Research and Development, and president of the Carnegie Institution of Washington.

Dr. Karl T. Compton, Chief of the Office of Field Service in the Office of Scientific Research and Development, and president of the Massachusetts Institute of Technology.

Dr. James B. Conant, Chairman of the National Defense Research Committee, and president of Harvard University.

The discussions of the committee ranged over the whole field of atomic energy, in its political, military, and scientific aspects. That part of its work which particularly concerns us here relates to its recommendations for the use of atomic energy against Japan, but it should be borne in mind that these recommendations were not made in a vacuum. The committee's work included the drafting of the statements which were published immediately after the first bombs were dropped, the drafting of a bill for the domestic control of atomic energy, and recommendations looking toward the international control of atomic energy. The Interim Committee was assisted in its work by a Scientific Panel whose members were the following: Dr. A. H. Compton, Dr. Enrico Fermi, Dr. E. O. Lawrence, and Dr. J. R. Oppenheimer. All four were nuclear physicists of the first rank; all four had held positions of great importance in the atomic project from its inception. At a meeting with the Interim Committee and the Scientific Panel on May 31, 1945, I urged all those present to feel free to express themselves on any phase of the subject, scientific or political. Both General Marshall and I at this meeting expressed the view that atomic energy could not be considered simply in terms of military weapons but must also be considered in terms of a new relationship of man to the universe.

On June 1, after its discussions with the Scientific Panel, the Interim Committee unanimously adopted the following recommendations:

(1) The bomb should be used against Japan as soon as possible.

(2) It should be used on a dual target—that is, a military installation or war plant surrounded by or adjacent to houses and other buildings most susceptible to damage, and

(3) It should be used without prior warning [of the nature of the weapon]. One member of the committee, Mr. Bard, later changed his view and dissented from recommendation (3).

In reaching these conclusions the Interim Committee carefully considered such alternatives as a detailed advance warning or a demonstration in some uninhabited area. Both of these suggestions were discarded as impractical. They were not regarded as likely to be effective in compelling a surrender of Japan, and both of them involved serious risks. Even the New Mexico test would not give final proof that any given bomb was certain to explode when dropped from an airplane. Quite apart from the generally unfamiliar nature of atomic explosives, there was the whole problem of exploding a bomb at a predetermined height in the air by a complicated mechanism which could not be tested in the static test of New Mexico. Nothing would have been more damaging to our effort to obtain surrender than a warning or a demonstration followed by a dud—and this was a real possibility. Furthermore, we had no bombs to waste. It was vital that a sufficient effect be quickly obtained with the few we had.

The Interim Committee and the Scientific Panel also served as a channel through which suggestions from other scientists working on the atomic project were forwarded to me and to the President. Among the suggestions thus forwarded was one memorandum which questioned using the bomb at all against the enemy. On June 16, 1945, after consideration of that memorandum, the Scientific Panel made a report, from which I quote the following paragraphs:

> The opinions of our scientific colleagues on the initial use of these weapons are not unanimous: they range from the proposal of a purely technical demonstration to that of the military application best designed to induce surrender. Those who advocate a purely technical demonstration would wish to outlaw the use of atomic weapons, and have feared that if we use the weapons now our position in future negotiations will be prejudiced. Others emphasize the opportunity of saving American lives by immediate military use, and believe that such use will improve the international prospects, in that they are more concerned with the prevention of war than with the elimination of this special weapon. We find ourselves closer to these latter views; *we can propose no technical demonstration likely to bring an end to the war; we see no acceptable alternative to direct military use.* [Italics mine]

With regard to these general aspects of the use of atomic energy, it is clear that we, as scientific men, have no proprietary rights. It is true that we are among the few citizens who have had occasion to give thoughtful consideration to these problems during the past few years. We have, however, no claim to special competence in solving the political, social, and military problems which are presented by the advent of atomic power.

The foregoing discussion presents the reasoning of the Interim Committee and its advisers. I have discussed the work of these gentlemen at length in order to make it clear that we sought the best advice that we could find. The committee's function was, of course, entirely advisory. The ultimate responsibility for the recommendation to the President rested upon me, and I have no desire to veil it. The conclusions of the committee were similar to my own, although I reached mine independently. I felt that to extract a genuine surrender from the Emperor and his military advisers, they must be administered a tremendous shock which would carry convincing proof of our power to destroy the Empire. Such an effective shock would save many times the number of lives, both American and Japanese, that it would cost. [...]

I wrote a memorandum for the President, on July 2, which I believe fairly represents the thinking of the American government as it finally took shape in action. This memorandum was prepared after discussion and general agreement with Joseph C. Grew, Acting Secretary of State, and Secretary of the Navy Forrestal, and when I discussed it with the President, he expressed his general approval.

July 2, 1945.

Memorandum for the President.

PROPOSED PROGRAM FOR JAPAN

1. The plans of operation up to and including the first landing have been authorized and the preparations for the operation are now actually going on. This situation was accepted by all members of your conference on Monday, June 18.

2. There is reason to believe that the operation for the occupation of Japan following the landing may be a very long, costly, and arduous struggle on our part. The terrain, much of which I have visited several times, has left the impression on my memory of being

one which would be susceptible to a last ditch defense such as has been made on Iwo Jima and Okinawa and which of course is very much larger than either of those two areas. According to my recollection it will be much more unfavorable with regard to tank maneuvering than either the Philippines or Germany.

3. If we once land on one of the main islands and begin a forceful occupation of Japan, we shall probably have cast the die of last ditch resistance. The Japanese are highly patriotic and certainly susceptible to calls for fanatical resistance to repel an invasion. Once started in actual invasion, we shall in my opinion have to go through with an even more bitter finish fight than in Germany. We shall incur the losses incident to such a war and we shall have to leave the Japanese islands even more thoroughly destroyed than was the case with Germany. This would be due both to the difference in the Japanese and German personal character and the differences in the size and character of the terrain through which the operations will take place.

4. A question then comes: Is there any alternative to such a forceful occupation of Japan which will secure for us the equivalent of an unconditional surrender of her forces and a permanent destruction of her power again to strike an aggressive blow at the "peace of the Pacific"? I am inclined to think that there is enough such chance to make it well worthwhile our giving them a warning of what is to come and a definite opportunity to capitulate. As above suggested, it should be tried before the actual forceful occupation of the homeland islands is begun and furthermore the warning should be given in ample time to permit a national reaction to set in.

We have the following enormously favorable factors on our side—factors much weightier than those we had against Germany:

Japan has no allies.

Her navy is nearly destroyed and she is vulnerable to a surface and underwater blockade which can deprive her of sufficient food and supplies for her population.

She is terribly vulnerable to our concentrated air attack upon her crowded cities, industrial and food resources.

She has against her not only the Anglo-American forces but the rising forces of China and the ominous threat of Russia.

We have inexhaustible and untouched industrial resources to bring to bear against her diminishing potential.

We have great moral superiority through being the victim of her first sneak attack.

The problem is to translate these advantages into prompt and economical achievement of our objectives. I believe Japan is susceptible to reason in such a crisis to a much greater extent than is indicated by our current press and other current comment. Japan is not a nation composed wholly of mad fanatics of an entirely different mentality from ours. On the contrary, she has within the past century shown herself to possess extremely intelligent people, capable in an unprecedentedly short time of adopting not only the complicated technique of Occidental civilization but to a substantial extent their culture and their political and social ideas. Her advance in all these respects during the short period of sixty or seventy years has been one of the most astounding feats of national progress in history—a leap from the isolated feudalism of centuries into the position of one of the six or seven great powers of the world. She has not only built up powerful armies and navies. She has maintained an honest and effective national finance and respected position in many of the sciences in which we pride ourselves. Prior to the forcible seizure of power over her government by the fanatical military group in 1931, she had for ten years lived a reasonably responsible and respectable international life.

My own opinion is in her favor on the two points involved in this question:

a. I think the Japanese nation has the mental intelligence and versatile capacity in such a crisis to recognize the folly of a fight to the finish and to accept the proffer of what will amount to an unconditional surrender; and

b. I think she has within her population enough liberal leaders (although now submerged by the terrorists) to be depended upon for her reconstruction as a responsible member of the family of nations. I think she is better in this last respect than Germany was. Her liberals yielded only at the point of the pistol and, so far as I am aware, their liberal attitude has not been personally subverted in the way which was so general in Germany.

On the other hand, I think that the attempt to exterminate her armies and her population by gunfire or other means will tend to produce a fusion of race solidity and antipathy which has no analogy in the case of Germany. We have a national interest in creating, if possible, a condition wherein the Japanese nation may live as a peaceful and useful member of the future Pacific community.

5. It is therefore my conclusion that a carefully timed warning be given to Japan by the chief representatives of the United States, Great Britain, China, and, if then a belligerent, Russia by calling upon Japan to surrender and permit the occupation of her country in order to insure its complete demilitarization for the sake of the future peace.

This warning should contain the following elements:

The varied and overwhelming character of the force we are about to bring to bear on the islands.

The inevitability and completeness of the destruction which the full application of this force will entail.

The determination of the Allies to destroy permanently all authority and influence of those who have deceived and misled the country into embarking on world conquest.

The determination of the Allies to limit Japanese sovereignty to her main islands and to render them powerless to mount and support another war.

The disavowal of any attempt to extirpate the Japanese as a race or to destroy them as a nation.

A statement of our readiness, once her economy is purged of its militaristic influence, to permit the Japanese to maintain such industries, particularly of a light consumer character, as offer no threat of aggression against their neighbors, but which can produce a sustaining economy, and provide a reasonable standard of living. The statement should indicate our willingness, for this purpose, to give Japan trade access to external raw materials, but no longer any control over the sources of supply outside her main islands. It should also indicate our willingness, in accordance with our now established foreign trade policy, in due course to enter into mutually advantageous trade relations with her.

The withdrawal from their country as soon as the above objectives of the Allies are accomplished, and as soon as there has been established a peacefully inclined government, of a character representative of the masses of the Japanese people. I personally think that if in saying this we should add that we do not exclude a constitutional monarchy under her present dynasty, it would substantially add to the chances of acceptance.

6. Success of course will depend on the potency of the warning which we give her. She has an extremely sensitive national pride and, as we are now seeing every day, when actually locked with the enemy will fight to the very death. For that reason the warning must be tendered before the actual invasion has occurred and while the impending destruction, though clear beyond peradventure, has not yet reduced her to fanatical despair. If Russia is a part of the threat, the Russian

attack, if actual, must not have progressed too far. Our own bombing should be confined to military objectives as far as possible.

It is important to emphasize the double character of the suggested warning. It was designed to promise destruction if Japan resisted, and hope, if she surrendered.

It will be noted that the atomic bomb is not mentioned in this memorandum. On grounds of secrecy the bomb was never mentioned except when absolutely necessary, and furthermore, it had not yet been tested. It was of course well forward in our minds, as the memorandum was written and discussed, that the bomb would be the best possible sanction if our warning were rejected. [...]

On July 28 the Premier of Japan, Suzuki, rejected the Potsdam ultimatum by announcing that it was "unworthy of public notice." In the face of this rejection we could only proceed to demonstrate that the ultimatum had meant exactly what it said when it stated that if the Japanese continued the war, "the full application of our military power, backed by our resolve, will mean the inevitable and complete destruction of the Japanese armed forces and just as inevitably the utter devastation of the Japanese homeland."

For such a purpose the atomic bomb was an eminently suitable weapon. The New Mexico test occurred while we were at Potsdam, on July 16. It was immediately clear that the power of the bomb measured up to our highest estimates. We had developed a weapon of such a revolutionary character that its use against the enemy might well be expected to produce exactly the kind of shock on the Japanese ruling oligarchy which we desired, strengthening the position of those who wished peace, and weakening that of the military party.

Because of the importance of the atomic mission against Japan, the detailed plans were brought to me by the military staff for approval. With President Truman's warm support I struck off the list of suggested targets the city of Kyoto. Although it was a target of considerable military importance, it had been the ancient capital of Japan and was a shrine of Japanese art and culture. We determined that it should be spared. I approved four other targets including the cities of Hiroshima and Nagasaki.

Hiroshima was bombed on August 6, and Nagasaki on August 9. These two cities were active working parts of the Japanese war effort. One was an army center; the other was naval and industrial. Hiroshima was the headquarters of the Japanese Army defending southern Japan and was a major military storage and assembly point. Nagasaki was a major seaport and it contained several large industrial plants of great wartime importance. We believed that our attacks had struck cities which must certainly be important to the Japanese military leaders, both Army and Navy, and we waited for a result. We waited one day. [...]

The two atomic bombs which we had dropped were the only ones we had ready, and our rate of production at the time was very small. Had the war continued until the projected invasion on November 1, additional fire raids of B-29's would have been more destructive of life and property than the very limited number of atomic raids which we could have executed in the same period. But the atomic bomb was more than a weapon of terrible destruction; it was a psychological weapon. In March 1945 our Air Force had launched its first great incendiary raid on the Tokyo area. In this raid more damage was done and more casualties were inflicted than was the case at Hiroshima. Hundreds of bombers took part and hundreds of tons of incendiaries were dropped. Similar successive raids burned out a great part of the urban area of Japan, but the Japanese fought on. On August 6 one B-29 dropped a single atomic bomb on Hiroshima. Three days later a second bomb was dropped on Nagasaki and the war was over. So far as the Japanese could know, our ability to execute atomic attacks, if necessary by many planes at a time, was unlimited. As Dr. Karl Compton has said, "it was not one atomic bomb, or two, which brought surrender; it was the experience of what an atomic bomb will actually do to a community, *plus the dread of many more*, that was effective."

The bomb thus served exactly the purpose we intended. The peace party was able to take the path of surrender, and

the whole weight of the Emperor's prestige was exerted in favor of peace. When the Emperor ordered surrender, and the small but dangerous group of fanatics who opposed him were brought under control, the Japanese became so subdued that the great undertaking of occupation and disarmament was completed with unprecedented ease. [...]

As I read over what I have written, I am aware that much of it, in this year of peace, may have a harsh and unfeeling sound. It would perhaps be possible to say the same things and say them more gently. But I do not think it would be wise. As I look back over the five years of my service as Secretary of War, I see too many stern and heartrending decisions to be willing to pretend that war is anything else than what it is. The face of war is the face of death; death is an inevitable part of every order that a wartime leader gives. The decision to use the atomic bomb was a decision that brought death to over a hundred thousand Japanese. No explanation can change that fact and I do not wish to gloss it over. But this deliberate, premeditated destruction was our least abhorrent choice. The destruction of Hiroshima and Nagasaki put an end to the Japanese war. It stopped the fire raids, and the strangling blockade; it ended the ghastly specter of a clash of great land armies.

In this last great action of the Second World War we were given final proof that war is death. War in the twentieth century has grown steadily more barbarous, more destructive, more debased in all its aspects. Now, with the release of atomic energy, man's ability to destroy himself is very nearly complete. The bombs dropped on Hiroshima and Nagasaki ended a war. They also made it wholly clear that we must never have another war. This is the lesson men and leaders everywhere must learn, and I believe that when they learn it they will find a way to lasting peace. There is no other choice.

GERTRUDE STEIN: A SELF-PORTRAIT

BY KATHERINE ANNE PORTER

DECEMBER 1947

[…] I want to say that just today I met Miss Hennessy and she was carrying, she did not have it with her, but she usually carried a wooden umbrella. This wooden umbrella is carved out of wood and looks like a real one even to the little button and the rubber string that holds it together. It is all right except when it rains. When it rains it does not open and Miss Hennessy looks a little foolish but she does not mind because it is after all the only wooden umbrella in Paris. And even if there were lots of others it would not make any difference.

GERTRUDE STEIN, *EVERYBODY'S AUTOBIOGRAPHY*

Wen Kahnweiler the picture dealer told Miss Stein that Picasso had stopped painting and had taken to writing poetry, she confessed that she had "a funny feeling" because "things belonged to you and writing belonged to me. I know writing belongs to me, I am quite certain," but still it was a blow. "…No matter how certain you are about anything belonging to you if you hear that somebody says it belongs to them it gives you a funny feeling."

Later she buttonholed Picasso at Kahnweiler's gallery, shook him, kissed him, lectured him, told him that his poetry was worse than bad, it was offensive as a Cocteau drawing and in much the same way, it was unbecoming. He defended himself by reminding her that she had said he was an extraordinary person, and he believed an extraordinary person should be able to do anything. She said that to her it was a repellent sight when a person who could do one thing well dropped it for something else he could not do at all. Convinced, or defeated, he promised to give back writing to its natural owner.

Writing was no doubt the dearest of Miss Stein's possessions, but it was not the only one. The pavilion atelier in rue de Fleurus was a catch-all of beings and created objects, and everything she looked upon was hers in more than the usual sense. Her weighty numerous divans and armchairs covered with dark, new-looking horsehair; her dogs, Basket and Pépé, conspicuous, special, afflicted as neurotic children; her clutter of small tables each with its own clutter of perhaps valuable but certainly treasured objects; her Alice B. Toklas; her visitors; and finally, ranging the walls from floor to ceiling, giving the impression that they were hung three deep, elbowing each other, canceling each other's best effects in the jealous way of pictures, was her celebrated collection of paintings by her collection of celebrated painters. These were everybody of her time whom Miss Stein elected for her own, from her idol Picasso (kidnapped bodily from brother Leo, who saw him first) to miniscule Sir Francis Rose, who seems to have appealed to the pixy in her.

Yet the vaguely lighted room where things accumulated, where they appeared to have moved in under a compulsion to be possessed once for all by someone who knew how to take hold firmly, gave no impression of disorder. On the contrary, an air of solid comfort, of inordinate sobriety and permanence, of unadventurous middle-class domesticity—respectability is the word, at last—settled around the shoulders of the guest like a Paisley shawl, a borrowed shawl of course, something to be worn and admired for a moment and handed back to the owner. Miss Stein herself sat there in full possession of herself, the scene, the spectators, wearing thick no-colored shapeless woolen clothes and honest woolen stockings knitted for her by Miss Toklas, looking extremely like a handsome old Jewish patriarch who had backslid and shaved off his beard.

Surrounded by her listeners, she talked in a slow circle in her fine deep voice, the word "perception" occurring again and again and yet again like the brass ring the children snatch for as their hobby horses whirl by. She was in fact at one period surrounded by snatching children, the literary young, a good many of them American, between two wars in a falling world. […]

Serious young men who were having a hard time learning to write realized with relief that there was nothing at all to it if you just relaxed and put down the first thing that came into your head. She gave them a romantic name, the Lost Generation, and a remarkable number of them tried earnestly if unsuccessfully to live up to it. A few of them were really lost, and disappeared, but others had just painted themselves into a very crowded corner. She laid a cooling hand upon their agitated brows and asked with variations, What did it matter? There were only a few geniuses, after all, among which she was one, only the things a genius said made any difference, the rest was "just there," and so she disposed of all the dark questions of life, art, human relations, and death, even eternity, even God, with perfect Stein logic, bringing the scene again into its proper focus, upon herself.

Some of the young men went away, read a book, began thinking things over, and became the best writers of their time. Humanly, shamefacedly, they then jeered at their former admiration, and a few even made the tactical error of quarreling with her. She enjoyed their discipleship while it lasted, and dismissed them from existence when it ended. It is easy to see what tremendous vitality and direction there was in the arts all over the world; for not everything was happening only in France, for life was generated in many a noisy seething confusion in many countries. Little by little the legitimate line of succession appeared, the survivors emerged each with his own shape and meaning, the young vanguard became the Old Masters and even old hat.

In the meantime our heroine went on talking, vocally or on paper, and in that slow swarm of words, out of the long drone and mutter and stammer of her lifetime monologue, often there emerged a phrase of ancient native independent wisdom, for she had a shrewd deep knowledge of the commoner human motives. Her judgments were neither moral nor intellectual, and least of all aesthetic, indeed they were not even judgments, but simply her description from observation of acts, words, appearances giving her view; limited, personal in the extreme, prejudiced without qualification, based on assumptions founded in the void of pure unreason. For example, French notaries' sons have always something strange about them—look at Jean Cocteau. The Spaniard has a natural center of ignorance, all except Juan Gris. On the other hand, Dali had not only the natural Spanish center of ignorance, but still another variety, quite malignant, of his own. Preachers' sons do not turn out like other people—E. E. Cummings, just for one. Painters are always little short round

men—Picasso and a crowd of them. And then she puts her finger lightly on an American peculiarity of our time: "...so perhaps they are right the Americans in being more interested in you than in the work you have done, although they would not be interested in you if you had not done the work you had done." And she remarked once to her publisher that she was famous in America not for her work that people understood but for that which they did not understand. That was the kind of thing she could see through at a glance.

It was not that she was opposed to ideas, but that she was not interested in anybody's ideas but her own, except as material to put down on her endless flood of pages. Like writing, opinion also belonged to Miss Stein, and nothing annoyed her more—she was easily angered about all sorts of things—than for anyone not a genius or who had no reputation that she respected, to appear to be thinking in her presence. Of all those GI's who swarmed about her in her last days, if any one showed any fight at all, any tendency to question her pronouncements, she smacked him down like a careful grandmother, for his own good. Her GI heroes Brewsie and Willie are surely as near to talking zombies as anything ever seen in a book, and she loved, not them, but their essential zombiness.

Like all talkers, she thought other people talked too much, and there is recorded only one instance of someone getting the drop on her—who else but Alfred Stieglitz? She sat through a whole session at their first meeting without uttering one word, a feat which he mentioned with surprised approval. If we knew nothing more of Stieglitz than this we would know he was a great talker. She thought that the most distressing sound was that of the human voice, other peoples' voices, "as the hoot owl is almost the best sound," but in spite of this she listened quite a lot. When she was out walking the dogs, if workmen were tearing up the streets she would ask them what they were doing and what they would be doing next. She only stopped to break the monotony of walking, but she remembered their answers. When a man passed making up a bitter little song against her dog and his conduct vis-à-vis lamp posts and house walls, she put it all down, and it is wonderfully good reporting. Wise or silly or nothing at all, down everything goes on the page with the air of everything being equal, unimportant in itself, important because it happened to her and she was writing about it.

She had not always been exactly there, exactly that. There had been many phases, all in consistent character, each giving way in turn for the next, of her portentous being. Ford Madox Ford described her, in earlier Paris days, as trundling through the streets in her high-wheeled American car, being a spectacle and being herself at the same time. And this may have been near the time of Man Ray's photograph of her, wearing a kind of monk's robe, her poll clipped, her granite front and fine eyes displayed at their best period.

Before that, she was a youngish stout woman, not ever really young, with a heavy shrewd face between a hard round pompadour and a round lace collar, looking more or less like Picasso's earliest portrait of her. What saved her then from a good honest husband, probably a stockbroker, and a houseful of children? The answer must be that her envelope was a tricky disguise of Nature, that she was of the company of Amazons which nineteenth-century America produced among its many prodigies: not-men, not-women, answerable to no function in either sex, whose careers were carried on, and how successfully, in whatever field they chose: they were educators, writers, editors, politicians, artists, world travelers, and international hostesses, who lived in public and by the public and played out their self-assumed, self-created rôles in such masterly freedom as only a few early medieval queens had equaled. Freedom to them meant precisely freedom from men and their stuffy rules for women. They usurped with a high hand the traditional masculine privileges of movement, choice, and the use of direct, personal power. They were few in number and they were not only to be found in America, and Miss Stein belonged with them, no doubt of it, in spite of a certain temperamental passivity which was Oriental, not feminine. With the top of her brain she was a modern girl, a New Woman, interested in scientific experiment, historical research, the rational view; for a time she was even a medical student, but she could not deceive herself for long. Even during her four years at Radcliffe, where the crisp theories of higher education battled with the womb-shaped female mind (and they always afterward seemed foolish to her at Radcliffe) she worried and worried, for worrying and thinking were synonyms to her, about the meaning of the universe, the riddle of human life, about time and its terrible habit of passing, God, death, eternity, and she felt very lonely in the awful singularity of her confusions. Added to this, history taught her that whole civilizations die and disappear utterly, "and now it happens again," and it gave her a great fright. She was sometimes frightened afterward, "but now well being frightened is something less frightening than it was," but her

ambiguous mind faced away from speculation. Having discovered with relief that all knowledge was not her province, she accepted rightly, she said, every superstition. To be in the hands of fate, of magic, of the daemonic forces, what freedom it gave her not to decide, not to act, not to accept any responsibility for anything—one held the pen and let the mind wander. One sat down and somebody did everything for one.

Still earlier she was a plump solemn little girl abundantly upholstered in good clothes, who spent her allowance on the work of Shelley, Thackeray, and George Eliot in fancy bindings, for she loved reading and *Clarissa Harlowe* was once her favorite novel. These early passions exhausted her; in later life she swam in the relaxing bath of detective and murder mysteries, because she liked somebody being dead in a story, and of them all Dashiell Hammett killed them off most to her taste. Her first experience of the real death of somebody had taught her that it could be pleasant for her too. "One morning we could not wake our father." This was in East Oakland, California. "Leo climbed in by the window and called out that he was dead in his bed and he was." It seems to have been the first thing he ever did of which his children, all five of them, approved. Miss Stein declared plainly they none of them liked him at all: "As I say, fathers are depressing but our family had one," she confessed, and conveys the notion that he was a bore of the nagging, petty sort, the kind that worries himself and others into the grave.

Considering her tepid, sluggish nature, really sluggish like something eating its way through a leaf, Miss Stein could grow quite animated on the subject of her early family life, and some of her stories are as pretty and innocent as lizards running over tombstones on a hot day in Maryland. It was a solid, getting-on sort of middle-class Jewish family of Austrian origin, Keyser on one side, Stein on the other: and the Keysers came to Baltimore about 1820. All branches of the family produced their individual eccentrics—there was even an uncle who believed in the Single Tax—but they were united in their solid understanding of the value of money as the basis of a firm stance in this world. There were incomes, governesses, spending money, guardians appointed when parents died, and Miss Stein was fascinated from childhood with stories about how people earned their first dollar. When, rather late, she actually earned some dollars herself by writing, it changed her entire viewpoint about the value of her work and of her own personality. It came to her as revelation that the only difference between men and four-footed animals is that men can count, and when they count, they like best to count money. In her first satisfaction at finding she had a commercial value, she went on a brief binge of spending money just for the fun of it. But she really knew better. Among the five or six of the seven deadly sins which she practiced with increasing facility and advocated as virtues, avarice became her favorite. Americans in general she found to be rather childish about money: they spent it or gave it away and enjoyed wastefully with no sense of its fierce latent power. [...]

There are the tones of sloth, of that boredom which is a low-pressure despair, of monotony, of obsession, in this portrait; she went walking out of boredom, she could drive a car, talk, write, but anything else made her nervous. People who were doing anything annoyed her: to be doing nothing, she thought, was more interesting than to be doing something. The air of deathly solitude surrounded her; yet the parade of names in her book would easily fill several printed pages, all with faces attached which she could see were quite different from each other, all talking, each taking his own name and person for granted—a thing she could never understand. Yet she could see what they were doing and could remember what they said. She only listened attentively to Picasso—for whose sake she would crack almost any head in sight—so she half-agreed when he said Picabia was the worst painter of all; but still, found herself drawn to Picabia because his name was Francis. She had discovered that men named Francis were always elegant, and though they might not know anything else, they always knew about themselves. This would remind her that she had never found out who she was. Again and again she would doubt her own identity, and that of everyone else. When she worried about this aloud to Alice B. Toklas, saying she believed it impossible for anyone ever to be certain who he was, Alice B. Toklas made, in context, the most inspired remark in the whole book. "It depends on who you are," she said, and you might think that would have ended the business. Not at all.

These deep-set, chronic fears led her to a good deal of quarreling, for when she quarreled she seems to have felt more real. She mentions quarrels with Max Jacobs, Francis Rose, with Dali, with Picabia, with Picasso, with Virgil Thomson, with Braque, with Breton, and how many others, though she rarely says just why they quarreled or how they made it up. Almost nobody went away and stayed, and the awful inertia of habit in friendships oppressed her. She was sometimes discouraged at the prospect of having to go on seeing certain persons to the end, merely because she had once seen them. The world seemed smaller every day, swarming with people perpetually in movement, full of restless notions which, once examined by her, were inevitably proved to be fallacious, or at least entirely useless. She found that she could best get rid of them by putting them in a book. "That is very funny if you write about any one they do not exist any more, for you, so why see them again. Anyway, that is the way I am."

But as she wrote a book and disposed of one horde, another came on, and worried her afresh, discussing their ludicrous solemn topics, trying to understand things, and being unhappy about it. When Picasso was fretful because she argued with Dali and not with him, she explained that "one discusses things with stupid people but not with sensible ones." Her true grudge against intelligent people was that they talked "as if they were getting ready to change something." Change belonged to Miss Stein, and the duty of the world was to stand still so that she could move about in it comfortably. Her top flight of reasoning on the subject of intelligence ran as follows: "The most actively war-like nations could always convince the pacifists to become pro-German. That is because pacifists were such intelligent beings they could follow what any one is saying. If you follow what any one is saying then you are a pacifist you are a pro-German...therefore understanding is a very dull occupation."

Intellectuals, she said, always wanted to change things because they had an unhappy childhood. "Well, I never had an unhappy childhood, what is the use of having an unhappy anything?" Léon Blum, then Premier of France, had had an unhappy childhood, and she inclined to the theory that the political uneasiness of France could be traced to this fact.

There was not, of course, going to be another war (this was in 1937!), but if there was, there *would* be, naturally; and she never tired of repeating that dancing and war are the same thing "because both are forward and back," while revolution, on the contrary, is up and down, which is why it gets nowhere. Sovietism was even then going rapidly out of fashion in her circles, because they had discovered that it is very conservative, even if the Communists do not think so.

Saul Steinberg

Anarchists, being rarities, did not go out of fashion so easily. The most interesting thing that ever happened to America was the Civil War; but General Lee was severely to be blamed for leading his country into that war, just the same, because he must have known they could not win; and to her, it was absurd that any one should join battle in defense of a principle in face of certain defeat. For practical purposes, honor was not even a word. Still it was an exciting war and gave an interest to America which that country would never have had without it. "If you win you do not lose and if you lose you do not win." Even as she was writing these winged words, the Spanish Civil War, the Republicans against the Franco-Fascists, kept obtruding itself. And why?

"Not because it is a revolution, but because I know so well the places they are mentioning and the things there they are destroying." When she was little in Oakland, California, she loved the big, nice American fires that had "so many horses and firemen to attend them," and when she was older, she found that floods, for one thing, always read worse in the papers than they really are; besides how can you care much about what is going on if you don't see it or know the people? [...] And when she asked Dashiell Hammett why so many young men authors were writing novels about tender young male heroines instead of the traditional female ones, he explained that it was because as women grew more and more self-confident, men lost confidence in themselves, and turned to each other, or became their own subjects for fiction. This, or something else, reminded her several times that she could not write a novel, therefore no one could any more, and no one should waste time trying.

Somehow by such roundabouts we arrive at the important, the critical event in all this eventful history. Success. Success in this world, here and now, was what Miss Stein wanted. She knew just what it was, how it should look and feel, how much it should weigh and what it was worth over the counter. It was not enough to be a genius if you had to go on supporting your art on a private income. To be the center of a recondite literary cult, to be surrounded by listeners and imitators and seekers, to be mentioned in the same breath with James Joyce, and to have turned out bales of titles by merely writing a half-hour each day: she had all that, and what did it amount to? There was a great deal more and she must have it. As to her history of the human race, she confessed: "I have always been bothered...but mostly...because after all I do as simply as it can, as commonplacely as it can say, what everybody can and does do; I never know what they can do, I really do not know what they are, I do not think that any one can think because if they do, then who is who?"

It was high time for a change, and yet it occurred at hazard. If there had not been a beautiful season in October and part of November 1932, permitting Miss Stein to spend that season quietly in her country house, the *Autobiography of Alice B. Toklas* might never have been written. But it was written, and Miss Stein became a best seller in America; she made real money. With Miss Toklas, she had a thrilling tour of the United States and found crowds of people eager to see her and listen to her. And at last she got what she had really wanted all along: to be published in the *Atlantic Monthly* and the *Saturday Evening Post*.

Now she had everything, or nearly. For a while she was afraid to write any more, for fear her latest efforts would not please her public. She had never learned who she was, and yet suddenly she had become somebody else. "You are you because your little dog knows you, but when your public knows you and does not want to pay you, and when your public knows you and does want to pay you, you are not the same you."

This would be of course the proper moment to take leave, as our heroine adds at last a golden flick of light to her self-portrait. "Anyway, I was a celebrity." The practical result was that she could no longer live on her income. But

she and Alice B. Toklas moved into an apartment once occupied by Queen Christina of Sweden, and they began going out more, and seeing even more people, and talking, and Miss Stein settled every question as it came up, more and more. But who wants to read about success? It is the early struggle which makes a good story.

She and Alice B. Toklas enjoyed both the wars. The first one especially being a lark with almost no one getting killed where you could see, and it ended so nicely too, without changing anything. The second was rather more serious. She lived safely enough in Bilignin throughout the German occupation, and there is a pretty story that the whole village conspired to keep her presence secret. She had been a citizen of the world in the best European tradition; for though America was her native land, she had to live in Europe because she felt at home there. In the old days people paid little attention to wars, fought as they were out of sight by professional soldiers. She had always liked the notion, too, of the gradual Orientalization of the West, the peaceful penetration of the East into European culture. It had been going on a great while, and all Western geniuses worth mentioning were Orientals: look at Picasso, look at Einstein. Russians are Tartars, Spaniards are Saracens—had not all great twentieth-century painting been Spanish? And her cheerful conclusion was, that "Einstein was the creative philosophic mind of the century, and I have been the creative literary mind of the century also, with the Oriental mixing with the European." She added, as a casual afterthought, "Perhaps Europe is finished."

That was in 1938, and she could not be expected to know that war was near. They had only been sounding practice *alertes* in Paris against expected German bombers since 1935. She spoke out of her natural frivolity and did not mean it. She liked to prophesy, but warned her hearers that her prophecies never came out right, usually the very opposite, and no matter what happened, she was always surprised. She was surprised again: as the nations of Europe fell, and the Germans came again over the frontiers of France for the third time in three generations, the earth shook under her own feet, and not somebody else's. It made an astonishing difference. Something mysterious touched her in her old age. She got a fright, and this time not for ancient vanished civilizations, but for this civilization, this moment; and she was quite thrilled with relief and gay when the American Army finally came in, and the Germans were gone. She did not in the least know why the Germans had come, but they were gone, and so far as she could see, the American Army had chased them out. She remembered with positive spread-eagle patriotism that America was her native land. At last America itself belonged to Miss Stein, and she claimed it, in a formal published address to other Americans. Anxiously she urged them to stay rich, to be powerful and learn how to use power, not to waste themselves; for the first time she used the word "spiritual." Ours was a spiritual as well as a material fight; Lincoln's great lucid words about government of the people by the people for the people suddenly sounded like a trumpet through her stammering confession of faith, she wanted nothing now to stand between her and her newly discovered country. By great good luck she was born on the winning side and she was going to stay there. And we were not to forget about money as the source of power; "Remember the depression, don't be afraid to look it in the face and find out the reason why, if you don't find out the reason why you'll go poor and my God, how I would hate to have my native land go poor."

The mind so long shapeless and undisciplined could not now express any knowledge out of its long willful ignorance. But the heart spoke its crude urgent language. She had liked the doughboys in the other war well enough, but this time she fell in love with the whole American Army below the rank of lieutenant. She "breathed, ate, drank, lived GI's," she told them, and inscribed numberless photographs for them, and asked them all to come back again. After her flight over Germany in an American bomber, she wrote about how, so often, she would stand staring into the sky watching American war planes going over, longing to be up there again with her new loves, in the safe, solid air. She murmured, "Bless them, bless them." She had been impatient with many of them who had still been naïve enough to believe they were fighting against an evil idea that threatened everybody; some of them actually were simple enough to say they had been—or believed they had been—fighting for democratic government. "What difference does it make what kind of government you have?" she would ask. "All governments are alike. Just remember you won the war." But still, at the end, she warned them to have courage and not be just yes or no men. And she said, "Bless them, bless them."

It was the strangest thing, as if the wooden umbrella feeling the rain had tried to forsake its substance and take on the nature of its form; and was struggling slowly, slowly, much too late, to unfold.

Anywhere in Europe

by Anne Morrow Lindbergh

April 1948

There is a new type of habitat in Europe today. It varies slightly from place to place. It may be the headquarters where you get your ration books, or the office where you apply for a visa, or the bureau where you pay your electricity bill, or ask for a permit for extra milk for a sick child, or for materials to mend a leaking roof. But it is essentially the same in color, odor, feeling. There is an archetype of this abode of applications, this palace of permits, this spider's nest of red tape, this hourglass of officialdom, through which life filters today in Europe—a Europe of shortages, barriers, suspicions, paralysis.

Because of the lack of houses, these official spiders' nests often settle in old mansions, stripped of their former trappings, but still redolent of the elegance of another day. There is a faint aroma of nostalgia about them, a backward look, a quality of hope in reverse, so to speak—the perfect setting for the transient occupants who file through them, those patient, humble petitioners, trying to find a normality, an order, a pattern to life that is gone forever.

One hurries through the usual tunnel-like entrance, past the curtained door of the concierge, a dark cave in which she sits endlessly knitting, like one of the blind spinners of fate. If you should stop and ask your way, she is just as likely to go right on knitting, impervious to interruption. "Pardon, Madame?" you might insist. Then looking up pettishly, "Can't you see that I'm busy?" she is apt to fling at you. Everyone is busy in these spiders' nests, only one is not quite sure what they are spinning.

You go on to the closed court behind, where the light is subdued, as though sifted through water to the bottom of an aquarium. The single chestnut tree, its roots under worn cobbles, is already dropping its leaves, dried up and tinged with brown, although it is only August. The old house rises before you, four stories high, to its genteel mansard roof, missing a few tiles here and there. Its long casement windows open onto grillwork balconies, dingy with rust. The paint is peeling off the slender, accordion-pleated shutters, and the formal cornices have a slightly decayed look—like cheese. The grand entrance door, where carriages once drove up, is covered with an ornate *porte-cochère*, a glass parasol of a roof. Several petals of the parasol are knocked out, which gives an odd toothless grin to the otherwise respectable, if faded, face of the house.

Up the broad steps trickles a line of people, hatless, coatless, barelegged, carrying their dusty leather portfolios, their bulging string shopping bags, their shapeless brown paper parcels. They are standing in line, in a vague sort of way; but the line has collapsed, gone slack with waiting, so that the separate figures seem purposeless, as if standing around for nothing. Actually, it is not a purpose they lack, but simply hope. They know already what lies before them.

The trickle leads up the stone steps into the once elegant reception hall, its polished parquetry floors now dusty with many shuffling feet, its pale, embossed, paneled walls grimy from many pencil-smudged hands, or damp shoulders that have leaned against them in weariness.

Desks barricade the hall at intervals, like hurdles in an obstacle race, but there are no chairs. Next to the front door reposes a dilapidated red plush sofa, moved out from one of the former salons. (Monsieur's private study, no doubt.) People stand around and half lean against its graceful curved back. No one sits on it. Why not? Ah—yes, it has been sat on too much; one end has collapsed to the floor. Then why don't they remove it? Nobody knows. At the back of the hall is a high bookcase, its shelves stuffed with old files, old papers, yellow with age and gritty with dust. Some of them have belched out of the jammed shelves, onto the floor where they lie in crumpled confusion. No one bothers to pick them up. There is a stale all-pervading odor of dust, ink, old newspapers, and humanity. Chiefly humanity.

For it is humanity, in the dejected trickle of applicants, that is slowly seeping by the desks. Those desks, that mean nothing once they are passed. Those officials, in threadbare pavement-colored suits, who stop you and ask you questions, but who cannot help you. Those myriad doors that honeycomb the hall, all marked "Private! Absolutely forbidden to enter!" But the signs are make-believe, like the scribbled signs of children playing house. It is an illusion only that they give, of privacy, of importance, of activity. Nothing will be accomplished when you finally break through and find inside still another line, still another desk. "You must have your paper stamped, Madame, by the Colonel— The Colonel is out for lunch—Well, he is usually back at three...." It is now four. The voice of a Kafka novel echoes in your mind, "You will miss him, whether you stay or whether you go!"

But one stays; one stands around; one waits. Here is a man with emaciated arms, white as macaroni sticks, protruding from a limp shirt. He is leaning against a baroque marble mantel. Above his head is a painted panel, left there from other days. (This must have been Madame's boudoir.) It is Venus, reposing on a bed of roses. He does not look up to see it. None of these people look up. They are only intent on getting past the desks, past the officials, past the doors marked "Absolutely Private," to that last desk (God's Desk, to them); there they can tell their unique, tiny, personal story to a questionnaire that is interested only in statistics.

"You have written, Monsieur?... Then I can only say, Monsieur, they do not consider your request of sufficient importance... If you wish, you may fill out this form."

Oh, those forms—those forms that do not fit you or your life. Those printed boxes that cannot contain a living man. Those questions that seem always directed at someone else over your shoulder—not you. *"Where is your present domicile?"* Where indeed? "You know, Monsieur, it is so hard to get a room, nowadays...I am staying with my mother-in-law—but it is very crowded—we are two families in four rooms—we keep hoping to find another...." The forms are not interested. *"What is your present occupation?"* "Well, I am supposed to be a scientist, but there is no money in it—with food so expensive, you see...so I mend watches in my cousin's shop.... But I might get another job—next week, perhaps...." The desk is not interested. *"Where is your present domicile?" "What is your present occupation?"* Simple enough questions; but the applicants find them difficult to answer. They feel in a kind of numb desperation that they do not fit into these boxes, where they are being perma-

Ben Shahn

nently nailed. They know, dumbly but instinctively, that their warm, vivid, flowing, particular story will not stay on those straight black lines. But they do not protest. They are so used to being filed in cabinets, numbered in rows, and nailed in boxes. Nobody protests.

Yes, the Americans still protest. "But, God damn it, I've been waiting four months!" an American business man explodes at the desk in front of me. "I'm sick of waiting and getting pushed all over the place. I'm not a schoolboy any more—I went to school thirty years ago. It wasn't so bad to get pushed around then, but—by God—I'm a lot older now, and I can't go back to school again. To hell with it— I'm through!"

Suddenly, the door opens—the door of this super-private inner office, this "Absolutely-forbidden-to-enter" sanctum. An American soldier comes in. He does not slip in unobtrusively like most people, awed to find themselves at last in the holy of holies. He blows in like a breeze off Lake Michigan. He seems oblivious of everyone else in the room, and, in fact, he towers above them. His neat khaki uniform fits his easy erect frame. His arms are not through at the elbows, and his trousers are not baggy at the knees. His shoulders are broad and square, not bent with waiting; and his clean-cut face has the good, ruddy color of oak leaves in October. Everyone looks up.

There is an expectant hush in the room. All sounds cease for an instant; the shuffling feet, the rustle of papers, the colorless monotone of complaints (like the minor drone of insects on a summer day). Even the telephone, by some miracle of tact, stops ringing.

He strides over to the main desk (God's Desk) and sticks out his hand. "I just wanted to say, thanks a lot," his voice rings out in the unnatural stillness. (Ah—he has got what he wanted! Each frustrated applicant in the room is pleased—not envious, just pleased. Then it is possible to break through—the American has done it. It is possible, then.) "Well," he laughs. "I guess you'll be glad to see the last of me," he flings over his shoulder as he wheels around and goes out again. Everyone looks after him; the man with the macaroni arms, the woman in the corner, slumped over her string shopping bag, the spectacled watch-mender with a hundred fine lines in his forehead.

There is a look on their faces that is difficult to define. It is the expression one sometimes sees on the winter-dulled faces of people sitting on a park-bench on a March morning. The dirty snow still covers frozen playground mud; the naked branches of trees are still black and bony against a hard blue sky. But there is something in the quality of increased light, in the warmth felt through to shoulder bones, in the green-house humidity of melting snow, that brings an openness to people's faces. It is possible, then, they feel for the first time—they knew it before in their minds but their bodies had ceased to believe it—spring really is possible.

The faces following the American out of the inner office have this same expression of openness. It is a little too hungry to be called happiness; and a little too happy to be called hunger. It might be described as expectancy, a possibility of belief, an early March forerunner of hope.

Is it this, then, I think, as the plaintive drone of insects starts again, that we have to give Europe?

ART FOR ART'S SAKE

BY E. M. FORSTER

AUGUST 1949

I believe in art for art's sake. It is, as you know, an unfashionable belief, and some of my statements must be of the nature of an apology. Fifty years ago I should have faced you with more confidence. A writer or a speaker who chose "Art for Art's Sake" for his theme fifty years ago could be sure of being in the swim, and could feel so confident of success that he sometimes dressed himself in aesthetic costumes suitable to the occasion—in an embroidered dressing gown, perhaps, or a blue velvet suit with a Lord Fauntleroy collar; or a toga, or a kimono, and carried a poppy or a lily or a long peacock's feather in his medieval hand. Times have changed. Not thus can I present either myself or my theme today. My aim rather is to ask you quietly to reconsider for a few minutes a phrase which has been much misused and much abused, but which has, I believe, great importance for us—has, indeed, eternal importance.

Now we can easily dismiss those peacock's feathers and other affectations—they are but trifles—but I want also to dismiss a more dangerous heresy, namely the silly idea that only art matters, an idea which has somehow got mixed up with the idea of art for art's sake, and has helped to discredit it. Many things, besides art, matter. It is merely one of the things that matter, and high though the claims are that I make for it, I want to keep them in proportion. No one can spend his or her life entirely in the creation or the appreciation of masterpieces. Man lives, and ought to live, in a complex world, full of conflicting claims, and if we simplified them down into the aesthetic he would be sterilized. Art for art's sake does not mean that only art

"A Sunday on La Grande Jatte," by Georges Seurat.

matters, and I would also like to order out such phrases as, "The Life of Art," "Living for Art," and even, "Art's High Mission." They confuse and mislead.

What does the phrase mean? Instead of generalizing, let us take a specific instance—Shakespeare's *Macbeth*, for example, and pronounce the words, "*Macbeth* for *Macbeth's* sake." What does that mean? Well, the play has several aspects—it is educational, it teaches us something about legendary Scotland, something about Jacobean England, and a good deal about human nature and its perils. We can study its origins, and study and enjoy its dramatic technique and the music of its diction, as Edith Sitwell has. All that is true. But *Macbeth* is furthermore a world of its own, created by Shakespeare and existing in virtue of its own poetry. It is in this aspect *Macbeth* for *Macbeth's* sake, and that is what I intend by the phrase "art for art's sake." A work of art—whatever else it may be—is a self-contained entity, with a life of its own imposed on it by its creator. It has internal order. It may have external form. That is how we recognize it.

Take for another example that picture of Seurat's which I saw two years ago in Chicago—"*La Grande Jatte.*" Here again there is much to study and to enjoy: the pointillism, the charming face of the seated girl, the nineteenth-century Parisian Sunday sunlight, the sense of motion in immobility. But here again there is something more; "*La Grande Jatte*" forms a world of its own, created by Seurat and existing by virtue of its own poetry: "*La Grande Jatte*" *pour "La Grande Jatte*": *l'art pour l'art.* Like *Macbeth* it has internal order and internal life.

It is to the conception of order that I would now turn. This is important to my argument, and I want to make a digression, and glance at order in daily life, before I come to order in art.

In the world of daily life, the world which we perforce inhabit, there is much talk about order, particularly from statesmen and politicians. They tend, however, to confuse order with orders, just as they confuse creation with regulations. Order, I suggest, is something evolved from within, not something imposed from without; it is an internal stability, a vital harmony, and, in the social and political category, it has never existed except for the convenience of historians. Viewed realistically, the past is really a series of *disorders*, succeeding one another by discoverable laws, no doubt, and certainly marked by an increasing growth of human interference, but disorders all the same. So that, speaking as a writer, what I hope for today is for disorder which will be more favorable to artists than is the present one, and which will provide them with fuller inspirations and better material conditions. It will not last—nothing lasts—but there have been some advantageous disorders in the past—for instance, in ancient Athens, in Renaissance Italy, eighteenth-century France, periods in China and Persia—and we may do something to accelerate the next one. But let us not again fix our hearts where true joys are not to be found. We were promised a new order after the first world war through the League of Nations. It did not come, nor have I faith in present promises, by whomsoever endorsed. The implacable offensive of Science forbids. We cannot reach social and political stability for the reason that we continue to make scientific discoveries and to apply them, and thus to destroy the arrangements which were based on more elementary discoveries. If Science would discover rather than apply—if, in other words, men were more interested in knowledge than in power—mankind would be in a far safer position, the stability statesmen talk about would be a possibility, there could be a new order based on vital harmony, and the earthly millennium might approach. But Science shows no signs of doing this: she gave us the internal combustion engine, and before we had digested and assimilated it with terrible pains into our social system, she harnessed the atom, and destroyed any new order that seemed to be evolving. How can man get into harmony with his surroundings when he is constantly altering them? The future of our race is, in this direction, more unpleasant than we care to admit, and it has sometimes seemed to me

that its best chance lies through apathy, uninventiveness, and inertia. Universal exhaustion might promote that Change of Heart which is at present so briskly recommended from a thousand pulpits. Universal exhaustion would certainly be a new experience. The human race has never undergone it, and is still too perky to admit that it may be coming and might result in a sprouting of new growth through the decay.

I must not pursue these speculations any further—they lead me too far from my terms of reference and maybe from yours. But I do want to emphasize that order in daily life and in history, order in the social and political category, is unattainable under our present psychology.

Where is it attainable? Not in the astronomical category, where it was for many years enthroned. The heavens and the earth have become terribly alike since Einstein. No longer can we find a reassuring contrast to chaos in the night sky and look up with George Meredith to the stars, the army of unalterable law, or listen for the music of the spheres. Order is not there. In the entire universe there seem to be only two possibilities for it. The first of them—which again lies outside my terms of reference—is the divine order, the mystic harmony, which according to all religions is available for those who can contemplate it. We must admit its possibility, on the evidence of the adepts, and we must believe them when they say that it is attained, if attainable, by prayer. "O thou who changest not, abide with me," said one of its poets. *"Ordina questo amor, o tu che m'ami,"* said another: "Set love in order thou who lovest me." The existence of a divine order, though it cannot be tested, has never been disproved.

The second possibility for order lies in the aesthetic category, which is my subject here: the order which an artist can create in his own work, and to that we must now return. A work of art, we are all agreed, is a unique product. But why? It is unique not because it is clever or noble or beautiful or enlightened or original or sincere or idealistic or useful or educational—it may embody any of those qualities—but because it is the only material object in the universe which may possess internal harmony. All the others have been pressed into shape from outside, and when their mold is removed they collapse. The work of art stands up by itself, and nothing else does. It achieves something which has often been promised by society, but always delusively. Ancient Athens made a mess—but the *Antigone* stands up. Renaissance Rome made a mess—but the ceiling of the Sistine got painted. James I made a mess—but there was *Macbeth*. Louis XIV—but there was *Phèdre*. Art for art's sake? I should just think so, and more so than ever at the present time. It is the one orderly product which our muddling race has produced. It is the cry of a thousand sentinels, the echo from a thousand labyrinths; it is the lighthouse which cannot be hidden: *c'est le meilleur témoignage que nous puissions donner de notre dignité. Antigone* for *Antigone*'s sake, *Macbeth* for *Macbeth*'s, *"La Grande Jatte" pour "La Grande Jatte."*

If this line of argument is correct, it follows that the artist will tend to be an outsider in the society to which he has been born, and that the nineteenth-century conception of him as a Bohemian was not inaccurate. The conception erred in three particulars: it postulated an economic system where art could be a full-time job, it introduced the fallacy that only art matters, and it overstressed idiosyncrasy and waywardness—the peacock-feather aspect—rather than order. But it is a truer conception than the one which prevails in official circles on my side of the Atlantic—I don't know about yours: the conception which treats the artist as if he were a particularly bright government advertiser and encourages him to be friendly and matey with his fellow citizens, and not to give himself airs.

Estimable is mateyness, and the man who achieves it gives many a pleasant little drink to himself and to others. But it has no traceable connection with the creative impulse, and probably acts as an inhibition on it. The artist who is seduced by mateyness may stop himself from doing the one thing which he, and he alone, can do—the making of something out of words or sounds or paint or clay or marble or steel or film which has internal harmony and presents order to a permanently disarranged planet. This seems worth doing, even at the risk of being called uppish by journalists. I have in mind an article which was published some years ago in the London *Times*, an article called "The Eclipse of the Highbrow," in which the "Average Man" was exalted, and all contemporary literature was censured if it did not toe the line, the precise position of the line being naturally known to the writer of the article. Sir Kenneth Clark, who was at that time director of our National Gallery, commented on this pernicious doctrine in a letter which cannot be too often quoted. "The poet and the artist," wrote Clark, "are important precisely because they are not average men; because in sensibility, intelligence, and power of invention they far exceed the average." These memorable words, and particularly the words "power of

Saul Steinberg

invention," are the Bohemian's passport. Furnished with it, he slinks about society, saluted now by a brickbat and now by a penny, and accepting either of them with equanimity. He does not consider too anxiously what his relations with society may be, for he is aware of something more important than that—namely the invitation to invent, to create order, and he believes he will be better placed for doing this if he attempts detachment. So round and round he slouches, with his hat pulled over his eyes, and maybe with a louse in his beard, and—if he really wants one—with a peacock's feather in his hand.

If our present society should disintegrate—and who dare prophesy that it won't?—this old-fashioned and démodé figure will become clearer: the Bohemian, the outsider, the parasite, the rat—one of those figures which have at present no function either in a warring or a peaceful world. It may not be dignified to be a rat, but many of the ships are sinking, which is not dignified either—the officials did not build them properly. Myself, I would sooner be a swimming rat than a sinking ship—at all events I can look around me for a little longer—and I remember how one of us, a rat with particularly bright eyes called Shelley, squeaked out, "Poets are the unacknowledged legislators of the world," before he vanished into the waters of the Mediterranean.

What laws did Shelley propose to pass? None. The legislation of the artist is never formulated at the time, though it is sometimes discerned by future generations. He legislates through creating. And he creates through his sensitiveness and his power to impose form. Without form the sensitiveness vanishes. And form is as important today, when the human race is trying to ride the whirlwind, as it ever was in those less agitating days of the past, when the earth seemed solid and the stars fixed, and the discoveries of science were made slowly, slowly. Form is not tradition. It alters from generation to generation. Artists always seek a new technique, and will continue to do so as long as their work excites them. But form of some kind is imperative. It is the surface crust of the internal harmony, it is the outward evidence of order.

My remarks about society may have seemed too pessimistic, but I believe that society can only represent a fragment of the human spirit, and that another fragment can only get expressed through art. And I wanted to take this opportunity, this vantage ground, to assert not only the existence of art but its pertinacity. Looking back into the past, it seems to me that that is all there has ever been: vantage grounds for discussion and creation, little vantage grounds in the changing chaos, where bubbles have been blown and webs spun, and the desire to create order has found temporary gratification, and the sentinels have managed to utter their challenges, and the huntsmen, though lost individually, have heard each other's calls through the impenetrable wood, and the lighthouses have never ceased sweeping the thankless seas. In this pertinacity there seems to me, as I grow older, something more and more profound, something which does in fact concern people who do not care about art at all.

In conclusion, let me summarize the various categories that have laid claim to the possession of Order.

(1) The social and political category. Claim disallowed on the evidence of history and of our own experience. If man altered psychologically, order here might be attainable; not otherwise.

(2) The astronomical category. Claim allowed up to the present century, but now disallowed on the evidence of the physicists.

(3) The religious category. Claim allowed on the evidence of the mystics.

(4) The aesthetic category—the subject of this article. Claim allowed on the evidence of various works of art, and on the evidence of our own creative impulses, however weak these may be, or however imperfectly they may function. Works of art, in my opinion, are the only objects in the material universe to possess internal order, and that is why, though I don't believe that only art matters, I do believe in Art for Art's Sake.

Vega

by John Cheever

December 1949

Vega Shouisky was given her curious and romantic forename as the result of an unusual series of affections and circumstances that crowded into the life of her parents shortly before Vega's birth in 1932. Her parents—Ella and Stanley Shouisky—were the children of Russians who had immigrated to the United States at the turn of the century and settled in the mill village of Hiems in northern New Hampshire. Ella and Stanley were born and raised in mill tenements, and they followed their parents into the cotton mill when they finished grade school. Stanley became a loom-fixer and Ella worked as a weaver until her marriage to him in 1930. When they married, the Harvey Company, who owned the mill, offered them space in a tenement, but they refused this offer and rented a farm in the hills at the edge of town. Ella got pregnant a year after their marriage and at about this time the Harvey Company suffered critical reverses and fired many of its workers and cut the wages of those they kept on.

There was no railroad station in Hiems, no main roads touched the town, and its life was dominated by the Harvey Mill. The Harveys themselves lived in a large house outside the town. They gave stained-glass windows to the church, beds to the hospital, and books to the library; and while they were a conscientious and bounteous family, the business reverses of the thirties went beyond their understanding. They knew that the people they discharged could find no other work, but they felt that they were helpless to stop the spread of misery. The isolation of the community, the appearance of hunger and raggedness on its streets, and the large house in which the Harveys lived with their servants, made a preternaturally clear distinction between the rich and the poor, the good and the evil, the worker and the parasite; and some organizers came up from New York to take advantage of these distinctions and precipitate a strike.

Stanley Shouisky was one of the workers then kept on at the mill. This was in recognition of his industry and his intelligence, and for these same reasons the organizers approached Stanley with an offer of leadership. They came to his house and talked with him; and their ideas, their reasoning, the thought of actively protesting the unjust hardships that seemed to lie inevitably before himself, his wife, and the life she was carrying, struck him with the force of a revelation, and he felt that he had been given a key to all the mystifying inequalities of the world he knew. Stanley took a position on the union committee, and when negotiations with the bewildered Harveys were stalemated, plans were made to call a strike in the first days of September.

Fewer than a hundred workers were employed by the Harveys then and all but twenty of these went out. Added to the picket lines were the more than two hundred workers the mill had laid off. They demonstrated at the mill gates at seven in the morning and again at four in the afternoon. The mill itself was a long brick building which had been raised before the Civil War in a spirit of profit and enlightenment. Forthright, homely, pridefully decorated with a steeple and an iron fence around its roof, it spoke bluntly across the river of the benefits of patriarchal employment. The strike began when the trees were green and the weather was fine, and went on into the winter. The sympathies of the town were divided and more than half of the tradespeople extended credit to the strikers. In the third month of the strike the Harveys began to evict the workers from the mill tenements. The Harveys' own agents set fire to one of these tenements

Andy Warhol

and two of the strikers were indicted for arson and sent to Concord for trial. Unfamiliar and criminal faces began to appear on the streets, and several of the strikers, walking home from the picket line, were singled out and beaten.

This use of force brought a reporter from New York to Hiems to report on the strike for a magazine. He wrote an eloquent story of the Harveys' mendacity and the courage of the underpaid workers. The simplicity of the situation, the dark line drawn between good and evil, and the fact that this struggle went on under the wine-glass elms of a New England mountain village, had its appeal. Contributions of over five hundred dollars were sent by magazine-readers to the strike committee. The organizers decided to take advantage of this flood of sympathy and planned a mass meeting. The Grange Hall was one of the few pieces of real estate in Hiems over which the Harveys did not have some kind of control and plans were made to hold the mass meeting there. Fifty sympathizers were expected to come up from New York, and student organizations at Bennington and Dartmouth Colleges had agreed to send delegations. It was winter by this time and Hiems was buried deep in snow.

The hardships under which the strikers were living then were extreme. They didn't have adequate food, their houses were cold, and their children lacked clothing or shoes to wear to school, but the thought that the eyes of the world, as the organizers put it, were recognizing the injustice of their sufferings, made their lives endurable and in some cases exciting. The hungry and ragged women decorated the Grange Hall with colored paper and offered their spare rooms to the New York delegation, most of whom, as it happened, chose to stay at the inn in Wellsford, thirty miles down the road. Late one afternoon cars with New York license plates began to appear on the streets. There was a meeting that afternoon in the Grange Hall and among the people who had come from New York were a famous artist, an opera singer, and a novelist. The New Yorkers took over the management of this meeting and arranged to send telegrams to the state Department of Labor, the state Department of Health, the Governor, the Harveys, the Secretary of Labor, the Secretary of the Interior, and the President of the United States himself. This roll-call of great titles in the rude Grange Hall excited Stanley Shouisky and he looked with astonishment at the handsome and powerful friends their protest had made for them. He and Ella were expecting one of the delegates to spend the night with them, and when the meeting ended he walked home through the miserable streets, cold and light-headed with hunger and excitement.

Ella was waiting. She was in the fifth month of her pregnancy, and because she had not had enough to eat, the child she was carrying had taxed her strength. She had scoured the three rooms they lived in, that day, in preparation for their guest. They were small and ugly rooms, lighted by a kerosene lamp. A little after dark they heard a car on the frozen snow outside their house. Stanley went to the window. He saw the headlights of a car extinguished, and with this light still on his retina he could not make out the features of the stranger who came towards the house. He opened the door to a young man. The delegate thrust out his hand and stared so intently into Stanley's eyes that he made it seem as if this handshake were a furtive and momentous pact. "I'm Randall Newhall," he said, in an unusually deep and hoarse voice, a voice that contrasted with his slight frame. "I'm with the Dartmouth delegation..." Then he went across the kitchen to the stove where Ella was working, wrung her hand, and stared at her in the same way. The fact that he went to college and drove a car made him as strange to the Shouiskys as if he had fallen into Hiems from off a star, as strange and as fascinating, and they watched him take off his ski-cap and his Mackinaw as if there were some mysterious significance in these movements. They had been waiting supper for him and as soon as he had washed at the pump they sat down. "They told me about you people at strike headquarters," Newhall said solemnly. "I'm honored to be with you."

His pompousness escaped them. They were enthralled by the aggravating notes of his voice, by his thin, sallow, and clever face, even by the way that he ate his bread. He asked them for details of the strike and he was deeply gratified by all the evidence of the Harveys' mendacity that they gave him. He told them they were heroic. The struggle they were leading was not confined to Hiems, he said. People knew about the Shouiskys in Berlin, London, Paris, Prague. Then he asked suddenly if anyone else could hear him. The Shouiskys told him that the farm was isolated. He went to the window to make sure. Then he said that he was a member of the Communist party. He returned to the table, lighted his pipe, and began. . . .

As he spoke he gestured awkwardly and broadly, like a green politician, but the undercurrent of hysteria in his voice transfixed the Shouiskys. A less simple couple might have been offended by his patronizing manner and his words, but the Shouiskys were half-strangers to the language themselves, and all of his references to the "toiling masses," to the "perfidious rainbow promises of capitalism," to "fascistization" and "chauvinism" moved them with the power of obscure poetry. He spoke to them condescendingly; he literally aimed his voice down at them as if he were standing on the platform of some Workers' Temple—between the lectern and the battered upright piano—and they were sitting way below him on the folding chairs. "Where has this disaster come from?" he asked Stanley angrily and he shot a finger at him. "What is it that knocked the bottom out from under your feet? What will you do to help yourselves? Only the Communist party has consistently organized and led the resistance to fascistization and capitalist attacks. The party needs workers to bring light to the dark corners where the toiling millions are oppressed by hatred, despair, hunger, and war. The bloodthirsty enemies of the Communist party try to scare away the toiling workers and the toiling farmers by screaming that the Communist party is interested only in revolution. They do this in order to hide the fact that they, one and all, pursue the single policy of saving the profits of the capitalists."

He spoke of racial equality, self-criticism, and the divine authority of Leninist theory as interpreted by the Central Committee. As he spoke the lamp smoked; the room got cold. He railed until his voice broke with hoarseness and the Shouiskys, whose response to his relentless and doctrinaire harangue was physical, were exhausted. It was after midnight when they said goodnight and lighted Newhall into the freezing spare room off the kitchen. They shook hands again. Stanley couldn't speak. Standing in the cold air and the sallow lamplight, he saw a vision of the brotherhood of man. It seemed to both the Shouiskys, although they would not have said so, that they were in the presence of a saint.

The next day was cold and the members of the delegation, coming up from the inn in Wellsford, were late for the mass meeting. The workers sat on the floor of the Grange Hall while the splendid strangers filed onto the platform. The speeches began at one and went on until three, when there was a pause for fund-raising. The response was disappointing but most of the strangers had already contributed to the original five hundred dollars. After the fund-raising ended the speeches began again, but the mood on the platform had changed, and as the light outside the Grange Hall deepened and got blue and as the cold increased and promised the intense cold of the night that was beginning, some restiveness, something oddly like homesickness overtook the adults on the stage. They looked apprehensively at the signs of night outside the windows and began to search in their pockets and pocketbooks for timetables and to consult in whispers with one another about the chances of driving to Boston or Albany that night, very much as the guests at a funeral begin to wonder whether or not it would be unsuitable if they avoided the trip to the cemetery. Several of them left the platform during the closing speeches and their cars could be heard starting and driving off. More of them left before the meeting ended. The comings and goings of the New Yorkers were so mysterious to the people of Hiems that they were not offended by these departures, but by dark all the New Yorkers had vanished, and, with the exception of Newhall, they were never heard from again.

A few weeks after the mass meeting the Harveys closed the mill and sold the looms to a firm in Alabama. Trucks came into the town early one morning and left at night, carting away the vitals of the place. A "For Rent" sign was hung on the mill building itself. Many of the workers left Hiems and moved to the cities near Boston, but Stanley was able to get work in a lumber mill in Hiems and he stayed on. Some time after the mass meeting he received in the mail from Randall Newhall a simple textbook of revolutionary doctrine and he and Ella studied this at night. One evening in the early spring they heard a car outside their house, and when Stanley went to the window he saw Randall Newhall and a girl coming up the walk. Stanley met them at the door. Ella was in the kitchen. When she saw Newhall's sallow and intelligent face and remembered those transcendent months, she began to cry. "I wanted to come over as soon as I heard that the strike was ended," he said. "I . . ."

"It was all right," Ella said. "What could you do?"

"This is Mary LeMaire."

"How do you do," Stanley said.

"We're glad to have you here," Ella said.

Mary was a thin, dark-haired girl. Her features were coarse. "Mary and I are going to be married," Randall said. "I'm going to leave college. Mary's from White River. She comes from the working class."

They went out of the dark kitchen onto the porch and Stanley brought a chair for Ella. It was a mild evening and it had the extraordinary force of vernal mildness in a part of the country where the winters are cruel. Everything was wet. Puddles in the undrained fields reflected the sky. The men talked together. Randall was going to leave college to work. He was going to Buffalo on a project to organize the steel workers. The women talked together. Mary asked the older woman when she was going to have her child. "Next month," Ella said. "I'm frightened for this child." She covered the younger woman's hand with hers. "We are so poor."

"She'll see it," Randall said, "your child will see it, Ella. Do you realize that? She'll see everything that you and Stanley have worked for. You really haven't lost the strike at all. The resolution and the courage you people have shown— the vision—these are things I'll always remember. You should be proud of the child you're bearing, Ella, proud and happy, and if you ever need help, if things go slower than we hope for, you get in touch with me. We'll take care of your child, won't we, Mary?"

"Sure, sweetie," Mary said.

"That's a promise," Randall said. "If you ever want help for your child write me a letter. I don't care where I am. If I'm in jail Mary will take care of it."

He spoke facing the sky. There were some clouds there of a gentle gray and where they had parted there was a piece of blue. As this faded the stars began to shine.

"What will you name the child?" Mary asked.

"We don't know."

"Name her Vega if it's a girl," Randall said. "There's Vega there in the sky. That beautiful star. Name her Vega."

"Which is Vega? Which star?"

"That one. See? There. Do you see?"

"Yes," Ella said, "yes. If we have a girl we'll name her Vega."

Vega was born in April in one of the farmhouse bedrooms. Stanley continued to work at the lumber mill after the birth of his daughter, and Ella raised chickens and vegetables. Their lives were contented and simple. But there are months, summers, journeys in our time during which we give and receive such intense happiness and excitement that our reluctance to see them end, our refusal sometimes to realize that they have ended, lingers with us and damages us as personalities; and Stanley's memory of the excitements and privations of the strike would dominate the rest of his life. He remained a clever and responsible workman, but some of his resilience and most of his humor seemed to have been spent on the picket line. He still held his belief in the

communism that he had been introduced to by Randall Newhall and gave his daughter lessons in revolutionary theory. Vega was much more interested in birds' nests. In her small bedroom she had a collection of more than thirty pestiferous and smelly nests.

When Vega was eleven, Ella was taken ill. It was hard for her to breathe and she complained of a pain in her back. Stanley and Vega tried to nurse her and a doctor from the village, an old man, came twice to see her and prescribed medicines. Late one night Vega was awakened by her father calling her mother's name. At first Vega thought he was protesting something Ella had done. She must have got out of bed, Vega thought, or said something that angered him. "Ella, Ella, Ella," he shouted, and because this was all he said and because he kept shouting her name again and again, Vega got out of bed and crossed the kitchen into her parents' room. Her mother was lying on the bed and her father was shouting as if he wanted to wake her. He stood by the bed crying, and now and then he would lean over to shake her shoulders, to kiss her on the face and the throat, to rub her hands in his, and all the time he cried, "Ella, Ella, Ella." He did not seem to recognize his daughter when he saw her. He looked back at the woman on the bed. He behaved as if the pain he was suffering were physical and now he stooped over, roaring with it; now he clapped his hand to his shoulder as if he had broken his shoulder in a fall. He went out of the room, pushing past the girl, out of the house and down the grass to a pile of stones at the edge of Ella's garden where he lay with his knees against his chest, racked with the excruciating realization that he no longer had a wife.

The frightened girl stayed in the kitchen until he returned to her. In the morning he made the arrangements for Ella's burial, and when the funeral was over, Vega returned to school and Stanley took up the life of a widower with a child. On his way home from the lumber mill he would stop in the village to buy something to eat. Either he or Vega would cook the miserable meal and they would eat it in the kitchen. Vega sensed her father's helplessness; after supper she would wash and dry the dishes and she tried to keep the house as orderly as her mother had kept it. Vega then wore her hair in long plaits that Ella had brushed and braided every morning. It had pleased Ella to dress her daughter's hair and she had never taught the girl to do it herself. On the Saturday after Ella died Vega sat by the kitchen table with a towel over her shoulders and newspapers at her feet and Stanley cut off her braids.

The problem of Vega was on Stanley's mind much of the time. The girl missed her mother in every way. She missed the attentions Ella had given her father and she tried to imitate these. She would come home as soon as school closed and struggle with the wash, the housework, and the cooking. She could not manage this nor could she manage her own appearance. She was coming of age in a bankrupt mill-town, and for this she would need guidance, Stanley knew, that he could not give her. He cast round in his mind for the name of someone who could help him, and because of the impediment in his memory that made the strike seem like something that had happened recently, he thought at once of the Newhalls. He stopped at the telephone office on his way home from the lumber mill one night and looked up their address in the New York directory. After supper he wrote a letter to Randall and Mary Newhall. He mailed this in the morning and received a reply from Mary a week later. She enclosed a check for twenty-five dollars and said that she would love to have Vega come and stay with her. Any time would be convenient and Stanley should wire when Vega was arriving. Mrs. Newhall would not meet her at the train. Vega could take a taxi to the house.

"I want you to leave here," he told the girl that night after supper. "I want you to go away from Hiems. This isn't a good place. I've talked to you about the Newhalls—he's a great working-class leader—and they've written a letter and said they'd like to have you come and live with them. They live in New York. They'll take good care of you. They'll send you to a good school. Then you can amount to something."

The stunned child began to cry. Grief enveloped her wholly, and like a much younger child who has never felt diffidence or the need to compose sorrow, she screamed and wailed and expressed loudly all the fear and confusion his suggestion gave her. She threw her arms around him. She buried her face in his shirt. She held to him as if they were going to be separated by force. The storm lasted ten minutes and when it had spent itself he began again quietly: "Mrs. Newhall has sent us twenty-five dollars. That will pay for your ticket. I want you to leave here, Vega . . ." She began to cry again.

By the end of the week Stanley had convinced her that she should go. It would be an exciting life, he told her, and he described to her the way he supposed the Newhalls lived. Then it was arranged for her to leave on a Sunday. Stanley rode with her on the train to Boston, crossed Boston with her, and said goodby to her in the South Station after he had put her on a New York train. He advised her not to speak to strangers or to buy anything, kissed her, and walked away. The station was crowded, the air smelled of gas; all around him were large bright signs calling his attention to the distinctions of whiskey, newspapers, and chewing gum; and to Stanley, who had lost his wife, and now his daughter, the lights, the gaseous air, and the crowds were bewildering. He took the train to the junction, the bus to Hiems, and walked back to the farm.

When Vega's train approached New York, the size and complexity of the lighted city intimidated her, and when she followed the crowds out of the waiting room onto the street the height of the buildings made her feel faint. She saw a cab-driver with a pleasant face and gave him a slip of paper with the Newhalls' address on it. Her drive through the gigantic and alien city excited memories of everything that she thought familiar—the streets of Hiems, her father, her father's principles—and she held to these memories and hoped that at the Newhalls' she would find something to connect with them. The taxi stopped at a doorway between two stores. She paid her fare and put her heavy suitcase on the sidewalk.

It was dark. A double row of tenements and brownstones reached in either direction, lighted harshly and spottily by street lamps, and children were playing in the light. Sensing her bewilderment, several people turned and watched to see what she would do. Then she heard a window thrown open, way above her, and someone called: "Vega, Vega, Vega, is that you, sweetheart? Come up. We're on the top floor. Come on up." Vega opened the door and stepped into a narrow and smelly passage. It was as cold as a cellar there and the change made her sneeze. She began to climb the stairs, stopping at every landing to catch her breath and rest from the weight of her suitcase. "Can you make it, sweetie?" Mrs. Newhall asked, as she neared the summit. "It's a terrible climb. I ought to know. I have to make it four or five times a day myself." She met Vega at the top of the last flight and embraced her. "Oh you cute little sweetheart," she said. "Come in, come in, you're going to have the back room but I haven't had time to fix it up yet. We'll do that after supper. Let me look at you, let me look at you." She held the girl away from her and they looked at each other.

Vega saw a haggard woman. Why had her father told her that she would be young? Her hair was gray and there was no contentment or youth left in her anxious face.

"You know you look just like your mother," Mrs. Newhall said. "I suppose a lot of people have told you that. You look just like your mother, your poor mother. You know I had a friend carried off like that, the week before last? Martha Prichard. I guess you wouldn't know her. The only reason I'm mentioning it is because she probably had the same thing your mother had. Here is life, and there, a step away, is death. But I don't suppose your mother had proper medical care, did she? Did she? Oh those doctors in those towns and those terrible country hospitals! I suppose her life might have been saved. Sit down, sit down. This is the kitchen but we use it for everything in the winter, the other rooms are so cold. Keats! Shelley!" she screamed at two cats who jumped off the table and fled. "Sit down, sit down, sweetheart. Do you want some coffee? Do you want to go to the bathroom? I guess you'd rather have milk than coffee. Would you like a glass of milk?"

"Yes, please," Vega said.

"I'll get you a glass of milk and I'll have a little drink. I thought I'd wait until you came."

The room seemed to be a kitchen but there was a bookshelf against one wall and a desk in the corner, beside a steel file cabinet. The gas oven was flaming, but with nothing in it.

"Oh you sweetheart, you little sweetheart," Mrs. Newhall said when she gave Vega her milk and she bent down and embraced and kissed her again. "I can't have any children of my own, you know," she said. "The doctors don't know why. I'm RH positive but I've had six miscarriages. My friends say that I ought to be analyzed but Randall says that I'm not worth reconstructing. I had a friend who had three miscarriages and then went to an analyst and had two perfectly beautiful children. Oh!" Mrs. Newhall sighed, when she heard the brakes of a car in the street below and she ran to the window. "Every time I hear that noise I think one of those children has been run over," she said. "I wish their mothers wouldn't let them play out there after dark. One of them was run over last year. His legs were broken. His father drives a laundry truck. I only mention this because it's important to my story. He was out there playing stick-ball after dark and he got hit. It broke both legs. His mother doesn't speak English. They're Italians. She has pierced ears and a mustache. What was I going to tell you?"

Mrs. Newhall took a drink of her whiskey. "Well, tell me all about yourself," she said. "I ought to clean this place up but I never seem to get around to it and Randall won't let me touch his papers. Are you sure you don't want to go to the bathroom? We won't have supper until Randall comes in, but he'll be home in a minute. We're going to have lamb, cold lamb. Do you like lamb? Did you have any lunch? Tell me all about your father. You know I only saw your folks once. That was after the strike. I drove over there with Randall. We got lost somewhere between Plymouth and Concord. The only reason I mention this is because it's important. We got lost. Randall stopped at a gas station and asked the way and they'd never heard of Hiems, so then we kept on going toward Plymouth and we got there."

There were footsteps in the hall and a key turned in the lock. These sounds seemed to dismay Mrs. Newhall. "Here's Randall now."

He opened the door, and as if Vega had inherited this affection from her father she responded to him at once. He hardly seemed to notice her. He took a searching look at the kitchen and asked his wife if anyone had telephoned.

"This is Vega," Mrs. Newhall said uneasily. "This is Vega Shouisky, Randall. She's going to stay with us for a little while. We're not using the back room for anything and she can stay there, can't she? I didn't tell you about it because I knew you wouldn't mind."

"Hello, Vega," he said. Then he turned to his wife. "I asked you if anyone telephoned."

"Three people called," Mrs. Newhall said. "I put all their names on the pad by the telephone. That's what you told me to do. They all called this morning. There weren't any calls this afternoon excepting a wrong number. The phone rang at about three o'clock. The only reason I'm mentioning this is because it's important," she said as a look of impatience began to constrict her husband's features. "The phone rang at about three o'clock and when I answered it a man asked me if this was that Hungarian restaurant on Third Avenue, and this is the fourth or fifth time this has happened and I think you ought to call the telephone company and tell them."

"When will supper be ready?" Newhall asked.

"In a minute," Mrs. Newhall said. "I can have it ready in a minute."

They ate cold meat and canned vegetables. Mrs. Newhall talked a lot as the meal began but her husband's silence intimidated her and she became silent herself. He said nothing. When supper was finished he spoke to Vega for the first time since he had said hello.

"What did you say your name was?"

"Vega," she said. "I'm named after a star called Vega because you asked my mother to name me after this star. My mother is dead. We live in Hiems. You told my mother and father..."

"Oh that strike, you mean that strike when I was in college," he said gently and he put a hand on his forehead. To piece the memory together took him a minute. "I remember now," he said, "I remember your parents. But what are you doing here?"

"Mrs. Newhall said I could come."

"I knew you wouldn't mind, Randall. You know how lonely it is for me here. Do you want any more supper? Do you want anything more, Vega? That oven gives me a headache."

"How is your father?" Newhall asked.

"He's all right," Vega said. "He works in the lumber mill now. They don't have a cotton mill in Hiems any more."

"Is he still a communist?"

"Yes," Vega said.

"That's incredible," Randall said. "I have some things here he ought to read." He went to the file cabinet, rolled open one of its drawers, and looked through a store of articles, torn from magazines. "Here's a piece I did on the Kirov assassination," he said, and he handed the sheets to Vega. The paper was yellow and turning at the edges to dust. "And here's a piece I did on the Moscow trials. You say he's still a communist. That's incredible. Spain. Spain. Here's a piece I did on POUM." He passed her another article. "Here's a piece on China. Here's a review of Souvarine's book. Here's a piece on Finland. Here's a piece I did in Mexico when we went down for Trotsky's trial. Here's a piece on Trotsky's assassination. Here's a piece on Tresca's assassination. Here's a piece on Stalinism and art. Here's a piece I did on the Bishops' Conference in Kansas City before I was confirmed. Here's a piece on Saint Augustine that I did after I'd left the church. Here's a piece on Saint Paul. Here's a piece on the Concept of Dread." He rolled the file shut and looked up thoughtfully. "Tell him to read those. You say he's still a communist?"

"Yes," Vega said.

"They probably don't get anything to read up there," Mrs. Newhall said.

"We get the *Daily Worker* almost every day," Vega said.

"Are you a communist?"

"I don't know," Vega said. "I'm mostly interested in ornithology."

"I was interested in birds when I was a girl," Mrs. Newhall exclaimed. Her husband left the table and went to the window. "I had a tame robin," she said. "He fell out of the nest and hurt himself and I nursed him and fed him and for a whole summer he lived in our woodshed. You know I haven't been back to New Hampshire for ten years. It isn't that I don't want to go back, but you lose touch. I don't know anybody at home any more."

"I need some cigarettes, Mary," Newhall said. "Will you go out and get them?"

She slipped on a coat and went out. He closed the door after her. The chill of a spring night had begun to penetrate the tenement and to ally itself to the everlasting damp in the halls, and the gas fire only staled the air. Newhall said nothing and the silence made Vega uneasy.

"You look awful tired, Mr. Newhall."

"What?"

"I said you look awful tired."

"How old are you, Vega?"

"Twelve."

"Is that the truth?"

"I'll be thirteen in May," she said, "if that's what you mean."

"Who sent you?"

"Daddy sent me," she said. She knew that this was not what he wanted, that from the portentous tone of his voice he expected some larger answer from her, but she couldn't think of one.

"Who sent you, Vega?"

"Daddy."

"I don't mean that. Who sent you? Which of his friends?"

"Nobody."

"They're stupid," he said. "I always forget how stupid they are. I always forget that brutes are stupid. They don't understand their own theories. I used to be a communist, Vega," he said. "When I left the party I took with me an invaluable sense of political reality. I recognize my enemies. I think you're one of them. I know that your father and his friends are cutthroats and murderers. For ten years I've watched them and their allies encircle the world—the Balkans, the Baltic, Bessarabia, Bucovina, Poland, Finland, Mongolia, China.

"Millions of toiling workers," he said, sounding a phrase he had sounded for her parents before she was born, "have been starved, enslaved, exiled, and murdered by these filthy beasts. They and their brutish police have exacerbated every human freedom and virtue. They've killed my good friends and they would like to kill me. I dream about their executioners. Now," he said, "who sent you?" He came around to where she was sitting. "Who sent you and what did they ask you to find?"

"Nobody sent me."

"Who sent you?"

"Nobody, nobody."

"Who sent you?" He reached into the chair where she sat, seized her right arm and wrenched it. This threw her forward into the chair and as he increased the pressure the pain drove her to her knees. "Who sent you," he shouted, "who sent you and what did they tell you to do?"

"Leave me alone. Leave me alone. Leave me alone. I don't know," the girl said and as he pulled on her arm she screamed with pain and then put her face in the dirt of the floor and pressed her cheek and her mouth to it, despairingly. He dropped her arm. Then she heard Mrs. Newhall's voice and felt the woman's hands on her shoulders, but she could not move to get up or raise her head.

Now, on every summer Saturday night, at about seven o'clock, a horse and carriage comes down the road from the hills into Hiems. The carriage is the last vehicle of its kind in use in that part of New Hampshire; the passengers are Vega and Stanley, and this appearance is their last contact with the community. Stanley lost his job at the lumber mill and Vega's meeting with Newhall had the same effect on her that her father's meeting with him had had before her birth. His cruelty impressed her with the rightness of the principles he had abandoned. She was left as devout a communist as her simple father. She returned to school when she came back from New York but after her trip she was always in trouble and when her father lost his job she withdrew with him from the life of the village, and—twice blessed with the attentions of an intellectual—these two lead a solitary life, taking advantage of the license dying rural communities give to eccentricity. Stanley lives as a farmer now and they are poor. He wears overalls. Vega's clothes are ragged.

They stop the carriage by the cash market between diagonal white lines that have been painted on the road for automobiles. Vacationists, killing time before the movie begins, or anyone else who is not familiar with the vehicle will point to it and laugh. Stanley takes a crate of eggs into the store. Vega never leaves her seat in the carriage.

By the time Stanley has been paid for his eggs the day is over. The fragrant gloom in the elms between the streetlights and the starlight is dense; the movie has begun. Stanley hangs a kerosene lamp at the back of the carriage and they start home. As they travel they look around them at the frivolous lights of the movie house and the single restaurant with scorn, for they know that the world will never share one mind and heart until the workers shape it to their needs, and while their carriage and their lantern, their rags and their mare, make them appear to belong to some rural past, they think themselves to be the prophets of the brotherhood of man.

1950's

THE CENTURY

BY BERNARD DEVOTO

OCTOBER 1950

The past, we think, was slower. The United States from 1940 to 1950 is a disc spinning so fast that we can barely cling to it or stay on our feet. But a century seems in retrospect to have moved at a measured, tranquil pace. Change in earlier days was not our master but our servant; season grew to season and the crop came to harvest. This is the visual illusion that makes a body seem to move the more slowly as we get farther away from it. History needs some such device as that by which the movies show a plant growing from slip to leaf to flower in fifty feet of film. It would correct the parallax and show that in all ten decades the motions of American society have been close to cataclysmic. We could then see for ourselves that all but one of them have been contained....

East of Lake Ontario, there may have been debatable ground: which area was truly Canada, which truly the United States? But westward there was not much margin. You could move the boundary a few miles north of the 49th Parallel or a few miles south of it without encountering much difference. But only a few miles: geography, climate, the flow of rivers, the architecture of mountain ranges divided one nation from the other as if by blueprint.

Along the southern edge, as three hundred years of Spain in North America demonstrated, the margin was even narrower: one area was the United States and the other Mexico by natural fiat. Earth's creation had surveyed and staked a continental domain between the Atlantic and the Pacific, between Canada and Mexico, for a single people, a single economic system, a single political organization. One determinant of our society is that the United States is a nation which occupies a continental unit. Another one is this: the United States is an empire whose imperial and national boundaries are the same.

A minor but clear-seeing prophet said, "Disunion and Civil War are synonymous terms. The Mississippi, source and mouth, must be controlled by one government." That was in December 1860. In December of 1862 a major prophet repeated what he had said at his inauguration: "Physically speaking we cannot separate. We cannot remove our respective sections from each other nor build an impassable wall between them," and added that the people of the American heartland must forever "find their way to Europe by New York, to South America and Africa by New Orleans, and to Asia by San Francisco." These men were proclaiming the necessity of economic and political unity in a unified geographical system. Thomas Jefferson had anticipated them in 1803, but so had Robert Cavalier, Sieur de la Salle, in 1682.

With an explosive heightening of energy the nation completed the occupation of its continent in a two-year period, 1846–1848. Mexico and Great Britain ceased to be illogical and irrelevant sovereignties in the American geographical system. The event brought to an end the imperial contention for the Great Valley and the Far West that had begun in the seventeenth century, if not indeed in the sixteenth. The Spanish and Russian Empires had been merely peripheral forces in this struggle but there had been a full century of conflict between the French and British Empires to possess and politically unify the American continent. By the time this struggle ended in victory for the British it had created the American empire. For the people whose representatives met in Philadelphia in 1775 and again in 1787 to make a nation were already an imperial people. As they made the nation they entered a half-century of conflict with Great Britain for the same great stake, the richest area in the world. That conflict settled itself along the lines laid down, leaving only the two illogicalities in the West that vanished before mid-century.

The attainment of our continental boundaries precipitated the crisis which gave the nation its final shape and pattern, and which made the nation and the empire the same thing. The United States into which Volume I, Number 1, of *Harper's New Monthly Magazine* issued in June of 1850 was already committed to the final testing. A self-governing people had created a democratic republic: was the system strong enough and flexible enough to maintain itself in a whole continent? Could the conflicting interests, feelings, and beliefs of irrational man in society adapt themselves to the rationality of natural conditions? Was there a self-limiting contradiction within the democratic forms? Could American society govern itself in the single system that the continent demanded, or was that demand too strong for government, admittedly man's weakest capacity? Must that weakness falsify the American experience and mock the continental unity by a process of Balkanization that would produce societies smaller and illogical but within man's capacity for government? In that same June of 1850 delegates from nine Southern states met in convention at Nashville to set up an experimental test. By November, convinced that they could predict the outcome, they were proposing to declare the American experience a failure and to dissolve the United States. The proposal was both too early and too late. Between June and November the resources of the political system proved it able, through the compromise of 1850, to preserve the nation and the empire for an undetermined time. Ultimately the period proved to be ten years. Just long enough.

It was a decade of steadily growing tension, passion, and turbulence. The surface was chaotic but realities beneath the surface were shaping a demand that evasions, ambiguities, and contradictions in the society be faced and resolved. The acquisition of the West revealed the inexorable fact that the Southern political hegemony would now be extinguished. Political dictation by the minority must end and government must pass to the majority. The Southern hegemony had never had financial dominance; Southern economists were aware that their section was in fact bankrupt and the new territory confirmed their diagnosis. The section's obsolete labor system had managed to keep its economy alive by a process of exhausting soils and then abandoning them for virgin land, but the labor system could not possibly be applied to the virgin land now acquired. Finally, the unresolved contradiction and untreated disease at the core of our social system, Negro slavery, had reached the stage of fatality. Outside the South, an intense moral horror no more to be discounted than that which our generation has felt about forced labor or genocide was now demanding that the spread of slavery be stopped short and some process of elimi-

nating it be invented. The Southern minority responded in the tradition of dying oligarchies, by demanding absolute immunity from control and by convincing itself that financial bankruptcy, political fallacy, and embedded social evil manifested the will of God. Both sections moved toward Lincoln's conclusion that the nation could not exist half slave and half free.

One great American said that God was sifting out the hearts of men before his judgment seat, another that one volume of our history had closed and a new one had opened of which no man could foresee the end, a third that irresistible if unnamable influences had begun to unfold a new destiny. The spinning disc was performing its function of constantly remaking the nation. We see easily enough, today, that the political system was hardening and the cleavage in the social system deepening. But in order to get these motions in focus we need the movies' device to throw on the screen condensed images of other motions. One would show the shaded area on the population map moving constantly westward across the blank area. Another would show a web of railroads being spun east of the Mississippi; others would show the steady multiplication of factory chimneys, the increase of emigration from Europe, the increase of wealth, the increase of mechanical power. Such images reveal why, in the event, ten years were enough.

Our generation has twice had proved to it that sometimes final decisions have to be reached and that if they cannot be reached in any other way then they must be fought out. "Both parties deprecated war, but one of them would *make* war rather than let the nation survive, and the other would *accept* war rather than let it perish, and the war came." The last four words have the greatest solemnity of our history. Bernard Shaw has said that it "was more clearly than any other war of our time a war for an idea," but it was tragedy to the uttermost. In all history there are no greater ironies than these: that secession belied and repudiated the entire experience of the American people, that the South which forced the war never had a chance to win it, that the Confederacy was an anachronism as society and an unworkable fallacy as government, that if the American system had been broken the European system would have been restored.

The war effected the political decision, "teaching men that what they cannot take by an election, neither can they take by war." It ended the fatal disease of slavery, though the sequelae, some of them only less evil, have not yet been cured. And it freed the nation forever to develop its empire as a single people in a continental unit. Now there would never be the Balkan States of North America.

No war ends as the same war it was when it began. The lightning of the terrible swift sword revealed again the deepest meaning and the highest aspiration of American life—perhaps they are to be glimpsed only in a lightning flash—and they found their supreme expression in the Gettysburg Address and the Second Inaugural. But if the fires of civil war purified much and forged much into its permanent form, they also destroyed much we should not have lost and they left scars that have proved permanent. But gigantic energies had been loosed. The United States came out of the war with a productive system more diverse, more integrated, and enormously more powerful than it had been in 1860—and politically entrenched. The expansion of that system, which was without parallel in human experience, was the focus of American history for the next generation. [...]

And who were the American people? They were the product of the American continent: a new people in a new world. No one understands them who does not understand that the words mean what they say: this is the New World. They were, for instance, the first people in history who had ever had enough to eat. The first people who were able to build a government and a society from the ground up—and on unencumbered ground. The first people whose society had the dynamics of political freedom and political equality, a class system so flexible that it could not stratify into a caste system, and a common wealth so great that it made economic opportunity a birthright. All this makes a difference. It makes so great a difference that the pattern of their neural paths is radically different from any developed in response to the Old World.

They are hopeful and empirical. In their spring morning, those who made the nation did not doubt that it was the hope of the world. Mankind, they thought, must necessarily come to recognize the superiority of American institutions and, insofar as it could, must adopt or imitate them. They were neither visionaries nor utopians. They were realistic, hard-headed men who understood the dynamics of freedom and saw that if they were loosed in any empty continent an augmentation would follow for which nothing in the past could be an adequate gauge. From then on, not the past but the future has counted in the United States. If it doesn't work, try something else; tomorrow is another day;

don't sell America short; the sky is the limit; rags to riches; canalboat boy to President.

That is what has denied the town dump decisive importance. No one has ever set up Utopia here, our utopian literature has always been clearly understood as promotional, and the dump is hideous with brutality, exploitation, failure, and human wreckage. The actual line where men meet in society is always a line of blood and struggle. It is perfectly feasible to write American history in terms of blood and struggle, injustice, fraud, desperation. They are on a scale appropriate to the map; they are monstrous. But the difference is that tomorrow is another day. It has always proved to be. No estimate of what the United States could achieve in population, power, comfort, wealth, or living standard has ever proved adequate. When tomorrow came, the expectation proved to have been too moderate, the achievement invariably outran the prophecy. The United States and the American people are the greatest success story in history.

Europeans came here by the million for a hundred and twenty years. Their expectation was simple and concrete. They expected a better life than had been open to them at home. More food, more comfort, a job, a farm. Citizenship, a stake in society, acknowledged individual integrity, development according to their capacities, a chance to better themselves, a chance to give their children a still better chance. It sums up not as the kingdom of heaven but as somewhat more favorable odds. The majority vote is that on the whole they got it. They kept on coming.

What kept happening is what made the neural paths different. It is a different consciousness, a different cast of thought. And it is very misleading to Europe. American bumptiousness has always been offensive but the abasement that goes with it is worse, for it has been deceptive. The instinctive generosity of the Americans is curiously linked with rapacity, their kindliness with cruelty, their violence with fear of disorder. They are warm-hearted and cold-blooded, their assertive self-confidence is mingled with self-criticism, and their conservatism is the other lobe of an unparalleled recklessness. Yet the most serious mistake of Europe has always been to misunderstand their romanticism, which is the consequence of having lived a Cinderella story. It has been repeatedly mistaken for softness, gullibility, decadence. Their smile is childlike and bland; they affect an innocence and credulity which the European mind has accepted as real. Yet from Franklin and John Jay on, their negotiators have usually come back not only with all

"Civilization is a race between those who destroy and those who build"

You can put your confidence in —

GENERAL ⚙ ELECTRIC

IN THIS BARN was founded the General Electric Research Laboratory, first in industry devoted to fundamental research.

FLUORESCENT LAMPS, first introduced by General Electric ten years ago, were another step in providing more light at less cost.

TURBOSUPERCHARGER. America's fastest airliner depends on G-E turbosuperchargers to step up speed at high altitudes.

BETTER TURBINES helped electric utilities to produce three times the power from the same amount of coal that they did 25 years ago.

FIRST GAS TURBINE LOCOMOTIVE in U.S. is now undergoing tests. From this new-type motive power may come better locomotives.

GIANT X-RAY for industry finds hidden flaws in castings. General Electric has pioneered x-ray for both industry and medicine.

ATOMIC RESEARCH. Complex tools like this mass spectrometer are helping to harness nuclear energy for industrial power.

that the adept cynicism of their opponents undertook to take from them with a cold deck, but with the scarf pins, cuff links, and pocket watches of the cynical as well. For the romanticism is the thinnest possible veneer. There have been no such realists since the Romans and they are the hardest empiricists of the modern world.

The national experience, that is, has justified the national optimism. The premises on which the hardheaded fathers established the American order were, philosophically, optimistic to the verge of fantasy; but the experience of the nation has been that the fantastic premises pay off. That the rights proclaimed in the Declaration, enacted in the Constitution, and buttressed by the Bill of Rights make a system which works more efficiently and has a higher potential than any other. That freedom is power, liberates power, generates power. That individual, social, and political freedom are the health of society. That protection of the individual human being's dignity, his freedom of movement, choice, criticism, communication, publication, and participation in government have pragmatically proved their social strength. They enable the organism to resist infections, they give it the equilibrium to develop resistance against destructive pressures—and this, the empiricists have found, gets work done, increases power, and can be trusted. They understand their history as proving that the fantastic system works. [...]

The fact that dwarfs all others, however, is this: the United States now knows that there is no way of not using power. It is true that no nation ever came so reluctantly to be the foremost nation of the world, but it is also true that none ever accepted the implications so quickly. Our traditional, no longer humorous quirk makes us present ourselves as bumpkins easily to be outguessed, outmaneuvered, and bilked by the Marxian slickers. Still it was not naïveté that, with the nonchalance of a man who holds four aces, tossed the Marshall Plan into a struggle which seemed more than half lost, or with a calculation of risks superbly vindicated by the outcome, launched the first flight of the Berlin airlift, let the chips fall where they might. The illusion of nearness presents us to ourselves as divided, irresolute, vacillating, and at random—which is the close-up image of any democratic system feeling its way. From the perspective of the east-

ern shore of the Atlantic we look otherwise. The image of the United States there has always been ogreish, anarchic, or revolutionary, and foolish if not mad; but something new has come into it. The Europeans waste no love on us, we give them adequate reason to resent and distrust us, and only the Russians keep the rest of Europe from feeling about us in the twentieth century as it felt about Spain in the sixteenth century or France in the seventeenth. But there is the new ingredient that fulfills quite literally what was laid down: the revolution has gone on and in the awareness of Western Europe we are, however fumbling, however resented, the last, best hope of earth.

There can be no disposition to understate the turbulence, horror, and alarm of the world in which the centennial number of *Harper's* issues. At the moment when man's greatest scientific achievement has unlocked a basic secret of matter, there is no word but Banquo's: fears and scruples shake us, in the great hand of God we stand. It will not be tragedy, it will not even be irony but only farce, if man, mastering nature, fails to govern himself. If he does fail, then the destruction of mankind will cleanse the earth for the convenience of organisms which may learn to create peaceful societies. But to those who have decided that the American people do not understand how desperate their estate is, the answer may be that with death hanging in the balance they trust their experience. They have never seen yesterday win over tomorrow. They believe that history is on their side and that they are on the side of the future.

No one has ever known what the next hour might bring forth but we have always made our bet. There came a moment when Mr. Lincoln quoted Scripture: a house divided against itself cannot stand. He went on to say, "I believe this government cannot endure permanently half slave and half free." Either our experience has meaning, as we believe, or else it hasn't. If it has, the world cannot exist permanently half slave and half free.

And mark Lincoln's next words: "I do not expect the Union to be dissolved, I do not expect the house to fall, but I do expect it will cease to be divided." He stood at the height of land between two eras and declared what he understood to be the meaning of history. The empirical people know that, as it turned out, he was right.

Evangelist

by Joyce Cary

November 1952

John Pratt, fifty-five, on holiday at the sea, gets up one sunny morning, looks from the window, says, "It won't last," and picks from his seven suits the only dark one. He dresses himself with care, and eats for breakfast one piece of dry toast.

"A touch of liver," he says to himself, takes his umbrella and a bowler, and goes for his morning walk along the Parade.

"Why the bowler?" he asks himself. "I'm not going back to town." And suddenly it strikes him that he is bored. "Impossible," he says; "I've only been here a week and my regular time is always a fortnight."

He looks about him to discover some usual source of pleasure in this charming old place; and immediately he is seized, possessed, overwhelmed with boredom, with the most malignant and hopeless of all boredoms, holiday boredom. It rises from his stomach, it falls from the lukewarm air. Everything in sight is instantly perceived as squalid, mercenary, debased by mean use and vulgar motives. The Regency façades whose delicate taste he has so much admired, which bring him year after year to a place neither smart nor quiet, seem to leer at him with the sly, false primness of old kept women on the lookout for some city lecher, willing to set off cracked plaster against lewd dexterity.

He looks at the sea for freshness. But it appears thick, greasy: he murmurs with horror, "The cesspool of the whole earth." He sees the drains discharging from a million towns, the rubbish unbucketed from ten thousand years of ships, wrecks full of corpses; the splash of glitter beyond the pier is like the explosion of some hidden corruption. The ozone comes to his nose like a stench.

He sees from the distance a friend, the Colonel in his light gray suit, stepping briskly. He is whirling his stick—it is plain that he is in his usual high spirits.

Pratt crosses the road to avoid him. A taxi hoots in an angry and distracted manner, but he does not hurry, he would rather be killed than betray the dignity of his despair. The taxi's brakes squawk like Donald Duck—it comes to a stop at his elbow—a furious young man with upstanding black hair and red-rimmed eyes thrusts out his neck and bawls insults. Bystanders laugh and stare. Pratt does not turn his head or quicken his walk. He accepts these humiliations as appropriate to such a morning in such a world.

Edward Gorey

man is in a fluster. Has Mr. Pratt seen the news? Is there going to be a war, is this it? Should he sell out his investments and pay his debts; should he fetch back his family from abroad?

Pratt draws himself up and out of mere wrath at this intrusion, utters in severe tones such banalities as amaze his own ears. If war comes, he says, it will come, and if not, then not. There are good arguments on both sides of the question. If we believe our freedom is worth defending, then we should be ready to defend it at all costs. For faith is not faith, not what we truly believe, unless we are prepared to die for it. And in a conflict of faith those alone who are prepared to die for what they believe deserve to win. As for bombs, one can die but once. One will die anyhow and possibly much worse than by a bomb.

And all these panic-mongers, are they not more than foolish? Panic is not only useless, it is a treachery—a

The shopping housewives with their predatory eyes and anxious wrinkled foreheads fill him with a lofty and scornful pity, as for insects generated by a conspiracy of gases and instinct to toil in blind necessity for the production of more insects.

Yes, he thinks, humanity is like the maggots on a perishing carcass. Its history is the history of maggots; the fly, the buzz, the coupling of flies, the dropping of their poison on every clean thing, the hunt for some ordure, some corpse, the laying of eggs, and another generation of maggots. Foulness upon foulness. Tides of disgust and scorn rise in his soul; he stalks more grandly; he has become a giant for whom all history is meaner than the dust on his boot soles.

Suddenly he is accosted by a red-faced man, an hotel acquaintance, who starts out of a shop and seizes him by the hand—impossible to avoid this person. The red-faced

defeat—an invitation to the enemy within as well as without.

The red-faced man is taken aback by this rigmarole of eloquence. He listens with surprised attention in his green eyes—then with respect. Pratt's unmoved solemnity, his severe tone born of scornful indifference, impress him. He ejaculates murmurs of approval. He says that this is just what he himself has always thought. And this is probably true. He could scarcely have escaped such reflections.

At last he is greatly moved. He turns even redder, his gooseberry eyes shine. He grasps Pratt's hand with fervor and a glance that means, "This is an important, a solemn occasion. You are a bigger man than I took you for. Men of sense and courage, like ourselves, should be better acquainted." He departs exalted.

Pratt walks on alone, his step is still majestic but full of spring. He is exhilarated; he looks at the sea and it appears to him noble in its vastness, transcendent in its unconcern, venerable in its intimation of glorious deeds. The houses are like veteran soldiers in line, meeting with stoic pride the injuries of time. The housewives, striving, saving for their families, wear the brows of angels; the battered angels roughly carved on some primitive church. He salutes with heroic elation a world made for heroes. He perceives with joy that it is going to be a fine day, that he is hungry. He whirls his umbrella.

THE SILENT GENERATION

BY THORNTON WILDER

APRIL 1953

A younger generation has been calling attention to itself again. These crises in the public appraisal of the young used to occur at longer intervals; now, with the acceleration of social changes, they appear with increasing frequency. Some of us remember the Jazz Age; this was followed by the Lost Generation; now we are in a state of alarm about the Silent Generation.

I have been given an article on "The Younger Generation" which appeared in *Time* magazine on November 5, 1951, and have been asked to comment on it. There I read that these young people "do not issue manifestoes, make speeches, or carry posters...do not want to go into the Army.... Their ambitions have shrunk.... They want a good secure job...either through fear, passivity, or conviction, they are ready to conform.... They are looking for a faith."

All this I recognize. I propose that we read the manifestations differently.

The Jazz Age preceded and accompanied the first world war. There was a breaking of windows and great scandal. It made evident to all that the American home or the patriarchal pattern had come to an end. The young people won the latchkey. Then the young men went off to the war. That made them heroes. As heroes they acquired more liberties than they had seized as rebellious bad boys. The Lost Generation was the generation that did not know what to do with its new liberties. The younger generation of today is facing the too-long delayed task of consolidating its liberty and of impressing upon it a design, a meaning, and a focus. No wonder they strike us as silent.

An even greater task rests on their shoulders. They are fashioning the Twentieth Century Man. They are called upon to illustrate what the Germans call a "life-style" for our times. This work is usually done by men and women of middle age, but in the accelerated tempo of these war-punc-

tuated years a man or woman of forty-five is out of date. He does not respect or despise the same institutions as an intelligent person in the middle twenties, does not read the same books, admire the same art, nor agree on the same social or cultural premises. The Silent Generation (loquacious enough among its contemporaries) holds its tongue because it cannot both explore itself and explain itself.

The first charge against these young people is apathy. They do not fling themselves into causes; they are not easily moved to enthusiasm; the expression on their faces is impassive, is "dead pan."

But I know where they learned this impassivity. They learned it at home, as adolescents, guarding themselves against their parents. Guardedness is not apathy. In all my reading I have discovered no age in which there was so great a gulf between parent and child. A seismic disturbance has taken place in the home. Within forty years America has ceased to be a patriarchy; it is moving toward a matriarchy but has not yet recognized and confirmed it. There is nothing wrong with a matriarchy; it does not connote any emasculation of men; it is merely a shift of balance. What is woeful for all parties is the time of transition. These young people grew up in the fluctuating tides of indeterminate authority. A father was no longer held to be, *ex officio*, wise and unanswerable. The mother had not yet learned the rules of supporting and circumscribing her new authority. Father, mother, and children have had daily to improvise their roles. This led to a constant emotional racket in the air. The child either learned a silent self-containment or fell into neurosis.

The second change is that they "aim low"—they want a good secure job. The article in *Time* says that, as far as their domestic life is concerned, they look forward to a "suburban idyll."

What they want, at all cost, is not to find themselves in "false situations." Life is full of false situations, especially

American life today. The most frequent and glaring of them is incompetence in high places. My generation saw a great deal of this in government, in the Army, in culture, and in education. We exercised our wit upon it, but we were ourselves (not yet free of patriarchal influence) still vaguely respectful of rank and office and status. This generation is not impressed by any vested authority whatever. And their freedom to judge authority is accompanied by their willingness to be judged. Their caution reposes upon their unwillingness to exercise any authority or responsibility for which they do not feel themselves to be solidly prepared and adequate. They hate the false and they shrink from those conspicuous roles which all but inevitably require a certain amount of it. I find this trait very promising. Plato was the first to say that high place is best in the hands of those who are reluctant to assume it.

I have said that the Silent Generation is fashioning the Twentieth Century Man. It is not only suffering and bearing forward a time of transition, it is figuring forth a new mentality.

In the first place, these young people will be the first truly international men and women. At last it has ceased to be a mere phrase that the world is one. Compared to them my generation was parochial. Their experience and their reading—their newspapers as well as their textbooks—have impressed upon them that the things which all men hold in common are more important and more productive than the things which separate them. In the Twenties and Thirties one felt oneself to be one among millions; these young people feel themselves to be one among billions. They know it not as a fact learned, but as a self-evident condition; they know it in their bones. On the one hand the

Knee-free coeds of Baldwin-Wallace College and their escorts parade in shorts across campus, 1955.

individual has shrunk; on the other, the individual has been driven to probe more deeply within himself to find the basis for a legitimate assertion of the claim of self. This conviction is new and its consequences are far-reaching—in international relations, in religion, in social reform, in art, and in the personal life.

For instance, we went to war against and among "foreigners" and "enemies." That attitude was narrow; henceforward all wars are civil wars. This generation goes forward not to punish and destroy, but to liberate oppressed and misguided brothers. The Army authorities go into anxious huddles over the unabashed candor with which young men can be heard exploring ways of avoiding military service. The Army—like the church, like the university—is an echoing gallery of out-dated attitudes and sentiments. It still thinks soldiers can be coerced and it still thinks that the primary qualifications of a soldier are courage and obedience. In a machine warfare, the soldier is a kind of engineer; his primary virtue is technical skill and his function is co-operation, not obedience.

Most of us were Protestants; the beliefs held by others were the objects of our all but condescending anthropological curiosity. Today these young people are interested in the nature of belief itself. Some of us in the previous generations hurled ourselves into social reform and social revolution; we did it with a personal passion that left little room for deliberation and long-time planning. To correct one abuse we were ready to upset many a benefit. It was of such crusaders that the Sidney Webbs were finally driven to say, "We hate moral indignation." The emerging International Man will move less feverishly in his enlarged thought-world. This generation is silent because these changes call not for argument but for rumination. The mistakes of the previous generations are writ large over the public prints.

These young people are setting new patterns for the relation of the individual to the society about him. The condition of being unimpressed by authorities and elders has thrown them back more resolutely on themselves. They are similarly unimpressed by time-honored conventions. For instance, young married couples today make few concessions to the more superficial aspects of social life. In my generation young brides suffered if their street address was not "right" and if their table silver was not distinguished. Young men were very conscious of influential connections, commissions in the Army, membership in good clubs. Members of this generation exhibit a singular insistence on wishing to be appraised for themselves alone. How often I have known them to conceal sedulously the fact that they come of privileged family. This insistence on being accepted as an individual produces an unprecedented candor. A college girl said to me: "You know I've always been an awful liar. I'm trying to get over it." A veteran, in the presence of his stricken parents, informed a mixed company that he had been a "psycho" for six months after the war. Such expressions reveal the consolidations of a liberty—the liberty of belonging to oneself and not to a social fiction.

These paragraphs have been part description, part explanation, part testimony of faith. Faith is in constant correspondence with doubt. It may be that these young people have been injured by the forces which have been sweeping across the world in their formative years. It may be that what I have called their self-containment is rather a cautious withdrawal from the demands of life. It may be that they lack passion and the constructive imagination. My faith returns, however, with each new encounter. I have just crossed the ocean with a boatload of choice young "Fulbrights" (all hail to the Senator!). The traits I have been describing reappear constantly. They have two orientations well in hand, to themselves and to the larger ranges of experience. It is toward those middle relationships that they are indifferent—current opinion and social usage and the imperatives of traditional religion, patriotism, and morality. Their parents wring their hands over them; their professors find them lukewarm or cool; the Army grows anxious; we older friends are often exasperated. These impatiences are provoked by the fact that they wish to live correctly by their lights and not by ours. In proportion as we are free we must accord them that.

LAMB TO THE SLAUGHTER

BY ROALD DAHL

SEPTEMBER 1953

The room was warm and clean, the curtains drawn, the two table lamps alight—hers and the one by the empty chair opposite. On the sideboard behind her, two tall glasses, soda water, whisky. Fresh ice cubes in the Thermos bucket.

Mary Maloney was waiting for her husband to come home from work.

Now and again, she would glance up at the clock, but without anxiety, merely to please herself with the thought that each minute gone by made it nearer the time when he would come. There was a slow smiling air about her, and about everything she did. The drop of the head as she bent over her sewing was curiously tranquil. Her skin—for this was her sixth month with child—had acquired a rather wonderful translucent quality, the mouth was soft, and the eyes, with their new placid look, seemed larger, darker than before.

When the clock said ten minutes to five, she began to listen, and a few moments later, punctually as always, she heard the tires on the gravel outside, and the car door slamming, the footsteps passing the window, the key turning in the lock. She laid aside her sewing, stood up, and went forward to kiss him as he came in.

"Hullo darling," she said.

"Hullo," he answered.

She took his coat and hung it in the closet. Then she walked over and made the drinks, a strongish one for him, a very weak one for herself; and soon she was back again in her chair with the sewing, and he in the other opposite, holding the tall glass with both his hands, rocking it so the ice cubes tinkled against the side.

For her, this was always a blissful time of day. She knew he didn't want to speak much until the first drink was finished, and she, on her side, was content to sit quietly, enjoying his company after the long hours alone in the house.

She loved to luxuriate in the presence of this man, and to feel—almost as a sunbather feels the sun—that warm male glow that came out of him to her when they were alone together. She loved him for the way he sat loosely in a chair, for the way he came in a door, or moved slowly across the room with long strides. She loved the intent, far look in his eyes when they rested on her, the funny shape of the mouth, and especially the way he remained silent about his tiredness, sitting still with himself until the whisky had taken some of it away.

"Tired darling?"

"Yes," he said. "I'm tired." And as he spoke, he did an unusual thing. He lifted his glass and drained it in one swallow although there was still half of it, at least half of it, left. She wasn't really watching him, but she knew what he had done because she heard the ice cubes falling back against the bottom of the empty glass when he lowered his arm. He paused a moment, leaning forward in the chair, then he got up and went slowly over to fetch himself another.

"I'll get it!" she cried, jumping up.

"Sit down," he said.

When he came back, she noticed that the new drink was dark amber with the quantity of whisky in it.

"Darling, shall I get your slippers?"

"No."

She watched him as he began to sip the dark yellow drink, and she could see little oily swirls in the liquid because it was so strong.

"I think it's a shame," she said, "that when a policeman gets to be as senior as you, they keep him walking about on his feet all day long."

He didn't answer, so she bent her head again and went on with her sewing; but each time he lifted the drink to his lips, she heard the ice cubes clinking against the side of the glass.

"Darling," she said. "Would you like me to get you some cheese? I haven't made any supper because it's Thursday."

"No," he said.

"If you're too tired to eat out," she went on, "it's still not too late. There's plenty of meat and stuff in the freezer, and you can have it right here and not even move out of the chair."

Her eyes waited on him for an answer, a smile, a little nod, but he made no sign.

"Anyway," she went on, "I'll get you some cheese and crackers first."

"I don't want it," he said.

She moved uneasily in her chair, the large eyes still watching his face. "But you *must* have supper. I can easily do it here. I'd like to do it. We can have lamb chops. Or pork. Anything you want. Everything's in the freezer."

"Forget it," he said.

"But darling, you *must* eat! I'll fix it anyway, and then you can have it or not, as you like."

She stood up and placed her sewing on the table by the lamp.

"Sit down," he said. "Just for a minute, sit down."

It wasn't till then that she began to get frightened.

"Go on," he said. "Sit down."

She lowered herself back slowly into the chair, watching him all the time with those large, bewildered eyes. He had finished the second drink and was staring down into the glass, frowning.

"Listen," he said. "I've got something to tell you."

"What is it, darling? What's the matter?"

He had now become absolutely motionless, and he kept his head down so that the light from the lamp beside him fell across the upper part of his face, leaving the chin and mouth in shadow. She noticed there was a little muscle moving near his left eye.

"This is going to be a bit of a shock to you, I'm afraid," he said. "But I've thought about it a good deal, and I've decided the only thing to do is tell you right away. I hope you won't blame me too much."

And he told her. It didn't take long, four or five minutes at most, and she sat very still through it all, watching him with a kind of dazed horror as he went further and further away from her with each word.

"So there it is," he added. "And I know it's kind of a bad time to be telling you, but there simply wasn't any other way. Of course, I'll give you money and see you're looked after. But there needn't really be any fuss. I hope not anyway. It wouldn't be very good for my job."

Adolf Hallman

Her first instinct was not to believe any of it, to reject it all. It occurred to her that perhaps he hadn't even spoken, that she herself had imagined the whole thing. Maybe, if she went about her business and acted as though she hadn't been listening, then later, when she sort of woke up again, she might find none of it had ever happened.

"I'll get the supper," she managed to whisper, and this time he didn't stop her.

When she walked across the room, she couldn't feel her feet touching the floor. She couldn't feel anything at all—except a slight nausea and a desire to vomit. Everything was automatic now—down the steps to the cellar, the light switch, the freezer, the hand inside the cabinet taking hold of the first object it met. She lifted it out, and looked at it. It was wrapped in paper, so she took off the paper and looked at it again.

A leg of lamb.

All right then, they would have lamb for supper. She carried it upstairs, holding the thin bone-end of it with both her hands, and as she went through the living-room, she saw him standing over by the window with his back to her, and she stopped.

"For God's sake," he said, hearing her, but not turning round, "don't make supper for me. I'm going out."

At that point, Mary Maloney simply walked up behind him, and without any pause, she swung the big frozen leg of lamb high in the air and brought it down as hard as she could on the back of his head.

She might just as well have hit him with a steel club.

She stepped back a pace, waiting, and the funny thing was that he remained standing there for at least four or five seconds, gently swaying. Then he crashed to the carpet.

The violence of the crash, the noise, the small table overturning, helped bring her out of the shock. She came out slowly, feeling cold and surprised, and she stood for a while, blinking at the body, still holding the ridiculous piece of meat tight with both hands.

All right, she told herself. So I've killed him.

It was extraordinary, now, how clear her mind became all of a sudden. She began thinking very fast. As the wife of a detective, she knew quite well what the penalty would be. That was fine. It made no difference to her. In fact, it would be a relief. On the other hand, what about the child? What were the laws about murderers with unborn children? Did they kill them both—mother and child? Or did they wait until the tenth month? What did they do?

Mary Maloney didn't know. And she certainly wasn't prepared to take a chance, in this instance.

She carried the meat into the kitchen, placed it in a pan, turned the oven on high, and shoved it inside. Then she washed her hands, and ran upstairs to the bedroom. She sat down before the mirror, tidied her hair, touched up her lips and face. She tried a smile. It came out rather peculiar. She tried again.

"Hullo Sam," she said brightly, aloud.

The voice sounded peculiar too.

"I want some potatoes please, Sam. Yes, and I think a can of peas."

That was better. Both the smile and the voice were coming out better now. She rehearsed it several times more. Then she ran downstairs, took her coat, went out the back door, down the garden, into the street.

It wasn't six o'clock yet and the lights were still on in the grocery shop.

"Hullo Sam," she said brightly, smiling at the man behind the counter.

"Why, good evening, Mrs. Maloney. How're *you?*"

"I want some potatoes please, Sam. Yes, and I think a can of peas."

The man turned and reached up behind him on the shelf for the peas.

"Patrick's decided he's tired and doesn't want to eat out tonight," she told him. "We go out Thursdays, and now he's caught me without any vegetables in the house."

"Then how about meat, Mrs. Maloney?"

"No, I've got meat, thanks. I got a nice leg of lamb from the freezer."

"Ah."

"I don't much like cooking it frozen, Sam, but I'm taking a chance on it this time. You think it'll be all right?"

"Personally," the grocer said, "I don't believe it makes any difference. You want these Idaho potatoes?"

"Oh yes, that'll be fine. Two of those."

"Anything else?" The grocer cocked his head on one side, looking at her pleasantly. "How about afterward? What you going to give him for afterward?"

"Well—what would you suggest, Sam?"

The man glanced around his shop. "How about a nice big slice of cheesecake? I know he likes that."

"Perfect," she said. "He loves it."

And when it was all wrapped and she had paid, she put on her brightest smile and said, "Thank you, Sam. Good night."

"Good night, Mrs. Maloney. And thank *you.*"

And now, she told herself as she hurried back, all she was doing now, she was returning home to her husband and he was waiting for his supper; and she must cook it good, and make it as tasty as possible because the poor man was tired; and if, when she entered the house, she happened to find anything unusual, or tragic, or terrible, then naturally it would be a shock and she'd become frantic with grief and horror. Mind you, she wasn't *expecting* to find anything. She was just going home with the vegetables. Mrs. Patrick Maloney going home with the vegetables on Thursday evening to cook supper for her husband.

That's the way, she told herself. Do everything right and natural. Keep things absolutely natural and there'll be no need for any acting at all.

Therefore, when she entered the kitchen by the back door, she was humming a little tune to herself, and smiling.

"Patrick!" she called. "How are you, darling?"

She put the parcel down on the table, and went through into the living room; and when she saw him lying there on the floor with his legs doubled up and one arm twisted back underneath his body, it really was rather a shock.

All the old love and longing for him welled up inside her, and she ran over to him, knelt down beside him, and began to cry her heart out. It was easy. No acting was necessary.

A few minutes later, she got up and went to the phone. She knew the number of the police station, and when the man at the other end answered, she cried to him, "Quick! Come quick! Patrick's dead!"

"Who's speaking?"

"Mrs. Maloney. Mrs. Patrick Maloney."

"You mean Patrick Maloney's dead?"

"I think so," she sobbed. "He's lying on the floor and I think he's dead."

"Be right over," the man said.

The car came very quickly, and when she opened the front door, two policemen walked in. She knew them both—she knew nearly all the men at that precinct—and she fell right into Jack Noonan's arms, weeping hysterically. He put her gently into a chair, then went over to join the other one, who was called O'Malley, kneeling by the body.

"Is he dead?" she cried.

"I'm afraid he is. What happened?"

Briefly, she told her story about going out to the grocer and coming back to find him on the floor.

While she was talking, crying and talking, Noonan discovered a small patch of congealed blood on the dead man's head. He showed it to O'Malley, who got up at once and hurried to the phone.

Soon, other men began to come into the house. First a doctor, then two detectives, one of whom she knew by name. Later, a police photographer arrived and took pictures, and a man who knew about fingerprints. There was a great deal of whispering and muttering beside the corpse, and the detectives kept asking her a lot of questions. But they always treated her kindly. She told her story again, this time right from the beginning, when Patrick had come in, and she was sewing, and he was tired, so tired he hadn't wanted to go out for supper. She told how she'd put the meat in the oven—"it's there now, cooking"—and how she'd slipped out to the grocer for vegetables, and come back to find him lying on the floor.

"Which grocer?" one of the detectives asked.

She told him, and he turned and whispered something to the other detective, who immediately went outside into the street.

In fifteen minutes he was back with a page of notes, and there was more whispering, and through her sobbing she heard a few of the whispered phrases—". . . acted quite normal . . . very cheerful . . . wanted to give him a good supper . . . peas . . . cheesecake . . . impossible that she . . ."

After a while, the photographer and the doctor departed, and two other men came in and took the corpse away on a stretcher. Then the fingerprint man went away. The two detectives remained, and so did the two policemen. They were exceptionally nice to her, and Jack Noonan asked if she wouldn't rather go somewhere else, to her sister's house perhaps, or to his own wife who would take care of her and put her up for the night.

No, she said. She didn't feel she could move even a yard at the moment. Would they mind awfully if she stayed just where she was until she felt better. She didn't feel too good at the moment, she really didn't.

Then hadn't she better lie down on the bed? Jack Noonan asked.

No, she said. She'd like to stay right where she was, in this chair. A little later, perhaps, when she felt better, she would move.

So they left her there while they went about their business, searching the house. Occasionally, one of the detectives asked her another question. Sometimes Jack Noonan spoke to her gently as he passed by. Her husband, he told her, had been killed by a blow on the back of the head administered with a heavy blunt instrument, almost certainly a large piece of metal. They were looking for the weapon. The murderer may have taken it with him, but on the other hand, he may've thrown it away or hidden it somewhere on the premises.

"It's the old story," he said. "Get the weapon, and you've got the man."

Later, one of the detectives came up and sat beside her. Did she know, he asked, of anything in the house that could've been used as the weapon? Would she mind having a look around to see if anything was missing—a very big spanner or a heavy metal vase.

They didn't have any heavy metal vases, she said.

"Or a big spanner?"

She didn't think they had a big spanner. But there might be some things like that in the garage.

The search went on. She knew that there were other policemen in the garden all around the house. She could hear their footsteps on the gravel outside, and sometimes she saw the flash of a torch through a chink in the curtains. It began to get late, nearly nine, she noticed by the clock on the mantle. The four men searching the rooms seemed to be growing weary, a trifle exasperated.

"Jack," she said, the next time Sergeant Noonan went by. "Would you mind giving me a drink?"

"Sure I'll give you a drink. You mean this whisky?"

"Yes please. But just a small one. It might make me feel better."

He handed her the glass.

"Why don't you have one yourself," she said. "You must be awfully tired. Please do. You've been very good to me."

"Well," he answered. "It's not strictly allowed, but I might take just a drop to keep me going."

One by one, the others came in and were persuaded to take a little nip of whisky. They stood around rather awkwardly with the drinks in their hands, uncomfortable in her presence, trying to say consoling things to her. Sergeant Noonan wandered into the kitchen, came out quickly, and said, "Look, Mrs. Maloney. You know that oven of yours is still on, and the meat still inside."

"Oh *dear* me!" she cried. "So it is!"

"I better turn it off for you, hadn't I?"

"Will you do that, Jack. Thank you so much."

When the sergeant returned the second time, she looked at him with her large, dark, tearful eyes. "Jack Noonan," she said.

"Yes?"

"Would you do me a small favor—you and these others?"

"We can try, Mrs. Maloney."

"Well," she said. "Here you all are, and good friends of dear Patrick's too, and helping to catch the man who killed him. You must be terrible hungry by now because it's long past your suppertime, and I know Patrick would never forgive me, God bless his soul, if I allowed you to remain in his house without offering you decent hospitality. Why don't you eat up that lamb that's in the oven. It'll be cooked just right by now."

"Wouldn't dream of it," he said.

"Please," she begged. "Please eat it. Personally I couldn't touch a thing, certainly not what's been in the house when he was here. But it's all right for you. It'd be a favor to me if you'd eat it up. Then you can go on with your work again afterward."

There was a good deal of hesitating among the four policemen, but they were clearly hungry, and in the end she was able to persuade them to go into the kitchen and help themselves.

The woman stayed where she was, listening to them through the open door, and she could hear them speaking among themselves, their voices thick and sloppy because their mouths were full of meat.

"Have some more, Charlie?"

"No. Better not finish it."

"She *wants* us to finish it. She said so. Be doing her a favor."

"Okay then. Give me some more."

"That's a hell of a big club the guy must've used to hit poor Patrick," one of them was saying. "The doc says his skull was smashed all to pieces just like from a sledge hammer."

"That's why it ought to be easy to find."

"Exactly what I say."

"Whoever done it, they're not going to be carrying a thing like that around with them longer than they need."

One of them belched.

"Personally, I think it's right here on the premises."

"Probably right under our very noses. What you think, Jack?"

And in the other room, Mary Maloney began to giggle.

THE GREAT WALL STREET CRASH

BY JOHN KENNETH GALBRAITH

OCTOBER 1954

Senator Couzens: Did Goldman, Sachs, & Co. organize the Goldman Sachs Trading Corporation?

Mr. Sachs: Yes, sir.

Senator Couzens: And it sold its stock to the public?

Mr. Sachs: A portion of it. The firm invested originally in 10 per cent of the . . . issue.

Senator Couzens: And the other 90 per cent was sold to the public?

Mr. Sachs: Yes, sir.

Senator Couzens: At what price?

Mr. Sachs: At 104 . . . the stock was [later] split two for one.

Senator Couzens: And what is the price of the stock now?

Mr. Sachs: Approximately 1¾.

— HEARINGS BEFORE SENATE COMMITTEE
ON BANKING AND CURRENCY ON STOCK
EXCHANGE PRACTICES. MAY 20, 1932.

A case can readily be made that, with the single exception of the Civil War, no event of the past hundred years so deeply impressed itself upon the thoughts, attitudes, and voting behavior of the American people as the Great Depression. This importance is hardly reflected in the dignity with which history treats of the tragedy. The climactic stock-market crash which launched the depression—and which was considerably more important in relation to what followed than the shots at Sumter—occurred only twenty-five years ago this month, but it has already receded far into the mists of memory. One measure of this neglect is the widespread and quite erroneous assumption that there was one day in October 1929 when the great crash occurred. Another indication is the total absence of agreement as to what day it was. Thus Thursday, October 24, the first day on which panic seized the market, has regularly been cited as the Black Thursday of the crash. But the professionals have always leaned to the following Monday or Tuesday, when the losses were far greater and when the volume of trading reached its all-time incredible high. Others have picked still other days. In a book explaining the debacle, Professor Irving Fisher of Yale—Professor Fisher as the acknowledged prophet of the boom was left with much explaining to do—singled out October 21 as the day of the catastrophe. (On that day trading was very heavy but the declines relatively modest.) The authorized biographers of Herbert Hoover, in 1935, refused to settle on any one day but—along with the twenty-ninth—picked October 23 and October 26. (The twenty-third was the day preceding Black Thursday; the twenty-sixth was a Saturday when things were tolerably quiet.) Not, certainly, since the siege of Troy has the chronology of a great event been so uncertain.

As a matter of fact, economic history, even at its most violent, has a much less exciting tempo than military or even political history. Days are rarely important. All of the autumn of 1929 was a terrible time, and all of that year was one of climax. With the invaluable aid of hindsight it is possible to see that throughout all of the early months the stage was being set for the final disaster. [. . .]

Thursday, October 24, is the first of the days which history—such as it is on the subject—identifies with the panic of 1929. Measured by disorder, fright, and confusion, it deserves to be so regarded. 12,894,650 shares changed hands that day, most of them at prices which shattered the dreams and the hopes of those who had owned them. Of all the mysteries of the stock exchange there is none so impenetrable as why there should be a buyer for everyone who seeks to sell. October 24, 1929 showed that what is mysterious is not inevitable. Often there were no buyers, and only after wide vertical declines could anyone be induced to bid.

The morning was the terrible time. The opening was unspectacular, and for a little prices were firm. Volume,

404 ◆ AN AMERICAN ALBUM

Thousands crowd the streets around the New York Stock Exchange, October 24, 1929.

however, was large and soon prices began to sag. Once again the ticker dropped behind the market. Prices fell farther and faster, and the ticker lagged more and more. By eleven o'clock what had been a market was only a wild scramble to sell. In the crowded board rooms across the country the ticker told of a frightful collapse. But the selected quotations coming in over the bond ticker also showed that current values were far below the ancient history of the tape. The uncertainty led more and more people to try to sell. Others, no longer able to respond to margin calls, were sold. By 11:30, panic, pure and unqualified, was in control.

Outside on Broad Street a weird roar could be heard. A crowd gathered and Police Commissioner Grover Whalen dispatched a special police detail to Wall Street to insure the peace. A workman appeared to accomplish some routine repairs atop one of the high buildings. The multitude, assuming he was a would-be suicide, waited impatiently for him to jump. At 12:30 the visitors' gallery of the Exchange was closed on the wild scenes below. One of the visitors who had just departed was displaying his customary genius for being on hand with history. He was the former Chancellor of the Exchequer, Mr. Winston Churchill. It was he in 1925 who returned Britain to a gold standard that substantially

over-valued the pound. To help relieve the subsequent strain the Federal Reserve eased money rates and, in the conventional though by no means unimpeachable view, it thereby launched the bull market. However, there is no record of anyone's that day having reproached Winston for the trouble he was causing. It is most unlikely that he reproached himself. Economics was never his strong point.

At noon, however, things took a turn for the better. At last came the long-awaited organized support. The heads of the National City Bank, Chase, Guaranty Trust, and Bankers Trust met with Thomas W. Lamont, the senior Morgan partner, at 23 Wall Street. All quickly agreed to come to the support of the market and to pool substantial resources for this purpose. Lamont then met with reporters and, in what Frederick Lewis Allen in his superb account of the day's events in *Only Yesterday* described as "one of the most remarkable understatements of all time," said: "There has been a little distress selling on the Stock Exchange." He added that this passing inconvenience was "due to a technical situation rather than any fundamental cause," and he told the newsmen the situation was "susceptible to betterment."

Meanwhile, word had reached the Exchange floor that the bankers were meeting and succor was on the way. These

Wall Street speculator trying to raise cash.

were the nation's most potent financiers; they had not yet been pilloried and maligned by the New Dealers. Prices promptly firmed and rose. Then at 1:30 Richard Whitney, widely known as a floor broker for Morgan's, walked jauntily to the post where Steel was traded and left with the specialist an order for 10,000 shares at several points above the current bids. He continued the rounds with this largesse. Confidence was wonderfully revived, and the market actually boomed upward. In the last hour the selling orders which were still flooding in turned it soft again, but the net loss for the day—about twelve points on the *Times* industrial averages—was far less than the day before. Some issues, Steel among them, were actually higher on the day's trading.

However, this recovery was of distant interest to the tens of thousands who had sold or been sold out during the decline and whose dreams of opulence had gone glimmering along with most of their merchantable possessions. It was eight and a half minutes past seven that night before the ticker finished recording the day's misfortunes. In the board rooms speculators who had been sold out since early morning sat silently watching the tape. The habit of months or

years, however idle it had now become, could not be broken at once. Then, as the final trades were registered, they made their way out into the gathering night.

In Wall Street itself lights blazed from every office as clerks struggled to come abreast of the day's business. Messengers and board-room boys, caught up in the excitement and untroubled by losses, went skylarking through the streets until the police arrived to quell them. Representatives of thirty-five of the largest wire houses assembled at the offices of Hornblower and Weeks and told the press on departing that the market was "fundamentally sound" and "technically in better condition than it has been in months." The host firm dispatched a market letter which stated that "commencing with today's trading the market should start laying the foundation for the constructive advance which we believe will characterize 1930." [...]

A Boston investment trust took space in the *Wall Street Journal* to say, "S-T-E-A-D-Y Everybody! Calm thinking is in order. Heed the words of America's greatest bankers." A single dissonant note, though great in portent, went completely unnoticed. Speaking in Poughkeepsie, Governor Franklin D. Roosevelt criticized the "fever of speculation."

On Sunday there were sermons suggesting that a certain measure of divine retribution had been visited on the Republic and that it had not been entirely unmerited. It was evident, however, that almost everyone believed that this heavenly knuckle-rapping was over and that speculation could be now resumed in earnest. The papers were full of the prospects for next week's market. Stocks, it was agreed, were again cheap and accordingly there would be a heavy rush to buy. Numerous stories from the brokerage houses, some of them possibly inspired, told of a fabulous volume of buying orders which was piling up in anticipation of the opening of the market. In a concerted advertising campaign in Monday's papers, stock-market firms urged the wisdom of buying stocks promptly. On Monday the real disaster began. [...]

Tuesday, October 29, was the most devastating day in the history of the New York stock market, and it may have been the most devastating in the history of markets. Selling began at once and in huge volume. The air holes, which the bankers were to close, opened wide. Repeatedly and in many issues there was a plethora of selling orders and no buyers at all. Once again, of course, the ticker lagged—at the close it was two and a half hours behind. By then 16,410,030 shares had been known to have been traded—more than three times the number that had once been considered a fabulously big day. (On an average good day last summer sales were running about three million shares.) Despite a closing rally on dividend news, the losses were again appalling. The *Times* industrial averages were down 43 points, canceling all of the huge gains of the preceding twelve months. Losses on individual issues were far greater. By the end of trading, members were near collapse from strain and fatigue. Office staffs, already near the breaking point, now had to tackle the greatest volume of transactions yet. By now, also, there was no longer quite the same certainty that things would get better. Perhaps they would go on getting worse. [...]

No feature of the Great Crash was more remarkable than the way it passed from climax to anticlimax to destroy again and again the hope that the worst had passed. Even on the thirtieth the worst was still to come, although henceforth it came more slowly. Day after day during the next two weeks prices fell with monotonous regularity. At the close of trading on October 29 the *Times* industrial average stood at 275.

In the rally of the next two days it gained more than fifty points, but by November 13 it was down to 224 for a further net loss of fifty points.

And these levels were wonderful compared with what were to follow. On July 8, 1932, the average of the closing levels of the *Times* industrials was 58.46. This was not much more than the amount by which the average dropped on the single day of October 28, and considerably less than a quarter of the closing values on October 29. By then, of course, business conditions were no longer sound, fundamentally or otherwise.

What might be called the everyday or utility-style history book tells of the Great Depression of the thirties which began with the great stock-market crash of 1929. Among sophisticates—professional students of the business cycle in particular—there has long been a tendency to decry the importance that this attributes to the stock-market crash as a cause of the depression. The crash was part of the froth, rather than the substance of the situation. A depression, it was pointed out, had been in the making since midsummer of 1929, when numerous of the indexes began to turn down.

In this matter the history books are almost certainly right. The market crash (and, of course, the speculation that set the stage) was of profound importance for what followed. It shrank the supply of investment funds and, at the same time, it shocked the confidence on which investment expenditure depends. The crash also reduced personal expenditures and deeply disrupted international capital flows and international trade. The effect of all this on economic activity was prompt and very real. Nothing else is a fraction so important for explaining the severity of the depression that followed.

Since it was important, the question inevitably arises whether a similar cycle of speculation and collapse could again occur. The simple answer is of course! Laws have been passed to outlaw some of the more egregious behavior which contributed to the big bull market of the twenties. Nothing has been done about the seminal lunacy which possesses people who see a chance of becoming rich. On the assumption that history does not repeat itself precisely, we may never again see the particular lunacy of the late twenties. But if we survive to suffer such things, we can undoubtedly count on some variation. The time to worry will be when important people begin to explain that it cannot happen because conditions are fundamentally sound.

The Sound of Moorish Laughter

by Harold Brodkey

May 1956

Across the street from my house was a Catholic church. It was really a parochial school, rather drab and old, built of dried-blood-color brick with white trim; but inside, it had a chapel, and every Sunday, cars filled our quiet suburban street, bells rang—small, almost shrill bells—and women dressed in stiff little hats and gloves stood and talked on the school steps. The school was sort of an eyesore in our neighborhood, which had been built, somewhat hopefully, in the closing years of the 'twenties and which consisted of a number of small one-family houses. My mother didn't like living so close to a parochial school and quondam church, because of the noise and traffic on Sundays and the lack of privacy. Also, our street, Courtney Avenue, had been designed to have a parkway running down its middle, like a boulevard, but the church had asked to have that space left for parking. My mother (my father was dead) had bought our house thinking there was going to be a parkway in front of it, and she was sullen about the church and the nuns and the brisk, athletic priest that ran it.

During the week when the church was a school, the noise was almost worse. Children played in the yard of the school (that yard was a shame, my mother always said; it had hardly any grass; and its seesaws and jungle-gym and swings were old and unsightly) and sometimes they chased their balls right up to our front steps and trampled my mother's flower borders. Sometimes too the nuns would raise their voices or a child would cry and the noise, disquieting and alien, would upset my mother and fill my grandmother with rage. My grandmother was seventy-eight years old; she was fierce and unreconciled; she despised most of her seven children and so far as I could tell liked only two of her fourteen grandchildren, both pretty girls. My grandmother didn't like me but she had the grace not to hide behind her age, and she fought me man to man with a kind of virulent hatred that was almost as good as affection. She used to pinch me and give me sandwiches for lunch that I didn't like—I hated boloney, for instance, but boloney I had four days out of five. But then on the other hand, when I called her names or talked back to her she never told on me. She merely shook one bony finger and warned me that I'd come to no good end and that she'd get even.

Anyway, grandmother hated the church. She had left Russia shortly after the 1888 pogrom in Odessa, and while she never spoke specifically of the horrors she had undergone, she sometimes would speak of how awful it had been, "with the priests leading the mob, flying their banners, and mocking at the poor dying Jews."

I didn't believe her. She was a dreadful liar.

The priest across the street was very young and athletic. Sometimes, coming home from school, I would see him with his gown tucked in, playing ball with some of the older boys of his school. The priest was dark-haired and rosy-lipped; after a few minutes of baseball, he would grow flushed and excited, and he would shout as loudly as any of the boys. Sometimes he would dance around the sidelines when his side got a hit or worked a man around into scoring position. Usually the opposing team was totally disheartened by all this; they seemed to feel they were playing against the blessed side. Sometimes, though, they'd set their faces, accept a league with the devil, and play with a kind of wild intensity—usually this was after considerable goading from the priest—and their air of defiance was enormous and moving.

At times, my mother would send me to the store and I would cut across the parochial school's playground to a Kroger's grocery store on the corner of Peabody and Corcoran. I would dawdle on the path watching the baseball game over one shoulder. There was something mysterious in the priest's relationship to the boys, something powerful and paternal and unquestioned. I wondered what it was in the priest that made the boys so docile. And often, I heard the boys call him Father.

One day, our neighborhood was in an uproar. My mother came home from her office early, and she and our neighbors and I stood on our front steps and watched workmen finish putting up a six-foot-high wire-mesh fence around the school's playground. Inside the mesh was a steam shovel.

"By God, they're going to put up a church," my mother said. "This is the end of the block."

Mr. Morgan, who lived on the corner, said he thought it might be a parking lot for the present chapel; perhaps the city had forced them to stop using the street. "Goodness knows," he said, "We've all complained often enough to the city manager."

My mother said she hoped Mr. Morgan was right but she would bet Mr. Morgan was wrong. My grandmother sitting by her window was stiff with rage when I went inside. "They'll be out burning our houses next," she said darkly.

"Don't be stupid, Grandma," I said, purposefully shoving her rocking chair a little. "There's a law against that."

"Who wants a cross hanging over their house all day long?" my grandmother said, but she was only talking, making noise because she was lonely; she had outlived everybody she cared about; and she was surprised still, after fifty years in this country, that things were so comparatively peaceful and uninteresting.

In the cold weather, I used to wear a bright red lumber jacket an older cousin had passed on to me. It was made out of a Hudson Bay blanket or out of the same material, and since I was particularly subject to colds and it was the warmest coat I had ever had, I wore it every day. It was an object of envy and mockery to my classmates, but the little boys at the parochial school were absolutely fascinated. They used to crowd to their fence and watch me walk by.

Sometimes they created incidents. One afternoon, coming home from school, I was waylaid by five or six of the parochial school boys. They jumped out of the bushes at the end of the block and surrounded me. I raised my book—I was carrying a large geography book—over my head and began to curse them. My blasphemy so startled them, they gave way and I ran down the street and got safely home.

But these incidents didn't happen often. Once, on a cold, late November evening, I sat idly on one of the swings in the parochial school's yard. The foundation for the church had been dug and covered over already for the winter. I was swinging with my eyes half-closed, trying to imagine the piles of dirt around the foundation were mountains. I had never seen mountains. Two boys from the school were playing desultorily at the other end of the yard, passing a football back and forth. The evening was drawing in and a cold wind nipped and twisted. The Father came out of the school and walked down to inspect the foundation; on the way back, my red jacket caught his eye—it was a very bright red—and he came over and asked me who I was. I told him, shyly, that I lived across the street; I asked him if he was building a big church. He was even handsomer up close than from a distance; he had a cleft in his chin and a perfect shave; he had sad dark eyes with thick lashes; his mouth had

Bob Pinkwater

a curiously lonely expression as if he had never quite gotten used to his responsibilities or to the quality of life in our lonely suburb. He said, amiably enough, that it was going to be a medium-sized church. He felt my jacket and said, "That's quite a coat you have there."

"It's the warmest coat in the world," I burst out. The Father patted my head and went away.

That was how I came to fall in love with him.

I took to waiting on our front steps in the cold December afternoons and when the priest came out of his school, I'd smile and wave at him. Then I would go and hide in the basement. I wasn't capable of bearing two waves in one afternoon.

Later, I hid in the attic, away from my grandmother, and stared out the dusty window at the school. I kept my passion an absolute secret. But I could not resist asking my mother one evening what she would do if a Father talked to her; I had to be prepared.

"Be polite," she said. "Why? Has the priest across the street been after you?" She looked at me sharply.

"No, no," I cried. "But if he had, would it be wrong?"

"Well, he would try to convert you," my mother said. She was watching me very closely. "You must be careful. Don't trust him an inch."

When spring came, I built a tree house in the maple that hung over our driveway. I could sit in the tree house and watch the school across the street. Often the priest came out and inspected the work the men were doing on the church. He beamed at them—which was a good thing; but often, he gave orders—which was not such a good thing; but he never saw me which was the best thing of all.

Without having the Father to think about, that would have been a terrible year for me. My best friend, Harry Bucker, had moved to California, and I had no other close friends. The other boys who were left were a dull crew. Listlessly I played war games; I patiently sat through games of torture, even though Johnny Parsons had once tied me to a chair and burned my sweater with a heated soldering iron and my mother had blamed me. I was bored.

I was difficult to play with. I enjoyed marbles, but I liked to win; I only played with boys I could beat. Over the years I won more than three hundred marbles. I kept count. When I played cops and robbers, those of us who were shot had to lie down and wait to be buried before they could get up and join the game again.

"You can't leave bodies all over the lawn," I'd argue disgustedly; "it brings the plague."

In the middle of a conversation I might yank a toy plane out of my pocket and bomb my companion. If he didn't immediately fall shrieking to the ground, I wouldn't play with him again. I would fall to the ground, if I was bombed, and it was bad for my health.

That left the Father, and he was my delight for almost six months. I even used to hover by the wire-mesh fence when he was playing baseball with his boys. I would hang on the fence with one hand and sort of spin back and forth until someone looked at me and then I'd go away.

The church was rising by leaps and bounds. My mother thought it was hideous. I liked it. It was a big building of gray stone with a high tower on which there was going to be a concrete statue of Jesus. The façade of the church was covered with a scaffolding, and I used to play on that with some of the other boys in the neighborhood. We climbed, daring

each other, all the way to the top of the tower. We ran up and down the ramps where the workmen wheeled barrows of mortar. We played tag on all fours on the half-finished roof.

One day when I was alone on the scaffolding—it was a Saturday, a warm sunny day, in June—the priest came to look at his building. He saw me perched up near the tower (as a matter of fact I was looking at the statue of Jesus which lay in the blocks on the roof) and called to me to come down. When I climbed down, he proceeded to lecture me on how dangerous that was and that I must never do it again or he would tell my parents. I got tears in my eyes. Then suddenly, he saw them, smiled, rather embarrassedly, and asked me if I liked his church. He wanted to console me for his bawling out. I said it was beautiful. He asked me if I wanted to see the inside. I said I did. He took my hand, while my heart palpitated, and led me into the church.

It was actually the first church I had ever been in. Shadows hung along the walls as thick as curtains. The pews gleamed newly; I thought the confessional booths were marvelous. I thought they were where shy women sat so they wouldn't be seen.

The interior was mostly completed. There was a small lobby and then doors and then a little vestibule marked off from the main part of the church by fluted concrete columns.

"We'll replace those with marble ones some day," the priest said briskly. He had a habit of striding forward, while I ran to keep up, then stopping suddenly, dropping his head to look at me, firing his sentences, and then striding on. He reminded me a good deal of my mother when she was being businesslike, except that he was holding my hand, and his voice would occasionally slip into a booming theatrical register that made me feel as if I were hanging on in a high wind. With two more athletic strides—closer to leaps really—he had me next to the water basin.

"Holy water," he barked. "The basin's Italian marble, real Italian marble."

"I think that's wonderful," I whispered shyly.

"Acanthus leaves," he said pointing to a carved frieze that ran around the edge. "Grapes. Pitchers of milk and honey."

I sighed admiringly, as I had heard my mother do when seeing a friend's new house. "They look very expensive."

The priest's eyebrows went up; his eyes fastened on my face. "You like such things?" he asked tersely.

"Yes, sir." I could tell that he was very lonely. The look on his face was a mixture of hope, and of the wariness that had come from a number of rebuffs in the past.

He sat down in a pew and pulled me down next to him. He told me that I shouldn't call him sir, I should call him Father. This seemed nearly blasphemy to me, a terrible and wicked pleasure, that I ought to avoid. I told him I didn't believe in him; did calling him Father mean that I believed?

He explained to me the hierarchy of the church, dwelling with a kind of loving eagerness on the titles of monsignor and bishop, archbishop and cardinal. When he went on to try to explain what such titles meant, his face grew flushed, and his voice stumbled searching for terms of sufficient glory to describe them. He even stammered a little in his excitement.

Then we talked about me. He asked me, as he studied me with his extraordinarily young and vivacious eyes, how old I was and if I prayed at night and if I liked school. It seemed to me he was growing to like me and I became uneasy. I decided to warn him now, rather than have him learn it later when it would hurt me more. "I'm a difficult child," I blurted out.

The priest's eyes kindled. "Well, I guessed that," he murmured. "I can see you're a regular Tartar. But it's quite all right with me."

Originally, of course, the priest had only meant to be kind. He had started to bawl me out and I had nearly cried, and his gentleness had led him—his gentleness and his embarrassment—to show me the church, to distract me, and that, by showing me what he took such pride in. But I had seen the church and showed no signs of wanting to leave, and I was staring at him with widened eyes; it was adoration, almost, but he couldn't guess that. He thought perhaps it might be religion.

He asked me, "Do you believe in God?"

"Oh yes, sir—Father."

"Do you know who Jesus was?"

"Yes, Father."

"Who?"

"The man who preached and started the Catholics."

"He wasn't a man, child. He was the Son of God."

"Oh, I don't believe that," I cried.

The priest sat there, perplexed. He couldn't quite comprehend then what I wanted; but at last a light grew in his eyes. "It's architecture you're interested in?" he asked me joyfully.

I didn't know quite what he was talking about, but I said yes.

"Would you like to see my treasures?"

"Oh, yes, Father."

"I haven't shown them to many people," he said, taking my hand, and striding toward the back of the church. "I am said to have a problem with spiritual pride." He shook his head briskly. "But it simply isn't true. I believe that worship should be grand, don't you?" Then he recollected who I was and smiled at himself. "Of course, you don't even know what spiritual pride is," he cried exultantly. "And now just look at that stained glass window! French. It's French. Have you ever seen such a crimson? Or such a blue?" His voice dropped to a whisper. "It's St. Thomas. And that one," raising his voice, "is St. George slaying the dragon."

"They're grand, they're grand," I said eagerly.

"And now to the storeroom!" the Father cried, in the voice with which he shouted at baseball games. We flew down a short curving corridor, the Father's cassock whipping against my legs and tangling them hopelessly. The Father produced a key and unlocked a door, switched on an overhead light, and released my hand.

"There!" he cried. All around the room were objects of gold and silver, some half in boxes, others standing on boxes with shreds of excelsior hanging to them, sticking in their filigree. "These are for the church," the Father said briskly. "They were inordinately expensive...." His breath escaped in a long sigh. "Mortgages, mortgages," he murmured. Around the walls were tacked blueprints, not ordinary blue and white blueprints, but ones of black lines on heavy white paper and under each sheet were small ink drawings of façades and altars and interiors, of doors and stained glass windows, even of pews and the water spout. I knew with sudden clairvoyance that the Father had drawn the pictures. I asked him and he nodded.

"However, I was not allowed to build that church!" he said with some bitterness. He led me to a table at one end of the room and among a pile of bills and receipts brought out an architect's drawing of a façade. It was high and narrow.

"I don't suppose it matters what kind of house you build to worship God in," the priest said with heavy sarcasm, his voice theatrical and pulsing, "but this suburb is ugly enough without planning on its turning into slum fifty years from now."

A chill ran up my back, a sensation of a malevolent world watching me. Slum? In fifty years? My home? What would happen to me? The Father was saying,

"After all, I raised the money...." He sat on one of the packing cases and put his head in his hands.

I realized that something had gone wrong. I said nothing. I blinked and then I walked around the room and saw a statue of a woman holding an infant. The statue was painted, and it was larger than I was. "Who's this?" I asked.

The Father raised his head but kept his hands in front of the lower part of his face; it was a curiously childlike gesture, though theatrical with his raised black eyebrows and piercing eyes staring over the tips of his fingers.

"The Virgin and the Infant Jesus." He kept his hands raised, as if he feared he was going to be laughed at. "Do you like it?"

"Yes," I said, enthusiastically.

"It's Italian." He rose and came over. "Genuine Italian work. Have you ever seen such a blue?" The Virgin had a blue cape. "Now, look closely. Do you see the tiny silver stars inlaid in the wood? Have you ever seen anything like that?" He was growing brighter by the minute. "It's going to stand in a little chapel under a blue window. Won't that be wonderful with those stars? And come look at this censer, it's true Spanish work, from Mexico. I have another one just like it, but it's not unpacked yet. In another hundred years, these will all be treasures. And come see the altar screen. It's gold-leafed. Here's the flight from Egypt: Israelites," he said, beaming at me, "just like you. And there's the Sermon on the Mount. Isn't that fish border marvelous?"

The fish spilled in golden profusion, sporting delicate, nearly transparent fins, out of a cornucopia that Jesus held above his head; on the cornucopia was engraved the word Charity. One fish twisted its head roguishly and bent adoring eyes on the figure of Jesus. I clapped my hands.

"Yes, the fish are heavenly. Now, look at this chasuble. The Bishop gave me this three years ago when I first came, to encourage me in getting a church built. You see, it's the garden of Eden." I saw the trees and a naked man and woman and a serpent.

"They're naked," I said.

"Sssh," the Father said, half-laughing, "you're not supposed to notice that at your age. And these are the cedar boards one of my parishioners gave me to make two closets in the rectory."

"Two," I cried, "whatever for?"

"They keep moths out," the Father said to me, "but it's the smell that's so glorious. Smell them."

He was right, the smell was glorious. I looked at him in delight. "Two!" I cried.

"Two!" he murmured with mild modesty.

Now, there was nothing left to look at. Silence descended. I stood with my head lowered, waiting patiently for the Father to begin the ritual grown-ups usually followed in getting rid of a child: he would ask me if it wasn't my dinnertime.

But the Father stood with his hands clasped behind his back. The excitement hadn't left his face. Slowly he opened his mouth. "Two thousand years of Christ," he said and slowly raised his head until his eyes were fixed on the ceiling, "and we are still building churches that look like gymnasiums. It maddens me, maddens me.... For the Lord who

died for us we will not build a decent tabernacle—if this is spiritual pride, I will gladly take my penance. Gladly!" he roared and took a quick look at me, a little surprised, probably, at how small I was.

"I'm not a Catholic, sir," I said weakly.

"I know, child. But who would want to be and worship in a gray warehouse across the street? If you only knew how beautiful churches can be! I suppose you've never seen Milan.

Milan," he sighed, "is nearly blasphemous. And Notre Dame? Notre Dame may be a little heavy and over-logical, but it has spirit, esprit, soul. . . . Chartres, I don't even mention. I won't discuss Chartres. Chartres is a miracle. This is not the age of miracles. What kind of Chartres could there be in St. Louis? No, I don't mention Chartres."

Idly I took three pieces of excelsior and tried to braid them.

"God is beautiful," the Father said. "His churches should be beautiful."

"Father, if you want a nicer church, why don't you build one? Who would stop you? Why do you let people boss you around?"

"Stop me? Let them?" He smiled; his eyebrows shot up; but then his face melted back, and he looked saddened and defeated. "Let my Bishop boss me . . . that's quite a novel thought, a charming thought. . . ." His voice trailed off.

"Sir," I said in a low voice. "I'm very sorry if I said something wrong. . . ." The priest looked at me; our glances met on a sharp incline; and it was one of those moments, when an emotion stands clear, easily recognizable, even in a child, even between two strangers. The priest gave an audible gasp. He had not even imagined what my feelings were or thought to wonder why he talked so freely to me. But at that moment, he realized everything. He had responded to the presence of love. He had warmed himself in it, even though it came from a ten-year-old child. In a spasm of embarrassment, he began to cough; he covered his mouth and coughed for several minutes, while I stood there nervously.

"My father's dead," I said, at last; I felt I had to explain. The priest could not help smiling, not because of any pleasure he felt, but because it was the only gesture he could allow himself. The smile played about his lips as if it were a small bird. "I have to go home," I said, miserable with shyness, "it's my dinnertime."

"Ah," the priest murmured. He stood up in a sudden flutter of his cassock. "Well, you come back and visit me again. . . ."

"I—" I began; I was trembling a little. "I'd have . . . I'd have to sneak in. . . ." I was sorry now the priest had guessed my secret, that he had to consider what was possible and what was not. . . . It was humiliating, and I felt the dim stirring of anger.

"Perhaps," the priest murmured, "I might talk to your mother and explain—" But I was shaking my head violently, and he paused. His eyes glittered. I think the love I felt for him must have seemed attractive; in every man there must exist somewhere the urge to be a father, or to play at it for a little while. . . . He gazed at me, probably wondering at himself for having such feelings. "You have a high sense of loyalty," he said at last, a faint shade of rebuke in his voice, "to your mother, don't you?"

I nodded.

"I've enjoyed your visit very much," the priest said and held out his hand; he had lapsed into sheerly masculine dignity.

I thanked him for showing me the church. "I appreciate it very much. It was very kind of you."

"Kind?" he said; he raised his arms, perplexed. "I try to be, child . . . I try to be. . . ."

The whole episode, so much of it taking place in gesture, so embarrassing and odd, had lasted only a few minutes. When I left the priest, he was standing in the middle of the storeroom, pulling idly at his ear.

I was furious with myself for giving everything away. I ran out the back door and then turned and gave it a kick; then I ran around the block and down Courtney Avenue to my house.

The clear June day was ending with a tumultuous sunset. An extraordinary effulgence of light blistered gold streaks on the bottom of fat-bellied clouds, cast out tangled streamers of lavender and crimson. The dazzling light flowed down Courtney street, gleamed along the docile fronts of the modest houses and set a pinkish flush on the gray stone of the uncompleted church. Now, the street was a river of light; now, the clouds began to plunge into the gap in the western sky. I wasn't old enough to have heard, faint in the distance, the sound of laughter from within the courtyards of Islam, among pierced walls and blossoming almond trees, where philosophers know there is no God but Allah.

That June day, as the sun set, I stood on the front steps of my house and gazed wonderingly at the parochial school. I heard my grandmother fling open her window (she hated fresh air) and stick her angry head out into the cool flush of evening: "What are you standing there for? You want to catch your death of cold? You want the Catholics to think you're admiring their church? You come inside. . . ." I made a face at her, hands to my ears, my tongue out, nose wrinkled. I wonder if the Father saw me. At any rate, my grandmother slammed the window down and I ran inside to do battle with her.

On Fear: The South in Labor

by William Faulkner

June 1956

Immediately after the Supreme Court decision abolishing segregation in schools, the talk began in Mississippi of ways and means to increase taxes to raise the standard of the Negro schools to match the white ones. I wrote the following letter to the open forum page of our most widely-read Memphis paper:

We Mississippians already know that our present schools are not good enough. Our young men and women themselves prove that to us every year by the fact that, when the best of them want the best of education which they are entitled to and competent for, not only in the humanities but in the professions and crafts—law and medicine and engineering—too, they must go out of the state to get it. And quite often, too often, they don't come back.

So our present schools are not even good enough for white people; our present state reservoir of education is not of high enough quality to assuage the thirst of even our white young men and women. In which case, how can it possibly assuage the thirst and need of the Negro, who obviously is thirstier, needs it worse, else the federal government would not have had to pass a law compelling Mississippi (among others of course) to make the best of our education available to him.

That is, our present schools are not even good enough for white people. So what do we do? Make them good enough, improve them to the best possible? No. We beat the bushes, rake and scrape to raise additional taxes to establish another system at best only equal to that one which is already not good enough, which therefore won't be good enough for Negroes either; we will have two identical systems neither of which are good enough for anybody.

A few days after my letter was printed in the paper, I received by post the carbon copy of a letter addressed to the same forum page of the Memphis paper. It read as follows:

When Weeping Willie Faulkner splashes his tears about the inadequacy of Mississippi schools...we question his gumption in these respects, etc.

From there it went on to cite certain facts of which all Southerners are justly proud: that the seed-stock of education in our land was preserved through the evil times following the Civil War when our land was a defeated and occupied country, by dedicated teachers who got little in return for their dedication. Then, after a brief sneer at the quality of my writing and the profit motive which was the obvious reason why I was a writer, he closed by saying: "I suggest that Weeping Willie dry his tears and work up a little thirst for knowledge about the basic economy of his state."

Later, after this letter was printed in the Memphis paper in its turn, I received from the writer of it a letter addressed to him by a correspondent in another small Mississippi town, consisting in general of a sneer at the Nobel Prize which was awarded me, and commending the Weeping Willie writer for his promptness in taking to task anyone traitorous enough to hold education more important than the color of the educatee's skin. Attached to it was the Weeping Willie writer's reply. It said in effect:

In my opinion Faulkner is the most capable commentator on Southern facts of life to date.... If we could insult him into acquiring an insight into the basic economy of our region, he could [sic] do us a hell of a lot of good in our fight against integration.

My answer was that I didn't believe that insult is a very sound method of teaching anybody anything, of persuading anyone to think or act as the insulter believes they should. I repeated that what we needed in Mississippi was the best possible schools, to make the best possible use of the men and women we produced, regardless of what color they were. And even if we could not have a school system which would do that, at least let us have one which would make no distinction among pupils except that of simple ability, since our principal and perhaps desperate need in America today was that all Americans at least should be on the side of America; that if all Americans were on the same side, we would not need to fear that other nations and ideologies would doubt us when we talked of human freedom. [. . .]

[W]hat the Negro threatens is not the Southern white man's social system but the Southern white man's economic system—that economic system which the white man knows and dares not admit to himself is established on an obsolescence—the artificial inequality of man—and so is itself already obsolete and hence doomed. He knows that only three hundred years ago the Negro's naked grandfather was eating rotten elephant or hippo meat in an African rain-forest, yet in only three hundred years the Negro produced Dr. Ralph Bunche and George Washington Carver and Booker T. Washington. The white man knows that only ninety years ago not one per cent of the Negro race could own a deed to land, let alone read that deed; yet in only ninety years, although his only contact with a county courthouse is the window through which he pays the taxes for which he has no representation, he can own his land and farm it with inferior stock and worn-out tools and gear—equipment which any white man would starve with—and raise children and feed and clothe them and send them North where they can have equal scholastic opportunity, and end his life holding his head up because he owes no man, with even enough over to pay for his coffin and funeral.

That's what the white man in the South is afraid of: that the Negro, who has done so much with no chance, might do so much more with an equal one that he might take the white man's economy away from him, the Negro now the banker or the merchant or the planter and the white man the sharecropper or the tenant. That's why the Negro can gain our country's highest decoration for valor beyond all call of duty for saving or defending or preserving white lives on foreign battlefields, yet the Southern white man dares not let that Negro's children learn their ABC's in the same classroom with the children of the white lives he saved or defended. [. . .]

What are we Mississippians afraid of? Why do we have so low an opinion of ourselves that we are afraid of people who by all our standards are our inferiors?—economically: i.e., they have so much less than we have that they must work for us not on their terms but on ours; educationally: i.e., their schools are so much worse than ours that the federal government has to threaten to intervene to give them equal conditions; politically: i.e., they have no recourse in law for protection from nor restitution for injustice and violence.

Why do we have so low an opinion of our blood and traditions as to fear that, as soon as the Negro enters our house by the front door, he will propose marriage to our daughter and she will immediately accept him?

Our ancestors were not afraid like this—our grandfathers who fought at First and Second Manassas and Sharpsburg and Shiloh and Franklin and Chickamauga and Chancellorsville and the Wilderness; let alone those who survived that and had the additional and even greater courage and endurance to resist and survive Reconstruction, and so preserved to us something of our present heritage. Why are we, descendants of that blood and inheritors of that courage, afraid? What are we afraid of? What has happened to us in only a hundred years?

For the sake of argument, let us agree that all white Southerners (all white Americans maybe) curse the day when the first Briton or Yankee sailed the first shipload of manacled Negroes across the Middle Passage and auctioned them into American slavery. Because that doesn't matter now. To live anywhere in the world today and be against equality because of race or color, is like living in Alaska and being against snow. We have already got snow. And as with the Alaskan, merely to live in armistice with it is not enough. Like the Alaskan, we had better use it. [. . .]

We, the Western white man who does believe that there exists an individual freedom above and beyond this mere equality of slavedom, must teach the non-white peoples this while there is yet a little time left. We, America, who are the strongest national force opposing Communism and monolithicism, must teach all other peoples, white and non-white, slave or (for a little while yet) still free. We, America, have the best opportunity to do this because we can begin here, at home; we will not need to send costly freedom task forces into alien and inimical non-white places which are already convinced that there is no such thing as freedom and liberty and equality and peace for non-white people too, or we would practice it at home. Because our non-white minority is already on our side; we don't need to sell the Negro on America and freedom because he is already sold; even when ignorant from inferior or no education, even despite the record of his history of inequality, he still believes in our concepts of freedom and democracy.

That is what America has done for the Negro in only three hundred years. Not done *to* them: done *for* them, because to our shame we have made little effort so far to teach them to be Americans, let alone to use their capacities and capabilities to make us a stronger and more unified America. These are the people who only three hundred years ago lived beside one of the largest bodies of inland water on earth and never thought of sail, who yearly had to move by whole villages and tribes from famine and pestilence and enemies without once thinking of the wheel; yet in three hundred years they have become skilled artisans and craftsmen capable of holding their own in a culture of technocracy. The people who only three hundred years ago were eating the carrion in the tropical jungles have produced the Phi Beta Kappas and the Doctor Bunches and the Carvers and the Booker Washingtons and the poets and musicians. They have yet to produce a Fuchs or Rosenberg or Gold or Burgess or Maclean or Hiss, and for every Negro Communist or fellow traveler there are a thousand white ones.

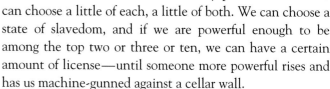

William H. Johnson

The Bunches and Washingtons and Carvers and the musicians and the poets, who were not just good men and women but good teachers too, taught him—the Negro—by precept and example what a lot of our white people have not learned yet: that to gain equality, one must deserve it, and to deserve equality, one must understand what it is: that there is no such thing as equality *per se*, but only equality *to*: equal right and opportunity to make the best one can of one's life within one's capacity and capability, without fear of injustice or oppression or violence. If we had given him this equality ninety or fifty or even ten years ago, there

would have been no Supreme Court ruling about segregation in 1954.

But we didn't. We dared not; it is our Southern white man's shame that in our present economy the Negro must not have economic equality; our double shame that we fear that giving him more social equality will jeopardize his present economic status; our triple shame that even then, to justify our stand, we must becloud the issue with the bugaboo of miscegenation. What a commentary that the one remaining place on earth where the white man can flee and have his uncorrupted blood protected and defended by law, is in Africa—Africa: the source and origin of the threat whose present presence in America will have driven the white man to flee it.

Soon now all of us—not just Southerners nor even just Americans, but all people who are still free and want to remain so—are going to have to make a choice, lest the next (and last) confrontation we face will be, not Communists against anti-Communists, but simply the remaining handful of white people against the massed myriads of all the people on earth who are not white. We will have to choose not between color nor race nor religion nor between East and West either, but simply between being slaves and being free. And we will have to choose completely and for good; the time is already past now when we can choose a little of each, a little of both. We can choose a state of slavedom, and if we are powerful enough to be among the top two or three or ten, we can have a certain amount of license—until someone more powerful rises and has us machine-gunned against a cellar wall.

But we cannot choose freedom established on a hierarchy of degrees of freedom, on a caste system of equality like military rank. We must be free not because we claim freedom, but because we practice it; our freedom must be buttressed by a homogeny equally and unchallengeably free, no matter what color they are, so that all the other inimical forces everywhere—systems political or religious or racial or national—will not just respect us because we practice freedom, they will fear us because we do.

THE FARMER'S WIFE
BY ANNE SEXTON

MAY 1959

From the hodge porridge
of their country lust,
their local life in Illinois,
where all their acres look
like a spouting broom factory,
they name just ten years now
that she has been his habit,
as again tonight he'll say
honey-bunch let's go
and she will not say how there
must be more to living
than this brief bright bridge
of the raucous bed or even
the slow braille touch of him
like a heavy god grown light;
that old pantomime of love
that she wants although

it leaves her still alone,
built back again at last,
minds apart from him, living
her own self in her own words
and hating the sweat of the house
they keep when they finally lie
unbuckled from their happy bones,
each in separate dreams
and then how she watches him
still strong in the blowzy bag
of his usual sleep while
her young years bungle past
their same marriage bed
and she wishes him cripple,
  or poet,
or even lonely, or sometimes,
better, my lover, dead.

RECOLLECTIONS FROM

Beyond the Last Rope

by Philip Roth

July 1959

Joel Szasz

As a child I was carried each summer to a small seaside city in New Jersey called Bradley Beach. Over the years, my mother, my brother, and I lived from July Fourth to Labor Day in a large furnished room (with kitchen privileges) or two rooms (with kitchen privileges) or—when my father discovered in May two hundred mysteriously extra dollars in the bank—in a small house of some six or seven rooms which we rented with three other families. In Newark, during the rest of the year, my brother and I lived in comfort and ease; my father might have been struggling to pay bills, my mother juggling so as to make ends meet, but it was all hidden from their two children, masked by the spotless house, the starchily fresh linens, and the full, well-cooked meals. At the shore it was different. Had I not been convinced by ten months of good living that we were "rich," I would from our summer quarters have thought us members of another social class.

Our vacation lodgings were small, sandy, and unprivate, and no matter to which of Bradley's many rooming houses we moved over the years, we were always greeted and farewelled by that same seashore smell, not so much musty as it was cementy and cool, like our cellar at home. Unlike home, however, were the chairs you settled into at the shore, chairs whose arms were always faintly damp, as though someone had just been seated upon them in a wet bathing suit. Sand crackled everywhere—under foot when you walked in the living room, between your sheets when you tossed in bed, and in your mouth when you ate. And, surrounding our family, there were always strangers—strangers eating in our dining-room, strangers closing the door behind them to our bathroom, and soapy strangers, washing and singing, their hairy limbs showing beneath the wooden door of our outdoor shower. Everything that was so preciously and naturally our own at home, was held in common at the seashore, a concept of ownership that had as much appeal to me as a child as it would to a member of the NAM. After all, what was Mrs. Blum from Bayonne doing at *our* refrigerator? The question plagued me, and beneath their forced smiles and their ear-splitting "Good morning!" it plagued the ten or so women who shared the rooming-house kitchen. Though each was assigned a compartment of the huge icebox at the start of the summer, the confusion as to who owned what was well under way by the second week of July.

As a young child, I remember, it was disturbing for me to watch my mother so often engaged in battle, especially in the kitchen, where I had understood her to be monarch by divine right. She could hardly act like royalty, however, with someone else's soup boiling on our burner and someone else's wrinkled old grandfather mumbling Anglo-Yiddish as he picked through our icebox. After a while the only way to restrain moral and domestic chaos was to issue commands, promise punishments, and make entreaties to others just as though they were your own. This communal authoritarianism must have had its appeal, for it quickly spread beyond the kitchen, and it was not unusual to find some strange woman cautioning me, the nearest child, not to go in swimming after lunch, not to go out over my head in the water, and not to eat my dinner in a wet suit.

Despite all the strain of this Brooke Farm atmosphere, I think it must have been reassuring to have any stray mother instruct me as my own mother would. If there was any comfort to be had in being forbidden to do pleasant things, it was in the discovery that kids from places as far as Jersey City and New Brunswick were forbidden to do them too. In part, what makes these summers stick in my memory is that each summer one or another of the paternal strictures was relaxed, either with or without paternal consent. For when we could swim, who could *keep* us from going over our heads? When we were old enough to see that what our parents labeled hygienic—"You want to get arthritis in the joints?"—was also comfortable, who *wanted* to sit around in a wet bathing suit?

Each year, ten months after Labor Day, we would meet at Bradley to discover that through the fall, winter, and spring we had all of us, in our separate camps, been slowly sabotaging the guardianship of our parents. Returning to Bradley every summer was like having a notch carved head-high in the woodwork. One summer your father brought home the badge needed to get you on the beach; the next he took you with him when he bought it; the next you were given the money, your hand was wrapped fiercely around it, and you were sent off to buy it yourself. You performed the old chores, played the same games in the sea, but in different postures, with different muscles and emotions, and so you always felt the full weight of time's passage. In the winter the rust stain on your bathing suit where you'd worn your badge all summer was always the same color; it was July and August that were different.

Now, in my memory, it seems that not only were the notches carved during the summer, but all the growing the notches stood for took place in summer as well. When I think back on the rest of the year, it always seems that outside of the classroom it was cloudy and dark; school was the

long sleep during which I rested—my season of sunlight was summer. On that oceanside speck of over-crowdedness and kitchen privileges I think I learned not only to swim and float and dive, but to flirt, to drink, to pose, to swindle, to do everything. It was right there, on the dark of the beaches, that my Coke-trained stomach had its first bout with beer, and there too that I was allowed my initial examination of someone else's body. And after that first time, how I pleaded for a second! Into ears of the unwilling, I would pour, alternately, reason and passion. I preached moral relativism, downright hedonism, Philip Wylie-ism, plain simple *love*, just to be allowed access to the hardly budded breasts of my schoolmates. Vaughan Monroe sang background music to my entreaties, and there was a brief portion of my life when my most hot-breathed fantasies were summoned up by only a few bars of "Racing with the Moon."

Girls, girls, girls. One summer I walked out on the hot tarry street, along the splintering boardwalk, down onto the beach, and there were only girls. The women in the kitchen must still have been arguing over whose cottage cheese belonged to whom, but I no longer heard them. So my mother wasn't queen of the kitchen. So what. There were girls—girls from home, cocoa-colored from the sun, glistening in their bathing suits. And other Jewish girls, strange as princesses because they came from Perth Amboy, or that most exotic-sounding of New Jersey towns, Bogota.

And more exotic yet, there was a family of Syrians, a clan of them who lived in Bradley all year round, and whose cocoa-colored skin was that color all year round. The men and the women and the children were all dark, smooth, faintly-mustached, and, to me, somehow sinister. The two young girls, who looked like twins but were cousins, wore two piece bathing suits of the sort that Betty Grable was making fashionable; they had pierced ears, and dark down on their cheeks and bellies, and they never bothered to learn the names of the summer people. At least they never bothered to learn mine, though my stomach trembled at the sight of them. The brothers (or cousins) played in our clandestine blackjack games, which were conducted to everyone's knowledge in the damp shade back under the boardwalk. I always played cautiously when one of the Syrians was dealer. And though it was a point of pride to have a friend who was a native of Bradley, I never sought such a prize from amongst the Syrians. About the men there actually seemed to me the possibility of knives flashing suddenly, and bloodshed; and about the women, the suggestion of swishing skirts, tiny bells, and hot-headed dancing. They knew a great deal about the tides, and hurricanes, and when the striped bass were running, and at about the age of eleven I began to suspect them of some secrets of passion and lust that I would forever be denied. And all they did to earn my fascination and fear was to stand around being dark. They were supposed to be Jews, but I never believed it. I still don't.

In cahoots with girls I learned many things—among them, dancing. It was easier than I thought it would be, easier at any rate than it was with my mother when we practiced on the kitchen linoleum in the winter. At Bradley it wasn't so much dancing as swaying to all the weepy summer songs sung by the crooners, or by the saddened females— the "Pattis" and "Maggies" and "Frans"—so smitten that they had to be jacked up from behind by humming choral groups. All summer long in the white, pillared pavilions that squared off the boardwalk toward the water, we danced close as we could to the Top Ten Tunes. It was different from dancing in winter, for at night you could smell the sea in the girl's hair—or perhaps it was just that the pavilion itself smelled of the waves that pounded the great wooden pillars driven in the sand beneath us. Early in June, if you had a good ear, you could spot the song that was to be the summer's favorite. It had to be slow enough for our feet to scrape inch-by-inch along the pavilion floor. It had to have a few good climactic moments for "dips." There had to be some words of poetry in it, words like *dusk, wish, remember,* words slightly forlorn. Above all, it had to have that breadth which is banality: it had to be applicable to *each* of our lives. Then we could serenade one another while we danced, give to the song a private meaning, make it do for our own kisses and uncertainties, our own dusks, wishes, and remembrances. We responded to it like undergraduate poets to their own verse. What raised the goose-pimples was that it was *ours ours!* It was always playing while we kissed and we kissed and we kissed. I think I kissed more kisses between the ages of thirteen and seventeen than I will kiss the rest of my life. And I'm only talking about summers.

For entire summers kissing was like baseball: an end in itself. But then one summer kissing was suddenly a prelude. Everything was a prelude, kissing, dancing, dipping—especially dipping—dressing, washing, my whole life seemed a prelude to those few minutes at the end of the night when I would seek to realize what had, for various reasons, been unrealizable all those summers before. I was just old enough

to drive and I would park on a dark street—whiffing the sea through the open window—and even if it meant running down my father's battery, I would leave the radio on. It was a great comfort to have Vaughan Monroe there in the car with me. I remember how there would be a flash of despair when I had turned the radio dial right down to the end and couldn't find any good music. Good music softens them, somehow it makes straps less complicated, hooks and eyes more unclaspable. It encourages girls to do what in silence they won't. Vaughan Monroe, Billy Eckstine, Frank Sinatra, Nat "King" Cole—all guilty of softening the morals of the young, and of giving us a style. The beat of draggy ballads, I'm sure of it, became the rhythm of my advances; I would be struggling to hold my own in an embrace, with one eye on Ray McKinley's baton. The music played on and on, so as to keep the *mood*. The girls changed, but the mood was constant.

Before my fingers had quite brailled out the angles of the object itself, I was busy learning the right responses. I sighed, I mooned; when rebuffed, I was terribly hurt. I would try to show off in beach games, or else exhibit all my brazen potency by tossing a tennis ball back and forth. It was all in how languid you could look. The real athlete looks languid. During the winter in the dark cellar of our house, I would practice pitching a taped-up baseball against an old carpet attached from ceiling to floor. What I was practicing was not curves, not hooks and drops, but languidness. In the kitchen above, I'm sure my mother did not know that with each thud the ball made in the carpet, I was thinking about those sunny days beyond the snowfalls and the meltings, when I would be standing in my bathing suit at the water's edge, tossing a ball back and forth before an audience in which there would be girls.

I practiced not only throwing but standing, waiting, retrieving. I knew exactly what I wanted to look like, and it was some years after I'd stopped vacationing at Bradley that I saw in Florence what I'd had in mind—it was Michelangelo's David. He would have knocked the girls at Bradley for a loop. Imagine that what he is holding up to his breast is not a sling, but a glove; imagine in that throwing arm, loose but ready at his side, not a rock but a baseball; see the way each joint picks up the weight from the one above; see how he peers down for the signals beneath those brows. See all that, and you'll see what I was trying for in my cellar all winter long.

My last few summers at Bradley I had *a* girl, and all those things I had done in previous years with boy friends, I did with her. We would swim together at Bradley, fish lazily for blow fish at Shark River, and stroll along the boardwalk to Asbury in the evenings, the sea still vaguely lit on our right, as we strolled out, and roaring invisibly to our left, coming home at night. On the beach my parents' friends would spot the two of us walking hand-in-hand toward the water to swim, and they would wink at me. On weekends when my father appeared he would be in the water, knee-high, talking to another insurance man, and see us pass by. He would flash me the signal with his eyes:

"Ah, so you're with a girl..."

Then he would turn back to his friend and I would overhear one or another of the old magic words. The words carried me all the way back: *premium, fifty-payment life, accident and health, the colored debit*. Insurance words—they circle my childhood. I'll bet some nights with the conversation from the kitchen still locked in my ears. I said them in my sleep to no one. *The colored debit*. That one had the most power for me; it was like a vase covered with pictures of black people in various poses. The colored debit was where my father had a great deal of trouble and got very tired trying to collect insurance money from colored people. It seemed that they had no idea of the importance of insurance; they committed the fatal sin: they let it *lapse*. It was the insurance man's burden to penetrate the dark-milling jungle of Prince and Spruce Streets, carrying the word from the Metropolitan, the Prudential, making, among the blacks, converts to security. What a task! Cecil Rhodes, Albert Schweitzer, my father, and his friends. I can still see them, Friday nights, sitting in our kitchen playing pinochle—the missionary's night off. They kibitz so loud and long that I am kept awake, while down in their grimy houses on Prince Street the colored people sit around letting their insurance lapse....

As I enter the water with my girl I look back at my father and his friend, and feel the undertow of despair that drags at me from knowing that if I am old enough for her, my parents are suddenly older than I like to imagine them. In their bathing suits you can see they are inching up on my grandparents. Suddenly, the girl dives, and the last I see of her are heels touching for a moment above the water, and then they slide away too. I start after her, past the series of poles and ropes that fences in the shallower water, protecting the innocent and the decrepit from the dangers of the sea. Finally, I am at the last rope. It is green, and tough, and hairy; I feel it graze over my back, and there I am! Past the

last rope! "Don't go out past the last rope," my mother would say. "Watch him!" my grandmother would whisper to the adult nearest to me, "he goes out past the last rope." "Be careful," my father says, "the undertow is treacherous. The last rope..." But suddenly there is one summer when there is nothing they can do about it. I raise my legs, arch my body, point my head down, and now I am below the water and absolutely alone. The shock of the water kills and kindles my senses all at once. I open my eyes, and see the floor of the Atlantic Ocean. "How he loves the water, you can't get him out of it." I hear this despite the fact that water is closing off my ears. "Look how purple his lips are, he's been in all afternoon." "You get a worse burn in the water than on the beach—watch your shoulders." "You have a little cough—don't stay in too long." "You can't get him out—he's a fish!" I *was* a fish—now I'm a man. I swim out to where the girl waits, the water so buoyant with salt it's like my father's hand under my belly teaching me the dead man's float. Together the girl and I move easily our arms and legs, a dance no one ever performed on land. We stay afloat, dancing, no music necessary.

Beyond where the waves break, where there is only swell from time to time, are the Serious Swimmers. Back and forth, back and forth, all day long. Among them are the non-languid athletes, out there to build up their shoulders and pectorals. On the beach these same fellows spend a fair amount of their time tightening their stomach muscles. If they should want only to turn the dial on a portable radio, they approach the task with such a passionate masculinity that they stiffen all the way up to their jaws. I see one now, beyond my companion and me, pounding hell out of the sea. After a while we move back toward the last rope, and I feel the sun so bright on my shoulders that I imagine you can see in its intensity every one of my cells. My mother was right—you *can* get a worse burn in the water. "Didn't I tell you?" she would say, as I lay belly down on the bed and she poured vinegar into my raw back. "Didn't I tell you?" I would have to sleep pajamaless and even the soft sheets pained my flesh. And in the next bed, with the supercilious tone of one who has carefully nurtured his tan, my brother would complain, "You stink."

Sometimes in these childhood summers I would carry the smell of vinegar with me even after my shoulders healed. It perfumed my sheets and towels for days, and in the winter there would be an evening when we would be eating something pickled for dinner, and for all the frost in the corners of the windows, I would ask, "When are we going to the shore this year?" "I thought maybe for a change you'd go to the mountains this summer," my father would say. "It might be nice," my mother says, "the shore is gloomy now."

She meant by that that the war was still on and the boardwalk blacked out at night. On the beach in the early 'forties there were areas fenced off, where machine-gun positions had been dug. Sailors patrolled at night, and it *was* gloomy. There was a great deal of talk about German subs—we children saw periscopes at least fifteen times a day. Often when we came out of the water our feet were black with tar, and at home we used my mother's nail polish remover to get them clean again. The tar, we were told, meant that a ship had been torpedoed, and we believed it when in the mornings we saw the planks of wood, the chunks of debris, that had slid up on our beach during the night. I remember having a terrible fear that some day I would emerge from under a wave and the bodies of dead sailors would be floating around me. I was nine then, and still young enough to fear the dead more than death itself.

Each summer we came back to the ocean the guns were in position and the lights were out. But then one August it was over—I was twelve and the atomic bomb had been dropped on Japan. "Wait," my father says, "now everything will be atomic—soap suds, breakfast cereals, movie stars. . . ." That night it was as though the poorest man in the world had married off his ugliest daughter. I've always felt a tremor of joy upon reading in books, "People danced in the streets." But there was more than a tremor in seeing it. Besides, it wasn't *people* who danced in the streets, it was Mrs. Blum from Bayonne and old man Klein from Hillside. Eventually all of Bradley had spilled its way up on to the boardwalk, and we children formed a conga line and conga-ed all the way from Ocean Grove to Avon-by-the-Sea, past the Pokerino, past the dance pavilions, the salt water baths, the hot dog joints, past the dark-buckling ocean, which would never be tar-blackened again. What would it be like with the war over, with everything atomic? It would be all good, we imagined—perhaps not dancing, but the serene equivalent of it. We imagined this until way down the boardwalk, in a neony ice-cream parlor, we saw a woman of about fifty, all dressed up in a gaudy print dress and a gala hat, eating a double-sized banana split, and crying so quietly and intensely that our hands fell from each other's hips and our celebration ended.

In bed I could still hear all the music from all the tiny bands that had appeared on the streets. I never realized so many people packed away instruments to take on vacations—there were violins, harmonicas, drums, kazoos, cornets, and an accordion that near the end of the night played "Johnny Got a Zero," as though it were the blues. Those who hadn't packed instruments sat in their cars and from time to time pressed down on their horns. No one with sleeping children was exasperated with them. Eventually the accordion player tired, and the car-owners locked their cars, and I heard my parents and their friends squeaking their rockers into the soft wood of the porch. I huddled near the front window, so as to hear—from where I crouched I could see clear out to the ocean. On the porch my father said, "I only wish Roosevelt were alive to see it." The words were soft; it wasn't a miracle my father was asking for—only to wake Roosevelt a minute, whisper, "F. D. R.—it's over," and then let him return to nothingness again.

"I wish *Hitler* were alive to see it," someone said harshly. "You don't think he is?" a man asked. "I'd bet a thousand dollars he's down in Buenos Aires now, living like a king." "That's right," someone added, "there's no *proof* he's dead." And then, after a long pause, I heard the hushed voice of Mrs. Ratnick, a very simple and uncertain woman. "In the grocery . . . I saw a man . . . who looked just like him—with his mustache shaved off. . . ."

Later that week I too saw a man who looked like Hitler, but I reported the incident to no one. I had by this time discovered that more and more my childhood fibs and inventions were being put down—as they hadn't been only last week—by the impatient skepticism of adults, and so rather than submit to my parents' suspicious look, I let Hitler go free.

I suppose that if my father was present on the porch the night of VJ-Day, then he was on vacation. Usually he took off the last week of July and the first in August; otherwise he would stay in the city during the week and drive down on weekends. Sometimes, though, our old Pontiac would pull up at LaReine Avenue smack in the middle of the week: the city was too hot. "You can't even breathe," he tells my mother. "The humidity," she'd say.

On these surprise visits he would usually arrive about seven-thirty without having had dinner. But dinner would wait—despite the protest of my mother—while he tossed away his wrinkled city clothes and changed into a bathing suit. I carried his towel for him as he headed down the

MUSHROOMS

BY SYLVIA PLATH

JULY 1960

Overnight, very
Whitely, discreetly,
Very quietly

Our toes, our noses
Take hold on the loam,
Acquire the air.

Nobody sees us,
Stops us, betrays us;
The small grains make room.

Soft fists insist on
Heaving the needles,
The leafy bedding,

Even the paving.
Our hammers, our rams,
Earless and eyeless,

Perfectly voiceless,
Widen the crannies,
Shoulder through holes. We

Diet on water,
On crumbs of shadow,
Bland-mannered, asking

Little or nothing.
So many of us!
So many of us!

We are shelves, we are
Tables, we are meek,
We are edible,

Nudgers and shovers
In spite of ourselves.
Our kind multiplies:

We shall by morning
Inherit the earth.
Our foot's in the door.

VERMONT

BY JOHN UPDIKE

JULY 1961

*H*ere green is king again,
Usurping honest men.
Like Brazilian cathedrals gone under to creepers,
Gray silos mourn their keepers.

Ski tows
And shy cows
Alone pin the ragged slopes to the earth
Of profitable worth.

Hawks, professors,
And summering ministers
Roost on the mountainsides of poverty
And sniff the poetry,

And every year
The big black bear,
Slavering through the woods with scrolling mouth,
Comes further south.

THE DANGEROUS ROAD BEFORE MARTIN LUTHER KING

BY JAMES BALDWIN

FEBRUARY 1961

I first met Martin Luther King, Jr. nearly three years ago now, in Atlanta, Georgia. He was there on a visit from his home in Montgomery. He was "holed up," he was seeing no one, he was busy writing a book— so I was informed by the friend who, mercilessly, at my urgent request, was taking me to King's hotel. I felt terribly guilty about interrupting him but not guilty enough to let the opportunity pass. Still, having been raised among preachers, I would not have been surprised if King had cursed out the friend, refused to speak to me, and slammed the door in our faces. Nor would I have blamed him if he had, since I knew that by this time he must have been forced to suffer many an admiring fool.

But the Reverend King is not like any preacher I have ever met before. For one thing, to state it baldly, I liked him. It is rare that one *likes* a world-famous man—by the time they become world-famous they rarely like themselves, which may account for this antipathy. Yet King is immediately and tremendously winning, there is really no other word for it; and there he stood, with an inquiring and genuine smile on his face, in the open door of his hotel room. Behind him, on a desk, was a wilderness of paper. He looked at his friend, he looked at me, I was introduced; he smiled and shook my hand and we entered the room.

I do not remember much about that first meeting because I was too overwhelmed by the fact that I was meeting him at all. There were millions of questions that I wanted to ask him, but I feared to begin. Besides, his friend had warned me not to "bug" him, I was not there in a professional capacity, and the questions I wanted to ask him had less to do with his public role than with his private life. When I say "private life" I am not referring to those maliciously juicy tidbits, those meaningless details, which clutter up the gossip columns and muddy everybody's mind and obliterate the humanity of the subject as well as that of the reader. I wanted to ask him how it felt to be standing where

he stood, how he bore it, what complex of miracles had prepared him for it. But such questions can scarcely be asked, they can scarcely be answered.

And King does not like to talk about himself. I have described him as winning, but he does not give the impression of being particularly outgoing or warm. His restraint is not, on the other hand, of that icily uneasy, nerve-racking kind to be encountered in so many famous Negroes who have allowed their aspirations and notoriety to destroy their identities and who always seem to be giving an uncertain imitation of some extremely improbable white man. No, King impressed me then and he impresses me now as a man solidly anchored in those spiritual realities concerning which he can be so eloquent. This divests him of the hideous piety which is so prevalent in his profession, and it also saves him from the ghastly self-importance which, until recently, was all that allowed one to be certain one was addressing a Negro leader. King cannot be considered a chauvinist at all, not even incidentally, or part of the time, or under stress, or subconsciously. What he says to Negroes he will say to whites; and what he says to whites he will say to Negroes. He is the first Negro leader in my experience, or the first in many generations, of whom this can be said; most of his predecessors were in the extraordinary position of saying to white men, *Hurry*, while saying to black men, *Wait*. This fact is of the utmost importance. It says a great deal about the situation which produced King and in which he operates; and, of course, it tells us a great deal about the man.

"He came through it all," said a friend of his to me, with wonder and not a little envy, "really unscarred. He never went around fighting with himself, like we all did." The "we" to whom this friend refers are all considerably older than King, which may have something to do with this lightly sketched species of schizophrenia; in any case, the fact that King really loves the people he represents and has—*therefore*—no hidden, interior need to hate the white people who oppose him has had and will, I think, continue to have the most far-reaching and unpredictable repercussions on our racial situation. It need scarcely be said that our racial situation is far more complex and dangerous than we are prepared to think of it as being—since our major desire is not to think of it at all—and King's role in it is of an unprecedented difficulty.

He is not, for example, to be confused with Booker T. Washington, whom we gratefully allowed to solve the racial problem singlehandedly. It was Washington who assured us, in 1895, one year before it became the law of the land, that the education of Negroes would not give them any desire to become equals; they would be content to remain—or, rather, after living for generations in the greatest intimacy with whites, to become—separate. It is a measure of the irreality to which the presence of the Negro had already reduced the nation that this utterly fantastic idea, which thoroughly controverts the purpose of education, which has no historical or psychological validity, and which denies all the principles on which the country imagines itself to have been founded, was not only accepted with cheers but became the cornerstone of an entire way of life. And this did not come about, by the way, merely because of the venom or villainy of the South. It could never have come about at all without the tacit consent of the North; and this consent robs the North, historically and actually, of any claim to moral superiority. The failure of the government to make any realistic provision for the education of tens of thousands of illiterate former slaves had the effect of dumping this problem squarely into the lap of one man—who knew, whatever else he may not have known, that the education of Negroes had somehow to be accomplished. Whether or not Washington believed what he said is certainly an interesting question. But he *did* know that he could accomplish his objective by telling white men what they wanted to hear. And it has never been very difficult for a Negro in this country to figure out what white men want to hear: he takes his condition as an echo of their desires.

There will be no more Booker T. Washingtons. And whether we like it or not, and no matter how hard or how long we oppose it, there will be no more segregated schools, there will be no more segregated anything. King is entirely right when he says that segregation is dead. The real question which faces the Republic is just how long, how violent, and how expensive the funeral is going to be; and this ques-

tion it is up to the Republic to resolve, it is not really in King's hands. The sooner the corpse is buried, the sooner we can get around to the far more taxing and rewarding problems of integration, or what King calls community, and what I think of as the achievement of nationhood, or, more simply and cruelly, the growing up of this dangerously adolescent country.

I saw King again, later that same evening, at a party given by this same friend. He came late, did not stay long. I remember him standing in the shadows of the room, near a bookcase, drinking something nonalcoholic, and being patient with the interlocutor who had trapped him in this spot. He obviously wanted to get away and go to bed. King is somewhat below what is called average height, he is sturdily built, but is not quite as heavy or as stocky as he had seemed to me at first. I remember feeling, rather as though he were a younger, much-loved, and menaced brother, that he seemed very slight and vulnerable to be taking on such tremendous odds.

I was leaving for Montgomery the next day, and I called on King in the morning to ask him to have someone from the Montgomery Improvement Association meet me at the airport. It was he who had volunteered to do this for me, since he knew that I knew no one there, and he also probably realized that I was frightened. He was coming to Montgomery on Sunday to preach in his own church.

Montgomery is the cradle of the Confederacy, an unlucky distinction which no one in Montgomery is allowed to forget. The White House which symbolized and housed that short-lived government is still standing, and "people," one of the Montgomery ministers told me, "walk around in those halls and cry." I do not doubt it, the people of Montgomery having inherited nothing less than an ocean of spilt milk. The boycott had been over for a year by the time I got there, and had been ended by a federal decree outlawing segregation in the busses. Therefore, the atmosphere in Montgomery was extraordinary. I think that I have never been in a town so aimlessly hostile, so baffled and demoralized. Whoever has a stone to fling, and flings it, is then left without any weapons; and this was (and remains) the situation of the white people in Montgomery.

I took a bus ride, for example, solely in order to observe the situation on the busses. As I stepped into the bus, I suddenly remembered that I had neglected to ask anyone the price of a bus ride in Montgomery, and so I asked the driver. He gave me the strangest, most hostile of looks, and turned his face away. I dropped fifteen cents into the box and sat down, placing myself, delicately, just a little forward of the center of the bus. The driver had seemed to feel that my question was but another Negro trick, that I had something up my sleeve, and that to answer my question in any way would be to expose himself to disaster. He could not guess what I was thinking, and he was not going to risk further personal demoralization by trying to. And this spirit was the spirit of the town. The bus pursued its course, picking up white and Negro passengers. Negroes sat where they pleased, none very far back; one large woman, carrying packages, seated herself directly behind the driver. And the whites sat there, ignoring them, in a huffy, offended silence.

This silence made me think of nothing so much as the silence which follows a really serious lovers' quarrel: the whites, beneath their cold hostility, were mystified and deeply hurt. They had been betrayed by the Negroes, not merely because the Negroes had declined to remain in their "place," but because the Negroes had refused to be controlled by the town's image of them. And, without this image, it seemed to me, the whites were abruptly and totally lost. The very foundations of their private and public worlds were being destroyed.

I had never heard King preach, and I went on Sunday to hear him at his church. This church is a red brick structure, with a steeple, and it directly faces, on the other side of the street, a white, domed building. My notes fail to indicate whether this is the actual capitol of the state or merely a courthouse; but the conjunction of the two buildings, the steepled one low and dark and tense, the domed one higher and dead white and forbidding, sums up, with an explicitness a set designer might hesitate to copy, the struggle now going on in Montgomery.

At that time in Montgomery, King was almost surely the most beloved man there. I do not think that one could have entered any of the packed churches at that time, if King was present, and not have felt this. Of course, I think that King would be loved by his congregations in any case, and there is always a large percentage of church women who adore the young male pastor, and not always, or not necessarily, out of those grim, psychic motives concerning which everyone today is so knowledgeable. No, there was a feeling in this church which quite transcended anything I have ever felt in a church before. Here it was, totally familiar and yet completely new, the packed church, glorious with the Sunday finery of the women, solemn with the touching,

gleaming sobriety of the men, beautiful with children. Here were the ushers, standing in the aisles in white dresses or in dark suits, with arm bands on. People were standing along each wall, beside the windows, and standing in the back. King and his lieutenants were in the pulpit, young Martin—as I was beginning to think of him—in the center chair.

When King rose to speak—to preach—I began to understand how the atmosphere of this church differed from that of all the other churches I have known. At first I thought that the great emotional power and authority of the Negro church was being put to a new use, but this is not exactly the case. The Negro church was playing the same role which it has always played in Negro life, but it had acquired a new power.

Until Montgomery, the Negro church, which has always been the place where protest and condemnation could be most vividly articulated, also operated as a kind of sanctuary. The minister who spoke could not hope to effect any objective change in the lives of his hearers, and the people did not expect him to. All they came to find, and all that he could give them, was the sustenance for another day's journey. Now, King could certainly give his congregation that, but he could also give them something more than that, and he had. It is true that it was *they* who had begun the struggle of which he was now the symbol and the leader; it is true that it had taken all of *their* insistence to overcome in him a grave reluctance to stand where he now stood. But it is also true, and it does not happen often, that once he had accepted the place they had prepared for him, their struggle became absolutely indistinguishable from his own, and took over and controlled his life. He suffered with them and, thus, he helped them to suffer. The joy which filled this church, therefore, was the joy achieved by people who have ceased to delude themselves about an intolerable situation, who have found their prayers for a leader miraculously answered, and who now know that they can change their situation, if they will.

And, surely, very few people had ever spoken to them as King spoke. King is a great speaker. The secret of his greatness does not lie in his voice or his presence or his manner, though it has something to do with all these; nor does it lie in his verbal range or felicity, which are not striking; nor does he have any capacity for those stunning, demagogic flights of the imagination which bring an audience cheering to its feet. The secret lies, I think, in his intimate knowledge of the people he is addressing, be they black or white, and in the forthrightness with which he speaks of those things which hurt and baffle them. He does not offer any easy comfort and this keeps his hearers absolutely tense. He allows them their self-respect—indeed, he insists on it.

"We know," he told them, "that there are many things wrong in the white world. But there are many things wrong in the black world, too. We can't keep on blaming the white man. There are many things we must do for ourselves."

He suggested what some of these were:

"I know none of you make enough money—but save some of it. And there are some things we've got to face. I know the situation is responsible for a lot of it, but do you know that Negroes are 10 per cent of the population of St. Louis and are responsible for 58 per cent of its crimes? We've got to face that. And we have to do something about our moral standards. And we've got to stop lying to the white man. Every time you let the white man think *you* think segregation is right, you are co-operating with him in doing *evil*.

"The next time," he said, "the white man asks you what you think of segregation, you tell him, Mr. Charlie, I think it's wrong and I wish you'd do something about it by nine o'clock tomorrow morning!"

This brought a wave of laughter and King smiled, too. But he had meant every word he said, and he expected his hearers to act on them. They also expected this of themselves, which is not the usual effect of a sermon; and that they are living up to their expectations no white man in Montgomery will deny.

There was a dinner in the church basement afterwards, where, for the first time, I met Mrs. King—light brown, delicate, really quite beautiful, with a wonderful laugh—and watched young Martin circulating among church members and visitors. I overheard him explaining to someone that bigotry was a disease and that the greatest victim of this disease was not the bigot's object, but the bigot himself. And these people could only be saved by love. In liberating oneself, one was also liberating them. I was shown, by someone else, the damage done to the church by bombs. King did not mention the bombing of his own home, and I did not bring it up. Late the next night, after a mass meeting in another church, I flew to Birmingham.

I did not see King again for nearly three years. I saw him in Atlanta, just after his acquittal by a Montgomery court of charges of perjury, tax evasion, and misuse of public funds.

He had moved to Atlanta and was co-pastor, with his father, of his father's church. He had made this move, he told me, because the pressures on him took him away from Montgomery for such excessively long periods that he did not feel that he was properly fulfilling his ministerial duties there. An attempt had been made on his life—in the North, by a mysterious and deranged Negro woman; and he was about to receive, in the state of Georgia, for driving without a resident driver's license, a suspended twelve-month sentence.

And, since I had last seen him, the Negro student movement had begun and was irresistibly bringing about great shifts and divisions in the Negro world, and in the nation. In short, by the time we met again, he was more beleaguered than he had ever been before, and not only by his enemies in the white South. Three years earlier, I had not encountered very many people—I am speaking now of Negroes—who were really critical of him. But many more people seemed critical of him now, were bitter, disappointed, skeptical. None of this had anything to do—I want to make this absolutely clear—with his personal character or his integrity. It had to do with his effectiveness as a leader. King has had an extraordinary effect in the Negro world, and therefore in the nation, and is now in the center of an extremely complex cross fire.

He was born in Atlanta in 1929. He has Irish and Indian blood in his veins—Irish from his father's, Indian from his mother's side. His maternal grandfather built Ebenezer Baptist Church, which, as I have said, young Martin now co-pastors with his father. This grandfather seems to have been an extremely active and capable man, having been one of the NAACP leaders in Atlanta thirty or forty years ago, and having been instrumental in bringing about the construction of Atlanta's first Negro high school. The paternal grandfather is something else again, a poor, violent, and illiterate farmer who tried to find refuge from reality in drinking. He clearly had a great influence on the formation of the character of Martin, Sr., who determined, very early, to be as unlike his father as possible.

Martin, Sr. came to Atlanta in 1916, a raw, strapping country boy, determined, in the classic American tradition, to rise above his station. It could not have been easy for him in the Deep South of 1916, but he was, luckily, too young for the Army, and prices and wages rose during the war, and his improvident father had taught him the value of thrift. So he got his start. He studied in evening school, entered Atlanta's Morehouse College in 1925, and graduated in June of 1930, more than a year after Martin was born. (There are two other children, an older girl who now teaches at Spelman College, and a younger boy, pastor of a church in Noonan, Georgia.) By this time, Martin, Sr. had become a preacher, and was pastor of two small churches; and at about this time, his father-in-law asked him to become the assistant pastor of Ebenezer Baptist Church, which he did.

His children have never known poverty, and Martin, Sr. is understandably very proud of this. "My prayer," he told me, "was always: Lord, grant that my children will not have to come the way I did." They didn't, they haven't, the prayers certainly did no harm. But one cannot help feeling that a person as single-minded and determined as the elder Reverend King clearly is would have accomplished anything he set his hand to, anyway.

"I equipped myself to give them the comforts of life," he says. "Not to waste, not to keep up with the Joneses, but just to be comfortable. We've never lived in a rented house—and never ridden *too* long in a car on which payment was due."

He is naturally very proud of Martin, Jr. but he claims to be not at all surprised. "He sacrificed to make himself ready"—ready, that is, for a trial, or a series of trials, which might have been the undoing of a lesser man. Yet, though he is not surprised at the extraordinary nature of his son's eminence, he *was* surprised when, at college, Martin decided that he was called to preach. He had expected him to become a doctor or a lawyer because he always spoke of these professions as though he aspired to them.

As he had; and since, as I have said, King is far from garrulous on the subject of his interior life, it is somewhat difficult to know what led him to make this switch. He had already taken pre-medical and law courses. But he had been raised by a minister, an extremely strong-minded one at that, and in an extraordinarily peaceful and protected way. "Never," says his father, "has Martin known a fuss or a fight or a strike-back in the home." On the other hand, there are some things from which no Negro can really be protected, for which he can only be prepared; and Martin, Sr. was more successful than most fathers in accomplishing this strenuous and delicate task. "I have never believed," he says, "that anybody was better than I." That this is true would seem to be proved by the career of his son, who *"never went around fighting with himself, like we all did."*

Here, speculation is really on very marshy ground, for the father must certainly have fought in himself some of the battles from which young Martin was protected. We have only to consider the era, especially in the South, to realize that this must be true. And it must have demanded great steadiness of mind, as well as great love, to hide so successfully from his children the evidence of these battles. And, since salvation, humanly speaking, is a two-way street, I suggest that, if the father saved the children, it was, almost equally, the children who saved him. It would seem that he was able, with rare success, to project onto his children, or at least onto one of them, a sense of life as he himself would have liked to live it, and somehow made real in their personalities principles on which he himself must often have found it extremely dangerous and difficult to act. Martin, Sr. is regarded with great ambivalence by both the admirers and detractors of his son, and I shall, alas, shortly have more to say concerning his generation; but I do not think that the enormous achievement sketched above can possibly be taken away from him.

Again, young Martin's decision to become a minister has everything to do with his temperament, for he seems always to have been characterized by his striking mixture of steadiness and peace. He apparently did the normal amount of crying in his childhood, for I am told that his grandmother "couldn't stand to see it." But he seems to have done very little complaining; when he was spanked, "he just stood there and took it"; he seems to have been incapable of carrying grudges; and when he was attacked, he did not strike back.

From King's own account, I can only guess that this decision was aided by the fact that, at Morehouse College, he was asked to lead the devotions. The relationship thus established between himself and his contemporaries, or between himself and himself, or between himself and God, seemed to work for him as no other had. Also, I think it is of the utmost importance to realize that King loves the South; many Negroes do. The ministry seems to afford him the best possible vehicle for the expression of that love. At that time in his life, he was discovering "the beauty of the South"; he sensed in the people "a new determination"; and he felt that there was a need for "a new, courageous witness."

But it could not have occurred to him, of course, that *he* would be, and in such an unprecedented fashion, that witness. When Coretta King—then Coretta Scott—met him in Boston, where he was attending Boston University and she was studying at the New England Conservatory of Music, she found him an earnest, somewhat too carefully dressed young man. He had gone from Morehouse to Crozer

Martin Luther King leading a prayer march in defiance of an injunction, Birmingham, 1963.

Theological Seminary in Pennsylvania; the latter institution was interracial, which may have had something to do with his self-consciousness. He was fighting at that time to free himself from all the stereotypes of the Negro, an endeavor which does not leave much room for spontaneity. Both he and Coretta were rather lonely in Boston, and for similar reasons. They were both very distinguished and promising young people, which means that they were also tense, self-conscious, and insecure. They were inevitably cut off from the bulk of the Negro community and their role among whites had to be somewhat ambiguous, for they were not being judged merely as themselves—or, anyway, they could scarcely afford to think so. They were responsible for the good name of all the Negro people.

Coretta had perhaps had more experience than Martin in this role. The more I spoke to her, the more I realized how her story illuminates that of her husband. She had come from Lincoln High in Marion, Alabama, to Antioch College in Ohio, part of one of the earliest groups of Negro students accepted there. She was thus, in effect, part of an experiment, and though she took it very well and can laugh about it now, she certainly must have had her share of exasperated and lonely moments. The social mobility of a Negro girl, especially in such a setting, is even more severely circumscribed than that of a Negro male, and any lapse or error on her part is far more dangerous. From Antioch, Coretta eventually came to Boston on a scholarship and by this time a certain hoydenish, tomboy quality in her had begun, apparently, to be confirmed. The atmosphere at Antioch had been entirely informal, which pleased Coretta; I gather that at this time in her life she was usually to be seen in sweaters, slacks, and scarves. It was a ferociously formal young man and a ferociously informal young girl who finally got together in Boston.

Martin immediately saw through Coretta's disguise, and informed her on their first or second meeting that she had all the qualities he wanted in a wife. Coretta's understandable tendency was to laugh at this; but this tendency was checked by the rather frightening suspicion that he meant it; if he had not meant it, he would not have said it. But a great deal had been invested in Coretta's career as a singer, and she did not feel that she had the right to fail all the people who had done so much to help her. "And I'd certainly never intended to marry a *minister*. It was true that he didn't seem like any of the ministers I'd met, but—still—I thought of how circumscribed my life might become." By circumscribed, she meant dull; she could not possibly have been more mistaken.

What had really happened, in Coretta's case, as in so many others, was that life had simply refused to recognize her private timetable. She had always intended to marry, but tidily, possibly meeting her husband at the end of a triumphant concert tour. However, here he was now, exasperatingly early, and she had to rearrange herself around this fact. She and Martin were married on June 18, 1953. By now, naturally, it is she whom Martin sometimes accuses of thinking too much about clothes. "People who are doing something don't have time to be worried about all that," he has informed her. Well, he certainly ought to know.

Coretta King told me that from the time she reached Boston and all during Martin's courtship, and her own indecision, she yet could not rid herself of a feeling that all that was happening had been, somehow, preordained. And one does get an impression, until this point in the King story at least, that inexorable forces which none of us really know anything about were shaping and preparing him for that fateful day in Montgomery. Everything that he will need has been delivered, so to speak, and is waiting to be used. Everything, including the principle of nonviolence. It was in 1950 that Dr. Mordecai W. Johnson of Howard University visited India. King heard one of the speeches Johnson made on his return, and it was from this moment that King became interested in Gandhi as a figure, and in nonviolence as a way of life. Later, in 1957, he would visit India himself.

But, so far, of course, we are speaking after the fact. Plans and patterns are always more easily discernible then.

This is not so when we try to deal with the present, or attempt speculations about the future.

Immediately after the failure, last June, of Montgomery's case against him, King returned to Atlanta. I entered, late, on a Sunday morning, the packed Ebenezer Baptist Church, and King was already speaking.

He did not look any older, and yet there was a new note of anguish in his voice. He was speaking of his trial. He described the torment, the spiritual state of people who are committed to a wrong, knowing that it is wrong. He made the trials of these white people far more vivid than anything he himself might have endured. They were not ruled by hatred, but by terror; and, therefore, if community was ever to be achieved, these people, the potential destroyers of the person, must not be hated. It was a terrible plea—to the people; and it was a prayer. In *Varieties of Religious Experience*, William James speaks of vastation—of *being*, as opposed to merely regarding, the monstrous creature which came to him in a vision. It seemed to me, though indeed I may be wrong, that something like this had happened to young Martin Luther—that he had looked on evil a long, hard, lonely time. For evil is in the world: it may be in the world to stay. No creed and no dogma are proof against it, and indeed no person is; it is always the naked person, alone, who, over and over and over again, must wrest his salvation from these black jaws. Perhaps young Martin was finding a new and more somber meaning in the command: "Overcome evil with good." The command does not suggest that to overcome evil is to eradicate it.

King spoke more candidly than I had ever heard him speak before, of his bitterly assaulted pride, of his shame, when he found himself accused, before all the world, of having used and betrayed the people of Montgomery by stealing the money they had entrusted to him. "I knew it wasn't true—but who would believe me?"

He had canceled a speaking trip to Chicago, for he felt that he could not face anyone. And he prayed; he walked up and down in his study, alone. It was borne in on him, finally, that he had no right *not* to go, no right to hide. "I called the airport and made another reservation and went on to Chicago." He appeared there, then, as an accused man, and gave us no details of his visit, which did not, in any case, matter. For if he had not been able to face Chicago, if he had not won that battle with himself, he would have been defeated long before his entrance into that courtroom in Montgomery.

When I saw him the next day in his office, he was very different, kind and attentive, but far away. A meeting of the Southern Christian Leadership Conference was to begin that day, and I think his mind must have been on that. The beleaguered ministers of the Deep South were coming to Atlanta that day in order to discuss the specific situations which confronted them in their particular towns or cities, and King was their leader. All of them had come under immensely greater local pressure because of the student sit-in movement. Inevitably, they were held responsible for it, even though they might very well not have known until reading it in the papers that the students had carried out another demonstration. I do not mean to suggest that there is any question of their support of the students—they may or may not be responsible *for* them but they certainly consider themselves responsible *to* them. But all this, I think, weighed on King rather heavily.

He talked about his visit to India and its effect on him. He was hideously struck by the poverty, which he talked about in great detail. He was also much impressed by Nehru, who had, he said, extraordinary qualities of "perception and dedication and courage—far more than the average American politician." We talked about the South. "Perhaps 4 or 5 per cent of the people are to be found on either end of the racial scale"—either actively for or actively against desegregation; "the rest are passive adherents. The sin of the South is the sin of conformity." And he feels, as I do, that much of the responsibility for the situation in which we have found ourselves since 1954 is due to the failure of President Eisenhower to make any coherent, any guiding statement concerning the nation's greatest moral and social problem.

But we did not discuss the impending conference, which, in any case, he could scarcely have discussed with me. And we did not discuss any of the problems which face him now and make his future so problematical. For he could not have discussed these with me, either.

That white men find King dangerous is well known. They can say so. But many Negroes also find King dangerous, but cannot say so, at least not publicly. The reason that the Negroes of whom I speak are trapped in such a stunning silence is that to say what they really feel would be to deny the entire public purpose of their lives.

Now, the problem of Negro leadership in this country has always been extremely delicate, dangerous, and complex. The term itself becomes remarkably difficult to define, the moment one realizes that the real role of the Negro leader, in the eyes of the American Republic, was not to make the Negro a first-class citizen but to keep him content as a second-class one. This sounds extremely harsh, but the record bears me out. And this problem, which it was the responsibility of the entire country to face, was dumped into the laps of a few men. Some of them were real leaders and some of them were false. Many of the greatest have scarcely ever been heard of.

The role of the genuine leadership, in its own eyes, was to destroy the barriers which prevented Negroes from fully participating in American life, to prepare Negroes for first-class citizenship, while at the same time bringing to bear on the Republic every conceivable pressure to make this status a reality. For this reason, the real leadership was to be found everywhere, in law courts, colleges, churches, hobo camps; on picket lines, freight trains, and chain gangs; and in jails. Not everyone who was publicized as a leader really was one. And many leaders who would never have dreamed of applying the term to themselves were considered by the Republic—when it knew of their existence at all—to be criminals. This is, of course, but the old and universal story of poverty in battle with privilege, but we tend not to think of old and universal stories as occurring in our brand-new and still relentlessly parochial land.

The real goal of the Negro leader was nothing less than the total integration of Negroes in all levels of the national life. But this could rarely be stated so baldly; it often could not be stated at all; in order to begin Negro education, for example, Booker Washington had found it necessary to state the exact opposite. The reason for this duplicity is that the goal contains the assumption that Negroes are to be treated, in all respects, exactly like all other citizens of the Republic. This is an idea which has always had extremely rough going in America. For one thing, it attacked, and attacks, a vast complex of special interests which would lose money and power if the situation of the Negro were to change. For another, the idea of freedom necessarily carries with it the idea of sexual freedom: the freedom to meet, sleep with, and marry whom one chooses. It would be fascinating, but I am afraid we must postpone it for the moment, to consider just why so many people appear to be convinced that Negroes would then immediately meet, sleep with, and marry white women; who, remarkably enough, are only protected from such undesirable alliances by the majesty and vigilance of the law.

The duplicity of the Negro leader was more than matched by the duplicity of the people with whom he had to deal. They, and most of the country, felt at the very bottom of their hearts that the Negro was inferior to them and, therefore, merited the treatment that he got. But it was not always politic to say this, either. It certainly could never be said over the bargaining table, where white and black men met.

The Negro leader was there to force from his adversary whatever he could get: new schools, new schoolrooms, new houses, new jobs. He was invested with very little power because the Negro vote had so very little power. (Other Negro leaders were trying to correct *that*.) It was not easy to wring concessions from the people at the bargaining table, who had, after all, no intention of giving their power away. People seldom do give their power away, forces beyond their control take their power from them; and I am afraid that much of the liberal cant about progress is but a sentimental reflection of this implacable fact. (Liberal cant about love and heroism also obscures, not to say blasphemes, the great love and heroism of many white people. Our racial story would be inconceivably more grim if these people, in the teeth of the most fantastic odds, did not continue to appear; but they were almost never, of course, to be found at the bargaining table.) Whatever concession the Negro leader carried away from the bargaining table was won with the tacit understanding that he, in return, would influence the people he represented in the direction that the people in power wished them to be influenced. Very often, in fact, he did not do this at all, but contrived to delude the white men (who are, in this realm, rather easily deluded) into believing that he had. But very often, too, he deluded himself into believing that the aims of white men in power and the desires of Negroes out of power were the same.

It was altogether inevitable, in short, that, by means of the extraordinary tableau I have tried to describe, a class of Negroes should have been created whose loyalty to their class was infinitely greater than their loyalty to the people from whom they had been so cunningly estranged. We must add, for I think it is important, that the Negro leader knew that he, too, was called "nigger" when his back was turned. The great mass of the black people around him were illiterate, demoralized, in want, and incorrigible. It is not hard to see that the Negro leader's personal and public frustrations would almost inevitably be turned against these people, for their misery, which formed the cornerstone of his peculiar power, was also responsible for his humiliation. And in Harlem, now, for example, many prominent Negroes ride to and from work through scenes of the greatest misery. They do not see this misery, though, because they do not want to see it. They defend themselves against an intolerable reality, which menaces them, by despising the people who are trapped in it.

The criticism, therefore, of the publicized Negro leadership—which is not, as I have tried to indicate, always the real leadership—is a criticism leveled, above all, against this class. They are, perhaps, the most unlucky bourgeoisie in the world's entire history, trapped, as they are, in a no man's land between black humiliation and white power. They cannot move backwards, and they cannot move forward, either.

One of the greatest vices of the white bourgeoisie on which they have modeled themselves is its reluctance to think, its distrust of the independent mind. Since the Negro bourgeoisie has so many things *not* to think about, it is positively afflicted with this vice. I should like at some other time to embark on a full-length discussion of the honorable and heroic role played by the NAACP in the national life, and point out to what extent its work has helped create the present ferment. But, for the moment, I shall have to confine my remarks to its organ, *The Crisis*, because I think it is incontestable that this magazine reveals the state of mind of the Negro bourgeoisie. *The Crisis* has the most exciting subject matter in the world at its fingertips, and yet manages to be one of the world's dullest magazines. When the Reverend James Lawson—who was expelled from Vanderbilt University for his sit-in activities—said this, or something like it, he caused a great storm of ill feeling. But he was quite right to feel as he does about *The Crisis*, and quite right to say so. And the charge is not answered by referring to the history of the NAACP.

Now, to charge *The Crisis* with dullness may seem to be a very trivial matter. It is not trivial, though, because this dullness is the result of its failure to examine what is really happening in the Negro world—its failure indeed, for that matter, to seize upon what is happening in the world at large. And I have singled it out because this inability is revelatory of the gap which now ominously widens between what we shall now have to call the official leadership and the young people who have begun what is nothing less than a moral revolution.

It is because of this gap that King finds himself in such a difficult position. The pressures on him are tremendous, and they come from above and below. He lost much moral credit, for example, especially in the eyes of the young, when he allowed Adam Clayton Powell to force the resignation of his (King's) extremely able organizer and lieutenant, Bayard Rustin. Rustin, also, has a long and honorable record as a fighter for Negro rights, and is one of the most penetrating and able men around. The techniques used by Powell— we will not speculate as to his motives—were far from sweet; but King was faced with the choice of defending his organizer, who was also his friend, or agreeing with Powell; and he chose the *latter* course. Nor do I know of anyone satisfied with the reasons given for the exclusion of James Lawson from the Southern Christian Leadership Conference. It would seem, certainly, that so able, outspoken, and energetic a man might prove of great value to this organization: why, then, is he not a part of it?

And there are many other questions, all of them ominous, and too many to go into here. But they all come, finally, it seems to me, to this tremendous reality: it is the sons and daughters of the beleaguered bourgeoisie—supported, in the most extraordinary fashion, by those old, work-worn men and women who were known, only yesterday, as "the country niggers"—who have begun a revolution in the consciousness of this country which will inexorably destroy nearly all that we now think of as concrete and indisputable. These young people have never believed in the American image of the Negro and have never bargained with the Republic, and now they never will. There is no longer any basis on which to bargain: for the myth of white supremacy is exploding all over the world, from the Congo to New Orleans. Those who have been watched and judged and described for so long are now watching and judging and describing for themselves. And one of the things that this means, to put it far too simply and bluntly, is that the white man on whom the American Negro has modeled himself for so long is vanishing. Because this white man was, himself, very largely a mythical creation: white men have never been, here, what they imagined themselves to be. The liberation of Americans from the racial anguish which has crippled us for so long can only mean, truly, the creation of a new people in this still-new world.

But the battle to achieve this has not ended, it has scarcely begun. Martin Luther King, Jr., by the power of his personality and the force of his beliefs, has injected a new dimension into our ferocious struggle. He has succeeded, in a way no Negro before him has managed to do, to carry the battle into the individual heart and make its resolution the province of the individual will. He has made it a matter, on both sides of the racial fence, of self-examination; and has incurred, therefore, the grave responsibility of continuing to lead in the path he has encouraged so many people to follow. How he will do this I do not know, but I do not see how he can possibly avoid a break, at last, with the habits and attitudes, stratagems and fears of the past.

No one can read the future, but we do know, as James has put it, that "all futures are rough." King's responsibility, and ours, is to that future which is already sending before it so many striking signs and portents. The possibility of liberation which is always real is also always painful, since it involves such an overhauling of all that gave us our identity. The Negro who will emerge out of this present struggle— whoever, indeed, this dark stranger may prove to be—will not be dependent, in any way at all, on any of the many props and crutches which help form our identity now. And neither will the white man. We will need every ounce of moral stamina we can find. For everything is changing, from our notion of politics to our notion of ourselves, and we are certain, as we begin history's strangest metamorphosis, to undergo the torment of being forced to surrender far more than we ever realized we had accepted.

MIAMI NOTEBOOK: CASSIUS CLAY AND MALCOLM X

BY GEORGE PLIMPTON

JUNE 1964

The press was incensed at Cassius Clay's behavior before the Liston fight. You could feel it. They wanted straight answers, and they weren't getting them. Usually, particularly with fighters, the direct question of extreme simplicity—which is of great moment to the sportswriters—will get a reply in kind. "Champ," asks the sportswriter, "how did you sleep last night and what did you have for breakfast?" When the champ considers the matter and says he slept real fine and had six eggs and four glasses of milk, the sportswriter puts down, "*gd sleep 6 eggs 4 gl milk,*" on his pad, and a little while later the statistic goes out over Western Union.

But with Clay, such a question simply served to unleash an act, an entertainment which included poetry, the brandishing of arms and canes, a chorus thrown in—not a dull show by any standard, even if you've seen it a few times before. The press felt that the act—it was constantly referred to as an "act"—was born of terror or lunacy. What *should* have appealed, Cassius surely being the most colorful, if bizarre, heavyweight since, well, John L. Sullivan or Jack Johnson, none of this seemed to work at all. The press's attitude was largely that of the lip-curling disdain the Cambridge police have toward the antics of students heeling for the *Harvard Lampoon.*

One of the troubles, I think—it occurred to me as I watched Clay at his last press conference on February 24 before the fight—is that his appearance does not suit his manner. His great good looks are wrong for the excessive things he shouts. Archie Moore used the same sort of routine as Clay to get himself a shot at both the light-heavyweight and heavyweight championships—self-promotion, gags, bizarre suits, a penchant for public speaking—but his character was suited to it, his face with a touch of slyness in it, and always humor. So the press was always very much in his support, and they had much to do with Moore's climb from obscurity. At his training camp outside San Diego—the Salt

Mines it is called, where Cassius himself did a tour at the start of his career—Moore has built a staircase in the rocks, sixty or seventy steps, each with a reporter's name painted in red to symbolize the assistance the press gave him. Clay's face, on the other hand, does not show humor. He has a fine grin, but his features are curiously deadpan when the self-esteem begins, which, of course, desperately needs humor as a softening effect. Clay himself bridled at the resentment he caused. It must have puzzled him to be cast as the villain in a fight with Liston, who, on the surface at least, had absolutely no flair or panache except as a symbol of destructiveness.

Clay made a short, final address to the newspapermen. "This is your last chance," he said. "It's your last chance to get on the bandwagon. I'm keeping a list of all you people. After the fight is done, we're going to have a roll call up there in the ring. And when I see so-and-so said this fight was a mismatch, why I'm going to have a little ceremony and some *eating* is going on—eating of words." His manner was that of the admonishing schoolteacher. The press sat in their rows at the Miami Auditorium staring balefully at him. It seemed incredible that a smile or two wouldn't show up on a writer's face. It was so wonderfully preposterous. But I didn't see any. [...]

Each fighter had his spiritual adviser, his *guru* at hand. In Liston's camp was Father Murphy, less a religious adviser than a confidant and friend of the champion. In Clay's camp was Malcolm X, who was then one of the high officials of the Black Muslim sect, indeed its most prominent spokesman, though he has since defected to form his own black nationalist political movement. For months he had been silent. Elijah Muhammad, the supreme leader, the Messenger of Allah, had muzzled him since November for making intemperate remarks after the assassination of President Kennedy. But he had been rumored to be in Miami, and speculation was strong that he was there to bring Cassius Clay into the Muslim fold.

I was riding in a car just after the weigh-in with Archie Robinson, who is Clay's business manager and closest friend—a slightly built young man, not much older than Clay, one would guess, very polite and soft-spoken—and he asked me if I'd like to meet Malcolm X. I said yes, and we drove across Biscayne Bay to the Negro-clientele Hampton House Motel in Miami proper—a small-town hotel compared to the Babylon towers across the Bay, with a small swimming pool, a luncheonette, a pitch-dark bar where you had to grope to find a chair, with a dance floor and a band which came on later, and most of the rooms in balconied barracks-like structures out back. It was crowded and very lively with people in town not only for the fight but also for an invitation golf tournament.

I waited at a side table in the luncheonette. Malcolm X came in after a while, moving by the tables very slowly. Elijah Muhammad's ministers—Malcolm X was one of them—are said to emulate him even to the speed of his walk, which is considerable. But the luncheonette was not set up for a swift entrance. The tables were close together, and Malcolm X came by them carefully—a tall, erect man in his thirties, a lean, intelligent face with a long pronounced jaw, a wide mouth set in it which seems caught in a perpetual smile. He was carrying one of the Cassius Clay camp's souvenir canes, and with his horn-rimmed glasses, his slow stately walk, and with Robinson half a step behind him, guiding him, I thought for a second that he'd gone blind. He sat down, unwrapped a package of white peppermints which he picked at steadily, and began talking. Robinson sat with us for a while, but he had things to attend to.

I took notes from time to time, scratching them down on the paper tablecloth, then in a notebook. Malcolm X did not seem to mind. He said he was going to be unmuzzled in March, which was only five days away. He himself wrote on the tablecloth once in a while—putting down a word he wanted to emphasize. He had an automatic pen-and-pencil set in his shirt pocket—the clasps initialed FOI on one (Fruit of Islam, which is the military organization within the Muslim temple) and ISLAM on the other. He wore a red ring with a small crescent.

Malcolm X's voice is gentle, and he often smiles broadly, but not with humor, so that the caustic nature of what he is saying is not belied. His manner is distant and grave, and he asks, mocking slightly, "Sir?" when a question is not heard or understood, leaning forward and cocking his head. His answers are always skilled, with a lively and effec- tive use of image, and yet as the phrases came I kept think- ing of Cassius Clay and *his* litany—the fighter's is more lim- ited, and a different sort of thing, but neither of them ever *stumbles* over words, or ideas, or appears balked by a ques- tion, so that one rarely has the sense of the brain actually working but rather that it is engaged in rote, simply a recording apparatus playing back to an impulse. Thus he is truly intractable—Malcolm X—absolutely dedicated, self- assured, self-principled, with that great energy...the true revolutionary. He does not doubt.

When give-and-take of argument is possible, when what Malcolm X says can be doubted, his assurance and position as an extremist give him an advantage in debate. He appreciates that this is so, and it amuses him. "The extremist," he said, "will always ruin the liberals in debate— because the liberals have something too nebulous to sell, or too impossible to sell—like the Brooklyn Bridge. That's why a white segregationalist—what's his name, Kilpatrick—will destroy Farmer, and why William Buckley makes a fool of Norman Mailer, and why Martin Luther King would lose a debate with me. Why King? Because integration is ridicu- lous, a dream. I am not interested in dreams, but in the nightmare. Martin Luther King, the rest of them, they are thinking about dreams. But then really King and I have nothing to debate about. We are both indicting. I would say to him: 'You indict and give them hope. I'll indict and give them no hope.'"

I asked him about the remarks that had caused him his muzzling by Elijah Muhammad. His remarks about the assas- sination had been taken out of context, he said, though it would be the sheerest hypocrisy to suggest that Kennedy was a friend to the Negro. Kennedy was a politician (he wrote down the word on the paper tablecloth with his FOI pencil and circled it)—a "cold-blooded politician" who trans- formed last year's civil-rights march on Washington into a "crawl" by endorsing the march, joining it, though it was supposed to be a protest against the country's leaders...a politician's trick which tamped out the fuse though the powder keg was there. Friend of the Negro? There never had been a politician who was the Negro's friend. Power cor- rupts. Lincoln? A crooked, deceitful hypocrite, claiming championship to the cause of the Negro who, one hundred years later, finds himself singing "We Shall Overcome." The Supreme Court? Its decision is nothing but an act of hypocrisy...nine Supreme Court justices expert in legal phraseology tangling the words of their decision in such a

LeRoy Neiman

way that lawyers can dilly-dally over it for years—which of course they will continue to do...

I scribbled these phrases, and others, on the paper tablecloth, mildly surprised to see the Muslim maxims in my own handwriting. We talked about practicality, which is the weakest area of the Muslim plans, granted the fires of resentment are justifiably banked. Malcolm X was not particularly concerned. What may be illogical or impractical in the long run is dismissed as not being pertinent to the *moment*—which is what the Negro must concern himself with. He could sense my frustration at this. It is not easy to dismiss what is practical. He had a peppermint and smiled.

I changed the subject and asked him what he did for exercise.

"I take walks," he said. "Long walks. We believe in exercise, physical fitness, but as for commercial sport, that's a racket. Commercial sport is the pleasure of the idle rich. The vice of gambling stems from it." He wrote down the word "Promoter" on the tablecloth with his FOI pencil and

circled it. "The Negro never comes out ahead—never *one* in the history of sport."

"Clay perhaps."

"Perhaps." He liked talking about Clay. "I'm interested in him as a human being," he said. He tapped his head. "Not many people know the quality of the mind he's got in there. He fools them. One forgets that though a clown never imitates a wise man, the wise man can imitate the clown. He is sensitive, very humble, yet shrewd—with as much untapped mental energy as he has physical power. He should be a diplomat. He has that instinct of seeing a tricky situation shaping up—my own presence in Miami, for example—and resolving how to sidestep it. He knows how to handle people, to get them functioning. He gains strength from being around people. He can't stand being alone. The more people around, the better—just as it takes water to prime a country well. If the crowds are big in there tonight in the Miami Auditorium, he's likely to beat Liston. But they won't be. The Jews have heard he's a Muslim and they won't show up."

"Perhaps they'll show up to see him taken," I said.

"Sir?" he said, with that slight cock of the head.

"Perhaps..."

"When Cassius said, 'I am a man of race,'" Malcolm X went on, "it pleased the Negroes. He couldn't eliminate the color factor. But the press and the white people saw it another way. They saw him, suddenly, as a threat. Which is why he has become the villain—why he is booed, the outcast." He seemed pleased with this.

Wasn't it possible, I asked, that the braggart, the loudmouth was being booed, not necessarily the Black Muslim? After all, Clay had been heartily booed during the Doug Jones fight in Madison Square Garden, and that was before his affiliation with the Muslims was known.

"You, *you* can't tell," replied Malcolm X. "But a Negro can feel things in sounds. The booing at the Doug Jones fight was good-natured—I was there—but the booing is now different... defiant... inflamed by the columnists, all of them, critical of Cassius for being a Muslim."

"And as a fighter?"

"He has tremendous self-confidence," said Malcolm X. "I've never heard him mention fear. Anything you're afraid of can whip you. Fear magnifies what you're afraid of. One thing about our religion is that it removes fear. Christianity is based on fear."

I remarked that the Muslim religion, since it has its taboos and promises and threats, is also based on fear—one remembers that British soldiers extracted secrets from terrified Muslim captives by threatening to sew them up for a while in a pig's skin.

Malcolm X acknowledged that the Muslims had to adapt Islam to their purposes. "We are in a cage," he said. "What must be taught to the lion in a cage is quite different from what one teaches the lion in the jungle. The Mohammedan abroad believes in a heaven and a hell, a hereafter. Here we believe that heaven and hell are on this earth, and that we are in the hell and must strive to escape it. If we can adapt Islam to this purpose, we should. For people fighting for their freedom there is no such thing as a bad device."

He snorted about peaceful methods. "The methods of Gandhi?" Another snort. "The Indians are hypocrites. Look at Goa. Besides, they are the most helpless people on earth. They succeeded in removing the British only because they outnumbered them, out*weighed* them—a big dark elephant sitting on a white elephant. In this country the situation is different. The white elephant is huge. But we will catch him. We will catch him when he is asleep. The mice will run up his trunk when he is asleep.

"Where? They will come out of the alley. The revolution always comes from the alley—from the man with nothing to lose. Never the bourgeois. The poor Negro bourgeois, with his golf clubs, his golfing hat"—he waved at the people in the lunchroom—"he's so much more frustrated than the Negro in the alley; he gets the doors slapped shut in his face every day. But the explosion won't come from him. Not from the pickets either, or the nonviolent groups—these masochists...they *want* to be beaten—but it will come from the people *watching*—spectators for the moment. They're different. You don't know. It is dangerous to suggest that the Negro is non-violent.

"There *must* be retribution. It is proclaimed. If retribution came to the Pharoah for his enslavement of six hundred thousand, it will come to the white American who enslaved twenty million and robbed their minds."

"And retribution, that is in the Koran?"

"Sir?"

"The Koran...?"

He said, "Chapter 22, verse 102."

I put the numbers down, thinking to catch him out; I looked later. The verse reads: "*The day when the trumpet is blown. On that day we assemble the guilty white-eyed (with terror).*"

"These are the things you are teaching Cassius?"

"He will make up his own mind."

He popped a peppermint in his mouth. We talked a little longer, somewhat aimlessly. He had an appointment with someone, he finally said, and he stood up. The noise of conversation dropped noticeably in the luncheonette as he stood up and walked out, erect and moving slowly, holding his gaudy souvenir cane out in front of him as he threaded his way between the tables; the people in the golfing hats watched him go.

I went out into the lobby of the hotel, just standing around there feeling low. A phrase from Kafka, or rather the *idea* of

some phrases from *The Trial* came to me. I looked them up the other day: "But I'm not guilty, said K. It's a mistake. Besides, how can a man be guilty? We're all men. True, said the priest: but that's how the guilty talk."

The lobby was crowded. I didn't feel comfortable. I went out to the street and stood *there*, watching the traffic. The cars came by going at sixty, none of them taxis. I went back to the lobby. The armchairs, not more than four or five, were occupied. I wouldn't have sat down anyway.

Then a fine thing happened. I was talking into the desk telephone, trying to find Archie Robinson, and a Negro, a big fellow, came up and said softly, "Hello, man, how's it?"—smiling somewhat tentatively, as if he wasn't quite sure of himself. I thought he was talking to someone else, but when I glanced up again, his eyes were still fixed on me. "We looked for you in New York when we came through," he said.

I recognized him, the great defensive back on the Detroit Lions, Night Train Lane, a good friend. "Train!" I shouted. I could sense people turn. It crossed my mind that Malcolm X might be one of them. "Hey!" I said. "*Hey!*" Lane looked a little startled. He hadn't remembered me as someone who indulged in such effusive greetings. But he asked me to come back to his room where he had friends, most of them from the golf tournament, dropping in for drinks and beans. I said that would be fine.

We went on back. Everyone we passed seemed to know him. "Hey man," they'd call, and he'd grin at them—a strong presence, an uncomplicated confidence, absolutely trusting himself. He had the room next to mine at the Detroit Lions' training camp (I was out there, an amateur among the pros, trying to play quarterback and write a book about it) and it was always full of teammates, laughing and carrying on. A record player, set on the floor, was always going in his room—Dinah Washington records. He had married her earlier in the year, her ninth or tenth husband, I think. The volume was always up, and if you came up from the practice field late, her voice would come at you across the school grounds. She had died later that year.

His room was small and full of people. I sat quietly. Train offered me some beans, but I wasn't hungry. He said, "What's wrong with you, man?"

"I'm fine," I said.

"Hey!" someone called across the room. "Was that you in the lunchroom? What you doin' talking to that guy X?"

"Well, I was listening to him," I said.

"They were telling around," this man said, "that X had a vision—he seen Cassius win in a *vision*."

Someone else said that in a fight they'd rather be supported by a Liston left jab than a Malcolm X vision. A big fine hoot of laughter went up, and Night Train said it was the damnedest co-in-ci-dence but a *horse* named Cassius had won one of the early races at Hialeah that afternoon—perhaps *that* was Malcolm X's vision.

They talked about him this way, easily, matter-of-factly. They could take him or leave him, which for a while I'd forgotten. Malcolm X had said about them: "They all know I'm here in the motel. They come and look at me through the door to see if I got horns...and you can see them turning things over in their minds."

The day after he beat Liston, Cassius turned up at a news conference at the Miami Beach Auditorium. The rumor was that he had gone to Chicago for the Muslim celebrations there, and the press was surprised when he appeared—and even more so at his behavior, which was subdued. Since a microphone system had gone out, his voice was almost inaudible. Cries went up which one never expected to hear in Clay's presence: "What's that, Clay? Speak up, Cassius!"

Archie Robinson took me aside and told me that he and Clay had dropped in on the celebrations at the Hampton House Motel after the fight, but it had been too noisy, so they'd gone home. It was quieter there, and they had been up until 4:00 A.M. discussing Cassius' "new image."

I remarked that this was a rare kind of evening to spend after winning the heavyweight championship. I'd met a young singer named Dee Something-or-other who had been waiting for Clay outside his dressing room after the fight. She had some idea she was going to help Cassius celebrate. She was very pretty. She had a singing engagement at a nightclub called the Sir John. Her mother was with her. She was very anxious, and once in a while when someone would squeeze in or out of the dressing room she'd call out: "Tell Cassius that Dee..." The girl was calm. "I call him Marcellus," she said. "A beautiful name. I can say it over and over."

The newspapermen waiting to get into the dressing room looked admiringly at her. "Clay's little fox," they called her, using Clay's generic name for girls—"foxes"—which is half affectionate and half suspicious; he feels that girls can be "sly" and "sneaky" and are to be watched warily. When the new champion finally emerged from his dressing room in a heavy press of entourage, photographers, and

newspapermen, he seemed subdued and preoccupied. He didn't glance at Dee, who was on her toes, waving shyly in his direction. "Marcellus," she called. The crowd, packed in tight around him, moved down the corridor, the photobulbs flashing. The mother looked quite put out.

The living accommodations for Liston and Clay were as different as their fighting styles. Liston had a big place on the beach, a sixteen-room house next to the Yankees' owner, Dan Topping, reportedly very plush, wall-to-wall carpeting, and each room set up like a golf-club lounge—a television set going interminably, perhaps someone in front of it, perhaps not, and then invariably a card game.

Clay's place was on the mainland, in North Miami, in a low-rent district—a small plain tater-white house with louvered windows, a front door with steps leading up to a little porch with room for one chair, a front yard with more chairs set around and shaded by a big ficus tree with leaves dusty from the traffic on Fifth Street. His entire entourage stayed there, living dormitory-style, two or three to a room. Outside the yard was almost worn bare. There wasn't a neighborhood child on his way home from school who didn't pass by to see if anything was up. Films were shown there in the evening, outside, the children sitting quietly until the film started. Then the questions and the exclamations would come, Clay explaining things, and you could hardly hear the soundtrack. Only one film kept them quiet. That was the favorite film shown two or three times, *The Invasion of the Body Snatchers*...watched wide-eyed in the comforting sounds of the projector and the traffic going by occasionally on Fifth Street. When the big moths would show up in the light beam, almost as big as white towels they seemed, a yelp or two would go up, particularly if a body was being snatched at the time, and the children would sway for one another.

The children were waiting for Clay when he drove up from his press conference the day after the fight. So was Malcolm X, a camera slung from his neck; his souvenir cane was propped against the ficus tree. The children came for the car, shouting, and packing in around so that the doors had to be opened gingerly. Clay got out, towering above them as he walked slowly for a chair in the front yard. The litany started almost as soon as he sat down, the children around him twelve deep, Malcolm X at the periphery, grinning as he snapped pictures.

"Who's the king of kings?"

"Cassius Clay!"

"Who shook up the world?"

"Cassius Clay!"

"Who's the ugly bear?"

"Sonny Liston!"

"Who's the prettiest?"

"Cassius Clay!"

Sometimes a girl, a bright girl, just for a change would reply *"me,"* pointing a finger at herself when everyone else was shouting *"Cassius Clay,"* or she might shout *"Ray Charles,"* and the giggling would start around her, and others would join in until Clay, with a big grin, would have to hold up a hand to reorganize the claque and get things straightened out. Neither he nor the children tired of the litany. They kept at it for an hour at a time. Malcolm X left after awhile. There were variations, but it was essentially the same, and it never seemed to lack for enthusiasm. The noise carried for blocks.

We went inside while this was going on. The main room, with an alcove for cooking, had sofas along the wall. The artifacts of the psychological campaign against Liston were set around—signs which read "settin' traps for the Big Bear," which had been brandished outside his training headquarters, and a valentine, as tall as a man, complete with cherubs, which had been offered Liston and which he had refused. It stood in a corner, next to an easel. Newspapers were flung around—there had been some celebrating the night before—and someone's shoes were in the middle of the room. Souvenir canes were propped up by the side of the stove in the cooking alcove. It was fraternity-house clutter.

I was standing next to Howard Bingham, Clay's "official" photographer. "It was fun, wasn't it?" I asked.

"Oh my," he said. "We have the *best* time here."

He had joined up with Clay after the George Logan fight in California, about Clay's age, younger perhaps, and shy. He stutters a bit, and he told me that he didn't take their kidding lying down. He said: "I walk around the house and sc...sc...scare people, jump out at them. Or they d...doze off on the c...couch, and I sneak around and tickle them on the nose, y'know, with a piece of string. Why I was agitating C...C...Cassius for half an hour once when he was dozing off. And I give the hot f...f...feet around here, a lot of that. We had a high time."

I asked what Cassius' winning the championship meant for him.

"Well, of course, that must make me the greatest ph...ph...photographer in the world." He couldn't keep a straight face. "Oh please," he said. His shoulders shook. "Well, I'll tell you. I'm going to get me a mo...mo...mohair wardrobe, that's one thing."

At the kitchen table Archie Robinson was sorting telegrams, stacked up in the hundreds. He showed me some of them—as impersonal as an injunction, from the long sycophantic messages from people they had to scratch around to remember, to the tart challenges from fighters looking to take Clay's title away from him. Clay wasn't bothering with them. He was going strong outside—his voice rising above the babble of children's voices: "Who shook up the world?"

"Cassius Clay!"

I wandered back to his room. It was just large enough for a bed, the mattress bare when I looked there, an armchair, with clothes including his Bear Huntin' jacket thrown across it, and a plain teak-colored bureau which had a large-size bottle of Dickinson's witch hazel standing on it. A tiny oil painting of a New England harbor scene was on one wall, with a few newspaper articles taped next to it, illustrated, describing Clay at his most flamboyant. A training schedule was taped to the mirror over the bureau. It called for "all" to rise at 5:00 A.M. The bedclothes were in a corner. One corner of the mattress was covered with Cassius Clay's signature in a light-blue ink, flowery with the Cs tall and graceful, along with such graffiti as: "Cassius Clay Is Next Champ"; "Champion of the World"; "Liston Is Finished"; "The Next Champ: Cassius Clay"...

Outside, it had all come true. His voice and the answers were unceasing. "You," he was calling to the children, "you all are looking...at...the...champion...of...the...whole...wide...world."

The Paranoid Style in American Politics
by Richard Hofstadter

November 1964

American politics has often been an arena for angry minds. In recent years we have seen angry minds at work mainly among extreme right-wingers, who have now demonstrated in the Goldwater movement how much political leverage can be got out of the animosities and passions of a small minority. But behind this I believe there is a style of mind that is far from new and that is not necessarily right-wing. I call it the paranoid style simply because no other word adequately evokes the sense of heated exaggeration, suspiciousness, and conspiratorial fantasy that I have in mind. In using the expression "paranoid style" I am not speaking in a clinical sense, but borrowing a clinical term for other purposes. I have neither the competence nor the desire to classify any figures of the past or present as certifiable lunatics. In fact, the idea of the paranoid style as a force in politics would have little contemporary relevance or historical value if it were applied only to men with profoundly disturbed minds. It is the use of paranoid modes of expression by more or less normal people that makes the phenomenon significant.

Of course this term is pejorative, and it is meant to be; the paranoid style has a greater affinity for bad causes than good. But nothing really prevents a sound program or demand from being advocated in the paranoid style. Style has more to do with the way in which ideas are believed and advocated than with the truth or falsity of their content. I am interested here in getting at our political psychology through our political rhetoric. The paranoid style is an old and recurrent phenomenon in our public life which has been frequently linked with movements of suspicious discontent.

Here is Senator McCarthy, speaking in June 1951 about the parlous situation of the United States:

How can we account for our present situation unless we believe that men high in this government are concerting to deliver us to disaster? This must be the product of a great conspiracy on a scale so immense as to dwarf any previous such venture in the history of man. A conspiracy of infamy so black that, when it is finally exposed, its principals shall be forever deserving of the maledictions of all honest men.... What can be made of this unbroken series of decisions and acts contributing to the strategy of defeat? They cannot be attributed to incompetence.... The laws of probability would dictate that part of... [the] decisions would serve the country's interest.

Now turn back fifty years to a manifesto signed in 1895 by a number of leaders of the Populist party:

As early as 1865–66 a conspiracy was entered into between the gold gamblers of Europe and America.... For nearly thirty years these conspirators have kept the people quarreling over less important matters while they have pursued with unrelenting zeal their one central purpose.... Every device of treachery, every resource of statecraft, and every artifice known to the secret cabals of the international gold ring are being used to deal a blow to the prosperity of the people and the financial and commercial independence of the country.

Next, a Texas newspaper article of 1855:

...It is a notorious fact that the Monarchs of Europe and the Pope of Rome are at this very moment plotting our destruction and threatening the extinction of our political, civil, and religious institutions. We have the best reasons for believing that corruption has found its way into our Executive Chamber, and that our Executive head is tainted with the infectious venom of Catholicism.... The Pope has recently sent his ambassador of state to this country on a secret commission, the effect of which is an extraordinary boldness of the Catholic Church throughout the United States.... These minions of the Pope are boldly insulting our Senators; reprimanding our Statesmen; propagating the adulterous union of Church and State; abusing with foul calumny all governments but Catholic; and spewing out the bitterest execrations on all Protestantism. The Catholics in the United States receive from abroad more than $200,000 annually for the propagation of their creed. Add to this the vast revenue collected here....

These quotations give the keynote of the style. In the history of the United States one finds it, for example, in the anti-Masonic movement, the nativist and anti-Catholic movement, in certain spokesmen of abolitionism who regarded the United States as being in the grip of a slaveholders' conspiracy, in many alarmists about the Mormons, in some Greenback and Populist writers who constructed a great conspiracy of international bankers, in the exposure of a munitions makers' conspiracy of World War I, in the popular left-wing press, in the contemporary American right wing, and on both sides of the race controversy today, among White Citizens' Councils and Black Muslims. I do not propose to try to trace the variations of the paranoid style that can be found in all these movements, but will confine myself to a few leading episodes in our past history in which the style emerged in full and archetypal splendor.

I begin with a particularly revealing episode—the panic that broke out in some quarters at the end of the eighteenth century over the allegedly subversive activities of the Bavarian Illuminati. This panic was a part of the general reaction to the French Revolution. In the United States it was heightened by the response of certain men, mostly in New England and among the established clergy, to the rise of Jeffersonian democracy. Illuminism had been started in 1776 by Adam Weishaupt, a professor of law at the University of Ingolstadt. Its teachings today seem to be no more than another version of Enlightenment rationalism, spiced with the anticlerical atmosphere of eighteenth-century Bavaria. It was a somewhat naïve and utopian movement which aspired ultimately to bring the human race under the rules of reason. Its humanitarian rationalism appears to have acquired a fairly wide influence in Masonic lodges.

Americans first learned of Illuminism in 1797, from a volume published in Edinburgh (later reprinted in New York) under the title, *Proofs of a Conspiracy Against All the Religions and Governments of Europe, Carried on in the Secret Meetings of Free Masons, Illuminati, and Reading Societies.* Its author was a well-known Scottish scientist, John Robison, who had himself been a somewhat casual adherent of Masonry in Britain, but whose imagination had been inflamed by what he considered to be the far less innocent Masonic movement on the Continent. Robison seems to have made his work as factual as he could, but when he came to estimating the moral character and the political influence of Illuminism, he made the characteristic paranoid leap into fantasy. The association, he thought, was formed "for the express purpose of ROOTING OUT ALL RELIGIOUS ESTABLISHMENTS, AND OVERTURNING ALL THE EXISTING GOVERNMENTS OF EUROPE." It had become "one great and wicked project fermenting and working all over Europe," and to it he attributed a central role in bringing about the French Revolution. He saw it as a libertine, anti-Christian movement, given to the corruption of women, the cultivation of sensual pleasures, and the violation of property rights. Its members had plans for making a tea that caused abortion—a secret substance that "blinds or kills when spurted in the face," and a device that sounds like a stench bomb—a "method for filling a bedchamber with pestilential vapours."

These notions were quick to make themselves felt in America. In May 1798, a minister of the Massachusetts Congregational establishment in Boston, Jedidiah Morse, delivered a timely sermon to the young country, which was then sharply divided between Jeffersonians and Federalists, Francophiles and Anglomen. Having read Robison, Morse was convinced that the United States too was the victim of a Jacobinical plot touched off by Illuminism, and that the country should be rallied to defend itself. His warnings were heeded throughout New England wherever Federalists brooded about the rising tide of religious infidelity or Jeffersonian democracy. Timothy Dwight, the president of Yale, followed Morse's sermon with a Fourth-of-July discourse on *The Duty of Americans in the Present Crisis,* in which he held forth against the Antichrist in his own glowing rhetoric. Soon the pulpits of New England were ringing with denunciations of the Illuminati, as though the country were swarming with them.

The anti-Masonic movement of the late 1820s and the 1830s took up and extended the obsession with conspiracy.

At first, this movement may seem to be no more than an extension or repetition of the anti-Masonic theme sounded in the outcry against the Bavarian Illuminati. But whereas the panic of the 1790s was confined mainly to New England and linked to an ultraconservative point of view, the later anti-Masonic movement affected many parts of the northern United States, and was intimately linked with popular democracy and rural egalitarianism. Although anti-Masonry happened to be anti-Jacksonian (Jackson was a Mason), it manifested the same animus against the closure of opportunity for the common man and against aristocratic institutions that one finds in the Jacksonian crusade against the Bank of the United States.

The anti-Masonic movement was a product not merely of natural enthusiasm but also of the vicissitudes of party politics. It was joined and used by a great many men who did not fully share its original anti-Masonic feelings. It attracted the support of several reputable statesmen who had only mild sympathy with its fundamental bias, but who as politicians could not afford to ignore it. Still, it was a folk movement of considerable power, and the rural enthusiasts who provided its real impetus believed in it wholeheartedly.

As a secret society, Masonry was considered to be a standing conspiracy against republican government. It was held to be particularly liable to treason—for example, Aaron Burr's famous conspiracy was alleged to have been conducted by Masons. Masonry was accused of constituting a separate system of loyalty, a separate imperium within the framework of federal and state governments, which was inconsistent with loyalty to them. Quite plausibly it was argued that the Masons had set up a jurisdiction of their own, with their own obligations and punishments, liable to enforcement even by the penalty of death. So basic was the conflict felt to be between secrecy and democracy that other, more innocent societies such as Phi Beta Kappa came under attack.

Since Masons were pledged to come to each other's aid under circumstances of distress, and to extend fraternal indulgence at all times, it was held that the order nullified the enforcement of regular law. Masonic constables, sheriffs, juries, and judges must all be in league with Masonic criminals and fugitives. The press was believed to have been so "muzzled" by Masonic editors and proprietors that news of Masonic malfeasance could be suppressed. At a moment when almost every alleged citadel of privilege in America was under democratic assault, Masonry was attacked as a fraternity of the privileged, closing business opportunities and nearly monopolizing political offices.

Certain elements of truth and reality there may have been in these views of Masonry. What must be emphasized here, however, is the apocalyptic and absolutistic framework in which this hostility was commonly expressed. Anti-Masons were not content simply to say that secret societies were rather a bad idea. The author of the standard exposition of anti-Masonry declared that Freemasonry was "not only the most abominable but also the most dangerous institution that ever was imposed on man.... It may truly be said to be HELL'S MASTER PIECE."

Fear of a Masonic plot had hardly been quieted when the rumors arose of a Catholic plot against American values. One meets here again the same frame of mind, but a different villain. The anti-Catholic movement converged with a growing nativism, and while they were not identical, together they cut such a wide swath in American life that they were bound to embrace many moderates to whom the paranoid style, in its full glory, did not appeal. Moreover, we need not dismiss out of hand as totally parochial or mean-spirited the desire of Yankee Americans to maintain an ethnically and religiously homogeneous society nor the particular Protestant commitments to individualism and freedom that were brought into play. But the movement had a large paranoid infusion, and the most influential anti-Catholic militants certainly had a strong affinity for the paranoid style. [...]

Anti-Catholicism has always been the pornography of the Puritan. Whereas the anti-Masons had envisaged drinking bouts and had entertained themselves with sado-masochistic fantasies about the actual enforcement of grisly Masonic oaths,* the anti-Catholics invented an immense lore about libertine priests, the confessional as an opportunity for seduction, licentious convents and monasteries. Probably the most widely read contemporary book in the United States before *Uncle Tom's Cabin* was a work supposedly written by one Maria Monk, entitled *Awful Disclosures*, which appeared in 1836. The author, who purported to have escaped from the Hotel Dieu nunnery in Montreal after five years there as novice and nun, reported her

---

* Many anti-Masons had been fascinated by the penalties invoked if Masons failed to live up to their obligations. My own favorite is the oath attributed to a royal archmason who invited "having my skull smote off, and my brains exposed to the scorching rays of the sun."

convent life in elaborate and circumstantial detail. She reported having been told by the Mother Superior that she must "obey the priests in all things"; to her "utter astonishment and horror," she soon found what the nature of such obedience was. Infants born of convent liaisons were baptized and then killed, she said, so that they might ascend at once to heaven. Her book, hotly attacked and defended, continued to be read and believed even after her mother gave testimony that Maria had been somewhat addled ever since childhood after she had rammed a pencil into her head. Maria died in prison in 1849, after having been arrested in a brothel as a pickpocket.

Anti-Catholicism, like anti-Masonry, mixed its fortunes with American party politics, and it became an enduring factor in American politics. The American Protective Association of the 1890s revived it with ideological variations more suitable to the times—the depression of 1893, for example, was alleged to be an intentional creation of the Catholics who began it by starting a run on the banks. Some spokesmen of the movement circulated a bogus encyclical attributed to Leo XIII instructing American Catholics on a certain date in 1893 to exterminate all heretics, and a great many anti-Catholics daily expected a nationwide uprising. The myth of an impending Catholic war of mutilation and extermination of heretics persisted into the twentieth century.

If, after our historically discontinuous examples of the paranoid style, we now take the long jump to the contemporary right wing, we find some rather important differences from the nineteenth-century movements. The spokesmen of those earlier movements felt that they stood for causes and personal types that were still in possession of their country—that they were fending off threats to a still established way of life. But the modern right wing, as Daniel Bell has put it, feels dispossessed: America has been largely taken away from them and their kind, though they are determined to try to repossess it and to prevent the final destructive act of subversion. The old American virtues have already been eaten away by cosmopolitans and intellectuals; the old competitive capitalism has been gradually undermined by socialist and communist schemers; the old national security and independence have been destroyed by treasonous plots, having as their most powerful agents not merely outsiders and foreigners as of old but major statesmen who are at the very centers of American power. Their predecessors had dis-

covered conspiracies; the modern radical right finds conspiracy to be betrayal from on high.

Important changes may also be traced to the effects of the mass media. The villains of the modern right are much more vivid than those of their paranoid predecessors, much better known to the public; the literature of the paranoid style is by the same token richer and more circumstantial in personal description and personal invective. For the vaguely delineated villains of the anti-Masons, for the obscure and disguised Jesuit agents, the little-known papal delegates of the anti-Catholics, for the shadowy international bankers of the monetary conspiracies, we may now substitute eminent public figures like Presidents Roosevelt, Truman, and Eisenhower, Secretaries of State like Marshall, Acheson, and Dulles, Justices of the Supreme Court like Frankfurter and Warren, and the whole battery of lesser but still famous and vivid alleged conspirators headed by Alger Hiss.

Events since 1939 have given the contemporary right-wing paranoid a vast theatre for his imagination, full of rich and proliferating detail, replete with realistic cues and undeniable proofs of the validity of his suspicions. The theatre of action is now the entire world, and he can draw not only on the events of World War II, but also on those of the Korean War and the Cold War. Any historian of warfare knows it is in good part a comedy of errors and a museum of incompetence; but if for every error and every act of incompetence one can substitute an act of treason, many points of fascinating interpretation are open to the paranoid imagination. In the end, the real mystery, for one who reads the primary works of paranoid scholarship, is not how the United States has been brought to its present dangerous position but how it has managed to survive at all.

The basic elements of contemporary right-wing thought can be reduced to three: First, there has been the now-familiar sustained conspiracy, running over more than a generation, and reaching its climax in Roosevelt's New Deal, to undermine free capitalism, to bring the economy under the direction of the federal government, and to pave the way for socialism or communism. A great many right-wingers would agree with Frank Chodorov, the author of *The Income Tax: The Root of All Evil*, that this campaign began with the passage of the income-tax amendment to the Constitution in 1913.

The second contention is that top government officialdom has been so infiltrated by Communists that American policy, at least since the days leading up to Pearl Harbor, has been dominated by men who were shrewdly and consistently selling out American national interests.

Finally, the country is infused with a network of Communist agents, just as in the old days it was infiltrated by Jesuit agents, so that the whole apparatus of education, religion, the press, and the mass media is engaged in a common effort to paralyze the resistance of loyal Americans.

Perhaps the most representative document of the McCarthyist phase was a long indictment of Secretary of State George C. Marshall, delivered in 1951 in the Senate by Senator McCarthy, and later published in a somewhat different form. McCarthy pictured Marshall as the focal figure in a betrayal of American interests stretching in time from the strategic plans for World War II to the formulation of the Marshall Plan. Marshall was associated with practically every American failure or defeat, McCarthy insisted, and none of this was either accident or incompetence. There was a "baffling pattern" of Marshall's interventions in the war, which always conduced to the well-being of the Kremlin. The sharp decline in America's relative strength from 1945 to 1951 did not "just happen"; it was "brought about, step by step, by will and intention," the consequence not of mistakes but of a treasonous conspiracy, "a conspiracy on a scale so immense as to dwarf any previous such venture in the history of man."

Today, the mantle of McCarthy has fallen on a retired candy manufacturer, Robert H. Welch, Jr., who is less strategically placed and has a much smaller but better organized following than the Senator. A few years ago Welch proclaimed that "Communist influences are now in almost complete control of our government"—note the care and scrupulousness of that "almost." He has offered a full scale interpretation of our recent history in which Communists figure at every turn: They started a run on American banks in 1933 that forced their closure; they contrived the recognition of the Soviet Union by the United States in the same year, just in time to save the Soviets from economic collapse; they have stirred up the fuss over segregation in the

Senator Joseph McCarthy and, to his left, Roy Cohn.

South; they have taken over the Supreme Court and made it "one of the most important agencies of Communism."

Close attention to history wins for Mr. Welch an insight into affairs that is given to few of us. "For many reasons and after a lot of study," he wrote some years ago, "I personally believe [John Foster] Dulles to be a Communist agent." The job of Professor Arthur F. Burns as head of Eisenhower's Council of Economic Advisers was "merely a cover-up for Burns's liaison work between Eisenhower and some of his Communist bosses." Eisenhower's brother Milton was "actually [his] superior and boss within the Communist party." As for Eisenhower himself, Welch characterized him, in words that have made the candy manufacturer famous, as "a dedicated, conscious agent of the Communist conspiracy"—a conclusion, he added, "based on an accumulation of detailed evidence so extensive and so palpable that it seems to put this conviction beyond any reasonable doubt."

The paranoid spokesman sees the fate of conspiracy in apocalyptic terms—he traffics in the birth and death of whole worlds, whole political orders, whole systems of human values. He is always manning the barricades of civilization. He constantly lives at a turning point. Like religious millennialists he expresses the anxiety of those who are living through the last days and he is sometimes disposed to set a date for the apocalypse. ("Time is running out," said Welch in 1951. "Evidence is piling up on many sides and from many sources that October 1952 is the fatal month when Stalin will attack.")

As a member of the avant-garde who is capable of perceiving the conspiracy before it is fully obvious to an as yet unaroused public, the paranoid is a militant leader. He does not see social conflict as something to be mediated and compromised, in the manner of the working politician. Since what is at stake is always a conflict between absolute good and absolute evil, what is necessary is not compromise but the will to fight things out to a finish. Since the enemy is thought of as being totally evil and totally unappeasable, he must be totally eliminated—if not from the world, at least from the theatre of operations to which the paranoid directs his attention. This demand for total triumph leads to the formulation of hopelessly unrealistic goals, and since these goals are not even remotely attainable, failure constantly heightens the paranoid's sense of frustration. Even partial success leaves him with the same feeling of powerlessness with which he began, and this in turn only strength-

ens his awareness of the vast and terrifying quality of the enemy he opposes.

This enemy is clearly delineated: he is a perfect model of malice, a kind of amoral superman—sinister, ubiquitous, powerful, cruel, sensual, luxury-loving. Unlike the rest of us, the enemy is not caught in the toils of the vast mechanism of history, himself a victim of his past, his desires, his limitations. He wills, indeed he manufactures, the mechanism of history, or tries to deflect the normal course of history in an evil way. He makes crises, starts runs on banks, causes depressions, manufactures disasters, and then enjoys and profits from the misery he has produced. The paranoid's interpretation of history is distinctly personal: decisive events are not taken as part of the stream of history, but as the consequences of someone's will. Very often the enemy is held to possess some especially effective source of power: he controls the press; he has unlimited funds; he has a new secret for influencing the mind (brainwashing); he has a special technique for seduction (the Catholic confessional).

It is hard to resist the conclusion that this enemy is on many counts a projection of the self; both the ideal and the unacceptable aspects of the self are attributed to him. The enemy may be the cosmopolitan intellectual, but the paranoid will outdo him in the apparatus of scholarship, even of pedantry. Secret organizations set up to combat secret organizations give the same flattery. The Ku Klux Klan imitated Catholicism to the point of donning priestly vestments, developing an elaborate ritual and an equally elaborate hierarchy. The John Birch Society emulates Communist cells and quasi-secret operation through "front" groups, and preaches a ruthless prosecution of the ideological war along lines very similar to those it finds in the Communist enemy. Spokesmen of the various fundamentalist anti-Communist "crusades" openly express their admiration for the dedication and discipline the Communist cause calls forth.

On the other hand, the sexual freedom often attributed to the enemy, his lack of moral inhibition, his possession of especially effective techniques for fulfilling his desires, give exponents of the paranoid style an opportunity to project and express unacknowledgeable aspects of their own psychological concerns. Catholics and Mormons—later, Negroes and Jews—have lent themselves to a preoccupation with illicit sex. Very often the fantasies of true believers reveal strong sado-masochistic outlets, vividly expressed, for example, in the delight of anti-Masons with the cruelty of Masonic punishments.

A special significance attaches to the figure of the renegade from the enemy cause. The anti-Masonic movement seemed at times to be the creation of ex-Masons; certainly the highest significance was attributed to their revelations, and every word they said was believed. Anti-Catholicism used the runaway nun and the apostate priest; the place of ex-Communists in the avant-garde anti-Communist movements of our time is well known. In some part, the special authority accorded the renegade derives from the obsession with secrecy so characteristic of such movements: the renegade is the man or woman who has been in the arcanum, and brings forth with him or her the final verification of suspicions which might otherwise have been doubted by a skeptical world. But I think there is a deeper eschatological significance that attaches to the person of the renegade: in the spiritual wrestling match between good and evil which is the paranoid's archetypal model of the world, the renegade is living proof that all the conversions are not made by the wrong side. He brings with him the promise of redemption and victory.

A final characteristic of the paranoid style is related to the quality of its pedantry. One of the impressive things about paranoid literature is the contrast between its fantasied conclusions and the almost touching concern with factuality it invariably shows. It produces heroic strivings for evidence to prove that the unbelievable is the only thing that can be believed. Of course, there are highbrow, lowbrow, and middlebrow paranoids, as there are likely to be in any political tendency. But respectable paranoid literature not only starts from certain moral commitments that can indeed be justified but also carefully and all but obsessively accumulates "evidence." The difference between this "evidence" and that commonly employed by others is that it seems less a means of entering into normal political controversy than a means of warding off the profane intrusions of the secular political world. The paranoid seems to have little expectation of actually convincing a hostile world, but he can accumulate evidence in order to protect his cherished convictions from it. [...]

The paranoid style is not confined to our own country and time; it is an international phenomenon [...] more or less constantly affecting a modest minority of the population. But certain religious traditions, certain social structures and national inheritances, certain historical catastrophes or frustrations may be conducive to the release of such psychic energies, and to situations in which they can more readily be built into mass movements or political parties. In American experience ethnic and religious conflict have plainly been a major focus for militant and suspicious minds of this sort, but class conflicts also can mobilize such energies. Perhaps the central situation conducive to the diffusion of the paranoid tendency is a confrontation of opposed interests which are (or are felt to be) totally irreconcilable, and thus by nature not susceptible to the normal political processes of bargain and compromise. The situation becomes worse when the representatives of a particular social interest— perhaps because of the very unrealistic and unrealizable nature of its demands—are shut out of the political process. Having no access to political bargaining or the making of decisions, they find their original conception that the world of power is sinister and malicious fully confirmed. They see only the consequences of power—and this through distorting lenses—and have no chance to observe its actual machinery. A distinguished historian has said that one of the most valuable things about history is that it teaches us how things do *not* happen. It is precisely this kind of awareness that the paranoid fails to develop. He has a special resistance of his own, of course, to developing such awareness, but circumstances often deprive him of exposure to events that might enlighten him—and in any case he resists enlightenment.

We are all sufferers from history, but the paranoid is a double sufferer, since he is afflicted not only by the real world, with the rest of us, but by his fantasies as well.

Mississippi: The Fallen Paradise

by Walker Percy

April 1965

little more than one hundred years ago, a Mississippi regiment dressed its ranks and started across a meadow toward Cemetery Ridge, a minor elevation near Gettysburg. There, crouched behind a stone wall, the soldiers of the Army of the Potomac waited and watched with astonishment as the gray-clads advanced as casually as if they were on parade. The Mississippians did not reach the wall. One soldier managed to plant the regimental colors within an arm's length before he fell. The University Grays, a company made up of students from the state university, suffered a loss of precisely one hundred per cent of its members killed or wounded in the charge.

These were good men. It was an honorable fight and there were honorable men on both sides of it. The issue was settled once and for all, perhaps by this very charge. The honorable men on the losing side, men like General Lee, accepted the verdict.

One hundred years later, Mississippians were making history of a different sort. If their record in Lee's army is unsurpassed for valor and devotion to duty, present-day Mississippi is mainly renowned for murder, church-burning, dynamiting, assassination, night-riding, not to mention the lesser forms of terrorism. The students of the university celebrated the Centennial by a different sort of warfare and in the company of a different sort of General. It is not frivolous to compare the characters of General Edwin Walker and General Lee, for the contrast is symptomatic of a broader change in leadership in this part of the South. In any event, the major claim to fame of the present-day university is the Ole Miss football team and the assault of the student body upon the person of one man, an assault of bullying, spitting, and obscenities. The bravest Mississippians in recent years have not been Confederates or the sons of Confederates but rather two Negroes, James Meredith and Medgar Evers. [...]

No ex-Mississippian is entitled to write of the tragedy which has overtaken his former state with any sense of moral superiority. For he cannot be certain in the first place that if he had stayed he would not have kept silent—or worse. And he strongly suspects that he would not have been counted among the handful, an editor here, a professor there, a clergyman yonder, who not only did not keep silent but fought hard.

What happened to this state? Assuredly it faced difficult times after the Supreme Court decision of 1954 and subsequent court injunctions which required painful changes in customs of long standing. Yet the change has been made peacefully in other states of the South. In Georgia over 39 per cent of Negroes of voting age are registered to vote. In Mississippi the figure is around 6 per cent.

What happened is both obvious and obscure. What is obvious is that Mississippi is poor, largely rural, and has in proportion the largest Negro minority in the United States. But Georgia shares these traits. Nor is it enough to say that Mississippi is the state that refused to change, although this is what one hears both inside and outside the state. On the contrary, Mississippi has changed several times since the Civil War. [...]

Two significant changes have occurred in the past generation. The most spectacular is the total defeat of the old-style white moderate and the consequent collapse of the alliance between the "good" white man and the Negro, which has figured more or less prominently in Mississippi politics since Reconstruction days. Except for an oasis or two like Greenville, the influential white moderate is gone. To use Faulkner's *personae*, the Gavin Stevenses have disappeared and the Snopeses have won. What is more, the Snopeses' victory has surpassed even the gloomiest expectations of their creator. What happened to men like Gavin Stevens? With a few exceptions, they have shut up or been exiled or they are running the local White Citizens' Council. Not even Faulkner foresaw the ironic denouement of the tragedy: that the Compsons and Sartorises should not

beach for a dip. I would be dressed, the salt and sun showered off me, and my hair parted and slicked down. There was a roughened iron rail that ran the length of the boardwalk, and I sat on the edge of it and watched him down below as he stepped into the water.

He entered slowly, lingering a long while with the water licking up at his knees. Then he would make a cup with his hands and in the thin after-supper dimness he would pour the water on his face and down the back of his neck. All my ideas of how difficult it was to be a man, to work and support a family, seem to me to have come not so much from being told about the difficulties, as from observing the kinds of relaxation the difficulties led you into: as for work, it made you want to pour a handful of cool water on your face and neck, it made such a simple thing a pleasure. I could tell that by the way he rubbed the water on his arms and massaged it into his shoulders. He would take so much time just getting *ready* to enter the water that I knew a lot of policies must have lapsed or almost lapsed that day. I had no clear idea, however, of how he prevented them from lapsing, of what exactly he did. What did he do during the day? and when we were away, what did he do at night? Who did he listen to the radio with? He missed us—I was sure of that—and though he would never indulge his loneliness, it must have pleased him when the day's temperature and humidity became so unbearable that he felt justified in fleeing the city for the night. He paid, most of the time, however, in money and loneliness for our comfort. The heat in the summer was the enemy of women and children—*we* had to be saved from it. . . . Finally I would watch him lower himself into the water to swim, and then to turn over and float on his back. Behind us the sun was perfect and red, and when its light broke out on the water I knew I was seeing something beautiful. My father floated so still—he worked so hard—and then he came in and was glowing, like the sea, from those last pure spikes of light.

When we got back I sat at the dining-room table drinking a glass of milk while my mother served his dinner; the other tables in the big dining-room were empty, most people having eaten hours before. In a way it was like *our* dining-room again. I sat and listened. In Newark you can't breathe, I learned once more, and what's worse, there're fifteen new cases of polio. In an instant I would check myself: sore throat? headache? nausea? stiff neck? If we continued coming to the shore every summer, I was pretty sure I would make it through childhood without getting it. . . . When the

meal ended, my father would try to convince my mother to leave the dishes in the sink, unwashed, and come for a walk; and when she was willing to do that, I knew how lonely *she* had been. So we would go out to the boardwalk, where the old grandparents would be seated on the green benches on either side, and where there would be other wives walking with other husbands, and all of them telling each other how awful it was in the city and how the Newark *News* said there was no end in sight. No end in sight! How marvelous for us women and children.

The end, when it did come, didn't come suddenly. Many times during those last few teenage summers I realized my vacations at Bradley were almost over. All I had to do, really, was look about the beach and note the absence of some of the old familiar faces. Where, for instance, were "the older guys"? Where was Mutzie Leibowitz of Irvington, Warren Gottlieb of Rahway, Morty Shuster of Teaneck? I asked someone. "Where's Morty Shuster from Teaneck?" The answer nearly knocked me over. Morty Shuster was in the trucking business. I couldn't believe it. Morty Shuster *owned* trucks. Morty Shuster, who on the beach and the boards I'd seen engaged in the very activities I myself was to engage in four years later, Morty Shuster was in business and married *and* had a baby on the way. No longer, I realized, would his years run from September to June—no longer would June be the end for him and summer Time Out. Poor Morty, I knew he must be surprised. For I was sure that Morty had believed as I did: that summer was What's Coming to You. "What are you doing next summer?" "Where are we going to stay next summer?" Autumn after autumn, grade school teachers would resume the inquisition: what did *you* do last summer? They knew it too, summer was for doing *different* things. But, God, in the trucking business...and with a wife and child, one summer would be like the last. Summer, in fact, would be like winter. No longer would it be the season to carve notches in. Probably there would be other ways to keep track of time's passage, but who could tell what they would be like. Years would begin to march endlessly by, with no Time Outs, endlessly until the end.

It was, truly, a frightening thought, for it carried with it rumors of my own mortality, and I remember that upon hearing of Morty's fate I swore that I would never get stuck in the trucking business. As it happens, I have managed to avoid that particular fate—and yet it also happens, that like Morty Shuster of Teaneck, all I have left of those summers at Bradley is what I can remember of them.

only be defeated by the Snopeses but that in the end they should join them.

Faulkner lived to see the defeat of his Gavin Stevens—the old-style good man, the humanist from Harvard and Heidelberg—but he still did not despair because he had placed his best hope in the youth of the state. Chick Mallison in *Intruder in the Dust*, a sort of latter-day Huck Finn, actually got the Negro Lucas Beauchamp out of jail while Gavin Stevens was talking about the old alliance. But this hope has been blasted, too. The melancholy fact is the Chick Mallisons today are apt to be the worst lot of all. Ten years of indoctrination by the Citizens' Councils, racist politicians, and the most one-sided press north of Cuba has produced a generation of good-looking and ferocious young bigots.

The other change has been the emigration of the Negro from Mississippi, reducing the Negro majority to a minority for the first time in a hundred years. At the same time great numbers of Negroes from the entire South were settling in Northern ghettos. The chief consequence has been the failure of the great cities of the North to deal with the Negro when he landed on their doorstep, or rather next door. Mississippi has not got any better, but New York and Boston and Los Angeles have got worse.

Meanwhile there occurred the Negro revolution, and the battle lines changed. For the first time in a hundred and fifty years, the old sectional division has been blurred. It is no longer "North" versus "South" in the argument over the Negro. Instead there has occurred a diffusion of the Negro and a dilution of the problem, with large sections of the South at least tolerating a degree of social change at the very time Northern cities were beginning to grumble seriously. It seems fair to describe the present national mood as a grudging inclination to redress the Negro's grievances—with the exception of a few areas of outright defiance like north Louisiana, parts of Alabama, and the state of Mississippi.

It is only within the context of these social changes, I believe, that the state can be understood and perhaps some light shed upon a possible way out. For, unfavorable as these events may be, they are nevertheless ambiguous in their implication. The passing of the moderate and the victory of the Snopeses may be bad things in themselves. Yet history being the queer business that it is, such a turn of events may be the very condition of the state's emergence from its long nightmare.

During the past ten years Mississippi as a society reached a condition which can only be described, in an analogous but exact sense of the word, as insane. The rift in its character between a genuine kindliness and a highly developed individual moral consciousness on the one hand, and on the other a purely political and amoral view of "states' rights" at the expense of human rights led at last to a sundering of its very soul. Kind fathers and loving husbands, when they did not themselves commit crimes against the helpless, looked upon such crimes with indifference. Political campaigns, once the noblest public activity in the South, came to be conducted by incantation. The candidate who hollers nigger loudest and longest usually wins.

The language itself has been corrupted. In the Mississippi standard version of what happened, noble old English words are used, words like *freedom, sacredness of the individual, death to tyranny,* but they have subtly changed their referents. After the Oxford riot in 1962, the Junior Chamber of Commerce published a brochure entitled *A Warning for Americans,* which was widely distributed and is still to be found on restaurant counters in Jackson along with the usual racist tracts, mammy dolls, and Confederate flags. The pamphlet purports to prove that James Meredith was railroaded into Ole Miss by the Kennedys in defiance of "normal judicial processes"—a remarkable thesis in itself considering that the Meredith case received one of the most exhaustive judicial reviews in recent history. The "warning" for Americans was the usual contention that states' rights were being trampled by federal tyranny. "Tyranny is tyranny," reads the pamphlet. "It is the duty of every American to be alert when his freedom is endangered."

Lest the reader be complacent about Mississippi as the only state of double-think, the pamphlet was judged by the *national* Jay Cees to be the "second most worthy project of the year."

All statements become equally true and equally false, depending on one's rhetorical posture. In the end even the rhetoric fails to arouse. When Senator Eastland declares, "There is no discrimination in Mississippi," and, "All who are qualified to vote, black or white, exercise the right of suffrage," these utterances are received by friend and foe alike with a certain torpor of spirit. It does not matter that there is very little connection between Senator Eastland's utterances and the voting statistics of his home county: that of a population of 31,020 Negroes, 161 are registered to vote. Once the final break is made between language and reality, arguments generate their own force and lay out their own logical rules. The current syllogism goes something like this: (1) There is no ill-feeling in Mississippi between the races; the Negroes like things the way they are; if you don't believe it, I'll call my cook out of the kitchen and you can ask her. (2) The trouble is caused by outside agitators who are communist-inspired. (3) Therefore, the real issue is between atheistic communism and patriotic God-fearing Mississippians.

Once such a system cuts the outside wires and begins to rely on its own feedback, anything becomes possible. The dimensions of the tragedy are hard to exaggerate. The sad and still incredible fact is that many otherwise decent people, perhaps even the majority of the white people in Mississippi, honestly believed that President John F. Kennedy was an enemy of the United States, if not a communist fellow-traveler.

How did it happen that a proud and decent people, a Protestant and Anglo-Saxon people with a noble tradition of freedom behind them, should have in the end become so deluded that it is difficult even to discuss the issues with them because the common words of the language no longer carry the same meanings? How can responsible leadership have failed so completely when it did not fail in Georgia, a state with a similar social and ethnic structure?

The answer is far from clear, but several reasons suggest themselves. For one thing, as James Dabbs points out in his recent book *Who Speaks for the South?*, Mississippi was part of the wild west of the Old South. Unlike the seaboard states, it missed the liberal eighteenth century altogether. Its tradition is closer to Dodge City than to Williamsburg. For another, the Populism of the eastern South never amounted to much here; it was corrupted from the beginning by the demagogic racism of Vardaman and Bilbo. Nor did Mississippi have its big city which might have shared, for good and ill, in the currents of American urban life. Georgia had its Atlanta and Atlanta had the good luck or good sense to put men like Ralph McGill and Mayor Hartsfield in key positions. What was lacking in Mississippi was the new source of responsible leadership, the political realists of the matured city. The old moderate tradition of the planter-lawyer-statesman class had long since lost its influence. The young industrial interests have been remarkable chiefly for their discretion. When, for example, they did awake to the folly of former Governor Barnett's two-bit rebellion, it was too late. And so there was no one to head off the collision

between the civil-rights movement and the racist coalition between redneck, demagogue, and small-town merchant. The result was insurrection.

The major source of racial moderation in Mississippi even until recent times has been, not Populism, but the white conservative tradition with its peculiar strengths and, as it turned out, its fatal weakness. There came into being after Reconstruction an extraordinary alliance, which persisted more or less fitfully until the last world war, between the Negro and the white conservative, an alliance originally directed against the poor whites and the Radical Republicans. The fruits of this "fusion principle," as it is called, are surprising. Contrary to the current mythology of the Citizens' Councils, which depicts white Mississippians throwing out the carpetbaggers and Negroes and establishing our present "way of life" at the end of Reconstruction, the fact is that Negroes enjoyed considerably more freedom in the 1880s than they do now. A traveler in Mississippi after Reconstruction reported seeing whites and Negroes served in the same restaurants and at the same bars in Jackson.

This is not to say that there ever existed a golden age of race relations. But there were bright spots. It is true that the toleration of the Old Captains, as W. J. Cash called them, was both politically motivated and paternalistic, but it is not necessarily a derogation to say so. A man is a creature of his time—after all, Lincoln was a segregationist—and the old way produced some extraordinary men. There were many felicities in their relation with the Negro—it was not all Uncle Tomism, though it is unfashionable to say so. In any case they lost; segregation was firmly established around 1890 and lynch law became widespread. For the next fifty years the state was dominated, with a few notable exceptions, by a corrupt Populism.

What is important to notice here is the nature of the traditional alliance between the white moderate and the Negro, and especially the ideological basis of the former's moderation, because this spirit has informed the ideal of race relations for at least a hundred years. For, whatever its virtues, the old alliance did not begin to have the resources to cope with the revolutionary currents of this century. Indeed the world view of the old-style "good" man is almost wholly irrelevant to the present gut issue between the Negro revolt and the Snopes counterrevolution.

For one thing, the old creed was never really social or political but purely and simply moral in the Stoic sense: if

Bob Adelman

you are a good man, then you will be magnanimous toward other men and especially toward the helpless and therefore especially toward the Negro. The Stoic creed worked very well—if you were magnanimous. But if one planter was just, the next might charge 80 per cent interest at the plantation store, the next take the wife of his tenant, the next lease convict labor, which was better than the sharecropper system because it did not matter how hard you worked your help or how many died.

Once again in recent years dissent became possible. During the depression of the 'thirties and afterward there were stirrings of liberal currents not only in the enthusiasm for the economic legislation of the Roosevelt Administration but also in a new awareness of the plight of the Negro. Mississippi desperately needed the New Deal and profited enormously from it. Indeed, the Roosevelt farm program succeeded too well. Planters who were going broke on ten cent cotton voted for Roosevelt, took federal money, got rich, lived to hate Kennedy and Johnson and vote for Goldwater—while still taking federal money. Yet there was something new in the wind after the war. Under the leader-

ship of men like Hodding Carter in the Delta, a new form of racial moderation began to gather strength. Frank Smith, author of the book *Congressman from Mississippi*, was elected to Congress. Described by Edward Morgan as "a breath of fresh air out of a political swamp," Smith was one of the few politicians in recent years who tried to change the old racial refrain and face up to the real problems of the state. But he made the mistake of voting for such radical measures as the Peace Corps and the United Nations appropriation, and he did not conceal his friendship with President Kennedy. What was worse, he addressed mail to his constituents with a Mr. and Mrs., even when they were Negroes. Smith was euchred out of his district by the legislature and defeated in 1962 by the usual coalition of peckerwoods, super-patriots, and the Citizens' Councils.

But the most radical change has occurred in the past few years. As recently as fifteen years ago, the confrontation was still a three-cornered one, among the good white man, the bad white man, and the Negro. The issue was whether to treat the Negro well or badly. It went without saying that you could do either. Now one of the parties has been eliminated and the confrontation is face to face. "I assert my right to vote and to raise my family decently," the Negro is beginning to say. His enemies reply with equal simplicity: "We'll kill you first."

Yet the victory of the Snopeses is not altogether a bad thing. At least the choice is clarified. It would not help much now to have Gavin Stevens around with his talk about "man's struggle to the stars."

The old way is still seductive, however, and evokes responses from strange quarters. Ex-Governor Ross Barnett was recently revealed as mellow emeritus statesman in the old style, even hearkening to the antique summons of noblesse oblige. A newspaper interview reported that the Governor was a soft touch for any Negro who waylaid him in the corridor with a "Cap'n, I could sho use a dollar." The Governor, it was also reported, liked to go hunting with a Negro friend. "We laugh and joke," the Governor reminisced, "and he gets a big kick out of it when I call him Professor. There's a lot in our relationship I can't explain." No doubt, mused the interviewer, the Governor would get up at all hours of the night to get Ol' Jim out of jail. It is hard to imagine what Gavin Stevens would make of this new version of the old alliance. Unquestionably something new has been added. When Marse Ross dons the mantle of Marse Robert, Southern history has entered upon a new age. And perhaps it is just as well. Let Governor Barnett become the new squire. It simplifies matters further.

Though Faulkner liked to use such words as "cursed" and "doomed" in speaking of his region, it is questionable that Mississippians are very different from other Americans. It is increasingly less certain that Minnesotans would have performed better under the circumstances. There is, however, one peculiar social dimension wherein the state does truly differ. It has to do with the distribution, as Mississippians see it, of what is public and what is private. More precisely it is the absence of a truly public zone, as the word is understood in most places. One has to live in Mississippi to appreciate it. No doubt it is the mark of an almost homogeneous white population, a Protestant Anglo-Saxon minority (until recently), sharing a common tragic past and bound together by kinship bonds. This society was not only felicitous in many ways; it also commanded the allegiance of Southern intellectuals on other grounds. Faulkner saw it as the chief bulwark against the "coastal spew of Europe" and "the rootless ephemeral cities of the North." In any case, the almost

familial ambit of this society came to coincide with the actual public space which it inhabited. The Negro was either excluded, shoved off into Happy Hollow, or admitted to the society on its own terms as good old Uncle Ned. No allowance was made—it would have been surprising if there had been—for a truly public sector, unlovely as you please and defused of emotional charges, where black and white might pass without troubling each other. The whole of the Delta, indeed of white Mississippi, is one big kinship lodge. You have only to walk into a restaurant or a bus station to catch a whiff of it. There is a sudden kindling of amiability, even between strangers. The salutations, "What you say now?" and "Yall be good," are exchanged like fraternal signs. The presence of fraternity and sorority houses at Ole Miss always seemed oddly superfluous.

One consequence of this peculiar social structure has been a chronic misunderstanding between the state and the rest of the country. The state feels that unspeakable demands are being made upon it while the nation is bewildered by the response of rage to what seem to be the ordinary and minimal requirements of the law. Recall, for example, President Kennedy's gentle appeal to the university the night of the riot when he invoked the tradition of L.Q.C. Lamar and asked the students to do their duty even as he was doing his. He had got his facts straight about the tradition of valor in Mississippi. But unfortunately, the Kennedys had no notion of the social and semantic rules they were up against. When they entered into negotiations with the Governor to get Meredith on the campus, they proceeded on the reasonable assumption that even in the arena of political give and take—i.e., deals—words bear some relation to their referents. Such was not the case. Governor Barnett did not double-cross the Kennedys in the usual sense. The double cross, like untruth, bears a certain relation to the truth. More serious, however, was the cultural confusion over the word "public." Ole Miss is not, or was not, a public school as the word is usually understood. In Mississippi as in England a public school means a private school. When Meredith finally did walk the paths at Ole Miss, his fellow students cursed and reviled him. But they also wept with genuine grief. It was as if he had been quartered in their living room.

It is this hypertrophy of pleasant familial space at the expense of a truly public sector which accounts for the extraordinary apposition in Mississippi of kindliness and unspeakable violence. Recently a tourist wrote the editor of the Philadelphia, Mississippi, newspaper that, although he expected the worst when he passed through the town, he found the folks in Philadelphia as nice as they could be. No doubt it is true. The Philadelphia the tourist saw is as pleasant as he said. It is like one big front porch.

How can peace be restored to Mississippi? One would like to be able to say that the hope lies in putting into practice the Judeo-Christian ethic. In the end, no doubt, it does. But the trouble is that Christendom of a sort has already won in Mississippi. There is more church news in the Jackson papers than news about the Ole Miss football team. Political cartoons defend God against the Supreme Court. On the outskirts of Meridian a road sign announces: "The Largest Percentage of Churchgoers in the World." It is a religion, however, which tends to canonize the existing social and political structure and to brand as atheistic any threat of change. "The trouble is they took God out of everything," said W. Arsene Dick of Summit, Mississippi, founder of Americans for the Preservation of the White Race. A notable exception to the general irrelevance of religion to social issues is the recent action of Millsaps College, a Methodist institution in Jackson, which voluntarily opened its doors to Negroes.

It seems more likely that progress will come about—as indeed it is already coming about—not through the impact of the churches upon churchgoers but because after a while the ordinary citizen gets sick and tired of the climate of violence and of the odor of disgrace which hangs over his region. Money has a good deal to do with it too; money, urbanization, and the growing concern of politicians and the business community with such things as public images. Governor Johnson occasionally talks sense. Last year the Mayor and the business leaders of Jackson defied the Citizens' Councils and supported the token desegregation of the schools. It could even happen that Governor Johnson, the man who campaigned up and down the state with the joke about what NAACP means (niggers, alligators, apes, coons, possums), may turn out to be the first Governor to enforce the law. For law enforcement, it is becoming increasingly obvious, is the condition of peace. It is also becoming more likely every day that federal intervention, perhaps in the form of local commissioners, may be required in places like Neshoba County where the Ku Klux Klan is in control and law enforcement is a shambles. Faulkner at last changed his mind about the durability of the old alliance and came to

prefer even enforced change to a state run by the Citizens' Councils and the Klan. Mississippians, he wrote, will not accept change until they have to. Then perhaps they will at last come to themselves: "Why didn't someone tell us this before? Tell us this in time?"

Much will depend on the residue of good will in the state. There are some slight signs of the long overdue revolt of the ordinary prudent man. There must be a good many of this silent breed. Hazel Brannon Smith, who won a Pulitzer Prize as editor of the Lexington *Advertiser*, recently reported that in spite of all the abuse and the boycotts, the circulation of the paper continues to rise. The Mississippi Economic Council, the state's leading businessmen's group, has issued a statement urging compliance with the Civil Rights Act and demanding that registration and voting laws be "fairly and impartially administered for all."

It is not difficult to make a long-range prophecy about the future of the state. The short-term outlook is certainly dark. Most thoughtful Mississippians agree that things are going to get worse before they get better. The vote in the national election, with its bizarre seven-to-one margin in favor of Senator Goldwater, attests to the undiminished obsession with race. It would not have mattered if Senator Goldwater had advocated the collectivization of the plantations and open saloons in Jackson; he voted against the Civil Rights Bill and that was that. Yet there is little doubt that Mississippi is even now beginning to feel its way to what might be called the American Settlement of the racial issue, a somewhat ambiguous state of affairs which is less a solution than a more or less tolerable impasse. There has come into being a whole literature devoted to an assault upon the urban life wherein this settlement is arrived at, and a complete glossary of terms, such as alienation, depersonalization, and mass man. But in the light of recent history in Mississippi, the depersonalized American neighborhood looks more and more tolerable. A giant supermarket or eighty thousand people watching a pro ball game may not be the most creative of cultural institutions, but at least they offer a *modus vivendi*. People generally leave each other alone.

A Southerner may still hope that some day the Southern temper, black and white, may yet prove to be the sociable yeast to leaven the American lump. Meanwhile he'll settle for the Yankee *pax* and be glad of it. I believe a Negro has as much right to be alienated as anyone else. It is at least a place to start.

Long View: Negro

by Langston Hughes

April 1965

100 years—Emancipation:
Sighted through the
Telescope of dreams
The end result looms larger,
So much larger, so it seems,
Than truth can be.

But turn it around,
Look through the larger end—
And wonder why
What is so large
Becomes so small again.

THE CELEBRATION

BY JAMES DICKEY

JUNE 1965

All wheels; a man breathed fire,
Exhaling like a blowtorch down the road
And burnt the stripper's gown
Above her moving-barely feet.
A condemned train climbed from the earth
Up stilted nightlights zooming in a track.
I ambled along in that crowd

Between the gambling wheels
At carnival time with the others
Where the Dodgem cars shuddered, sparking
On grillwire, each in his vehicle half
In control, half helplessly power-mad
As he was in the traffic that brought him.
No one blazed at me; then I saw

My mother and my father, he leaning
On a dog-chewed cane, she wrapped to the nose
In the fur of exhausted weasels.
I believed them buried miles back
In the country, in the faint sleep
Of the old, and had not thought to be
On this of all nights compelled

To follow where they led, not losing
Sight, with my heart enlarging whenever
I saw his crippled Stetson bob, saw her
With the teddy bear won on the waning
Whip of his right arm. They laughed;
She clung to him; then suddenly
The Wheel of wheels was turning

The colored night around.
They climbed aboard. My God, they rose
Above me, stopped themselves and swayed
Fifty feet up; he pointed
With his toothed cane, and took in
The whole Midway till they dropped,
Came down, went from me, came and went

Faster and faster, going up backward,
Cresting, out-topping, falling roundly.
From the crowd I watched them,
Their gold teeth flashing,
Until my eyes blurred with their riding
Lights, and I turned from the standing
To the moving mob, and went on:

Stepped upon sparking shocks
Of recognition when I saw my feet
Among the others, knowing them given,
Understanding the whirling impulse
From which I had been born,
The great gift of shaken lights,
The being wholly lifted with another,

All this having all and nothing
To do with me. Believers, I have seen
The wheel in the middle of the air
Where old age rises and laughs,
And on Lakewood Midway became
In five strides a kind of loving,
A mortal, a dutiful son.

History by the Ounce

by Barbara W. Tuchman

July 1965

At a party given for its reopening last year, the Museum of Modern Art in New York served champagne to five thousand guests. An alert reporter for the *Times*, Charlotte Curtis, noted that there were eighty cases which, she informed her readers, amounted to 960 bottles or 7,680 three-ounce drinks. Somehow through this detail the Museum's party at once becomes alive; a fashionable New York occasion. One sees the crush, the women eyeing each other's clothes, the exchange of greetings, and feels the gratifying sense of elegance and importance imparted by champagne—even if, at one and a half drinks per person, it was not on an exactly riotous scale. All this is conveyed by Miss Curtis' detail. It is, I think, the way history as well as journalism should be written. It is what Pooh-Bah, in *The Mikado,* meant when, telling how the victim's head stood on its neck and bowed three times to him at the execution of Nanki-poo, he added that this was "corroborative detail intended to give artistic verisimilitude to an otherwise bald and unconvincing narrative." Not that Miss Curtis' narrative was either bald or unconvincing; on the contrary, it was precise, factual, and a model in every way. But what made it excel, made it vivid and memorable, was her use of corroborative detail.

Pooh-Bah's statement of the case establishes him in my estimate as a major historian or, at least, as the formulator of a major principle of historiography. True, he invented his corroborative detail, which is cheating if you are a historian and fiction if you are not; nevertheless what counts is his recognition of its importance. He knew that it supplies verisimilitude, that without it a narrative is bald and unconvincing. Neither he nor I, of course, discovered the principle; historians have for long made use of it beginning with Thucydides, who insisted on details of topography, "the appearance of cities and localities, the description of rivers and harbors, the peculiar features of seas and countries and their relative distances." I know exactly what he means by that reference to relative distances; it was the need to acquire a feel of them that led me to drive through Belgium and northern France before attempting to write about battles that took place there.

Corroborative detail is the great corrective. Without it historical narrative and interpretation, both, may slip easily into the invalid. It is a disciplinarian. It forces the historian who uses and respects it to cleave to the truth, or as much as he can find out of the truth. It keeps him from soaring off the ground into theories of his own invention. On those Toynbeean heights the air is stimulating and the view is vast but people and houses down below are too small to be seen. However persuaded the historian may be of the validity of the theories he conceives, if they are not supported and illustrated by corroborative detail they are of no more value as history than Pooh-Bah's report of the imagined execution.

It is wiser, I believe, to arrive at theory by way of the evidence rather than the other way around, like Hegel and all the later Hegels; it saves one from being waylaid by that masked highwayman, the categorical imperative. It is more rewarding, in any case, to assemble the facts first and, in the process of arranging them in narrative form, to discover a theory or a historical generalization emerging of its own accord. This to me is the excitement, the built-in treasure hunt, of writing history. In the book I am working on now, which deals with the twenty-year period before 1914 (and the reader must forgive me if all my examples are drawn from my own work but that, after all, is the thing one knows best), I have been writing about a moment during the Dreyfus Affair in France when on the day of the reopening of Parliament, everyone expected the Army to attempt a coup d'etat. English observers predicted it, troops were brought into the capital, the Royalist pretender was summoned to the frontier, mobs hooted and rioted in the streets, but when the day had passed, nothing had happened; the Republic still stood. By this time I had assembled so much corroborative detail pointing to a coup d'etat that I had to explain why it had not occurred. Suddenly I had to stop and think. After a while I found myself writing, "The Right lacked that necessary chemical of a coup—a leader. It had its small, if loud, fanatics but to upset the established government in a democratic country requires either foreign help or the stuff of a dictator." That is a historical generalization, I believe; a modest one to be sure, but my size. I had arrived at it out of the necessity of the material and felt immensely pleased and proud. These moments do not occur every day; sometimes no more than one a chapter, if that, but when they do they leave one with a lovely sense of achievement.

I am a disciple of the ounce because I mistrust history in gallon jugs whose purveyors are more concerned with establishing the meaning and purpose of history than with what happened. Is it necessary to insist on a purpose? No one asks the novelist why he writes novels or the poet what is his purpose in writing poems. The lilies of the field, as I remember, were not required to have a demonstrable purpose. Why cannot history be studied and written and read for its own sake, as the record of human behavior, the most fascinating subject of all? Insistence on a purpose turns the historian into a prophet—and that is another profession.

To return to my own: corroborative detail will not produce a generalization every time but it will often reveal a historical truth, besides keeping one grounded in historical reality. When I was investigating General Mercier, the Minister of War who was responsible for the original condemnation of Dreyfus and who in the course of the Affair became the hero of the Right, I discovered that at parties of the *haut monde* ladies rose to their feet when General Mercier entered the room. That is the kind of detail which to me is worth a week of research. It illustrates the society, the people, the state of feeling at the time more vividly than anything I could write and in shorter space, too, which is an additional advantage. It epitomizes, it crystallizes, it visualizes. The reader can see it; moreover it sticks in his mind; it is memorable. [...]

The absence of corroborative detail when one is looking for it can be very irritating. Describing William Howard Taft, Governor General of the Philippines at that time, I did not want merely to write that he was a very large, very fat man, a general statement which could apply to any oversize person. I wanted to be able to write specifically that he was six foot so-many inches tall and weighed 280 or 290—or whatever it was—pounds. Stated in figures a weight becomes vis-

ible and besides would give more impact to the story about Taft's telegram to Elihu Root after an illness, saying that he had been out horseback riding and was feeling fine, to which Root wired back, "How is the horse feeling?" Nowhere, however, in Taft's biography, a large two-volume work by Henry Pringle, who won the Pulitzer Prize for his life of Theodore Roosevelt, could I find any statement of Taft's weight. It may appear that I am making a fuss here over nothing but the point is that a weight of over 300 pounds (a figure that I found eventually in a magazine article after a prolonged hunt) is surely a major factor in a man's life, affecting his character, prospects, health, career, and personal relations. It is a fact which, it seems to me, a reader has a right to know.

Failing to know such details, one can be led astray. In 1890 Congress authorized the building of the first three American battleships, and, two years later, a fourth. Shortly thereafter, in 1895, this country plunged into a major quarrel with Great Britain, known as the Venezuelan crisis, in which there was much shaking of fists and chauvinist shrieking for war. Three years later we were at war with Spain. She was no longer a naval power equal to Britain, of course, but still not negligible. One would like to know what exactly was American naval strength at the time of both these crises. How many, if any, of the battleships authorized in 1890 were actually at sea five years later? When the jingoes were howling for war in 1895, what ships did we have to protect our coasts, much less to take the offensive? It seemed to me this was a piece of information worth knowing.

To my astonishment, on looking for the answer in textbooks on the period, I could not find it. The historians of America's rise to world power, of the era of expansion, of American foreign policy, or even of the Navy have not concerned themselves with what evidently seems to them an irrelevant detail. It was hardly irrelevant to policy makers of the time who bore the responsibility for decisions of peace or war. Text after text in American history is published every year, each repeating on this question more or less what his predecessor has said before, with no further enlightenment. To find the facts I finally had to write to the Director of Naval History at the Navy Department in Washington.

My point is not how many battleships we had on hand in 1895 and '98 (which I now know) but why this hard, physical fact was missing from the professional historians' treatment. "Bald and unconvincing," said Pooh-Bah of narrative without fact, a judgment in which I join.

When I come across a generalization or a general statement in history unsupported by illustration I am instantly on guard; my reaction is, "Show me." If a historian writes that it was raining heavily on the day war was declared, that is a detail corroborating a statement, let us say, that the day was gloomy. But if he writes merely that it was a gloomy day without mentioning the rain, I want to know what is his evidence: what made it gloomy. Or if he writes, "The population was in a belligerent mood," or, "It was a period of great anxiety," he is indulging in general statements which carry no conviction to me if they are not illustrated by some evidence. [. . .]

Even if corroborative detail did not serve a valid historical purpose, its use makes a narrative more graphic and intelligible, more pleasurable to read, in short more readable. It assists communication, and communication is after all the major purpose. History written in abstract terms communicates nothing to me. I cannot comprehend the abstract and, since a writer tends to create the reader in his own image, I assume my reader cannot comprehend it either. No doubt I underestimate him. Certainly many serious thinkers write in the abstract and many people read them with interest and profit and even, I suppose, pleasure. I respect this ability but I am unable to emulate it.

My favorite visible detail in *The Guns of August,* for some inexplicable reason, is the one about the Grand Duke Nicholas who was so tall (six foot six) that when he established headquarters in a railroad car his aide pinned up a fringe of white paper over the doorway to remind him to duck his head. Why this insignificant item, after several years' work and out of all the material crammed into a book of 450 pages, should be the particular one to stick most sharply in my mind I cannot explain, but it is. I was so charmed by the white paper fringe that I constructed a whole paragraph describing Russian headquarters at Baranovici in order to slip it in logically.

In another case the process failed. I had read that the Kaiser's birthday gift to his wife was the same every year: twelve hats selected by himself which she was obliged to wear. There you see the value of corroborative detail in revealing personality; this one is worth a whole book about the Kaiser—or even about Germany. It represents, however, a minor tragedy of *The Guns,* for I never succeeded in working it in at all. I keep my notes on cards and the card about the hats started out with those for the first chapter. Not having been used, it was moved forward to a likely place in Chapter 2, missed again, and continued on down through all the chapters until it emerged to a final resting place in a packet marked "Unused."

A detail about General Haig, equally revealing of personality or at any rate of contemporary customs and conditions in the British officer corps, did find a place. This was the fact that during the campaign in the Sudan in the 'nineties he had "a camel laden with claret" in the personal pack train that followed him across the desert. Besides being a vivid bit of social history the phrase itself, "a camel laden with claret," is a thing of beauty, a marvel of double and inner alliteration. That, however, brings up another whole subject, the subject of language, which needs an article of its own for adequate discussion.

Having inadvertently reached it, I will only mention that the independent power of words to affect the writing of history is

William Howard Taft

a thing to be watched out for. They have an almost frightening autonomous power to produce in the mind of the reader an image or idea that was not in the mind of the writer. Obviously, they operate this way in all forms of writing but history is particularly sensitive because one has a duty to be accurate, and careless use of words can leave a false impression one had not intended. Fifty per cent at least of the critics of *The Guns* commented on what they said was my exposé of the stupidity of the generals. Nothing of the kind was in my mind when I wrote. What I meant to convey was that the generals were in the trap of the circumstances, training, ideas, and national impulses of their time and their individual countries; that there but for the grace of God go we. I was not trying to convey stupidity but tragedy, fatality. Many reviewers understood this, clearly intelligent perceptive persons (those who understand one always are), but too many kept coming up with that word "stupidity" to my increasing dismay.

This power of words to escape from a writer's control is a fascinating problem which, since it was not what I started out to discuss, I can only hint at here. One more hint before I leave it: for me the problem lies in the fact that the art of writing interests me as much as the art of history (and I hope it is not provocative to say that I think of history as an art, not a science). In writing I am seduced by the sound of words and by the interaction of their sound and sense. Recently, at the start of a paragraph I wrote, "Then occurred the intervention which irretrievably bent the twig of events." It was intended as a kind of signal to the reader. (Every now and then, in a historical narrative after one has been explaining a rather complicated background, one feels the need of waving a small red flag that says, "Wake up, Reader; something is going to happen.") Unhappily, after finishing the paragraph, I was forced to admit that the incident in question had *not* irretrievably bent the twig of events. Yet I hated to give up such a well-made phrase. Should I leave it in because it was good writing or take it out because it was not good history? History governed and it was lost to posterity (although, you notice, I have rescued it here). Words are seductive and dangerous material, to be used with caution. Am I writer first or am I historian? The old argument starts inside my head. Yet there need not always be dichotomy or dispute. The two functions need not be, in fact should not be, at war. The goal is fusion. In the long run the best writer is the best historian. [...]

Silences: When Writers Don't Write

by Tillie Olsen

October 1965

Literary history and the present are dark with silences: some the silences for years by our acknowledged great; some silences hidden; some the ceasing to publish after one work appears; some the never coming to book form at all.

What is it that happens with the creator, to the creative process in that time? What *are* creation's needs for full functioning? Without intention of or pretension to literary scholarship, I have had special need to learn all I could of this over the years, myself so nearly remaining mute and having let writing die over and over again in me.

These are not *natural* silences, what Keats called *agonie ennuyeuse* (the tedious agony), that necessary time for renewal, lying fallow, gestation, in the natural cycle of creation. The silences I speak of here are unnatural; the unnatural thwarting of what struggles to come into being, but cannot. In the old, the obvious parallels: when the seed strikes stone; the soil will not sustain; the spring is false; the time is drought or blight or infestation; the frost comes premature.

The very great have known such silences—Thomas Hardy, Melville, Rimbaud, Gerard Manley Hopkins. They tell us little as to why or how the creative working atrophied and died in them—if it ever did.

"Less and less shrink the visions then vast in me," writes Thomas Hardy in his thirty-year ceasing from novels after the Victorian vileness to his *Jude the Obscure*. ("So ended his prose contributions to literature, his experiences having killed all his interest in this form"—the official explanation.) But the great poetry he wrote to the end of his life was not sufficient to hold, to develop, the vast visions which for twenty-five years had had scope in novel after novel. People, situations, interrelationships, landscape—they cry for this larger life in poem after poem.

It was not visions shrinking with Hopkins, but a different torment. For seven years he kept his religious vow to refrain from writing poetry, but the poet's eye he could not shut, nor win "elected silence to beat upon [his] whorléd ear." "I had *long* had haunting my ear the echo of a poem which now I realized on paper," he writes of the first poem permitted to end the seven years' silence. But poetry ("to hoard unheard; be heard, unheeded") could be only the least and last of his heavy priestly responsibilities. Nineteen poems were all he could produce in his last nine years—fullness to us, but torment pitched past grief to him, who felt himself become "time's eunuch, never to beget."

Silence surrounds Rimbaud's silence. Was there torment of the unwritten; haunting of rhythm, of visions; anguish at dying powers; the seventeen years after he abandoned the unendurable literary world? We know only that the need to write continued into his first years of vagabondage, and that on his deathbed he spoke again like a poet-visionary.

Melville's stages to his thirty-year prose silence are clearest. The presage is in his famous letter to Hawthorne, as he had to hurry *Moby Dick* to an end:

I am so pulled hither and thither by circumstances. The calm, the coolness, the silent grass growing mood in which a man ought always to compose, that can seldom be mine. Dollars damn me. What I feel most moved to write, that is banned, it will not pay. Yet altogether, write the other way I cannot. So the result is a final hash.

Reiterated in *Pierre* (Melville himself), writing "that book whose unfathomable cravings drink his blood . . .

when at last the idea obtruded that the wiser and profounder he should grow, the more he lessened his chances for bread.

To have to try final hash; to have one's work met by "drear ignoring"; to be damned by dollars into a Customs House job; to have only occasional weary evenings and Sundays left for writing—

How bitterly did unreplying Pierre feel in his heart that to most of the great works of humanity, their authors had given not weeks and months, not years and years, but their wholly surrendered and dedicated lives.

Is it not understandable why Melville began to burn work, then refused to write it, "immolating" it, "sealing in a fate subdued"? Instead he turned to sporadic poetry, manageable in a time sense, "to nurse through night the ethereal spark" where once had been "flame on flame." A thirty-year night. He was nearly seventy before he could quit the Customs dock and again have full time for writing, start back to prose. "Age, dull tranquilizer," and devastation of "arid years that filed before" to work through before he could restore the creative process. Three years of trying before he felt capable of beginning *Billy Budd* (the kernel waiting half a century); three years more, the slow, painful, never satisfied writing and rewriting of it.

Kin to these years-long silences are the *hidden* silences; work aborted, deferred, denied—hidden by the work which does come to fruition. Hopkins' last years rightfully belong here, as does Kafka's whole writing life, that of Mallarmé, Olive Schreiner, probably Katherine Anne Porter, and many other contemporary writers.

Censorship silences. Deletions, omissions, abandonment of the medium (as with Thomas Hardy). Self-censorship, like Mark Twain's. Publishers' censorship, refusing subject matter or treatment. Religious, political censorship—sometimes spurring inventiveness—most often (read Dostoevski's letters) a wearing attrition.

The extreme of this: those writers physically silenced by governments. Isaac Babel, the years of imprisonment, what took place in him with what wanted to be written? Or in Oscar Wilde, who was not permitted even a pencil until the last months of his imprisonment?

Other silences. The truly memorable poem, story, or book, then the writer never heard from again. Was one work all the writer had in him, and he respected literature too much to repeat himself? Was there the kind of paralysis psychiatry might have helped? Were the conditions not present for establishing the habits of creativity (a young Colette who lacked a Willy to lock her in her room each day? or other claims, other responsibilities so writing could not be first)? It is an eloquent commentary that this one-book silence is true of most Negro writers; only eleven, these last hundred years, have published more than twice.

There is a prevalent silence I pass by quickly, the absence of creativity where it once had been; the ceasing to create literature, though the books keep coming out, year after year. That suicide of the creative process Hemingway describes so accurately in *The Snows of Kilimanjaro:*

He had destroyed his talent himself—by not using it, by betrayals of himself and what he believed in, by drinking so much that he blunted the edge of his perceptions, by laziness, by sloth, by snobbery, by hook and by crook; selling vitality, trading it for security, for comfort.

No, not Scott Fitzgerald. His not a death of creativity, not silence, but what happens when (his words) there is "the sacrifice of talent, in pieces, to preserve its essential value."

Almost unnoted are the foreground silences, *before* the achievement. (Remember when Emerson hailed Whitman's genius, he guessed correctly, "which yet must have had a long *foreground* for such a start.") George Eliot, Joseph Conrad, Isak Dinesen, Sherwood Anderson, Elizabeth Madox Roberts, Joyce Cary—all close to, or in, their forties before they became writers; Lampedusa, Maria Dermout (*The Ten Thousand Things*), Laura Ingalls Wilder, the "children's writer," in their sixties. Their capacities evident early in the "being one on whom nothing is lost." Not all struggling and anguished, like Anderson, the foreground years; some needing the immobilization of long illness or loss, or the sudden lifting of responsibility to make writing necessary, make writing possible; others waiting circumstances and encouragement (George Eliot, her Henry Lewes; Laura Wilder, a daughter's insistence that she transmute her storytelling gift onto paper).

Very close to this last grouping are the silences where the lives never came to writing. Among these, the mute inglorious Miltons: those whose waking hours are all struggle for existence; the barely educated; the illiterate; women. Their silence the silence of centuries as to how life was, is, for most of humanity. Traces of their making, of course, in folk song, lullaby, tales, language itself, jokes, maxims, superstitions, but we know nothing of the creators or how it was with them. In the fantasy of Shakespeare born in deepest Africa (as at least one Shakespeare must have been), was the ritual, the oral storytelling a fulfillment? Or was there restlessness, indefinable yearning, a sense of restriction? Was it as Virginia Woolf in *A Room of One's Own* guesses—about women?

Genius of a sort must have existed among them, as it existed among the working classes, but certainly it

never got itself onto paper. When, however, one reads of a woman possessed by the devils, of a wise woman selling herbs, or even a remarkable man who had a remarkable mother, then I think we are on the track of a lost novelist, a suppressed poet, or some Emily Brontë who dashed her brains out on the moor, crazed with the torture her gift had put her to.

Rebecca Harding Davis whose work sleeps in the forgotten (herself as a woman of a century ago so close to remaining mute) also guessed about the silent in that time of the twelve-hour-a-day, six-day work week. She writes of the illiterate ironworker in "Life in the Iron Mills" who sculptured great shapes in the slag, "his fierce thirst for beauty, to know it, to create it, to *be* something other than he is—a passion of pain." *Margaret Howth* in the textile mill:

> There were things in the world, that like herself, were
> marred, did not understand, were hungry to know....
> Her eyes quicker to see than ours, delicate or grand
> lines in the homeliest things.... Everything she saw
> or touched, nearer, more human than to you or me.
> These sights and sounds did not come to her common;
> she never got used to living as other people do.

She never got used to living as other people do. Was that one of the ways it was?

So some of the silences, incomplete listing of the incomplete, where the need and capacity to create were of a high order.

Now, what *is* the work of creation and the circumstances it demands for full functioning—as told in the journals and notes of the practitioners themselves: Henry James, Katherine Mansfield, Gide, Virginia Woolf; the letters of Flaubert, Rilke, Conrad; Thomas Wolfe's *Story of a Novel*, Valéry's *Course in Poetics*. What do they explain of the silences?

"Constant toil is the law of art, as it is of life," says (and demonstrated) Balzac:

> To pass from conception to execution, to produce, to
> bring the idea to birth, to raise the child laboriously
> from infancy, to put it nightly to sleep surfeited, to kiss
> it in the mornings with the hungry heart of a mother,
> to clean it, to clothe it fifty times over in new garments which it tears and casts away, and yet not revolt

against the trials of this agitated life—this unwearying maternal love, this habit of creation—this is execution and its toils.

"Without duties, almost without external communication," Rilke specifies, "unconfined solitude which takes every day like a life, a spaciousness which puts no limit to vision and in the midst of which infinities surround."

Unconfined solitude as Joseph Conrad experienced it:

For twenty months I wrestled with the Lord for my creation...mind and will and conscience engaged to the full, hour after hour, day after day...a lonely struggle in a great isolation from the world. I suppose I slept and ate the food put before me and talked connectedly on suitable occasions, but I was never aware of the even flow of daily life, made easy and noiseless for me by a silent, watchful, tireless affection.

So there is a homely underpinning for it all, the even flow of daily life made easy and noiseless.

"The terrible law of the artist"—says Henry James—"the law of fructification, of fertilization. The old, old lesson of the art of meditation. To woo combinations and inspirations into being by a depth and continuity of attention and meditation."

"That load, that weight, that gnawing conscience," writes Thomas Mann—

That sea which to drink up, that frightful task.... The will, the discipline and self-control to shape a sentence or follow out a hard train of thought. From the first rhythmical urge of the inward creative force towards the material, towards casting in shape and form, from that to the thought, the image, the word, the line, what a struggle, what Gethsemane.

Does it become very clear what Melville's Pierre so bitterly remarked on, and what literary history bears out, why most of the great works of humanity have come from wholly surrendered and dedicated lives? How else sustain the constant toil, the frightful task, the terrible law, the continuity? Full self, this means, full time for the work. (That time for which Emily Dickinson withdrew from the world.)

But what if there is not that fullness of time, let alone totality of self? What if the writer, as in some of these

silences, must work regularly at something besides his own work—as do nearly all in the arts in the United States today?

I know the theory (kin to starving in the garret makes great art) that it is this very circumstance which feeds creativity. I know, too, that for the beginning young, for some who have such need, the job can be valuable access to life they would not otherwise know. A few (I think of the doctors, Chekhov and William Carlos Williams) for special reasons sometimes manage both. But the actuality testifies: substantial creative work demands time, and with rare exceptions only full-time workers have created it. Where the claims of creation cannot be primary, the results are atrophy; unfinished work; minor effort and accomplishment; silences. (Desperation which accounts for the mountains of applications to the foundations for grants—undivided time—in the strange breadline system we have worked out for our artists.)

Twenty years went by on the writing of *Ship of Fools*, while Katherine Anne Porter, who needed only two years, was "trying to get to that table, to that typewriter, away from my jobs of teaching and trooping this country and of keeping house." "Your subconscious needed that time to grow the layers of pearl," she was told. Perhaps, perhaps, but I doubt it. Subterranean forces can make you wait, but they are very finicky about the kind of waiting it has to be. Before they will feed the creator back, they must be fed, passionately fed, what needs to be worked on. "We hold up our desire as one places a magnet over a composite dust from which the particle of iron will suddenly jump up," says Paul Valéry. A receptive waiting, that means, not demands which prevent "an undistracted center of being." And when the response comes, availability to work must be immediate. If not used at once, all may vanish as a dream; worse, future creation be endangered, for only the removal and development of the material frees the forces for further work.

There is a life in which all this is documented: Franz Kafka's. For every one entry from his diaries here, there are fifty others which testify as unbearably to the driven strategems for time, the work lost (to us), the damage to the creative powers (and the body) of having to deny, interrupt, postpone, put aside, let work die.

"I cannot devote myself completely to my writing," Kafka explains (in 1911). "I could not live by literature, if only, to begin with, because of the slow maturing of my work and its special character." So he worked as an official in a state insurance agency, and wrote when he could.

These two can never be reconciled.... If I have written something one evening, I am afire the next day in the office and can bring nothing to completion. Outwardly I fulfill my office duties satisfactorily, not my inner duties however, and every unfulfilled inner duty becomes a misfortune that never leaves. What strength it will necessarily drain me of.

[1911] No matter how little the time or how badly I write, I feel approaching the imminent possibility of great moments which could make me capable of anything. But my being does not have sufficient strength to hold this to the next writing time. During the day the visible world helps me; during the night it cuts me to pieces unhindered.... Calling forth such powers which are then not permitted to function.

Which are then not permitted to function.

[1912] When I begin to write after such a long interval, I draw the words as if out of the empty air. If I capture one, then I have just this one alone, and all the toil must begin anew.

[1914] Yesterday for the first time in months, an indisputable ability to do good work. And yet wrote only the first page. Again I realize that everything written down bit by bit rather than all at once in the course of the larger part is inferior, and that the circumstances of my life condemn me to this inferiority.

[1915] My constant attempt by sleeping before dinner to make it possible to continue working [writing] late into the night, senseless. Then at one o'clock can no longer fall asleep at all, the next day at work insupportable, and so I destroy myself.

[1917] Distractedness, weak memory, stupidity.... Always this one principal anguish—if I had gone away in 1911 in full possession of all my powers. Not eaten by the strain of keeping down living forces.

Eaten into tuberculosis. By the time he won through to self and time for writing, his body could live no more. He was forty-one.

I think of Rilke who said: "If I have any responsibility, I mean and desire it to be responsibility for the deepest and innermost essence of the loved reality [writing] to which I am inseparably bound"; and who also said: "Anything alive, that makes demands, arouses in me an infinite capacity to give it its due, the consequences of which completely use me up." These were true with Kafka, too, yet how different their lives. When Rilke wrote that about responsibility, he is explaining why he will not take a job to support his wife and baby, nor live with them (years later will not come to his daughter's wedding nor permit a two-hour honeymoon visit lest it break his solitude where he awaits poetry). The "infinite capacity" is his explanation as to why he cannot even bear to have a dog. Extreme—and justified. He protected his creative powers.

Kafka's, Rilke's "infinite capacity" and all else that has been said here of the needs of creation, illuminate women's silence of centuries. I will not repeat what is in Virginia Woolf's *A Room of One's Own*, but talk of this last century and a half in which women have begun to have voice in literature. (It has been less than that time in Eastern Europe, and not yet, in many parts of the world.)

In the last century, of the women whose achievements endure for us in one way or another, nearly all never married (Jane Austen, Emily Brontë, Christina Rossetti, Emily Dickinson, Louisa May Alcott, Sarah Orne Jewett) or married late in their thirties (George Eliot, Elizabeth Barrett Browning, Charlotte Brontë, Olive Schreiner). I can think of only three (George Sand, Harriet Beecher Stowe, and Helen Hunt Jackson) who married and had children as young women. All had servants.

In our century, until very recently, it has not been so different. Most did not marry (Lagerlöf, Cather, Glasgow, Gertrude Stein, Sitwell, Gabriela Mistral, Elizabeth Madox Roberts, Charlotte Mew, Welty, Marianne Moore) or, if married, have been childless (Undset, Wharton, Woolf, Katherine Mansfield, H. H. Richardson, Bowen, Dinesen, Porter, Hellman, Dorothy Parker). Colette had one child. If I include Kay Boyle, Pearl Buck, Dorothy Canfield Fisher, that will make a small group who had more than one child. Nearly all had household help.

Am I resaying the moldy theory that women have no need, some say no capacity, to create art, because they can create babies? And the additional proof is precisely that the few women who have created it are nearly all childless? No.

The power and the need to create, over and beyond reproduction, is native in both men and women. Where the gifted among women (*and men*) have remained mute, or have never attained full capacity, it is because of circumstances, inner or outer, which oppose the needs of creation.

Wholly surrendered and dedicated lives; time as needed for the work; totality of self. But women are traditionally trained to place others' needs first, to feel these needs as their own (the "infinite capacity"); their sphere, their satisfaction to be in making it possible for others to use their abilities. This is what Virginia Woolf meant when, already a writer of achievement, she wrote in her diary:

Father's birthday. He would have been 96, 96, yes, today; and could have been 96, like other people one has known; but mercifully was not. His life would have entirely ended mine. What would have happened? No writing, no books;—inconceivable.

It took family deaths to free more than one woman writer into her own development. Emily Dickinson freed herself, denying all the duties expected of a woman of her social position except the closest family ones, and she was fortunate to have a sister, and servants, to share those. How much is revealed of what happened to their own talents in the diaries of those sisters of great men, Dorothy Wordsworth, Alice James.

And where there is no servant or relation to assume the responsibilities of daily living? Listen to Katherine Mansfield in the early days of her relationship with John Middleton Murry, when they both dreamed of becoming great writers:

The house seems to take up so much time.... I mean when I have to clean up twice over or wash up extra unnecessary things, I get frightfully impatient and want to be working [writing]. So often this week you and Gordon have been talking while I washed dishes. Well someone's got to wash dishes and get food. Otherwise "there's nothing in the house but eggs to eat." And after you have gone I walk about with a mind full of ghosts of saucepans and primus stoves and "will there be enough to go around?" And you calling, whatever I am doing, writing, "Tig, isn't there going to be tea? It's five o'clock."

I loathe myself today. This woman who superintends you and rushes about slamming doors and slopping water and shouts "You might at least empty the pail and wash out the tea leaves." O Jack, I wish that you would take me in your arms and kiss my hands and my face and every bit of me and say, "It's all right, you darling thing, I understand."

A long way from Conrad's favorable circumstance for creation: the flow of daily life made easy and noiseless.

And, if, in addition to the infinite capacity, to the daily responsibilities, there are children?

Balzac, you remember, described creation in terms of motherhood. Yes, in intelligent passionate motherhood there are similarities, and in more than the toil and patience. The calling upon total capacities; the re-living and new using of the past; the comprehensions; the fascination, absorption, intensity. All almost certain death to creation.

Not because the capacities to create no longer exist, or the need (though for a while, as in any fullness of life, the need may be obscured) but because the circumstances for sustained creation are almost impossible. The need cannot be first. It can have at best, only part self, part time. (Unless someone else does the nurturing. Read Dorothy Fisher's "Babushka Farnham" in *Fables for Parents*.) More than in any human relationship, overwhelmingly more, motherhood means being instantly interruptible, responsive, responsible. Children need one *now* (and remember, in our society, the family must often be the center for love and health the outside world is not). The very fact that these are needs of love, not duty, that one feels them as one's self; that there is no one else to be responsible for these needs, gives them primacy. It is distraction, not meditation, that becomes habitual; interruption, not continuity; spasmodic, not constant toil. The rest has been said here. Work interrupted, deferred, postponed, makes blockage—at best, lesser accomplishment. Unused capacities atrophy, cease to be.

When H. H. Richardson, who wrote the Australian classic *Ultima Thule*, was asked why she—whose children, like all her people, were so profoundly written—did not herself have children, she answered: "There are enough women to do the childbearing and childrearing. I know of none who can write my books." I remember thinking rebelliously, yes, and I know of none who can bear and rear my children either. But literary history is on her side. Almost no mothers—as almost no part-time, part-self persons—have created enduring literature—so far.

If I talk now quickly of my own silences—almost presumptuous after what has been told here—it is that the individual experience may add.

In the twenty years I bore and reared my children, usually had to work on a job as well, the simplest circumstances for creation did not exist. Nevertheless writing, the hope of it, was "the air I breathed, so long as I shall breathe at all." In that hope, there was conscious storing, snatched reading, beginnings of writing, and always "the secret rootlets of reconnaisance."

When the youngest of our four was in school, the beginnings struggled toward endings. This was a time, in Kafka's words, "like a squirrel in a cage: bliss of movement, desperation about constriction, craziness of endurance."

Bliss of movement. A full extended family life; the world of my job (transcriber in a dairy-equipment company); and the writing, which I was somehow able to carry around within me through work, through home. Time on the bus, even when I had to stand, was enough; the stolen moments at work, enough; the deep night hours for as long as I could stay awake, after the kids were in bed, after the household tasks were done, sometimes during. It is no accident that the first work I considered publishable began: "I stand here ironing, and what you asked me moves tormented back and forth with the iron."

In such snatches of time I wrote what I did in those years, but there came a time when this triple life was no longer possible. The fifteen hours of daily realities became too much distraction for the writing. I lost craziness of endurance. What might have been, I don't know, but I asked for, and received, eight months' writing time. There was still full family life, all the household responsibilities, but I did not have to go out on a job. I had continuity, three full days, sometimes more, and it was in those months I made the mysterious turn and became a writing writer.

Then had to return to the world of work, someone else's work, nine hours, five days a week.

This was the time of festering and congestion. For a few months I was able to shield the writing with which I was so full against the demands of jobs on which I had to be competent, through the joys and responsibilities of family. For a few months. Always roused by the writing, always denied. "I could not go to write it down. It convulsed and died in me. I will pay." My work died. What demanded to be written, did not; it seethed, bubbled, clamored, peopled me. At last moved into the hours meant for sleeping. I worked now full time on temporary jobs, a Kelly, a Western Agency girl (girl!), wandering from office to office, always hoping we could manage two, three writing months ahead. Eventually there was time.

I had said: always roused by the writing, always denied. Now, like a woman made frigid, I had to learn response, to trust this possibility for fruition that had not been before.

Any interruption dazed and silenced me. It took a long while of surrendering to what I was trying to write, of invoking Henry James's "passion, piety, patience," before I was able to reestablish work.

When again I had to leave the writing, I lost consciousness. A time of anesthesia. There was still an automatic noting that did not stop, but it was as if writing had never been. No fever, no congestion, no festering. I ceased being peopled, slept well and dreamlessly, took a "permanent" job. The few pieces which had been published seemed to have vanished like the not-yet-written. I wrote someone, unsent: "So long they fed each other—my life, the writing; the writing or hope of it, my life—and now they destroy each other." I knew, but did not feel the destruction.

A Ford grant in literature, awarded me on nomination by others, came almost too late. Time granted does not necessarily coincide with time that can be most fully used, as the congested time of fullness would have been. Still, it was two years.

Drowning is not so pitiful as the attempt to rise, says Emily Dickinson. I do not agree, but I know of what she speaks. For a long time I was that emaciated survivor trembling on the beach, unable to rise and walk. Said differently, I could manage only the feeblest, shallowest growth on that devastated soil. Weeds, to be burnt like weeds, or used as compost. When the habits of creation were at last rewon, one book went to the publisher, and I dared to begin my present work. It became my center, engraved on it: "Evil is whatever distracts." (By now, had begun a cost to our family life, to my own participation in life as a human being.) I shall not tell the "rest, residue, and remainder" of what I was "leased, demised, and let unto" when once again I had to leave work at the flood to return to the Time Master, to business-ese and legalese. This most harmful of all my silences has ended, but I am not yet recovered, may still be a one-book instead of a hidden and foreground silence.

However that will be, perhaps we are in a time of more and more hidden and foreground silences, men *and* women. Denied full writing life, more may try to "nurse through night" (that part-time, part-self night) "the ethereal spark," but it seems to me there would almost have had to be "flame on flame" first, and time as needed afterwards, and enough of the self, the capacities, undamaged for the rebeginnings on the frightful task. I would like to believe this for what has not yet been written into literature. But it cannot reconcile for what is lost by unnatural silences.

THE PLAYER PIANO

BY RANDALL JARRELL

FEBRUARY 1967

I ate pancakes one night in a Pancake House
Run by a lady my age. She was gay.
When I told her that I came from Pasadena
She laughed and said, "I lived in Pasadena
When Fatty Arbuckle drove the El Molino bus."

I felt that I had met someone from home.
No, not Pasadena, Fatty Arbuckle.
Who's that? Oh, something that we had in common
Like—like—the false armistice. Piano rolls.
She told me her house was the first Pancake House

East of the Mississippi, and I showed her
A picture of my grandson. Going home—
Home to the hotel—I began to hum,
"Smile a while, I bid you sad adieu,
When the clouds roll back I'll come to you."

Let's brush our hair before we go to bed,
I say to the old friend who lives in my mirror.
I remember how I'd brush my mother's hair
Before she bobbed it. How long has it been
Since I hit my funnybone? had a scab on my knee?

Here are Mother and Father in a photograph,
Father's holding me.... They both look so young.
I'm so much older than they are. Look at them,
Two babies with their baby. I don't blame you,
You weren't old enough to know any better;

If I could I'd go back, sit down by you both,
And sign our true armistice: you weren't to blame.
I shut my eyes and there's our living room.
The piano's playing something by Chopin,
And Mother and Father and their little girl

Listen. Look, the keys go down by themselves!
I go over, hold my hands out, play I play—
If only, somehow, I had learned to live!
The three of us sit watching, as my waltz
Plays itself out a half-inch from my fingers.

MIAMI BEACH AND CHICAGO

BY NORMAN MAILER

NOVEMBER 1968

The Amphitheatre was the best place in the world for a convention. Relatively small, it had the packed intimacy of a neighborhood fight club. The entrances to the gallery were narrow as hallway tunnels, and the balcony seemed to hang over each speaker. The colors were black and gray and red and white and blue, bright powerful colors in support of a ruddy beef-eating Democratic sea of faces. The standards in these cramped quarters were numerous enough to look like lances. The aisles were jammed. The carpets were red. The crowd had a blood in their vote which had traveled in unbroken line from the throng who cheered the blood of brave Christians and ferocious lions. It could have been a great convention, stench and all—politics in an abattoir was as appropriate as license in a boudoir. There was *bottom* to this convention: some of the finest and some of the most corrupt faces in America were on the floor. Cancer jostled elbows with acromegaly, obesity with edema, arthritis with alcoholism, bad livers sent curses to bronchias, and quivering jowls beamed bad cess to puffed-out paunches. Cigars curved mouths which talked out of the other corner to cauliflower ears. The leprotic took care of the blind. And the deaf attached their hearing aid to the voice-box of the dumb. The tennis players communicated with the estate holders, the Mob talked bowling with the Union, the principals winked to the principals, the honest and the passionate went hoarse shouting through dead mikes.

Yet the night was in trouble and there was dread in the blood, the air of circus was also the air of the slaughterhouse. Word ripped through delegations of monstrosities unknown. Before the roll call was even begun, Peterson of Wisconsin, Donald Peterson, McCarthy man from the winning primary in Wisconsin, was on his feet, successful in obtaining the floor. (Since he was surrounded by TV, radio, and complements of the Press, the Chair knew it would be easier to accede than to ignore his demand for a voice.) Peterson wanted... Peterson wanted to have the convention postponed for two weeks and moved to another hall in some city far away, because of the "surrounding violence" and the "pandemonium in the hall." Before a mighty roar could even get off the ground, the Chair had passed to other business, and nominations were in order and so declared to a round of boos heavy as a swell of filthy oil. The sense of riot would not calm. Delegates kept leaving the floor to watch films on TV of the violence. McCarthy was reported to have witnessed the scene from his window and called it "very bad." McGovern described the fighting he saw as a "blood bath" which "made me sick to my stomach." He had "seen nothing like it since the films of Nazi Germany."

But that was the mood which hung over the hall, a revel of banquetry, huzzah and horror, a breath of gluttony, a smell of blood. The party had always been established in the mansions and slaughterhouses of society; Hyde Park and the take from policy, social legislation and the lubricating jelly of whores had been at the respective ends of its Democratic consensus, the dreams and the nose for power of aristocrat and gentry were mixed with beatings in the alley, burials at sea in concrete boots, and the poll tax with the old poll-tax rhetoric. The most honorable and the most debauched had sat down at table for Democratic luncheons. Now, the party was losing its better half, and the gang in the gashouse couldn't care less. They were about to roll up their sleeves and divide the pie, the local pie—who cared that the big election was dead? They had been pallbearers to moral idealism for too many years. Now they would shove it in the ground. The country was off its moorings and that was all right with them—let the ship of state drift into its own true berth: let patriotism and the fix cohabit in the comfort for which they were designed and stop these impossible collaborations.

So episodes popped up all over the place. The police dragged a delegate from the floor when a sergeant-at-arms told him to return to his seat and the delegate refused and exchanged words. Paul O'Dwyer, candidate for the Senate from New York, was pulled from the hall as he hung onto him. Mike Wallace of CBS was punched on the jaw when he asked some questions—they went out in a flurry of cops quickly summoned, and rumors raced into every corner. Clear confidence in the location of the seat of power was gone. A delegate had now to face the chimera of arrest by the police, then incarceration. Who would get him out? Did Daley have the power or Johnson? Would Humphrey ever be of use? Should one look for the U.S. Marines? A discomfiture of the fundamental cardinal points of all location was in the rumblings of the gut. A political man could get killed in this town by a cop, was the general sentiment, and who would dare to look the Mayor in the eye? If politics was property, somebody had tipped the plot: West was now up in the North! To the most liberal of the legislators and delegates on the floor must have come the real panic of wondering: was this how it felt with the Nazis when first they came in, the fat grin on the face of that cigar who had hitherto been odious but loyal? Hard suppressed guffaws of revelry

rumbled among the delegates with the deepest greed and the most steaming bile. There was the sense of all centers relocated, of authority on a ride.

The nominations took place in muted form. The Democrats had declared there would be no demonstrations at their convention. The Democrats! Famous for their demonstrations. But they were afraid of maniacal outbursts for McCarthy, fist fights on the floor, whole platoons of political warriors grappling rivals by the neck. So each candidate would merely be put in nomination, his name then cheered, seconding speeches would follow, the roll would be called, the next nominated.

McCarthy was put in by Governor Harold Hughes of Iowa, Humphrey by Mayor Alioto of San Francisco. Let us listen to a little of each—they are not uncharacteristic of their men. Hughes said:

"We are in the midst of what can only be called a revolution in our domestic affairs and in our foreign policy as well.

"And as the late President Kennedy once said: 'Those who would make peaceful revolution impossible make violent revolution inevitable.'

An anti-Humphrey demonstrator confronts a policeman in Chicago.

"...We must seek a leader who can arrest the polarization in our society, the alienation of the blacks from the whites, the haves from the have-nots and the old from the young.

"We must choose a man with the wisdom and the courage to change the direction of our foreign policy before it commits us for an eternity to a maze of foreign involvements without clear purpose or moral justification.

"But most of all the man we nominate must embody the aspirations of all those who seek to lift mankind to its highest potential. He must have that rare intangible quality that can lift up our hearts and cleanse the soul of this troubled country.

"Gene McCarthy is such a man."

Mayor Alioto said:

"I came here to talk to you about the man who has been for twenty years, right up to the present time, the articulate exponent of the aspirations of the human heart— for the young, for the old, and for those of us in between.

"I'm not going to read to you, but I am going to ask you to project yourselves to Jan. 20, 1969, to project yourselves to the steps of the great Capitol of Washington, and in your mind's eyes to picture a man standing on those steps with his hands raised pledging that he will execute the office of the President of the United States and that he will in accordance with his ability preserve, protect and defend the Constitution of the United States, so help him God.

"That man will look down on a country that is gripped in an earnest desire to find its way out of the confusion and the frustration that now infect this country. And the people at that moment will be looking for a decisive leader.

"Let me put it directly to you—that man on Jan. 20 of 1969 is going to have to be an extraordinary man. And if he isn't an extraordinary man, the burdens of that office will crack him and the turbulence of the times will overwhelm us."

McGovern was nominated by Ribicoff, Senator Abraham Ribicoff of Connecticut, formerly Governor, a Kennedy man for many years—his career had prospered with the Kennedys. He was not a powerful looking man. He had wings of silver gray hair, dark eyebrows, a weak mouth which spoke of the kind of calculation which does not take large chances. He had a slim frame with a hint of paunch. He was no heavyweight. He had gotten along by getting along, making the right friends. He was never famous as a speaker, but he began by saying, "Mr. Chairman...as I look at the confusion in this hall and watch on television the turmoil and violence that is competing with this great convention for the attention of the American people, there is something else in my heart tonight, and not the speech that I am prepared to give."

It was a curious beginning, but as he went on, the speech became boring despite the force of a few of the phrases: "500,000 Americans in the swamps of Vietnam." Ribicoff droned, he had no flair, he was indeed about as boring as a Republican speaker. There were yawns as he said:

"George McGovern is not satisfied that in this nation of ours, in this great nation of ours, our infant mortality rate is so high that we rank twenty-first in all the nations of the world.

"We need unity and we can only have unity with a new faith, new ideas, new ideals. The youth of America rally to the standards of men like George McGovern like they did to the standards of John F. Kennedy and Robert Kennedy.

"And with George McGovern as President of the United States we wouldn't have those Gestapo tactics in the streets of Chicago.

"With George McGovern we wouldn't have a National Guard."

Seconds had elapsed. People turned to each other. Did he say, "Gestapo tactics in the streets of Chicago"? But he had. His voice had quavered a hint with indignation and with fear, but he had said it, and Daley was on his feet, Daley was shaking his fist at the podium, Daley was mouthing words. One could not hear the words, but his lips were clear. Daley seemed to be telling Ribicoff to go have carnal relations with himself.

There was a roundhouse of roars from the floor, a buzz from the gallery. Daley glowered at Ribicoff and Ribicoff stared back, his ordinary face now handsome, dignified with some possession above itself. Ribicoff leaned down from the podium, and said in a good patrician voice, "How hard it is to accept the truth."

Perhaps it was Ribicoff's finest moment. Later, backstage, in McGovern Headquarters, he looked less happy, and consid-

Policeman sprays mace at a crowd, Chicago.

erably less in possession of himself as people came up to congratulate him for his speech. Indeed, Ribicoff had the winded worried heart-fatigued expression of a lightweight fighter who had just dared five minutes ago in the gym to break off a jab which broke the nose of a middleweight champ who had been working out with him. Now the lightweight would wake up in the middle of the night, wondering how they were going to pay him in return. Let us think of the man rather in his glory.

The balloting was finally begun. There were no surprises expected and none arrived. North Dakota actually said, "North Dakota which modestly admits to being cleaner and greener in the summer and brighter and whiter in the winter, casts 25 votes, 18 for Hubert Humphrey, 7 for Gene McCarthy." Then Ohio gave 94, Oklahoma was 37^1/$_2$, the floor began to shout. Pennsylvania offered up 103^3/$_4$ of 130 and Humphrey was in. It was the state where McCarthy had gotten 90% of the primary vote. The deed was completed. The future storefront of the Mafia was now nominated to run against the probable prince of the corporation. In his hotel suite at the Hilton, Humphrey kissed Mrs. Fred R. Harris, wife of the Oklahoma Senator and co-chairman of his campaign; then as if to forestall all rumors, and reimpose propriety in its place, he rushed to the television screen and kissed the image of his own wife, which was then appearing on the tube. He was a politician; he could kiss babies, rouge, rubber, velvet, blubber and glass. God had not given him oral excellence for nothing.

Then the phone calls came. President Johnson, to whom Humphrey said with Southern grace, "Bless your heart," Mrs. Johnson, Lynda Bird and Luci; then Dick Nixon who congratulated him for winning the nomination earlier on the roll call than himself. Nixon was reported to have said that he enjoyed watching Mrs. Humphrey and the Humphrey family on television.

The vote when tabulated went like this: Humphrey 1,761¾; McCarthy 601; McGovern 146½; Channing Philips (first Negro to be nominated for the Presidency) 67½; Dan Moore 17½; Edward Kennedy (without nomination) 12¾; James H. Gray ½; Paul E. "Bear" Bryant, coach of Alabama, 1½; and George C. Wallace ½. George C. Wallace would do a lot better in November. [...]

EDITOR'S EASY CHAIR
SURVIVAL U

PROSPECTUS FOR A REALLY RELEVANT UNIVERSITY

BY JOHN FISCHER

~~OCTOBER~~ 1969
SEPTEMBER

It gets pretty depressing to watch what is going on in the world and realize that your education is not equipping you to do anything about it.
— FROM A LETTER BY A
UNIVERSITY OF CALIFORNIA SENIOR

She is not a radical, and has never taken part in any demonstration. She will graduate with honors, and profound disillusionment. From listening to her—and a good many like-minded students at California and East Coast campuses—I think I am beginning to understand what they mean when they say that a liberal-arts education isn't relevant.

They mean it is incoherent. It doesn't cohere. It consists of bits and pieces which don't stick together, and have no common purpose. One of our leading Negro educators, Arthur Lewis of Princeton, recently summed it up better than I can. America is the only country, he said, where youngsters are required "to fritter away their precious years in meaningless peregrination from subject to subject...spending twelve weeks getting some tidbits of religion, twelve weeks learning French, twelve weeks seeing whether the history professor is stimulating, twelve weeks seeking entertainment from the economics professor, twelve weeks confirming that one is not going to be able to master calculus."

These fragments are meaningless because they are not organized around any central purpose, or vision of the world. The typical liberal arts college has no clearly defined goals. It merely offers a smorgasbord of courses, in hopes that if a student nibbles at a few dishes from the

"Anthology," by Michelle Barnes.

humanities table, plus a snack of science, and a garnish of art or anthropology, he may emerge as "a cultivated man"—whatever that means. Except for a few surviving church schools, no university even pretends to have a unifying philosophy. Individual teachers may have personal ideologies—but since they are likely to range, on any given campus, from Marxism to worship of the scientific method to exaltation of the irrational (*à la* Norman O. Brown), they don't cohere either. They often leave a student convinced at the end of four years that any given idea is probably about as valid as any other—and that none of them has much relationship to the others, or to the decisions he is going to have to make the day after graduation.

Education was not always like that. The earliest European universities had a precise purpose: to train an elite for the service of the Church. Everything they taught was focused to that end. Thomas Aquinas had spelled it all out: what subjects had to be mastered, how each connected with every other, and what meaning they had for man and God.

Later, for a span of several centuries, Oxford and Cambridge had an equally clear function: to train administrators to run an empire. So too did Harvard and Yale at the time they were founded; their job was to produce the clergymen, lawyers, and doctors that a new country needed. In each case, the curriculum was rigidly prescribed. A student learned what he needed, to prepare himself to be a competent priest, district officer, or surgeon. He had no doubts about the relevance of his courses—and no time to fret about expanding his consciousness or currying his sensual awareness. [...]

For a long while some of our less complacent academics have been trying to restore coherence to American education. When Robert Hutchins was at Chicago, he tried to use the Great Books to build a comprehensible framework for the main ideas of civilized man. His experiment is still being carried on, with some modifications, at St. John's—but it has not proved irresistibly contagious. Sure, the thoughts of Plato and Machiavelli are still pertinent, so far as they go—but somehow they don't seem quite enough armor for a world beset with splitting atoms, urban guerrillas, nineteen varieties of psychotherapists, amplified guitars, napalm, computers, astronauts, and an atmosphere polluted simultaneously with auto exhaust and TV commercials.

Another strategy for linking together the bits-and-pieces has been attempted at Harvard and at a number of other universities. They require their students to take at least two years of survey courses, known variously as core studies, general education, or world civilization. These too have been something less than triumphantly successful. Most faculty members don't like to teach them, regarding them as superficial and synthetic. (And right they are, since no survey course that I know of has a strong unifying concept to give it focus.) Moreover, the senior professors shun such courses in favor of their own narrow specialties. Consequently, the core studies which are meant to place all human experience—well, at least the brightest nuggets—into One Big Picture usually end up in the perfunctory hands of resentful junior teachers. Naturally the undergraduates don't take them seriously either.

Any successful reform of American education, I am now convinced, will have to be far more revolutionary than anything yet attempted. At a minimum, it should be:

1. Founded on a single guiding concept—an idea capable of knotting together all strands of study, thus giving them both coherence and visible purpose.

2. Capable of equipping young people to do something about "what is going on in the world"—notably the things which bother them most, including war, injustice, racial conflict, and the quality of life.

Maybe it isn't possible. Perhaps knowledge is proliferating so fast, and in so many directions, that it can never again be ordered into a coherent whole, so that molecular biology, Robert Lowell's poetry, and highway engineering will seem relevant to each other and to the lives of ordinary people. Quite possibly the knowledge explosion, as Peter F. Drucker has called it, dooms us to scholarship which grows steadily more specialized, fragmented, and incomprehensible. [...]

Is it conceivable, then, that we might hit upon another idea which could serve as the organizing principle for many fields of scholarly inquiry; which is relevant to the urgent needs of our time; and which would not, on the other hand, impose an ideological strait jacket? [...]

Just possibly it could be done. For the last two or three years I have been probing around among professors, college administrators, and students—and so far I have come up with only one idea which might fit the specifications. It is simply the idea of survival.

For the first time in history, the future of the human race is now in serious question. This fact is hard to believe, or even think about—yet it is the message which a growing number of scientists are trying, almost frantically, to get across to us. Listen, for example, to Professor Richard A. Falk of Princeton and of the Center for Advanced Study in the Behavioral Sciences:

> The planet and mankind are in grave danger of irreversible catastrophe...Man may be skeptical about following the flight of the dodo into extinction, but the evidence points increasingly to just such a pursuit.... There are four interconnected threats to the planet—wars of mass destruction, overpopulation, pollution, and the depletion of resources. They have a cumulative effect. A problem in one area renders it more difficult to solve the problems in any other area.... The basis of all four problems is the inadequacy of the sovereign states to manage the affairs of mankind in the twentieth century.

Similar warnings could be quoted from a long list of other social scientists, biologists, and physicists, among them such distinguished thinkers as Rene Dubos, Buckminster Fuller, Loren Eiseley, George Wald, and Barry Commoner. They are not hopeless. Most of them believe that we still have a chance to bring our weapons, our population growth, and the destruction of our environment under control before it is too late. But the time is short, and so far there is no evidence that enough people are taking them seriously.

That would be the prime aim of the experimental university I'm suggesting here: to look seriously at the interlinking threats to human existence, and to learn what we can do to fight them off.

Let's call it Survival U. It will not be a multiversity, offering courses in every conceivable field. Its motto—emblazoned on a life jacket rampant—will be: "What must we do to be saved?" If a course does not help to answer that question, it will not be taught here. Students interested in musicology, junk sculpture, the Theater of the Absurd, and the literary *dicta* of Leslie Fiedler can go somewhere else.

Neither will our professors be detached, dispassionate scholars. To get hired, each will have to demonstrate an emotional commitment to our cause. Moreover, he will be expected to be a moralist; for this generation of students, like no other in my lifetime, is hungering and thirsting after righteousness. What it wants is a moral system it can believe in—and that is what our university will try to provide. In every class it will preach the primordial ethic of survival.

The biology department, for example, will point out that it is sinful for anybody to have more than two children. It has long since become glaringly evident that unless the earth's cancerous growth of population can be halted, all other problems—poverty, war, racial strife, uninhabitable cities, and the rest—are beyond solution. So the department naturally will teach all known methods of birth control, and much of its research will be aimed at perfecting cheaper and better ones.

Its second lesson in biological morality will be: "Nobody has a right to poison the environment we live in." This maxim will be illustrated by a list of public enemies. At the top will stand the politicians, scientists, and military men—of whatever country—who make and deploy atomic weapons; for if these are ever used, even in so-called defensive systems like the ABM, the atmosphere will be so contaminated with strontium 90 and other radioactive isotopes that human survival seems most unlikely. Also on the list will be anybody who makes or tests chemical and biological weapons—or who even attempts to get rid of obsolete nerve gas, as our Army recently proposed, by dumping the stuff in the sea. [...]

Before he finishes this course, a student may begin to feel twinges of conscience himself. Is his motorcycle exhaust adding carbon monoxide to the smog we breathe? Is his sewage polluting the nearest river? If so, he will be reminded of two proverbs. From Jesus: "Let him who is without sin among you cast the first stone." From Pogo: "We have met the enemy and he is us."

In like fashion, our engineering students will learn not only how to build dams and highways, but where *not* to build them. Unless they understand that it is immoral to flood the Grand Canyon or destroy the Everglades with a jetport, they will never pass the final exam. Indeed, our engineering graduates will be trained to ask a key question about every contract offered them: "What will be its effect on human life?" That obviously will lead to other questions which every engineer ought to comprehend as thoroughly as his slide rule. Is this new highway really necessary? Would it be wiser to use the money for mass transit—or to decongest traffic by building a new city somewhere else? Is an offshore oil well really a good idea? [...]

Our engineering faculty also will specialize in training men for a new growth industry: garbage disposal. Americans already are spending $4.5 billion a year to collect and get rid of the garbage which we produce more profusely than any other people (more than five pounds a day for each of us). But unless we are resigned to stifling in our own trash, we are going to have to come up with at least an additional $835 million a year.[*] Any industry with a growth rate of 18 per cent offers obvious attractions to a bright young man—and if he can figure out a new way to get rid of our offal, his fortune will be unlimited. [...]

Survival U's Department of Earth Sciences will be headed—if we are lucky—by Dr. Charles F. Park, Jr., now professor of geology and mineral engineering at Stanford. He knows as well as anybody how fast mankind is using up the world's supply of raw materials. In a paper written for the American Geographical Society he punctured one of America's most engaging (and pernicious) myths: our belief that an ever-expanding economy can keep living standards rising indefinitely.

It won't happen; because, as Dr. Park demonstrates, the tonnage of metal in the earth's crust won't last indefinitely. Already we are running short of silver, mercury, tin, and cobalt—all in growing demand by the high-technology industries. Even the commoner metals may soon be in short supply. The United States alone is consuming one ton of iron and eighteen pounds of copper every year, for each of its inhabitants. Poorer countries, struggling to industrialize, hope to raise their consumption of these two key materials to something like that level. If they should succeed—and if the globe's population doubles in the next forty years, as it

[*] *According to Richard D. Vaughn, chief of the Solid Wastes Program of HEW, in his recent horror story entitled "1968 Survey of Community Solid Waste Practices."*

will at present growth rates—then the world will have to produce, somehow, *twelve times* as much iron and copper every year as it does now. Dr. Park sees little hope that such production levels can ever be reached, much less sustained indefinitely. The same thing, of course—doubled in spades—goes for other raw materials: timber, oil, natural gas, and water, to note only a few.

Survival U, therefore, will prepare its students to consume less. This does not necessarily mean an immediate drop in living standards—perhaps only a change in the yardstick by which we measure them. Conceivably Americans might be happier with fewer automobiles, neon signs, beer cans, supersonic jets, barbecue grills, and similar metallic fluff. But happy or not, our students had better learn how to live The Simpler Life, because that is what most of them are likely to have before they reach middle age.

To help them understand how very precious resources really are, our mathematics department will teach a new kind of bookkeeping: social accounting. It will train people to analyze budgets—both government and corporate—with an eye not merely to immediate dollar costs, but to the long-range costs to society.

By conventional bookkeeping methods, for example, the coal companies strip-mining away the hillsides of Kentucky and West Virginia show a handsome profit. Their ledgers, however, show only a fraction of the true cost of their operations. They take no account of destroyed land which can never bear another crop; of rivers poisoned by mud and seeping acid from the spoil banks; of floods which sweep over farms and towns downstream, because the ravaged slopes can no longer hold the rainfall. Although these costs are not borne by the mining firms, they are nevertheless real. They fall mostly on the taxpayers, who have to pay for disaster relief, flood-control levees, and the resettlement of Appalachian farm families forced off the land. As soon as our students (the taxpayers of tomorrow) learn to read a social balance sheet, they obviously will throw the strip miners into bankruptcy. [...]

Our students will keep that in mind when they walk across campus to their government class. Its main goal will be to discover why our institutions have done so badly in their efforts (as Dr. Falk put it) "to manage the affairs of mankind in the twentieth century." This will be a compulsory course for all freshmen, taught by professors who are capable of looking critically at every political artifact, from the Constitution to the local county council. They will start by pointing out that we are living in a state of near-anarchy, because we have no government capable of dealing effectively with public problems.

Instead we have a hodgepodge of 80,000 local governments—villages, townships, counties, cities, port authorities, sewer districts, and special purpose agencies. Their authority is so limited, and their jurisdictions so confused and overlapping, that most of them are virtually impotent. The states, which in theory could put this mess into some sort of order, usually have shown little interest and less competence. When Washington is called to help out—as it increasingly has been for the last thirty-five years—it often has proved ham-handed and entangled in its own archaic bureaucracy. The end result is that nobody in authority has been able to take care of the country's mounting needs. Our welfare rolls keep growing, our air and water get dirtier, housing gets scarcer, airports jam up, road traffic clots, railways fall apart, prices rise, ghettos burn, schools turn out more illiterates every year, and a war nobody wants drags on and on. Small wonder that so many young people are losing confidence in American institutions. In their present state, they don't deserve much confidence.

The advanced students of government at Survival U will try to find out whether these institutions can be renewed and rebuilt. They will take a hard look at the few places—Jacksonville, Minnesota, Nashville, Appalachia—which are creating new forms of government. Will these work any better, and if so, how can they be duplicated elsewhere? Can the states be brought to life, or should we start thinking about an entirely different kind of arrangement? Ten regional prefectures, perhaps, to replace the fifty states? Or should we take seriously Norman Mailer's suggestion for a new kind of city-state to govern our great metropolises? (He merely called for New York City to secede from its state; but that isn't radical enough. To be truly governable, the new Republic of New York City ought to include chunks of New Jersey and Connecticut as well.) Alternatively, can we find some way to break up Megalopolis, and spread our population into smaller and more livable communities throughout the continent? Why should we keep 70 per cent of our people crowded into less than 2 per cent of our land area, anyway?

Looking beyond our borders, our students will be encouraged to ask even harder questions. Are nation-states actually feasible, now that they have power to destroy each other in a single afternoon? Can we agree on something else to take their place, before the balance of terror becomes unstable? What price would most people be willing to pay for a more durable kind of human organization—more taxes, giving up national flags, perhaps the sacrifice of some of our hard-won liberties?

All these courses (and everything else taught at Survival U) are really branches of a single science. Human ecology is one of the youngest disciplines, and probably the most important. It is the study of the relationship between man and his environment, both natural and technological. It teaches us to understand the consequences of our actions—how sulfur-laden fuel oil burned in England produces an acid rain that damages the forests of Scandinavia, why a well-meant farm subsidy can force millions of Negro tenants off the land and lead to Watts and Hough. A graduate who comprehends ecology will know how to look at "what is going on in the world," and he will be equipped to do something about it. Whether he ends up as a city planner, a politician, an enlightened engineer, a teacher, or a reporter, he will have had a relevant education. All of its parts will hang together in a coherent whole.

And if we can get enough such graduates, man and his environment may survive a while longer, against all the odds.

My Lai 4

by Seymour M. Hersh

May 1970

Charlie Company, First Battalion, Twentieth Infantry, came to Vietnam in December 1967. Its men, like GIs in all combat units, considered themselves to be part of the best and toughest outfit in the newly formed Eleventh Brigade. Since December 1966, the brigade had been readying itself for Vietnam at Schofield Barracks, Hawaii; when the orders came to move out, Charlie Company was named to lead the advance party.

Captain Ernest L. Medina, the thirty-three-year-old former enlisted man who was the company's commanding officer, was proud of his men. "We became the best company in the battalion. We took every award—athletics, the company-of-the-month trophy." Medina's hustle had earned him the nickname "Mad Dog," a term that many of his company would use later when complaining about the captain's love of marching and field duty. [...]

The captain was enthusiastic about killing Viet Cong, even in mock battles. He was anxious to go to Vietnam to help win a war he believed in. But there was a personal reason, too—his career. A Mexican-American, he was born into poverty at Springer, New Mexico, in 1936. His mother died when he was an infant and he was raised in a hard-working ranching and farming community in Montrose, Colorado, on the western slope of the Colorado Mountains. When he was sixteen, he lied about his age to enlist in the National Guard, and then the Army; from the very first he wanted to make the military a career. In 1964, after eight years in the infantry, he became an officer, graduating with honors from the Officers' Candidate School at Fort Benning, Georgia, and stayed on for two years to serve as an instructor. He wrote a school paper on "Meteorological Effects on the 4.2-in. Mortar Shell." In 1966 he was promoted to captain and made a company commander. By all accounts he was an excellent officer. Lieutenant Colonel Edward C. Beers, who served above Medina as commanding

officer of the First Battalion in Hawaii and in Vietnam, personally considered him the most outstanding officer in his command. "He is a good Army man."

Medina's promotion to captain had been quick and easy, but rising to major would be more difficult because, as he said, he "didn't have enough education." Vietnam offered him his best chance, and he wanted to make the most of it.

He was off to a good start. Putting together a first-rate fighting unit was no easy feat in 1966. As always, the men assigned to infantry units were those who, upon entering service, performed poorly on the various Army qualification and aptitude examinations. GIs scoring average and above were most usually assigned to a support or training unit to become, for example, clerk-typists, or computer technicians. In Vietnam, there were as many as eight support troops for each combat soldier in the field. Most of the men in Charlie Company had volunteered for the draft; only a few had gone to college for even one year. Nearly half were black, with a few Mexican-Americans. Most were eighteen to twenty-two years old. The favorite reading matter of Charlie Company, like that of other line infantry units in Vietnam, was comic books. Thirteen of the 130 men had not done well enough in the Army's basic intelligence tests to qualify for service, but had been accepted under a new program, Project 100,000, endorsed by Secretary of Defense Robert S. McNamara, which provided remedial education for those who would otherwise not be eligible for the Army. But as it worked out, none of the Project 100,000 men in Charlie Company had been exposed to any further education before getting shipped to Vietnam.

There was a decided advantage for Medina in not having a group of college graduates under his command: Charlie Company was a "grunt" unit; its men were the foot soldiers, the "GI Joes," who understood they were to take orders, not question them. In Hawaii, Medina had been fair but tough, handing out disciplinary penalties when needed but sticking up for his men on many occasions. Charlie Company respected and admired its captain. "He did everything for his men," Henry Pedrick Jr., of Alameda, California, said. "When we had chow in the field, the enlisted men ate before the officers... all the time. His men always came first." Michael Bernhardt of Franklin Square, New York, was impressed by Medina's "tremendous grip on his men. He was so hard-core." Medina could outwalk anybody in the company. "He was hard," William Wyatt of Oklahoma City said. "That's the way you got to do it."

Nobody in the unit, however, admired Medina as much as William L. Calley, Jr., then a twenty-four-year-old second lieutenant from Miami who was serving as a platoon leader. Medina was swarthy, powerfully built, and commanded respect; Calley was boyish-looking, five-foot, three-inches tall, and unsure of himself. No sergeant would dare cross Medina in public; but Calley's chief noncommissioned officer, Sergeant Isaiah Cowen, a thirteen-year veteran from Columbia, South Carolina, was always arguing with Calley in front of the men.

Despite these differences, Calley and Medina had much in common: they both wanted to make the military a career. Calley had flunked out of Palm Beach Junior College in 1963 after earning four Fs. By his own admission, he came from an emotionally cold family, one that had never been close. His high-school friends had called him "Rusty," a nickname that stayed with him. There was nothing relaxed about him; he began smoking three to four packages of cigarettes a day and by the age of nineteen he was treated for a stomach ulcer. After leaving college, Calley worked as a bellhop and then briefly as a restaurant dishwasher before becoming a switchman for the then strike-bound East Coast Railway. He made the local newspapers in 1964 when police in Fort Lauderdale, Florida, arrested him for allowing a forty-seven-car freight train to block traffic for nearly thirty minutes during rush hour at several downtown intersections. He was later exonerated. Facing a bleak future, he saved some money, bought a car, and in 1965 left Florida, heading west. His friends didn't hear from him again for nearly three years; some thought he was dead. He wandered around for a year—one of his jobs then was taking photographs for an insurance-adjustment agency—before enlisting in the Army in July 1966 while in Albuquerque, New Mexico. He quickly found roots as an enlisted man, and was pleased when the Army—despite his poor academic record—decided he would make good officer material.

He graduated from the Officers' Candidate School at Fort Benning without learning how to read a map properly.

If there is any consensus among former members of Calley's platoon in Vietnam, it is amazement that the Army considered Calley officer material. Allen Boyce of Bradley Beach, New Jersey, an eighteen-year-old rifleman at the time of the massacre, said that "everybody used to joke about Calley. He was one of those guys they just take off the street." Rennard Doines of Fort Worth, Texas, thought that Calley constantly tried to impress Medina. "He was always trying to be the big man; always would be the one to beat them [the Vietnamese] up. He didn't know what was going on half the time." Charles W. Hall of Columbus, Ohio, was one of Calley's machine gunners: "Calley also reminded me of a kid, a kid trying to play war." [...]

Many men in the company said that the captain would sometimes refer to Calley as "Sweetheart"; some thought it was a mocking reference, others described it as just a nickname. Gary Garfolo of Stockton, California, recalled that Medina "didn't show any respect for Calley; it was kind of hard for anybody else to show respect." Roy L. Wood of Richmond, Virginia, a rifleman in Calley's platoon, believed that "Medina didn't like Calley. Calley was always doing things wrong... never right. I wondered sometimes how he got through OCS; he couldn't read no darn map and a compass would confuse his ass." Robert E. Maples of Freehold, New Jersey, said that Calley was always trying to "do things that would make him out to be a hero. That's what he tried to do—be a good boy in front of the captain. I just couldn't make it out... why he always had to try to make something out of himself he wasn't. He was always trying to be the first one."

Daniel E. Zeigler of Santa Barbara, California, served with Calley's platoon until he, Zeigler, was seriously injured in a mine accident in mid-February. He remembers that the men in his platoon mocked the young officer, but followed his orders. A favorite Calley expression was "I'm the boss." Sergeant Cowen, a Negro who bitterly argued about tactics with Calley throughout their stay in Vietnam, later commented that Calley "was my superior officer and I had to follow him whether I wanted to or not. Personal opinions don't enter into it; you can't have any ifs, ands, or buts about it, you have to go with your officers."

The other key sergeant in the first platoon, David Mitchell of St. Francisville, Louisiana, was also a Negro. Mitchell was widely disliked in his platoon, however, for his arrogance.

Lieutenant William L. Calley, Jr.

In Charlie Company, the whites and blacks usually kept to themselves, as happened in most units in Vietnam. To Roy Wood, a black Southerner, "it seemed like some of those whites didn't want to be bothered too much with us." Other Negroes noted that Medina surrounded himself with whites in his headquarters group who manned radios and helped to run the company. Harry Stanley, born in Gulfport, Mississippi, a quick-witted Negro, had learned Vietnamese on his own while in Vietnam; in fact, he was convinced that he could speak Vietnamese more fluently than white members of the company who had studied it in Army language school. Yet, it was not until Medina left the company in July 1968 that Stanley got a chance to demonstrate this ability. On the whole, however, Charlie Company saved its antagonism for the Vietnamese. "There wasn't any prejudice in that whole company," said Herbert Carter of Houston, Texas, a Negro. "The government ought to take some pictures of us and say: 'Hey, these guys got along good—at least they killed together.'"

If there was any reason for what began to happen to Charlie Company, it was not too much combat—but too little. The company had conducted some search-and-destroy missions around Eleventh Brigade headquarters at Duc Pho shortly after arriving in Vietnam, with no real enemy contact. Its expectations rose when the brigade, with more units arriving every day from Hawaii, took over responsibility from the South Korean Marines for monitoring an area 40 miles to the north. The 150-square-mile area included parts of the embattled Quang Ngai Province east of Highway One to the South China Sea coast. To continue search-and-destroy operations in the zone, the brigade set up Task Force Barker, a tiny ad hoc unit composed of one company from each of the three battalions in the brigade. The ultimate parent unit of this force, headed by and named after Lieutenant Colonel Frank A. Barker, Jr., was the Americal Division operating out of Chu Lai to the south. Medina's company was assigned to the task force, and relocated on January 26, 1968, at Landing Zone Dotti, one of the three artillery bases from which the three companies worked and bivouacked in the area.

One of the task force's main objectives would be keeping pressure on an area a few miles northeast of Quang Ngai City known as Pinkville, the name deriving from the fact that its higher population density caused it to appear in red on Army maps. The operation was given the code name "Muscatine."

"We were informed that the Viet Cong had been in the area for twenty to twenty-five years," Medina later recalled. "The inhabitants in the outlying villages had all been moved at one time or another. The area was a permanent free-fire zone." The captain said he routinely explained to his troops that if they received fire from a hamlet, they could return it, taking care not to fire at unarmed citizens who posed no seeming threat. At least one soldier recalled other advice. Gary Garfolo remembered that "Medina used to always tell us about the grenade bit. If you shoot a gook and check him out and find he's got an ID [identification card indicating he is not a Viet Cong]—plant a grenade on him."

But nothing happened. "We seemed to be blessed," Ronald Grzesik of Holyoke, Massachusetts, remarked later. "I could walk along a street and not draw a shot—and other companies would come along the same street and get into a good firefight. Other guys would be getting like, you know, hero treatment."

Occasionally the company, still new to Vietnam, was stunned by the evidence of the almost barbarous attitudes veterans displayed toward the Vietnamese people. Gregory Olsen of Portland, Oregon, remembered that soon after they were in Vietnam they saw an American troop carrier drive by with "about twenty human ears tied to the antenna. It was kind of hard to believe. They actually had ears on the antenna."

Charlie Company wanted some action. It began to make a little of its own. Daniel Zeigler remembered that at first there was very little manhandling of civilian suspects. "It started off easy, then it got rough." Both Medina and Calley began trying to convince the company that most of the suspects in the area were Viet Cong. "Once Grzesik gave a prisoner something to eat, and they got mad." Zeigler never understood why Medina or Calley would beat a prisoner to try to get information in a language they couldn't understand anyway. "Whenever we got to a village, there were usually no males of military age around. So if they found one, they would just assume he was a VC. That is, if he wasn't an old man or a little teeny kid."

After many weeks of no combat, the company began to systematically beat its prisoners, and it began to be less discriminating about who was—or was not—a VC. Michael Bernhardt thought that as far as Medina was concerned, "Everything that walked and didn't wear any uniform was a VC.... He was as much of a nut as anybody else. He was pissed off at the people and had no respect for them." The lack of respect was apparently infectious. "On the lower level," Charles Hall said, "squad leaders and platoon leaders didn't enforce the rules—like for beating people. This happened every day; every day there was disregard for the people. There were a few people who made a habit of this." [. . .]

During these weeks [at Landing Zone Dotti], Medina said later, Charlie Company was learning that "this was a dangerous area." Mines and booby traps, often placed by women and children, were everywhere. This was a prevalent belief among GIs in Vietnam, including Charlie Company, yet not one member of Charlie Company to whom I put the question was ever able to cite a specific act of terror by either a woman or child. Such incidents most certainly did occur throughout Vietnam, and still do, but they weren't happening to Charlie Company. When one of its men got hurt, there was usually one reason: carelessness.

One of the first casualties at LZ Dotti was Zeigler: "We were coming back from a night ambush, and I stepped off the trail and got wounded." The date was February 14, 1968. Zeigler decided that what happened to him "could be considered dumb in a way. We were using a well-worn trail and that would be dumb." Something else dumb happened that day: there was no medic around. Calley, who was leading the operation, had forgotten to take one along. "It was our first night patrol, and we asked him for one. I guess he just didn't think it was necessary." Zeigler suffered twenty-one punctures in his body from mine fragments, including a collapsed lung. Luckily, the incident took place a few hundred yards from Dotti, and medical help came before he could bleed to death.

A few days later, Medina led his men into Song My, establishing a blocking position on a stream to the north while other Task Force Barker units sought the Viet Cong's crack 48th Battalion, then operating in the Song My area. By this time, the three platoons of Charlie Company were patrolling on a rotating basis. The second platoon was in the field cautiously making its way toward the river when it made contact with the enemy. It was a tough fight, Medina remarked later, with intense small-arms and rocket fire. Michael Bernhardt's squad was a few hundred meters behind the other squads. "Somebody yelled 'incoming'—it was in front of us. I sat down on a dike, lit a cigarette, and watched the battle going on. I saw these guys shooting; I couldn't figure it out; it was really confusing. Nobody knew what was going on." But Bernhardt watched as one nearby GI reacted to the attack by firing his M16 rifle at a group of Vietnamese civilians crouching in a rice paddy fifteen feet in front of the men. "The moment the rounds were incoming, this guy let the people have it.... They fell down right fast." After firing, the GI closed in on them. "They were holding their ID cards over their heads. Then he said, 'Okay,' and the people walked away." It had been a family of four—a mother, father, child, and infant. The infant was left behind in the field; it had been struck by one of the GI's bullets.

A few soldiers in the squad near the river were hit by rifle fire from the well-entrenched Viet Cong on the other side. The second platoon was further shaken when mortar shells, flinging showers of shrapnel, injured a few more men. Gunships were called in. "They held them under fire and we took off," Bernhardt recalled, "running back for a mile or so. Then we kind of pulled ourselves together and walked the rest of the way." Gary Crossley of San Marcos, Texas, another member of the second platoon, confirmed that his unit had been overwhelmed. "We had to take off running," he said. "We didn't have a chance." Bernhardt blamed the company officers for the debacle. "It was always ridiculous. They'd sit down and try to figure out what to do next, and it would be over before they figured it out." [...]

By this time the men had been living in the field for nearly three weeks without relief; they were tired, confused, and morale was low. Olsen remembered that the company "always seemed to get the dirty job. Everybody thought that we were getting the short end of the stick." Some were beginning to wonder whether they were being volunteered for additional search-and-destroy duty by Captain Medina, who told the men that the Viet Cong were afraid of Charlie Company and knew what a good unit it was; that's why they had yet to come out and engage it in a firefight. The men of Charlie Company were getting more violent, Olsen recalled, routinely kicking away the Vietnamese children who would come begging for gum or money when the unit went through villages and hamlets. [...]

Michael Terry, a Mormon from Orem, Utah, said that the company simply treated the Vietnamese "like animals. A lot of guys didn't feel that they were human beings." Charles Sledge of Batesville, Mississippi, knew why the Vietnamese were beginning to show increasing hostility to the young GIs. "We did it ourselves. We would go through a village, tearing up stuff, kicking it over, burning it down—I know. I did it."

The company was taking its cue from Captain Medina, who was quick to beat and terrorize suspected Viet Cong soldiers or civilian sympathizers in his attempt to gain intelligence information. John T. Paul of Cherry Hills, New Jersey, one of Medina's radiomen, described the captain's interrogation technique: "He thought that if you could instill fear in a prisoner, you'd most likely get them to talk. He wanted to put a point across right away on these people—'We're not fucking around with you.'" Sometimes Medina's antics brought laughs. Paul recalled that Medina

once hid behind a large rock after hearing that one of the platoons was bringing up an old man—a "papa-san"—for questioning. "He told us to 'watch this' and then jumped out with a roar and grabbed the guy in a bear hug from behind. They started rolling on the ground. The old man was screaming." He already had been gashed on the head with the gunsight from a rifle. The old man defecated in fear, much to the merriment of the company. With another prisoner, Medina suddenly pulled out "his survival knife and cut the guy a little behind the ear." The old man wasn't a Viet Cong, so the company medic patched him up, gave him a cigarette and sent him on his way. [...]

The atrocities began with Carter. About February 15, Charlie Company was assigned another patrol mission in the task-force area. As they filed through a hamlet, Carter offered a "papa-san" a cigarette. As the man took it, Carter suddenly began to club him with his rifle butt. He broke his jaws and ribs. Most of the company watched; some "were mad as hell," Olsen remembered, but no one said anything. Nor was Carter reprimanded. Later that day, the first platoon separated to reconnoiter on its own. By this time, Harry Stanley recalled, the platoon had the idea that "if they wanted to do something wrong, it was always right with Calley. He didn't try to stop them." A few hours later two men in the platoon suddenly began firing at a figure walking across a field. They said he was carrying something. It took a dozen shots with an M16 rifle before he fell. They ran forward and shot again. The victim turned out to be a woman farmer who was carrying the deed to her land in a tube. Stanley translated the writing for Lieutenant Calley, and then listened as the lieutenant radioed Captain Medina and told him his men had killed a Viet Cong.

A few minutes later, two men, possibly Viet Cong guerrillas, were brought in to Calley. He turned this time to Grzesik, who had had 350 hours of Vietnamese language instruction while the company was in Hawaii, to interpret. But before he could begin, Grzesik recalled, "somebody brought in an old man. He was a farmer; there was no doubt in my mind." Grzesik questioned the man, quickly found that he had an identification card. "I told Calley I didn't think he was a VC." But it didn't matter; the first platoon hadn't had any contact with the enemy in weeks. Calley motioned Grzesik away with his M16. "Why are you going to kill him?" Grzesik asked. Calley told him to "get moving." But before Calley could fire, Herbert Carter moved forward.

Harry Stanley was ten feet away. During an interrogation in October 1969, he told the Army's main police unit, the Criminal Investigating Division (CID), what happened next: "Carter hit the old man into a well, but the old man spread his legs and arms and held on and didn't fall.... Then Carter hit the old man in his stomach with his rifle stock. The old man's feet fell into the well, but he continued to hold on with his hands. Carter hit the man's fingers, trying to make him fall ... and Calley shot the man with his M16." [...]

According to Grzesik, Calley then radioed Captain Medina and told him that "an old man jumped in a well and we got him." Calley told his commanding officer the man was a Viet Cong guerrilla. Medina promptly asked Calley to have the well carefully searched to make sure it wasn't part of an enemy tunnel system. No one in the company would crawl into the—by now—bloody well. Calley reported it was not part of a tunnel complex. [...]

On February 25, Charlie Company suffered its worst day. Six men were killed and twelve seriously wounded when it ran into a well-laid minefield north of Pinkville. Most of the casualties were in the first and third platoons. Medina earned the Silver Star, the Army's third-highest medal for valor, for his role in rescuing the wounded. "I lost some of my best men that day," Medina has said. The incident stunned the company. Carter recalled that "the guys were confused. They said, 'Okay, you guys [the Viet Cong] want to be tough. We can be tough right with them.' The VC were blowing us up with mines—sending little kids with grenades. It was getting ridiculous."

The shock of the incident was increased for a few by the nagging thought that perhaps it could have been avoided. Allen Boyce remembered that it happened when "we was in a hurry and had to move through the minefield." Sergeant Cowen was leading the platoon that day and Boyce thought he could have taken his time and gone around the minefield, which was marked on the maps. "A whole lot of guys were mad about it, mad at Sergeant Cowen." Michael Bernhardt remembered something else: the task force was operating in an area that formerly was the responsibility of the South Korean Marines. He was convinced the mine that ruptured the company had been emplaced by the Koreans. "We all knew it, you see"—meaning that the Koreans didn't always clear their minefields or report them, as regulations required. The incident happened, Bernhardt continued, "in a place where the Koreans had laid mines out in their perimeter. But

the guys in the company didn't want to know the sad truth. They were all for the Army; all gung ho. Someone you can blame is the Viet Cong or the Vietnamese. Somebody you can't blame are the big men in the Army. They [the men in Charlie Company] didn't want to believe it.... They knew it. We all talked about it. The truth is that the Koreans had set up a base camp and surrounded it with mines. And we walked into the area that they had set up." [...]

Medina and his men continued their fruitless routine of search-and-destroy missions until the second week in March. [...] On March 14, two days before the mission to My Lai 4, a small squad from the third platoon ran into a booby trap. Gary Garfolo watched Sergeant George Cox lead a patrol into a cluster of trees. Suddenly, he heard Cox call over the radio that he'd found something. "Next thing—kaBOOM—big mushroom cloud, everybody hits the ground. We went over there—this big ruin of a place—and found everybody tore up." Richard Pendleton [of Richmond, California] arrived seconds after the booby trap went off. "Somebody that was injured said Cox picked the bomb up before it went off. He was kind of curious about those things." Cox was killed and one GI lost his eyes, an arm, and a leg. There were screams and calls for medics. Michael Terry, also on the patrol, remembered: "It was a kind of gruesome thing. We were good and mad."

The wounded and dead were lifted away by helicopters and the remaining men in the squad—about eight—began marching back to LZ Dotti. En route, they stole a radio while walking through a small hamlet. "We stole it because we wanted it," Gary Garfolo explained. "They had it and we wanted it—we figured, 'What the hell, they're gooks, they caused Cox's death.'" "Everybody was just taking things," said Pendleton. "They knew that people here might have something to do with it." The squad wanted more revenge. Moments after leaving the hamlet, a GI shouted, "Something's moving in the bushes." Lieutenant Jeffrey La Crosse of the third platoon ordered them to find out what it was. Someone yelled, "He's got a weapon. He's got a weapon," and the squad opened up with M16 rifle fire. The suspect fell, and the squad came running after him. William Doherty [of Reading, Massachusetts] saw what happened next: "I ran there. I was the first to get there. I kicked her, and then I saw she was a woman, so I stopped. But some of the other guys kept on." Michael Terry yelled in protest as he came up to the group. The woman was still alive. Someone suggested calling in a helicopter to evacuate her to a hospital. "She don't need no medivac," one GI suddenly exclaimed, and shot her in the chest. Someone else stole her ring.

The murder and the theft of the radio and ring angered the residents of the hamlet, a secure area near LZ Dotti. They called in the Vietnamese national police. The police began asking around at the LZ; eventually they found their way to Charlie Company and Medina. "Medina was really hot," Garfolo remembered. "Not because we did it, but because it got to him—we got caught." Garfolo didn't remember whether the ring or radio were returned. No charges were filed.

Medina later had a much different version of what had happened. He told a reporter that the booby trap was detonated by remote control and that his company found a fifteen-year-old girl hidden nearby with her hand still on the plunger. His men then killed her, Medina said. He did not mention any theft charges. "Captain Medina just kind of hushed that up," Michael Terry said of the shooting of the woman, "but something like that's a war crime, just out and out a war crime." [...]

On the day after the mine incident, Charlie Company held a brief funeral service for Sergeant George Cox. By all accounts, it was a moving occasion. "The men were hurt real bad, real bad," Henry Pedrick said. "The company was very upset. The company was also very angry. It had revenge on its mind." Like other members of the company, Pedrick came close to tears as he talked about it.

After the chaplain's service, Medina got up to speak. The men were quiet. Charles West [of Chicago, a member of the third platoon] remembered what the captain said: "He knew it was hard on them, but it was just as hard on him. Maybe he didn't show it because he was held responsible for being a leader but that was no reason for the guys to hold back. He said to let it out, let it go." At this point, West said, many of the men of Charlie Company cried.

Medina then began to tell his men about the next day's mission. As Medina described it later, he and Colonel Barker had begun planning the mission early in the day. At one point, they flew from LZ Dotti in a helicopter for a peek at My Lai 4, 11 kilometers to the south, being careful not to get too close and alert the enemy. Barker told Medina that elements of the 48th Viet Cong Battalion, one of the enemy's best units with a strength of 250 to 280 men, was in My Lai 4. The colonel said intelligence reports predicted that the

hamlet's women and children would be gone by 7:00 A.M., en route to the weekly markets in Quang Ngai City or Son Tinh Districts. Charlie Company's mission was to destroy the 48th Battalion as well as My Lai 4. Medina was ordered to burn houses and blow up bunkers and tunnels, along with killing the livestock. Normally, killing the animals was not done, Medina said, but he didn't think it was unusual. "The idea was to destroy the village so the 48th VC would be forced to move. It looked like a tough fight," he said. The captain claimed that his men would be out-numbered at least two-to-one by the Viet Cong during the assault, but added that he did not expect heavy casualties. "I have a lot of faith in the firepower that the American infantryman has. The helicopter pilots and the gunship pilots do a tremendous job in supporting the infantryman on the ground."*

His objective in the pep talk after the funeral that night, he later explained, was to "fire them up to get them ready to go in there. I did not give any instructions as to what to do with women and children in the village."

There were sharply conflicting opinions among the company over what Medina did order. Many thought the captain had ordered them to kill every person in the hamlet. Others thought that he had given routine—if more emotional—orders for a search-and-destroy mission. A few felt that Medina had been vague, as if to leave the interpretation of his orders for the next day to the feelings and conscience of the individual soldier.

Harry Stanley later told the CID that Medina "ordered us to 'kill everything in the village.' The men in my squad talked about this among ourselves that night," Stanley said, "because the order...was so unusual. We all agreed that Medina meant for us to kill every man, woman, and child in the village." Charles West remembered hearing the captain saying that when Charlie Company left the area, "nothing

---

* Despite Medina's confidence in the ability of helicopter gunships, there is a puzzling aspect to Charlie Company's mission as outlined by Medina. Most military tacticians, especially those in Vietnam, agree that an attacking force must have a manpower superiority of at least three-to-one over a well-armed enemy force defending fortified positions. Only 70 to 75 GIs from Charlie Company took part in the assault against the expected 250 to 280 Viet Cong guerrillas. Charlie Company thus would actually have been outnumbered four-to-one. Even more puzzling, then, were Medina's eventual decisions to attack the hamlet by initially sending in only two platoons, and to land the company less than 200 yards from My Lai 4, well within range of enemy rifle fire. The inevitable question left begging is: did Medina really expect to find Viet Cong troops in My Lai 4?

would be walking, growing, or crawling." He also recalled the captain saying that the women and children would be out of the area. Herbert Carter told the CID he thought Medina had been explicit. "Well, boys," he said the captain told them, "this is your chance to get revenge on these people. When we go into My Lai, it's open season. When we leave, nothing will be living. Everything's going to go." [...]

But Gregory Olsen was sure Captain Medina did not order the killing of women and children: "He did say—he did make the statement—that we had a score to even up. He did tell us that we were to go there and destroy the food supply and hamlet. He said it was known that VC sympathizers were in My Lai 4 and that it was harboring VCs. He told us to shoot the enemy." At this point someone asked, "Who was the enemy?" Olsen said Medina then defined "the enemy as anybody that was running from us, hiding from us, or who appeared to us to be the enemy. If a man was running, shoot him; sometimes even if a woman with a rifle was running, shoot her. He never at any time said, 'Slaughter the people.'" Ron Grzesik agreed with Olsen. He heard Medina tell the men "to go in and destroy the village; to make it uninhabitable," but did not recall an order to destroy the inhabitants.

Perhaps the best answer to what was said or what was believed has been supplied by Henry Pedrick: "The orders could be interpreted in different ways to different persons according to their emotional structure.... One person just might interpret it to kill if he wanted to." The question about who was the enemy was asked by Michael Terry. He thought the captain was in an awkward position because of the charged atmosphere following the funeral service. "Guys were asking when they would have a chance to fight instead of marching around and getting blown up. Some of the guys were all shook up, and like a good captain he was trying to appease them." The net result, Terry said, was that Medina "gave the impression—he never specifically said it—that they could kill the people...that they could kill anybody they saw. I remember paying attention to how he was handling the situation. It seemed like there would be a whole lot of killing the next day."

Most significantly, Lieutenant William Calley thought so, too. "Every time we got hit [in the Pinkville area] it was from the rear," Calley recalled later. "So the third time in there the order came down to go in there and make sure no one was behind us. Just to clear the area. It was a typical combat assault tactic. We came in hot [firing], with a cover

of artillery in front of us, came down the line, and destroyed the village." [...]

For Ron Grzesik, My Lai 4 was the end of a vicious circle that had begun months earlier. "It was like going from one step to another, worse one," he says. "First, you'd stop the people, question them, and let them go. Second, you'd stop the people, beat up an old man, and let them go. Third, you'd stop the people, beat up an old man, and then shoot him. Fourth, you go in and wipe out a village."

Nobody saw it all. Some, like Roy Wood, didn't even know the extent of the massacre until the next day. Others, like Charles Sledge, who served that day as Calley's radioman, saw more than they want to remember.

But they all remember the fear that morning as they climbed onto helicopters at LZ Dotti for the assault on Pinkville. They all remember the sure knowledge that they would meet face-to-face for the first time with the enemy.

Calley and his platoon were the first to board the large black Army assault helicopters. The men were heavily armed, each carrying twice the normal load of rifle and machine-gun ammunition. Leading the way was Calley, who had slung an extra belt of M16 rifle bullets over his shoulder. There were nine helicopters in the first lift-off, more than enough for the whole first platoon—about twenty-five men—and Captain Medina and his small headquarters unit of three radiomen, some liaison officers, and a medic. It was sunny and already hot when the first helicopter started its noisy flight to My Lai 4. The time was 7:22 A.M.; it was logged by a tape recorder at brigade headquarters. A brief artillery barrage had already begun; the My Lai 4 area was being "prepped" in anticipation of that day's search-and-destroy mission. A few heavily armed helicopters were firing thousands of small-caliber bullets into the area by the time Calley and his men landed in a soggy rice paddy 150 meters west of the hamlet. It was harvest season; the fields were thick with growth.

The first platoon's mission was to secure the landing zone and make sure no enemy troops were left to fire at the second wave of helicopters—by then already airborne from LZ Dotti. As the flight of helicopters hovered over the landing area, the door gunners began spraying protective fire to keep the enemy—if he was there—busy. One of the helicopter pilots had reported that the LZ was "hot," that is, Viet Cong were waiting below. The first platoon came out firing. But, after a moment, some men noticed that there was no return fire. "I didn't hear any bullets going past me," recalled Charles Hall, a machine gunner that day. "If you want to consider an area hot, you got to be fired on."

The platoon quickly formed a perimeter and secured the landing zone. [...] After about twenty minutes, the second flight of helicopters landed, and the forty men of the second and third platoons jumped off. Gary Garfolo heard the helicopter blades make sharp crackling sounds as they changed pitch for the landing. "It was a pop, pop, pop sound like a rifle. Lots of us never even heard a hot LZ before. We knew we were going into a hot place. This got their adrenaline going." The men were quickly assembled. Calley's first platoon and Lieutenant Stephen Brooks' second platoon would lead the sweep into the hamlet, Calley to the south and Brooks to the north. The third platoon, headed by Lieutenant Jeffrey La Crosse, would be held in reserve and move in on the heels of the other men. Captain Medina and his headquarters unit would move with the third platoon and then set up a command post (CP) inside to monitor the operation and stay in touch with other units. Charlie Company was not alone in its assault; the other two companies of Task Force Barker set up blocking positions to the north and south. They were there to prevent the expected Viet Cong troops from fleeing.

The My Lai 4 assault was the biggest thing going in the Americal Division that day. To get enough airlift, Task Force Barker had to borrow helicopters from other units throughout the division. The air lanes above the action were carefully allotted to high-ranking officers for observation. Barker monitored the battle from the 1,000-foot level. Major General Samuel W. Koster, commanding general of the division, was allotted the air space at 2,000 feet. His helicopter was permanently stationed outside his door at division headquarters 21 miles to the north waiting to fly him to the scene of any action within minutes. Oran K. Henderson, commander of the Eleventh Brigade, was given the top spot—at 2,500 feet. All of the helicopters were to circle counterclockwise over the battle area. Flying low, beneath the 1,000-foot level, would be the gunships, heavily armed helicopters whose mission was to shoot down any Viet Cong soldiers attempting to escape.

Brigade headquarters, sure that there would be a major battle, sent along two men from the Army's 31st Public Information Detachment to record the event for history. Jay Roberts of Arlington, Virginia, a reporter, and photographer Ronald L. Haeberle of Cleveland, Ohio, arrived with the second wave of helicopters and immediately attached themselves to the third platoon, which was bringing up the rear.

The hamlet itself had a population of about 700 people, living either in flimsy thatch-covered huts—"hootches," as the GIs called them—or in solidly made red-brick homes, many with small porches in front. There was an east-west footpath just south of the main cluster of homes in My Lai 4: a few yards further south was a loose surface road that marked a hamlet boundary. A deep drainage ditch and then a rice paddy marked the eastern boundary. To the south of My Lai 4 was a large center, or plaza area—clearly the main spot for mass meetings. The foliage was dense: there were high bamboo trees, hedges, and plant life everywhere. Medina couldn't see 30 feet into the hamlet from the landing zone.

The first and second platoons lined up carefully to begin the 100-meter advance into the hamlet. Walking in line is an important military concept; if one group of men gets too far in front, it could be hit by bullets from behind—those fired by colleagues. Yet even this went wrong. Ron Grzesik was in charge of a small first-platoon team of riflemen and a machine gunner that day; he took his job seriously. His unit was supposed to be on the right flank, protecting Calley and his men. But Grzesik's group ended up on Calley's left.

As Brooks' second platoon cautiously approached the hamlet, a few Vietnamese began running across a field several hundred meters on the left. They may have been Viet Cong, or they may have been civilians fleeing the artillery shelling or the bombardment from the helicopter gunships. Vernado Simpson, Jr. of Jackson, Mississippi, told reporters he saw a man he identified as a Viet Cong soldier running with what seemed to be a weapon. A woman and small child were running with him. Simpson fired...again and again. He killed the woman and the baby. The man got away. Reporter Roberts saw a squad of GIs jump off a helicopter and begin firing at a group of people running on a nearby road. One was a woman with her children. Then he saw them "shoot two guys who popped up from a rice field. They looked like military-age men...when certain guys pop up from rice fields, you shoot them." This was the young reporter's most dangerous assignment. He had never been in combat before. "You're scared to death out there. We just wanted to go home."

The first two platoons of Charlie Company, still unfired upon, entered My Lai 4. Behind them, still in the rice paddy, were the third platoon and Captain Medina's command group. Calley and some of his men walked into the plaza area in the southern part of My Lai 4. None of the villagers was running away; they knew that U.S. soldiers would assume that anyone running was a Viet Cong and shoot to kill. There was no immediate sense of panic. The time was after 8:00 A.M. Grzesik and his fire team were a few meters north of Calley; they couldn't see each other because of the dense vegetation. Grzesik and his men began their usual job of pulling people from their homes, interrogating them, and searching for Viet Cong. The villagers were gathered up, and Grzesik sent Paul Meadlo, [an easygoing farm boy from Terre Haute, Indiana,] who was in his unit, to take them to Lieutenant Calley for further questioning. Grzesik didn't see Meadlo again for more than an hour.

Some of Calley's men recalled thinking it was breakfast time as they walked in; a few families were gathered in front of their homes cooking rice over a small fire. Without a direct order, the first platoon also began rounding up the villagers. There still was no sniper fire, no sign of a large enemy unit. Sledge remembered thinking that "if there were VC around, they had plenty of time to leave before we came in. We didn't tiptoe in there."

The killings began without warning. Harry Stanley told the CID that one young member of Calley's platoon took a civilian into custody and then "pushed the man up to where we were standing and then stabbed the man in the back with his bayonet.... The man fell to the ground and was gasping for breath." The GI then "killed him with another bayonet thrust or by shooting him with a rifle.... There were so many people killed that day it is hard for me to recall exactly how some of the people died." The youth next "turned to where some soldiers were holding another forty- or fifty-year-old man in custody." He "picked this man up and threw him down a well. Then [he] pulled the pin from a M26 grenade and threw it in after the man." Moments later Stanley saw "some old women and some little children—fifteen or twenty of them—in a group around a temple where some incense was burning. They were kneeling and crying and praying and various soldiers... walked by and executed these women and children by shooting them in the head with their rifles. The soldiers killed all fifteen or twenty of them...."

There were few physical protests from the people; about eighty of them were taken quietly from their homes and herded together in the plaza area. A few hollered out, "No VC. No VC." But that was hardly unexpected. Calley left Meadlo, Boyce, and a few others with the responsibility of guarding the group. "You know what I want you to do with them," he told Meadlo. Ten minutes later—about 8:15 A.M.—he returned and asked, "Haven't you got rid of them yet? I want them dead." Radioman Sledge, who was trailing Calley, heard the officer tell Meadlo to "waste them." Meadlo followed orders: "We stood about 10 to 15 feet away from them and then he [Calley] started shooting them. Then he told me to start shooting them. I started to shoot them. So we went ahead and killed them. I used more than a whole clip—used four or five clips." There are seventeen M16 bullets in each clip. Boyce slipped away, to the northern side of the hamlet, glad he hadn't been asked to shoot. Women were huddled against their children, vainly trying to save them. Some continued to chant "No VC." Others simply said, "No. No. No." [...]

The few Viet Cong who had chosen to stay near the hamlet were safely hidden. Nguyen Ngo, a former deputy commander of a Viet Cong guerrilla platoon operating in the My Lai area, ran to his hiding place 300 meters away when the GIs came in shooting, but he could see that "they shot everything in sight." His mother and sister hid in ditches and survived because bodies fell on top of them. Pham Lai, a former hamlet security guard, climbed into a bunker with a bamboo top and heard but did not see the shootings. His wife, hidden under a body, survived the massacre.

By this time, there was shooting everywhere. Dennis I. Conti, a GI from Providence, Rhode Island, later explained to CID investigators what he thought had happened. "We were all psyched up, and as a result when we got there the shooting started, almost as a chain reaction. The majority of us had expected to meet VC combat troops, but this did not turn out to be so. First we saw a few men running... and the next thing I knew we were shooting at everything. Everybody was just firing. After they got in the village, I guess you could say that the men were out of control."

Brooks and his men in the second platoon to the north had begun to ransack the hamlet systematically and slaughter the people, kill the livestock, and destroy the crops. Men poured rifle and machine-gun fire into huts without knowing—or seemingly caring—who was inside. [...]

Once the first two platoons had disappeared into the hamlet, Medina ordered the third platoon to start moving. He and his men followed. Gary Garfolo was caught up in the confusion: "I could hear heavy shooting all the time. Medina was running back and forth everywhere. This wasn't no organized deal." So Garfolo did what most GIs did when they could get away with it. "I took off on my own." He ran south; others joined him. Terrified villagers, many carrying personal belongings in wicker baskets, were running everywhere to avoid the carnage in the hamlet. In most cases it didn't help. The helicopter gunships circling above cut them down, or else an unfortunate group ran into the third platoon. Charles A. West sighted and shot six Vietnamese, some with baskets, on the edge of My Lai 4. "These people were running into us, away from us, running every which way. It's hard to distinguish a mama-san from a papa-san when everybody has on black pajamas."

West and his men may have thought that those Vietnamese were Viet Cong. Later they knew better. West's first impression upon reaching My Lai 4: "There were no people in the first part.... I seen bodies everywhere. I knew that everyone was being killed." His group, no longer burdened by questions of differentiation, quickly joined in.

Medina—as any combat officer would do during his unit's first major engagement—decided to move from the rice paddy nearer to the hamlet. John Paul, one of Medina's radiomen, figured that the time was about 8:15 A.M. West remembered that "Medina was right behind us" as his platoon moved inside the hamlet. There are serious contradictions about what happened next. Medina later said he did not enter the hamlet proper until well after 10:00 A.M. and did not see anyone kill a civilian. John Paul didn't think that Medina ever entered the hamlet. But Herbert Carter told the CID that Medina did some of the shooting of civilians as he moved into My Lai 4.

Carter testified that soon after the third platoon moved in, a woman was sighted. Somebody knocked her down and then, Carter said, "Medina shot her with his M16 rifle. I was 50 to 60 feet away and saw this. There was no reason to shoot this girl." The men continued on, making sure no one was escaping. "We came to where the soldiers had collected fifteen or more Vietnamese men, women, and children in a group. Medina said, 'Kill every one. Leave no one standing.'" A machine gunner began firing into the group. Moments later, one of Medina's radio operators slowly "passed among them and finished them off." Medina did not personally shoot any of them, according to Carter, but moments later, the captain "stopped a seventeen- or eighteen-year-old man with a water buffalo. Medina told the boy to make a run for it,"

Carter told the CID. "He tried to get him to run but the boy wouldn't run, so Medina shot him with his M16 rifle and killed him.... I was 75 or 80 meters away at the time and I saw it plainly." At this point in Carter's interrogation, the Army investigator warned him that he was making very serious charges against his commanding officer. "What I'm telling is the truth," Carter replied, "and I'll face Medina in court and swear to it."

If Carter is correct, Medina walked first into the north side of My Lai 4, then moved south with the CP to the hamlet plaza, and arrived there at about the time Paul Meadlo and Lieutenant Calley were executing the first group of villagers. Meadlo still wonders why Medina didn't stop the shooting, "if it was wrong." Medina and Calley "passed each other quite a few times that morning, but didn't say anything. I don't know if the CO [company commander] gave the order to kill or not, but he was right there when it happened.... Medina just kept marching around."

Roberts and Haeberle also moved in just behind the third platoon. Haeberle watched a group of ten to fifteen GIs methodically pump bullets into a cow until it keeled over. A woman then poked her head out from behind some brush; she may have been hiding in a bunker. The GIs turned the fire from the cow to the woman. "They just kept shooting at her. You could see the bones flying in the air chip by chip." No one had attempted to question her; men inside the hamlet also were asking no questions. Before moving on, the photographer took a picture of the dead woman. Haeberle took many more pictures that day; he saw about thirty GIs kill at least a hundred Vietnamese civilians.

When the two correspondents entered the hamlet, they saw dead animals, dead people, burning huts and homes. A few GIs were going through victims' clothing, looking for piasters. Another GI was chasing a duck with a knife; others stood around watching a GI slaughter a cow with a bayonet.

Haeberle noticed a man and two small children walking toward a group of GIs. "They just kept walking toward us.... You could hear the little girl saying, 'No, no....' All of a sudden, the GIs opened up and cut them down." Later, on his left, he watched a machine gunner suddenly open fire on a group of civilians—women, children, and babies—who had been collected in a big circle. "They were trying to run. I don't know how many got out." He saw a GI with an M16 rifle fire at two young boys walking along a road; the older of the two—about seven or eight years old—fell over the first to protect him. The GI kept on firing until both were dead.

Haeberle and Roberts walked further into the hamlet, and Medina came up to them. Eighty-five Viet Cong had been killed in action thus far, the captain told them, and twenty suspects had been captured. Roberts jotted down the captain's information in his note pad. [...]

Now it was nearly 9:00 A.M. and all of Charlie Company was in My Lai 4. Most families were being shot inside their homes, or just outside their doorways. Those who had tried to flee were crammed by GIs into the many bunkers built throughout the hamlet for protection—once the bunkers became filled, hand grenades were lobbed in. Everything became a target. Gary Garfolo borrowed someone's M79 grenade launcher and fired it point-blank at a water buffalo. "I hit that sucker right in the head; went down like a shot. You don't get to shoot water buffalo with an M79 every day." Others fired the weapon into the bunkers full of people. [...]

Grzesik and his men, meanwhile, had been slowly working their way through the hamlet. The young GI was having problems controlling his men; he was anxious to move on to the rice paddy in the east. About three-quarters of the way through, he suddenly saw Meadlo again. The time was now after 9:00 A.M. Meadlo was crouched, head in his hands, sobbing like a bewildered child. "I sat down and asked him what happened." Grzesik felt responsible; after all, he was supposed to be a team leader. Meadlo told him Calley had made him shoot people. "I tried to calm him down," Grzesik says, but the squad leader didn't stay long. He had to move on; his men still hadn't completed their sweep.

Those Vietnamese who were not killed on the spot were being shepherded by the first platoon to a large drainage ditch at the eastern end of the hamlet. After Grzesik left, Meadlo and a few others gathered seven or eight villagers in one hut and were preparing to toss in a hand grenade when an order came to take them to the ditch where they found Calley, along with a dozen other first platoon members, and perhaps seventy-five Vietnamese, mostly women, old men, and children.

Not far away, invisible in the brush and trees, the second and third platoons were continuing their search-and-destroy operations in the northern half of the hamlet. Ron Grzesik and his fire team had completed a swing through the hamlet and were getting ready to turn around and walk back to see what was going on. And just south of the plaza Michael Bernhardt had attached himself to Medina and his command post. Shots were still being fired, the helicopters were still whirring overhead, and the enemy was still nowhere in sight.

One of the helicopters was piloted by Chief Warrant Officer Hugh C. Thompson of Decatur, Georgia. For him, the mission had begun routinely enough. He and his two-man crew in a small observation helicopter from the 123rd Aviation Battalion had arrived at the area around 9:00 A.M. and immediately reported what appeared to be a Viet Cong soldier armed with a weapon heading south. Although his mission was simply reconnaissance, Thompson directed his crew men to fire at and attempt to kill the Viet Cong as he wheeled the helicopter after him. They missed. Thompson flew back to the hamlet and it was then, as he told the Army Inspector General's office in June 1969, that he began seeing wounded and dead Vietnamese civilians all over the hamlet, with no sign of an enemy force.

The pilot thought that the best thing he could do would be to mark the location of wounded civilians with smoke so that the GIs on the ground could move over and begin treating some of the many injured persons. "The first one that I marked was a girl that was wounded," Thompson told the Inspector General (IG), "and they came over and walked up to her, put their weapon on automatic and let her have it." The man who did the shooting was a captain, Thompson said. Later he identified the officer as Ernest Medina.

Flying with Thompson that day was Lawrence M. Colburn of Mount Vernon, Washington, who remembers that the girl was about twenty years old and was lying on the edge of a dike outside of the hamlet with part of her body in a rice paddy. "She had been wounded in the stomach, I think, or the chest," Colburn told the IG. "This captain was coming down the dike and he had men behind him. They were sweeping through and we were hovering a matter of feet away from them. I could see this clearly and he emptied a clip into her."

Medina and his men immediately began moving south toward the Viet Cong sighted and reported by Thompson. En route they saw the young girl in the rice paddy who had been marked by the smoke. Bernhardt had a ground view of what happened next: "He [Medina] was just going alone... he shot the woman. She seemed to be busy picking rice, but rice was out of season. What she really was doing was trying to pretend that she was picking rice. She was 100 meters away with a basket.... If she had a hand grenade, she would have to have a better arm than me to get us.... Medina lifted the rifle to his shoulder, looked down the barrel and pulled the trigger. I saw the woman drop. He just took a potshot...he wasn't a bad shot. Then he walked up. He got up real close, about three or six feet, and shot at her a couple times and finished her off. She was a real clean corpse.... She wasn't all over the place, and I could see her clothing move when the bullets hit.... I could see her twitch, but I couldn't see any holes...he didn't shoot her in the head." A second later, Bernhardt remembered, the captain "gave me a look, a dumb shit-eating grin."

By now, it was past 9:30 A.M. and the men of Charlie Company had been at work for more than two hours. A few of them flung off their helmets, stripped off their heavy gear, flopped down, and took a smoke break.

Hugh Thompson's nightmare had only begun with the shooting of the girl. He flew north back over My Lai 4 and saw a small boy bleeding along a trench. Again he marked the spot so that the GIs below could provide some medical aid. Instead, he saw a lieutenant casually walk up and empty a clip into the child. He saw yet another wounded youngster; again he marked it, and this time it was a sergeant who came up and fired his M16 at the child. [...]

Thompson was furious. He tried unsuccessfully to radio the troops on the ground to find out what was going on. He then reported the wild firings and unnecessary shootings to brigade headquarters. All of the command helicopters flying overhead had multichannel radios and could monitor most conversations. Lieutenant Colonel Barker apparently intercepted the message and called down to Medina at the CP just south of the plaza. John Kinch of the mortar platoon heard Medina answer that he "had a body count of 310." The captain added, "I don't know what they're doing. The first platoon's in the lead. I am trying to stop it." A moment later, Kinch said, Medina called Calley and ordered, "That's enough for today."

Harry Stanley was standing a few feet away from Calley near some huts at the drainage ditch when the call came from Medina. He had a different recollection: "Medina called Calley and said, 'What the fuck is going on?' Calley said he got some VC, or some people that needed to be checked out." At this point Medina cautioned Calley to tell his men to save their ammunition because the operation still had a few more days to run.

It is not clear how soon or to whom Medina's order was given, but Stanley told the CID what Calley did next:

"There was an old lady in a bed and I believe there was a priest in white praying over her.... Calley told me to ask about the VC and NVA and where the weapons were. The priest denied being a VC or NVA." Charles Sledge watched with horror as Calley pulled the old man outside: "He said a few more words to the monk. It looked like the monk was pleading for his life. Lieutenant Calley then took his rifle and pushed the monk into a rice paddy and shot him point-blank."

Calley then turned his attention back to the crowd of Vietnamese and issued an order: "Push all those people in the ditch." Three or four GIs complied. Calley struck a woman with a rifle as he pushed her down. Stanley remembered that some of the civilians "kept trying to get out. Some made it to the top...." Calley began the shooting and ordered Meadlo to join in. Meadlo told about it later: "So we pushed our seven to eight people in with the big bunch of them. And so I began shooting them all. So did Mitchell, Calley.... I guess I shot maybe twenty-five or twenty people in the ditch...men, women, and children. And babies." Some of the GIs switched from automatic fire to single shot to conserve ammunition. Herbert Carter watched the mothers "grabbing their kids and the kids grabbing their mothers. I didn't know what to do." Calley then turned again to Meadlo and said, "Meadlo, we've got another job to do." Meadlo didn't want any more jobs. He began to argue with Calley. Sledge watched Meadlo once more start to sob. Calley turned next to Robert Maples and said, "Maples, load your machine gun and shoot these people." Maples replied, as he told the CID, "I'm not going to do that." He remembered that "the people firing into the ditch kept reloading magazines into their rifles and kept firing into the ditch and then killed or at least shot everyone in the ditch." William C. Lloyd of Tampa, Florida, told the CID that some grenades were also thrown into the ditch. Dennis Conti noticed that "a lot of women had thrown themselves on top of the children to protect them, and the children were alive at first. Then the children who were old enough to walk got up and Calley began to shoot the children."

One further incident stood out in many GIs' minds: seconds after the shooting stopped, a bloodied but unhurt two-year-old boy miraculously crawled out of the ditch, crying. He began running toward the hamlet. Someone hollered, "There's a kid." There was a long pause. Then Calley ran back, grabbed the child, threw him back in the ditch, and shot him.

Moments later, Thompson, still in his helicopter, flew by. He told the IG what had happened next: "I kept flying around and across a ditch... and it... had a bunch of bodies in it and I don't know how they got in the ditch. But I saw some of them were still alive." Captain Brian W. Livingston was piloting a large helicopter gunship a few hundred feet above. He had been monitoring Thompson's agonized complaints and went down to take a look for himself. He told a military hearing: "There were bodies lying in the trenches.... I remembered that we remarked at the time about the old Biblical story of Jesus turning water into wine. The trench had a gray color to it, with the red blood of the individuals lying in it."

By now Thompson was almost frantic. He landed his small helicopter near the ditch, and asked a soldier there if he could help the people out: "He said the only way he could help them was to help them out of their misery." Thompson took off again and noticed a group of mostly women and children huddled together in a bunker near the drainage ditch. He landed a second time. "I don't know," he explained, "maybe it was just my belief, but I hadn't been shot at the whole time I had been there and the gunships following hadn't...." He then saw Calley and the first platoon; the same group that had shot two of the wounded civilians he had earlier marked with smoke. "I asked him if he could get the women and kids out of there before they tore it [the bunker] up and he said the only way he could get them out was to use hand grenades." "You just hold your men right here," Thompson told the equally angry Calley, "and I will get the women and kids out." [...]

Before climbing out of his aircraft, Thompson had ordered Colburn and his crew chief to stay alert. "He told us that if any of the Americans opened up on the Vietnamese, we should open up on the Americans," Colburn recalled. Thompson walked back to the ship and called in two helicopter gunships to rescue the civilians. While waiting for them to land, Colburn said, "he stood between our troops and the bunker. He was shielding the people with his body. He just wanted to get those people out of there." [...] The helicopters landed, with Thompson still standing between the GIs and the Vietnamese, and rescued nine persons—two old men, two women, and five children. One of the children later died en route to the hospital. Calley did nothing to stop Thompson, but later stormed up to Sledge, his radioman, and complained that the pilot "doesn't like the way I'm running the show, but I'm the boss." [...]

Grzesik had seen the helicopter carrying some wounded Vietnamese take off from the area a moment earlier; much later he concluded that Calley—furious with Thompson's intervention—wanted to make sure there were no more survivors in the ditch. Calley told Grzesik to gather his team to do the job. "I really believed he expected me to do it," Grzesik said later, with some amazement. Calley asked him again and Grzesik again refused. The lieutenant then angrily ordered him to take his team and help burn the hootches. Grzesik headed for the hamlet plaza.

Thompson continued to fly over the ditch and noticed that some of the children's bodies had no heads. He landed a third time after his crew chief told him that he had seen some movement in the mass of bodies and blood below. The crew chief and Colburn walked toward the ditch. "Nobody said anything," Colburn said. "We just got out." They found a young child still alive. No GIs were in the immediate area. The crew chief climbed into the ditch. "He was knee-deep in people and blood." The child was quiet, buried under many bodies. "He was still holding onto his mother," Colburn said. "But she was dead." The child, clinging desperately, was pried loose. He still did not cry. Thompson later told the Inspector General: "I don't think this child was even wounded at all, just down there among all the other bodies, and he was terrified." Thompson and his men flew the baby to Quang Ngai Hospital and safety.

In other parts of My Lai 4, GIs were taking a break, or loafing. Others were systematically burning those remaining homes and huts and destroying food. Some villagers—still alive—were able to leave their hiding places and walk away. Charles West recalled that one member of his squad who simply wasn't able to slaughter a group of children asked for and received permission from an officer to let them go.

West's third platoon went ahead, nonetheless, with the killing. They gathered a group of about ten women and children, who huddled together in fear a few feet from the plaza, where dozens of villagers already had been slain. West and his squad had finished their mission in the north and west of the hamlet, and were looking for new targets. They drifted south toward the CP. Jay Roberts and Ron Haeberle, who had spent the last hour watching the slaughter in other parts of the hamlet, stood by—pencil and cameras at the ready. A few men now singled out a slender Vietnamese girl of about fifteen. They tore her from the group and started to pull at her blouse. They attempted to fondle her breasts. The old women and children were screaming and crying. One GI yelled, "Let's see what she's made of." Another said, "VC boom, boom," meaning she was a Viet Cong whore. Jay Roberts thought that the girl was good-looking. An old lady began fighting with fanatical fury, trying to protect the girl. Roberts said, "She was fighting off two or three guys at once. She was fantastic. Usually they're pretty passive.... They hadn't even gotten that chick's blouse off when Haeberle came along." One of the GIs finally smacked the old woman with his rifle butt; another booted her in the rear.

Grzesik and his fire team watched the fight develop as they walked down from the ditch to the hamlet center. Grzesik was surprised: "I thought the village was cleared.... I didn't know there were that many people left." He knew trouble was brewing, and his main thought was to keep his team out of it. He helped break up the fight. Some of the children were desperately hanging onto the old lady as she struggled. Grzesik was worried about the cameraman. He may have yelled, "Hey, there's a photographer." He remembered thinking: "Here's a guy that you've never seen before standing there with a camera." Then somebody said, "What do we do with them?" A GI answered "Waste them." Suddenly there was a burst of automatic fire from many guns. Only a small child survived. Somebody then carefully shot him, too. A photograph of the woman and child, with the young Vietnamese girl tucking in her blouse, was later published in *Life*. Roberts tried to explain later: "It's just that they didn't know what they were supposed to do; killing them seemed like a good idea, so they did it. The old lady who fought so hard was probably a VC." He thought a moment and added: "Maybe it was just her daughter." [...]

By now it was nearly 10:30 A.M. and most of the company began drifting aimlessly toward the plaza and the command post a few yards to the south. Their work was largely over; a good part of the hamlet was in flames. [...]

Herb Carter and Harry Stanley had shed their gear and were taking a short break at the CP. Near them was a young Vietnamese boy, crying, with a bullet wound in his stomach. Stanley watched one of Captain Medina's three radio operators walk along a trail toward them; he was without his radio gear. As Stanley later told the CID, the radio operator went up to Carter and said, "Let me see your pistol." Carter gave it to him. The radio operator "then stepped within two feet of the boy and shot him in the neck with a pistol. Blood gushed from the child's neck. He then tried to walk off, but he could only take two or three steps. Then he fell onto the ground. He lay there and took four or five deep breaths and then he stopped breathing." The radio operator turned to Stanley and said, "Did you see how I shot that son of a bitch?" Stanley told him, "I don't see how anyone could just kill a kid." Carter got his pistol back; he told Stanley, "I can't take this no more...." Moments later Stanley heard a gun go off and Carter yell. "I went to Carter and saw he had shot himself in the foot," Stanley remembered. "I think Carter shot himself on purpose."

Other children were also last-minute targets. After the scene with the women and children, West noticed a small boy, about seven years old, staring dazedly beside a footpath. He had been shot in the leg. "He was just standing there staring; I don't think he was crying. Somebody asked, 'What do we do with him?'" At this point West had remembered there had been an order from Captain Medina to stop the shooting. "I just shrugged my shoulders," West recalled, "and said, 'I don't know,' and just kept walking." Seconds later he heard some shots, turned around and saw the boy no longer standing on the trail.

Haeberle and Roberts were walking together on the edge of the hamlet when they also noticed the wounded child with the vacant stare. In seconds, Roberts said, "Haeberle, envisioning the war-torn-wounded-waif picture of the year, got within five feet of the kid for a close-up. He was focusing when some guy, just walking along, leveled his rifle, fired three times, and walked away." Haeberle saw the shooting through the lens of his camera. "He looked up in shock," Roberts added. "He just turned around and stared. I think that was the thing that stayed in our mind. It was so close, so real; we just saw some kid blown away."

By then a helicopter had landed near the command post, under Medina's supervision, to fly out the wounded Carter. [...] One of Haeberle's photographs shows the company medic bandaging Carter, with Medina and a radio operator, Rodger Murray of Waukegan, Illinois, in the background near a partially destroyed red-brick house. Medina was on the radio. William Wyatt remembered the scene; that was the first time he'd seen Medina that morning. Roy Wood also saw him then for the first time. Others recalled, however, that the captain had left his command post south of the plaza many times during the late morning to tour the northern and western sections, urging the men to stop the shooting and get on with the job of burning down the buildings. Some GIs from the second platoon, under Lieutenant Brooks, found three men still alive. Gary Crossley heard the

GIs ask Brooks, "What do we do now?" The lieutenant relayed the question by radio to Medina. "Don't kill them," the captain said. "There's been too much of that already." Gary Garfolo remembered that Medina seemed frantic at times, dashing about the hamlet: "He was telling everybody, 'Let's start getting out—let's move out of here.'" [...]

Most of the shooting was over by the time Medina called a break for lunch, shortly after 11:00 A.M. By then, Roberts and Haeberle had grabbed a helicopter and cleared out of the area, their story for the day far bigger than they wanted. Calley, Mitchell, Sledge, Grzesik, and a few others went back to the command post west of My Lai 4 to take lunch with Captain Medina and the rest of his headquarters crew. Grzesik recalled that at that point he had thought there couldn't be a survivor left in the hamlet. But two little girls showed up, about ten and eleven years old. John Paul said they came in from one of the paddies where they apparently had waited out the siege. "We sat them down with us [at the command post]," Paul recounts "and gave them some cookies and crackers to eat." When a CID interrogator later asked Charles Sledge how many civilians he thought had survived, he answered: "Only two small children who had lunch with us."

In the early afternoon, the men of Charlie Company mopped up to make sure all the houses and goods in My Lai 4 were destroyed. Medina ordered the underground tunnels in the hamlet blown up; most of them already had been blocked. Within another hour, My Lai 4 was no more; its red-brick buildings demolished by explosives, its huts burned to the ground, its people dead or dying.

Michael Bernhardt later summarized the day: "We met no resistance and I only saw three captured weapons. We had no casualties. It was just like any other Vietnamese village—old papa-sans, women, and kids. As a matter of fact, I don't remember seeing one military age male in the entire place, dead or alive. The only prisoner I saw was in his fifties."

The three platoons of Company C pulled out shortly after noon, rendezvousing in the rice paddies east of the hamlet. Lieutenant Brooks' second platoon had about eighty-five villagers in tow; it kept those of military age with them and told the rest to begin moving south. Following his original orders, Medina then marched the GIs a few hundred meters northeast through the deserted hamlets of My Lai 5 and My Lai 6, ransacking and burning as they went. In one of the hamlets, Medina ordered the residents gathered, and then told Sergeant Phu, the regular company interpreter, to tell them, as Phu later told Vietnamese investiga-

tors, that "they were to go away or something will happen to them—just like what happened at My Lai 4."

By nightfall, the Viet Cong were back in My Lai 4, helping the survivors bury the dead. It took five days. Most of the funeral speeches were made by the Communist guerrillas. Nguyen Bat was not a Communist at the time of the massacre, but the incident changed his mind. "After the shooting," he said, "all the villagers became Communists."

When Army investigators reached the barren area in November 1969, in connection with the My Lai probe in the United States, they found mass graves at three sites, as well as a ditch full of bodies. It was estimated that between 450 and 500 people—most of them women, children, and old men—had been slain and buried there.

Specialist 5 Jay Roberts carried his reporter's note pad and a pencil with him when he took the helicopter from Eleventh Brigade headquarters at Duc Pho that morning. But whatever he wrote could not be used. The Army had decided the night before that the Viet Cong were in My Lai 4; nothing that happened in the next twenty-four hours officially changed that view.

A Saigon report of Charlie Company's battle sent to the Pentagon the night of March 16 noted that initial "contact with the enemy force" occurred at 7:50 A.M., about the time Lieutenant Calley and his platoon had secured the landing zone and shot an unarmed old man. The military message added that a second combat company had been airlifted into the area by 9:10 A.M. and that both units reported "sporadic contact" with the enemy as they moved toward a rendezvous. The companies had support from "Army artillery and helicopter gunships." [...]

A report of the My Lai 4 invasion, based on the official version supplied newsmen in Saigon, was published on the front page of the *New York Times*, as well as in many other newspapers, on March 17. It said that two Americal Division companies had caught a North Vietnamese unit in a pincer movement, killing 128 enemy soldiers. "The United States soldiers were sweeping the area," the *Times* said. "The operation is another American offensive to clear enemy pockets still threatening the cities. While the two companies of United States soldiers moved in on the enemy force from opposite sides, heavy artillery barrages and armed helicopters were called in to pound the North Vietnamese soldiers." The report said two American GIs were killed and ten wounded during the day-long fight six miles northeast of

Quang Ngai, even though Medina's company had only sustained one casualty—Carter. There was no mention of civilian casualties. [...]

Charlie Company's apparent victory did not go unnoticed. A few days after the battle, General William C. Westmoreland, then commander of U.S. forces in Vietnam, sent the following message: "Operation Muscatine [the code name for the My Lai 4 assault] contact northeast of Quang Ngai City on 16 March dealt enemy heavy blow. Congratulations to officers and men of C-1-20 [Charlie Company, First Battalion, Twentieth Infantry] for outstanding action."

Hours after it was over, most members of Charlie Company were still keyed up. There was a lot of talk; much of it bragging about how many gooks had been killed that day. Harry Stanley said that three members of the company had staged a contest at My Lai 4 to see who would kill the most people there. Charles West got angry at all the loose talk and joking after the incident. "It was bad enough that we did this, but some guys were telling how many people they had killed.... This didn't make no sense. The guys wasn't unhappy until after we came out; until they stopped to think about what they did." [...]

Later that night, Medina told his men that a helicopter pilot had filed a complaint and there was the possibility of an investigation. Bernhardt remembered Medina promising that he would back them up in case of trouble: "He said he would say that there was a gunfight and that we did a lot of shooting." The captain urged his men not to talk about it. "The guys weren't worried," Bernhardt added. "They had absolute faith in him."

Charlie Company heard no more officially about My Lai 4 that day. But they talked among themselves. Mike Terry shared his dinner that night with Gregory Olsen and Michael Bernhardt. They were all upset about what had happened. "We talked about the way the Army was going to cover it by saying it was such a good thing...a big victory," Terry recalled. All three thought that field-grade officers must have known about it. Bernhardt heard talk of a body-count of "over three hundred" in My Lai; he also heard that only those old enough to walk were tallied. Young children and infants were not. Paul Meadlo was deeply disturbed about what he had done. [...]

Back at Duc Pho, Captain Charlie R. Lewellen, assistant intelligence officer for Task Force Barker, was just getting to sleep after an exhausting day. He liked to tape radio

transmissions during combat: "It's one thing to tell a man what combat's like, it's another to play a tape." He had set up his equipment at the communications center at Duc Pho early in the morning. The first words recorded, he said later, showed that the "lift ships were getting off the ground at 7:22 A.M." The tape played continuously during the day, transcribing all of the complaints made by Thompson and the transmissions between Medina and others in the Eleventh Brigade. Lewellen kept the Japanese-made recorder going until "I checked out and went to bed."

Charlie Company spent that night in a Vietnamese graveyard, their sleeping bags and pup tents flung amidst shrines and burial mounds. [...]

Sometime in the afternoon of March 17, Medina got a call from Task Force Barker headquarters informing him that Colonel Henderson, the brigade commander, was en route for a visit. The colonel, accompanied by two other officers, landed and told Medina he had been accused of shooting a woman at My Lai 4. The colonel said he was conducting an informal investigation. "He asked me if there had been any war crimes at My Lai 4, and I told him no," Medina recalled. Henderson left. By this time, word of Charlie Company's victory at My Lai 4 was on the front page of the *New York Times* and General Westmoreland's office was readying his routine message of congratulations.

But Medina was worried. John Smail of Renton, Washington, a squad leader in the third platoon, remembered thinking that "somebody gave him a good ass-chewing." Smail and Medina got along well; the GI said that "Medina liked to bullshit with me, but he just wasn't himself" after Henderson's visit. "He was sweating about something," Smail said. "He walked around real nervously, and kept on saying, 'Sergeant Smail, what can I do?' I asked him, 'What do you mean, sir?'"

The next day, Charlie Company returned to LZ Dotti, its mission a success. Some of the men were quizzed by Colonel Henderson about My Lai 4 as they climbed off the helicopters onto the landing pad, but all denied seeing a massacre. For most of the GIs, that was the last they would hear about My Lai 4 from their officers or brigade headquarters.

Michael Bernhardt, however, wanted to do something about what he had seen. But he was afraid to speak out. He had watched as Colonel Henderson asked his questions, and he felt sure nothing would come of it. He thought, too, that the helicopter pilot who had reported the incident had been killed in action the next day. Not many could speak, he figured, without implicating themselves, and if they did, no one knew how the Army would react. Bernhardt felt he had no place to go. He decided he could, perhaps, write his Congressman about the shooting. He apparently mentioned his ideas to other members of his platoon; the word got to the platoon leader, Lieutenant Stephen Brooks. Brooks passed it on to Medina. The captain accosted Bernhardt in a mess hall, and told the rifleman, "You can write your Congressman if you want to. But you will create a big stink. The matter is being investigated." Medina did not spell out just what could be reported to the Congressman, but it was clear to both men what they were talking about. Bernhardt denied that he had any such plan; Medina then emphasized that it would be unwise to send such a letter. An Army investigation concluded more than a year later that Medina had not really threatened the youth; he had merely "encouraged" him not to write any letters.

A few days after Charlie Company's invasion of My Lai 4, Ronald L. Ridenhour, a GI from Phoenix, Arizona, then serving as a helicopter door gunner in the Eleventh Brigade, flew over the stricken area: "The hamlet was completely desolate. There were no people around, no signs of life anywhere." The pilot, Warrant Officer Gilbert Honda, hovered the craft over a rice paddy near the hamlet. Ridenhour saw a body below. The helicopter flew down to investigate. "It was a woman," Ridenhour remembered, "spread-eagled as if on display. She had an Eleventh Brigade patch between her legs—as if it were some type of display, some badge of honor. We just looked; it was obviously there so people would know the Eleventh Brigade had been there. We just thought, 'What in the hell's wrong with these guys? What's going on?'"

The pilot banked the helicopter so its prop wash caught the patch and blew it away. Moments later Ridenhour spotted a number of possible Viet Cong suspects walking together in the My Lai 4 area. The men ran and jumped into a bunker when the helicopter approached. Ridenhour wanted to flush them out with a white phosphorous grenade to determine if they were enemy troops. "They were obviously bad guys," he recalled. But Honda seemed reluctant, and halfheartedly flew the helicopter over the bunker—at far too high an altitude to hit it with a grenade. Ridenhour was angry: "What in hell's going on, sir?" Honda told him cryptically that "these people around here have had a pretty rough time the last few days." The helicopter flew off.

Within hours, word of what had happened in My Lai 4 had spread throughout the helicopter units of the Eleventh Brigade. "We just rapped about it," Larry Colburn recalled. "Guys in the 123rd Aviation saw it and got mad. Thompson was so pissed he wanted to turn in his wings."

Charlie Company quickly settled back into its routine of search-and-destroy missions that continued until its year in Vietnam was over. There were only a few reminders of what had happened. Somehow other companies in the First Battalion of the Eleventh Brigade had learned about My Lai 4. "They'd say, 'Yeah, we heard you killed a whole lot of women and children—and then reported 128 VC killed,'" West recalled. Charles Sledge also remembered, with unhappiness, the fact that other companies "would razz us about it." [...]

No one had stepped forward in protest, and most of the men started brooding about the incident only after they left the company or returned to their homes in the United States. Larry Colburn later bumped into some GIs at Fort Hood, Texas, who had served in other units of Task Force Barker at the time of My Lai 4. He talked to them about it. "They heard that Charlie Company had a turkey shoot," Colburn recalled.

At least one GI, however, had second thoughts while still with Medina's company in Vietnam. Ron Grzesik remembered that he wasn't immediately distressed by what he saw that day. Four days after My Lai he wrote a friend back home without even mentioning the shooting. But the following week he sent another letter, this one describing the massacre and concluding that every man in Charlie Company "should be sent to jail."

The Army defines the shooting of unarmed civilians as a "Grave Breach" of the Geneva Convention of August 12, 1949, for the protection of war victims. A 1968 directive published by the United States Command in Saigon is explicit about what to do: "It is the responsibility of all military personnel having knowledge or receiving a report of an incident or of an act thought to be a war crime to make such incident known to his commanding officer as soon as possible...."

March 16, 1968, was Colonel Oran K. Henderson's first day on his new job as commanding officer of the Eleventh Brigade. It should have been a happy day. But things began going wrong for Henderson right from the start. Shortly after 9:00 A.M., the colonel, cruising above the battle in My Lai 4, noticed two men fleeing the hamlet. He thought they might be Viet Cong and ordered Warrant Officer Thompson, below him in a small observation helicopter, to stop them. After this was done, Henderson landed and personally interrogated the suspects. They turned out to be, Thompson later told the IG, not Viet Cong but two members of the Saigon government's local militia, who had apparently been held captive in My Lai 4.

Sometime in that same hour, Thompson filed his complaint to brigade headquarters about the "wild shooting by men on the ground and by helicopters in the area." He specifically cited the shooting of a woman by a captain. Upon learning of the complaint, Henderson said later, "I reported it to division headquarters [at Chu Lai] right away." He told them that he would make an inquiry. Henderson already had had some hints of wild shooting at My Lai 4 before he heard from Thompson. In the fall of 1969 Henderson told a reporter that on an earlier helicopter fly-by, he had seen the bodies of "five or six" civilians, two of which appeared to be men.

But the colonel, testifying in the spring of 1969 in private at the Pentagon about the incident, had had a different recollection: he had observed the bodies of only one woman and two children, both killed—he believed—by artillery. The IG subsequently asked Thompson about that statement, and the warrant officer—who had landed his helicopter in the same area at the same time—disagreed.

Henderson gave a third version of what he saw. He told a group of radio and television newsmen in November 1969 that he had flown over My Lai 4 and had seen no evidence of a massacre. By the end of the next day, March 17, Henderson said, he had questioned the men of Charlie Company and they had proclaimed their innocence.

There is yet another version of Henderson's involvement. Larry Colburn decided to tell somebody what he had witnessed in My Lai 4. After returning in the afternoon to brigade headquarters at Duc Pho, he walked over to Henderson's office. "I told him what happened that day," Colburn said. "He took a few notes and then I just never heard anything about it." The colonel seemed "nonchalant" about the whole affair. Colburn wasn't surprised: "I never thought anything would come of it anyway. I'd seen it happen before, but just not with that many people." Thompson accompanied his young crew member to the colonel's quarters. Colburn recalled that the pilot also spoke to Henderson that day. [...]

It took twenty months for the American public to learn what Charlie Company had done in a few hours at My Lai 4. Why, and how, the deliberate murder of hundreds of civilians remained a secret so long is difficult to understand, especially because so many knew about it—and so many had participated in it. Dozens of Charlie Company GIs had transferred to other units; many chose, perhaps deliberately, the most dangerous job in South Vietnam—long-range reconnaissance patrols into enemy territory. GIs talk, and brag; the 250 men in the other two companies of Task Force Barker learned within days about what had happened in My Lai 4. A number of officers in the brigade had listened with fascination to a tape recording of the events at the hamlet. At least sixty Army men in a dozen helicopters saw firsthand what was going on in My Lai 4; the gunships had been assigned by the American Division to help Charlie Company overcome the expected Viet Cong resistance. And there were the survivors, unknown in number, of My Lai 4 itself.

Details of the massacre had been published twice in France: in the May 15, 1968, edition of the French-language publication *Sud Vietnam en Lutte*, and in *Bulletin du Vietnam*, published by the North Vietnamese delegation to the Paris peace talks. The issue was raised again in a report to the July meeting in Grenoble, France, of the World Conference of Jurists for Vietnam.

By the early summer of 1968, Paul Meadlo was home in Terre Haute, Indiana, his right foot gone, along with his self-respect. And by early 1969, most of Charlie Company was gone from Vietnam, back on the job or at school in cities across the nation. Ron Haeberle was busy in Ohio showing slide photographs of the My Lai 4 massacre to Rotary Club luncheons and the like; no one in his audiences apparently cared, or believed, enough to find out how he had managed to take such pictures. None of the GIs seemed to consider his experiences worth telling about.

But at that time a twenty-two-year-old ex-GI in Phoenix, Arizona, was in the midst of preparing a letter that would eventually prompt an Army investigation of the massacre. Ronald Ridenhour had flown over My Lai 4 a few days after the shootings. He noticed the complete desolation, but did not find out what caused it until he joined a long-range reconnaissance unit operating out of Duc Pho, where he heard accounts of the massacre from five eyewitnesses. Ridenhour drove to the American Division headquarters in Chu Lai and confirmed that Charlie Company had indeed been at My Lai 4 on March 16. Ridenhour was cautious as he gathered information in Vietnam; he did not even make written notes for fear of his safety.

Ridenhour was discharged and returned to Phoenix in early December 1968, intent on doing something about the shootings at My Lai 4. He had served well in Vietnam, both as a helicopter door-gunner and as a team leader of long-range patrol groups. He earned the usual medals, and did nothing that would mark him as an antiwar protester. He kept his outrage to himself. But "I wanted to get those people," Ridenhour said. "I wanted to reveal what they did. My God, when I first came home, I would tell my friends about this and cry—literally cry. As far as I was concerned it was a reflection on me, on every American, on the ideals that we supposedly represent. It completely castrated the whole posture of America." [...]

He turned to Arthur A. Orman, one of his former high-school teachers who had also taught him creative writing during the one year he attended Phoenix College before getting drafted. Along with his moral indignation, Ridenhour had another motivation: he'd always wanted to be a writer, and he knew he would never find a better story with which to begin. Orman, however, convinced the ex-GI not to try to sell his story to a magazine. Instead, he argued, Ridenhour should give his information to those government agencies that were equipped to investigate such matters. "I thought it would cheapen what he was doing if he tried to sell the story," Orman recalled. [...]

Then came the critical decision to approach Congress. The two men agreed that letters should be sent to leading members of the House and Senate, and not just to the White House, Pentagon, and State Department. The letter described in detail what Ridenhour had learned about My Lai 4, but he was careful to make clear he was reporting what he heard, and not what he saw. [...]

Nine letters—sent by registered mail—were addressed to: President Nixon; three Democratic Senators who were then the leading anti-Vietnam war spokesmen in Congress—Eugene J. McCarthy of Minnesota, J. W. Fulbright of Arkansas, and Edward M. Kennedy of Massachusetts; and the five members of the Arizona Congressional delegation—Republican Senators Barry M. Goldwater and Paul J. Fannin, House members Sam Steiger and John J. Rhodes, both Republicans, and Democrat Morris K. Udall. Letters were also sent by ordinary air mail to the Pentagon, State Department, Joint Chiefs of Staff, thirteen other members of the Senate, three members of the House, including Chairman L. Mendel Rivers of the Armed Services Committee, and to the House and Senate Chaplains.

Twenty-two of the offices later said they had no record of ever receiving Ridenhour's letter. The Reverend Edward Gardiner Latch, Chaplain of the House, read the Xeroxed letter, but said later he did not answer it because "I don't answer letters of that kind." Five legislators—Congressmen Rhodes and Steiger of Arizona, and Senators Edward W. Brooke of Massachusetts and Goldwater and Fannin of Arizona—routinely referred it to the Army.

Only two men, Representatives Morris Udall, a liberal from Arizona, and L. Mendel Rivers, a conservative from South Carolina, took a personal interest in the letter. In both cases, their concern was the result of alert staff work.

When Ridenhour's letter arrived at the office of the Armed Services Committee, it was read by Frank Slatinshek, a staff lawyer, who took it to his superior, chief counsel John R. Blandford. "We couldn't brush it off," Blandford recalled later. "It had too many facts. There was too much of a germ of truth in it." A letter was drafted for Rivers' signature, urging the Department of the Army to investigate the matter, and Rivers signed it April 7, only three days after it was received by the committee.

One factor behind Rivers' quick action may have been Udall. Ridenhour had included Udall on his list of thirty largely because he represents his home state, and to a lesser degree because of Udall's political views. Both factors were important to what happened next. Udall was especially impressed by Ridenhour's letter, which was brought to his attention by Roger Lewis, an aide. "It just had a ring to it," Lewis said. "Furthermore, he was an Arizonan."

Udall wrote a letter to Secretary of Defense Melvin A. Laird about Ridenhour's charges, and took the unusual step of sending a copy to Rivers. Udall knew that any military investigation would have a better chance of being held if Rivers pushed it, and he thought Rivers might just—out of legislative courtesy—push. "He likes me," Udall said of Rivers. Udall's letter reached the Armed Services Committee April 7, the same day on which Rivers forwarded his letter to the Department of the Army.

There was additional pressure on the Army—from Secretary of Defense Laird, who later told newsmen he read Ridenhour's letter on April 4, three days before Rivers' request for an investigation was mailed. Laird recognized that it was "more than a routine letter," an aide said, and forwarded it to the Department of the Army for handling. Laird's personal reading of the letter—one of thousands that arrive every day at the Pentagon—wasn't unusual, the aides explained; he often dealt directly with citizen complaints.

Thus, by the end of the first week in April, the Army had received a total of six Congressional referrals enclosing the Ridenhour letter; clearly it had to do something to avoid another public black eye. [...]

On April 23 General Westmoreland, then Army Chief of Staff, officially turned over the case to the office of the Inspector General, the Army's main investigatory agency for administrative and procedural complaints and directed it to make a full-scale inquiry. Colonel William Vickers Wilson, a Southerner, was assigned the task of building the Army's case.

Wilson began at the beginning: he flew into Phoenix April 29 with a court reporter to question Ridenhour. He told Ridenhour, as he would tell others he interrogated, that he was conducting a special investigation for General Westmoreland. Wilson and Ridenhour carefully went over the allegations in an interview lasting an hour and a half. The former GI was told that if Wilson could find corroboration of the charges from just one other witness, a more intensive investigation would be ordered—with the ultimate aim of filing criminal charges against those responsible.

Wilson, operating in official secrecy, then began a cross-country journey. He interviewed Michael Terry in Orem, Utah, immediately after seeing Ridenhour; Terry told how he had shot and killed some wounded Vietnamese civilians in the drainage ditch at My Lai 4. [...] He saw Michael Bernhardt May 8 in Washington, and received further confirmation of the details in Ridenhour's letter. He called on others in the Inspector General's office for help, and statements from other Charlie Company members began flooding in. On May 13, Wilson himself flew to Fort Benning, Georgia, and interrogated Captain Medina. Medina was stunned; he was then in the midst of a nine-month career officers' advanced course that would enable him to get his promotion to major. Since leaving Charlie Company, Medina had been marked for advancement, handling key staff assignments with the First Battalion in Vietnam and later with the American Division's tactical-operations center. He had left Charlie Company, he said later, thinking, "We had a good combat record."

While Wilson worked, Ridenhour worried. He wondered if any of the witnesses named in his letter would confirm the essential details of the massacre. He had reason to believe that most of the persons quoted in his letter were implicated in some manner in the killings. His star witness, he thought, would be Michael Bernhardt. When they had talked in Chu Lai, where Bernhardt was recovering from a severe case of jungle rot on his feet, Ridenhour had sought assurance that

Bernhardt would verify his story at the proper time. The GI said he would. Ridenhour began placing collect calls to Colonel Wilson, asking what was going on. He called sometimes twice a week during April and May, and learned that Bernhardt had told all he knew to Wilson on May 10. But nothing happened. In Ridenhour's eyes, Wilson had not kept his word and he took the colonel's reassurance as a stall for time while the Army sought a means of covering up the incident. His trust shaken, Ridenhour decided the only thing to do then was to try to make the details of My Lai 4 public.

On May 29, Ridenhour picked up a writer's guide to literary agents and found one whose blurb seemed sympathetic, Michael Cunningham, then a twenty-two-year-old part-time literary agent in Hartford, Connecticut. Ridenhour mailed Cunningham a copy of his letter with this comment: "It is my belief that the U.S. Army will, if at all possible, cover up this incident hoping that it will fade away and be forgotten. I believe very strongly that this should not be allowed to happen."

Ridenhour was basing his belief about a cover-up on flimsy evidence, fed in part by the Army's inability—or unwillingness—to brief him fully on the progress of its investigation. Since Cunningham did not personally know many editors or publishers, he sent telegrams over the next six weeks to a number of magazines. Only *Ramparts* responded, but Ridenhour did not want to be associated with the violently anti-Vietnam war politics of the magazine.

Ridenhour's persistent inquiries resulted in another report from the Pentagon, this one informing him that about 70 per cent of the persons cited in his letter had been interviewed. Ridenhour was not reassured by that information: only eight persons had been named in all in his letter. The Pentagon also noted that "the investigation is requiring considerable time and travel." To Ridenhour, it seemed like another stall. He got in touch with Udall's office and complained that the Army was burying the case. Udall's aide, Roger Lewis, began to think—it was now early June—that he might have been mistaken in assuming that Ridenhour was not a crackpot. "We still had nothing from the military," Lewis explained later, "no way of knowing. And the fact that it hadn't broken led one to wonder whether Ridenhour's information was good." Surely a massacre of that magnitude, and a Pentagon investigation of it, would have been leaked to the Washington press corps by then. Lewis decided to telephone Captain Medina. Medina was polite but firm; he couldn't discuss the case. Lewis then called Bernhardt and was told that the GI had been interrogated by the Inspector General's office. The aide decided that the Army was trying its best to investigate the Ridenhour charges, whether they were accurate or not.

By then, Colonel Wilson had been working full-time on the case for nearly five weeks.

At 8:30 A.M. on June 13, 1969, the Inspector General's office of the Army staged a police lineup at the new Forrestal Defense Building in Southwest Washington. One of the officers in the lineup was Lieutenant William L. Calley, Jr.

Calley had been abruptly pulled out of Vietnam in early June—at least one month before his tour of duty was over—and shipped home overnight to Fort Benning, Georgia, with special orders to report to Washington. Calley had been forewarned of trouble when the Army turned down his request to extend his tour of duty in Vietnam for a third time. He knew then, he recalled later, that something was up.

The lineup was called by Colonel Wilson to enable a key witness to the massacre—Warrant Officer Hugh C. Thompson of the 123rd Aviation Battalion—to identify the young officer who was directing operations at the bloody drainage ditch at My Lai 4. [...] Thompson picked out Calley as the officer at the drainage ditch in My Lai 4 on March 16, 1968. That fact was duly recorded by an Army stenographer. Thompson also had reported seeing a captain shoot a woman at close range during the same day. Wilson now turned to that charge. He had received Medina's explanation of the event during his interview with the captain on May 13 at Fort Benning.

"Could you identify the man who shot the girl?" Wilson asked.

"I think it was a captain, sir..."

Without mentioning Medina by name, Wilson then read the pilot Medina's version of the shooting. "Now could this have happened?" he asked.

"Nothing is impossible," Thompson said. He added that he saw Medina back at LZ Dotti two days after My Lai 4. "He asked me how everything was going and I said, 'Everything is going just fine,' and saluted him and walked away." He said nothing else to Medina, Thompson said, "because I didn't care anything about talking to him."*

---

* On October 15, 1969, four months after his testimony at the Pentagon, Thompson was awarded the Distinguished Flying Cross for heroism in the line of duty at My Lai 4. The citation credited Thompson with "disregarding his own safety" to rescue fifteen children hiding in a bunker "between Viet Cong positions and advancing friendly forces."

On June 19, Wilson heard testimony from Larry Colburn, who corroborated Thompson's testimony and also identified Medina and Calley as the officers involved in the shootings. Colburn picked out the Charlie Company officers from photographs shown by Wilson; the ex-GI also was shown detailed aerial maps of My Lai 4. Wilson next began interrogating Medina's radiomen and others in the command group who had knowledge of the captain's movements that day.

Colonel Wilson and other officers in the Inspector General's office had interrogated thirty-six witnesses by the end of July, ranging from Colonel Henderson, the Eleventh Brigade commander, to Paul Meadlo. [...] The evidence mounted swiftly against Calley and on July 23, Wilson was able to order Colonel James D. Kiersey, chief of staff at Fort Benning, to "flag" Calley's records, an Army procedure freezing any promotion or transfer for a soldier. Wilson's lengthy report was submitted to General Westmoreland, and on August 4, Westmoreland responded by ordering the Inspector General's office to turn over the results of its investigation to the Provost Marshal's office of the Army and its Criminal Investigation Division to determine whether there was enough evidence to file criminal charges against Calley and others in the company.

Once the CID took over the case, its men retraced Colonel Wilson's steps and began to interrogate all of the available members of Charlie Company to determine how many GIs or ex-GIs were involved. Many of the investigators became personally involved in the investigation. Michael Bernhardt said that he was visited three times by CID agents who were trying to pry out the truth about Medina's shooting of the woman.

On August 25, the CID agents found Ronald L. Haeberle in Cleveland, and he gave them a set of his color photographs of the shooting. Haeberle had been discharged shortly after the My Lai 4 incident; upon his return to the States he had assembled his best photographs into a slide show which he screened, upon request, for civic organizations in Cleveland. Haeberle's series of photographs began with the Eleventh Brigade in training at Schofield Barracks in Hawaii, and moved with the unit to Vietnam. Then, amidst pictures of smiling peasants and GIs came the scenes from My Lai 4. "They caused no commotion," he said. "Nobody believed it. They said Americans wouldn't do this." Haeberle also told the military police agents that, as far as he knew, his unprinted rolls of black-and-white film were still lying around the public-information office of brigade headquarters. The CID sent someone to check; the film was there.

By the end of August, interrogations of former Charlie Company members were being conducted all over the United States and Vietnam.* Many witnesses were quizzed a second time and shown the Haeberle photographs. The photos jogged memories and the GIs began recalling what happened in more detail. [...]

It was now clear that the Army was going to institute proceedings against Calley. [...] In late August, Defense Secretary Laird, who had been kept abreast of the case by the Department of Army, flew to the Summer White House at San Clemente, California, and handed over a detailed summary of Colonel Wilson's findings to the President. Nixon was reportedly angered by the Army's delay in finding out about and investigating the massacre.

The Army cautiously waited for the President to study the documents and react—if he chose to. [...] On September 4, two days before Calley was to be released from the Army, Fort Benning officials were told to go ahead and file the charges, if they were so determined. "It's all yours," a general told Colonel Kiersey. "You are not receiving any instructions."

On the next day, charges were formally preferred against Calley. Six specifications of premeditated murder were drawn up, accusing Calley of killing a total of 109 "Oriental human beings, occupants of the village of My Lai 4, whose names and sexes are unknown, by means of shooting them with a rifle." Preparing the charge sheet had been a difficult task: at one time the Army planned to charge Calley with only four specifications. The officer who wrote the charges, Colonel Robert M. Lathop, chief legal official at Fort Benning, had flown to Washington in August to get assistance in drafting the language. Lathop later recalled that the information for many of the specific charges came from Paul Meadlo's statement.*

Once the charges were filed, the Army immediately began an Article 32 hearing to determine whether the charges were justified. The hearing is a phenomenon of military law, roughly equivalent to a grand-jury proceeding, in which the evidence against a suspect is weighed to determine whether or not he should stand trial. At that time Calley refused to testify against Captain Medina, his commanding officer, and continued to refuse in subsequent legal proceedings. Asked later to explain this refusal, he said cryptically, "Because I don't scare easily." Sergeant Isaiah Cowen, one of Calley's sergeants in the first platoon, was a witness at the Article 32 hearing and also refused to testify against Medina "because he was the company commander."

Calley's refusal to testify against Medina was apparently based on his strong sense of loyalty, both to Medina and to the military, but the Army thought there might be a different reason. Calley later said that Major Kenneth A. Raby of Fort Benning, his appointed military legal officer, unsuccessfully tried on at least one or two occasions to persuade him to take a sanity test.

The House Armed Services Committee was also told at the same time by the Department of the Army of its action against Calley. "We are exercising utmost caution," a communiqué said, "to avoid any public discussion which could prejudice the continuing investigation or the rights of Lieutenant Calley."

The Pentagon, well aware of the potential impact of the story, debated how to release it to the public. It found a way that managed to bring no credit either to the military—or to the press.

The first public hint of the My Lai 4 massacre was a blandly worded news release issued to the Georgia press on Friday afternoon, September 5, by the public information office at Fort Benning. [...] A reporter in Georgia for the Associated Press asked for more information and was referred to the Pentagon, where he was told that no further details were available. The AP's subsequent dispatch did no more than repeat

---

* The CID interviewed more than 75 witnesses by November 26, 1969. Many of them recalled being asked about the use of marijuana in Charlie Company; that question seemed to be of special interest to the investigators. The GIs all acknowledged that many members of the company smoked or otherwise made use of marijuana, which is plentiful in South Vietnam, but none believed it was in any way a significant factor in what happened at My Lai 4.

---

* The charges were later reduced to 102 on February 6, 1970, after Calley's lawyer protested that they were too broadly drawn. The Army also made clear in subsequent pretrial hearings that it was not accusing Calley personally of killing each of the Vietnamese victims, but with killing some and "causing others" to kill them.

the essential facts as released by Fort Benning. The wire-service story was published in dozens of newspapers over the weekend, but none gave it prominence. The *New York Times*, for example, published an edited version of the AP story at the bottom of page 38 of its September 8 editions.

Officers in the Pentagon were prepared for a flood of questions that weekend from all news media—but it didn't come. "I was amazed that it didn't get picked up—just amazed," said one colonel. Secretary of Defense Melvin A. Laird later revealed that he had ordered the news wires monitored to see if the announcement would spark immediate controversy.

Five days after the original announcement, the news of Calley's arrest was telecast on the Huntley-Brinkley nightly evening news show. Robert Goralski, NBC's Pentagon correspondent, told the millions of viewers that Calley "has been accused of premeditated murder of a number of South Vietnamese civilians. The murders are alleged to have been committed a year ago and the investigation is continuing. A growing number of such cases is coming to light and the Army doesn't know what to do about them."

For weeks there was nothing more in the press about Calley, but the Army continued to gather evidence for his court-martial. Paul Meadlo, the most important prosecution witness, was interviewed for a third time by CID agents on September 18 at his home in Terre Haute. And Captain Lewellen decided at about that time to turn over his tapes of the radio traffic above My Lai 4 to the prosecution at Fort Benning. He kept a few copies for himself, however. (Later Lewellen explained that he was planning to sell the tape to the highest bidder as soon as the court proceedings against Charlie Company were completed. "It paints a picture," Lewellen said of his recordings.)

Ridenhour became convinced that the Army's failure to publicize details of the case against Calley meant not only that "Calley was going to get hung as a scapegoat" but higher-ranking officers who passed down the order to Calley would get off without a reprimand. He also suspected that the Army would make a deal with Calley through his lawyers, "to keep him quiet." On October 13, the Army again wrote Ridenhour, telling him that Calley's Article 32 hearing on the murder charges would begin that month, and noting: "It is not appropriate to report details of the allegations to news media. Your continued cooperation in this matter is acknowledged." On October 22 Michael Cunningham, his agent, wrote Ridenhour conceding defeat:

"Quite frankly, Ron, I am doubtful of my ability to be of much more help. I honestly feel the matter is best handled at this stage by waiting until your next response from the Army."

Details of the charges against Calley were now known to dozens of officials—Senator John C. Stennis and his shocked Senate Armed Forces Committee were given a private briefing that fall—yet nothing reached the press. Despite the widespread official knowledge of the Calley case a few Pentagon officers actually thought Calley could be court-martialed without attracting any significant public attention. The opinion was far from unanimous, however. Perhaps anticipating a future furor over My Lai 4, General Westmoreland included these unusual words during a speech October 14 to the annual meeting of the Association of the U.S. Army in Washington: "Recently, a few individuals involved in serious incidents have been highlighted in the news. Some would have these incidents reflect on the Army as a whole. They are, however, the actions of a pitiful few. Certainly the Army

Thirteen-year-old My Lai survivor at press conference.

cannot and will not condone improper conduct or criminal acts—I personally assure you that I will not."

The Calley case remained dormant as far as the news was concerned until the inevitable Washington tipsters got to work. The *New York Times* heard something about a massacre case being tried at Fort Gordon, Georgia. It was the right case, but the wrong base. The *Washington Post* queried the Pentagon about some officer's being charged with more than 150 civilian murders in connection with a Vietnam operation. One *Post* reporter even managed to locate George W. Latimer, Calley's attorney, at his Salt Lake City office and ask him about the case. Latimer begged off, saying, "I'm hoping maybe we can come up with some kind of resolution that won't make it necessary for this to be public. I can't see it would do any good to anybody." No news story was written.

I was in the midst of completing research for a book on the Pentagon when I received a telephone tip on October 22. "The Army's trying to court-martial some guy in secret at Fort Benning for killing 75 Vietnamese civilians," the source said. At that time, in fact, the Army had done nothing more than prefer charges and it was still trying to keep any word about the events at My Lai 4 out of the newspapers.

It took two days and twenty-five telephone calls before somebody told me about the AP story on Calley. From there, it was a short step to Latimer, and on October 29, a Monday, I flew from Washington to Salt Lake City to interview the lawyer. Before leaving Washington, I had received confirmation of the essential facts of the story from a government source. Latimer confirmed them, adding that "whatever killing there was was in a firefight in connection with an operation. To me," Latimer said, "the thing that's important is this: why do we prosecute our own people while on a search-and-destroy mission and they kill some people, be they civilian or not? Is there a point in the chain of command at which somebody could be tried? I think not."

On November 11, a Tuesday, I decided to fly down to Fort Benning and find Calley. But Calley's name did not appear anywhere in the Fort Benning telephone book, nor did the file of tenants in the bachelor officers' quarters list him. It was ten hours afterward and very late at night before I found a warrant officer, who was a downstairs neighbor of Calley's, at one of the officers' quarters. As we were talking, he suddenly hollered at a slight young man walking toward us—"Rusty, come over here and meet this guy." Impatient, I began to leave. "No, wait a second," the officer said. "That's Calley."

Calley was apprehensive. All he wanted in life was to stay in the Army and be a good soldier. He reminded me of an earnest freshman one might find at an agricultural college, anxious about making a fraternity. We went to a party at a friend's apartment, and had some drinks. I wanted to leave. Calley wanted me to stay. He knew what was coming and he knew I was the last reporter with whom he would talk, and drink, for many months. He told me, that evening, a little bit about the operation; he also told me how many people he had been accused of killing. I flew back to Washington the next day and began to write my story. I did it somewhat hesitantly, my thought being that Calley, perhaps, was as much of a victim as those infants he and his men murdered at My Lai 4. [...]

Once I had completed my research on My Lai 4, I tried to get it published. *Life* and *Look* magazines weren't interested. With some hesitation, I turned over my story to the Dispatch News Service, a small news agency run by David Obst of Washington. Fifty newspapers were offered the initial Dispatch story by cable on November 12; more than thirty—including many of the leading newspapers in the nation—published it the next day, a remarkably high number. [...]

As yet there was little investigative reporting on the part of the American press to determine exactly what had happened, perhaps because newspapers did not try to locate former members of Charlie Company. By Friday, November 21, I had found Paul Meadlo in Terre Haute, Indiana. Meadlo agreed also to tell his story on television, and David Obst and the Dispatch lawyers arranged to produce him—for a fee—on the CBS evening news with Walter Cronkite. His confession, later published in newspapers around the world, stunned the nation. "Many of us sat in sheltered living rooms," wrote columnists Richard Harwood and Laurence Stern of the *Washington Post*, "perhaps starting in on a dinner martini as Meadlo's face showed on the screen.... From the vantage point of those living rooms Meadlo was the American 'gook'—the scapegoat and the buffer between the torn bodies in open graves at My Lai and ourselves." That Sunday the *Post* devoted three full pages to the story. At the least, Meadlo's CBS appearance made the American press finally face up to the fact that something very terrible indeed happened at My Lai 4. [...]

Is There a Place for Morality in Foreign Affairs?
by Arthur Schlesinger, Jr.

August 1971

For centuries, theologians have distinguished between just and unjust wars, jurists have propounded rules for international conduct, and moralists have worried whether their own nation's course in foreign affairs was right or wrong. Yet the problem of the relationship between morality and international politics remains perennially unsettled. It is particularly difficult and disturbing for Americans today. The Indochina war was first widely justified on moral grounds and is now widely condemned on moral grounds. Both judgments cannot be right. This contradiction and, even more, of course, the shame and horror of the war must surely compel us to look again at the moral question in its relation to foreign policy. [...]

People who respond to international politics divide temperamentally into two schools: those who see policies as wise or foolish, and those (evidently in the majority today) who see them as good or evil. One cannot claim an ultimate metaphysical difference here. No one can escape perceptions of good and evil, and no policy can achieve a total separation of political and moral principles. Nor in the impenetrability of one's heart can one easily know when political motives are moral motives in disguise or when moral motives are political motives in disguise. Still the choice of disguise reveals something about temperament and philosophy.

In this time, when both Right and Left yield with relish to the craving for moral judgment, it may be useful to set forth a minority view. Should—as both supporters and critics of the Indochina war have asserted—overt moral principles decide issues of foreign policy? Required to give a succinct answer, I am obliged to say: as little as possible. If, in the management of foreign affairs, decisions can be made and questions disposed of on other grounds, so much the better. Moral values in international politics—or so, at least, my temperament enjoins me to believe—should be

decisive only in questions of last resort. One must add that questions of last resort do exist.

How to define right and wrong in dealings among sovereign states? The moralist of foreign affairs relies on the moral code most familiar to him—the code that governs dealings among individuals. He contends that states should be judged by principles of individual morality. As Woodrow Wilson put it in his address to Congress on the declaration of war in 1917: "We are at the beginning of an age in which it will be insisted that the same standards of conduct and of responsibility for wrong done shall be observed among nations and their governments that are observed among the individual citizens of civilized states." John Foster Dulles said it even more bluntly, or naïvely, in the midst of the second world war: "The broad principles that should govern our international conduct are not obscure. They grow out of the practice by the nations of the simple things Christ taught."

The argument for the application of moral principles to questions of foreign policy is thus that there is, or should be, an identity between the morality of individuals and the morality of states. The issues involved here are not easy. Clearly, there are cases in foreign affairs where moral judgment is possible and necessary. But I suggest that these are extreme cases and do not warrant the routine use of moral criteria in making foreign-policy decisions. It was to expose such indiscriminate moralism that Reinhold Niebuhr wrote *Moral Man and Immoral Society* forty years ago. The passage of time has not weakened the force of his analysis.

Niebuhr insisted on the distinction between the moral behavior of individuals and of social groups. The obligation of the individual was to obey the law of love and sacrifice; "from the viewpoint of the author of an action, unselfishness must remain the criterion of the highest morality." But nations cannot be sacrificial. Governments are not individuals. They are trustees for individuals. Niebuhr quotes Hugh

Cecil's argument that unselfishness "is inappropriate to the action of a state. No one has a right to be unselfish with other people's interests." Alexander Hamilton made the same point in the early years of the American republic: "The rule of morality... is not precisely the same between nations as between individuals. The duty of making its own welfare the guide of its actions is much stronger upon the former than upon the latter. Existing millions, and for the most part future generations, are concerned in the present measures of a government; while the consequences of the private action of an individual ordinarily terminate with himself, or are circumscribed with a narrow compass."

In short, the individual's duty of self-sacrifice and the nation's duty of self-preservation are in conflict; and this makes it impossible to measure the action of nations by a purely individualistic morality. "The Sermon on the Mount," said Churchill, "is the last word in Christian ethics.... Still, it is not on those terms that Ministers assume their responsibilities of guiding states." Saints can be pure, but statesmen must be responsible. As trustees for others, they must defend interests and compromise principles. In politics, practical and prudential judgment must have priority over moral verdicts. [...]

This is not to say we cannot discern the rudiments of an international consensus. Within limits, mankind has begun to develop standards for conduct among nations—defined, for example, in the Hague Conventions of 1899 and 1907; in the Geneva Protocol of 1925 and the Geneva Conventions of 1949; in the Charter and Covenants of the United Nations; in the Charter, Judgment, and Principles of the Nuremberg Tribunal, and so on. Such documents outlaw actions that the world has placed beyond the limits of permissible behavior. Within this restricted area a code emerges that makes moral judgment in international affairs possible up to a point. And within its scope this rudimentary code deserves, and must have, the most unflinching and rigorous enforcement.

But these international rules deal with the limits rather than with the substance of policy. They seek to prevent abnormalities and excesses in the behavior of states, but they do not offer ground for moral judgment and sanction on normal international transactions (including, it must be sorrowfully said, war itself, so long as war does not constitute aggression and so long as the rules of warfare are faithfully observed). They may eventually promote a world moral consensus. But, for the present, national, ideological, ethi-

cal, and religious divisions remain as bitterly intractable as ever.

Moreover, few problems in international politics call for unequivocal ethical approval or disapproval. Most foreign-policy decisions are self-evidently matters of prudence and maneuver, not of good and evil. "I do not think we can conclude," George Kennan noted a decade ago, "that it matters greatly to God whether the free trade area or the Common Market prevails in Europe, whether the British fish or do not fish in Icelandic territorial waters, or even whether Indians or Pakistani run Kashmir. It might matter, but it is hard for us, with our limited vision, to know." The raw material of foreign affairs is, most of the time, morally neutral or ambiguous. In consequence, for the great majority of foreign-policy transactions, moral principles cannot be decisive.

But this is not all. It is not only that moral principles are of limited use in the conduct of foreign affairs. It is also that the compulsion to see foreign policy in moral terms may have, with the noblest of intentions, the most ghastly of consequences. The moralization of foreign affairs encourages, for example, a misunderstanding of the nature of foreign policy. Moralists tend to prefer symbolic to substantive politics. They tend to see foreign policy as a means not of influencing events but of registering virtuous attitudes. One has only to recall the attempt, made variously by Right and by Left, to make recognition policy an instrument of ethical approval or disapproval.

A deeper trouble is inherent in the very process of pronouncing moral judgment on foreign policy. For the man who converts conflicts of interest and circumstance into conflicts of good and evil necessarily invests himself with moral superiority. Those who see foreign affairs as made up of questions of right and wrong begin by supposing they know better than other people what is right for them. The more passionately they believe they are right, the more likely they are to reject expediency and accommodation and seek the final victory of their principles. Little has been more pernicious in international politics than excessive righteousness.

Moral absolutism may strike at any point along the political spectrum. From the standpoint of those who mistrust self-serving ethical stances, the heirs of John Foster Dulles and the disciples of Noam Chomsky are equal victims of the same malady. Both regard foreign policy as a branch of ethics. They end up as mirror images of each other. In the process of moral self-aggrandizement, each loses the humility which is the heart of human restraint. [...]

Moralism in foreign policy ends up in fanaticism, and the fanatic, as Mr. Dooley put it, "does what he thinks th' Lord wud do if He only knew th' facts in th' case." Abroad it leads to crusades and the extermination of the infidel; at home it perceives mistakes in political judgment as evidence of moral obliquity. The issue becomes not self-delusion or stupidity but criminality and treachery; ferreting out the reprobate as traitors or war criminals becomes the goal. Those who are convinced of their own superior righteousness should recall Chekhov's warning: "You will not become a saint through other people's sins."

If moral principles have only limited application to foreign policy, then we are forced to the conclusion that decisions in foreign affairs must generally be taken on other than moralistic grounds. What are these other grounds? I believe that where the embryonic international community cannot regulate dealings among nations, the safest basis for foreign policy lies not in attempts to determine what is right or wrong but in attempts to determine the national interest.

Though the idea is an old and honorable one, "national interest," despite the valiant efforts through the years of Walter Lippmann, George Kennan, and Hans Morgenthau, has become an alarming phrase in America in the 1970s. Mention it before students, and the audience shudders. The words should alarm no one. A moment's thought will show that every nation *must* respond to some sense of its national interest, for a nation that rejects national interest as the mainspring of its policy cannot survive. Without the magnetic compass of national interest, there would be no regularity and predictability in international affairs. George Washington called it "a maxim founded on the universal experience of mankind that no nation is to be trusted farther than it is bound by its interest." [...]

Obviously a government can take a greedy as well as an enlightened view of its nation's interest. Greed tends to become the dominant motive when there is disparity of power between nations: thus the history of imperialism. But national interest has a self-limiting factor. It cannot, unless transformed by an injection of moral righteousness, produce ideological crusades for unlimited objectives. Any consistent defender of the idea of national interest must concede that other nations have legitimate interests too, and this sets bounds on international conflict. "You can compromise interests," Hans Morgenthau has reminded us, "but you cannot compromise principles."

This self-limiting factor does not rest only on the perception of other nations' interests. It is reinforced by self-correcting tendencies in the power equilibrium which, at least when the disparity of power is not too great, prevent national interest from billowing up into unbridled national egoism. History has shown how often the overweening behavior of an aggressive state leads to counteraction on the part of other states determined to restore a balance of power. This means that uncontrolled national egoism generally turns out to be contrary to long-term national interest. Can it be persuasively held, for example, that Hitler's foreign policy was in the national interest of Germany? The imperialist states of nineteenth-century Europe have generally been forced to revise their notions as to where national interest truly lies. National interest, realistically construed, will promote enlightened rather than greedy policy. So a realist like Hamilton said (my emphasis) that his aim was not "to recommend a policy absolutely selfish or interested in nations; but to show, that a policy regulated by their own interest, *as far as justice and good faith permit*, is, and ought to be, their prevailing one." And a realist like Theodore Roosevelt could say: "It is neither wise nor right for a nation to disregard its own needs, and it is foolish—and may be wicked—to think that other nations will disregard theirs. But it is wicked for a nation only to regard its own interest, and foolish to believe that such is the sole motive that actuates any other nation. It should be our steady aim to raise the ethical standard of national action just as we strive to raise the ethical standard of individual action." [...]

As moral men, we prefer to feel that our actions spring from profound ethical imperatives. The Anglo-American tradition, in particular, has long been addicted to the presentation of egoism in the guise of altruism. And if one has an honest sense of moral concern or moral outrage, it seems idle—indeed, false—to deny this when supporting or censuring a foreign policy. For better or worse, moreover, democratic opinion rebels at the idea of the domination of policy by self-interest. "Let the people get it into their heads that a policy is selfish and they will not follow it," A. J. P. Taylor has wisely written. "...A democratic foreign policy has got to be idealistic; or at the very least it has to be justified in terms of great general principles."

Nor is this cynicism. It may well be that the instinct among nearly all nations to justify their actions in terms of abstract moral principle is an involuntary tribute to the existence of a world public opinion, a latent international consensus, that we must all hope will one day be crystallized in law and institutions. [...]

Thus an irrepressible propensity to moral judgment in the field of foreign affairs exists. Nor, despite the perils of moral absolutism, is it without value. It may provide an indispensable reminder that all policies are imperfect and all statesmen capable of self-deception. Indeed, the truly Christian perspective offers the best antidote to the moralistic fallacy of transforming expedients into absolutes. John C. Bennett tells us of the meeting of a delegation from the World Council of Churches with President Kennedy in 1962. The delegation brought a message to heads of states from the New Delhi Assembly of the Council; a paragraph called for the cessation of nuclear tests. When Kennedy read this passage, he responded by discussing his own dilemma: what should the United States do to assure its own security in view of the resumption of tests by the Soviet Union? Impressed, a member of the delegation said, "Mr. President, if you do resume tests, how can we help you?" Kennedy turned to him and said, "Perhaps you shouldn't." Not all statesmen thus recognize the value of separating ultimate from immediate considerations and of preserving ideals in a world of distasteful compromise; if more did, the world would be spared much trouble.

In addition, there are certain problems in foreign policy with so clear-cut a moral character that moral judgment must control political judgment—questions of war crimes and atrocities, of the nuclear arms race, of colonialism, of racial justice, of world poverty. Some have already been defined in international documents. Others define themselves when the consequences of decision transcend the interests of individual nations and threaten the very future of humanity. Modern weapons technology has notably enlarged the number of problems demanding moral priority, for the nuclear bomb, the ICBM and MIRV, by virtue of their unimaginable powers of indiscriminate destruction, have gone far beyond the limits of prudential decision. Still other essentially moral problems arise when civilized values of tolerance and human dignity are menaced by powerful armed fanaticisms whose victory would abolish intellectual and civil freedom. I have in mind such movements as Nazism and Stalinism. [...]

It is through the idea of national interest that moral values enter most effectively into the formation of foreign policy. The moral question arises particularly in a state's observance or nonobservance of its own best standards. Foreign policy is the face a nation wears to the world. If a course in foreign affairs implies moral values incompatible with the ideals of the national community, either the nation will refuse after a time to sustain the policy, or else it must abandon its ideals. A people is in bad trouble when it tries to keep two sets of books—when it holds one scale of values for its internal polity and applies another to its conduct of foreign affairs. The consequent moral schizophrenia is bound to convulse the homeland. This is what happened to France during the Algerian war. It is what is happening to the United States because of the Indochina war.

In order to condemn this horrid conflict it is not necessary to deliver a moral judgment on it. If our policy had been founded on a sober and deliberate calculation of the national interest, we could hardly have sunk so deeply and unthinkingly into a situation where our commitment so far exceeds any rational involvement of that interest or any demonstrable threat to our national security. This is why the analysts who have most consistently invoked the idea of the national interest—Lippmann, Kennan, and Morgenthau—have been skeptical about the Indochinese adventure from the start.

I do not suggest that its advocates did not have a national-interest argument too. This argument in its most sophisticated version was that, with the establishment of nuclear balance between America and Russia, the main source of world instability lay in Third World wars—the kind that Khrushchev called "national liberation" wars in the truculent speech of January 1961 which had so unfortunate an effect on the Kennedy Administration. If the United States proved its ability to deal with such wars, then the world could look forward to an age of peace. Unhappily, this argument assumed that Communist activity everywhere occurred at the behest of and for the benefit of the Soviet Union. It gravely underestimated the strength of national Communism, and it wildly overestimated the capacity of the United States to win guerrilla wars.

Moreover, the argument was thereafter translated into a crude series of political propositions. Our national interest was involved, we were soon given to understand, because the Vietcong and Hanoi were the spearheads of a planned system of Chinese expansion. Therefore, by fighting in Vietnam, we were holding the line against an aggressive Red China. If we did not fight, we would, like Chamberlain at

Munich, invite further aggression; and a billion Chinese armed with nuclear weapons (a specter invoked with relish by Secretary [Dean] Rusk) would overrun Asia and turn the world balance of power permanently in favor of Communism. "The threat to world peace," as Vice President [Herbert H.] Humphrey summed up this fantasy as late as October 1967, "is militant, aggressive Asian communism, with its headquarters in Peking, China.... The aggression of North Vietnam is but the most current and immediate action of militant Asian communism."

The argument that Asian Communism was a monolithic movement run out of Peking was preposterous at the time. It is more preposterous in these days of Ping-Pong diplomacy. As even William Buckley has managed to discern, President Nixon's China policy abolishes the major strategic argument for the Indochina war.

Since it is painful to charge our national leaders with stupidity, one must suppose that this foolish analysis was only a secondary motive for our involvement in Indochina. The primary motive, it seems probable in retrospect, had little to do with national interest at all. It was, rather, a precise consequence of the belief that moral principles should govern decisions of foreign policy. It was the insistence on seeing the civil war in Vietnam as above all a moral issue that led us to construe political questions in ethical terms, local questions in global terms, and relative questions in absolute terms. [...]

Other pressure hastened the Indochina catastrophe— above all, the momentum of the military machine, with its institutional conviction that political problems have military solutions; its institutional desire to try out weapons, tactics, and personnel; and its institutional capacity for self-delusion about the ability of just one more step of escalation to assure military success. Still, the opportunity seized with such avidity by the military was created by those who believed that America was in Vietnam on a moral mission—who applauded when President Johnson cried in 1965:

> History and our own achievements have thrust upon us the principal responsibility for protection of freedom on earth.... No other people in no other time has had so great an opportunity to work and risk for the freedom of all mankind.

The Indochina war was a morality trip, and moral absolutism was the final stop. As early as 1965, the *New York Times* quoted an American pilot: "I do not like to hit a village. You know you are hitting women and children. But you've got to decide that your cause is noble and that the work has to be done." In this anointed spirit we conceived ourselves the world's judge, jury, and executioner and did our work in Indochina.

The moralistic cant of Presidents Johnson and Nixon helped delude a lot of pilots into supposing they were doing God's work. Unfortunately, instead of strengthening the national-interest wing of the opposition to the war, Vietnam seems to have incited an equally moralistic outburst on the part of the war's most clamorous critics. Too many people on both sides of the Indochina debate feel they know exactly what the Lord would do if He only knew the facts in the case.

Yet may not these critics, emotional and extravagant as they often are, have a point? Are not even those quite satisfied to oppose the war as contrary to our national interest still obliged to face the question of whether it may not be an immoral as well as a stupid war? I think they are, if we are ever to extract the full and awful lesson from this catastrophe.

My own answer to the question is yes, it is an immoral war, and it became so, ironically, when our moralistic zeal burst the limitations of national interest. Our original presence in South Vietnam hardly seems immoral, since we were there at the request of the South Vietnam government. Nor does it seem necessarily contrary to our national interest; conceivably it might have been worth it to commit, say, 20,000 military advisers if this could preserve an independent South Vietnam. But at some point the number of troops, and the things they were instructed to do, began to go beyond the requirements of national interest. This point was almost certainly the decision taken in early 1965 to send our bombers to North Vietnam and our combat units to South Vietnam and thus to Americanize the war.

Theologians talk about the principle of proportionality—the principle that means must have a due and rational relationship to ends. The Indochina war became, in my view, what can properly be called an immoral war when the means employed and the destruction wrought grew out of any conceivable proportion to the interests involved and the ends sought.

Enjoined by our leaders as to the sublimity of the mission, we cast ourselves as saviors of human freedom, misconceived the extremely restricted character of our national stake in Indochina, and, step by step, intensified senseless terror till we stand today as a nation disgraced before the world and before our own posterity.

How will our descendants ever understand the mood in which ordinary GIs, inflamed with the belief that anything Americans did was right, virtuously massacred Indochinese women and children—or in which such crimes were condoned, if not concealed, by the theater command? How will they understand the mood in which some American citizens hailed an hysterical killer [Lieutenant William L. Calley] as a national hero and proposed that, instead of conviction by a military court-martial, he should receive the Congressional Medal of Honor? How will historians explain national decisions, piously taken by God-fearing men in air-conditioned offices in Washington, that resulted in the detonation over this weak and hapless land of six million tons of explosives— three times as much as we dropped on Germany, Italy, and Japan during the second world war?

For years we averted our eyes from what we were doing in Indochina—from the search-and-destroy missions and the free-fire zones; from the defoliation and the B-52s; from the noncombatants slaughtered; the villages laid waste; the crops and forests destroyed; the refugees, one-third of the population of South Vietnam, huddled in unimaginable squalor; from the free and continuous violations of the laws of war. For years we even refrained from pursuing the question of why we were fighting in Indochina—the question that will mystify future historians as they try to figure out what threat to national security, what involvement of national interest, conceivably justified the longest war in American history, the systematic deception of the American people, and the death of thousands of Americans and hundreds of thousands of Vietnamese. [...]

At the very least, a full inquiry into the causes and consequences of the war, as recently suggested by the *New Republic*, would force the nation to contemplate the things we must do to provide reparation for our acts and safeguards against their repetition. But such an inquiry, one must trust, will not result in the vindication of the moral approach to foreign policy. One must hope, rather, that it would increase skepticism about moral judgments promiscuously introduced into international politics. One must hope the Indochina experience will inoculate the nation against the perversion of policy by moralism in the future. An intelligent regard for one's own national interest joined to unremitting respect for the interest of others seems more likely than the invocation of moral absolutes to bring about greater restraint, justice, and peace among nations.

Cathy Hull

EVERYDAY USE

BY ALICE WALKER

APRIL 1973

I will wait for her in the yard that Maggie and I made so clean and wavy yesterday afternoon. A yard like this is more comfortable than most people know. It is not just a yard. It is like an extended living room. When the hard clay is swept clean as a floor and the fine sand around the edges lined with tiny, irregular grooves, anyone can come and sit and look up into the elm tree and wait for the breezes that never come inside the house.

Maggie will be nervous until after her sister goes: she will stand hopelessly in corners, homely and ashamed of the burn scars down her arms and legs, eyeing her sister with a mixture of envy and awe. She thinks her sister has held life always in the palm of one hand, that "no" is a word the world never learned to say to her.

You've no doubt seen those TV shows where the child who has "made it" is confronted, as a surprise, by his own mother and father, tottering in weakly from backstage. (A pleasant surprise, of course: what would they do if parent and child came on the show only to curse out and insult each other?) On TV mother and child embrace and smile into each other's faces. Sometimes the mother and father weep, the child wraps them in his arms and leans across the table to tell how he would not have made it without their help. I have seen these programs.

Sometimes I dream a dream in which Dee and I are suddenly brought together on a TV program of this sort. Out of a dark and soft-seated limousine I am ushered into a bright room filled with many people. There I meet a smiling, gray, sporty man like Johnny Carson who shakes my hand and tells me what a fine girl I have. Then we are on the stage and Dee is embracing me with tears in her eyes. She pins on my dress a large orchid, even though she has told me once that she thinks orchids are tacky flowers.

In real life I am a large big-boned woman with rough, man-working hands. In the winter I wear flannel night-gowns to bed and overalls during the day. I can kill and clean a hog as mercilessly as a man. My fat keeps me hot in zero weather. I can work outside all day, breaking ice to get water for washing; I can eat pork liver cooked over the open fire minutes after it comes steaming from the hog. One winter I knocked a bull calf straight in the brain between the eyes with a sledgehammer and had the meat hung up to chill before nightfall. But of course all this does not show on television. I am the way my daughter would want me to be; a hundred pounds lighter, my skin like an uncooked barley pancake. My hair glistens in the hot bright lights. Johnny Carson has much to do to keep up with my quick and witty tongue.

But that is a mistake. I know even before I wake up. Who ever knew a Johnson with a quick tongue? Who can even imagine me looking a strange white man in the eye? It seems to me I have talked to them always with one foot raised in flight, with my head turned in whichever way is farthest from them. Dee, though. She would always look anyone in the eye. Hesitation was no part of her nature.

"How do I look, Mama?" Maggie says, showing just enough of her thin body enveloped in pink skirt and red blouse for me to know she's there almost hidden by the door.

"Come out into the yard," I say.

Have you ever seen a lame animal, perhaps a dog run over by some careless person rich enough to own a car, sidle up to someone who is ignorant enough to be kind to him? That is the way my Maggie walks. She has been like this, chin on chest, eyes on ground, feet in shuffle, ever since the fire that burned the other house to the ground.

Dee is lighter than Maggie, with nicer hair and a fuller figure. She's a woman now, though sometimes I forget. How long ago was it that the other house burned? Ten, twelve years? Sometimes I can still hear the flames and feel Maggie's arms sticking to me, her hair smoking and her dress falling off her in little black papery flakes. Her eyes seemed stretched open, blazed open by the flames reflected in them. And Dee. I see her standing off under the sweetgum tree she used to dig gum out of; a look of concentration on her face as she watched the last dingy gray board of the house fall in toward the red-hot brick chimney. Why don't you do a dance around the ashes? I'd wanted to ask her. She had hated the house that much.

I used to think she hated Maggie too. But that was before we raised the money, the church and me, to send her to Augusta to school. She used to read to us without pity; forcing words, lies, other folks' habits, whole lives upon us two, sitting trapped and ignorant underneath her voice. She washed us in a river of make-believe, burned us with a lot of knowledge we didn't necessarily need to know. Pressed us to her with the serious way she read, to shove us away, like dimwits, at just the moment we seemed about to understand.

Dee wanted nice things. A yellow organdy dress to wear to her graduation from high school; black pumps to match a green suit she'd made from an old suit somebody gave me. She was determined to stare down any disaster in her efforts. Her eyelids would not flicker for minutes at a time. Often I fought off the temptation to shake her. At sixteen she had a style of her own: and knew what style was.

I never had an education myself. After second grade the school was closed down. Don't ask me why: in 1927 colored asked fewer questions than they do now. Sometimes Maggie reads to me. She stumbles along good-naturedly but can't see well. She knows she is not bright. Like good looks and money, quickness passed her by. She will marry John Thomas (who has mossy teeth in an earnest face), and then I'll be free to sit here and I guess just sing church songs to myself. Although I never was a good singer. Never could carry a tune. I was always better at a man's job. I used to love to milk till I was hooked in the side in '49. Cows are soothing and slow and don't bother you, unless you try to milk them the wrong way.

I have deliberately turned my back on the house. It is three rooms, just like the one that burned, except the roof is tin; they don't make shingle roofs anymore. There are no real windows, just some holes cut in the sides, like the portholes in a ship, but not round and not square, with rawhide holding the shutters up on the outside. This house is in a pasture too, like the other one. No doubt when Dee sees it she will want to tear it down. She wrote me once that no matter where we "choose" to live, she will manage to come

see us. But she will never bring her friends. Maggie and I thought about this and Maggie asked me, "Mama, when did Dee ever *have* any friends?"

She had a few. Furtive boys in pink shirts hanging about on washday after school. Nervous girls who never laughed. Impressed with her they worshipped the well-turned phrase, the cute shape, the scalding humor that erupted like bubbles in lye. She read to them.

When she was courting Jimmy T she didn't have much time to pay to us, but turned all her fault-finding power on him. He *flew* to marry a cheap city girl from a family of ignorant flashy people. She hardly had time to recompose herself.

When she comes I will meet . . . but there they are!

Maggie attempts to make a dash for the house, in her shuffling way, but I stay her with my hand. "Come back here," I say. And she stops and tries to dig a well in the sand with her toe.

It is hard to see them clearly through the strong sun. But even the first glimpse of leg out of the car tells me it is Dee. Her feet were always neat looking, as if God himself had shaped them with a certain style. From the other side of the car comes a short, stocky man. Hair is all over his head a foot long and hanging from his chin like a kinky mule tail. I hear Maggie suck in her breath. "Uhnnnh," is what it sounds like. Like when you see the wriggling end of a snake just in front of your foot on a road. "Uhnnnh."

Dee, next. A dress down to the ground, in this hot weather. A dress so loud it hurts my eyes. There are yellows and oranges enough to throw back the light of the sun. I feel my whole face warming from the heat waves it throws out. Earrings gold too, and hanging down to her shoulders. Bracelets dangling and making noises when she moves her arm up to shake the folds of the dress out of her armpits. The dress is loose and flows, and as she walks closer, I like it. I hear Maggie go "Uhnnnh" again. It is her sister's hair. It stands straight up like the wool on a sheep. It is black as night and around the edges are two long pigtails that rope about like small lizards disappearing behind her ears.

"Wa-su-zo-Tean-o!" she says, coming on in that gliding way the dress makes her move. The short stocky fellow with the hair to his navel is all grinning and he follows up with, "Asalamalakim, my mother and sister!" He moves to hug Maggie but she falls back, right up against the back of my chair. I feel her trembling there, and when I look up I see the perspiration falling off her skin.

"Don't get up," says Dee. Since I am stout it takes something of a push. You can see me trying to move a second or two before I make it. She turns, showing white heels through her sandals, and goes back to the car. Out she peeks next with a Polaroid. She stoops down quickly and snaps off picture after picture of me sitting there in front of the house with Maggie cowering behind me. She never takes a shot without making sure the house is included. When a cow comes nibbling around the edge of the yard she snaps it and me and Maggie *and* the house. Then she puts the Polaroid on the back seat of the car, and comes up and kisses me on the forehead.

Meanwhile Asalamalakim is going through motions with Maggie's hand. Maggie's hand is as limp as a fish, and probably as cold, despite the sweat, and she keeps trying to pull it back. It looks like Asalamalakim wants to shake hands but wants to do it fancy. Or maybe he don't know how people shake hands. Anyhow, he soon gives up on Maggie.

"Well," I say. "Dee."

"No, Mama," she says. "Not 'Dee,' Wangero Leewanika Kemanjo!"

"What happened to 'Dee'?" I wanted to know.

"She's dead," Wangero said. "I couldn't bear it any longer, being named after the people who oppress me."

"You know well as me you was named after your aunt Dicie," I said. Dicie is my sister. She named Dee. We called her "Big Dee" after Dee was born.

"But who was *she* named after?" asked Wangero.

"I guess after Grandma Dee," I said.

"And who was she named after?" asked Wangero.

"Her mother," I said, and saw Wangero was getting tired. "That's about as far back as I can trace it," I said. Though, in fact, I probably could have carried it back beyond the Civil War through the branches.

"Well," said Asalamalakim, "there you are."

"Uhnnnh," I heard Maggie say.

"There I was not," I said, "before 'Dicie' cropped up in our family, so why should I try to trace it that far back?"

He just stood there grinning, looking down on me like somebody inspecting a Model A car. Every once in a while he and Wangero sent eye signals over my head.

"How do you pronounce this name?" I asked.

"You don't have to call me by it if you don't want to," said Wangero.

"Why shouldn't I?" I asked. "If that's what you want us to call you, we'll call you."

"I know it might sound awkward at first," said Wangero.

"I'll get used to it," I said. "Ream it out again."

Well, soon we got the name out of the way. Asalamalakim had a name twice as long and three times as hard. After I tripped over it two or three times he told me to just call him Hakim-a-barber. I wanted to ask him was he a barber, but I didn't really think he was, so I didn't ask.

"You must belong to those beef cattle peoples down the road," I said. They said "Asalamalakim" when they met you too, but they didn't shake hands. Always too busy: feeding the cattle, fixing the fences, putting up salt-lick shelters, throwing down hay. When the white folks poisoned some of the herd, the men stayed up all night with rifles in their hands. I walked a mile and a half just to see the sight.

Hakim-a-barber said, "I accept some of their doctrines, but farming and raising cattle is not my style." They didn't tell me, and I didn't ask, whether Wangero (Dee) had really gone and married him.

We sat down to eat and right away he said he didn't eat collards and pork was unclean. Wangero, though, went on through the chitlins and corn bread, the greens and everything else. She talked a blue streak over the sweet potatoes. Everything delighted her. Even the fact that we still used the benches her daddy made for the table when we couldn't afford to buy chairs.

"Oh, Mama!" she cried. Then turned to Hakim-a-barber. "I never knew how lovely these benches are. You can feel the rump prints," she said, running her hands underneath her and along the bench. Then she gave a sigh and her hand closed over Grandma Dee's butter dish. "That's it!" she said. "I knew there was something I wanted to ask you if I could have." She jumped up from the table and went over in the corner where the churn stood, the milk in it clabber by now. She looked at the churn and looked at it.

"This churn top is what I need," she said. "Didn't Uncle Buddy whittle it out of a tree you all used to have?"

"Yes," I said.

"Uh huh," she said happily. "And I want the dasher too."

"Uncle Buddy whittle that too?" asked the barber.

Dee (Wangero) looked up at me.

"Aunt Dee's first husband whittled the dash," said Maggie so low you almost couldn't hear her. "His name was Henry, but they called him Stash."

"Maggie's brain is like an elephant's," Wangero said, laughing. "I can use the churn top as a centerpiece for the alcove table," she said, sliding a plate over the churn, "and I'll think of something artistic to do with the dasher."

When she finished wrapping the dasher the handle stuck out. I took it for a moment in my hands. You didn't even have to look close to see where hands pushing the dasher up and down to make butter had left a kind of sink in the wood. In fact, there were a lot of small sinks; you could see where thumbs and fingers had sunk into the wood. It was beautiful light yellow wood, from a tree that grew in the yard where Big Dee and Stash had lived.

After dinner Dee (Wangero) went to the trunk at the foot of my bed and started rifling through it. Maggie hung back in the kitchen over the dishpan. Out came Wangero with two quilts. They had been pieced by Grandma Dee, and then Big Dee and me had hung them on the quilt frames on the front porch and quilted them. One was in the Lone Star pattern. The other was Walk Around the Mountain. In both of them were scraps of dresses Grandma Dee had worn fifty and more years ago. Bits and pieces of Grandpa Jarrell's paisley shirts. And one teeny faded blue piece, about the size of a penny matchbox, that was from Great Grandpa Ezra's uniform that he wore in the Civil War.

"Mama," Wangero said sweet as a bird. "Can I have these old quilts?"

I heard something fall in the kitchen, and a minute later the kitchen door slammed.

"Why don't you take one or two of the others?" I asked. "These old things was just done by me and Big Dee from some tops your grandma pieced before she died."

"No," said Wangero. "I don't want those. They are stitched around the borders by machine."

"That'll make them last better," I said.

"That's not the point," said Wangero. "These are all pieces of dresses Grandma used to wear. She did all this stitching by hand. Imagine!" She held the quilts securely in her arms, stroking them.

"Some of the pieces, like those lavender ones, come from old clothes her mother handed down to her," I said, moving up to touch the quilts. Dee (Wangero) moved back just enough so that I couldn't reach the quilts. They already belonged to her.

"Imagine!" she breathed again, clutching them closely to her bosom.

"The truth is," I said, "I promised to give them quilts to Maggie, for when she marries John Thomas."

She gasped, like a bee had stung her.

"Maggie can't appreciate these quilts!" she said. "She'd probably be backward enough to put them to everyday use."

"I reckon she would," I said. "God knows I been saving 'em for long enough with nobody using 'em. I hope she will!" I didn't want to bring up how I had offered Dee (Wangero) a quilt when she went away to college. Then she had told me they were old-fashioned, out of style.

"But they're *priceless*!" She was saying now, furiously; for she has a temper. "Maggie would put them on the bed and in five years they'd be in rags. Less than that!"

"She can always make some more," I said. "Maggie knows how to quilt."

Dee (Wangero) looked at me with hatred. "You just will not understand. The point is these quilts, *these* quilts!"

"Well," I said, stumped, "what would *you* do with them?"

"Hang them," she said. As if that was the only thing you *could* do with quilts.

Maggie, by now, was standing in the door. I could almost hear the sound her feet made as they scraped over each other.

"She can have them, Mama," she said, like somebody used to never winning anything, of having anything reserved for her. "I can 'member Grandma Dee without the quilts."

I looked at her hard. She had filled her bottom lip with checkerberry snuff, and it gave her face a kind of dopey, hang-dog look. It was Grandma Dee and Big Dee who taught her how to quilt herself. She stood there with her scarred hands hidden in the folds of her skirt. She looked at her sister with something like fear, but she wasn't mad at her. This was Maggie's portion. This was the way she knew God to work.

When I looked at her like that something hit me in the top of my head and ran down to the soles of my feet. Just like when I'm in church and the spirit of God touches me and I get happy and shout. I did something I never had done before: hugged Maggie to me, then dragged her on into the room, snatched the quilts out of Miss Wangero's hands and dumped them into Maggie's lap. Maggie just sat there on my bed with her mouth open.

"Take one or two of the others," I said to Dee.

But she turned without a word and went out to Hakim-a-barber.

"You just don't understand," she said, as Maggie and I came out to the car.

"What don't I understand?" I wanted to know.

"Your heritage," she said. And then she turned to Maggie, kissed her, and said, "You ought to try to make something of yourself too, Maggie. It's really a new day for us. But from the way you and Mama still live you'd never know it."

She put on some sunglasses that hid everything above the tip of her nose and her chin.

Maggie smiled; maybe at the sunglasses. But a real smile, not scared. After we watched the car dust settle I asked Maggie to bring me a dip of snuff. And then the two of us sat there just enjoying, until it was time to go in the house and go to bed.

The Death of Salvador Allende

by Gabriel García Márquez

Translated by Gregory Rabassa

March 1974

It was toward the end of 1969 that three generals from the Pentagon dined with five Chilean military officers in a house in the suburbs of Washington. The host was then Lt. Col. Gerardo López Angulo, assistant air attaché of the Chilean Military Mission to the United States, and the Chilean guests were his colleagues from the other branches of service. The dinner was in honor of the new director of the Chilean Air Force Academy, Gen. Carlos Toro Mazote, who had arrived the day before on a study mission. The eight officers dined on fruit salad, roast veal, and peas, and drank the warm-hearted wines of their distant homeland to the south where birds glittered on the beaches while Washington wallowed in snow, and they talked mostly in English about the only thing that seemed to interest Chileans in those days: the approaching presidential elections of the following September. Over dessert, one of the Pentagon generals asked what the Chilean army would do if the candidate of the Left, someone like Salvador Allende, were elected. Gen. Toro Mazote replied: "We'll take Moneda Palace in half an hour, even if we have to burn it down."

One of the guests was Gen. Ernesto Baeza, now Director of National Security in Chile, the one who led the attack on the Presidential palace during the coup last September and gave the order to burn it. Two of his subordinates in those earlier days were to become famous in the same operation: Gen. Augusto Pinochet, President of the military junta, and Gen. Javier Palacios. Also at the table was Air Force Brig. Gen. Sergio Figueroa Gutiérrez, now Minister of Public Works and the intimate friend of another member of the military junta, Air Force Gen. Gustavo Leigh, who ordered the rocket bombing of the Presidential palace. The last guest was Adm. Arturo Troncoso, now naval governor of Valparaiso, who carried out the bloody purge of progressive naval officers and was one of those who launched the military uprising of September 11.

That dinner proved to be a historic meeting between the Pentagon and high officers of the Chilean military services. On other successive meetings, in Washington and Santiago, a contingency plan was agreed upon, according to which those Chilean military men who were bound most closely, heart and soul, to United States interests would seize power in the event of Allende's Popular Unity party victory in the elections.

The plan was conceived cold-bloodedly, as a simple military operation, and was not a consequence of pressure brought to bear by International Telephone and Telegraph. It was spawned by much deeper reasons of world politics. On the North American side, the organization set in motion was the Defense Intelligence Agency of the Pentagon, but the one in actual charge was the Naval Intelligence Agency, under the higher political direction of the CIA, and the National Security Council. It was quite the normal thing to put the Navy and not the Army in charge of the project, for the Chilean coup was to coincide with Operation Unitas, which was the name given to the joint maneuvers of American and Chilean naval units in the Pacific. Those maneuvers were held at the end of each September, the same month as the elections, and the appearance on land and in the skies of Chile of all manner of war equipment and men well trained in the arts and sciences of death was natural.

During that period Henry Kissinger had said in private to a group of Chileans: "I am not interested in, nor do I know anything about, the southern portion of the world from the Pyrenees on down." By that time the contingency plan had been completed to its smallest details, and it is impossible to suppose that Kissinger or President Nixon himself was not aware of it.

Chile is a narrow country, some 2,660 miles long and an average of 119 wide, and with 10 million exuberant inhabitants, almost 3 million of whom live in the metropolitan area of Santiago, the capital. The country's greatness is not derived from the number of virtues it possesses, but, rather, from its many singularities. The only thing it produces with any absolute seriousness is copper ore, but that ore is the best in the world, and its volume of production is surpassed only by that of the United States and the Soviet Union. It also produces wine as good as the European varieties, but not much of it is exported. Its per capita income of $650 ranks among the highest in Latin America, but, traditionally, almost half the gross national product has been accounted for by fewer than 300,000 people. In 1932 Chile became the first socialist republic in the Americas and, with the enthusiastic support of the workers, the government attempted the nationalization of copper and coal. The experiment lasted only thirteen days. Chile has an earth tremor on the average of once every two days and a devastating earthquake every Presidential term. The least apocalyptic of geologists think of Chile not as a country of the mainland, but as a cornice of the Andes in a misty sea, and believe that the whole of its national territory is condemned to disappear in some future cataclysm.

Chileans are very much like their country in a certain way. They are the most pleasant people on the continent, they like being alive, and they know how to live in the best way possible and even a little more; but they have a dangerous tendency toward skepticism and intellectual speculation. A Chilean once told me on a Monday that "no Chilean believes tomorrow is Tuesday," and he didn't believe it either. Still, even with that deep-seated incredulity, or thanks to it, perhaps, the Chileans have attained a degree of natural civilization, a political maturity, and a level of culture that sets them apart from the rest of the region. Of the three Nobel Prizes in literature that Latin America has won, two have gone to Chileans, one of whom, Pablo Neruda, was the greatest poet of this century.

Henry Kissinger may have known this when he said that he knew nothing about the southern part of the world. In any case, United States intelligence agencies knew a great deal more. In 1965, without Chile's permission, the nation became the staging center and a recruiting locale for a fantastic social and political espionage operation: Project Camelot. This was to have been a secret investigation which would have precise questionnaires put to people of all social levels, all professions and trades, even in the farthest reaches of a number of Latin-American nations, in order to establish in a scientific way the degree of political development and the social tendencies of various social groups. The questionnaire destined for the military contained the same question that the Chilean officers would hear again at the dinner in Washington: what will their position be if Communism comes to power? It was a wily query.

Chile had long been a favored area for research by North American social scientists. The age and strength of its popular movement, the tenacity and intelligence of its leaders, and the economic and social conditions themselves afforded a glimpse of the country's destiny. One didn't require the findings of a Project Camelot to venture the belief that Chile was a prime candidate to be the second socialist republic in Latin America after Cuba. The aim of the United States, therefore, was not simply to prevent the government of Salvador Allende from coming to power in order to protect American investments. The larger aim was to repeat the most fruitful operation that imperialism has ever helped bring off in Latin America: Brazil.

On September 4, 1970, as had been foreseen, the socialist and Freemason physician Salvador Allende was elected President of the republic. The contingency plan was not put into effect, however. The most widespread explanation is also the most ludicrous: someone made a mistake in the Pentagon and requested 200 visas for a purported Navy chorus, which, in reality, was to be made up of specialists in government overthrow; however, there were several admirals among them who couldn't sing a single note. That gaffe, it is to be supposed, determined the postponement of the adventure. The truth is that the project had been evaluated in depth: other American agencies, particularly the CIA, and the American Ambassador to Chile felt that the contingency plan was too strictly a military operation and did not take current political and social conditions in Chile into account.

Indeed, the Popular Unity victory did not bring on the social panic U.S. intelligence had expected. On the contrary, the new government's independence in international affairs and its decisiveness in economic matters immediately created an atmosphere of social celebration. During the first year, forty-seven industrial firms were nationalized along with most of the banking system. Agrarian reform saw the expropriation and incorporation into communal property of six million acres of land formerly held by the large landowners. The inflationary process was slowed, full employment was attained, and wages received a cash rise of 30 percent.

The previous government, headed by the Christian Democrat Eduardo Frei, had begun steps toward nationalizing copper, though he called it Chileanization. All the plan did was to buy up 51 percent of U.S.-held mining properties, and for the mine of El Teniente alone it paid a sum greater than the total book value of that facility. Popular Unity, with a single legal act supported in Congress by all of the nation's political parties, recovered for the nation all copper deposits worked by the subsidiaries of American companies Anaconda and Kennecott. Without indemnification: the government having calculated that the two companies during a period of fifteen years had made a profit in excess of $800 million.

The petit bourgeoisie and the middle class, the two great social forces which might have supported a military coup at that moment, were beginning to enjoy unforeseen advantages, and not at the expense of the proletariat, as had always been the case, but, rather, at the expense of the financial oligarchy and foreign capital. The armed forces, as a social group, have the same origins and ambitions as the middle class, so they had no motive, not even an alibi, to back the tiny group of coup-minded officers. Aware of that reality, the Christian Democrats not only did not support the barracks plot at that time, but resolutely opposed it, for they knew it was unpopular among their own rank and file.

Their objective was something else again: to use any means possible to impair the good health of the government so as to win two-thirds of the seats in Congress in the March 1973 elections. With such a majority they could vote the constitutional removal of the President of the republic.

The Christian Democrats make up a huge organization cutting across class lines, with an authentic popular base among the modern industrial proletariat, the small and middle rural landowners, and the petit bourgeoisie and middle class of the cities. Popular Unity, while also interclass in its makeup, was the expression of workers of the less-favored proletariat, the agricultural proletariat, and the lower middle class of the cities.

The Christian Democrats, allied with the extreme right-wing National party, controlled the Congress and the courts; Popular Unity controlled the executive. The polarization of these two parties was to be, in fact, the polarization of the country. Curiously, the Catholic Eduardo Frei, who doesn't believe in Marxism, was the one who took best advantage of the class struggle, the one who stimulated it and brought it to a head, with an aim to unhinge the government and plunge the country into the abyss of demoralization and economic disaster.

The economic blockade by the United States, because of expropriation without indemnification, did the rest. All kinds of goods are manufactured in Chile, from automobiles to toothpaste, but this industrial base has a false identity: in the 160 most important firms, 60 percent of the capital was foreign and 80 percent of the basic materials came from abroad. In addition, the country needed 300 million dollars a year in order to import consumer goods and another 450 million to pay the interest on its foreign debt. Credits advanced by the socialist countries could not remedy the fundamental lack of replacement parts, for much of Chilean industry, agriculture, and transportation is based on American equipment. The Soviet Union had to buy wheat in Australia to send to Chile because it had none of its own, and through the Commercial Bank of Northern Europe in Paris it made several substantial loans in cash and in dollars. But Chile's urgent needs were extraordinary and went much deeper. The merry ladies of the bourgeoisie, under the pretext of protesting rationing, galloping inflation, and the demands made by the poor, took to the streets beating their empty pots and pans. It wasn't by chance, quite the contrary; it was very significant that that street spectacle of silver foxes and flowered hats took place on the same afternoon that Fidel Castro was ending a thirty-day visit, a visit that had brought an earthquake of social mobilization of government supporters.

President Allende understood then, and he said so, that the people held the government but they did not hold the power. The phrase was more bitter than it seemed, and also more alarming, for inside himself Allende carried a legalist germ that held the seed of his own destruction: a man who fought to the death in defense of legality, he would have been capable of walking out of Moneda Palace with his head held high if the Congress had removed him from office within the bounds of the constitution.

The Italian journalist and politician Rossana Rossanda, who visited Allende during that period, found him aged, tense, and full of gloomy premonitions as he talked to her from the yellow cretonne couch where, seven months later, his riddled body was to lie, the face crushed in by a rifle butt. Then, on the eve of the March 1973 elections, in which his destiny was at stake, he would have been content with 36 percent of the vote for Popular Unity. And yet, in spite of runaway inflation, stern rationing, and the pot-and-pan concert of the merry wives of the upper-class districts, he received 44 percent. It was such a spectacular and decisive victory that when Allende was alone in his office with his friend and confidant, the journalist Augusto Olivares, he closed the door and danced a *cueca* all by himself.

For the Christian Democrats it was proof that the process of social justice set in motion by the Popular Unity party could not be turned back by legal means, but they lacked the vision to measure the consequences of the actions they then undertook. For the United States the election was a much more serious warning and went beyond the simple interests of expropriated firms. It was an inadmissible precedent for peaceful progress and social change for the peoples of the world, particularly those of France and Italy, where present conditions make an attempt at an experiment along the lines of Chile possible. All forces of internal and external reaction came together to form a compact bloc.

On the other side, the parties making up Popular Unity, with internal rifts much deeper than has been admitted, were unable to reach an agreement in their analysis of the March vote. The government found itself facing demands from one extreme to take advantage of the evident radicalization of the masses which the election had revealed and make a decisive leap forward in the area of social change, while from the more moderate wing, which feared the specter of civil war, there was pressure to have faith in a regressive agreement with the Christian Democrats. It is quite obvious now that those feelers on the part of the opposition were simply a distraction in order to win more time.

The truck owners' strike was the final blow. Because of the wild geography of the country, the Chilean economy is at the mercy of its transport. To paralyze trucking is to paralyze the country. It was easy for the opposition to coordinate the strike, for the truckers' guild was one of the groups most affected by the scarcity of replacement parts and, in addition, it found itself threatened by the government's small pilot program for providing adequate state trucking services in the extreme south of the nation. The stoppage lasted until the very end without a single moment of relief because it was financed with cash from outside. "The CIA flooded the country with dollars to support the strike by the bosses, and that foreign capital found its way down into the formation of a black market," Pablo Neruda wrote a friend in Europe. One week before the coup, oil, milk, and bread had run out.

During the last days of Popular Unity, with the economy unhinged and the country on the verge of civil war, the maneuvering of the government and the opposition centered on the hope of changing the balance of power in the armed forces in favor of one or the other. The final move was hallucinatory in its perfection: forty-eight hours before the coup, the opposition managed to disqualify all high officers supporting Salvador Allende and to promote in their places, one by one, in a series of inconceivable gambits, all of the officers who had been present at the dinner in Washington.

At that moment, however, the political chess game had got out of the control of its players. Dragged along by an irreversible dialectic, they themselves ended up as pawns in a much larger game of chess, one much more complex and politically more important than any mere scheme hatched in conjunction by imperialism and the reaction against the government of the people. It was a terrifying class confrontation that was slipping out of the hands of the very people who had provoked it, a cruel and fierce scramble by counter-

Allende waves to crowd after hearing election results, September 1970.

poised interests, and the final outcome had to be a social cataclysm without precedent in the history of the Americas.

A military coup under those conditions could not be bloodless. Allende knew it. "You don't play with fire," he had told Rossana Rossanda. "If anyone thinks that a military coup in Chile will be like those in other countries of America, with a simple changing of the guard at Moneda Palace, he is flatly mistaken. If the army strays from the bounds of legality here, there will be a bloodbath. It will be another Indonesia." That certainty had a historical basis.

The Chilean armed forces, contrary to what we have been led to believe, have intervened in politics every time that their class interests have seemed threatened, and they have done so with an inordinately repressive ferocity. The two constitutions which the country has had in the past hundred years were imposed by force of arms, and the recent military coup has been the sixth uprising in a period of fifty years.

The blood lust of the Chilean army is part of its birthright, coming from that terrible school of hand-to-hand combat against the Auracanian Indians, a struggle which lasted 300 years. One of its forerunners boasted in 1620 of having killed more than 2,000 people with his own hand in a single action. Joaquín Edwards Bello relates in his chronicles that during an epidemic of exanthematic typhus the army dragged sick people out of their houses and killed them in a poison bath in order to put an end to the plague. During a seven-month civil war in 1891, 10,000 died in a series of gory encounters. The Peruvians assert that during the occupation of Lima in the War of the Pacific, Chilean soldiers sacked the library of Don Ricardo Palma, taking the books not for reading, but for wiping their backsides.

Popular movements have been suppressed with the same brutality. After the Valparaiso earthquake of 1906, naval forces wiped out the longshoremen's organization of 8,000 workers. In Iquique, at the beginning of the century, demonstrating strikers tried to take refuge from the troops and were machine-gunned: within ten minutes there were 2,000 dead. On April 2, 1957, the army broke up a civil disturbance in the commercial center of Santiago and the number of victims was never established because the government sneaked the bodies away. During a strike at the El Salvador mine during the government of Eduardo Frei, a military patrol opened fire on a demonstration to break it up and killed six people, among them some children and a pregnant woman. The post commander was an obscure fifty-two-year-old general, the father of five children, a geography teacher, and the author of several books on military subjects: Augusto Pinochet.

The myth of the legalism and the gentleness of that brutal army was invented by the Chilean bourgeoisie in their own interest. Popular Unity kept it alive with the hope of changing the class makeup of the higher cadres in its favor. But Salvador Allende felt more secure among the Carabineros, an armed force that was popular and peasant in its origins and that was under the direct command of the President of the republic. Indeed, the junta had to go six places down the seniority list of the force before it found a senior officer who would support the coup. The younger officers dug themselves in at the junior officers' school in Santiago and held out for four days until they were wiped out in an aerial bombardment.

That was the best-known battle of the secret war that broke out inside military posts on the eve of the coup. Officers who refused to support the coup and those who failed to carry out the orders for repression were murdered without pity by the instigators. Entire regiments mutinied, both in Santiago and in the provinces, and they were suppressed without mercy, with their leaders massacred as a lesson for the troops. The commandant of the armored units in Viña del Mar, Colonel Cantuarias, was machine-gunned by his subordinates. A long time will pass before the number of victims of that internal butchery will ever be known, for the bodies were removed from military posts in garbage trucks and buried secretly. All in all, only some fifty senior officers could be trusted to head troops that had been purged beforehand.

The story of the intrigue has to be pasted together from many sources, some reliable, some not. Any number of foreign agents seem to have taken part in the coup. Clandestine sources in Chile tell us that the bombing of Moneda Palace—the technical precision of which startled the experts—was actually carried out by a team of American aerial acrobats who had entered the country under the screen of Operation Unitas to perform in a flying circus on the coming September 18, National Independence Day. There is also evidence that numerous members of secret police forces from neighboring countries were infiltrated across the Bolivian border and remained in hiding until the day of the coup, when they unleashed their bloody persecution of political refugees from other countries of Latin America.

Brazil, the homeland of the head gorillas, had taken charge of those services. Two years earlier she had brought off the reactionary coup in Bolivia which meant the loss of substantial support for Chile and facilitated the infiltration of all manner and means of subversion. Part of the loans made to Brazil by the United States was secretly transferred to Bolivia to finance subversion in Chile. In 1972 a U.S. military advisory group made a trip to La Paz, the aim of which has not been revealed. Perhaps it was only coincidental, however, that a short time after that visit, movements of troops and equipment took place on the frontier with Chile, giving the Chilean military yet another opportunity to bolster their internal position and carry out transfer of personnel and promotions in the chain of command that were favorable to the imminent coup. Finally, on September 11, while Operation Unitas was going forward, the original plan drawn up at the dinner in Washington was carried out, three years behind schedule but precisely as it had been conceived: not as a conventional barracks coup, but as a devastating operation of war.

It had to be that way, for it was not simply a matter of overthrowing a regime, but one of implanting the hell-dark seeds brought from Brazil, with all of the machines of terror, torture, and death, until in Chile there would be no trace of the political and social structures which had made Popular Unity possible. The harshest phase, unfortunately, has only just begun.

In that final battle, with the country at the mercy of uncontrolled and unforeseen forces of subversion, Salvador Allende was still bound by legality. The most dramatic contradiction of his life was being at the same time the congenital foe of violence and a passionate revolutionary. He believed that he had resolved the contradiction with the hypothesis that conditions in Chile would permit a peaceful evolution toward socialism under bourgeois legality. Experience taught him too late that a system cannot be changed by a government without power.

That belated disillusionment must have been the force that impelled him to resist to the death, defending the flaming ruins of a house that was not his own, a somber mansion that an Italian architect had built to be a mint and which ended up as a refuge for Presidents without power. He resisted for six hours with a submachine gun that Fidel Castro had given him and was the first weapon that Salvador Allende had ever fired. Around four o'clock in the afternoon, Maj. Gen. Javier Palacios managed to reach the second floor with his adjutant, Captain Gallardo, and a group of officers. There, in the midst of the fake Louis XV chairs, the Chinese dragon vases, and the Rugendas paintings in the red parlor, Salvador Allende was waiting for them. He was in shirtsleeves, wearing a miner's helmet and no tie, his clothing stained with blood. He was holding the submachine gun, but he had run low on ammunition.

Allende knew General Palacios well. A few days before he had told Augusto Olivares that this was a dangerous man with close connections to the American Embassy. As soon as he saw him appear on the stairs, Allende shouted at him: "Traitor!" and shot him in the hand.

According to the story of a witness who asked me not to give his name, the President died in an exchange of shots with that gang. Then all the other officers, in a caste-bound ritual, fired on the body. Finally, a noncommissioned officer smashed in his face with the butt of his rifle. A photograph exists: Juan Enrique Lira, a photographer for the newspaper *El Mercurio*, took it. He was the only one allowed to photograph the body. It was so disfigured that when they showed the body in its coffin to Señora Hortensia Allende, his wife, they would not let her uncover the face.

He would have been sixty-four years old last July and he was a perfect Leo: tenacious, firm in his decisions, and unpredictable. "What Allende thinks, only Allende knows," one of his cabinet ministers had told me. He loved life, he loved flowers, he loved dogs, and he was a gallant with a touch of the old school about him, perfumed notes and furtive rendezvous. His greatest virtue was following through, but fate could grant him only that rare and tragic greatness of dying in armed defense of the anachronistic booby of bourgeois law, defending a Supreme Court of Justice which had repudiated him but would legitimize his murderers, defending a miserable Congress which had declared him illegitimate but which was to bend complacently before the will of the usurpers, defending the freedom of opposition parties which had sold their souls to fascism, defending the whole moth-eaten paraphernalia of a shitty system which he had proposed abolishing, but without a shot being fired. The drama took place in Chile, to the greater woe of the Chileans, but it will pass into history as something that has happened to us all, children of this age, and it will remain in our lives forever.

THE SOUND OF TINKLING BRASS

BY MURRAY KEMPTON

AUGUST 1974

Sometimes one has to decide that the proper tone for the recollections of journalists is Samuel Beckett's, which is the voice of an old man endlessly evoking forgotten occasions he is unable to explain. The most exquisite pleasures of our vocation all seem to have to do with the companionship of waiting. I remember once in Albany when Governor Rockefeller and Mayor Lindsay were writhing in combat over which of them was to have an important place in history, and no one yet permitted himself to imagine that neither would have much. But then, the practice of journalism, like the trade of politics, requires first of all the suspension of the sense of proportion.

Rockefeller and Lindsay wrangled all night, while the journalists commissioned to exaggerate the consequence of their quarrel waited on the lawn outside. It was one of those times when each of us could indulge his private weakness: the drinkers to drink, the compulsive monologuists to talk, the dreamers to lose themselves in dreams. At last, the spokesmen for these barely recollected titans came out to announce whatever official pretense had been devised to paper over their differences; and we shook ourselves and went back to work, and just before we did Robert Alden of the *New York Times* looked across the Governor's lawn at the cold, squalid, and emerging daylight and said, "You know, journalism is a terrible profession, but it's a great job." Four or five years later, Robert Alden died from the exhaustion of covering one of those United Nations disputes which are settled only by being forgotten. The true heroes are those who die for causes they cannot quite take seriously, being persons of the rare sort that care more for the voyage than the destination.

Now Bob Woodward and Carl Bernstein of the *Washington Post* have made newspapers a force of history again; and, even so, I cannot hear the tale they tell without being so caught up in how they journeyed that I care not where

they got. What in their story, after all, is quite so compelling as the image of two young men set adrift on a raft and coming ashore each night to forage for food among strangers? Still, their arrival turned out to be consequential enough to make us wonder about pretentious matters like puzzles of history. How could Woodward and Bernstein complete a trip that their elders in experience did not even bother to try? Why are governments so seldom really overthrown except by persons whose faces the Governors have never seen before? The answer, I am afraid, is that journalism *is* a terrible profession because it is one of those in which the more you know, the less lastingly useful you are.

As a general proposition, the faults of virtuous men have always seemed to me a richer subject for speculation than the sins of vicious ones. In the case of journalists the faults are not so much matters of corruption as of simple domesticity. I refer of course to the coupling of the newspaperman and the institution he covers, a relationship that is less parasitical than symbiotic, and in which each draws considerable nutriment and comfort from the other.

The symbiotic pattern begins very early and is a basic model for the education, not of the inferior, but of the very best journalists in our tradition. Persons beginning on newspapers are sent most often to the police beat—this is preparatory to learning to type—and very soon they make the acquaintance of its oldest inhabitant, a police reporter left long enough in that backwater—because of some deficiency or other in grace or articulation—to have become the familiar of its every weed and mud-bank. His frustrations have left him remarkably free from envy or spite—fraternity is the purest thing about his craft—and he truly enjoys helping the apprentice to learn everything he knows.

Unfortunately, everything this man knows is confined pretty much to what policemen think. I have a pretty high opinion of the thought processes of policemen—they do get about rather more than the rest of us do—but life has also made me quite aware of the limitations of any specialized cast of mind. And the longer the police reporter stays in the shack, the more what are in many cases merely the opinions of policemen become for him the facts and are printed in his newspaper as the facts, which, by the standards of newspapers, they may very well be, since they can be credited to a source and to an official one.

When the apprentice becomes the journeyman and makes his escape from the police shack he will move, if he is grave and serious enough for a role not without its ambassadorial aspects, to represent his paper on a specialized beat. It is superficially most sensible for newspapers to be attracted to the notion of the specialist. A great deal of what newspapers print is an explanation of events they were unable to predict, and the explanation is usually least absurd when provided by someone on the staff with some familiarity with the names and faces of the players. [...]

[T]he longer the reporter spends seeing the same things the men he covers see, the more likely it is that they and he will all see with the same eye. Tom Winship, the editor of the *Boston Globe*, has reminded us that some 1,500 journalists reside in Washington and that only two of them, Carl Bernstein and Bob Woodward, demonstrated any curiosity remotely passionate about the Watergate burglaries until six months after they had happened. Woodward and Bernstein were among the least experienced soldiers in that road-bound army; and while they were scurrying hot-eyed about alleys, their seniors were traveling with Senator McGovern and making fun of the desperation that had reduced him to peddling nonsense like his assertion that the Nixon Administration was the most corrupt since Grant's.

Watergate is in fact a quite typical illustration of one immutable law of journalism: the newspaper investigations that give the profession its occasional opportunities to congratulate itself are almost never produced by journalists who cover the institutions in which the scandals arise. Police reporters mention police corruption no more frequently than automotive reporters noticed the safety defects of the Corvair before Ralph Nader scared pretty much everyone else in the country about it. To me, whose tastes are confessedly exotic, the noblest activity within a journalist's power is helping an innocent man get out of jail. But in every case I know, the reporter who rescued the innocent began his effort as an absolute stranger to the District Attorney who put the poor man there. What familiarity really breeds is the most disabling respect; there are apparently a lot of men who are heroes only to their valets. The journalist is, by habit and necessity, increasingly dependent for his rations upon government officials who are more and more inclined to lie, if only because their own habits and necessities make them more and more prone to believe their own lies. Unpleasant truths are a most unpalatable diet for any governor. Even so, the affairs of government are more rigorously scrutinized in the newspapers these days than they have been. But I think we owe this happier condition less to the pertinacity of journalists than to the sudden disarray of government itself. The events of the past decade, especially in Vietnam, cast more Americans than ever before toward thoughts that used to be accounted treasonable, and this mass disaffection could hardly have exempted from its contagion great numbers of servants of government. Journalists are to be commended for giving wide currency to the results of this particular treason of the clerks, but they would give themselves too much credit if they claimed to have been responsible for its inception.

Few of the great revelations that have discomfited government of late were initiated by investigative journalism; large and unexceptionably busy as the press cadre in Vietnam was, our 1969 bombing of Cambodia might well have remained a secret if a master sergeant had not written a Senator about it. We know about My Lai because an ex-soldier persisted in talking about it; he might, it is true, have gone unheard if Seymour Hersh, a free-lance writer, had not kept after and documented his story. [...]

What history the investigative journalist makes is owed less often to the official servant tortured in his conscience than to the bureaucrat disturbed in his comfort. When we examine the techniques of the best investigative reporters, we are wise to remember what Shaw once said of Shakespeare—that nobody equaled him in telling a story providing only that someone had told it to him first. Even the highest forms of journalism do not often earn compliments any more deserved than this one. We almost have to assume, then, that, well as Woodward and Bernstein told their story, someone had to tell it to them first. When we commence to wonder who that guide could have been, we enter the domain which its detractors call surmise but which I prefer to designate more elegantly as the historical imagination.

Who of Mr. Nixon's 18 million servants knew enough and was disaffected enough to tell Woodward and Bernstein his story? The most plausible institutional candidate that the historical imagination can summon up becomes the Federal Bureau of Investigation. J. Edgar Hoover's FBI was a city-state whose director needed to worry about deferring to the President almost as seldom as twelfth-century Florence had to be troubled by any sense of responsibility toward the Holy Roman Empire. But then J. Edgar Hoover died and was replaced by L. Patrick Gray, whose many unappreciated virtues did not alter the condition that formally he was Mr. Nixon's creature and had risen—to the degree that so humble a fellow could be said to have risen—outside the Bureau. Gray began by affronting its traditions with a directive that FBI agents would henceforth be permitted to wear colored shirts, a meager cosmetic change to most of us but an affront to the relicts of Mr. Hoover. Then the Watergate investigation was thrust on the FBI, and its agents watched their new director defer to the pallid young man who was the President's counsel and saw him falter between his impulses to be a free man and his habits of being a servant. To the members of the FBI's permanent party, servitude to Hoover had been a vocation, but the idea of servitude to an exterior sovereign, however sanctified by the Constitution, was an indignity. They had their resentments, and they had the evidence they had gone on gathering in their remorseless and routine fashion. It is very difficult to imagine men this proud and this used to intrigue not putting together their sense of affront with the means of avenging it, and not leaking what they had found out to Woodward and Bernstein.

It cannot be said with absolute assurance that, if poor Patrick Gray had shown due respect for J. Edgar Hoover's inhibitions about haberdashery the FBI might have tamely commenced to move toward some comity with the White House and that the flames now rising around Mr. Nixon might have been, if not suppressed, at least dampened down to proportions well below the heights at which they are now raging. Still the idea is not implausible, and it reminds us again that the armed resistance of the bureaucrat against any intrusion upon his comfort and self-interest is one great reason that government is so seldom able to

accomplish either the good its friends hope or the evil its enemies fear.

The pall of suspicion that is creeping upon persons whose respectability was taken for granted is, in most ways, a quite salutary one. I have always felt that the single greatest deficiency of journalism as a reflection of social reality was the cold and suspicious treatment it gave disreputable persons and the tenderness of its approach to officially reputable ones. Our newspapers have always operated like those policemen in Graham Greene's pre-Castro Cuba who divided society into two classes of citizens, the ones you can get away with torturing and the ones you cannot.

When Vito Genovese gave up the ghost, and the issue arose of who might inherit the tattered robe of the Boss of All Bosses, the newspapers were filled with speculations about the rivals for the estate, their schemes, and their motives, all, of course, highly speculative. But the speculators never suggest that the subject of these quarrels was anything but private ambition; no one entertained the notion that any capo might be moved by his dedication to the Mafia as an institution, or some concept of its place in the nation's service. There were no intimations of any motive except greed and selfishness. Yet the eye, so sharp when it comes to the Mafia, is covered with clouds when it approaches persons whose status decrees their respectability.

It is almost thirty years since President Roosevelt's funeral train rolled toward Hyde Park, but only now are we getting the diaries of some of those who rode with it, and we can begin to sense how selfish some of their thoughts were—the dead President's old retainers worrying about their old jobs and their old friends tasting their approaching new jobs and their new power. All quite venomous, really; men's thoughts in moments of high state crisis are not all lofty and selfless. There is in politics, as in all other branches of life, an element of the cruelly personal. And yet journalism cannot quite exempt itself from the habit of treating private quarrels as if they were disputes over the national welfare. A public figure is granted the longest possible range before he crosses the shadow line that separates the man assumed to have some decency of motive and the man dismissed as having no decency at all.

The trick in Brecht's *Threepenny Opera* is that he dared to write about gangsters and crooked cops as though they were respectable businessmen. I would not quite argue that newspapers should write about businessmen as though they were gangsters or crooked cops; still, some quotient of the skepticism that covers every sort of pariah might quite usefully be extended to the many varieties of priesthood whose anointment as managers of our affairs have made them sacred in our journalism.

We have, it is true, reached some such point of skepticism in the press treatment of Mr. Nixon. The press's approach to a President is normally pretty much a branch of sacred studies of the first magistrate of the land. But now, unfortunately, Mr. Nixon is the first first magistrate of the land who, not inconceivably, might someday face a magistrate. Mr. Nixon has passed that shadow line which separates the nontorturable from the torturable classes. The consequences would be rather more satisfying if the nontorturable class, despite this singular loss in its ranks, did not remain otherwise intact, and if whoever succeeds Mr. Nixon as President will not most assuredly take his place on its side of the line.

For Mr. Nixon's position as displaced sacred object is a most special one. He has become the subject of the curiosity of criminal investigators. In that condition, he must suffer all the torments the press is free to inflict upon anyone who is damaged goods. He can be assigned no motive that is not some calculation of his own interest and the public's expense.

Consider, for example, a headline the *New York Times* printed the day after Mr. Nixon gave Southern California the boon of whatever grandeur and majesty attend his presence there:

"Nixon, After Making Secret Plans, Flies to California on Commercial Jet for Holiday at San Clemente."

Observe the elements of that summary of an event which, if sin at all, must be accounted as, by Mr. Nixon's standards, a sin too minor for the attention of the recording angel.

"Secret plans"—he moves by stealth. "San Clemente"—he sneaks to places whose very name reminds us of the scandals around him. "Holiday"—he is careless of our sufferings. Even the expression "commercial jet," while entirely precise, comes to me—who may, of course, be undergoing sympathetic pains of paranoia with my President—with a sound almost sinister; somehow Mr. Nixon's whole round seems so unremittingly commercial.

I wish I did not have to mention the *Times* in my criticisms, but it is our bible and even its sins represent our highest standards of virtue. Still, in January, the *Times* printed on its front page on a Sunday a report that Mr. Nixon had fired Archibald Cox, his own special prosecutor, because Cox had planned to name Mr. Nixon as a co-conspirator—although not as a defendant—in a general indictment for obstruction of justice in the Watergate case. Mr. Cox's denial that he had ever considered doing anything this portentous showed up two days later in decent obscurity among the girdle ads.

Journalism has entered upon that historic function which it has always, to my bafflement, conceived as its duty—doing the prosecutor's job for him, helping him sweat the suspect just outside his net. The prosecutor's gossip has no purpose except to make the suspect of whose guilt the evidence is insufficient think that the prosecutor knows more than he really does.

We are in a very old game; there is more of duty than malice in it and more of habit than passion. Mr. Nixon's is a special case. It will have its gaudy moments, but there is more heat than electricity in this lightning. We are doing what we generally have done to persons in trouble, and, when this is all over, we will have a President who is out of trouble, and we will do with him what we generally do with persons out of trouble.

Things are likely to be what they were. It is curious, but at moments like these I think upon what has always been my own wistful hope for what the journalist might be. It is, of course, Yeats's epitaph: "Cast a cold eye/On life, on death./Horseman, pass by!" I have always amended that—badly, I concede—to: "Cast the same eye/Upon friend, upon stranger,/Upon rich, upon poor,/Upon winner, upon loser,/Horseman, pass by."

It is a code that I myself have never kept very well, and I do not expect it to pass into general usage. But oh, how I wish it would.

Innocence in the Galápagos

by Annie Dillard

May 1975

First there was nothing, and although you know with your reason that nothing is nothing, it is easier to visualize it as a limitless slosh of sea— say, the Pacific. Then energy contracted into matter, and although you know that even an invisible gas is matter, it is easier to visualize it as a massive squeeze of volcanic lava spattered inchoate from the secret pit of the ocean and hardening mute and intractable on nothing's lapping shore—like a series of islands, an archipelago. Like: the Galápagos. Then a softer strain of matter began to twitch. It was a kind of shaped water; it flowed, hardening here and there at its tips. There were blue-green algae; there were tortoises; there were men.

The ice rolled up, the ice rolled back, and I knelt on a plain of lava boulders in the islands called Galápagos, stroking a giant tortoise's neck. The tortoise closed its eyes and stretched its neck to its greatest height and vulnerability. I rubbed that neck, and when I pulled away my hand, my palm was green with a slick of single-celled algae. I stared at the algae, and at the tortoise, the way you stare at any life on a lava flow, and thought, Well—here we all are.

Being here is being here on the rocks. These Galapagonian rocks, one of them seventy-five miles long, dried under the equatorial sun between 500 and 600 miles west of the South American continent, at the latitude of the Republic of Ecuador, to which they belong.

There is a way a small island rises from the ocean affronting all reason. It is a chunk of chaos pounded into visibility *ex nihilo*, here rough, here smooth, shaped just so by a matrix of physical necessities too weird to contemplate, here instead of there, here instead of not at all. It is a fantastic utterance, as though I were to open my mouth and emit a French horn, or a vase, or a knob of tellurium. It smacks of folly, of first causes.

I think of the island called Daphnecita, little Daphne, on which I never set foot. It's in half of my few photographs, though, because it obsessed me: a dome of gray lava like a pitted loaf, the size of the Plaza Hotel, glazed with guano and crawling with red-orange crabs. Sometimes I attributed to this island's cliff face a surly, infantile consciousness, as though it were sulking in the silent moment after it had just shouted, to the sea and the sky, I didn't ask to be born. Or sometimes it aged to a raging adolescent, a kid who's just learned that the game is fixed, demanding, What did you have me for, if you're just going to push me around? Daphnecita: again, a wise old island, mute, leading the life of pure creaturehood open to any antelope or saint. After you've blown the ocean sky-high, what's there to say? What if we the people had sense or grace to live as cooled islands in an archipelago live, with dignity, passion, and no comment?

It is worth flying to Guayaquil, Ecuador, and then to Baltra in the Galápagos to see only the rocks. But these rocks are animal gardens. They are home to a Hieronymus Bosch assortment of windblown, stowaway, castaway, flotsam and shipwrecked creatures. Most exist nowhere else on earth. These reptiles and insects, small mammals and birds evolved unmolested on the various islands on which they were cast into unique species adapted to the boulder-wrecked shores, the cactus deserts of the lowlands, or the elevated jungles of the large island's interiors. You come for the animals. You come to see the curious shapes soft proteins can take, to impress yourself with their reality, and to greet them.

You walk among clattering four-foot marine iguanas heaped on the shore lava, and on each other, like slag. You swim with penguins; you watch flightless cormorants dance beside you, ignoring you, waving the black nubs of their useless wings. Here are nesting blue-footed boobies, real birds with real feathers, whose legs and feet are nevertheless patently fake, manufactured by Mattel. The tortoises you touch are as big as stoves. The enormous land iguanas at your feet change color in the sunlight, from gold to blotchy red as you watch.

There is always some creature going about its beautiful business. I missed the boat back to my ship, and was left behind momentarily on uninhabited South Plaza Island because I was watching the Audubon's shearwaters. These dark pelagic birds flick along pleated seas in stitching flocks, flailing their wings rapidly—because if they don't, they'll stall. A shearwater must fly fast, or not at all. Consequently it has evolved two nice behaviors which serve to bring it into its nest alive. The nest is a shearwater-sized hole in the lava cliff. The shearwater circles over the water, ranging out from the nest a quarter of a mile, and veers gradually toward the cliff, making passes at its nest. If the flight angle is precisely right, the bird will fold its wings at the hole's entrance and stall directly onto its floor. The angle is perhaps seldom right, however; one shearwater I watched made a dozen suicidal-looking passes before it vanished into a chink. The other, alternative, behavior is spectacular. It involves choosing the nest hole in a site below a prominent rock with a downward-angled face. The shearwater comes careering in full tilt, claps its wings, stalls itself into the rock, and the rock, acting as a backboard, banks it home.

The animals are tame. They have not been persecuted, and show no fear of man. You pass among them as though you were wind, spindrift, sunlight, leaves. The songbirds are tame. On Hood Island I sat beside a nesting waved albatross while a mockingbird scratched in my hair, another mockingbird jabbed at my fingernail, and a third mockingbird made an exquisite progression of pokes at my bare feet up the long series of eyelets in my basketball shoes. The marine iguanas are tame. One settler, Carl Angermeyer, built his house on the site of a marine iguana colony. The gray iguanas, instead of moving out, moved up on the roof, which is corrugated steel. Twice daily on the patio, Angermeyer feeds them a mixture of boiled rice and tuna fish from a plastic basin. Their names are all, unaccountably, Annie. Angermeyer beats on the basin with a long-handled spoon, calling Here AnnieAnnieAnnieAnnie—and the spiny reptiles, fifty or sixty strong, click along the steel roof, finger their way down the lava boulder and mortar walls, and swarm round his bare legs to elbow into the basin and be elbowed out again smeared with a mash of boiled rice on their bellies and on their protuberant, black, plated lips.

The wild hawk is tame. The Galápagos hawk is related to North America's Swainson's hawk; I have read that, if you take pains, you can walk up and pat it. I never tried. We people don't walk up and pat each other; enough is enough.

The animals' critical distance and mine tended to coincide, so we could enjoy an easy sociability without threat of violence or unwonted intimacy. The hawk, which is not notably sociable, nevertheless endures even a blundering approach, and is apparently as content to perch on a scrub tree at your shoulder as anyplace else.

In the Galápagos, even the flies are tame. Although most of the land is Ecuadorian national park, and as such rigidly protected, I confess I gave the evolutionary ball an offsides shove by dispatching every fly that bit me, marveling the while at its pristine ignorance, its blithe failure to register a flight trigger at the sweep of my descending hand—an insouciance that was almost, but not quite, disarming. After you kill a fly, you pick it up and feed it to a lava lizard, a bright-throated four-inch creature that scavenges everywhere in the arid lowlands. And you walk on, passing among the innocent mobs on every rock hillside; or you sit, and they come to you.

We are strangers and sojourners, soft dots on the rocks. You have walked along the strand and seen where birds have landed, walked, and flown; their tracks begin in sand, and go, and suddenly end. Our tracks do that: but we go down. And stay down. While we're here, during the seasons our tents are pitched in the light, we pass among each other crying "greetings" in a thousand tongues, and "welcome," and "goodbye." Inhabitants of uncrowded colonies tend to offer the stranger famously warm hospitality—and such are the Galápagos sea lions. Theirs is the greeting the first creatures must have given Adam—a hero's welcome, a universal and undeserved huzzah. Go, and be greeted by sea lions.

I was sitting under a ledge of pewter cloud with Soames Summerhays, the ship's naturalist, on a sand beach under cliffs on uninhabited Hood Island. The white beach was a havoc of lava boulders black as clinkers, sleek with spray, and lambent as brass in the sinking sun. To our left a dozen sea lions were body-surfing in the long green combers that rose, translucent, half a mile offshore. When the combers broke, the shoreline boulders rolled. I could feel the roar in the rough rock on which I sat; I could hear the grate inside each long backsweeping sea, the rumble of a rolled million rocks muffled in splashes and the seethe before the next wave's heave.

To our right, a sea lion slipped from the ocean. It was a young bull; in another few years he would be more dangerous, bellowing at intruders and biting off great dirty chunks of the ones he catches. Now this young bull, which weighed maybe 120 pounds, sprawled silhouetted in the late light, slick as a drop of quicksilver, his glistening whiskers radii of gold like any crown. He hauled his packed bulk toward us up the long beach; he flung himself with an enormous surge of fur-clad muscle onto the boulder where I sat. "Soames," I said—very quietly—"he's here because *we're* here, isn't he?" The naturalist nodded. I felt water drip on my elbow behind me, then the fragile scrape of whiskers, and finally the wet warmth and weight of a muzzle, as the creature settled to sleep on my arm. I was catching on to sea lions.

Walk into the water. Instantly sea lions surround you, even if none has been in sight. To say that they come to play with you is not especially anthropomorphic. Animals play. The bull sea lions are off patrolling their territorial shores; these are the cows and young, which range freely. A five-foot sea lion peers intently into your face, then urges her muzzle gently against your underwater mask and searches your eyes without blinking. Next she rolls upside down and slides along the length of your floating body, rolls again, and casts a long glance back at your eyes. You are, I believe, supposed to follow, and think up something clever in return. You can play games with sea lions in the water using shells, or bits of leaf, if you are willing. You can spin on your vertical axis, and a sea lion will swim circles around you, keeping his face always six inches from yours, as though he were tethered. You can make a game of touching their back flippers, say, and the sea lions will understand at once; somersaulting conveniently before your clumsy hands, they will give you an excellent field of back flippers.

And when you leave the water, they follow. They porpoise to the shore, popping their heads up when they lose you and casting about, then speeding to your side and emitting a choked series of vocal notes. If you won't relent, they disappear, barking; but if you sit on the beach with so much as a foot in the water, two or three will station with you, floating on their backs and saying, Urr.

Few people come to the Galápagos. Buccaneers used to anchor in the bays to avoid pursuit, to rest, and to lighter on fresh water. The world's whaling ships stopped here as well, to glut their holds with fresh meat in the form of giant tortoises. The whalers used to let the tortoises bang around on deck for a few days to empty their guts; then they stacked

them below on their backs to live—if you call that living—without food or water for a year.

Early inhabitants in the islands were a desiccated assortment of grouches, cranks, and ship's deserters. These hardies shot, enslaved, and poisoned each other off, leaving behind a fecund gang of feral goats, cats, dogs, and pigs whose descendants skulk in the sloping jungles and take their tortoise hatchlings neat. Now scientists at the Charles Darwin Research Station, on the island of Santa Cruz, rear the tortoise hatchlings for several years until their shells are tough enough to resist the crunch; then they release them in the wilds of their respective islands. Some few thousand people live on three of the islands; settlers from Ecuador, Norway, Germany, and France make a livestock or pineapple living from the rich volcanic soils. The settlers themselves seem to embody a high degree of courteous and conscious humanity, perhaps because of their relative isolation.

On the island of Santa Cruz, eleven fellow passengers and I climb into an open truck and bump for an hour up the Galápagos's only long road to visit Alf Kastdalen. Where the road's ascent ends, native villagers leave their muddy soccer game to provide horses, burros, and mules which bear us lurching up a jungle path to a mountain clearing, to the isolate Kastdalen farm.

Alf Kastdalen came to the islands as a child with his immigrant parents from Norway. Now a broad, blond man in his late forties, he lives with his mother and his Ecuadorian wife and their children in a solitary house of finished timbers imported from the mainland, on 400 acres he claimed from the jungle by hand. He raises cattle. He walks us round part of his farm, smiling expansively and meeting our chatter with a willing, open gaze and kind words. The pasture looks like any pasture—but the rocks under the grass are round lava, the copses are a tangle of thorny bamboo and bromeliads, and the bordering trees dripping in epiphytes are breadfruit, papaya, avocado, and orange.

Kastdalen's house is heaped with books in three languages. He knows animal husbandry; he also knows botany and zoology. He feeds us soup, chicken worth chewing for, green naranjilla juice, noodles, pork in big chunks, marinated mixed vegetables, rice, and bowl after bowl of bright mixed fruits.

And his white-haired Norwegian mother sees us off; our beasts are ready. We will ride down the mud forest track to the truck at the Ecuadorian settlement, down the long, long road to the boat, and across the bay to the ship. I lean down to catch her words. She is gazing at me with enormous warmth. "Your hair," she says softly. I am blonde. Adios.

Charles Darwin came to the Galápagos in 1835, on the *Beagle*; he was twenty-six. He threw the marine iguanas as far as he could into the water; he rode the tortoises and sampled their meat. He noticed that the tortoise's carapaces varied wildly from island to island; so also did the forms of various mockingbirds. He made collections. Nine years later he wrote in a letter, "I am almost convinced (quite contrary to the opinion I started with) that species are not (it is like confessing a murder) immutable." In 1859 he published *On the Origin of Species*, and in 1871 *The Descent of Man*. It is fashionable now to disparage Darwin's originality; not even the surliest of his detractors, however, faults his painstaking methods or denies his impact.

Darwinism today is more properly called neo-Darwinism. It is organic evolutionary theory informed by the spate of new data from modern genetics, molecular biology, paleobiology—from the new wave of the biologic revolution which spread after Darwin's announcement like a tsunami. The data are not all in. Crucial first appearances of major invertebrate groups are missing from the fossil record—but these early forms, sometimes modified larvae, tended to be fragile either by virtue of their actual malleability or by virtue of their scarcity and rapid variation into "hardened," successful forms. Lack of proof in this direction doesn't worry scientists. What neo-Darwinism seriously lacks, however, is a precise description of the actual mechanism of mutation in the chromosomal nucleotides.

In the larger sense, neo-Darwinism also lacks, for many, sheer plausibility. The triplet splendors of random mutation, natural selection, and Mendelian inheritance are neither energies nor gods; the words merely describe a gibbering tumult of materials. Many things are unexplained, many discrepancies unaccounted for. Appending a very modified neo-Lamarckism to Darwinism would solve many problems—and create new ones. Neo-Lamarckism holds, without any proof, that certain useful acquired characteristics may be inherited. Read C. H. Waddington, *The Strategy of the Genes*, and Arthur Koestler, *The Ghost in the Machine*. The Lamarckism/Darwinism issue is not only complex, hinging perhaps on whether DNA can be copied from RNA, but also emotionally and politically hot. The upshot of it all is that while a form of Lamarckism recently held sway in Russia, neo-Darwinism is supreme in the West, and its basic assumptions, though variously modified, are not overthrown.

Fundamentalist Christians, of course, still reject Darwinism because it conflicts with the creation account in Genesis. Fundamentalist Christians have a very bad press. Ill-feeling surfaces when, from time to time in small Southern towns, they object again to the public schools' teaching evolutionary theory. Tragically, these people feel they have to make a choice between the Bible and modern science. They live and work in the same world we do, and know the derision they face from people whose areas of ignorance are perhaps different, who dismantled their mangers when they moved to town and threw out the baby with the straw.

Even less appealing in their response to the new evolutionary picture were, and are, the social Darwinists. Social Darwinists seized Herbert Spencer's phrase "the survival of the fittest," applied it to capitalism, and used it to sanction ruthless and corrupt business practices. A social Darwinist is unlikely to identify himself by the term; social Darwinism is, as the saying goes, not a religion but a way of life. A modern social Darwinist wrote the slogan "If you're so smart, why ain't you rich?" The notion still obtains, I believe, wherever people seek power: that the race is to the swift, that everybody is *in* the race, with varying and merited degrees of success or failure, and that reward is its own virtue.

Philosophy reacted to Darwin with unaccustomed good cheer. William Paley's fixed and harmonious universe was gone, and with it its meticulous watchmaker god. Nobody mourned. Instead, philosophy shrugged and turned its attention from first and final causes to analysis of certain values here in time. "Faith in progress," the man-in-the-street philosophy, collapsed in two world wars. Philosophers were more guarded; pragmatically, they held a very refined "faith in process"—which, it would seem, could hardly lose. Christian thinkers, too, outside of Fundamentalism, examined with fresh eyes the world's burgeoning change. Some Protestants, taking their cue from Whitehead, posited a dynamic god who lives alongside the universe, himself charged and changed by the process of becoming. The Catholic Pierre Teilhard de Chardin, a paleontologist, examined the evolution of species itself, and discovered in that flow a surge toward complexity and consciousness, a free ascent capped with man and propelled from within and attracted from without by god, the holy freedom and awareness that is creation's beginning and end. And so forth. Like tortoises, like languages, ideas evolve. And they evolve, as Arthur Koestler suggests, not from hardened final forms, but from the softest plasmic germs in a cell's heart, in the nub of a word's root, in the supple flux of an open mind.

Darwin gave us time. Before Darwin (and Huxley, Wallace, et al.) there was in the nineteenth century what must have been a fairly unsettling period in which people knew about fossils of extinct species, but did not yet know about organic evolution. They thought the fossils were litter from a series of past creations. At any rate, for many, this creation, the world as we know it, had begun in 4004 B.C., a date set by the Irish Archbishop James Ussher in the seventeenth century. We were all crouched in a small room against the comforting back wall, awaiting the millennium which had been gathering impetus since Adam and Eve. Up there was a universe, and down here would be a small strip of man come and gone, created, taught, redeemed, and gathered up in a bright twinkling, like a sprinkling of confetti torn from colored papers, tossed from windows, and swept from the streets by morning.

The Darwinian revolution knocked out the back wall, revealing eerie lighted landscapes as far back as we can see. Almost at once, Albert Einstein and astronomers with reflector telescopes and radio telescopes knocked out the other walls and the ceiling, leaving us sunlit, exposed, and drifting—leaving us puckers, albeit evolving puckers, on the inbound curve of space-time.

It all began in the Galápagos, with these finches. The finches in the Galápagos are called Darwin's finches; they are everywhere in the islands, sparrow-like, and almost identical but for their differing beaks. At first Darwin scarcely noticed their importance. But by 1839, when he revised his journal of the *Beagle* voyage, he added a crucial sentence about the finches' beaks: "Seeing this gradation and diversity of structure in one small, intimately related group of birds, one might really fancy that from an original paucity of birds in this archipelago, one species had been taken and modified for different ends."

And so it was.

The finches come when called. I don't know why it works, but it does. Scientists in the Galápagos have passed down the call: you say psssssh psssssh psssssh psssssh psssssh until you run out of breath; then you say it again until the island runs out of birds. You stand on a flat of sand by a shallow lagoon rimmed in mangrove thickets and call the birds right out of the sky. It works anywhere, from island to island.

Once, on the island of James, I was standing propped against a leafless palo santo tree on a semiarid inland slope when the naturalist called the birds.

From other leafless palo santo trees flew the yellow warblers, speckling the air with bright bounced sun. Gray mockingbirds came running. And from the green prickly pear cactus, from the thorny acacias, sere grasses, bracken, and manzanilla, from the loose black lava, the bare dust, the fern-hung mouths of caverns, or the tops of sunlit logs—came the finches. They fell in from every direction like colored bits in a turning kaleidoscope. They circled and homed to a vortex, like a whirlwind of chips, like draining water. The tree on which I leaned was the vortex. A dry series of puffs hit my cheeks. Then a rough pulse from the tree's thin trunk met my hand and rang up my arm—and another, and another. The tree trunk agitated against my palm like a captured cricket: I looked up. The lighting birds were rocking the tree. It was an appearing act: before there were barren branches; now there were birds like leaves.

Darwin's finches are not brightly colored; they are black, gray, brown, or faintly olive. Their names are even duller: the large ground finch, the medium ground finch, the small ground finch; the large insectivorous tree finch; the vegetarian tree finch; the cactus ground finch, and so forth. But the beaks are interesting, and the beaks' origins even more so.

Some wield chunky parrot beaks modified for cracking seeds. Some have slender warbler beaks, short for nabbing insects, long for probing plants. One sports the long chisel beak of a woodpecker; it bores wood for insect grubs and often uses a twig or cactus spine, like a pickle fork, when the grub won't dislodge. They have all evolved, fanwise, from one ancestral population.

The finches evolved in isolation. So did everything else on earth. With the finches, you can see how it happened. The Galápagos Islands are near enough to the mainland that some strays could hazard there; they are far enough away that those strays could evolve in isolation from parent species. And the separate islands are near enough to each other for further dispersal, further isolation, and the eventual reassembling of distinct species. (In other words, finches blew to the Galápagos, blew to various islands, evolved into differing species, and blew back together again.) The tree finches and the ground finches, the woodpecker finch and the warbler finch, veered into being on isolated rocks. The witless green sea shaped those beaks as surely as it shaped the beaches. Now on the finches in the palo santo tree you see adaptive radiation's results, a fluorescent splay of horn. It is as though an archipelago were an arpeggio, a rapid series of distinct but related notes. If the Galápagos had been one unified island, there would be one dull note, one super-dull finch.

Now let me carry matters to an imaginary, and impossible, extreme. If the earth were one unified island, a smooth ball, we would all be one species, a tremulous muck. The fact is that when you get down to this business of species formation, you eventually hit some form of reproductive isolation. Cells tend to fuse. Cells tend to engulf each other; primitive creatures tend to move in on each other and on us, to colonize, aggregate, blur. (Within species, individuals have evolved immune reactions, which help preserve individual integrity; you might reject my liver—or, someday, my brain.) As much of the world's energy seems to be devoted to keeping us apart as was directed to bringing us here in the first place. All sorts of different creatures can mate and produce fertile offspring: two species of snapdragon, for instance, or mallard and pintail ducks. But they don't. When you scratch the varying behaviors and conditions behind reproductive isolation, you find, ultimately, geographical isolation. Once the isolation has occurred, of course, forms harden out, enforcing reproductive isolation, so that snapdragons will never mate with pintail ducks.

Geography is the key, the crucial accident of birth. A piece of protein could be a snail, a sea lion, or a systems analyst, but it had to start somewhere. This is not science; it is metaphor. And the landscape in which the protein "starts" shapes its end as surely as bowls shape water.

We have all, as it were, blown back together like the finches, and it's hard to imagine the isolation from parent species in which we evolved. The frail beginnings of great phyla are lost in the crushed histories of cells. Now we see the embellishments of random chromosomal mutations selected by natural selection and preserved in geographi-

cally isolate gene pools as faits accomplis, as the differentiated fringe of brittle knobs that is life as we know it. The process is still going on, but there is no turning back. It happened, in the cells; geographical determination is not the cow-caught-in-a-crevice business I make it seem. I'm dealing in imagery, working toward a picture.

Geography is life's limiting factor. Speciation—life itself—is ultimately a matter of warm and cool currents, rich and bare soils, deserts and forests, fresh and salt waters, deltas and jungles and plains. Species arise in isolation. A plaster cast is as intricate as its mold; life is a gloss on geography. And if you dig your fists into the earth and crumble geography, you strike geology. Climate is the wind of the mineral earth's rondure, tilt, and orbit modified by local geological conditions. The Pacific Ocean, the Negev Desert, and the rain forest of Brazil are local geological conditions. So are the slow carp pools and splashing trout riffles of any backyard creek. It is all, God help us, a matter of rocks.

The rocks shape life like hands around swelling dough. In Virginia, the salamanders vary from mountain ridge to mountain ridge; so do the fiddle tunes the old men play. These are not merely anomalous details. This is what life is all about: salamanders, fiddle tunes, you and me and things, the split and burr of it all, the fizz into particulars. No mountains and one salamander, one fiddle tune, would be a lesser world. No continents, no fiddlers. The earth, without form, is void.

The mountains are time's machines; in effect, they roll out protoplasm like printer's rollers pressing out news. But life is already part of the landscape, a limiting factor in space; life, too, shapes life. Geology's rocks and climate have already become Brazil's rain forest, yielding shocking bright birds. To say that all life is an interconnected membrane, a weft of linkages like chain mail, is truism. But in this case, too, the Galápagos Islands afford a clear picture.

On Santa Cruz Island, for instance, the saddleback carapaces of tortoises enable them to stretch high and reach the succulent pads of prickly pear cactus. But the prickly pear cactus on that island,

Martim Avillez

and on other tortoise islands, has evolved a tall treelike habit; those lower pads get harder to come by. Without limiting factors, the two populations could stretch right into the stratosphere.

Ça va. It goes on everywhere, tit for tat, action and reaction, triggers and inhibitors ascending in a spiral like spatting butterflies. Within life, we are pushing each other around. How many animal forms have evolved just so because there are, for instance, trees? We pass the nitrogen around, and other vital gases; we feed and nest, plucking this and that and planting seeds. The protoplasm responds, nudged and nudging, bearing the news.

And the rocks themselves shall be moved. The rocks themselves are not pure necessity, given, like vast, complex molds around which the rest of us swirl. They heave to their own necessities, to stirrings and prickings from within and without.

The mountains are no more fixed than the stars. Granite, for example, contains much oxygen and is relatively light. It "floats." When granite forms under the earth's crust, great chunks of it bob up, I read somewhere, like dumplings. The continents themselves are beautiful pea-green boats. The Galápagos archipelago as a whole is surfing toward Ecuador; South America is sliding toward the Galápagos; North America, too, is sailing westward. We're on floating islands, shaky ground.

So the rocks shape life, and then life shapes life, and the rocks are moving. The completed picture needs one more element: life shapes the rocks.

Life is more than a live green scum on a dead pool, a shimmering scurf like slime mold on rock. Look at the planet. Everywhere freedom twines its way around necessity, inventing new strings of occasions, lassoing time and putting it through its varied and spirited paces. Everywhere live things lash at the rocks. Softness is vulnerable, but it has a will; tube worms bore and coral atolls rise. Lichens in delicate lobes are chewing the granite mountains; forests in serried ranks trammel the hills. Man has more freedom than other live things; anti-entropically, he batters a bigger dent in the given, damming the rivers, planting the plains, drawing in his mind's eye dotted lines between the stars.

The old ark's a moverin'. Each live thing wags its home waters, rumples the turf, rearranges the air. The rocks press out protoplasm; the protoplasm pummels the rocks. It could be that this is the one world, and that world a bright snarl.

Like boys on dolphins, the continents ride their crustal plates. New lands shoulder up from the waves, and old lands buckle under. The very landscapes heave; change burgeons into change. Gray granite bobs up, red clay compresses, yellow sandstone tilts, surging in forests, incised by streams. The mountains tremble, the ice rasps back and forth, and the protoplasm furls in shock waves, up the rock valleys and down, ramifying possibilities, riddling the mountains. Life and the rocks, like spirit and matter, are a fringed matrix, lapped and lapping, clasping and held. It is like hand washing hand. It is like hand washing hand and the whole tumult hurled. The planet spins, rapt inside its intricate mists. The galaxy is a flung thing, loose in the night, and our solar system is one of its many dotted campfires ringed with tossed rocks. What shall we sing?

What shall we sing, while the fire burns down? We can sing only specifics, time's rambling tune, the places we have seen, the faces we have known. I will sing you the Galápagos Islands, the sea lions soft on the rocks. It's all still happening there, in real light, the cool currents upwelling, the finches falling on the wind, the shearwaters looping the waves. I could go back, or I could go on; or I could sit down, like Kubla Khan:

> *Weave a circle round him thrice,*
> *And close your eyes with holy dread,*
> *For he on honey-dew hath fed,*
> *And drunk the milk of Paradise.*

To the Disney Station

by Michael Harrington

January 1979

On October 1, 1978, the President of the United States and the Secretary-General of the United Nations met to discuss war and peace in the Middle East; later in the afternoon they went to an amusement park for what the *Miami Herald* described as "an economic summit for private enterprise."

Jimmy Carter stood before Cinderella's Castle, the turreted fantasy-come-true that overlooks the 2,700-acre "Magic Kingdom" built by Walt Disney and his heirs in central Florida. He told the 2,500 businessmen who had come there for the 26th Congress of the International Chamber of Commerce (the first such gathering not held in a capital city) of his deep capitalist faith. Then, whimsically referring to one of the nearby theme parks, the President remarked, "I looked forward to seeing Fantasyland because it is the source of inspiration for my economic advisers."

The artificiality of the event no doubt was familiar to the President's audience. Hoopla. Photo Opportunities. Free-Enterprise Ritual. Obligatory Presidential Wit. Even an Amy Story. The President was turning fifty-four in Florida, and he had phoned his daughter to tell her that they would be celebrating the birthday of one of "the world's greatest and most admired leaders." "Yes, I know, Daddy," she had said. "This is Mickey Mouse's fiftieth birthday."

On reading the accounts of this spectacle I couldn't help thinking that the President had found the appropriate forum in which to present his vision of the American future. Disney World is a corporate utopia, a pretentious and socially conscious fun house that, for all of its evident superficiality, embodies the current dream of American business. Moreover, Carter explicitly identified himself with that dream in his speech, to the extent that it seemed to me plausible that when he described Fantasyland as "the source of inspiration for my economic advisers" he was only half joking. That is why I propose to take Disney's capitalist fairy tale seriously. It is possible that Amy is not the only citizen in the White House who believes in Mickey Mouse.

At first glance, Disney World seems to have nothing to do with politics. It is a sophisticated and frivolous carnival that has been seen and enjoyed by more than 80 million people since 1971. The rides and attractions delight adults—who make up two-thirds of the crowd—as well as children. Who by now is not familiar with at least the photographs of a fraudulently neat Main Street, with an ice cream parlor, a silent movie, and horse-drawn cars followed by sanitation workers plodding ever onward toward Cinderella's Castle and then to Adventureland, Frontierland, Fantasyland, and Tomorrowland?

The less obvious aspects of Disney World are not so easy to see, yet they have been discovered by a fair number of thoughtful observers who have come to admire the futuristic technology, the air-conditioned, electric-powered Monorail that silently circles the place, and the trash disposal system that sucks refuse through underground tubes at sixty miles an hour to a central disposal point. This is the Disney World that captivated Peter Blake, the architecture critic, and James Rouse, the creator of a new city in Maryland. As a German commentator, Dankwart Grube, last year put this socially conscious interpretation of Disney World, "German builders, architects, and, above all, city planners should be forced, in chains if need be, to find out from the Mickey Mouse people how one can create an 'environment' in which laughter flourishes and well-being is produced."

Mr. Carter and the International Chamber also had a chance to see this second Disney World. As the President finished his speech a tropical rain began to fall on the buglers in medieval costume who were playing "Hail to the Chief." Carter and Amy retreated into Cinderella's Castle, and, the *Economist* of London reported, "2,500 tycoons were saved from pneumonia by the incredible instant efficiency of the young people who do the work in Disney's fantasyland."

The *Economist* is usually reserved, even dyspeptic, in such matters, and it did note that the Presidential address was a speech of "monumental wetness." Even so, the magazine was deeply impressed by the automation and crime prevention, and concluded, "If Mickey Mouse were everywhere elected mayor, the efficiency of local government round the world would rise by several hundred per cent." This Disney World of the city planners does indeed exist and it even has a humane potential, as we will see. But it is a much more ambiguous vision than most of its devotees realize. Perhaps this is because the technological Disney World is encapsulated within the invisible structure of a corporate utopia. The "Magic Kingdom" is designed by "Imagineers"—as Disney Speak calls them—who construct escapist diversions on computers programmed according to a sophisticated calculus of profit. They aim at nothing less than the total control of a physical and human environment of forty-three square miles, which is twice the area of Manhattan. Toward that end, they have banished politics, competition, and excessive individualism from their monopolist's Shangri-La, thus fulfilling the daydream of the American board room. In their more ecstatic moments they persuade themselves that their fun-filled Brave New World is, and will be, an Experimental Prototype Community of Tomorrow (EPCOT in Disney Speak).

This, of course, is a fairy tale, and yet, if that gingerbread Main Street does not really lead into the twenty-first century, as its designers believe, it does embody one of the most powerful desires of the late Seventies: that it is possible to reach apolitical, anti-intellectual, corporate, and technocratic solutions to the problems of society. Faced with a simultaneous inflation and recession that none of the established theories can deal with, reading the reports of tax revolts from California and elsewhere, the President of the United States is turning into a born-again free entrepreneur. It was perfectly appropriate that he should give witness to this faith in front of Cinderella's Castle, which is one of its cathedrals.

Let us begin with the life of the saint. Walt Disney's formative years were spent, predictably enough, on a farm near a small Missouri town with a real-life Main Street. He moved to California and, after a number of vicissitudes—including a fight with Eastern bankers who took his first cartoon character away from him—established himself as a leading Hollywood artist. Success came—but so did a union movement that shattered the paternal calm of the Disney Studios. In 1941 Disney faced a picket line with signs asking, "Are We Mice Or Men?" Bitter and disillusioned, he became more conservative. During the Forties, he was involved in the Motion Picture Alliance for the Preservation of American Ideals, a center for blacklisters and the rest of the Hollywood Right. Later on, in 1964, when Disney received the Medal of Freedom from Lyndon Johnson he wore a Goldwater button in his lapel.

In 1948 Disney began to dream of a new kind of amusement park. Facing financial difficulties, he borrowed against his life insurance and in 1955 opened Disneyland, in Anaheim, California. It was an instant success. But there were problems. The core of the Disneyland site was formerly an orange grove, a mere 160-acre lot. That meant that Disney could not dominate his own surroundings. "The one thing I learned from Disneyland," he was to comment later on, "was to control the environment. Without that we get blamed for the things that someone else does. When they come here [to Disney World] they're coming because of an integrity we've established over the years, and they drive for hundreds of miles and the little hotels on the fringe would jump their rates three times."

Control. That is the key to Disney World and the future it envisions. When Disney was working on his plans for the project, he talked, characteristically, of the need to proceed without any interference from the politicians. Embittered by his experience with Disneyland, the founder decided to insulate his new world in Florida from any outside influences. He managed to buy more than 27,000 acres, of which only 3,000 are currently developed. So competitors and parasites (which is to say, other free-entrepreneurs) are kept miles away. That, however, is only the beginning of the control in Disney World. There are no peanuts in the Magic Kingdom, no chewing gum and no cotton candy. These things are messy, and Disney didn't want them fouling up his fantasy. There are no saloons, either, even though that venerable institution played its part on some of the Main Streets of America (liquor is, however, available in the hotels on the property, and the general stores sell beer and wine). One result is that there is practically no drunken brawling and very little crime.

It was more than a little ironic that President Carter chose this setting for a denunciation of protectionism. "Hardly a week goes by," he said, "but what I have some businessman come to see me and ask for some form of protectionism while deploring the protectionism of others." This was proclaimed in a Magic Kingdom expertly and explicitly designed on the principles of a state monopoly. Walt Disney and his associates, exactly like those anti-protectionist protectionists whom Carter assailed, were, and are, deeply committed to free enterprise everywhere but in their own market. Their dominion extends beyond the economy and controls human beings as well as commodities.

The whole place is run by relentlessly smiling young people, who are, it seems to me, disproportionately blond and blue-eyed. They are uniformed in Disney designs made by Disney workers and coached as actors on a stage. Long hair and moustaches, predictably, are not allowed. So far, one could rightly say, there is nothing particularly ominous about these conditions. If Walt Disney and his heirs thought it good business to keep out chewing gum, to restrict drinking and drunks, and to hire stereotypes, what's wrong with that? Indeed, the Magic Kingdom has to be neater, cleaner, and less raucous than any amusement park for thousands of people that one could imagine.

Things become more complex as soon as one takes a few steps behind this idyllic facade. Just inside the gate of the Magic Kingdom there is a City Hall. Downstairs is an information center, upstairs the publicity office. For the politicians have been banished from this kingdom, just as Disney hoped. Sovereignty resides in the Reedy Creek Improvement District. Under Florida law, an "improvement district" has no police or judicial power, but it can legislate with regard to water, building codes, and fire protection. When the planners were dealing with this problem, Disney chose the improvement district rather than a municipal charter, in part because a city would have to deal with civil rights.

So Disney World is under the police and judicial authority of the counties (Orange and Osceola) in which it is located, but in all other matters the Reedy Creek Improvement District remains sovereign. It is democratically run by the forty or fifty people who live within Disney World—all of whom are employees of the company that, in their political persona, they are supposed to regulate. The Disney people admit that this arrangement is not designed to promote adversary relationships, but they insist that Reedy Creek is truly independent of the corporation. They also note that there has never been a serious quarrel between them.

All of this comes fairly close to Disney's dream of EPCOT: "It will be a planned, controlled community, a showcase for American industry and research, schools, cultural and educational opportunities. In EPCOT there will be no slum areas because we won't let them develop. There will be no landowners and therefore no voting control. People will rent houses instead of buying them, and at modest rentals. There will be no retirees. Everyone must be employed. One of our requirements is that the people who live in EPCOT must help keep it alive."

In that statement—which is still Holy Writ in Disney World—the totalitarian character of this utopia begins to show itself. If you can invest $700 million in a domain roughly the size of Liechtenstein, and if you allow only a handful of employee-citizens to live in that corporate kingdom, then you can ban slums, retirees, and most of the rest of social reality. But what relevance, prototypical or otherwise, such an exercise has to any possible world of tomorrow is unclear. Moreover, even this attempt at utopia has not achieved the total control of which the founder dreamed.

In July, when I was last there, pickets from the Hotel and Restaurant Employees Union shuffled back and forth in front of the Royal Plaza Hotel, an inn that leases from, but is not run by, Disney World. This was the first strike within the Magic Kingdom, but, if the *Economist* is right, it may well not be the last. The "pay is low and jobs often part time," the *Economist* noted in July. "Many workers have long journeys because, although villas and tree houses have been built as well as hotels, Disney has built no low-cost housing for its employees." And the stand of the black women picketing, the *Economist* noted shrewdly, "took some courage in a place where the employer pays the police."

The hired help are not the only ones made to endure the indignities appropriate to commodities. So do the paying customers, and their plight casts some doubt upon the vaunted efficiency of the place. The Magic Kingdom has been fulsomely praised for the Monorail; its "people mover system" has been awarded a grant by the Department of Transportation. True enough, inside the park, where transportation efficiency is necessary for quick, paying circulation, things move relatively fast. But when it is a question of access to Disney World from one of the independently run hotels on the property (which are not, like the Disney-owned operations, hooked into the Monorail), there is another story. Crowded buses, sometimes with their air conditioning out of order in the middle of the humid summer, carry people from the periphery to the Magic Kingdom.

Once past this inconvenience, things become easier—and also profitable for the system. At one time last July, it took me an hour to get from my hotel, on the Disney property, to the gates of the park, and the experience was reminiscent of the decaying central-city present, not of the urban future.

That same point applies to children, who, in theory at least, might be thought central to an enterprise built upon their devotion for more than half a century. That children are routinely shoved out of vantage points for the various parades by adult bullies can hardly be blamed on the Disney people. It is, after all, just the reality of American society that, for all of its stated veneration of kids, it pushes them around given half the chance. But the officials I talked to didn't seem to take a great interest in the problem or to respond to suggestions that they might take some steps to guarantee that the kids have access to what is supposed to be a kid's show. That access cannot be fed into a computer and quantified as contributing to profits; it does not, therefore, exist as a concern.

So Disney World is not a company town; it is a company state. Free of the pressures of democracy, it treats employees, customers, and children as so many pawns on the corporate game board. But isn't that just one more—vivid, perhaps bizarre—manifestation of some classic capitalist contradictions? Don't all competitors want to succeed so well as to drive out the competition, the Department of Justice to the contrary notwithstanding? And in the late Sixties, American business spent $45 billion a year on advertising and other sales promotion (which was slightly less than the nation's outlays for health or education). Wouldn't every corporation like to dictate to the sovereign consumer in the name of free enterprise? Disney's only innovation, it might be argued, is that he bought enough land to make his the only voice in a tiny kingdom.

These objections, however, miss the implications of the corporate utopia in Florida. It is not just that Disney World has turned those priorities into a seemingly coherent philosophy. More to the point, that philosophy states (and anticipated) the fashionable corporate ideology of the late

Paul Richer

Seventies. To be sure, that philosophy is as absurd as the idea of locating Shangri-La in a real corner of Florida rather than in the imaginary Himalayas. But these utopian themes are playing a significant part in American politics. So I treat the pretensions of EPCOT with a provisional seriousness.

Let me return to the beginnings. Walt Disney was not simply a small-town boy turned successful businessman who became conservative and virulently anti-Communist when unions disrupted his paternal studio. That obviously relates to the corporate side of Disney World. But the founder was also the son of a socialist, and that, it seems to me, has something to do with his futurism and that of his disciples.

One may be quite speculative. Elias Disney was a turn-of-the-century American radical. When he and his family were living near that small Missouri town, for instance, he tried to organize the local farmers into an American Society of Equity that would focus their hatreds of the middlemen and the railroads. He voted for Debs and he read the *Appeal to Reason*, the famous radical paper published in Kansas and

reaching a mass audience of the Left. And even in the Thirties, not long before his death, he told his son that he was not sorry that all of the candidates for whom he had voted had lost. "We have won," he told Walt. "We've won a lot. I've found out that things don't always come out in the way you have advocated. But you keep fighting and they come about in some way or another. Today, everything I fought for in those early days has been absorbed into the platform of both major parties. Now I feel pretty good about that."

Those sentiments are in the Norman Thomas tradition and they are hardly sinister. But there is another aspect of American socialist history that is much more ambiguous: it sometimes expresses a warmhearted, futuristic authoritarianism. That sentiment, which was completely alien to Thomas, can be seen in Edward Bellamy's *Looking Backward*, a book that was much more influential in defining socialism for many Americans of Elias Disney's generation than *Das Kapital*. It presents a neat, rational, crisis-free society with distributional justice—and without any visible democratic noise, conflict, or argument.

Was Walt Disney influenced by that misunderstanding of socialism that prepared the way in some instances for an acceptance of Stalinism? The evidence I have seen permits only a deductive guess. But the possibility is fascinating, since Disney's EPCOT is a curious mixture of planner's futurism and free-enterprise faith, i.e., it seems to yoke two conflicting aspects of Disney's heritage. [...]

[W]hen I went to the "presentation" on EPCOT, I did not know whether to laugh or cry. The preview of the Disney future was held in an air-conditioned auditorium across the street from "City Hall," i.e., the publicity office. There was a huge mock-up of the entire park, with the EPCOT addition, and a smaller model of EPCOT itself. At the proper moment someone pushed a button and the exhibit sank with electronic grace as a screen came down to present the posthumous voice and person of the founder. All of this reminded me of a Strangelovian war room, only it had to do with expanding an amusement park rather than with World War III. It was as if George Orwell had written *Alice in Wonderland.*

EPCOT, we were told, will have two major sections. There will be Future World—science-fiction writer Ray Bradbury is working on a script for it—and the World Showcase. The whole thing will be financed by corporations and governments and will cost in the neighborhood of $500 million (which will bring the investment in the Florida plant to more than $1 billion). The companies and the governments will get the chance to present their message in return for paying the bills. But, and this is a critical element of the whole undertaking, politics and ideological conflict will be kept out. This will be so despite the fact that "Communicore," "the global marketplace of new ideas, will be the communications center of EPCOT. Here, *industry and public* will participate in a 'hands on' exchange of new and exciting ideas, systems, products, and technologies" (emphasis added). But as the enterprise is now projected, "industry" will speak, the "public" will listen, and the controversial will be filtered out.

Indeed, the "ideas" in the Communicore, as now planned, will be mainly technological gimmickry. There will be an "electronic travel port where visitors can 'dial-in' their travel interests and other itinerary requirements and watch an 'instant preview' of their upcoming vacation." A "Casino of Information" will use a game-playing format to update the penny arcade and make it relevant to the "information age." And so on. Exactly how this will promote "the

advancement of international understanding and the solution of the problems of people everywhere through the communication of ideas" is left marvelously unclear. Back in 1933, Disney boasted that Mickey Mouse was the one thing on which the Chinese and the Japanese agreed, and the naive hope in that thought—which ignores the fact that those admirers of the mouse then tried to annihilate one another—is alive and well in Florida right now.

In this non-ideological environment—which, as we will see, is a profoundly ideological concept—Exxon has already signed on to present the problems and solutions of the energy future. General Motors will lend its benevolent expertise to the challenge of twenty-first-century transportation. And there will be an exhibit on the seas. Guests will board the clipper ship *Spirit of Mankind,* and after a simulated journey through the deep will arise at "Sea Base Alpha," where they will "experience an authentic ocean environment with marine life, an undersea restaurant, and a showcase of oceanographic exhibits and displays."

Will there be a word of the debate that has been going on for more than ten years on the law of the sea? Will there be a discussion of the relative merits of the American corporate proposal for the private mining of the wealth of the oceans and the counterposed notion that the deeps are "the common heritage of mankind"? The answer is clearly no. Indeed, the American Adventure, the attraction that will link Future World and the World Showcase, is going to give an uncontroversial—which is to say, necessarily bowdlerized—version of this country's past. This is all the more amazing when one realizes that the chronicle will be dominated by "animatronic" figures (full-scale talking, moving models invented by Disney and currently on display in Disney World's Hall of the Presidents) of Ben Franklin, Mark Twain, and Will Rogers. How those witty, contentious, sometimes bitter and acerb Americans will do that job is difficult to imagine.

The World Showcase is supposed to be a sort of permanent international exposition where the various nations can communicate with the millions who come to Disney World. But here, again, there is a ban on ideology. Of course, most of the countries that have thus far shown an interest in the scheme—Iran, Canada, West Germany, Japan, Mexico, some Arab states, Costa Rica, and Morocco—are safely on the corporate side of the world divide. But just to be sure, the exhibitors will have to confine themselves to presenting their culture. The Arabs and Israelis have been told that they cannot speak of their rivalries, and the young people who come from various lands to work on the project will be expected to live together in a World Village.

This anti-ideology is, of course, an ideology. It is the key to Disney World and, more importantly, to much of the American political mentality of recent years. The bias appears throughout the spectrum of political debate, in the dreams of urban planners sponsored by the Ford Foundation as well as in the moral blueprints designed by the sociologists in the universities. Corporate technology, we are told in stunning television commercials and newspaper ads designed to look like serious comment, can solve our social problems—if only the bumbling politicians and regulators will leave the businessmen alone. There is an objective, one-best-way to do things, and it is the private property of the experts at General Motors and Exxon. Conventional academic wisdom says much the same thing in learned journals and the popular press.

There is a surface plausibility to these claims, which is why they convince so many people. That is vividly in evidence at Disney World. The entire park is built over a system of tunnels—Utilidors, in Disney Speak. All of the air-conditioning apparatus, the utility lines, and the like are down there, easily accessible for repairs and never requiring that the streets be torn up. Garbage, as we have seen, is collected through that sixty-mile-an-hour evacuation system. On the back lot, the Reedy Creek Utility Company has constructed a building in which solar collectors are the roof and the energy collected provides all of the air conditioning and all of the heat for the offices.

Disney even used futuristic technology to build his park. The Contemporary Hotel is the most famous hostelry in Disney World, not the least because the Monorail runs through its gigantic lobby. The Contemporary's huge A-frame was constructed as a shell, and then prefabricated rooms—which, not so incidentally, also fit into the pseudo-Oceanic Polynesian Hotel—were inserted by cranes. An even more interesting innovation is found in the Magic Kingdom's power system. Two huge jet turbines do the generating, and their waste heat stokes boilers that yield hot water, which is then fed into four cooling machines and used for air conditioning in the hotels. The water left over from the whole process is purified and piped out to the tree farm where Disney World produces eucalyptus trees. Small wonder that various urban planners have gone starry-eyed in the presence of so many prodigies.

Given this recycling technology, it is also not surprising that "Spaceship Earth" is "the major theme show and introduction to the concept and meaning of EPCOT." But, on second thought, what is an environmental concept like "Spaceship Earth" doing in a corporate-dominated exhibit at a time when business daily tells us that environmental and safety regulations are undermining our productivity and thereby threatening the entire system? The answer is relatively simple. Disney World is going to "communicate ideas" and ban controversy and ideology at the same time. The communicators will be big businesses, and they will present themselves, not as profit maximizers, but as problem solvers. Only their "objective" solutions will conceal a highly controversial, very partisan corporate self-interest. [...]

And yet, this reactionary ideology can be given a liberal surface. The fraudulent nineteenth-century charm of Main Street is the front for a fraudulent twenty-first-century version of the future. Therefore, Disney World can claim to be forward-looking, progressive, even utopian. The hero of its Hall of Presidents show is an animatronic Abraham Lincoln (surrounded by animatrons of all the other Presidents, including Jimmy Carter). And in the Small World attraction—originally designed for UNICEF at the New York World's Fair in 1964—one rides in boats along a waterway bordered by animatronic dolls of all colors and races singing of the unity of humankind. In EPCOT itself there will be the World Showcase and the World Village. Why this liberal gloss in a corporate, technocratic enterprise?

Because the multinational corporation is, in one of its most important modes, internationalist and even pacifist. To the organizers of the World Showcase, the Arab-Israeli dispute is an inconvenience, and therefore the Arabs and the Israelis in EPCOT will not be allowed to mention the unfortunate fact of its very existence. Anything that disrupts the global factory is considered intolerable since it disturbs business-as-usual. To be sure, radical democratic change, as in Allende's Chile, calls forth countermeasures seeking the law and order of a graveyard. That, however, only illuminates the basic point that disruption is to be avoided at all costs. So the Imagineers exclude the political differences between countries from their "world," much as they ban the politics of technology in favor of corporate objectivity. What remains is cultural charm and business expertise. [...]

[I]f Disney World is not the wave of the future it is a portent of the present. Jimmy Carter, like Walt Disney, is a business executive from a small town who believes in science and is an antipolitics politician. And he is in the process of adapting the world view that is fantasized in Florida. It asks government to socialize the costs of business, and to turn the planning of the future over to the executives, even to the point of granting political sovereignty to private corporations. This system of administered and controlled markets is then legitimated in the name of free enterprise. Only the capitalist Imagineers don't really believe in their own dreams any more than the Disney World people do. Right now they, too, are awash with capital, and uncertain and afraid about investing it; they, too, talk of innovation, but they have come up with few serious new ideas. All these things are writ small in the Magic Kingdom and large in the American economy.

1980's

LIBERTY UNDER SIEGE

BY WALTER KARP

NOVEMBER 1985

The Reagan Administration came to power firm in its resolve to liberate corporate enterprise from government regulation, to free the economy from the incubus of the welfare system, and to reduce the government's role in the life of the country. It never said that these far-reaching goals could not be achieved by the ordinary methods of democratic persuasion and the established procedures of congressional lawmaking. The Administration never contended in public, and perhaps not even in private, that the exercise of liberty gave its enemies an unfair advantage, or that the traditional sources of public information kept the electorate too well informed, or that popular government in general was a hindrance to its aims. Only once did any ranking member of the Administration publicly admit that the "Reagan Revolution" included—indeed necessitated—a program of drastic political change. This occurred in late 1981, when David Stockman, the White House budget director, said that the new Administration's success "boils down to a political question, not of budget policy, or economic policy, but whether we can change the habits of the political system." After Stockman's outburst of perilous candor, the curtain came abruptly down. It has not risen again on the political intentions of the Reagan Administration, for the habits the Administration has striven to change have been, by and large, the habits of freedom.

"What we are witnessing," said the American Civil Liberties Union in November 1981, "is a systematic assault on the concept of government accountability and deterrence of illegal government conduct." Alas, "we," the people, were not witnessing a thing, and have not been witnessing a thing for almost five years. In politics, what is seen is what is talked about, and the "systematic assault" has not been talked about—not by the Administration, not by Congress, not by the opposition party, not by the press.

Nothing is more important, however, than what public men prefer *not* to discuss. For nearly five years now the Reagan Administration has been engaged in an unflagging campaign to exalt the power of the presidency and to undermine the power of the law, the courts, the Congress, and the people. That is what our politicians have not discussed with us, and what lies hidden behind the screen of political rhetoric and the smile of a popular President.

What follows is a chronicle of that campaign, told simply by means of recounting the deeds that comprise it. This chronicle is not the secret history of an alleged secret plot. Most of the events have been duly reported in the daily newspapers. The chronicle is simply a matter of paying attention to public deeds that have been largely ignored or made light of outside the confines of congressional hearings. The chronicle is remorseless because the campaign is remorseless, and it is shocking because the campaign is shocking. When a concerted assault on the habits of freedom ceases to shock us, there will be no further need to assault them, for they will have been uprooted once and for all.

I. 1981

The newly elected Reagan Administration promised to "hit the ground running" and it does—like a company of commandos fanning out in a hostile country that just happens to be its own.

What it besieges at once is the old, unsung bulwark against overweening presidential power: the open, garrulous, decentralized executive branch itself. Bureaucrats practiced in rudeness and evasion are put in place of helpful press officers. Telephone requests for information are suddenly given short shrift. Press briefings become so grudging, notes one veteran reporter, that a State Department spokesman says "no comment" and "I can't say" more than thirty times in the course of one forty-five-minute session. Pentagon officials are warned that the polygraph test—which accuses the guilty and the innocent alike—will be used to identify those who "leak" classified information to the press.

In late April the President declares a moratorium on the preparation and dissemination of government publications, and the huge, habitual outflow of official reports, bulletins, and pamphlets is quickly brought under control. The Administration's stated goal is the "elimination of wasteful spending on government periodicals." Dropped in the moratorium is a government booklet on bedbugs, which Edwin Meese III, counselor to the President, brandishes for reporters with a hearty chuckle, as well as Central Intelligence Agency reports on "U.S.-Soviet Military Dollar-Cost Comparisons," which disappear unbrandished. Meanwhile, the White House musters every specious argument it can find to justify the biggest arms buildup in history. Something considerably more important than thrift lies behind this moratorium.

Whatever can be hidden the Administration hides. "The White House is structuring key advisory panels," reports the *New York Times* in July, "so that they do not fall under the public meeting rules of the Advisory Committee Act." Under the direction of the White House the agencies of the executive branch evade the public accountability provisions of the Administrative Procedure Act. New regulations are issued as "guidelines" so that the public need not be notified. Existing regulations are altered by internal memorandums.

On June 6 the *Washington Post* runs a story under the headline "Administration Attempting to Stem Information Flow to Trickle." This is only the beginning, however, for the President is determined to redress the balance between, in his words, "the media's right to know and the government's right to confidentiality."

This latter "right" is a figment of the official imagination: in America the governed have rights, not the government. But one reason the Administration is determined to uphold it becomes clear on July 8 when a legal analysis of the gravest importance begins circulating in the House Committee on Energy and Commerce. Prepared for the committee by the American Law Division of the Library of Congress, it describes a far-reaching seizure of power carried out by the President on February 17 when he signed Executive Order 12291. That order, says the report, "sets up a framework for [presidential] management of the rule-making process that is undeniably unprecedented in scope and substance," one that "does not appear to draw its authority from any specific con-

gressional enactment." It "provides no explicit safeguards to protect the integrity of the process or the interest of the public against secret, undisclosed, and unreviewable contacts... the Order, on its face, deprives participants of essential elements of fair treatment required by due process." Most important, the order threatens to make "cost-benefit principles," imposed and manipulated by the White House, supreme over the statutory mission given by Congress to the executive agencies of the government—in violation of the doctrine of separation of powers. The warning falls into the public arena as noiselessly as a feather.

The Administration's most ambitious efforts to censor and suppress lie in the future, but even in mid-1981 it begins to choke off various sources of objectionable opinions.

Cuba is one such source. On July 10 the secretary of the Treasury notifies 30,000 subscribers of the Communist Party weekly *Granma,* which was impounded by Treasury agents in May, that "it will be necessary for you to obtain a specific import license from this office" in order to "import" Cuban periodicals in the future. The maximum penalty for subscribing without a license is ten years in prison and a $10,000 fine under the Trading With the Enemy Act of 1917; this act has never before been applied to periodicals, owing to the longstanding national "habit" of distinguishing printed matter from merchandise. By treating Cuban periodicals like Cuban cigars the Administration claims control over a hitherto free activity—until it is stopped by a First Amendment lawsuit brought by the ACLU. This is not the last time, however, that the Administration will try to use commercial regulations to suppress non-commercial activity.

Political refugees from friendly tyrannies are another source of objectionable opinions: they know too much about the regimes they fled. After seeing its February white paper on El Salvador, which presented "evidence" that the Salvadoran guerrillas were being heavily armed by Cuba and the Soviet Union, exposed as a pack of lies, the Administration begins to deport Salvadorans en masse. In August, the tortured corpse of one deportee turns up by a Salvadoran roadside.

To the Administration, however, the most dangerous source of objectionable opinions are its own documents. On October 15 the White House submits legislation to Congress that would keep these documents out of the public's hands by "reforming" the Freedom of Information Act into oblivion. Politically, this is the Administration's first truly perilous moment, for the act is no ordinary piece of legislation. It has behind it the entire weight and authority of the democratic tradition in America: the sovereignty of the people, the accountability of government, the old republican distrust of official secrecy and bureaucratic caprice. "The Freedom of Information Act is a blessing for those who value a check on Government snooping," William Safire, the conservative columnist for the *Times,* wrote in May when the White House, testing the waters, first indicated its hostility to the law. "Individuals can now find out what the FBI file says about them. Even better, individuals can force the Federal bureaucracy to disgorge rulings made without public scrutiny, and documents more politically embarrassing than secret."

Yet one "improvement" in the Administration's Freedom of Information Improvement Act of 1981 would put out of the public's reach precisely those documents that give the governed their "check on government snooping." Another "improvement" would make it difficult to discover how the agencies of the executive branch are enforcing the health, safety, and environmental laws that the White House is bent on subjecting to cost-benefit analysis. A third improvement would make it dauntingly expensive for the act to be used by those who inform the public—scholars, writers, newspaper reporters, public-interest organizations—the very users that, under the unimproved act, pay little or nothing.

"Freedom of information is not cost-free. It is not an absolute good," Jonathan C. Rose, an assistant attorney general in charge of abridging the freedom of information, would say a year later. But the Administration's cant about thrift rings false. "If the Freedom of Information Act is rescinded or crippled," says Kurt Vonnegut at a symposium on the FOIA, "the American people will have been treated as spies for a foreign enemy." An Administration which prates about getting the government off the backs of the people has revealed its real ambition: to get the people off the back of the government.

On October 14 that ambition could scarcely be plainer, as the President invokes "executive privilege" to withhold from Congress thirty-one documents, many of them unsigned memorandums, prepared by junior officials in the Department of Interior. In the most sweeping assertion of executive secrecy in our history, the President declares that all information that is "part of the executive branch deliberative process" lies beyond the oversight of Congress. President Reagan, who invents his own constitution as he goes

along, has expanded the confidentiality of the Oval Office to cloak the entire executive branch. In the space of twenty-four hours he has proposed to cut off the government not only from the people but from their elected representatives as well.

By October 15 Congress has every reason to ask—and loudly—on what meat doth this our Caesar feed. But Congress asks nothing. The opposition leaders are silent; "liberals" are as mute as "conservatives." The elected representatives of the people apparently prefer to deal privately with the White House rather than awaken the sleeping electorate. Quietly, Congress will preserve the Freedom of Information Act, and quietly it will challenge "executive privilege"; but the Administration's assault on accountability it will not make known to the people.*

On December 4 the President signs an executive order authorizing the CIA for the first time to collect "foreign intelligence" in the United States by surreptitiously questioning the citizenry. It also authorizes the CIA to employ the entire local police force of the country in this undercover questioning, which can take place in a barroom, a barbershop, or the aisle of a K-Mart—as if the U.S. government needed to monitor the unguarded conversations of private citizens to keep itself informed about foreign countries. Getting the government off the backs of the people is the very last thing this Administration wants.

II. 1982

On January 7, at the annual meeting of the American Association for the Advancement of Science in Washington, the Administration opens an assault on the old, slack habits of scientific freedom. The "hemorrhage of the country's technology" overseas is so severe, says Admiral Bobby Inman, deputy director of central intelligence, that the government must step in to "control" the public dissemination of private research. If the nation's scientists do not submit voluntarily to such censorship, Admiral Inman warns the assembled audience, a "tidal wave" of public outrage "could well cause the federal government to overreact" against the liberties of

---

* *The Administration's FOIA bill never came to a vote. Other legislation incorporating many of the Administration's proposals passed in the Senate but stalled in the House. In late 1981, the House Committee on Energy and Commerce cited Interior Secretary James Watt for contempt; the documents at issue were subsequently turned over.*

science. Anger and indignation sweep the meeting. What the government wants "is clearly more compatible with a dictatorship than a democracy," says Peter Denning, a computer scientist from Purdue University, in a sharp rebuttal to Inman. The Administration mistakes the very source of the "hemorrhage," reports the March issue of the *Bulletin of the Atomic Scientists. Commerce* is what transfers technology abroad, according to a 1979 study made by the Pentagon itself, and commerce is what the 1979 Export Administration Act was designed to control.

To all arguments against censorship, however, the Administration is deaf. As Lawrence J. Brady, an assistant secretary of commerce, tells the press in March, the government is determined to combat "a strong belief in the academic community that they have an inherent right...to conduct research...free of government review and oversight." Accordingly, the Commerce Department informs universities across the country that any faculty member who lectures on advanced technology to even a single foreign student may be considered a "U.S. exporter" under the 1979 law and fined $100,000 for exporting technical data without a government license. At a scientific conference in August, 100 optical engineers are forced to withdraw their research papers at the last minute when government agents warn them that they may violate export control regulations. Once again, an Administration which regards the lawful regulation of commerce as unwarranted oppression uses commercial regulations to suppress non-commercial activity. Yet about the transfer of technology overseas the Administration evidently cares little. Due to its slack enforcement of the *real* export control laws, California's Silicon Valley, in the words of an FBI official, is "as leaky as a sieve."

The pretexts are shifted around like the three shells in the shell game—efficiency, thrift, and national security—but the aim is always the same: to give the White House the power to withhold from the American people whatever the President thinks it best for the people not to know.

On February 4 the President shows Congress the final draft of an executive order on "classified information." The order betrays an appetite for secrecy so wanton that the White House declines to send a representative to defend it at a congressional hearing. Under the order, a bureaucracy which already withholds from the public about 16 million documents each year is instructed to resolve all doubts about secrecy in favor of public ignorance. The order creates a new category of technical data ("vulnerabilities or capabil-ities of systems, installations, projects, or plans relating to the national security") so vast and so vague that it enables the government for the first time to classify private technical research—thereby giving the White House another way to clamp down on the campus and the laboratory and the Freedom of Information Act. The new category has the additional advantage of greatly thickening the wall of secrecy surrounding the Administration's wasteful, fraud-ridden military buildup.

The new secrecy order treats history itself as a menace to national security. The systematic declassification of documents, begun by President Eisenhower in 1953, is brought to a virtual halt, and its unprecedented antithesis—reclassification—is introduced in its place. Under the new order government officials can reach into the public domain and re-conceal what is already public. After high-ranking officials use classified information to present their version of events, the government can now deny that information to others. "We are encouraging the distortion of history," says Anna K. Nelson, representing the American Historical Association at the March 10 hearings. "The knowledge that documents and records are equally available to all has kept many a participant an honest observer. This provision has no place in a representative democracy."

The one-day hearing makes no public stir. But the White House is still anxious to preserve its "conservative" reputation. At a meeting of the National Newspaper Association on March 14, Ed Meese blames the draft order on "overzealous bureaucrats"; but the President signs it just the same. On April 1, armed with their new authority to suppress private research, Pentagon officials telephone the technical journal *Spectrum* and order an editor to start shredding a manuscript about high-tech Army weapons systems "immediately."

The White House in 1982 is steadily consolidating its new legislative powers. Under Executive Order 12291, which elevates cost-benefit principles over acts of Congress, a new mode of lawmaking is being set up before our unseeing eyes. Under this new system, Congress continues to enact legislation after years of study and deliberation. And it continues to delegate to the appropriate agency the authority to issue regulations carrying out the aims of each law. But after that, a few dozen clerks in the White House budget office virtually dictate the promulgation of any new regulations, thereby nullifying acts of Congress that the President considers too costly. "The result is a return, to some extent, to autocratic government," says Kenneth Culp

Davis, one of the country's leading experts on administrative law, writing in the April issue of the *Tulane Law Review*.

And what is the purpose of inserting autocracy into the American republic? To "reduce the burdens of existing and future regulations," says the White House, but that is all it dares say in public. Like the arms buildup, like domestic snooping, this "good," too, thrives best out of sight of the electorate. Under the direction of the budget office the Nuclear Regulatory Commission in June suspends some of its most important safety regulations without the knowledge of the millions of people who live near nuclear power plants. Under the control of the White House the Environmental Protection Agency turns into a massive conspiracy against the environmental protection laws. The *Times*, reporting on the 1983 congressional testimony of John E. Daniel, the second-ranking official at the EPA, notes that the budget office "tried to dictate regulations to the agency, threatened reprisals, urged that cost factors be built into health rules when the law prohibited them and showed proposed rules changes to officials of the industries being regulated before the changes were available to the public." With the White House acting as an influence-peddler—exactly what the American Law Division's report on Executive Order 12291 had warned of a year earlier—a field report on dioxin contamination is altered to delete a sentence reading: "Dow's discharge represents the major source, if not the only source, of TCDD contamination" in Saginaw Bay, Michigan. EPA field officials are ordered not to submit a new report until Dow "endorsed" it.

These are public benefactions so desperately in need of public inattention that when a congressional subcommittee subpoenas EPA documents on October 21, the President is compelled once again to invoke his personal constitution. On November 30 he declares that "the Constitutional doctrine of separation of powers" obliges him to withhold from Congress the documentary evidence of the agency's efforts to give America "cost-effective" toxic waste dumps. The "dissemination of such documents outside the Executive Branch," says the President, "would impair my solemn responsibility to enforce the law."

Under White House control the Department of Labor nullifies the occupational safety laws by cutting down on inspections, reducing fines, weakening the old rules, and delaying the enactment of needed new ones. The department also quietly undermines a law ensuring fair employment opportunities for Vietnam veterans by suspending key

regulations without public notice or comment. According to the department it is "unnecessary and contrary to the public interest" to let the American people know how their President treats the veterans of a war he is trying to glorify.

In June the Department of Health and Human Services proposes that all changes in rules affecting the aged, the poor, the young, and the disabled henceforth be promulgated without public notice or comment. A cost-benefit analysis has persuaded the department that the "delay" caused by public participation in the rule-making process "outweigh[s] the benefits of receiving public comment." Alas for democracy, it cannot make the poor run on time.

A few weeks before making its secrecy proposal the department had direct experience of the utter incompatibility of democracy and cost-benefit analysis. In May it tried unsuccessfully to save nearly $1 billion by gutting a program that provides preventive medical checkups to 2 million poor children. When this came to public notice, the shysters of "cost-effectiveness" had a hard time explaining why an ounce of prevention was no longer worth a pound of cure, this being the well-known result of a cost-benefit analysis made by humanity at large and not readily rescinded except in the dark. What an enemy of the "good" is common humanity!

As long as a free people can bring the executive to court, however, presidential power is under constraint, for the courts do not yet recognize the new legislative system. In July, Federal District Judge Harold Greene stops the Department of Labor from nullifying two laws it considers too costly to enforce. "It is not for the Secretary of Labor or his subordinates to make that judgment," wrote Judge Greene. "Under our constitutional system, policy decisions are not made by Government administrators; they are made by the Congress." What an enemy of the "good" is the old Constitution!

To free arbitrary power from the constraints of the courts, the Administration tries to cut off the courts from the people. To prevent the citizenry from enforcing the civil rights laws themselves, the Administration will try in 1983 (in vain) to amend those provisions that allow people to sue the government in order to compel it to enforce those laws. To make it financially difficult for the public-spirited to uphold the law against lawless bureaucracy the Administration will also try in 1983, again in vain, to curtail government payment of fees to lawyers who vindicate the law. To weaken the "habit" of judicial review the Administration rails at the federal courts for what Attorney General William French Smith calls "constitutionally dubious and unwise intrusions into the legislative domain"—the domain which the White House itself has lawlessly invaded. To put the old, the young, the poor, and the disabled beyond the protection of the courts the Department of Health and Human Services announces in June that in the future the internal rules it issues to administer its programs will not create any rights or benefits that are "enforceable" in court.*

To deprive the poor of their legal rights, the White House asks Congress in November to abolish the Legal Services Corporation, which provides the poor with counsel to help them protect their rights in court. When Congress refuses, the White House installs its own agents at the corporation. In late November they unfurl their handiwork: pettifogging rules (later dropped) that make it almost impossible for Legal Services lawyers to sue on behalf of large groups of people, the single most efficient weapon in vindicating the legal rights of the poor. And what is the "cost-effectiveness" of compelling the victims of official injustice to sue for their rights one at a time? The inestimable "benefit" of liberating lawless power from the constraints of the law.

III. 1983

On January 24 the budget office proposes a change in its Circular A-122—"Cost Principles for Nonprofit Organizations." What is proposed are new accounting rules for the thousands of private organizations that receive federal grants to carry out government functions in lieu of an extended bureaucracy. The new rules say, in effect, that all such organizations—from the Girl Scouts and the Izaak Walton League to the Association for Retarded Citizens—must forfeit federal funds if they speak out on public affairs.

The new rules "would inhibit the free flow of information between these parties and all levels of government," says an angry Chamber of Commerce. "Operated in tandem, the scope and inherent vagueness of the terms 'political advocacy' and 'unallowable costs' can easily become a giant pincers for the stifling of the free and unfettered exercise of First Amendment rights," says the National Association of Manufacturers, which finds itself puzzled at the spectacle of the White House discouraging "citizen involvement in the

political process." Representatives of both organizations testify on March 1 before the one forum left in Washington for a republican opposition to arbitrary power: the House Government Operations Committee, under the chairmanship of Jack Brooks of Texas.

Frank Horton of New York, the senior Republican on the committee, cannot hide his anger or his shame. "We are talking about what a citizen can do with his own money on time not paid for by the Government.... [The revision] says that if he receives any money through an award based on cost, he cannot express an opinion on public matters and still be compensated. Mr. Chairman, this is positively outrageous. I cannot believe that this could possibly be the intent of the Administration, and yet the language is painfully clear."

Two weeks after issuing its proposed revision of A-122 (which will be only slightly modified before being adopted in April 1984), the President signs an executive order banning "any organization that seeks to influence...the determination of public policy" from participating in the federal government's lucrative on-the-job charity drives. A month later, the White House calls for the elimination of postal subsidies for the blind, libraries, schools, and other nonprofit organizations.

Why does the White House wish to silence so many thousands of public-spirited people who have firsthand knowledge of the effects of its policies? The question answers itself: so that the American people cannot judge for themselves the costs and benefits of those policies, and so cannot hold the Administration accountable. That is why the Administration stops funding the publication of the *Survey of Income and Program Participation*, which assesses the effects of its welfare policies; stops publishing the *Annual Survey of Child Nutrition* and the *Annual Housing Survey*; stops publishing several bulletins on occupational health hazards; stops issuing warnings about newly discovered toxics; withholds health care data from local officials; and eliminates or reduces "at least 50 major statistical programs," the Government Operations Committee reports, on such matters as nursing homes, medical care expenditures, monthly department store sales, and labor turnover.

According to Administration spokesmen, the "free market" will attend to these things, so the government need not inform the electorate about them. But how can the American people judge the merits of the "free market" if they are kept in ignorance of its effects? This question, too,

---

* Although a final regulation was never published, this proposal, as well as the one stipulating that the department's rules be promulgated in secret, remains on the agenda.

Ronald Reagan   *Philip Burke*

answers itself. The market is not for the American people to judge. Although it is the highest good of all, the market, too, apparently thrives best in darkness.

On a radio program devoted to "Defunding Anti-Family Organizations," Michael Horowitz, general counsel of the budget office and mastermind of the A-122 revision, describes the kind of Americans the White House favors: "Americans who live in real-world communities, have real-world jobs, real-world concerns, who are not political in character."

Under Justice Department guidelines issued on March 7, Americans who are "political in character" are put within easy reach of police surveillance. In addition to permitting FBI agents to infiltrate political organizations in the cause of "domestic security," the new guidelines allow the Bureau to collect "publicly available information" on any American it chooses to monitor for any reason whatever. Thanks to an Administration which pretends to oppose official oppression, any citizen who emerges from "real-world" obscurity now falls within the purview of, and possibly into the files of, the federal police power.

On March 11 the White House attempts to do for national security affairs what A-122 was meant to do for domestic affairs: stop up the mouths of those who know too much. Under the President's National Security Decision Directive 84, all government employees with access to "sensitive compartmentalized information" must sign contracts which subject them to an extraordinary system of official censorship. If they wish to publish a book, an article, or even submit a letter to the editor containing "any information" related to "intelligence"—a category vast enough to take in most of the domain of national security—they must first show it to the government for review, and, if need be, alteration, not only while in office but for the rest of their lives.*

The White House does not give a clear-cut justification for this system of lifetime censorship, possibly because there is none. The Administration's statement accompanying the directive describes it as both a harmless effort to give government policy "a greater consistency" and an urgent effort to prevent the unauthorized disclosure of important state secrets. The press briefing at the Justice Department borders on the theater of the absurd.

"How many employees are you talking about here?" a reporter asks an official.

"SCI access is given out only to a handful of employees."

"Hundreds, thousands?"

"It would probably be classified."

"Can you provide one or two examples of concrete damage to national security" from unauthorized disclosures?

No, he cannot: "When we officially confirm information that has been disclosed in this manner, it compounds the damage."

The truth comes out later and the truth is devastating. The "handful" is 128,000 officials. And, according to the State Department, the total number of damaging "leaks" conveyed through the writings of government officials during the preceding five years is *none*, not one.

"Well, I just can't believe it," says Lucas A. Powe Jr., a professor of law at the University of Texas, in testimony before a Government Operations subcommittee. "It is as if in coming up with the proposal the Administration weighed censorship in the balance as a positive good instead of a presumptively unconstitutional evil."

---

* On February 17, 1984, the President orders the censorship provisions of NSDD-84 "held in abeyance" but does not revoke them.

That their highest officials might be the enemies of their freedom Americans find hard to believe, but such is the case. On a pretext so false its falsity cries out to heaven, the White House is determined to censor the writings of the only class of citizens who can effectively challenge a president in affairs of state—all those retired State and Defense Department officials whose character and patriotism cannot be impugned and whose judgments command attention even when they run counter to a president's. The Administration is apparently bent on turning the White House into the unopposable voice of Authority.

On February 24 a prizewinning Canadian film about the horrors of nuclear war is labeled "political propaganda" by the Justice Department and placed under the restrictions of the Foreign Agents Registration Act of 1938. The name of every organization and individual to whom the film is distributed must be filed with the government. On March 3 the State Department denies a visa to Salvador Allende's widow, who had been invited to address church groups in San Francisco. It is "prejudicial to United States interests," says the department, to let a few Americans hear, perhaps, that the present Chilean regime is a tyranny.

On April 1 the Department of Energy introduces a new kind of official secret. According to the department's proposed regulations, which were later modified, a vast mass of published books, articles, and reports must henceforth be concealed from the public if they could possibly contribute to "nuclear terrorism." Any library that lets such "unclassified controlled nuclear information" fall into unauthorized hands could be fined up to $100,000 for failing to help the government achieve what Stanford University, in a stinging rejoinder, calls "the futile and repugnant object of making known and unclassified information secret."*

On May 25 the President fires three members of the six-person Civil Rights Commission—something no other president has ever done—for daring to monitor the Administration's non-enforcement of the civil rights laws. At a single stroke the commission's statutory independence is destroyed, but the White House has little patience for contrary voices. Americans have a right to speak out about

their "concerns," says the President at a press conference in mid-June, "but let us always remember, with that privilege goes a responsibility to be right."

On September 12 the White House takes another step toward centralizing control of government information. The budget office proposes that all government agencies must consider that "information is not a free good but a resource of substantial economic value and should be treated as such." In light of this, they must submit to the White House clear proof that any information they make public passes the supreme test of "cost-benefit analysis."* Half in shock, half in anguish, the American Library Association asks how such an analysis can properly be made. "What is the dollar benefit of an informed citizenry?"

"You can't let your people know" what the government is doing, the President explains at an October 19 press conference, "without letting the wrong people know—those who are in opposition to what you're doing." (On October 20 the Senate votes 56 to 34 against lifetime censorship for government officials.) Reporters are so inured to the President's artless press conference remarks that nobody asks him why the people's right to know chiefly benefits "the wrong people."

The meaning of the President's remarks becomes clear on October 25, when U.S. forces invade the island of Grenada and the American press is barred from the scene at gunpoint, forced to huddle on a nearby island, and compelled to transmit to the public only official lies and evasions. This wanton act of government censorship reveals "a certain mind-set" among the nation's leaders, *Time* angrily observes: "the notion that events can be shaped by their presentation, that truth should be a controlled substance." Indeed so, but this flaunting of censorship reveals something more than a "mind-set": it reveals a determination to habituate a free people to official news and to regarding a free press as the national enemy. "It seems as though the reporters are always against us. They're always seeking to report something that's going to screw things up," says Secretary of State George Shultz, "pandering," writes Safire on December 18, "to the most dangerous I-Am-the-State instincts of his boss."

And who is "us," Secretary Shultz is asked. "Our side militarily—in other words, all of America."

---

* The final regulations, passed in April 1985, allow the DOE to restrict access to such information only if it is contained in material acquired by a library after that date.

* Although formal guidelines were never issued, this has become the Administration's de facto policy.

IV. January–October 1984

In early January the Administration makes its first crude attempt to revive seditious libel—the ancient crime of speaking ill of the government. On January 3 Justice Department officials obtain a court order barring a publisher from printing a legal opinion of a Colorado judge because the department thinks it is "slanderous" to three of its lawyers. Three weeks later the sear of notoriety forces the U.S. Court of Appeals in Denver to recollect what country it is in, but America has had its first inkling of a future in which the executive may punish with prior restraint the sin of slandering the state.

In January, too, the Administration experiments with new ways to deter government officials from disclosing classified information to the public. "Leaks are consensual crimes," says Acting Assistant Attorney General Richard Willard. Willard shows Senate aides the draft of unprecedented legislation that would authorize the federal government to punish with crushing financial penalties any person with access to classified information—more than 4 million people—who divulges the most trivial fact concealed within the bloated empire of national security.*

The Administration takes a parallel step against leaks in late January, when two Air Force investigators approach Professor Jeffrey Richelson of American University an hour before he is to deliver a technical paper on arms control verification to an academic audience in Los Angeles. They warn Richelson that if he delivers his paper, he could be prosecuted under the 1917 Espionage Act.**

On February 3 the *Washington Post* reports that FBI agents have warned two former National Security Agency officials that their research into the downing of the Korean Air Lines jet "technically violated" the Espionage Act.

The word "technically" betrays the Administration's intention. It seeks to turn a law aimed at the transfer of vital secrets to a foreign power with the intent to harm the country into an instrument for prosecuting those who transfer

---

* *The White House never formally proposed this legislation, in large part because the details of Willard's draft were reported in the press, generating widespread public opposition.*

** *Richelson delivered his paper anyway. He later provided the Justice Department with evidence that it was based on published information, and a decision was made not to prosecute.*

information to the public with the intent to help the country. The great advantage of this law over other methods of stopping leaks, notes a confidential White House memorandum circulated in 1982, is that it "could also be used to prosecute a journalist who knowingly receives and publishes classified documents or information."

Behind the President's "leakomania," as Safire calls it, lies the force of a very practical necessity. Ordinary means of concealment can no longer hide the scandalous truth about the Administration's trillion-dollar military buildup; it is a colossal squandering of the public wealth. The established secrecy rules are good enough to silence time-servers, but they cannot prevent men of honor from supplying Congress, the press, and the public with the sordid evidence of wanton waste—the evidence that "the vast majority of money we put into major weapons systems is pure waste and inefficiency," according to Senator Charles E. Grassley, a conservative Iowa Republican; the evidence that "we are not buying airplanes, we are buying the contractors' costs," according to A. Ernest Fitzgerald, the Air Force official who gave "whistle-blowing" a good name; the evidence that the entire weapons buildup "had nothing to do with a strategy, nothing to do with a program of what we needed for defense," according to Richard A. Stubbing, who served in the budget office as deputy chief of national security during the first years of the buildup.

To help it conceal this hideous engine of waste from the American people, Congress has quietly handed the Department of Defense extensive new secrecy powers. Slipped into the voluminous folds of the Omnibus Defense Authorization Act of 1984 is a provision that gives the Pentagon statutory authority "to withhold from public disclosure any technical data with military or space application" that could not be released to a foreigner without obtaining an export license. After all, why should Americans have a right to know any more than foreigners? We are a thousand times more dangerous than foreigners. This *congressional* assault on accountable government gives the executive the authority to conceal the entire domain of national defense from the American people. But the Pentagon waits until after the election to exercise its new powers.

Secrecy rules are one thing; enforcing them is another. Hence the importance the Administration places on expanding the Espionage Act.

On October 1 the Administration takes the next step toward the act's expansion when it arrests a civilian Navy official for selling three classified satellite photographs of a Soviet aircraft carrier under construction to a venerable British military magazine. There is no question of disclosing information damaging to our national security. The Defense Department releases satellite photographs whenever it suits the Administration's purposes. Nor is there anything surreptitious about the sale: the arrested official, Samuel Loring Morison, is an editor of *Jane's Fighting Ships,* and the photographs were duly published in August. The only question is whether the Administration can find a judge willing to rule that the Espionage Act is in fact an official secrets act under which no one has been convicted in sixty-seven years.

V. NOVEMBER 1984–NOVEMBER 1985

The President's great popular victory in November does not reconcile the Administration to the habits of freedom and popular government. It merely gives the President and his faction greater power to besiege and subvert them.

On November 20 the Defense Department exercises its new statutory power to conceal itself from the country. It issues a directive stating that every Pentagon official must henceforth withhold from the public all "technical data," including any pertaining to "contractor performance evaluation"—fraud—and "results of test and evaluation of... military hardware"—waste—if such data "are likely to be disseminated outside the Department of Defense." In other words, if the American people want to know about something, then, for that very reason, it must be kept from their knowledge. That is the plain English of the regulations. The maximum penalty for enlightening the country is ten years' imprisonment and a $100,000 fine for violating the export control laws, now distorted beyond recognition.

The great Administration engine for squandering the public wealth, the machine which generates crushing budget deficits, which in turn serve as a permanent force for reducing "social spending," has at last become what it so desperately needs to be: a single, all-embracing secret of state. Wanton waste, under heavy concealment, will enforce needless sacrifice, and the sovereignty of a free people will be crushed under a fabricated necessity. Social programs will be abolished, public benefits reduced, social services left to decay; and a blinded electorate will no more understand why their country has grown so impoverished than a savage can understand why the sun rolls around in the heavens.

Also in the aftermath of the election the Administration reveals what the President means by "the responsibility to be right." It will try to make falsehood a federal crime. A writer named Antoni Gronowicz has published a book about Pope John Paul II, *God's Broker,* containing extensive interviews with the pontiff which the Vatican says are fictitious. This is gross falsehood—the pope says so—and this the White House is determined to punish. An Administration which thinks it is oppressive to prevent corporations from poisoning the air thinks it is the government's duty to prevent an author from misleading a few readers. The Justice Department seeks a grand jury investigation in Philadelphia, hoping to have Gronowicz indicted, not precisely for publishing a book containing falsehoods but for violating the mail fraud statutes.*

In late November the Administration finds a still more potent way to curtail the freedom of the press in America. The CIA files a complaint with the Federal Communications Commission against the American Broadcasting Company that could result in the loss of its broadcast licenses for airing a false charge, later retracted, against the agency. Since the CIA's unprecedented suit has the backing of the White House, the FCC proves obliging. Even though it eventually rules against the CIA, the FCC declares that any agency of the government henceforth has the right to file such a complaint against a broadcaster (under the Fairness Doctrine) if it feels it has been unfairly abused on the airwaves. Thus has the FCC reinvented seditious libel. By bureaucratic fiat, it is now an offense punishable by the threat of extinction for any broadcaster to treat the executive branch unfairly—in the judgment of the executive branch.

As long as Americans still cherish a free press, however, the Administration cannot successfully subjugate the news media. Accordingly, the Administration renews its effort to turn the people against their own newspapers. Another flaunted drama of censorship provides the instrument. On December 17 the Defense Department calls in the press to announce that the scheduled January 23 flight of the space shuttle *Discovery* will be treated as a military secret of the gravest kind. The public learns that Secretary of Defense Caspar Weinberger has personally asked the Associated

---

* *A grand jury was convened, and ordered Gronowicz to turn over his notes. He refused, and has asked the Supreme Court to overturn lower court rulings ordering that he do so.*

Caspar Weinberger

Press, NBC News, and *Aviation Week & Space Technology* to suppress their stories about the shuttle mission in the interests of "national security"—and that the three organizations have dutifully complied. The public learns, too, that even "speculation" about the purpose of the flight is forbidden and will be punished by a full-out investigation of the offender—a truly extraordinary threat.

This sudden, officious announcement stuns the Washington press corps. There is simply no warrant for such elaborate secrecy. The military purpose of the shuttle flight has been publicly available information for months. To kill a news story merely because the government orders it would set a "dangerous precedent," warns John Chancellor on the *NBC Nightly News.* True enough, but the Administration evidently wants something more than that servile precedent. Its insolent warning against "speculation" is a goad to defiance, "an enticement for people to go after what the mission was about and then to publish what they found out," as former Defense Secretary James R. Schlesinger tells the press.

Taking up the gauntlet, the *Washington Post* refuses to keep secret what is not a secret and publishes a story about the shuttle flight based on information from available sources. Secretary Weinberger denounces the paper for daring to "violate requests" from the Pentagon. Disobedience to a government decree, he says, "can only give aid and comfort to the enemy." This is more than mere calumny; it is the precise wording of the constitutional definition of treason, and it suggests a motive for the shuttle affair. What the Administration has done is stage a little morality play before the eyes

of the country, a corrupting drama in which the servility of the press appears in the bright garb of patriotism and the freedom of the press in the black hues of treason.

Some weeks later the Administration stages a second act of the vicious play when the *Times* publishes a second-hand story by Leslie Gelb against the wishes of the State Department. The department's Bureau of Politico-Military Affairs orders Gelb ostracized and ostentatiously denounces him for "willingly, willfully, and knowingly" publishing information "harmful and damaging to the country." That the information has been previously published is irrelevant, the department explains. "The Secretary of Defense and Secretary of State and National Security Adviser were against printing it," and this alone makes it treasonable conduct in the new tyrannized republic. As Floyd Abrams, the famed constitutional lawyer, observes, the Administration is "attacking the legitimacy of the press, not its performance."

Under the Administration's powerful assault the press grows timid. The Morison case passes through various preliminary stages but the public hears almost nothing about it. Tyranny is not "news." That is the new rule of American journalism. The truth is, the press is too frightened to write about what frightens it. It cowers in dread of being called "too powerful." For the myth of media power, which the media never contested in their salad days, is now being used by the enemies of liberty to incite the people against a free press.

On January 4, without the slightest public notice, the White House issues an executive order that concentrates still greater legislative power in the hands of its budget office. Under Executive Order 12498 the White House gives itself the formal power not only to impose cost-benefit analysis but to review, control, approve, or suppress any agency activity "that may influence, anticipate, or could lead to the commencement of rule-making proceedings at a later date." Regardless of the laws they are supposed to implement, the executive agencies of government can now do virtually nothing the White House disapproves of. For the first time in American history a president has the formal power to turn acts of Congress into mere husks for secret White House legislation. Under the new executive order the president also has the unprecedented power to bar any executive agency from even studying anything the White House prefers to leave unstudied. No official information that might allow the American people to question the wisdom of a president may be collected without that president's permission—which will be given or withheld in secret. Under this new dispensation the old, decentralized executive branch stands on the verge of extinction. The traditional bulwark against presidential despotism has been reduced to silence and servility.

On March 12 a federal judge in Baltimore, deciding a motion in the Morison case, rules that the Espionage Act applies to unauthorized disclosures of classified information to the press. According to Judge Joseph H. Young, "the danger to the United States is just as great when this information is released to the press as when it is released to an agent of a foreign government." For decades it was plain to Congress and the courts that the vital secrets of 1917 bear little resemblance to the half-billion "classified" documents concealed by the modern security establishment. For decades it was evident to everybody that informing the American people is different from informing a foreign government, that the wish to enlighten the country is different from the intent to harm it. But this Administration believes that an enlightened citizenry is a menace to the state. Thanks to Judge Young's ruling, patriotic officials may no longer menace the great engine of Pentagon waste. Morison himself faces up to forty years in prison for putting three harmless photographs into a well-known magazine.

Imagine a faction that would throw honorable men into prison so that it could impoverish the public treasury with impunity and bend a sovereign people to its will, not just this year and the next but long after it has fallen from power. Imagine a venerable republic, the hope of the world, where the habits of freedom are besieged, where self-government is assailed, where the vigilant are blinded, the well informed gagged, the press hounded, the courts weakened, the government exalted, the electorate degraded, the Constitution mocked, and laws reduced to a sham so that, in the fullness of time, corporate enterprise may regain the paltry commercial freedom to endanger the well-being of the populace. Imagine a base-hearted political establishment, "liberal" as well as "conservative," Democratic as well as Republican, watching with silent, protective approval this lunatic assault on popular government. Imagine a soft-spoken demagogue, faithful to nothing except his own faction, being given a free hand to turn Americans into the enemies of their own ancient liberties. Imagine this and it becomes apparent at last how a once-great republic can be despoiled in broad daylight before the unseeing eyes of its friends.

THE SOCCER WAR

BY RYSZARD KAPUŚCIŃSKI

JUNE 1986

This spring at Oxford's St. Antony's College (where I have been lecturing on the Third World) I met several people from Latin America. We met the day after my arrival, at lunch, which is eaten here in a large hall, at long tables which afford the opportunity of general conversation. As always with Latins, one can discuss endlessly. The talk turned quickly to Central America. Because of the events in Nicaragua, but also because of the tensions in Honduras and El Salvador, there is more discussion today of these small countries than of the Latin American giants—Brazil and Argentina.

We agreed that there has never been peace in Central America, or in any event that it has never lasted long. Revolts, upheavals, interventions—there's no rest in that region's history. As we talked we gave examples, and I of course brought up the war seventeen years ago between Honduras and El Salvador, the famous soccer war, which once caught world attention. I say "of course" because I witnessed that war, lived through it, and then wrote about it. Later, traveling around the world, I realized that many people learned of the existence of Honduras and El Salvador only because of that war, and I thought of the tragedy of such small states, spoken of only when they spill blood.

For me that war held a great and still relevant lesson. It erupted over something trivial—a soccer match. But if a minor incident can start a major conflict (domestic or international), it means that the situation, the climate of the place, is brimming with dramatic tensions, that the powder keg is chock-full, and any spark will suffice to set off the conflagration. Such is the climate of Central America. The atmosphere is electric, unbalanced, because in the countries of that region there have accumulated an unusually large number of social contradictions, age-old conflicts, grievances, inveterate quarrels, unredressed wrongs. It is difficult to sort it all out, yet without the effort, without the desire to know this world that is Central America, it is impossible to grasp a most important point—that these conflicts and grievances are *their affair*, that they constitute a local reality which in itself most frequently bears no relation to any extraregional one. Being in the soccer war, I was in their world. I saw how for them no other world exists, how all their thoughts are circumscribed by the borders of their national consciousness, because nationalism is finally the only ideology of these societies, at least the only ideology authentically experienced.

Nationalism is their only value, and sometimes their only wealth. This is because in moments of euphoria (in times of war, for example), nationalism gives rise to social equality in these hierarchical societies, and all (at least for a while) become brothers, the rich and the poor suddenly equal, all feeling needed by one another. Talk is only of the nation. To restore the nation's dignity, to protect the nation's borders, to create a strong nation—it's a language understood by all and accepted by all. *Patria* is the key word, the all-embracing concept, the highest principle.

Now, as I read press reports and commentaries from Central America, I'm struck by how everything there is seen exclusively in terms of East-West relations, how little attention is paid to the fact that these people have their own ways of thinking, their own ideals. If things get to the stage of open conflict, it is only the rivalry of the great powers that gives this conflict its ideological dimension, its international character. For without such external interference, it would only be a question of their own great game, their own, next soccer war.

Luis Suarez said there was going to be a war, and I believed whatever Luis said. We were staying together in Mexico. Luis was giving me a lesson in Latin America: what it is and how to understand it. He could foresee many events. Long before the return of Perón he believed that the old *caudillo* would again become president of Argentina; he foretold as well the sudden death of the Haitian dictator François Duvalier, at a time when everybody said Papa Doc had many years left. Luis knew how to pick his way through the shifting sands of Latin politics, in which amateurs like me bogged down and blundered with each step.

This time Luis announced his opinion about the impending war after laying down the newspaper in which he had read a report on the soccer match between the Honduran and Salvadoran national teams. The two countries were playing for the right to take part in the 1970 World Cup in Mexico.

The first match was held on Sunday, June 8, 1969, in the Honduran capital, Tegucigalpa.

Nobody in the world paid any attention.

The Salvadoran team arrived in Tegucigalpa on Saturday and spent a sleepless night in their hotel. The players could not sleep because they were the target of psychological warfare waged by the Honduran fans. A swarm of people encircled the hotel. The crowd threw stones at the windows and beat sheets of tin and empty barrels with sticks. They set off one string of firecrackers after another. They leaned on the horns of cars parked in front of the hotel. The fans whistled, screamed, and set up hostile chants. This went on all night. The idea was that a sleepy, edgy, exhausted team would be bound to lose. In Latin America these are standard practices that surprise no one.

The next day Honduras defeated the Salvadoran squad, 1–0.

Eighteen-year-old Amelia Bolanios was sitting in front of her television in San Salvador when Roberto Cardona, the Honduran forward, scored the winning goal in the final minute. She got up, ran to the desk, opened the drawer containing her father's pistol, and committed suicide by shooting herself in the heart. "The young girl could not bear to see her fatherland brought to its knees," wrote the Salvadoran newspaper *El Nacional* the next day. The whole capital took part in the televised funeral of Amelia Bolanios. An army honor guard marched with a flag at the head of the procession. The president of the republic and his ministers walked behind the flag-draped coffin. Behind them came the Salvadoran soccer eleven, who, booed, laughed at, and spat on at the Tegucigalpa airport, had returned to the country on a special flight that morning.

The return match of the home-and-home series took place in San Salvador, in the beautifully named Flor Blanca

stadium, a week later. This time it was the Honduran team that spent a sleepless night. The screaming crowd of fans broke all the windows in their hotel and threw rotten eggs, dead rats, and stinking rags inside. The Honduran players were transported to the stadium in armored cars of the First Salvadoran Mechanized Division—which saved them from bloodshed at the hands of the mob that lined the route, holding up portraits of the national heroine Amelia Bolanios.

The army surrounded the stadium. Around the field stood a cordon of soldiers from a crack National Guard regiment, with submachine guns ready to fire. During the playing of the Honduran national anthem the stadium roared and whistled. Next, instead of raising the Honduran flag— which had been burned before the eyes of the spectators, driving them mad with joy—the hosts ran a dirty, tattered dishrag up the flagpole. Under such conditions the players from Tegucigalpa did not, understandably, have their minds on the game.

El Salvador prevailed, 3–0.

The same armored cars carried the Honduran team straight from the playing field to the airport. A worse fate awaited the visiting fans. Kicked and beaten, they fled toward the Honduran border. Two of them died. Scores landed in the hospital. A hundred and fifty of the visitors' cars were burned. The border between the two states was closed a few hours later.

Luis read about all of this in the newspaper and said that there was going to be a war. He had been a reporter for a long time and he knew his beat.

In Latin America, he said, the line between soccer and politics is extremely tenuous. The list of governments that have fallen or been overthrown by the army after the defeat of the national team is long. Players on the losing side are denounced in the press as traitors to the nation. When Brazil won the 1970 World Cup, a colleague of mine, a Brazilian political exile, was heartbroken: "The military right wing," he said, "can be sure of at least five more years of peaceful rule." On the way to the title, Brazil beat England. In an article headlined "Jesus Defends Brazil," the Rio de Janeiro paper *Jornal dos Esportes* explained the reasons for the win this way: "Whenever the ball flew toward our goal and a score seemed inevitable, Jesus reached his foot out of the clouds and cleared the ball." Drawings illustrating this supernatural spectacle accompanied the article.

Anyone who goes to a stadium can lose his life. Take the match in 1969 that Mexico lost to Peru, 2–1. An embittered Mexican fan shouted in an ironic tone, "Viva Mexico!" A moment later he was dead, massacred by the crowd. But sometimes the heightened emotions find another outlet. After a match once in which Mexico downed Belgium, 1–0, Augusto Mariaga, the warden of a maximum-security prison in Chilpancingo, became delirious with joy and ran around waving a pistol, firing into the air and shouting "Viva Mexico!" He opened all the cells, releasing 142 dangerous criminals. A court acquitted him since, as the verdict read, "he acted in patriotic exultation."

"Do you think it's worth going to Honduras?" I asked Luis, who was then editing the serious and influential weekly *Siempre*.

"I think it's worth it," he answered. "Something's bound to happen." I was in Tegucigalpa the next morning.

At dusk an airplane flew over the city and dropped a bomb. Everybody heard it go off. The neighboring mountains echoed the violent blast of bursting metal; some said later that it had been a whole series of bombs. Panic swept the city. Merchants closed their shops. Cars stood abandoned in the middle of the street. Then everything became still, as though the city had died. Soon the lights went out and Tegucigalpa sank into darkness.

I hurried to my hotel, burst into my room, fed a piece of paper into the typewriter, and tried to write a dispatch to Warsaw. I was trying to move fast because I knew that at that moment I was the only foreign correspondent in the city, and that I could be the first to inform the world about the outbreak of war in Central America.

But it was pitch dark in the room and I couldn't see anything. I felt my way downstairs to the reception desk, where they lent me a candle. I went back upstairs, lit the candle, and turned on my transistor radio. The announcer was reading a communiqué from the Honduran government about the commencement of hostilities with El Salvador. Then came the news that the Salvadoran army was attacking Honduras all along the front line.

I began to write:

TEGUCIGALPA (HONDURAS) PAP JULY 14 VIA TROPICAL RADIO RCA TODAY AT 6 PM WAR BEGAN BETWEEN EL SALVADOR AND HONDURAS STOP SALVADORAN AIR FORCE BOMBARDED FOUR HONDURAN CITIES STOP AT SAME TIME SALVADORAN ARMY CROSSED HONDURAN BORDER ATTEMPTING TO PENETRATE DEEP INTO COUN-

TRY STOP IN RESPONSE TO AGGRESSION HONDURAN AIR FORCE BOMBARDED IMPORTANT SALVADORAN INDUS-TRIAL AND STRATEGIC TARGETS AND GROUND FORCES BEGAN DEFENSIVE ACTION

At this moment someone in the street started shouting "Apaga la luz!" over and over, sounding more nervous and serious each time, so I had to blow out the candle. I went on typing blind, by touch, striking a match over the keys every now and then.

RADIO REPORTS FIGHTING UNDERWAY ALONG FULL LENGTH OF FRONT AND THAT HONDURAN ARMY IS INFLICTING HEAVY LOSSES ON SALVADORAN ARMY STOP GOVERNMENT HAS CALLED WHOLE POPULATION TO DEFENSE OF ENDANGERED NATION AND APPEALED TO UN FOR CONDEMNATION OF ATTACK

I carried the dispatch downstairs, found the owner of the hotel, and asked him to find someone to lead me to the post office. It was my first day there and I did not know Tegucigalpa at all. The owner wanted to help but he had no one to send with me, and I was in a hurry. In the end he called the police. Nobody at the police station had time. So he called the fire department. Three firemen arrived in full gear, wearing helmets and carrying axes. We greeted each other in the dark; I could not see their faces. I begged them to lead me to the post office. I know Honduras well, I lied, and I know that its people are renowned for hospitality. I was sure they would not refuse me. It was very important that the world find out the truth about who started the war, who shot first, and so on, and I wanted to assure them that I had written the honest truth. The main thing at the moment was time, and we had to hurry.

We left the hotel. I could see only the outlines of the street. I do not know why we spoke in whispers. I counted my steps, trying to remember the way. I was getting close to a thousand when the firemen stopped. One of them knocked on a door. A voice from inside asked what we wanted. Then the door opened, but only for a minute, so that too much light wouldn't get out. Now I was inside. They ordered me to wait. In all of Honduras there was only one telex machine, and the president of the republic was using it. The president was carrying on an exchange of views with the Honduran ambassador in Washington, whom he was directing to apply to the American government for military assistance. This went on for a long time, since the president and the ambassador were using uncommonly flowery language; besides, the connection would break every so often. After midnight I finally made contact with Warsaw.

I awoke in my hotel the next morning and found that the city was preparing for a siege. People had been digging trenches and putting up barricades for hours. Women were laying in supplies and crisscrossing their windows with masking tape. People scurried aimlessly through the streets; an atmosphere of panic reigned. Student brigades were painting outsized slogans on walls and fences. A bubble full of poetry had burst over Tegucigalpa, and within hours thousands of verses covered the walls:

ONLY AN IMBECILE WORRIES:
NOBODY BEATS HONDURAS

PICK UP YOUR GUNS AND LET'S GO GUYS
CUT THOSE SALVADORANS DOWN TO SIZE

WE SHALL AVENGE 3–0

PORFIRIO RAMOS SHOULD BE ASHAMED OF HIMSELF FOR
LIVING WITH A SALVADORAN WOMAN

ANYONE SEEING RAIMUNDO GRANDOS CALL THE POLICE
HE'S A SALVADORAN SPY

Latins generally have an obsession with spies, conspiracies, and plots. Now, in wartime conditions, they regarded everyone as a fifth-column diversionist. My own situation did not look good. Official propaganda on both sides had featured wild campaigns blaming communists for every misfortune, and in the whole region I was the only correspondent from a socialist country. They could expel me.

I went to the post office and invited the telex operator for a beer. He was in terror, because although he had a Honduran father, his mother was a citizen of El Salvador. As a mixed national, he found himself among the suspected. He did not know what would happen next. All morning the police had been herding Salvadorans into provisional camps, most often in stadiums. Throughout Latin America, stadiums play a double role: in peacetime they are sports venues, and in times of war they turn into prisons.

In the afternoon forty correspondents, my colleagues, arrived from Mexico. Because the airport in Tegucigalpa was closed, they flew into Guatemala and hired a bus there. They all wanted to drive to the front. We went to the presidential palace to try to arrange permission. It was an ugly turn-of-the-century building, painted bright blue, in the very center of the town. There were machine-gun nests, covered with sandbags, set up around the palace. Antiaircraft guns stood in the courtyard. Inside, in the corridors, soldiers were dozing or lolling around in full battle dress. It was quite a mess.

Every war is a horrible mess and a great waste of life and property. People have been making war for thousands of years, but it looks each time as if they were starting from scratch, as if the first war in the world were being held.

A captain appeared and said he was the army press spokesman. He told us that they were winning all along the front and that the enemy was suffering heavy losses.

"O.K.," said the man from AP. "And we want to see."

We always sent the Americans first, because this was their sphere of influence—they commanded obedience and could arrange all sorts of things. The captain said we could go to the front the next day.

We drove to a place where two artillery pieces stood under some trees. Cannons were firing and stacks of ordnance were lying around. Ahead of us we could see the road that led to El Salvador. Swamp stretched along both sides of the road and dense green bush began past the belt of swamp.

The sweaty, unshaven major charged with holding the road said we could go no farther. Beyond this point both armies were in action, and it was hard to tell who was who or what belonged to which side. The bush was too thick to see anything. Two opposing units often noticed each other only at the last moment, when, wandering through the overgrowth, they met face to face. In addition, since both armies wore the same uniforms, carried the same equipment, and spoke the same language, it was difficult to distinguish friend from foe.

The major advised us to return to Tegucigalpa, because advancing might mean getting killed without even knowing who had done it. (As if that mattered, I thought.) But the television cameramen said they had to push forward, to the front line, to film soldiers in action, firing, dying. Gregor Straub of NBC said he had to have a close-up of a soldier's face dripping sweat. Rodolfo Carillo of CBS said he had to catch a despondent commander sitting under a bush and weeping because he had lost his whole unit. A French cameraman wanted a panorama shot with a Salvadoran unit charging a Honduran unit from one side, or vice versa. Somebody else wanted to capture the image of a soldier carrying his dead comrade. The radio reporters sided with the cameramen. One wanted to record the cries of a casualty summoning help, growing weaker and weaker, until he breathed his last breath. Charles Meadows of Radio Canada wanted the voice of a soldier cursing war amid a hellish racket of gunfire. Naotake Mochida of Radio Japan wanted the bark of an officer shouting to his commander over the roar of artillery—using a Japanese field telephone.

Many others also decided to go forward. Competition is a powerful incentive. Since American television was going, the American wire services had to go as well. Since the Americans were going, Reuters had to go. Excited by patriotic ambition, I decided, as the only Pole on the scene, to attach myself to the group that intended the desperate

march. Those who said they had bad hearts, or professed to be uninterested in particulars since they were writing general commentaries, we left behind, under a tree.

There might have been twenty of us who set out along an empty road bathed in intense sunlight. The risk, or even the madness, of the march lay in the fact that the road ran along the top of an embankment: we were perfectly visible to both of the armies hiding in the bush that began about a hundred yards away. One good burst of machine-gun fire in our direction would be enough.

At the beginning everything went well. We heard intense gunfire and the detonation of artillery shells but it was a mile or so away. To keep our spirits up we were all talking (nervously and without necessarily making sense). But soon fear began to take its toll. It is, indeed, a rather unpleasant feeling to walk with the awareness that at any moment a bullet can find you. No one, however, acknowledged fear openly. First, somebody simply proposed we take a rest. So

Honduran troops view the bodies of slain Salvadoran soldiers.

we sat down and caught our breath. Then, when we started again, two began lagging behind—apparently immersed in conversation. Then somebody spotted an especially interesting group of trees that deserved long, careful inspection. Then two others announced that they had to go back because they had forgotten the filters they needed for their cameras. We took another rest. We rested more and more often, and the pauses grew longer. There were ten of us left.

In the meantime, nothing was happening in our vicinity. We were walking along an empty road in the direction of El Salvador. The air was wonderful. The sun was setting. That very sun helped us extricate ourselves. The television men suddenly pulled out their light meters and stated that it was already too dark to film. Nothing could be done—not long shots, nor close-ups, nor action shots, nor stills. And it was a long way to the front line yet. By the time we got there it would be night.

The whole group started back. The ones who had heart trouble, who were going to write general commentaries, who had turned back earlier because they had forgotten their filters, were waiting for us under the tree, beside the two artillery pieces.

The sweaty, unshaven major (his name was Policarpio Paz) found an army truck to carry us to our quarters for the night, in a village behind the line called Nacaome. There we held a conference and decided that the Americans would phone the president to request permission to see the whole front, to go into the very midst of the fighting.

In the morning they sent a plane to take us to the far end of the front, where heavy fighting was in progress. A night rain had turned the grass airstrip at Nacaome into a rust-colored quagmire. The dilapidated DC-3, black with exhaust smoke, stuck up out of the water like a hydroplane. It had been shot up the previous day by a Salvadoran fighter and there were holes patched with rough boards in its fuselage. The sight of these ordinary, simple boards frightened those who had said they had bad hearts. They stayed behind and later returned to Tegucigalpa.

We were to fly to Santa Rosa de Copán. On its takeoff run the plane trailed as much smoke and flame as a rocket starting for the moon. In the air it screeched, groaned, and reeled like a drunk swept along in a hurricane. The cabin—this aircraft usually carried freight—contained no seats or benches of any kind. We gripped curved metal handholds to avoid being thrown against the walls.

In Santa Rosa de Copán, a sleepy hamlet filled just then with soldiers, a truck carried us through muddy streets to the barracks. The barracks stood in the old Spanish fort, surrounded by a gray, moisture-swollen wall. When we went inside we could hear three prisoners in the courtyard.

"Talk!" the interrogating officer was shouting at them. "Tell me everything!"

The prisoners mumbled. They were weak from loss of blood. They stood stripped to the waist, the first with a belly wound, the second with a shoulder wound, the third with part of his hand shot away. The one with the belly wound wouldn't last long. He groaned, turned as if executing a dance step, and fell to the ground. The remaining two went silent and looked at their colleague, with the blunt gaze of landed fish.

An officer led us to the garrison commander. The commander, pale and tired, did not know what to do with us. He ordered that we be given military shirts. He ordered his aide to bring coffee. He was worried that Salvadoran units might arrive at any moment. Santa Rosa lay along the enemy's main line of attack—that is, along the road connecting the Atlantic and the Pacific. El Salvador, lying on the Pacific, dreamed of conquering Honduras, lying on the Atlantic. In this way little El Salvador would suddenly become a two-ocean power. Salvadoran armor had already penetrated deep into Honduran territory. The Salvadorans were moving: push through to the Atlantic, push through to Europe, push through to the world!

Their radio repeated:

A LITTLE SHOUTING AND NOISE
AND THAT'S THE END OF HONDURAS

Weaker and poorer, Honduras was defending itself fiercely. Through the open barracks window we could see officers readying their units for the front. Young conscripts stood in scraggly ranks. They were small dark boys, Indians all, with tense faces, terrified—but ready to fight. The officers said something and pointed at the distant horizon. Afterward a priest appeared and sprinkled holy water on the platoons.

In the afternoon we left for the front in an open truck. The first twenty miles or so passed without incident. The road led through higher and higher country, through green heights covered with thick tropical bush. Empty clay huts, some of them burned out, clung to the mountain slopes. At one point we passed a whole village straggling along the edge of the road, carrying bundles. Later a crowd of peasants in white shirts and sombreros flourished machetes and shotguns as we passed.

Suddenly there was a commotion in the road. We had reached a triangular clearing in the forest where casualties were brought. Some were lying on stretchers, others right on the grass. A few soldiers and two orderlies moved among them. There was no doctor. Nearby, four soldiers were digging a hole. The wounded lay there calmly, patiently, and the most amazing thing was that patience, the unimaginable superhuman endurance of pain so characteristic of Indians. No one was crying out, no one was calling for help. The soldiers brought them water and the orderlies applied primitive dressings as well as they could. What I saw there staggered me. One of the orderlies, with a lancet in his hand, was going from one casualty to another and digging the bullets out of them, as if he were coring apples. The other orderly poured iodine on the wounds and then pressed on a bandage.

Later a wounded boy came in on a truck. A Salvadoran. He had taken a bullet in the knee. He was ordered to lie down on the grass. The boy was barefoot, pale, spattered with blood. The orderly poked around in his knee, looking for the bullet. The boy moaned.

"Quiet, you poor bastard," the orderly said. "You're distracting me."

He used his fingers to pull out the bullet. Then he poured iodine on the wound and wrapped it in a bandage.

"Stand up and go to the truck," said one of the soldiers.

The boy picked himself up off the grass and hobbled to the vehicle. He didn't say a word, didn't make a sound.

"Climb in," the soldier commanded. We rushed to give the boy a hand up, but the soldier waved us away with his rifle. This soldier had something under his skin—he'd been at the front; his nerves were jangly. The boy rested himself on the high tailgate and dragged himself in. His body hit the bed of the truck with a thud. I thought he was finished. But a moment later his gray, naive, quizzical face appeared, waiting humbly for the next stroke of destiny.

"How about a smoke?" he asked us in a quiet, hoarse voice. We all tossed whatever cigarettes we had into the truck.

Now the orderlies were administering intravenous glucose to a dying soldier. This drew a crowd of interested onlookers. Some were sitting around the stretcher where he was lying, others were leaning on their rifles. He might have been, say, twenty. He had taken eleven rounds. An older, weaker man hit by those eleven would have been dead long ago. But the bullets had ripped into a young, strong, powerfully built body, and death was meeting resistance. The wounded man lay unconscious, already on the other side of existence, but some remnant of life was putting up a last desperate fight. The soldier was stripped to the waist, and everyone could see his muscles contracting and the sweat beading up on his sallow skin. The tense muscles and streams of sweat let everyone appreciate what a fierce battle it is when life goes against death. Everybody was interested in that struggle; they wanted to know how much strength there is in life and how much strength there is in death.

"Doesn't anybody know him?" one of the soldiers asked eventually.

The wounded man's heart was working at maximum effort; we could sense its feverish thumping.

"Nobody," another soldier answered.

A truck was climbing the road, its motor complaining.

"Is he ours or theirs?" a soldier sitting by the stretcher asked.

"Nobody knows," said the orderly after a moment's quiet.

"He's his mother's," a soldier standing nearby said.

"He's God's now," added another after a pause. He took off his cap and hung it on the barrel of the rifle.

The man on the stretcher shivered, and his muscles pulsed under his glossy yellowish skin.

Everyone was silent, concentrating on the sight of the wounded man. He was drawing breath more slowly now, and his head had tilted back. The soldiers sitting near him clasped their hands around their knees and hunched up, as if the fire were burning low and the cold creeping in. In the end—it would be a while yet—somebody said: "He's gone. All he was is gone."

They stayed there for some time, looking fearfully at the dead man, and afterward, when they saw that nothing else would happen, they began walking away.

We drove on. The road snaked through forested mountains. Past the village of San Francisco a series of curves began, one after another, and suddenly, around one curve, we ran into the maw of the war. Soldiers were running and firing, bullets whizzed overhead, long bursts of machine-gun fire ripped along both sides of the road. The driver braked suddenly and at that instant a shell exploded in front of us. Sweet Jesus, I thought, this is it. What felt like the wing of a typhoon swept through the truck. Everybody dove for it, one on top of another, just to make it to the ground, to hit the ditch, to vanish.

I plunged forward in the direction that struck me as being quietest; I threw myself into the bushes, down, down, as far as I could get from that curve where we had been hit, downhill, along bare ground, skating across slick clay, and then into the bush, deep into the bush, but I didn't run far because suddenly there was shooting right in front of me, bullets were flying around, branches were fluttering, a machine gun was roaring. I fell to the ground.

When I came to and opened my eyes I could see a piece of soil and ants crawling over that soil.

They were walking along their paths, one after another, in various directions. It wasn't exactly the time to be observing ants, but the very sight of them marching along, the sight of another world, another reality, brought me back to consciousness. An idea came into my head: If I could control my fear enough to stop my ears for a moment and look only at the wandering insects, I could begin to think with some sort of sense. I lay among the thick bushes, plugging my ears with all my might, nose in the dirt, watching the ants.

How long it went on like that, I don't know. When I raised my head, I was looking into the eyes of a soldier.

I froze. Falling into the hands of the Salvadorans was what I feared most, because the only thing I could look forward to then was certain death. They were a brutal army, blind with fury, shooting whomever they got hold of in the madness of the war. In any case, having been fed Honduran propaganda, that is what I thought. An American or an Englishman might have a chance, although not necessarily. In Nacaome, the day before, we had been shown an American missionary killed by the Salvadorans.

The soldier was taken by surprise, too. Crawling through the bush, he hadn't noticed me until the last moment. He adjusted his helmet, which was adorned with grass and leaves. He had a dark, skinny, furrowed face. In his hands there was an old Hauser.

"Who are you?" he asked.

"And what army are you from?" I responded.

"Honduras," he said; he could tell right off that I was a foreigner, neither his nor theirs.

"Honduras! Dear brother!" I rejoiced and pulled a piece of paper out of my pocket. It was the document from the Honduran high command, from Colonel Ramirez Ortega, permitting me to enter the region of military activity. Each newsman had received an identical document in Tegucigalpa before leaving for the front.

I told the soldier that I had to get to Santa Rosa and then to Tegucigalpa so that I could send a dispatch to Warsaw. The soldier was happy; he was already thinking that with an order from the general staff (the document commanded all subordinates to assist me), he could withdraw to the rear along with me.

"We will go together, Señor," the soldier said. "Señor will say that he has commanded me to accompany him."

He was a recruit, a dirt farmer; he had been called up the week before. He didn't know the army, the war meant nothing to him. He was trying to figure an angle that would permit him to survive.

Shells were slamming around us. Far, far away we could hear shooting. Cannons were firing. The smell of powder and smoke was in the air. There were machine guns behind us and on both sides.

His company had been crawling forward through the bushes, up this hill, when our truck came around the corner and drove into the turmoil of war and was abandoned. From where we lay, pressing against the ground, we could see the thick-ribbed gum soles of his company, only their soles, as the men crawled through the grass. Then the soles of their boots stopped, then they moved ahead, one-two-one-two, a few yards forward, and then they stopped again.

The soldier nudged me: "Señor, mira cuantos zapatos!" (Look at all those shoes!)

He kept looking at the shoes of his company as the men crawled forward. He blinked, he weighed something in his mind, and at last he said hopelessly, "Toda mi familia anda descalza." (My whole family goes barefoot.) We started crawling through the forest.

The shooting let up for a moment and the soldier, fatigued, stopped. In a hushed voice he told me to wait while he went back to where his company had been fighting. He said that the living had certainly kept moving forward, because their orders were to pursue the enemy to the very border; the dead would remain on the battlefield, and for them, boots were now superfluous. He would strip a few of the dead of their boots, hide them under a bush, and mark the place. When the war was over, he would come back here and have boots enough for his whole family. He had already calculated that he could trade one pair of army boots for three pairs of children's shoes; there were nine little ones back home.

It crossed my mind that he was going mad, so I told him that I was putting him under my orders and that we should keep crawling. But the soldier did not want to listen. He was driven by thoughts of footwear, and he would throw himself into the front line in order to secure for himself the property lying there in the grass, rather than let it be buried with the dead. Now the war had meaning for him, a point of reference and a goal. Now he knew what he wanted.

I was certain that if he left me we would be separated, and would never meet again. The last thing I wanted was to be left alone in that forest, because I did not know who controlled it or which army was where or which direction I should set off in. There is nothing worse than finding yourself alone in somebody else's country, in somebody else's war. So I crawled after the soldier toward the battlefield. We crept to where the forest gave out, where the fresh scene of combat could be observed through the stumps and bushes. The front had moved off laterally: shells were bursting behind an elevation that rose up to the left of us, and somewhere to the right—underground, it seemed, but it must have been in a ravine—machine guns were muttering. An abandoned mortar stood in front of us, and in the grass lay dead soldiers.

I told my companion that I was going no farther. He could do what he had to do, as long as he didn't get lost and returned quickly. He left his rifle with me and bolted ahead. I was too worried to watch him: worried that someone would catch us there, worried that someone would pop up from behind the bushes or throw a grenade. I felt sick lying there with my head on the wet dirt, dirt smelling of rot and smoke. If only we don't get encircled, I thought, if only we can crawl closer to a peaceful world. This soldier of mine, I thought, is satisfied now. The clouds have parted above his head and the heavens are raining manna—he will return to the village, dump a sackful of boots on the floor, and watch his children jump for joy.

The soldier came back dragging his booty and hid it in the bushes. He wiped the sweat off his face and looked around to fix the spot in his mind. We moved back into the depth of the forest. It was drizzling, and fog lay in the clearing. We walked in no specific direction, just keeping as far as possible from the tumult of the war. Somewhere, not far from there, it must have been Guatemala. And farther, Mexico. And farther still, the United States. But for us at that moment, all those countries were on a different planet. The inhabitants of that other planet had their own lives and thought about entirely different problems. Perhaps they did not know that we had a war here. No war can be conveyed over a distance. Somebody sits eating dinner and watching television: pillars of earth blown into the air—cut—the tracks of a charging tank—soldiers falling and writhing in pain. And the man watching television gets angry and curses because while he was gaping at the screen he over-salted his soup. War becomes a spectacle, a show, when it is seen from a distance and expertly reshaped in the cutting room. In reality, a soldier sees no farther than his own nose, shoots at random, and clings to the ground like a mole. Above all, he is frightened. The front line soldier says little: If questioned he might not respond at all, or a shrug of his shoulders might be his whole answer. As a rule he walks around hungry and tired, not knowing what the next order will be or what will become of him in an hour. War provides an opportunity for constant familiarity with death. This experience sinks deep into the memory. Afterward, in old age, a man reaches back more and more to his war memories, as if recollections of the front expand with time, as if he had spent his whole life in a foxhole.

I asked the soldier why his country was fighting with El Salvador. He replied that he did not know, that those are government affairs. I asked him how he could fight when he did not know what he was spilling blood in the name of. He answered that when you live in a village it's better not to ask questions, because asking questions arouses the suspicion of the mayor. Later, the mayor volunteers him for the road gang. While he's working on the roads a farmer has to neglect his farm and his family, and then the hunger waiting for him is greater. And isn't the everyday poverty enough as it is? A man has to live in such a way that his name never reaches the ears of authority. When the authorities hear a name, they write it down immediately, and that man is in for a lot of trouble. Government matters are not fit for the mind of a village farmer; the government understands such things, but nobody's going to let a dirt farmer understand anything.

At sunset we came to a small village plastered together out of clay and straw: Santa Teresa. An infantry battalion, decimated in the all-day battle, was billeted there. Exhausted and stunned by the experience of the front line, soldiers wandered among the huts. It was drizzling, and everybody was dirty, smeared with clay.

The people from the guardpost at the edge of the village led us to the battalion commander. He sat in an abandoned hut, listening to the radio. The announcer was reading a string of communiqués from the front. Next we heard that a wide range of states from both hemispheres wanted to begin mediation to bring the war between Honduras and El Salvador to an end. The countries of Latin America, along with many from Europe and Asia, had already issued statements about the war. Africa was expected to take a stand presently. Communiqués about the attitudes of Australia and Oceania were also anticipated. The silence of China was provoking interest, and so was that of Canada.

Then the announcer read a report that the Apollo 11 rocket had been launched from Cape Kennedy. Three astronauts, Armstrong, Aldrin, and Collins, were flying to the moon. Man was drawing closer to the stars, opening new worlds, soaring into the infinite galaxies. Congratulations were pouring into Houston from all corners of the world, the announcer informed us, and all humanity was rejoicing at the triumph of rationality and precise thinking.

Finished off by the day's hardships, my soldier dozed in a corner. At dawn I woke him up and said we were leaving. Still half asleep, the exhausted battalion driver took us to Tegucigalpa in a jeep.

The soccer war lasted 100 hours. Its victims: 6,000 dead, more than 12,000 wounded. About 50,000 people lost their homes and fields. Many villages were destroyed.

The two countries ceased military action as a result of intervention by various Latin American states, but to this day there are exchanges of gunfire along the Honduras-El Salvador border, and people die, and villages are burned.

But both governments were satisfied with the war, because for several days Honduras and El Salvador occupied the front pages of the world press and were the object of international concern. Small countries from the third, fourth, and fifth worlds have a chance to evoke lively interest only when they decide to shed blood. This is a sad truth, but so it is.

THE MOMENT BEFORE THE GUN WENT OFF

BY NADINE GORDIMER

AUGUST 1988

Marais Van der Vyver shot one of his farm laborers, dead. An accident, there are accidents with guns every day of the week—children playing a fatal game with a father's revolver in the cities where guns are domestic objects, nowadays, hunting mishaps like this one, in the country—but these won't be reported all over the world. Van der Vyver knows his will be. He knows that the story of the Afrikaner farmer—regional leader of the National Party and commandant of the local security commando—shooting a black man who worked for him will fit exactly *their* version of South Africa, it's made for them. They'll be able to use it in their boycott and divestment campaigns, it'll be another piece of evidence in their truth about the country. The papers at home will quote the story as it has appeared in the overseas press, and in the back and forth he and the black man will become those crudely drawn figures on anti-apartheid banners, units in statistics of white brutality against blacks quoted at the United Nations—he, whom they will gleefully be able to call "a leading member" of the ruling Party.

People in the farming community understand how he must feel. Bad enough to have killed a man, without helping the Party's, the government's, the country's enemies as well. They see the truth of that. They know, reading the Sunday papers, that when Van der Vyver is quoted saying he is "terribly shocked," he will "look after the wife and children," none of those Americans and English, and none of those people at home who want to destroy the white man's power will believe him. And how they will sneer when he even says of the farm boy (according to one paper, if you can trust any of those reporters), "He was my friend, I always took him hunting with me." Those city and overseas people don't know it's true: farmers usually have one particular black boy they like to take along with them in the lands; you could call it a kind of friend, yes, friends are not only your own white people,

like yourself, whom you take into your house, pray with in church, and work with on the Party committee. But how can those others know that? They don't want to know it. They think all blacks are like the big-mouth agitators in town. And Van der Vyver's face in the photographs, strangely opened by distress—everyone in the district remembers Marais Van der Vyver as a little boy who would go away and hide himself if he caught you smiling at him, and everyone knows him now as a man who hides any change of expression round his mouth behind a thick, soft mustache, and in his eyes by always looking at some object in hand, a leaf or a crop fingered, pen or stone picked up, while concentrating on what he is saying, or while listening to you. It just goes to show what shock can do; when you look at the newspaper photographs you feel like apologizing, as if you had stared in on some room where you should not be.

There will be an inquiry; there had better be, to stop the assumption of yet another case of brutality against farm workers, although there's nothing in doubt—an accident, and all the facts fully admitted by Van der Vyver. He made a statement when he arrived at the police station with the dead man in his *bakkie*. Captain Beetge knows him well, of course; he gave him brandy. He was shaking, this big, calm, clever son of Willem Van der Vyver, who inherited the old man's best farm. The black was stone dead, nothing to be done for him. Beetge will not tell anyone that after the brandy Van der Vyver wept. He sobbed, snot running onto his hands, like a dirty kid. The captain was ashamed for him, and walked out to give him a chance to recover himself.

Marais Van der Vyver left his house at three in the afternoon to cull a buck from the family of kudu he protects in the bush areas of his farm. He is interested in wildlife and sees it as the farmers' sacred duty to raise game as well as cattle. As usual, he called at his shed to pick up Lucas, a twenty-year-old farmhand who had shown mechanical aptitude and whom Van der Vyver himself had taught to maintain tractors and other farm machinery. He hooted, and Lucas followed the familiar routine, jumping onto the back of the truck. He liked to travel standing up there, spotting game before his employer did. He would lean forward, bracing against the cab below him.

Van der Vyver had a rifle and .30 caliber ammunition beside him in the cab. The rifle was one of his father's, because his own was at the gunsmith's in town. Since his father died (Beetge's sergeant wrote "passed on") no one had used the rifle, and so when he took it from a cupboard he was sure it was not loaded. His father had never allowed a loaded gun in the house, he himself had been taught since childhood never to ride with a loaded weapon in a vehicle. But this gun was loaded. On a dirt track, Lucas thumped his fist on the cab roof three times to signal: look left. Having seen the white-ripple-marked flank of a kudu, and its fine horns raking through disguising bush, Van der Vyver drove rather fast over a pothole. The jolt fired the rifle. Upright, it was pointing straight through the cab roof at the head of Lucas. The bullet pierced the roof and entered Lucas's brain by way of his throat.

That is the statement of what happened. Although a man of such standing in the district, Van der Vyver had to go through the ritual of swearing that it was the truth. It has gone on record, and will be there in the archive of the local police station as long as Van der Vyver lives, and beyond that, through the lives of his children, Magnus, Helena, and Karel—unless things in the country get worse, the example of black mobs in the town spreads to the rural areas and the place is burned down as many urban police stations have been. Because nothing the government can do will appease the agitators and the whites who encourage them. Nothing satisfies them, in the cities: blacks can sit and drink in white hotels now, the Immorality Act has gone, blacks can sleep with whites... It's not even a crime anymore.

Van der Vyver has a high, barbed security fence round his farmhouse and garden which his wife, Alida, thinks spoils completely the effect of her artificial stream with its tree ferns beneath the jacarandas. There is an aerial soaring like a flagpole in the backyard. All his vehicles, including the truck in which the black man died, have aerials that swing their whips when the driver hits a pothole: they are part of the security system the farmers in the district maintain, each farm in touch with every other by radio, twenty-four hours out of twenty-four. It has already happened that infiltrators from over the border have mined remote farm roads, killing

Greg Voth

white farmers and their families out on their own property for a Sunday picnic. The pothole could have set off a land mine, and Van der Vyver might have died with his farm boy. When neighbors use the communications system to call up and say they are sorry about "that business" with one of Van der Vyver's boys, there goes unsaid: it could have been worse.

It is obvious from the quality and fittings of the coffin that the farmer has provided money for the funeral. And an elaborate funeral means a great deal to blacks; look how they will deprive themselves of the little they have, in their lifetime, keeping up payments to a burial society so they won't go in boxwood to an unmarked grave. The young wife is pregnant (of course) and another little one, a boy wearing red shoes several sizes too large, leans under her jutting belly. He is too young to understand what has happened, what he is witnessing that day, but neither whines nor plays about; he is solemn without knowing why. Blacks expose small children to everything, they don't protect them from the sight of fear and pain the way whites do theirs. It is the young wife who rolls her head and cries like a child, sobbing on the breast of this relative and that. All present work for Van der Vyver or are the families of those who work; in the weeding and harvest seasons, the women and children work for him too, carried at sunrise to the fields, wrapped in their blankets, on a truck, singing. The dead man's mother is a woman who can't be more than in her late thirties (they start bearing children at puberty), but she is heavily mature in a black dress, standing between her own parents, who were already working for old Van der Vyver when Marais, like their daughter, was a child. The parents hold her as if she were a prisoner or a crazy woman to be restrained. But she says nothing, does nothing. She does not look up; she does not look at Van der Vyver, whose gun went off in the truck, she stares at the grave. Nothing will make her look up; there need be no fear that she will look up, at him. His wife, Alida, is beside him. To show the proper respect, as for any white funeral, she is wearing the navy blue and cream hat she wears to church this summer. She is always support-ive, although he doesn't seem to notice it; this coldness and

reserve—his mother says he didn't mix well as a child—she accepts for herself but regrets that it has prevented him from being nominated, as he should be, to stand as the Party's parliamentary candidate for the district. He does not let her clothing, or that of anyone else gathered closely, make con-tact with him. He, too, stares at the grave. The dead man's mother and he stare at the grave in communication like that between the black man outside and the white man inside the cab the moment before the gun went off.

The moment before the gun went off was a moment of high excitement shared through the roof of the cab, as the bullet was to pass, between the young black man outside and the white farmer inside the vehicle. There were such moments, without explanation, between them, although often around the farm the farmer would pass the young man without returning a greeting, as if he did not recognize him. When the bullet went off what Van der Vyver saw was the kudu stumble in fright at the report and gallop away. Then he heard the thud behind him, and past the window saw the young man fall out of the vehicle. He was sure he had leapt up and toppled—in fright, like the buck. The farmer was almost laughing with relief, ready to tease, as he opened his door, it did not seem possible that a bullet passing through the roof could have done harm.

The young man did not laugh with him at his own fright. The farmer carried him in his arms, to the truck. He was sure, sure he could not be dead. But the young black man's blood was all over the farmer's clothes, soaking against his flesh as he drove.

How will they ever know, when they file newspaper clippings, evidence, proof, when they look at the pho-tographs and see his face—guilty! guilty! they are right!—how will they know, when the police stations burn with all the evidence of what has happened now, and what the law made a crime in the past? How could they know that *they do not know*. Anything. The young black callously shot through the negligence of the white man was not the farmer's boy; he was his son.

UNTIME OF THE IMAM

BY SALMAN RUSHDIE

DECEMBER 1988

Gibreel Farishta, for fifteen years the biggest star in the history of the Indian movies, had spent the greater part of his unique career incarnating, with absolute conviction, the countless deities of the subcontinent in the popular genre films known as theologicals. Then, during a near-fatal illness, he used every conscious minute to call upon God, without success; until he lost his faith. On the day he was discharged from the hospital, he told the driver to take him to the Taj hotel, where in the great dining room he devoured a loaded plateful of the forbidden flesh of the swine; rashers of bacon, pork sausages, hams. And after he ate the pigs the retribution began, a nocturnal retribution, a punishment of dreams. In these visions he was always present, not as himself but as his namesake, the archangel Gibreel, large as life. And every time he went to sleep the dreams started up from the point at which they had stopped; they were serial visions, inexorable, impossible to escape. Gibreel, fleeing his old life and arriving in London, brought the visions with him.

This, for instance, has started coming: a mansion block built in the Dutch style in a part of London, which he will subsequently identify as Kensington, to which the dream flies him at high speed past Barkers department store and the small gray house with double bay windows where Thackeray wrote *Vanity Fair* and the square with the convent where the little girls in uniform are always going in, but never come out, and the house where Talleyrand lived in his old age when after a thousand and one chameleon changes of allegiance and principle he took on the outward form of the French ambassador to London, and there it is, a seven-story corner block with green wrought-iron balconies up to the fourth, and now the dream rushes him up the outer wall of

Editors' Note: This story appeared in slightly different form in Rushdie's novel The Satanic Verses.

the house and on the fourth floor it pushes aside the heavy curtains at the living-room window and finally there he sits, unsleeping as usual, eyes wide in the dim yellow light, staring into the future, the bearded and turbaned Imam.

Who is he? An exile. Which must not be confused with, allowed to run into, all the other words that people throw around: émigré, expatriate, refugee, immigrant, silence, cunning. Exile is a dream of glorious return. Exile is a vision of revolution: Elba, not St. Helena. It is an endless paradox: looking forward by always looking back. The exile is a ball hurled high into the air. He hangs there, frozen in time, translated into a photograph; denied motion, suspended impossibly above his native earth, he awaits the inevitable moment at which the photograph must begin to move, and the earth reclaim its own. These are the things the Imam thinks. His home is a rented flat. It is a waiting room, a photograph, air.

The thick wallpaper, olive stripes on a cream ground, has faded a little, enough to emphasize the brighter rectangles and ovals that indicate where pictures used to hang. The Imam is the enemy of images. When he moved in, the pictures slid noiselessly from the walls and slunk from the room, removing themselves from the rage of his unspoken disapproval. Some representations, however, are permitted to remain. On the mantelpiece he keeps a small group of postcards bearing conventional images of his homeland, which he calls simply Desh: a mountain looming over a city; a picturesque village scene beneath a mighty tree; a mosque. But in his bedroom, on the wall facing the hard cot where he lies, there hangs a more potent icon, the portrait of a woman of exceptional force, famous for her profile of a Grecian statue and the black hair that is as long as she is high. A powerful woman, his enemy, his other: he keeps her close. Just as, far away in the palaces of her omnipotence, she will be clutching his portrait beneath her royal cloak or hiding it in a locket at her throat. She is the Empress, and her name

is—what else?—Ayesha. On this island, the exiled Imam, and at home in Desh, She. They plot each other's deaths.

The curtains, thick golden velvet, are kept shut all day, because otherwise the evil thing might creep into the apartment: foreignness. Abroad, the alien nation. The harsh fact that he is here and not There, upon which all his thoughts are fixed. On those rare occasions when the Imam goes out to take the Kensington air, at the center of a square formed by eight young men in sunglasses and bulging suits, he folds his hands before him and fixes his gaze upon them, so that no element or particle of this hated city—this sink of iniquities which humiliates him by giving him sanctuary, so that he must be beholden to it in spite of the lustfulness, greed, and

vanity of its ways—can lodge itself, like a dust speck, in his eyes. When he leaves this loathed exile to return in triumph to that other city beneath the postcard mountain, it will be a point of pride to be able to say that he remained in complete ignorance of the Sodom in which he had been obliged to wait; ignorant, and therefore unsullied, unaltered, pure.

And another reason for the drawn curtains is that of course there are eyes and ears around him, not all of them friendly. The orange buildings are not neutral. Somewhere across the street there will be zoom lenses, video equipment, jumbo mikes; and always the risk of snipers. Above and below and beside the Imam are the safe apartments occupied by his guards, who stroll the Kensington streets disguised as women in shrouds and silvery beaks; but it is as well to be too careful. Paranoia, for the exile, is a prerequisite of survival.

A fable, which he heard from one of his favorites, the American convert, formerly a successful singer, now known as Bilal X. In a certain nightclub to which the Imam is in the habit of sending his lieutenants to listen in to certain other persons belonging to certain opposed factions, Bilal met a young man from Desh, also a singer of sorts, so they fell to talking. It turned out that this Mahmood was scared within an inch of his life. He had recently *shacked up* with a *gori*, a long red woman with a big figure, and then it turned out that the previous lover of his beloved Renata was the exiled boss of the SAVAK torture organization of the Shah of Iran. The number one Grand Panjandrum himself, not some minor sadist with a talent for extracting toenails or setting fire to eyelids, but the great *haramzada* in person. The day after Mahmood and Renata moved into their new apartment a letter arrived for Mahmood. *Okay, shit-eater, you're fucking my woman, I just wanted to say hello.* The next day a second letter arrived. *By the way, prick, I forgot to mention, here is your new telephone number.* At that point Mahmood and Renata had asked for a new ex-directory listing but had not as yet been given their number by the telephone company. When it came through two days later and was exactly the same as the one on the letter, Mahmood's hair fell out all at once. When he saw it lying on the pillow he joined his hands together in front of Renata and begged, "Baby, I love you, but you're too hot for me, please go somewhere, far far." When the Imam was told this story he shook his head and said, that whore, who will touch her now, in spite of her lust-creating body? She put a stain on herself worse than leprosy; thus human beings do mutilate themselves. But the true moral of the fable was the need for external vigilance. London was a city in which the ex-boss of SAVAK had great connections in the telephone company and the Shah's ex-chef ran a thriving restaurant in Hounslow. Such a welcoming city, such a refuge, they take all types. Keep the curtains drawn.

Floors three to five of this block of mansion flats are, for the moment, all the homeland that the Imam possesses. Here there are rifles and shortwave radios and rooms in which the sharp young men in suits sit and speak urgently into several telephones. There is no alcohol here, nor are playing cards or dice anywhere in evidence, and the only woman is the one hanging on the old man's bedroom wall. In this surrogate homeland, which the insomniac saint thinks of as his waiting room or transit lounge, the central heating is at full blast night and day, and the windows are tightly shut. The exile cannot forget, and must therefore simulate, the dry heat of Desh, the once and future land where even the moon is hot and dripping like a fresh, buttered chapati. O that longed-for part of the world where the sun and moon are male but their hot sweet light is named with female names. At night the exile parts his curtains and the alien moonlight sidles into the room, its coldness striking his eyeballs like a nail. He winces, narrows his eyes. Loose-robed, frowning, ominous, awake; this is the Imam.

Exile is a soulless country. In exile, the furniture is ugly, expensive, all bought at the same time in the same store and in too much of a hurry: shiny silver sofas with fins like old Buicks DeSotos Oldsmobiles, glass-fronted bookcases containing not books but clippings files. In exile the shower goes scalding hot whenever anybody turns on a kitchen tap, so that when the Imam goes to bathe, his entire retinue must remember not to fill a kettle or rinse a dirty plate, and when the Imam goes to the toilet his disciples leap scalded from the shower. In exile no food is ever cooked; the dark-spectacled bodyguards go out for takeaway. In exile all attempts to put down roots look like treason: they are admissions of defeat.

The Imam is the center of a wheel.

Movement radiates from him, around the clock. His son, Khalid, enters his sanctum bearing a glass of water, holding it in his right hand with his left palm under the glass. The Imam drinks water constantly, one glass every five minutes, to keep himself clean; the water itself is cleansed of impurities, before he sips, in an American filtration machine. All the young men surrounding him are well aware of his famous monograph on water, whose purity, the Imam believes, communicates itself to the drinker, its thinness and simplicity, the ascetic pleasures of its taste. "The Empress," he points out, "drinks wine." Burgundies, clarets, hocks mingle their intoxicating corruptions within that body both fair and foul. The sin is enough to condemn her for all time without hope of redemption. The picture on his bedroom wall shows the Empress Ayesha holding, in both hands, a human skull filled with a dark red fluid. The Empress drinks blood, but the Imam is a water man. "Not for nothing do the peoples of our hot lands offer it reverence," the monograph proclaims. "Water, preserver of life.

No civilized individual can refuse it to another. A grandmother, be her limbs ever so arthritically stiff, will rise at once and go to the tap if a small child should come to her and ask, *pani, nani.* Beware all those who blaspheme against it. Who pollutes it, dilutes his soul."

The Imam has often vented his rage upon the memory of the late Aga Khan, as a result of being shown the text of an interview in which the head of the Ismailis was observed drinking vintage champagne. *O, sir, this champagne is only for outward show. The instant it touches my lips, it turns to water.* Fiend, the Imam is wont to thunder. Apostate, blasphemer, fraud. When the future comes such individuals will be judged, he tells his men. Water will have its day and blood will flow like wine. Such is the miraculous nature of the future of exiles: what is first uttered in the impotence of an overheated apartment becomes the fate of nations. Who has not dreamed this dream, of being a king for a day? But the Imam dreams of more than a day; feels, emanating from his fingertips, the arachnid strings with which he will control the movement of history.

No, not history.

His is a stranger dream.

His son, water-carrying Khalid, bows before his father like a pilgrim at a shrine, informs him that the guard on duty outside the sanctum is Salman Farsi. Bilal is at the radio transmitter, broadcasting the day's message, on the agreed frequency, to Desh.

The Imam is a massive stillness, an immobility. He is living stone. His great gnarled hands, granite-gray, rest heavily on the wings of his high-backed chair. His head, looking too large for the body beneath, lolls ponderously on the surprisingly scrawny neck that can be glimpsed through the gray-black wisps of beard. The Imam's eyes are clouded; his lips do not move. He is pure force, an elemental being; he moves without motion, acts without doing, speaks without uttering a sound. He is the conjurer and history is his trick.

No, not history: something stranger.

The explanation of this conundrum is to be heard, at this very moment, on certain surreptitious radio waves, on which the voice of the American convert Bilal is singing the Imam's holy song. Bilal the muezzin: his voice enters a ham radio in Kensington and emerges in dreamed-of Desh, transmuted into the thunderous speech of the Imam himself. Beginning with ritual abuse of the Empress, with lists of her crimes, murders, bribes, sexual relations with lizards, and

so on, he proceeds eventually to issue in ringing tones the Imam's nightly call to his people to rise up against the evil of her state. "We will make a revolution," the Imam proclaims through him, "that is a revolt not only against a tyrant but against history." For there is an enemy beyond Ayesha, and it is History herself. History is the blood-wine that must no longer be drunk. History, the intoxicant, the creation and possession of the Devil, of the great Shaitan, the greatest of the lies—progress, science, rights—against which the Imam has set his face. History is a deviation from the Path, knowledge is a delusion, because the sum of knowledge was complete on the day Al-Lah finished his revelation to Mahound. "We will unmake the veil of history," Bilal declaims into the listening night, "and when it is unraveled, we will see Paradise standing there, in all its glory and light." The Imam chose Bilal for this task on account of the beauty of his voice, which in its previous incarnation succeeded in climbing the Everest of the hit parade, not once but a dozen times, to the very top. The voice is rich and authoritative, a voice in the habit of being listened to; well nourished, highly trained, the voice of American confidence, a weapon of the West turned against its makers, whose might upholds the Empress and her tyranny. In the early days Bilal X protested at such a description of his voice. He, too, belonged to an oppressed people, he insisted, so that it was unjust to equate him with the Yankee imperialists. The Imam answered, not without gentleness: Bilal, your suffering is ours as well. But to be raised in the house of power is to learn its ways, to soak them up, through that very skin that is the cause of your oppression. The habit of power, its timbre, its posture, its way of being with others. It is a disease, Bilal, infecting all who come too near it. If the powerful trample over you, you are infected by the soles of their feet.

Bilal continues to address the darkness. "Death to the tyranny of the Empress Ayesha, of calendars, of America, of time! We seek the eternity, the timelessness, of God, His still waters, not her flowing wines." Burn the books and trust the Book; shred the papers and hear the Word, as it was explicated by your interpreter and Imam. "Ameen," Bilal said, concluding the night's proceedings. While, in his sanctum, the Imam sends a message of his own: and summons, conjures up, the archangel, Gibreel.

Gibreel sees himself in the dream: no angel to look at, just a man in his ordinary street clothes, gaberdine and trilby over outsize trousers held up by braces, a fisherman's woolen pullover, billowy white shirt. This dream-Gibreel, so like the waking one, stands quaking in the sanctum of the Imam, whose eyes are white as clouds.

Gibreel speaks, querulously, to hide his fear.

"Why insist on archangels? Those days, you should know, are gone."

The Imam closes his eyes, sighs. The carpet extrudes long hairy tendrils, which wrap themselves around Gibreel, holding him fast.

"You don't need me," Gibreel emphasizes. "The revelation is complete. Let me go."

The other shakes his head, and speaks, except that his lips do not move, and it is Bilal's voice that fills Gibreel's ears, even though the broadcaster is nowhere to be seen, *tonight's the night*, the voice says, *and you must fly me to Jerusalem*.

Then the apartment dissolves and they are standing on the roof beside the water tank, because the Imam, when he wishes to move, can remain still and move the world around him. His beard is blowing in the wind. It is longer now; if it were not for the wind that catches at it as if it were a flowing chiffon scarf, it would touch the ground by his feet; he has red eyes, and his voice hangs around him in the sky. *Take me*. Gibreel argues: Seems you can do it easily by yourself, but the Imam, in a single movement of astonishing rapidity, slings his beard over his shoulder, hoists up his skirts to reveal two spindly legs with an almost monstrous covering of hair, and leaps high into the night air, twirls himself about, and settles on Gibreel's shoulders, clutching onto him with fingernails that have grown into long, curved claws. Gibreel feels himself rising into the sky, bearing the old man of the sea, the Imam with hair that grows longer by the minute, streaming in every direction, his eyebrows like pennants in the wind.

Jerusalem, he wonders, which way is that?—And then, it's a slippery word, Jerusalem, it can be an idea as well as a place: a goal, an exaltation. Where is the Imam's Jerusalem? "The fall of the harlot," the disembodied voice resounds in his ears. "Her crash, the Babylonian whore."

They zoom through the night. The moon is heating up, beginning to bubble like cheese under a grill; he, Gibreel, sees pieces of it falling off from time to time, moon-drips that hiss and bubble on the sizzling griddle of the sky. Land appears below them. The heat grows intense.

It is an immense landscape, reddish, with flat-topped trees. They fly over mountains that are also flat-topped; even the stones, here, are flattened by the heat. Then they come to a high mountain of almost perfectly conical dimensions, a mountain that also sits postcarded on a mantelpiece far away; and in the shadow of the mountain, a city, sprawling at its feet like a supplicant, and on the mountain's lower slopes, a palace, the palace, her place: the Empress, whom radio messages have unmade. This is a revolution of radio hams.

Gibreel, with the Imam riding him like a carpet, swoops lower, and in the steaming night it looks as if the streets are alive, they seem to be writhing, like snakes; while in front of the palace of the Empress's defeat a new hill seems to be growing, *while we watch, baba, what's going on here?* The Imam's voice hangs in the sky: "Come down. I will show you Love."

They are at rooftop level when Gibreel realizes that the streets are swarming with people. Human beings, packed so densely into those snaking paths that they have blended into a larger composite entity, relentless, serpentine. The people move slowly, at an even pace, down alleys into lanes, down lanes into side streets, down side streets into highways, all of them converging upon the grand avenue, twelve lanes wide and lined with giant eucalyptus trees, that leads to the palace gates. The avenue is packed with humanity; it is the central organ of the new, many-headed being. Seventy abreast, the people walk gravely toward the Empress's gates. In front of which her household guards are waiting in three ranks, lying, kneeling, and standing, with machine guns at the ready. The people are walking up the slope toward the guns; seventy at a time, they come into range; the guns babble, and they die, and then the next seventy climb over the bodies of the dead, the guns giggle once again, and the hill of the dead grows higher. Those behind it commence, in their turn, to climb. In the dark doorways of the city there are mothers with covered heads, pushing their beloved sons into the parade, go, *be a martyr, do the needful, die*. "You see how they love me," says the disembodied voice. "No tyranny on earth can withstand the power of this slow, walking love."

"This isn't love," Gibreel, weeping, replies. "It's hate. She has driven them into your arms." The explanation sounds thin, superficial.

"They love me," the Imam's voice says, "because I am water. I am fertility and she is decay. They love me for my habit of smashing clocks. Human beings who turn away from God lose love and certainty and also the sense of his boundless time that encompasses past, present, and future; the timeless time, that has no need to move. We long for the eternal, and I am eternity. She is nothing: a tick or tock. She looks in her mirror every day and is terrorized by the idea of age, of time passing. Thus she is the prisoner of her own nature; she, too, is in the chains of Time. After the revolution there will be no clocks; we'll smash the lot. The word *clock* will be expunged from our dictionaries. After the revolution there will be no birthdays. We shall all be born again, all of us the same unchanging age in the eye of Almighty God."

He falls silent now because below the great moment has come: the people have reached the guns. Which are silenced in their turn, as the endless serpent of the people, the gigantic python of the risen masses, embraces the guards, suffocating them, strangling, and silences the lethal chuckling of their weapons. The Imam sighs heavily. "Done."

The lights of the palace are extinguished as the people walk toward it, at the same measured pace as before. Then, from within the darkened palace, there rises a hideous sound, beginning as a high, thin, piercing wail, then deepening into a howl, an ululation loud enough to fill every cranny of the city with its rage. Then the golden dome of the palace bursts open like an egg, and rising from it, glowing with blackness, is a mythological apparition with vast black wings, her hair streaming loose, as long and black as the Imam's is long and white: Al-Lat, Gibreel understands, bursting out of Ayesha's shell.

"Kill her," the Imam commands.

Gibreel sets him down on the palace's ceremonial balcony, his arms outstretched to encompass the joy of the people, a sound that drowns even the howls of the goddess and rises up like a song. And then he is being propelled into the air, having no option, he is a marionette going to war; and she, seeing him coming, turns, crouches in air, and, moaning dreadfully, comes at him with all her might. Gibreel understands that the Imam, fighting by proxy as usual, will sacrifice him as readily as he did the hill of corpses at the palace gate, that he is a suicide soldier in the service of the cleric's cause. I am weak, he thinks, I am no match for her, but she, too, has been weakened by her defeat. The Imam's strength moves Gibreel, places thunderbolts in his hands, and the battle is joined; he hurls lightning spears into her feet and she plunges comets into his groin, *we are killing each other,* he thinks, *we will die and there will be two new constellations in space: Al-Lat and Gibreel.* Like exhausted warriors on a corpse-littered field, they totter and slash. Both are failing fast.

She falls.

Down she tumbles, Al-Lat queen of the night; crashes upside down to earth, crushing her head to bits; and lies, a headless black angel with her wings ripped off, by a little wicket gate in the palace gardens, all in a crumpled heap. And Gibreel, looking away from her in horror, sees the Imam grown monstrous, lying in the palace forecourt with his mouth yawning open at the gate; as the people march through the gates he swallows them whole.

The body of Al-Lat has shriveled on the grass, leaving behind only a dark stain; and now every clock in the capital city of Desh begins to chime, and goes on unceasingly, beyond twelve, beyond twenty-four, beyond one thousand and one, announcing the end of Time, the hour that is beyond measuring, the hour of the exile's return, of the victory of water over wine, of the commencement of the Untime of the Imam.

WHEN YOU'RE A CRIP (OR A BLOOD)

MARCH 1989

The drive-by killing is the sometime sport and occasional initiation rite of city gangs. From the comfort of a passing car, the itinerant killer simply shoots down a member of a rival gang or an innocent bystander. Especially common among L.A.'s Bloods and Crips, the drive-by killing is the parable around which every telling of the gang story revolves. Beyond that lies a haze of images: million-dollar drug deals, ominous graffiti, and colorfully dressed marauders armed with Uzis. The sociologists tell us that gang culture is the flower on the vine of single-parent life in the ghetto, the logical result of society's indifference. It would be hard to write a morality play more likely to strike terror into the hearts of the middle class.

Many questions, though, go unasked. Who, really, are these people? What urges them to join gangs? What are their days like? To answer these questions, *Harper's Magazine* recently asked Léon Bing, a journalist who has established relations with the gangs, to convene a meeting between two Bloods and two Crips and to talk with them about the world in which the drive-by killing is an admirable act.

The following forum is based on a discussion held at the Kenyon Juvenile Justice Center in south central Los Angeles. Parole Officer Velma V. Stevens assisted in the arrangements. Léon Bing served as moderator.

LÉON BING is a Los Angeles-based journalist. She is currently writing a book about teenage life in Los Angeles.

LI'L MONSTER was a member of the Eight-Trey Gangsters set of the Crips. He is twenty-three years old and currently on probation; he has served time for first-degree murder, four counts of attempted murder, and two counts of armed robbery.

RAT-NECK was a member of the 107-Hoover Crips. He is twenty-eight years old and currently on probation after serving time for attempted murder, robbery with intent to commit grave bodily harm, assault and battery, burglary, and carrying concealed weapons.

TEE RODGERS founded the first Los Angeles chapter of the Chicago-based Blackstone Rangers, affiliated with the Bloods. He is currently the resident "gangologist" and conflict specialist at Survival Education for Life and Family, Inc., and an actor and lecturer.

B-DOG is a pseudonym for a twenty-three-year-old member of the Van Ness Gangsters set of the Bloods. After this forum was held, his telephone was disconnected, and he could not be located to supply biographical information.

LÉON BING: Imagine that I'm a thirteen-year-old guy, and I want to get into a gang. How do I go about it? Am I the right age?

LI'L MONSTER: There's no age limit. It depends on your status coming into it. It's like, some people get jumped in, some people don't.

BING: Jumped in?

LI'L MONSTER: Beat up.

B-DOG: Either beat up or put some work in.

RAT-NECK: Put some work in, that's mandatory, you know, a little mis [misdemeanor]—small type of thing, you know.

It's like this: say I get this guy comin' up and he says, "Hey, Cuz, I wanna be from the set." Then I'm like, "Well, what you *about*, man? I don't know you—you might be a punk." So I might send him somewhere, let him go and manipulate, send him out on a burg' or—

BING:—is that a burglary?

LI'L MONSTER: Yeah. But then, you might know some person who's got a little juice, and, like, I might say, "You don't got to go through that, come on with me. You *from the* set."

TEE RODGERS: If you click with somebody that's already from a set, then you clicked up, or under his wing, you his protégé, and you get a ride in. Now, even though you get a ride in, there's gonna come a time when you got to stand alone and hold your own.

BING: Stand alone and hold your own? Does that mean I might have to steal a car or beat up somebody or commit a burglary?

RAT-NECK: Right.

BING: Is there another way?

RAT-NECK: You can be good from the shoulders.

LI'L MONSTER: Yeah. Fighting.

TEE: That's one of *the* best ways. A homeboy says:
I'm young and mean and my mind's more keen
And I've earned a rep with my hands
And I'm eager to compete with the bangers on the street
'Cause I've got ambitious plans.

LI'L MONSTER: See, when Tee was comin' up—he's *first* generation and we *second* generation. Now, if he saw me, he wouldn't be comin' from the pants pocket with a gat or a knife, he'd be comin' from his shoulders like a fighter. That's what it was established on. Then, later on, come a whole bunch of cowards that *can't* come from the shoulders, so they come from the pocket—

RAT-NECK:—he unloads!

BING: What's the most popular weaponry?

B-DOG: Whatever you get your hands on.

TEE: Keep in mind we don't have no target ranges and shit where we get prolific with these guns.

B-DOG: Shoot 'til you out of bullets, then back up.

RAT-NECK: Bullet ain't got no name, hit whatever it hit.

TEE: Wait a minute! That was a hell of a question, 'cause the mentality of the people that gonna read this be thinkin'—

LI'L MONSTER:—every gang member walks around with that type of gun—

TEE:—and I can hear the police chief saying, "That's why we need bazookas!" Look, put it on the record that everybody ain't got a mother-fuckin' bazooka—or an Uzi. Okay?

BING: It's all on the record.

B-DOG: There *are* some people still believe in .22s.

TEE: Or ice picks. And don't forget the bat.

RAT-NECK: And the lock in the sock!

BING: Are there little peewees, say, nine- to ten-year-olds, in the sets?

RAT-NECK: Yeah, but we say "Li'l Loc" or "Li'l Homie" or "Baby Homie." We never use "peewee" because then people think you're a Mexican. Mexicans say "peewee."

TEE: If it's a Blood set, they use a *k* instead of a *c*. Li'l Lok with a *k*. See, Bloods don't say *c*'s and Crips don't say *b*'s. To a Blood, a cigarette is a "bigarette." And Crips don't say "because," they say "cecause."

BING: What prompted you to join, Li'l Monster?

LI'L MONSTER: Say we're white and we're rich. We're in high school and we been buddies since grammar school. And we all decide to go to the same *college*. Well, *we* all on the same street, all those years, and we all just decide to—

RAT-NECK:—join the gang.

TEE: What I think is formulating here is that human nature wants to be accepted. A human being gives less of a damn what he is accepted into. At that age—eleven to seventeen—all kids want to belong. They are un-people.

BING: If you move—can you join another set?

LI'L MONSTER: A couple weeks ago I was talking to a friend 'bout this guy—I'll call him "Iceman." He used to be from Eight-Trey, but he moved to Watts. Now he's a Bounty Hunter.

B-DOG: Boy, that stinks, you know?

BING: He went from the Crips to the Bloods?

LI'L MONSTER: Yeah. And he almost lost his life.

TEE: When you switch sets, when you go from Cuz to Blood, or Blood to Cuz, there's a jacket on you, and you are really pushed to prove yourself for that set. Sometimes the set approves it, and other times they cast you out. If you don't have loyalty to the *first* set you belong to, what the fuck makes us think that you gonna be loyal to us? That's just too much *information*. Shit, we kickin' it, we hangin', bangin', and slangin'. But who the fuck are you, and where are you *really* at? Where your *heart* at?

B-DOG: Perpetrated is what he is!

BING: What does that mean?

TEE: A perpetrator is a fraud, a bullshitter.

BING: How can someone prove himself?

LI'L MONSTER: All right, like the cat Iceman. They might say, "To prove yourself as a Bounty Hunter you go hit somebody from Eight-Trey."

B-DOG: If you got that much love.

BING: Hit somebody from the very set he was in?

RAT-NECK: Yeah. Then his loyalty is there.

BING: But is it really? Wouldn't someone say, "Hey, he hit his homeboy, what's to say he won't hit us if he changes his mind again?"

TEE: Look, when he changes sets, he's already got a jacket on his ass. And when he goes back and takes somebody else out, that cuts all ties, all love.

B-DOG: Can't go to no 'hood. Can't go nowhere.

RAT-NECK: There it is.

TEE: The highest honor you can give for your set is death. When you die, when you go out in a blaze of glory, you are respected. When you kill for your set, you earn your stripes—you put work in.

RAT-NECK: But once you a Crip—no matter what—you can't get out. No matter what, woo-wah-wham, you still there. I can leave here for five years. Then I gets out of jail, I gets a new haircut, new everything. Then, "Hey, there goes Rat-Neck!" You can't hide your face. You can't hide nothin'! All that immunity stuff—that's trash. Nobody forgets you.

TEE: That's how it goes. Just like L.A.P.D.—once he retire and shit, that fool still the police! He's still strapped, carrying a gun. He's *always* a cop. Same with us. If you know the words, sing along: "When you're a Jet, you're a Jet all the way, from your first cigarette to your last dying day."

LI'L MONSTER: There you go.

BING: Once you're a Blood or a Crip, do you dress differently? We hear about guys with their jeans riding low, their underwear showing up top, wearing colors, and having a certain attitude.

TEE: See, a lot of that is media shit. A brother will get up, take his time, spray his hair, put his French braids in, fold his rag, press his Pendleton or his khaki top, put creases in his pants, lace his shoes, and hit the streets.

LI'L MONSTER: He's dressed to go get busy!

TEE: He's dressed, pressed, he's down!

BING: Is that the way you dress after you're in?

TEE: The reason a lot of brothers wear khaki and house slippers and shit like that is because it's cheap and comfortable.

B-DOG: Ain't no dress code nowadays.

LI'L MONSTER: Look, Rat-Neck got on a blue hat, I got on this hat, we Crips. B-Dog's a Blood: he got red stripes on his shoes, and *that* is that. Now I can be in the mall, look at his shoes, and know he's a Blood. He can look at *my* shoes—these B-K's I got on—and say, "He's a Crip."

RAT-NECK: But then again, might be none of that. Might just be ordinary guys.

BING: I've always thought that B-K stands for "Blood Killers" and that's why Crips wear them.

LI'L MONSTER: It stands for British Knights. I don't buy my clothes because they blue. My jacket and my car is red

L.A. gang members.

and white. I wear the colors I want to wear. I don't have no blue rag in my pocket. I don't have no blue rubber bands in my hair. But I can be walking down the street and, nine times out of ten, the police gonna hem me up, label me a gangbanger—

RAT-NECK:—or a dope dealer.

LI'L MONSTER: There's only one look that you got to have. Especially to the police. You got to look black. *That's* the look. Now B-Dog here's a Blood, and he doesn't even have to be gangbanging because if I'm in a mall with some of my homeboys, nine times out of ten we gonna look at him *crazy*. That's how you know. He don't have to have no red on, we gonna look at him crazy. *That's* the mentality.

TEE: Let me give up this, and you correct me if I'm wrong: police officers can recognize police officers, athletes can recognize athletes, gay people can recognize gay people. Well, we can recognize each other. It's simple.

BING: When someone insults you, what happens?

LI'L MONSTER: Depends on what he saying.

BING: Say he calls you "crab" or "E-ricket." Or, if you're a Blood, he calls you a "slob." These are fighting words, aren't they?

RAT-NECK: It's really just words. Words anybody use. But really, a lot of that word stuff don't get people going nowadays.

LI'L MONSTER: That's right.

TEE: There was a time when you could say something about somebody's mama, and you got to fight. Not so anymore.

LI'L MONSTER: Now just ignore the fool.

TEE: But if somebody say, "Fuck your dead homeboys," oh, *now* we got a problem.

LI'L MONSTER: Yeah, that's right.

TEE: Somebody call me "oo-lah" or "slob," fuck 'em. My rebuttal to that is "I'm a super lok-ed out Blood." There's always a cap back, see what I'm saying? But when you get down to the basics, like, "Fuck your dead homeboy," and you *name* the homeboy, that is death. Oh man, we got to take *this* to the grave.

BING: Well, let's say you're with your homeboys and someone does say, "Fuck your dead homeboys." What happens then?

B-DOG: That's it. The question of the matter is on, right there, *wherever* you at.

LI'L MONSTER: He's dead. And if he's not, he's gonna—

B-DOG:—wish he was.

BING: What does that mean?

TEE: I cannot believe the readers of this magazine are that naive. The point of the matter is, if he disrespects the dead homeboys, his ass is gonna get got. Period. Now let your imagination run free; Steven Spielberg does it.

BING: Why this intensity?

TEE: Because there's something called dedication that we got to get into—dedication to the gang mentality—and understanding where it's coming from. It's like this: there's this barrel, okay? All of us are in it together, and we all want the same thing. But some of us are not so highly motivated to be educated. So we have to get ours from the blood, the sweat, and the tears of the street. And if a homeboy rises up—and it is not so much jealousy as it is the fear of him *leaving* me—I want to come up *with* him, but when he reaches the top of the barrel, I grab him by the pants leg and I—

TEE and LI'L MONSTER:—pull him back down.

TEE: It's not that I don't want to see you go home, but *take me with you!* As a man, I'm standing alone as an individual. But I can't say that to him! I got that manly pride that won't let me break down and say, "Man, I'm scared! Take me with you—I want to go with you!" Now, inside this barrel, we are in there so tight that every time we turn around we are smelling somebody's ass or somebody else's stinky breath. There's so many people, I got to leave my community to change my fuckin' mind!

RAT-NECK: Yeah!

TEE: That's how strong peer pressure is! It's that crab-in-the-barrel syndrome. We are just packed in this motherfucker, but I want to feel good. So how? By bustin' a nut. So I fuck my broad, she get pregnant, and now I got *another* baby. So we in there even tighter. In here, in this room, we can relax, we can kick it, we can laugh, we can say, "Well, shit—homeboy from Hoover's all right." Because we in a setting now, and nobody's saying, "FUCK HIM UP, BLOOD! FUCK HIS ASS! I DON'T LIKE HIM—*KICK HIS ASS!*" You know what I'm saying? That's *bullshit!* We can't just sit down and enjoy each other and say, "Are you a man? Do you wipe your ass like I wipe my ass? Do you cut? Do you bleed? Do you cry? Do you die?" There's nowhere where we can go and just experience each other as *people*. And then, when we *do* do that, everybody's strapped.

RAT-NECK: Seems like nothin' else . . .

BING: You make it sound inescapable. What would you tell someone coming along? What would you tell a younger brother?

RAT-NECK: I had a younger brother, fourteen years old. He's dead now, but we never did talk about it. He was a Blood and I am a Crip, and I *know* what time it is. I couldn't socialize with him on what he do. All he could do is ask me certain things, like, "Hey, bro, do you think I'm doing the right thing?" And, well, all I could say is, "Hey, man, choose what you wanna be. What can I do? I love you, but what do I look like, goin' to my mama, tellin' her I *smoked* you, *smoked* my brother? What I look like? But why should I neglect you because you from there? Can't do that. You my love." And if I don't give a fuck about my love, and I don't give a fuck about my brother, then I don't give a fuck about my mama. And then your ass out, when you don't give a fuck about your mama.

Like some people say, "I don't give a fuck, I'll *smoke* my mama!" Well, you know, that's stupidity shit.

BING: I realize that loyalty is paramount. But what I want to know is, if a rival set has it out for someone, does it always mean death?

LI'L MONSTER: Before anybody go shooting, it's going to be, "What is the problem?" Then we are going to find the root of the problem. "Do you personally have something against Eight-Trey?" You say, "No, I just don't like what one of your homeboys did." Then you all beat him up.

B-DOG: Beat him up, yeah.

LI'L MONSTER: Just head it up. Ain't nobody else going to get in this.

BING: Head it up?

LI'L MONSTER: Fight. One on one. You know, head up. And then it's over.

BING: Are you friends after that?

LI'L MONSTER: Well, you not sending each other Christmas cards.

BING: What if you just drive through another gang's turf? Are you in danger?

LI'L MONSTER: Yeah. I mean, I could be sitting at a light, and somebody say, "That's that fool, Li'l Monster," and they start shooting. That could be anywhere. Bam! Bam! Bam!

BING: Are you targeted by reputation?

LI'L MONSTER: Yeah. That's my worst fear, to be sitting at a light.

B-DOG: That's one of mine, too.

LI'L MONSTER: So I don't stop. I don't pull up right behind a car. And I am always looking around.

B-DOG: Always looking.

LI'L MONSTER: That's my worst fear because *we* did so much of it. You know, you pull up, man, block him in, and—

B-DOG: —that was it.

LI'L MONSTER: They put in work. That is my worst fear. And if you ever ride with me, you notice I always position myself where there is a curb. That middle lane is no-man's-land.

B-DOG: That's dangerous.

LI'L MONSTER: You know how they say, "Look out for the other guy"? Well, I *am* the other guy. Get out of my way. Give me the starting position. You know, because I can— phew! Claustrophobia. I seen that shit happenin', man. I *be* that shit happenin', man, and I don't *never* want that to happen to me, just to be sitting at the light and they take your whole head off.

BING: Say everybody's fired up to get somebody from an enemy set, but there's this young kid who says, "I can't do that. I don't feel right about it—this is a friend of mine." What's going to happen?

LI'L MONSTER: There's many ways that it can be dealt with. Everybody can disown him, or everybody can just say, "Okay, *fine*, but you gotta do something else." See what I'm saying?

B-DOG: But he's gonna be disciplined one way or the other.

RAT-NECK: 'Cause he know everything, man, and he think he gonna ride on up outta here? LI'L MONSTER: So you go home and say, "Yeah, mama. I got out, mama. Everything's cool." And mama looking at *you* like—"Son, are you sure?" 'Cause she knows damn well those motherfuckers ain't gonna let you go that easy.

TEE: Now that's the flip side to those motherfuckers who say, "I smoke *anybody*—I'll smoke my mama!" We, as home-boys, look at him and say, "Your mama carried you nine months and shitted you out, and if you'll kill your mama, I know you don't give two shakes of a rat's rectum about me!"

RAT-NECK: He'll kill me. He'll smoke me.

BING: What's going to happen in 1989? Los Angeles has the highest body count ever. More deaths than in Ireland.

RAT-NECK: Not more than New York. In New York they kill you for just a penny. I took a trip to New York one time. This guy wanted me to see what it was like.

BING: You mean gang life in New York City?

RAT-NECK: No, to see how people live—gang life, the whole environment, the whole everything. I was there for two days, right? He took us to Queens, Harlem, the Bronx— everywhere. We talked about going out strapped. He said, "What the fuck, you can't go out there strapped! What's wrong with you?" But I say I gotta let 'em know what time it is and carry *something*, you know, 'cause we don't really know what's going on in New York. But we hear so *much* about New York, how they operate, how rough it's supposed to be. So, okay, we decide we gonna carry a buck knife— something. So we kickin', walkin', cruisin' the street, everything. And then I see a homeboy standin' right here next to me.

And he come up to us and do some shit like this: he take three pennies, shake 'em, and throw 'em down in front of his shoe. We, like, what the fuck is this? Is it, you got a beef? Like, he knew we weren't from there. So we not lookin' at him, but, like, why the fuck he throw three pennies down there? Like, was it, "Get off our turf"? But we didn't understand his language. Out here, it's like, "What's happenin'? What's up, Cuz? What's up, Blood?" But in New York, you lookin' at the damn pennies, and maybe he come back and hit you. Maybe if you pick up the pennies, then you got a beef with him. Maybe if you don't pick 'em up, then you supposed to walk off. But shit, we lookin' at the pennies, and lookin' at him, and it's like god*damn!* So we walks off and leaves the Bronx and goes to Harlem.

Oh, man—*that's* what you call a gutter. You get to lookin' around there and thinking, "God*damn*, these my people? Livin' like *this?* Livin' in a cardboard box?" I mean, skid row got it goin' *on* next to Harlem. Skid row look like *Hollywood* to them.

BING: Did you vote in the last election?

TEE: Yeah, I voted. But look at the choice I had: Bush bastard and Dumb-kakis.

RAT-NECK: A bush and a cock.

BING: Why didn't you vote for Jesse in the primary?

TEE: I truly believe that shit rigged. Everybody I know voted for Jesse, but—

B-DOG:—Jesse was out.

RAT-NECK: It's different for us. Like, what's that guy's name shot President Reagan? What happened to that guy? *Nothin'!*

BING: He's in prison.

LI'L MONSTER: Oh no he's not. He's in a *hospital.*

TEE: They're *studyin'* him.

RAT-NECK: See, they did that to cover his ass. They say he retarded or something.

B-DOG: See, if I had shot Reagan, would they have put *me* in a mental facility?

RAT-NECK: They would have put you away right there where you shot him. Bam—judge, jury, executioner.

TEE: Why is it they always study white folks when they do heinous crimes, but they never study us? *We* got black psychiatrists.

BING: What about all this killing, then?

TEE: I'm gonna shut up now, because the way the questions are coming, you portray us as animals. Gangbanging is a way of life. You got to touch it, smell it, feel it. Hearing the anger, the frustration, and the desperation of all of us only adds to what the media's been saying—and it's worse, coming out of *our* mouths. There has to be questions directed with an understanding of our point of view. Sorry.

BING: All right. Ask one.

TEE: It's not my interview.

BING: I'm trying to understand your motives. Let me ask a different question: If a homeboy is killed, how is the funeral conducted?

TEE: You got four different sets here in this room, and each set has its own rules and regulations.

RAT-NECK: Okay, like, my little brother just got killed. You talkin' funeralwise, right? At this funeral, Bloods *and* Crips was there. But didn't nobody wear nothin', just suits. *Every* funeral you go to is not really colors.

TEE: Thank you! Yeah!

RAT-NECK: You just going to give your last respect. Like my little brother, it really tripped me out, the way I seen a big "B" of flowers with red roses in it, and one tiny *blue* thing they brought. And these were *Bloods!*—goddamn! Like one of my homeboys asked me, "What's happenin', Rat?" and I said, "Hey, man—you tell *me*." And I looked around, saw some other guys there, you know? They ain't *us*, but they came and showed respect, so—move back. Couple of them walked by us, looked at us, and said, "That's our homeboy, that's Rat-Neck's brother."

When he got killed, you know, I had a whole lot of animosity. I'd smoke any damn one of 'em, but one thing—one thing about it—*it wasn't black people who did it.* That's the one thing that didn't make me click too much. Now, if a black person woulda did it, ain't no tellin' where I'd be right now, or what I'd do, or how I'd feel. I'd be so confused I might just straight out fuck my job, my wife, my kid, whatever, and say, "I don't give a fuck about you—bro got killed!"

BING: How did he get killed?

RAT-NECK: I don't really know the whole rundown.

TEE: What Rat-Neck's saying is the respect. We buried three of our own yesterday, and for each one we went to the mother to see how *she* wanted it—

LI'L MONSTER:—how she wanted it! That's it!

TEE: 'Cause the mother carried that baby for nine months—that's her *child.* It's *her* family, and we're the extended family. She got the first rights on what goes on there. It's the respect factor that lies there, and if the mother says there's no colors, you better believe ain't no colors!

RAT-NECK: And no cartridges in the coffin.

TEE: If he went out in a blaze of glory, and his mama say, "You all bury him like you want to bury him"—oh, then we *do* it.

BING: How would that be?

TEE: If he was a baller—you know what I'm saying—then everybody get suited and booted.

BING: Do you mean a sea of colors?

EVERYONE: *NO!* Suits and ties! Shined shoes!

LI'L MONSTER: Jump in the silk!

TEE: We own suits, you know! Brooks Brothers, C and R Clothiers! And some of the shit is tailored!

BING: You mention your mothers a lot, and I sense a love that's very real. If you do love your moms so much and you kill each other, then it has to be the mothers who ultimately suffer the worst pain. How do you justify that?

B-DOG: Your mother gonna suffer while you living, anyway. While you out there gang-banging, she's suffering. My mother's suffering right now. All my brothers in jail.

RAT-NECK: My mother's sufferin', sittin' in her living room, and maybe there's a bullet comin' in the window.

BING: What do you say to your mother when she says, "All your brothers are in jail, and you're out there in danger"?

B-DOG: We don't even get *into* that no more.

RAT-NECK: She probably don't think about that at all—just so she can cope with it.

B-DOG: Me and my mother don't discuss that no more, because I been into this for so long, you know. When me and my mother be together, we try to be happy. We don't talk about the gang situation.

Spud the Blood and Gangster Todd of the Crips.

LI'L MONSTER: Me and my mother are real tight, you know? We talk like sister and brother. I don't try to justify myself to her—any more than she tries to justify *her* work or how she makes her money to me. What I do *may* come back to hurt her, but what *she* does may also come back to hurt me. Say I'm thirteen and I'm staying with my mother, and she goes off on her boss and loses her job—how does she justify that to *me*?

BING: Well, the loss of a job is not quite the same as an actively dangerous life-style in the streets, wouldn't you agree?

TEE: "An actively dangerous life-style"—that really fucks me up. Okay, here we go. "Woman" is a term that means "of man." *Wo-man.* My mother raised me, true

enough. Okay? And she was married. There was a male figure in the house. But I never accepted him as my father. My mother can only teach me so much 'bout being a man-child in the Promised Land. If, after that, there is nothing for me to take pride in, then I enter into manhood asshole backwards, and I stand there, a warrior strong and proud. But there is no outlet for that energy, for me or my brothers, so we *turn on each other.*

So, Mom sends us to the show, and all we get is Clint Eastwood, *Superfly,* and *Sweet Sweet Bad Ass.* Now what goes up on the silver screen comes down into the streets, and now you got a homeboy. And mama says, "I don't want you to go to your grave as a slave for the minimum wage." So you say, "I am going to go get us something, make this better, pay the rent."

The first thing a successful athlete does—and you can check me out—is buy his mama a big-ass house. That's what we want. And if we have to get it from the streets, that's where we go.

BING: Why?

TEE: It's the same *everywhere.* A sorority, a fraternity, the Girl Scouts, camping club, hiking club, L.A.P.D., the Los Angeles Raiders, are all the same. Everything that you find in those groups and institutions you find in a gang.

BING: So are you saying there's no difference between the motives of you guys joining a gang and, say, a young WASP joining a fraternity?

RAT-NECK: You got a lot of gangbangers out there who are smart. They want it. They *got* what it takes. But the difference is they got no money.

TEE: I know a homie who had a scholarship to USC. But he left school because he found prejudice *alive* in America, and it cut him out. He said, "I don't have to stand here and take this. As a matter of fact, you owe my great-grandfather forty acres and a mule."

LI'L MONSTER: Forget the mule, just give me the forty acres.

TEE: So he took to the streets. He got a Ph.D. from SWU. That's a Pimp and Hustler Degree from Sidewalk University.

A GANGBANGER'S GLOSSARY

Baller: a gangbanger who is making money; also *high roller*

Cap: a retort

Click up: to get along well with a homeboy

Crab: insulting term for a Crip; also *E-ricket*

Cuz: alternative name for a Crip; often used in a greeting, e.g., "What's up, Cuz?"

Down: to do right by your homeboys; to live up to expectations; to protect your turf, e.g., "It's the job of the homeboys to be down for the 'hood"

Gangbanging: the activities of a gang

Gat: gun

Give it up: to admit to something

Hangin', bangin', and slangin': to be out with the homeboys, talking the talk, walking the walk; slangin' comes from "slinging" or selling dope

Head up: to fight someone one-on-one

Hemmed up: to be hassled or arrested by the police

'Hood: neighborhood; turf

Homeboy: anyone from the same neighborhood or gang; a friend or an accepted person; in a larger sense, a person from the inner city; also *homie*

Jacket: a record or a reputation, both within the gang and at the police station

Jumped in: initiated into a gang; getting jumped in typically entails being beaten up by the set members

Kickin' it: kicking back, relaxing with your homeboys

Loc-ed out: also *lok-ed out;* from "loco," meaning ready and willing to do anything

Make a move: commit a crime; also *manipulate*

Mark: someone afraid to commit a crime; also *punk*

O.G.: an abbreviation for Original Gangster; i.e., a gang member who has been in the set for a long time and has made his name

Oo-lah: insulting term for a Blood; also *slob*

Perpetrate: betray your homeboys; bring shame on yourself and your set

Put in work: any perilous activity from fighting to murder that benefits the set or the gang

Set: any of the various neighborhood gangs that fit within the larger framework of Bloods and Crips

Smoke: to kill someone

Top it off: to get along well with someone; reach an understanding

BING: If it went the other way, what would your life be like?

RAT-NECK: I'm really a hardworking man. I make bed mattresses now, but I would like to straight out be an engineer, or give me a daycare center with little kids coming through, and get me the hell away as far as I can. All I want to do is be myself and not perpetrate myself, try not to perpetrate my black people. Just give me a job, give me a nice house—everybody dream of a nice home—and just let me deal with it.

BING: And how do drugs figure into this?

LI'L MONSTER: Wait a minute. I just want to slide in for a minute. I want to set the record straight. People think gangs and drugs go hand in hand, but they don't. If I sell drugs, does that make me a gangbanger? No. If I gangbang, does that make me sell drugs? No. See, for white people—and I am not saying for all white people, just like what I say about black people is not for all black people—they go for college, the stepping-stone to what they want to get. And some black people look to drugs as a stepping-stone to get the same thing.

B-DOG: They want to live better. To buy what they want. To get a house.

RAT-NECK: Not worry about where the next meal come from.

TEE: To live comfortable and get a slice of American Pie, the American Dream.

B-DOG: There it is.

TEE: The Army came out with a hell of a slogan: "Be all you can be." And that's it.

We all want the same thing. We've been taught by television, the silver screen, to grow up and have a chicken in every pot, two Chevys, 2.3 kids in the family. So we have been taught the same thing that you have been taught, but there is certain things that we can hold on to and other things that—we see them, but we just cannot reach them. Most of us are dealing with the reality of surviving as opposed to, "Well, my dad will take care of it."

BING: Are you saying that gangbanging is just another version of the American Dream?

LI'L MONSTER: It's like this. You got the American Dream over there, and you reaching for it. But you can't get it. And you got dope right here, real close. You can grab it easy. Dealing with the closer one, you might possibly make enough money to grab the other one. Then you throw away the dope. That's a big *if* now.

BING: Seriously, does anybody ever stop dealing?

B-DOG: If you was making a million dollars off of drugs, you know what I'm saying, are you gonna give that up for a legitimate business?

TEE: This goes back to it. You started out for need, and now you stuck in it because of greed. That's when you play your life away. There comes a time when you have to stop playing, but as far as the streets go, you are a *street player*. Now there may come a time when you say, all right, I've played, I've had time in the gang, now I got to raise up. But if you is so greedy that you cannot smell the coffee, then you're cooked.

BING: But if you do get out, do you always have to come back when your homeboys call?

LI'L MONSTER: It ain't like you gonna be called upon every month.

B-DOG: But if you gets called, then you must be needed, and you must come.

LI'L MONSTER: It's like this—and I don't care who you are, where you started, or how far you got—you *never* forget where you come from.

TEE: That's it.

B-DOG: You *never* forget where you come from.

Users, Like Me

by Gail Regier

May 1989

Profiles of typical drug users, in the newspapers and on TV, obscure the fact that many users aren't typical. I used to do coke with a violinist who was the most sheltered woman I've ever known. My mushroom connection was a fifty-year-old school-bus driver. And one of my high-school buddies, who moved $1,000 worth of drugs a day in and out of his girlfriend's tattoo shop, would always extend credit to transients and welfare moms— debts he'd let slide after a while when they weren't paid.

It's easy to start thinking all users are media stereotypes: ghetto trash, neurotic child stars, mutinous suburban adolescents. Users, the media imagine, can't hold jobs or take care of their kids. Users rob liquor stores.

Real users, for all their chilly scorn of the straight world, buy into the same myths, but turn them inside out. The condescension becomes a kind of snobbery: we are different from the straight people, we are special, we are more free. We are spiritual adventurers. When I was twenty-four, which was not that long ago, my friends and I thought nothing was more hip than drugs, nothing more depraved, nothing more elemental. When we were messed up, we seemed to become exactly who we were, and what could be more dangerous and splendid? Other vices made our lives more complicated. Drugs made everything simple and pure.

Anyone who hangs around drugs learns not to think too much about all this, learns to watch the bent spoon in the water glass.

Some of the users I knew were people with nothing left to lose. The rest of us were in it only a little for the money, more than a lot for the nights we would drive to one place after another, in and out of people's parties, looking for a connection. It was a kind of social life, and we weren't in any hurry.

What we had in common was drugs. Getting high bound us together against outsiders, gathered us into a common purpose. No one else understood us and we understood each other so well.

New Year's eve 1979: We're riding around trying to cop some speed. My poet friend Brian* is driving and in the backseat is Guy, who is on probation and very uptight because we keep telling him the car is stolen. "You mothers are rounding me," he keeps saying. He doesn't believe us, but the game makes him real paranoid. We make some parties but the speed is always gone before we arrive, so we head for the truck stop where I used to work. The high-school kids who work there always have grass and pills. Their stuff is not so hot, but it's real cheap. Restaurant people have a high rate of casual use; the work's so menial you can't stand it without getting high.

Lynne Bushman

The place is full of tired truck drivers and travelers with whiny kids. The hookers wear miniskirts and army jackets and all have colds. Our favorite waitress, Sherry, combines two parties to get us a booth. She's telling some truckers at the counter about her sexual problems with her husband. They tell her to wear leather panties and she sighs and says that doesn't work.

Fleetwood Mac songs shake the jukebox. Sherry slings us coffee and asks, What's the scam? Brian puts thumb and forefinger to his lips and mimes a toke from a joint. She goes back to the kitchen, and when she comes back tells us that

---

* I have changed the names of those mentioned here for obvious reasons.

Larry is holding. We take our coffee with us through the door marked AUTHORIZED PERSONNEL. Everybody in the kitchen is drunk. Two of the girls are playing the desert-island game: If you could have only two drugs for the rest of your life, what would they be? Sherry pours us some cold duck from a bottle that was in the walk-in cooler.

There was a time when the rap here was all baseball and dates, but not anymore. Tonight the drizzle of abstractions is as vacuous as any graduate seminar. The kids say the owner gives them shit for coming to work stoned. They need their jobs but they know how they want to live. I tell them that the Church of Drugs has its own rituals and rules, and its members are a martyred elite. Brian tells Sherry about acid and stained glass. Guy tells the dishwasher how to tell if it's his starter or his alternator that's bad. The kids listen. They are impressed by us. They want to be like us.

Drug dealers on TV are vampires: oily, smooth, psychotic, sexy, human paradigms of the narcotics they sell. Larry is a skinny punk who is studying auto body at the vo-tech high school. Wearing a GMC cap and a long, stained apron, he stands behind a grease-blackened grill covered with steaks and bacon and skillets asizzle with eggs.

"Watch this shit," he tells another aproned kid, and motions to us to follow him. The kid protests that he'll get behind. Larry leads us back to the storeroom, past shelves of #10 cans and signs that read ALL DELIVERIES C.O.D. and ABSOLUTELY NO FIREARMS ALLOWED ON THESE PREMISES. He takes a baggie from his gym bag and shows us some speeders he says are pharmaceutical. The black capsules have the right markings on them, but they unscrew too easily and the bone-white powder inside isn't bitter enough. We tell him no thanks, but buy a joint from him for a dollar.

When I was selling drugs I made a lot of money, but I usually got stoned on the profits. It was black money and it seemed the highs I bought with it were free and therefore sweeter. I was a college dropout with a kid and a nervous wife. I worked as a cook in a Mexican café fifty hours a week and brought home $200. For that $200 I could buy half a kilo of sinsemilla, break it down into finger bags, and double my money. Selling meant I always had drugs—though we didn't that New Year's eve. Dealing, with its arcana of mirrors and scales, was a guild mystery, a secret, forbidden craft. It was a ticket to places I couldn't get to any other way. I got to know guys who drove Cadillacs and carried forged passports, guys who cooked acid and smack in basement labs, women who wore lots of rings and called every man Jones.

Brian and I smoke the joint on the back porch of the truck stop. The rain, we decide, is very righteous. Eighteen-wheelers grind and hiss their gaudy lights onto the interstate. Diane, a sloe-eyed, peach-skinned fifteen-year-old, comes out and vamps us for a couple of hits. I tell her about those cocaine nights when the room fills with snowflakes sifting down slow as if they were under water. She's kissing Brian and I've got my hand up her short skirt, but she refuses to get in the car with us.

Downtown by the hospital, we get in a confusion with some ambulance guys with their cherry top on. Bald tires skid on the wet pavement. Brian decides to let me drive. We stop at my house, where my wife is watching *Dick Clark's New Year's Rockin' Eve*. Her eyes are red from crying, but she tries to smile.

"Dan and Jan were here," she says. "Don't you remember we invited them?"

I look in the refrigerator for wine. There isn't any.

"Brian and Guy are in the car," I say. "I've got to run them home."

"Then will you come back?"

"Come with us if you want." I know she won't. Our son's asleep upstairs.

"Don't get speed," she says.

"We're not."

"You get mean when you do speed."

I want to get wired. I head for the door.

We make the Steak N' Ale. In a real city there would be black guys pushing stuff on the sidewalk out front, but this is Springfield, Missouri, and we can't score. The manager, our connection, isn't around. At the bar we order shots of whiskey. The place is full of pretty girls, and even the ones who don't drink are drunk, but we're not looking for girls.

Guy says, "We should go see Casey." Casey is an old guy who sold black-market penicillin in post-war Europe. Brian doesn't know Casey but he knows he's expensive, and he fusses about that. But Guy and I are studying on how good Casey's crystal meth is and how Casey could get us a set of points so we could hit it.

On our way we boost three wine glasses and a bottle of Korbel from somebody's table. Sitting in the car, we drink to ourselves and the dying year. Brian wets his fingertip in the champagne and strokes it gently round and round the rim of his glass, making space noises rise from the crystal. We all do it, but then the noises turn spooky and we get paranoid. We drop the glasses out the window and drive.

Prudence is sitting on the front porch watching the rain. She kisses me and I taste her tongue. I introduce my friends and she kisses them.

"Casey's inside."

"Has he got meth?"

She shrugs. The business is Casey's gig. Prudence is twenty and has a cat named Lenin and a one-year-old baby. She's kept the job she had before she moved in with Casey: evening attendant at a laundry near the college. Her place is the cleanest in town. My buddies and I would drop in to wash some jeans and score a little pot, and end up hanging around all evening eating candy bars and flirting with Prudence.

On the weekends Prudence ran a perpetual carport sale, things she made and stuff taken in barter from customers with cash-flow problems. Clothes and belt buckles, pipes and bottles, bootleg eight-tracks and cassettes with typed labels, old skin mags, car stereos and CB radios trailing cut wires.

The living room is brightly lit as always; Prudence leaves her pole lamps on twenty-four hours a day. Casey is sprawled among pillows on an old couch ripe with cigarette scars, culling sticks and seeds from some dope on the glass-topped coffee table. Framed beneath the glass are large-denomination bills from several South American countries. Casey's favorite objects litter the shelf below: brass pipes with small screw fittings, ceramic ashtrays from the commune at Ava, a rifle scope he uses to case visitors coming up the rutted driveway.

A candy dish holds pills—speckled birds and bootleg ludes coloring a base of Tylenol with codeine, bought over-the-counter in Canada. Casey offers us some, and I sift thumb and forefinger carefully through the pile and pick out two black beauties for tomorrow. Brian starts to take a handful and I sign him not to. Casey scarfs codeine the whole time we talk.

Prudence and I go to the kitchen to mix a fruit jar of gin and orange juice, stay there a little while to touch and neck. She has painted everything in the kitchen white, walls and floors and cabinets and fixtures, and in the glare of many bare bulbs the room is stark as a laboratory. White-painted plaster peels off the walls in loops and splinters. There are no dishes or pans; Prudence buys only things she can cook in her toaster oven.

Last time I was over, Casey went after Prudence with a ratchet wrench and I had to talk him down. As we mix the drinks she tells me how she and Casey dropped acid together and now things are better. He's even starting to like the boy. I tell her how my four-year-old thinks acid is the best trick going, because when I'm tripping I play with him so much. We take baths together, drenching the floor with our bathtub games, while my wife sits on the toilet lid, watching us with her bright blue eyes.

On the floor, Lenin and the baby take turns peekabooing and pouncing. I'm surprised the baby isn't scared. I've changed my mind and dropped one of the beauties and I'm feeling edgy and fast and tricky. Lenin rubs himself against my ankles and I grow paranoid.

"You want to help me water the plants?" Prudence asks.

We climb the rungs nailed to the closet wall, push up the trapdoor, and crawl into the attic. Gro-lights illuminate twenty marijuana plants set in plastic tubs. Casey has run a hose up through the wall. I turn the water on and off for her as she crawls back and forth across the rafters on her hands and knees.

Downstairs, I can hear Brian on a rap. "Radiation will be the next great vice. They already use it with chemo to kill cancer. Soon they'll discover wavelengths that reproduce the effects of every known drug. The cops will be able to spot users easy 'cause we'll all be bald."

Prudence digs out a Mamas and Papas tape and plays "Straight Shooter." Casey tells us how some junkies will put off shooting-up until the craving starts, like getting real hungry before a steak dinner. I listen, but to me the addict world is as mythical as Oz. I've met junkies, but they were in town only accidentally and soon moved on to Kansas City or New Orleans. Like a symphony orchestra or a pro sports team, a junkie population needs a large urban center to support it.

Casey says that the word "heroin" is a corruption of the German word *heroisch*, meaning "powerful, even in small amounts." I cruise the bookshelf. A rogues' gallery: Henry Miller, Cocteau, Genet, de Sade's *Justine* in scarlet leather, *Story of O*. Casey explains a William Burroughs story he's just read, about a secret society dedicated to discovering the Flesh Tree described in an ancient Mayan codex. This is the rare and sacred plant from which human life originally derived. According to Burroughs, flesh is really a vegetable, and the human system of reproduction is a perversion of its true nature.

working hard to slip this through. You must really listen if this gets by the censors and everything, because I have limited time and fewer words than I'd like. I would dearly love to be there soon for breakfast and see that cussed little Willie come downstairs grumping like he always does till he's got a touch of coffee in him. I would even like to hear the Claxtons' roosters sounding off again. I remember Poppa, God rest him, saying as how other men kept hens for eggs but the Claxtons kept roosters for their noise and it was our ill-luck to draw such fools as neighbors! The old man that wrote you of my end had the finest gray-white beard and finest speaking voice I ever met with, finer even than Parson Brookes we set such store by. The man who wrote you was here most days after lunch, even ones I now recall but parts of. He brought ward C our first lilacs in late April, great purple ones he stuck into a bedpan near my pillow. Their smell worked better on me than the laudanum that our army chemists so sadly ran out of. He read to us from Scripture and once, my hand resting on his safe-feeling leg, I asked him for a ditty and he said one out that sounded fine like Ecclesiastes but concerned our present war, my war. I told him it was good and asked him who had wrote it and he shrugged and smiled, then he nodded along the double row of cots set in our tent here, like showing me that every wounded fellow'd had a hand in setting down the poem. He was so pleasing-looking and kind-spoken and affectionate, I myself liked him very much. Ice cream he brought us more than once—a bigger vat of it I've not seen even at the Bucks County Fair. Him and our lady nurses kept making funny jokes, bringing around the great melting buckets of it and the spoons, and he himself shoveled a good bit of it into my gullet—grateful, it felt, all the way down. "Now for some brown," he gave me samples, "now pink, but best for you is this, Frank. You've heard Mrs. Howe's line 'In the beauty of the lilies Christ was born across the sea'? This vanilla's that white, white as your arm here. That makes vanilla cool the deepest, my brave Pennsylvania youth." How I ate it. Cold can be good. If you hurt enough, cold can be so good. Momma? I do not love Lavinia like I was forever saying. I do not know how I got into being so mistruthful. Maybe it was how her Poppa was Mayor and I liked the idea of pleasing you with our family's possible new station or how everybody spoke of Miss Lavinia's attainments and her skills at hostessing. It is my second cousin Emily I loved and love. She knew and knows, and it was just like Em to bide that. Em met whatever gaze I sent her with such a quiet wisdom

that it shamed and flattered me, the both. Once, at that Fourth of July picnic where the Claxtons' rowboat exploded from carrying more firecrackers than the *Merrimack* safely could, I noticed Emily near Doanes' Mill Creek gathering lilacs for to decorate our picnic quilt later. You were bandaging Willie's foot where he stepped on a nail after you told him he must wear shoes among that amount of fireworks but he didn't. I wandered down where Emily stood. She had a little silver pair of scissors in her skirt's pocket and I recall remarking how like our Em that was, how homely and prepared and how like you she was that way, Momma. She was clipping flowers when I drew up. I commenced shivering, that fearful of my feelings for her after everybody on earth seemed to think Lavinia had decided on me long since. "Frank," Emily said. I spoke her name and when she heard how I said it, she stopped in trimming a heavy branch of white blooms (you know that place by the waterwheel where there are two bushes, one white, one purple, grown up side by side together and all mixed?). Emily's hands were still among the flowers when she looked back over her shoulder at me. Tears were in her eyes but not falling, just held in place, and yet I saw the light on their water tremble with each pulse from her. It was then, Momma, I understood she knew my truest feelings, all.

"Why is it we're cousins and both poor?" I asked her. "Why could it not be just a little different so things'd fall into place for us more, why, Emily?" and she lifted one shoulder and turned her head aside. She half-fell into the sweet bushes then, white and green and purple, but caught herself and looked away from me. Em finally spoke but I half-heard with all the Roman candles going off and Willie bawling. She said quiet, looking out toward water through the beautiful branches, "We will always know, Frank, you and me will. Hearing as how you understand it, that already gives me so much, Frank. Oh, if you but guessed how it strengthens me just to say your name at night, Frank, Franklin Horatio Irwin Jr., how I love to say it out, sir." Lavinia was calling that same name but different and I turned, fearful of being caught here by her, me unfaithful to the one that loved me if not strongest then loudest, public-like. "Excuse me, Cousin Emily," said I and walked off and then soon after got mustered in, then snagged the minié that cost the leg then the rest of it, me, and no one knowing my real heart.—Mother? I never even kissed her. Momma? Treat her right. Accord my cousin Emily such tender respects as befit the young widow of a man my age, for she is that to me and not Lavinia that made such a show at the funeral and is ordering more styles of black crepe from a Boston catalogue even now, Momma. Have Emily to dinner often as you can afford it, and encourage her to look around at other boys, for there's not much sense in wasting two lives, mine and hers, for my own cowardly mistakes. That is one thing needs saying out.

I used to speak to my bearded visitor about brother Willie and all of you and I thought up things I'd tell my kid brother who has so bad a temper but is funny throughout. I'd want Will to be brave and not do what the town said he should, like pay court on a girl who's snooty and bossy just because of who her kin is and their grand home. I would tell Willie to hide in a cave and not sign up like I did, with the bands and drums and the setting off of all the fireworks not burned up in the Claxtons' calamity rowboat—but, boy, it sure did look pretty going down, didn't it, Momma? My doctor took some time and pains with me and, near the end, got like Lavinia in telling me how fine a looking young man I was. That never pleased me much since I didn't see it all that clear myself and had not personally earned it and so felt a little guilty, not that any of it matters now. The lady from Baltimore combed my hair and said nice things and I am sorry that she never got the watch and the daguerreotypes to you. She is a confidence artist who makes tours of hospitals, promising to take boys' valuables home but never does and sells them in the shops. Still, at the time, I trusted her, her voice was so refined and hands real soft and brisk and I felt good for days after she left, believing Willie'd soon have Poppa's gold watch in hand, knowing it had been with me at the end.

Just before they shot me, Momma, I felt scared to where I considered, for one second, running. No one ever knew of this but I must tell you now because just thinking on my failing cost me many inward tribulations at the last. "I could jump out of this hole and run into that woods and hide and then take off forever." So the dreadful plan rushed forth, and then how I stifled it, choked it practically. I never in my life was thought capable of even thinking such a thing, and here I'd said it to myself! Then, like as punishment, not six minutes after looking toward that peaceful-seeming woods, I moved to help another fellow from Bucks County (Ephraim's second cousin, the youngest Otis boy from out New Hope way) and felt what first seemed an earthquake that'd knocked the entire battle cockeyed but that narrowed to a nearby complaint known just as the remains of my left

leg. It felt numb till twenty minutes later when I seriously noticed. It takes that kind of time sometimes to feel. It takes a delay between the ending and knowing what to say of that, which is why this reaches you six weeks after my kind male nurse's news, ma'am. I asked him once why he'd quit the newspaper business to come visit us, the gimps and bullet-catchers, us lost causes.

He leaned nearer and admitted a secret amusement: Said he was, from among the thousands of Northern boys and Reb prisoners he'd seen, recasting Heaven. Infantry angels, curly-headed all. "And Frank," said he, "I don't like to tease you with the suspense but it's between you and two other fellows, a three-way heat for the Archangel Gabriel." I laughed, saying how the others had my blessings for that job just yet. He kept close by me during the amputation part especially. They said that if the leg was taken away, then so would all my troubles go. And I trusted them, Momma. And everybody explained and was real courteous and made me feel manly, like the loss of the leg could be my choice and would I agree? "Yes," I said.

My doctor's name was Dr. Bliss and during the cutting of my leg, others kept busting into the tent, asking him stuff and telling him things and all calling him by name—Bliss, Bliss, Bliss, they said. It helped me to have that name and word drifting over the table where they worked on me so serious, and I thanked God that neither you nor Emily would be walking in to see me spread out like this, so bare and held down helpless, like some boy. Afterwards, my friend the nurse trained me to pull the covers back, he taught me I must learn to look at it. But I couldn't bear to yet. They'd tried but I had wept when asked to stare at the left leg above where the knee once was. It'd been *left* all right! Walt (my nurse's name was Walt), he said we would do it together. He held my hand and counted then—one, two, three...I did so with him and it was like looking at what was there and what was not at once, just like my lost voice is finding you during this real dawn, ma'am. He told me to cheer up, that it could've been my right leg, and only later did I see he meant that as a little joke and I worried I had let him down by not catching on in time. I have had bad thoughts, lustful thoughts and evil. I fear I am yet a vain person and always have been secretly, Momma. You see, I fretted how it'd be to live at home and go downtown on crutches and I knew Lavinia's plan would change with me a cripple. Lavinia would not like that. And even after everything, I didn't know if I could choose Emily, a seamstress after all, over so grand a place on Summit Avenue as the Mayor'd already secretly promised Lavinia and me (it was the old Congers mansion, Momma).

It seems to me from here that your Frank has cared way too much for how others saw him. It was Poppa's dying early that made me want to do so much and seem so grown and that made me join up when you had your doubts, I know. You were ever strict with me but I really would've turned out all right in the end... if it hadn't been for this.

Momma, by late April, I could feel the bad stuff moving up from the leg's remains, like some type of chemical, a kind of night or little army set loose in me and taking all the early lights out, one by one, lamp by lamp, farm by farm, house by house it seemed. The light in my head, don't laugh, was the good crystal lantern at your oilclothed kitchen table. That was the final light I worried for—and knew, when that went, it all went. But, through chills and talking foolish sometimes, I tried keeping that one going, tried keeping good parts separate, saved back whole. I felt like if I could but let you hear me one more time, it'd ease you some. Your sleeping so poorly since... that's just not like you, Ma, and grieves me here. Dying at my age is an embarrassment, on top of everything else! It was just one shot in the knee, but how could I have stopped it when it started coming up the body toward the last light in the kitchen in my head? You told me not to enlist. You said, as our household's one breadwinner, I could stay home. But the braided uniform and the party that Lavinia promised tipped me over. Fevered, I imagined talking to Willie and all the younger cousins lined up on our front porch's seven steps, and me wagging my finger and striding to and fro in boots like our lieutenant's beautiful English leather boots, such as I never owned in life. I talked bold and I talked

"Young Soldier," by Winslow Homer.

grand and imagined Emily was in the shady house beside you, listening, approving my sudden wisdom that'd come on me with the suffering, and on account of the intestine cramps, and after the worst convulsion Walt got me through, still that lead was coming up the thigh into my stomach, then greeting and seizing the chest and then more in the throat and that was about all of it except for the great gray beard and those knowing eyes that seemed to say, "Yes, yes, Frank," even to my need to be done with it, the pain (the last white pain of it, I do not mind telling you, was truly something, Momma). I couldn't have held out much longer anyway and the idea of choosing between my two loves, plus living on a crutch for life, it didn't set right with vain me.

What I am telling you should include that I hid the five-dollar gold piece I won for the History Prize at the Academy commencement up inside the hollowed left headpost of my bedstead. Get Willie to go upstairs with you and help lift the whole thing off the floor and out the coin will fall. Use it for your and Emily's clothes. Bonnets might be nice with it. Buy nothing but what's extra, that is how I want it spent. I should've put it in your hand before I left, but I planned to purchase my getting-home gifts out of that and never thought I wouldn't. Selfish, my keeping it squirreled back and without once suspecting the prize'd go unspent. But then maybe all people are vain. Maybe it's not just your Frank, right?

If you wonder at the color you are seeing now, Momma, the pink-red like our fine conch shell on the parlor's hearth, you are seeing the backs of your own eyelids, Momma. You will soon hear the Claxtons' many crowers set up their alarum yet again and will catch a clinking that is McBride's milk wagon pulled by Bess, who knows each house on old McBride's route. Your eyes are soon to open on your room's whitewash and July's yellow light in the dear place. You will wonder at this letter of a dream, ma'am, and, waking, will look toward your bedside table and its often-unfolded letter from the gentleman who told you of my passing. His letter makes this one possible. For this is a letter toward your loving Franklin Horatio Irwin Jr., not only from him. It is your voice finding ways to smooth your mind. This is for letting you get on with what you have to tend, Momma. You've always known I felt Lavinia to be well-meaning but right silly, and that our sensible and deep Emily was truly meant as mine from her and my childhoods onward. You've guessed where the coin is stowed, as you did ever know such things, but have held back on account of honoring the privacy of me even dead. Go fetch it later today, and later today spend it on luxuries you could not know otherwise. This is the rich echo that my bearded nurse's voice allows. It is mostly you. And when the pink-and-red opens, and morning's here already, take your time in dressing, go easy down the stairs, let Willie doze a little longer than he should, and build the fire and start a real big breakfast. Maybe even use the last of Poppa's maple syrup we tapped that last winter he was well. Use it up and then get going on things, new things, hear? That is the wish of your loving eldest son, Frank. That is the wish of the love of your son Frank who is no deader than anything else that ever lived so hard and wanted so so much, Mother.

Something holy will stand before you soon, ma'am. Cleave to that. Forget me. Forget me by remembering me. Imagine what a boy like me would give now for but one more breakfast (ever my favorite meal—I love how it's most usually the same) and even Willie's crabbiness early, or the Claxtons' rooster-house going off every which way like their rowboat did so loud. I know what you know, ma'am, and what you doubt, and so do you. But be at peace in this: Everything you suspect about your missing boy is true. So, honor your dear earned civilian life. Nights, sleep sounder. Be contained. In fifty seconds you will refind waking and the standing light. Right away you'll feel better, without knowing why or even caring much. You will seem to be filling,

brimming with this secret rushing-in of comfort, ma'am. Maybe like some bucket accustomed to a mean purpose— say, a hospital slop pail—but one suddenly asked to offer wet life to lilacs unexpected here. Or maybe our dented well-bucket out back, left daily under burning sun and daily polished by use and sandy winds, a bucket that's suddenly dropped far beneath even being beneath the ground and finally striking a stream below all usual streams and one so dark and sweet and ice-cream cold. Your eyes will open and what you'll bring to light, ma'am, is that fine clear over-sloshing vessel. Pulled back. Pulled back up to light. Be refreshed. Feel how my secrets and your own (I know a few of yours too, ma'am, oh yes I do) are pooling here, all mixed now, cool, and one.

I am not the ghost of your dead boy. I'm mostly you. I am just your love for him, left stranded so unnaturally alive—a common enough miracle. And such fineness as now reaches you in your half-sleep is just the echo of your own best self. Which is very very good.

Don't give all your credit to your dead. Fineness stays so steady in you, ma'am, and keeps him safe, keeps him lit continually. It's vain of Frank but he is now asking: Could you, and Willie and Em, please hold his spot for him for just a little longer? do. And Mother? know I rest. Know that I am in my place here. I feel much easement, Ma, in having heard you say this to yourself.

There, worst worrying's done. Here, accepting it begins.

All right. Something holy now stands directly before you. How it startles, waiting so bright at the foot of your iron bedstead. Not to shy away from it. I will count to three and we will open on it, please. Then we'll go directly in, like, hand in hand, we're plunging. What waits is what's still yours, ma'am, which is ours.

—Such brightness, see? It is something very holy.

Mother? Everything will be in it.

It is a whole day.

—One two three, and light.

—Now, we move toward it.

—Mother? Wake!

Stalking the Billion-Footed Beast

by Tom Wolfe

November 1989

May I be forgiven if I take as my text the sixth page of the fourth chapter of *The Bonfire of the Vanities*? The novel's main character, Sherman McCoy, is driving over the Triborough Bridge in New York City in his Mercedes roadster with his twenty-six-year-old girlfriend, not his forty-year-old wife, in the tan leather bucket seat beside him, and he glances triumphantly off to his left toward the island of Manhattan. "The towers were jammed together so tightly, he could feel the mass and stupendous weight. Just think of the millions, from all over the globe, who yearned to be on that island, in those towers, in those narrow streets! There it was, the Rome, the Paris, the London of the twentieth century, the city of ambition, the dense magnetic rock, the irresistible destination of all those who insist on being *where things are happening*—"

To me the idea of writing a novel about this astonishing metropolis, a big novel, cramming as much of New York City between covers as you could, was the most tempting, the most challenging, and the most obvious idea an American writer could possibly have. I had first vowed to try it in 1968, except that what I had in mind then was a nonfiction novel, to use a much-discussed term from the period. I had just written one, *The Electric Kool-Aid Acid Test*, about the psychedelic, or hippie, movement, and I had begun to indulge in some brave speculations about nonfiction as an art form. These were eventually recorded in a book called *The New Journalism*. Off the record, however, alone in my little apartment on East Fifty-eighth Street, I was worried that somebody out there was writing a big realistic fictional novel about the hippie experience that would blow *The Electric Kool-Aid Acid Test* out of the water. Somebody? There might be droves of them. After all, among the hippies were many well-educated and presumably, not to mention avowedly, creative people. But one, two, three, four years went by, and to my relief, and then my bafflement, those novels never appeared. (And to this day they remain unwritten.)

Meantime, I turned to the proposed nonfiction novel about New York. As I saw it, such a book should be a novel *of the city*, in the sense that Balzac and Zola had written novels *of Paris* and Dickens and Thackeray had written novels *of London*, with the city always in the foreground, exerting its relentless pressure on the souls of its inhabitants. My immediate model was Thackeray's *Vanity Fair*. Thackeray and Dickens had lived in the first great era of the metropolis. Now, a century later, in the 1960s, certain powerful forces had converged to create a second one. The economic boom that had begun in the middle of the Second World War surged through the decade of the Sixties without even a mild recession. The flush times created a sense of immunity, and standards that had been in place for millennia were swept aside with a merry, rut-boar abandon. One result was the so-called sexual revolution, which I always thought was a rather prim term for the lurid carnival that actually took place.

Indirectly, the boom also triggered something else: overt racial conflict. Bad feelings had been rumbling on low boil in the cities ever since the great migrations from the rural South had begun in the 1920s. But in 1965 a series of race riots erupted, starting with the Harlem riot in 1964 and the Watts riot in Los Angeles in 1965, moving to Detroit in 1967, and peaking in Washington and Chicago in 1968. These were riots that only the Sixties could have produced. In the Sixties, the federal government had created the War on Poverty, at the heart of which were not alms for the poor but setups called CAPs: Community Action Programs. CAPs were something new in the history of political science. They were official invitations from the government to people in the slums to improve their lot by rising up and rebelling against the establishment, including the government itself. The government would provide the money, the headquarters, and the advisers. So people in the slums obliged. The riots were merely the most sensational form the strategy took, however. The more customary form was the confrontation. *Confrontation* was a Sixties term. It was not by mere coincidence that the most violent of the Sixties confrontational groups, the Black Panther Party of America, drew up its ten-point program in the North Oakland poverty center. That was what the poverty center was there for.

Such was the backdrop one day in January of 1970 when I decided to attend a party that Leonard Bernstein and his wife, Felicia, were giving for the Black Panthers in their apartment at Park Avenue and Seventy-ninth Street. I figured that here might be some material for a chapter in my nonfiction *Vanity Fair* about New York. I didn't know the half of it. It was at this party that a Black Panther field marshal rose up beside the north piano—there was also a south piano—in Leonard Bernstein's living room and outlined the Panthers' ten-point program to a roomful of socialites and celebrities, who, giddy with *nostalgie de la boue*, entertained a vision of the future in which, after the revolution, there would no longer be any such thing as a two-story, thirteen-room apartment on Park Avenue, with twin grand pianos in the living room, for one family.

All I was after was material for a chapter in a nonfiction novel, as I say. But the party was such a perfect set piece that I couldn't hold back. I wrote an account of the evening for *New York* magazine entitled "Radical Chic" and, as a companion piece, an article about the confrontations the War on Poverty had spawned in San Francisco, "Mau-mauing the Flak Catchers." The two were published as a book in the fall of 1970. Once again I braced and waited for the big realistic novels that were sure to be written about this phenomenon that had played such a major part in American life in the late 1960s and early 1970s: racial strife in the cities. Once again the years began to roll by, and these novels never appeared.

This time, however, my relief was not very profound. I still had not written my would-be big book about New York. I had merely put off the attempt. In 1972 I put it off a little further. I went to Cape Canaveral to cover the launch of *Apollo 17*, the last mission to the moon, for *Rolling Stone*. I ended up writing a four-part series on the astronauts, then decided to spend the next five or six months expanding the material into a book. The five or six months stretched into a year, eighteen months, two years, and I began to look over my shoulder. Truman Capote, for one, had let it be known that he was working on a big novel about New York entitled

Answered Prayers. No doubt there were others as well. The material was rich beyond belief and getting richer every day.

Another year slipped by...and, miraculously, no such book appeared.

Now I paused and looked about and tried to figure out what was, in fact, going on in the world of American fiction. I wasn't alone, as it turned out. Half the publishers along Madison Avenue—at that time, publishing houses could still afford Madison Avenue—had their noses pressed against their thermopane glass walls scanning the billion-footed city for the approach of the young novelists who, surely, would bring them the big novels of the racial clashes, the hippie movement, the New Left, the Wall Street boom, the sexual revolution, the war in Vietnam. But such creatures, it seemed, no longer existed.

The strange fact of the matter was that young people with serious literary ambitions were no longer interested in the metropolis or any other big, rich slices of contemporary life. Over the preceding fifteen years, while I had been immersed in journalism, one of the most curious chapters in American literary history had begun. (And it is not over yet.) The story is by turns bizarre and hilarious, and one day some lucky doctoral candidate with the perseverance of a Huizinga or a Hauser will do it justice. I can offer no more than the broadest outline.

After the Second World War, in the late 1940s, American intellectuals began to revive a dream that had glowed briefly in the 1920s. They set out to create a native intelligentsia on the French or English model, an intellectual aristocracy—socially unaffiliated, beyond class distinctions—active in politics and the arts. In the arts, their audience would be the inevitably small minority of truly cultivated people as opposed to the mob, who wished only to be entertained or to be assured they were "cultured." By now, if one need edit, the mob was better known as the middle class.

Among the fashionable European ideas that began to circulate was that of "the death of the novel," by which was meant the realistic novel. Writing in 1948, Lionel Trilling gave this notion a late-Marxist twist that George Steiner and others would elaborate on. The realistic novel, in their gloss, was the literary child of the nineteenth-century industrial bourgeoisie. It was a slice of life, a cross section, that provided a true and powerful picture of individuals and society—as long as the bourgeois order and the old class system were firmly in place. But now that the bourgeoisie was in a state of "crisis and partial rout" (Steiner's phrase) and the old class system was crumbling, the realistic novel was pointless. What could be more futile than a cross section of disintegrating fragments?

The truth was, as Arnold Hauser had gone to great pains to demonstrate in *The Social History of Art*, the intelligentsia have always had contempt for the realistic novel—a form that wallows so enthusiastically in the dirt of everyday life and the dirty secrets of class envy and that, still worse, is so easily understood and obviously relished by the mob, i.e., the middle class. In Victorian England, the intelligentsia regarded Dickens as "the author of the uneducated, undiscriminating public." It required a chasm of time—eighty years, in fact—to separate his work from its vulgar milieu so that Dickens might be canonized in British literary circles. The intelligentsia have always preferred more refined forms of fiction, such as that longtime French intellectual favorite, the psychological novel.

By the early 1960s, the notion of the death of the realistic novel had caught on among young American writers with the force of revelation. This was an extraordinary turnabout. It had been only yesterday, in the 1930s, that the big realistic novel, with its broad social sweep, had put American literature up on the world stage for the first time. In 1930 Sinclair Lewis, a realistic novelist who used reporting techniques as thorough as Zola's, became the first American writer to win the Nobel Prize. In his acceptance speech, he called on his fellow writers to give America "a literature worthy of her vastness," and, indeed, four of the next five Americans to win the Nobel Prize in literature—Pearl Buck, William Faulkner, Ernest Hemingway, and John Steinbeck—were realistic novelists. (The fifth was Eugene O'Neill.) For that matter, the most highly regarded new novelists of the immediate postwar period—James Jones, Norman Mailer, Irwin Shaw, William Styron, Calder Willingham—were all realists.

Yet by 1962, when Steinbeck won the Nobel Prize, young writers, and intellectuals generally, regarded him and his approach to the novel as an embarrassment. Pearl Buck was even worse, and Lewis wasn't much better. Faulkner and Hemingway still commanded respect, but it was the respect you give to old boys who did the best they could with what they knew in their day. They were "squares" (John Gardner's term) who actually thought you could take real life and spread it across the pages of a book. They never comprehended the fact that a novel is a sublime literary game.

All serious young writers—*serious* meaning those who aimed for literary prestige—understood such things, and they were dismantling the realistic novel just as fast as they could think of ways to do it. The dividing line was the year 1960. Writers who went to college after 1960 . . . *understood*. For a serious young writer to stick with realism after 1960 required contrariness and courage.

Writers who had gone to college before 1960, such as Saul Bellow, Robert Stone, and John Updike, found it hard to give up realism, but many others were caught betwixt and between. They didn't know which way to turn. For example, Philip Roth, a 1954 graduate of Bucknell, won the National Book Award in 1960 at the age of twenty-seven for a collection entitled *Goodbye, Columbus*. The title piece was a brilliant novella of manners—brilliant . . . but, alas, highly realistic. By 1961 Roth was having second thoughts. He made a statement that had a terrific impact on other young writers. We now live in an age, he said, in which the imagination of the novelist lies helpless before what he knows he will read in tomorrow morning's newspaper. "The actuality is continually outdoing our talents, and the culture tosses up figures daily that are the envy of any novelist."

Even today—perhaps especially today—anyone, writer or not, can sympathize. What novelist would dare concoct a plot in which, say, a Southern television evangelist has a tryst in a motel with a church secretary from Babylon, New York—Did you have to make it *Babylon*?—and is ruined to the point where he has to sell all his worldly goods at auction, including his air-conditioned doghouse—*air-conditioned doghouse?*—whereupon he is termed a "decadent pompadour boy" by a second television evangelist, who, we soon learn, has been combing his own rather well-teased blond hair forward over his forehead and wearing headbands in order to disguise himself as he goes into Louisiana waterbed motels with combat-zone prostitutes—Oh, *come on*—prompting a third television evangelist, who is under serious consideration for the Republican presidential nomination, to charge that the damning evidence has been leaked to the press by the Vice President of the United States . . . while, meantime, the aforesaid church secretary has now bared her chest to the photographers and has thereby become an international celebrity and has gone to live happily ever after in a castle known as the Playboy Mansion . . . and her erstwhile tryst mate, evangelist No. 1, was last seen hiding in the fetal position under his lawyer's couch in Charlotte, North Carolina . . .

What novelist would dare dream up such crazy stuff and then ask you to suspend your disbelief?

The lesson that a generation of serious young writers learned from Roth's lament was that it was time to avert their eyes. To attempt a realistic novel with the scope of Balzac, Zola, or Lewis was absurd. By the mid-1960s the conviction was not merely that the realistic novel was no longer possible but that American life itself no longer deserved the term *real*. American life was chaotic, fragmented, random, discontinuous; in a word, *absurd*. Writers in the university creative writing programs had long, phenomenological discussions in which they decided that the act of writing words on a page was the real thing and the so-called real world of America was the fiction, requiring the suspension of disbelief. *The so-called real world* became a favorite phrase.

New types of novels came in waves, each trying to establish an avant-garde position out beyond realism. There were Absurdist novels, Magical Realist novels, and novels of Radical Disjunction (the novelist and critic Robert Towers's phrase) in which plausible events and plausible characters were combined in fantastic or outlandish ways, often resulting in dreadful catastrophes that were played for laughs in the ironic mode. Irony was the attitude supreme, and nowhere more so than in the Puppet-Master novels, a category that often overlapped with the others. The Puppet-Masters were in love with the theory that the novel was, first and foremost, a literary game, words on a page being manipulated by an author. Ronald Sukenick, author of a highly praised 1968 novel called *Up*, would tell you what he looked like while he was writing the words you were at that moment reading. At one point you are informed that he is stark naked. Sometimes he tells you he's crossing out what you've just read and changing it. Then he gives you the new version. In a story called "The Death of the Novel," he keeps saying, à la Samuel Beckett, "I can't go on." Then he exhorts himself, "Go on," and on he goes. At the end of *Up* he tells you that none of the characters was real: "I just make it up as I go along."

The Puppet-Masters took to calling their stories *fictions*, after the manner of Jorge Luis Borges, who spoke of his *ficciones*. Borges, an Argentinian, was one of the gods of the new breed. In keeping with the cosmopolitan yearnings of the native intelligentsia, all gods now came from abroad: Borges, Nabokov, Beckett, Pinter, Kundera, Calvino, García Márquez, and, above all, Kafka; there was a whole rash of stories with characters named H or V or K or T or P (but, for some reason, none named A, B, D, or E). It soon reached the point where a creative writing teacher at Johns Hopkins held up Tolstoy as a master of the novel—and was looked upon by his young charges as rather touchingly old-fashioned. As one of them, Frederick Barthelme, later put it, "He talked Leo Tolstoy when we were up to here with Laurence Sterne, Franz Kafka, Italo Calvino, and Gabriel García Márquez. In fact, Gabriel García Márquez was already *over* by then."

By the 1970s there was a headlong rush to get rid of not only realism but everything associated with it. One of the most highly praised of the new breed, John Hawkes, said: "I began to write fiction on the assumption that the true enemies of the novel were plot, character, setting, and theme." The most radical group, the Neo-Fabulists, decided to go back to the primal origins of fiction, back to a happier time, before realism and all its contaminations, back to myth, fable, and legend. John Gardner and John Irving both started out in this vein, but the peerless leader was John Barth, who wrote a collection of three novellas called *Chimera*, recounting the further adventures of Perseus and Andromeda and other characters from Greek mythology. *Chimera* won the 1972 National Book Award for fiction.

Other Neo-Fabulists wrote modern fables, à la Kafka, in which the action, if any, took place at no specific location. You couldn't even tell what hemisphere it was. It was some nameless, elemental terrain—the desert, the woods, the open sea, the snowy wastes. The characters had no backgrounds. They came from nowhere. They didn't use realistic speech. Nothing they said, did, or possessed indicated any class or ethnic origin. Above all, the Neo-Fabulists avoided all big, obvious sentiments and emotions, which the realistic novel, with its dreadful Little Nell scenes, specialized in. Perfect anesthesia; that was the ticket, even in the death scenes. Anesthetic solitude became one of the great motifs of serious fiction in the 1970s. The Minimalists, also known as the K-Mart Realists, wrote about real situations, but very tiny ones, tiny domestic ones, for the most part, usually in lonely Rustic Septic Tank Rural settings, in a deadpan prose composed of disingenuously short, simple sentences—with the emotions anesthetized, given a shot of novocaine. My favorite Minimalist opening comes from a short story by Robert Coover: "In order to get started, he went to live alone on an island and shot himself."

Many of these writers were brilliant. They were virtuosos. They could do things within the narrow limits they had set for themselves that were more clever and amusing than anyone could have ever imagined. But what was this lonely island they had moved to? After all, they, like me, happened to be alive in what was, for better or for worse, the American century, the century in which we had become the mightiest military power in all history, capable of blowing up the world by turning two cylindrical keys in a missile silo but also capable, once it blew, of escaping to the stars in spaceships. We were alive in the first moment since the dawn of time in which man was able at last to break the bonds of Earth's gravity and explore the rest of the universe. And, on top of that, we had created an affluence that reached clear down to the level of mechanics and tradesmen on a scale that would have made the Sun King blink, so that on any given evening even a Neo-Fabulist's or a Minimalist's electrician or air-conditioner mechanic or burglar-alarm repairman might very well be in Saint Kitts or Barbados or Puerto Vallarta wearing a Harry Belafonte cane-cutter shirt, open to the sternum, the better to reveal the gold chains twinkling in his chest hair, while he and his third wife sit on the terrace and have a little designer water before dinner...

What a feast was spread out before every writer in America! How could any writer resist plunging into it? I couldn't.

In 1979, after I had finally completed my book about the astronauts, *The Right Stuff*, I returned at last to the idea of a novel about New York. I now decided the book would not be a nonfiction novel but a fictional one. Part of it, I suppose, was curiosity or, better said, the question that rebuked every writer who had made a point of experimenting with nonfiction over the preceding ten or fifteen years: Are you merely ducking the big challenge—The Novel? Consciously, I wanted to prove a point. I wanted to fulfill a prediction I had made in the introduction to *The New Journalism* in 1973; namely, that the future of the fictional novel would be in a highly detailed realism based on reporting, a realism more thorough than any currently being attempted, a realism that would portray the individual in intimate and inextricable relation to the society around him.

One of the axioms of literary theory in the Seventies was that realism was "just another formal device, not a permanent method for dealing with experience" (in the words of the editor of the *Partisan Review*, William Phillips). I was convinced then—and I am even more strongly convinced now—that precisely the opposite is true. The introduction

of realism into literature in the eighteenth century by Richardson, Fielding, and Smollett was like the introduction of electricity into engineering. It was not just another device. The effect on the emotions of an everyday realism such as Richardson's was something that had never been conceived of before. It was realism that created the "absorbing" or "gripping" quality that is peculiar to the novel, the quality that makes the reader feel that he has been pulled not only into the setting of the story but also into the minds and central nervous systems of the characters. No one was ever moved to tears by reading about the unhappy fates of heroes and heroines in Homer, Sophocles, Molière, Racine, Sydney, Spenser, or Shakespeare. Yet even the impeccable Lord Jeffrey, editor of the *Edinburgh Review*, confessed to having cried—blubbered, boohooed, snuffled, and sighed—over the death of Little Nell in *The Old Curiosity Shop*. For writers to give up this power in the quest for a more up-to-date kind of fiction—it is as if an engineer were to set out to develop a more sophisticated machine technology by first of all discarding the principle of electricity, on the grounds that it has been used ad nauseam for a hundred years.

One of the specialties of the realistic novel, from Richardson on, was the demonstration of the influence of society on even the most personal aspects of the life of the individual. Lionel Trilling was right when he said, in 1948, that what produced great characters in the nineteenth-century European novel was the portrayal of "class traits modified by personality." But he went on to argue that the old class structure by now had disintegrated, particularly in the United States, rendering the technique useless. Again, I would say that precisely the opposite is the case. If we substitute for *class*, in Trilling's formulation, the broader term *status*, that technique has never been more essential in portraying the innermost life of the individual. This is above all true when the subject is the modern city. It strikes me as folly to believe that you can portray the individual in the city today without also portraying the city itself.

Asked once what three novels he would most recommend to a creative writing student, Faulkner said (or is said to have said): "*Anna Karenina, Anna Karenina,* and *Anna Karenina.*" And what is at the core of not only the private dramas but also the very psychology of *Anna Karenina*? It is Tolstoy's concept of the heart at war with the structure of society. The dramas of Anna, Vronsky, Karenin, Levin, and Kitty would be nothing but slow-moving romances without the panorama of Russian society against which Tolstoy

Tullio Pericoli

places them. The characters' electrifying irrational acts are the acts of the heart brought to a desperate edge by the pressure of society.

If Trilling were here, he would no doubt say, But of course: "class traits modified by personality." These are substantial characters (*substantial* was one of Trilling's favorite terms) precisely because Russian society in Tolstoy's day was so clearly defined by social classes, each with its own distinctive culture and traditions. Today, in New York, Trilling could argue, Anna would just move in with Vronsky, and people in their social set would duly note the change in their Scully & Scully address books; and the arrival of the baby, if they chose to have it, would occasion no more than a grinning snigger in the gossip columns. To which I would say, Quite so. The status structure of society has changed, but it has not disappeared for a moment. It provides an infinite number of new agonies for the Annas and Vronskys of the Upper East Side, and, as far as that goes, of Leningrad. Anyone who doubts that need only get to know them.

American society today is no more or less chaotic, random, discontinuous, or absurd than Russian society or French society or British society a hundred years ago, no matter how convenient it might be for a writer to think so. It is merely more varied and complicated and harder to

define. In the prologue to *The Bonfire of the Vanities*, the mayor of New York delivers a soliloquy in a stream of consciousness as he is being routed from a stage in Harlem by a group of demonstrators. He thinks of all the rich white New Yorkers who will be watching this on television from within the insulation of their cooperative apartments. "Do you really think this is *your* city any longer? Open your eyes! The greatest city of the twentieth century! Do you think *money* will keep it yours? Come down from your swell co-ops, you general partners and merger lawyers! It's the Third World down there! Puerto Ricans, West Indians, Haitians, Dominicans, Cubans, Colombians, Hondurans, Koreans, Chinese, Thais, Vietnamese, Ecuadorians, Panamanians, Filipinos, Albanians, Senegalese, and Afro-Americans! Go visit the frontiers, you gutless wonders! Morningside Heights, St. Nicholas Park, Washington Heights, Fort Tryon—*por qué pagar más!* The Bronx—the Bronx is finished for you!"—and on he goes. New York and practically every other large city in the United States are undergoing a profound change. The fourth great wave of immigrants—this one from Asia, North Africa, Latin America, and the Caribbean—is now pouring in. Within ten years political power in most major American cities will have passed to the nonwhite majorities. Does that render these cities incomprehensible, fragmented beyond the grasp of all logic, absurd, meaningless to gaze upon in a literary sense? Not in my opinion. It merely makes the task of the writer more difficult if he wants to know what truly presses upon the heart of the individual, white or nonwhite, living in the metropolis in the last decade of the twentieth century.

That task, as I see it, inevitably involves reporting, which I regard as the most valuable and least understood resource available to any writer with exalted ambitions, whether the medium is print, film, tape, or the stage. Young writers are constantly told, "Write about what you know." There is nothing wrong with that rule as a starting point, but it seems to get quickly magnified into an unspoken maxim: The only valid experience is personal experience.

Emerson said that every person has a great autobiography to write, if only he understands what is truly his own unique experience. But he didn't say every person had *two* great autobiographies to write. Dickens, Dostoyevski, Balzac, Zola, and Sinclair Lewis *assumed* that the novelist had to go beyond his personal experience and head out into society as a reporter. Zola called it documentation, and his documenting expeditions to the slums, the coal mines, the races, the *folies*, department stores, wholesale food markets, newspaper offices, barnyards, railroad yards, and engine decks, notebook and pen in hand, became legendary. To write *Elmer Gantry*, the great portrait of not only a corrupt evangelist but also the entire Protestant clergy at a time when they still set the moral tone of America, Lewis left his home in New England and moved to Kansas City. He organized Bible study groups for clergymen, delivered sermons from the pulpits of preachers on summer vacation, attended tent meetings and Chautauqua lectures and church conferences and classes at the seminaries, all the while doggedly taking notes on five-by-eight cards.

It was through this process, documentation, that Lewis happened to scoop the Jim Bakker story by sixty years—and to render it totally plausible, historically and psychologically, in fiction. I refer to the last two chapters of *Elmer Gantry*. We see Elmer, the great evangelist, get caught in a tryst with…the church secretary (Hettie Dowler is her name)…who turns out to be in league with a very foxy lawyer…and the two of them present Elmer with a hefty hush-money demand, which he is only too eager to pay…. With the help of friends, however, Elmer manages to turn the tables, and is absolved and vindicated in the eyes of humanity and the press. On the final page, we see Elmer on his knees beside the pulpit on Sunday morning before a packed house, with his gaze lifted heavenward and his hands pressed together in Albrecht Dürer mode, tears running down his face, loudly thanking the Lord for delivering him from the vipers. As the book ends, he looks toward the choir and catches a glimpse of a new addition, "a girl with charming ankles and lively eyes…"

Was it reporting that made Lewis the most highly regarded American novelist of the 1920s? Certainly not by itself. But it was the material he found through reporting that enabled Lewis to exercise with such rich variety his insights, many of them exceptionally subtle, into the psyches of men and women and into the status structure of society. Having said that, I will now reveal something that practically every writer has experienced—and none, as far as I know, has ever talked about. The young person who decides to become a writer because he has a subject or an issue in mind, because he has "something to say," is a rare bird. Most make that decision because they realize they have a certain musical facility with words. Since poetry is the music of language, outstanding young poets are by no means rare. As he grows older, however, our young genius keeps running into this damnable problem of *material*, of what to write about, since by now he realizes that literature's main arena is prose, whether in fiction or the essay. Even so, he keeps things in proportion. He tells himself that 95 percent of literary genius is the unique talent that is secure inside some sort of crucible in his skull and 5 percent is the material, the clay his talent will mold.

I can remember going through this stage myself. In college, at Washington and Lee, I decided I would write crystalline prose. That was the word: *crystalline*. It would be a prose as ageless, timeless, exquisite, soaring, and transparently dazzling as Scarlatti at his most sublime. It would speak to the twenty-fifth century as lucidly as to my own. (I was, naturally, interested to hear, years later, that Iris Murdoch had dreamed of the same quality and chosen the same word, *crystalline*, at a similar point in her life.) In graduate school at Yale, I came upon the Elizabethan books of rhetoric, which isolated, by my count, 444 figures of speech, covering every conceivable form of wordplay. By analyzing the prose of writers I admired—De Quincey, I remember, was one of them—I tried to come up with the perfect sequences of figures and make notations for them, like musical notes. I would flesh out this perfect skeleton with some material when the time came.

Such experiments don't last very long, of course. The damnable beast, material, keeps getting bigger and more obnoxious. Finally, you realize you have a choice. Either hide from it, wish it away, or wrestle with it. I doubt that there is a writer over forty who does not realize in his heart of hearts that literary genius, in prose, consists of proportions more on the order of 65 percent material and 35 percent of the talent in the sacred crucible.

I never doubted for a moment that to write a long piece of fiction about New York City I would have to do the same sort of reporting I had done for *The Right Stuff* or *Radical Chic & Mau-mauing the Flak Catchers*, even though by now I had lived in New York for almost twenty years. By 1981, when I started work in earnest, I could see that Thackeray's *Vanity Fair* would not be an adequate model. *Vanity Fair* deals chiefly with the upper orders of British society. A book about New York in the 1980s would have to deal with New York high and low. So I chose Wall Street as the high end of the scale and the South Bronx as the low. I knew a few more people on Wall Street than in the South Bronx, but both were terrae incognitae as far as my own experience was concerned. I headed forth into I knew not exactly what. Any big book about New York, I figured, should have at least one subway scene. I started riding the subways in the Bronx. One evening I looked across the car and saw someone I knew sitting there in a strange rig. He was a Wall Street broker I hadn't seen for nine or ten years. He was dressed in a business suit, but his pants legs were rolled up three or four hitches, revealing a pair of olive green army surplus socks, two bony lengths of shin, and some decomposing striped orthotic running shoes. On the floor between his feet was an A&P shopping bag made of slippery white polyethylene. He had on a dirty raincoat and a greasy rain hat, and his eyes were darting from one end of the car to the other. I went over, said hello, and learned the following. He and his family lived in the far North Bronx, where there are to this day some lovely, leafy Westchester-style neighborhoods, and he worked on Wall Street. The subways provided fine service, except that lately there had been a problem. Packs of young toughs had taken to roaming the cars. They would pick out a likely prey, close in on his seat, hem him in, and ask for money. They kept their hands in their pockets and never produced weapons, but their leering, menacing looks were usually enough. When this fellow's turn came, he had capitulated, given them all he had—and he'd been a nervous wreck on the subway ever since. He had taken to traveling to and from Wall Street in this pathetic disguise in order to avoid looking worth robbing. In the A&P shopping bag he carried his Wall Street shoes and socks.

I decided I would use such a situation in my book. It was here that I began to run into not Roth's Lament but Muggeridge's Law. While Malcolm Muggeridge was editor of *Punch*, it was announced that Khrushchev and Bulganin were coming to England. Muggeridge hit upon the idea of a mock itinerary, a lineup of the most ludicrous places the two paunchy, pear-shaped little Soviet leaders could possibly be paraded through during the solemn business of a state visit. Shortly before press time, half the feature had to be scrapped. It coincided exactly with the official itinerary, just released, prompting Muggeridge to observe: We live in an age in which it is no longer possible to be funny. There is nothing you can imagine, no matter how ludicrous, that will not promptly be enacted before your very eyes, probably by someone well known.

This immediately became my problem. I first wrote *The Bonfire of the Vanities* serially for *Rolling Stone*, producing a chapter every two weeks with a gun at my temple. In the third chapter, I introduced one of my main characters, a thirty-two-year-old Bronx assistant district attorney named Larry Kramer, sitting in a subway car dressed as my friend had been dressed, his eyes jumping about in a bughouse manner. This was supposed to create unbearable suspense in the readers. What on earth had reduced this otherwise healthy young man to such a pathetic state? This chapter appeared in July of 1984. In an installment scheduled for April of 1985, the readers would learn of his humiliation by a wolfpack, who had taken all his money plus his little district attorney's badge. But it so happened that in December of 1984 a young man named Bernhard Goetz found himself in an identical situation on a subway in New York, hemmed in by four youths who were, in fact, from the South Bronx. Far from caving in, he pulled out a .38-caliber revolver and shot all four of them and became one of the most notorious figures in America. Now, how could I, four months later, in April of 1985, proceed with my plan? People would say, This poor fellow Wolfe, he has no imagination. He reads the newspapers, gets these obvious ideas, and then gives us this wimp Kramer, who caves in. So I abandoned the plan, dropped it altogether. The *Rolling Stone* readers' burning thirst, if any, to know what accounted for Assistant D.A. Kramer's pitiful costume and alarming facial tics was never slaked.

In one area, however, I was well ahead of the news, and this lent the book a curious kind of alter-life. The plot turns on a severe injury to a black youth in an incident involving a white couple in an automobile. While the youth lies in a coma, various forces close in on the case—the press, politicians, prosecutors, real estate brokers, black activists—each eager, for private reasons, to turn the matter into a racial Armageddon. Supreme among them is Reverend Bacon, a Harlem minister, a genius at handling the press who soon has the entire city throbbing to the young man's outrageous fate. In the book, the incident casts its shadow across the upcoming elections and threatens to cost the white mayor City Hall.

The Bonfire of the Vanities reached bookstores in October of 1987, a week before the Wall Street crash. From the start, in the press, there was a certain amount of grumbling, some of it not very nice, about my depiction of Reverend Bacon. He was a grotesque caricature of a black activist, grotesque or worse. Then, barely three months later, the Tawana Brawley case broke. At the forefront of the Brawley case appeared an activist black minister, the Reverend Al Sharpton, who was indeed a genius at handling the press, even when he was in the tightest corners. At one point the New York *Post* got a tip that Sharpton was having his long Byronic hair coiffed at a beauty parlor in Brooklyn. A reporter and photographer waited until he was socketed in under the dryer, then burst in. Far from throwing up his hands and crying out about invasion of privacy, Sharpton nonchalantly beckoned to his stalkers. "Come on in, boys, and bring your cameras. I want you to see how...a real man...gets his hair done." Just like that!—another Sharpton media triumph, under the heading of "Masculinity to Burn." In fact, Sharpton was so flamboyant, the grumbling about Reverend Bacon swung around 180 degrees. Now I heard people complain, This poor fellow Wolfe, he has no imagination. Here, on the front page of every newspaper, are the real goods—and he gives us this little divinity student, Reverend Bacon.

But I also began to hear and read with increasing frequency that *The Bonfire of the Vanities* was "prophetic." The Brawley case turned out to be only one in a series of racial incidents in which young black people were, or were seen as, the victims of white brutality. And these incidents did, indeed, cast their shadow across the race for mayor in New York City. As in the prologue to the book, the mayor, in real life, was heckled, harassed, and shouted down by demonstrators in Harlem, although he was never forced to flee the podium. And perhaps these incidents were among the factors that cost the white mayor City Hall. But not for a moment did I ever think of *The Bonfire of the Vanities* as prophetic. The book only showed what was obvious to anyone who had done what I did, even as far back as the early Eighties, when I began; anyone who had gone out and looked frankly at the new face of the city and paid attention not only to what the voices said but also to the roar.

This brings me to one last point. It is not merely that reporting is useful in gathering the *petits faits vrais* that create verisimilitude and make a novel gripping or absorbing, although that side of the enterprise is worth paying attention to. My contention is that, especially in an age like this, they are essential for the very greatest effects literature can achieve. In 1884 Zola went down into the mines at Anzin to do the documentation for what was to become the novel *Germinal*. Posing as a secretary for a member of the French Chamber of Deputies, he descended into the pits wearing his city clothes, his frock coat, high stiff collar, and high stiff hat (this appeals to me for reasons I won't delay you with), and carrying a notebook and pen. One day Zola and the miners who were serving as his guides were 150 feet below the ground when Zola noticed an enormous workhorse, a Percheron, pulling a sled piled with coal through a tunnel. Zola asked, "How do you get that animal in and out of the mine every day?" At first the miners thought he was joking. Then they realized he was serious, and one of them said, "Mr. Zola, don't you understand? That horse comes down here *once*, when he's a colt, barely more than a foal, and still able to fit into the buckets that bring *us* down here. That horse grows up down here. He grows blind down here after a year or two, from the lack of light. He hauls coal down here until he can't haul it anymore, and then he dies down here, and his bones are buried down here." When Zola transfers this revelation from the pages of his documentation notebook to the pages of *Germinal*, it makes the hair on your arms stand on end. You realize, without the need of amplification, that the horse is the miners themselves, who descend below the face of the earth as children and dig coal down in the pit until they can dig no more and then are buried, often literally, down there.

The moment of The Horse in *Germinal* is one of the supreme moments in French literature—and it would have been impossible without that peculiar drudgery that Zola called documentation. At this weak, pale, tabescent moment in the history of American literature, we need a battalion, a brigade, of Zolas to head out into this wild, bizarre, unpredictable, Hog-stomping Baroque country of ours and reclaim it as literary property. Philip Roth was absolutely right. The imagination of the novelist is powerless before what he knows he's going to read in tomorrow morning's newspaper. But a generation of American writers has drawn precisely the wrong conclusion from that perfectly valid observation. The answer is not to leave the rude beast, the material, also known as the life around us, to the journalists but to do what journalists do, or are supposed to do, which is to wrestle the beast and bring it to terms.

Of one thing I am sure. If fiction writers do not start facing the obvious, the literary history of the second half of the twentieth century will record that journalists not only took over the richness of American life as their domain but also seized the high ground of literature itself. Any literary person who is willing to look back over the American literary terrain of the past twenty-five years—look back candidly, in the solitude of the study—will admit that in at least four years out of five the best nonfiction books have been *better literature* than the most highly praised books of fiction. Any truly candid observer will go still further. In many years, the most highly praised books of fiction have been overshadowed *in literary terms* by writers whom literary people customarily dismiss as "writers of popular fiction" (a curious epithet) or as genre novelists. I am thinking of novelists such as John le Carré and Joseph Wambaugh. Leaving the question of talent aside, Le Carré and Wambaugh have one enormous advantage over their more literary confreres. They are not only willing to wrestle the beast; they actually love the battle.

In 1973, in *The New Journalism*, I wrote that nonfiction had displaced the novel as American literature's "main event." That was not quite the same as saying that nonfiction had dethroned the novel, but it was close enough. At the time, it was a rash statement, but *como Fidel lo ha dijo*, history will absolve me. Unless some movement occurs in American fiction over the next ten years that is more remarkable than any detectable right now, the pioneering in nonfiction will be recorded as the most important experiment in American literature in the second half of the twentieth century.

I speak as a journalist, with some enthusiasm, as you can detect, a journalist who has tried to capture the beast in long narratives of both nonfiction and fiction. I started writing *The Bonfire of the Vanities* with the supreme confidence available only to a writer who doesn't know quite what he is getting into. I was soon plunged into despair. One very obvious matter I had not reckoned with: In nonfiction you are very conveniently provided with the setting and the characters and the plot. You now have the task—and it is a huge one—of bringing it all alive as convincingly as the best of realistic fiction. But you don't have to concoct the story. Indeed, you can't. I found the sudden freedom of fiction intimidating. It was at least a year before I felt comfortable enough to use that freedom's advantages, which are formidable. The past three decades have been decades of tremendous and at times convulsive social change, especially in large cities, and the tide of the fourth great wave of immigration has made the picture seem all the more chaotic, random, and discontinuous, to use the literary clichés of the recent past. The economy with which realistic fiction can bring the many currents of a city together in a single, fairly simple story was something that I eventually found exhilarating. It is a facility that is not available to the journalist, and it seems more useful with each passing month. Despite all the current talk of "coming together," I see the fast-multiplying factions of the modern cities trying to insulate themselves more diligently than ever before. However brilliant and ambitious, a nonfiction novel about, say, the Tawana Brawley case could not get all of New York in 1989 between two covers. It could illuminate many things, most especially the press and the workings of the justice system, but it would not reach into Wall Street or Park Avenue, precincts even the resourceful Al Sharpton does not frequent. In 1970 the Black Panthers *did* turn up in Leonard Bernstein's living room. Today, there is no chic, radical or otherwise, in mixing colors in the grand salons.

So the doors close and the walls go up! It is merely another open invitation to literature, especially in the form of the novel. And how can any writer, in fiction or nonfiction, resist going to the beano, to the rout! At the end of *Dead Souls*, Gogol asks, "Whither art thou soaring away to, then, Russia? Give me an answer!" Russia gives none but only goes faster, and "the air, rent to shreds, thunders and turns to wind," and Gogol hangs on, breathless, his eyes filled with wonder. America today, in a headlong rush of her own, may or may not truly need a literature worthy of her vastness. But American novelists, without any doubt, truly need, in this neurasthenic hour, the spirit to go along for that wild ride.

1990's

CHRONICLE OF A DEBACLE FORETOLD

BY L. J. DAVIS

SEPTEMBER 1990

Ever since the first Florentine loaned his first ducat to his first Medici, it has been one of the most shopworn clichés of the financial industry that the best way to rob a bank is to own one. This maxim, like all maxims, is rooted in a basic truth about human nature: To wit, if criminals are given easy access to large sums of money, they will steal, and under such tempting circumstances even honest men may be corrupted. To forget this is to invite madness and ruin. In our time, such madness and ruin has visited in the form of the savings and loan scandal.

Perhaps a thorough understanding of the scandal—and, in particular, an understanding of the fact that the scandal will cost American taxpayers an estimated $500 billion, though this latest figure is entirely untrustworthy and may well be higher—will aid our powers of recall should there be a next time, as the runs on banks that followed the stock market crash of 1929 no doubt quickened the concentration of Franklin Delano Roosevelt. Roosevelt, at least compared with the politicians of our moment, understood the nature of man, notably Banking Man. He had seen for himself the failure of more than 1,700 of the country's 12,000 or so S&Ls and had glimpsed as well the unwillingness of depositors to return their savings to the S&Ls—where they had lost millions—despite the 1932 signing into law by Herbert Hoover of the Federal Home Loan Bank Act, which for the first time brought the S&L industry under the watchful eye of federal examiners.

To bolster confidence in the system, Roosevelt eventually acquiesced in a plan, urged by populists in Congress, to have the federal government guarantee deposits of up to $5,000 placed in an S&L. The Federal Savings and Loan Insurance Corporation (FSLIC) would build its fund with modest premiums paid by member thrifts. But if, somehow, too many banks should fail, and the fund become exhausted, it would be the taxpayers who would pick up the bill, because

the FSLIC was eventually backed by the full faith and credit of the federal government. Roosevelt therefore insisted on strict regulation and monitoring of any bank so insured.

"We do not wish to make the United States government liable for the mistakes and errors of individual banks," he declared, "and put a premium on unsound banking in the future." Less delicately put, Roosevelt didn't want the fiduciary classes to begin each business day with the wild sense of freedom and confidence that somehow seems to take hold when one is gambling with someone else's—in this case, the federal government's—money. After all, bankers loaning and investing money that they, in effect, *could not lose* were capable of... Well, what *weren't* they capable of?

In the 1980s, in the Washington of Ronald Reagan, such a phrase came to be uttered not with suspicion but rather with wonderment: *Why, with the government off his back, what couldn't a hardworking banker do?* In all too many ways, the S&L debacle is the story of what happened when Washington came to a wholly new and different understanding of Banking Man. Beginning in the late 1970s, there emerged the belief—hardened to a conviction during the Reagan years—that the banker might well be God's chief lieutenant on earth. Warren Buffett, the self-made Omaha billionaire, once put it to me this way, with ill-concealed disdain: Yes, he said, the new maxim in Washington was that "a banker is born good and gets better."

This was the understanding of Congress, which merrily undid regulation after regulation. This was also the understanding of Ronald Reagan's secretary of the treasury, Donald Regan, who seemed to regard the United States of America as a branch office of his old brokerage firm, Merrill Lynch Pierce Fenner & Smith. Our current President, like his predecessor, had once boldly subscribed to the new estimation of Banking Man. In Washington in the 1980s, anyone believing otherwise maintained a discreet silence or found himself talking to a wall.

The story of how this faith in bankers begat the S&L mess is neither brief nor happy—though there are numerous instances of comedy bordering on the lunatic. It is a mess for which we will be paying, however, for many years, in the form of higher interest rates on loans and higher taxes on income. And it may have as its sequel the total irrelevance of a bankrupt United States in the next phase of world history: Ask a German or a Japanese. Or ask one of the bank regulators who are just beginning to understand the most astounding financial scandal the nation has ever witnessed—not simply a debacle but a series of debacles that made a few people preposterously rich and will leave most of us significantly poorer.

I. THE SAVINGS DEBACLE

The U.S. banking system is divided into two main parts: the commercial banks, with origins in the late Middle Ages, and the savings and loan institutions, patterned on a British model, that began to appear in America in 1831. Historically, the two had been very different. The commercial banks are given great flexibility in managing their money. They are permitted to take deposits from the general citizenry and to issue home mortgages, and many of them do; but their main business, both foreign and domestic, consists of large, relatively short-term loans to underwrite commercial and governmental activity, resulting in a high turnover

Ronald Searle

in their so-called asset portfolios, where the loans are kept. (It should be noted that, where money is concerned, the thinking of bankers is a mirror image of the thinking of the average citizen. To a banker, a loan is an asset, because it usually—if everything works right—produces income in the form of interest payments; whereas a deposit is a liability, because it is the bank that owes the interest to the depositor.) The commercial banks, therefore, have been able to adjust over the years to changing circumstances—fluctuations in interest rates, deadbeat debtors, gyrations in the business cycle (provided they were not too extreme), and the banks' own abundant mistakes (such as all those billions in loans to Brazil)—with some rapidity, although they have not always done it well.

The nation's savings and loan companies and savings banks have had a somewhat different purpose, and also a different constituency. Called "thrifts" because they were deliberately designed to promote saving among the laboring classes and to finance the purchase of single-family homes and modest apartments for its depositors, the S&Ls, in the years following the Depression, became an ideal 3-6-3 business: Its executives paid out 3 percent interest to attract deposits, lent the deposits out at 6 percent, and headed for the golf course at 3 in the afternoon. Overseeing their activities since the days of the New Deal was the Federal Home Loan Bank Board, the FHLBB—or "flub," for short—which in recent times consists of a presidentially appointed chairman, usually from the president's party, and two board members, one Republican and one Democrat. In return for accepting this supervision, the thrifts, like the big, national, commercial banks in their separate system, received federal deposit insurance, which meant that a depositor who kept his or her account below a certain level—by the 1970s this level had risen to $40,000—would lose no money in the unlikely but not unprecedented event that the thrift failed, because the federal insurance system would automatically make the depositor whole. (By an historical quirk peculiar to the United States, there was also a state-chartered thrift system that operated under somewhat more liberal rules but, often, under the supervision of a superior regulatory force. These state-chartered thrifts were also eligible for federal insurance.)

As long as interest rates remained stable—and from 1934 until well into the 1960s interest rates remained remarkably stable—running a thrift (and supervising one) was an undemanding task, and the industry was literally as sound as the dollar: People would give up many things

before they gave up their mortgaged homes, and loan defaults were few. Between the thrift executives and their depositors, therefore, a simple social compact existed: The depositors forked over their money, in return for a small profit, and the thrift executives gave it back, at a modest profit, in the form of much needed loans for homes. The return on the investment was slow—many mortgages ran for thirty years—but it was steady. And Americans, at an unprecedented rate, got to own what they lived in.

Thanks to the social compact, Americans saved and Americans bought homes and bankers puttered (and putted) along. But in the late 1960s, through no fault of the thrift industry, the social compact began to unravel.

First, Lyndon Johnson tried to fight a land war in Southeast Asia while simultaneously encouraging a civilian boom at home through the simple expedient of printing a great deal of money, thus creating a persistent, intractable inflation. Next, in a related step, both Johnson and Richard Nixon separated the currency from its firm anchor in the gold supply; long the world's most stable currency, the dollar began to flit about like a butterfly, its short-term value changing daily and its long-term value subject to wild fluctuations.

Not long after, in the mid-1970s, the Arabs and Iranians decided that the petroleum beneath their sands was worth a king's ransom and charged accordingly, an event that temporarily blasted the price of virtually everything else in the world into the stratosphere. Last, as confusion reigned and inflation rose into the double digits in 1979 and 1980, Paul Volcker's Federal Reserve decided to bring the situation under control by sharply restricting the money supply. This had the immediate effect of sending interest rates rocketing after prices. The easily predicted result, by the spring of 1980, was double-digit inflation accompanied by double-digit interest rates.

During a previous, but much milder, inflationary period in the 1960s, Congress—worried over the increasing cost of money, and thus of homes—had passed legislation stating that all federally chartered thrifts could pay an interest rate on deposits no more than one-quarter of 1 percent higher than the interest paid by the much more flexible commercial banks. The reasoning was that if the S&Ls didn't have to pay too much for deposits, they wouldn't have to charge much for loans—although, under this system, they would still be able to offer deposit rates just high enough to give them a slight edge on the commercial banks.

But by the late 1970s, the S&Ls were losing depositors by the thousands as customers abandoned the S&Ls, locked into paying 5.5 percent on deposits with inflation at 13 percent, in favor of uninsured money market accounts, newly available to the public from major Wall Street brokerage houses and mutual funds. (By 1982, there was more than $200 billion in these new accounts.) With their tangible net worth—the amount of actual money they had on hand—shrinking rapidly, some beleaguered thrifts could measure their life span in a handful of years or even months.

Creatures of Congress all, thanks to the supervisory and regulatory systems they had voluntarily accepted by joining the federal insurance system, the S&Ls naturally looked to their legislative parent for help. In return, they received a masterpiece of fiduciary humor. The most rudimentary economic wisdom suggested that the solution to the problem was a simple one. No economic trend—boom, bust, inflation—is permanent; all trends become their opposites as the business cycle, ideally at least, turns with the regularity of the tide. In the short term, the sickest thrifts, not numerous, should have been allowed to merge with stronger partners or close their doors, with the depositors reimbursed by the insurance system, the FSLIC.

Or the interest the thrifts charged for their mortgages could have been deregulated, allowing the rates to rise to market levels, which eventually would have reversed the outward flow of money and slowly returned the surviving thrifts to profitability. This would have to have been done carefully, however. In the trade, mortgages are called "slow assets," because they are paid off over a very long period of time. The thrifts would have had to be granted a breathing space of at least several years to attract new, market-rate mortgages and retire the older, low-paying mortgages, thus enabling them to make a modest amount of money from their assets (loans) before the interest rates on their liabilities (deposits) were raised. Indeed, if no such adjustment period was permitted, an unprecedented catastrophe would inevitably occur: The thrifts would find themselves paying generous market-rate interest to their depositors that the income from their slow assets would not come close to covering. In other words, the thrifts would find themselves shoveling money out the door.

This, of course, is precisely what happened. Consumer advocates, led by the Gray Panthers and groups under the influence of Ralph Nader, regarded cheap home mortgages as a God-given right of the American people—even people earning 12 percent (or higher) interest in money markets. Moreover, these advocates said so, not once but several times, and very loudly. Beginning in 1980 with the Depository Institutions Deregulation and Monetary Control Act, a panicky Congress commenced to deregulate the thrifts—but did it *backward*. Mortgage rates were frozen at the old levels, which meant, in practice, that almost no mortgages would be written, because they made no money. On the other hand, the thrifts were now allowed to pay market rates on deposits.

It would have been one thing—and we would be reeling from a smaller disaster—if this change had been all. But this was not all. At the very moment—March 1980—that Congress gave the thrifts the green light to raise the interest rates they could pay on deposits, Congress also raised the FSLIC insurance coverage on deposits from $40,000 per account to $100,000. No hearing was held on this move; there was no debate. It now seems clear that, at the time, most of the legislators had no idea of what they were doing. The more than doubling of insurance coverage was apparently suggested to the lawmakers hammering out the Depository Institutions Deregulation and Monetary Control Act at a late-night session by a certain Glen Troop, Washington lobbyist for the muscular U.S. League of Savings Institutions. One House staffer later called the change an "afterthought." But it was not an afterthought for the key Democratic member of the House who pushed it, Fernand St. Germain, of Woonsocket, Rhode Island. He was the chairman of the House Banking Committee and had maintained a comfortable residency in the S&L industry's pocket.

The boost in deposit insurance was nothing less than a subsidy—a safety net under every bad loan and mad investment an S&L made—and in the first years of the Reagan administration, thrift owners and directors quickly figured out how to exploit it. The financial device that would bring big money back into the thrifts was something called a "brokered deposit." A brokered deposit worked this way: Wall Street brokerage houses and investment banks took billions of dollars they attracted from big-money investors (pension funds, insurance companies, oil-rich Arab nations, and eventually mobsters and other money launderers) and parceled this money into neat, $100,000 packets. Each morning, these brokers scoured the nation for the highest rate being offered that day by the thrifts on their "jumbo" ($100,000) certificates of deposit (CDs)—deposits fully insured by the federal government. The brokers had struck a bonanza: They could offer their investors a high rate of return and, at the same time, assure them they would not lose a dime. The brokers moved their money around constantly from bank to bank (their deposits came to be called "hot" money), seeking the best rates for their clients, who owned shares in the funds. To attract these big deposits, the thrifts bid against one another, offering higher and higher rates of interest—rates they could not possibly afford to pay, but with the full faith and credit of the federal government behind them . . . well, you get the picture.

Even if *this* had been all, we would be in the grip of a significant but not calamitous S&L scandal. But this, alas, was not all either. In 1963, having noticed thrifts were gorging themselves on brokered deposits (but not too dangerously: FSLIC insurance at the time was only $10,000 per account), the FHLBB had moved in with a new regulation: The amount of brokered deposits a thrift could hold was limited to 5 percent of its total deposits. In 1980, this regulation was quietly repealed by the FHLBB.

By 1984, there was more than $34 billion worth of brokered deposits held by FSLIC-insured institutions. It was not uncommon for an S&L to have nearly half its deposits comprised of this "hot" money; in a couple thrifts, "hot" money constituted the entire deposit base.

As early as 1982, there were regulators who were urgently calling for a return to the 5 percent brokered-deposit limit. But by then Donald Regan was secretary of the treasury and a most influential man in the Reagan administration. Regan saw nothing wrong with the S&Ls getting out of the mundane business of slow-return mortgages and into the bracing world of venture capital, the world in which he had spent much of his life. He liked brokered deposits and didn't want to hear from the regulators that, say, one of the country's principal deposit brokerages, the First United Fund of Garden City, Long Island, was owned by Mario Renda, a former tap-dance instructor with shadowy ties to both Adnan Khashoggi, the international arms merchant, and the Lucchese crime family. It may or may not have chagrined Donald Regan that when the Brooklyn Organized Crime Strike Force finally raided Mario Renda's headquarters they found, among many other things, the sheet music for two company songs, "The Twelve Days of Bilking" and "Bilkers in the Night." If confronted with such alarming information, Regan would no doubt have felt compelled to note that his old firm, Merrill Lynch, was doing quite well as a result of brokered deposits—that it was doing more business in brokered deposits, in fact, than any-

one else. Regan might also have mentioned, quite proudly, that he was credited on Wall Street with being the father of the brokered deposit.

II. The Loan Debacle

By 1982—that is, two years into the deregulatory "reforms" advanced by Washington—the S&L industry, representing some 3,300 thrifts, was effectively broke. In 1980 these institutions had a collective net worth of $32.2 billion; by December 1982 the figure was $3.7 billion. Paying 12 and 13 percent for their deposits while receiving a pittance in income from their mortgage portfolios, the thrifts had managed to virtually wipe themselves out.

Yet salvation of a sort was at hand; it only required a little patience together with a willingness on the part of the thrifts to swallow a little bad-tasting medicine. The draconian policies of Paul Volcker's Federal Reserve had finally broken the back of the inflationary spiral. Free-market interest rates were falling; S&L depositors' interest rates would inevitably follow. The industry could expect to be making money again soon. Of course, a number of thrifts would fall by the wayside. But closing them was a simple and straightforward matter that would cost the FSLIC a few billion dollars. This would strain the fund—a fund, remember, built of moneys drawn from the *thrifts themselves*—but not destroy it. Were the industry to take its losses now, it would cost the taxpayers *nothing*.

There was only one problem with this scenario. The U.S. League of Savings Institutions, the industry's principal lobbying group, refused to buy it. And it was common knowledge in Washington that Freddy St. Germain, chairman of the House Banking Committee, did anything the U.S. League wanted him to. So did the Federal Home Loan Bank Board. Instead of a mild purge followed by renewed profitability on the economy's upswing, it was decided that much of the thrift industry would be permitted to *pretend* that it was making a great deal of money. In such a way, the fully insured brokered deposits would continue to flow into the thrifts, and the thrift owners and officials, in turn, could continue to do with them the creative things we have come to call (belatedly) scandalous.

With the blessing of Congress, and flying in the face of everything that had been known about banking for hundreds of years, the Bank Board, under the leadership of Jimmy Carter appointee Jay Janis and then of Reagan appointee Richard Pratt, did what it could to destroy every vestige of capital discipline at the thrifts. Before the Bank Board began this tinkering, a thrift, like a commercial bank, was required to maintain reserves—real money, cash on hand—equal to 5 percent of its assets. If the mortgage portfolio grew, the reserves also grew; if it was impossible to set aside sufficient reserves, growth was impossible: Thus was the system self-limiting. It has long been a truism in Washington, however, that when economic reality collides with an official agenda, the official agenda survives. Unremarked by virtually anybody outside the financial community, the FHLBB proceeded to lower the reserve requirement to 3 percent, meaning that a thrift needed to keep only half as much real money in its vaults. With the proverbial stroke of the pen, sick thrifts were instantly returned to a state of ruddy health, while thrifts that only a moment before had been among the dead who walk were now reclassified as merely enfeebled.

The Bank Board also made esoteric changes in the industry's accounting practices. The changes were hard to understand; they were almost impenetrable by laymen and by much of the financial press, who consequently ignored them. But by abandoning Generally Accepted Accounting Principles, which were themselves notoriously subject to a certain amount of creative manipulation, the board allowed a rapidly expanding S&L to show a handsome profit even if it was disastrously run, and the S&L could continue to show handsome profits until it was utterly looted by its owner.

Looted by its owner? Weren't most thrifts owned by you and me and the guy down the block, little guys like in *It's a Wonderful Life*? Well, yes, they were, and no, they were no longer to be.

At the time the Reaganauts landed in Washington, most federally chartered thrifts were still mutual associations, owned by their depositors. But, thanks to a little-noticed reform of the 1970s, a few of them were joint-stock companies operating under severe restrictions designed to protect the small depositors while keeping out the real-estate developers, whose hunger for money—to finance development schemes—could be expected to empty the coffers in short order. No thrift could have fewer than 400 stockholders, no single stockholder could own more than 10 percent of the shares, no control group or family could own more than 25 percent, and all stockholders had to live within 125 miles of the main office. Now, in 1982—its thinking addled by crisis and also by the deregulation Zeit-

geist of the 1980s—the Bank Board decided that anyone who had the money could buy or start a thrift.

New S&Ls started springing up everywhere, and many others changed hands. Traditionally, to obtain a thrift charter had been a slow and complicated task, requiring widespread local support and the clear articulation of a need for the institution within the community. This was all by way of buffering and controlling the zeal of the type of man who might confuse a thrift charter with a license to make piles of money for himself. In the early 1980s, however, this was precisely the kind of man Washington wanted in charge of an S&L. He was to be called an entrepreneur. And to make it easier for him to purchase an S&L, regulators, in the fullness of their wisdom, would allow him to start his thrift not only with money—with cash—but also with "noncash" assets, such as the 1,000 acres of dry, useless scrubland he could arrange to have a friend appraise in the millions.

Still, our rugged, bold, brash entrepreneurs could not do as they pleased with the funds they now had access to as a result of owning thrifts. Those billions in brokered deposits were still expected to be offered to Mr. and Mrs. Home-buyer, though not necessarily Mr. and Mrs. Homebuyer from down the street. Thrifts, beginning in 1982, could make loans not only in their markets (as had long been the case) but anywhere. Moreover, thrifts would no longer have to require a down payment from the borrower—not a big deal, really, as long as the borrower was seeking a thirty-year, $100,000 mortgage. But the mortgage business was precisely what the new thrift owners wanted out of.

The interest to be gotten from mortgages, as has been shown, could not begin to meet that being offered for brokered deposits. This loan crisis—the thrifts' inability to earn money—was a direct result of Congress's failed attempt to stanch the savings crisis—the thrifts' inability to attract capital in the late 1970s. Now, in the midst of all the Bank Board deregulation, the politicians were ready to confront the loan crisis. It was time, went the thinking on Capitol Hill and in the White House, to let the thrifts earn money in ways that might allow them to meet the interest payments on those jumbo CDs. It was time to turn a manageable crisis into a half-trillion-dollar (at least) catastrophe.

This most diabolical of changes came in 1982 as a result of a bill named after its sponsors, Democratic Representative Freddy St. Germain (once again) and Republican Senator Jake Garn of Utah, a member of the Senate Banking Committee. Much of the bill was written by Garn's staff director, M. Danny Wall—we will meet him again, in another guise—and many of its provisions were benign and even sound, allowing honest if troubled thrifts to stay in business. But a number of its provisions would be greeted with wide smiles by the new roguish thrift owners. There was a provision, for example, allowing thrifts to invest up to 40 percent of their assets in nonresidential real-estate lending. A thrift could also make consumer loans of up to 30 percent of its assets. Which is to say, as of October 15, 1982—the day Ronald Reagan signed the Garn–St. Germain Depository Institutions Act, hailing it as "the most important legislation for financial institutions in the last fifty years"—thrift owners by and large could all but abandon the business of home mortgages their thrifts were designed to provide.

Yet perhaps history will record that Garn–St. Germain managed to do its greatest damage indirectly, in the even worse state-level legislation it quickly spawned. California thrifts, responding to the liberal provisions of Garn–St. Germain, began to abandon their state charters and join the federal system, an event that immediately attracted the attention of alarmed legislators in Sacramento. Various reasons have been advanced for the peculiar two-tier arrangement—state and federal—of the American banking and thrift industries, but it actually serves a perfectly simple purpose. In return for the more liberal provisions of state law, the state-chartered banks and thrifts are expected to make handsome campaign contributions to the men and women who have made the liberal provisions possible. But with the passage of Garn–St. Germain, it was now the federal system that was the more liberal of the two, and faced with the defections of the state thrifts, the California legislature reacted with blinding speed.

On the last night of California's 1982 legislative session, a bill named for a prominent Republican assemblyman, Pat Nolan, cleared its final hurdle and passed in twenty seconds with not a hint of debate. Under the Nolan Bill, a California-chartered thrift could invest *100 percent* of its deposits in any venture it chose. A California thrift could purchase stocks and bonds; it could become a corporate raider and practice greenmail. It could buy mushroom farms and Antarctic real estate; it could invest in junk bonds and perpetual-motion machines. The California thrifts, in short, were permitted to become perfect venture capitalists—high-fliers, indeed, but with full knowledge that beneath them spread the safety net of federal deposit insurance. The Nolan

Bill was quickly copied in Texas and Florida. And what happened next was remarkably similar to what might have occurred if Nicolae Ceauşescu had gotten control of the thrift industry rather than Romania.

III. The Looting Debacle

Robbing an S&L is not among the more difficult challenges faced by humankind as it climbs the slippery slope of evolution. To rob a thrift stupidly, one has merely to don a ski mask and brandish a Winchester or perhaps a threatening note, which generally nets the thief a bag containing a few thousand dollars that will, in our day, shortly explode, covering him with dye. But to deftly rob a thrift suddenly required only a fountain pen, a circle of close personal friends in the real-estate and financial businesses, and the perfect freedom provided by the absence of regulation. Even so, there are only a limited number of ways that the trick may be performed, and in the S&L catastrophe they were played again and again, until they became as depressingly commonplace as those other hallmarks of the Reagan years, homelessness and debt.

The old mutual savings associations, owned by their depositors and managed for their depositors' benefit, had traditionally been among the soundest financial institutions in the land, but the rogue thrifts of the 1980s typically were controlled by a single dominant and unscrupulous individual who ran the institution for his personal benefit; in the late 1980s, the General Accounting Office surveyed the wreckage of the American thrift industry and found the pattern in virtually every failed thrift it examined. For example, Empire Savings and Loan in suburban Mesquite, Texas, whose failure eventually cost the taxpayers some $300 million, appeared to be run by a banker with impeccable credentials, Spencer H. Blain Jr. But Blain's strings were pulled by a prominent though illiterate developer named D. L. ("Danny") Faulkner, who held court (and gave out Rolex watches) at the Wise Circle Grill and seemed to regard Empire's deposits as his personal checking account. Bold, brash banking was conducted this way: Faulkner and his associates would essentially sit around a table doing a "land flip"—i.e., trading a piece of property at ever escalating prices. (No real cash ever changed hands during a flip.) Every time a piece of property was sold, the thrift made a new loan to cover the purchase price. Each time a loan was made, the thrift owner or owners pocketed fees—loan fees for negotiating the deal, origination fees for preparing the documents—all of which provided him or them with a handsome and ever increasing income. Nor was repayment a problem when a bad loan finally came due. In many cases, Empire and like-minded institutions advanced the borrower money to service the debt, usually for a period of two years, whereupon the deal could be refinanced and yet more fees pocketed.

The actual, market-determined value of the land was irrelevant and often ignored; a corrupt thrift frequently neglected to obtain an independent appraisal of the property or to make any appraisal at all. At Charles H. Keating Jr.'s now notorious Lincoln Savings and Loan, whose failure may cost the taxpayers in excess of $2 billion, such loans were sometimes given without an application, a credit check, or any paperwork whatever. Anticipating that the federal examiners would eventually demand to see Lincoln's loan records, a team from the thrift's outside accountant, the Big Eight firm of Arthur Andersen, quickly stuffed the files with bogus documentation—but so amateurishly that Lincoln's inside counsel was forced to admit that the documentation had been placed there solely for the examiners to find. At Lincoln, too, no loan manual existed until the examiners demanded to see one, whereupon a manual was created; Lincoln, it turned out, had given millions in undocumented loans with no guidelines whatever. It had also purchased billions of dollars' worth of junk bonds with a similar cavalier disregard for paperwork; much of the junk was purchased from the Wall Street firm Drexel Burnham Lambert, which, by an amazing coincidence, was Charles Keating's undisclosed partner in Lincoln. Apparently, Lincoln was buying any junk Drexel told it to.

At Empire, as elsewhere, there was remarkably little interest in the fate of the money the thrift loaned after it departed the vault, although Faulkner and his associates found it necessary to justify at least some of the borrowing by indulging in a building frenzy along the I-30 corridor east of Dallas. Most of these condominiums simply remained empty. Siding was warped. Windows were broken. Some structures had been burned to the ground and others had been hauled away, leaving only their foundations—"Martian landing pads," a federal attorney later called them. It was not the soundness of a thrift's loans that meant profits to the thrift owner or directors. It was the number and size of the loans—specifically, the fees these large and numerous loans generated.

Because many of the loans given by corrupt thrifts were senseless, these thrifts sometimes fell into recognizable default despite the "flips," interpretative accounting, etc. But this proved to be no insurmountable difficulty. One had only to exercise the "daisy chain," whereby bad loans are passed on to a network of other corrupt thrifts, or to exercise the "dead horse – dead cow swap," wherein bad loans were exchanged with those of another corrupt thrift and both were refinanced (more fees). And if, for some reason, it was deemed necessary for the land purchaser to appear to make a large down payment, the money could simply be advanced to him through one of the corrupt thrift's subsidiaries—of which corrupt thrifts, eager to confuse their pursuers, often had many—and the trail could be concealed by lending the money to a third party. True, the thrift was only lending itself its own money, minus (in many cases) a substantial sum that the sham purchaser kept for his own use, but as long as fresh brokered funds could be attracted to make up the shortfall, the game could continue indefinitely. (In its circa 1983 heyday, although it was being looted hollow, Empire appeared to be the most profitable thrift in the country.)

Senseless? Mad? There was more. For example, there was something called an ADC—a loan for acquisition, development, and construction—which was actually a direct investment but which, counted as a loan, also yielded fees. Loans to gambling casinos were another possibility, particularly loans to the Dunes Hotel and Casino in Las Vegas, owned by the elderly Morris Shenker, a friend, counsel, and confidant of the presumably late Jimmy Hoffa, who disappeared in 1975. In the new age of the thrift industry, the Dunes became a popular destination for S&L executives, one of whom miraculously "won" $200,000 at the gaming tables and deposited the sum in a secret account; by an amazing coincidence, his thrift had advanced some $1.6 million to the Shenker interests.

But by far the simplest way to make it in the thrift business was to pay yourself vast sums of money in the traditional form of a salary. This, not surprisingly, became a fairly common practice, perfected (as were so many other practices) by Charles Keating. At his peak, Keating deemed his own services to be worth some $3.2 million a year. Further, Keating hired virtually his entire immediate family, including his son, Charles III, a college dropout whose previous experience consisted of busing tables at his father's country club and later managing it. Young Keating was nonetheless deemed sufficiently talented to ascend to the very chairmanship of Lincoln, where he received more than a million dollars in his best year. Regulators now believe that in return for their long and prudent hours devoted to Lincoln during the 1980s, the Keating family took home a minimum of $34 million.

With so little effort required to make such money, time and energy could be devoted to spending it. Keating kept a company refrigerator stocked with Dom Pérignon. He once gave the women on his legal staff $500 each—but only twenty minutes—to buy clothing at a nearby upscale mall; another woman—his female employees were called "Charlie's Angels"—was given $5,000 to replace a pair of shoes she had ruined in his service.

In Texas, Vernon Savings and Loan chairman Don Dixon and his wife, Dana, took a modest trip to Europe in 1983, paid for with Vernon's federally insured funds. They had flown there by privately chartered jet. Because the Dixons had it in mind to open a world-class French restaurant, it was necessary for them to dine thoroughly and well in the greatest eateries of France with Philippe Junot, the former husband of Princess Caroline of Monaco, as their well-paid guide. In Lyons, Paul Bocuse lined up his twelve sous-chefs for the Dixons' inspection. They rested from their labors, tired but happy, in the finest hotels. It was, Dana Dixon wrote in her memoir, "a flying house party…a gastronomique-fantastique!" As it happened, her wedding had also been paid for by Vernon. (On a second, Vernon-subsidized trip to Europe, Don Dixon gave a $40,000 oil painting to the pope. As far as the thrift regulators could figure out, the picture had been bought by Vernon. It hangs in the Vatican Museum.) To move Dixon and his associates around the country, the thrift maintained a fleet of five airplanes and a helicopter. (Charles Keating also bought an air force for Lincoln.)

About the S&L scandal there are few things safe to say, but surely one thing is that we will never know exactly how much money—taxpayers' money, I am moved to repeat—went where for what. We know that CenTrust chairman David L. Paul had at home a $13.2 million Rubens. We know that in Dallas, Sunbelt Savings and Loan Association's Ed McBirney III, who would later be charged with seventeen counts of bank fraud, financed the purchase of eighty-four Rolls-Royces from the Bhagwan Shree Rajneesh. It may be that that other symbol of the 1980s, the United States–backed Contra army, also received funds looted from

thrifts. Anything seemed possible, and perhaps there is no better proof of this than the fact that at one point Lamar Savings and Loan of Austin, Texas, applied to open a branch on the moon.

IV. THE REGULATORY DEBACLE

One may well ask at this point, and so we will: How could all of this fraud—it is now estimated that 60 percent of the failed S&Ls were up to no good—go so perfectly unnoticed for so long?

Answer: It *did not* go unnoticed. It simply went unchallenged.

Of course, the thrift owners and officers *hoped* their doings would go unnoticed and took steps to foster such blindness. For example, with the torrents of federally guaranteed cash generated by brokered funds and bogus loans, it was possible to buy the loyalty of employees who knew too much. At Lincoln's apogee in the late 1980s, eight of the seventeen highest-paid executives in Arizona worked for Keating. His personal secretary made a reported $200,000; another secretary, on twenty-four-hour call, received $70,000.

In much the same spirit, Keating hired Alan Greenspan, then an economist in private practice, to go before Congress and testify to what a splendid idea the new S&Ls were; of the seventeen S&Ls the future Federal Reserve chairman chose as his examples, sixteen failed, and the survivor was not an S&L. Keating also hired Lincoln's chief outside auditor, Jack D. Atchison of the accounting firm of Arthur Young, and paid him $930,000, more than triple his old salary, for less than a year's work. Making an accountant rich, many felt, was an excellent way of obtaining a clean annual audit to wave under the nose of pesky examiners.

But a few men saw through this—even Edwin Gray, who would seem to have been a man to see nothing of the sort. In June 1983, a month after he was sworn in as the new head of the Federal Home Loan Bank Board, Gray was in Dallas to deliver a pep talk about deregulation. A stocky, square-faced man of forty-seven, Gray was a Reaganaut to his fingertips. He had been drawn into the inner circle when his employer seconded him to Reagan's gubernatorial transition team. Eventually rising to the post of press secretary, he left to handle public relations for a thriving thrift in San Diego, a post that eminently qualified him to become Reagan's second Bank Board chairman and, it was widely believed, the willing flack for the U.S. League of Savings Institutions.

Knowing something, but not much, about the thrift system made him the ideal choice, an impression that was powerfully reinforced by his personality. Around the Bank Board offices, he became known (among those familiar with TV history) as the genial "Mr. Ed," a pleasant, undemanding chair warmer in the finest tradition of the post. Like most of the Reaganauts, he was also an avid fan of deregulation in all its forms—as a San Diego banker, or kind of banker, he had enthusiastically lobbied for it—and as one of his first official acts he proposed to take the gladsome news of Garn-St. Germain to the S&L owners of north Texas. The title of his speech, delivered in Dallas, was "A Sure Cure for What Ails You."

But although Ed Gray was not a great man for noticing things, a few details in Dallas caught his attention. One of his hosts, Spencer Blain, the chairman of Empire Savings and Loan, wore a $5,000 Rolex watch and drove a blue Rolls-Royce. Gray wondered how an officer of an S&L could possibly afford them. And Linwood Bowman III, then the Texas state savings and loan commissioner, took Gray aside and told him that something peculiar seemed to be going on in Blain's operations—specifically, at Blain's huge new condominium developments to the east of the city. Someone, Bowman said, was parking junked cars there, to make the units look as though they were occupied.

To Ed Gray, who was not paid to think, the odd events in Texas suggested nothing until the end of the summer, when his regulatory staff in Washington informed him of an equally odd new problem. Thanks to Garn-St. Germain, lax oversight, and liberalized state laws, the problem at the thrifts no longer centered on the negative spread between the cost of paying interest on deposits and the inadequate income derived from the mortgage portfolio. The problem, said the staff, now revolved around all the terrible loans—the "land flips," the "dead horse–dead cow swaps," the ADCs, and so on—that the thrifts were making with their huge new brokered deposits. And the problem had suddenly become immense.

In Washington, Gray scanned the field reports from his overworked, underpaid staff of examiners and tried to tell Treasury Secretary Donald Regan's people about the expensive cars and watches. But to Regan this only proved that the Reaganauts' plan was working. As promised, they had gotten the government out of the pocket of the American

businessman. Entrepreneurial energies had been unleashed; the just rewards for daring and hard work were big cars and expensive watches.

"If the thrifts had problems, Don Regan and his people didn't care," Gray told me. "Suddenly, in Don Regan's eyes, I was this awful reregulator."

If he wanted to get to the bottom of things—to thoroughly examine the thrifts—Gray was on his own.

It would not be easy. Because of a seemingly minor historical fluke, the thrift examiners, unlike their commercial-bank counterparts, were paid through the White House Office of Management and Budget. OMB also determined how many examiners there would be. With deregulation, and with David Stockman heading up OMB, there were to be even fewer of them than there had been before—eliminating regulators was an essential part of the Reaganaut agenda.

In 1983, the year Ed Gray assumed his post, a starting thrift examiner was paid $14,000 a year. Turnover was immense, with the average examiner having only two years on the job, and there were fewer than 800 of them to cover the entire country. Meanwhile, the examiners in the Ninth District, covering Mississippi, Louisiana, Arkansas, New Mexico, and Texas, were shifting their headquarters from Little Rock, Arkansas, to Dallas. Only fourteen members of the district office's supervisory staff agreed to make the move, and only two were supervisors. Until the Ninth District rebuilt its staff, Texas was wide open.

But even if a thrift examiner, untrained as he was for the new age of deregulation, detected fraud—and, for example, the Texas examiners were onto the situation at Empire virtually from the beginning—there was depressingly little likelihood that a case would ever make it to court. Federal prosecutors loathe cases involving banks and thrifts; such cases sometimes take years to unravel, and they tend to be so fiendishly complex that there is no guarantee that a bewildered jury will return a conviction. Federal prosecutors have been known to simply refuse to consider such cases.

With too few regulators to work with, and too little interest in rectifying this among those in the Reaganaut executive branch, one might think Gray could turn to Congress, where Democrats were not in short supply. One might go so far as to reason that this is why we have two political parties and three branches of government. But then one only has to be reminded that the St. Germain of Garn-St. Germain was a Democrat—*was*, I write, because in 1988 his constituents apparently tired of his many thrift-funded junkets and S&L-backed nights about town and voted him out. But St. Germain was not a maverick on the Hill in his fondness for the nation's newly deregulated thrifts. And the thrifts' owners and officers were not content to merely keep their employees quiet and happy with their abundant new funds.

To take but one example, Vernon's Don Dixon, for whom no excess was too wretched, purchased the sister ship of the presidential yacht *Sequoia*, named it *High Spirits*, anchored it in the Tidal Basin, and made it available to Congressman Tony Coelho of California, the majority whip and chairman of the Democratic Congressional Campaign Committee, who held fund-raising events on the vessel eleven times in 1985 and 1986. But because Coelho's mind was evidently clouded by affairs of state, he seemed not to notice that Dixon and Vernon never billed him the $2,000 half-day charter fee; when the oversight was pointed out to him by Gray's weary examiners, Coelho and the campaign committee reimbursed Vernon to the tune of $48,450. Other voyagers included House Majority Leader Jim Wright and his fellow Texas Democrats J. J. Pickle and Jim Chapman. When Congressman Chapman was questioned about his parties aboard the vessel, his staff replied by pointing out that Texas thrift lobbyist Durward Curlee often lived on the yacht when he was in town and that election law allowed him to donate the use of his residence.

By 1984, Ed Gray began to resemble a man shouting into a barrel. With disasters igniting everywhere in the thrift system, with Congress refusing to listen to him, with the examiners depleted, and with the secretary of the treasury refusing to return his phone calls, he decided to take action on his own. The twelve regional Home Loan banks reported to Washington, but, by another quirk of the law, they were not overseen by OMB—their salaries were paid directly by the Bank Board system. Moreover, a loop hole in Garn-St. Germain allowed Gray to transfer his OMB-supervised examination staff to the regionals. To Ed Gray, it was the answer to a prayer. As 1984 came to an end, with the Reaganauts returned to Washington by the voters, he had just 700 examiners or so and a turnover rate of 30 percent.

Gray began transferring examiners to the regionals in July 1985. He also raised wages and recruited more foot soldiers. He was able to attract the services of H. Joe Selby, a regulator with thirty-one distinguished years of experience. Selby was sent to Dallas, the heart of the problem. Gray was also able to persuade another crack examiner, Mike Patriarca, to take charge of the investigations of the San Francisco office, which had jurisdiction over Keating's Lincoln. Before the bolstering of the examination staff, Ed Gray had known that he had a terrible problem on his hands, possibly the worst financial disaster in American history, but the story had arrived in fragments; now he began to find out just how large the problem was. By September 1986, at least

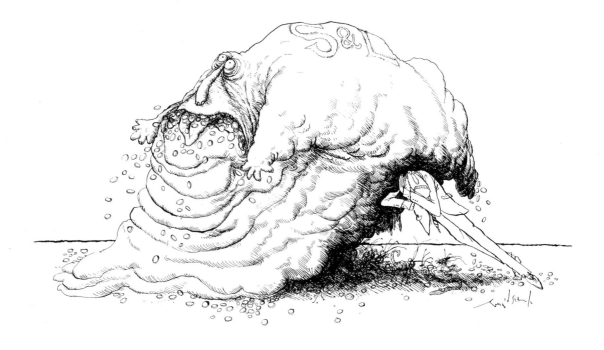

252 thrifts with assets of almost $95 billion were in serious trouble.

The FSLIC had only $2.5 billion. It was essential to recapitalize the fund with an infusion of taxpayer money—Gray thought he needed at least $15 billion—but the only way to obtain the necessary funds was to apply to Congress. Applying to Congress meant that Gray would have to deal with Congressman Jim Wright of Texas, who became speaker of the House in January 1987. And Jim Wright, a man who owed certain political debts, had his own ideas.

Wright repeatedly called Gray in for a series of tongue-lashings. Wright was concerned about Craig Hall, a Dallas real-estate syndicator, who was more than $500 million in the hole; if he went under thanks to Selby's "Gestapo," Hall claimed, he would take twenty-nine thrifts with him. (Gray, against the strenuous advice of his staff, arranged to give Hall some breathing room.) Wright was also deeply concerned about Tom Gaubert, who had been removed from the helm of the Independent American Savings Association of Irving, a Dallas suburb. Gaubert, whose home shooting gallery featured a picture of Ed Gray, chaired a fund-raising event that produced a million-dollar campaign contribution for... yes, Jim Wright.

There was no way Gray was going to let Gaubert back into his thrift. There was no way Wright, with considerable assistance from House Banking Committee chairman St. Germain, was going to bring the FSLIC recapitalization bill to the floor for a vote. In Dallas, Selby, who in 1986 alone had slapped thrifts with no fewer than 100 supervisory actions, heard that plans were afoot to have him kidnapped. Wright, in turn, accused Selby of running a ring of homosexual lawyers. Unable to close rogue thrifts, Gray was reduced to placing them in a management-consignment program, assigning executives from soundly run thrifts to try and clean up the mess. But the executives in the consignment program found that the only way to keep the walking wounded alive was to continue to solicit the brokered funds that had caused the trouble in the first place. Sound business practices could no longer save them.

Meanwhile, Don Regan—now the White House chief of staff—and Charles Keating tried to pack Gray's Bank Board. Its two members, Mary Grigsby and Don Hovde, had left. (Gray, left alone, could make administrative decisions but, without a board, was unable to make policy.) Professor Lawrence J. White of New York University was appointed to the Democratic slot, a surprisingly good appointment.

The Republican slot was filled by a Georgia lawyer named Lee Henkel. In 1980 he had been the East Coast campaign manager for the abortive presidential campaign of John Connally, the former Texas governor and treasury secretary; Charles Keating had been Connally's national campaign chairman and later, as de facto head of Lincoln, one of his principal creditors as well as the employer of Connally's son, Mark. As it turned out, real-estate interests in which Henkel had involved himself owed Lincoln Savings and Loan at least $97.9 million, and at least one of the loans was chronically delinquent. Henkel left the board when William Proxmire, the chairman of the Senate Banking Committee, learned of his Lincoln loans.

In the early months of 1987, Ed Gray may have been the most embattled official in Washington. His insurance fund was broke; the recapitalization was stalled by Wright. The Bank Board was paralyzed again; White felt that no major decisions should be made until Gray was replaced by a new chairman at the end of his term in June 1987. The country was focused on Iran-Contra, if on anything. Congress was gearing up to unmask that scandal, not his.

But some men on Capitol Hill had Ed Gray on their minds. In April 1987, Gray was summoned to the office of Senator Dennis DeConcini, Democrat of Arizona. With DeConcini were Senators John McCain (Rep., Ariz.), Alan Cranston (Dem., Calif.), and John Glenn (Dem., Ohio). (This was the Four Senator Meeting, to be followed shortly by the Five Senator Meeting, with Michigan Democrat Donald Riegle joining the regathered four.) All had received handsome campaign contributions from Charles Keating and his associates. (The thrift industry, during the 1980s, is believed to have made $11 million in direct contributions to elected officials.) And there were other favors as well: McCain's wife and father-in-law had invested $395,000 in one of Keating's Phoenix shopping centers; and McCain himself had enjoyed three vacations at Keating's Bahamas estate. Keating had made James Grogan, Glenn's former legislative assistant, a vice president of one of Lincoln's subsidiaries. Cranston, who had received $39,000 in direct contributions, got considerably more after the meetings with Gray: Three California voter-registration projects controlled by him and his son received $850,000, and the California Democratic Party got $85,000.

DeConcini received a comparatively beggarly $48,100 in direct contributions, but concerning Senator DeConcini there were other interesting matters. Federal prosecutors, at last aroused from their torpor and now extremely interested in Lincoln, discovered what they believed to be a sham $30 million real-estate transaction between Lincoln and an entity called RA Homes, and they concluded that Lincoln would probably never recover its money. In other words, the investigators believed that RA Homes had, in effect, stolen $30 million from Lincoln with Lincoln's complicity. Two of the principals of RA Homes were close political associates of Dennis DeConcini's.

It should come as no surprise, therefore, that the senators, four and then five, wanted to know why Gray and his people were being so hard on Keating. DeConcini, perhaps hoping to bring a bit of levity to the initial gathering, assured Gray that Keating wanted nothing more than to get back to the sound business of lending prudent amounts of money to first-time buyers of ranch homes. In the year following Keating's acquisition of Lincoln in 1984, the S&L, which had twenty-six branches, originated precisely eleven mortgages. Four were for employees.

V. THE BAILOUT DEBACLE

It must be said again, for it has not been said enough, that had Washington understood the nature of Banking Man, had the Reagan administration let even the few regulators it kept around do a modicum of regulating, had our key elected officials on Capitol Hill spent more time watching out for the taxpayer's dollar than the thrift owner's millions—had all or any of the aforementioned come to pass, the S&L bailout would not be costing each and every American at least $2,000 in the years to come. Had Washington allowed the numerous broke S&Ls to simply close in 1982, the FSLIC insurance fund could have handled the tab at the cost to taxpayers of not a dime. In the years Ed Gray spent getting doors slammed in his face, the cost ballooned beyond what the insurance fund could handle, but it remained manageable: $15 or $20 billion. By the time Gray's term as Bank Board chairman expired in June 1987, the problem had fattened, snowballed, pyramided into a multibillion-dollar colossus. And Washington late in 1987—that is, just a bit more than one year from the November 1988 election—was agreed on how to go about confronting it. It was to be carefully, skillfully ignored.

To get Ronald Reagan (who never once as president publicly mentioned the S&L mess) out of town before the roof fell in and to allow George Bush to go before the tax-

payers without having to explain how he had chaired the administration's 1984 task force on financial deregulation—which gazed upon the thrifts and saw capitalism working—was the job of M. Danny Wall: Ed Gray's successor, Jake Garn's protégé (Wall's wife was Garn's secretary), former staff director of the Senate Banking Committee, principal author of Garn-St. Germain, and a man who either could not read a balance sheet or didn't want to. In one of his first official acts, Wall threw Bill Crawford, the crusty California thrift regulator (and a dedicated foe of Charles Keating's) off the Federal Home Loan Advisory Board. Although Wall's own Washington analysts, examining the San Francisco office's findings at Lincoln, had agreed that the thrift would almost certainly fail by 1991 at the latest, Wall pulled San Francisco off the case.

The Bank Board also managed to *not* get around to closing Denver's Silverado Banking, Savings and Loan until December 9, 1988. Silverado's losses from bad loans and real-estate deals will cost taxpayers about $1 billion. One of Silverado's directors was Neil Bush, son of George Bush, who stood for election on November 8.

Wall repeated to anyone and everyone that whatever the problems of the S&L industry, there was no crisis and there would be no need for tax money in the solution—an opinion that earned him the nickname, among officials at the Federal Deposit Insurance Corporation, of M. Danny Isuzu. Still he stuck gamely to his opinions, turning a deaf ear to horrified investigators and sending those with figures on thrift losses double or triple his own back to their calculators. (Wall also conducted a government fire sale of failing thrifts, called the Southwest Plan: underpricing troubled S&Ls, oversubsidizing the deals with taxpayers' dollars, and involving, in at least one case, a business executive indicted for securities fraud.) Thus was George Bush able to fill the silence created for him with talk of flags and points of light.

Michael Dukakis embraced competence, but of competently run thrifts—and the lack thereof—he had absolutely nothing to say. Robert Shapiro, who advised him on economic policy, says that the Dukakis camp was told not to bring it up—that what was a bad issue for George Bush was also a bad issue for Jim Wright, Tony Coelho, and many other congressional Democrats putting themselves before the voters. Dukakis thereby, and with typical maladroitness, avoided an issue that might have won him . . . well, votes.

His election secured, his inaugural speech behind him, President Bush promptly turned his attention to the series of

S&L debacles he had so artfully avoided. He unveiled a bailout plan in February 1989, and in August 1989 he signed a bailout plan into law. The Bank Board was abolished, as was the FSLIC, and a new entity specifically devoted to resolving troubled thrifts—the Resolution Trust Corporation—was created. And so commenced the bailout debacle.

Like so many aspects of the S&L crisis itself, the bailout was from the beginning to be kept from full public scrutiny. Funding for the bailout was to be kept "off-budget," so that those in the White House and on Capitol Hill could not be said to have added to the federal deficit by having remained so blind and so mum for so long. Of course, funding the bailout in this way—through the sale of thirty- and forty-year Resolution Trust bonds—has added enormously to its cost. (*Three fifths* of the estimated $500 billion cost of the bailout is to pay for interest.) And should interest rates rise, a half-trillion dollars could someday look like a bargain.

In the months and years to come, one can expect the Resolution Trust to make any number of sweetheart deals as it moves quickly to sell off the real estate accumulated by the busted thrifts. The government itself acknowledged earlier this summer that a certain amount of fraud is inevitable. That the buyers of these properties might number among them the very gentlemen who got the country into the mess in the first place should not be discounted, and already certain individuals with cash-filled suitcases have made their appearance. Who knows more about the true value of the properties the government intends to sell off than the developers and the thrift owners who defaulted on the properties?

That the vast majority of these swindlers are not in danger of spending a few years behind bars is quite clear, as Washington has shown little sign beyond the symbolic of committing the proper time or resources to the task. The FBI is said to have on file 7,000 major bank-fraud referrals nationwide. The Bush Justice Department announced in July that it has selected 100 savings institutions for priority investigation. The spread in the numbers is the spread between action and the *appearance* of action.

The bailout, of course, is not designed to prevent a commercial-bank debacle or an insurance-industry debacle, both of which may be in the offing—and neither of which is unrelated to the S&L mess. Then there is the cleanup at the nuclear-weapons plants, the astronomical national debt run up during the Reagan years, and the trade deficit. It may not be going too far to say that the United States is broke. And because the country may be broke, the future is hard to read, because the United States has never been broke before.

Still, it is interesting to note that the United States, once everybody's generous (and, as a consequence, influential) rich uncle, finds itself increasingly shut out of the complex events now unfolding in Eastern Europe, where our vastly more solvent allies are taking pride of place. It may not be wild to speculate that America has not bought itself into the game because it cannot afford to, and that may be the truest and most lasting legacy of the Charles Keatings: the United States having no role in the 1990s save as a (shaky) guarantor of government bonds.

Late Victorians

by Richard Rodriguez

October 1990

St. Augustine writes from his cope of dust that we are restless hearts, for earth is not our true home. Human unhappiness is evidence of our immortality. Intuition tells us we are meant for some other city.

Elizabeth Taylor, quoted in a magazine article of twenty years ago, spoke of cerulean Richard Burton days on her yacht, days that were nevertheless undermined by the elemental private reflection: This must end.

On a Sunday in summer, ten years ago, I was walking home from the Latin Mass at St. Patrick's, the old Irish parish downtown, when I saw thousands of people on Market Street. It was San Francisco's Gay Freedom Day parade—not the first, but the first I ever saw. Private lives were becoming public. There were marching bands. There were floats. Banners blocked single lives thematically into a processional mass, not unlike the consortiums of the blessed in Renaissance paintings, each saint cherishing the apparatus of his martyrdom: GAY DENTISTS. BLACK AND WHITE LOVERS. GAYS FROM BAKERSFIELD. LATINA LESBIANS. From the foot of Market Street they marched, east to west, following the mythic American path toward optimism.

I followed the parade to Civic Center Plaza, where flags of routine nations yielded sovereignty to a multitude. Pastel billows flowed over all.

Five years later, another parade. Politicians waved from white convertibles. Dykes on Bikes revved up, thumbs upped. But now banners bore the acronyms of death. AIDS. ARC. Drums were muffled as passing, plum-spotted young men slid by on motorized cable cars.

Though I am alive now, I do not believe that an old man's pessimism is truer than a young man's optimism simply because it comes after. There are things a young man knows that are true and are not yet in the old man's power to recollect. Spring has its sappy wisdom. Lonely teenagers

still arrive in San Francisco aboard Greyhound buses. The city can still seem, I imagine, by comparison to where they came from, paradise.

Four years ago on a Sunday in winter—a brilliant spring afternoon—I was jogging near Fort Point while overhead a young woman was, with difficulty, climbing over the railing of the Golden Gate Bridge. Holding down her skirt with one hand, with the other she waved to a startled spectator (the newspaper next day quoted a workman who was painting the bridge) before she stepped onto the sky.

To land like a spilled purse at my feet.

Serendipity has an eschatological tang here. Always has. Few American cities have had the experience, as we have had, of watching the civic body burn even as we stood, out of body, on a hillside, in a movie theater. Jeanette MacDonald's loony scatting of "San Francisco" has become our go-to-hell anthem. San Francisco has taken some heightened pleasure from the circus of final things. To Atlantis, to Pompeii, to the Pillar of Salt, we add the Golden Gate Bridge, not golden at all but rust red. San Francisco toys with the tragic conclusion.

For most of its brief life, San Francisco has entertained an idea of itself as heaven on earth, whether as Gold Town or City Beautiful or Treasure Island or Haight-Ashbury.

San Francisco can support both comic and tragic conclusions because the city is geographically *in extremis*, a metaphor for the farthest-flung possibility, a metaphor for the end of the line. Land's end.

To speak of San Francisco as land's end is to read the map from one direction only—as Europeans would read or as the East Coast has always read it. In my lifetime, San Francisco has become an Asian city. To speak, therefore, of San Francisco as land's end is to betray parochialism. Before my parents came to California from Mexico, they saw San Francisco as the North. The West was not west for them.

I cannot claim for myself the memory of a skyline such as the one César saw. César came to San Francisco in middle age; César came here as to some final place. He was born in South America; he had grown up in Paris; he had been everywhere, done everything; he assumed the world. Yet César was not condescending toward San Francisco, not at all. Here César saw revolution, and he embraced it.

Whereas I live here because I was born here. I grew up ninety miles away, in Sacramento. San Francisco was the nearest, the easiest, the inevitable city, since I needed a city. And yet I live here surrounded by people for whom San Francisco is a quest.

I have never looked for utopia on a map. Of course, I believe in human advancement. I believe in medicine, in astrophysics, in washing machines. But my compass takes its cardinal point from tragedy. If I respond to the metaphor of spring, I nevertheless learned, years ago, from my Mexican parents, from my Irish nuns, to count on winter. The point of Eden for me, for us, is not approach but expulsion.

After I met César in 1984, our friendly debate concerning the halcyon properties of San Francisco ranged from restaurant to restaurant. I spoke of limits. César boasted of freedoms.

It was César's conceit to add to the gates of Jerusalem, to add to the soccer fields of Tijuana, one other dreamscape hoped for the world over. It was the view from a hill, through a mesh of electrical tram wires, of an urban neighborhood in a valley. The vision took its name from the protruding wedge of a theater marquee. Here César raised his glass without discretion: To the Castro.

There were times, dear César, when you tried to switch sides if only to scorn American optimism, which, I remind you, had already become your own. At the high school where César taught, teachers and parents had organized a campaign to keep kids from driving themselves to the junior prom in an attempt to forestall liquor and death. Such a scheme momentarily reawakened César's Latin skepticism.

Didn't the Americans know? (His tone exaggerated incredulity.) Teenagers will crash into lampposts on their way home from proms, and there is nothing to be done about it. You cannot forbid tragedy.

By California standards I live in an old house. But not haunted. There are too many tall windows, there is too much salty light, especially in winter, though the windows rattle, rattle in summer when the fog flies overhead, and the house creaks and prowls at night. I feel myself immune to any confidence it seeks to tell.

To grow up homosexual is to live with secrets and within secrets. In no other place are those secrets more closely guarded than within the family home. The grammar of the gay city borrows metaphors from the nineteenth-century house. "Coming out of the closet" is predicated upon family laundry, dirty linen, skeletons.

I live in a tall Victorian house that has been converted to four apartments; four single men.

Neighborhood streets are named to honor nineteenth-century men of action, men of distant fame. Clay. Jackson. Scott. Pierce. Many Victorians in the neighborhood date from before the 1906 earthquake and fire.

Architectural historians credit the gay movement of the 1970s with the urban restoration of San Francisco. Twenty years ago this was a borderline neighborhood. This room, like all the rooms of the house, was painted headache green, apple green, boardinghouse green. In the 1970s homosexuals moved into black and working-class parts of the city, where they were perceived as pioneers or as blockbusters, depending.

Two decades ago some of the least expensive sections of San Francisco were wooden Victorian sections. It was thus a coincidence of the market that gay men found themselves living with the architectural metaphor for family. No other architecture in the American imagination is more evocative of family than the Victorian house. In those same years—the 1970s—and within those same Victorian houses, homosexuals were living rebellious lives to challenge the foundations of domesticity.

Was "queer-bashing" as much a manifestation of homophobia as a reaction against gentrification? One heard the complaint, often enough, that gay men were as promiscuous with their capital as otherwise, buying, fixing up, then selling and moving on. Two incomes, no children, described an unfair advantage. No sooner would flower boxes begin to appear than an anonymous reply was smeared on the sidewalk out front: KILL FAGGOTS.

The three- or four-story Victorian house, like the Victorian novel, was built to contain several generations and several classes under one roof, behind a single oaken door. What strikes me is the confidence of Victorian architecture. Stairs, connecting one story with another, describe the confidence

Michael Nichols

ened austerity of an expensive sort—black-and-white marble floors and faux masonry. A man comes in the afternoons to texture the walls with a sponge and a rag and to paint white mortar lines that create an illusion of permanence, of stone.

The renovation of Victorian San Francisco into dollhouses for libertines may have seemed, in the 1970s, an evasion of what the city was actually becoming. San Francisco's rows of storied houses proclaimed a multigenerational orthodoxy, all the while masking the city's unconventional soul. Elsewhere, meanwhile, domestic America was coming undone.

Suburban Los Angeles, the prototype for a new America, was characterized by a more apparently radical residential architecture. There was, for example, the work of Frank Gehry. In the 1970s Gehry exploded the nuclear-family house, turning it inside out intellectually and in fact. Though, in a way, Gehry merely completed the logic of the postwar suburban tract house—with its one story, its sliding glass doors, Formica kitchen, two-car garage. The tract house exchanged privacy for mobility. Heterosexuals opted for the one-lifetime house, the freeway, the birth-control pill, minimalist fiction.

The age-old description of homosexuality is of a sin against nature. Moralistic society has always judged emotion literally. The homosexual was sinful because he had no kosher place to stick it. In attempting to drape the architecture of sodomy with art, homosexuals have lived for thousands of years against the expectations of nature. Barren as Shakers and, interestingly, as concerned with the small effect, homosexuals have made a covenant against nature. Homosexual survival lay in artifice, in plumage, in lampshades, sonnets, musical comedy, couture, syntax, religious ceremony, opera, lacquer, irony.

I once asked Enrique, an interior decorator, if he had many homosexual clients. "*Mais non,*" said he, flexing his eyelids. "Queers don't need decorators. They were born knowing how. All this A.S.I.D. stuff—tests and regulations—as if you can confer a homosexual diploma on a suburban housewife by granting her a discount card."

A knack? The genius, we are beginning to fear in an age of AIDS, is irreplaceable—but does it exist? The question is whether the darling affinities are innate to homosexuality or whether they are compensatory. Why have so many homosexuals retired into the small effect, the ineffectual career,

that bound generations together through time—confidence that the family would inherit the earth.

If Victorian houses exude a sturdy optimism by day, they are also associated in our imaginations with the Gothic—with shadows and cobwebby gimcrack, long corridors. The nineteenth century was remarkable for escalating optimism even as it excavated the backstairs, the descending architecture of nightmare—Freud's labor and Engels's.

I live on the second story, in rooms that have been rendered as empty as Yorick's skull—gutted, unrattled, in various ways unlocked, added skylights and new windows, new doors. The hallway remains the darkest part of the house.

This winter the hallway and lobby are being repainted to resemble an eighteenth-century French foyer. Of late we had walls and carpet of Sienese red; a baroque mirror hung in an alcove by the stairwell. Now we are to have enlight-

the stereotype, the card shop, the florist? *Be gentle with me?* Or do homosexuals know things others do not?

This way power lay: Once upon a time the homosexual appropriated to himself a mystical province, that of taste. Taste, which is, after all, the insecurity of the middle class, became the homosexual's licentiate to challenge the rule of nature. (The fairy in his blood, he intimated.)

Deciding how best to stick it may be only an architectural problem or a question of physics or of engineering or of cabinetry. Nevertheless, society's condemnation forced the homosexual to find his redemption outside nature. *We'll put a little skirt here.* The impulse is not to create but to re-create, to sham, to convert, to sauce, to rouge, to fragrance, to prettify. No effect is too small or too ephemeral to be snatched away from nature, to be ushered toward the perfection of artificiality. *We'll bring out the highlights there.* The homosexual has marshaled the architecture of the straight world to the very gates of Versailles—that great Vatican of fairyland—beyond which power is converted to leisure.

In San Francisco in the 1980s the highest form of art became interior decoration. The glory hole was thus converted to an eighteenth-century French foyer.

I live away from the street, in a back apartment, in two rooms. I use my bedroom as a visitor's room—the sleigh bed tricked up with shams into a sofa—whereas I rarely invite anyone into my library, the public room, where I write, the public gesture.

I read in my bedroom in the afternoon because the light is good there, especially now, in winter, when the sun recedes from the earth.

There is a door in the south wall that leads to a balcony. The door was once a window. Inside the door, inside my bedroom, are twin green shutters. They are false shutters, of no function beyond wit. The shutters open into the room; they have the effect of turning my apartment inside out.

A few months ago I hired a man to paint the shutters green. I wanted the green shutters of Manet—you know the ones I mean—I wanted a weathered look, as of verdigris. For several days the painter labored, rubbing his paints into the wood and then wiping them off again. In this way he rehearsed for me decades of the ravages of weather. Yellow enough? Black?

The painter left one afternoon, saying he would return the next day, leaving behind his tubes, his brushes, his sponges and rags. He never returned. Someone told me he has AIDS.

Repainted facades extend now from Jackson Street south into what was once the heart of the black "Mo"—black Fillmore Street. Today there are watercress sandwiches at three o'clock where recently there had been loudmouthed kids, hole-in-the-wall bars, pimps. Now there are tweeds and perambulators, matrons and nannies. Yuppies. And gays.

The gay male revolution had greater influence on San Francisco in the 1970s than did the feminist revolution. Feminists, with whom I include lesbians—such was the inclusiveness of the feminist movement—were preoccupied with career, with escape from the house in order to create a sexually democratic city. Homosexual men sought to reclaim the house, the house that traditionally had been the reward for heterosexuality, with all its selfless tasks and burdens.

Leisure defined the gay male revolution. The gay political movement began, by most accounts, in 1969, with the Stonewall riots in New York City, whereby gay men fought to defend the nonconformity of their leisure.

It was no coincidence that homosexuals migrated to San Francisco in the 1970s, for the city was famed as a playful place, more Catholic than Protestant in its eschatological intuition. In 1975 the state of California legalized consensual homosexuality, and about that same time Castro Street, southwest of downtown, began to eclipse Polk Street as the homosexual address in San Francisco. Polk Street was a string of bars. The Castro was an entire district. The Castro had Victorian houses and churches, bookstores and restaurants, gyms, dry cleaners, supermarkets, and an elected member of the Board of Supervisors. The Castro supported baths and bars, but there was nothing furtive about them. On Castro Street the light of day penetrated gay life through clear plate-glass windows. The light of day discovered a new confidence, a new politics. Also a new look—a noncosmopolitan, Burt Reynolds, butch-kid style: beer, ball games, Levi's, short hair, muscles.

Gay men who lived elsewhere in the city, in Pacific Heights or in the Richmond, often spoke with derision of "Castro Street clones," describing the look, or scorned what they called the ghettoization of homosexuality. To an older generation of homosexuals, the blatancy of sexuality on Castro Street threatened the discreet compromise they had negotiated with a tolerant city.

As the Castro district thrived, Folsom Street, south of Market, also began to thrive, as if in counterdistinction to the utopian Castro. The Folsom Street area was a warehouse district of puddled alleys and deserted streets. Folsom Street offered an assortment of leather bars, an evening's regress to the outlaw sexuality of the Fifties, the Forties, the nineteenth century, and so on—an eroticism of the dark, of the Reeper-bahn, or of the guardsman's barracks.

The Castro district implied that sexuality was more crucial, that homosexuality was the central fact of identity. The Castro district, with its ice-cream parlors and hardware stores, was the revolutionary place.

Into which carloads of vacant-eyed teenagers from other districts or from middle-class suburbs would drive after dark, cruising the neighborhood for solitary victims.

The ultimate gay basher was a city supervisor named Dan White, ex-cop, ex-boxer, ex-fireman, ex-altar boy. Dan White had grown up in the Castro district; he recognized the Castro revolution for what it was. Gays had achieved power over him. He murdered the mayor and he murdered the homosexual member of the Board of Supervisors.

Katherine, a sophisticate if ever there was one, nevertheless dismisses the two men descending the aisle at the Opera House: "All so sleek and smooth-jowled and silver-haired— they don't seem real, poor darlings. It must be because they don't have children."

Lodged within Katherine's complaint is the perennial heterosexual annoyance with the homosexual's freedom from child-rearing, which places the homosexual not so much beyond the pale as it relegates the homosexual outside "responsible" life.

It was the glamour of gay life, after all, as much as it was the feminist call to career, that encouraged heterosexuals in the 1970s to excuse themselves from nature, to swallow the birth-control pill. Who needs children? The gay bar became the paradigm for the single's bar. The gay couple became the paradigm for the selfish couple—all dressed up and everywhere to go. And there was the example of the gay house in illustrated life-style magazines. At the same time that suburban housewives were looking outside the home for fulfillment, gay men were reintroducing a new generation in the city—heterosexual men and women—to the complacencies of the barren house.

Puritanical America dismissed gay camp followers as Yuppies; the term means to suggest infantility. Yuppies were obsessive and awkward in their materialism. Whereas gays arranged a decorative life against a barren state, Yuppies sought early returns—lives that were not to be all toil and spin. Yuppies, trained to careerism from the cradle, wavered in their pursuit of the northern European ethic—indeed, we might now call it the pan-Pacific ethic—in favor of the Mediterranean, the Latin, the Catholic, the Castro, the Gay.

The international architectural idioms of Skidmore, Owings & Merrill, which defined the city's skyline in the 1970s, betrayed no awareness of any street-level debate concerning the primacy of play in San Francisco nor of any human dramas resulting from urban redevelopment. The repellent office tower was a fortress raised against the sky, against the street, against the idea of a city. Offices were hives where money was made, and damn all.

In the 1970s San Francisco was divided between the interests of downtown and the pleasures of the neighborhoods. Neighborhoods asserted idiosyncrasy, human scale, light. San Francisco neighborhoods perceived downtown as working against their influence in determining what the city should be. Thus neighborhoods seceded from the idea of a city.

The gay movement rejected downtown as representing "straight" conformity. But was it possible that heterosexual Union Street was related to Castro Street? Was it possible that either was related to the Latino Mission district? Or to the Sino-Russian Richmond? San Francisco, though complimented worldwide for holding its center, was in fact without a vision of itself entire.

In the 1980s, in deference to the neighborhoods, City Hall would attempt a counter-reformation of downtown, forbidding "Manhattanization." Shadows were legislated away from parks and playgrounds. Height restrictions were lowered beneath an existing skyline. Design, too, fell under the retrojurisdiction of the city planner's office. The Victorian house was presented to architects as a model of what the city wanted to uphold and to become. In heterosexual neighborhoods, one saw newly built Victorians. Downtown, postmodernist prescriptions for playfulness advised skyscrapers to wear party hats, buttons, comic mustaches. Philip Johnson yielded to the dollhouse impulse to perch angels atop one of his skyscrapers.

In the 1970s, like a lot of men and women in this city, I joined a gym. My club, I've even caught myself calling it.

In the gay city of the 1970s, bodybuilding became an architectural preoccupation of the upper middle class. Bodybuilding is a parody of labor, a useless accumulation of the laborer's bulk and strength. No useful task is accomplished. And yet there is something businesslike about the habitués, and the gym is filled with the punch-clock logic of the workplace. Machines clank and hum. Needles on gauges toll spent calories.

The gym is at once a closet of privacy and an exhibition gallery. All four walls are mirrored.

I study my body in the mirror. Physical revelation—nakedness—is no longer possible, cannot be desired, for the body is shrouded in meat and wears itself.

The intent is some merciless press of body against a standard, perfect mold. Bodies are "cut" or "pumped" or "buffed" as on an assembly line in Turin. A body becomes so many extrovert parts. Delts, pecs, lats.

I harness myself in a Nautilus cage.

Lats become wings. For the gym is nothing if not the occasion for transcendence. From homosexual to autosexual...

I lift weights over my head, baring my teeth like an animal with the strain.

...to nonsexual. The effect of the over-developed body is the miniaturization of the sexual organs—of no function beyond wit. Behold the ape become Blakean angel, revolving in an empyrean of mirrors.

The nineteenth-century mirror over the fireplace in my bedroom was purchased by a decorator from the estate of a man who died last year of AIDS. It is a top-heavy piece, confusing styles. Two ebony-painted columns support a frieze of painted glass above the mirror. The frieze depicts three bourgeois Graces and a couple of free-range cherubs. The lake of the mirror has formed a cataract, and at its edges it is beginning to corrode.

Thus the mirror that now draws upon my room owns some bright curse, maybe—some memory not mine.

As I regard this mirror, I imagine St. Augustine's meditation slowly hardening into syllogism, passing down through centuries to confound us: Evil is the absence of good.

We have become accustomed to figures disappearing from our landscape. Does this not lead us to interrogate the landscape?

With reason do we invest mirrors with the superstition of memory, for they, though glass, though liquid captured in a bay, are so often less fragile than we are. They—bright ovals or rectangles or rounds—bump down unscathed, unspilled through centuries, whereas we...

The man in the red baseball cap used to jog so religiously on Marina Green. By the time it occurs to me that I have not seen him for months, I realize he may be dead—not lapsed, not moved away. People come and go in the city, it's true. But in San Francisco in 1990, death has become as routine an explanation for disappearance as Allied Van Lines.

AIDS, it has been discovered, is a plague of absence. Absence opened in the blood. Absence condensed into the fluid of passing emotion. Absence shot through opalescent tugs of semen to deflower the city.

And then AIDS, it was discovered, is a non-metaphorical disease, a disease like any other. Absence sprang from substance—a virus, a hairy bubble perched upon a needle, a platter of no intention served round: fever, blisters, a death sentence.

At first I heard only a few names—names connected, perhaps, with the right faces, perhaps not. People vaguely remembered, as through the cataract of this mirror, from dinner parties or from intermissions. A few articles in the press. The rumored celebrities. But within months the slow beating of the blood had found its bay.

One of San Francisco's gay newspapers, the *Bay Area Reporter*, began to accept advertisements from funeral parlors and casket makers, inserting them between the randy ads for leather bars and tanning salons. The *Reporter* invited homemade obituaries—lovers writing of lovers, friends remembering friends and the blessings of unexceptional life.

Peter. Carlos. Gary. Asel. Perry. Nikos.

Healthy snapshots accompany each annal. At the Russian River. By the Christmas tree. Lifting a beer. In uniform. A dinner jacket. A satin gown.

He was born in Puerto La Libertad, El Salvador.

He attended Apple Valley High School, where he was their first male cheerleader.

From El Paso. From Medford. From Germany. From Long Island.

I moved back to San Francisco in 1979. Oh, I had had some salad days elsewhere, but by 1979 I was a wintry man. I came here in order not to be distracted by the ambitions or, for that matter, the pleasures of others but to pursue my own ambition. Once here, though, I found the company of men who pursued an earthly paradise charming. Skepticism became my demeanor toward them—I was the dinner-party skeptic, a firm believer in Original Sin and in the limits of possibility.

Which charmed them.

He was a dancer.

He settled into the interior-design department of Gump's, where he worked until his illness.

He was a teacher.

César, for example.

César could shave the rind from any assertion to expose its pulp and jelly. But César was otherwise ruled by pulp. César loved everything that ripened in time. Freshmen. Bordeaux. César could fashion liturgy from an artichoke. Yesterday it was not ready (cocking his head, rotating the artichoke in his hand over a pot of cold water). Tomorrow will be too late (Yorick's skull). Today it is perfect (as he lit the fire beneath the pot). We will eat it now.

If he's lucky, he's got a year, a doctor told me. If not, he's got two.

The phone rang. AIDS had tagged a friend. And then the phone rang again. And then the phone rang again. Michael had tested positive. Adrian, well, what he had assumed were shingles . . . Paul was back in the hospital. And César, dammit, César, even César, especially César.

That winter before his death César traveled back to South America. On his return to San Francisco he described to me how he had walked with his mother in her garden—his mother chafing her hands as if she were cold. But it was not cold, he said. They moved slowly. Her summer garden was prolonging itself this year, she said. The cicadas will not stop singing.

When he lay on his deathbed, César said everyone else he knew might get AIDS and die. He said I would be the only one spared—"spared" was supposed to have been chased with irony, I knew, but his voice was too weak to do the job. "You are too circumspect," he said then, wagging his finger upon the coverlet.

So I was going to live to see that the garden of earthly delights was, after all, only wallpaper—was that it, César? Hadn't I always said so? It was then I saw that the greater sin against heaven was my unwillingness to embrace life.

It was not as in some Victorian novel—the curtains drawn, the pillows plumped, the streets strewn with sawdust. It was not to be a matter of custards in covered dishes, steaming pos-

sets, *Try a little of this, my dear.* Or gathering up the issues of *Architectural Digest* strewn about the bed. Closing the biography of Diana Cooper and marking its place. Or the unfolding of discretionary screens, morphine, parrots, pavilions.

César experienced agony.

Four of his high school students sawed through a Vivaldi quartet in the corridor outside his hospital room, prolonging the hideous garden.

In the presence of his lover Gregory and friends, Scott passed from this life . . .

He died peacefully at home in his lover Ron's arms.

Immediately after a friend led a prayer for him to be taken home and while his dear mother was reciting the Twenty-third Psalm, Bill peacefully took his last breath.

I stood aloof at César's memorial, the kind of party he would enjoy, everyone said. And so for a time César lay improperly buried, unconvincingly resurrected in the conditional: would enjoy. What else could they say? César had no religion beyond aesthetic bravery.

Sunlight remains. Traffic remains. Nocturnal chic attaches to some discovered restaurant. A new novel is reviewed in the *New York Times*. And the mirror rasps on its hook. The mirror is lifted down.

A priest friend, a good friend, who out of naïveté plays the cynic, tells me—this is on a bright, billowy day; we are standing outside—"It's not as sad as you may think. There is at least spectacle in the death of the young. Come to the funeral of an old lady sometime if you want to feel an empty church."

I will grant my priest friend this much: that it is easier, easier on me, to sit with gay men in hospitals than with the staring old. Young men talk as much as they are able.

But those who gather around the young man's bed do not see spectacle. This doll is Death. I have seen people caressing it, staring Death down. I have seen people wipe its tears, wipe its ass; I have seen people kiss Death on his lips, where once there were lips.

Chris was inspired after his own diagnosis in July 1987 with the truth and reality of how such a terrible disease could bring out the love, warmth, and support of so many friends and family.

Sometimes no family came. If there was family, it was usually mother. Mom. With her suitcase and with the torn flap of an envelope in her hand.

Brenda. Pat. Connie. Toni. Soledad.

Or parents came but then left without reconciliation, some preferring to say cancer.

But others came. Sissies were not, after all, afraid of Death. They walked his dog. They washed his dishes. They bought his groceries. They massaged his poor back. They changed his bandages. They emptied his bedpan.

Men who sought the aesthetic ordering of existence were recalled to nature. Men who aspired to the mock-angelic settled for the shirt of hair. The gay community of San Francisco, having found freedom, consented to necessity—to all that the proud world had for so long held up to them, withheld from them, as "real humanity."

And if gays took care of their own, they were not alone. AIDS was a disease of the entire city; its victims were as often black, Hispanic, straight. Neither were Charity and Mercy only white, only male, only gay. Others came. There were nurses and nuns and the couple from next door, co-workers, strangers, teenagers, corporations, pensioners. A community was forming over the city.

Cary and Rick's friends and family wish to thank the many people who provided both small and great kindnesses.

He was attended to and lovingly cared for by the staff at Coming Home Hospice.

And the saints of this city have names listed in the phone book, names I heard called through a microphone one cold Sunday in Advent as I sat in Most Holy Redeemer Church. It might have been any of the churches or community centers in the Castro district, but it happened at Most Holy Redeemer at a time in the history of the world when the Roman Catholic Church still pronounced the homosexual a sinner.

A woman at the microphone called upon volunteers from the AIDS Support Group to come forward. One by one, in twos and threes, throughout the church, people stood up, young men and women, and middle-aged and old, straight, gay, and all of them shy at being called. Yet they came forward and assembled in the sanctuary, facing the congregation, grinning self-consciously at one another, their hands hidden behind them.

I am preoccupied by the fussing of a man sitting in the pew directly in front of me—in his seventies, frail, his iodine-colored hair combed forward and pasted upon his forehead. Fingers of porcelain clutch the pearly beads of what must have been his mother's rosary. He is not the sort of man any gay man would have chosen to become in the 1970s. He is probably not what he himself expected to become. Something of the old dear about him, wizened butterfly, powdered old pouf. Certainly he is what I fear becoming. And then he rises, this old monkey, with the most beatific dignity, in answer to the microphone, and he strides into the sanctuary to take his place in the company of the Blessed.

So this is it—this, what looks like a Christmas party in an insurance office and not as in Renaissance paintings, and not as we had always thought, not some flower-strewn, some sequined curtain call of grease-painted heroes gesturing to the stalls. A lady with a plastic candy cane pinned to her lapel. A Castro clone with a red bandanna exploding from his hip pocket. A perfume-counter lady with an Hermès scarf mantled upon her left shoulder. A black man in a checkered sports coat. The pink-haired punkess with a jewel in her nose. Here, too, is the gay couple in middle age, wearing interchangeable plaid shirts and corduroy pants. Blood and shit and Mr. Happy Face. These know the weight of bodies.

Bill died.

… Passed on to heaven.

… Turning over in his bed one night and then gone.

These learned to love what is corruptible, while I, barren skeptic, reader of St. Augustine, curator of the earthly paradise, inheritor of the empty mirror, I shift my tailbone upon the cold, hard pew.

Ladies and Gentlemen:

by Joyce Carol Oates

December 1990

L adies and gentlemen: a belated but heartfelt welcome aboard our cruise ship S.S. *Ariel*; it's a true honor and a privilege for me, your captain, to greet you all on this lovely sun-warmed January day—as balmy, isn't it, as any June morning back north? I wish I could claim that we of the *Ariel* arranged personally for such splendid weather, as compensation of sorts for the, shall we say, somewhat rocky weather of the past several days, but, at any rate, it's a welcome omen indeed and bodes well for the remainder of the cruise and for this morning's excursion, ladies and gentlemen, to the island you see us rapidly approaching, a small but remarkably beautiful island the natives of these waters call the "Island of Tranquillity"— or, as some translators prefer, the "Island of Repose." For those of you who've become virtual sailors with a keen eye for navigating, you'll want to log our longitude at 155 degrees east and our latitude at 5 degrees north, approximately 1,200 miles north and east of New Guinea. Yes, that's right! We've come so far! And as this is a rather crucial morning, and your island adventure an important event not only on this cruise but in your lives, ladies and gentlemen, I hope you will quiet just a bit—just a bit!—and give me, your captain, your fullest attention. Just for a few minutes—I promise! Then you will disembark.

As to the problems some of you have experienced: Let me take this opportunity, as your captain, ladies and gentlemen, to apologize, or at least to explain. It's true, for instance, that certain of your staterooms are not *precisely* as the advertising brochures depicted them; the portholes are not quite so large, in some cases the portholes are not in evidence. This is not the fault of any of the *Ariel* staff; indeed, this has been a sore point with us for some years, a matter of misunderstandings and embarrassments out of our control, yet I, as your captain, ladies and gentlemen, offer my apologies and my profoundest sympathies. Though I am a bit your junior in age, I can well understand the special

disappointment, the particular hurt, outrage, and dismay that attend one's sense of having been cheated on what, for some of you, probably, is perceived as being the last time you'll be taking so prolonged and exotic a trip. Thus, my profoundest sympathies! As to the toilets that have been reported as malfunctioning, or out of order entirely, and the loud throbbing or "tremors" of the engines that have been keeping some of you awake, and the negligent or even rude service, the over- or undercooked food, the high tariffs on mineral water, alcoholic beverages, and cigarettes, the reported sightings of rodents, cockroaches, and other vermin on board ship—perhaps I should explain, ladies and gentlemen, that this is the final voyage of the S.S. *Ariel*, and it was the owners' decision, and a justifiably pragmatic decision, to cut back on repairs, services, expenses, and the like. Ladies and gentlemen, I am sorry for your inconvenience, but the *Ariel* is an old ship, bound for dry dock in Manila and the fate of many a veteran seagoing vessel that has outlived her time. God bless her! We'll not see her likes again, ladies and gentlemen!

Ladies and gentlemen, may I have some quiet? *Please?* Just five minutes more, before the stewards help you prepare for your disembarkment? Thank you.

Yes, the *Ariel* is bound for Manila next. But have no fear: You won't be aboard.

Ladies and gentlemen, *please*. This murmuring and muttering begins to annoy.

(Yet, as your captain, I'd like to note that, amid the usual whiners and complainers and the just plain bad-tempered, it's gratifying to see a number of warm, friendly, *hopeful* faces; and to know that there are men and women determined to enjoy life, not quibble and harbor suspicions. Thank *you!*)

Now to our business at hand: Ladies and gentlemen, do you know what you have in common?

You can't guess?

You *can* guess?

No? Yes?

No?

Well—yes, sir, it's true that you are all aboard the S.S. *Ariel*; and yes, sir—excuse me, *ma'am*—it's certainly true that you are all of "retirement" age. (Though "retirement" has come to be a rather vague term in the past decade or so, hasn't it? For the youngest among you are in your late fifties—the result, I would guess, of especially generous early-retirement programs; and the eldest among you are in your mid-nineties. Quite a range of ages!)

Yes, it's true you are all Americans. You have expensive cameras, even, in some cases, video equipment for recording this South Seas adventure; you have all sorts of tropical-cruise paraphernalia, including some extremely attractive bleached-straw hats; some of you have quite a supply of sun-protective lotions; and most of you have a considerable quantity, and variety, of pharmacological supplies. And quite a store of paperbacks, magazines, cards, games, and crossword puzzles. Yet there is one primary thing you have in common, ladies and gentlemen, which has determined your presence here this morning, at longitude 155 degrees east and latitude 5 degrees north; your fate, as it were. Can't you guess?

Ladies and gentlemen: *your children.*

Yes, you have in common the fact that this cruise on the S.S. *Ariel* was originally your children's idea; and that they arranged for it, if you'll recall. (Though you have probably paid for your own passages, which weren't cheap.) Your children, who are "children" only technically, for of course they are fully grown, fully adult; a good number of them parents themselves (having made you proud grandparents—yes, haven't you been proud!); these sons and daughters, who, if I may speak frankly, are *very* tired of waiting for their inheritances.

Yes, and *very* impatient, some of them, very angry, waiting to come into control of what they believe is their due.

Ladies and gentlemen, please!—I'm asking for quiet, and I'm asking for respect. As captain of the *Ariel*, I am not accustomed to being interrupted.

I believe you did hear me correctly, sir. And you too, sir.

Yes, and you, ma'am. And *you*. (Most of you aren't nearly so deaf as you pretend!)

Let me speak candidly. While your children are in many or at least in some cases genuinely fond of you, they are simply impatient with the prospect of waiting for your "natural" deaths. Ten years, fifteen? Twenty? With today's medical technology, who knows, you might outlive them!

Of course it's a surprise to you, ladies and gentlemen. It's a *shock*. Thus you, sir, are shaking your head in disbelief, and you, sir, are muttering just a little too loudly, "Who does that fool think he is, making such bad jokes!" and you, ladies, are giggling like teenage girls, not knowing what to think. But remember: Your children have been living lives of their own, in a very difficult, very competitive corporate America; they are, on the face of it, "well-to-do," even affluent; yet they want, in some cases desperately need, *your* estates—not in a dozen years but *now*.

That is to say, as soon as your wills can be probated, following our "act of God" in these tropical seas.

For, however your sons and daughters appear in the eyes of their neighbors, friends, and business colleagues, even in the eyes of their own offspring, you can be sure that *they have not enough money*. You can be sure that they suffer keenly certain financial jealousies and yearnings. And who dares calibrate another's suffering? Who dares peer into another's heart? Without betraying anyone's confidence, I can say that there are several youngish men, beloved sons of couples in your midst, ladies and gentlemen, who are nearly bankrupt; men of integrity and "success" whose worlds are about to come tumbling about their heads—unless they get money, or find themselves in the position of being able to borrow money against their parents' estates, *fast*. Investment bankers, lawyers, a college professor or two—some of them already in debt. Thus, they decided to take severe measures.

Ladies and gentlemen, it's pointless to protest. As captain of the *Ariel*, I merely expedite orders.

And you must know that it's pointless to express disbelief or incredulity; to roll your eyes, as if I (of all people) were a bit cracked; to call out questions or demands; to shout, weep, sob, beg, rant and rave, and mutter, "If this is a joke it isn't a very funny joke!" "As if my son/daughter would ever do such a thing to me/us"—in short, it's pointless to express any and all of the reactions you're expressing and have been expressed by other ladies and gentlemen on past *Ariel* voyages to the South Seas.

Yes, it's the best thing, to cooperate. Yes, in an orderly fashion. It's wisest not to provoke the stewards (whose nerves are a bit ragged these days—the crew is only human, after all) into using force.

Ladies and gentlemen, these *are* lovely azure waters,

David Johnson

without exception, you showered love upon your sons and daughters, who knew themselves, practically in the cradle, to be privileged. The very best, the most exclusive nursery schools—private schools—colleges, universities. Expensive toys and gifts of all kinds, closets of clothing, ski equipment, stereo equipment, racing bicycles, tennis lessons, riding lessons, snorkeling lessons, private tutoring, trips to the Caribbean, to Mexico, to Tangier, to Tokyo, to Switzerland, junior years abroad in Paris, in Rome, in London. Yes, and their teeth were perfect, or were made to be; yes, and they had cosmetic surgery if necessary or nearly necessary; yes, and you gladly paid for their abortions or their tuition for law school, medical school, business school; yes, and you paid for their weddings; yes, and you loaned them money "to get started," certainly you helped them with their mortgages, or their second cars, or their children's orthodontist bills. Nothing was too good or too expensive for them, for what, ladies and gentlemen, would it have been?

And, always, the more you gave your sons and daughters the more you seemed to be holding in reserve; the more generous you displayed yourself the more generous you were hinting you might be, in the future. But so far in the future—when your wills might be probated, after your deaths!

Ladies and gentlemen, you rarely stopped to consider your children as other than *your* children—as men and women growing into maturity, distinct from you. Rarely did you pause to see how patiently they were waiting to inherit their due—and then, by degrees, how impatiently. What anxieties besieged them, what nightmare speculations? For what if you squandered your money on medical bills? Nursing-home bills? The melancholic impedimenta of age in America? What if—worse yet!—addlebrained, suffering from Alzheimer's disease (about which they'd been reading suddenly, it seemed, everywhere), you turned against them? Disinherited them? Remarried someone younger, healthier, more cunning than they? Rewrote your wills, as elderly fools are always doing?

Ladies and gentlemen, your children declare that they want only *what's theirs*.

They say, laughingly, *they* aren't going to live forever.

(Well, yes: I'll confide in you, off-the-cuff, in several instances it was an *in-law* who looked into the possibility of a cruise on the S.S. *Ariel;* your own son or daughter merely cooperated, after the fact, as it were. Of course, that isn't the same thing!)

exactly as the brochures promised! But shark-infested, so take care.

Ah yes, those dorsal fins slicing the waves, just beyond the surf—observe them closely.

No, we're leaving no picnic baskets with you today. Nor any bottles of mineral water, Perrier water, champagne.

For why delay what's inevitable? Why, cruelly, protract anguish?

Ladies and gentlemen, maybe it's a simple thing, maybe it's a self-evident thing, but consider: You are the kind of civilized men and women who brought babies into the world not by crude, primitive, anachronistic chance but by systematic *deliberation*. You planned your futures, you planned, as the expression goes, your parenthood. You are all of that American economic class called upper-middle; you are educated, you are cultured, you are stable; nearly

Ladies and gentlemen, as your captain, about to bid you farewell, let me say: I *am* sympathetic with your plight. Your stunned expressions, your staggering-swaying gait, your damp eyes, working mouths—"This is a bad joke!" "This is intolerable!" "This is a nightmare!" "No child of mine could be so cruel, inhuman, monstrous," etc.—all this is touching, wrenching to the heart, altogether *natural*. One might almost say *traditional*. Countless others, whose bones you may discover, should you have the energy and spirit to explore the "Island of Tranquillity" (or "Repose"), reacted in more or less the same way.

Thus, do not despair, ladies and gentlemen, for your emotions, however painful, are time-honored; but do not squander the few precious remaining hours of your life, for such emotions are futile.

Ladies and gentlemen: The "Island of Tranquillity" upon which you now stand shivering in the steamy morning heat is approximately six kilometers in circumference, ovoid in shape, with a curious archipelago of giant metamorphic rocks trailing off to the north, a pounding hallucinatory surf, and horizon, vague, dreamy, and distant, on all sides. Its soil is an admixture of volcanic ash, sand, rock, and pear; its jungle interior is pocked with treacherous bogs of quicksand.

It *is* a truly exotic island! But most of you will quickly become habituated to the ceaseless winds that ease across the island from several directions simultaneously, air as intimate and warmly stale as exhaled breaths, caressing, narcotic. You'll become habituated to the ubiquitous sand fleas, the glittering dragonflies with their eighteen-inch iridescent wings, the numerous species of snakes (the small quicksilver orange-speckled baja snake is the most venomous, you'll want to know); the red-beaked carnivorous macaw and its ear-piercing shriek; bullfrogs the size of North American jackrabbits; 200-pound tortoises with pouched, thoughtful eyes; spider monkeys as playful as children; tapir; tarantulas; most colorful of all, the comical cassowary birds with their bony heads, gaily hued wattles, stunted wings—these ungainly birds whom millions of years of evolution, on an island lacking mammal-predators, have rendered flightless.

And orchids: Some of you have already noticed the lovely, bountiful orchids growing everywhere, dozens of species, every imaginable color, some the size of grapes and others the size of a man's head, unfortunately inedible.

And the island's smells—are they fragrances or odors? Is it rampant fresh-budding life or jungle-rancid decay? Is there a difference?

By night (and the hardiest among you should survive numerous nights, if past history prevails) you'll contemplate the tropical moon, so different from our North American moon, hanging heavy and luminous in the sky like an overripe fruit; you'll be moved to smile at the sport of fiery-phosphorescent fish frolicking in the waves; you'll be lulled to sleep by the din of insects, the cries of nocturnal birds, your own prayers perhaps.

Some of you will cling together, like terrified herd animals; some of you will wander off alone, dazed, refusing to be touched, even comforted by a spouse of fifty years.

Ladies and gentlemen, I, your captain, speak for the crew of the S.S. *Ariel*, bidding you farewell.

Ladies and gentlemen, your children have asked me to assure you that they *do* love you—but circumstances have intervened.

Ladies and gentlemen, your children have asked me to recall to you those years when they were, in fact, *children*—wholly innocent as you imagined them, adoring you as gods.

Ladies and gentlemen, I now bid farewell to you as children do, waving good-bye not once but numerous times, solemn, reverential—good-bye, good-bye, good-bye.

THE RAKE

BY DAVID MAMET

JUNE 1992

There was the incident of the rake and there was the incident of the school play, and it seems to me that they both took place at the round kitchen table.

The table was not in the kitchen proper but in an area called "the nook," which held its claim to that small measure of charm by dint of a waist-high wall separating it from an adjacent area known as the living room.

All family meals were eaten in the nook. There was a dining room to the right, but, as in most rooms of that name at that time and in those surroundings, it was never used.

The round table was of wrought iron and topped with glass; it was noteworthy for that glass, for it was more than once and rather more than several times, I am inclined to think, that my stepfather would grow so angry as to bring some object down on the glass top, shattering it, thus giving us to know how we had forced him out of control.

And it seems that most times when he would shatter the table, as often as that might have been, he would cut some portion of himself on the glass, or that he or his wife, our mother, would cut their hands on picking up the glass afterward, and that we children were to understand, and did understand, that these wounds were our fault.

So the table was associated in our minds with the notion of blood.

The house was in a brand-new housing development in the southern suburbs. The new community was built upon, and now bordered, the remains of what had once been a cornfield. When our new family moved in, there were but a few homes in the development completed, and a few more under construction. Most streets were mud, and boasted a house here or there, and many empty lots marked out by white stakes.

The house we lived in was the development's Model Home. The first time we had seen it, it had signs plastered on the front and throughout the interior telling of the various conveniences it contained. And it had a lawn, and was one of the only homes in the new community that did.

My stepfather was fond of the lawn, and he detailed me and my sister to care for it, and one fall afternoon we found ourselves assigned to rake the leaves.

Why this chore should have been so hated I cannot say, except that we children, and I especially, felt ourselves less than full members of this new, cobbled-together family, and disliked being assigned to the beautification of a home that we found unbeautiful in all respects, and for which we had neither natural affection nor a sense of proprietary interest.

We went to the new high school. We walked the mile down the open two-lane road on one side of which was the just-begun suburban community and on the other side of which was the cornfield.

The school was as new as the community, and still under construction for the first three years of its occupancy. One of its innovations was the notion that honesty would be engendered by the absence of security, and so the lockers were designed and built both without locks and without the possibility of attaching locks. And there was the corresponding rash of thievery and many lectures about the same from the school administration, but it was difficult to point with pride to any scholastic or community tradition supporting the suggestion that we, the students, pull together in this new, utopian way. We were, in school, in an uncompleted building in the midst of a mud field in the midst of a cornfield. Our various sports teams were called The Spartans; and I played on those teams, which were of a wretchedness consistent with their novelty.

Meanwhile my sister interested herself in the drama society. The year after I had left the school she obtained the lead in the school play. It called for acting and singing, both of which she had talent for, and it looked to be a signal triumph for her in her otherwise unremarkable and enjoyed school career.

On the night of the play's opening she sat down to dinner with our mother and our stepfather. It may be that they ate a trifle early to allow her to get to the school to enjoy the excitement of the opening night. But however it was, my sister had no appetite, and she nibbled a bit at her food, and then she got up from the table to carry her plate back to scrape it in the sink, when my mother suggested that she sit down, as she had not finished her food. My sister said she really had no appetite, but my mother insisted that, as the meal had been prepared, it would be good form to sit and eat it.

My sister sat down with the plate and pecked at her food and she tried to eat a bit, and told my mother that, no, really, she possessed no appetite whatever, and that was due, no doubt, not to the food, but to her nervousness and excitement at the prospect of opening night.

My mother, again, said that, as the food had been cooked, it had to be eaten, and my sister tried and said that she could not; at which my mother nodded. She then got up from the table and went to the telephone and looked the number up and called the school and got the drama teacher and identified herself and told him that her daughter wouldn't be coming to school that night, that, no, she was not ill, but that she would not be coming in. Yes, yes, she said, she knew that her daughter had the lead in the play, and, yes, she was aware that many children and teachers had worked hard for it, et cetera, and so my sister did not play the lead in her school play. But I was long gone, out of the house by that time, and well out of it. I heard that story, and others like it, at the distance of twenty-five years.

In the model house our rooms were separated from their room, the master bedroom, by a bathroom and a study. On some weekends I would go alone to visit my father in the city and my sister would stay and sometimes grow frightened or lonely in her part of the house. And once, in the period when my grandfather, then in his sixties, was living with us, she became alarmed at a noise she had heard in the night; or perhaps she just became lonely, and she went out of her room and down the hall, calling for my mother, or my stepfather, or my grandfather, but the house was dark, and no one answered.

And, as she went farther down the hall, toward the living room, she heard voices, and she turned the corner, and saw a light coming from under the closed door in the master bed-

room, and heard my stepfather crying, and the sound of my mother weeping. So my sister went up to the door, and she heard my stepfather talking to my grandfather and saying, "Jack. Say the words. Just say the words…" And my grandfather, in his Eastern European accent, saying, with obvious pain and difficulty, "No. No. I can't. Why are you making me do this? Why?" And the sound of my mother crying convulsively.

My sister opened the door, and she saw my grandfather sitting on the bed, and my stepfather standing by the closet and gesturing. On the floor of the closet she saw my mother, curled in a fetal position, moaning and crying and hugging herself. My stepfather was saying, "Say the words. Just say the words." And my grandfather was breathing fast and repeating, "I can't. She knows how I feel about her. I can't." And my stepfather said, "Say the words, Jack. Please. Just say you love her." At which my mother would moan louder.

And my grandfather said, "I can't."

My sister pushed the door open farther and said—I don't know what she said, but she asked, I'm sure, for some reassurance, or some explanation, and my stepfather turned around and saw her and picked up a hairbrush from a dresser that he passed as he walked toward her, and he hit her in the face and slammed the door on her. And she continued to hear "Jack, say the words."

Gwyn Stramler

She told me that on weekends when I was gone my stepfather ended every Sunday evening by hitting or beating her for some reason or other. He would come home from depositing his own kids back at their mother's house after their weekend visitation, and would settle down tired and angry, and, as a regular matter on those evenings, would find out some intolerable behavior on my sister's part and slap or hit or beat her.

Years later, at my mother's funeral, my sister spoke to our aunt, my mother's sister, who gave a footnote to this behavior. She said when they were young, my mother and my aunt, they and their parents lived in a small flat on the West Side. My grandfather was a salesman on the road from dawn on Monday until Friday night. Their family had a fiction, and that fiction, that article of faith, was that my mother was a naughty child. And each Friday, when he came home, his first question as he climbed the stairs was, "What has she done this week…?" At which my grandmother would tell him the terrible things that my mother had done, after which she, my mother, was beaten.

This was general knowledge in my family. The footnote concerned my grandfather's behavior later in the night. My aunt had a room of her own, and it adjoined her parents' room. And she related that each Friday, when the house had gone to bed, she, through the thin wall, heard my grandfather pleading for sex. "Cookie, please." And my grandmother responding, "No, Jack." "Cookie, please." "No, Jack." "Cookie, please."

And once, my grandfather came home and asked, "What has she done this week?" and I do not know, but I imagine that the response was not completed, and perhaps hardly begun; in any case, he reached and grabbed my mother by the back of the neck and hurled her down the stairs.

And once, in our house in the suburbs there had been an outburst by my stepfather directed at my sister. And she had, somehow, prevailed. It was, I think, that he had the facts of the case wrong, and had accused her of the commission of something for which she had demonstrably had no opportunity, and she pointed this out to him with what I can imagine, given the circumstances, was an understandable, and, given my prejudice, a commendable degree of freedom. Thinking the incident closed she went back to her room to study, and, a few moments later, saw him throw open her door, bat the book out of her hands, and pick her up and throw her against the far wall, where she struck the back of her neck on a shelf.

She was told, the next morning, that her pain, real or pretended, held no weight, and that she would have to go to school. She protested that she could not walk, or, if at all, only with the greatest of difficulty and in great pain; but she was dressed and did walk to school, where she fainted, and was brought home. For years she suffered various headaches; an X ray taken twenty years later for an unrelated problem revealed that when he threw her against the shelf he had cracked her vertebrae.

When we left the house we left in good spirits. When we went out to dinner, it was an adventure, which was strange to me, looking back, because many of these dinners ended with my sister or myself being banished, sullen or in tears, from the restaurant, and told to wait in the car, as we were in disgrace.

These were the excursions that had ended, due to her or my intolerable arrogance, as it was then explained to us.

The happy trips were celebrated and capped with a joke. Here is the joke: My stepfather, my mother, my sister, and I would exit the restaurant, my stepfather and mother would walk to the car, telling us that they would pick us up. We children would stand by the restaurant entrance. They would drive up in the car, open the passenger door, and wait until my sister and I had started to get in. They would then drive away.

They would drive ten or fifteen feet, and open the door again, and we would walk up again, and they would drive away again. They sometimes would drive around the block. But they would always come back, and by that time the four of us would be laughing in camaraderie and appreciation of what, I believe, was our only family joke.

We were raking the lawn, my sister and I. I was raking, and she was stuffing the leaves into a bag. I loathed the job, and my muscles and my mind rebelled, and I was viciously angry, and my sister said something, and I turned and threw the rake at her and it hit her in the face.

The rake was split bamboo and metal, and a piece of metal caught her lip and cut her badly.

We were both terrified, and I was sick with guilt, and we ran into the house, my sister holding her hand to her mouth, and her mouth and her hand and the front of her dress covered in blood.

We ran into the kitchen where my mother was cooking dinner, and my mother asked what happened.

Neither of us, myself out of guilt, of course, and my sister out of a desire to avert the terrible punishment she knew I would receive, neither of us would say what occurred.

My mother pressed us, and neither of us would answer. She said that until one or the other answered, we would not go to the hospital; and so the family sat down to dinner where my sister clutched a napkin to her face and the blood soaked the napkin and ran down onto her food, which she had to eat; and I also ate my food and we cleared the table and went to the hospital.

I remember the walks home from school in the frigid winter, along the cornfield that was, for all its proximity to the city, part of the prairie. The winters were viciously cold. From the remove of years, I can see how the area might and may have been beautiful. One could have walked in the stubble of the cornfields, or hunted birds, or enjoyed any of a number of pleasures naturally occurring.

THE 400-POUND CEO

BY GEORGE SAUNDERS

FEBRUARY 1993

A t noon another load of raccoons comes in and Claude takes them out back of the office and executes them with a tire iron. Then he checks for vitals, wearing protective gloves. Then he drags the cage across 209 and initiates burial by dumping the raccoons into the pit that's our little corporate secret. After burial comes prayer, a personal touch that never fails to irritate Tim, our ruthless CEO. Before founding Humane Raccoon Alternatives, Tim purposely backed his car over a frat boy and got ten-to-twelve for manslaughter. In jail he earned his MBA by designing and marketing a line of light-up Halloween lapel brooches. Now he gives us the brooches as performance incentives and sporadically trashes a bookshelf or two to remind us of his awesome temper and of how ill-advised we would be to cross him in any way whatsoever.

Post-burial, I write up the invoices and a paragraph or two on how overjoyed the raccoons were when we set them free. Sometimes I'll throw in something about spontaneous mating beneath the box elders. No one writes a better misleading letter than me. In the area of phone inquiries I'm also unsurpassed. When a client calls to ask how their release went, everyone in the office falls all over themselves transferring the call to me. I'm reassuring and joyful. I laugh until tears run down my face at the stories I make up regarding the wacky things their raccoon did upon gaining its freedom. Then, as per Tim, I ask if they'd mind sending back our promotional materials. The brochures don't come cheap. They show glossies of raccoons in the wild, contrasted with glossies of poisoned raccoons in their death throes. You lay that on a housewife with perennially knocked-over trash cans and she breathes a sigh of relief. Then she hires you. Then you get a 10 percent commission.

These days commissions are my main joy. I'm too large to attract female company. I weigh four hundred. I don't like it but it's beyond my control. I've tried running and rowing the stationary canoe and hatha-yoga and belly staples and even a muzzle back in the dark days when I had it bad for Freeda, our document placement and retrieval specialist. When I was merely portly it was easy to see myself as a kind of exuberant sportsman who overate out of lust for life. Now no one could possibly mistake me for a sportsman.

When I've finished invoicing I enjoy a pecan cluster. Two, actually. Claude comes in all dirty from the burial and sees me snacking and feels compelled to point out that even my sub-rolls have sub-rolls. He's right but still it isn't nice to say. Tim asks did Claude make that observation after having wild sex with me all night. That's a comment I'm not fond of. But Tim's the boss. His T-shirt says: I HOLD YOUR PURSE STRINGS IN MY HOT LITTLE HAND.

"Ha, ha, Tim," says Claude. "I'm no homo. But if I was one, I'd die before doing it with Mr. Lard."

"Ha, ha," says Tim. "Good one. Isn't that a good one, Jeffrey?"

"That's a good one," I say glumly.

What a bitter little office.

My colleagues leave hippo refrigerator magnets on my seat. They imply that I'm a despondent virgin, which I'm not. They might change their tune if they ever spoke with Ellen Burtomly regarding the beautiful night we spent at her brother Bob's cottage. I was by no means slim then but could at least buy pants off the rack and walk from the den to the kitchen without panting. I remember her nude at the window and the lovely seed helicopters blowing in as she turned and showed me her ample front on purpose. That was my most romantic moment. Now for that kind of thing it's the degradation of Larney's Consenting Adult Viewing Center. Before it started getting to me I'd bring bootloads of quarters and a special bottom cushion and watch hours and hours of Scandinavian women romping. It was shameful. Finally last Christmas I said enough is enough, I'd rather be sexless than evil. And since then I have been. Sexless and

Anthony Russo

good, but very very tense. Since then I've tried to live above the fray. I've tried to minimize my physical aspects and be a selfless force for good. When mocked, which is nearly every day, I recall Christ covered with spittle. When filled with lust, I remember Gandhi purposely sleeping next to a sexy teen to test himself.

After work I go home, watch a little TV, maybe say a rosary or two.

Thirty more years of this and I'm out of it without hurting anybody or embarrassing myself.

But still. I'm a human being. A little companionship would be nice. My colleagues know nothing of my personal life. They couldn't care less that I once had a dog named Woodsprite who was crushed by a backhoe. They couldn't care less that my dad died a wino in the vicinity of the Fort Worth stockyards. In his last days he sent me a note filled with wonder:

"Son," he wrote, "are you fat, too? It came upon me suddenly and now I am big as a house. Beware, perhaps it's in our genes. I wander cowboy sidewalks of wood, wearing a too-small hat, filled with remorse for the many lives I failed to lead. Adieu. In my mind you are a waify-looking little fellow who never answered when I asked you a direct question. But I loved you as best I could."

What do my colleagues know of Dad? What do they know of me? What kind of friend gets a kick out of posting in the break room a drawing of you eating an entire computer? What kind of friend jokes that someday you'll be buried in a specially built container after succumbing to heart strain?

I'm sorry, but I feel that life should offer more than this.

As a child my favorite book was *Little Red-faced Cop on the Beat*. Everyone loved the Little Red-faced Cop. He knew what was what. He donned his uniform in a certain order every morning. He chased bad guys and his hat stayed on. Now I'm surrounded by kooks. I'm a kook myself. I stoop down and tell raccoons to take it like a man. I drone on and on to strangers about my weight. I ogle salesgirls. I double back to pick up filthy pennies. When no one's around I dig and dig at my earwax, then examine it. I'm huge, and terrified of becoming bitter.

Sometimes I sense deep anger welling up, and have to choke it back.

Sadly, I find my feelings for Freeda returning. I must have a death wish. Clearly I repulse her. Sometimes I catch her looking at my gut overhangs with a screwed-up face. I see her licking her lips while typing, and certain unholy thoughts go through my head. I hear her speaking tenderly on the phone to her little son, Len, and can't help picturing myself sitting on a specially reinforced porch swing while she fries up some chops and Len digs in the muck.

Today as we prepare mailers she says she's starting to want to be home with Len all the time. But there's the glaring problem of funds. She makes squat. I've seen her stub. There's the further problem that she suspects Mrs. Rasputin, Len's baby-sitter, is a lush.

"I don't know what to do," Freeda says. "I come home after work and she's sitting there tipsy in her bra, fanning herself with a *Racing Form*."

"I know how you feel," I say. "Life can be hard."

"It has nothing to do with life," she says crossly. "It has to do with my drunken baby-sitter. Maybe you haven't been listening to me."

Before I know what I'm saying I suggest that perhaps we should go out for dinner and offer each other some measure of comfort. In response she spits her Tab out across her cubicle. She says now she's heard it all. She goes to fetch Tim and Claude so they can join her in guffawing at my nerve. She faxes a comical note about my arrogance to her girl-friend at the DMV. All afternoon she keeps looking at me with her head cocked.

Needless to say, it's a long day.

Then at five, after everyone else is gone, she comes shyly by and says she'd love to go out with me. She says I've always been there for her. She says she likes a man with a little meat on his bones. She says pick her up at eight and bring something for Len. I'm shocked. I'm overjoyed.

My knees are nearly shaking my little desk apart.

I buy Len a football helmet and a baseball glove and an aquarium and a set of encyclopedias. I basically clean out my pitiful savings. Who cares. It's worth it to get a chance to observe her beautiful face from across a table without Claude et al. hooting at me.

When I ring her bell someone screams come in. Inside I find Len behind the home entertainment center and Mrs. Rasputin drunkenly poring over her grade-school yearbook with a highlighter. She looks up and says: "Where's that kid?" I feel like saying: How should I know? Instead I say: "He's behind the home entertainment center."

"He loves it back there," she says. "He likes eating the lint balls. They won't hurt him. They're like roughage."

"Come out, Len," I say. "I have gifts."

He comes out. One tiny eyebrow cocks up at my physical appearance. Then he crawls into my lap holding his MegaDeathDealer by the cowl. What a sweet boy. The Dealer's got a severed human head in its hand. When you pull a string the Dealer cries, "You're dead and I've killed you, Prince of Slime," and sticks its Day-Glo tongue out. I give Len my antiviolence spiel. I tell him only love can dispel hate. I tell him we were meant to live in harmony and give one another emotional support. He looks at me blankly, then flings his DeathDealer at the cat.

Freeda comes down looking sweet and casts a baleful eye on Mrs. Rasputin and away we go. I take her to Ace's Volcano Island. Ace's is an old service station now done up Hawaiian. They've got a tape loop of surf sounds and some Barbies in grass skirts climbing a papier-mâché mountain. I'm known there. Every Friday night I treat myself by taking up a whole booth and ordering the Broccoli Rib Luau. Ace is a gentle aging beatnik with mild Tourette's. When the bad words start flying out of his mouth you never saw someone so regretful. One minute he'll be quoting the Bhagavad Gita and the next roughly telling one of his patrons to lick their own bottom. We've talked about it. He says he's tried pills. He's tried biting down on a pencil eraser. He's tried picturing himself in the floodplain of the Ganges with a celestial being stroking his hair. Nothing works. So he's printed up an explanatory flier. Shirleen the hostess hands it out pre-seating. There's a cartoon of Ace with lots of surprise marks and typographic symbols coming out of his mouth.

"My affliction is out of my hands," it says. "But please know that whatever harsh words I may direct at you, I truly treasure your patronage."

He fusses over us by bringing extra ice water and sprinting into the back room whenever he feels an attack looming. I purposely starve myself. We talk about her life philosophy. We talk about her hairstyle and her treasured childhood memories and her paranormally gifted aunt. I fail to get a word in edgewise, and that's fine. I like listening. I like learning about her. I like putting myself in her shoes and seeing things her way.

I walk her home. Kids in doorways whistle at my width. I handle it with grace by shaking my rear. Freeda laughs. A kiss seems viable. It all feels too good to be true.

Then on her porch she shakes my hand and says great, she can now pay her phone bill, courtesy of Tim. She shows me their written agreement. It says: "In consideration of your consenting to be seen in public with Jeffrey, I, Tim, will pay you, Freeda, the sum of fifty dollars."

She goes inside. I take a week of vacation and play Oil Can Man nonstop. I achieve Level Nine. I master the Hydrocarbon Dervish and the Cave of Dangerous Lubrication. I cream Mr. Grit and consistently prohibit him from inflicting wear and tear on my Pistons. There's something sick about the amount of pleasure I take in pretending Freeda's Mr. Grit as I annihilate him with Bonus Cleansing Additives. At the end of night three I step outside for some air. Up in the sky are wild clouds that make me think of Tahiti and courageous sailors on big sinking wooden ships. Meanwhile here's me, a grown man with a joystick-burn on his thumb.

So I throw the game cartridge in the trash and go back to work. I take the ribbing. I take the abuse. Someone's snipped my head out of the office photo and mounted it on a bride's body. Tim says what the heck, the thought of the visual incongruity of our pairing was worth the fifty bucks.

"Do you hate me?" Freeda asks.

"No," I say. "I truly enjoyed our evening together."

"God, I didn't," she says. "Everyone kept staring at us. It made me feel bad about myself that they thought I was actually with you. Do you know what I mean?"

I can't think of anything to say, so I nod. Then I retreat moist-eyed to my cubicle for some invoicing fun. I'm not a bad guy. If only I could stop hoping. If only I could say to my heart: Give up. Be alone forever. There's always opera. There's angel-food cake and neighborhood children caroling, and the look of autumn leaves on a wet roof. But no. My heart's some kind of idiotic fishing bobber.

My invoices go very well. The sun sinks, the moon rises, round and pale as my stupid face.

I minimize my office time by volunteering for the Carlisle entrapment. The Carlisles are rich. A poor guy has a raccoon problem, he sprinkles poison in his trash and calls it a day. Not the Carlisles. They dominate bread routes throughout the city. Carlisle supposedly strong-armed his way to the top of the bread heap, but in person he's nice enough. I let him observe me laying out the rotting fruit. I show him how the cage door coming down couldn't hurt a flea. Then he goes inside and I wait patiently in my car.

Just after midnight I trip the wire. I fetch the Carlisles and encourage them to squat down and relate to the captured raccoon. Then I recite our canned speech congratulating them for their advanced thinking. I describe the wilderness where the release will take place, the streams and fertile valleys, the romp in the raccoon's stride when it catches its first whiff of pristine air.

Mr. Carlisle says thanks for letting them sleep at night sans guilt. I tell him that's my job. Just then the raccoon's huge mate bolts out of the woods and tears into my calf. I struggle to my car and kick the mate repeatedly against my wheel well until it dies with my leg in its mouth. The Carlisles stand aghast in the carport. I stand aghast in the driveway, sick at heart. I've trapped my share of raccoons and helped Claude with more burials than I care to remember, but I've never actually killed anything before.

I throw both coons in the trunk and drive myself to the emergency room, where I'm given the first of a series of extremely painful shots. I doze off on a bench post-treatment and dream of a den of pathetic baby raccoons in V-neck sweaters yelping for food.

When I wake up I call in. Tim asks if I'm crazy, kicking a raccoon to death in front of clients. Couldn't I have gently lifted it off, he asks, or offered it some rotting fruit? Am I proud of my ability to fuck up one-car funerals? Do I or do I not recall Damian Flaverty?

Who could forget Damian Flaverty? He'd been dipping into the till to finance his necktie boutique. Tim black-jacked him into a crumpled heap on the floor and said: Do you think I spent nine years in the slammer only to get out and be fleeced by your ilk? Then he broke Damian's arm with an additional whack. I almost dropped my mug.

I tell Tim I'm truly sorry I didn't handle the situation more effectively. He says the raccoon must've had a sad last couple of minutes once it realized it had given up its life for the privilege of gnawing on a shank of pure fat. That hurts. Why I continue to expect decent treatment from someone who's installed a torture chamber in the corporate basement is beyond me. Down there he's got a Hide-A-Bed and a whip collection and an executioner's mask with a built-in Walkman. Sometimes when I'm invoicing late he'll bring in one of his willing victims. Usually they're both wasto. I get as much of me under my desk as I can. Talk about the fall of man. Talk about some father somewhere being crestfallen if he knew what his daughter was up to. Once I peeked out as they left and saw a blonde with a black eye going wherever Tim pointed and picking up his coat whenever he purposely dropped it.

"You could at least take me for coffee," she said.

"I'd like to spill some on your bare flesh," Tim said.

"Mmm," she said. "Sounds good."

How do people get like this, I thought. Can they change back? Can they learn again to love and be gentle? How can they look at themselves in the mirror or hang Christmas ornaments without overflowing with self-loathing?

Then I thought: I may be obese but at least I'm not cruel to the point of being satanic.

Next day Tim was inducted into Rotary and we all went to the luncheon. He spoke on turning one's life around. He spoke on the bitter lessons of incarceration. He sang the praises of America, and joked with balding sweetheart ophthalmologists, and after lunch hung his Rotary plaque in the torture chamber stairwell and ordered me to Windex it daily or face extremely grim consequences.

Tuesday, as Claude and I approach the burial pit with the Carlisle raccoons, a car pulls up. We drag the cage into a shrub and squat, panting. Claude whispers that I smell. He whispers that if he weighed four hundred he'd take into account the people around him and go on a diet. The sky's the purple of holy card crucifixion scenes, the rending of the

firmament and all that. A girl in a sari gets out of the car and walks to the lip of the pit. She paces off the circumference and scribbles in a notebook. She takes photos. She slides down on her rear and comes back up with some coon bones in a Baggie.

After she leaves we rush back to the office. Tim's livid and starts baby-oiling his trademark blackjack. He says no more coons in the pit until further notice. He says we're hereby in crisis mode and will keep the coons on blue ice in our cubicles and if need be wear nose clips. He says the next time she shows up he may have to teach her a bitter lesson about jeopardizing our meal ticket. He says animal rights are all well and good but there's a substantive difference between a cute bunny or cat and a disgusting raccoon that thrives on carrion and trash and creates significant sanitation problems with its inquisitiveness.

"Oh, get off it," Claude says, with affection for Tim shining from his dull eyes. "You'd eliminate your own mother if there was a buck in it for you."

"Undeniably," Tim says. "Especially if she knocked over a client trash can or turned rabid."

Then he hands me the corporate Visa and sends me to HardwareNiche for coolers. At HardwareNiche you can get a video of *Bloodiest Crimes of the Century Re-enacted*. You can get a video of great bloopers made during the filming of *Bloodiest Crimes of the Century Re-enacted*. You can get a bird feeder that plays "How Dry I Am" while electronically emitting a soothing sensation birds love. You can get a Chill'n'Pray, an overpriced cooler with a holographic image of a famous religious personality on the lid. I opt for Buddha. I can almost hear Tim sarcastically comparing our girths and asking since when has cost control been thrown to the wind. But the Chill'n'Prays are all they've got. I'm on Tim's shit list if I do, and on Tim's shit list if I don't. He has an actual shit list. Freeda generated it and enhanced it with a graphic of an angry piece of feces stamping its feet.

I buy the coolers, hoping in spite of myself that he'll applaud my decisiveness. When I get back to the office everyone's gone for the night. The Muzak's off for a change and loud whacks and harsh words are floating up from the basement via the heat ducts. Before long Tim tromps up the stairs swearing. I hide pronto. He shouts thanks for nothing, and says he could have had more rough-and-tumble fun dangling a cat over a banister, and that there's nothing duller than a clerk with the sexual imagination of a grape.

"Document placement and retrieval specialist," Freeda says in a hurt tone.

"Whatever," Tim says, and speeds off in his Porsche.

I emerge overwhelmed from my cubicle. Over her shoulder and through the plate glass is a shocked autumnal moon. Freeda's cheek is badly bruised. Otherwise she's radiant with love. My mouth hangs open.

"What can I say?" she says. "I can't get enough of the man."

"Good night," I say, and forget about my car, and walk the nine miles home in a daze.

All day Wednesday I prepare to tell Tim off. But I'm too scared. Plus he could rightly say she's a consenting adult. What business is it of mine? Why defend someone who has no desire to be defended? Instead I drop a few snots in his coffee cup and use my network access privileges to cancel his print jobs. He asks can I work late and in spite of myself I fawningly say sure. I hate him. I hate myself. Everybody else goes home. Big clouds roll in. I invoice like mad. Birds light on the Dumpster and feed on substances caked on the lid. What a degraded cosmos. What a case of something starting out nice and going bad.

Just after seven I hear him shout: "You, darling, will rot in hell, with the help of a swift push to the grave from me!" At first I think he's pillow talking with Freeda by phone. Then I look out the window and see the animal rights girl at the lip of our pit with a Camcorder.

Admirable dedication, I think, wonderful clarity of vision.

Tim runs out the door with his blackjack unsheathed.

What to do? Clearly he means her harm. I follow him, leaving behind my loafers to minimize noise. I keep to the shadows and scurry in my socks from tiny berm to tiny berm. I heave in an unattractive manner. My heart rate's in the ionosphere. To my credit I'm able to keep up with him. Meanwhile she's struggling up the slope with her hair in sweet disarray, backlit by a moon the color of honey, Camcorder on her head like some kind of Kenyan water jug.

"Harlot," Tim hisses, "attempted defiler of my dream," and whips his blackjack down. Am I quick? I am so quick. I lunge up and take it on the wrist. My arm bone goes to mush, and my head starts to spin, and I wrap Tim up in a hug the size of Tulsa.

"Run," I gasp to the girl, and see in the moonlight the affluent white soles of her fleeing boat-type shoes.

I hug hard. I tell him drop the jack and to my surprise he does. Do I then release him? To my shame, no. So much sick rage is stored up in me. I never knew. And out it comes in one mondo squeeze, and something breaks, and he goes limp, and I lay him gently down in the dirt.

I CPR like anything. I beg him to rise up and thrash me. I do a crazy little dance of grief. But it's no good.

I've killed Tim.

I sprint across 209 and ineffectually drag my bulk around Industrial Grotto, weeping and banging on locked corporate doors. United KneeWrap's having a gala. Their top brass are drunkenly lip-synching hits of the Fifties en masse and their foot soldiers are laughing like subservient fools, so no one hears my frantic knocking. I prepare to heave a fake boulder through the plate glass. But then I stop. By now Tim's beyond help. What do I gain by turning myself in? Did I or did I not save an innocent girl's life? Was he or was he not a cruel monster? What's done is done. My peace of mind is gone forever. Why spend the remainder of my life in jail for the crime of eliminating a piece of filth?

And standing there outside the gala I learn something vital about myself: When push comes to shove, I couldn't give a crap about lofty ideals. It's me I love. It's me I want to protect.

Me.

I hustle back to the office for the burial gear. I roll Tim into the pit. I sprinkle on lime and cover him with dirt. I forge a letter in which he claims to be going to Mexico to clarify his relationship with God via silent meditation in a rugged desert setting.

"My friends," I write through tears in his childish scrawl. "You slave away for minimal rewards! Freedom can be yours if you open yourself to the eternal! Good health and happiness to you all. I'm truly sorry for any offense I may have given. Especially to you, Freeda, who deserved a better man than the swine I was. I am a new man now, and Freeda dear, I suggest counseling. Also: I have thought long and hard on this, and have decided to turn over the reins to Jeffrey, whom I have always wrongly maligned. I see now that he is a man of considerable gifts, and ask you all to defer to him as you would to me."

I leave the letter on Claude's chair and go out to sleep in my car. I dream of Tim wearing a white robe in a Mexican cantina. A mangy dog sits on his lap explaining the rules of the dead. No weeping. No pushing the other dead. Don't bore everyone with tales of how great you were. Tim smiles sweetly and rubs the dog behind the ears. He sees me and says no hard feelings and thanks for speeding him on to the realm of bliss.

I wake with a start. The sun comes up, driving sparrows before it, turning the corporate reflective windows wild with orange. I roll out of my car and brush my teeth with my finger.

My first day as a killer.

I walk to the pit in the light of fresh day, hoping it was all a dream. But no. There's our scuffling footprints. There's the mound of fresh dirt, under which lies Tim. I sit on a paint can in a patch of waving weeds and watch my colleagues arrive. I weep. I think sadly of the kindly bumbler I used to be, bleary-eyed in the morning, guiltless and looking forward to coffee.

When I finally go in, everyone's gathered stunned around the microwave.

"El Presidente," Claude says disgustedly.

"Sorry?" I say.

I make a big show of shaking my head in shock as I read and reread the note I wrote. I ask if this means I'm in charge. Claude says, with that kind of conceptual grasp we're not exactly in for salad days. He asks Freeda if she had an inkling. She says she always knew Tim had certain unplumbed depths but this is ridiculous. Claude says he smells a rat. He says Tim never had a religious bone in his body and didn't speak a word of Spanish. My face gets red. Thank God Blamphin, that toady, pipes up.

"I say in terms of giving Jeffrey a chance, we should give Jeffrey a chance, inasmuch as Tim was a good manager but a kind of a mean guy," he says.

"Well put," Claude says cynically. "And I say this fatty knows something he's not telling."

I praise Tim to the skies and admit I could never fill his shoes. I demean my organizational skills and leadership abilities but vow to work hard for the good of all. Then I humbly propose a vote: Do I assume leadership or not? Claude says he'll honor a quorum, and then via a show of hands I achieve a nice one.

I move my things into Tim's office. Because he'd always perceived me as a hefty Milquetoast with no personal aspirations he trusted me implicitly. So I'm able to access the corporate safe. I'm able to cater in prime rib and a trio of mustachioed violinists, who stroll from cubicle to cubicle hoping for tips. Claude's outraged. Standing on his chair, he demands to know whatever happened to the profit motive.

Everyone ignores him while munching on my prime rib and enjoying my musicians. He says one can't run a corporation on good intentions and blatant naïveté. He pleads that the staff fire me and appoint him CEO. Finally Blamphin proposes I can him. Torson from Personnel seconds the motion. I shrug my shoulders and we vote, and Claude's axed. He kicks the watercooler. He gives me the finger. But out he goes, leaving us to our chocolate mousse and cocktails.

By nightfall the party's kicked into high gear. I bring in jugglers and a comedian and drinks, drinks, drinks. My staff swears their undying loyalty. We have drunken toasts to my health, and theirs. I tell them we'll kill no more. I tell them we'll come clean with the appropriate agencies and pay all relevant fines. Henceforth we'll relocate the captured raccoons as we've always claimed to be doing. The company will be owned by us, the employees, who will come and go as we please. Beverages and snacks will be continually on hand. Insurance will be gratis. Day care will be available on-site.

Freeda brightens and sits on the arm of my chair.

Muzak will give way to personal stereos in each cubicle. We will support righteous charities, take troubled children under our collective wing, enjoy afternoons off when the sun is high and the air sweet with the smell of mown grass, treat one another as family, send one another fond regards on a newly installed electronic mail system, and, when one of us finally has to die, we will have the consolation of knowing that, aided by corporate largess, our departed colleague has known his or her full measure of power, love, and beauty, and arm in arm we will all march to the graveyard, singing sad hymns.

Just then the cops break in, led by Claude, who's holding one of Tim's shoes.

"If you went to Mexico," he shouts triumphantly, "wouldn't you take your Porsche? Would you be so stupid as to turn your life's work over to this tub of lard? Things started to add up. I did some literal digging. And there I found my friend Tim, with a crushed rib cage that broke my heart, and a look of total surprise on his face."

"My Timmy," Freeda says, rising from my chair. "This disgusting pig killed my beautiful boy."

They cuff me and lead me away.

In court I tell the truth. The animal rights girl comes out of the woodwork and corroborates my story. The judge says he appreciates my honesty and the fact that I saved a life. He wonders why, having saved the life, I didn't simply release Tim and reap the laurels of my courage. I tell him I lost control. I tell him a lifetime of scorn boiled over. He says he empathizes completely. He says he had a weight problem himself when a lad.

Then he gives me fifty, as opposed to life without parole.

So now I know misery. I know the acute discomfort of a gray jail suit pieced together from two garments of normal size. I know the body odor of Vic, a Chicago kingpin who's claimed me for his own and compels me to wear a feminine hat with fruit on the brim for nightly interludes. Do my ex-colleagues write? No. Does Freeda? Ha. Have I achieved serenity? No. Have I transcended my horrid surroundings and thereby won the begrudging admiration of my fellow cons? No. They exult in hooting at me nude during group showers. They steal my allotted food portions. Do I have a meaningful hobby that makes the days fly by like minutes? No. I have a wild desire to smell the ocean. I have a sense that God is unfair and preferentially punishes his weak, his dumb, his fat, his lazy. I believe he takes more pleasure in his perfect creatures, and cheers them on like a brainless dad as they run roughshod over the rest of us. He gives us a need for love, and no way to get any. He gives us a desire to be liked, and personal attributes that make us utterly unlikable. Having placed his flawed and needy children in a world of exacting specifications, he deducts the difference between what we have and what we need from our hearts and our self-esteem and our mental health.

This is how I feel. These things seem to me true. But what's there to do but behave with dignity? Keep a nice cell. Be polite but firm when Vic asks me to shimmy while wearing the hat. Say a kind word when I can to the legless man doing life, who's perennially on toilet duty. Join in at the top of my lungs when the geriatric murderer from Baton Rouge begins his nightly spiritual.

Maybe the God we see, the God who calls the daily shots, is merely a subGod. Maybe there's a God above this subGod who's busy for a few Godminutes with something else, and will be right back, and when he gets back will take the subGod by the ear and say: Now look. Look at that fat man. What did he ever do to you? Wasn't he humble enough? Didn't he endure enough abuse for a thousand men? Weren't the simplest tasks hard? Didn't you sense him craving affection? Were you unaware that his days unraveled as one long bad dream? And maybe as the subGod slinks away, the true God will sweep me up in his arms, saying: My sincere apologies, a mistake has been made. Accept a new birth, as token of my esteem.

And I will emerge again from between the legs of my mother, a slighter and more beautiful baby, destined for a different life, in which I am masterful, sleek as a deer, a winner.

The Last Shot

by Darcy Frey

April 1993

AUGUST 1991

Russell Thomas places his right sneaker one inch behind the three-point line, considers the basket with a level gaze, cocks his wrist to shoot, then suddenly looks around. Has he spotted me, watching from the corner of the playground? No, something else is up: he is lifting his nose to the wind like a spaniel, he is gauging air currents. He waits until the wind settles, bits of trash feathering lightly to the ground. Then he sends a twenty-five-foot jump shot arcing through the soft summer twilight. It drops without a sound through the dead center of the bare iron rim. So does the next one. So does the one after that. Alone in the gathering dusk, Russell works the perimeter against imaginary defenders, unspooling jump shots from all points. Few sights on Brooklyn playgrounds stir the hearts and minds of the coaches and scouts who recruit young men for college basketball teams quite like Russell's jumper; they have followed its graceful trajectory ever since he made varsity at Abraham Lincoln High School, in Coney Island, two years ago. But the shot is merely the final gesture, the public flourish of a private regimen that brings Russell to this court day and night. Avoiding pickup games, he gets down to work: an hour of three-point shooting, then wind sprints up the fourteen flights in his project stairwell, then back to the court, where (much to his friends' amusement) he shoots one-handers ten feet from the basket while sitting in a chair.

At this hour Russell usually has the court to himself; most of the other players won't come out until after dark, when the thick humid air begins to stir with night breezes and the court lights come on. But this evening is turning out to be a fine one—cool and foggy. The low, slanting sun sheds a feeble pink light over the silvery Atlantic a block away, and milky sheets of fog roll off the ocean and drift in tatters along the project walkways. The air smells of sewage and saltwater. At the far end of the court, where someone has torn a hole in the chicken-wire fence, other players climb through and begin warming up.

Like most of New York's impoverished and predominantly black neighborhoods, Coney Island does not exactly shower its youth with opportunity. In the early 1960s, urban renewal came to Coney Island in the form of a vast tract of housing projects, packed so densely along a twenty-block stretch that a new skyline rose suddenly behind the boardwalk and amusement park. The experiment of public housing, which has isolated the nation's urban poor from the hearts of their cities, may have failed here in even more spectacular fashion because of Coney Island's utter remoteness. In this neighborhood, on a peninsula at the southern tip of Brooklyn, there are almost no stores, no trees, no police; just block after block of gray cement projects—hulking, prison-like, and jutting straight into the sea.

Most summer nights an amorphous unease settles over Coney Island as apartments become too stifling to bear and the streets fall prey to the gangs and drug dealers. Options are limited: to the south is the stiff gray meringue of the Atlantic; to the north, more than ten miles away, are the Statue of Liberty and the glass-and-steel spires of Manhattan's financial district. Officially, Coney Island is considered a part of the endless phantasmagoria that is New York City. But on nights like these, as the dealers set up their drug marts in the streets and alleyways, and the sounds of sirens and gunfire keep pace with the darkening sky, it feels like the end of the world.

Yet even in Coney Island there are some uses to which a young man's talent, ambition, and desire to stay out of harm's way may be put: there is basketball. Hidden behind the projects are dozens of courts, and every night they fill with restless teenagers, there to remain for hours until exhaustion or the hoodlums take over. The high-school dropouts and the aging players who never made it to college usually show up for a physical game at a barren strip of courts by the water known as Chop Chop Land, where bruises and minutes played are accrued at a one-to-one ratio. The younger kids congregate for rowdy games at Run-and-Gun Land. The court there is short and the rims are low, so everyone can dunk, and the only pass ever made is the one inbounding the ball. At Run-and-Gun, players stay on the move for another reason: the court sits just below one of the most dreaded projects, where Coney Island's worst hoodlums sometimes pass a summer evening "getting hectic," as they say—tossing batteries and beer bottles onto the court from apartment windows fifteen stories above.

The neighborhood's best players—the ones, like Russell, with aspirations—practice a disciplined, team-driven style of basketball at this court by the O'Dwyer projects, which has been dubbed the Garden after the New York Knicks' arena. In a neighborhood ravaged by the commerce of drugs, the Garden offers a tenuous sanctuary. A few years ago, community activists petitioned the housing authority to install night lights. And the players themselves resurfaced the court and put up regulation-height rims that snap back after a player dunks. Russell may be the only kid at the Garden who practices his defensive footwork while holding a ten-pound brick in each hand, but no one here treats the game as child's play. Even the

James Hamilton

hoodlums decline to vandalize the Garden, because in Coney Island the possibility of transcendence through basketball is an article of faith.

Most evenings this summer I have come to the Garden to watch Russell and his friends play ball. The notion that basketball can liberate dedicated players like these from the grinding daily privations of the ghetto has become a cherished parable, advanced by television sportscasters, college basketball publicists, and sneaker companies proselytizing the work ethic and $120 high-tops. And that parable is conveyed directly to the players at the Garden by the dozens of college coaches who arrive in Coney Island each year with assurances that even if a National Basketball Association contract isn't in the cards, a player's talent and tenacity will

at least reward him with a free college education, a decent job, and a one-way ticket out of the neighborhood. But how does this process actually unfold? And what forces stand in its way? How often is basketball's promise of a better life redeemed? It was questions like these that drew me to this court, between Mermaid and Surf avenues.

"Just do it, right?" I glance to my left and there is Corey Johnson, smiling mischievously, eyes alight. He nods toward the court—players stretching out, taking lay-ups—and it does, in fact, resemble a sneaker commercial. "Work hard, play hard, buy yourself a pair of Nikes, young man," Corey intones. Corey is a deft mimic and he does a superb white TV announcer. "They get you where you want to go, which is out of the ghet-to!" He laughs, we shake hands, and he takes up an observation post by my side.

Corey is Russell's best friend and one of Lincoln High's other star seniors. He, too, expects to play college ball. But he specializes in ironic detachment and normally shows up courtside with his Walkman merely to watch for girls beneath his handsome, hooded eyes. Tonight he is wearing a fresh white T-shirt, expertly ripped along the back and sleeves to reveal glimpses of his sculpted physique; denim shorts that reach to his knees; and a pair of orange sneakers that go splendidly with his lid—a tan baseball cap with orange piping, which he wears with the bill pointing skyward. From his headphones come the sounds of Color Me Badd, and Corey sings along: *I—wanna—sex—you—up* ... He loops his fingers around the chicken-wire fence and says, "I tell you, Coney Island is like a disease. Of the mind. It makes you lazy. You relax too much. 'Cause all you ever see is other guys relaxing."

Although a pickup game has begun at the basket nearest us, Russell still commands the other. As the last light drains from the sky, he finishes with three-pointers and moves on to baby hooks: fifteen with the left hand, fifteen with the right; miss one and start all over again. Corey smiles at his friend's hair-shirt discipline. Russell, it is hoped, will play next year in the Big East, one of the nation's top college conferences, in which Seton Hall, St. John's, Georgetown, Syracuse, and others compete. [...]

Basketball newsletters and scouting reports are constantly scrutinizing the players, and practically every day some coach shows up—appraising, coaxing, negotiating, and, as often as not, making promises he never keeps. Getting [a] scholarship offer is every player's dream—in anticipation, no one steps outside in Coney Island without a Syracuse cap or a St. John's sweatshirt. But in reality only a handful of the neighborhood's players have ever made it to such top four-year programs; most have been turned back by one obstacle or another in high school. Others who have enrolled in college never saw their dream to completion. The list is grim: there was Eric "Spoon" Marbury, who played for the University of Georgia but never graduated, and ended up back in Coney Island working construction; his younger brother Norman "Jou-Jou" Marbury, who lost his scholarship to highly ranked Tennessee because of academic problems in high school; and now David "Chocolate" Harris, a talented player who never even graduated from high school. He dropped out of Lincoln after his freshman year and became a small-time drug dealer. Earlier this summer police found him in an abandoned lot, his hood pulled over his head and a bullet through his skull. He was seventeen. Some of the players warming up at the Garden have written on the tongues of their sneakers, CHOCOLATE: R.I.P.

The orange court lights have come on now, displacing the encroaching darkness. Two players on either end of the court climb the fence and sit atop the backboards, hanging nets—a sign that a serious game is about to begin. Suddenly a ferocious grinding noise fills the air. It gets louder and louder, and then a teenage kid riding a Big Wheel careers onto the court. He darts through the playground crowd, leaving a wake of pissed-off players, then hops off his ride and watches it slam into the fence. "Ah, yes, Stephon Marbury," Corey says dryly, "future of the neighborhood."

Stephon—Eric and Norman Marbury's kid brother—is barely fourteen, has yet to begin high school, but already his recruiting has begun. At least one college coach is known to have sent him fawning letters, in violation of National Collegiate Athletic Association rules; street agents, paid under the table by colleges to bring top players to their programs, have begun cultivating Stephon; and practically every high-school coach in the city is heaping him with free gear—sneakers, caps, bags—in an attempt to lure him to his school. At first glance, Stephon doesn't look like the future of anything: he's diminutive, barely five feet nine, with the rounded forehead and delicate features of an infant. He sports a stylish razor cut and a pierced ear, and the huge gold stud seems to tilt his tiny bald head off its axis. Caught somewhere between puberty and superstardom, he walks around with his sneakers untied, the ends of his belt drooping suggestively from his pants, and half a Snickers bar extruding from his mouth.

With Stephon here, Corey wanders onto the court. Russell, too, is persuaded to give up his solo regimen. Basketball, it is commonly said, is a game of pure instinct, but the five-on-five contest that begins here is something else. Corey and Stephon are cousins, and Russell is as good as family—the three of them have played together since they were in grade school. They seem to move as if the spontaneous, magical geometry of the game had all been rehearsed in advance. Stephon, the smallest by far, is doing tricks with the ball as though it were dangling from his hand by a string, then gunning it to his older teammates with a series of virtuoso no-look passes: behind-the-back passes, sidearm passes, shovel passes. Corey is lulling defenders with his sleepy eyes, then exploding to the basket, where he casually tosses the ball through the hoop. Russell is sinking twenty-footers as if they were six-inch putts.

The game has just begun when a crowd starts to form: sidelined players, three deep, waiting their turn. A prostitute trolling for clients. A drunk yelling maniacally, "I played with Jordan, I played with Jabbar. They ain't shit. And neither are *you!*" A buffed-out guy in a silk suit and alligator shoes arrives, swigging from a bottle of Courvoisier. An agent? A scout? The crowd gives him elbow room. A couple of teenage mothers with strollers come by; they get less elbow room.

Basketball is so inextricably woven into the fabric of Coney Island life that almost everyone here can recite a complete oral history of the neighborhood's players. People remember the exact scores of summer tournament games played at this court ten years ago, or describe in rapturous detail the perfect arc that Carlton "Silk" Owens put on his jumper before he was shot in the elbow in 1982. Dog-eared copies of a ten-year-old University of Georgia catalogue with a picture of Spoon Marbury playing with future NBA great Dominique Wilkins get passed around like samizdat.

Russell, Corey, and Stephon are the natural heirs to this vaunted tradition. But this is a complicated business: given the failures that have preceded them, the new crew is watched by the neighborhood with a certain skittishness, a growing reluctance to care too deeply. Yet Coney Island offers its residents little else on which to hang their pride. So the proceedings here take on a desperate, exalted quality, and by unspoken agreement the misfortunes of bygone players are chalked up to either a lack of will or plain bad luck—both of which make possible the continuance of hope. Silk didn't go pro, it is said, "because that was the year they cut the college draft from three rounds to two." Another player, the explanation goes, had that pro game, went to the hoop both ways, "but he was done in by a shyster agent."

Still, the suspicion lingers that something larger and less comprehensible may be at work. Ten years ago, the Long Island City projects in Queens produced New York's best players, but the drug industry and the collapse of that neighborhood into violence, broken families, and ever-greater poverty put an end to its dynasty. In recent years the torch has passed to Coney Island, which struggles to avoid a similar fate.

It's past midnight now, and the ambient glow of Manhattan's remote skyscrapers has turned the sky a metallic blue. Standing courtside, we can see only the darkened outlines of the projects, looming in every direction, and the shirtless players streaking back and forth, drenched in a pool of orange light. For Russell, Corey, and Stephon, the hard labor of winning their scholarships lies ahead; for now this game is enough. Corey, sprinting downcourt, calls out, "Homeboy! Homeboy!" Standing under his own basket, Stephon lets fly with a long, improbable pass that Corey somehow manages to catch and dunk in one balletic leap. The game is stopped on account of pandemonium: players and spectators are screaming and staggering around the court—knees buckling, heads held in astonishment. Even Mr. Courvoisier loses his cool. Stephon laughs and points to the rim, still shuddering fearfully from its run-in with Corey's fists. "Yo, cuz," he yells. "Make it bleed!" Then he raises his arms jubilantly and dances a little jig, rendered momentarily insane by the sheer giddy pleasure of playing this game to perfection.

SEPTEMBER

Abraham Lincoln High School is a massive yellow-brick building of ornate stonework and steel-gated windows a few blocks north of the boardwalk. As Coney Island has deterio-

rated, so has Lincoln High, though the school itself sits about a mile from the projects at the end of Ocean Parkway, a stately, tree-lined boulevard. Across the parkway are Brighton Beach and several other Jewish neighborhoods, but the kids from those areas are usually sent elsewhere for their education, as Lincoln has become, little by little, a ghetto school for the projects.

A malaise has set in at Lincoln, as it has at so many inner-city public schools. Students regularly walk in and out of class, sleep at their desks, throw projectiles through doorways at friends in the hall. In the teachers' cafeteria, conversation often reverts to pension plans and whether the 2,500 Lincoln kids are as bad as last year or worse. The first day I dropped by, there was much commotion because the locker of a student was found to contain a handgun. On my second visit, the weapon in question was a six-inch knife. After one student was sent to the hospital with a neck wound requiring forty stitches, even some of the most peaceable kids began carrying X-Acto knives for protection. [...]

Into this chaos walk the college coaches—pin-striped and paisley-tied, bearing four-color photos of sold-out college arenas and statistics on how many games their teams play on national television. Usually they precede their visits by dropping the players brief notes, like the one from a Fordham coach to a Lincoln player describing how one of the college's basketball stars became rich beyond his wildest dreams. "This could be you someday," the coach wrote. "See how Fordham can change your life?" The coach signed off with the salutation, "Health, Happine$$, and Hundred$."

Most of the coaches are leery of Corey right now; he spends too much time with girls and, despite his intelligence, his grades are among the worst on the team. Stephon is, as far as the NCAA rules are concerned, off-limits for the next three years. So they come to see Russell. In the first week of school, Wichita State, St. Bonaventure, and the University of Delaware have paid him visits. After school today he sits down with Rod Baker, the head coach at the University of California at Irvine.

"My apologies for not coming to see you before, but the fact is one of our players just dropped out and suddenly we need another guard." Coach Baker is a trim, handsome black man wearing a natty blue suit, tasseled loafers, and a gleaming gold NCAA ring. "And the first person we thought of was Russell Thomas. I'm not bull-shitting you. Frankly, I think you're an impact player, a franchise player.

Five years from now, I wouldn't be surprised if people were saying, 'Remember when Russell Thomas came in and changed the fortunes of Cal-Irvine?'" Baker runs a finger down each side of his well-groomed mustache. Russell smiles uncertainly.

"Now let me tell you about California. Ever been there?" Russell shakes his head. "Well, you're gonna think you died and went to heaven. I'm serious. What is it today—seventy degrees? Nice and sunny? In California this is a shitty day in December. That's the God's truth. And the other thing about going to school on the West Coast…"

[…] After Coach Baker leaves, Russell and I walk out to the football field behind the school, a lovely, tree-lined expanse of green in an otherwise barren urban setting. It's one of those crystalline September afternoons, with fall in the air but the sun pulsing down on the aluminum bleachers where we sit with the last warmth of summer. (Weather like this may ruin a Californian's day, but in Brooklyn this is as good as it gets.) "I was impressed with Coach Baker. I felt he was definitely leveling with me," Russell declares. "But I'm going to wait and see. Hear what they all have to say. Then decide. Try not to be pressured. Just take it one day at a time." Russell's initial comments after a recruiting session often mimic the solemn coach-speak to which he is subjected every day. So many people—high-school and college coaches and free-lance street agents—want a piece of Russell and try to influence where he will sign that it often takes him a while to locate his own thoughts. "They say it's the second-biggest decision I gotta make in my life—after I pick my wife." He looks around the field, swatting imaginary flies. "But I'm doing good, I'm handling it." He locates some gum on the bottom rung of the bleachers, picks it free, rolls it between two fingers, and flips it onto the grass. "It's normal to be confused, right?" Now the elastic of his right sock receives his complete attention as he performs a series of micro-adjustments to get the folds just right. "That's only human, isn't it? […] You know, I used to say that I couldn't wait to be a senior," he says. "But I got to worry about classes, the season, recruiting, the SATs. That's *a lot* of pressure." According to NCAA rules, students who want to play sports at a four-year, Division I school, those with the nation's top athletic programs, must enter college having maintained at least a 70 average in high school and having received a combined score of 700 on the math and verbal sections of the SATs—the last an insurmountable obstacle to many black players with poor educations and little expe-

rience taking standardized tests. Failing that, a player must earn a two-year degree at a junior college before moving on to a four-year school. Many Division I coaches, however, refuse to recruit junior-college players, considering them damaged goods. So players who don't go directly to a four-year school often never get to play top college ball or earn their bachelor's degrees.

The first time Russell took the SATs, he received a combined score somewhere in the mid-500s. (You receive 400 points for signing your name.) This year he gave up his lunch period to study, and lately he's been carrying around a set of vocabulary flash cards, which he pulls out whenever there isn't a basketball in his hands. By dint of tremendous effort, Russell had also brought his average up to 78—the highest on the team. These are extraordinary developments for someone whose schooling over the years has been so bad that he had never, until recently, finished a book or learned the fundamentals of multiplication, even as he was being called upon to answer reading-comprehension and algebra questions on the SATs. "I used to think there were smart people and dumb people, but that's not true," Russell says forcefully. "Everybody's got the same brain. They say a human mind can know a thousand words—it's like a little computer! But you got to practice." He pauses. "But how come it's always the guys who don't study who get their 700s? Seems like the guys who work hard always get screwed. But oh, well."

From across the football field, the chants and cries of cheerleading practice travel toward us with perfect clarity. Russell shades his eyes with his hands and watches a tumble of cartwheels. "It's nice out here, isn't it? All the trees and everything? Out where I live there's nothing but total corruption and evilness, drugs and stolen cars. All my friends be getting arrested, shot at…" It is not too much to say that basketball saved Russell. In junior high he was trouble, sometimes leaving home for long stretches to hang out on the streets with his friends. But he was spotted playing ball in the parks by one of Lincoln's unofficial recruiters, who persuaded him to enroll. In high school he gained confidence and won the hearts of teachers who admired his efforts while growing increasingly appalled by what he had never been taught. Now after school, while certain of his classmates walk over to Brighton Beach to hold up pensioners at gunpoint, Russell goes straight home, takes his vitamins, does his push-ups, and combs through college-recruiting brochures until bedtime. His dream is not to become a pro, he tells me, but "to graduate college, start me a nice little family, and get me a nice little job as a registered nurse." [. . .]

All of [the players] have improved since I saw them in August. Russell, once a stationary jump shooter, is shooting off the dribble, driving with authority to the hoop. For years, Russell had gotten a rap for "playing white"—taking a lay-up when he could have dunked. "No one thinks I can dunk 'cause I never dunked in public," he told me over the summer. "But between you and me, I dunk in the park all the time—when no one's looking." I was tempted to ask if this was a riddle (is a dunk really a dunk if no one is around to see it?), but Russell wasn't smiling. "I'm going to dunk this year. Trust me." And he does. At practice, Russell drives the lane and goes straight over Corey for an emphatic jam. The whole place erupts—guys are chanting his name, yelling, "He flushed it *good!*" Russell, ignoring the cheers, walks over to me and grips my shoulder. "See, it's all part of the plan," he says. "Just like the shoes." Now what the hell does *that* mean?

As for Corey, he seems to have added an extra cylinder for the coming season. At six feet one, Corey is so fast he doesn't even bother to fake; he just wastes his man on the first step and springs into the air as if coming off a trampoline. "Do the 360!" someone yells from the bleachers and Corey obliges, performing a gyrating dunk. "Statue of Liberty!" comes the next request, and Corey takes off near the foul line, soars toward the basket, and then—legs split, arm extended, ball held high like a torch—throws down a thunderous, backboard-rattling jam. Corey knows how to work a crowd, sometimes too well. Last year, in one of the season's crucial games, Corey was all alone under the basket, tried a fancy lay-up, and blew it. The coaches rose to their feet, howling in rage. Corey jogged downcourt shrugging, palms turned toward the ceiling. "Relax, guys," he said, nonchalance itself. "It's just *basketball.*"

And then there is Stephon. He is making his debut as a high-school player today, but he takes the court as he always does—ever confident, leaning forward onto the balls of his feet in happy anticipation, arms jangling at his sides. "Mission day," he announces with a clap. "Time to get busy." Within moments he is making quick work of his competition, stunning the crowded, noisy gym into a reverential silence. Here he is, out by the three-point line. He does a stutter step to freeze the defense, then drives the lane. En route, he encounters the team's six-foot-seven center in

midair, so he changes direction, shifts the ball from right hand to left, and sinks a reverse lay-up. I hear one of the coaches mutter, "Holy shi—," not even finishing the thought because here Stephon is again, off to the left. He drives, sees too many bodies in the paint, and pulls up for a jumper. He is way out of position, his lithe body still floating toward the basket, so he calculates his velocity, takes a little something off the ball, and banks it gently off the glass.

"Jesus, this kid's the real thing! Do you realize Stephon could keep us in TV tournaments for the next four years?" Bobby Hartstein, head coach of the Lincoln team, sounds overjoyed—and vastly relieved. Lincoln has had great players before, but never a virtual child prodigy like Stephon. All summer long, Coach Hartstein held his breath as other schools tried to lure his incoming star with promises of a starting position and a guaranteed supply of his favorite sneakers. One Brooklyn coach presented Stephon with a new uniform and treated him and his father to a series of extravagant dinners. A coach in the Bronx was rumored to have offered cash up front. But Lincoln had the edge. Stephon's three older brothers—Eric, Donnie, and Norman— had all starred at the school. And to close the sale, Hartstein made Stephon an extraordinary offer: the forty-two-year-old coach promised the fourteen-year-old player that he'd turn down any college coaching offer to personally shepherd Stephon through high school.

After practice the players all tumble down the school's front steps. Stephon walks up to me and says, "Take me to Mickey D's. I'm hungry. I could eat three Big Macs. You got any cash?" I've already agreed to drive Russell and Corey home, so I tell Stephon to hop in. "This is your ride?" Stephon stares slack-jawed at my ten-year-old Toyota. "When I get to college, I'm gonna get me a white Nissan Sentra—that shit is *milk!*"

"Just get in the damn car," Russell says. In the last few weeks, some schools that had recruited Russell aggressively in September have backed off, and Russell is taking it hard. No sooner had Russell made up his mind to sign with Cal-Irvine than Coach Baker called to say they were no longer interested—the guard they thought was leaving decided to come back. Meanwhile, other schools seem convinced that Russell won't ever pass his SATs. (Coaches somehow learn of Russell's test scores before he's even had time to show them to his mother.) With every school that courts and then abandons him, Russell goes through the full cycle of infatuation, falling in love, rejection, and recuperation; each time he survives with a little less of the spirit to forge on with the school year. Stephon wants the front seat of my car, but Russell says gruffly, "Six foot three gets the front. Five foot nine goes in back." Corey wisely stays out of it. He puts his Walkman on, pops the hatch, and climbs in the far back, draping his legs over the bumper.

Autumn is arriving quickly this year. For weeks now the sky has been a study in gray, and the trees along Ocean Parkway are already bare. On the drive to McDonald's we splash through piles of fallen leaves. "If you crash and I get injured, Coach is gonna kill you," Stephon advises me. Then he announces, to no one in particular, "When I go to college, I'm going to Syracuse or Georgia Tech."

"How come?" I ask.

"Because at Syracuse you play in front of 32,820 people every home game—it's crazy-loud in there," he says, meaning the Syracuse Carrier Dome. "And because Georgia Tech knows how to treat its point guards." Stephon is no doubt thinking of Kenny Anderson—the player he is most often compared with—who left Georgia Tech after his sophomore year to sign a five-season, $14.5 million contract with the NBA's New Jersey Nets. Anderson's salary is a figure Stephon knows as precisely as the seating capacity of the Carrier Dome.

Driving along, we pass beneath the elevated tracks over Stillwell Avenue, where four of New York City's subway lines come to an end. The Coney Island peninsula begins here; beyond the tracks are the projects. Few store owners will risk doing business out there, and the McDonald's near Stillwell is the last outpost of junk food before the streets plunge into the shadow of the high rises. We order our food to go and pile back into my car. Stephon, hungrily consuming his first burger, wedges himself between the two front seats in order to speak directly into his friend's ear. "So, Russell. What are they offering you?" Russell snatches his head away and stares out the window. "You mean you're just gonna sign?" Stephon goes on. "And then when you get to campus and see all them players driving those nice white Nissan Sentras, what are you gonna say to yourself? 'Oh well, I guess they got them from their *mothers'?*"

We ride along in hostile silence. As we drive down Mermaid Avenue toward the projects, the trees, shops, and pedestrians become scarcer, block by block. During the urban-renewal years, the city knocked down storefronts all along this stretch, but it abandoned much of its commer-

cial-redevelopment plan after moving tenants into the projects. Now the only signs of life along some blocks are the drunks leaning against the plywood of boarded-up buildings and the mangy dogs scavenging vacant lots.

Russell says, "By the way, Stephon, the NCAA does *not* allow players to get cars."

"Ha! You think the NCAA gives a fuck about *cars?*" Stephon, still with his head next to Russell's, gives a shrill little laugh. "Why do you think the best players go where they go? 'Cause the schools promise to take care of them and their families. They say the magic word: *money.*"

It's no secret where Stephon gets his head for business. Last summer, while I was watching Stephon play ball, his father, Donald Marbury, approached me. "You the guy writing about Lincoln?" he asked. "And you haven't even interviewed Mr. Lincoln himself?" We shook hands, and when I told him how much I wanted to speak to him, a sly smile crossed his creased and handsome face. "Well in that case I expect there will be some gratuities for me and my family." I must have looked surprised because Mr. Marbury snapped angrily, "Oh come on now! If it weren't for me and my boys, Lincoln wouldn't even be worth writing about!"

The Marbury story *is* a good one, though it may never be written to the father's liking. After starring at Lincoln, Eric went on to play for the University of Georgia, but he failed to graduate before his scholarship ran out and was now back in Coney Island. Donnie, the second son, displayed even greater promise, but he didn't have a 70 average in high school and had to do time at two junior colleges. After two years, he moved on to Texas A&M, where he led the Southwest Conference in scoring. But he too never graduated and was passed over in the college draft; now he's out in Utah, at another college, trying to finish his degree. Then came Norman. If ever Coney Island had produced pro material, it was he. The first public-school player in New York ever to be named all-city three years in a row, Norman was a dazzler—fast, strong, with a deadly outside shot and the ability, on drives to the basket, to take on the largest foes. He had his pick of top programs and eventually signed with Tennessee, which had assured him that if he chose their school, he could still attend for free even if he didn't make 700; he would simply have to sit out his freshman season, as the NCAA rules require. But in the summer of 1990, just weeks before he was set to leave for Knoxville, he came up 40 points short of 700 on his final SAT attempt. Tennessee broke its promise and withdrew its offer. Norman, Coney Island's finest product to date, packed his bags for a junior college in Florida. (He now plays for a Salt Lake City junior college.)

For years Donald Marbury had watched his boys fall short. Now he was down to his last—and most talented—son. "You want information, I expect that you will have the money to pay for it," he said to me last summer. I told him that wasn't possible and he shrugged dismissively. "I'm not like all them other Coney Island guys—too stupid to know the value of what they're sitting on." He tapped his brow. "This is a business—ain't nothing but. And if I don't receive satisfaction, I will take my business somewhere else."

Among the coaches who are now recruiting Stephon, it is said, as one did recently, that Donald Marbury "just won't stop dining out on his son's talent." As for Stephon, the coaches complain that he's a player always looking to "get over," to take advantage of any situation. But how *should* they act? The entire basketball establishment has been trying to buy Stephon for years: summer-league teams pay his way to tournaments around the country (last summer found him in Arizona); street agents take Stephon into the Nets' locker room for chats with the pros; basketball camps give him wardrobes full of free gear; and coaches are constantly laying on hands and giving him awkward little hugs, hoping to win his affection.

And the Marbury family knows only too well, from witnessing the fates of Eric, Donnie, and Norman, how abruptly the coaches will withdraw their largess. So the Marbury policy, as Stephon explains it to Russell in my car, has become quite simple: "If you don't ask, you don't get. Like if I wasn't getting my burn"—his playing time—"here at Lincoln? I'd be up and out with quickness."

By the time I reach the tag end of the peninsula, where Corey, Russell, and Stephon live, everyone has finished his burgers and fries, and I swing by their buildings to drop them off. It's not yet 6:00 P.M., but the drug dealers are already out. Russell spots a kid he used to play with at the Garden loping down the street with a rangy gait and his Georgetown cap on backward. "Look at him. Just doing the same ol' same ol'. Shoot 'em up. Bang bang." Dealers and players make up the principal social groups among young men in Coney Island, although there's cross-pollination, with washed-up players joining the gangs and dealers dis-

rupting games to show off their playground moves. One major difference, however, is that the dealers own white Nissan Sentras whereas players like Stephon just talk about them.

Russell, Corey, and Stephon have never been involved with the gangs, but that leaves them broke most of the time, with few options for making money besides hawking sodas on the boardwalk during the summer. It's hard work, lugging a case of Cokes from the nearest supermarket a mile away, then selling them one by one in the blazing heat. For their trouble, they usually get a summons from the police. Later on those summer evenings, when the athletes start their workouts, the dealers often gather at the sidelines to jeer. "They ain't doing nothing with their lives, so they don't want you to be doing nothing either," Russell explains. He climbs out of my car with a pile of SAT review books under his arm. "Man, I hate Coney Island. After I get to college, I'm *never* coming back. Until then, boys"—he gives us a weary salute—"I'm staying inside."

I drive down the block to drop off Stephon and Corey. They live on the fourth and fifth floors of the same building, directly over the Garden. After leaning into the window to slap my hand, Stephon starts walking with that King Marbury stride toward his building. I watch as he swaggers across the deserted playground, trailing his hand along the jungle gym. All the guys drinking their afternoon beers call out to him as he goes by.

I've spent some time in Stephon's building, and it's not the most pleasant place to come home to after a long practice. It's fourteen stories high and the elevator never works. The long halls stink of urine, and the dark stairwells, where the dealers lurk, echo with the low rumble of drug transactions. The apartment doors don't even have numbers on them, though they must have had at one time because just outside the Marburys' apartment someone has scrawled violently across the wall, I WANNA FUCK THE GIRL IN 3B CAUSE SHE SUCKS DICK GOOD.

Everyone is hoping that Stephon will keep his head together as his notoriety grows throughout his high-school career and that, more to the point, he or his father won't accept some "gratuity" that raises the interest of the NCAA enforcement division. Given the family's circumstances, however, and the lessons they have learned about how this recruiting game is played, one can hardly blame Stephon and his father for wanting theirs—and wanting it now.

Heading toward Thanksgiving, Lincoln could not have asked for greater success. The team was undefeated, making headlines in all the major New York City dailies, and had received an invitation to play in San Diego in a Christmas tournament of the country's top high-school teams. Lincoln didn't just win its games either; the team routed its opponents by such lopsided scores that opposing coaches often shook their heads and remarked, "Those guys were *high-school* players?" Russell was scoring at will—in the team's first scrimmage he turned in an outrageous 46-point performance, missing only three of twenty-four field-goal attempts, then kept to that pace for the next several games. *The Hoop Scoop*, a recruiting newsletter, ranked him the sixth-best player in New York City, and he earned an honorable mention in the magazine *Street & Smith's* nationwide basketball roundup.

Meanwhile Stephon was getting his burn, and then some. He started the season's first game (fifteen points, twelve assists) and every one thereafter. *New York Newsday*, under a half-page picture of the Lincoln team holding their smiling young point guard in their arms, announced the beginning of "the era of Stephon Marbury." Scouting reports were giving Stephon their top rating, and an assistant from Providence College showed up in Coney Island to watch Stephon practice one day, waving discreetly to the freshman—violating the intent, if not the letter, of NCAA rules designed to protect underclassmen from recruiters. "It's never too early to start showing interest," the coach whispered. Word of Stephon's prowess even reached a TV production company, which contacted Stephon about making a commercial, though when the NCAA informed the Marburys that accepting a fee might violate its rules, his father declined.

Off the court, however, there were some unwelcome developments. Stephon was working hard in his classes, hoping to break the pattern of academic failure set by his brothers, but his teachers were noticing that his book reports rarely included a period or a capital letter—not a good omen for the verbal portion of the SATs. As for Russell, he was scoring well on practice SAT exams, but when test day arrived he would panic and forget all his last-minute cramming, shaking his faith that hard work would eventually win the day. Years of bad schooling are coming back to haunt Russell just when he needs his education the most.

Leaving the school building now, he looks exhausted, defeated, like a sullen factory worker at the end of a long shift. [...]

The days are getting shorter now. By the time [the afternoon] practice is over, the sun has long since dropped into its slot behind the Verrazano Narrows Bridge and the sky at twilight is covered with brooding clouds. Corey's older brother Willie owns a barbershop just off Flatbush Avenue in central Brooklyn, twenty minutes away. After practice Russell, Corey, and Stephon like to hang out there, and I usually give them a lift on my way home. As we drive past the brightly lit bodegas and rice-and-beans joints on Flatbush Avenue, fires rage out of metal drums, circled by hooded men trying to keep warm. Corey looks out the window and says in a high, fragile voice, "Oh no. I just *hate* it when the Negroes wear those hoods. Scary! Oh! So scary!" Everyone laughs and Corey lifts his own hood over his head. He knows that when he too walks around like that, cops will stop him and pedestrians will turn away from him in fear. "Only in America," he says.

I have yet to hear Corey talk much about colleges, so I ask him where he wants to play. "Oh, I'm thinking about some southern schools: Florida State, North Carolina, maybe Virginia. I hate it when it gets sharp and brisk out like this. My one rule is, I won't go anyplace where I got to wear one of them Eskimo coats." Corey's recruiting hasn't even begun, but he's already established the proper hedonistic frame of mind.

"Still got to pass those SATs," Russell warns.

"I'm not scared," Corey replies. "I do well on tests. Anyway, this should be our year to relax."

"That test is *hard*," says Stephon from the backseat. "I looked at it once and almost fainted. I read somewhere that David Robinson got a 1300. Is that possible?"

"I heard there are players who get other guys to take the test for them," Russell says. "How do they get away with that? Find someone who looks like them?"

This is not a good sign. One of Russell's friends [...], who had scored lower than he on practice tests, suddenly got his 700 and signed with a top program. Some Lincolnites have begun wondering whether [other high school] players are using stand-ins to take the test.

The NCAA and the college basketball industry have done much soul-searching in recent years over the SAT requirement, as well they should. A combined score of 700 may not seem like a terribly rigorous standard, but given the

quality of the Lincoln players' schooling, it's not surprising that they don't know a synonym for *panache* or how to make the most of what they do know; they've never been told, for example, to avoid guessing and answer only the questions they're sure of—the kinds of test-taking tips suburban kids learn on their first day in a Stanley Kaplan review course. Russell's school average, now over 80, says a lot more about his determination to succeed, but that alone will get him nowhere.

Business is brisk tonight at Willie's shop—either that or a lot of guys are using the place to keep warm. Willie and his partner are cutting with dispatch and still a half dozen guys are hanging out. Willie keeps a basketball in the shop that everyone passes around while watching sitcom reruns on the TV. It's a homey place: taped to the mirrors are photos of the Johnson clan—Corey, Willie, and their six siblings. (The Johnsons are one of the only intact families I know in Coney Island: the father lives at home and all the children out of high school have jobs.) A T-shirt commemorating Lincoln's championship last year is pinned to the wall, next to a painting of Jesus, a bust of Nefertiti, and four portraits

of Martin Luther King. Willie has also slapped up an assortment of bumper stickers: MORE HUGGING, LESS MUGGING and TO ALL YOU VIRGINS...THANKS FOR NOTHING. Outside, darkness has fallen like a black curtain against the shop window, but inside Willie's it's bright and warm.

Corey, whistling the theme song to *The Andy Griffith Show*, grabs a razor and stands next to Russell, trimming his right sideburn. (When Russell began dressing for success this season, Corey would remain in the locker room to troubleshoot in case Russell hit any snags knotting his tie.) [...] Most Coney Island kids feel utterly lost outside their neighborhood, but Corey goes club-hopping in Manhattan and every time he shows up for a game—no matter where in the city it is—some girl in the bleachers is calling out his name. His shrewdness on a variety of topics—dating, churchgoing, cooking, writing poetry—has earned him the nickname "Future," because, as Russell once explained, "Corey's a future-type guy, crazy-smart, a walking genius. There are no limits to what he can do."

One day in study hall, I watched Corey sitting in the back, bent over his desk, while all around him his classmates wreaked havoc, throwing spitballs and jumping from desk to desk. At the end of the period I asked what he had accomplished and he handed me a poem about life in Coney Island that ended, "A place meant for happiness, sweet love and care—/Something any human desires to share./Yet it seems to haunt instead of praise/The foundation and center of our bitter days."

When I had finished reading, Corey said to me, "I'm going to be a writer—you know, creative writing, poetry, free-associative stuff. I just play ball to take up time." Corey was tremendously prolific, dashing off a new poem for every girl he met. But having successfully merged his twin passions—writing and romance—he never left time for his homework. He did the assignments he liked, ignored the rest, and, though he never caused trouble in class, had a 66 average and was one failed test away from losing his high-school eligibility. Already Division I coaches had identified him as a gifted player whose grades could be his undoing. [...] Willie is cutting Stephon's hair, but mostly he's been keeping a weather eye on his brother. "Corey's smart, but he's stupid too," Willie says to me. "You know what I mean? In junior high, he was a virgin with a 90 average. Now he's got a 65. You tell me." I laugh, but Willie says, "No, I'm *serious*, man. I try to talk to him. I say, 'Don't you want to go to college? Don't you know you got to sacrifice for things you want?' " Willie is clipping Stephon's hair with growing agitation, and Stephon has sunk low in his chair, hoping to avoid a scalping. "At home Corey's on the phone all night, talking to girls. I say, 'You got a personal problem? Just tell me.' "

Willie is speaking in code now. What he's hinting at is the Johnson family's fear that Corey will get one of his girlfriends pregnant. In Coney Island, girls and the distractions of friends represent such a threat to a college career that the neighborhood's talented athletes are often urged to give up the rights and privileges of adolescence and attend a high school far from home. They will be lonely, but they will stay on the straight and narrow. Corey's older brother Louis took this strategy one step further, going into seclusion at an all-boys school, then spending an extra year at a prep school that serves as a sort of academic rehab clinic for basketball players. Not coincidentally, he passed his SATs and became the first of the six Johnson boys to make it to a Division I program, the University of Buffalo.

Louis was so dedicated to his craft that he would practice his shot under the Garden lights until 4:00 A.M. Everyone wishes Corey were equally single-minded. But Corey's

sensibility is too quirky for that, and therein lies a danger. If Corey lived twenty-five miles north in, say, Scarsdale, he'd play the offbeat writer whose poor grades earn him a four-year sentence at Colgate, to be served while his classmates all go Ivy. But Corey fools around in an arena where there are no safety schools or safety nets. All of which presents a sad bit of irony: inner-city kids are always accused of doing nothing but throwing a ball through a hoop. Then along comes someone like Corey, who takes pleasure in a million other things. (When the Lincoln team runs wind sprints on the outdoor track, Corey gladly takes the outside lane so he can run his hands through the canopy of leaves above his head.) In Coney Island, however, you ignore your basketball talent at great risk—athletic scholarships being significantly easier to come by than those for ghetto poets.

By the time Russell and Corey submit themselves to Willie's shears, it's already late, so I agree to drive them home. All three are tired, and we ride along in a rare moment of quiet. Finally, Russell turns to me and says, "What do you know about Rob Johnson?"

Oh boy.

Johnson is a street agent, a middleman, a flesh peddler. He makes his living getting chummy with high-school players and then brokering them to colleges for a fee—though the coaches who pay it swear they've never heard of him. Lately, Johnson has become entangled in an NCAA investigation, but it hasn't kept him from showing up regularly at the Lincoln gym—a tall black man with an enormous gut, Day-Glo Nikes, and a thick gold chain around his wrist. After practice, he lingers around the players, offering to drive them home or take them to the movies—a particularly appealing figure to broke and fatherless kids like Russell.

"Has Rob offered to be your agent?" I ask. Russell looks out the window and says, "He called me last night. Said he liked the way I played. A *lot*." I tell Russell he might want to check out Rob's reputation, but Russell says, "It don't matter. I've decided to sign with South Carolina. They really want me." Having announced this unexpected decision, Russell pulls out a paper bag with his customary after-practice snack: a plain bagel and a carton of Tropicana.

"You should visit before you make up your mind," Corey advises. He's stretched luxuriously across the backseat.

"But I already know I want to go there," Russell says between mouthfuls.

"Russell, you've never been outside Coney Island! How the hell are you gonna know? Look"—Corey lowers his voice and tries to speak in tones of unimpeachable reasonableness—"Russell, say you're going to marry someone. You going to marry the first girl you sleep with? No. Of course not. You're going to look around, see what the other girls can do for you, and *then* make your decision. Same with colleges. You got to go up there and have a careful look around."

"Nobody can make me take visits if I don't want to."

Corey laughs. "Nobody's gonna *make* you do anything. But you might as well let them show you a good time. Let them wine you and dine you. When my recruiting starts, I'm going to have me some fun."

Russell, having finished his snack, balls up the paper bag and tosses it out the window with an air of finality: "I don't want to be wined and dined."

As much as he hates Coney Island, Russell has never lived anywhere else, and he often fears that his dark complexion (Corey and Stephon are lighter-skinned) will get him into trouble outside his home turf. That may explain why he doesn't want to take any visits. But something else is up. Corey notes this and changes strategy. "What's your reason? You got to have a reason."

"I'm not like everybody else," Russell replies.

"Yes," Corey says slowly. "This is true."

"Look, all the best players sign in the fall. Only the scrubs wait until spring."

"I'm not telling you to sign in the spring," Corey says, "I'm just saying you change your mind every day."

"I'm telling *you*, Corey, I'm having a great season. And when those schools that lost interest in me come back in the spring, I'm gonna be, like, 'Too late, *sucka!*' I'm gonna be throwing it all year! Tomahawk jams!" Russell starts thrashing about in the front seat, dunking his orange-juice carton into the ashtray of my car, and now I finally get it—that his decision to dunk in public, like his policy of wearing nice shoes, and now his intention to abruptly sign at a school he's never seen, is Russell's way of propping up his identity, of seizing some measure of control, now that he has realized how easily exchangeable he is for a player with better test scores. Recruiting may be the most important thing in Russell's life, but to the coaches it's just a yearly ritual.

"Man, you are one *crazy* nigger!" Corey says. "I'm not talking about dunking! I'm talking about whether you should sign at some school you never even seen in your life!"

"Don't matter. It's my decision. And part of growing up is learning to live with your decisions. Even if it turns out to be a nightmare."

"But why?"

"Don't push me, Corey." Russell's voice has begun to rise up the scale.

"But *why?*"

"Because I don't want to talk about it."

"That's not a reason."

"BECAUSE I HATE ALL THIS FUCKING RECRUITING!" Russell screams. "All right?"

Corey leans back against his seat, defeated. "Okay, well, at least that's a reason."

DECEMBER

Coney Island never looks quite so forlorn as it does just before Christmas. The amusement park is shuttered, the boardwalk littered with broken glass and crack vials. The cold weather has swept the streets clean of everyone but the most hardened criminals. At night, Christmas lights blink on and off from the top floors of the projects, but few people are around to enjoy them. No one simply passes through Coney Island on the way to somewhere else.

Tonight, Russell and I walk into the deserted lobby of his building and he says, his eyes cast down by shame, "Welcome to the old ghetto." Russell's building is identical in design to the one in which Corey and Stephon live, just a block away—an X-shaped slab of concrete rising fourteen stories into the air. I have always assumed it was no better or worse than theirs. But Russell assures me that looks are deceiving. By the way he peers around the elevator door before getting in, I believe him.

Upstairs, his family's apartment is tiny: a living room, kitchenette, and two bedrooms. His mother has one bedroom, Russell and his two younger sisters share the other. It's Russell's room, though: basketball posters cover the walls from top to bottom and trophies crowd the floor. [...]

[We're looking at] photos when Russell hears a key in the front door. He grabs the pictures from my hand and shoves them back in the scrapbook, snapping it shut just as his mother walks through the door.

"You come home right after practice?" she asks anxiously. He nods, and she smiles in my direction. "Russell thinks I'm overprotective, but I have to know where he's at. If he's at practice or at Willie's, okay. But just hanging out on the street? No!" She plunks down a bag of groceries on the kitchen table and lets out a long sigh. The neighborhood's only supermarket is fifteen blocks away. "This is a hard neighborhood, *wicked*, nothing but drugs out there," says Mrs. Thomas. "Most of Russell's friends are just wasting their lives. You've got to have a strong and powerful will not to go in that direction."

Joyce Thomas certainly has that. She is tall and thin like Russell, and moves around her apartment with fierce efficiency. A burst of what sounds like gunfire erupts outside, but Mrs. Thomas doesn't react. "I always tell Russell, it takes that much"—she spreads two fingers an inch apart—"to get into trouble, and that much"—now two hands shoulder-width apart—"to get out of it." She looks over to her son, but he has vanished from the room. "So far Russell's okay." She raps twice on her kitchen table. "So far."

I start to say something, but Mrs. Thomas cuts me off. "When Russell messes up, I knock him out. I *do*. I tell him, 'Don't you dog me, boy, I'm all you got!'" She is looking at me forcefully, without blinking. "I don't care how big he is or how much ball he plays, I'll put a ball in his head!"

Russell reappears, this time with his Walkman on and a strange, stricken look on his face. He starts to sing aloud to a slow love song coming from his Walkman—though all we can hear, of course, is Russell's crooning. [...]

She speaks with seeming indifference, though it's not hard to hear what lies beneath it: a desperation to get Russell away from Coney Island. [...] "He's got a lot of decisions ahead of him. Important decisions. *Business* decisions. Without that scholarship, he's nothing. *Nothing!*" Mrs. Thomas looks to her son to gauge his reaction, but Russell has checked out completely. He's turned his Walkman up to full volume, and he's singing as loud as he can.

A few nights later, Russell, Stephon, Corey, and I are all in my car, making the usual rounds to Willie's. Stephon announces that he's going to get an X shaved into the back of his scalp. Russell is considering a center part like Larry Johnson's, the star of the Charlotte Hornets. As we approach the barbershop Corey says, "Don't be wasting time, all right?" When I ask why, he tells me a gang from a nearby project has been roaming lately. Last week a woman was hit by a stray bullet right outside the shop, so they all want to get their cuts and be gone.

To me, Coney Island's desolate project walkways and stairwells have always seemed more threatening than the raucous street life here along Flatbush Avenue. And, in fact, the few Lincoln players who live "across town"—Flatbush or Crown Heights or East New York—won't be caught dead in the Coney Island high rises ever since one of them spent the night at Corey's apartment and someone blew up a car right outside his window. But I am given to understand that in the patchwork of highly distinct neighborhoods that make up Brooklyn, a group of black teenagers will always be at risk outside their own turf. Wherever they go, the three are always scanning to see who might be coming up to them. One of their teammates was shot in the hand a few months ago. Another classmate was stabbed at a party recently; he's still in intensive care. "Something's happening, boy, every day, every day," says Russell.

As planned, they're in and out of Willie's in a flash and happy to be heading home in my car. Russell has been unusually quiet all evening. When I ask if something is bothering him, he tells me his mother has forbidden him to speak to me anymore. Apparently, she doesn't think it wise for him to talk to a reporter while his recruiting hangs in the balance. I tell Russell that this story won't appear until he's already off to college, but he says, "You don't understand. My mother's *crazy!*"

Stephon pipes in with some advice for me. "Just greet her at the door and hit her with a hundred. She'll change her mind." He snickers knowingly. "She's no different than my father. He wants to make sure he gets some loot." Lately, Mr. Marbury has been threatening to keep Stephon from talking to me unless I cut him a deal.

At first I think Stephon is missing the point—that Mrs. Thomas's suspicion of me and her desperation to get Russell out of Coney Island are entirely different from Mr. Marbury's demand for money. But Corey sees the connection: "Damn," he says, "your parents must have had a hard life."

"Still do," Stephon replies. "Your father got himself a whole plumbing business. My father and Russell's mother got nothing." Stephon looks at me out of the corner of his eye and says, "You're thinking, *What a bunch of niggers, right?*"

The word just hangs in the air. I can't think of a thing to say. Over the last five months, I realize, I have tried to ignore our racial differences in an attempt at some broader understanding. Stephon's comment may be his way of telling me that understanding *begins* with race. "You got to think like a black man," he goes on, "got to learn how to say, 'Fuck it, fuck everybody, *fuck the whole damn thing.*' Now *that's* life in the ghetto."

"It's true!" Russell exclaims, his mood improving for the first time all evening. "My mother *is* a nigger! She's a black woman who does not give a damn."

"Man, I'm *tired* of all this shit!" Stephon slams his hands down hard on his book bag. "Somebody's *got* to make it, somebody's *got* to go all the way. How come this shit only happens to us Coney Island niggers?" He shakes his head wildly and laughs. "My father and Russell's mother—yeah, they're crazy, but it's about time there was a little something for the niggs."

"Something for the niggs!" Russell repeats the line with a hoot. "Yeah, Steph! Time to get outspoken!"

"You got it," Stephon says, and laughs again. Then Corey joins in. And they're all three whooping and slapping their knees—laughing at their parents and also, I imagine, at the absurdity of this whole situation.

Here they are, playing by all the rules: They stay in school—though their own school hardly keeps its end of the bargain. They say no to drugs—though it's the only fully employed industry around. They don't get into trouble with the NCAA—though its rules seem designed to foil them, and the coaches who break the rules go unpunished. They even heed their parents' wishes—and often pay a stiff price.

Of course none of them is perfect: Russell panics about his SATs and the choices he must make, and has trouble owning up to it; Corey won't apply himself and kids himself into thinking it won't matter; Stephon has—what shall we call it?—an attitude that needs some adjustment. But they operate in an environment that forgives none of the inevitable transgressions of adolescence and bestows no second chances.

Which makes this process of playing for a scholarship not the black version of the American dream, as some would suggest, but a cruel parody of it. In the classic parable you begin with nothing and slowly accrue your riches through hard work in a system designed to help those who help themselves. Here you begin with nothing but one narrow, treacherous path and then run a gauntlet of obstacles that merely reminds you of how little you have: recruiters pass themselves off as father figures, standardized tests humiliate you and reveal the wretchedness of your education, the promise of lucrative NBA contracts reminds you of what it feels like to have nothing in this world.

Jou-Jou, Silk, Chocolate, Spoon, Spice, Ice, Goose, Tiny, T, Stretch, Space, Sky: all of them great Coney Island players, most of them waiting vainly for a second chance, hanging out in the neighborhood, or dead. And here come Russell, Corey, and Stephon in my car, riding down Mermaid Avenue in the bone chill and gloom of this December night, still laughing about "the niggs," hoping for the best, and knowing that in this particular game failure is commonplace, like a shrug, and heartbreak the order of the day.

EPILOGUE: WINTER 1993

In the spring of 1992, near the end of his senior year, Russell signed with Philadelphia's Temple University, whose team in recent years has regularly been among the nation's top twenty. But on his final SAT attempt, his score went down and Temple withdrew its scholarship offer. Rob Johnson brokered Russell into a Texas junior college known on the street as a "bandit" school, where his teammates seemed to carry more guns than schoolbooks. Desperately unhappy, Russell transferred after a week to a junior college near Los Angeles. There, this past winter, he was averaging twenty-six points per game and hoping that after two years he would be recruited by a four-year school and earn his degree.

Corey fell short of a 700 on his SATs by ten points. He planned to spend a year at a prep school to brush up on his academics but filed his application for financial aid too late. He went to another junior college in Texas. Away from his girlfriends, Corey earned four B's and two A's in his first semester. He hopes to move on to a four-year school himself.

Stephon is now in his sophomore year. In the summer of 1992, he was among the four youngest players invited to the Nike all-American camp, an all-expenses-paid jamboree in Indianapolis for the 120 top high-school stars in the country. His play, before every Division I coach in the country, looked like a highlight film. Now four inches taller and dunking the ball, he should have his pick of top programs in his senior year, provided he can score 700 on the SATs and that neither he nor his father violates any recruiting rules.

And at the Garden, some of Coney Island's elders have organized nighttime shooting drills for the neighborhood's schoolchildren—eight years old and up—to prepare them for the road ahead.

ON NOT BEING A VICTIM

BY MARY GAITSKILL

MARCH 1994

In the early 1970s, I had an experience that could be described as acquaintance rape. Actually, I have had two or three such experiences, but this one most dramatically fits the profile. I was sixteen and staying in the apartment of a slightly older girl I'd just met in a seedy community center in Detroit. I'd been in her apartment for a few days when an older guy she knew came over and asked us if we wanted to drop some acid. In those years, doing acid with complete strangers was consistent with my idea of a possible good time, so I said yes. When I started peaking, my hostess decided she had to go see her boyfriend, and there I was, alone with this guy, who, suddenly, was in my face.

He seemed to be coming on to me, but I wasn't sure. My perception was quite loopy, and on top of that he was black and urban-poor, which meant that I, being very inexperienced and suburban-white, did not know how to read him the way I might have read another white kid. I tried to distract him with conversation, but it was hard, considering that I was having trouble with logical sentences, let alone repartee. During one long silence, I asked him what he was thinking. Avoiding my eyes, he answered, "That if I wasn't such a nice guy you could really be getting screwed." The remark sounded to me like a threat, albeit a low-key one. But instead of asking him to explain himself or to leave, I changed the subject. Some moments later, when he put his hand on my leg, I let myself be drawn into sex because I could not face the idea that if I said no, things might get ugly. I don't think he had any idea how unwilling I was—the cultural unfamiliarity cut both ways—and I suppose he may have thought that all white girls just kind of lie there and don't do or say much. My bad time was made worse by his extreme gentleness; he was obviously trying very hard to please me, which, for reasons I didn't understand, broke my heart. Even as inexperienced as I was, I sensed that in his own way he intended a romantic encounter.

For some time afterward I described this event as "the time I was raped." I knew when I said it that the statement wasn't quite accurate, that I hadn't, after all, said no. Yet it *felt* accurate to me. In spite of my ambiguous, even empathic feelings for my unchosen partner, unwanted sex on acid is a nightmare, and I did feel violated by the experience. At times I even flat-out lied about what had happened, grossly exaggerating the violence and the threat—not out of shame or guilt, but because the pumped-up version was more congruent with my feelings of violation than the confusing facts. Every now and then, in the middle of telling an exaggerated version of the story, I would remember the actual man and internally pause, uncertain of how the memory squared with what I was saying or where my sense of violation was coming from—and then I would continue with my story. I am ashamed to admit this, both because it is embarrassing to me and because I am afraid the admission could be taken as evidence that women lie "to get revenge." I want to stress that I would not have lied that way in court or in any other context that might have had practical consequences; it didn't even occur to me to take my case to court. My lies were told not for revenge but in service of what I felt to be the metaphorical truth.

I remember my experience in Detroit, including its aftermath, every time I hear or read yet another discussion of what constitutes "date rape." I remember it when yet another critic castigates "victimism" and complains that everyone imagines himself or herself to be a victim and that no one accepts responsibility anymore. I could imagine telling my story as a verification that rape occurs by subtle threat as well as by overt force. I could also imagine telling it as if I were one of those cry-babies who want to feel like victims. Both stories would be true and not true. The complete truth is more complicated than most of the intellectuals who have written scolding essays on victimism seem willing to accept. I didn't understand my own story fully until I described it to an older woman many years later, as a proof of the unreliability of feelings. "Oh, I think your feelings were reliable," she returned. "It sounds like you were raped. It sounds like you raped yourself." I immediately knew that what she said was true, that in failing even to try to speak up for myself, I had, in a sense, raped myself.

I don't say this in a tone of self-recrimination. I was in a difficult situation: I was very young, and he was aggressive. But my inability to speak for myself—to *stand up* for myself—had little to do with those facts. I was unable to stand up for myself because I had never been taught how.

When I was growing up in the 1960s, I was taught by the adult world that good girls never had sex and bad girls did. This rule had clarity going for it but little else; as it was presented to me, it allowed no room for what I actually might feel, what I might want or not want. Within the confines of this rule, I didn't count for much, and I quite vigorously rejected it. Then came the less clear "rules" of cultural trend and peer example that said that if you were cool you wanted to have sex as much as possible with as many people as possible. This message was never stated as a rule, but, considering how absolutely it was woven into the social etiquette of the day (at least in the circles I cared about), it may as well have been. It suited me better than the adults' rule—it allowed me my sexuality, at least—but again it didn't take into account what I might actually want or not want.

The encounter in Detroit, however, had nothing to do with being good or bad, cool or uncool. It was about someone wanting something I didn't want. Since I had been taught only how to follow rules that were somehow more important than I was, I didn't know what to do in a situation where no rules obtained and that required me to speak up on my own behalf. I had never been taught that my behalf mattered. And so I felt helpless, even victimized, without really knowing why.

My parents and my teachers believed that social rules existed to protect me and that adhering to these rules constituted social responsibility. Ironically, my parents did exactly what many commentators recommend as a remedy

Anthony Russo

for victimism. They told me they loved me and that I mattered a lot, but this was not the message I got from the way they conducted themselves in relation to authority and social convention—which was not only that I didn't matter but that *they* didn't matter. In this, they were typical of other adults I knew as well as of the culture around them. When I began to have trouble in school, both socially and academically, a counselor exhorted me to "just play the game"—meaning to go along with everything from school policy to the adolescent pecking order—regardless of what I thought of "the game." My aunt, with whom I lived for a short while, actually burned my jeans and T-shirts because they violated what she understood to be the standards of decorum. A close friend of mine lived in a state of war with her father because of her hippie clothes and hair—which were, of course, de rigueur among her peers. Upon discovering that she was smoking pot, he had her institutionalized.

Many middle-class people—both men and women—were brought up, like I was, to equate responsibility with obeying external rules. And when the rules no longer work, they don't know what to do. [...] If I had been brought up to reach my own conclusions about which rules were congruent with my internal experience of the world, those rules would have had more meaning for me. Instead, I was usually given a series of static pronouncements. For example, when I was thirteen, I was told by my mother that I couldn't wear a short skirt because "nice girls don't wear skirts above the knee." I countered, of course, by saying that my friend Patty wore skirts above the knee. "Patty is not a nice girl," returned my mother. But Patty *was* nice. My mother is a very intelligent and sensitive person, but it didn't occur to her to define for me what she meant by "nice," what "nice" had to do with skirt length, and how the two definitions might relate to what I had observed to be nice or not nice—and then let me decide for myself. It's true that most thirteen-year-olds aren't interested in, or much capable of, philosophical discourse, but that doesn't mean that adults can't explain themselves more completely to children. Part of becoming responsible is learning how to make a choice about where you stand in respect to the social code and then holding yourself accountable for your choice. In contrast, many children who grew up in my milieu were given abstract absolutes that were placed before us as if our thoughts, feelings, and observations were irrelevant.

Recently I heard a panel of feminists on talk radio advocating that laws be passed prohibiting men from touching or making sexual comments to women on the street. Listeners called in to express reactions both pro and con, but the one I remember was a woman who said, "If a man touches me and I don't want it, I don't need a law. I'm gonna beat the hell out of him." The panelists were silent. Then one of them responded in an uncertain voice, "I guess I just never learned how to do that." I understood that the feminist might not want to get into a fistfight with a man likely to be a lot bigger than she, but if her self-respect was so easily shaken by an obscene comment made by some slob on the street, I wondered, how did she expect to get through life? She was exactly the kind of woman whom the cultural critics Camille Paglia and Katie Roiphe have derided as a "rape-crisis feminist"— puritans, sissies, closet-Victorian ladies who want to legislate the ambiguity out of sex. It was very easy for me to feel self-righteous, and I muttered sarcastically at my radio as the panel yammered about self-esteem.

I was conflicted, however. If there had been a time in my own life when I couldn't stand up for myself, how could I expect other people to do it? It could be argued that the grown women on the panel should be more capable than a sixteen-year-old girl whacked out on acid. But such a notion presupposes that people develop at a predictable rate or react to circumstances by coming to universally agreed-upon conclusions. This is the crucial unspoken presumption at the center of the date-rape debate as well as of the larger discourse on victimism. It is a presumption that in a broad but potent sense reminds me of a rule.

Feminists who postulate that boys must obtain a spelled-out "yes" before having sex are trying to establish rules, cut in stone, that will apply to any and every encounter and that every responsible person must obey. The new rule resembles the old good girl/bad girl rule not only because of its implicit suggestion that girls have to be protected but also because of its absolute nature, its iron-fisted denial of com-plexity and ambiguity. I bristle at such a rule and so do a lot of other people. But should we really be so puzzled and indignant that another rule has been presented? If people have been brought up believing that to be responsible is to obey certain rules, what are they going to do with a can of worms like "date rape" except try to make new rules that they see as more fair or useful than the old ones?

But the "rape-crisis feminists" are not the only absolutists here; their critics play the same game. Camille Paglia, author of Sexual Personae, has stated repeatedly that any girl who goes alone into a frat house and proceeds to tank up is cruising for a gang bang, and if she doesn't know that, well, then she's "an idiot." The remark is most striking not for its crude unkindness but for its reductive solipsism. It assumes that all college girls have had the same life experiences as Paglia, and have come to the same conclusions about them. By the time I got to college, I'd been living away from home for years and had been around the block several times. I never went to a frat house, but I got involved with men who lived in rowdy "boy houses" reeking of dirty socks and rock and roll. I would go over, drink, and spend the night with my lover of the moment; it never occurred to me that I was in danger of being gang-raped, and if I had been, I would have been shocked and badly hurt. My experience, though some of it had been bad, hadn't led me to conclude that boys plus alcohol equals gang bang, and I was not naive or idiotic. Katie Roiphe, author of The Morning After: Fear, Sex, and Feminism on Campus, criticizes girls who, in her view, create a myth of false innocence: "But did these twentieth-century girls, raised on Madonna videos and the six o'clock news, really trust that people were good until they themselves were raped? Maybe. Were these girls, raised on horror movies and glossy Hollywood sex scenes, really as innocent as all that?" I am sympathetic to Roiphe's annoyance, but I'm surprised that a smart chick like her apparently doesn't know that people process information and imagery (like Madonna videos and the news) with a complex subjectivity that doesn't in any predictable way alter their ideas about what they can expect from life.

Roiphe and Paglia are not exactly invoking rules, but their comments seem to derive from a belief that everyone except idiots interprets information and experience in the same way. In that sense, they are not so different in attitude from those ladies dedicated to establishing feminist-based rules and regulations for sex. Such rules, just like the old rules, assume a certain psychological uniformity of experience, a right way.

The accusatory and sometimes painfully emotional rhetoric conceals an attempt not only to make new rules but also to codify experience. The "rape-crisis feminists" obviously speak for many women and girls who have been raped or have *felt* raped in a wide variety of circumstances. They would not get so much play if they were not addressing a widespread and real experience of violation and hurt. By asking, "Were they really so innocent?" Roiphe doubts the veracity of the experience she presumes to address because it doesn't square with hers or with that of her friends. Having not felt violated herself—even though she says she has had an experience that many would now call date rape—she cannot understand, or even quite believe, that anyone else would feel violated in similar circumstances. She therefore believes all the fuss to be a political ploy or, worse, a retrograde desire to return to crippling ideals of helpless femininity. In turn, Roiphe's detractors, who have not had her more sanguine "morning after" experience, believe her to be ignorant and callous, or a secret rape victim in deep denial. Both camps, believing their own experience to be the truth, seem unwilling to acknowledge the emotional truth on the other side.

It is at this point that the "date-rape debate" resembles the bigger debate about how and why Americans seem so eager to identify themselves and be identified by others as victims. Book after article has appeared, written in baffled yet hectoring language, deriding the P.C. goody-goodies who want to play victim and the spoiled, self-centered fools who attend twelve-step programs, meditate on their inner child, and study pious self-help books. The revisionist critics have all had a lot of fun with the recovery movement, getting into high dudgeon over those materially well-off people who describe their childhoods as "holocausts" and winding up with a fierce exhortation to return to rationality. Rarely do such critics make any but the most superficial attempt to understand why the population might behave thus.

In a fussing, fuming essay in these pages ("Victims, All?" October 1991) that has almost become a prototype of the genre, David Rieff expressed his outrage and bewilderment that affluent people would feel hurt and disappointed by life.

He angrily contrasted rich Americans obsessed with their inner children to Third World parents concerned with feeding their actual children. On the most obvious level, the contrast is one that needs to be made, but I question Rieff's idea that suffering is one definable thing, that he knows what it is, and that since certain kinds of emotional pain don't fit this definition they can't really exist. This idea doesn't allow him to have much respect for other people's experience—or even to see it. It may be ridiculous and perversely self-aggrandizing for most people to describe whatever was bad about their childhood as a "holocaust," but I suspect that when people talk like that they are saying that as children they were not given enough of what they would later need in order to know who they are or to live truly responsible lives. Thus they find themselves in a state of bewildering loss that they can't articulate, except by wild exaggeration—much like I defined my inexplicable feelings after my Detroit episode. "Holocaust" may be a grossly inappropriate exaggeration. But to speak in exaggerated metaphors about psychic injury is not so much the act of a crybaby as it is a distorted attempt to explain one's own experience. I think the distortion comes from a desperate desire to make one's experience have consequence in the eyes of others, and that such desperation comes from a crushing doubt that one's own experience counts at all. [...]

If thousands of Americans say that they are in psychic pain, I would not be so quick to write them off as self-indulgent fools. A metaphor like "the inner child" may be silly and schematic, but it has a fluid subjectivity, especially when projected out into the world by such a populist notion as "recovery." Ubiquitous recovery-movement phrases like "We're all victims" and "We're all co-dependent" may not seem to leave a lot of room for interpretation, but they are actually so vague that they beg for interpretation and projection. Such phrases may be fair game for ridicule, but it is shallow to judge them on their face value, as if they hold the same meaning for everyone. What is meant by an "inner child" depends on the person speaking, and not everyone will see it as a metaphor for helplessness. I suspect that most inner-child enthusiasts use the image of themselves as children not so that they can *avoid* being responsible but to learn responsibility by going back to the point in time when they *should* have been taught responsibility—the ability to think, choose, and stand up for themselves—and were not. As I understand it, the point of identifying an "inner child" is to locate the part of yourself that didn't develop into adulthood and then to develop it yourself. Whether or not this works is an open question, but it is an attempt to accept responsibility, not to flee it.

When I was in my late teens and early twenties, I could not bear to watch movies or read books that I considered demeaning to women in any way; I evaluated everything I saw or read in terms of whether it expressed a "positive image" of women. I was a very P.C. feminist before the term existed, and, by the measure of my current understanding, my critical rigidity followed from my inability to be responsible for my own feelings. In this context, being responsible would have meant that I let myself feel whatever discomfort, indignation, or disgust I experienced without allowing those feelings to determine my entire reaction to a given piece of work. In other words, it would have meant dealing with my feelings and what had caused them, rather than expecting the outside world to assuage them. I could have chosen not to see the world through the lens of my personal unhappiness and yet maintained a kind of respect for my unhappiness. For example, I could have decided to avoid certain films or books because of my feelings without blaming the film or book for making me feel the way I did. [...]

As I've grown older, I've become more confident of myself and my ability to determine what happens to me, and, as a result, those images no longer have such a strong emotional charge. I don't believe they will affect my life in any practical sense unless I allow them to do so. I no longer feel that misogynistic stories are about me or even about women (whether they purport to be or not) but rather are about the kinds of experience the authors wish to render—and therefore are not my problem. I consider my current view more balanced, but that doesn't mean my earlier feelings were wrong. The reason I couldn't watch "disrespect to women" at that time was that such depictions were too close to my own experience (most of which was not unusual), and I found them painful. I was displaying a simplistic self-respect by not subjecting myself to something I was not ready to face. Being unable to separate my personal experience from what I saw on the screen, I was not dealing with my own particular experience—I think, paradoxically, because I hadn't yet learned to value it. It's hard to be responsible for something that isn't valuable. Someone criticizing me as dogmatic and narrow-minded would have had a point, but the point would have ignored the truth of my unacknowledged experience, and thus ignored me.

Many critics of the self-help culture argue against treating emotional or metaphoric reality as if it were equivalent to objective reality. I agree that they are not the same. But emotional truth is often bound up with truth of a more objective kind and must be taken into account. This is especially true of conundrums such as date rape and victimism, both of which often are discussed in terms of unspoken assumptions about emotional truth anyway. Sarah Crichton, in a cover story for *Newsweek* on "Sexual Correctness," described the "strange detour" taken by some feminists and suggested that "we're not creating a society of Angry Young Women. These are Scared Little Girls." The comment is both contemptuous and superficial; it shows no interest in *why* girls might be scared. By such logic, anger implicitly is deemed to be the more desirable emotional state because it appears more potent, and "scared" is used as a pejorative. It's possible to shame a person into hiding his or her fear, but if you don't address the cause of the fear, it won't go away. Crichton ends her piece by saying, "Those who are growing up in environments where they don't have to figure out what the rules should be, but need only follow what's been prescribed, are being robbed of the most important lesson there is to learn. And that's how to live." I couldn't agree more. But unless you've been taught how to think for yourself, you'll have a hard time figuring out your own rules, and you'll feel scared—especially when there is real danger of sexual assault.

One reason I had sex with strangers when I didn't really want to was that part of me wanted the adventure, and that tougher part ran roughshod over the part of me that was scared and uncertain. I'll bet the same thing happened to many of the boys with whom I had these experiences. All people have their tough, aggressive selves as well as their more delicate selves. If you haven't developed these characteristics in ways that are respectful of yourself and others, you will find it hard to be responsible for them. I don't think it's possible to develop yourself in such ways if you are attuned to following rules and codes that don't give your inner world enough importance. I was a strong-willed child with a lot of aggressive impulses, which, for various reasons, I was actively discouraged from developing. They stayed hidden under a surface of extreme passivity, and when they did appear it was often in a wildly irresponsible, almost crazy way. My early attraction to aggressive boys and men was in part a need to see *somebody* act out the distorted feelings I didn't know what to do with, whether it was destructive or not. I suspect that boys who treat girls with disrespectful aggression have failed to develop their more tender, sensitive side and futilely try to regain it by "possessing" a woman. Lists of instructions about what's nice and what isn't will not help people in such a muddled state, and it's my observation that many people are in such a state to a greater or lesser degree.

I am not idealistic enough to hope that we will ever live in a world without rape and other forms of sexual cruelty; I think men and women will always have to struggle to behave responsibly. But I think we could make the struggle less difficult by changing the way we teach responsibility and social conduct. To teach a boy that rape is "bad" is not as effective as making him see that rape is a violation of his own masculine dignity as well as a violation of the raped woman. It's true that children don't know big words and that teenage boys aren't all that interested in their own dignity. But these are things that children learn more easily by example than by words, and learning by example runs deep.

A few years ago I invited to dinner at my home a man I'd known casually for two years. We'd had dinner and comradely drinks a few times. I didn't have any intention of becoming sexual with him, but after dinner we slowly got drunk and were soon floundering on the couch. I was ambivalent not only

because I was drunk but because I realized that although part of me was up for it, the rest of me was not. So I began to say no. He parried each "no" with charming banter and became more aggressive. I went along with it for a time because I was amused and even somewhat seduced by the sweet, junior-high spirit of his manner. But at some point I began to be alarmed, and then he did and said some things that turned my alarm into fright. I don't remember the exact sequence of words or events, but I do remember taking one of his hands in both of mine, looking him in the eyes, and saying, "If this comes to a fight you would win, but it would be very ugly for both of us. Is that really what you want?"

His expression changed and he dropped his eyes; shortly afterward he left.

I consider that small decision to have been a responsible one because it was made by taking both my vulnerable feelings and my carnal impulses into account. When I spoke, my words came from my feeling of delicacy as well as from my capacity for aggression. And I respected my friend as well by addressing both sides of his nature. It is not hard for me to make such decisions now, but it took me a long time to get to this point. I only regret that it took so long, both for my young self and for the boys I was with, under circumstances that I now consider disrespectful to all concerned.

NOTEBOOK
MORTE DE NIXON

BY LEWIS H. LAPHAM

JULY 1994

*A frivolous society can acquire dramatic significance only
through what its frivolity destroys.*

— EDITH WHARTON

When Richard Nixon resigned the office of the
presidency twenty years ago this summer, I thought it possible that in his own peculiar and crooked way he might have
done his countrymen an honest service. It wasn't the one
that he had in mind, and honesty was never a trait for
which he had much liking or use, but by so conspicuously
attempting to suborn the Constitution and betray every
known principle of representative government, he had
allowed the American people to see what could become of
their democracy in the hands of a thoroughly corrupt politician bent upon seizing the prize of absolute power. The
civics lesson was conducted in plain sight over a period of
eighteen months on network television and memorably
illustrated by the singular ugliness of Nixon's character. The
more obvious aspects of that character (its hypocrisy and
self-pitying rage) had been made, as he so often said, "perfectly clear" during his prior years in public office, but the
congressional hearings preliminary to his certain impeachment showed that he was also vindictive, foulmouthed, and
determined to replace the rule of law with corporate despotism. Nixon's distrust of any and all forms of free speech was
consistent with his ambition to shape the government of
the United States in his own resentful image, and when he
left for the beach at San Clemente, as grudgingly as a dog
giving up its bone, I remember watching his helicopter rise
for the last time from the White House lawn and thinking
that his fellow citizens wouldn't soon forget the constitutional moral of the tale.

The assumption was mistaken. When Nixon died on
April 22 in New York City, at the age of eighty-one, the
national news media pronounced him a great American and
told the story of his life as sentimental melodrama. The
assembled dignitaries on the weekend television shows
solemnly mourned the passing of a benevolent sage, a figure
of "historic proportions" and "towering size," who had
weathered the storms of obloquy and defeat and so proved
the theorem of an American success. The Sunday newspaper sermons reiterated the theme of redemption, and
William Safire, the *New York Times* columnist who had once
served as Nixon's speechwriter, provided the middle A to
which the rest of the media orchestra tuned their instruments: "Richard Nixon...proved there is no political wrongdoing so scandalous that it cannot be expiated by years of
useful service; no humiliation so painful that it cannot be
overcome by decades of selfless sagacity..."

The sentence deliberately shifts the weight of judgment from the public to the private man, from the realm of
law (in which magistrates uphold sworn oaths) to the
realm of conscience (in which citizens answer only to their
good intentions and their aerobics instructors), from the
political forum to *Oprah*. The choir of sound opinion
hummed the requiem in an arrangement by Lawrence
Welk: "An Indomitable Man, An Incurable Loneliness"—
the *New York Times*; "He would have been a great, great
man had somebody loved him"—Hugh Sidey; "Figure of
gentle pathos...impossible not to feel, simply, sorry for
him"—*The New Yorker*; "So much kin to the rest of us that
I never felt the faintest impulse to apologize for liking
him"—Murray Kempton; "Inspired and inflamed the
American imagination for half a century...a giant, right
up there with Citizen Kane and Moby Dick"—the *New
York Times*.

Stray voices of dissent appeared in *The Nation* and *The
New Republic*, but for the most part nobody addressing a
large audience said more than a few polite words about the
Vietnam War or the deceased's manifest contempt for the
American people. The prominent eulogists spoke of Nixon's

"triumph over adversity," not of the numberless dead in Indochina; of Nixon as "the comeback kid," not of the damage he had inflicted on the nation's political culture; of Nixon's youth and early sorrows, his loneliness, his "vulnerable awkwardness" and "longing for respect." All present agreed that what Nixon had done he had done for the most American of reasons—because, as he himself once said to somebody who asked him why he told so many lies, "I had to win. That's the thing you don't understand. The important thing is to win." Unable to contradict so patriotic a truism (offered by one of the news magazines as a further proof of the former president's subtle grasp of world affairs), the eulogists absolved Nixon of his sins and pardoned his crimes because he had worked so hard to commit them, thus demonstrating, in another of Safire's sophisms, "a gutsy engagement with life."

The flattering sentiment accompanied Nixon's body west to California, and on the Tuesday that it was brought to Yorba Linda the dispatch in the New York Times began with a flourish of Shakespearean trumpets and drums: "In a scene worthy of 'King Lear,' the usually sunny California sky unleashed thunder, lightning, rain and hail today as Richard M. Nixon's body returned to his birthplace in a plain wooden coffin covered by a flag." At the burial service on Wednesday afternoon the illusion of grandeur was somewhat more difficult to sustain, possibly because so many of the well-manicured mourners at the grave resembled the guests at a Mafia funeral, but a military band played "Victory at Sea," the tune that comforted Nixon during his last paranoid months in the White House in the summer of 1974, and the speeches expressed the proper sense of pious grief. Henry Kissinger, on the verge of tears, praised Nixon for his "visionary dream" of a new world order intended "to give new hope to mankind"; Senator Robert Dole, also in tears, proclaimed the second half of the twentieth century "The Age of Nixon" and said that "in the end what matters is that you have always lived life to the hilt"; President Clinton, who, at a banquet the previous Saturday in Washington, had said of Nixon that "he taught me what it means to be an American," observed that the dearly departed would have enjoyed the proceedings and approved the subsequent press releases.

The service ended with the playing of "The Battle Hymn of the Republic" and "America the Beautiful," and as a bugler played taps and a flight of air force planes passed overhead in the missing-man formation, I wondered what had become of our historical memory and why so many people were so eager to award Richard Nixon the headline of an apotheosis. Even in the best of times Nixon's performance in the national political theater tottered precariously close to the comic and grotesque. Look at him askew or in an odd light, and it was always frighteningly easy to mistake him for an old vaudevillian who had stumbled into a production of Macbeth, an inspired clown traipsing around the stage declaiming stately gibberish.

I could understand President Clinton wishing to divert the media's attention from his own misdemeanors by so charitably overlooking Nixon's felonies; I could understand Kissinger justifying a failed foreign policy that was, in point of fact, his own; I could understand Dole wanting to present himself, in time for the next Republican National Convention, as a man of the people; and I could understand a reluctance on the part of the ladies and gentlemen of the fourth estate to admit that they spend their time dressing up thugs and mountebanks in costumes signifying high and noble deeds. But even when taken all together, the several specific motives and agendas don't account for the grace bestowed on so wooden and paltry a politician as Richard Nixon, and I suspect that his translation into a statue follows from our common wish to declare, now and forever, world without end, our collective innocence. If Nixon is innocent, we are all innocent; if Nixon can murder nearly 1 million people in Indochina (among them 21,000 American kids) to no purpose other than his own self-aggrandizement, then who among us cannot cheat our children, or falsify our tax returns, or swindle the customers, bribe the judge, and abandon the girl. Forgive Nixon, and we forgive ourselves. Why else go to the trouble of transforming the lying congressman and the disgraced president into the elder statesman and wise diplomat remarkable for his telling of geopolitical truths?

Certainly it was a metamorphosis accomplished against long and heavy odds. Nixon's incompetence as a president shows up on almost every page of the published record, and a close reading of the small print suggests that his gifts as a statesman can best be compared to John Grisham's genius as a novelist or Madonna's talent for dancing. It's true that as president, Nixon pursued the opening to China, which, given the circumstances, was a feat of diplomacy comparable to conceding the existence of the Pacific Ocean, and it's also true that most of the time he knew which telephones to tap, but with respect to the more difficult questions confronting his administration (most especially the ones in Indochina), Nixon was consistently and pitiably wrong. He believed in the chimera of the domino theory, and he thought that the United States could win the Vietnam War if only the air force dropped another twelve tons of explosives on another four peasants. He was wrong about the effects of the secret bombing and the subsequent invasion of Cambodia—the North Vietnamese sanctuaries that he meant to destroy didn't exist. At the end he was even wrong about the character of the American people. Thinking that they would applaud his cleverness and what he was pleased to imagine as his striking resemblance to both Teddy Roosevelt and Charles de Gaulle, he never understood why so many college students hated the sound of his voice.

Nor did Nixon's record on domestic affairs provide the iconographers with many proofs of "historic proportions" and "towering size." As ignorant as Kissinger about the economic consequences of his foreign policies and indifferent to the concerns of the American electorate, Nixon (again for reasons having solely to do with his own reelection) set in motion a corrosive inflation as well as a divisive racial politics from which the country has yet to recover.

The publicists also encountered various technical difficulties washing the laundry of Nixon's gangsterism. Whenever possible he substituted palace intrigues for candid debate, and the standard biographies suggest that he felt freely at ease only in the company of his own toadying courtiers or in the presence of military despots like Ferdinand Marcos and the Shah of Iran, and I think it probable that he envied the Soviets their freedom of criminal maneuver.

He was constantly scribbling furious directives in the margins of the daily press summaries, instructing his henchmen to rid him of enemies both real and imagined. His verbs were always violent—"Get someone to hit him," "Fire him," "Freeze him," "Cut him," "Knock him down," "Dump him." His hatred of free speech was apparent in his every gesture and expression, and when confronted with an obstacle to his will, he invariably exhibited the autocrat's instinct to coerce, break in, lie, and suppress. On one of the tape recordings impounded by the Watergate investigation, Nixon speaks to Chuck Colson about the great task of chastising the legion of his enemies in a voice hard to reconcile with the image of the benevolent sage: "One day we will get them . . . Get them on the floor and step on them,

crush them, show no mercy. And we'll stick our heels in, step on them hard and twist . . . right, Chuck, right?"

Although by the summer of 1987 the standard iconographies routinely mentioned Nixon's "brilliant" intellect and "enigmatic" character, neither adjective is easy to align with the noun. As Nixon's national security adviser, Kissinger used to make fun of Nixon's "meatball mind." He often telephoned his more sardonic confederates to read aloud from the president's memoranda, laughing at the pomposity of the language that glossed over the threadbare emptiness of the thought. Nixon's several books extend and annotate the joke. The writing is poor, the arguments trite, the author's voice as sententious as that of a latter-day Polonius. Fond of belaboring the obvious and very pleased with himself in his wizard's hat, Nixon is forever telling his readers that the Russians cannot be trusted, that a surprising number of people exist in a state of poverty, and that war isn't a game of Parcheesi.

Nor does the record show Nixon among the more complex, let alone enigmatic, figures appearing on the American political stage over the last thirty-odd years. Although he was unstable, he was also tiresomely predictable. His principal biographers unanimously attest to the rigidity of his character and its uncanny lack of development; even his mother said of him, "I never knew a person to change so little." Loyal only to his invincible selfishness, Nixon in any and all circumstances could be counted upon to adhere to three inflexible rules of procedure: (1) To tell the expedient and self-serving lie, (2) To ask only one important question of the other people at the table (i.e., "What's in it for Richard Nixon?"), (3) To unctuously proclaim his own innocence.

Bryce Harlow, another of Nixon's counselors, once compared him to "a cork . . . push him down and he pops right back up." Precisely like a cork or a mechanical toy, Nixon is forever saying, "I am not a crook," or "When the President does it, that means it is not illegal," and because it always turns out that he is a crook (or a liar, or a shill, or a cheat) the story is never very interesting. Neither are the adventures of a cork.

Corks, however, possess the virtue of predictably rising and falling like the caricatures made for afternoon soap opera, forever scaling the battlements of melodrama and falling back into the moat of bathos, and it was in his capacity as an actor temporarily on loan from *As the World Turns*

that Nixon served the purposes of the mass media. Reassuringly incapable of further development, he never failed to come up with the *cliché juste* (about his wife's "respectable Republican cloth coat" or "the little cocker spaniel dog, Checkers"), and he was always there, as he once famously said, "to kick around" like a cheap toy or a stuffed bear.

Like most everything else made by and for the mass media, Nixon was a collaboration, a product of the corporate imagination in the manner of a Broadway musical, a Hollywood action film, or the CBS evening news. He was cast as the suspect wanted for the murder of everyone's brightest hopes and best instincts, and the caricature was so broadly drawn that it could absorb or blot out very high quotients of guilt, fear, and self-loathing. Diverted by the melodrama of Richard M. Nixon, the lonely urchin from

Whittier, California, who found fame and fortune in the nation's capital (found it and lost it and then found it again), we could forget what it was that he did—forget what was at risk in the Watergate conspiracies and Indochina, forget how many people died. The bias of the mass media favors the personal over the impersonal, the actor over the act, and the caricature of Nixon allowed us to preserve the innocence of the American dream by transforming a bleak and terrible tragedy into prime-time situation comedy.

As is the habit of actors, Nixon brooded over the worth and beauty of his image in the press, often peering through the newspapers for two and three hours at a time, and when I listened to Washington reporters talk about his obsessive marking up of their copy I thought of the mechanical toy reading the label on its box, trying to figure out what it was that the manufacturers had in mind. I'm not sure that he ever fully understood the instructions, which possibly explains why he so often mistook his own character or felt compelled, especially in his later years, to speak of himself in the third person. Prior to his first meeting with Russian Premier Leonid Brezhnev in the spring of 1972, Nixon directed Kissinger, who preceded him to Moscow, to announce him as a man who was "direct, honest, strong." He was, in fact, devious, dishonest, and weak, but Kissinger at the time was still wearing the White House livery and let the remark pass without amendment. On the eve of another of his departures to Moscow, Nixon compared himself both with Dwight Eisenhower on the morning of D-day and with William the Conqueror on the afternoon prior to the Norman invasion of England in the eleventh century.

Among the reported sightings of Nixon impersonating a public statue, the most recent appeared in *The New Yorker* on May 9, in Michael Korda's breathlessly admiring account of an August 1989 dinner party at Nixon's house in Saddle River, New Jersey. Nixon always liked to conduct impromptu seminars on the topics of geography and world history, and while the brandy was being handed around, he took it into his head to enlighten and improve two Chinese diplomats recently arrived from Beijing. Meaning for his words to be carried grandly back to China (as if they were emeralds on a velvet cushion), Nixon, speaking very slowly, very solemnly, said, "When Nixon was President and Leader of the Free World, he found that *firmness paid*. You tell them that." Somewhat later in the evening, while showing his guests around the house, he opened the door to his study and announced, "This is where Nixon works." "This is the desk at which Nixon wrote all his books."

The next question, "Who wrote Nixon?" Korda was too polite to ask, but if I had to answer it, I would guess that we all wrote Nixon. Even citizens as nominally liberal as Tom Wicker and Murray Kempton found in the caricature the hope of redemption. Wicker's biography of Nixon, *One of Us,* derives its melancholy and elegiac tone from the author's sense of his own failures, and Kempton, writing his maudlin farewell on the occasion of Nixon's death, said, "His sheer vulnerability so fills the memory as to expel all musings about his place in history." No wonder the media were so loud with lamentation. So many of us have so much for which we wish to be forgiven that I wouldn't be surprised if in the not-too-distant future President Clinton suggests naming a national holiday in Nixon's honor.

Ticket to the Fair

by David Foster Wallace

July 1994

August 5, 1993,
Interstate 55, westbound, 8:00 a.m.

Today is Press Day at the Illinois State Fair in Springfield, and I'm supposed to be at the fairgrounds by 9:00 A.M. to get my credentials. I imagine credentials to be a small white card in the band of a fedora. I've never been considered press before. My real interest in credentials is getting into rides and shows for free. I'm fresh in from the East Coast, for an East Coast magazine. Why exactly they're interested in the Illinois State Fair remains unclear to me. I suspect that every so often editors at East Coast magazines slap their foreheads and remember that about 90 percent of the United States lies between the coasts, and figure they'll engage somebody to do pith-helmeted anthropological reporting on something rural and heartlandish. I think they asked me to do this because I grew up here, just a couple hours' drive from downstate Springfield. I never did go to the state fair, though—I pretty much topped out at the county-fair level. Actually, I haven't been back to Illinois for a long time, and can't say I've missed it.

The heat is all too familiar. In August it takes hours for the dawn fog to burn off. The air is like wet wool. Eight A.M. is too early to justify turning on the car's AC. The sun is a blotch in a sky that isn't so much cloudy as opaque. The corn starts just past the breakdown lanes and goes right to the sky's hem. August corn in Illinois is as tall as a tall man. With all the advances in fertilization, it's now knee-high by June 1. Locusts chirr in every field, a brassy electric sound that Dopplers oddly inside the speeding car. Corn, corn, soybeans, corn, exit ramp, corn, and every few miles an outpost way off on a reach in the distance—house, tree with tire swing, barn, satellite dish. Grain silos are the only skyline. A fog hangs just over the fields. It is over eighty degrees and climbing with the sun. It'll be over ninety degrees by 10:00 A.M. There's that tightening quality to the air, like it's drawing itself in and down for a siege. The interstate is dull and pale. Occasional other cars look ghostly, their drivers' faces humidity-stunned. [...]

9:05 a.m.

The man processing print-press credentials has a mustache and short-sleeve knit shirt. In line before me are newshounds from *Today's Agriculture*, the *Decatur Herald & Review*, *Illinois Crafts Newsletter*, *4-H News*, and *Livestock Weekly*. Credentials are just a laminated mug shot with a gator clip for your pocket. Not a fedora in the house. Two older ladies behind me from a local horticulture organ engage me in shoptalk. One lady is the unofficial historian of the Illinois State Fair: she gives slide shows on the fair at nursing homes and Rotary lunches. She begins to emit historical data at a great rate—the fair started in 1853; there was a fair during the Civil War but not during WWII, and not in 1893, because Chicago was hosting the World's Columbian Exposition; the governor has failed to cut the ribbon personally on opening day only twice; etc. It occurs to me that I ought to have brought a notebook. I'm also the only person in the room in a T-shirt. It is a fluorescent-lit cafeteria in something called the Illinois Building Senior Center, uncooled. The local TV crews have their equipment spread out on tables and are lounging against walls. They all have mustaches and short-sleeve knit shirts. In fact, the only other males in the room without mustaches and golf shirts are the local TV reporters, four of them, all in suits. They are sleek, sweatless, deeply blue-eyed. They stand together up by the dais, which has a podium and a flag and a banner reading "Give Us a Whirl"—this year's theme. Middle-management types enter. A squelch of feedback on a loudspeaker brings the official Press Welcome & Briefing to order. It's dull. The words "excited," "proud," and "opportunity" are used repeatedly. Ms. Illinois County Fairs, tiara bolted to the tallest coiffure I've ever seen (bun atop bun, multiple layers, a ziggurat of hair), is proudly excited to have the opportunity to present two corporate guys, sweating freely in suits, who report the excited pride of McDonald's and Wal-Mart to have the opportunity to be this year's corporate sponsors.

9:50 A.M.

Under way at 4 mph on the Press Tour, on a kind of flatboat with wheels and a lengthwise bench so queerly high that everybody's feet dangle. The tractor pulling us has signs that say "ethanol" and "agripowered." I'm particularly keen to see the carnies setting up the rides in the fairgrounds' "Happy Hollow," but we head first to the corporate and political tents. Most every tent is still setting up. Workmen crawl over structural frames. We wave at them; they wave back; it's absurd: we're only going 4 mph. One tent says "Corn: Touching Our Lives Every Day." There are massive many-hued tents courtesy of McDonald's, Miller Genuine Draft, Morton Commercial Structures Corp., the Land of Lincoln Soybean Association ("Look Where Soybeans Go!"), Pekin Energy Corp. ("Proud of Our Sophisticated Computer-Controlled Processing Technology"), Illinois Pork Producers, the John Birch Society. Two tents that say "Republican" and "Democrat." Other, smaller tents for various Illinois officeholders. It is well up in the nineties and the sky is the color of old jeans.

We go over a system of crests to Farm Expo—twelve acres of wicked-looking needle-toothed harrows, tractors, seeders, harvesters. Then back around the rear of the big permanent Artisans' Building, Illinois Building Senior Center, Expo Center, passing tantalizingly close to Happy Hollow, where half-assembled rides stand in giant arcs and rays and shirtless guys with tattoos and wrenches slouch around them, fairly oozing menace and human interest, but on at a crawl up a blacktop path to the livestock buildings. By this time, most of the press is off the tram and walking in order to escape the tour's PA speaker, which is tinny and brutal. Horse Complex. Cattle Complex. Swine Barn. Sheep Barn. Poultry Building and Goat Barn. These are all long brick barracks open down both sides of their length. Some contain stalls; others have pens divided into squares with aluminum rails. Inside, they're gray cement, dim and yeasty, huge fans overhead, workers in overalls and waders hosing

everything down. No animals yet, but the smells still hang from last year—horses' odors sharp, cows' rich, sheep's oily, swine's unspeakable. No idea what the Poultry Building smelled like because I couldn't bring myself to go in. Traumatically pecked once, as a child, at the Champaign County Fair, I have a long-standing phobic thing about poultry. [...]

AUGUST 13, 9:25 A.M.

Official opening. Ceremony, introductions, verbiage. Big brass shears, for cutting the ribbon across the main gate. It is cloudless and dry, but forehead-tighteningly hot. Noon will be a kiln. No anthropologist worth his pith helmet would be without the shrewd counsel of a colorful local, and I've lured a Native Companion here for the day with the promise of free admission, unlimited corn dogs, and various shiny trinkets. Knit-shirt press and rabid early fairgoers are massed from the gate all the way out to Springfield's Sangamon Avenue, where home-owners with plastic flags invite you to park on their front lawn for five dollars. We stand near the back. I gather that "Little Jim" Edgar, the governor, isn't much respected by the press. Governor Edgar is maybe fifty and greyhound-thin, with steel glasses and hair that looks carved out of feldspar. He radiates sincerity, though. After the hacks introduce him, he speaks sanely and, I think, well. He invites everybody to get in there and have a really good time and to revel in watching everybody else also having a good time—a kind of reflexive exercise in civics. The press corps seems unmoved.

But this fair, the idea and now the reality of it, does seem to have something uniquely to do with state-as-community, a grand-scale togetherness. And it is not just the claustrophobic mash of people waiting to get inside. The fair occupies space, and there's no shortage of empty space in downstate Illinois. The fairgrounds take up 300-plus acres on the north side of Springfield, a depressed capital of 109,000 where you can't spit without hitting a Lincoln-site plaque. The fair spreads itself out, and visually so. The main gate is on a rise, and through the two sagged halves of ribbon you get a specular vantage on the whole thing—virgin and sun-glittered, even the tents looking freshly painted. It seems garish and endless and aggressively special. Kids are having little epileptic fits all around us, frenzied with a need to take in everything at once. I suspect that part of the self-conscious community thing here has to do with space. Rural Midwesterners live surrounded by unpopulated land, marooned in a space whose emptiness is both physical and spiritual. It is not just people you get lonely for. You're alienated from the very space around you, for here the land is not an environment but a commodity. The land is basically a factory. You live in the same factory you work in. You spend an enormous amount of time with the land, but you're still alienated from it in some way. I theorize to Native Companion (who worked detasseling

The largest-boar contest.

summer corn with me in high school) that the state fair's animating thesis involves some kind of structured, decorated interval of communion with both neighbor and space—the sheer *fact* of the land is to be celebrated here, its yields ogled and its stock groomed and paraded. A special vacation from alienation, a chance, for a moment, to love what real life out here can't let you love. Native Companion gives me a look, then rummages for her cigarette lighter, quite a bit more interested in that. [...]

11:50 A.M.

Since Native Companion was lured here for the day by the promise of free access to high-velocity rides, we make a quick descent into Happy Hollow. Most of the rides aren't even twirling hellishly yet. Guys with ratchet wrenches are still cranking away, assembling the Ring of Fire. The Giant Gondola Wheel is only half-built, and its seat-draped lower half resembles a hideous molary grin. It is over 100 degrees in the sun, easy.

Happy Hollow's dirt midway is flanked by carnival-game booths and ticket booths and rides. There's a merry-go-round and a couple of tame kiddie rides, but most of the rides look like genuine Near-Death Experiences. The Hollow seems to be open only technically, and the ticket booths are unmanned, though little heartbreaking jets of AC air are blowing out through the money slots in the booths' glass. Attendance is sparse, and I notice that none of the ag-pro or farm people are anywhere in sight down here. A lot of the carnies slouch and slump in the shade of awnings. Every one of them seems to chain-smoke. The Tilt-a-Whirl operator has got his boots up on his control panel reading a motorcycle-and-naked-girl magazine while guys attach enormous rubber hoses to the ride's guts. We sidle over for a

chat. The operator is twenty-four and from Bee Branch, Arkansas, and has an earring and a huge tattoo of a flaming skull on his triceps. He's far more interested in chatting with Native Companion than with me. He's been at this gig five years, touring with this one here same company here. Couldn't rightly say if he liked it or not. Broke in on the Toss-a-Quarter-Onto-the-Plates game and got, like, transferred over to the Tilt-a-Whirl in '91. He smokes Marlboro 100's but wears a cap that says "Winston."

All the carny game barkers have headset microphones; some are saying "Testing" and reciting their pitch lines in tentative warm-up ways. A lot of the pitches seem frankly sexual: You got to get it up to get it in. Take it out and lay 'er down, only a dollar. Make it stand up. Two dollars, five chances. Make it stand up. Rows of stuffed animals hang by their feet in the booths like game put out to cure. It smells like machine grease and hair tonic down here, and there's already a spoiled, garbagy smell. The media guide says Happy Hollow is contracted to "one of the largest owners of amusement attractions in the country," one Blomsness-Thebault Enterprises, of Crystal Lake, Illinois, near Chicago. But the carnies are all from the middle South—Tennessee, Arkansas, Oklahoma. They are visibly unimpressed by the press credentials clipped to my shirt. They tend to look at Native Companion like she's food, which she ignores. I lose four dollars trying to "get it up and in," tossing miniature basketballs into angled baskets in such a way that they don't bounce out. The game's barker can toss them behind his back and get them to stay, but he's right up next to the baskets. My shots carom out from eight feet away; the straw baskets look soft, but their bottoms make a suspicious steely sound when hit.

It's so hot that we move in quick vectors between areas of shade. I'm reluctant to go shirtless because there'd be no way to display my credentials. We zigzag gradually westward. One of the fully assembled rides near the Hollow's west end is something called the Zipper. It's riderless as we approach, but in furious motion, a kind of Ferris wheel on amphetamines. Individual caged cars are hinged to spin on their own axes as they go around in a tight vertical ellipse. The machine looks less like a Zipper than the head of a chain saw. It sounds like a shimmying V-12 engine, and it is something I'd run a mile in tight shoes to avoid riding.

Native Companion starts clapping and hopping, though. The operator at the controls sees her and shouts down to git on over and git some, if she's a mind. He claims they want to test it somehow. He's elbowing a colleague next to him in a way I don't much care for. We have no tickets, I point out, and none of the cash-for-ticket booths are manned. "Ain't no sweat off my balls," the operator says without looking at me. The operator's colleague conducts Native Companion up the waffled-steel steps and straps her into a cage, upping a thumb at the operator, who pulls a lever. She starts to ascend. Pathetic little fingers appear in the cage's mesh. The Zipper's operator is ageless and burnt-brown and has a mustache waxed to wicked points like a steer's horns, rolling a Drum cigarette with one hand as he nudges levers upward and the ellipse of cars speeds up and the individual cars themselves start to spin on their hinges. Native Companion is a blur of color inside her cage, but operator and colleague (whose jeans have worked down his hips to the point that the top of his butt-crack is visible) watch studiously as Native Companion's spinning car and the clanking empty cars circle the ellipse once a second. I can barely watch. The Zipper is the color of unbrushed teeth, with big scabs of rust. The operator and colleague sit on a little steel deck before a panel of black-knobbed levers. The colleague spits Skoal into a can he holds and tells the operator, "Well then take her up to eight then you pussy." The Zipper begins to whine and the thing to spin so fast that a detached car would surely be hurled into orbit. The colleague has a small American flag folded into a bandanna around his head. The empty cars shudder and clank as they whirl and spin. One long scream, wobbled by changes in vector, is coming from Native Companion's cage, which is going around and around on its hinges while a shape inside tumbles like stuff in a clothes dryer. My neurological makeup (extremely sensitive: carsick, airsick, heightsick) makes just watching this an act of great personal courage. The scream goes on and on; it is nothing like a swine's. Then the operator stops the ride abruptly with her car at the top, so she's hanging upside down inside the cage. I call up—is she okay? The response is a strange high-pitched noise. I see the two carnies gazing upward very intently, shading their eyes. The operator is stroking his mustache contemplatively. The cage's inversion has made Native Companion's dress fall up. They're ogling her nethers, obviously.

Now the operator is joggling the choke lever so the Zipper stutters back and forth, forward and backward, making Native Companion's top car spin around and around on its hinges. His colleague's T-shirt has a stoned Ninja Turtle on it, toking on a joint. There's a distended A-sharp scream from the whirling car, as if Native Companion is being slow-roasted. I summon saliva to step in and really say something stern, but at this point they start bringing her down. The operator is deft at his panel; the car's descent is almost fluffy. His hands on the levers are a kind of parody of tender care. The descent takes forever—ominous silence from Native Companion's car. The two carnies are laughing and slapping their knee. I clear my throat twice. Native Companion's car descends, stops. Jiggles of movement in the car, then the door's latch slowly turns. I expect whatever husk of a person emerges from the car to be hunched and sheet-white, dribbling fluids.

Instead she bounds out. "That was fucking *great*! Joo *see* that? Son of a bitch spun that car *sixteen times*, did you see?" This woman is native Midwestern, from my hometown. My prom date a dozen years ago. Her color is high. Her dress looks like the world's worst case of static cling. She's still got her *chewing gum* in, for God's sake. She turns to the carnies: "You sons bitches, that was fucking *great*." The colleague is half-draped over the operator; they're roaring with laughter. Native Companion has her hands on her hips, but she's grinning. Am I the only one who's in touch with the sexual-harassment element in this whole episode? She takes the steel stairs several at a time and starts up the hillside toward the food booths. Behind us the operator calls out, "They don't call me King of the Zipper for nuthin', sweet thang!"

She snorts and calls back over her shoulder, "Oh, *you.*"

I'm having a hard time keeping up. "Did you hear that?" I ask her.

"Jesus I thought I bought it for sure, that was so great. Assholes. But did you *see* that one spin up top at the end, though?"

"Did you hear that Zipper King comment?" I protest. She has her hand around my elbow and is helping me up the hillside's slick grass. "Did you sense something kind of sexual-harassmentish going on through that whole sick little exercise?"

"Oh for fuck's sake, it was fun—son of a bitch spun that car *sixteen times.*"

"They were looking up your *dress.* You couldn't see them, maybe. They hung you upside down at a great height and made your dress fall up and ogled you. They shaded their eyes and commented to each other."

"Oh for Christ's sake."

I slip a bit and she catches my arm. "So this doesn't bother you? As a Midwesterner, you're unbothered? Or did you just not have a sense of what was going on?"

"So if I noticed or didn't, why does it have to be *my* deal? What, because there's assholes in the world I don't get to ride the Zipper?"

"This is potentially key," I say. "This may be just the sort of regional eroto-political contrast the East Coast magazine is keen for. The core value informing a kind of eroto-willed political stoicism on your part is your prototypically Midwestern appreciation of fun—"

"Buy me some pork skins, you dipshit."

"—whereas on the East Coast, eroto-political indignation *is* the fun. In New York a woman who'd been hung upside down and ogled would get a whole lot of other women together and there'd be this frenzy of eroto-political indignation. They'd confront the guy. File an injunction. The management would find themselves litigating—violation of a woman's right to non-harassed fun. I'm telling you. Personal and political fun merge somewhere just east of Cleveland, for women."

Native Companion kills a mosquito without looking. "And they all take Prozac and stick their finger down their throat too out there. They ought to try just climbing on and spinning and saying, 'Fuck 'em.' That's pretty much all you can do with assholes."

12:35 P.M.

Lunchtime. The fairgrounds are a Saint Vitus' dance of blacktop footpaths, the axons and dendrites of mass spectation, connecting buildings and barns and corporate tents. Each path is flanked, pretty much along its whole length, by booths hawking food, and I realize that there's a sort of digestive subtheme running all through the fair. In a way, we're all here to be swallowed up. The main gate's maw admits us, and tightly packed slow masses move peristaltically along complex systems of branching paths, engage in complex cash-and-energy transfers at the villi alongside the paths, and are finally, both filled and depleted, expelled out of exits designed for heavy-flow expulsion. And then, of course, the food itself. There are tall Kaopectate-colored shacks that sell Illinois Dairy Council milk shakes for an off-

the-scale $2.50—though they're mind-bendingly good milk shakes, silky and so thick they don't even insult your intelligence with a straw or spoon, giving you instead a kind of plastic trowel. There are uncountable pork options— Paulie's Pork Out, The Pork Patio, Freshfried Pork Skins, The Pork Avenue Cafe. The Pork Avenue Cafe is a "100 Percent All-Pork Establishment," says its loud-speaker. [...] And it is at least ninety-five degrees in the shade, and due east of Livestock the breeze is, shall we say, fragrant. But food is being bought and ingested at an incredible clip all up and down the path. Everyone's packed in, eating and walking, moving slowly, twenty abreast, sweating, shoulders rubbing, the air spicy with armpits and Coppertone, cheek to jowl, a peripatetic feeding frenzy. Fifteen percent of the female fairgoers here have their hair in curlers. Forty percent are clinically fat. By the way, Midwestern fat people have no compunction about wearing shorts or halter tops. The food booths are ubiquitous, and each one has a line before it. Zipper or no, Native Companion is "*storved*," she says, "to *daith*." She puts on a parodic hick accent whenever I use a term like "peripatetic."

There are Lemon Shake-Ups, Ice Cold Melon Man booths, Citrus Push-Ups, and Hawaiian Shaved Ice you can suck the syrup out of and then crunch the ice. But a lot of what's getting bought and gobbled is not hot-weather food at all: bright-yellow popcorn that stinks of salt; onion rings as big as leis; Poco Peños Stuffed Jalapeño Peppers; Zorba's Gyros; shiny fried chicken; Bert's Burritos—"Big As You're [sic] Head"; hot Italian beef; hot New York City beef; Jojo's Quick Fried Doughnuts; pizza by the shingle-sized slice; and chitlins and crab Rangoon and Polish sausage. There are towering plates of "Curl Fries," which are pubic-hair-shaped and make people's fingers shine in the sun. Cheez-Dip hot dogs. Pony pups. Hot fritters. Philly steak. Ribeye BBQ Corral. Joanie's Original ½-lb. Burgers booth's sign says "2 Choices—Rare or Mooin'." I can't believe people eat this stuff in this kind of heat. There's the green reek of fried tomatoes. The sky is cloudless and galvanized, and the sun fairly pulses. The noise of deep fryers forms a grisly sound-carpet all up and down the paths. The crowd moves at one slow pace, eating, densely packed between the rows of booths. The Original 1-lb. Butterfly Pork Chop booth has a sign: "Pork: The Other White Meat"— the only discernible arm wave to the health-conscious. This is the Midwest: no nachos, no chili, no Evian, nothing Cajun. But holy mackerel, are there sweets: fried dough,

black walnut taffy, fiddlesticks, hot Crackerjack. Caramel apples for a felonious $1.50. Angel's Breath, known also as Dentist's Delight. There's All-Butter Fudge, Rice Krispie–squarish things called Krakkles. Angel Hair cotton candy. There are funnel cakes: cake batter quick-fried to a tornadic spiral and rolled in sugared butter. Another artery clogger: elephant ears, an album-sized expanse of oil-fried dough slathered with butter and cinnamon-sugar—cinnamon toast from hell. No one is in line for ears except the morbidly obese.

1:10 P.M.

"Here we've got as balanced in dimension a heifer as any you'll see today. A high-volume heifer, but also solid on mass. Good to look at in terms of rib length to depth. Depth of forerib. Notice the depth of flank on the front quarter. We'd like to see maybe perhaps a little more muscle mass on the rear flank. Still, an outstanding heifer."

We're in the Jr. Livestock Center. The ring of cows moves around the perimeter of the dirt circle, each led by an ag-family kid. The "Jr." apparently refers to the owners, not the animals. Each cow's kid holds a long poker with a right-angled tooth at its end and prods the cow into the center of the ring to move in a tighter circle. The beef-show official is dressed just like the kids in the ring—dark new stiff jeans, check shirt, bandanna around neck. On him it doesn't look goofy. Plus he's got a stunning white cowboy hat. While Ms. Illinois Beef Queen presides from a dais decked with flowers sent over from the horticulture show, the official stands in the arena itself, his legs apart and his thumbs in his belt, 100 percent man, radiating livestock savvy. "Okay this next heifer, a lot of depth of rib but a little tighter in the fore flank. A bit tighter-flanked, if you will, from the standpoint of capacity."

The owners—farm kids, deep-rural kids from back-of-beyond counties like Piatt, Moultrie, Vermilion, all here because they're county-fair winners—are earnest, nervous, pride-puffed. Dressed rurally up. Straw-colored crewcuts. High number of freckles per capita. Kids remarkable for a kind of classic Rockwellian USA averageness, the products of balanced diets, vigorous daily exertion, and solid GOP upbringings. The Jr. Livestock Center bleachers are half-full, and it is all ag-people, parents mostly, many with video cameras. Cowhide vests and ornate dress-boots and simply amazing hats. Illinois farmers are rural and inarticulate, but they are not poor. Just the amount of revolving credit you need to capitalize a hundred-acre operation—seed and herbicides, heavy equipment and crop insurance—makes a lot of them millionaires on paper. Media dirges notwithstanding, banks are no more keen to foreclose on Midwestern farms than they are on Third World nations; they're in that deeply. Nobody here wears sunglasses; everyone's in long pants and tanned in an earth-tone, all-business way. And if the fair's ag-pros are also stout, it is in a harder, squarer, somehow more *earned* way than the tourists on the paths outside. The fathers in the bleachers have bushy brows and simply enormous thumbs, I notice. Native Companion keeps making growly throat noises about the beef official. The Jr. Livestock Center is cool and dim and spicy with livestock. The atmosphere is good-natured but serious. Nobody's eating any booth-food, and nobody's carrying the fair's complimentary "Governor Edgar" shopping bags.

"An excellent heifer from a profile standpoint."

"Here we have a low-volume heifer, but with exceptional mass in the rear quarter."

I can't tell whose cow is winning.

"Certainly the most extreme heifer out here in terms of frame to depth."

Some of the cows look drugged. Maybe they're just superbly trained. You can imagine these farm kids getting up so early they can see their breath and leading their cows in practice circles under the cold stars, then having to do their chores. I feel good in here. The cows all have colored ribbons on their tails. They are shampooed and mild-eyed and lovely, incontinence notwithstanding. They're also assets. The ag-lady beside us says her family's operation will "realize" perhaps $2,500 for the Hereford in the Winners Auction coming up. Illinois farmers call their farms "operations," rarely "farms" and never "spreads." The lady says $2,500 is "maybe about around half" what the ag-family has spent on the heifer's breeding and care. "We do this for pride," she says. This is more like it—pride, care, selfless expense. The little boy's chest puffs out as the official tips his blinding hat.

Farm spirit. Oneness with crop and stock. The ag-lady says that the official is a beef buyer for a major Peoria packing plant and that the bidders in the upcoming auction (five brown suits and three string ties on the dais) are from McDonald's, Burger King, White Castle, etc. Meaning that the mild-eyed winners have been sedulously judged as meat. The ag-lady has a particular bone to pick with McDonald's, " 'cause they always come in and overbid high on the champions and don't care about nothing else. Mess up the pricing." Her husband confirms they got "screwed back to front" on last year's bidding. [...]

4:05 P.M.

We're about 100 yards shy of the Poultry Building when I break down. I've been a rock about the prospect of poultry all day, but now my nerve goes. I can't go in there. *Listen* to the thousands of sharp squawking beaks in there, I say. Native Companion not unkindly offers to hold my hand, talk me through it. It is 100 degrees and I have pygmy-goat shit on my shoe and am almost crying with fear and embarrassment. I have to sit down on a green bench to collect myself. The noise of the Poultry Building is horrifying. I think this is what insanity must sound like. No wonder madmen clutch their heads. There's a thin stink. Bits of feather float. I hunch on the bench. We're high on a ridge overlooking the carnival rides. When I was eight, at the Champaign County Fair, I was pecked without provocation, flown at and pecked by a renegade fowl, savagely, just under the right eye.

Sitting on the bench, I watch the carnies way below. They mix with no one, never seem to leave Happy Hollow. Late tonight, I'll watch them drop flaps to turn their booths into tents. They'll smoke cheap dope and drink peppermint schnapps and pee out onto the midway's dirt. I guess they're the gypsies of the rural United States—itinerant, insular, swarthy, unclean, not to be trusted. You are in no way drawn to them. They all have the same blank hard eyes as people in the bathrooms of East Coast bus terminals. They want your money and maybe to look up your skirt; beyond that you're just blocking the view. Next week they'll dismantle and pack and haul up to the Wisconsin State Fair, where they'll never set foot off the midway they pee on.

While I'm watching from the bench, an old withered man in an Illinois Poultry Association cap careers past on one of those weird three-wheeled carts, like a turbocharged wheelchair, and runs neatly over my sneaker. This ends up being my one unassisted interview of the day, and it's brief. The man keeps revving his cart's engine like a biker. "*Traish*," he calls the carnies. "Lowlifes." He gestures down at the twirling rides. "Wouldn't let my own kids go off down there on a goddamn bet." He raises pullets down near Olney. He has something in his cheek. "Steal you blind. Drug-addicted and such. Swindle you nekked them games. Traish. Me, I ever year we drive up, I carry my wallet like this here." He points to his hip. His wallet's on a big steel clip attached to a wire on his belt; the whole things looks vaguely electrified. Q: "But do they want to? Your kids? Hit the Hollow?" He spits brownly. "*Hail* no. We all come for the shows." He means the livestock competitions. "See some folks, talk stock. Drink a beer. Work all year round raising 'em for show birds. It's for pride. And to see folks. Shows're over Tuesday, why, we go on home." He looks like a bird himself. His face is mostly nose, his skin loose and pebbly like poultry's. His eyes are the color of denim. "Rest of this here's for city people." Spits. He means Springfield, Decatur, Normal. "Walk around, stand in line, eat junk, buy soovneers. Give their wallet to the traish. Don't even know there's folks come here to work up here." He gestures up at the barns, then spits again, leaning way out over the cart to do it. "We come up to work, see some folks. Drink a beer. Bring our own goddamn food. Mother packs a hamper. Hail, what we'd want to go on down there for? No folks we know down there." He laughs. Asks my name. "It is good to see folks," he says before leaving me and peeling out in his chair, heading for the chicken din. "We all stayin' up to the *motel*. Watch your wallet, boy."

AUGUST 14, 6:00 A.M.

The dawn is foggy. The sky looks like soap. It rained in brutal sheets last night, damaged tents, tore up corn near my motel. Midwestern thunderstorms are real Old Testament temple clutchers: Richter-scale thunder, big zigzags of cartoon lightning. Happy Hollow is a bog as I walk along the midway, passing an enfilade of snores from the booths and tents. Native Companion went home last night. My sneakers are already soaked. Someone behind the flaps of the Shoot-2D-Ducks-With-an-Air-Rifle booth is having a wicked coughing fit, punctuated with obscenities. Distant sounds of garbage Dumpsters being emptied. The Blomsness-Thebault management trailer has a blinky electric burglar alarm on it. The goddamn roosters in the Poultry Building are at it already. Thunder-mutters way off east over Indiana. The trees shudder and shed drops in the breeze. The paths are empty, eerie, shiny with rain.

6:20 A.M.

Sheep Barn. I am looking at legions of sleeping sheep. I am the only waking human in here. It is cool and quiet. Sheep excrement has an evil vomity edge to it, but olfactorily it is not too bad in here. One or two sheep are upright but silent. No fewer than four ag-pros are also in the pens, sleeping right up next to their sheep, about which the less speculation the better as far as I'm concerned. The roof in here is leaky and most of the straw is sopping. In here are yearling ewes, brood ewes, ewe lambs, fall lambs. There are signs on every pen. We've got Corriedales, Hampshires, Dorset Horns, Columbias. You could get a Ph.D. just in sheep, from the looks of it. Rambouillets, Oxfords, Suffolks, Shropshires, Cheviots, Southdowns. Outside again, undulating ghosts of fog on the fairground paths. Everything set up but no one about. A creepy air of hasty abandonment.

8:20 A.M.

Press room, fourth floor, Illinois Building. I'm the only credentialed member of the press without a little plywood cubbyhole for mail and press releases. Two guys from an ag-newspaper are trying to hook a fax machine up to a rotary-phone jack. A state-fair PR guy arrives for the daily press briefing. We have coffee and unidentifiable muffinish

6:30 A.M. at the cow barn.

things, compliments of Wal-Mart. This afternoon's highlights: Midwest Truck and Tractor Pull, the "Bill Oldani 100" U.S.A.C. auto race. Tonight's Grandstand show is to be the poor old doddering Beach Boys, who I suspect now must make their entire living from state fairs. The special guest is America, another poor old doddering group. The PR guy cannot give away all his free press passes to the concert. I learn that I missed some law-and-order dramatics yesterday: two Zipper-riding minors were detained last night when a vial of crack fell from the pocket of one of them and direct-hit a state trooper alertly eating a Lemon Push-Up on the midway below. Also reported: a rape or date rape in Parking Lot 6, assorted buncos and D&D's. Two reporters also vomited on from great heights in two separate incidents under two separate Near-Death-Experience rides, trying to cover the Hollow. [...]

9:30 A.M.

I'm once again at the capacious McDonald's tent, at the edge, the titanic inflatable clown presiding. There's a fair-sized crowd in the basketball bleachers at one side and rows of folding chairs on another. It's the Illinois State Jr. Baton-Twirling Finals. A metal loudspeaker begins to emit disco, and little girls pour into the tent from all directions, gamboling and twirling in vivid costumes. In the stands, video cameras come out by the score, and I can tell it's pretty much just me and a thousand parents.

The baroque classes and divisions, both team and solo, go from age three(!) to sixteen, with epithetic signifiers—the four-year-olds compose the Sugar 'N' Spice division, and so on. I'm in a chair up front behind the competition's judges, introduced as "varsity twirlers" from (oddly) the University of Kansas. They are four frosted blondes who smile a lot and blow huge grape bubbles.

The twirler squads are all from different towns. Mount Vernon and Kankakee seem especially rich in twirlers. The twirlers' spandex costumes, differently colored for each team, are paint-tight and brief in the legs. The coaches are grim, tan, lithe-looking women, clearly twirlers once, on the far side of their glory now and very serious-looking, each with a clipboard and whistle. The teams go into choreographed routines, each routine with a title and a designated disco or show tune, full of compulsory baton-twirling maneuvers with highly technical names. A mother next to me is tracking scores on what looks almost like an astrology

chart, and is in no mood to explain anything to a novice baton watcher.

The routines are wildly complex, and the loud-speaker's play-by-play is mostly in code. All I can determine for sure is that I've bumbled into what has to be the most spectator-hazardous event at the fair. Missed batons go all over, whistling wickedly. The three-, four-, and five-year-olds aren't that dangerous, though they do spend most of their time picking up dropped batons and trying to hustle back into place—the parents of especially fumble-prone twirlers howl in fury from the stands while the coaches chew gum grimly. But the smaller girls don't really have the arm strength to endanger anybody, although one judge takes a Sugar 'N' Spice's baton across the bridge of the nose and has to be helped from the tent.

But when the sevens and eights hit the floor for a series of "Armed Service medleys" (spandex with epaulets and officers' caps and batons over shoulders like M16's), errant batons start pin-wheeling into the ceiling, tent's sides, and crowd, all with real force. I myself duck several times. A man just down the row takes one in the solar plexus and falls out of his metal chair with a horrid crash. The batons are embossed "Regulation Length" on the shaft and have white rubber stoppers on each end, but it is that hard dry kind of rubber, and the batons themselves aren't light. I don't think it's an accident that police nightsticks are also called service batons.

Physically, even within same-age teams, there are marked incongruities in size and development. One nine-year-old is several heads taller than another, and they're trying to do a complex back-and-forth duet thing with just one baton, which ends up taking out a bulb in one of the tent's steel hanging lamps, showering part of the stands with glass. A lot of the younger twirlers look either anorexic or gravely ill. There are no fat baton twirlers.

A team of ten-year-olds in the Gingersnap class have little cotton bunny tails on their costume bottoms and rigid papier-mâché ears, and they can do some serious twirling. A squad of eleven-year-olds from Towanda does an involved routine in tribute to Operation Desert Storm. To most of the acts there's either a cutesy ultrafeminine aspect or a stern butch military one, with little in between. Starting with the twelve-year-olds—one team in black spandex that looks like cheesecake leotards—there is, I'm afraid, a frank sexuality that begins to get uncomfortable. Oddly, it's the cutesy feminine performances that result in the serious audience casualties. A dad standing up near the top of the stands with a Toshiba video camera to his eye takes a tomahawking baton directly in the groin and falls over on somebody eating a funnel cake, and they take out good bits of several rows below them, and there's an extended halt to the action, during which I decamp. As I clear the last row of chairs yet another baton comes *wharp-wharping* cruelly tight over my shoulder, caroming viciously off big Ronald's inflated thigh.

11:05 A.M.

The Expo Building, a huge enclosed mall-like thing, AC'd down to eighty degrees, with a gray cement floor and a hardwood mezzanine overhead. Every interior inch is given over to commerce of a special and lurid sort. Just inside the big east entrance, a man with a headset mike is slicing up a block of wood and then a tomato, standing on a box in a booth that says "SharpKut," hawking these spin-offs of Ginsu knives, "As Seen on TV." Next door is a booth offering personalized pet-ID tags. Another for the infamous mail-order-advertised Clapper, which turns on appliances automatically at the sound of two hands clapping (but also at the sound of a cough, sneeze, or sniff, I discover; *caveat emptor*). There's booth after booth, each with an audience whose credulity seems sincere. A large percentage of the booths show signs of hasty assembly and say "As Seen on TV" in bright brave colors. The salesmen all stand on raised platforms; all have headset mikes and rich neutral media voices.

The Copper Kettle All-Butter Fudge booth does a brisk air-conditioned business. There's something called a Full Immersion Body Fat Analysis for $8.50. A certain Compu-Vac, Inc., offers a $1.50 Computerized Personality Analysis. Its booth's computer panel is tall and full of blinking lights and reel-to-reel tapes, like an old bad sci-fi-film computer. My own Personality Analysis, a slip of paper that protrudes like a tongue from a red-lit slot, says, "Your Boldness of Nature Is Ofset [sic] with the Fear of Taking Risk." There's a booth that offers clock faces superimposed on varnished photorealist paintings of Christ, John Wayne, Marilyn Monroe. There's a Computerized Posture Evaluation booth. A lot of the headsetted vendors are about my age or younger. Something overscrubbed about them suggests a Bible-college background. It is just cool enough in here for a sweat-soaked shirt to get clammy. One vendor recites a

pitch for Ms. Suzanne Somers's Thighmaster while a woman in a leotard demonstrates the product, lying on her side on the fiberboard counter. I'm in the Expo Building almost two hours, and every time I look up the poor woman's still at it with the Thighmaster. Most of the vendors won't answer questions and give me beady looks when I stand there making notes. But the Thighmaster lady, cheerful, friendly, violently cross-eyed, informs me she gets an hour off for lunch at 2:00 P.M., then goes another eight hours to closing at 11:00 P.M. I say her thighs must be pretty darn well Mastered by now, and her leg sounds like a banister when she raps her knuckle against it. We both have a laugh, until her vendor asks me to scram.

Booth after booth. A Xanadu of chintzola. Obscure non-stick cookware. "Eye Glasses Cleaned Free." A booth with anti-cellulite sponges. Dippin' Dots futuristic ice cream. A woman with Velcro straps on her sneakers gets fountain-pen ink out of a linen tablecloth with a Chapsticky-looking spot remover whose banner says "As Seen on TV's 'Amazing Discoveries,'" a late-night infomercial I'm kind of a fan of. A booth that for $9.95 will take a photo and superimpose your face on either an FBI Wanted poster or a *Penthouse* cover. An "MIA—Bring Them Home!" booth staffed by women playing Go Fish. An anti-abortion booth called Lifesavers that lures you over with little candies. Sand art. Shredded-ribbon art. A booth for "Latest Advance! Rotary Nose Hair Clippers" whose other sign reads (I kid you not), "Do Not Pull Hair From Nose, May Cause Fatal Infection." Two different booths for collectible sports-star cards, "Top Ranked Investment of the Nineties." And tucked way back on one curve of the mezzanine's ellipse—*yes*—black-velvet paintings, including—*yes*—several of Elvis in pensive poses.

Also on display is the expo's second economy—the populist evangelism of the rural Midwest. It is not your cash they want but to "Make a Difference in Your Life." And they make no bones about it. A Church of God booth offers a Computerized Bible Quiz. Its computer is CompuVacish in appearance. I go eighteen for twenty on the quiz and am invited behind a chamois curtain for a "person-to-person faith exploration," which no thanks. The conventional vendors get along fine with the Baptists and Jews for Jesus who operate booths right near them. They all laugh and banter back and forth. The SharpKut guy sends all the vegetables he's microsliced over to the Lifesavers booth, where they put them out with the candy. The scariest spiritual booth is right up near the west exit, where something called Covenant Faith Triumphant Church has a big hanging banner that asks, "What Is the ONE Man Made Thing Now in Heaven?" and I stop to ponder, which with charismatics is death, because a heavy-browed woman is out around the booth's counter like a shot and into my personal space. She says, "Give up? Give up do you?" She's looking at me very intensely, but there's something about her gaze: it is like she's looking *at* my eyes rather than *in* them. "What one man-made thing?" I ask. She puts a finger to her palm and makes screwing motions. Signifying coitus? I don't say "coitus" out loud, though. "Not but one thing," she says. "The holes in Christ's palms," screwing her finger in. Except isn't it pretty well known that Roman crucifees were nailed at the wrists, since palm-flesh won't support weight? But now I've been drawn into the dialogue, going so far as to let her take my arm and pull me toward the booth's counter. "Lookee here for a second now," she says. She has both hands around my arm. A Midwestern child of humanist academics gets trained early on to avoid these weird-eyed eager rural Christians who accost your space, to say "Not interested" at the front door and "No thanks" to mimeoed pamphlets, to look right through streetcorner missionaries like they were stemming for change. But the woman drags me toward the Covenant Faith counter, where a fine oak box rests, a sign propped on it: "Where Will YOU Be When YOU Look Like THIS?" "Take a look-see in here," the woman says. The box has a hole in its top. I peek. Inside the box is a human skull. I'm pretty sure it's plastic. The interior lighting is tricky, but I'm pretty sure the skull isn't genuine. I haven't inhaled for several minutes. The woman is looking at the side of my face. "Are you *sure*? is the question," she says. I manage to make my straightening-up motion lead right into a backing-away motion. "Are you a hunderd percent *sure*?" Overhead, on the mezzanine, the Thighmaster lady is still at it, smiling cross-eyed into space.

1:36 P.M.

I'm on a teetery stool watching the Illinois Prairie Cloggers competition in a structure called the Twilight Ballroom that's packed with ag-folks and well over 100 degrees. I'd nipped in here only to get a bottle of soda pop on my way to the Truck and Tractor Pull. By now the pull's got to be nearly over, and in half an hour the big U.S.A.C. dirt-track auto race starts. But I cannot tear myself away from the

scene in here. I'd imagined goony Jed Clampett types in tattered hats and hobnail boots, a-stompin' and a-whoopin', etc. I guess clogging, Scotch-Irish in origin and the dance of choice in Appalachia, did used to involve actual clogs and boots and slow stomps. But clogging has now miscegenated with square dancing and honky-tonk boogie to become a kind of intricately synchronized, absolutely kick-ass country tap dance.

There are teams from Pekin, Le Roy, Rantoul, Cairo, Morton. They each do three numbers. The music is up-tempo country or dance-pop. Each team has anywhere from four to ten dancers. Few of the women are under thirty-five, fewer still under 175 pounds. They're country mothers, red-cheeked gals with bad dye jobs and big pretty legs. They wear western-wear tops and midiskirts with multiple ruffled slips underneath; and every once in a while they grab handfuls of cloth and flip the skirts up like cancan dancers. When they do this they either yip or whoop, as the spirit moves them. The men all have thinning hair and cheesy rural faces, and their skinny legs are rubberized blurs. The men's western shirts have piping on the chest and shoulders. The teams are all color-coordinated—blue and white, black and red. The white shoes all the dancers wear look like golf shoes with metal taps clamped on.

Their numbers are to everything from Waylon and Tammy to Aretha, Miami Sound Machine, Neil Diamond's "America." The routines have some standard tap-dance moves—sweep, flare, chorus-line kicking. But it is fast and sustained and choreographed down to the last wrist-flick. And square dancing's genes can be seen in the upright, square-shouldered postures on the floor, and there's a kind of florally enfolding tendency to the choreography, some of which uses high-speed promenades. But it is methedrine-paced and exhausting to watch because your own feet move; and it is erotic in a way that makes MTV look lame. The cloggers' feet are too fast to be seen, really, but they all tap out the exact same rhythm. A typical routine is something like: ta*tatatatatatatatatata*. The variations around the basic rhythm are baroque. When they kick or spin, the two-beat absence of tap complexifies the pattern.

The audience is packed in right to the edge of the portable hardwood flooring. The teams are mostly married couples. The men are either rail-thin or have big hanging guts. A couple of the men on a blue-and-white team are great fluid Astaire-like dancers, but mostly it is the women who compel. The men have constant smiles, but the women look orgasmic; they're the really serious ones, transported. Their yips and whoops are involuntary, pure exclamation. They are arousing. The audience claps savvily on the back-beat and whoops when the women do. It is almost all folks from the ag and livestock shows—the flannel shirts, khaki pants, seed caps and freckles. The spectators are soaked in sweat and extremely happy. I think this is the ag-community's special treat, a chance here to cut loose a little while their animals sleep in the heat. The transactions between cloggers and crowd seem synecdochic of the fair as a whole: a culture talking to itself, presenting credentials for its own inspection, bean farmers and herbicide brokers and 4-H sponsors and people who drive pickup trucks because they really need them. They eat non-fair food from insulated hampers and drink beer and pop and stomp in perfect time and put their hands on neighbors' shoulders to shout in their ears while the cloggers whirl and fling sweat on the crowd.

There are no black people in the Twilight Ballroom, and the awakened looks on the younger ag-kids' faces have this astonished aspect, like they didn't realize their race could dance like this. Three married couples from Rantoul, wearing full western bodysuits the color of raw coal, weave an incredible filigree of high-speed tap around Aretha's "R-E-S-P-E-C-T," and there's no hint of racial irony in the room; the song has been made this people's own, emphatically. This Nineties version of clogging does have something sort of pugnaciously white about it, a kind of performative nose-thumbing at M.C. Hammer. There's an atmosphere in the room—not racist, but aggressively *white*. It's hard to describe—the atmosphere is the same at a lot of rural Midwest events. It is not like a black person who came in would be ill treated; it's more like it would just never occur to a black person to come here.

I can barely hold the tablet still to scribble journalistic impressions, the floor is rumbling under so many boots and sneakers. The record player is old-fashioned, the loudspeakers are shitty, and it sounds fantastic. Two of the dancing Rantoul wives are fat, but with great legs. Who could practice this kind of tapping as much as they must and stay fat? I think maybe rural Midwestern women are just congenitally big. But these people clogging get *down*. And they do it as a troupe, a collective, with none of the narcissistic look-at-me grandstanding of great dancers in rock clubs. They hold hands and whirl each other around and in and out, tapping like mad, their torsos upright and almost formal, as if only

incidentally attached to the blur of legs below. It goes on and on. I'm rooted to my stool. Each team seems the best yet. In the crowd's other side across the floor I can see the old poultry farmer, he of the carny hatred and electrified wallet. He's still got his poultry cap on, making a megaphone of his hands to whoop with the women, leaning way forward in his geriatric scooter, body bobbing like he's stomping in time, while his little cowboy boots stay clamped in their stays. [...]

6:00 P.M.

Back again at the seemingly inescapable Club Mickey D's. The tent is now set up for Illinois Golden Gloves Boxing. Out on the floor is a square of four boxing rings. The rings are made out of clothesline and poles anchored by cement-filled tires, one ring per age division: Sixteens, Fourteens, Twelves, Tens(!). Here's another unhyped but riveting spectacle. If you want to see genuine violence, go check out a Golden Gloves tourney. None of your adult pros' silky footwork or Rope-a-Dope defenses here. Here human asses are thoroughly kicked in what are essentially playground brawls with white-tipped gloves and brain-shaped head guards. The combatants' tank tops say things like "Peoria Jr. Boxing" and "Elgin Fight Club." The rings' corners have stools for the kids to sit on and get worked over by their teams' coaches. The coaches are clearly dads: florid, blue-jawed, bull-necked, flinty-eyed men who oversee sanctioned brawls. Now a fighter's mouth guard goes flying out of the Fourteens' ring, end over end, trailing strings of spit, and the crowd around that ring howls. In the Sixteens' ring is a local Springfield kid, Darrell Hall, against a slim fluid Latino, Sullivano, from Joliet. Hall outweighs Sullivano by a good twenty pounds. Hall also looks like every kid who ever beat me up in high school, right down to the wispy mustache and upper lip's cruel twist. The crowd around the Sixteens' ring is all his friends—guys with muscle shirts and gym shorts and gelled hair, girls in cutoff overalls and complex systems of barrettes. There are repeated shouts of "Kick his *ass*, Darrell!" The Latino sticks and moves. Somebody in this tent is smoking a joint, I can smell. The Sixteens can actually box. The ceiling's lights are bare bulbs in steel cones, hanging cockeyed from a day of batons. Everybody here pours sweat. The reincarnation of every high-school cheerleader I ever pined for is in the Sixteens' crowd. The girls cry out and frame their faces with their hands when Darrell gets hit. I do not know why cut-off overall shorts have evaded the East Coast's fashion ken; they are devastating. The fight in Fourteens is stopped for a moment to let the ref wipe a gout of blood from one kid's glove. Sullivano glides and jabs, orbiting Hall. Hall is implacable, a hunched and feral fighter, boring in. Air explodes through his nose when he lands a blow. He keeps trying to back the Latino against the clothesline. People cool themselves with wood-handled fans from the Democratic Party. Big hairy mosquitoes work the crowd. The refs keep slapping at their necks. The rain has been heavy, and the mosquitoes are the bad kind, field-bred and rapacious. I can also see the Tens from this vantage, a vicious free-for-all between two tiny kids whose head guards make their skulls look too big for their bodies. Neither ten-year-old has any interest in defense. Their shoes' toes touch as they windmill at each other, scoring at will. Scary dads chew gum in their corners. One kid's mouth guard keeps falling out. Now the Sixteens' crowd explodes as their loutish Hall catches Sullivano with an uppercut that puts him on his bottom. Sullivano gamely rises, but his knees wobble and he won't face the ref. Hall raises both arms and faces the crowd, disclosing a missing incisor. The girls betray their cheerleading backgrounds by clapping and jumping up and down at the same time. Hall shakes his gloves at the ceiling as several girls call his name, and you can feel it in the air's very ions: Darrell Hall is going to get laid before the night's over.

The digital thermometer in the Ronald-Buddha's left hand reads ninety-three degrees at 6:30 P.M. Behind him, big ominous scoop-of-coffee-ice-cream clouds are massing at the western horizon, but the sun's still above them and very much a force. People's shadows on the paths are getting pointy. It's the part of the day when little kids cry from what their parents naively call exhaustion. Cicadas chirr in the grass by the tent. The ten-year-olds stand toe to toe and whale the living shit out of each other. It is the sort of savage mutual beating you see in black-and-white films of old-time fights. Their ring now has the largest crowd. The fight will be all but impossible to score. But then it is over in an instant at the second intermission, when one of the little boys, sitting on his stool, being whispered to by a dad with tattooed forearms, suddenly throws up. Prodigiously. For no apparent reason. Maybe a stomach punch recollected in tranquillity. It is kind of surreal. Vomit flies all over. Kids in the crowd go "Eeeyuuu." The sick fighter starts to cry. His scary coach and the ref wipe him down and help him from

the ring, not ungently. His opponent, watching, tentatively puts up his arms.

7:30 P.M.

So the old heave-ho is the last thing I see at Golden Gloves Boxing and then the first thing I see at Happy Hollow, right at sunset. Standing on the midway looking up at the Ring of Fire—a set of flame-colored train cars sent around and around the inside of a 100-foot neon hoop, the operator stalling the train at the top and hanging the patrons upside down, jackknifed over their seat belts, with loose change and eyeglasses raining down—looking up, I witness a thick coil of vomit arc from a car; it describes a 100-foot spiral and lands with a meaty splat between two young girls, who look from the ground to each other with expressions of slapstick horror. And when the flame train finally brakes at the ramp, a mortified-looking little kid wobbles off, damp and pale, staggering over toward a Lemon Shake-Up stand.

This is my last day at the fair, and I've put off a real survey of the Near-Death Experiences until my last hour. I want to get everything catalogued before the sun sets. I've already had some distant looks at the nighttime Hollow and have an idea that being down here in the dark, amid all this rotating neon and the mechanical clowns and plunging machinery's roar and jagged screams and barkers' pitches and high-volume rock, would be like the depiction of a bum acid trip in a bad Sixties movie. It strikes me hardest in the Hollow that I'm not spiritually Midwestern anymore, and no longer young—I do not like crowds, screams, amplified noise, or heat. I'll endure them if I have to, but they're sure not my idea of a magic community-interval. The crowds in the Hollow, though—mostly high-school couples, local toughs, and kids in single-sex packs, as the demographics of the fair shift to prime time—seem radically happy, vivid, somehow awakened, sponges for sensuous data, not bombarded by the stimuli but feeding on it. It is the first time I've felt really lonely at the fair.

Nor do I understand why some people will pay money to be careened and suspended and dropped and whipped back and forth at high speeds and hung upside down until somebody vomits. It seems to me like paying to be in a traffic accident. I do not get it; never have. It's not a regional or cultural thing. I think it's a matter of neurological makeup. The world divides into those who like the managed induction of terror and those who don't. I do not find terror exciting. I find it terrifying. [...]

It nevertheless seems journalistically irresponsible to try to describe the Hollow's rides without experiencing at least one firsthand. The Kiddie Kopter is a carousel of miniature Sikorsky prototypes rotating at a sane and dignified clip. The propellers on each helicopter rotate as well. My copter is a bit snug, admittedly, even with my knees drawn up to my chest. I get kicked off the ride, though, when the whole machine's tilt reveals that I weigh quite a bit more than the maximum 100 pounds; and I have to say that both the little kids on the ride and the carny in charge were unnecessarily snide about the whole thing. Each ride has its own PA speaker with its own discharge of adrenalizing rock; the Kiddie Kopter's speaker is playing George Michael's "I Want Your Sex." The late-day Hollow itself is an enormous sonic mash from which different sounds take turns protruding—mostly whistles, sirens, calliopes, heavy-metal tunes, human screams hard to distinguish from recorded screams.

Both the Thunderboltz and the Octopus hurl free-spinning modular cars around a topologically complex plane; the Thunderboltz's sides reveal further evidence of gastric distress. Then there's the Gravitron, basically a centrifuge—an enclosed, top-shaped structure inside which is a rubberized chamber that spins so fast you're mashed against the wall like a fly on a windshield. A small boy stands on one foot tugging the Gravitron operator's khaki sleeve, crying that he lost a shoe in there. The best description of the carnies' tan is that they're somehow *sinisterly* tanned. I notice that many of them have the low brow and prognathous jaw one associates with fetal alcohol syndrome. The carny operating the Scooter—bumper cars that are fast, savage, underinsulated, a sure trip to the chiropractor—has been slumped in the same position in the same chair every time I've seen him, staring past the frantic cars and tearing up used ride-tickets with the vacant intensity of someone on a locked ward. I lean casually against his platform's railing so that my credentials dangle and ask him in a neighborly way how he keeps from going out of his freaking mind with the boredom of his job. He turns his head very slowly, revealing a severe facial tic: "The fuck you talkin' 'bout?"

The same two carnies as before are at the Zipper's controls, in the exact same clothes, looking up into the full cars and elbowing each other. The midway smells of machine oil and fried food, smoke and Cutter repellent and mall-bought adolescent perfume and ripe trash in the bee-swarmed cans. The very Nearest-to-Death ride looks to be the Kamikaze, way down at the western end by the Zyklon roller coaster.

Its neon sign has a skull with a headband and says "Kamikaze." It is a 70-foot pillar of white-painted iron with two 50-foot hammer-shaped arms hanging down, one on either side. The cars are at the ends of the arms, twelve-seaters enclosed in clear plastic. The two arms swing ferociously around, as in 360 degrees, vertically, and in opposite directions, so that twice on every rotation it looks like your car is going to get smashed up against the other car, and you can see faces in the other car hurtling toward you, gray with fear and squishy with G's. An eight-ticket, four-dollar waking nightmare.

Then I find the worst one. It wasn't even here yesterday. The Sky Coaster stands regally aloof at the Hollow's far western edge, just past the Uphill-Bowling-for-Dinnerware game, in a kind of grotto formed by trailers and dismantled machinery. It is a 175-foot construction crane, one of the really big mothers, with a tank's traction belts instead of wheels, a canary-yellow cab, and a long proboscis of black steel, towering, canted upward at maybe 70 degrees. This is half the Sky Coaster. The other half is a 100-foot tower assembly of cross-hatched iron that's been erected about two football fields to the north of the crane. There's a folding table in front of the clothesline cordoning off the crane, and a line of people at the table. The woman taking their money is fiftyish and a compelling advertisement for sunscreen. Behind her on a vivid blue tarp are two meaty blond guys in Sky Coaster T-shirts helping the next customer strap himself into what looks like a combination straitjacket and utility belt, bristling with hooks and clips. From here the noise of the Hollow behind is both deafening and muffled. My media guide, sweated into the shape of my butt pocket, says, "If you thought bungee jumping was a thrill, wait until you soar high above the Fairgrounds on Sky Coaster. The rider is fastened securely into a full-body harness that hoists them [sic] onto a tower and releases them to swing in a pendulum-like motion while taking in a spectacular view of the Fairgrounds below." The signs at the folding table are more telling: "$40.00 AMEX Visa MC. No Refunds. No Stopping Half Way Up." The two guys are leading the customer up the stairs of a rolling platform maybe ten feet high. One guy is at each elbow, and I realize they're helping hold the customer up. Who would pay $40 for an experience requiring you to be held up as you walk toward it? There's also something off about the customer, odd. He's wearing tinted aviator glasses. No one in the rural Midwest wears aviator glasses, tinted or otherwise. Then I see what it really is. He's wearing $400 Banfi loafers. Without socks. This guy, now lying prone on the platform below the crane, is *from the East Coast*. He's a ringer. I almost want to shout it. A woman is on the blue tarp, already in harness, wobbly kneed, waiting her turn. A steel cable descends from the tip of the crane's proboscis, on its end a fist-sized clip. Another cable leads from the crane's cab to the tower, up through ring-tipped pitons all up the tower's side, and over a pulley at its top, another big clip on the end. One of the guys waves the tower's cable down and brings it over to the platform. The clips of both cables are attached to the back of the East Coast guy's harness, fastened and locked. The guy is trying to look around behind him to see what-all's attached as the two big blonds leave the platform. Another blond man in the yellow cab throws a lever, and the tower's cable pulls tight in the grass and up the tower's side and down. The crane's cable stays slack as the guy is lifted into the air by the tower's cable. The harness covers his shorts and top, so he looks babe-naked as he rises. The one cable sings with tension as the East Coaster is pulled slowly to the top of the tower. He's still stomach-down, limbs wriggling. At a certain height he starts to look like livestock in a sling. You can tell he's trying to swallow until his face gets too small to see. Finally he's all the way up at the top of the tower, his ass against the pulley, trying not to writhe.

I can barely take notes. They cruelly leave him up there a while, slung, a smile of slack cable between him and the crane's tip. I am constructing a mental list of the personal violations I would undergo before I'd let anyone haul me ass-first to a great height and swing me like high-altitude beef. One of the blond guys has a bullhorn and he's playing to the crowd's suspense, calling up to the slung East Coaster: "Are. You. *Ready*." The East Coaster's response noises are more bovine than human. His tinted aviator glasses hang askew from just one ear; he doesn't bother to fix them. I can see what's going to happen. They're going to throw a lever and detach the tower-cable's clip, and the man in sockless Banfis will free-fall for what will seem forever, until the slack of the crane's cable is taken up and the line goes taut behind him and swings him way out over the grounds to the south, his upward arc almost as high as the crane's tip, and then back, and then forth, the man prone at the arc's bottom and seeming to stand on either side, swinging back and forth against a rare-meat sunset. And just as the cab man reaches for his lever and everyone inhales, I lose my nerve and disappear into the crowd.

9:15 P.M.

Walking aimlessly. Seas of fairgoing flesh, plodding, elbowing, looking, still eating. They stand placidly in long lines. No East Coast games of Beat the Crowd. Midwesterners lack a certain public cunning. No one gets impatient. Don't the fairgoers mind the crowds, lines, noise? But the state fair is deliberately about the crowds and jostle, the noise and overload of sight and event. At last an overarching theory blooms inside my head: megalopolitan East Coasters' summer treats and breaks are literally "getaways," flights-from—from crowds, noise, heat, dirt, the stress of too many sensory choices. Hence the ecstatic escapes to glassy lakes, mountains, cabins, hikes in silent woods. Getting away from it all. They see more than enough stimulating people and sights Monday through Friday, thank you, stand in enough lines, elbow enough crowds. Neon skylines. Grotesques on public transport. Spectacles at every urban corner practically grab you by the lapels, commanding attention. The East Coast existential treat is escape from confines and stimuli—quiet rustic vistas that hold still, turn inward, turn away. Not so in the rural Midwest. Here you're pretty much away all the time. The land is big here—board-game flat, horizons in every direction. See how much farther apart the homes are, how broad the yards: compare with New York or Boston or Philly. Here a seat to yourself on all public transport, parks the size of airports, rush hour a three-beat pause at a stop sign. And the farms themselves are huge, silent, vacant: you can't see your neighbor. Thus the urge physically to commune, melt, become part of a crowd. To see something besides land and grass and corn and cable TV and your wife's face. Hence the sacredness out here of spectacle, public event: high-school football, Little League, parades, bingo, market day, fair. All very big deals, very deep down. Something in a Midwesterner sort of *actuates*, deep down, at a public event. The faces in the sea of faces are like the faces of children released from their rooms. Governor Edgar's state-spirit rhetoric at the ribbon-cutting rings true. The real spectacle that draws us here is us.

WHERE WORLDS COLLIDE

BY PICO IYER

AUGUST 1995

They come out, blinking, into the bleached, forgetful sunshine, in Dodgers caps and Rodeo Drive T-shirts, with the maps their cousins have drawn for them and the images they've brought over from *Cops* and *Terminator 2*; they come out, dazed, disoriented, heads still partly in the clouds, bodies still several time zones—or centuries—away, and they step into the Promised Land.

In front of them is a Van Stop, a Bus Stop, a Courtesy Tram Stop, and a Shuttle Bus Stop (the shuttles themselves tracing circuits A, B, and C). At the Shuttle Bus Stop, they see the All American Shuttle, the Apollo Shuttle, Celebrity Airport Livery, the Great American Stageline, the Movie Shuttle, the Transport, Ride-4-You, and forty-two other magic buses waiting to whisk them everywhere from Bakersfield to Disneyland. They see Koreans piling into the Taeguk Airport Shuttle and the Seoul Shuttle, which will take them to Koreatown without their ever feeling they've left home; they see newcomers from the Middle East disappearing under the Arabic script of the Sahara Shuttle. They see fast-talking, finger-snapping, palm-slapping jive artists straight from their TV screens shouting incomprehensible slogans about deals, destinations, and drugs. Over there is a block-long white limo, a Lincoln Continental, and, over there, a black Chevy Blazer with Mexican stickers all over its windows, being towed. They have arrived in the Land of Opportunity, and the opportunities are swirling dizzily, promiscuously, around them. [...]

Above them in the Los Angeles International Airport terminal, voices are repeating, over and over, in Japanese,

Steve Lehman

Spanish, and unintelligible English, "Maintain visual contact with your personal property at all times." Out on the sidewalk, a man's voice and a woman's voice are alternating an unending refrain: "The white zone is for loading and unloading of passengers only. No parking." There are "Do Not Cross" yellow lines cordoning off parts of the sidewalk and "Wells Fargo Alarm Services" stickers on the windows; there are "Aviation Safeguard" signs on the baggage carts and "Beware of Solicitors" signs on the columns; there are even special phones "To Report Trouble." More male and female voices are intoning, continuously, "Do not leave your car unattended" and "Unattended cars are subject to immediate tow-away." There are no military planes on the tarmac here, the newcomers notice, no khaki soldiers in fatigues, no instructions not to take photographs, as at home; but there are civilian restrictions every bit as strict as in many a police state.

"This Terminal Is in a Medfly Quarantine Area," says the sign between the terminals. "Stop the Spread of Medfly!" If, by chance, the new Americans have to enter a parking lot on their way out, they will be faced with "Cars left over 30 days may be impounded at Owner's Expense" and "Do not enter without a ticket." It will cost them $16 if they lose their parking ticket, they read, and $56 if they park in the wrong zone. Around them is an unending cacophony of antitheft devices, sirens, beepers, and car-door openers; lights are flashing everywhere, and the man who fines them $16 for losing their parking ticket has the tribal scars of Tigre across his forehead.

The blue skies and palm trees they saw on TV are scarcely visible from here: just an undifferentiated smoggy haze, billboards advertising Nissan and Panasonic and Canon, and beyond those an endlessly receding mess of gray streets. Overhead, they can see the all-too-familiar signs of Hilton and Hyatt and Holiday Inn; in the distance, a sea of tract houses, mini-malls, and high-rises. The City of Angels awaits them.

It is a commonplace nowadays to say that cities look more and more like airports, cross-cultural spaces that are a gathering of tribes and races and variegated tongues; and it has always been true that airports are in many ways like miniature cities, whole, self-sufficient communities, with their own chapels and museums and gymnasiums. Not only have airports colored our speech (teaching us about being

Police arrest at LAX.

upgraded, bumped, and put on standby, coaching us in the ways of fly-by-night operations, holding patterns, and the Mile High Club); they have also taught us their own rules, their own codes, their own customs. We eat and sleep and shower in airports; we pray and weep and kiss there. Some people stay for days at a time in these perfectly convenient, hermetically sealed, climate-controlled duty-free zones, which offer a kind of caesura from the obligations of daily life.

Airports are also, of course, the new epicenters and paradigms of our dawning post-national age—not just the bus terminals of the global village but the prototypes, in some sense, for our polyglot, multicolored, user-friendly future. And in their very universality—like the mall, the motel, or

the McDonald's outlet—they advance the notion of a future in which all the world's a multiculture. If you believe that more and more of the world is a kind of mongrel hybrid in which many cities (Sydney, Toronto, Singapore) are simply suburbs of a single universal order, then Los Angeles's LAX, London's Heathrow, and Hong Kong's Kai Tak are merely stages on some great global Circle Line, shuttling variations on a common global theme. Mass travel has made L.A. contiguous to Seoul and adjacent to São Paulo, and has made all of them now feel a little like bedroom communities for Tokyo.

And as with most social trends, especially the ones involving tomorrow, what is true of the world is doubly true of America, and what is doubly true of America is quadruply true of Los Angeles. L.A., legendarily, has more Thais than any city but Bangkok, more Koreans than any city but Seoul, more El Salvadorans than any city outside of San Salvador, more Druze than anywhere but Beirut; it is, at the very least, the easternmost outpost of Asia and the northernmost province of Mexico. When I stopped at a Traveler's Aid desk at LAX recently, I was told I could request help in Khamu, Mien, Tigrinya, Tajiki, Pashto, Dari, Pangasinan, Pampangan, Waray-Waray, Bambara, Twi, and Bicolano (as well, of course, as French, German, and eleven languages from India). LAX is as clear an image as exists today of the world we are about to enter, and of the world that's entering us.

For me, though, LAX has always had a more personal resonance: it was in LAX that I arrived myself as a new immigrant, in 1966; and from the time I was in the fourth grade, it was to LAX that I would go three times a year, as an "unaccompanied minor," to fly to school in London—and to LAX that I returned three times a year for my holidays. Sometimes it seems as if I have spent half my life in LAX. For me, it is the site of my liberation (from school, from the Old World, from home) and the place where I came to design my own new future.

Often when I have set off from L.A. to some distant place—Havana, say, or Hanoi, or Pyongyang—I have felt that the multicultural drama on display in LAX, the interaction of exoticism and familiarity, was just as bizarre as anything I would find when I arrived at my foreign destination. The airport is an Amy Tan novel, a short story by Bharati Mukherjee, a Henry James sketch set to an MTV beat; it is a cross-generational saga about Chang Hsieng meeting his daughter Cindy and finding that she's wearing a nose ring now and is shacked up with a surfer from Berlin. The very best kind of airport reading to be found in LAX these days is the triple-decker melodrama being played out all around one—a complex tragicomedy of love and war and exile, about people fleeing centuries-old rivalries and thirteenth-century mullahs and stepping out into a fresh, forgetful, born-again city that is rewriting its script every moment.

Not long ago I went to spend a week in LAX. I haunted the airport by day and by night, I joined the gloomy drinkers listening to air-control-tower instructions on earphones at the Proud Bird bar. I listened each morning to Airport Radio (530 AM), and I slept each night at the Airport Sheraton or the Airport Hilton. I lived off cellophaned crackers and Styrofoam cups of tea, browsed for hours among Best Actor statuettes and Beverly Hills magnets, and tried to see what kinds of America the city presents to the new Americans, who are remaking America each day.

It is almost too easy to say that LAX is a perfect metaphor for L.A., a flat, spaced-out desert kind of place, highly automotive, not deeply hospitable, with little reading matter and no organizing principle. (There are eight satellites without a center here, many international arrivals are shunted out into the bleak basement of Terminal 2, and there is no airline that serves to dominate LAX as Pan Am once did JFK.) Whereas "SIN" is a famously ironical airline code for Singapore, cathedral of puritanical rectitude, "LAX" has always seemed perilously well chosen for a city whose main industries were traditionally thought to be laxity and relaxation. LAX is at once a vacuum waiting to be colonized and a joyless theme park—Tomorrowland, Adventureland, and Fantasyland all at once.

The postcards on sale here (made in Korea) dutifully call the airport "one of the busiest and most beautiful air facilities in the world," and it is certainly true that LAX, with thirty thousand international arrivals each day— roughly the same number of tourists that have visited the Himalayan country of Bhutan in its entire history—is not uncrowded. But bigger is less and less related to better: in a recent survey of travel facilities, *Business Traveller* placed LAX among the five worst airports in the world for customs, luggage retrieval, and passport processing.

LAX is, in fact, a surprisingly shabby and hollowed-out kind of place, certainly not adorned with the amenities one might expect of the world's strongest and richest power.

When you come out into the Arrivals area in the International Terminal, you will find exactly one tiny snack bar, which serves nine items; of them, five are identified as Cheese Dog, Chili Dog, Chili Cheese Dog, Nachos with Cheese, and Chili Cheese Nachos. There is a large panel on the wall offering rental-car services and hotels, and the newly deplaned American dreamer can choose between the Cadillac Hotel, the Banana Bungalow (which offers a Basketball Court, "Free Toast," "Free Bed Sheets," and "Free Movies and Parties"), and the Backpacker's Paradise (with "Free Afternoon Tea and Crumpets" and "Free Evening Party Including Food and Champagne").

Around one in the terminal is a swirl of priests rattling cans, Iranians in suits brandishing pictures of torture victims, and Japanese girls in Goofy hats. "I'm looking for something called Clearasil," a distinguished-looking Indian man diffidently tells a cashier. "Clearasil?" shouts the girl. "For your face?"

Upstairs, in the Terrace Restaurant, passengers are gulping down "Dutch Chocolate" and "Japanese Coffee" while students translate back and forth between English and American, explaining that "soliciting" loses something of its cachet when you go across the Atlantic. A fat man is nuzzling the neck of his outrageously pretty Filipina companion, and a few Brits are staring doubtfully at the sign that assures them that seafood is "cheerfully served at your table!" Only in America, they are doubtless thinking. A man goes from table to table, plunking down on each one a key chain attached to a globe. As soon as an unsuspecting customer picks one up, touched by the largesse of the New World and convinced now that there is such a thing as a free lunch in America, the man appears again, flashes a sign that says "I Am a Deaf," and requests a dollar for the gift. [...]

Yet for all these grounding reminders of the world outside, everywhere I went in the airport I felt myself in an odd kind of twilight zone of consciousness, that weightless limbo of a world in which people are between lives and between selves, almost sleepwalking, not really sure of who or where they are. Light-headed from the trips they've taken, ears popping and eyes about to do so, under a potent foreign influence, people are at the far edge of themselves in airports, ready to break down or through. You see strangers pouring out their life stories to strangers here, or making new life stories with other strangers. Everything is at once intensified and slightly unreal. One L.A. psychiatrist advises shy women to practice their flirting here, and religious groups circle in the hope of catching unattached souls.

Airports, which often have a kind of perpetual morning-after feeling (the end of the holiday, the end of the affair), are places where everyone is ruled by the clock, but all the clocks show different times. These days, after all, we fly not only into yesterday or this morning when we go across the world but into different decades, often, of the world's life and our own: in ten or fifteen hours, we are taken back into the twelfth century or into worlds we haven't seen since childhood. And in the process we are subjected to transitions more jolting than any imagined by Oscar Wilde or Sigmund Freud: if the average individual today sees as many images in a day as a Victorian saw in a lifetime, the average person today also has to negotiate switches between continents inconceivable only fifty years ago. Frequent fliers like Ted Turner have actually become ill from touching down and taking off so often; but, in less diagnosable ways, all of us are being asked to handle difficult suspensions of the laws of Nature and Society when moving between competing worlds.

This helps to compound the strange statelessness of airports, where all bets are off and all laws are annulled—modern equivalents, perhaps, to the hundred yards of no-man's-land between two frontier crossings. In airports we are often in dreamy, floating, out-of-body states, as ready to be claimed as that suitcase on Carousel C. Even I, not traveling, didn't know sometimes if I was awake or asleep in LAX, as I heard an announcer intone, "John Cheever, John Cheever, please contact a Northwest representative in the Baggage Claim area. John Cheever, please contact a service representative at the Northwest Baggage Claim area."

As I started to sink into this odd, amphibious, bipolar state, I could begin to see why a place like LAX is a particular zone of fear, more terrifying to many people than anywhere but the dentist's office. Though dying in a plane is, notoriously, twenty times less likely than dying in a car, every single airline crash is front-page news and so dramatic—not a single death but three hundred—that airports are for many people killing grounds. Their runways are associated in the mind's (televisual) eye with hostages and hijackings; with bodies on the tarmac or antiterrorist squads storming the plane.

That general sense of unsettledness is doubtless intensified by all the people in uniform in LAX. There are ten different security agencies working the Tom Bradley Terminal

alone, and the streets outside are jam-packed with Airport Police cars, FBI men, and black-clad airport policemen on bicycles. All of them do as much, I suspect, to instill fear as to still it. "People are scared here," a gloomy Pakistani security guard told me, "because undercover are working. Police are working. You could be undercover, I could be undercover. Who knows?" [...]

One reason airports enjoy such central status in our imaginations is that they play such a large part in forming our first (which is sometimes our last) impression of a place; this is the reason that poor countries often throw all their resources into making their airports sleek, with beautifully landscaped roads leading out of them into town. L.A., by contrast, has the bareness of arrogance, or simple inhospitability. Usually what you see as you approach the city is a grim penitential haze through which is visible nothing but rows of gray buildings, a few dun-hued warehouses, and ribbons of dirty freeway: a no-colored blur without even the comforting lapis ornaments of the swimming pools that dot New York or Johannesburg. (Ideally, in fact, one should enter L.A. by night, when the whole city pulses like an electric grid of lights—or the back of a transistor radio, in Thomas Pynchon's inspired metaphor. While I was staying in LAX, Jackie Collins actually told *Los Angeles* magazine that "Flying in [to LAX] at night is just an orgasmic thrill.") You land, with a bump, on a mess of gray runways with no signs of welcome, a hangar that says "T ans W rld Airlines," another broken sign that announces "Tom Bradl y International Ai port," and an air-control tower under scaffolding.

The first thing that greeted me on a recent arrival was a row of Asians sitting on the floor of the terminal, under a sign that told them of a $25,000 fine for bringing in the wrong kinds of food. As I passed through endless corridors, I was faced with almost nothing except long escalators (a surprisingly high percentage of the accidents recorded at airports comes from escalators, bewildering to newcomers) and bare hallways. The other surprise, for many of my fellow travelers, no doubt, was that almost no one we saw looked like Robert Redford or Julia Roberts or, indeed, like anyone belonging to the race we'd been celebrating in our in-flight movies. As we passed into the huge, bare assembly hall that is the Customs and Immigration Center here, I was directed into one of the chaotic lines by a Noriko and formally admitted to the country by a C. Chen. The man waiting to transfer my baggage (as a beagle sniffed around us in a coat that said "Agriculture's Beagle Brigade" on one side and "Protecting American Agriculture" on the other) was named Yoji Yosaka. And the first sign I saw, when I stepped into America, was a big board being waved by the "Executive Sedan Service" for one "Mr. T. Ego."

For many immigrants, in fact, LAX is quietly offering them a view of their own near futures: the woman at the Host Coffee Shop is themselves, in a sense, two years from now, and the man sweeping up the refuse is the American dream in practice. The staff at the airport seems to be made up almost entirely of recent immigrants: on my very first afternoon there, I was served by a Hoa, an Ephraim, and a Glinda; the wait-people at a coffee shop in Terminal 5 were called Ignacio, Ever, Aura, and Erick. Even at the Airport Sheraton (where the employees all wear nameplates), I was checked in by Viera (from "Bratislavia") and ran into Hasmik and Yovik (from Ethiopia), Faye (from Vietnam), Ingrid (from Guatemala City), Khrystyne (from Long Beach, by way of Phnom Penh, I think), and Moe (from West L.A., she said). Many of the bright-eyed dreamers who arrive at LAX so full of hope never actually leave the place.

The deeper drama of any airport is that it features a kind of interaction almost unique in our lives, wherein many of us do not know whom we are going to meet or whom others are going to meet in us. You see people standing at the barriers outside the Customs area looking into their pasts, while wide-open newcomers drift out, searching for their futures. Lovers do not know if they will see the same person who kissed them good-bye a month ago; grandparents wonder what the baby they last saw twenty years ago will look like now.

In L.A. all of this has an added charge, because unlike many cities, it is not a hub but a terminus: a place where people come to arrive. [...] And the newcomers pour in in astonishing numbers. A typical Sunday evening, in a single hour, sees flights arriving from England, Taiwan, the Philippines, Indonesia, Mexico, Austria, Germany, Spain, Costa Rica, and Guatemala; and each new group colors and transforms the airport: an explosion of tropical shades from Hawaiian Air, a rash of blue blazers and white shirts around the early flight from Tokyo. Red-haired Thais bearing pirated Schwarzenegger videos, lonely Africans in Aerial Assault sneakers, farmers from changeless Confucian cultures peering into the smiles of a Prozac city, children whose parents can't pronounce their names. Many of them are

returning, like Odysseus, with the spoils of war: young brides from Luzon, business cards from Shanghai, boxes of macadamia nuts from Oahu. And for many of them the whole wild carnival will feature sights they have never seen before: Japanese look anxiously at the first El Salvadorans they've ever seen, and El Salvadorans ogle sleek girls from Bangkok in thigh-high boots. All of them, moreover, may not be pleased to realize that the America they've dreamed of is, in fact, a land of tacos and pita and pad thai—full, indeed, of the very Third World cultures that other Third Worlders look down upon.

One day over lunch I asked my Ethiopian waitress about her life here. She liked it well enough, she said, but still she missed her home. And yet, she added, she couldn't

Vietnamese refugee at LAX.

go back. "Why not?" I asked, still smiling. "Because they killed my family," she said. "Two years back. They killed my father. They killed my brother." "They," I realized, referred to the Tigreans—many of them working just down the corridor in other parts of the hotel. So, too, Tibetans who have finally managed to flee their Chinese-occupied homeland arrive at LAX to find Chinese faces everywhere; those who fled the Sandinistas find themselves standing next to Sandinistas fleeing their successors. And all these people from ancient cultures find themselves in a country as amnesiac as the morning, where World War II is just a rumor and the Gulf War a distant memory. Their pasts are escaped, yes, but by the same token they are unlikely to be honored.

It is dangerously tempting to start formulating socioeconomic principles in the midst of LAX: people from rich countries (Germany and Japan, say) travel light, if only because they are sure that they can return any time; those from poor countries come with their whole lives in cardboard boxes imperfectly tied with string. People from poor countries are often met by huge crowds—for them each arrival is a special occasion—and stagger through customs with string bags and Gold Digger apple crates, their addresses handwritten on them in pencil; the Okinawan honeymooners, by contrast, in the color-coordinated outfits they will change every day, somehow have packed all their needs into a tiny case.

If airports have some of the excitement of bars, because so many people are composing (and decomposing) selves there, they also have some of the sadness of bars, the poignancy of people sitting unclaimed while everyone around them has paired off. A pretty girl dressed in next to nothing sits alone in an empty Baggage Claim area, waiting for a date who never comes; a Vietnamese man, lost, tells an official that he has friends in Orange County who can help him, but when the friends are contacted, they say they know no one from Vietnam. I hear of a woman who got off and asked for "San Mateo," only to learn that she was meant to disembark in San Francisco; and a woman from Nigeria who came out expecting to see her husband in Monroe, Louisiana, only to learn that someone in Lagos had mistaken "La." on her itinerary for "L.A."

The greetings I saw in the Arrivals area were much more tentative than I had expected, less passionate—as ritualized in their way as the kisses placed on Bob Barker's cheek—and much of that may be because so many people are meeting strangers, even if they are meeting people they once knew. Places like LAX—places like L.A.—perpetuate the sense that everyone is a stranger in our new floating world. I spent one afternoon in the airport with a Californian blonde, and I saw her complimented on her English by a sweet Korean woman and asked by an Iranian if she was Indian. Airports have some of the unsteady brashness of singles bars, where no one knows quite what is expected of them. "Mike, is that you?" "Oh, I didn't recognize you." "I'd have known you anywhere." "It's so kind of you to come and pick me up." And already at a loss, a young Japanese girl and a broad, lonely-looking man head off toward the parking lot, not knowing, in any sense, who is going to be in the driver's seat.

The driving takes place, of course, in what many of the newcomers, primed by video screenings of *L.A. Law*

and *Speed*, regard as the ultimate heart of darkness, a place at least as forbidding and dangerous as Africa must have seemed to the Victorians. They have heard about how America is the murder capital of the world; they have seen Rodney King get pummeled by L.A.'s finest; they know of the city as the site of drive-by shootings and freeway snipers, of riots and celebrity murders. The "homeless" and the "tempest-tost" that the Statue of Liberty invites are arriving, increasingly, in a city that is itself famous for its homeless population and its fires, floods, and earthquakes.

In that context, the ideal symbol of LAX is, perhaps, the great object that for thirty years has been the distinctive image of the place: the ugly white quadruped that sits in the middle of the airport like a beached white whale or a jet-age beetle, featuring a 360-degree circular restaurant that does not revolve and an observation deck from which the main view is of twenty-three thousand parking places. The Theme Building, at 201 World Way, is a sad image of a future that never arrived, a monument to Kennedy-era idealism and the thrusting modernity of the American empire when it was in its prime; it now has the poignancy of an abandoned present with its price tag stuck to it. When you go there (and almost nobody does) you are greeted by photos of Saturn's rings and Jupiter and its moons, by a plaque laid down by L.B.J. and a whole set of symbols from the time when NASA was shooting for the heavens. Now the "landmark" building, with its "gourmet-type restaurant," looks like a relic from a time long past, when it must have looked like the face of the future. [...]

Yet just as I was about to give up on L.A. as yesterday's piece of modernity, I got on the shuttle bus that moves between the terminals in a never-ending loop. The seats next to me were taken by two tough-looking dudes from nearby South Central, who were riding the free buses and helping people on and off with their cases (acting, I presumed, on the safe assumption that the Japanese, say, new to the country and bewildered, had been warned beforehand to tip often and handsomely for every service they received). In between terminals, as a terrified-looking Miss Kudo and her friend guarded their luggage, en route from Nagoya to Las Vegas, the two gold-plated sharks talked about the Raiders' last game and the Lakers' next season. Then one of them, without warning, announced, "The bottom line is the spirit is with you. When you work out, you chill out and, like, you meditate in your spirit. You know what I mean?

Meditation is recreation. Learn math, follow your path. That's all I do, man, that's all I live for: learnin' about God, learnin' about Jesus. I am *possessed* by that spirit. You know, I used to have all these problems, with the flute and all, but when I heard about God, I learned about the body, the mind, and the flesh. People forget, they don't know, that the Bible isn't talkin' about the flesh, it's talkin' about the spirit. And I was reborn again in the spirit."

His friend nodded. "When you recreate, you meditate. Recreation is a spiritually uplifting experience."

"Yeah. When you do that, you allow the spirit to breathe."

"Because you're gettin' into the physical world. You're lettin' the spirit flow. You're helpin' the secretion of the endorphins in the brain."

Nearby, the Soldiers of the Cross of Christ Church stood by the escalators, taking donations, and a man in a dog collar approached another stranger.

I watched the hustlers allowing the spirit to breathe, I heard the Hare Krishna devotees plying their wares, I spotted some Farrakhan flunkies collecting a dollar for a copy of their newspaper, *The Final Call*—redemption and corruption all around us in the air—and I thought: welcome to America, Miss Kudo, welcome to L.A.

Beyond Belief

by Fenton Johnson

September 1998

What we have to be is what we are.
— Thomas Merton

The chapter room at Our Lady of Gethsemani, the Kentucky abbey where Thomas Merton wrote, is on this pleasant evening of July 1996 filled with monks. Along the right wall, and under an image of the risen Christ, stand the Trappist hosts—the "white monks," dressed in white robes covered with a black hooded scapular and cinched at the waist with a broad leather belt; next to them stand the Benedictines—the "black monks," the more publicly engaged of Catholic monastics. Among these monks are scattered a few women, most dressed in the white blouse and below-the-knee gray skirt favored by post–Vatican II nuns. Along the left wall, under a batik banner of the seated Buddha, stand the Buddhist monks—the Mahayanists of Tibet wearing maroon, the Southeast Asian Theravadans wearing saffron. A lone Japanese monk wears dove-gray robes trimmed in black and white; a lone Taiwanese nun wears saffron, peach fuzz sprouting from her shaven head. Among these Asians mingle American Buddhists—what are those nice Jewish women and men doing wearing black Zen robes? Except that some aren't Jewish and some aren't Zen, some are wearing street clothes, and some of the Asians are Americans, immigrant priests and monks whose Buddhist congregations increasingly include white Americans. The Christians and the American Buddhists are almost all Caucasian; the Asians range from Japanese ivory to Sri Lankan browned butter. Timothy Kelly, abbot of Gethsemani, and the exiled Dalai Lama of Tibet stand at front center, the focal point for this international convocation of Buddhist and Christian monks, nuns, and contemplatives.

Geography is destiny: European and Asian ways of being first mingled in the aptly named Middle East, which served as incubator of the West's great spiritual traditions. Judaism and its children, Christianity and Islam, were all three influenced by Asian philosophies (such as Zoroastrianism and Buddhism) transported, along with silk and spices, over the great trade routes. Now in America the "circle [is] almost circled," to quote Walt Whitman, and the two great ways of being meet again: The westward-migrating, Judeo-Christian–rooted democratic idealism of eighteenth-century Europe is encountering the eastward-migrating ways of Buddhism; the Enlightenment is encountering enlightenment; the religion of the Word is encountering the philosophy of silence. Observing from the back of the room, I am brought to ask if the encounter of these Western and Eastern disciplines may hold the key to a legitimately American faith.

Faith: not at all the same as belief. Zen philosopher Alan Watts explains the difference: "Belief... is the insistence that the truth is what one would 'lief' or wish it to be.... Faith... is an unreserved opening of the mind to the truth, whatever it may turn out to be. Faith has no preconceptions; it is a plunge into the unknown. Belief clings, but faith lets go... faith is the essential virtue of science, and likewise of any religion that is not self-deception."

My travels among American monasteries have brought me to write not about belief but about faith; not about doctrine (the Virgin birth, the infallible pope, reincarnation) but about the subsuming of self to the greater order. Watts contends that belief in God is antithetical to faith, because God, conceived as omnipotent power, necessarily stands between ourselves and complete letting go. To argue as much is to ignore the role of belief as a means to the end of faith. Usually expressed in metaphor (the burning bush, the resurrected Christ, the reincarnated essence of being), belief challenges the imagination to conceive and embrace a universe larger than what we immediately perceive. It engages a community in a collective imaginative act, one of the most powerful ways of binding a people into a shared identity.

Which is where the trouble begins. When communities use belief not as an aid to faith but as a means to establish identity, sooner or later the guns appear. Catholic, Jew, Protestant, Sikh, Buddhist, Hindu, Muslim—these are powerful labels, easily used to identify and take up arms against the Other. This is the challenge facing institutionalized religions if they are to be vehicles for peace: the teaching of belief as the outer garment to faith, a means to the end but not to be mistaken for (and finally not essential to) the real thing.

But what is the real thing? The question is central, the path of this journey: for skeptical Americans, children of a nation born of the union of religious idealists and Enlightenment rationalists, what does it mean to have faith?

And so I return to the monks, the keepers of faith.

After eight children my parents ran out of ideas for names, so they gave me over for naming to the Trappist monks at the Abbey of Gethsemani, a crow's mile across the Kentucky hills. In the 1950s, the Trappists more rigidly observed the rules of silence and mortification of the flesh. They spoke only at prayer or in emergency; they slept on straw pallets in unheated rooms; they fasted on not much more than bread and water throughout Lent and on all Fridays. My father, a maintenance worker at a local distillery, delivered to the monastery the bourbon the monks used in the fruitcakes they baked and sold to raise money. The monks appreciated my father's studied casualness in counting the bottles; for his part, my father preferred their company to the responsibilities of parenting his sprawling brood.

Within months of their acquaintance, some of those monks became regulars at our dining table. Through various subterfuges they slipped from the abbey to make their ways to our house, managing to arrive just before supper. *They* got pork chops, *we* got fried baloney, but still as children we adored their company. For the most part they were educated men, Yankees from impossibly exotic places (Cleveland, Buffalo), who stayed late into the evening drinking beer, smoking cigarettes, watching football on television, and talking, talking, talking.

One brother was fond of a grass skirt someone had sent my mother from Hawaii. When the moon was right and the whiskey flowing he donned the skirt and some hot pink plastic leis, then hoisted my mother to the tabletop and climbed up after her. There she sang "Hard Hearted Hannah" ("the vamp of Savannah, G.A.!") while her partner

swayed his hips and waved his hands in mock hula. Later he launched into Broadway tunes, warbling in falsetto with his arms thrown around one or more of his brethren.

Brother Fintan, my namesake, was a baker who made elaborate cakes for each of my birthdays until I was five. Then he left the monastery and disappeared from our lives, for reasons I would not learn for many years.

Monasticism is among the oldest of human archetypes. Like the family, like marriage, like the complex rituals of sexual desire, it predates recorded history. It is less a manifestation of any particular religious tradition than an outgrowth of the imperative to ask why. It is the practice (practice: the methodical pursuit of perfection) of the search for a state of integration with the whole of being that Buddhists call nirvana, that Christians call a state of grace. It offers a discipline to govern and assist the search for faith.

Theologian Ewert Cousins speculates that monasticism arose almost simultaneously with the individuation of consciousness: as soon as humans perceived themselves as individuals apart from their community, a few panicked at the notion of a fate distinct from that of their tribe or clan. They ran for the hills and the caves, to give their lives over to contemplation of the mystery of being alive and alone. Monasticism does not exist in cultures (tribal Africa, New Guinea, Native America) where individual identity is subsumed to the community. It emerges when and where cultures recognize the possibility of an individual consciousness and destiny apart from the communal whole.

That monasticism is so ancient complicates the definition of the term; across history the word "monk" has been used to describe a wide range of individuals and practices. In the West, our words "monk" and "monastic" contain and express solitude (from ancient Greek *monos*, "one alone").* And yet in both West and East, the practice evolved from the earliest, wandering hermits ("eremites") to become communal ("cenobitic"). In the West, the Benedictine orders (of which the Trappists are a subset) abide by the Rule of St. Benedict, composed in the sixth century with a presumption of cenobitic life. In the East, Buddhist monastics observe the precepts of the vinaya, with its roots in the

---

* *Following the practice of many contemplatives, I use the term "monastic" to include both men and women, and "monasticism" to include all contemplative orders, regardless of the gender of their members.*

earliest Buddhist teachings and similarly oriented toward a collective life. Still, the essence of the practice springs from an ongoing engagement with the terrifying, liberating knowledge that finally we each face our gods and demons by ourselves. Thousands of years into the history of monasticism, the newly arrived Trappist enters the walled-in enclosure at Gethsemani under an engraved lintel reading GOD ALONE.

In various forms and at various times some version of the ascetic life has manifested itself in all major contemporary religions, but it achieved its apotheosis in Buddhist and Christian monasticism. Buddhism evolved directly out of monasticism: Siddhartha Gautama, the sixth-century B.C. Indian prince commonly referred to as "the Buddha," first conveyed his philosophy to one of the bands of mendicant ascetics who roved (and rove) the subcontinent. Even today traditional Buddhism posits that enlightenment—defined as triumph over *samsara*, the endless cycle of desire and dissatisfaction—may be achieved only within the *sangha*, a word broadly translated to mean the monastic community.

In contrast, the Bible (Old or New Testament) contains no explicit references to monasticism. Christian monks describe their lives as an attempt to imitate the life of Christ, but the first monks of the Sinai deserts, who lived as hermits, had as much in common with distant Indian ascetics as with the infant hierarchy of Roman Catholicism. The history of the Western evolution of the practice is complex, but a simplified version has the hermits' students establishing communities so as to live near their teachers; from these communities eventually evolved the powerful abbeys that became tools for the advancement of the Vatican's temporal ambitions, and that in the Middle Ages were often synonymous with politics and intrigue.

Considered in their kindest light, however, monasteries have offered both West and East a model of a simple, contemplative life to inspire the larger secular world. They are communistic communities where property is shared and time freed by collective labor given to contemplation and prayer; exemplars of a life lived not for the future but in the here and now, a life built on and lived by faith. [...]

Monasticism is the archetypal manifestation of the impulse to mystery, an institutionalized response to the intuitive need to construct and dwell in sacred time. What's remarkable is that, although separated by vast gaps of geography and history and culture, both Western and traditional Eastern monastics lead lives committed to poverty, celibacy,

and obedience, addressing the three great obstacles to faith, the cornerstones of secular culture—money, sex, and power.

The first great principle of Buddhism also explains the success of the consumer economy: humanity is born to *dukkha*, "dissatisfaction" (often translated as "suffering"). Stated simply: we are born to want what we do not have; if we get what we want, we transfer our desire to a less attainable object. Starting from this principle, Buddhism teaches how to recognize and defend against human weakness; capitalism focuses our intelligence and creativity on its exploitation.

At a panel on the explosion of Buddhist references in pop culture, graphic designer Milton Glaser posed the question: "In a culture where every image or idea can and will be used for commerce, how can anything remain sacred?" And if nothing sacred remains, why not lie and steal? When we're barraged with messages equating personal worth with material wealth, when the poorest poor can buy a gun, what's astonishing is not that America has so much violence but that it has so little—testimony both to some elemental longing for virtue and to our willingness to fund a police state as the price of prosperity. Meanwhile, fundamentalist movements grow here and abroad, as people seek to find or restore value in lives that corporate capitalism perceives as another resource to be exploited, exhausted, and trashed.

Monasteries as repositories for the sacred—it's a charming if slightly desperate hope, at least if one compares the numbers of monasteries and Wal-Marts on the American landscape. Then I spent time in monasteries, to discover that they're less islands in the culture than microcosms of it: whatever is happening "over the wall" is generally epitomized inside it.

As its mainstream culture, the technology that severed Trappists from their roots has enabled them to prosper, to the point that a Gethsemani Trappist told me, "We have too much money. We've become the worst possible thing for men of faith—we're bourgeois, respectable men of substance, making a living." [...]

In the weeklong Gethsemani convocation of people dedicated to contemplation, many of whom have committed themselves to celibacy, the subject that most frequently recurs: anger. The subject that never occurs: sex. Might there be a connection between the obsession with the first and the evasion of the second? [...]

Possibly more than any other aspect of monastic life, celibacy intrigues, mystifies, and (often) repels lay people, and for good reason. In the knees, in the heart, in the head, sex renders us weak—the wisest and strongest among us understands what it means to be a fool for desire—and to be weak is to be comically, tragically, poignantly human. To remove oneself from sex is arguably to separate oneself from one's humanity, to place oneself in a class apart and above. Power inheres to the party who says no; unless undertaken within a larger discipline, celibacy is a kind of power play, and the institutions of religion—East and West—have historically used it to that end.

Which is too bad, because monasticism in both traditions can speak eloquently to matters of sexual morality and discipline. Most of us, most of the time, have sex not to make babies but to assuage desire—not just physical desire but the desire to love and be loved, for union with the whole, for an end to the aloneness inherent in being alive. During sex, to invoke a Christian metaphor, we die to ourselves, however briefly; to invoke a Buddhist principle, we have a moment of surcease from *samsara*, from the endless cycle of dissatisfaction. We are one with ourselves, with another, with the other; we triumph over solitude, even over death. And then it's finished, and we're alone, and dissatisfaction returns.

Monasticism seeks not to triumph over aloneness but to embrace it (GOD ALONE), and in so doing to transform the short-lived triumph of orgasm into an ongoing triumph of consciousness, an enduring acceptance of and union with the whole great roundness of being—including birth, growth, love, insecurity, loss, aging, suffering, death. This is the place where desire becomes faith, springboard for the poetry of St. John of the Cross and Sor Juana Inés de la Cruz—both mendicants, both mystics, troublesome to their traditions while alive, valued once dead, writers of poetry that invokes spirit and flesh, in which faith is another manifestation of the crazy, fooling energy that drives the heart (among other organs). [...]

"Chastity does not mean abstention from sexual wrong," wrote the British novelist and Catholic G. K. Chesterton, "it means something flaming, like Joan of Arc." I prefer the Buddhist concept of "right conduct" to Chesterton's "chastity," but the point remains the same: what finally is at stake is not sex but love, and celibacy is or ought to be not about punishing that but sacralizing it, celebrating it, bowing down before its power in an effort to channel and focus that power to constructive ends.

Traditional monasticism is very good at disciplining the power of the mind; in the face of the power of the body, it has resorted to proscriptions more arcane in traditional Buddhism than even in Catholicism. The rise of feminism and the concurrent consciousness of the body has rendered that contempt for the flesh no longer possible. East and West, monasticism faces a fork in the road: in one direction lies reaction and fundamentalism; in the other, the labor of reforming the practice of celibacy to acknowledge and respect the body and its desires.

Among the official participants at the Gethsemani convocation, men greatly outnumber women; among the observers—sitting in the rear but not allowed to participate—women significantly outnumber men. Excepting the American Buddhists, the assembly presents a picture postcard of religious hierarchy, East or West: the men elevated on the dais, the women below and to the rear. Later in this week a Sri Lankan Buddhist priest takes the microphone. "To be sure I understand," he says. "In your tradition, women are considered inferior to men." A Trappist priest illustrates with a gesture, not judgmental but merely graphic: hands extended, one at his shoulder, the other at his waist.

Jesus Christ and the Buddha share this: they based their teachings in universal democratic principles. Athens' democracy limited citizenship to free-born men; Jesus Christ and the Buddha preached philosophies equally available and applicable to all—men, women, rich, poor, citizen, slave, saint, sinner. The Buddha transcended the rigid castes of his native India; Jesus welcomed not just lepers and pagans but (most astounding for the time) women. True democracy begins in the West when Jesus emphasizes the equality of women, in the East when the Buddha accepts his stepmother's plea to permit women to form monasteries.

Their revolution remained intact for as long as it took for their teachings to be institutionalized. Although the Buddha eventually yielded to his stepmother's plea, he insisted on conditions that made clear that nuns occupied secondary status to monks; later Buddhist precepts codified those conditions. The persecution of Christians in the West kept Christian doctrine and structure fluid (and remarkably egalitarian) until Constantine's acceptance of Christianity in A.D. 312. But with official sanction came institutionalization, with Augustine, Western history's other most famous monk, as its architect.

Susan Saas

ments—it's difficult to accomplish the letting go that is faith's sine qua non; the more we have to lose, the greater the challenge. To find genuine faith—to find those who dwell in the world as it is, rather than as they would have it be—one must look among the poor, among the dispossessed, among the outsiders to power.

Sister Maricela García was born in Mexico to a poor family and spent years in a teaching order before seeking out the Trappistines. Olive-skinned, dark-eyed, a García Lorca woman, she shines with a fierceness that brought her to be transferred from her Trappistine monastery in northern California to Gethsemani for three months that became three years, in which she lived as the only woman among an enclosed, cloistered community of seventy men. "What are we doing to awaken a questioning attitude in the people who come to us?" she asked me then. "We wear a dress from the twelfth century that stands up because it's so dirty, but we can't take it off because we'll be naked. That's us not wanting to change, fearing change and not understanding our own worth. Change is always uncomfortable. To me the obvious issue is: We're dying out. We're no longer a living tradition. Younger people are thirsting for a spiritual life, and we're not doing our job in offering it to them." [...]

As single-gender communities, monasteries East and West have offered opportunities for women that existed nowhere else. But both traditions have operated within, and helped sustain, a patriarchal culture that regards nuns, like women in general, as second-class citizens. Buddhist or Catholic, monasteries have historically functioned as organized economic units that have served the ends of power (which is to say, the religious patriarchy) as much as those of faith.

The bloody severance of church and state accomplished in revolutionary France and the secularization of government throughout Western Europe all but wiped out monasteries. However brutally accomplished, the removal of monastics from political influence was surely the most beneficial modern development for monasticism. Because Christian and American Buddhist monastics are removed from temporal power, they represent their traditions' best opportunities to explore faith, for power and faith do not comfortably cohabit. Belief—that is, dogma and doctrine—may serve the ends of power, but faith is the province of individuals, not institutions. So long as individuals have something to lose—the Buddhists would say, so long as we have attach-

Shortly after I turned sixteen, my namesake, Brother Fintan, returned to visit my family and his old friends at Gethsemani. We received him and his handsome companion with the usual hospitality and food and drink. Monks came over. There was dancing on the table; we trotted out the grass skirt and plastic leis for my mother's dancing partner, now in need of a stool to climb to the tabletop but otherwise as sinuous and campy as ever.

Afterward I listened for the customary post-party gossip. Had Fintan arrived with a woman, the household would have been abuzz: *Who is she? Might they get married?* Had he brought a mere friend, there would have been idle chatter: *Nice man. Needs a haircut.* But: nothing. My namesake and his companion might never have sat at our table.

In my small town, among garrulous Southerners only one subject invoked a silence so vast and deliberate. That night I went to bed understanding that Fintan and his companion were lovers. Which meant that I was perhaps not the freak of nature I had believed myself to be; I was not alone.

Each of us must find for himself or herself the wellspring of faith. To judge from their devotion to the Virgin Mary, many women find that place through their gender; for me it resides in the source of my otherness, my homosexuality.

Father Matthew Kelty, one of Gethsemani's older and most popular chaplains and openly gay, speculates that "gays have always been attracted to the religious life because it was a viable way of living. I would think that in the Middle Ages many monastics were gay, though they didn't call it that. Look at the monasteries of the Middle Ages, which were centers of art, culture, peace." Instead of "gay" a younger speaker than Father Kelty might use the word "queer"—persons who may be homosexual or heterosexual but who define themselves as outsiders, who dwell on the margins of power, who haven't the luxury to assume a world the way they would have it be and so must construct a philosophy for embracing it as it is.

Of course not all those who live responsibly at the margins of power are gays or lesbians. The point is that (as repeatedly noted in Old and New Testaments) the outsider has special access to faith, if only because he or she grapples daily with limitations imposed by circumstances, whether of class, race, gender, sexual orientation, or physical, psychological, or intellectual limitations. Because a healthy society recognizes the need to moderate hubris, it takes care to protect and listen to its outsiders, who function as a combination of court jesters and advance scouts (cf. Sophocles or Shakespeare) for the culture as a whole.

In its earliest incarnations, this was one role of monasticism: to act as an institutionalized contradiction of and conscience for power. [...]

Monasticism is like art—in a very real sense it is art, the hours of life shaped to an ideal, never achieved but always present as a place to which to aspire. Like art it must be an end unto itself; its beauty and its truth reside in its being explicitly nonutilitarian. It is about making time sacred, removing from it any possibility of a price. But like all that is sacred, contemplatives dwell in the real, physical world, and a vital monasticism is committed to ways of bringing its truths to that life.

Thomas Merton's greatest achievement may lie not in his books but in his lifelong, largely successful battle to shift the focus of the Trappists, from penitence and asceticism to the preservation and enhancement of the sacred. In keeping with his aspirations, the goal of monastic reform should be to rediscover, not reinvent, in their purest forms the permanent ideals of monasticism, which may act as a model for a more materially frugal, spiritually engaged life—a living out not of doctrine but of faith.

I like to think that an American faith would define the place where skepticism may coexist and collaborate with a respect for mystery. I like to think that faith, in its infinitude of expressions, is that quality that might keep us humble in the face of our inevitable hubris; it enables the transformation of knowledge into wisdom. I like to think of monasteries as repositories of faith and so as both models and catalysts, to which we can look for inspiration in shaping the vessels of our lives.

This is the great contradiction between our economics and our political and spiritual aspirations: capitalism excels in offering choice, but liberty fulfills itself not in choice but in discipline. Life is like water: it takes the shape of the vessel into which it's poured; remove the vessel and it's lost. What we are seeking are vessels into which to pour the chaos of life; what we are seeking are models of discipline.

Not that contemporary culture has no models to offer. Corporate capitalism offers the considerable discipline of making money, and the government offers the discipline of military life, which is still available to young people (excluding homosexuals unwilling to lie). But both military and corporate disciplines rely on what philosopher William James called "the need of crushing weaker peoples," whether they are the assemblers of silicon chips in the Philippines or the strawberry pickers of California or the leftists of Grenada. Whereas monasticism based in agriculture or in cottage industry offers a model of a sustainable discipline.

New millennium or no, the mass of people is no more likely to flock to monasteries now than in the time of Augustine. The rare young man who joins the Trappists today is likely to have been raised in those few remaining American pockets of fervent Catholicism, and is likely to be more conservative than his elders. Among the American Buddhists, the monastic at Tassajara, the contemplative retreat of the San Francisco Zen Center, is likely to be a college-educated liberal with an income, if not to burn at least to sacrifice. At both institutions non-white persons are notable for their absence.

But ideas percolate through society in mysterious ways: consider how Zen concepts have permeated popular culture even as its practitioners remain a tiny minority. The Benedictine monks of the Middle Ages expressed their faith through the discipline of the illuminated manuscript, their love of the Word rendered incarnate. Looking from the cliff above the organic farm at the San Francisco Zen Center's Green Gulch, I see in its meticulously patterned fields of vegetables and flowers a twentieth-century equivalent to those pages, the love of the earth given form and substance. I am dogged by the memory of that farm, and by the young people who told me how it drew them to Buddhism before they knew anything of its practice or philosophy.

Might the Abbey of Gethsemani's acres of Kentucky bottomland—much of it now leased out to neighboring farmers—be turned to a similar end, with young people brought to reconnect with the earth? Could the hundred-plus Christian monasteries scattered across the American countryside act as loci for a revitalized discipline of a particularly American faith, incorporating the wisdom of the Federalists, the feminists, the activists for human rights and dignity, and functioning as places of collaboration between skepticism and spirituality? I would like to think that the revitalization of American Christian monasticism might incorporate some return to the Trappists' historical roots in agriculture, or to the Benedictines' roots as cultivators of culture. These are the literal incarnations, after all, of the roundness of being, offering a contemporary version of a discipline of faith.

This is a big demand of small institutions whose populations are shrinking and elderly. [...] But in East and West, the history of monasticism is a repeating pattern of spiritual engagement followed by decadence followed by reform and renewed engagement. I like to think that the ideal of the American Buddhist contemplatives—exploring sustainable living based in but evolved from an ancient tradition—might inspire the American Trappists not to imitation but to a new reform. Working from the Cistercian history of agricultural innovation, the Trappists could offer a model of a Western version of an engaged, contemplative, American faith, incorporating democratic principles while de-emphasizing doctrine, integrating body and spirit while bringing to the forefront the veneration of the simple mystery of being.

In his profile of the encounter of Jews and Buddhists, *The Jew in the Lotus*, Rodger Kamenetz suggests that Buddhism might revitalize Judaism. Might it serve Christianity in the same fashion? The Western spiritual tradition needs not a wholesale conversion to Eastern traditions but a return to its authentic, egalitarian, faith-based roots as articulated in all the Gospels, stripped of the institutionalized Church's obsession with temporal power and prestige.

This is the continuing gift of the New World—the breathing space to challenge the old ways of being and doing. Emerson, the great prophet of the American faith, asks, "Why should not we also enjoy an original relation to the universe?... Let us demand our own works and laws and worship." Transcendentalism, Emerson's early ideal, withered on the vine, even as its Eastern-influenced principles significantly shaped American spirituality.

Like Emerson, monasticism poses an ideal—a community of people identifying a discipline and attempting to live it out. The practical effect of American multiculturalism, however, has been to challenge the old shared values without offering viable substitutes—in effect, to fracture the big-picture ideal without providing an alternative. Instead of looking to turn the calendar back, might Christian monasticism, influenced by the American Buddhists, propose a new ideal: a discipline of faith lived in respect of and in collaboration with the disciplines of skepticism? I pose the question to Christian monasticism because it is of the West and because it is our rich and entirely adequate cultural heritage.

Literary critic Harold Bloom argues persuasively for the existence of the American religion, the product of the American imagination. But American religion without American faith is fundamentalism—religion grounded not in faith but in belief. I argue for aspiring not to an American religion but to an American faith, founded in and cherishing of the old wisdom, but actively testing that wisdom in the crucible of the present moment, our present nation so far removed in history and character from its worthy roots. Already, every established denomination in the United States (including Judaism, Catholicism, and Buddhism, and soon, I suspect, Islam) sustains a practice distinct if not separate from its Old World origins. In this American faith, belief—that is, doctrine and dogma—takes a distant back seat to faith in oneself, in one's place in and responsibility to the workings of the great order (if one insists on a word: God), in the ongoing task of the preservation and enhancement of the sacred.

Speaking before a congress of monks in Bangkok a few hours before his death, Thomas Merton argued, "What is essential in the monastic life is not embedded in buildings, is not embedded in clothing, is not necessarily embedded even in a rule. It is concerned with this business of total inner transformation. All other things serve that end.... I believe that by openness to Buddhism, to Hinduism, and to these great Asian traditions, we stand a wonderful chance of learning more about the potentiality of our own traditions…"

I first undertook to write about faith in my thirties, but each time I was assaulted by bitterness at the thought of all those lives ruined or deformed in the name of organized religion. As I grew older I was better able to embrace the gift my church gave me—an appreciation of mystery, the experience of awe. But it was meditation, learned from the Buddhists, that brought me to some kind of forgiveness. These days I set aside a half hour daily as sacred time; these days I am beginning to imagine what it means to have faith. I have taken years to begin to become familiar with Eastern traditions, and those years have educated me into the vastness of my ignorance as well as the preeminence of my right and responsibility to work to shape the Western tradition into which I was born to my place and moment in history. With time I may be able to name myself, if not a Catholic, at least a Christian.

Several months after the Gethsemani convocation I talked with Norman Fischer, co-abbot of the San Francisco Zen Center. "A fully developed imagination enables us to live in a world that's ennobling without dwelling in some fantasyland," he said. "For a Buddhist, enlightenment is the development of the faculty of imaginative vision that enables us to see the world in a transfigured way." He looked up from his black Zen robes. "That's what a Catholic Mass is about, right?"

The Mass: you enter the Gethsemani abbey church, high and long and narrow, whitewashed brick, plain as an empty hand whose lines direct your eyes forward to the dais, on which sit two vertical blocks of black granite topped by a horizontal slab, lit from above by a spotlight. Behind this altar stands the starkest of thrones: six flat planes (a back, a seat, two arms, two armrests) of polished oak. To either side: ranks of monastics, robed and cowled.

You have entered the theater of faith. The setting prepares you for blood sacrifice; what you get is art. It is 1,998 years into the Christian era, six thousand years into the era of self-consciousness, and we are here to bear witness to the triumph of the imagination, the great human achievement: the acting out of mystery in metaphor instead of in fact. Transubstantiation: the bread becomes flesh, the wine becomes blood, we eat the flesh and drink the blood and so reenact the violent heart of the mystery of being.

To teach literal transubstantiation as the focal point of this genuine miracle is to take the narrowest view on the greatest work of ongoing performance art Western civilization has conceived. It is to collude with secularism in assigning the miraculous to the past, when in fact the spark of the divine resides in the present imagination, in the leap of faith required to conceive and achieve science, art, the Catholic Mass. It is that facility and faculty of imagination that is the genuine and continuing miracle, that organized religion so often quashes as antithetical to the ends of institutionalized power.

I take an imaginative leap here, to see consciousness as evolving from those first hermit monks through Plato, who understood unity with the whole of being as the soul's aspiration and goal. We move from the era of prophets who ascribe the mystery of being to external agents (gods and demons) to prophets (Buddha, Jesus) who direct us to the sacred place within. We move from an era when the acknowledgment of mystery demanded blood sacrifice (less than five hundred years ago, the Aztecs built a civilization around it) to an era in which we are clever enough to substitute bread and wine and understand it as the real thing. The quality we draw upon to accomplish this imaginative leap—this act of confidence in our human right and responsibility to shape the terms of our encounter with the divine, as well as confidence in the greater order in which our search takes place—we give the name of faith.

Anita Kunz

Must rationalism obviate faith? "Science without religion is lame," wrote Einstein. "Religion without science is blind." Contemporary physics is rediscovering the revelation that mystical, often monastic writers repeatedly present as the culminating fact of the contemplative life: the understanding that science and art lead to mystery. Finally we can only glimpse the great unity, with an understanding increasingly supported by scientific evidence but sustained by a leap of faith. Immersed in and part of this great river of energy, we live every instant the precise analogue of the moment of transubstantiation in the Catholic Mass, in which the divine order is at once revealed and concealed. Seen in this light, faith does not divide but unifies body and spirit, perception and miracle, science and spirituality.

Faith is first among the cardinal virtues because everything proceeds from it, including and especially love. Faith is the leap into the unknown—the entering into an action or a person knowing only that you will emerge changed, with no preconceptions of what that change will be. Its antonym is fear. In the prosperous 1990s America is a fearful society (consider our obsession with security, whether national or international, or in our financial, professional, emotional, and spiritual lives) because we are a faithless society. Without faith, without that willingness to embrace life, including its uncertainty and pain and mortality and mystery, the soul becomes stagnant—possibly the only aspect of the universe that can resist change, and in so doing possibly the only aspect of the universe that can really die.

Faith accepts that we cannot know everything and can control only a little. If we can bring that acceptance to science—if we can recognize science as existing on a continuum with art, if we can embrace both not as means to the accumulation of money, sex, and power but as done for the sake of the love of knowledge, which is to say the love of beauty, which is to say the love of truth—we will have reason to hope.

In paling darkness the *shuso* makes her circuit through the Tassajara canyon, ringing the wake-up bell with the self-satisfaction of a young woman awake and given the pleasure of rousing everyone else. In silence your neighbors struggle into their black robes. Outside a waning moon sets over the dark ragged line of the mountains, egg into nest, the moonlight knits shadows of branches on a glistening carpet of wet leaves. The black-robed monks hurry to the meditation hall, where later you will join them, but on this particular morning you walk past the hall and up the canyon, beyond the kerosene lamps. You follow your nose past sage and under California bay laurel to the sulfurous spring, heated in the bowels of the earth. You drop your clothes and step in.

An early-sprouting big-leaf maple drips catkins into the chill. A middle-aged man (pudgy at the waist, thinning at the crown) rises from the pool. He arches a hand over his head, first to the right, then to the left, then he bends at the waist, then straightens, stacking his vertebra one at a time until his head lolls back, to one side, then another. He raises his arms and you see stiffness rising from his ruddy steaming skin, crepuscular light passes through the curling steam, and it's as if an angel has stepped from the cold rushing stream below through the heated waters and into the brightening dappling light, and for a moment you are given to understand that you are that man, that angel above the rushing water, that here and now you are made in the image of the divine, that paradise is a mirror in which you see yourself, that what we have to become is what we already are.

NOTEBOOK

EXORCISM

BY LEWIS H. LAPHAM

MARCH 1999

Take but degree away, untune that string,
And, hark, what discord follows! Each thing meets
In mere oppugnancy. The bounded waters
Should lift their bosoms higher than the shores
And make a sop of all this solid globe.
— WILLIAM SHAKESPEARE,
Troilus and Cressida

Early in the afternoon of January 7 the Chief Justice of the Supreme Court converted the members of the Senate into a jury fit to pass judgment on the President of the United States, and during the half hour required to perform the ceremony it was possible to believe, even from the skeptical height of the periodical press gallery, that nothing important to the country's political history and character had been irretrievably lost. The nineteenth-century furnishings of the Senate chamber—the oval ceiling, the antique desks, the mahogany paneling on the doors—evoked the memory of the successful American past, and the ritual dignity of the proceeding invested the actors in it with the solemnity of figures moving in a world out of time.

Each senator in turn rose to swear, "so help me God," that he or she would "do impartial justice" with respect to the Articles of Impeachment placed before them by the House of Representatives, and then, again in turn, they stepped forward to inscribe their names on the clerk's register, testifying with their signatures to the sacred honor of their spoken word. Mindful of the stateliness of the occasion, the senators walked the short distance from their desks in nearly perfect silence, glancing neither right nor left, omitting the customary exchanges of idle pleasantry and reassuring gesture. For a full thirty minutes they sustained the illusion of *gravitas* once prized by Cicero and Cato the Elder—the United States Senate alone with its conscience,

gathered by constitutional directive under the marble busts of Aaron Burr and Andrew Johnson, making good on Dan Rather's promise of an historic moment.

Not, however, a moment made for television. The ceremony took too much time, and although the mood and feeling evident in the chamber possibly could be expressed in words, the sense of it didn't segue into a quick series of lively camera shots. Cut the scene into videotape, and on the screen it comes up dull and slow—a dreary crowd of middle-aged lawyers with bad haircuts and missing teeth, wandering aimlessly around a static set without a script, and no music on the soundtrack.

The lack of charismatics in the scene also could be inferred from the absence of broadcast people in the press galleries. For three weeks the network talking heads had been awarding their gaudiest hyperbole ("amazing," "heady drama," "astounding," "beyond fiction") to a trial billed as the equal to O. J. Simpson's, but the day was given over to parliamentary formalities—Representative Henry Hyde of Illinois, chairman of the House Judiciary Committee, shuffling into the well of the Senate with his twelve fellow prosecutors and their two indictments; Chief Justice William Rehnquist, resplendent in a black robe tricked up with gold stripes on the sleeves, administering the oath of impartiality; various prominent senators making various misleading statements of procedural intent—and why would anybody squander footage on a history lesson?

Because the calendar was long on ceremony and short on news, I had time to pursue the thought about the differences between the modus operandi of the print and electronic media. Remembering Marshall McLuhan's observation that the habits of mind derived from the latter deconstruct the texts of the civilization founded on the premises of the former, it occurred to me that maybe the argument at the root of the impeachment trial was epistemological, not moral. Content follows form, and new systems of communication give rise to new structures of feeling and thought. The linear order of the printed page aligns itself with perceptions of the world biased in favor of sequence, composition, narrative, hierarchy, classification, continuity, cause and effect; perceptions of the world associated with the electronic media tend toward discontinuity, improvisation, intuition, repetition, simultaneity, and incantation.

The disagreement between the two languages and the two ways of thinking offered at least the beginning of an answer to the question why the President was on trial for misrepresenting the character (and falsely reporting the actions) of his penis. Sympathetic to a pagan rather than a Christian appreciation of the world, the camera sees but doesn't think; it cares only for the sensation of the moment, for any tide of emotion strong enough to draw a paying crowd. A plane crash in the mountains of Peru commands the same slack-jawed respect as Mick Jagger in a divorce court, Monica Lewinsky eating Belgian chocolate, cruise missiles falling on Baghdad.

Because the camera doesn't know how to make distinctions—between treason and fellatio, between the moral and the amoral, between an important senator and an important ape—its insouciance works against the operative principle of a democratic republic. Such a government requires of both its politicians and its citizens a high degree of literacy, also a sense of history, and, at least in the American context, an ethics derived from the syllabus of the Bible. None of those requirements carry any weight in the Kingdom of the Eternal Now governed by the rule of images. Bring narrative to Jay Leno, or hierarchy to Howard Stern, and you might as well be speaking Homeric Greek.

December's impeachment debate in the House of Representatives suggested some of the difficulties in translation. The Republican majority defended the realm of Christian print against the pagan worship of celebrity. Invoking the names of God and Alexander Hamilton (also Benjamin Franklin, Abraham Lincoln, and the truth), the captains of Henry Hyde's crusade cast themselves as rescuers of the nation's children and implacable upholders of "the rule of law." When briefly at a loss for another calumny to slop upon the head of President Clinton, they deplored "the politics of personal destruction."

What was remarkable about the Republican argument in the House was the utter lack of self-awareness on the part of the congressmen who dressed up their attempt at political assassination in the rhetoric of high-minded conscience. Themselves creatures of the electronic media, they behaved in the manner of the people whom they professed to despise. How else had they come to Washington if not by the "politics of personal destruction"? Who else had armed them with the weapon of impeachment if not the lawless special prosecutor, Kenneth Starr? Where else did they find the texts for their snow-white sermons if not in the men's room of a singles bar?

The vocabulary of the electronic media is necessarily primitive, rendering argument as gossip and history as fable, and the time available to the defenders of coherent narrative and Roman eloquence ("the gentleman from Oklahoma is recognized for one minute") didn't permit the kind of oratory that opened the Oregon Trail or won the Civil War. Even when granted the privilege of three minutes, the members could muster little more than repetitions (incantatory and discontinuous) of ornamental cliché—"this is God's country, and I know He will bless America," "Catch the falling flag as we keep our appointment with history," etc. The Democrats could do no better than the Republicans. Several of them sought to characterize the impeachment of President Clinton as a right-wing "coup d'état," but within the parameters of the vicious sound bite and the twelve-second slander they couldn't give meaning to the plot.

On Thursday, January 14, the network cameras showed up in force. So did a large crowd of spectators waiting patiently in a cold rain behind the ropes on the west front of the Capitol. Here at last was the day on which the House prosecutors would make their opening arguments on behalf of the Magna Carta and against what several of them condemned as the "divine-right-of-kings theory of governance." Another historic moment, and for the first hour the anticipation in the press gallery compared favorably with the excitement of a train wreck or the glamour of the Academy Awards.

In a voice heavy with unctuous piety, Representative Hyde began by reminding the Senate of its grave duty and summoned the departed spirit of Sir Thomas More, lord chancellor of England during the reign of Henry VIII, who had chosen to die under the headsman's ax rather than swear an oath that he deemed heretical and false. Making the point about the sanctity of oaths—the one sworn by

The chamber where on Thursday, December 15, 1998, the House of Representatives began its impeachment session.

President Clinton to uphold the Constitution, the one sworn by each of the hundred senators to do impartial justice—Hyde quoted the line given to the blessed Sir Thomas in the film *A Man for All Seasons*: "When a man takes an oath, Meg, he's holding his own self in his hands like water, and if he opens his fingers, then he needn't hope to find himself again."

The twelve Apostles who followed Hyde to the rostrum over the next three days presented a set of variations on the theme of a man being as good as his word. Any man, but especially the President of the United States, the exemplar of the nation's honor, the living embodiment of the rule of law. All the speeches dwelled on the same precept—no man above the law, truth-telling the foundation stone of the American republic—and they all reviewed, and re-reviewed and then reviewed again, the familiar narrative of the Presi-

dent's dalliance with Monica Lewinsky. Yes, the circumstances were private and not public, and yes, what we've been talking about here in this august chamber is the President of the United States accepting the compliment of a blow job—eleven of them to be precise, together with some stuffed animals and a ceramic frog—but the man lied, lied to his wife, lied to his friends and cabinet ministers, lied to the American people. Perjury discolors and poisons the stream of justice, subverts and undermines the integrity of government. Fail to remove the President from the body politic (as one would remove a cancer or a festering sore) and you desecrate the American flag and everything for which it stands.

The managers told a more coherent story than the one told in the House, but the points had been made so often over the past year that after the first three hours several senators clearly were finding it hard to stay awake. In the corridors behind the press gallery the reporters were talking mostly about Michael Jordan, whose retirement from basketball had played as bigger news on the front page of that morning's *New York Times* than had the commencement of the President's impeachment trial. At least 500 correspondents had crowded into Chicago's United Center; not as many as 100 were seated in the Senate.

The deference to Jordan accurately reflected the society's order of value, which was why, as I understood after listening to the last of the speeches in the Senate early Saturday afternoon, the Republican managers had brought their Grand Remonstrance against the pagan, Clinton. They objected to the society's order of value and wished to overturn it. It was the government, the majesty of the law, and possibly the editors of *The Weekly Standard* that deserved the nation's affection and respect, not a sum of ratings points or the roaring of the mob. Representative Charles Canady of Florida cited the wisdom of Judge Louis Brandeis: "Our government is the potent, the omnipresent teacher. For good or ill, it teaches the whole people by its example."

But what if it doesn't? Suppose the citizenry looks elsewhere for instruction. Not to Congress or the White House, not to the state capitol in Tallahassee or to San Francisco's city hall, but to Giants Stadium and *Entertainment Tonight*, to a brute wrestler elected governor of Minnesota or Hulk Hogan telling Jay Leno about his forthcoming presidential campaign, to the pornographer Larry Flynt, who chased Representative Robert Livingston out of Washington (almost as soon as he was elected speaker of the House of Representatives), to Dick Morris, columnist and talk-show host, transformed into a sage by virtue of his long and patient study of a prostitute's toes.

The electronic media believe, and believe passionately, in "the divine-right-of-kings theory of governance," also in Dionysus and the great god Pan. They invest authority in persons, not in institutions, and the identity of the state comes to be embodied in a small repertory company of miraculous mandarins dressed up by publicists in the wardrobe of immortality. Celebrities who can hold the interest of the camera receive the emblems of divinity once assigned to Zeus and Aphrodite. It doesn't matter who they are (Monica Lewinsky, Michael Jordan, Cindy Crawford, Saddam Hussein); what they say (about lipstick or Tibet); how they acquired their fame (in a baseball park or a brothel, by heal-ing the sick or murdering the poor); whether they favor the teachings of Zoroaster or L. Ron Hubbard. Once possessed of the sovereign power to sponsor perfume or sell basketball shoes, all the names are royal.

Not a pleasing prospect for the admirers of Alexander Hamilton or the friends of Henry Hyde. The accelerated technologies of electronic media apparently were carrying the country backward into the forests of pagan superstition, and somebody had to be called to account. Lacking the subpoena power to impeach the Internet or the Super Bowl, the Republican majority in the House directed its entire flow of fear and rage into the empty reservoir otherwise known as William Jefferson Clinton. Who better to bear the blame for everything else that has gone so badly wrong in the once happy land of Christian print? Both product and personification of the television screen, not a man for all seasons but a man for a thousand cable channels, polymorphous and perverse, the President's character lends itself to the project—a natural-born catch basin and as hollow as an abandoned mine, the apple of every salesman's eye, a free-range appetite happy to devour anything on offer (all the limelight, every loaf of scandal), the great American consumer who, if asked, probably could drink the Colorado River.

Saturday's speeches rose to the pitch of exorcism, Congressman Hyde delivering the final peroration in language as Victorian as the drapery on the Senate walls. The President, he said, had dishonored his noble office, broken his sacred covenant with the American people, impaired their freedoms, injured their history, debased their trust. Thus had his low crimes become high crimes, and the time had come for him to go. Go and take with him all the other evils of which he was both proof and symbol—not only his saxophone and his bandleader's smile, but also every homosexual bartender in Santa Monica, every new-made billionaire in New York.

Calling upon a long list of the country's most heroic victories (Bunker Hill, Lexington, Flanders fields, Normandy, Iwo Jima), the congressman offered his speech as a prayer for the safe return of an imaginary American past, and when he finished, the nearly perfect silence in the Senate chamber again brought to mind the ritual stillness of a world out of time. For a long moment none of the senators moved in their chairs, and in the periodical press gallery skepticism was temporarily in short supply. The evening-news broadcasts cut the scene to what seemed like a very long twenty seconds.

INDEX

Page references in italics indicate illustrations

Abbey, Edwin A., *100*
Adam (Biblical figure), 146–50
Adams, John Quincy, 13
Adelman, Bob, *455*
African-Americans. *See* Blacks
Age/aging, 219–24
AIDS, 620–27
Airports, 683–89
Alden, Henry Mills, *xvii*, xvii–xxi
Ali, Muhammad. *See* Clay, Cassius
Allen, Frederick Lewis, xxiv–xxiii, 312
Allende, Salvador, 520–25, *523*
American character, 166–67
American language, 290–94
American Mercury magazine, *293*
American slums, 205–9
American women, 302–7
Anarchism, 115–16, 285–89
Andersen, Hans Christian, 47
Anderson, Sherwood, viii, 197
Anti-Catholicism, 445–51
Anti-Communism, 445–51
Antietam, Battle of, 42–46, *45*
Anti-Masonic movement, 445–51
Arapaho Indians, 20–28
Art for art's sake, 375–78, *377*
Atkinson, Fort. *See* Fort Atkinson
Atomic bombs, decision to use on Japan, *359*, 359–64, *361*, *363*
Aviation, 241–42

Baby boom generation, 396–98
Baldwin, James, 428
Barnes, Michelle, *478*
Basketball, 643–56
Battles. *See* Civil War; Wars/battles; World War II; *and specific battles, e.g.,* Antietam, Battle of
Benét, Stephen Vincent, 270
Bing, Léon, 577–85
Blacks, 12–16, 332–35, 428–44, 458
   In Coney Island, 643–56, *652*
   Emancipation of, 452–58
   Racial integration in the South, 414–16

Bloods (gang), 577–85, *583*
Boswell, James, 17–19
Brace, C. L., 84
Brodkey, Harold, 408
Buck, Pearl S., 302
Bureaucracy in Europe, 372–74
Burke, Philip, *552*, *556*

Calley, William L., Jr., 485–508, *486*
Carroll, Lewis, 175, *176*
Cary, Joyce, 393
Cather, Willa Sibert, 189
Central America, 558–67
Character, American, 166–67
Charlie Company, 484–508
Cheever, John, 379
Chicago, 115–16
Chicago Seven, 473–77, *474*, *476*
Child labor in New York City, 84–86, *85*
Chile, 520–25
Cistercian monasteries, 690–98
Civil War
   Antietam, Battle of, 42–46, *45*
   Hooker, Joseph, 43–44, 46
   McClellan, George B., 42, 45
   Meade, George G., 44, 46
   Trade boom during, 53–56
Clay, Cassius, 438–44, *440–41*
Clemens, Samuel. *See* Twain, Mark
Cleveland, Grover, 166, *167*
Clinton, Bill, impeachment of, 699–702
Cohn, Roy, *449*. *See also* McCarthy, Joseph
Comstock, Sarah, 243
Concord, Massachusetts, 308–10
Coney Island, 643–56
Confederate States of America, 42–46
Congress, 29–39
Conrad, Joseph, 178
Constitution, 12–16, 29–39
Country doctors, 210–16
Country newspapers, 201–4
Countryside in Pennsylvania, 251–55
Cowles, John, Jr., xxv, xxvii
Cowley, Malcolm, 251
Crane, Stephen, viii, 140

Crime, 230–34
　Drive-by shootings, 577–85
　Organized crime, 231
Crips (gang), 577–85, 583
Cuba, 133–39
Curtis, George William, xvi, xix, 72, 81, 98, 106, 113

Dahl, Roald, 399
Daley, Richard J., 473–77
Darrow, Clarence S., 230
Date rape, 657–62
Davis, L. J., 606
Davis, Richard Harding, xi
Death, 219–24
Democratic Party Convention, 1968, 473–77
De Vere, M. Schele, 59
DeVoto, Bernard, viii, xxiv, xxv, 388
Dickens, Charles, *72*, 72–73
Dickey, James, 459, *459*
Dillard, Annie, 530
Disney, Walt, 537–44
Doctors, country, 210–16
Dos Passos, John, 336
Douglas, Stephen A., 29, *32*
Dreiser, Theodore, viii, 210
Drive-by shootings, 577–85
Drug abuse, 586–89
Durant, Will, 235
Dust Bowl migrant, *298*

East Side ghetto, New York City, 205–9, *207*
"Easy Chair" (monthly column), xvi, xviii, xix, xxiii, xxiv, xxv
Economic boom, during Civil War, 53–56
Education, higher, 478–82
El Salvador, 558–67
English language, 290–94
Europe
　Bureaucracy in, 372–74
　Traveling in, 241–42
Eve (Biblical figure), 151–57, *153*

Fairs. *See* Illinois State Fair
Fascism, 280–84
Faulkner, William, 414
Federal and local authority, 29–39
Fellows, Stan, *326*
Fiction writing, 595–604
Financial crises, 87–92
Fischer, John, viii, xxiii, xxiv, xxv, 478
Foreign affairs, 509–14
Forster, E. M., 375
Fort Atkinson, siege of, 20–28

Freedmen, 59–67
Freedom, 235–39
Frey, Darcy, 643
Friedman, Benno, *517*
Frost, Robert, viii, 228, *228*

Gaitskill, Mary, 657
Galápagos Islands, 530–36
Galbraith, John Kenneth, 404
Gangs, in Los Angeles, *572*, 577–85, 583
Gays, in San Francisco, 620–27
Generations, "baby boom" and "silent," 396–98, *397*
Georgia, 31
Germany, 280–84
Gethsemani, Abbey of, 690–98
Ghettos, Lower East Side, New York, 205–9, *207*
Gibson, Charles Dana, *144*
Goldman, Emma, 285, *287*
Gordimer, Nadine, 568
Gorey, Edward, *393, 394*
Gould, Jay, 91
Grant, Ulysses S., 113–14
　Funeral of, *113*
Great Plains, 68–70
Greeley, Horace, 68
Guernsey, Albert, xvii
Gurganus, Allan, 590

Hallman, Adolf, *400, 403*
Harding, Warren, xxi
Hardy, Thomas, viii, 196, *196*
Harper, Fletcher, xii, *xiii*, xiv–xvi
Harper, James, xii, *xiii*, xiv–xvi
Harper, John, xii, *xiii*, xiv–xvi
Harper, Joseph Wesley, xii, *xiii*, xiv–xvi
Harper & Brothers, xii, *xiii*, xiv–xvi
Harper's Magazine, viii–ix, xi–xxxi
　Centennial issue (1950), 388–89, *392*
　Covers for, by Edward Penfield, *following page 144*
　Harper's New Monthly Magazine, viii–xxxi
　Harper's Weekly, xvi, xviii, xxi
　History and character of, viii–xxxi
　New York City and, viii–xxxi
　Readers of, *100*
Harrington, Michael, 537
Hartman, Lee Foster, xxiii
Hawthorne, Nathaniel, xvi, *17*, 17
Haymarket riot, 115–16
　John Most, *115*
Hersh, Seymour M., 484, 508
Historical writing, 461–64
Hitler, Adolf, 280–84, *281*

Hofstadter, Richard, 445
Homer, Winslow, 89, *593*
Homosexuals. *See* Gays
Honduras, 558–67, *562*
Hooker, Joseph, 43–44, 46
Hoover, Herbert, 262–66
    Hooverville, *263*
Hoover, J. Edgar, viii, 528
Hopper, Edward, *343*
Howells, William Dean, viii, xix, xxi, *219*, 219
Hughes, Langston, 458, *458*
Humphrey, Hubert, 473–77

Illinois State Fair, 668–82, *670*, *673*
Immigrants, Jewish, 205–9
Impeachment of Bill Clinton, 699–702, *701*
Indians, xviii, 20–28, *23*, 109, 111, 125–32
Intellect, 175–77
International politics, 509–14
Iwo Jima, Battle of, 346–51, *350*
Iyer, Pico, 683

Jackson, Thomas Jonathan (Stonewall), 43–44, 46
James, Henry, viii, xxi, 102, *102*
Japan
    Decision to use atomic bombs on, viii, *359*, 359–64, *361*, *363*
    Iwo Jima, Battle of, 346–51, *350*
    In World War II, 346–64, *347*, *350*, *355*
Japanese-Americans, relocation programs for, 352–58, *355*
Jarrell, Randall, 472, *472*
Jewett, Sarah Orne, 120
Jewish immigrants, 205–9
Johnson, Fenton, 690
Johnson, Lyndon, 473–77
Johnson, Samuel (Dr. Johnson), 17–19
Journalism, 201–4, 526–29

Kansas-Nebraska Act, 36
Kapuściński, Ryszard, 558–67
Karp, Walter, 546
Kazin, Alfred, 343
Kempton, Murray, 526
Kent, Rockwell, *153*, *237*
King, Martin Luther, 428–37, *433*
Kinsley, Michael, xxvii
Kipling, Rudyard, 226, *227*

Labor laws
    Child labor in New York City, 84–86, *85*
    New York State, 90–92

Land policy, 108–12
Language, American English, 290–94
Lapham, Lewis H., viii, xi, xxvii, xxx, xxxi, 663, 699
LAX (Los Angeles airport), 683–89, *684*, *687*
Lichfield (England), 17–19
Lindbergh, Anne Morrow, 372
Lindbergh, Charles, 241–42
Lippmann, Walter, 262
Literature, 465–71, 595–604. *See also* Writing
Local authority, 29–39
London, Jack, 168, *168*
Los Angeles airport, 683–89, *684*, *687*
Los Angeles gangs, *572*, 577–85, *583*
Lowell, James Russell, viii, 118, *119*
Lower East Side, New York, 205–9, *207*
Lynch, Anne C., xvi–xvii

MacIntyre, C. F., 301
MacIver, Loren, *334*
MacLeish, Archibald, 256, *256*
Mailer, Norman, 473
Malcolm X, 438–44
Mamet, David, 632
Marquand, John P., 346
Márquez, Gabriel García, 520
Marquis, Don, 217
Married life, 268–69, *269*
Martin, Edward S., xxiii, 241
Massachusetts, 31
McCarthy, Eugene, 473–77
McCarthy, Joseph/McCarthyism, viii, 445–51, *449*
McClellan, George B., 42, 45
McGovern, George, 473–77
McPherson, Aimee Semple, 243–50, *246*, *247*
Meade, George G., 44, 46
Medical research, 332–35
Medina, Ernest L., 484–508
Melville, Herman, 2, 57, *57*
Mencken, H. L., 290, *293*
Merton, Thomas, 695–96
Millay, Edna St. Vincent, 267, *267*
Milton, John, 229
Mississippi (state) 452–57
Mississippi River, 68–70, 74–80
Monastic and religious life (Trappist and Zen Buddhist), 690–98
Morality and international politics, 509–14
Morris, Willie, viii, xxv, xxvii
Most, John, *115*, 115–16
Mother Goose, *217*, 217–18
My Lai massacre, 484–508

Nast, Thomas, xvii, xviii, 98
Native Americans. *See* Indians
Nazis/Nazism, 280–84, 316–20
Negroes. *See* Blacks
Neiman, LeRoy, *440–41*
New Hampshire, 31
Newspapers, country, 201–4
New York City
    Child labor in, 84–86, *85*
    Coney Island, 643–56
    History of (*See Harper's Magazine,* history and
        character of)
    Hooverville, *263*
    Lower East Side ghetto, 205–9, *207*
New York Stock Exchange
    1873 panic, *87,* 87–92
    1929 crash, 404–7, *405, 406*
New York Times, xiv
Nichols, George Ward, 74
Nixon, Richard M., 529, 663–67, *666*
Nonfiction novels, 595–604
North Carolina, 30–31
Noyes, George F., 42

Oates, Joyce Carol, 628
Ohio River, 68–69
Old age, 219–24
Olsen, Tillie, 465
Organized crime, 231

Pacific Theater (World War II), 346–51, *347,* 353, 359–64
Paine, Veeder B., 108
Paranoia in politics, 445–51
Parrish, Maxfield, *260*
Party Convention, 1968, Democratic, 473–77, *474, 476*
Party Convention, 1968, Republican, 473–77
Penfield, Edward, *following page 144, 147*
Pennsylvania, 36, 251–55
Percy, Walker, 452
Pericoli, Tullio, *600*
Pinkwater, Bob, *409, 412*
Pinochet, Augusto, 520–25
Plath, Sylvia, *426,* 426
Plimpton, George, 438
Politics
    In America, 81–83
    International, 509–14
    Paranoia in, 445–51, *449*
Popular sovereignty, 29–39
Porter, Katherine Anne, 365
Prohibition, *312,* 312–14
Public land policy, 108–12

Pyle, Howard, *107, 194*

Rackham, Arthur, *217*
Ravage, M. E., 205
Raymond, Henry J., xiv, xix
Reagan, Ronald, 546–57, *552*
Real property, 108–12
Redwood trees, 93–96
Regier, Gail, 586
Reid, Robert, *259*
Religion, 690–98
Relocation of Japanese-Americans, 352–58, *355*
Remington, Frederic, 133, *134, 138*
Republican Party Convention, 1968, 473–77
Research, medical, 332–35
Revivalism, 243–50
Rhode Island, 31
Ribicoff, Abraham, 473–77
Rilke, Rainer Maria, 301, *301*
River steamers, 74–80, *77*
Rodriguez, Richard, 620
Roosevelt, Theodore, viii, 125
Rossetti, Christina, 97, *97*
Rostow, Eugene V., viii, 352
Roth, Philip, 418
Rushdie, Salman, 571

Sandburg, Carl, viii, 229, *229*
San Francisco, 620–27
San Juan Hill, Battle of, 139
Saturday Evening Post, xxi, xxviii
Saunders, George, 635
Savings & loan scandal, 606–19
Schlesinger, Arthur, Jr., viii, 509
Schnayerson, Robert, xxvii
Scott, Dred, 34–35
Searle, Ronald, *607, 616*
Senate, U.S., 699–702
Seurat, Georges, *375*
Sexton, Anne, 417, *417*
Shahn, Ben, *373*
Sherman, William Tecumseh, 57–58
Shipbuilding, for World War II, *336,* 336–42, *339–40*
Silent generation, 396–98, *397*
Slavery, 12–16, 29–39, 59–67
Slums, American, 205–9
Soccer War, 558–67
South Carolina, 30–31
Sovereignty, popular, 29–39
Spanish-American War, 133–39
Speakeasies. *See* Prohibition
St. Clair, Arthur, 125–32, *130, 132*

State Fair, Illinois, 668–82, *670, 673*
Stauber, K., *281*
Steamboats, 74–80, *77*
Stein, Gertrude, 365–71, *369*
Steinbeck, John, 295
Steinberg, Saul, *369, 377*
Stimson, Henry L., viii, 359
Stock Exchange. *See* New York Stock Exchange
Strikes, 115–16
Szasz, Joel, *418, 423*

Taft, William Howard, *463*
Tammany Ring, *98,* 98–99
Territories, 29–39
Thackeray, William Makepeace, xii
Thompson, Dorothy, 316
Thoreau, Henry David, xvi, 308–10, *310*
Thurber, James, 268, *269*
Tomes, Robert, 53
Trade boom, during Civil War, 53–56
Trappists, 690–98
Trees, redwood, 93–96
Trotsky, Leon, 280
Tuchman, Barbara W., 461
Twain, Mark, viii, 146, *147,* 151
Tweed, William M. (Boss Tweed), *98,* 98–99

United States. *See also* Civil War; Vietnam War;
    Wars/battles; World War II
  Congress, 29–39
  Constitution, 12–16, 29–39
  Federal and local authority, 29–39
  Foreign affairs of, 509–14
  History of, 1850-1950, 388–92 (*See also Harper's
    Magazine,* history and character of)
  Land policy, 108–12
  Politics of, 81–83
    International, 509–14
    Paranoia in, 445–51
  Popular sovereignty in, 29–39
  Senate, 699–702
  Territories, 29–39
Updike, John, 427, *427*
Urban life, 683–89
Uttoxeter (England), 17–19

Vanderbilt, Cornelius, 91
Vermont, 427
Vietnam War, 484–508
Virginia, 30

Walden Pond, 308–10, *310*

Walker, Alice, 515
Wallace, David Foster, 668
Wall Street. *See* New York Stock Exchange
Walpole, Sir Robert, 99
Warhol, Andy, *379, 385*
Wars/battles. *See also* Civil War; World War II
  Antietam, Battle of, 42–46, *45*
  San Juan Hill, Battle of, 139
  Iwo Jima, Battle of, 346–51, *350*
  Fort Atkinson, siege of, 20–28
  Soccer War, 558–67
  Spanish-American War, 133–39
  St. Clair's defeat, 125–32
  Vietnam War, 484–508
Weinberger, Caspar, 555–56, *556*
Wells, Thomas Bucklin, viii, xxi, xxiii
Welty, Eudora, 321
Wharton, Edith, viii, 158
White, E. B., 308
White, William Allen, 201
Whitman, Walt, *93,* 93
Wilder, Thornton, 396
Wilson, Woodrow, viii
Wister, Owen, xi
Wolfe, Tom, 595
Women, American, 302–7, 336–42
Women's rights, 106–7
Woolf, Virginia, 257
World War II, 336–42, 346–58, *355,* 359–64
  Atomic bombs on Japan, 359, 359–64, *361, 363*
  Japan in, 346–64, *347, 350*
  Pacific Theater in, 346–51, *347, 353,* 359–64
  Shipbuilding for, *336,* 336–42, *339–40*
Wright, Richard, 332
Writing, 465–71, 595–604
  Fiction writing, 595–604
  Historical writing, 461–64
  Writer's block, 465–71
Wyeth, Newell, *199*

Yellow Bear (Arapaho chief), 20–28
Youth gangs, Los Angeles, 577–85, *579, 583*

Zen Buddhists, 690–98

ILLUSTRATION CREDITS

Abbreviations
[Years refer to the relevant issue of *Harper's Magazine*.]
NYHS: © Collection of The New-York Historical Society.
C/B: Corbis/Bettmann. BB: Brown Brothers. CU: Solton
and Julia Engel Collection, Rare Book and Manuscript
Library, Columbia University.

"(see caption)" appears where artist's name has been stated
in the caption and no further credit is necessary.

Endpapers: Harper's Story Book, 1855
Page i: 1865. **ii:** NYHS, neg. #156. **vii:** 1920's. **xiii:** 75th
Anniversary Issue (1850–1935). **xv:** 1850. **xvii:** 1900 **xx** 1901,
1919. **xxii:** 1922, 1940. **xxvi:** 1949, 1957. **xxviii:** 1984, 1970.

1850's
Page 3: 1856. **13:** 1854. **17:** 1872. **23:** (both) 1856. **28:** 1855.
32: C/B. **39:** ~~1856~~. **40:** Centennial Issue.

JAN. 1857

1860's
Page 45: C/B. **48:** 1864. **50:** 1864. **56:** 1862. **57:** C/B. **58:**
1865. **65:** 1866. **69:** ~~1868~~. *JAN. 1869*

1870's
Page 72: 1871. **75:** 1870. **77:** 1870. **83:** 1870. **85:** 1873. **89:**
Harper's Weekly, Adventures of America 1857–1900,
133. **92:** 1874. **93:** BB. **96:** 1878. **97:** 1878. **98:** *Harper's
Weekly*, Adventures of America 1857–1900, # 138. **100:**
1875.

1880's
Page 102: Harper's Centennial Issue 1950. **107:** 1885. **110:**
1880. **113:** BB. **114:** 1883. **115:** *Harper's Weekly*, Adventures
of America 1857–1900, # 200.

1890's
Page 118: 1891. **119:** 1916. **121:** 1895. **124:** 1895. **130:**
1896. **132:** 1896. **134:** 1898. **138:** 1898. **143:** 1899. **144:**
1897.

Color Insert of Edward Penfields—unpaginated
Poster Calendar for 1897: CU. **January 1896:** NYHS, neg.
#133. **February 1895:** NYHS, neg. #119. **March 1899:** CU.
April 1899: CU. **May 1898:** CU. **June 1897:** CU. **July**

1898: CU. **August 1896:** NYHS, neg. #147. **September
1895:** NYHS, neg. #126. **October 1895:** NYHS, neg. #128.
November 1898: CU. **Christmas 1895:** NYHS, neg. #131.

1900's
Page 147: CU. **153:** Courtesy of The Rockwell Kent Legacies. **165:** 1902. **167:** 1921. **168:** 1921. **173:** 1905. **176:** BB.
186: 1906. **190:** 1909. **194:** 1900.

1910's
Page 196: C/B. **199:** Art Resource, NY. **203:** 1917. **207:**
1916. **216:** 1901. **218:** 1918. **219:** 1921. **224:** 1919.

1920's
Page 226: 1920. **227:** C/B. **228:** C/B. **229:** C/B. **231:** C/B.
234: 1921. **237:** Courtesy of The Rockwell Kent Legacies.
241: 1908. **246:** C/B. **247:** C/B. **251:** 1909. **256:** C/B. **259:**
National Museum of American Art,
Washington, DC/Art Resource, NY. **260:** 1921.

1930's
Page 263: BB. **267:** NYHS, neg. #70908 / Photo by Arnold
Genthe. **269:** From the book *Men, Women and Dogs* by
James Thurber. © 1943 by James Thurber. Copyright
renewed 1971 by Helen Thurber and Rosemary A. Thurber.
Reprinted by arrangement with Rosemary A. Thurber and
The Barbara Hogenson Agency. **279:** 1900. **281:** AKG :
London. **287:** AP/Wide World Photos. **293:** C/B. **298:** BB.
301: BB. **303:** 1937. **310:** BB. **312:** C/B.

1940's
Page 317: BB. **326:** Stan Fellows (see caption). **334:**
1945. **336:** 1940. **339:** Corbis/Hulton-Deutsch Collection.
340: Corbis/Hulton-Deutsch Collecton. **343:** Art
Resource, NY. **347:** AP/Wide World Photos. **350:**
AP/Wide World Photos. **355:** BB. **359:** BB. **361:** BB.
363: BB. **369:** © 2000 Estate of Saul Steinberg/Artists
Rights Society (ARS), New York. **373:** © Estate of Ben
Shahn/Licensed by VAGA, New York, NY. **375:** Helen
Birch Bartlett Memorial Collection, Photograph courtesy
of The Art Institute of Chicago. **377:** © 2000 Estate of
Saul Steinberg/Artists Rights Society (ARS), New York.
379: © 2000 Andy Warhol Foundation for the Visual Arts
/ ARS, New York. **385:** © 2000 Andy Warhol Foundation
for the Visual Arts / ARS, New York.

1950's

Page 391: Harper's Centennial Issue, 1950. **393, 394:** Edward Gorey (see caption). **397:** C/B. **400, 403:** A.Hallman (see caption). **405:** C/B. **406:** C/B. **409, 412:** Bob Pinkwater (see caption). **416:** National Museum of American Art, Washington, DC/Art Resource, NY. **417:** C/B. **418, 423:** Joel Szasz (see caption).

1960's

Page 426: C/B. **427:** C/B. **433:** C/B. **440, 441:** Leroy Nieman (see caption). **449:** BB. **455:** Bob Adelman(see caption). **458:** C/B. **459:** C/B. **463:** BB. **472:** C/B. **474:** C/B. **476:** AP/Wide World Photos. **478:** (see caption).

1970's

Page 486: C/B. **507:** Corbis/Hulton-Deutsch Collection. **514:** (see caption). **517:** (see caption). **523:** C/B. **528:** (see caption). **534:** (see caption). **535:** (see caption). **540–41:** (see caption).

1980's

Page 552: (see caption). **556:** (see caption). **562:** C/B. **569:** (see caption). **572:** (see caption). **579:** AP/Wide World Photos. **583:** AP/Wide World Photos. **586:** (see caption). **593:** Cooper-Hewitt Museum, Smithsonian Institution/Art Resrouce, NY. **600:** (see caption).

1990's

Page 607: (see caption). **616:** (see caption). **622:** Michael Nichols/Magnum Photos. **630:** (see caption). **633:** (see caption). **636:** (see caption). **644:** (see caption). **652:** (see caption). **658:** (see caption). **659:** (see caption). **662:** (see caption). **666:** SIPA PRESS/Art Resource, NY. **670:** © 1999 The State Journal Register. **673:** © 1999 The State Journal Register. **675:** © 1999 The State Journal Register. **683–84, 687:** Photo by Steve Lehman. **694:** (see caption). **697:** (see caption). **701:** AP/Wide World Photos.

COPYRIGHT ACKNOWLEDGMENTS